HANDBOOK OF
EATING DISORDERS AND OBESITY

Edited by

J. Kevin Thompson

WILEY

John Wiley & Sons, Inc.

This book is dedicated to my mother, Wilma Nichols Thompson.

Library of Congress Cataloging-in-Publication Data:

Handbook of eating disorders and obesity / edited by J. Kevin Thompson.
     p. cm.
   ISBN 0-471-23073-1 (cloth : alk. paper)
   1. Eating disorders—Handbooks, manuals, etc. 2. Obesity—Handbooks, manuals, etc. I. Thompson, J. Kevin.
   RC552.E18H362   2003
   616.85'26—dc21

                             2003002432

Printed in the United States of America.

10 9 8 7 6 5 4 3 2 1

Acknowledgments ──────────────────────────

This book would not have been possible without the creative input and unwavering faith of Cristina Wojdylo, acquisitions editor at Wiley. She approached me with the initial idea in the fall of 2001, and her constant support and direction were essential to the ultimate product. I would also like to thank Tom Cash for his close friendship and creative contribution to this volume and the entire field of body image. I'd also like to wish him good luck with his new journal, *Body Image: An International Journal of Research*. Thanks also to some good friends and collaborators for their work on the current book, including Leslie Heinberg, Stacey Dunn, Myles Faith, Linda Smolak, Michael Levine, Eleanor Wertheim, Susan Paxton, and Eric Stice. Thanks to my current students who were incredibly supportive during the process of editing this book: Megan Roehrig, Hemal Shroff, Sylvia Herbozo, Susan Himes, Guy Cafri, Yuko Yamamiya, Helene Keery, Robyn Birkeland, Patricia van den Berg, and Michael Boroughs.

Contributors

Liana B. Abascal, MA, SDSU/UCSD
Joint Doctoral Program
San Diego, California

David B. Allison, PhD
University of Alabama at Birmingham
Birmingham, Alabama

Drew A. Anderson, PhD
State University of New York at Albany
Albany, New York

Eileen P. Anderson-Fye, EdD
University of California at Los Angeles
Los Angeles, California

Anne E. Becker, MD, PhD
Massachusetts General Hospital
Boston, Massachusetts

Simone Blaney, BBSc (Hons)
La Trobe University
Bundoora, Victoria, Australia

Kelly D. Brownell, PhD
Yale University
New Haven, Connecticut

Cynthia M. Bulik, PhD
William and Jeanne Jordan Distinguished
    Professor of Eating Disorders
Department of Psychiatry

University of North Carolina at
    Chapel Hill
Chapel Hill, North Carolina

Thomas F. Cash, PhD
Old Dominion University
Norfolk, Virginia

Jordana Cooperberg
University of Pennsylvania School
    of Medicine
Philadelphia, Pennsylvania

Mark B. Cope, PhD
University of Alabama at Birmingham
Birmingham, Alabama

Canice E. Crerand, MA
Drexel University
Philadelphia, Pennsylvania

Scott J. Crow, MD
University of Minnesota
Minneapolis, Minnesota

Martina de Zwaan, MD
Friedrich-Alexander University
    Erlangen-Nuremberg
Erlangen, Germany

Michael J. Devlin, MD
Columbia University
New York, New York

Nikhil V. Dhurandhar, PhD
Wayne State University
Detroit, Michigan

Myles S. Faith, PhD
University of Pennsylvania School
    of Medicine
Philadelphia, Pennsylvania

José R. Fernández, PhD
University of Alabama at Birmingham
Birmingham, Alabama

Alison E. Field, ScD
Harvard Medical School
Boston, Massachusetts

Gary D. Foster, PhD
University of Pennsylvania School
    of Medicine
Philadelphia, Pennsylvania

Debra L. Franko, PhD
Northeastern University
Boston, Massachusetts

Jessica Gokee-LaRose, MS
University of Central Florida
Orlando, Florida

Angela S. Guarda, MD
Johns Hopkins School of Medicine
Baltimore, Maryland

Jess Haines, MHSc, RD
School of Public Health
University of Minnesota
Minneapolis, Minnesota

Kristen Harrison, PhD
University of Illinois
Urbana, Illinois

M. Ammar Hatahet, MD
Wayne State University
Detroit, Michigan

Leslie J. Heinberg, PhD
Johns Hopkins University School
    of Medicine
Baltimore, Maryland

Kathryn F. Henderson, PhD
Yale University
New Haven, Connecticut

David B. Herzog, MD
Massachusetts General Hospital
Boston, Massachusetts

Emily Hoffman, PhD
University of Texas at Austin
Austin, Texas

Joshua I. Hrabosky
Old Dominion University
Norfolk, Virginia

Karin Jasper, PhD, MEd
Hospital for Sick Children
Toronto, Canada

Maria C. LaVia, MD
Western Psychiatric Institute and Clinic
Pittsburgh, Pennsylvania

Michael P. Levine, PhD
Kenyon College
Gambier, Ohio

Deborah Little, MS
Northeastern University
Boston, Massachusetts

James Lock, MD, PhD
Stanford University School of Medicine
Stanford, California

Katharine L. Loeb, PhD
Columbia University
New York, New York

Kristine H. Luce, PhD
Stanford University School of Medicine
Stanford, California

Leanne Magee, BA
University of Pennsylvania School
  of Medicine
Philadelphia, Pennsylvania

Marsha D. Marcus, PhD
Western Psychiatric Institute and Clinic
Pittsburgh, Pennsylvania

Elizabeth Blocher McCabe, LSW
University of Pittsburgh Medical Center
Pittsburgh, Pennsylvania

Marita P. McCabe, PhD, FAPS
Deakin University
Burwood, Victoria, Australia

James E. Mitchell, MD
University of North Dakota
Fargo, North Dakota

Sarah K. Murnen, PhD
Kenyon College
Gambier, Ohio

**Dianne Neumark-Sztainer, PhD,
  MPH, RD**
School of Public Health
University of Minnesota
Minneapolis, Minnesota

Dasha Nicholls, MBBS, MD
Great Ormond Street Hospital
London

Roberto Olivardia, PhD
McLean Hospital/Harvard Medical
  School
Belmont, Massachusetts

Caroline A. Paulosky
State University of New York at Albany
Albany, New York

**Susan J. Paxton, BA (Hons), MPsych,
  PhD**
La Trobe University
Bundoora, Victoria, Australia

Alison Pepper
California State University at
  San Marcos
San Marcos, California

Carol B. Peterson, PhD
University of Minnesota
Minneapolis, Minnesota

Rachel D. Peterson, BA
University of Central Florida
Orlando, Florida

Suzanne Phelan, PhD
Brown Medical School
Providence, Rhode Island

Kathleen M. Pike, PhD
Columbia University
New York, New York

Leora Pinhas, MD, FRCP (C)
Southlake Regional Health Centre
New Market, Canada
Hospital for Sick Children
Toronto, Canada

Niva Piran, PhD, C Psych
Ontario Institutie for Studies in
  Education
University of Toronto
Toronto, Canada

Claire Pomeroy, MD, MBA
University of California at Davis
Davis, California

Lina A. Ricciardelli, PhD
Deakin University
Burwood, Australia

James L. Roerig, PharmD
Neuropsychiatric Research Institute
University of North Dakota School of
  Medicine and Health Sciences
Fargo, North Dakota

Sonia Y. Ruiz
California State University at
    San Marcos
San Marcos, California

David R. Sarwer, PhD
University of Pennsylvania School of
    Medicine
Philadelphia, Pennsylvania

Linda Smolak, PhD
Kenyon College
Gambier, Ohio

Tiffany M. Stewart
Pennington Biomedical Research Center
Baton Rouge, Louisiana

Eric Stice, PhD
University of Texas at Austin
Austin, Texas

Ruth H. Striegel-Moore, PhD
Wesleyan University
Middletown, Connecticut

Stacey Tantleff-Dunn, PhD
University of Central Florida
Orlando, Florida

J. Kevin Thompson, PhD
University of South Florida
Tampa, Florida

Kevin M. Thompson, PhD
North Dakota State University and
    Health Sciences
Fargo, North Dakota

Thomas A. Wadden, PhD
University of Pennsylvania School
    of Medicine
Philadelphia, Pennsylvania

**Eleanor H. Wertheim, BA, MA, PhD,
    FAPS**
La Trobe University
Bundoora, Victoria, Australia

Denise E. Wilfley, PhD
Washington Univesity School
    of Medicine
St. Louis, Missouri

Donald A. Williamson, PhD
Pennington Biomedical Research Center
Baton Rouge, Louisiana

Andrew J. Winzelberg, PhD
Stanford University School of Medicine
Stanford, California

Stephen A. Wonderlich, PhD
University of North Dakota School
    of Medicine
Fargo, North Dakota

Contents

Part II   Obesity

Section 1   Etiology, Risk, and Prevention

Section 2   Assessment and Diagnosis

Section 3   Treatment

Part III   Body Image Disturbances and Body Dysmorphic Disorder

Part IV   Special Topics

Preface

EATING DISORDERS AND OBESITY: DEFINITIONS, PREVALENCE, AND ASSOCIATED FEATURES

Eating disorders and obesity comprise two of the most frequently encountered clinical disorders and have morbidity and mortality rates that are among the highest of any psychological or health-related conditions. The range of problems that can be usefully captured under the phrase of "eating, weight, and shape-related" disorders is broad and includes not only the four *Diagnostic and Statistical Manual of Mental Disorders,* Fourth Edition, Text Revision (*DSM-IV-TR*) categories for eating disorders, but also the somatoform disorder of body dysmorphic disorder (American Psychiatric Association [APA], 2000). Obesity is not included per se as a *DSM* disorder, yet perhaps 10% to 20% of individuals with binge eating disorder are obese. Additionally, although obesity has not been found to be associated with general psychological dysfunction (depression appears to be strongly connected, however), the physical health consequences associated with obesity are rapidly emerging as a paramount public health issue. This introductory preface provides an overview of the accepted definitions of these eating and weight disorders, along with estimates of prevalence and the costs, both physical and psychological, that accompany these clinical problems.

The most widely used definitional schemes for the diagnosis of eating disorders, obesity, and body dysmorphic disorder are contained in Tables P.1 and P.2. Specific diagnostic and classification issues always engender debate among researchers, and some of these issues are explored in the chapters in this book. However, most epidemiological, etiological, and intervention studies adhere to these categories or some minor variant of the criteria contained in these schemes, and prevalence numbers are generally based on these nosologies.

A simple consideration of the prevalence statistics indicates that an enormous number of individuals are affected by one or more of these clinical problems. The most significant data shift in prevalence over the past few years has occurred with obesity; therefore, it may be most appropriate to begin with an examination of these numbers.

Recent evidence indicates that 65% of adult Americans are overweight and 31% are obese (Flegal, Carroll, Ogden, & Johnson, 2002), representing a dramatic increase over the past two decades (Centers for Disease Control [CDC], 2002). For childhood and adolescence, the figures are lower, but the trajectory is equally alarming. Thirteen percent of children (ages 6 to 11) and 14% of adolescents are obese, doubling the prevalence rates of the mid-1970s. Ethnicity is a critical issue in the examination of obesity

Table P.1   Categories of Eating Disorders from the *DSM-IV-TR*

Diagnostic criteria for Anorexia Nervosa

A. Refusal to maintain body weight at or above a minimally normal weight for age and height (e.g., weight loss leading to maintenance of body weight less than 85% of that expected; or failure to make expected weight gain during period of growth, leading to body weight less than 85% of that expected).

B. Intense fear of gaining weight or becoming fat, even though underweight.

C. Disturbance in the way in which one's body weight or shape is experienced, undue influence of body weight or shape on self-evaluation, or denial of the seriousness of the current low body weight.

D. In postmenarcheal females, amenorrhea (i.e., the absence of a least three consecutive menstrual cycles). A woman is considered to have amenorrhea if her periods occur only following hormone (e.g., estrogen, administration).

Specify type:

Restricting Type: During the current episode of Anorexia Nervosa, the person has not regularly engaged in binge-eating or purging behavior (i.e., self-induced vomiting or the misuse of laxatives, diuretics, or enemas).

Binge-Eating/Purging Type: During the current episode of Anorexia Nervosa, the person has regularly engaged in binge-eating or purging behavior (i.e., self-induced vomiting or the misuse of laxatives, diuretics, or enemas).

Diagnostic criteria for Bulimia Nervosa

A. Recurrent episodes of binge eating. An episode of binge eating is characterized by both of the following:

1. Eating, in a discrete period of time (e.g., within any 2-hour period), an amount of food that is definitely larger than most people would eat during a similar period of time and under similar circumstances.

2. A sense of lack of control over eating during the episode (e.g., a feeling that one cannot stop eating or control what or how much one is eating).

B. Recurrent inappropriate compensatory behavior in order to prevent weight gain, such as self-induced vomiting; misuse of laxatives, diuretics, enemas, or other medications; fasting; or excessive exercise.

C. The binge eating and inappropriate compensatory behaviors both occur, on average, at least twice a week for 3 months.

D. Self-evaluation is unduly influenced by body shape and weight.

E. The disturbance does not occur exclusively during episodes of Anorexia Nervosa.

Specify type:

Purging Type: During the current episode of Bulimia Nervosa, the person has regularly engaged in self-induced vomiting or the misuse of laxatives, diuretics, or enemas.

Nonpurging Type: During the current episode of Bulimia Nervosa, the person has used other inappropriate compensatory behaviors, such as fasting or excessive exercise, but has not regularly engaged in self-induced vomiting or the misuse of laxatives, diuretics, or enemas.

Table P.1   *(Continued)*

Research criteria for Binge-Eating Disorder

A. Recurrent episodes of binge eating. An episode of binge eating is characterized by both of the following:

  1. Eating, in a discrete period of time (e.g., within any 2-hour period), an amount of food that is definitely larger than most people would eat in a similar period of time under similar circumstances.

  2. A sense of lack of control over eating during the episode (e.g., a feeling that one cannot stop eating or control what or how much one is eating).

B. The binge-eating episodes are associated with three (or more) of the following:

  1. Eating much more rapidly than normal.

  2. Eating until feeling uncomfortably full.

  3. Eating large amounts of food when not feeling physically hungry.

  4. Eating alone because of being embarrassed by how much one is eating.

  5. Eating disgusted with oneself, depressed, or very guilty after overeating.

C. Marked distress regarding binge eating is present.

D. The binge eating occurs, on average, at least 2 days a week for 6 months.

  Note: The method of determining frequency differs from that used for Bulimia Nervosa; future research should address whether the preferred method of setting a frequency threshold is counting the number of days on which binges occur or counting the number of episodes of binge eating.

E. The binge eating is not associated with the regular use of inappropriate compensatory behaviors (e.g., purging, fasting, excessive exercise) and does not occur exclusively during the course of Anorexia Nervosa or Bulimia Nervosa.

Eating Disorder Not Otherwise Specified

The Eating Disorder Not Otherwise Specified category is for disorders of eating that do not meet the criteria for any specific Eating Disorder. Examples include:

  1. For females, all of the criteria for Anorexia Nervosa are met except that the individual has regular menses.

  2. All of the criteria for Anorexia Nervosa are met except that, despite significant weight loss, the individual's current weight is in the normal range.

  3. All of the criteria for Bulimia Nervosa are met except that the binge eating and inappropriate compensatory mechanisms occur at a frequency of less than twice a week or for a duration of less than 3 months.

  4. The regular use of inappropriate compensatory behavior by an individual of normal body weight after eating small amounts of food (e.g., self-induced vomiting after the consumption of two cookies).

  5. Repeatedly chewing and spitting out, but not swallowing, large amounts of food.

  6. Binge-eating Disorder: Recurrent episodes of binge eating in the absence of the regular use of inappropriate compensatory behaviors characteristic of Bulimia Nervosa.

(continued)

Table P.1   *(Continued)*

Body Dysmorphic Disorder

A. Preoccupation with an imagined defect in appearance. If a slight physical anomaly is present, the person's concern is markedly excessive.

B. The preoccupation causes clinically significant distress or impairment in social, occupational, or other important areas of functioning.

C. The preoccupation is not better accounted for by another mental disorder (e.g., dissatisfaction with body shape and size in Anorexia Nervosa).

From *Diagnostic and Statistical Manual of Mental Disorders,* Fourth Edition, Text Revision (2000). Note that binge eating disorder is included in the *DSM* on a provisional basis. Reprinted with permission of the American Psychiatric Association.

rates—a staggering 50% of African American women and 40% of Hispanic American women are obese, compared to 30% of Caucasian women (Flegal et al., 2002).

In contrast, the rates for eating disorders are much lower; however, even the low estimates for the various disorders, when summed, lead to the conclusion that many individuals, and a disproportionate number of women, suffer from some type of eating dysfunction. The *DSM-IV-TR* puts the prevalence rate for anorexia nervosa at approximately .5% and between 1.0% and 3.0% for bulimia nervosa (APA, 2000). Although the data for binge eating disorder are far less conclusive, it appears that the incidence may also be between 1.0% and 3.0% (see Thompson & Kinder, 2003). Many prevalence rate studies do not include the category of *eating disorder not otherwise specified,* which may add perhaps 50% more cases worthy of clinical intervention to these estimates (Nicholls, Chater, & Lask, 2000). One of the most comprehensive examinations of prevalence was reported by Lewinsohn (2001). Adolescent females were followed for more than 10 years and assessed periodically for the presence of eating disturbances. By age 24, 1.4% had anorexia nervosa and 2.8% had bulimia nervosa. Additionally, 4.4% met criteria for a partial syndrome, similar to the subclinical diagnosis of eating disorder not otherwise specified.

Table P.2   Classification of Overweight and Obesity by Body Mass Index (BMI)

	Obesity Class	BMI (kg/m2)
Underweight		<18.5
Normal		18.5–24.9
Overweight		25.0–29.9
Obesity	I	30.0–34.9
	II	35.0–39.9
Extreme Obesity	III	≥40.0

Note: From National Institutes of Health/NHLBI, 1998. A version of the formula with pounds and inches is: weight (lbs)/height (inches)^2 × 704.5.

Gender differences for anorexia nervosa and bulimia nervosa are prominent, with women outnumbering men by a 10 to 1 ratio (Thompson & Kinder, 2003). However, there appear to be few gender differences for binge eating disorder. Additionally, eating disorders and obesity overlap in the instance of perhaps 10% to 20% of individuals who are obese and who meet criteria for binge eating disorder (see Sarwer, Foster, & Wadden, Chapter 21 of this volume).

Body dysmorphic disorder (BDD) occurs at essentially the same rate as the individual eating disorders, affecting about 1% to 2% of the population (Phillips, 1996). Additionally, BDD is about equally common in males and females. Body image disturbances consisting of a general dissatisfaction with some aspect of appearance, not meeting the severity of a BDD diagnosis, are common (Thompson, Heinberg, Altabe, & Tantleff-Dunn, 1999). Several large-scale surveys indicate that approximately 40% to 60% of adolescent and adult females are dissatisfied with some aspect of their appearance. Also, recent studies indicate that level of dissatisfaction for men and boys appears to be increasing and is focused more on a muscularity than overall size dimension (Cafri, Strauss, & Thompson, 2002).

Psychological and health consequences of eating disorders, obesity, and body image problems represent a huge concern for researchers and clinicians. The Surgeon General recently released a report referring to the current rates of obesity as a "public health epidemic" (CDC, 2002). It has been estimated that 325,000 deaths each year could be attributed to obesity (Allison, Fontaine, Manson, Stevens, & Van Itallie, 1999). An overweight or obese status has been linked to a startling variety of health problems including heart disease, Type II diabetes, stroke, arthritis, cancer, sleep apnea, hypertension, gout, and gallstones (Field, Barnoya, & Colditz, 2002). Of additional concern is that most children and adolescents who are overweight or obese will also have significant weight problems in adulthood (Flegal, Carroll, Kuczmarski, & Johnson, 1998). Additionally, the psychosocial problems experienced by obese individuals, especially those in childhood and adolescence, have damaging interpersonal consequences (see Neumark-Stzainer & Haines, Chapter 18, this volume). Although obesity is not generally associated with increased risk for other psychiatric disorders, the exception is in the area of depression, where good prospective evidence indicates that it is associated with onset of depressive problems (Roberts, Strawbridge, Deleger, & Kaplan, 2002).

The medical and psychological complications of eating disorders are numerous and well documented (Agras, 2001; Pomeroy, Chapter 5, this volume). Anorexia nervosa has the highest mortality rate of any psychiatric disorder—one 21-year follow-up study found a death rate of 15.6% (Zipfel, Lowe, Deter, & Herzog, 2000). Comorbidity with other disorders, such as depression, obsessive-compulsive disorder, and personality disorders ranges from 30% to 50% (Agras, 2001). In one of the most extensive prospective studies, Johnson, Cohen, Kasen, and Brook (2002) followed a community sample of 717 adolescents for 10 years, finding that those with an eating disorder were at an increased risk for development of depressive and anxiety disorders, infectious diseases, suicide attempts, chronic pain, insomnia, neurological symptoms, and cardiovascular problems.

BDD and subclinical levels of body dissatisfaction are also associated with other disturbances. BDD is associated with severe depression, interpersonal difficulties, and frequent hospitalization (Phillips, 1996). Body dissatisfaction, even in the absence of an associated diagnosis of an eating disorder, obesity, or BDD, has been found to be associated with elevated levels of depression and low self-esteem and may dramatically affect an individual's level of social functioning (Thompson et al., 1999; Wertheim, Paxton, & Blaney, Chapter 23, this volume). Importantly, prospective work indicates that body dissatisfaction is one of the few consistent predictors of the onset of eating disturbances (Thompson & Smolak, 2001).

In summary, the sheer number of individuals who may suffer from some type of eating, weight, or shape disorder is staggering. Each of these problems, additionally, is associated with psychological and medical factors that have a negative impact on life expectancy, quality of life, and ability to function optimally in occupational and social settings. It is necessary to distill current work in the assessment and treatment of these disorders, as well as exploring the biological, social, and psychological factors that cause and maintain these conditions.

This book attempts to provide a contemporary exploration of the multiple areas of research and clinical practice that constitute the field of eating disorders and obesity. Sections within each category are devoted to etiology, risk, and prevention, assessment and diagnosis, and treatment. In addition, because of the tremendous relevance of body image concerns to both eating disorders and obesity (e.g., Thompson, 1996), a smaller separate section contains four chapters that extensively review the issues related to etiology, assessment, and treatment of BDD and other body image disturbances. A final section examines in detail special topics such as sexual abuse in eating disorders, the role of ethnicity in obesity and body dissatisfaction, and cosmetic surgery.

The content of chapters is directed at clinicians and researchers. Assessment, preventive, and treatment-related chapters contain not only a critical review of the empirically based literature, but also specific guidelines for implementing strategies in clinical practice. Often, clinical cases and clinically relevant anecdotes and commentary are provided to illustrate the application of treatment components in applied situations. The section on treatment of eating disorders offers a vast array, including chapters on the strategies that have received extensive analysis for many years (cognitive-behavioral, interpersonal, pharmacotherapy) and coverage of new treatment strategies that appear to offer a great deal of promise (e.g., dialectical behavior therapy, feminist therapies, integrative cognitive therapy, and family therapy).

Chapters on etiology, risk, and prevention offer crucial information for understanding the formative and maintaining influences for eating disorders, obesity, and body image disturbances. These chapters include a critical analysis and reinterpretation of available data, with an intent of directing future research endeavors and conceptualizations of the causes of these problems. These chapters are essential reading for anyone interested in conducting research in these areas, yet even the clinician will find the information has treatment relevance, particularly because so much of it is directly germane to prevention and early intervention work.

J. Kevin Thompson

REFERENCES

Agras, W. S. (2001). The consequences and costs of the eating disorders. *Psychiatric Clinics of North America, 24*, 371–379.

Allison, D. B., Fontaine, K. R., Manson, J. E., Stevens, J., & VanItallie, T. B. (1999). Annual deaths attributable to obesity in the United States. *Journal of the American Medical Association, 282,* 1530–1538.

American Psychiatric Association. (2000). *Diagnostic and statistical manual of mental disorders* (4th ed., text rev.). Washington, DC: Author.

Cafri, G., Strauss, J., & Thompson, J. K. (2002). Male body image: Satisfaction and its relationship to psychological functioning using the somatomorphic matrix. *International Journal of Men's Health, 1,* 215–231.

Centers for Disease Control. (2002). *Surgeon General's report on obesity.* Available from http://www.cdc.gov.

Field, A. E., Barnoya, J., & Colditz, G. A. (2002). Epidemiology and health and economic consequences of obesity. In T. A. Wadden & A. J. Stunkard (Eds.), *Handbook of obesity treatment* (pp. 3–18). New York: Guilford Press.

Flegal, K. M., Carroll, M. D., Kuczmarski, R. J., & Johnson, C. L. (1998). Overweight and obesity in the United States: Prevalence and trends, 1960–1994. *International Journal of Obesity, 22,* 39–47.

Flegal, K. M., Carroll, M. D., Odgen, C. L., & Johnson, C. L. (2002). Prevalence and trends in obesity among, U.S. adults, 1999–2000. *Journal of the American Medical Association, 288,* 1723–1727.

Johnson, J. G., Cohen, P., Kasen, S., & Brook, J. S. (2002). Eating disorders during adolescence and the risk for physical and mental disorders during early adulthood. *Archives of General Psychiatry, 59,* 545–552.

Lewinsohn, P. M. (2001, December). *The role of epidemiology in prevention science.* Paper presented at the annual meeting of the Eating Disorders Research Society, Bernalillo, NM.

Nicholls, D., Chater, R., & Lask, B. (2000). Children into *DSM* don't go: A comparison of classification systems for eating disorders in childhood and early adolescence. *International Journal of Eating Disorders, 28,* 317–324.

National Institutes of Health/NHLBI. (1998). Clinical guidelines on the identification, evaluation, and treatment of overweight and obesity in adults: The evidence report. *Obesity Research, 6,* 51S–209S.

Phillips, K. A. (1996). *The broken mirror: Understanding and treating body dysmorphic disorder.* New York: Oxford University Press.

Roberts, R. E., Strawbridge, W. J., Deleger, S., & Kaplan, G. A. (2002). Are the fat more jolly? *Annals of Behavioral Medicine, 24,* 169–180.

Thompson, J. K., Heinberg, L. J., Altabe, M. N., & Tantleff-Dunn, S. (1999). *Exacting beauty: Theory, assessment and treatment of body image disturbance.* Washington, DC: American Psychological Association.

Thompson, J. K., & Kinder, B. (2003). Eating disorders. In M. Hersen & S. Turner (Eds.), *Handbook of adult psychopathology* (4th ed., pp. 555–582). New York: Plenum Press.

Thompson, J. K., & Smolak, L. (Eds.). (2001). *Body image, eating disorders, and obesity in youth: Assessment, treatment and prevention.* Washington, DC: American Psychological Association.

Zipfel, S., Lowe, B., Deter, H. C., & Herzog, W. (2000). Long-term prognosis in anorexia nervosa: Lessons for a 21-year follow-up study. *Lancet, 355,* 721–722.

PART I

Eating Disorders

Anorexia Nervosa, Bulimia Nervosa, and Binge Eating Disorder

Chapter 1 ────────────────────────────────

GENETIC AND BIOLOGICAL RISK FACTORS

CYNTHIA M. BULIK

THE "OLD BIOLOGY OF EATING DISORDERS"

Historically, sociocultural and family theories of etiology have dominated the scientific literature on eating disorders. There was certain sound logic to the belief that the pervasive emphasis on thinness as a symbol of beauty and control somehow "caused" eating disorders or that certain family interaction patterns were more likely than others to bring food and eating-related issues to the fore as a center of familial conflict. These explanations had considerable face validity—they seemed like common sense. However, they were not rigorously tested as true prospective risk factors. For decades, biological researchers have been working in the background of the scientific community of eating disorders. A small but dedicated group of researchers has continued to forge ahead with the notion that biology plays a substantial causal role in the etiology of anorexia nervosa (AN) and bulimia nervosa (BN).

THE "NEW BIOLOGY OF EATING DISORDERS"

In the past decade, genetic and biological research has moved to the forefront of our expanding knowledge about eating disorders. The findings are not ignorable, and they are forcing each of us to reshape our conceptualization of these disorders. Components of the "new biology" include research in the areas of epidemiology, genetic epidemiology, molecular genetics, neurobiology of feeding, neurobiology of eating disorders, genetics of obesity and thinness, and neuroimaging studies. In this chapter, I address how research on genetic epidemiology and genetics of eating disorders is forcing us to refocus our understanding of the balance of the contributions of genetic and environmental factors to the etiology of anorexia nervosa and bulimia nervosa.

HOW HAS GENETIC EPIDEMIOLOGY CHANGED OUR UNDERSTANDING OF THE ETIOLOGY OF EATING DISORDERS?

Over the past decade, a burgeoning of family, twin, and molecular genetic studies of eating disorders has shed new light on etiological factors associated with AN and BN. These findings have been sufficiently strong and adequately replicated to warrant the recommendation that all individuals in the field consider developing at least a passing familiarity with their meaning and their implications for etiology, prevention, and treatment of eating disorders. This chapter outlines the background for understanding the genetic epidemiological and molecular genetic approaches, presents current findings relevant to eating disorders, and suggests implications for prevention and treatment.

The Methods of Genetic Epidemiology: Family, Twin, and Adoption Studies

Three major research designs in genetic epidemiology allow for the delineation and quantification of the relative contribution of genes and environment to the etiology of complex behavioral traits (see Table 1.1). The first step is to determine whether a trait or disorder aggregates in families. This question can be addressed by the traditional family study, which determines whether there is a statistically greater lifetime risk of eating disorders in biological relatives of individuals who have an eating disorder in comparison to relatives of individuals without eating disorders. If no increased risk is observed, probability that the disorder is genetically influenced is low. The primary limitation of the family design is that genetics and environment are confounded. Therefore, if you find that a disorder or trait runs in families, the family study does not allow you to determine to what extent that familial pattern is due to genes and to what extent it is due to environment.

Two additional designs are possible that enable the disentangling of genetic and environmental effects, namely adoption and twin designs. Adoption studies are a *social experiment* in which the degree of similarity between an adoptee and his or her biological versus adoptive parents is compared. A greater similarity to biological parents

Table 1.1   Research Designs in Genetic Epidemiology

	Method	Question	Resolve
Family	Case-control	Familial?	$\left[\dfrac{a^2 \ c^2}{e^2}\right]$
Adoption	Social experiment	Genes? Environment?	a^2 c^2 e^2
Twin	Biological experiment	Genes? Environment?	a^2 c^2 e^2

Note: a^2 = Additive genetic effects; c^2 = Common or shared environmental effects; e^2 = Unique environmental effects.

suggests genetic effects, whereas greater similarity to adoptive parents suggests environmental effects. Although these are powerful designs, adoption is rare and the method is complicated by a number of assumptions. Moreover, when studying rare complex traits such as eating disorders, prevalence of the disorders is often too low to draw meaningful conclusions from adoption studies.

Twin studies, in contrast, are a *biological experiment.* Monozygotic (MZ) or identical twinning occurs at some stage in the first two weeks after the first mitosis when the zygote separates and yields two genetically identical embryos. Therefore, any differences between MZ twins who—for most intents and purposes share all of their genes—provide strong evidence for the role of environmental influences (Plomin, DeFries, McClearn, & Rutter, 1994, pp. 171–172). Dizygotic (DZ) or fraternal twinning results from the fertilization of two ova by different spermatozoa. DZ twins are no more similar genetically than nontwin siblings and share—on average—half of their genes identical by descent. Thus, differences between DZ twins can result from genetic and/or environmental effects.

The goal of the classical twin study is to use the similarities and differences between MZ and DZ twin pairs to identify and delineate genetic and environmental causes for a particular trait. Twin studies are one of the few quasi-experimental means to accomplish this goal in humans and are often the only practical approach.

Using structural equation modeling techniques, liability can be parsed to a trait or disorder into three sources of variability: additive genetic effects (a^2), common or shared environmental effects (c^2), and unique environmental effects (e^2).

Additive Genetic Effects (Abbreviation A)

Although a number of different types of genetic influences can be studied in theory (e.g., dominance or epistatic effects), statistical power is usually low except for additive genetic effects (Neale, Eaves, & Kendler, 1994). Additive genetic effects result from the cumulative impact of many individual genes, each of small effect. The presence of A is inferred when the correlation between MZ twins is greater than the correlation between DZ twins. If a trait were entirely due to additive genetic effects and could be measured without error, the MZ:DZ correlation would be 1.0 and 0.5, respectively.

Common Environmental Effects (Abbreviation C)

Common environmental effects result from etiological influences to which both members of a twin pair are exposed regardless of zygosity. Thus, common environmental effects contribute equally to the correlation between MZ and between DZ twins. In the simplest case, if the correlations between MZ and DZ twins are both 1, the trait is entirely determined by common environmental effects. Examples include the social class and religious preference of the family of origin.

Individual-Specific Environmental Effects (Abbreviation E)

The second type of environmental effect results from etiological influences to which one member of a twin pair is exposed but not the other. Thus, individual-specific environmental effects decrease the magnitude of the correlation between both MZ and DZ twins. In the simplest case, if the correlation between both MZ and DZ twins is 0, the trait is entirely determined by individual-specific environmental effects. Examples include one member of a twin pair being exposed to a traumatic experience not shared with the co-twin.

Qualitative characterizations such as the presence of C or the absence of A are useful, but quantifying the contributions of A, C, and E is more relevant. It is straightforward to scale the total variance of a trait to one and to use twin pair correlations to describe the proportions of variance due to A, C, and E. The proportion of variance due to A (additive genetic effects) is a^2 (also known as *heritability* or, more correctly, as narrow heritability in liability). The proportion of variance due to C is c^2, and the proportion due to E is e^2. The value of e^2 also incorporates measurement error. The values of a^2, c^2, and e^2 must sum to the total variance of one.

What Is Heritability? What Isn't Heritability?

Perhaps because of unfamiliarity with the approach, twin studies can easily be misinterpreted. Heritability estimates are often quoted with little understanding of their meaning or of their limitations. Most importantly, there is not one true heritability estimate for any given trait or disorder. Heritability is a statistic that varies across populations and across time. Perhaps one of the most vivid examples of how heritability estimates of a trait can change over time emanates from a study of smoking behavior in male and female twins in Sweden. Kendler, Thornton, and Pedersen (2000) explored the pattern of twin resemblance for regular tobacco use in a population-based sample of Swedish twins. Results for males suggested both genetic and rearing-environmental effects, which, in the best-fit biometrical model, accounted for 61% and 20% of the variance in liability to regular tobacco use, respectively. For women, the pattern differed by birth cohort. In women born before 1925, rates of regular tobacco use were low and twin resemblance was influenced primarily by environmental factors. In later cohorts, rates of regular tobacco use in women increased substantially and heritability estimates were on par with those seen in men (63%). This study shows that heritable influences were detectable in females only after social constraints on female tobacco use were relaxed.

Allison and Faith (2000) outline a number of common misinterpretations of heritability. For example, a heritability of BN of 83% does *not* mean that 83% of the reason that people develop bulimia is genetic or that 83% of the people who have bulimia have a "genetic form" of bulimia. What it does mean is that approximately 80% (probably, more likely, 50% to 85% considering the confidence intervals) of the variance in liability to BN is due to genetic effects. More simply, your genes play a role in determining the extent to which you are liable to develop BN (or whatever the relevant trait may be).

LINKAGE AND ASSOCIATION STUDIES

If genetic effects appear to be important in the transmission of the disorder, linkage and association studies are next employed to determine the precise location, identity, and function of the genes that are implicated.

The two prominent molecular genetic designs are case-control association studies and linkage studies (Sham, 1998; Table 1.2). Case-control association studies are often

Table 1.2 Linkage versus Association Studies

	Linkage	Association
Samples	Families	Case/control
Statistical basis	Trait-genotype correlation within families	Allele frequency across groups
Power	Lower	Higher
Cost	Higher	Lower
Precision	Lower	Higher
Markers	Anonymous (400–600)	Candidate genes (1–20)
Hypothesis/prior knowledge	Unnecessary	Required

viewed as alternative or complementary to linkage studies, which have yet to be as richly fruitful in the study of complex psychiatric traits in neuropsychiatry as they have with Mendelian disorders (Moldin, 1997; Risch & Zhang, 1996). Linkage studies (Craddock & Owen, 1996; Lander & Schork, 1994; Ott, 1991; Sham, 1998; Terwilliger & Goring, 2000) investigate correlations between a disease and inheritance of specific chromosomal regions in families, whereas association studies focus on differences in the frequency of specific genetic markers in groups of affected versus unaffected individuals (see Table 1.2).

The standard approach to association studies is to ascertain cases with a trait of interest and controls without the trait, obtain DNA samples, and genotype all subjects for a genetic marker believed to be of etiological relevance. Statistical analysis compares allele or genotype frequencies (Sasieni, 1997) in cases versus controls (Sham, 1998). As with any case-control approach, there are numerous sources of bias (Sackett, 1979); considerable care must be taken to ensure the proper matching of cases and controls. Fundamentally, cases and controls should represent "identical" samples from a single population except for the diagnostic differences. Confidence in case-control association studies wavers (Crowe, 1993; Gambaro, Anglani, & D'Angelo, 2000; Kidd, 1993; Risch & Zhang, 1996; Sullivan, Eaves, Kendler, & Neale, 2001). Association designs are particularly useful and powerful when prior knowledge of the pathophysiology of a trait suggests a number of candidate genes. However, the use of this design is controversial because of the risk of false positive findings when studying a sample that contains individuals of evolutionary diverse ancestry (Kidd, 1993). More often than not, seemingly exciting findings from association studies in neuropsychiatry are followed rapidly by a series of nonreplications (Moldin, 1997; Risch & Zhang, 1996; Stoltenberg & Burmeister, 2000).

Linkage studies can be used in gene discovery with a sufficiently large number of multiplex pedigrees or extreme sibling pairs (Allison, Heo, Schork, Wong, & Elston, 1998). Anonymous genetic markers scattered across the genome can identify the chromosomal regions that may contain genes that contribute to the trait of interest. The strength of this design is tempered by the relatively low power (Risch & Merikangas,

1996) and resolution (Roberts, MacLean, Neale, Eaves, & Kendler, 1999) likely for linkage studies of complex traits. Given the size of the human genome, linkage studies allow narrowing down of regions of interest for a particular trait. Results of linkage studies can then be applied to the choice of rational candidate genes for association studies. The choice of candidate genes can then be based on function requiring knowledge of the function of the genes and proposed pathophysiology of the traits, as well as position (gene is located under the observed linkage peak).

Both association and linkage designs have been applied to the study of eating disorders, although genetic studies in the field are truly in their infancy.

APPLICATION OF GENETIC EPIDEMIOLOGY AND MOLECULAR GENETICS TO EATING DISORDERS

Family Studies of Eating Disorders

A series of large, well-controlled family studies of eating disorders now exists. The vast majority of controlled family studies (Gershon et al., 1983; Hudson, Pope, Jonas, Yurgelun-Todd, & Frankenburg, 1987; Kassett et al., 1989; Lilenfeld et al., 1998; Strober, Freeman, Lampert, Diamond, & Kaye, 2000; Strober, Lampert, Morrell, Burroughs, & Jacobs, 1990) have found a significantly greater lifetime prevalence of eating disorders among relatives of eating-disordered individuals in comparison to relatives of controls. Moreover, several studies have found increased rates of both AN and BN (i.e., coaggregation) in relatives of individuals with AN as well as individuals with BN, compared to rates among relatives of controls (Gershon et al., 1983; Hudson et al., 1987; Kassett et al., 1989; Strober et al., 1990, 2000), suggesting that AN and BN share transmissible risk factors. Moreover, relatives of individuals with AN and BN have also been found to have a significantly increased rate of subthreshold eating disorders compared to relatives of controls (Lilenfeld et al., 1998; Strober et al., 2000), suggesting that the eating disorders do not "breed true" but are expressed in families as a broad spectrum of eating-related pathology. Woodside, Field, Garfinkel, and Heinmaa (1998) showed a tendency for AN to cluster more in families of probands with AN, possibly suggesting some specificity of clustering for AN.

In summary, family study data reveal an elevation in the lifetime prevalence of eating disorders among the relatives of people with eating disorders. In addition, the coaggregation in families of AN, BN, and milder eating disturbances suggests shared etiologic factors across these conditions.

Twin Studies of Eating Disorders

The goal of the classical twin study is to qualify and quantify similarities and differences between MZ and DZ twin pairs to identify and quantify genetic and environmental causes for a particular trait. Given that MZ twins, for most purposes, share all of their genes and DZ twins share, on average, half of their genes, any excess concordance in MZ twins over DZ twins suggests a genetic contribution to liability to the disorder. Conversely, any differences between MZ twins provide strong evidence for the role of environmental influences (Plomin et al., 1994, pp. 171–172), whereas differences between DZ twins can result from genetic and/or environmental effects. More complicated statistical modeling allows parsing of the variance in liability to illness into three sources: additive genetic effects (a^2), shared environmental effects (c^2), and unique environmental effects (e^2). Additive genetic effects reflect the cumulative impact on a trait of many individual genes, each of which has a relatively small individual effect on the behavioral phenotype. The presence of a^2 is inferred when the correlation between MZ twins is greater than the correlation between DZ twins. By contrast, common environmental effects reflect etiological influences to which both members of a twin pair are exposed, regardless of zygosity. Examples of such effects include the social class and religious preference of the family of origin. Unique environmental effects, on the other hand, result from etiological influences to which one member of a twin pair is exposed but not the other and contribute to differences between members of a twin pair. Examples include one member of a twin pair being exposed to a traumatic experience not shared with the co-twin.

One of the key caveats to the twin study is the assumption of equal environments (EEA), which posits that MZ and DZ twins are equally correlated for their exposure to environmental influences that are of etiologic relevance to the trait under study (Plomin et al., 1994). That is, MZ twins are no more likely to have received similar exposure to an environmental factor that may play a causal role in eating disorders. We know that, in many cases, the environments shared by MZ twins are more similar than the environments shared by DZ twins. One vivid example is that MZ twins are more often dressed alike than DZ twins. Although this suggests a more correlated environment in MZ than DZ twins, the relevant point is that this dimension is not one that is assumed to be of etiological relevance to eating disorders. No extant data suggest that being dressed like your twin increases your risk of developing an eating disorder. Violations of the EEA are critical only when the violation occurs in domains that are relevant to the etiology of the trait.

If the EEA is violated, the greater resemblance of MZ twins in comparison to DZ twins could actually be due to environmental factors. A violation of the EEA does not necessarily invalidate the results of a twin study but may influence the magnitude of the estimated genetic and environmental components. Studies of the EEA concerning eating disorders suggest that this assumption has not been violated in twin studies (Bulik, Sullivan, Wade, & Kendler, 2000; Kendler, Neale, Kessler, Heath, & Eaves, 1993; Klump, Holly, Iacono, McGue, & Willson, 2000; Sullivan, Bulik, & Kendler, 1998).

Twin Studies of Anorexia Nervosa

Beyond isolated case reports, the first systematic study of clinically ascertained twins with AN (Holland, Hall, Murray, Russell, & Crisp, 1984; Holland, Sicotte, & Treasure, 1988; Treasure & Holland, 1989) found that the concordance for MZ twins was substantially greater than for DZ twins. Reanalyses of these data (assuming a population prevalence of AN of 0.75%) revealed evidence of familial aggregation with parameter estimates of 88% for a^2, 0 for c^2, and 12% for e^2. In short, the observed familial aggregation for AN appears to be influenced most strongly by additive genetic effects; however, the estimates were rather imprecise given the small sample size.

Population-based studies of AN are difficult to conduct given the relatively low prevalence of the disorder. There have been three twin studies of AN. Wade, Bulik, Neale, and Kendler (2000) derived heritability estimates for AN in the context of studying the nature of the comorbid relationship between AN and major depression. The heritability of AN was estimated to be 58%, although the authors could not rule out a contribution of shared environment to the liability to AN. Kortegaard, Hoerder, Joergensen, Gillberg, and Kyvik (2001) conducted a twin study on 34,142 Danish twins based on self-reported diagnosis of AN. They derived heritability estimates of 0.48 and 0.52 for narrow and broad definitions of AN. Finally, Klump, Miller, Keel, McGue, and Iacono (2001) estimated the heritability of broadly defined AN to be 0.74 in 17-year-old female twins, with the remaining variance accounted for by individual-specific environmental effects.

On balance, we can conclude from family studies (see Lilenfeld, Kaye, & Strober, 1997, for a review) that AN is familial. In addition, the preliminary twin studies, each of which carries its own unique shortcomings, suggest that the familiality is accounted for primarily by additive genetic effects. However, the jury is still out. The definitive resolution of the independent contribution of genetic and shared environmental factors to the observed familiality of AN will require more ambitious collaborative efforts to obtain larger sample sizes with sufficient statistical power.

Twin Studies of Bulimia Nervosa

Twin studies of BN have been more successful given the higher population prevalence of the disorder. Initial case series of twins with BN revealed consistently greater concordance for BN in MZ than DZ twin pairs (Fichter & Noegel, 1990; Hsu, Chesler, & Santhouse, 1990; Treasure & Holland, 1989). Pooling data from these case series for twin modeling and assuming a population prevalence of BN of 2.5% revealed evidence of familial aggregation with 47% of the variance accounted for by additive genetic effects, 30% by shared environmental effects, and 23% by unique environmental effects. However, the sample sizes were small and the estimates imprecise.

Population-based studies of BN have been conducted in the United States (Bulik, Sullivan, & Kendler, 1998; Kendler et al., 1991) and Australia (Wade, Neale, Lake, & Martin, 1999; Wade, Martin, et al., 1999) and via self-report diagnoses in Denmark (Kortegaard et al., 2001). The studies that have estimated the heritability of BN based on a single occasion of measurement suggest a moderate contribution of additive genetic effects, a negligible contribution of shared environmental effects, and a more substantial contribution of unique environmental effects to liability to BN (Bulik et al., 1998; Kendler et al., 1991; Kortegaard et al., 2001). Although a marked improvement over the clinical series, these studies still had limited statistical power given the relatively low population prevalence of BN and given that the reliability of the diagnosis of BN tends to be poor, which can lead to underestimation of both a^2 and c^2 (Bulik et al., 1998).

Two studies have boosted statistical power by incorporating more than one occasion of measurement into the twin model (Bulik et al., 1998; Wade, Martin, et al., 1999). This approach controls for unreliability of diagnosis, increases power to detect both a^2 and c^2, and, therefore, provides the most reliable information concerning the nature and magnitude of genetic and environmental contributions to BN. In short, these two studies reveal a markedly greater contribution of additive genetic effects to the liability to BN (59% and 83%, respectively), a negligible contribution of shared environment (0 in both studies), and a moderate contribution of unique environmental effects (41% and 17%). Although the parameter estimates for c^2 were 0, the confidence intervals did not completely rule out a contribution of shared environment. Results from these two studies confirm the central role of genetic factors in the observed familiality of BN.

In summary, from twin and family studies, we can conclude that BN is familial and that there appears to be a moderate to substantial contribution made by genetic factors and unique environmental factors to liability to the disorder. The contribution of shared environment is less certain but appears to be of lesser prominence than the effect of genes and of unique environment. A reasonable next step for twin studies is to determine the precise nature of the unique environmental effects that increase risk for developing BN.

LINKAGE AND ASSOCIATION STUDIES IN EATING DISORDERS

Given that family and twin studies point toward the involvement of genes in the etiology of eating disorders, it has been sensible to pursue linkage and association approaches to begin to identify relevant genes.

Several extensive reviews of association studies of eating disorders contain comprehensive coverage of this topic (Gorwood, Bouvard, Mouren-Simeoni, Kipman, & Ades, 1998; Hinney, Remschmidt, & Hebebrand, 2000; Tozzi, Bergen, & Bulik, 2002). In the absence of linkage information, the majority of association studies have chosen candidate genes based on function. Genes associated with systems that have been implicated in feeding and body weight regulation have been common targets—such as genes associated with serotonergic function, dopaminergic function, neuropeptides related to feeding function, and other genes related to control of energy expenditure and metabolic adaptation during fasting. Although several groups have pursued association studies in eating disorders and encouraging associations have been found, no single gene or set of genes has consistently emerged across studies as being strongly associated with either AN or BN.

Linkage studies of AN and BN have only begun to appear in the literature. Kaye et al. (2000) reported on a linkage study sponsored by the Price Foundation of 192 families with at least one affected relative pair with AN and related eating disorders. This study represented a collaborative effort across a number of clinical sites across North America and Europe. The initial scan of the entire sample yielded no significant linkage results. However, two additional approaches yielded significant linkage results. First, to reduce sample heterogeneity, the researchers restricted the linkage analysis to a subset of families in which at least two affected relatives had a diagnosis of restricting AN (severe food restriction without the presence of binge-eating or purging behavior). This approach was important because heterogeneity in a sample can reduce underlying linkage signals. In many ways, restricting AN represents a uniquely recognizable phenotype and one that is plausibly influenced by heritable biological factors. The restricting AN subset yielded evidence suggestive of the presence of an anorexia susceptibility locus on chromosome 1 (Grice et al., 2002).

In an additional novel approach, Devlin et al. (2002) incorporated selected behavioral covariates into the linkage analysis. The key covariates were drive for thinness and obsessionality. The inclusion of these covariates, providing an additional means to refine the phenotype, revealed several regions suggestive of linkage on chromosomes 1, 2, and 13.

A second multicenter, collaborative eating disorder study, also supported by the Price Foundation, recruited probands with purging-type BN and family members affected with either AN, BN, or ED-NOS (Bulik et al., 2003). When the entire sample (316 families) was analyzed, significant linkage was observed on chromosome 10; suggestive linkage was observed on chromosome 14. However, the clinical presentation of BN can vary substantially suggesting marked phenotypic heterogeneity. Of the core symptoms of BN, the frequency of vomiting has been shown to be a reliable (Wade et al., 2000) and heritable measure (Sullivan et al., 1998). Thus, the phenotypic heterogeneity of the sample was reduced by selecting families that had at least two individuals with an ED and with regular vomiting behavior. This phenotypic clarification resulted in an even stronger linkage signal on chromosome 10.

These two examples highlight the importance of our fully understanding the phenotypes we are using in genetic analyses. That is, it is highly unlikely that the human genome maps perfectly onto the diagnostic categories that currently exist in the *Diagnostic and Statistical Manual of Mental Disorders (DSM)* or the International Classification of Diseases (ICD). It is imperative that individuals familiar with the clinical syndromes continue to refine their definitions of the natural clusterings of traits and disturbances that make up these conditions. It is only through sophisticated and accurate phenotyping that we will be able to maximize the tools we have at hand for genetic analysis and move closer to identifying genes that contribute to liability to these conditions.

IMPLICATIONS OF THESE RESULTS FOR DETECTION AND PREVENTION

Although the implications of genetic epidemiological and genetic research on eating disorders for treatment may seem to rest far into the future, implications for prevention are more immediate. The clear data on the familiality of these disorders underscore the notion that offspring of individuals with eating disorders are indeed at greater risk than individuals in the general population for the development of eating disorders.

In general, global preventive efforts for eating disorders have been less than optimally successful. Although as yet untried, consideration should be given to the development of targeted prevention efforts aimed at individuals who are at known increased risk by virtue of their family history.

Although offspring of individuals with eating disorders may be at greater risk by virtue of their genes, the expression of that genetic predisposition is not inevitable. Whereas much research has focused on environmental factors that *contribute* to the development of AN and BN, we know much less about environmental factors that *inhibit* the expression of a genetic predisposition to eating disorders.

A particularly difficult issue for prevention of eating disorders in high-risk populations has to do with gene-environment correlations. Genotype-environment correlation arises when the exposure to positive or negative environmental influences is not randomly distributed with respect to genetic differences. For example, girls who are genetically more prone to body dissatisfaction may tend to evoke more appearance-related comments from their parents or peers (evocative gene-environment correlation) and actively seek peers or activities that reinforce their focus on appearance (e.g., cheerleading or modeling; active gene-environment correlation). Another type of gene-environment correlation ("passive" gene-environment correlation) reflects the fact that children receive genotypes that are correlated with their family environment. This latter form of gene-environment correlation may be particularly thorny when dealing with prevention. Stated in another way, you receive your genes from the same individuals who create your environment. Moreover, the environment that they create for you is in part determined by their genotype. Concretely, imagine a father with a subthreshold eating disorder who has passed on this genetic predisposition to his daughter. In addition, he has contributed to an environment in the family that is highly appearance focused, obsessed with low body fat, and perfectionistic. Thus, the daughter is not only dealing with the impact of her inherited genotype, but also being raised in an environment that may facilitate the expression of that genetic predisposition.

Given that many women with eating disorders continue to suffer from subthreshold symptoms and cognitions even after formal recovery from the eating disorder, the environment they create may contribute to expression. Research efforts to help understand how mothers with histories of eating disorders can create healthy environments for their offspring is essential—especially because problems have been identified in mothers with a history of eating disorders in terms of adequate nutrition during pregnancy, feeding styles, and parenting (e.g., Mitchell-Gieleghem, Mittelstaedt, & Bulik, 2002; Waugh & Bulik, 1999).

IMPLICATIONS OF THESE RESULTS FOR TREATMENT

The implications of twin and genetic research on treatment may be less immediate, but they can be conceptualized on two entirely different levels. The first level is how this information impacts patients' and their supporters' perception of the illness. Clinically, many patients find this type of information to be liberating—especially those individuals who may have been accused of having these disorders simply by "choice." In contrast, others may become mired in a sense of biological or genetic determinism and may find the struggle against the disorder harder knowing that there is a genetic component to its etiology.

An additional concern voiced by some parents is that genetics can be viewed as yet another form of "mother blaming"—one over which they have even less control. It is, therefore, important to develop a strategy for incorporating this knowledge in a helpful way into patients' understanding of their disorder. This often includes heavy emphasis on the fallacy of genetic determinism. It remains critical to underscore that the presence of a genetic predisposition in no way guarantees expression of the trait.

The second level on which genetic studies can influence treatment will result only when genes have been identified that actually influence susceptibility to the disorders. Such genes may highlight pathways of which we are already aware that influence feeding behavior, mood, or temperament (e.g., serotonergic pathways) or of yet-undiscovered biological pathways that may influence susceptibility to these disorders. The discovery of new pathways may then pave the way for new pharmacological agents to influence their function.

REFERENCES

Allison, D., & Faith, M. (2000). Genetic and environmental influences on human body weight: Implications for the behavior therapist. *Nutrition Today, 35,* 18–21.

Allison, D. B., Heo, M., Schork, N. J., Wong, S. L., & Elston, R. C. (1998). Extreme selection strategies in gene mapping studies of oligogenic quantitative traits do not always increase power. *Human Heredity, 48*(2), 97–107.

Bulik, C. M., Devlin, B., Bacanu, S. A., Thornton, L., Klump, K. L., Fichter, M. M., et al. (2003). Significant linkage on chromosome 10p in families with bulimia nervosa. *American Journal of Human Genetics, 72*(1), 200–207.

Bulik, C. M., Sullivan, P., Wade, T., & Kendler, K. (2000). Twin studies of eating disorders: A review. *International Journal of Eating Disorders, 27,* 1–20.

Bulik, C. M., Sullivan, P. F., & Kendler, K. S. (1998). Heritability of binge-eating and broadly defined bulimia nervosa. *Biological Psychiatry, 44*(12), 1210–1218.

Craddock, N., & Owen, M. J. (1996). Modern molecular genetic approaches to psychiatric disease. *British Medical Bulletin, 52,* 434–452.

Crowe, R. R. (1993). Candidate genes in psychiatry: An epidemiological perspective. *American Journal of Medical Genetics, 48,* 74–77.

Devlin, B., Bacanu, S. A., Klump, K. L., Bulik, C. M., Fichter, M. M., Halmi, K. A., et al. (2002). Linkage analysis of anorexia nervosa incorporating behavioral covariates. *Human Molecular Genetics, 11*(6), 689–696.

Fichter, M. M., & Noegel, R. (1990). Concordance for bulimia nervosa in twins. *International Journal of Eating Disorders, 9*(3), 255–263.

Gambaro, G., Anglani, F., & D'Angelo, A. (2000). Association studies of genetic polymorphisms and complex disease. *Lancet, 355,* 308–311.

Gershon, E., Schreiber, J., Hamovit, J., Dibble, E., Kaye, W., Nurnberger, J., et al. (1983). Anorexia nervosa and major affective disorders associated in families: A preliminary report. In S. B. Guze, F. J. Earls, & J. E. Barrett (Eds.), *Childhood psychopathology and development* (pp. 279–284). New York: Raven Press.

Gorwood, P., Bouvard, M., Mouren-Simeoni, M. C., Kipman, A., & Ades, J. (1998). Genetics and anorexia nervosa: A review of candidate genes. *Psychiatric Genetics, 8*(1), 1–12.

Grice, D. E., Halmi, K. A., Fichter, M. M., Strober, M., Woodside, D. B., Treasure, J., et al. (2002). Evidence for a susceptibility gene for anorexia nervosa on chromosome 1. *American Journal of Human Genetics, 70*(3), 787–792.

Hinney, A., Remschmidt, H., & Hebebrand, J. (2000). Candidate gene polymorphisms in eating disorders. *European Journal of Pharmacology, 410*(2/3), 147–159.

Holland, A. J., Hall, A., Murray, R., Russell, G. F. M., & Crisp, A. H. (1984). Anorexia nervosa: A study of 34 twin pairs and one set of triplets. *British Journal of Psychiatry, 145,* 414–419.

Holland, A. J., Sicotte, N., & Treasure, J. (1988). Anorexia nervosa: Evidence for a genetic basis. *Journal of Psychosomatic Research, 32*(6), 561–571.

Hsu, G. L. K., Chesler, B. E., & Santhouse, R. (1990). Bulimia nervosa in eleven sets of twins: A clinical report. *International Journal of Eating Disorders, 9*(3), 275–282.

Hudson, J. I., Pope, H. G., Jonas, J. M., Yurgelun-Todd, D., & Frankenburg, F. R. (1987). A controlled family history study of bulimia. *Psychological Medicine, 17,* 883–890.

Kassett, J., Gershon, E., Maxwell, M., Guroff, J., Kazuba, D., Smith, A., et al. (1989). Psychiatric disorders in the first-degree relatives of probands with bulimia nervosa. *American Journal of Psychiatry, 146,* 1468–1471.

Kaye, W. H., Lilenfeld, L. R., Berrettini, W. H., Strober, M., Devlin, B., Klump, K. L., et al. (2000). A search for susceptibility loci for anorexia nervosa: Methods and sample description. *Biological Psychiatry, 47*(9), 794–803.

Kendler, K. S., MacLean, C., Neale, M. C., Kessler, R. C., Heath, A. C., & Eaves, L. J. (1991). The genetic epidemiology of bulimia nervosa. *American Journal of Psychiatry, 148,* 1627–1637.

Kendler, K. S., Neale, M. C., Kessler, R. C., Heath, A. C., & Eaves, L. J. (1993). A test of the equal environment assumption in twin studies of psychiatric illness. *Behavior Genetics, 23,* 21–27.

Kendler, K. S., Thornton, L. M., & Pedersen, N. L. (2000). Tobacco consumption in Swedish twins reared apart and reared together. *Archives of General Psychiatry, 57*(9), 886–892.

Kidd, K. K. (1993). Associations of disease with genetic markers: Deja vu all over again. *American Journal of Medical Genetics, 48*(2), 71–73.

Klump, K. L., Holly, A., Iacono, W. G., McGue, M., & Willson, L. E. (2000). Physical similarity and twin resemblance for eating attitudes and behaviors: A test of the equal environments assumption. *Behavior Genetics, 30*(1), 51–58.

Klump, K. L., Miller, K. B., Keel, P. K., McGue, M., & Iacono, W. G. (2001). Genetic and environmental influences on anorexia nervosa syndromes in a population-based twin sample. *Psychological Medicine, 31*(4), 737–740.

Kortegaard, L. S., Hoerder, K., Joergensen, J., Gillberg, C., & Kyvik, K. O. (2001). A preliminary population-based twin study of self-reported eating disorder. *Psychological Medicine, 31*(2), 361–365.

Lander, E. S., & Schork, N. J. (1994). Genetic dissection of complex traits. *Science, 265*(5181), 2037–2048.

Lilenfeld, L., Kaye, W., Greeno, C., Merikangas, K., Plotnicov, K., Pollice, C., et al. (1998). A controlled family study of restricting anorexia and bulimia nervosa: Comorbidity in probands and disorders in first-degree relatives. *Archives of General Psychiatry, 55,* 603–610.

Lilenfeld, L., Kaye, W., & Strober, M. (1997). Genetics and family studies of anorexia nervosa and bulimia nervosa. *Baillière's Clinical Psychiatry, 3,* 177–197.

Mitchell-Gieleghem, A., Mittelstaedt, M. E., & Bulik, C. M. (2002). Eating disorders and childbearing: Concealment and consequences. *Birth, 29*(3), 182–191.

Moldin, S. (1997). The maddening hunt for madness genes. *Nature Genetics, 17,* 127–129.

Neale, M., Eaves, L., & Kendler, K. (1994). The power of the classical twin study to resolve variation in threshold traits. *Behavior Genetics, 24,* 239–258.

Ott, J. (1991). *Analysis of human genetic linkage.* Baltimore: Johns Hopkins University Press.

Plomin, R., DeFries, J. C., McClearn, G. E., & Rutter, M. (1994). *Behavioral genetics* (3rd ed.). New York: Freeman.

Risch, N., & Merikangas, K. (1996). The future of genetic studies of complex human diseases. *Science, 273,* 1516–1517.

Risch, N., & Zhang, H. (1996). Mapping quantitative trait loci with extreme discordant sib pairs: Sampling considerations. *American Journal of Human Genetics, 58,* 836–843.

Roberts, S. B., MacLean, C. J., Neale, M. C., Eaves, L. J., & Kendler, K. S. (1999). Replication of linkage studies of complex traits: An examination of variation in location estimates. *American Journal of Human Genetics, 65*(3), 876–884.

Sackett, D. L. (1979). Bias in analytic research. *Journal of Chronic Disease, 32,* 51–63.

Sasieni, P. D. (1997). From genotypes to genes: Doubling the sample size. *Biometrics, 53,* 1253–1261.

Sham, P. (1998). *Statistics in human genetics.* London: Arnold.

Stoltenberg, S. F., & Burmeister, M. (2000). Recent progress in psychiatric genetics: Some hope but no hype. *Human Molecular Genetics, 9,* 927–935.

Strober, M., Freeman, R., Lampert, C., Diamond, J., & Kaye, W. (2000). Controlled family study of anorexia nervosa and bulimia nervosa: Evidence of shared liability and transmission of partial syndromes. *American Journal of Psychiatry, 157*(3), 393–401.

Strober, M., Lampert, C., Morrell, W., Burroughs, J., & Jacobs, C. (1990). A controlled family study of anorexia nervosa: Evidence of familial aggregation and lack of shared transmission with affective disorders. *International Journal of Eating Disorders, 9*(3), 239–253.

Sullivan, P. F., Bulik, C. M., & Kendler, K. S. (1998). The genetic epidemiology of binging and vomiting. *British Journal of Psychiatry, 173,* 75–79.

Sullivan, P. F., Eaves, L. J., Kendler, K. S., & Neale, M. C. (2001). Genetic case-control association studies in neuropsychiatry. *Archives of General Psychiatry, 58*(11), 1015–1024.

Terwilliger, J. D., & Goring, H. H. (2000). Gene mapping in the 20th and 21st centuries: Statistical methods, data analysis, and experimental design. *Human Biology, 72,* 63–132.

Tozzi, F., Bergen, A., & Bulik, C. M. (2002). Candidate genes for anorexia and bulimia nervosa: State of the science. *Psychopharmacology Bulletin, 36,* 60–90.

Treasure, J., & Holland, A. (1989). Genetic vulnerability to eating disorders: Evidence from twin and family studies. In H. Remschmidt & M. Schmidt (Eds.), *Child and youth psychiatry: European perspectives* (pp. 59–68). New York: Hogrefe & Huber.

Wade, T. D., Bulik, C. M., & Kendler, K. S. (2000). Reliability of lifetime history of bulimia nervosa: Comparison with major depression. *British Journal of Psychiatry, 177,* 72–76.

Wade, T. D., Bulik, C. M., Neale, M., & Kendler, K. S. (2000). Anorexia nervosa and major depression: Shared genetic and environmental risk factors. *American Journal of Psychiatry, 157*(3), 469–471.

Wade, T. D., Martin, N., Neale, M., Tiggemann, M., Trealor, S., Heath, A., et al. (1999). The structure of genetic and environmental risk factors for three measures of disordered eating characteristic of bulimia nervosa. *Psychological Medicine, 29,* 925–934.

Wade, T., Martin, N. G., & Tiggemann, M. (1998). Genetic and environmental risk factors for the weight and shape concerns characteristic of bulimia nervosa. *Psychological Medicine, 28*(4), 761–771.

Wade, T. D., Neale, M. C., Lake, R. I. E., & Martin, N. G. (1999). A genetic analysis of the eating and attitudes associated with bulimia nervosa: Dealing with the problem of ascertainment. *Behavior Genetics, 29,* 1–10.

Waugh, E., & Bulik, C. (1999). Offspring of women with eating disorders. *International Journal of Eating Disorders, 25,* 123–133.

Woodside, D., Field, L. L., Garfinkel, P., & Heinmaa, M. (1998). Specificity of eating disorders diagnoses in families of probands with anorexia nervosa and bulimia nervosa. *Comprehensive Psychiatry, 39,* 261–264.

Chapter 2 ———————————————————

RISK FACTORS FOR EATING DISORDERS: AN EVALUATION OF THE EVIDENCE

ALISON E. FIELD

Many papers are published each year on disordered eating and eating disorders; nevertheless, little is known about the true risk factors for these outcomes. To determine true risk factors, longitudinal studies with sufficiently large sample sizes are needed to study the development of new cases. Although there are very few large longitudinal studies, many papers, as well as the *Diagnostic and Statistical Manual for Mental Disorders,* fourth edition (*DSM-IV;* American Psychiatric Association [APA], 1994), have implied that many risk factors are known. Some of those established risk factors may not be true risk factors, and the widespread belief that they are may be sending the field in the wrong direction (Kraemer, Yesavage, Taylor, & Kupfer, 2000).

THE DIFFERENCE AMONG TRUE RISK FACTORS, CONFOUNDERS, AND CORRELATES

Risk factors, correlates, and confounders all have an association with the outcome, but they are not the same (see Table 2.1). A true risk factor *predicts* the outcome, such as development of the eating disorder or, in clinical studies, recovery from the disorder. A correlate is *associated* with the outcome, but not necessarily a predictor of it. This is an extremely important distinction to make and one that is frequently not appreciated. With the exception of factors that do not change over time, such as race or gender, associations observed in cross-sectional studies can be misleading because they may be due to either distorted recall of past events (e.g., the correlate) or reverse temporal ordering (i.e., the suspected "risk factor" occurred after or because of the disorder of interest). You can be sure that being female predated the onset of the bulimic behaviors, but you cannot assume that the subject's having a poor relationship with her family predated the subject's anorexia nervosa. In fact, the disorder could cause a decline in family functioning, which would be an example of reverse temporal ordering. A prospective study design is needed to ascertain the temporal order of most associations.

Table 2.1   Relationship with the Study Outcome

Risk factor	*Predicts* the outcome.
✓ Correlate	Is *associated* with the outcome. It may cause or be caused by the outcome; *no assumptions about temporal order can be made.*
Confounder	Is *associated with both the risk factor and the outcome;* therefore, it distorts the association between the risk factor and the outcome. Unless the confounder is taken into consideration in the analysis, the results will be biased.

A *confounder* is a factor associated with *both* the true risk factor and the outcome (e.g., onset of symptoms, onset of the disorder, recovery; Rothman & Greenland, 1998).

The confounder, therefore, distorts the association because it mixes the association of the confounder and the outcome in with the association between the risk factor and the outcome. Confounding can result in either an under- or overestimation of the true risk factor, depending on the direction of the association the confounder has with the risk factor and the outcome. For risk factors that are only modest in magnitude (e.g., 1 < relative risk [RR] < 2), confounding can easily conceal the true increase in risk. Failure to consider both the confounder and the true risk factor in the statistical analysis will lead to drawing faulty inference. To illustrate the importance of controlling for confounding, consider the analysis conducted by Herzog and colleagues (1996) to investigate whether there was a difference in recovery rates between restrictor and bulimic anorexics. The sample was a prospective cohort of 225 treatment-seeking women with anorexia and/or bulimia nervosa. At the time they enrolled in the study, the bulimic anorexics had been ill significantly longer than the restrictor anorexics, thus duration of illness (the possible confounder) was associated with the risk factor of interest (e.g., subtype of anorexia; see Figure 2.1).

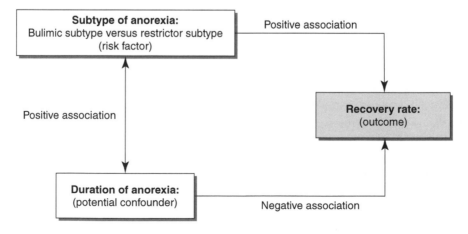

Figure 2.1   Cognitive Behavioral Model of Eating Disorders.

In unadjusted analyses, there was a suggestion that anorexics of the bulimic subtype were more likely than restrictor anorexics to recover (RR = 2.37, 95% confidence interval [CI] 0.59 to 9.55), but the confidence intervals were too wide to make any firm conclusions and were consistent with either a decrease or an increase in risk. However, after adjusting for duration of illness before enrollment in the study, the effect became much stronger and bordered on statistical significance (RR = 4.63, 95% CI 0.98 to 21.9). Moreover, adjusting for subtype of anorexia strengthened the association of duration of illness with recovery from anorexia. Thus, duration of anorexia was an important confounder. When the confounder was not adjusted for in the statistical analysis, it was difficult to ascertain whether there was a difference in "risk of recovery" between the subtypes of anorexia. Adjusting for the confounder made the difference between the two subtypes more apparent.

Confounders do not always result in an underestimation of the true risk factor. Positive confounding—when the confounder and risk factor have a positive association with each other and the outcome—results in overestimating the magnitude of the risk factor. For example, Field, Berkey, Rockett, and Colditz (2000) assessed whether dieting frequency predicted the development of overweight among children and adolescents in the Growing Up Today Study, a prospective cohort study of approximately 17,000 youth in the United States. *Overweight* was defined as having a body mass index (BMI, weight in kilograms/height in meters) at or above the 85th percentile for age and gender according to the latest Centers for Disease Control and Prevention (2002) and the National Center for Health Statistics standards (http://www.cdc.gov/growthcharts/). The closer a child was to the 85th percentile at baseline, the more likely he or she was to become overweight; therefore, baseline BMI was positively predictive of the outcome: becoming overweight. In addition, baseline BMI was positively associated with dieting frequency—the heavier a participant was at baseline, the more likely he or she was to diet. In analyses that did not control for the child's baseline BMI, it appeared that compared to females who never dieted, infrequent dieters were almost three times (odds ratio [OR] = 2.83) and frequent dieters six times (OR = 5.81) more likely to become overweight during one year of follow-up. After adjusting for baseline BMI, a positive confounder, the estimated risks associated with dieting were still statistically significant, but they were of lesser magnitude. The odds ratio comparing infrequent to never dieters decreased from 2.83 to 1.68, and the odds ratio comparing frequent to never dieters decreased from 5.81 to 4.21. As these examples show, failure to control for confounding can result in either an under- or overestimation of the true risk factor of interest.

Kraemer, Stice, Kazadin, Offord, and Kupfer (2001) have used a slightly different terminology, which helps to differentiate true risk factors from other types of correlates, including mediators and moderators. Using their terminology, confounders would be proxy risk factors, as opposed to true risk factors. Whether the potential confounder modifies the relationship between the true risk factor and the outcome should always be assessed. For example, among adult women, despite a greater prevalence in overweight among African American women, several studies have shown that they are more satisfied than White women with their current body weight (Cameron et al., 1996; Henriques, Calhoun, & Cann, 1996; Smith, Thompson, Raczynski, & Hilner, 1999). Thus, race/ethnicity might modify the relationship between body weight and body dissatisfaction or disordered eating. If a factor does modify the relationship, it is of inherent interest and the researcher should either conduct a stratified analysis (stratified on the moderator) or include interaction terms in the statistical model. A more detailed description of the moderators, as well as mediators, has been written by Kraemer and colleagues.

APPROPRIATE INFERENCE: IMPLICATIONS OF STUDY DESIGN, SAMPLE, AND TERMINOLOGY

Understanding and addressing confounding is necessary, but not sufficient, to ensure that appropriate inference can be drawn from a given study. The four main types of study designs—cross-sectional studies, case-control studies, cohort (prospective or retrospective) studies, and randomized clinical trials—each has their strengths, but it is imperative to be aware of the limitations of the respective study designs.

Cross-Sectional Studies

Cross-sectional studies are the easiest and cheapest type of study to conduct. Moreover, because no follow-up is done, surveys can be anonymous, thus allowing investigators to ask sensitive questions that subjects might feel uncomfortable answering if they had to provide identifying information. Large cross-sectional studies, such as the Epidemiologic Catchment Area (ECA) study ($n = 20,861$) and the National Health and Nutrition Survey III ($n = 16,681$), have provided valuable information on the prevalence of mental disorders, obesity, and many lifestyle factors (Regier et al., 1993; Troiano & Flegal, 1998). You must, however, be very cautious in drawing inference from cross-sectional studies because except for factors that do not change over time, such as gender, nothing can be assumed about the temporal order of the association. Unfortunately, the majority of studies of disordered eating and eating disorders have been cross-sectional. To study gender and race/ethnic differences, a cross-sectional design may be appropriate because these are fixed traits that clearly precede the outcome being studied. Moreover, disordered eating is much less common among males and some non-White race/ethnic groups; thus a very large sample size would be required to be able to detect any differences in incidence rates. However, when assessing relationships with factors that can change over time, you need to be cautious about interpreting results from cross-sectional studies.

Questionable Inference from Cross-Sectional Studies

The limitations of cross-sectional surveys are often forgotten; thus, there are plenty of examples of inappropriate inferences that have been made from cross-sectional data (Kraemer et al., 2000). The problems stem from assuming an incorrect temporal order between the factors and incorrectly assuming that the cross-sectional differences translate to longitudinal differences. The problem of failing to consider that the observed differences may be the result of characteristics of the sample applies to all study designs, including cross-sectional surveys.

Assuming an Incorrect Temporal Order   Several population-based studies have reported a positive association between weight and engaging in bulimic behaviors (Neumark-Sztainer et al., 1997; Shisslak et al., 1998; Striegel-Moore et al., 2000;

Wertheim et al., 1992). In addition, clinical studies have found that bulimics frequently report having been overweight before the onset of the disorder, thus some researchers have concluded that being overweight is a risk factor for bulimia nervosa (Beumont, George, & Smart, 1976; Garner, Garfinkel, & O'Shaughnessey, 1985). However, bulimic patients have usually been ill for at least several years before seeking treatment (Herzog, Keller, Lavori, & Ott, 1988). Unless past medical records are obtained, it is not possible in clinical studies to validate whether the report of having been overweight is accurate or a distorted self-perception; thus, it is unclear whether the association truly exists. Moreover, it is possible that the people who engage in bulimic behaviors gained weight and became obese, in part, because of their binge eating. In summary, the assumed temporal order of the association is questionable. Only prospective studies can assess whether obesity predicts the *development* of eating disorders or whether the cross-sectional association exists because of distorted self-perception of weight status (i.e., being overweight) or because binge eating causes the subjects to become overweight.

Assuming That the Cross-Sectional Differences Translate to Longitudinal Differences
Kraemer and colleagues (2000) have summarized the mathematical and statistical reasons that longitudinal inference from cross-sectional data, which occurs frequently, can be very misleading. It is a well-known phenomenon in epidemiology that cross-sectional age associations tend to be much stronger than prospective age associations; thus, age effects reported in much of the eating disorder literature are probably an overestimation. The problem of assuming that you can make longitudinal inference from cross-sectional studies is particularly troublesome in hospital-based studies where the subjects have had an eating disorder for varying lengths of time. Differences observed among types of patients are difficult to interpret because the subjects are being compared at different and arbitrary points in their illness. Cross-sectional differences in and of themselves are not important; rather, differences in clinical studies are important only if they support hypotheses that the disorders being studied have different etiologies, require different treatments from one another, and/or have different courses of illness. Unfortunately, making those inferences from cross-sectional data is unwarranted and frequently misleading.

To illustrate, consider the evolution of the diagnostic criteria of anorexia nervosa from the *Diagnostic and Statistical Manual for Mental Disorders,* third edition (*DSM-III-R*), to the fourth edition (*DSM-IV*; APA, 1994). Results from cross-sectional studies suggested that restrictor and bulimic anorexics differed on several baseline characteristics, such as the number of comorbidities, leading some researchers to conclude that anorexics with bulimic symptoms had a more persistent and serious disorder than restrictor anorexics (DaCosta & Halmi, 1992; Hsu, 1988). Therefore, it was argued that anorexia nervosa should be subtyped in the *DSM-IV* by the presence or absence of binge eating and/or purging behavior. Herzog and colleagues (1996) investigated whether subtyping was warranted by comparing the two subtypes of anorexia cross-sectionally, as well as assessing whether there was a difference between the subtypes in terms of recovery rates. They observed that the duration of the disorder was inversely associated with recovery, which was uncommon for both types of anorexics. Although anorexics with the bulimic subtype did present with more comorbidities, comorbid disorders were not predictive of recovery, nor was age of onset of the current disorder, age of onset of the first disorder, or engaging in impulse-related behaviors (kleptomania, suicide attempts, and drug abuse). Thus, in contrast to the argument made for subtyping, Herzog and colleagues observed that after controlling for duration of anorexia, anorexics with bulimic symptoms were *more* likely to recover than pure anorexics (relative risk [RR] = 4.6, 95% confidence interval [CI] 0.98 to 21.0). In summary, the inference made from cross-sectional studies that was used as evidence to support subtyping was incorrect.

Case-Control Studies

In case-control studies, subjects are selected based on their disease status. That is, one group is chosen because they have the disorder (e.g., anorexia nervosa), and another is chosen because they are similar to the cases, but without the disorder. The cases and controls are then asked to recall a variety of factors that occurred before the case was diagnosed. As Schulz and Grimes (2002) summarized, "Case-control designs also tend to be more susceptible to biases than other comparative studies. Although easier to do, they [case-control studies] are also easier to do wrong" (p. 431).

Recall Bias

One of the most important limitations of case-control studies is that it is assumed that people are able to accurately recall past information and that the degree of accuracy is not related to being a case or a control. *Recall bias* is the term used to describe when there is a difference between cases and controls in terms of the accuracy of recalled information. This type of differential misclassification can lead to an under- or overestimation of the true association. Recall bias is possible in all case-control studies, but studies focused on factors that people think might be related to the outcome are particularly prone to recall bias. For example, there is a widely held belief, not entirely supported by data, that high-fat diets increase a woman's risk of developing breast cancer. Giovannucci et al. (1993) assessed whether recall bias might explain why results from case-control studies supported the "fat hypothesis," but prospective studies did not. As part of the ongoing Nurses' Health Study, a prospective cohort study of 121,700 female registered nurses from across the United States, information on dietary intake during the past year was collected in 1986. Between 1986 and 1988, 398 women were diagnosed with breast cancer. In a case-control study nested in the prospective cohort study, 300 of these women (the cases) and 602 age-matched controls completed another food frequency questionnaire in 1989, but this one asked them to recall their diet in 1985. Thus, Giovannucci and colleagues had both prospective and retrospective assessments of dietary intake during the one-year period from 1985 to 1986. In the analysis using the prospectively collected dietary information, no associations between breast cancer incidence and fat intake were observed. In contrast, in the analysis, using the retrospective assessment suggested a positive association between fat intake and the risk of developing breast cancer. The difference in results reflects the differential ability of cases and controls in recalling their past diets. Moreover, the results highlight the fact that associations observed in case-control studies may reflect recall bias rather than true associations.

Characteristics of the Sample as the Source of Observed Differences

Eating disorders are relatively uncommon in the general population; thus, to study anorexia and bulimia nervosa, either a clinic- or hospital-based sample or an extremely large population-based sample is needed to ensure that there are enough cases to conduct meaningful analyses. There are, however, many potential problems with using clinic- or hospital-based samples. The largest problem in hospital-based case-control studies is figuring out the appropriate comparison or control group. In all case-control studies, the control should be just like the cases but without the disease. That is, if one of the controls had developed anorexia or bulimia nervosa, he or she would be a case in the study (i.e., they are in the catchment area). In practice, this is very difficult to accomplish in much of the United States because patients seeking treatment from a research hospital rarely come from one limited catchment area. In countries with socialized medicine and in areas where most people in a geographic area seek medical help from one hospital or system, such as an HMO, an appropriate control group can more easily be identified. Further complicating the problem is that many people with a psychiatric disorder, including an eating disorder, do not seek treatment (Wang, Demler, & Kessler, 2002). Thus, the controls should be people who, had they developed an eating disorder, would be among the minority who do seek treatment. One other word of caution: It is essential that the risk factors for the disease or medical condition that characterizes the control group be unrelated to the risk factors for developing the disease of interest (e.g., an eating disorder). If the patients in the control group had a disease with risk factors similar to the eating disorder of interest, the cases and controls would be too similar to one another to distinguish any risk factors. Alternatively, if a variable was a protective factor for the disease that controls had, but increased the risk of developing an eating disorder, it would not be identified as a risk factor in the case-control study because too few controls would have the factor.

Fairburn and colleagues have addressed this potential problem by conducting case-control studies with two control groups—one with another disease and one from the general population. For example, one study included adult women with bulimia nervosa, a comparison group of women with other psychiatric diagnoses, and another comparison group of healthy controls (Fairburn, Welch, Doll, Davies, & O'Connor, 1997). By having two groups of control subjects, they were able to empirically test whether the observed differences were a function of an inappropriate control group. It is a prudent design that other researchers conducting case-control studies would be wise to follow because Fairburn et al. did find numerous differences in the results when one control series was used rather than the other. In most cases, the use of general psychiatric controls lead to an underestimation of the magnitude of the risk factor. For example, cases of bulimia nervosa were more than 17 times (OR = 17.4) more likely than healthy controls to report major depression whereas cases of bulimia nervosa were only 2 times (OR = 2.3) more likely than general psychiatric controls to report depression.

Another challenge when using hospital-based samples of eating disorder patients is figuring out to whom the results are generalizable. This is an issue for hospital-based cohort studies, as well as case-control studies. Often, the patients may represent the most severe cases of anorexia or bulimia nervosa, so it is unclear whether the results are generalizable to less severe cases. This is a particularly important issue to consider when estimating the mortality rates (which will be overestimated if only the sickest patients are studied) or the effectiveness of treatments (which may be underestimated if only very sick patients are studied) for anorexia nervosa.

Patients with severe anorexia nervosa are often in need of immediate medical attention, but it is unclear what factors predict seeking treatment among patients who are not at immediate medical risk. It is important to understand these factors so that they are not mistakenly identified as risk factors. The relationship of socioeconomic status (SES) to eating disorders is one example of mistaking a factor associated with seeking treatment for a true risk factor. Until recently, it was a widely held belief that females of high SES were at the highest risk for an eating disorder; however, in population-based research, SES does not appear to be associated with having an eating disorder of clinical severity (Rogers, Resnick, Mitchell, & Blum, 1997; Warheit, Langer, Zimmerman, & Biafora, 1993). In a cross-sectional study of 17,571 adolescent girls, Rogers et al. observed that the prevalence of engaging in weight control behaviors was associated with SES, but the prevalence of meeting probable criteria for an eating disorder (e.g., more frequent use of weight control behaviors) was not associated with SES. Thus, high SES may be a predictor of seeking treatment if the person has an eating disorder, rather than a true risk factor. Alternatively, it is possible that SES is associated with developing anorexia nervosa, but not the other eating disorders, which are more common than anorexia nervosa in the population at large.

Cohort Studies

Cohort studies follow subjects over time and collect information before subjects become cases; therefore, temporal order can be assessed, and recall bias is not a problem. The difficulty with making inference from cohort studies is that caution must be taken in implying causality. Unlike randomized clinical trials, the investigators in cohort studies have no control over who has the potential risk or protective factor of interest. Therefore, there is always a possibility of unmeasured confounders explaining observed associations, and it is prudent to phrase results as "exposure X predicted the development of Y." Although randomized clinical trials are considered necessary to infer causality, many exposures could not be evaluated in randomized clinical trials. It would be unethical to randomize people to smoke, abuse alcohol, or suffer abuse; thus, cohort studies are the best option for studying the health impact of these types of factors.

Choice and Implications of Study Design

Although cohort studies and randomized clinical trials have the fewest limitations in terms of the inference that can be made, they are not always the best design to answer specific research questions. No one study design is best for addressing all research questions, except for research addressing the effectiveness of treatments for which randomized clinical trials are the superior study design. The choice of study design for other research topics should depend on the outcome and the primary exposure of interest, as well as the more practical issues of the amount of funding available and the length of time the researcher has to answer the question (see Table 2.2).

Table 2.2   Study Design Differences

	Cross-Sectional	Case-Control	Cohort	RCT
Able to discern temporality	No.	Yes, if no recall bias.	Yes.	Yes.
Cost	Can be inexpensive.	Can be inexpensive.	Expensive.	Expensive.
Appropriate outcomes	Weight concerns. Disordered eating. Full criteria eating disorders other than anorexia nervosa (if the sample is large).	Full criteria eating disorders.	Weight concerns. Disordered eating. Full criteria eating disorders other than anorexia nervosa (if the sample is large).	Partial and full criteria eating disorders.
Appropriate inference	Correlates. Risk factors *only* if the factor cannot change overtime (e.g., race).	Risk factors if recall bias can be ruled out.	Risk factors.	"Treatment" effects.

Outcome

To study rare disorders, such as full criteria anorexia nervosa, either an extremely large sample or a study design that allows oversampling of eating-disordered patients is needed. Case-control studies, where subjects are sampled based on their disease state (e.g., having an eating disorder), or hospital-based cohort studies may be the best study design options for studying full criteria eating disorders because they ensure enough cases for a meaningful analysis. The prevalence of anorexia nervosa among a general sample of adolescent females is approximately 0.1% to 1.0%. Lucas, Beard, O'Fallon, and Kurland (1991) estimated that the incidence rate among 15- to 19-year-old females was approximately 70 cases per 100,000 person years of follow-up. Using that estimated incidence rate, the researcher would need to follow a cohort of at least 40,000 young females for four or more years to have 90% power to detect if a relatively common factor (occurring in 20% of the sample) doubled the risk of developing anorexia nervosa. To have adequate power to detect a smaller relative risk, an even larger sample would be needed. For example, to have 80% power to detect if a factor occurring in 20% of the sample increased the risk of developing anorexia nervosa by 50% (i.e., RR = 1.5), 40,000 young females should be followed for nine years or 60,000 young females should be followed for six years. The difficulty in identifying and motivating 40,000 or more adolescent females to join a prospective study and the labor and cost involved in conducting a longitudinal study of that magnitude make it unlikely that the development of anorexia nervosa will be studied prospectively. Instead, case-control studies may be the best option. However, recall bias is a serious concern because distorted body perceptions and a refusal to acknowledge the seriousness of their low body weight are two symptoms of anorexia nervosa. It is unknown, but possible, whether the cases may have a distorted perception of past, as well as present, weight and body shape issues. Investigators planning case-control studies would be well advised to conduct at least small validation studies to determine whether the recalled data are sufficiently accurate and equally well recalled by cases and controls.

Case Definitions

Full Criteria Eating Disorders

Full criteria eating disorders are relatively uncommon in the general population. Approximately 1% to 4% of young women have bulimia nervosa (Drewnowski, Hopkins, & Kessler, 1988; Pemberton, Vernon, & Lee, 1996; Shisslak, Crago, & Estes, 1995; Striegel-Moore, Silberstein, Frensch, & Rodin, 1989; Warheit et al., 1993), and another 0.1% to 1% (Lewinsohn, Striegel-Moore, & Seeley, 2000; Lucas et al., 1991) suffer from anorexia nervosa. Although some researchers may desire to combine past and present cases or partial and full criteria cases in an effort to increase their sample size and statistical power, it may actually not help the researchers as much as believed. Risk factors may have a different or weaker association with past or partial cases than full cases. Therefore, by making the outcome a more inclusive category (e.g., full cases plus partial cases or past cases), the average of the two risks will be observed; thus, the true risk between the exposure and having a full criteria eating disorder may be underestimated. The ratio of past cases to current cases is frequently large. For example, Lewinsohn and colleagues prospectively studied a sample of approximately 900 adolescent girls. At each of the three assessments, 25% or fewer of the girls with a lifetime history of anorexia or bulimia nervosa were currently disordered. If a risk factor had an association with current, but not past, cases, unless the risk was very large, it would most likely be missed because the majority of the cases would be past, not current cases.

Partial Criteria Cases

Much of the population-based research, as well as some of the clinical research, focuses on individuals who meet some, but not all, criteria for an eating disorder. The interest in this group reflects the fact that the prevalence of partial criteria cases is greater than the prevalence of full criteria cases (Shisslak et al., 1995). Moreover, there is some empirical evidence to suggest a continuum of eating disorder pathology, and individuals with full criteria eating disorders are at one end of the spectrum (Drewnowski, Yee, Kurth, & Kann, 1994; Stice, Killen, Hayward, & Taylor, 1998). In addition, population-based researchers may not have the statistical power to study full criteria cases; therefore, focusing on partial or a combination of partial and full criteria cases seems prudent. One difficulty with making inference from studies on partial criteria eating disorders is lack of a uniform definition of *caseness*. As a result, it is extremely difficult to compare results across studies.

Although many studies are not sufficiently large to break partial cases into partial bulimia nervosa, partial anorexia nervosa, and partial binge eating disorder, combining all of the types into one category is not advisable because if the various types of subclinical or subthreshold disorders do not have the same risk factors, the nonshared risk factors will most likely be obscured due to combining all types of cases. For example, if history of childhood obesity is a risk factor for subclinical binge eating disorder, but not for subclinical anorexia or bulimia nervosa, combining all of the people with any type of subclinical disorder will dampen or completely obscure the relationship be-tween childhood obesity and risk of developing subclinical binge eating disorder.

Bulimic Behaviors and Dissatisfaction with Weight and Shape

If the aim of the research is to assess weight concerns, body dissatisfaction, or bulimic behaviors, a hospital-based sample would be a poor choice because it would represent a biased sample skewed toward the high end of pathology. Moreover, because body dis-satisfaction and bulimic behaviors are relatively common and exist on a continuum, a case-control design would not be advisable. Instead, cross-sectional or cohort studies would be the better study designs to use.

Because these outcomes occur on a continuum, it is important to clearly define the outcomes. Bulimic behaviors can be defined in terms of ever use, current use, or fre-quency of current use. Although commonly used in research studies, *ever use* is an unde-sirable outcome measure for several reasons. First, questions assessing ever use tend to give inflated prevalence estimates because they combine people who experimented with a behavior once with others who engaged in the behavior on a more regular basis. The former group is unlikely to be of scientific interest to the researcher but may account for a nontrivial proportion of the cases. The impact of using ever use versus use during the past week or month was illustrated by Serdula, Mokdad, Pamuk, Williamson, and Byers (1995), who observed that among 5,882 female students, the prevalence of vomiting was 3% when asking about the past week, but 14% when asking about ever use. The second problem with using ever use as the outcome is that it is impossible to determine whether the correlates assessed in the study occurred before, during, or after the period during which the subject engaged in bulimic behaviors.

Outcomes that occur on a continuum, such as weight concerns, body dissatisfaction, and Eating Disorder Inventory scores, present a challenge in terms of interpretation. Although they are attractive as outcomes because a large sample size is not needed to study differences in continuous outcomes, the results are rarely easy to interpret. For example, it is unclear what a one-unit difference on a scale means and whether the dif-ferences observed are clinically meaningful. If the mean score in group A is two units higher than the mean score in group B, but the prevalence of scoring above the thresh-old for caseness is the same in the two groups, is the two-unit difference in mean score important or interesting? Although statistical power is lost when a continuous measure is converted into a dichotomous one, it may be advisable for the sake of interpretabil-ity. Alternatively, investigators could present information on clinically relevant differ-ences and cut-off values.

Another challenge of using continuous measures is that frequently they have a skewed distribution. If the data can be transformed, such as by using a log transformation, what remains will be a measure that will perform well but will be very difficult to interpret (e.g., log body dissatisfaction score). Sometimes, however, the data are too heavily skewed or there are gaps in the distribution (e.g., very few people at the top or bottom of a scale). In these cases and some others, some investigators have opted to compare high scores to low scores by creating quintiles, quartiles, or tertiles of the variable and com-paring the extremes. Although this approach will guarantee enough subjects in the refer-ence and the group of interest, it renders the results difficult to interpret (on their own) and impossible to compare to other studies. The cut-off value for the highest tertile in one study may be the middle tertile in another study. Therefore, this approach is not advised unless it is coupled with information on cut-off values for the groups.

Risk Factor or Exposure of Interest

If the desire is to assess treatments, a randomized clinical trial is the appropriate study design to use. Results from observational studies (e.g., cohort or case-control studies) can be misleading because of confounding by indication. Confounding by indication occurs when people are on specific treatments because of severity of their illness or other personal factors that, regardless of the effectiveness of the treatment, predict outcome (e.g., recovery from the illness). In other words, even if the treatment offered no benefit or harm, one would expect to observe differences in outcome because of these personal factors that predict who gets which treatment. Therefore, randomized clinical trials are the best study design to assess treatment effects. It is important, however, to note that relatively large sample sizes are needed to assume that the randomization process will have made the distribution of the exposures in the two or more arms of the study equivalent.

If the effect of treatments is not being studied, the choice of study design should be influenced by whether people are able or willing to retrospectively recall the exposure of greatest importance to the study. In prospective cohort studies, where information is collected before the participant develops the outcome of interest, memory is less of an issue. Although adults appear to be able to accurately report past body weights (Field, Colditz, Herzog, & Heatherton, 1996; Troy et al., 1995), little is known about the ability to recall some of the commonly mentioned known risk factors for eating disorders, such as personal and family history of perfectionism (Hewitt, Flett, & Ediger, 1995), obsessive-compulsive disorder (Rasmussen & Eisen, 1992), childhood sexual abuse (Everill & Waller, 1995; Fairburn et al., 1997; Fairburn, Cooper, Doll, & Welch, 1999; Welch & Fairburn, 1994), anxiety disorders (Brewerton et al., 1995; Kendler, 1991), familial psychopathology (Fairburn et al., 1997; Rastam & Gillberg, 1991), childhood eating and digestive problems (Marchi & Cohen, 1990), and low self-esteem (Button, Sonuga-Barke, Davies, & Thompson, 1996; Kendler et al., 1991; Williams et al., 1993). Some data suggests that other known risk factors, such as substance (Krahn, 1991) and alcohol abuse (Timmerman, Wells, & Chen, 1990) and depression (Fairburn et al., 1997), are not well recalled (Aneshenel, Estrada, Hansell, & Clark, 1987; Bromet, Dunn, Connell, Drew, & Schulberg, 1986; Prustoff, Merikangas, & Weissman, 1988; Robins, 1985). The magnitude of the errors in recall can be substantial. For example, Aneshensel et al. found that 57.8% of the people who had reported a depressive episode during a three-year interval of study failed to report having had any episode of depression during their lifetime when they were questioned at the end of the four-year study. Moreover, there is an inverse association between the reliability of the diagnosis and the time interval between the episode and assessment (Bromet et al., 1986). Results suggest that studies that ask subjects to recall potential risk factors that occurred in the distant past may have substantial misclassification. Few of the known risk factors have been identified in prospective cohort studies, the study design that guards against these types of misclassification. Therefore, it is likely that some of these "known risk factors," which were identified through case-control or cross-sectional study designs, may reflect recall bias rather than be true risk factors.

Randomized clinical trials are considered by some the only design that allows causation to be proved; however, randomized clinical trials are not always feasible or ethical. It would not be ethical to randomize people to a low self-esteem or a substance use group, nor would it be feasible to randomize people to have a history of childhood sexual abuse or familial psychopathology. For many of the risk factors of greatest interest in eating disorder research, an observational study is the only viable study option.

Costs

Substantial cost and time differences are involved in conducting cross-sectional surveys, cohort studies, case-control studies, and randomized clinical trials. Cross-sectional studies can be relatively inexpensive to conduct because they do not require tracking subjects over time. Cohort studies, on the other hand, are expensive to conduct because maintaining contact with participants and maintaining high response rates over an extended time period is labor intensive and costly but essential for the results to be useful. The inference from a large prospective study with low follow-up rates would be problematic because it would be unclear whether the results were a function of a biased sample remaining in the cohort.

Another factor that makes cohort studies and randomized clinical trials very expensive and labor intensive is that the studies must be large so an adequate number of new cases will develop to be able to perform meaningful analyses. Moreover, the investigators need to wait for at least several years to observe the results of interest. The costs and time required for conducting prospective cohort studies are daunting, but to understand the development and course of disordered eating and eating disorders, more such studies are needed.

CONCLUSION

Eating disorders are difficult to treat, and prevention efforts have not been very successful; thus, more longitudinal research is needed to identify modifiable risk factors that can be the focus of prevention interventions. Although there is considerable literature on risk factors for eating disorders, some of the "established risk factors" may not be true risk factors. To move the field forward, large longitudinal cohort studies and rigorously designed case-control studies are needed to identify new modifiable risk factors, as well as confirm or refute whether the "established risk factors" are true risk factors. In addition, research is needed to better understand the ability or willingness of eating-disordered individuals to recall suspected risk factors and whether their ability differs from that of noneating-disordered individuals.

REFERENCES

American Psychiatric Association. (1994). *Diagnostic and statistical manual of mental disorders* (4th ed.). Washington, DC: Author.

Aneshensel, C. S., Estrada, A. L., Hansell, M. J., & Clark, V. A. (1987). Social psychological aspects of reporting behavior: Lifetime depressive episode reports. *Journal of Health and Social Behavior, 28,* 232–246.

Beumont, P. J. V., George, G. C. W., & Smart, D. E. (1976). "Dieters" and "vomiters and purgers" in anorexia nervosa. *Psychological Medicine, 6,* 617–622.

Brewerton, T. D., Lydiard, R. B., Herzog, D. B., Brotman, A. W., O'Neil, P. M., & Ballenger, J. C. (1995). Comorbidity of axis I psychiatric disorders in bulimia nervosa. *Journal of Clinical Psychiatry, 56,* 77–80.

Bromet, E. J., Dunn, L. O., Connell, M. M., Drew, M. A., & Schulberg, H. C. (1986). Long-term reliability of diagnosing lifetime major depression in a community sample. *Archives of General Psychiatry, 43,* 435–440.

Button, E. J., Sonuga-Barke, E. J. S., Davies, J., & Thompson, M. (1996). A prospective study of self-esteem in the prediction of eating problems in adolescent schoolgirls: Questionnaire findings. *British Journal of Clinical Psychology, 35,* 193–203.

Cameron, R. P., Grabill, C. M., Hofoll, S. E., Crowther, J. H., Ritter, C., & Lavin, J. (1996). Weight, self-esteem, ethnicity, and depressive symptomatology during pregnancy among inter-city women. *Health Psychology, 15,* 293–297.

Centers for Disease Control Growth Charts. (2002). Available from www.cdc.gov/growthcharts/.

DaCosta, M., & Halmi, K. A. (1992). Classification of anorexia nervosa: Question of subtypes. *International Journal of Eating Disorders, 11,* 305–313.

Drewnowski, A., Hopkins, S. A., & Kessler, R. C. (1988). The prevalence of bulimia nervosa in the U.S. college student population. *American Journal of Public Health, 78*(10), 1322–1325.

Drewnowski, A., Yee, D. K., Kurth, C. L., & Kann, D. D. (1994). Eating pathology and *DSM-III-R* bulimia nervosa: A continuum of behavior. *American Journal of Psychiatry, 151*(8), 1217–1219.

Everill, J. T., & Waller, G. (1995). Reported sexual abuse and eating psychopathology: A review of the evidence for a causal link. *International Journal of Eating Disorders, 18,* 1–11.

Fairburn, C. G., Cooper, Z., Doll, H. A., & Welch, S. L. (1999). Risk factors for anorexia nervosa: Three integrated case-control comparisons. *Archives of General Psychiatry, 56,* 468–476.

Fairburn, C. G., Welch, S. L., Doll, H. A., Davies, B. A., & O'Connor, M. E. (1997). Risk factors for bulimia nervosa: A community-based case-control study. *Archives of General Psychiatry, 54,* 509–517.

Field, A. E., Berkey, C. S., Rockett, H. R., & Colditz, G. A. (2000). Frequent dieting predicts the development of obesity among preadolescent and adolescent girls and boys. *Obesity Research, 8*(Suppl. 1), 37S.

Field, A. E., Colditz, G. A., Herzog, D., & Heatherton, T. (1996). Disordered eating: Can women accurately recall their binging and purging behaviors ten years later? *Obesity Research, 4,* 153–159.

Garner, D. M., Garfinkel, P. E., & O'Shaughnessey, M. (1985). The validity of the distinction between bulimia with and without anorexia nervosa. *American Journal of Psychiatry, 142*(5), 581–587.

Giovannucci, E., Stampfer, M. J., Colditz, G. A., Manson, J. E., Rosner, B. A., Longnecker, M., et al. (1993). A comparison of prospective and retrospective assessments of diet in the study of breast cancer. *American Journal of Epidemiology, 137*(5), 502–511.

Henriques, G. R., Calhoun, L. G., & Cann, A. (1996). Ethnic differences in women's body satisfaction: An experimental investigation. *Journal of Social Psychology, 136,* 689–697.

Herzog, D. B., Field, A. E., Keller, M. B., West, J. C., Robbins, W. M., Stanley, J., et al. (1996). Subtyping eating disorders: Is it justified? *Journal of the American Academy of Child and Adolescent Psychiatry, 35,* 928–936.

Herzog, D. B., Keller, M. B., Lavori, P. W., & Ott, I. L. (1988). Short-term prospective recovery in bulimia nervosa. *Psychiatry Research, 23,* 45–55.

Hewitt, P. L., Flett, G. L., & Ediger, E. (1995). Perfectionism traits and perfectionistic self-presentation in eating disorder attitudes, characteristics, and symptoms. *International Journal of Eating Disorders, 18,* 317–326.

Hsu, L. K. G. (1988). The outcome of anorexia nervosa: A reappraisal. *Psychological Medicine, 18,* 807–812.

Kendler, K. S., MacLean, C., Neale, M., Kessler, R., Heath, A., & Eaves, L. (1991). The genetic epidemiology of bulimia nervosa. *American Journal of Psychiatry, 148,* 1627–1637.

Kraemer, H. C., Stice, E., Kazadin, A., Offord, D., & Kupfer, D. (2001). How do risk factors work together? Mediators, moderators, and independent, overlapping, and proxy risk factors. *American Journal of Psychiatry, 158,* 848–856.

Kraemer, H. C., Yesavage, J. A., Taylor, J. L., & Kupfer, D. (2000). How can we learn among developmental processes from cross-sectional studies, or can we? *American Journal of Psychiatry, 157,* 163–171.

Krahn, D. D. (1991). The relationship of eating disorders and substance abuse. *Journal of Substance Abuse, 3,* 239–253.

Lewinsohn, P. M., Striegel-Moore, R. H., & Seeley, J. R. (2000). Epidemiology and natural course of eating disorders in young women from adolescence to young adulthood. *Journal of the American Academy of Child and Adolescent Psychiatry, 39*(10), 1284–1292.

Lucas, A. R., Beard, C. M., O'Fallon, W. M., & Kurland, L. T. (1991). 50-year trends in the incidence of anorexia nervosa in Rochester, Minn: A population-based study. *American Journal of Psychiatry, 148*(7), 917–922.

Marchi, M., & Cohen, P. (1990). Early childhood eating behaviors and adolescent eating disorders. *Journal of the American Academy of Child and Adolescent Psychiatry, 29,* 112–117.

Neumark-Sztainer, D., Story, M., French, S. A., Hannan, P. J., Resnick, M. D., & Blum, R. W. (1997). Psychosocial concerns and health-compromising behaviors among overweight and nonoverweight adolescents. *Obesity Research, 5,* 237–249.

Pemberton, A. R., Vernon, S. W., & Lee, E. S. (1996). Prevalence and correlates of bulimia nervosa and bulimic behaviors in a racially diverse sample of undergraduate students in two universities in southeast Texas. *American Journal of Epidemiology, 144*(5), 450–455.

Prustoff, B. A., Merikangas, K. R., & Weissman, M. M. (1988). Lifetime prevalence and age of onset of psychiatric disorders: Recall 4 years later. *Journal of Psychiatry Research, 22*(2), 107–117.

Rasmussen, S. A., & Eisen, J. L. (1992). The epidemiology and differential diagnosis of obsessive compulsive disorder. *Journal of Clinical Psychiatry, 53*(Suppl.), 4–101.

Rastam, M., & Gillberg, C. (1991). The family background in anorexia nervosa: A population-based study. *Journal of the American Academy of Child and Adolescent Psychiatry, 30,* 283–289.

Regier, D. A., Farmer, M. E., Rae, D. S., Myers, J. K., Kramer, M., Robins, L. N., et al. (1993). One-month prevalence of mental disorders in the United States and sociodemographic characteristics: The Epidemiologic Catchment Area study. *Acta Psychiatrica Scandinavica, 88*(1), 35–47.

Robins, L. N. (1985). Epidemiology: Reflections on testing the validity of psychiatric interviews. *Archives of General Psychiatry, 42,* 918–927.

Rogers, L., Resnick, M. D., Mitchell, J. E., & Blum, R. W. (1997). The relationship between socioeconomic status and eating-disordered behaviors in a community sample of adolescent girls. *International Journal of Eating Disorders, 22*(1), 15–23.

Rothman, K. J., & Greenland, S. (1998). *Modern epidemiology.* Philadelphia: Lippincott, Williams, & Wilkins.

Schulz, K. F., & Grimes, D. A. (2002). Case-control studies: Research in reverse. *Lancet, 359*(9304), 431–434.

Serdula, M. K., Mokdad, A. H., Pamuk, E. R., Williamson, D. F., & Byers, T. (1995). Effects of question order on estimates of the prevalence of attempted weight loss. *American Journal of Epidemiology, 142*(1), 64–67.

Shisslak, C. M., Crago, M., & Estes, L. S. (1995). The spectrum of eating disturbances. *International Journal of Eating Disorders, 18*(3), 209–219.

Shisslak, C. M., Crago, M., McKnight, K. M., Estes, L. S., Gray, N., & Parnaby, O. G. (1998). Potential risk factors associated with weight control behaviors among elementary and middle school girls. *Journal of Psychosomatic Research, 44,* 301–313.

Smith, D. E., Thompson, J. K., Raczynski, J. M., & Hilner, J. E. (1999). Body image among men and women in a biracial cohort: The CARDIA Study. *International Journal of Eating Disorders, 25,* 71–82.

Stice, E., Killen, J. D., Hayward, C., & Taylor, C. B. (1998). Support for the continuity hypothesis of bulimic pathology. *Journal of Consulting and Clinical Psychology, 66*(5), 784–790.

Striegel-Moore, R. H., Schreiber, G. B., Lo, A., Crawford, P., Obarzanek, E., & Rodin, J. (2000). Eating disorder symptoms in a cohort of 11 to 16-year-old black and white girls: The NHLBI growth and health study. *International Journal of Eating Disorders, 27*(1), 49–66.

Striegel-Moore, R. H., Silberstein, L. R., Frensch, P., & Rodin, J. (1989). A prospective study disordered eating among college students. *International Journal of Eating Disorders, 8*(5), 499–509.

Timmerman, M. G., Wells, L. A., & Chen, S. (1990). Bulimia nervosa and associated alcohol abuse among secondary school students. *Journal of the American Academy of Child and Adolescent Psychiatry, 29,* 118–122.

Troiano, R. P., & Flegal, K. M. (1998). Overweight children and adolescents: Description, epidemiology, and demographics. *Pediatrics, 101*(3, Pt. 2), 497–504.

Troy, L. M., Hunter, D. J., Manson, J. E., Colditz, G. A., Stampfer, M. J., & Willett, W. C. (1995). The validity of recalled weight among younger women. *International Journal of Obesity Research, 19,* 570–572.

Wang, P. S., Demler, O., & Kessler, R. C. (2002). Adequacy of treatment for serious mental illness in the United States. *American Journal of Public Health, 92,* 92–98.

Warheit, G. J., Langer, L. M., Zimmerman, R. S., & Biafora, F. A. (1993). Prevalence of bulimic behaviors and bulimia among a sample of the general population. *American Journal of Epidemiology, 137*(5), 569–576.

Welch, S. L., & Fairburn, C. G. (1994). Sexual abuse and bulimia nervosa: Three integrated case control comparisons. *American Journal of Psychiatry, 151,* 402–407.

Wertheim, E. H., Paxton, S. J., Maude, D., Szmukler, G. I., Gibbons, K., & Hiller, L. (1992). Psychosocial predictors of weight loss behaviors and binge eating in adolescent girls and boys. *International Journal of Eating Disorders, 12,* 151–169.

Williams, G. J., Power, K. G., Millar, H. R., Freeman, C. P., Yellowlees, A., Dowds, T., et al. (1993). Comparison of eating disorders and other dietary/weight groups on measures of perceived control, assertiveness, self-esteem, and self-directed hostility. *International Journal of Eating Disorders, 14,* 27–32.

Chapter 3

EATING DISORDER PREVENTION PROGRAMS

ERIC STICE AND EMILY HOFFMAN

Eating disorders, some of the most common psychiatric problems faced by females, are characterized by chronicity and relapse (Fairburn, Cooper, Doll, Norman, & O'Connor, 2000; Lewinsohn, Striegel-Moore, & Seeley, 2000). Eating disorders are marked by psychosocial impairment and comorbid psychopathology and have the highest levels of treatment seeking, inpatient hospitalization, suicide attempts, and mortality of common psychiatric syndromes (Newman et al., 1996; Wilson, Heffernan, & Black, 1996). Furthermore, eating pathology increases the risk for subsequent onset of obesity, depression, and substance abuse (Stice, Cameron, Killen, Hayward, & Taylor, 1999; Stice, Hayward, Cameron, Killen, & Taylor, 2000; Stice & Shaw, 2003).

Because most individuals with eating disorders never seek treatment (Fairburn et al., 2003; Newman et al., 1996) and treatment produces symptom remission for only 30% to 40% of patients (Agras, Walsh, Fairburn, Wilson, & Kraemer, 2000; Fairburn, Jones, Peveler, Hope, & O'Connor, 1993), much effort has been devoted to developing prevention programs. Indeed, there has been a profusion of prevention trials in the last few years. Because these recent findings have not been critically reviewed and synthesized, the aims of this chapter are to (1) provide a comprehensive review of eating disorder prevention programs, (2) discuss program content and design features associated with positive intervention effects, (3) consider theoretical, methodological, and statistical limitations of the trials, and (4) explore promising directions for future research.

Eating disorder prevention interventions can be classified into two broad categories: universal programs and targeted programs. Universal programs are directed at all consenting individuals in a given population, such as a given grade level in a school (Smolak, Levine, & Schermer, 1998a). Targeted programs focus only on subpopulations at elevated risk for eating pathology, such as individuals who possess a risk factor

Preparation of this manuscript was supported by a career award (MH01708) and a national research service award (MH64254) from the National Institute on Mental Health.

We are very grateful to Michael Levine for sharing the results of his literature search on eating disorder prevention trials. Thanks also go to the numerous authors who ran additional analyses when requested.

shown to predict onset of eating pathology (Kaminski & McNamara, 1996). In practice, however, the distinction between universal and targeted programs is often blurred. For example, most "universal" eating disorder prevention programs have focused solely on girls and women—and the female sex represents one of the most potent risk factors for eating pathology (Lewinsohn, Hops, Roberts, Seeley, & Andrews, 1993; Newman et al., 1996). In addition, most targeted programs allow participants to self-select into the intervention (e.g., Winzelberg et al., 2000), rather than using a screening measure, as is common in prevention programs for other psychiatric conditions (Clarke et al., 1995). Participants who self-select into programs designed to improve body acceptance or eating disturbances typically show elevations on risk factors for eating pathology, such as body dissatisfaction (Celio et al., 2000). Similarly, individuals who enroll in eating disorder classes at universities also appear to represent a high-risk group, despite the absence of an explicit screening measure (Stice & Ragan, 2002). Nonetheless, interventions delivered to all participants in intact classrooms and trials that do not mention the intervention objective during recruitment (to improve body dissatisfaction) were considered universal for this chapter. Those that screened participants for a risk factor or that used recruitment strategies that implicitly screened participants, such as advertisements for a body acceptance intervention, were considered targeted programs.

The defining feature of a successful eating disorder prevention program is that it reduces initial and/or future eating disorder symptoms or rates of clinically significant eating pathology relative to the changes in these outcomes observed in a control group. Reductions in initial symptoms signify a successful prevention program because there are nontrivial rates of subdiagnostic eating pathology in unselected samples that are associated with subjective distress and functional impairment (Lewinsohn et al., 2000; Patton, Selzer, Coffey, Carlin, & Wolfe, 1999; Stice, Killen, Hayward, & Taylor, 1998). Prevention programs for other psychiatric conditions, such as depression, have similarly focused on reducing both initial and future pathology (Clarke et al., 1995).

Some investigations have focused on reducing established risk factors for eating pathology that have been found to predict subsequent increases in eating disorder symptoms or onset of eating pathology in prospective studies. The rationale is that a reduction in an established risk factor should produce decreases in initial or future eating pathology. In other words, any intervention effects on eating pathology are putatively mediated by reductions in the risk factors. Thus, to be considered optimally successful, an eating disorder prevention program should reduce both the risk factor *and* eating pathology—even if the intervention focuses solely on reducing the risk factor.

This review focuses exclusively on eating disorder prevention programs that have been evaluated in controlled trials. These include trials in which participants are randomly assigned to an intervention or to a waitlist or measurement-only control condition, as well as trials in which some relevant comparison group is used (e.g., matched controls) in a quasi-experimental design. Randomization is optimal because it is the best approach to generating comparison groups that are equated on *any* potential confounding variables. Because many potential confounds are not known by investigators, random assignment to condition is preferable to the use of control groups that are matched to the intervention group on certain dimensions. Nonetheless, carefully selected comparison groups can permit useful inferences as to impact of intervention programs if the data analyses test for significant differences in change from pre- to postassessment across conditions. Studies without waitlist or measurement-only control groups were omitted because there is no way to determine whether any observed changes result from intervention or from the passage of time, regression to the mean, or measurement artifacts (pretest sensitization). In all, 14 studies were omitted because they did not include a no-intervention control group. Admittedly, the use of waitlist or measurement-only control groups does not permit ruling out the possibility that any observed effects are because of expectancies or demand characteristics. However, because only a handful of trials employed placebo control conditions (Baranowski & Hetherington, 2001; Dworkin & Kerr, 1987; Nicolino, Martz, & Curtin, 2001; Rosen, Saltzberg, & Srebnik, 1989; Stice, Presnell, Hoffman, & Trost, 2002), we did not require the use of a placebo control group for inclusion in this review.

This review also focused exclusively on studies that tested whether the change in the outcomes over time was significantly greater in the intervention group versus the control group. This can take the form of a time-by-condition interaction in a repeated-measures analysis of variance (ANOVA) model (Paxton, 1993). Alternatively, an analysis of covariance model (ANCOVA) that statistically controls for initial levels of the outcome variable (Celio et al., 2000) can be used. Similar approaches can be taken with growth curve or proportional hazards models that control for initial versions of the outcome (Winzelberg et al., 1998). Studies that tested for only significant changes *within* condition were excluded because this type of analysis does not permit valid inferences about intervention effects. This type of analysis provides no way to separate out the effects of the intervention versus those from alternative sources, such as the passage of time, regression to the mean, or measurement artifact. Authors of the prevention trials who did not test for significant differences in change in the outcomes across conditions were contacted and asked if they would provide the results of these additional analyses. Of six authors contacted, two provided the requested information so that their results could be included in this review.[1] Studies that included only posttest measures were also excluded because it is not possible to model *change* in the outcomes with this type of design. Hence, there is no way of ruling out the possibility that any observed findings resulted because random assignment failed to create equivalent groups at baseline. Three studies were excluded from this review because they did not include a pretest measure. Finally, studies that did not collect information that allowed them to pair pretest to posttest data were excluded because it is not possible to model change with unmatched data. One study was excluded because pretest and posttest data could not be matched.

We included trials that investigated interventions that were not originally considered eating disorder prevention programs if they examined body image and eating disturbance outcomes. For example, several studies that examined treatments for body dissatisfaction produced desirable effects (Butters & Cash, 1987). Because these interventions focused on women with initial elevations in body dissatisfaction, we considered them targeted interventions. Similarly, studies that attempted to promote healthy weight management behaviors were also reviewed if they included body image and eating disturbance outcome measures (Klem, Wing, Simkin-Silverman, & Kuller, 1997).

---

[1] Several authors who did not report the results of analyses testing whether there was significantly differential change across conditions in the original article provided this information when contacted (Franko, 1998; Martz & Bazzini, 1999).

However, studies that recruited participants with current eating pathology were excluded because it seemed that the interventions evaluated in such trials are better conceptualized as treatments.

Several procedures were used to retrieve published and unpublished articles. First, a computer search was performed on *PsychInfo* and *MedLine* for the years 1980 to 2002 using the following keywords: eating disorder, eating pathology, anorexia, anorexic, bulimia, bulimic, binge eating, prevention, and preventive. We performed independent searches to increase the odds that all relevant articles would be retrieved. Then, the products of both searches were reviewed to identify pertinent articles. Second, the tables of content for journals that commonly publish articles in this area were reviewed for the same period (e.g., *International Journal of Eating Disorders, Journal of Consulting and Clinical Psychology*). Third, reference sections of all identified articles, past reviews, and books in this area were examined. Finally, established eating disorder prevention researchers were contacted and asked for copies of in-press articles describing prevention trials. The literature search identified 37 published and unpublished studies, in which 33 eating disorder prevention programs were evaluated in 39 independent controlled trials (seven programs were evaluated in more than one trial, four trials evaluated two interventions simultaneously, and two reports described the results from two independent trials). The reports, methodological features of the trials, and intervention effects are summarized in Table 3.1.

In the sections to follow, universal and targeted eating disorder prevention programs that have been evaluated in controlled trials are reviewed. Table 3.1 summarizes the key methodological features of these trials and the findings. The effects summarized in the table reflect analyses performed on all samples used in these studies. Separate analyses performed on high-risk subgroups are described in a separate section. Only outcome measures examined in two or more trials are summarized in Table 3.1. Relevant outcomes that were examined in only one trial are noted in text when the trial findings are described. In addition, this review focused on the results from analyses of participants who provided complete data rather than on intent-to-treat analyses (wherein the last available data point for participants who drop out of the trial is carried forward). Intent-to-treat analyses may provide an overly liberal or overly conservative indication of program effects depending on when most participants dropped out and whether attrition favored the intervention or control group. If most participants dropped out before providing data at the termination of the program, intent-to-treat analyses may be conservative because the analyses assume that participants remain as symptomatic as they were at baseline. However, if most participants dropped out after providing termination data, intent-to-treat analyses may be overly liberal because the analyses assume that any intervention gains are preserved over follow-up (which is typically not the case with intervention effects). To complicate matters further, intent-to-treat analyses provide an overestimate of intervention effects if more participants drop out from the control group before providing termination data or more participants drop out from the intervention condition after providing termination data. Reflexively, intent-to-treat analyses provide an underestimate of intervention effects if more participants drop out from the intervention group before providing termination data or more participants drop out from the control condition after providing termination data.

Table 3.1 Results and Design Features of Controlled Eating Disorder Prevention Trials

Study	N	Mean Age	Randomized	Follow-Up Period (Months)	Type	Focus	Program Duration (Hours)	Outcomes — Knowledge	Healthy Lifestyle Improvements	Perfectionism	Thin-Ideal Internalization	Body Dissatisfaction	Dieting	Negative Affect	Eating Pathology	Body-Mass
Baranowski & Hetherington, 2001	29 F	11.5	No	6	Targ.	Inter.	7.5	—	—	—	—	No	Yes	No	No	—
Bearman et al., 2002	73 F	18.9	Yes	6	Targ.	Inter.	4	—	—	—	—	Yes	No	Yes	No	—
Buddeberg-Fischer et al., 1998	314 MF	16.1	No	0	Univ.	Didac.	4.5	—	—	—	—	—	—	—	—	No
Butters & Cash, 1987	31 F	21.3	Yes	0	Targ.	Inter.	6	—	—	—	—	Yes	—	Yes	—	—
Celio et al., 2000	76 F	19.6	Yes	6	Targ.	Inter.	5 Comp.	—	—	—	—	Yes	Yes	—	No	—
							24 Class.	—	—	—	—	No	No	—	No	—
Dalle Grave et al., 2001	106 MF	11.6	No	6	Univ.	Inter.	16	Yes	—	—	—	No	No	No	No	—
Dworkin & Kerr, 1987	79 F	—	Yes	0	Targ.	Inter.	1.5 CT	—	—	—	—	Yes	—	—	—	—
							1.5 CBT	—	—	—	—	Yes	—	—	—	—
Franko, 1998	19 F	—	No	0	Targ.	Inter.	2	—	—	—	No	Yes	—	—	No	—
Kaminski & McNamara, 1996	29 F	18.3	Yes	1	Targ.	Inter.	12	—	—	Yes	Yes	Yes	Yes	Yes	No	—
Kater et al., in press	206 F	10.0	No	0	Univ.	Didac.	11	Yes	No	—	No	No	—	No	—	—
	209 M	10.0	No	0	Univ.	Didac.	11	Yes	Yes	—	Yes	No	—	Yes	—	—
Killen et al., 1993	838 F	12.4	Yes	24	Univ.	Didac.	15	Yes	No	No	—	No	No	No	No	No
Klem et al., 1997	520 F	47.0	Yes	0	Targ.	Inter.	15	—	Yes	—	—	—	—	Yes	Yes	Yes
Mann et al., 1997	113 F	17.9	No	4	Univ.	Didac.	1.5	—	—	—	—	No	—	No	No	—
Martz & Bazzini, 1999	114 F	19.0	Yes	1	Univ.	Didac.	1	—	—	—	No	No	No	—	—	No
	77 F	19.0	Yes	1	Univ.	Didac.	1	—	—	—	No	No	No	—	—	No

(continued)

Table 3.1 *(Continued)*

Study	N	Mean Age	Randomized	Follow-Up Period (Months)	Type	Focus	Program Duration (Hours)	Knowledge	Healthy Lifestyle Improvements	Perfectionism	Thin-Ideal Internalization	Body Dissatisfaction	Dieting	Negative Affect	Eating Pathology	Body-Mass
												Outcomes				
McVey & Davis, 2002	263 F	10.9	No	12	Univ.	Inter.	5	—	—	—	—	No	—	—	No	—
McVey, Davis, et al., 2002	258 F	11.2	No	12	Univ.	Inter.	6	—	—	No	—	Yes	—	Yes	No	—
McVey, Lieberman, et al., 2002	214 F	12.5	No	3	Targ.	Inter.	10	—	—	—	—	Yes	Yes	No	Yes	—
Moreno & Thelen, 1993	104 F	13.7	No	1	Univ.	Didac.	0.5	Yes	—	—	—	—	—	—	—	—
	115 F	13.8	No	1	Univ.	Didac.	0.5	Yes	—	—	—	—	—	—	—	—
Neumark-Sztainer et al., 1995	269 F	15.3	No	24	Univ.	Inter.	10	Yes	Yes	—	—	No	Yes	No	Yes	—
Neumark-Sztainer et al., 2000	208 F	10.6	Yes	3	Univ.	Inter.	9	Yes	—	—	Yes	No	No	—	No	—
Nicolino et al., 2001	85 F	18.9	Yes	1	Univ.	Inter.	1	—	—	—	—	No	No	No	—	—
O'Dea & Abraham, 2000	470 FM	12.9	No	12	Univ.	Inter.	10	—	—	No	Yes	Yes	No	No	No	Yes
Paxton, 1993	136 F	14.1	No	11	Univ.	Inter.	10	—	—	—	No	No	No	No	No	No
Phelps et al., 2000	530 F	12.0	No	0	Univ.	Inter.	6	—	—	—	—	No	—	—	No	—
Presnell & Stice, 2003	81 F	20.0	Yes	1.5	Targ.	Inter.	3	—	—	—	—	—	Yes	Yes	Yes	Yes
Rosen et al., 1989	23 F	19.0	Yes	2	Targ.	Inter.	12	—	—	—	—	Yes	—	—	—	—
Santonastaso et al., 1999	308 F	16.1	No	12	Univ.	Inter.	16	—	—	No	No	No	No	No	No	No
Smolak et al., 1998a	222 FM	10.0	No	2	Univ.	Didac.	8	Yes	No	—	—	No	No	—	—	—

Study	Sample	Age			Program	Format	Length								
Smolak et al., 1998b	266 FM	9.0	No	0	Univ.	Didac.	8	Yes	No	—	No	No	No	—	—
Stewart et al., 2001	752 F	13.4	No	6	Univ.	Inter.	4.5	Yes	—	—	Yes	Yes	No	No	—
Stice, Mazotti, et al., 2000	30 F	18.0	No	1	Targ.	Inter.	3	—	—	Yes	Yes	No	Yes	Yes	—
Stice & Ragan, 2002	66 F	21.0	No	0	Targ.	Inter.	33	—	No	Yes	Yes	Yes	No	Yes	Yes
Stice et al., 2003	148 F	17.4	Yes	6	Targ.	Inter.	3 Diss.	—	—	No	No	No	Yes	Yes	—
							3 Health	—	—	No	No	No	Yes	Yes	—
Stice et al., 2002	193 F	17.0	Yes	6	Targ.	Inter.	3 Diss.	Yes	Yes	Yes	Yes	Yes	Yes	Yes	Yes
							3 Health	Yes	Yes	Yes	Yes	Yes	No	Yes	Yes
Varnado-Sullivan et al., 2001	157 F	12.0	No	0	Univ.	Inter.	2.5	—	—	Yes	No	No	No	No	—
	130 M	12.0	No	0	Univ.	Inter.	2.5	—	—	No	No	No	No	No	—
Winzelberg et al., 1998	57 F	19.7	Yes	3	Targ.	Didac.	5	No	—	—	Yes	—	Yes	No	No
Winzelberg et al., 2000	60 F	20.0	Yes	3	Targ.	Didac.	5	—	—	Yes	Yes	—	Yes	No	—

Note: F = Females; M = Males; CBT = Cognitive behavior therapy; Class. = Eating disorder course; Comp. = Computer-administered Intervention; CT = Cognitive therapy; Didac. = Didactic presentation; Diss. = Dissonance Intervention; Health = Healthy weight management Intervention; Inter = Interactive exercises; Targ. = Targeted program; Univ. = Universal program. All outcomes are for analyses on the whole sample, rather than subgroups at high risk. The tables report *any* positive program effects regardless of whether they occurred at termination or a subsequent follow-up assessment. A dash signifies that this outcome was not examined in the trial.

UNIVERSAL PREVENTION PROGRAMS

Universal Programs Evaluated in Randomized Controlled Trials

Our literature search identified four universal eating disorder prevention programs that have been evaluated in trials wherein participants were randomly assigned to condition. Studies for which the basis of random assignment was the classroom or school were considered randomized trials only if the data analytic technique reflected the fact that the unit of random assignment was not the individual (e.g., used hierarchical linear models).

The earliest trial evaluated a didactic psychoeducational intervention that provided information on the harmful effects of unhealthy weight control behaviors, promoted healthy weight control behaviors (good nutrition and regular moderate exercise), and taught coping skills to resist sociocultural pressures for thinness (Killen et al., 1993). Although this intervention resulted in increased knowledge at termination (postintervention), this effect was no longer significant at follow-up and the program did not produce significant change in healthy weight control behaviors, perfectionism, body dissatisfaction, dieting, negative affect, eating pathology, or body mass at termination or any follow-up assessment.

Martz and Bazzini (1999) evaluated a brief didactic psychoeducational intervention that distributed treatment referrals and provided information on eating disorders, putative causes of eating disorders, and healthy weight control behaviors. The authors first examined the effects of the intervention when a peer educator delivered the program (study 1). They next evaluated the effects of this intervention when a professional delivered an enhanced version of the program that included a guided imagery exercise to enhance body satisfaction (study 2). However, the intervention did not produce significant changes in thin-ideal internalization, body dissatisfaction, dieting, or body mass in either evaluation at termination or one-month follow-up.

The next trial examined an intervention that provided psychoeducational material on normative physical development, included exercises intended to promote self-esteem, and involved a variety of interactive exercises focused on helping adolescents become critical consumers of the thin-ideal media (Neumark-Sztainer, Sherwood, Coller, & Hannan, 2000). This intervention produced significant increases in knowledge at termination, but not three-month follow-up, and significant decreases in thin-ideal internalization at three-month follow-up, but not at termination. This intervention did not produce significant effects for body dissatisfaction, dieting, or eating pathology at either termination or three-month follow-up.

The last trial (Nicolino et al., 2001) evaluated an abbreviated version of the cognitive-behavioral intervention originally developed by Butters and Cash (1987). This brief intervention focused on emotional and behavioral precipitants and consequences of body image disturbances, behavioral rituals concerning appearance, challenging maladaptive cognitions concerning body dissatisfaction and other negative cognitions, and relapse prevention. A noteworthy aspect of this trial was its use of a placebo control group that provided education concerning body image and eating disorders. However, the intervention did not produce any significant reductions in body dissatisfaction, anxiety as to body shape, fear of fat, or dieting behavior at the one-month follow-up.

Universal Programs Evaluated in Controlled Trials

We located 16 universal eating disorder prevention programs that were evaluated in controlled trials that did not randomly assign participants to condition. The earliest program presented didactic psychoeducational information about sociocultural pressures, determinants of body size, nutrition, weight control methods, and emotional eating and allowed students to have interactive discussions about these topics in small groups (Paxton, 1993). However, this intervention did not produce any significant reductions in thin-ideal internalization, body dissatisfaction, dieting, negative affect, eating pathology, or body mass at 1-month or 12-month follow-ups.

Moreno and Thelen (1993) evaluated a brief didactic psychoeducational presentation that provided information on eating disorders, adverse consequences of eating pathology, putative causes of eating disorders, healthy weight control behaviors, and peer pressure resistance skills. The effects of this intervention were evaluated when it was delivered by a research assistant (study 1) and when it was delivered by a home economics teacher (study 2). This intervention produced a significant effect on knowledge and behavioral intentions to diet at termination and one-month follow-up, but no measures of risk factors for eating pathology or of eating pathology were included in this trial.

The next trial examined the effects of a didactic psychoeducational intervention that presented information on healthy weight control behaviors, body image, eating disorders, putative causes of eating disorders, and social pressure resistance skills (Neumark-Sztainer, Butler, & Palti, 1995). This intervention produced significant improvements in knowledge, healthy weight control behaviors, dieting, and binge eating at six-month follow-up, although only the effect for binge eating remained significant at the two-year follow-up. No significant changes were observed for body dissatisfaction and negative affect at either of the follow-up assessments.

Mann and associates (1997) examined a didactic psychoeducational intervention that provided information on eating disorders and consequences of eating disorders, as well as presentations from individuals in recovery from eating disorders concerning the course of their illness. However, this intervention produced no statistically significant changes in body dissatisfaction, negative affect, or eating pathology at either the one-month or three-month follow-up assessments.

The next trial evaluated a didactic psychoeducational intervention for fifth-grade students that provided information on nutrition, healthy weight control techniques, and diversity of body shapes and promoted critical evaluation of thin-ideal content in the media (Smolak et al., 1998a). Although the intervention produced some improvements in knowledge and attitudes toward overweight individuals at follow-up (one to four months), there were no significant effects on healthy weight control behaviors, body dissatisfaction, or dieting. Smolak, Levine, and Schermer (1998b) also evaluated this intervention when it was delivered to fourth-grade students. Whereas significant improvements were observed for knowledge at termination, there were no significant effects for attitudes toward overweight individuals, healthy weight control behaviors, body dissatisfaction, or dieting.

Another universal prevention trial evaluated a didactic intervention that provided information on normative physical development, nutrition, healthy weight control behaviors, eating disorders, and putative risk factors for eating disorders (Buddeberg-Fischer,

Klaghofer, Gnam, & Buddeberg, 1998). Unfortunately, there were no significant intervention effects on eating disorders symptoms, general psychiatric symptoms, or physical symptoms at termination.

Santonastaso and colleagues (1999) evaluated an intervention that provided psycho-educational information about normative physical development and eating disorders and allowed participants to engage in unstructured discussions about a variety of topics, including body image concerns, sociocultural pressures, and coping with life stressors. However, there were no significant intervention effects for perfectionism, thin-ideal internalization, body dissatisfaction, dieting, negative affect, eating pathology, or body mass at the one-year follow-up assessment.

The next intervention, which was interactive in nature, consisted of sessions focusing on promoting positive self-esteem, coping skills, and social skills (O'Dea & Abraham, 2000). Two exemplary design features of this study were: (1) the intervention and the questionnaires used to assess the intervention were presented as completely unrelated and (2) the teachers who delivered the intervention were not informed that the intervention was designed to improve body satisfaction and eating disturbances. These features putatively minimized the possibility that demand characteristics and expectancy effects could explain any observed intervention effects. This intervention produced significant reductions in thin-ideal internalization and unhealthy weight loss at 12-month follow-up, but not at termination, and reductions in body dissatisfaction at termination, but not at 12-month follow-up. There were no significant intervention effects for change in perfectionism, dieting, negative affect, or eating pathology at termination or follow-up.

Another trial evaluated an interactive program among middle school girls that focused on reducing thin-ideal internalization and body dissatisfaction and on promoting feelings of competence and healthy weight control behaviors (Phelps, Sapia, Nathanson, & Nelson, 2000). Unfortunately, there were no significant intervention effects on change in body satisfaction, self-esteem, or eating pathology at termination.

An additional trial evaluated an interactive program that focused on resisting cultural pressures for thinness, determinants of body weight, body acceptance, effects of cognitions on emotions, nature and consequences of eating disorders, self-esteem enhancement, stress management, and healthy weight control behaviors (Stewart, Carter, Drinkwater, Hainsworth, & Fairburn, 2001). This intervention produced significant improvements in knowledge and body dissatisfaction and decreases in dieting at termination, but not at six-month follow-up. There were no significant intervention effects for negative affect or eating disorder symptoms at termination or follow-up assessment.

The next trial evaluated an interactive intervention that provided information concerning eating disorders and the putative risk factors for eating disorders and attempted to reduce overvaluation of appearance and promote self-acceptance and healthy weight control behaviors (Dalle Grave, De Luca, & Campello, 2001). Significant intervention effects were observed for knowledge and eating concerns at termination and six-month follow-up, but no significant effects were observed for body dissatisfaction, dieting, negative affect, or eating pathology at either of these assessments.

Another trial evaluated an intervention that focused on the causes and consequences of body dissatisfaction (particularly cultural influences) and healthy weight control behaviors (Varnado-Sullivan et al., 2001). There were significant intervention effects at termination for thin-ideal internalization, but not for dieting, negative affect, or eating pathology for girls. No intervention effects were observed for boys.

McVey and Davis (2002) evaluated an interactive program that focused on fostering critical use of the media, body acceptance, healthy weight control behaviors, and stress management skills and that provided information concerning the determinants of body mass. However, this intervention did not produce any significant change in body dissatisfaction or eating pathology at termination or any of the follow-up assessments. McVey, Davis, Tweed, and Shaw (2002), in an independent evaluation of this intervention, found that the intervention produced significant improvements in body dissatisfaction and negative affect at termination but that these effects did not persist for any of the follow-up assessments. There were no significant program effects on perfectionism or eating pathology at termination or follow-up assessments.

The final trial evaluated a psychoeducational intervention that provided knowledge concerning the determinants of body shape and healthy weight control behaviors and sought to promote body acceptance, coping skills, and critical thinking concerning mass media (Kater, Rohwer, & Londre, in press). For girls, there were significant intervention effects for knowledge at termination, but not for healthy weight control behaviors, thin-ideal internalization, body satisfaction, and negative affect. For boys, there were significant intervention effects for knowledge, healthy weight control behaviors, thin-ideal internalization, and negative affect, but not body satisfaction.

TARGETED PREVENTION PROGRAMS

Targeted Programs Evaluated in Randomized Controlled Trials

Our literature review identified 13 targeted eating disorder prevention programs that have been evaluated in randomized trials. The earliest evaluated a cognitive and a cognitive-behavioral intervention designed to reduce body dissatisfaction among individuals with elevated body image disturbances (Dworkin & Kerr, 1987). The individually administered cognitive intervention focused exclusively on changing women's negative self-statements into more positive ones. The individually administered cognitive-behavioral intervention focused on changing negative self-statements, but also promoted self-reinforcement for cognitive restructuring and required participants to role-play being a confident person with an attractive body. There were significant reductions in body dissatisfaction at termination for both interventions relative to the placebo control condition, but no follow-up data were collected. No other outcome measures were included in this trial.

Butters and Cash (1987) evaluated another cognitive-behavioral intervention designed to promote body satisfaction among women with initial body image disturbances. This individually administered intervention focused on replacing negative self-statements about appearance with positive statements and used systematic desensitization to reduce anxiety about body dissatisfaction. This intervention produced significant reductions in body dissatisfaction and negative affect by termination. No other outcomes were examined and no follow-up data were collected.

The next trial compared a cognitive-behavioral intervention designed to reduce body image disturbances to a minimal-treatment control condition (Rosen et al., 1989). The cognitive-behavioral intervention was similar in content to that evaluated by Butters and Cash (1987), except it was delivered in a small group format, it provided corrective feedback as to body size misperception, and it attempted to reduce avoidance of behaviors that elicit body image concerns. The minimal-treatment placebo control condition covered only the didactic presentation of material covered in the cognitive-behavioral intervention and excluded the exercises designed to promote use of cognitive and behavioral skills for reducing body image disturbances. The cognitive-behavioral program produced significantly greater improvements in body size estimation, body dissatisfaction, and behavioral avoidance at termination and two-month follow-up relative to the minimal-treatment intervention.

Kaminski and McNamara (1996) examined an interactive intervention that provided information about eating disorders, putative risk factors for eating disorders, and healthy and unhealthy weight control; presented cognitive interventions for body image and eating disturbances; and taught affect regulation and communication skills. This intervention produced significant reductions in perfectionism, thin-ideal internalization, body dissatisfaction, dieting, and negative affect at termination. All of these effects except perfectionism were present at one-month follow-up. There were no significant intervention effects for eating pathology at either termination or follow-up.

The next trial evaluated a healthy weight management intervention that focused on reducing caloric overconsumption and increasing exercise among adult women at risk for weight gain by virtue of impending menopause (Klem, Wing, Simkin-Silverman, & Kuller, 1997). Participants assigned to this intervention, versus those in a measurement-only control condition, evidenced significant improvements in healthy lifestyle behaviors, negative affect, binge eating, and body mass at termination.

Franko (1998) evaluated an intervention that critically evaluated cultural pressures for thinness, presented healthy weight control skills, used cognitive-behavioral skills to challenge dysfunctional cognitions about body image, and introduced affect regulation skills. The intervention produced significant improvements in body dissatisfaction at termination but did not produce significant effects for thin-ideal internalization or bulimic symptoms.

Another trial (Winzelberg et al., 1998) evaluated a computer-administered eating disorder prevention program that was based on cognitive-behavioral interventions for body dissatisfaction (Butters & Cash, 1987; Rosen et al., 1989). This intervention provided information on eating disorders, healthy weight control behaviors, and nutrition. Participants also took part in an unstructured e-mail support interchange that allowed participants to talk about emotionally important material and reactions to the intervention. Although the intervention produced significant decreases in body dissatisfaction that persisted through the three-month follow-up assessment, there were no significant effects for knowledge, eating pathology, or body mass at termination or follow-up. The first follow-up study (Winzelberg et al., 2000) evaluated a refined version of this computer-administered intervention. This intervention produced significant reductions in body dissatisfaction at follow-up but not termination. There were no intervention effects on eating pathology at either termination or follow-up assessment. The second follow-up study (Celio et al., 2000) evaluated the third generation of the computer-administered intervention developed by Winzelberg and associates (1998) and an eating disorder class offered at a university. The computer-administered program was enhanced by including interactive cognitive-behavioral exercises, in-person meetings with a facilitator, weekly reading assignments, and critical reflection papers on the readings.

Relative to the control group, the computer-administered intervention produced significant improvements in body dissatisfaction at termination and six-month follow-up and significant improvements in dieting at six-month follow-up. No significant effects were observed for bulimic symptoms at termination or six-month follow-up. There were no significant intervention effects on these outcomes for the eating disorder class relative to the control group.

The next trial evaluated an interactive dissonance-based intervention and an interactive healthy weight management intervention relative to a waitlist control condition (Stice, Trost, & Chase, 2003). In the dissonance intervention, participants with elevated levels of thin-ideal internalization were asked to voluntarily take a stance against the thin ideal in a series of verbal, written, and behavioral exercises. The healthy weight management intervention, which asserted that body image disturbances are a product of unhealthy lifestyle behaviors, promoted lasting decreases in consumption of high-fat foods and increases in exercise. The dissonance intervention produced significant intervention effects for negative affect and eating pathology at termination and three-month follow-up, although both effects were no longer significant at the six-month follow-up. The healthy weight intervention produced significant effects for negative affect and eating pathology, and these effects were present at termination and all follow-up assessments. Neither intervention produced significant effects for thin-ideal internalization, body dissatisfaction, or dieting.

Another trial (Presnell & Stice, 2003) evaluated the effects of a low-calorie diet on nonobese women. The intervention was adapted from Brownell's (1997) obesity treatment program but spanned only a six-week period. The intervention produced significant reductions in interview-assessed bulimic pathology and weight loss, as well as marginally significant reductions in depressive symptoms, relative to the waitlist control group at termination.

An additional trial (Bearman, Stice, & Chase, 2002) evaluated an abbreviated four-session version of the cognitive-behavioral intervention for body dissatisfaction developed by Cash and Rosen (Butters & Cash, 1987; Rosen et al., 1989). There were significant intervention effects for body dissatisfaction at termination; these effects persisted to six-month follow-up relative to a waitlist control condition, as well as for negative affect at termination, but these effects persisted only to three-month follow-up. There were marginally significant effects for bulimic symptoms at termination; these effects persisted through three-month follow-up. However, there were no significant intervention effects for dieting.

The final trial (Stice et al., 2002), which is still ongoing (current $N = 193$), is providing a more rigorous test of the dissonance and healthy weight management interventions tested in a preliminary trial (Stice et al., 2003). Participants were randomly assigned to the dissonance intervention, the healthy weight management intervention, a writing-paradigm placebo control condition, or a measurement-only control condition. There were significant program effects for the dissonance intervention relative to the placebo and measurement-only control conditions for healthy weight control behaviors, thin-ideal internalization, body dissatisfaction, dieting, negative affect, and eating disorder symptoms at termination. However, the effects for healthy weight management behaviors and negative affect were no longer significant at the three-month and/or six-month follow-up assessment. The dissonance intervention produced significant program effects for body mass at follow-up assessments but not termination. There were significant intervention effects for the healthy weight management intervention relative to the placebo and measurement-only conditions for healthy weight control behaviors, thin-ideal internalization, body dissatisfaction, and eating pathology at termination, but effects for healthy weight control behaviors were no longer significant at the three-month and six-month follow-up assessments. There were significant effects for the healthy weight management intervention for body dissatisfaction and body mass at the three-month follow-up, but not at termination or six-month follow-up. It must be acknowledged that the power to detect effects at the three-month and six-month follow-up assessments was limited because of the relatively small sample size for these analyses at this point in the study.

Targeted Programs Evaluated in Nonrandomized Controlled Trials

Our literature search identified four targeted prevention programs that were evaluated in a controlled trial wherein the participants were not randomly assigned to condition. The first trial (Stice, Mazotti, Weibel, & Agras, 2000) was a preliminary evaluation of the dissonance intervention examined (Stice et al., 2003). This intervention produced significant reductions in thin-ideal internalization, body dissatisfaction, negative affect, and bulimic symptoms. All effects except that for negative affect persisted at the one-month follow-up. It was noteworthy that the intervention appeared to prevent the significant increases in bulimic symptoms that were observed in the control participants over the two-month study period.

The second targeted intervention to be evaluated in a nonrandomized controlled trial provided information on eating disorders, causes and consequences of eating disorders, body dissatisfaction, thin-ideal internalization, and negative affect (Baranowski & Hetherington, 2001). A noteworthy feature of this evaluation is that it used a placebo control group that promoted awareness of the benefits of eating fruits and vegetables. This intervention produced significantly greater reductions in dietary restraint at termination and follow-up than were observed in the placebo control group. However, there were no significant intervention effects for body dissatisfaction, negative affect, or eating pathology.

Stice and Ragan (2002) evaluated a psychoeducational eating disorder class offered at a university. The high rates of body image and eating disturbances among the participants who enrolled in the class suggest that this intervention is best conceptualized as targeted in nature. This interactive class presented psychoeducational information on eating disorders and obesity, putative causes of these disorders, and prevention and treatment programs for these disorders. This intervention produced significant decreases in thin-ideal internalization, body dissatisfaction, dieting, eating pathology, and body mass at termination, although effects were not observed for negative affect or healthy weight control behaviors. It was noteworthy that this intervention appeared to prevent the naturalistic increases in weight that were observed in the control group and reduced weight in the most overweight participants.

The final trial (McVey, Lieberman, Voorberg, Wardrope, & Blackmore, 2002) evaluated the interactive psychoeducational intervention examined by McVey and colleagues (McVey & Davis, 2002). This intervention was considered targeted because rather than offering it to all students in extant classes, it was offered only to participants who voluntarily signed up for a support group designed to prevent low body satisfaction and self-esteem, peer pressure to diet, and eating disturbances. The intervention produced significant improvements in body dissatisfaction, dieting, and bulimic symptoms relative to the measurement-only control group at both termination and three-month follow-up assessments. It was noteworthy that the effect for bulimic pathology appears to represent a classic prevention effect, wherein the intervention appeared to prevent the increases in bulimic symptoms that were observed in the measurement-only control group.

RESULTS FOR HIGH-RISK PARTICIPANTS

Several universal prevention trials also examined the effects of their intervention for subsets of participants at high-risk for eating pathology. These results are particularly important because they provide a within-study comparison of whether the intervention effects are stronger for the entire sample or high-risk subsamples. Killen and associates (1993) found an effect for change in body mass in a high-risk group characterized by initial body dissatisfaction that did not reach significance when the full sample was examined. However, there were still no intervention effects for healthy weight control behaviors, perfectionism, body dissatisfaction, dieting, negative affect, or eating pathology in the high-risk subsample. Buddeberg-Fischer and associates (1998) found intervention effects for physical symptoms, but not eating disorder symptoms or general psychiatric symptoms, among females with initial elevations in eating pathology (this effect was not significant in the full sample analyses). Stewart and colleagues (2001) found that decreases in dietary restraint were stronger for participants with initial elevations in this outcome. O'Dea and Abraham (2000) found that the intervention effects for body dissatisfaction persisted longer in the high-risk subsample compared to the complete sample. Even within targeted prevention trials, the intervention effects for body dissatisfaction are more pronounced for high-risk subjects characterized by particularly high levels of body image disturbances (Celio et al., 2000; Winzelberg et al., 2000). In contrast, two studies have not found that the intervention effects were stronger for high-risk subsamples (Santonastaso et al., 1999; Varnado-Sullivan et al., 2001). However, the sample sizes for the high-risk analyses for these two studies were particularly small, which may explain the anomalous results.

SUMMARY EFFECTS

Overall, this review suggests that a number of promising eating disorder prevention programs have been evaluated in controlled trials. Specifically, 22 (67%) of the prevention programs resulted in significant reductions in at least one established risk factor for eating pathology, such as body dissatisfaction. Even more exciting is the fact that 6 (18%) of the prevention programs resulted in significant reductions in eating pathology, including evidence that these interventions both reduce extant eating pathology and prevent increases in eating pathology that were observed in control groups. These promising findings represent a relatively new development, given that most of the more effective prevention programs have been evaluated in the past few years. The programs that produced intervention effects for eating pathology appear to primarily involve cognitive interventions that alter maladaptive attitudes, such as thin-ideal internalization or body dissatisfaction, and behavioral interventions that alter maladaptive behaviors, such as fasting and overeating. Nevertheless, there was a wide range of intervention effects, ranging from those that produced no effects on any outcomes to those that produced significant effects for all outcomes. Because positive intervention effects appeared to be systematically related to the type of prevention program, content of the intervention, and design features of the trials, it seemed most useful to describe intervention effects as a function of these moderating factors.

First, didactic interventions produced fewer effects than interactive interventions. Most of the programs that were coded as didactic in this review produced only changes in knowledge, with very few effects on eating pathology or established risk factors for eating pathology. It was particularly illustrative that none of the didactic interventions produced significant effects for eating pathology and that all of the interventions that produced effects for this key outcome were interactive. Parenthetically, prevention researchers in other areas have similarly concluded that psychoeducational didactic presentations are less effective than interventions that actively engage participants and teach new skills (Clarke, Hawkins, Murphy, & Sheeber, 1993; Moskowitz, 1989). An interactive format might be necessary to ensure that participants engage in the program material and learn to apply the concepts to their own lives.

Second, targeted prevention programs tended to produce more positive effects than universal interventions. Most of the universal programs did not produce effects for thin-ideal internalization, body dissatisfaction, dieting, negative affect, eating pathology, and adiposity, whereas most of the targeted interventions produced effects for these outcomes. A similar pattern of findings emerged for healthy weight control behaviors and perfectionism, although fewer programs included these outcomes. It was particularly noteworthy that seven of the eight interventions that produced effects for eating pathology were targeted. It was also striking that only targeted interventions prevented the future increases in eating pathology that were observed in control groups. This is important because it suggests that the intervention effects are not resulting merely because the programs decrease initial elevations in eating disturbances. Mirroring the pattern of findings across studies, there was also evidence from within data sets that supported this conclusion. Several universal prevention programs were more effective for high-risk participants than for the full sample. Prevention programs for depression (Clarke et al., 1995), anxiety (Lowry-Webster, Barrett, & Dadds, 2001), behavior problems (Stoolmiller, Eddy, & Reid, 2000), substance abuse (Murphy et al., 2001), and sexual coercion (Pacifici, Stoolmiller, & Nelson, 2001) also produce stronger effects for people with initially elevated symptoms. The levels of eating pathology and risk factors for eating pathology in unselected samples may be so low that they render it difficult to detect any significant intervention effects. Alternatively, unselected samples may not be sufficiently motivated to fully engage in the prevention program, which may attenuate the intervention effects.

Third, studies focusing on older participants tended to produce stronger prevention effects. Seven of the eight programs that produced effects on eating pathology focused on samples with a mean age of 15 or greater. In contrast, none of the programs focusing on participants younger than 12 years of age produced effects on eating pathology. The program that focused on the youngest sample (mean age of 9 years) did not produce any effects for risk factors for eating pathology (eating pathology was not assessed). Thus, the suggestion that past prevention programs have shown limited success because participants were too old when the program was delivered (Smolak et al., 1998a) was not supported. One possible explanation for this pattern of findings is that younger girls have such low levels of eating disturbances and risk factors for eating pathology, it attenuates statistical power to detect intervention effects. It may also be that younger participants have not struggled with body image and eating disturbances long enough for them to be sufficiently motivated to engage in prevention programs. It may be preferable to intervene immediately before the period of greatest risk for onset of eating pathology because this might maximize motivation to participate in the intervention and result in optimal prevention effects. Prospective studies suggest that binge eating and bulimic pathology typically emerge between the ages of 16 and 18, but that anorexic pathology often emerges a few years earlier (Lewinsohn et al., 2000; Stice et al., 1998).

There also appeared to be a trend for interventions that were not explicitly presented as eating disorder prevention programs to produce more positive effects. Among seven of the eight prevention programs that produced effects on eating pathology, participants were not informed that the intervention was hypothesized to decrease eating pathology. Most of these interventions were described as either body acceptance or weight control interventions. Such *covert prevention programs* may be more effective because they skirt defensiveness about disturbed eating behaviors. This conjecture accords with the evidence that targeted interventions that sought to recruit high-risk participants with eating disorder screening measures were ineffective (Shisslak, Crago, & Neal, 1990; Varnado-Sullivan et al., 2001). It is acknowledged that this observation is speculative because it was not always clear how the programs were described (but we were confident about the five trials from our research group that produced effects for eating pathology).

It is also important to note aspects of the intervention and experimental design that did *not* appear to be related to positive intervention effects. Surprisingly, length of the intervention was only weakly related to positive outcome, in that several of the longest interventions produced no effects on any outcome and a number of brief interventions produced potent effects. However, programs one hour or less in duration consistently produced no effects for established risk factors or eating pathology. In addition, sample size did not appear systematically related to positive intervention effects. The trial with the largest sample produced no effects for any eating disorder risk factor or eating pathology, whereas some studies with very small samples were able to produce marked effects on these same outcomes. There was also little evidence that length of follow-up was related to positive outcome. Programs that produced effects for eating pathology had follow-up periods ranging from 0 to 24 months—which is the exact range for prevention trials that failed to produce effects for this primary outcome. There were also instances wherein positive intervention effects were observed only at termination and other instances when the positive effects were observed only at long-term follow-up assessments. Thus, it seemed that session content and the sampling frame were more important than sheer duration of the intervention, the sample size, and the length of follow-up assessments. It is noteworthy, however, that the content of the successful prevention programs varied dramatically, including programs that focused on promoting media literacy and life skills, healthy weight management, and critical analysis of the thin ideal. This suggests that there may be multiple methods to successfully prevent eating pathology.

There is insufficient information to draw conclusions about a number of factors that might be predictors of positive intervention effects. First, it was not feasible to determine what specific types of program content are related to positive outcome. Because most programs focused on a number of topics and because there was substantial overlap in certain topics, we were not able to generate mutually exclusive groups of interventions with different program content. Because many interventions were not described in detail, it was difficult to determine program content that was associated with positive intervention effects. Second, although seven trials included both boys and girls (Buddeberg-Fischer et al., 1998; Dalle Grave et al., 2001; Kater et al., in press; O'Dea & Abraham, 2000; Smolak et al., 1998a, 1998b; Varnado-Sullivan et al., 2001), no study apparently tested whether sex moderated intervention effects. Thus, it was not possible to draw conclusions about the effects of participant sex on intervention effects. It is noteworthy, however, that the two studies that analyzed the intervention effects separately for boys and girls produced mixed findings: One found stronger effects for girls (Varnado-Sullivan et al., 2001), and one found stronger effects for boys (Kater et al., in press).

Theoretical Issues

Three main theoretical limitations appear to be hindering the development of more effective eating disorder prevention programs. First, etiologic models of eating pathology did not guide the design of most eating disorder prevention programs. Most of the early prevention programs focused on providing psychoeducational information about eating pathology, despite the fact that no etiologic model posits that a lack of information about eating disorders is a risk factor for development of these conditions. It seems preferable to design interventions to reduce factors that theoretically increase the risk for eating pathology onset.

A second theoretical limitation of the literature is that several of the interventions sought to reduce putative risk factors for eating pathology that have not yet been validated in prospective research or that have received meager support in prospective studies. Examples of the former types of programs are those that attempt to promote communication skills, coping skills, or media literacy. To our knowledge, these factors have not yet been found to predict subsequent development or increases in eating pathology (although some may eventually be shown to predict this outcome). Examples of the latter types of programs are those that focus on promoting self-esteem, which has generally been found not to predict future eating pathology (Keel, Fulkerson, & Leon, 1997; Vohs, Bardone, Joiner, Abramson, & Heatherton, 1999; Vohs et al., 2001). The payoff for prevention efforts would probably be greater if interventions targeted empirically established risk factors.

Another theoretical limitation is revealed by a vexing pattern of findings. Three of the successful eating disorder prevention programs *increased* a variable that is widely accepted to be a risk factor for eating pathology: dieting. Interventions that entailed either a low-calorie diet for weight loss purposes (Presnell & Stice, 2003) or lifestyle changes in caloric intake and exercise for weight maintenance purposes (Klem et al., 1997; Stice et al., 2002) resulted in significant *reductions* in bulimic pathology. These findings converge with the evidence from obesity treatment trials that low-calorie diets result in decreased binge eating (Goodrick, Poston, Kimball, Reeves, & Foreyt, 1998; Reeves et al., 2001). These findings raise serious questions about the accepted theory that dieting is a risk factor for eating pathology. Indeed, a literature review revealed no experimental evidence that dieting causes eating pathology. A broader implication is that we may be mistaken about the causal relation between other putative risk factors and eating pathology. This state of affairs underscores the importance of confirming the relation between risk factors and eating pathology that emerge in prospective studies with randomized experiments.

Methodological Limitations

There were a number of methodological limitations of this literature. Most importantly, many prevention trials did not include a control group. Without a waitlist control group or measurement-only control group, it is not possible to disentangle true intervention effects from the effects of passage of time, regression to the mean, or measurement artifacts. In this context, there appears to be little evidence that repeated administration of assessment measures produces artifactual decreases in scores (a.k.a. pretest sensitization). Experiments that tested whether completing measures once impacts how these scales are completed a second time with a Soloman four-group design have provided no evidence of pretest sensitization (Mann et al., 1997; Martz & Bazzini, 1999).

A second methodological limitation is that many prevention trials did not randomly assign participants to condition. More confidence can be placed in inferences from randomized prevention trials because they are in a better position to rule out any potential third-variable confounds (because all variables should be roughly equally distributed across conditions).

Third, only a handful of prevention trials used a placebo control condition. Without a placebo control group, there is no way to rule out the possibility that any observed decreases in the outcomes are due to demand characteristics or expectancy effects. On the one hand, the fact that most of the eating disorder prevention programs did not produce significant reductions in eating pathology suggests that demand characteristics and expectancy effects do not typically produce artifactual findings. On the other hand, the one study that included a placebo and a waitlist control condition found a small placebo response (3.6% of the variance explained for change eating disorder symptoms from pretest to posttest; Stice et al., 2002).[2] It must be acknowledged, however, that it can be difficult to identify a placebo intervention that is truly ineffective. It is also important to note that great care should be taken in selecting a placebo intervention because it

[2] Four trials compared an intervention to a placebo control group in the absence of a waitlist or measurement-only control group. However, this design provides little information as to whether there is a placebo response because nonsignificant differences between the intervention and placebo condition on the outcomes could result from a placebo response or because the intervention was not effective.

determines what inferences can be drawn as to potential confounds. For example, if the investigators think that nonspecific group factors are clinically important, they should select a placebo that does not contain these nonspecific factors.

Fourth, a surprising number of eating disorder prevention programs apparently did not assess eating pathology. This is troublesome because the defining feature of a successful eating disorder prevention program is that it reduces current or future eating disorder symptoms or syndromes. The assumption of interventions that target empirically established risk factors for eating pathology is that, by reducing the risk factors, consequent reductions in eating pathology should be observed. Such trials should include a measure of eating pathology so that this assumption can be directly tested.

Fifth, few studies have assessed clinically significant eating pathology. Several investigators used continuous symptom measures that do not map onto the diagnostic criteria for the eating disorders. Thus, there is no way of determining whether any reductions in these variables are clinically meaningful. It is preferable to use clinical interviews to ensure that only clinically significant eating pathology is recorded. This also helps minimize the false-positive problem that occurs with self-report measures of eating pathology (Fairburn & Beglin, 1994).

A final troublesome feature of previous trials is that they have sometimes used scales that do not tap a conceptually clear (unidimensional) construct (e.g., the drive for thinness scale, weight concerns scale, and the restraint scale). This state of affairs renders findings difficult to interpret unambiguously.

Statistical Limitations

The most serious statistical limitation of extant eating disorder prevention trials is that a large portion of the trials did not conduct appropriate inferential tests of intervention effects. Similar to randomized clinical trials, it is necessary to test whether there is *significantly greater change* (decreases or increases) on the outcome variable in the intervention versus control condition. This can be accomplished with repeated-measures ANOVA models or some sort of analysis of covariance models that control for initial levels of the outcome variables (as discussed previously). Some investigators simply tested for significant change in both intervention and control conditions without testing for significantly greater change in the intervention condition. If there was not significantly greater change, the effects are likely due to some alternative explanation (e.g., regression to the mean or measurement artifacts). Other investigators simply compared the mean levels of the outcome variables across the two groups at follow-up assessments without controlling for initial levels. The problem with this type of analysis is that any significant differences at follow-up might have been due to baseline differences between the two groups rather than a product of the intervention. Similar processes might obscure true intervention effects.

In this context, it is important to note that there is currently *no statistically reliable evidence of iatrogenic effects from eating disorder prevention programs.* Mann et al. (1997) found no evidence of any program effects in either a positive or negative direction when they analyzed their data correctly (what they refer to as a *conservative approach* in the article), that is, when they modeled change in the outcomes in the same participants over time. It was only when they compared follow-up data without controlling for initial levels of the outcome that they found what they interpreted as ia-trogenic effect. These latter analyses focused on data from chance groups of partici-pants who happened to complete their surveys at the various assessments—who did not even have to be the same subjects. Such findings could have been observed if a few more participants with eating disorders happened to complete the T2 assessment com-pared to the T1 and T3 assessment. It was remarkable that only 113 of the 597 provided data at all three assessments, leaving ample room for chance fluctuation in the compo-sition of the groups. The results from Carter, Stewart, Dunn, and Fairburn (1997) have also been interpreted by some as suggesting that prevention programs might do more harm than good. However, because this study did not include a control group, there is no way of ruling out the possibility that control participants would have shown similar, or even greater, increases in dieting over the same six-month period. Finally, some re-viewers have interpreted any evidence of symptom worsening among any participants in an intervention condition as indicative of an iatrogenic effect. However, care should be taken to distinguish statistically reliable evidence of greater symptom worsening in the intervention versus control group from chance fluctuation in symptoms. Only the former should be considered reliable evidence of iatrogenic effects—the latter reflects random noise. The premise of inferential statistics is that they help us differentiate re-liable patterns in the data from chance findings.

A second statistical limitation of the eating disorder prevention literature is that al-most no trials reported effect sizes (e.g., variance explained). This information is vital because it provides a clear indication of the clinical importance of prevention effects. For example, a prevention effect could be significant but might explain less than 1% of the variance in change in the outcome. Indexes such as correlations or variance ex-plained are the most useful effect size measures because of their ease of interpretation and because they are scale invariant.

CONCLUSIONS AND DIRECTIONS FOR FUTURE RESEARCH

This review revealed that a number of promising eating disorder prevention programs have been developed and evaluated in the last few years. The content of these interven-tions primarily involved cognitive interventions that alter maladaptive attitudes, such as thin-ideal internalization, and behavioral interventions that alter maladaptive be-haviors, such as fasting. Nonetheless, the heterogeneity in the content of the successful programs implies that there may be several approaches to effectively preventing eating disturbances. The pattern of findings revealed several factors associated with more positive intervention effects, including an interactive format, use of targeted interven-tions for high-risk individuals, and a focus on participants in middle to late adoles-cence. There was also some suggestive evidence that programs that are not explicitly presented as eating disorder prevention programs produced more positive effects.

It is hoped that the next generation of eating disorder prevention trials will build on the promising results emerging from this field and will attempt to address the concep-tual, methodological, and statistical limitations noted in this chapter. It is particularly important that future studies compare the more promising prevention programs in an effort to isolate the most potent interventions and to provide a forum for exploring the possibility of treatment-matching approaches that might improve the overall success rate of prevention efforts. Future studies will need to begin testing whether the successful interventions can be disseminated to a large number of individuals and eventually be self-sustaining in the community. With continued diligence, we may yet realize the goal of decreasing the overall prevalence of eating disorders in the population.

REFERENCES

Agras, W. S., Walsh, B. T., Fairburn, C. G., Wilson, G. T., & Kraemer, H. C. (2000). A multi-center comparison of cognitive-behavioral therapy and interpersonal psychotherapy for bulimia nervosa. *Archives of General Psychiatry, 57,* 459–466.

Baranowski, M. J., & Hetherington, M. M. (2001). Testing the efficacy of an eating disorder prevention program. *International Journal of Eating Disorders, 29,* 119–124.

Bearman, S. K., Stice, E., & Chase, A. (2002). Effects of body dissatisfaction on depressive and bulimic symptoms: A longitudinal experiment. *Behavior Therapy.*

Brownell, K. D. (1997). *The LEARN program for weight control.* Dallas, TX: American Health.

Buddeberg-Fischer, B., Klaghofer, R., Gnam, G., & Buddeberg, C. (1998). Prevention of disturbed eating behavior: A prospective intervention study in 14- to 19-year old Swiss students. *Acta Psychiatrica Scandinavica, 98,* 146–155.

Butters, J. W., & Cash, T. F. (1987). Cognitive-behavioral treatment of women's body-image dissatisfaction. *Journal of Consulting and Clinical Psychology, 55,* 889–897.

Carter, J. C., Stewart, D. A., Dunn, V. J., & Fairburn, C. G. (1997). Primary prevention of eating disorders: Might it do more harm than good? *International Journal of Eating Disorders, 22,* 167–172.

Celio, A. A., Winzelberg, A. J., Wilfley, D. E., Eppstein-Herald, D., Springer, E. A., Dev, P., et al. (2000). Reducing risk factors for eating disorders: Comparison of an Internet- and classroom-delivered psychoeducational program. *Journal of Consulting and Clinical Psychology, 68,* 650–657.

Clarke, G. N., Hawkins, W., Murphy, M., & Sheeber, L. (1993). School-based primary prevention of depressive symptomatology in adolescents: Findings from two studies. *Journal of Adolescent Research, 8,* 183–204.

Clarke, G. N., Hawkins, W., Murphy, M., Sheeber, L., Lewinsohn, P. M., & Seeley, J. R. (1995). Targeted prevention of unipolar depressive disorder in an at-risk sample of high school adolescents: A randomized trial of group cognitive intervention. *Journal of the American Academy of Child and Adolescent Psychiatry, 34,* 312–321.

Dalle Grave, R., De Luca, L., & Campello, G. (2001). Middle school primary prevention program for eating disorders: A controlled study with a twelve-month follow-up. *Eating Disorders, 9,* 327–337.

Dworkin, S. H., & Kerr, B. A. (1987). Comparison of interventions for women experiencing body image problems. *Journal of Counseling Psychology, 34,* 136–140.

Fairburn, C. G., & Beglin, S. J. (1994). Assessment of eating disorders: Interview or self-report questionnaire? *International Journal of Eating Disorders, 16,* 363–370.

Fairburn, C. G., Cooper, Z., Doll, H. A., Norman, P. A., & O'Connor, M. E. (2000). The natural course of bulimia nervosa and binge eating disorder in young women. *Archives of General Psychiatry, 57,* 659–665.

Fairburn, C. G., Jones, R., Peveler, R. C., Hope, R. A., & O'Connor, M. (1993). Psychotherapy and bulimia nervosa: Longer-term effects of interpersonal psychotherapy, behavior therapy, and cognitive behavior therapy. *Archives of General Psychiatry, 50,* 419–428.

Fairburn, C. G., Stice, E., Cooper, Z., Doll, H. A., Norman, P. A., & O'Connor, M. E. (2003). Understanding persistence of bulimia nervosa: A five-year naturalistic study. *Journal of Consulting and Clinical Psychology, 71,* 103–109.

Franko, D. L. (1998). Secondary prevention of eating disorders in college women at risk. *Eating Disorders, 6,* 29–40.

Goodrick, G. K., Poston, W. S., Kimball, K. T., Reeves, R. S., & Foreyt, J. P. (1998). Nondieting versus dieting treatments for overweight binge-eating women. *Journal of Consulting and Clinical Psychology, 66,* 363–368.

Kaminski, P. L., & McNamara, K. (1996). A treatment for college women at risk for bulimia: A controlled evaluation. *Journal of Counseling and Development, 74,* 288–294.

Kater, K. J., Rohwer, J., & Londre, K. (in press). Evaluation of an upper elementary school program to prevent body image, eating, and weight concerns. *Journal of School Psychology.*

Keel, P. K., Fulkerson, J. A., & Leon, G. R. (1997). Disordered eating precursors in pre- and early adolescent girls and boys. *Journal of Youth and Adolescence, 26,* 203–216.

Killen, J. D., Taylor, C. B., Hammer, L., Litt, I., Wilson, D. M., Rich, T., et al. (1993). An attempt to modify unhealthful eating attitudes and weight regulation practices of young adolescent girls. *International Journal of Eating Disorders, 13,* 369–384.

Klem, M. L., Wing, R. R., Simkin-Silverman, L., & Kuller, L. H. (1997). The psychological consequences of weight gain prevention in healthy, premenopausal women. *International Journal of Eating Disorders, 21,* 167–174.

Lewinsohn, P. M., Hops, H., Roberts, R. E., Seeley, J. R., & Andrews, J. A. (1993). Adolescent psychopathology. I: Prevalence and incidence of depression and other *DSM-II-R* disorders in high school students. *Journal of Abnormal Psychology, 102,* 133–144.

Lewinsohn, P. M., Striegel-Moore, R. H., & Seeley, J. R. (2000). Epidemiology and natural course of eating disorders in young women from adolescence to young adulthood. *Journal of the American Academy of Child and Adolescent Psychiatry, 39*(10), 1284–1292.

Lowry-Webster, H. M., Barrett, P. M., & Dadds, M. R. (2001). A universal prevention trial of anxiety and depressive symptomatology in childhood: Preliminary data from an Australian study. *Behavior Change, 18,* 36–50.

Mann, T., Nolen-Hoeksema, S., Huang, K., Burgard, D., Wright, A., & Hanson, K. (1997). Are two interventions worse than none? Joint primary and secondary prevention of eating disorders in college females. *Health Psychology, 16,* 215–225.

Martz, D., & Bazzini, D. (1999). Eating disorders prevention programming may be failing: Evaluation of two one-shot programs. *Journal of College Student Development, 40,* 32–42.

McVey, G. L., & Davis, R. (2002). A program to promote positive body image. A 1-year follow-up assessment. *Journal of Early Adolescence, 22,* 96–108.

McVey, G. L., Davis, R., Tweed, S., & Shaw, B. F. (2002). *Parental involvement in the prevention of eating disorders: Findings from a 1-year evaluation study.* Under review.

McVey, G. L., Lieberman, M., Voorberg, N., Wardrope, D., & Blackmore, E. (2002). *School-based peer support groups: A new approach to the prevention of disordered eating.* Manuscript submitted for publication.

Moreno, A. B., & Thelen, M. H. (1993). A preliminary prevention program for eating disorders in a junior high school population. *Journal of Youth and Adolescence, 22*(2), 109–124.

Moskowitz, J. M. (1989). The primary prevention of alcohol problems: A critical review of the research literature. *Journal of Studies on Alcohol, 50,* 54–88.

Murphy, J. G., Duchnick, J. J., Vuchinich, R. E., Davison, J. W., Karg, R. S., Olson, A. M., et al. (2001). Relative efficacy of a brief motivational intervention for college student drinkers. *Psychology of Addictive Behaviors, 15,* 373–379.

Neumark-Sztainer, D., Butler, R., & Palti, H. (1995). Eating disturbances among adolescent girls: Evaluation of a school-based primary prevention program. *Journal of Nutritional Education, 27,* 24–31.

Neumark-Sztainer, D., Sherwood, N. E., Coller, T., & Hannan, P. J. (2000). Primary prevention of disordered eating among preadolescent girls: Feasibility and short-term effect of a community-based intervention. *Journal of the American Dietetic Association, 100,* 1466–1473.

Newman, D. L., Moffitt, T. E., Caspi, A., Magdol, L., Silva, P. A., & Stanton, W. R. (1996). Psychiatric disorder in a birth cohort of young adults: Prevalence, comorbidity, clinical significance, and new case incidence from ages 11 to 21. *Journal of Consulting and Clinical Psychology, 64,* 552–562.

Nicolino, J. C., Martz, D. M., & Curtin, L. (2001). Evaluation of a cognitive-behavioral therapy intervention to improve body image and decrease dieing in college women. *Eating Behaviors, 2,* 353–362.

O'Dea, J. A., & Abraham, S. (2000). Improving the body image, eating attitudes, and behaviors of young male and female adolescents: A new educational approach that focuses on self-esteem. *International Journal of Eating Disorders, 28,* 43–57.

Pacifici, C., Stoolmiller, M., & Nelson, C. (2001). Evaluating a prevention program for teenagers on sexual coercion: A differential effectiveness approach. *Journal of Consulting and Clinical Psychology, 69,* 552–559.

Patton, G. C., Selzer, R., Coffey, C., Carlin, J. B., & Wolfe, R. (1999). Onset of adolescent eating disorders: Population based cohort study over 3 years. *British Medical Journal, 318,* 765–768.

Paxton, S. J. (1993). A prevention program for disturbed eating and body dissatisfaction in adolescent girls: A 1 year follow-up. *Health Education Research, 8,* 43–51.

Phelps, L., Sapia, J., Nathanson, D., & Nelson, L. (2000). An empirically supported eating disorder prevention program. *Psychology in the Schools, 37,* 443–452.

Presnell, K., & Stice, E. (2003). An experimental test of the effect of weight-loss dieting on bulimic pathology: Tipping the scales in a different direction. *Journal of Abnormal Psychology, 112,* 166–170.

Reeves, R. S., McPherson, R. S., Nichaman, M. Z., Harrist, R. B., Foreyt, J. P., & Goodrick, G. K. (2001). Nutrient intake of obese female binge eaters. *Journal of the American Dietetic Association, 101,* 209–215.

Rosen, J. C., Saltzberg, E., & Srebnik, D. (1989). Cognitive behavior therapy for negative body image. *Behavior Therapy, 20,* 393–404.

Santonastaso, P., Zanetti, T., Ferrara, S., Olivotto, M. C., Magnavita, N., & Savaro, A. (1999). A preventive intervention program in adolescent school girls: A longitudinal study. *Psychotherapy and Psychosomatics, 68,* 46–50.

Shisslak, C. M., Crago, M., & Neal, M. E. (1990). Prevention of eating disorders among adolescents. *American Journal of Health Promotion, 5,* 100–106.

Smolak, L., Levine, M., & Schermer, F. (1998a). A controlled evaluation of an elementary school primary prevention program for eating problems. *Journal of Psychosomatic Research, 44,* 339–353.

Smolak, L., Levine, M., & Schermer, F. (1998b). Lessons from lessons: An evaluation of an elementary school prevention program. In W. Vandereyeken & G. Noordenbos (Eds.), *The prevention of eating disorders* (pp. 137–172). London: Athlone.

Stewart, D. A., Carter, J. C., Drinkwater, J., Hainsworth, J., & Fairburn, C. G. (2001). Modification of eating attitudes and behavior in adolescent girls: A controlled study. *International Journal of Eating Disorders, 29,* 107–118.

Stice, E., Cameron, R., Killen, J. D., Hayward, C., & Taylor, C. B. (1999). Naturalistic weight reduction efforts prospectively predict growth in relative weight and onset of obesity among female adolescents. *Journal of Consulting and Clinical Psychology, 67,* 967–974.

Stice, E., Hayward, C., Cameron, R., Killen, J. D., & Taylor, C. B. (2000). Body image and eating related factors predict onset of depression in female adolescents: A longitudinal study. *Journal of Abnormal Psychology, 109,* 438–444.

Stice, E., Killen, J. D., Hayward, C., & Taylor, C. B. (1998). Support for the continuity hypothesis of bulimic pathology. *Journal of Consulting and Clinical Psychology, 66,* 784–790.

Stice, E., Mazotti, L., Weibel, D., & Agras, W. S. (2000). Dissonance prevention program decreases thin-ideal internalization, body dissatisfaction, dieting, negative affect, and bulimic symptoms: A preliminary experiment. *International Journal of Eating Disorders, 27,* 206–217.

Stice, E., Presnell, K., Hoffman, E., & Trost, A. (2002). *Dissonance and healthy weight control eating disorder prevention programs: Results from a randomized trial.* Manuscript in preparation.

Stice, E., & Ragan, J. (2002). A controlled evaluation of an eating disturbance psychoeducational intervention. *International Journal of Eating Disorders, 31,* 159–171.

Stice, E., & Shaw, H. (2003). Prospective relations of body image, eating, and affective disturbances to smoking onset in adolescent girls: How Virginia slims. *Journal of Consulting and Clinical Psychology, 71,* 129–135.

Stice, E., Trost, A., & Chase, A. (2003). Healthy weight control and dissonance-based eating disorder prevention programs: Results from a controlled trial. *International Journal of Eating Disorders, 33,* 10–21.

Stoolmiller, M., Eddy, J. M., & Reid, J. B. (2000). Detecting and describing preventive intervention effects in a universal school-based randomized trial targeting delinquent and violent behavior. *Journal of Consulting and Clinical Psychology, 68,* 296–306.

Varnado-Sullivan, P. J., Zucker, N., Williamson, D. A., Reas, D., Thaw, J., & Netemeyer, S. B. (2001). Development and implementation of the Body Logic Program for adolescents: A two-stage prevention program for eating disorders. *Cognitive and Behavioral Practice, 8,* 248–259.

Vohs, K. D., Bardone, A. M., Joiner, T. E., Abramson, L. Y., & Heatherton, T. F. (1999). Perfectionism, perceived weight status, and self-esteem interact to predict bulimic symptoms: A model of bulimic symptom development. *Journal of Abnormal Psychology, 108,* 695–700.

Vohs, K. D., Voelz, Z. R., Pettit, J. W., Bardone, A. M., Katz, J., Abramson, L. Y., et al. (2001). Perfectionism, body dissatisfaction, and self-esteem: An interactive model of bulimic symptom development. *Journal of Social and Clinical Psychology, 20,* 476–497.

Wilson, G. T., Heffernan, K., & Black, C. M. (1996). Eating disorders. In E. J. Mash & R. A. Barkley (Eds.), *Child psychopathology* (pp. 541–571). New York: Guilford Press.

Winzelberg, A. J., Eppstein, D., Eldredge, K. L., Wilfley, D., Dasmahapatra, R., Dev, P., et al. (2000). Effectiveness of an Internet-based program for reducing risk factors for eating disorders. *Journal of Consulting and Clinical Psychology, 68,* 346–350.

Winzelberg, A. J., Taylor, C. B., Sharpe, T., Eldredge, K. L., Dev, P., & Constantinou, P. S. (1998). Evaluation of a computer-mediated eating disorder intervention program. *International Journal of Eating Disorders, 24,* 339–349.

Chapter 4

DIAGNOSIS AND CLASSIFICATION OF EATING DISORDERS

DEBRA L. FRANKO, STEPHEN A. WONDERLICH,
DEBORAH LITTLE, AND DAVID B. HERZOG

In this chapter, we address current controversies and clinical and research questions related to the classification of eating disorders. In addition to examining the current diagnostic criteria, several areas are covered in depth: subtyping of anorexia nervosa (AN) and bulimia nervosa (BN), alternative methodologies for classifying eating disorders, and a detailed examination of current questions surrounding the categories of eating disorder not otherwise specified (EDNOS) and binge eating disorder (BED).

Why is the study of classification and diagnosis important? Simply put, classification systems influence research agendas, policy issues, funding initiatives, third-party reimbursement, and treatment strategies. Reliable and valid diagnoses provide a shorthand method of communication for clinicians and researchers and inform research initiatives and clinical interventions.

Both conceptual models and treatment interventions are heavily influenced by the existing classification schemes offered in the *Diagnostic and Statistical Manual of Mental Disorders,* fourth edition (*DSM-IV*; American Psychiatric Association [APA], 1994). The current system provides a qualitative distinction between AN and BN and divides each of these eating disorders into distinct subtypes. Although this conceptual approach is viable, there is much debate about the most appropriate way to classify these disorders (e.g., Bulik, Sullivan, & Kendler, 2000; Gleaves, Lowe, Green, Cororve, & Williams, 2000).

ANOREXIA NERVOSA

The criteria for AN from the *DSM-IV* have been somewhat controversial. One major area of concern is the weight criterion of less than 85% of expected body weight. Herzog and Delinsky (2001) note that this number appears somewhat arbitrary because it does not consider the wide range of weights in the population, pubertal growth changes, or cultural variability. Garfinkel and colleagues indicated that little is known about the predictive value of the weight criterion as to therapy outcome, medical status, health consequences, or prognosis (Garfinkel, Kennedy, & Kaplan, 1995). However, several studies have found that low discharge weight is related to poorer outcome, although the exact weight criterion for poor prognosis has not been determined (Baran, Weltzin, & Kay, 1995; Russell & Gross, 2000). Hebebrand, Wehmeier, and Remschmidt (2000) argue for a change to the 10th percentile of body mass index (BMI) as a cutoff for weight to address the issues of differential age and sex distributions and to provide an epidemiologically based weight criterion. However, as pointed out by others (Oehlschlaegel-Akiyoshi, Malewski, & Mahon, 1999), BMI is only an approximation for relative weight, does not take into account frame size, and differs depending on ethnicity. An inpatient study resulted in a call for a shift from a specific low weight criterion to a "more fundamental understanding of anorexia nervosa as a decrement between set-point and illness driven weight loss" (Andersen, Bowers, & Watson, 2001, p. 277).

Two additional criteria, the fear of weight gain and the absence of three consecutive menstrual periods, have been the source of considerable debate. Weight phobia has come under fire primarily based on the work of Lee and others (Lee, Ho, & Hsu, 1993; Walsh & Kahn, 1997), who have pointed out that this clinical characteristic typically seen in Western countries is often not present in patients with AN in other countries, such as Hong Kong. As a culture-bound criteria, they argue that it should not be mandatory for a diagnosis of AN. However, others (Habermas, 1996) have responded to this critique by noting that this cognitive symptom is important for both diagnostic specificity and the prediction of outcome. In a 10- to 15-year follow-up study, Strober and colleagues found that the group of anorexic patients without fear of gaining weight were less likely to have run a chronic course or engage in binge eating and more likely to have achieved full recovery (Strober, Freeman, & Morrell, 1997).

Amenorrhea as a diagnostic criteria has been questioned in part because some women at very low weights continue to have menstrual bleeding (Cachelin & Maher, 1998), and, further, amenorrhea sometimes occurs before significant weight loss (Garfinkel et al., 1996b). These two studies have found that women with AN with and without amenorrhea *do not* differ on measures of severity, body image disturbance, depression, or personality disorders. Similarly, Andersen et al. (2001) found no weight differences between anorexic inpatients with or without amenorrhea, except for a slightly lower lifetime maximum weight in the latter group. No differences were found between the two groups on current, high, or low BMI or length of illness. Amenorrhea as a diagnostic criterion is problematic for prepubescent girls and is not relevant for male patients with AN.

Based on a study of 397 hospital admissions and a close examination of the existing diagnostic criteria, Andersen and colleagues (2001) proposed a revision of the criteria for AN. The new criteria would focus on the core features of weight loss, drive for thinness, and an overvaluation of thinness and remove the 85% ideal body weight criterion, replacing it with "a substantial weight loss, usually greater than 20% of initial weight." Further, they suggested that the amenorrhea requirement is out of date and should be excluded as a criterion for diagnosis of AN.

In light of considerable controversy and existing empirical research, it appears that several of the diagnostic criteria for AN are in need of review.

BULIMIA NERVOSA

The diagnostic criteria for BN have also been the source of some debate. The area of greatest concern is the lack of specification of the terms "an episode of binge eating," and "an amount that is definitely larger than what most people would eat." Research finds great variability in the size of a typical binge (Rossiter & Agras, 1990), and there do not appear to be any meaningful differences based on the amount of food alone (Pratt, Niego, & Agras, 1998), with the exception of impulse control (Keel, Mayer, & Fischer, 2001). Herzog and Delinsky (2001) point out that other indicators, such as the level of mood disturbance, the degree of the sense of loss of control, and the quality of the binge, would better define a binge episode. In a recent study, Keel and her colleagues compared the caloric counts of binges from individuals with self-reported binge episodes to those of undergraduates who did not binge. They found that the largest amount of food consumed by the non-binge-eating college women ranged from 500 to 900 calories. Among self-identified binge eaters, 22% did not eat an amount that was "definitely larger" than what college women would eat. Among these individuals, 70% were engaging in inappropriate compensatory behaviors such as self-induced vomiting, laxative abuse, and excessive exercise. The authors suggested that there may be a substantial subpopulation of women who purge and have subjective binge episodes but who would not meet *DSM-IV* criteria for BN because the binges are not "large enough" (Keel, Cogley, Ghosh, & Lester, 2002).

The criteria based on time and frequency are also problematic. The *DSM-IV* states that the binge eating occur "in a discrete period of time" and offers "within any 2-hour period" by way of example. However, there is no data suggesting that longer or shorter binge episodes have any clinical utility in predicting course or outcome of BN. Further, the frequency criterion (behaviors must occur at least twice weekly for a three-month period) is problematic. Garfinkel and colleagues (1995) point out that this frequency minimum was not determined on the basis of empirical research. Conflicting results have been obtained as to whether degree of distress and impairment differs between those who binge on average twice a week and those who binge less often (Garfinkel et al., 1996a; Hay, 1998; Wilson & Eldredge, 1991). Andersen et al. (2001) reported no differences on the Eating Attitudes Test (Garner, Olmsted, Bohr, & Garfinkel, 1982), the Eating Disorders Inventory (Garner & Olmsted, 1984), or the Beck Depression Inventory (Beck, Ward, Mendelson, Mock, & Erbaugh, 1961) scores between BN patients who did or did not meet the frequency criterion. An early twin study ($n = 2,163$) compared subjects with subsyndromal and *DSM-III-R* BN and found no differences between the groups on any risk factor measures, including history of weight fluctuations, low self-esteem, and high levels of neuroticism, among others (Kendler et al., 1991). Based on this evidence, the authors concluded that "a bulimic-like syndrome with binge eating episodes less frequent than twice per week for 3 months may differ quantitatively but does *not* appear to differ qualitatively from the classic disorder of bulimia nervosa" (p. 1635).

Thus, several of the specific criteria concerning frequency and duration of binge episodes appear to have little empirical support, suggesting that their inclusion into the diagnostic criteria for BN should be reevaluated.

CROSSOVER BETWEEN ANOREXIA NERVOSA AND BULIMIA NERVOSA

DSM-IV is based on discrete categories of diagnoses—either an individual has AN *or* BN at a particular point in time. What the current diagnostic system does not take into account is that these disorders often vary in severity over time and, further, that many with BN have a history of AN and a majority of those with AN, if followed for long enough, develop symptoms of BN. Nearly one-quarter to one-third of those with BN have a history of AN (Braun, Sunday, & Halmi, 1994; Keel, Mitchell, Miller, Davis, & Crow, 2000); and in a 15.5-year follow-up study, 54% of women with AN developed bulimic symptoms (Bulik, Sullivan, Fear, & Pickering, 1997). Herzog and colleagues (1999) found that 16% of AN, restricting subtype, developed full *DSM-IV* criteria BN over the course of 7.5 years and 7% with BN developed full AN. Studies such as these raise the issue of whether eating disorders should be conceptualized as dimensions or discrete entities, an issue that is further described in the section on alternate classification strategies.

SUBTYPING

Given the tremendous degree of heterogeneity in patients with eating disorders, due to variability in both symptoms and psychiatric comorbidity, efforts to subclassify eating disorder patients have emerged in the past decade. One scheme for classifying individuals is the subtyping system introduced in the *DSM-IV*. If an individual meets the diagnostic criteria for AN and also binge eats and purges, either by self-induced vomiting or the misuse of laxatives, diuretics, or enemas, a diagnosis of AN, binge eating-purging (ANBP) type is given. Similarly, for BN, diagnosis can be either purging (BN-P) or nonpurging (BN-NP), depending on which type of compensatory behaviors are used. Subtypes were instituted based on evidence of differential outcome and medical risk, but since the publication of *DSM-IV*, a great deal of research has generated questions as to the utility and validity of these subtypes. For example, it remains unclear whether binge-purge anorexics represent a subtype of AN or a variation of BN (Gleaves, Lowe, Green, et al., 2000; Herzog et al., 1999). Similarly, questions have been raised as to the validity of the purging versus nonpurging subtype distinction in the *DSM* (Gleaves, Lowe, Snow, Green, & Murphy-Eberenz, 2000; Williamson et al., 2002). There may be subtypes within the AN and BN constructs based on personality differences and not on eating disorder symptom differences (Westen & Harnden-Fischer, 2001; Wonderlich & Mitchell, 2001) or affective dimensions (Stice & Agras, 1999). For example, there is evidence of a highly impulsive group of eating-disordered individuals. It is unclear whether such individuals represent a true subtype of AN or BN, an eating disorder with psychiatric comorbidity, or an entirely alternative form of psychopathology that happens to include eating disorder symptoms (e.g., substance use disorder, personality disorder; Wonderlich & Mitchell, 2001).

Studies of the *DSM* Subtypes for Anorexia Nervosa

The AN subtypes (i.e., restricting versus binge-purge) are based on early studies finding that anorexic women with bulimic symptoms showed considerably more comorbid psychopathology (e.g., depression, substance abuse, impulse control problems, personality disorders) than those anorexics who did not binge and purge (Dacosta & Halmi, 1992; Garner, Garner, & Rosen, 1993; Herzog, Keller, Sachs, Yeh, & Lavori, 1992). Garner's work in this area further implies that those anorexics who purge, but do not binge, are behaviorally more similar to binge-purge anorexics than they are to restricting anorexics (Garner et al., 1993). However, in a study of 245 adolescent inpatients with eating disorders, Minnesota Multiphasic Personality Inventory-Adolescent results did not distinguish restricting from binge-purge subtypes of AN (Cumella, Wall, & Kerr-Almedia, 1999).

More recent studies have also supported the idea that the binge-purge anorexic has a more complicated clinical course than restricting anorexics (Herzog & Delinsky, 2001; Herzog et al., 1999; Pryor, Wiederman, & McGilley, 1996). Results from a prospective longitudinal study of treatment-seeking anorexic women present a somewhat more complex picture of the relationship between restricting and binge-purge AN. Herzog et al. found no significant differences between binge-purge and restricting anorexics in rates of full recovery, partial recovery, or relapse at 7.5 years of follow-up. Additionally, binge-purge anorexic individuals reported less overall life satisfaction and reduced improvement in global functioning at five-year follow-up than did the restricting anorexic individuals.

A closer examination of subtyping of this same cohort found few differences between AN—restricting subtype (ANR) and AN binge-purge subtype (ANBP) groups. Prospective weekly data collected on the fluctuation of eating disorder symptomatology in a cohort of 136 ANs over a median of eight years of follow-up indicated few differences between the groups (Eddy et al., 2002). Intake comparisons between ANRs and ANBPs yielded no differences on measures of impulsivity, including history of alcohol abuse, drug abuse, kleptomania, suicidality, or borderline personality disorder diagnosis. By eight years of follow-up, 62% of ANRs crossed over to ANBP prospectively, and only 12% of ANs never reported regular binge-purge behaviors. With the longitudinal data, it was possible to determine that as the duration of follow-up increased, the number of ANRs who developed regular bingeing or purging also increased. In the majority of the ANR sample, ANR appeared to represent an earlier phase in the course of AN, which eventually progressed to ANBP. Indeed, among the ANs, only 16 (11.8%) did not report lifetime histories of regular binge-purge behavior by eight years of follow-up. The prospective crossover rates from ANR to ANBP of 62.2% at eight years and 51.5% at five years were higher in this sample than those reported by other investigators (Bulik et al., 1997; Eckert, Halmi, Marchi, Grove, & Crosby, 1995; Garfinkel, Moldofsky, & Garner, 1980; Strober et al., 1997). Strober et al. and Garfinkel et al. measured the onset of bingeing (29% and 44%, respectively) in AN groups that included women who were purging at intake, without separately considering when bingeing or purging began in ANs who did neither at intake. Neither Bulik et al. nor Eckert et al. measured whether the prospective binge-purge behavior occurred during an episode of AN, which may not accurately estimate the crossover rate from ANR to ANBP. The longitudinal data of

Eddy et al. suggest that the ANR-ANBP distinction may have more to do with where an individual is in the "lifetime" of the illness than accurately depicting two unique types of AN. Future research should focus on strategies for differentiating those who cross over from ANR to ANBP from those who do not, particularly as to clinical characteristics and effective treatment interventions.

Subtyping in Bulimia Nervosa

The *DSM* distinction between normal weight bulimic individuals who purge through vomiting and laxatives versus those who do not purge, but exercise or starve, has received considerably less empirical attention than the anorexic subtypes. An early twin study ($n = 2,163$) compared subjects with subsyndromal and *DSM-III-R* BN and found no differences between the groups on any risk factor measures, including history of weight fluctuations, low self-esteem, and high levels of neuroticism, among others (Kendler et al., 1991). Based on this evidence, the authors concluded that "a bulimic-like syndrome with binge eating episodes less frequent than twice per week for 3 months may differ quantitatively but does *not* appear to differ qualitatively from the classic disorder of bulimia nervosa" (p. 1635).

In a large epidemiologic study, Garfinkel et al. (1996a) reported differences in age of onset, comorbidity (e.g., affective and anxiety disorders, alcoholism), history of sexual abuse, and parental discord between purging and nonpurging subtypes of BN. Other studies provided evidence of differences in clinical features and response to treatment between the two groups (McCann, Rossiter, King, & Agras, 1991; Mitchell, 1992; Willmuth, Leitenberg, Rosen, & Cado, 1988). However, more recent studies have uniformly found few, if any, differences. Tobin and associates did not find support for the subtypes in a study of severity of eating pathology and comorbidity (Tobin, Griffing, & Griffing, 1997). Hay and Fairburn (1998) reported no differences between purging and nonpurging women with BN in eating disorder features, social adjustment, general psychopathology, and self-esteem. In a community-based study, Striegel-Moore and colleagues (2001) found no differences between purging and nonpurging BN on a large number of eating-related variables (e.g., age of onset, levels of shape or weight concern, BMI, prevalence of obesity, history of treatment for eating disorder or obesity, and history of AN). In addition, there were no differences in comorbidity based on the Structured Clinical Interview for *DSM-IV* Axis I disorders. Notably, only 14 of 212 women in the study (6.6%) were diagnosed with BN nonpurging type, which is consistent with the numbers reported by other researchers (Hay & Fairburn, 1998 [6%]; Tobin et al., 1997 [8%]). Striegel-Moore et al. suggested that BN-NP is a rare disorder, and recent research provides evidence that the diagnostic validity of this subtype should be reexamined.

Alternatives to Current *DSM-IV* Subtypes: Personality Profiles in Anorexia Nervosa and Bulimia Nervosa

Another approach to subtyping eating disorder patients is to classify personality-based subgroups that cut across the traditional eating disorder diagnostic categories. There is considerable evidence of heterogeneity within the AN and BN diagnostic constructs in terms of personality variables. For example, both AN and BN are characterized by a wide range of personality traits ranging from highly impulsive to compulsive descriptors *within* each category (Abbott, Wonderlich, & Mitchell, 2001; Westen & Harnden-Fischer, 2001; Wonderlich & Mitchell, 2001). Such heterogeneity suggests that personality differences within eating disorder diagnoses may serve as a potent subtyping strategy. Furthermore, personality-based categorizations have been shown to be more effective than symptom-based categorizations in predicting level of functioning, history of psychiatric hospitalization, histories of childhood adversity, and specific symptom constellations (Steiger & Stotland, 1996; Westen & Harnden-Fischer, 2001).

Two personality-based conceptual schemes have been most commonly used to describe the heterogeneity within the eating disorders. The first has been applied primarily to BN and suggests a subtype of bulimia that is characterized by multiple forms of behavioral impulsivity, frequently referred to as *multi-impulsive bulimia nervosa* (Fichter, Quadflieg, & Rief, 1994; Lacey, 1993). Fichter and colleagues found that bulimic subjects who reported at least three impulsive behaviors (i.e., suicide attempt, self-harm, stealing, severe alcohol abuse, sexual promiscuity, drug abuse) showed more general psychopathology, a distinct personality profile, and a worse prognosis than bulimic subjects without such behaviors (Fichter et al., 1994). Although one study suggested that rates of multi-impulsive bulimia were relatively low (i.e., Welch & Fairburn, 1996), a report using rigorous interviewing techniques found that nearly 40% of bulimic individuals display at least three forms of destructive impulsive behaviors (Crosby et al., 2001). Moreover, there is increasing evidence that extreme forms of impulsive self-destructive behaviors in BN are associated with increased likelihood of experiencing childhood abuse (Favaro & Santonastaso, 1998; Wonderlich et al., 2001). Considerably less is known about the prevalence of multiple forms of impulsivity in AN, but one study suggests that rates of multi-impulsivity are considerably higher in binge-purge anorexics than in restricting anorexics (Nagata, Kawarada, Kiriike, & Iketani, 2000).

A second scheme for modeling the personality heterogeneity as to impulsivity has been the measurement of borderline personality disorder in eating-disordered individuals. Studies fairly consistently show that when assessed by clinical interview, binge-purge anorexics and normal weight bulimics are more likely than restricting anorexics to meet criteria for borderline personality disorder (Zanarini et al., 1998). However, only a minority of bulimic and binge-purge anorexic individuals actually meet criteria for borderline or Cluster B diagnoses. In fact, both bulimic and binge-purge anorexic individuals also show elevations in Cluster C (anxious-fearful) personality styles (Nilsson, Gillberg, Gillberg, & Rastam, 1999; Rosenvinge, Martinussen, & Ostensen, 2000). Thus, considerable variability exists *within* eating disorder diagnoses in borderline personality functioning.

These differences in personality style appear related to clinical variables. Bulimic individuals with borderline personality disorder, or any *DSM-III* Cluster B personality disorder, display a poorer outcome across a range of therapeutic modalities, including individual and group therapy (Herzog et al., 1992), cognitive behavior therapy (Rossiter, Agras, Telch, & Schneider, 1993), and pharmacotherapy (Rossiter et al., 1993). Compared to bulimic individuals free of personality disturbance, those with Cluster B disorders show more general psychopathology, drug and alcohol use, self-destructive behavior, suicide attempts, histories of sexual or physical abuse, negative appraisals of family functioning, greater hospitalization rates, and higher use of psychotropic medication (Johnson, Tobin, & Dennis, 1990; Steiger & Stotland, 1996; Wonderlich & Swift, 1990).

Few longitudinal studies have examined eating disorder subtypes based on personality variables, but the available data suggest that impulsivity predicts a relatively negative course in bulimic individuals (Johnson et al., 1990; Steiger, Jabalpurwala, & Champagne, 1996; Wonderlich, Fullerton, Swift, & Klein, 1994). In the only longitudinal study that compared multi-impulsive subjects to nonimpulsive bulimic subjects (i.e., Fichter et al., 1994), multi-impulsive subjects had a worse course and outcome, in spite of baseline similarities in eating disorder symptoms.

Thus, while evidence does suggest that the presence of impulsivity, whether measured as a personality trait, disorder, or multi-impulsive syndrome, is associated with a poorer outcome in BN, these studies have been limited by inadequate assessments of impulsivity and short follow-up periods. Furthermore, most of the studies of multi-impulsivity and borderline personality disorder have been conducted with normal weight bulimics, in spite of the fact that binge-purge anorexics may display the highest level of this personality configuration (Rosenvinge et al., 2000). Future research should investigate the longitudinal predictive value of personality configurations across AN and BN.

CLUSTER ANALYTIC STUDIES OF PERSONALITY VARIABILITY

The idea that eating-disordered individuals may be composed of different subtypes with varying degrees of personality traits (e.g., impulsivity, compulsivity), self-destructive behavior, and other comorbid features of the eating disorders has received increased empirical attention in the last few years. Studies have consistently identified three to four separate clusters of eating-disordered individuals based on personality type (Johnson & Connors, 1987; Swift & Stern, 1982). Strober and colleagues (Strober, Salkin, Burroughs, & Morrell, 1982) cluster analyzed MMPI profiles of individuals with AN and found three types: a high-functioning group with high levels of conformity and a need for control but lacking severe personality pathology, a more socially avoidant and anxious group, and an impulsive group with poor coping strategies and a poor prognosis. Similarly, Goldner et al. (Goldner, Srikameswaran, Schroeder, Livesley, & Birmingham, 1999) cluster analyzed responses of eating disorder patients to the Dimensional Assessment of Personality Pathology (DAPP; Livesley, Jackson, & Schroeder, 1991). Three groups were identified: one with higher levels of compulsivity and interpersonal difficulties (49.3%); one with minimal personality pathology that differed little from controls (32.4%); and a third that seemed more psychopathic, neurotic, and impulsive (18.2%). Furthermore, in the study, bulimic subjects were not significantly linked to any particular personality-based cluster, again highlighting the variability in this eating disorder diagnostic construct. Finally, Westen and Harnden-Fischer (2001) cluster analyzed the clinician Q-sorts of personality traits in eating disorder patients and described three categories of patients: a high-functioning, perfectionistic group; a constricted and over-controlled group; and an emotionally dysregulated group. Moreover, each of the clusters was associated with a different pattern of etiological variables, symptomatic presentation, and level of adaptive functioning.

PSYCHOBIOLOGICAL STUDIES OF EATING DISORDERS: POSSIBLE SUBTYPES

In the past decade, there has been an increased interest in the relationship between eating disorders and various neurotransmitters and neurohormones. This line of investigation has recently become relevant to possible subtyping strategies, as eating-disordered individuals have shown considerable variability in serotonergic functioning.

The serotonergic neurotransmitter system has been studied in acutely ill and weight-recovered anorexic patients (Brewerton & Jimerson, 1996; Kaye & Weltzin, 1991). These studies suggest that anorexics display a reduction of basal CSF 5-HIAA, which returns to normal levels after weight restoration but appears to be elevated after more protracted recovery. Furthermore, challenge tests with serotonergic agonists find that anorexic individuals have blunting of plasma prolactin in the acute phase but that this disturbance resolves with recovery. Importantly, however, these findings may also have relevance to a personality-based subtyping system. For example, in long-term recovered anorexics, levels of serotonergic metabolites are positively associated with personality traits such as perfectionism and obsessionality (Kaye, 1997). Thus, even within the AN diagnostic category, there may be significant personality variation, which is associated with these biological variables.

Similarly, these biological variables may be useful in understanding personality-related variability in BN. Early studies were mixed about whether BN was associated with abnormal serotonergic functioning when measured in cerebrospinal fluid (Jimerson, Lesem, Kaye, & Brewerton, 1992; Kaye, Berrettini, Gwirtsman, & George, 1990). These studies did imply that individuals with more severe bulimic symptoms may have lower CSF 5-HIAA levels relative to less symptomatic patients. With increasing numbers of studies using pharmacologic challenge tests, clearer evidence of serotonergic dysfunction in bulimic individuals has been found. Regardless of the type of serotonin agonist studied, acutely ill bulimic individuals showed blunted prolactin responses (Brewerton, Lydiard, Laraia, Shook & Ballenger, 1992; Goldbloom, Hicks, & Garfinkel, 1990; Jimerson, Wolfe, Metzger, & Finkelstein, 1997; Levitan, Kaplan, Joffe, Levitt, & Brown, 1997). However, these differences appeared to be state related because recovered bulimic patients did not show significant 5HT dysfunction (Kaye et al., 1998; Wolfe et al., 2000).

Platelet measures, such as high platelet 5HT uptake, and decreased platelet ^{3}H-imipramine binding have also been reported in bulimic subjects (Goldbloom et al., 1990; Marazziti, Macchi, Rotondo, Placidi, & Cassano, 1988). These approaches were also used to study behavioral or personality dimensions, finding that platelet abnormalities indicative of serotonergic dysfunction might be particularly related to impulsivity traits within bulimic subjects and *not* BN in and of itself (Carrasco, Diaz-Marsa, Hollander, Cesar, & Saiz-Ruiz, 2000; Okamoto, Okamoto, Kagaya, Horiguchi, & Yamawaki, 1999).

Paralleling these studies, Steiger and colleagues have examined both paroxetine binding in platelets and prolactin responses following oral metachloraphenylpiperazine (m-CPP), both of which may be helpful in validating efforts to subtype BN. Bulimic symptoms were associated with reduced density of paroxetine binding sites and blunting of prolactin response and cortisol following m-CPP administration. However, closer examination of these data indicated that 5HT dysfunction was uniquely associated with self-harm behaviors (Steiger, Koerner, et al., 2001) or impulsivity (Steiger, Young, et al., 2001). Furthermore, additional analyses suggest that while 5HT indicators continue to be associated with BN, cortisol levels following m-CPP administration may be more specifically linked to child abuse than to bulimic status (Steiger, Gauvin, et al., 2001).

In summary, the available evidence suggests that BN and AN may be associated with disturbances in serotonergic functioning, although it remains unclear if this is a precursor or complication of eating disorder symptomatology. Moreover, these biological parameters have been shown to correlate with personality-related variability within the eating disorder constructs, which may be useful in terms of subtyping strategies.

ALTERNATIVE SUBTYPING STRATEGIES

An alternative approach to subtyping examined whether bulimic patients could be differentiated into a dietary restraint subtype and a negative affect subtype (Stice & Agras, 1999). The dual pathway model (Stice, 1994) proposes that bulimic behavior may be initiated either because of dieting or affective disturbance, or both. Using a sample of 265 women who met *DSM-III-R* criteria for BN, support was found for two subgroups, although the negative affect group showed both high dieting scores and depressive affect. The authors suggested that subtyping BN may inform treatment strategies. The high dieters/depressive affect group might benefit from interventions first directed at depression (using cognitive therapy and/or antidepressants) before addressing the eating pathology, whereas the high dieting alone group might best be treated with standard cognitive behavioral therapy for BN (Fairburn, 1985).

EMPIRICAL APPROACHES TO IDENTIFYING SUBTYPES OF ANOREXIA NERVOSA AND BULIMIA NERVOSA

Whether considering the empirical support for the *DSM*-based subtyping system or, alternatively, assessing the validity of subtyping strategies based on personality traits or other models, previously used data analytic strategies have been limited. Although factor analytic, cluster analytic, and longitudinal strategies provide useful information about variability within the AN and BN constructs, these techniques do not clarify whether a given subtype represents a discrete diagnostic class.

Bulik et al. (2000) examined interview data from more than 2,100 female twins using latent class analysis to develop an empirically based typology of eating disorders. While three classes were similar to the *DSM-IV* eating disorders (AN, BN, BED), the three remaining classes had different combinations of clinical features. Two classes showed low weight without clinical characteristics of eating disorders, and one class demonstrated distorted eating attitudes without low body weight. The classes closest to the *DSM* criteria showed more similarity in monozygotic than dizygotic twins and had comparable personality profiles.

Alternatively, a group of statistical procedures collectively referred to as *taxometrics* can be used to address questions of subtyping and diagnostic validity. These methodologies are designed to determine if a diagnostic entity is best viewed as a latent taxon or a latent dimension (Waldman & Lilienfeld, 2001). A *latent taxon* refers to a distinct category or type that is qualitatively different from another taxon. A *latent dimension* refers to an entity that occurs on a continuum, such as height or weight. Thus, the use of taxometrics to study eating disorders could clarify whether AN and BN are actually distinct categories (as in the current *DSM* conceptualization) or whether they are dimensional in nature. Taxometrics can also be used to determine if a given disorder has underlying subtypes or if two "apparently distinct disorders" are actually alternative manifestations of a single underlying condition or actually distinct and separate disorders (Waldman & Lilienfeld, 2001). Although various statistical strategies—including analysis of variance, confirmatory factor analysis, and cluster analysis—have been used in an effort to clarify nosological distinctions, they do not address whether diagnostic entities are dimensional or taxonic or if distinct subtypes exist (Gleaves, Lowe, Green, et al., 2000; Joiner & Schmidt, 2002). Taxometric analyses are better able to accomplish this goal. The value of taxometric analysis for addressing these types of nosologic questions has recently been highlighted in a series of studies on depression (J. Ruscio & Ruscio, 2000), worry (A. M. Ruscio, Borkovec, & Ruscio, 2001), and posttraumatic stress disorder (A. M. Ruscio, Ruscio, & Keane, 2002). In addition, a special section on comorbidity and taxometrics in *Clinical Psychology Science and Practice* (Waldman & Lilienfeld, 2001) and a series on the classification of eating disorders by Joiner (2000) and Gleaves, Lowe, Green, et al. (2000) in a special section of *Behavior Therapy* have described the utility of this approach in investigating nosological questions.

TAXOMETRIC STUDIES WITH EATING DISORDER SAMPLES

Several studies have used taxometric methods to address whether eating disorders reflect extreme points on a dimension of normal eating behavior or a true class (or taxon), which is qualitatively distinct from normal behaviors. For example, Gleaves and Eberenz (1995) conducted taxometric analyses on BN and concluded that the diagnostic construct differs qualitatively from lesser forms of weight and eating problems. In a similar study, Williamson, Gleaves, and Savin (1992) conducted taxometric analyses with a variety of eating disorder diagnoses as well as obesity and found that each group, including the obese, appeared to be qualitatively distinct from normality. Gleaves, Lowe, Green, et al. (2000) used Meehl's (1995) taxometric procedures to complete several analyses in a sample of 959 women (745 with clinically diagnosed eating disorders and 214 non-eating-disordered controls). The first question was whether BN differs qualitatively or quantitatively from normality; that is, is BN a latent taxon or a latent dimension? Both the purging and nonpurging forms of BN appeared to be taxonic in these analyses, suggesting they reflect a qualitative class that is different from normal. In a second analysis, these researchers assessed possible subtyping categorizations in the eating disorders and found that:

1. Dimensionality versus taxonicity for AN and BN could not be determined.
2. All eating disorders that include bingeing were different from restricting AN.

3. Normal weight bulimia and binge-purge AN appear to be separate points on the same dimension.

4. Purging versus nonpurging types of BN do not appear to reflect a true class distinction but more likely indicate quantitative differences along an underlying dimension.

These findings suggest that AN, binge eating-purging type, is more similar to normal weight bulimia than it is to restricting anorexia. Furthermore, restricting anorexia seems to represent a form of eating disorder that is truly distinct from other types. Finally, whether an individual with BN purges through vomiting or laxatives versus food restriction or exercise does not seem to represent a true taxonic class distinction.

Williamson and colleagues (2002) investigated three questions using taxometric techniques:

1. What are the latent features of eating disorder symptoms in AN, BN, and BED?

2. Are the three groups similar or different as to eating disorder symptoms?

3. Do eating disorders lie on a continuum or represent discrete categories?

To answer these questions, 201 women with eating disorders (ANR, ANBP, BN-P, BN-NP, EDNOS, and BED) were compared to 116 normal comparison subjects using an interview-based assessment of eating disorder symptoms. Factor analytic procedures revealed that three latent features described the symptoms encompassed by the *DSM-IV* eating disorder diagnoses: binge eating, fear of fatness/compensatory behaviors, and drive for thinness. Several findings from the taxometric analyses are of note. First, support was not found for the continuity hypothesis of eating disorders, similar to Gleaves, Lowe, Snow, et al. (2000). Instead, eating disorders were found to differ qualitatively from the behaviors of normal weight control women. Second, for BN and BED, evidence for a discrete syndrome (or latent taxon) was found. For AN, on the other hand, the findings were less clear and suggested that differences between AN and normal controls were quantitative rather than qualitative in nature. Support for the question of whether the eating disorders differ from one another was mixed, with some features identified to be latent categories and others latent dimensions.

In summary, several preliminary inferences can be drawn from these taxometric analyses. First, AN, binge eating-purging type, appears to be more similar to normal weight BN than it is to restricting anorexia. Second, restricting anorexia seems to represent an eating disorder that is truly distinct from other types but not clearly different from normal variations in eating pathology. Third, whether an individual with BN purges through vomiting or laxatives versus food restriction or exercise (purging vs. nonpurging BN) does not seem to represent a true taxonic class distinction.

DIAGNOSTIC CONSIDERATIONS FOR EATING DISORDER NOT OTHERWISE SPECIFIED

In addition to AN and BN, a third category of diagnosis in the *DSM-IV* consists of eating disorders that are clinically significant (in that the individual experiences social or occupational dysfunction and marked distress) but that do not meet the full criteria for a diagnosis of either AN or BN. A diagnosis of EDNOS is given when an individual: (1) lacks one of the diagnostic criteria (e.g., a patient who meets all of the AN criteria except that she still experiences regular menstrual bleeding or a patient who experiences amenorrhea but has not lost sufficient weight to be considered 15% below ideal body weight); (2) does not meet duration criteria (e.g., a patient who binges and engages in compensatory behavior but has done so for less than three months); or (3) does not meet frequency criteria (e.g., a patient who engages in binge and compensatory behavior but does so fewer than two times per week), in addition to all other atypical eating disorder cases. Also included in this category are those diagnosed with binge eating disorder (BED), which is discussed in greater detail in the next section.

What is particularly controversial about this category is that it is composed of what are thought to be less common forms of the disorder. This does not appear to be the case, however, because estimates of between 20% and 61% of all eating disorder cases treated fall within the EDNOS category (Andersen et al., 2001; Fairburn & Walsh, 2002). It has been estimated that between 4% and 6% of both genders in the general population have an EDNOS (Herzog & Delinsky, 2001), whereas only an estimated 1% to 2% of the population is diagnosed with AN and BN. Herzog, Hopkins, and Burns (1993) reported that more than 40% of women seeking treatment at an eating disorders clinic failed to meet full diagnostic criteria for AN or BN and would be characterized as EDNOS.

EDNOS is a much more common diagnosis than was once thought and should be a focus of research efforts for several reasons. It has been noted that some managed care companies do not cover treatment if the diagnosis of EDNOS is given (Andersen et al., 2001). Because of the large number of people diagnosed with this disorder, many may be left with little or no coverage. Little is known about the effective treatment of those disorders that fall into the EDNOS category. For this reason, therapists may be unsure about the most appropriate treatment, potentially resulting in ineffective care. Still another consideration is the belief by some that eating disorders that fall into this third category are somehow less severe, which may not always be the case. For example, women with an EDNOS report as much body dissatisfaction as women with clinical AN and BN and a significant amount of impairment and psychosocial stress (Herzog & Delinsky, 2001). Herzog et al. (1993) reported that a group of subdiagnostic patients had highly persistent symptoms over a four-year period and that nearly half eventually met *DSM-III-R* criteria for AN or BN during this time. It should be noted, however, that a diagnosis of EDNOS may indicate a more positive course of recovery than either full-fledged AN or BN, and in cases where recovery from AN or BN is minimal, these disorders often evolve into an EDNOS (Fairburn & Walsh, 2002). It is possible that EDNOS represents a more long-lasting or chronic form of an eating disorder, which waxes and wanes in approaching the diagnostic criteria for AN and BN. Additional investigations examining the course and outcome of those given the EDNOS diagnosis are needed.

With the exception of recent studies on binge eating disorder, very little empirical or systematic research has been conducted on the EDNOS category. However, studies have shown that a great deal of heterogeneity exists within the EDNOS diagnosis. Some diagnosed with EDNOS would be considered "partial syndromes," in that they are similar to AN or BN but do not meet all of the diagnostic criteria. Others might be considered "subthreshold" disorders because all criteria are met, but the symptoms are not severe enough to reach the necessary thresholds (Fairburn & Walsh, 2002). Despite the diversity, however, a common symptom of most cases that fall into the EDNOS category is the overconcern with eating, weight, and shape and the connection between physical appearance and self-evaluation. Future research efforts might be directed toward developing clearer and more specific criteria for EDNOS.

The heterogeneity of this group and the resemblance to AN and BN have led some researchers to ask if the diagnostic criteria for AN and BN should be broadened and, further, whether additional categories are needed. Such a reconceptualization might absorb some of the cases from an already too large and diverse group. Andersen and colleagues (2001) studied 397 consecutive admissions to the eating disorder unit of the University of Iowa Hospitals and Clinics from 1991 to 1998. Of this sample, 30% (119 of the total cases) were diagnosed with EDNOS on admission. The authors hypothesized that by broadening the diagnostic criteria for AN and BN slightly, only a few would be left in the EDNOS category, closer to the size that a true atypical category should be. After evaluation, it was found that 47% of those diagnosed EDNOS would meet all diagnostic criteria for AN but without amenorrhea (they called this group ANXA), 28% would meet all criteria for AN but with a body weight greater than 85% of ideal body weight yet less than 20% of starting weight (ANXW), 3% did not experience amenorrhea and weighed more than 85% of their ideal weight yet lacked binge behavior and could not be considered BN (ANXAW), and 3% met criteria for BN but with a binge frequency or duration that was too low (BNXFD). After removing these groups, only 18% of the original EDNOS group (which was only 5% of the original eating disorders sample) still remained with a diagnosis of EDNOS. The authors proposed that these four new categories (ANXA, ANXW, ANXAW, and BNWFD) be added to the current diagnostic system. As noted earlier, there is some empirical support from earlier studies for these suggestions. There may be little predictive value to the weight criterion in AN (Garfinkel et al., 1995), and amenorrhea has been questioned as a relevant diagnostic criterion (Cachelin & Maher, 1998; Garfinkel et al., 1996b). In BN, the duration, frequency minimum, and size of the binge may be arbitrary (Garfinkel et al., 1995; Keel et al., 2002). Thus, some rethinking along the lines proposed by Andersen and colleagues may be indicated before subsequent versions of the *DSM* are published.

Based on the fairly limited amount of research published to date, further empirical studies should be conducted to examine the validity and specificity of this category as well as to investigate effective treatments for patients diagnosed with EDNOS. Based on what is known about this population, it is important to remember that the diagnosis of EDNOS can be a serious form of an eating disorder and that more research is needed to determine effective treatment and optimal categorization of those classified as EDNOS.

BINGE EATING DISORDER—TO BE OR NOT TO BE A DIAGNOSIS?

Of all those eating disorders that fall into the EDNOS category, binge eating disorder (BED) has been the most studied. In the *DSM-IV*, BED is found as an example under the criteria for EDNOS, but it is also listed in Appendix B as one of the "criteria sets provided for further study."

In prevalence studies of community samples, it has been found that an estimated 2% to 3% of the general population may be diagnosed with BED. Those figures are much higher for the obese population (defined as weight greater than 30 kg/m^2), where between 5% and 10% may be diagnosed with this disorder (Grilo, 2002). Also of note is that, unlike AN and BN (where there is a much higher proportion of Caucasian females with these disorders), BED is not uncommon in males or minorities. BED also affects a much older population—the average age of onset for this disorder is between 30 and 50 years of age (Grilo, 2002).

Many researchers have examined the similarities and differences between BED and BN. Questions have been raised about diagnostic criteria, outcome, clinical characteristics, and subtypes. To meet the criteria for BED, a person must engage in binge activity at least two times a week for six consecutive months without any type of compensatory or purging behavior. There has been much speculation as to whether BED should be a separate category from BN, though there is substantial evidence that the two differ in some important ways (Herzog & Delinsky, 2001). First is the difference in binge episodes. Because there is no purging behavior to indicate the termination of a binge in BED, binges are measured by the number of days on which bingeing occurs, rather than as distinct episodes as in BN (Grilo, 2002). For those with BED, there is usually no dietary restriction during the day, but instead, daily overeating mixed with periods of binge activity. This is very different from BN, where everyday diet may be restricted except during binges.

Another difference that exists between BED and BN is in outcome. Individuals with BED appear to have a much more favorable outcome than those with BN, and it is not uncommon for BED patients to remit even without treatment (Herzog & Delinsky, 2001). Also of note are the differences in clinical characteristics between the two disorders. The age of onset for BED is much later than those with BN, and studies find significantly more obesity in BED and more self-injurious behaviors in BN (Grilo, 2002).

Masheb and Grilo (2000) examined 129 outpatients, 46 of whom met the criteria for BN and 83 who met the criteria for BED (51 were considered obese while 32 were considered nonobese). Based on the Eating Disorder Examination-Questionnaire (EDE-Q), BED and BN subjects were similar in binge frequency and in their levels of dysfunctional attitudes toward weight, eating, and shape. As a group, however, BED subjects scored much lower on dietary restraint than those with BN (Masheb & Grilo, 2000). Grilo (2002) further pointed out that the absence of cognitive features in the diagnostic criteria for BED is problematic because several studies have found similarities between BED and BN patients on this dimension.

Many studies have been criticized based on their inclusion of only those cases found in clinical settings. Of note are two studies using community samples. Striegel-Moore et al. (2001) found that their groups of BED ($n = 150$), BN purging type ($n = 48$), and BN nonpurging type ($n = 14$) did not vary significantly on self-report measures of shape and weight concern, even after adjusting for group differences in BMI. Sullivan (2001) found that a sample composed of BED and BN subjects differed on obesity and dietary restraint (those with BED were more likely to be obese and less likely to have high measures of dietary restraint) but were, again, similar on levels of weight and shape concern. A major strength of this study was that self-report (on the EDE-Q) was used in addition to a structured clinical interview (Sullivan, 2001).

Striegel-Moore and colleagues (Striegel-Moore, Dohm, et al., 2000) looked at a community sample of 44 women with BED, 44 with subthreshold BED (defined as a minimum frequency of one binge over a six-month period with the use of no inappropriate compensatory behavior), and 44 matched controls. It was found that the BED and subthreshold groups did not differ significantly on BMI ($M = 33.84$ and 31.45, respectively), though the control group had a mean BMI much lower than these two groups ($M = 25.53$). Using the EDE clinical interview, it was also determined that the BED and subthreshold BED groups were very similar on measures of eating and shape concern (after adjustments for BMI were made) as well as measures of psychiatric distress. These groups differed significantly on these measures from the controls. The findings are important because (1) AN and BN may not be the only disorders where there is significant shape and weight concern and (2) further research should be done to determine the validity of the frequency and duration criteria for BED because subthreshold cases of the disorder appear to be similar to those that meet clinical standards.

As with AN and BN, efforts have been made toward understanding possible subtypes within the BED category. Mizes and Sloan (1998) looked at 53 patients diagnosed with EDNOS who were being treated with psychotherapy. Using cluster analysis, two subgroups of patients were found. In one of the subgroups ($n = 11$), a group of overweight binge eaters were found to be distinct from the other EDNOS patients. This distinct group was significantly greater in BMI, highest adult weight, and number of binges per week. What was most noteworthy was that this overweight binge-eating group engaged in vomiting behavior just as much as the other EDNOS patients and also reported laxative use. This contradicts the current *DSM-IV* diagnostic criteria for BED, which strictly state that there should be no compensatory behavior to accompany the binges. The authors note the need for further research into both the diagnostic criteria and potential subtypes of BED (Mizes & Sloan, 1998).

Across three independent samples of women with interview-diagnosed BED, Stice and colleagues (Stice et al., 2001) found a dietary subtype and a dietary-depressive subtype. The latter group was found to have more overall psychopathology and greater impairments in social functioning and was more treatment resistant. In a replication study, Grilo, Masheb, and Wilson (2001) used cluster analyses to identify a pure dietary subtype and a negative affect subtype in a sample of 101 patients with BED, with the latter showing greater eating-related pathology and more overall psychological disturbance. These results were very similar to those of Stice et al., except that Grilo et al. did not find differences in binge frequency between the two subtypes. Considerable stability was found for the two subtypes over a four-week period.

Although there are similarities between BED and BN, several differences between them suggest they are distinct diagnostic categories. However, the distinction between BED and the nonpurging form of BN is not altogether clear. Because individuals with BED appear to have dysfunctional attitudes toward eating, shape, and weight comparable to other eating disorder groups, a cognitive component may be a necessary addition to the current diagnostic research criteria for BED. Moreover, existing data strongly suggest that subtypes exist in BED and are in need of additional study.

FUTURE RESEARCH

More research is needed into the validity of the diagnostic criteria across ethnic and cultural groups. The current *DSM* criteria may need to be reconsidered in light of studies with diverse groups, particularly Asians and potentially African Americans (Lee et al., 1993; Striegel-Moore, Wilfley, Pike, Dohm, & Fairburn, 2000), but this question has not been adequately addressed in the empirical literature. Additional studies are needed to better delineate the clinical and prognostic utility of alternate forms of subtyping (e.g., personality variables) for both AN and BN. Recent research has raised the question of whether ANBP is truly distinct from bulimic syndromes. The issue of subtyping within AN is of concern because it appears that the majority of those with ANR cross over to ANBP given enough time. We propose that combining several approaches to nosological research would be particularly useful in identifying subtypes of AN and BN and suggest that the following strategies offer a rigorous and efficient means of assessing the classification of eating disorders:

1. Taxometric analysis.
2. The longitudinal study of biological indicators focusing on serotonergic functioning.
3. Longitudinal studies of clinical course.

Taxometric analysis would help to identify if variability within eating disorders is related to a nonarbitrary class or taxon, which, if present, could then be further validated through comparison of biological variables and clinical course and outcome trajectories.

CONCLUSION

A great deal of progress has been made on clarifying the diagnostic criteria for anorexia nervosa and bulimia nervosa since the publication of *DSM-IV*. The validity and clinical utility of the specific weight loss criteria and amenorrhea for AN have been questioned by a number of researchers, particularly for adolescent and male populations. These criteria may be in need of reexamination for future editions of the *DSM*. The purging-nonpurging subtypes for BN appear to have little empirical support as distinct subtypes, and the differences between BN nonpurging subtype and BED are unclear. Questions have been raised concerning the diagnostic validity of the EDNOS and BED categories and the differentiation between these disorders and AN and BN. EDNOS, in particular, appears to be a disorder in need of clearer and more precise definition. Finally, newer approaches to classification, based on personality features and alternative methodologies such as taxometrics, provide promise for a more refined understanding of the diagnostic features of the eating disorders.

REFERENCES

Abbott, D. W., Wonderlich, S. A., & Mitchell, J. E. (2001). Treatment implications of comorbid personality disorders. In J. E. Mitchell (Ed.), *The outpatient treatment of eating disorders:*

A guide for therapists, dietitians and physicians (pp. 173–186). Minneapolis: University of Minnesota Press.

American Psychiatric Association. (1994). *Diagnostic and statistical manual of mental disorders* (4th ed.). Washington, DC: Author.

Andersen, A. E., Bowers, W. A., & Watson, T. (2001). A slimming program for eating disorders not otherwise specified: Reconceptualizing a confusing, residual diagnostic category. *Psychiatric Clinics of North America, 24,* 271–280.

Baran, S. A., Weltzin, T. E., & Kaye, W. H. (1995). Low discharge weight and outcome in anorexia nervosa. *American Journal of Psychiatry, 152,* 1070–1072.

Beck, A. T., Ward, C. H., Mendelson, M., Mock, J., & Erbaugh, J. (1961). An inventory for measuring depression. *Archives of General Psychiatry, 4,* 561–571.

Braun, D. L., Sunday, S. R., & Halmi, K. A. (1994). Psychiatric comorbidity in patients with eating disorders. *Psychological Medicine, 24,* 859–867.

Brewerton, T. D., & Jimerson, D. C. (1996). Studies of serotonin function in anorexia nervosa. *Psychiatry Research, 62,* 31–42.

Brewerton, T. D., Lydiard, R. B., Laraia, M. T., Shook, J. E., & Ballenger, J. C. (1992). CSF beta-endorphin and dynorphin in bulimia nervosa. *American Journal of Psychiatry, 149,* 1086–1090.

Bulik, C. M., Sullivan, P. F., Fear, J. L., & Pickering, A. (1997). Predictors of the development of bulimia nervosa in women with anorexia nervosa. *Journal of Nervous and Mental Diseases, 185,* 704–707.

Bulik, C. M., Sullivan, P. F., & Kendler, K. S. (2000). An empirical study of the classification of eating disorders. *American Journal of Psychiatry, 157,* 886–895.

Cachelin, F. M., & Maher, B. A. (1998). Is amenorrhea a critical criterion for anorexia nervosa? *Journal of Psychosomatic Research, 44,* 435–440.

Carrasco, J. L., Diaz-Marsa, M., Hollander, E., Cesar, J., & Saiz-Ruiz, J. (2000). Decreased platelet monoamine oxidase activity in female bulimia nervosa. *European Neuropsychopharmacology, 10,* 113–117.

Crosby, R. D., Wonderlich, S. A., Redlin, J., Engel, S., Simonich, H., Paxton-Jones, M., et al. (2001, November). *Impulsive behavior patterns in a sample of females with bulimia nervosa.* Paper presented at the annual meeting of the Eating Disorders Research Society, Bernalillo, NM.

Cumella, E. J., Wall, A. D., & Kerr-Almedia, N. (1999). MMPI-A in the inpatient assessment of adolescents with eating disorders. *Journal of Personality Assessment, 73,* 31–44.

DaCosta, M., & Halmi, K. A. (1992). Classification of anorexia nervosa: Question of subtypes. *International Journal of Eating Disorders, 11,* 305–311.

Eckert, E. D., Halmi, K. A., Marchi, P., Grove, W., & Crosby, R. (1995). Ten-year follow-up of anorexia nervosa: Clinical course and outcome. *Psychological Medicine, 25,* 143–156.

Eddy, K. T., Keel, P. K., Dorer, D. J., Delinsky, S. S., Franko, D. L., & Herzog, D. B. (2002). A longitudinal comparison of anorexia nervosa subtypes. *International Journal of Eating Disorders, 31,* 191–201.

Fairburn, C. G. (1985). Cognitive-behavioral treatment for bulimia. In D. M. Garner & P. E. Garfinkel (Eds.), *Handbook of psychotherapy for anorexia nervosa and bulimia* (pp. 160–192). New York: Guilford Press.

Fairburn, C. G., & Walsh, B. T. (2002). Atypical eating disorders (eating disorder not otherwise specified). In C. G. Fairburn & K. D. Brownell (Eds.), *Eating disorders and obesity: A comprehensive handbook* (pp. 171–177). New York: Guilford Press.

Favaro, A., & Santonastaso, P. (1998). Impulsive and compulsive self-injurious behavior in bulimia nervosa: Prevalence and psychological correlates. *Journal of Nervous and Mental Diseases, 186,* 157–165.

Fichter, M. M., Quadflieg, N., & Rief, W. (1994). Course of multi-impulsive bulimia. *Psychological Medicine, 24,* 591–604.

Garfinkel, P. E., Kennedy, S. H., & Kaplan, A. S. (1995). Views on classification and diagnosis of eating disorders. *Canadian Journal of Psychiatry, 40,* 445–456.

Garfinkel, P. E., Lin, E., Goering, P., Spegg, C., Goldbloom, D. S., Kennedy, S., et al. (1996a). Purging and nonpurging forms of bulimia nervosa in a community sample. *International Journal of Eating Disorders, 20,* 231–238.

Garfinkel, P. E., Lin, E., Goering, P., Spegg, C., Goldbloom, D. S., Kennedy, S., et al. (1996b). Should amenorrhea be necessary for the diagnosis of anorexia nervosa? Evidence from a Canadian community sample. *British Journal of Psychiatry, 168,* 500–506.

Garfinkel, P. E., Moldofsky, H., & Garner, D. M. (1980). The heterogeneity of anorexia nervosa: Bulimia as a distinct subgroup. *Archives of General Psychiatry, 37,* 1036–1040.

Garner, D. M., Garner, M. V., & Rosen, L. W. (1993). Anorexia nervosa "restrictors" who purge: Implications for subtyping anorexia nervosa. *International Journal of Eating Disorders, 13,* 171–186.

Garner, D. M., & Olmsted, M. P. (1984). *The Eating Disorder Inventory manual.* Odessa, FL: Psychological Assessment Resources.

Garner, D. M., Olmsted, M. P., Bohr, Y., & Garfinkel, P. E. (1982). The eating attitudes test: Psychometric features and clinical correlates. *Psychological Medicine, 12,* 871–878.

Gleaves, D. H., & Eberenz, K. P. (1995). Validating a multidimensional model of the psychopathology of bulimia nervosa. *Journal of Clinical Psychology, 51,* 181–189.

Gleaves, D. H., Lowe, M. R., Green, B. A., Cororve, M. B., & Williams, T. L. (2000). Do anorexia and bulimia nervosa occur on a continuum? A taxometric analysis. *Behavior Therapy, 31,* 195–219.

Gleaves, D. H., Lowe, M. R., Snow, A. C., Green, B. A., & Murphy-Eberenz, K. P. (2000). Continuity and discontinuity models of bulimia nervosa: A taxometric investigation. *Journal of Abnormal Psychology, 109,* 56–68.

Goldbloom, D. S., Hicks, L. K., & Garfinkel, P. E. (1990). Platelet serotonin uptake in bulimia nervosa. *Biological Psychiatry, 28,* 644–647.

Goldner, E. M., Srikameswaran, S., Schroeder, M. L., Livesley, W. J., & Birmingham, C. L. (1999). Dimensional assessment of personality pathology in patients with eating disorders. *Psychiatry Research, 85,* 151–159.

Grilo, C. M. (2002). Binge eating disorder. In C. G. Fairburn & K. D. Brownell (Eds.), *Eating disorders and obesity: A comprehensive handbook* (pp. 178–182). New York: Guilford Press.

Grilo, C. M., Masheb, R. M., & Wilson, G. T. (2001). Subtyping binge eating disorder. *Journal of Consulting and Clinical Psychology, 69,* 1066–1072.

Habermas, T. (1996). In defense of weight phobia as the central organizing motive in anorexia nervosa: Historical and cultural arguments for a culture sensitive psychological conception. *International Journal of Eating Disorders, 19,* 317–334.

Hay, P. (1998). The epidemiology of eating disorder behaviors: An Australian community-based survey. *International Journal of Eating Disorders, 23,* 371–382.

Hay, P., & Fairburn, C. (1998). The validity of the *DSM-IV* scheme for classifying bulimic eating disorders. *International Journal of Eating Disorders, 23,* 7–15.

Hebebrand, J., Wehmeier, P. M., & Remschmidt, H. (2000). Weight criteria for diagnosis of anorexia nervosa. *American Journal of Psychiatry, 157,* 1024.

Herzog, D. B., & Delinsky, S. S. (2001). Classification of eating disorders. In R. H. Striegel-Moore & L. Smolak (Eds.), *Eating disorders: Innovative directions for research and practice* (pp. 31–50). Washington, DC: American Psychological Association.

Herzog, D. B., Dorer, D. J., Keel, P. K., Selwyn, S. E., Ekeblad, E. R., Flores, A. T., et al. (1999). Recovery and relapse in anorexia and bulimia nervosa: A 7.5 year follow-up study. *Journal of the American Academy of Child and Adolescent Psychiatry, 38,* 829–837.

Herzog, D. B., Hopkins, J. D., & Burns, C. D. (1993). A follow-up study of 33 subdiagnostic eating disordered women. *International Journal of Eating Disorders, 14,* 261–267.

Herzog, D. B., Keller, M. B., Sachs, N. R., Yeh, C., & Lavori, P. W. (1992). Psychiatric comorbidity in treatment seeking anorexics and bulimics. *Journal of the American Academy of Child and Adolescent Psychiatry, 31,* 810–818.

Jimerson, D. C., Lesem, M. D., Kaye, W. H., & Brewerton, T. D. (1992). Low serotonin and dopamine metabolite concentrations in cerebrospinal fluid from bulimic patients with frequent binge episodes. *Archives of General Psychiatry, 49,* 132–138.

Jimerson, D. C., Wolfe, B. E., Metzger, E. D., & Finkelstein, D. M. (1997). Decreased serotonin function in bulimia nervosa. *Archives of General Psychiatry, 54,* 529–534.

Johnson, C., & Connors, M. E. (1987). *The etiology and treatment of bulimia nervosa: A biopsychosocial perspective.* New York: Basic Books.

Johnson, C., Tobin, D. L., & Dennis, A. (1990). Differences in treatment outcome between borderline and nonborderline bulimics at one-year follow-up. *International Journal of Eating Disorders, 9,* 617–627.

Joiner, T. E., Jr. (2000). Special series: Samples from four frontiers of eating disorders research overview. *Behavior Therapy, 31,* 187–193.

Joiner, T. E., Jr., & Schmidt, N. B. (2002). Taxometrics can do diagnostics right. In L. Neutler & M. Malik (Eds.), *Rethinking the DSM: A psychological perspective* (pp. 107–120). Washington, DC: American Psychological Association.

Kaye, W. H. (1997). Persistent alterations in behavior and serotonin activity after recovery from anorexia and bulimia nervosa. *Annals of the New York Academy of Science, 817,* 162–178.

Kaye, W. H., Berrettini, W., Gwirtsman, H., & George, D. T. (1990). Altered cerebrospinal fluid neuropeptide Y and peptide YY immunoreactivity in anorexia and bulimia nervosa. *Archives of General Psychiatry, 47,* 584–556.

Kaye, W. H., Greeno, C. G., Moss, H., Fernstrom, J., Fernstrom, M., Lilenfeld, L. R., et al. (1998). Alterations in serotonin activity and psychiatric symptoms after recovery from bulimia nervosa. *Archives of General Psychiatry, 55,* 927–935.

Kaye, W. H., & Weltzin, T. E. (1991). Neurochemistry of bulimia nervosa. *Journal of Clinical Psychiatry, 52,* 21–28.

Keel, P. K., Cogley, C. B., Ghosh, S., & Lester, N. (2002, April). *What constitutes an unusually large amount of food for defining binge episodes?* Paper presented at the Academy for Eating Disorders International Conference on Eating Disorders, Boston.

Keel, P. K., Mayer, S. A., & Fischer, J. H. (2001). Importance of size in defining binge eating episodes in bulimia nervosa. *International Journal of Eating Disorders, 29,* 294–301.

Keel, P. K., Mitchell, J. E., Miller, K. B., Davis, T. L., & Crow, S. J. (2000). Predictive validity of bulimia nervosa as a diagnostic category. *American Journal of Psychiatry, 157,* 136–138.

Kendler, K. S., MacLean, C., Neale, M., Kessler, R., Heath, A., & Eaves, L. (1991). The genetic epidemiology of bulimia nervosa. *American Journal of Psychiatry, 148,* 1627–1637.

Lacey, J. H. (1993). Self-damaging and addictive behavior in bulimia nervosa: A catchment area study. *British Journal of Psychiatry, 163,* 190–194.

Lee, S., Ho, T. P., & Hsu, L. K. G. (1993). Fat phobic and nonfat phobic anorexia nervosa: A comparative study of 70 Chinese patients in Hong Kong. *Psychological Medicine, 23,* 999–1017.

Levitan, R. D., Kaplan, A. S., Joffe, R. T., Levitt, A. J., & Brown, G. M. (1997). Hormonal and subjective responses to intravenous meta-chlorphenylpiperazine in bulimia nervosa. *Archives of General Psychiatry, 54,* 521–527.

Livesley, W. J., Jackson, D. W., & Schroeder, M. L. (1991). Dimensions of personality pathology. *Canadian Journal of Psychiatry, 36,* 557–562.

Marazziti, D., Macchi, E., Rotondo, A., Placidi, G. F., & Cassano, G. B. (1988). Involvement of the serotonin system in bulimia. *Life Sciences, 43,* 2123–2126.

Masheb, R. M., & Grilo, C. M. (2000). Binge eating disorder: A need for additional diagnostic criteria. *Comprehensive Psychiatry, 41,* 159–162.

McCann, U. D., Rossiter, E. M., King, R. J., & Agras, W. S. (1991). Nonpurging bulimia: A distinct subtype of bulimia nervosa. *International Journal of Eating Disorders, 10,* 679–687.

Meehl, P. E. (1995). Bootstraps taxometrics: Solving the classification problem in psychopathology. *American Psychologist, 50,* 266–275.

Mitchell, J. E. (1992). Subtyping of bulimia nervosa. *International Journal of Eating Disorders, 11,* 327–332.

Mizes, J. S., & Sloan, D. M. (1998). An empirical analysis of eating disorder, not otherwise specified: Preliminary support for a distinct group. *International Journal of Eating Disorders, 23,* 233–242.

Nagata, T., Kawarada, Y., Kiriike, N., & Iketani, T. (2000). Multi-impulsivity of Japanese patients with eating disorders: Primary and secondary impulsivity. *Psychiatric Research, 94,* 239–250.

Nilsson, E. W., Gillberg, C., Gillberg, I. C., & Rastam, M. (1999). Ten-year follow-up of adolescent-onset anorexia nervosa: Personality disorders. *Journal of the American Academy of Child and Adolescent Psychiatry, 38,* 1389–1395.

Oehlschlaegel-Akiyoshi, J., Malewski, P., & Mahon, J. (1999). How to define anorectic weight. *European Eating Disorders Review, 7,* 321–333.

Okamoto, Y., Okamoto, Y., Kagaya, A., Horiguchi, J., & Yamawaki, S. (1999). The relationship of the platelet 5-HT-induced calcium response to clinical symptoms in eating disorders. *Psychopharmacology, 142,* 289–294.

Pratt, E. M., Niego, S. H., & Agras, W. S. (1998). Does the size of a binge matter? *International Journal of Eating Disorders, 24,* 307–312.

Pryor, T., Wiederman, M. W., & McGilley, B. (1996). Clinical correlates of anorexia nervosa subtypes. *International Journal of Eating Disorders, 19,* 371–379.

Rosenvinge, J. H., Martinussen, M., & Ostensen, E. (2000). The comorbidity of eating disorders and personality disorders: A meta-analytic review of studies published between 1983 and 1998. *Eating and Weight Disorders, 5,* 52–61.

Rossiter, E. M., & Agras, W. S. (1990). An empirical test of the *DSM-III-R* definition of binge. *International Journal of Eating Disorders, 9,* 513–518.

Rossiter, E. M., Agras, W. S., Telch, C. F., & Schneider, J. A. (1993). Cluster B personality disorder characteristics predict outcome in the treatment of bulimia nervosa. *International Journal of Eating Disorders, 13,* 349–357.

Ruscio, A. M., Borkovec, T. D., & Ruscio, J. (2001). A taxometric investigation of the latent structure of worry. *Journal of Abnormal Psychology, 110,* 413–422.

Ruscio, A. M., Ruscio, J., & Keane, T. M. (2002). The latent structure of posttraumatic stress disorder: A taxometric investigation of reactions to extreme stress. *Journal of Abnormal Psychology, 111,* 290–301.

Ruscio, J., & Ruscio, A. M. (2000). Informing the continuity controversy: A taxometric analysis of depression. *Journal of Abnormal Psychology, 109,* 473–487.

Russell, J., & Gross, G. (2000). Anorexia nervosa and body mass index. *American Journal of Psychiatry, 157,* 2060.

Steiger, H., Gauvin, L., Israel, M., Koerner, N., Ng Ying Kin, N. M. K., Paris, J., et al. (2001). Association of serotonin and cortisol indices with childhood abuse in bulimia nervosa. *Archives of General Psychiatry, 58,* 837–843.

Steiger, H., Jabalpurwala, S., & Champagne, J. (1996). Axis II comorbidity and developmental adversity in bulimia nervosa. *Journal of Nervous and Mental Diseases, 184,* 555–560.

Steiger, H., Koerner, N., Engelberg, M. J., Israel, M., Ng Ying Kin, N. M. K., & Young, S. N. (2001). Self-destructiveness and serotonin function in bulimia nervosa. *Psychiatry Research, 103,* 15–26.

Steiger, H., & Stotland, S. (1996). Prospective study of outcome in bulimics as a function of Axis-II comorbidity: Long-term responses on eating and psychiatric symptoms. *International Journal of Eating Disorders, 20,* 149–161.

Steiger, H., Young, S. N., Ng Ying Kin, N. M. K., Koerner, N., Israel, M., Lageix, P., et al. (2001). Implications of impulsive and affective symptoms for serotonin function in bulimia nervosa. *Psychological Medicine, 31,* 85–95.

Stice, E. (1994). Review of evidence for a sociocultural model of bulimia nervosa and an exploration of the mechanisms of action. *Clinical Psychology Review, 14,* 633–661.

Stice, E., & Agras, W. S. (1999). Subtyping bulimic women along dietary restraint and negative affect dimensions. *Journal of Consulting and Clinical Psychology, 67,* 460–469.

Stice, E., Agras, W. S., Telch, C. F., Halmi, K. A., Mitchell, J. E., & Wilson, G. T. (2001). Subtyping binge eating-disordered women along dieting and negative affect dimensions. *International Journal of Eating Disorders, 30,* 11–27.

Striegel-Moore, R. H., Cachelin, F. M., Dohm, F. A., Pike, K. M., Wilfley, D. E., & Fairburn, C. G. (2001). Comparison of binge eating disorder and bulimia nervosa in a community sample. *International Journal of Eating Disorders, 29,* 157–165.

Striegel-Moore, R. H., Dohm, F. A., Solomon, E. E., Fairburn, C. G., Pike, K. M., & Wilfley, D. E. (2000). Subthreshold binge eating disorder. *International Journal of Eating Disorders, 27,* 270–278.

Striegel-Moore, R. H., Wilfley, D. E., Pike, K. M., Dohm, F. A., & Fairburn, C. G. (2000). Recurrent binge eating in black American women. *Archives of Family Medicine, 9,* 83–87.

Strober, M., Freeman, R., & Morrell, W. (1997). The long-term course of severe anorexia nervosa in adolescents: Survival analysis of recovery, relapse, and outcome predictors over 10–15 years in a prospective study. *International Journal of Eating Disorders, 22,* 339–360.

Strober, M., Salkin, B., Burroughs, J., & Morrell, W. (1982). Validity of the bulimia-restrictor distinction in anorexia nervosa: Parental personality characteristics and family psychiatric morbidity. *Journal of Nervous and Mental Disorders, 170,* 345–351.

Sullivan, K. A. (2001). The clinical features of binge eating disorder and bulimia nervosa: What are the differences? *Canadian Journal of Counseling, 35,* 315–328.

Swift, W. J., & Stern, S. (1982). The psychodynamic diversity of anorexia nervosa. *International Journal of Eating disorders, 2,* 17–35.

Tobin, D. L., Griffing, A., & Griffing, S. (1997). An examination of subtype criteria for bulimia nervosa. *International Journal of Eating Disorders, 22,* 179–286.

Waldman, I. D., & Lilienfeld, S. O. (2001). Applications of taxometric methods to problems of comorbidity: Perspectives and challenges. *Clinical Psychology Science and Practice, 8,* 520–527.

Walsh, B. T., & Kahn, C. B. (1997). Diagnostic criteria for eating disorders: Current Concerns and future directions. *Psychopharmacology Bulletin, 33,* 369–372.

Welch, S. L., & Fairburn, C. G. (1996). Impulsivity or comorbidity in bulimia nervosa: A controlled study of deliberate self-harm and alcohol and drug misuse in a community sample. *British Journal of Psychiatry, 169,* 451–458.

Westen, D., & Harnden-Fischer, J. (2001). Personality profiles in eating disorders: Rethinking the distinction between axis I and axis II. *American Journal of Psychiatry, 158,* 547–562.

Williamson, D. A., Gleaves, D. H., & Savin, S. S. (1992). Empirical classification of eating disorder not otherwise specified: Support for *DSM-IV* changes. *Journal of Psychopathology and Behavioral Assessment, 14,* 201–216.

Williamson, D. A., Womble, L. G., Smeets, M. A. M., Netemeyer, R. G., Thaw, J. M., Kutlesic, V., et al. (2002). Latent structure of eating disorder symptoms: A factor analytic and taxometric investigation. *American Journal of Psychiatry, 159,* 412–418.

Willmuth, M. E., Leitenberg, H., Rosen, J. C., & Cado, S. (1988). A comparison of purging and nonpurging normal weight bulimics. *International Journal of Eating Disorders, 7,* 825–835.

Wilson, G. T., & Eldredge, K. (1991). Frequency of binge eating in bulimia nervosa: Diagnostic validity. *International Journal of Eating Disorders, 10,* 557–561.

Wolfe, B. E., Metzger, E. D., Levine, J. M., Finkelstein, D. M., Cooper, T. B., & Jimerson, D. C. (2000). Serotonin function following remission from bulimia nervosa. *Neuropsychopharmacology, 22,* 257–263.

Wonderlich, S. A., Crosby, R., Mitchell, J. E., Thompson, K., Redlin, J., Demuth, G., et al. (2001). Pathways mediating sexual abuse and eating disturbances in children. *International Journal of Eating Disorders, 29,* 270–279.

Wonderlich, S. A., Fullerton, D., Swift, W. J., & Klein, M. H. (1994). Five-year outcome from eating disorders: Relevance of personality disorders. *International Journal of Eating Disorders, 15,* 233–243.

Wonderlich, S. A., & Mitchell, J. E. (2001). The role of personality in the onset of eating disorders and treatment implications. *Psychiatric Clinics of North America, 24,* 249–258.

Wonderlich, S. A., & Swift, W. J. (1990). Perceptions of parental relationships in eating disorders: The relevance of depressed mood. *Journal of Abnormal Psychology, 100,* 353–360.

Zanarini, M. C., Frankenburg, F. R., Dubo, E. D., Sickel, A. E., Trikha, A., Levin, A., et al. (1998). Axis I comorbidity of borderline personality disorder. *American Journal of Psychiatry, 155,* 1733–1739.

Chapter 5

ASSESSMENT OF MEDICAL STATUS AND PHYSICAL FACTORS

CLAIRE POMEROY

The eating disorders are associated with a variety of physical illnesses (Agras, 2001; Becker, Grinspoon, Klibanski, & Herzog, 1999; Brown & Mehler, 2000; Comerci, 1990; Herzog, Deter, Fiehn, & Petzold, 1997; Mitchell, Seim, Colon, & Pomeroy, 1987; Palla & Litt, 1988; Pomeroy & Mitchell, 1989; Powers & Santana, 2002; Roerig, Mitchell, Myers, & Glass, 2002; Sharp, & Freeman, 1993). Every patient should undergo a thorough baseline medical evaluation to determine physical condition and detect medical complications. Medical assessment provides the opportunity to confirm the diagnosis and rule out other illnesses that may mimic eating disorders. The baseline medical examination also forms the basis for the medical clinician's recommendations for ongoing management of the physical status of the patient. Medical conditions involving every major organ system in the body may complicate the course of patients with eating disorders. Recognition and management of these superimposed medical illnesses are a necessary part of the successful treatment program for the patient with anorexia nervosa, bulimia nervosa, or binge eating syndrome. Close collaboration between the medical physician and other members of the eating disorders team is critical. The goal is to maximize the opportunity for patients to undergo successful treatment of their eating disorder and to minimize long-term adverse health consequences.

MEDICAL HISTORY AND PHYSICAL EXAMINATION CLUES TO THE DIAGNOSES OF EATING DISORDERS

Physical abnormalities and medical diseases are important clues to the presence of an eating disorder. Health care providers must be aware that medical complications may be the first presentation of an eating disorder. Many patients with eating disorders are secretive about their abnormal eating patterns. Anorexics and bulimics often avoid seeking medical assistance from designated eating disorder specialists, especially those who practice in a psychiatric clinic or hospital. Therefore, primary care clinicians, medical specialists, or even emergency room physicians may be the first health care providers to evaluate patients with eating disorders (Mehler, 2001; Walsh, Wheat,

& Freund, 2000). In these settings, medical history and physical examination clues can provide critical evidence of an underlying eating disorder (see Table 5.1).

Patients with anorexia nervosa often deny the magnitude of their weight loss or its significance and, indeed, may go to dramatic lengths to conceal their low weight from medical care providers. Anorexics may present to their physician with vague complaints of fatigue, anxiety, depression, or stress. They may also seek care for evaluation of headaches resulting from hypoglycemia or poor nutritional status or abdominal discomfort and constipation because of ileus or poor gut peristalsis. Some patients express concern about hair loss, brittle hair and nails, or cold intolerance. Patients may also present emergently with complications such as fractures resulting from the osteoporosis that characterizes the disease. Careful and compassionate questioning may be necessary to elicit an accurate dietary history of caloric restriction or medical details such as absence of menses. The patient may be resistant to medical assessment, and significant attention should be paid to establishing a nonjudgmental and trusting physician-patient relationship.

Table 5.1   Medical History and Physical Examination Clues to the Eating Disorder

Eating Disorder	Medical History Clues	Physical Examination Clues
Anorexia nervosa	Denial of significance of illness/medical complications. Failure to acknowledge obvious weight loss. Reports of excessive exercise. Anxiety, depression, stress. Irritability, withdrawal. Fatigue. Headaches. Abdominal bloating/discomfort. Constipation. Hair loss. Cold intolerance. Fractures with minimal trauma.	Inanition. Bradycardia. Hypotension, orthostasis. Alopecia, hair loss. Lanugo hair formation. Low body temperature. Acrocyanosis. Dry skin. Brittle hair and nails. Peripheral edema. Carotenodermia (yellow-orange) skin, especially palms.
Bulimia nervosa	Denial of binge-purge behaviors. Anxiety, depression, stress. Fatigue, lethargy. Headaches. Abdominal bloating/discomfort. Constipation. Irregular menses.	Usually appear healthy. Parotid/salivary gland enlargement. Erosion of dental enamel. Russell's sign. Peripheral edema.
Binge eating disorder	Concern about overweight. Request for diet advice. Eating binges. Anxiety, depression, stress. Symptoms due to complications of obesity.	Usually overweight. Otherwise often appear healthy. Signs due to complications of obesity.

The physical examination in anorexia nervosa provides clues to the diagnosis of the eating disorder. Low weight and inanition are obvious signs to the clinician of significant illness, and anorexia nervosa should be included in the differential diagnosis. Vital signs often reveal slow pulse rates, low blood pressure, and orthostatic blood pressure changes. Alopecia, brittle hair, or acrocyanosis of the digits also suggest the diagnosis. Some patients have carotenodermia with a yellow-orange discoloration of the skin that is often especially obvious on the palms. It is the responsibility of the medical provider to recognize the significance of the weight loss and other physical examination clues. Too often, societal and family pressures perpetuate denial of the significance of the low weight.

Bulimic patients are usually secretive and embarrassed by the purging behaviors that characterize their illness and, therefore, are reluctant to share these details with the medical provider. Compassionate questioning and nonjudgmental responses are necessary. Patients may be more comfortable sharing this type of information with a nurse or social worker, rather than the physician. Patients often present with nonspecific complaints of fatigue, lethargy, anxiety, depression, or stress. Somatic complaints of abdominal bloating or pain and constipation may reflect gastrointestinal manifestations of recurrent vomiting or laxative abuse. Some patients may seek advice about irregular menses or infertility.

Some physical examination clues can be very helpful in suggesting a diagnosis of bulimia nervosa. Parotid and salivary gland enlargement can be caused by a number of conditions but should prompt consideration of a diagnosis of bulimia nervosa (Mandel & Kaynar, 1992). *Russell's sign* is defined as calluses or abrasions on the skin of the hand resulting from manual stimulation of the gag reflex to induce vomiting. Because dental exam may reveal evidence of enamel erosion due to recurrent vomiting, primary care providers should include oral evaluation in their screening evaluation, and dentists should be aware of their role in identifying the eating disorder (Milosevic, Brodie, & Slade, 1997; Simmons, Grayden, & Mitchell, 1986; Studen-Pavlovich & Elliott, 2001).

Binge-eating patients most commonly present to the medical care system with requests for dietary advice or for management of the complications of obesity. Patients may not volunteer information about bingeing, but a careful history can provide this essential clue. Obesity is obvious on physical examination, and there may be signs of complications of the increased weight, such as heart disease or degenerative arthritis.

Given the frequency of eating disorders and the problems with underdiagnosis, it is critical that all health care providers be familiar with the medical history and physical examination clues to the eating disorders. This facilitates early recognition and allows prompt institution of appropriate therapy. Intervention early in the disease course is now recognized as central to the successful management of these illnesses and the prevention of morbidity and mortality from associated medical complications.

INITIAL MEDICAL ASSESSMENT

After the diagnosis of an eating disorder, a medical assessment to detect physical manifestations is critical (Becker et al., 1999; Comerci, 1990; Mehler, 2001; Pomeroy & Mitchell, 1989; Powers & Santana, 2002; Sharp & Freeman, 1993; Walsh et al., 2000).

This medical evaluation should be performed by an internist, pediatrician, family practice clinician, or other physician or physician extender who is experienced in the care of patients with eating disorders. If the eating disorder team does not include such an individual, it is advisable to identify professionals to whom the team can refer patients for medical assessment. This facilitates the very important communication between the eating disorder specialists and the medical physician responsible for monitoring the physical condition of the patient.

During the initial clinic visit for medical assessment, a complete medical history and physical examination should be performed (American Academy of Pediatrics, 2003; Becker et al., 1999; Comerci, 1990; Mehler, 2001; Pomeroy & Mitchell, 1989; Powers & Santana, 2002; Sharp & Freeman, 1993; Walsh et al., 2000; see Table 5.2). In addition to the usual components of historical evaluation, particular attention should be focused on details that can be useful in defining the medical severity of the underlying eating disorder and identifying potential physical complications. A complete weight history including maximum and minimum weights should be obtained, and details about the duration of disordered eating should be ascertained. A diet history, including the use of weight loss medications and diets, should be documented. For women, a menstrual history is critical to help determine the risk of osteoporosis in underweight anorexics and to assist with assessment of fertility. Given the high rates of comorbid substance abuse and psychiatric illness, inquiries about illicit drug use and depression augment details obtained from the referring team. A medication history should include questioning about the use of over-the-counter medications, especially diuretics, laxatives, or ipecac. An exercise history identifies participation in sports activities associated with an increased risk for anorexia or bulimia nervosa or a sedentary lifestyle in overweight patients, including those with binge eating disorder.

Table 5.2   Initial Medical Assessment of Eating-Disordered Patients

Medical History	Physical Examination	Laboratory Evaluation
Weight history (maximum and minimum weights).	Weight, body habitus.	Guided by history and physical examination findings.
Diet history.	Vital signs.	Complete blood count.
Menstrual/obstetric history (women).	State of hydration-skin turgor, mucus membranes.	Serum electrolytes and urine.
Sexual history.	Dental/oral evaluation.	Liver enzymes tests.
Psychiatric history, including depression, substance abuse.	Standard organ system examination, including skin, cardiac, pulmonary, abdominal, musculoskeletal, and neurologic evaluations.	Renal function tests.
Medication history, including over-the-counter, alternative medications.		Urinalysis.
	Assessment of mental status and affect.	Thyroid function tests.
Use of diuretics, laxatives, diet pills, ipecac.		Stool guaiac.
Use of cigarettes, alcohol.	Gynecological examination (women).	Electrocardiogram.
Exercise history, especially participation in activities that encourage low weight.		Bone densitometry.

A complete physical examination is recommended for every patient diagnosed with an eating disorder (Becker et al., 1999; Comerci, 1990; Mehler, 2001; Pomeroy & Mitchell, 1989; Powers & Santana, 2002; Sharp & Freeman, 1993; Walsh et al., 2000). Particular attention should be paid to height and weight and obtaining accurate vital signs including pulse rate and blood pressure with testing for orthostatic changes. The state of hydration should be assessed by examination of skin turgor and moisture of mucus membranes. An oral examination should be emphasized, with special attention to integrity of the dental enamel in patients who may repeatedly engage in purging behaviors. Standard evaluations of the heart, lungs, abdomen, and musculoskeletal systems can detect other physical complications of the eating disorders. A thorough neurologic examination should be performed to eliminate neurologic diseases that mimic the eating disorders. Assessment of mental status and affect is an important part of the physical assessment. Finally, in women, gynecologic examination with particular attention to potential signs of delayed maturation and estrogen deficiency is required (see Table 5.2).

Laboratory testing is indicated to detect physical complications of the eating disorders. The extent of appropriate laboratory testing is driven by the findings on the medical history and physical examination (Mitchell et al., 1984; Pomeroy & Mitchell, 1989; Yager et al., 2000). Most patients should receive a complete blood count to detect evidence of anemia resulting from malnutrition or gastrointestinal blood loss. Testing of serum electrolytes is critical, especially in low-weight anorexics and in bulimic patients who are actively purging. Special attention should be paid to serum potassium levels, bicarbonate levels, and serum glucose in these patients. Consideration may be given to measuring serum magnesium, calcium, and phosphorus concentrations as well. Urine electrolytes have been identified as a useful marker of bulimia nervosa (Crow, Rosenberg, Mitchell, & Thuras, 2001). Renal function tests and urinalysis are appropriate screening tests to detect renal complications and to help evaluate the extent of dehydration. Liver enzymes are included in most standard laboratory batteries and are particularly important to obtain in obese binge-eating patients at risk for gallbladder disease and nonalcoholic steatohepatitis. Thyroid function tests are critical to rule out occult hypo- or hyperthyroidism that can mimic eating disorders. Serum lipid determinations are especially important in obese patients who are at increased risk of dyslipidemia. Albumin, prealbumin, or transferrin can provide evidence of nutritional status. Stool guaiac testing will detect evidence of gastrointestinal bleeding and is particularly important in bulimic patients.

An electrocardiogram is recommended to detect evidence of cardiac complications and arrhythmias in anorexics and bulimics and in obese binge-eating patients at risk of atherosclerotic disease. Bone densitometry should be performed in patients with anorexia nervosa and bulimics with a history of anorexia or significant caloric restriction. In some patients, urine or blood tests to detect surreptitious use of illicit drugs of abuse, diuretics, or laxatives may be appropriate. Additional tests may be prompted by findings on the history and physical examination. Specific concerns may necessitate the use of other procedures, such as chest or abdominal roentgenograms, electromyography, and computerized tomography of the brain, to assess diagnoses suggested by the screening examinations (Yager et al., 2000). ·

PHYSICAL MANIFESTATIONS

Importance of Associated Behaviors

Many of the medical complications that occur in eating-disordered patients are secondary to associated behaviors, especially purging activities in individuals with bulimia nervosa (see Table 5.3). Bulimics may abuse ipecac, diuretics, laxatives, diet pills, or thyroid hormone to control their weight (Mitchell, Pomeroy, & Huber, 1988). Clinicians should be aware of the frequency of these weight control methods, take a careful history to learn if the patient is engaging in these activities, and remain vigilant for the possibility of occult purging behaviors.

Bulimics use a wide variety of inventive means to augment weight loss by inducing vomiting, eliminating fluid, suppressing appetite, or minimizing food absorption (Mitchell, Pomeroy, & Huber, 1988). Frequent vomiting can be induced by manual stimulation of the gag reflex. Many bulimics learn to spontaneously vomit without manipulation. Others use a variety of purgatives, especially ipecac, to induce vomiting.

Ipecac is a serious drug of abuse in the eating disorders. Patients may repetitively ingest large amounts of the drug to induce vomiting and eliminate unwanted calories. The active ingredient in ipecac, emitine, has a very long half-life with slow elimination. As a result, large amounts of the drug can accumulate in the heart, skeletal muscle, and other body sites, leading to prolonged organ dysfunction. Patients may develop profound muscle weakness and may note difficulty climbing stairs or walking (Palmer & Guay, 1985). Life-threatening cardiomyopathy can necessitate prolonged cardiac support and may be fatal (Dresser, Massey, Johnson, & Bossen, 1992).

Other patients with bulimia nervosa ingest huge amounts of laxative drugs (Mitchell & Boutacoff, 1986; Turner, Batik, Palmer, Forbes, & McDermott, 2000). Both over-the-counter medications and those available by prescription may be abused. Doses far in excess of those recommended by the manufacturer may be taken. Some studies have suggested that as many as one-third of patients with bulimia nervosa abuse laxatives. Stimulant-type laxatives are most frequently used; these are easily available in many

Table 5.3   Behaviors Contributing to Physical Complications of Eating Disorders

Anorexia Nervosa	Bulimia Nervosa	Binge Eating Disorder
Restriction of calories—food/fluids.	Intermittent caloric restriction.	Very low calorie diets.
Excessive exercise.	Excessive exercise.	Alternative medicines used for weight loss.
Overaggressive caloric replacement causing refeeding syndrome.	Vomiting.	Other weight-loss "fads."
	Diuretic abuse.	
	Laxative abuse.	
	Enema abuse.	
	Diet pill abuse.	
	Thyroid hormone abuse.	
	Ipecac abuse.	
	Excess use of saunas.	
	If overweight—weight-loss fads.	

forms at the local drug store. Patients may frequent multiple retail outlets to purchase the medication to avoid notice. Other patients request and often receive prescriptions for laxatives from their physicians. It is ironic that laxative use is an ineffective form of weight loss. While an initial small weight loss may occur, the body quickly responds by stimulation of the renin-angiotensin-aldosterone system, and the consequent secondary hyperaldosteronism results in fluid retention. Of concern, chronic laxative abuse is associated with an array of gastrointestinal abnormalities, including loss of peristaltic function and bleeding. A vicious cycle can develop with patients taking ever larger doses of laxatives to stimulate colonic activity. Laxative dependency and cathartic colon can cause permanent loss of gastrointestinal function.

Other methods may be used by bulimic patients to induce gastrointestinal losses. Repeated enemas may be used to lose weight (Mitchell, Pyle, Hatsukami, & Eckert, 1991). Patients who surreptitiously use tap water or Fleet enemas as often as every day have been reported. Damage to the anal sphincter can result from repeated use of enemas.

Diuretic medications are also frequently used by bulimics to lose weight (Mitchell, Pomeroy, & Huber, 1988). Many over-the-counter medications designed for the relief of premenstrual symptoms contain agents such as pamabron with diuretic activity. Patients may take large doses to induce fluid loss. Other patients may obtain prescription diuretics and take excess amounts or misappropriate prescriptions meant for others. Bulimics who abuse hydrochlorothiazide, furosemide, and even spironolactone have been reported. Like laxatives, diuretic abuse results in stimulation of the renin-angiotensin-aldosterone system, and secondary hyperaldosteronism can cause reflex fluid accumulation if the patient attempts to discontinue diuretic use. Concerned about the edema formation, the patient often resumes use of the medication, usually in increased doses, perpetuating a cycle of diuretic abuse. Clinicians clearly should substantiate medical need before prescribing diuretics for patients at risk of or with eating disorders. Patients who abuse diuretics should be urged to discontinue their use and be supported during the period of withdrawal with suggestions of mild fluid restriction and use of support hose to minimize symptoms of edema.

Bulimic patients may also use diet pills to augment weight loss (Mitchell, Pomeroy, & Huber, 1988). Many drugs containing ingredients such as phenylpropanolamine are available without prescription. Use in excessive amounts has been associated with significantly adverse effects including anxiety, seizures, elevated blood pressure, intracranial hemorrhage, and cardiac arrhythmias. Some patients also abuse illicit amphetamines, which further predispose to these complications. Other patients may take unnecessary or excess thyroid hormone to induce weight loss. Clinicians should be vigilant to detect the use of these substances and counsel patients about the risks associated with their abuse.

Cardiovascular System

Cardiac manifestations frequently complicate the medical course of patients with eating disorders and represent a major cause of morbidity and mortality in anorexia and bulimia nervosa (Kreipe & Harris, 1992; see Table 5.4). For anorexics, cardiac illness can be the result of caloric restriction or can complicate refeeding (Cooke & Chambers, 1995). In bulimics, most serious cardiac abnormalities stem from the electrolyte disturbances occurring after purging behaviors. Patients with binge eating syndrome

Table 5.4   Major Cardiovascular Manifestations of Eating Disorders

Anorexia Nervosa	Bulimia Nervosa	Binge Eating Disorder
Bradycardia.	Orthostasis.	Atherosclerotic cardiovascular disease, including increased risk of myocardial infarction and cerebrovascular accident
Hypotension/orthostasis.	Cardiac arrhythmias, including life-threatening ventricular arrhythmias.	
Electrocardiogram abnormalities, especially sinus arrhythmia, prolonged QT interval.		
	Prolonged QT interval.	Hypertension.
Congestive heart failure.	Sudden cardiac death.	Congestive heart failure.
Decreased stroke volume.	Ipecac myocarditis.	
Increased recognition of mitral valve prolapse.	Reflex edema (after discontinuing laxatives, diuretics).	
Refeeding cardiomyopathy.		
Fluid accumulation during refeeding.		

experience cardiac complications predominantly as manifestations of the obesity consequent to their disordered eating.

The anorexic patient tends to have a low pulse rate and low blood pressure. These abnormal vital signs most often represent appropriate adaptive responses to the hypometabolic state of starvation and do not require specific therapy other than weight gain. An electrocardiogram should be obtained to rule out more serious arrhythmias but usually shows sinus bradycardia. In patients who severely restrict fluids, dehydration may also result in orthostasis. Cardiac function may be severely depressed in anorexia nervosa with loss of cardiac muscle and decreased stroke volume. Furthermore, an increased prevalence of mitral valve prolapse has been recognized in this population and has been attributed to the disproportion between the ventricle and the mitral valve that results when ventricular muscle mass is lost (Meyers, Starke, Pearson, Wilken, & Ferrell, 1987). Severe inanition may be associated with cardiac failure, ventricular arrhythmias, and death. However, in general, cardiac complications reverse with weight gain.

Anorexics are also at risk of cardiac complications as part of the refeeding syndrome (Swenne, 2000). The refeeding syndrome occurs in very low-weight patients if caloric replacement is too aggressive. In this instance, the patient has depleted total body phosphorus stores but has adapted during starvation. When calories are replaced, phosphorus enters the cells, further depleting serum levels, and life-threatening hypophosphatemia can result. A major consequence of the low serum phosphorus levels is congestive heart failure and ventricular arrhythmias. Other manifestations may include mental confusion, seizures, and respiratory failure. Although deaths were originally reported solely in patients receiving hyperalimentation, it is now clear that the refeeding syndrome can occur in patients who receive only intravenous fluids and even aggressive oral refeeding (Fisher, Simpser, & Schneider, 2000). Cautious replacement of calories with medical monitoring of serum phosphorus and other electrolytes can attenuate the risk of refeeding syndrome (Swenne, 2000).

Bulimics may have significant orthostatic changes in blood pressure if they are dehydrated secondary to purging behaviors. In addition, cardiac complications are common in bulimia nervosa. Hypokalemia predisposes the patient to potentially life-threatening ventricular arrhythmias, and sudden death is a feared outcome of bulimia nervosa. Careful attention to maintaining adequate serum potassium levels is critical to the medical management of this eating disorder. Some bulimics abuse ipecac and may recurrently ingest large doses of the drug to induce vomiting. These patients can develop cardiomyopathy, which may be fatal (Dresser et al., 1992). Because of the slow metabolism of ipecac, the drug accumulates in cardiac muscle tissue and can cause prolonged or even irreversible cardiac dysfunction.

The cardiac complications of binge eating disorder predominantly reflect the consequences of obesity. Overweight patients are at increased risk of hyperlipidemia and subsequent cardiovascular atherosclerotic disease. Therefore, increased rates of myocardial infarction and cerebrovascular accidents would be anticipated in this patient population.

Clinicians should pay close attention to the prevention and management of cardiac complications in eating-disordered patients. A baseline electrocardiogram is appropriate for most of these patients and should be repeated if the patient reports symptoms of palpitations, irregular heartbeats, or chest pain. Significant conduction abnormalities, rhythm disturbances, or a prolonged QT interval should prompt cardiac evaluation and careful monitoring. A prolonged QT interval is considered a major risk factor for ventricular arrhythmias. Holter monitoring may be needed to detect less frequent rhythm disturbances. Careful monitoring of the serum potassium and other electrolytes is important, especially in patients who actively engage in purging behaviors. Replacement of potassium is critical and may require correction of the fluid status to be successful.

Gastrointestinal System

Myriad gastrointestinal complications occur in patients with disordered eating (Cuellar & Van Thiel, 1986; McClain, Humphries, Hill, & Nickl, 1993; see Table 5.5). These conditions range from minor discomforts such as delayed gastric emptying to life-threatening illnesses such as refeeding pancreatitis or gastric rupture. Some of these

Table 5.5   Major Gastrointestinal Manifestations of Eating Disorders

Anorexia Nervosa	Bulimia Nervosa	Binge Eating Disorder
Delayed gastric emptying.	Parotid/salivary gland hypertrophy.	Nonalcoholic steatophepatitis.
Constipation.	Hyperamylasemia.	Cholelithiasis, cholecystitis.
Superior mesenteric artery syndrome.	Esophagitis.	Gastric dilatation/rupture.
Hypokalemic ileus.	Esophageal perforation.	
Refeeding pancreatitis.	Mallory-Weiss tears.	
	Hematemesis/gastrointestional bleeding.	
	Delayed gastric emptying.	
	Constipation.	
	Steatorrhea/protein-losing gastroenteropathy.	
	Cathartic colon/melanosis coli.	
	Hypokalemic ileus.	

diseases, such as cathartic colon resulting from laxative abuse, can cause permanent disability even if eating patterns are corrected.

Anorexic patients may develop delayed gastric emptying and prolonged gut transit times (Kamal et al., 1991). These patients often note abdominal bloating and discomfort, as well as constipation (Chiarioni et al., 2000). It is presumed that the symptoms are the result of chronic starvation and reflect the chronic hypometabolic state Anorexia nervosa can also be complicated by the superior mesenteric artery syndrome (Adson, Mitchell, & Trenkner, 1997). In this condition, severe inanition and loss of the normal intra-abdominal fat results in compression of the third portion of the duodenum by the overlying superior mesenteric artery. Patients suffer from abdominal pain that is exacerbated by eating. Resolution is dependent on weight gain.

A major gastrointestinal concern for patients with anorexia nervosa is the risk of pancreatitis that can develop during refeeding. Symptoms of pancreatitis, including abdominal pain, nausea, and vomiting, should prompt measurement of serum amylase and lipase. Treatment includes slowing of caloric replacement, bowel rest, and nasogastric suction under the supervision of an experienced physician.

Gastrointestinal manifestations are prominent in patients with bulimia nervosa (L. Anderson, Shaw, & McCargar, 1997). Parotid and salivary gland enlargement is a classic finding in patients with bulimia nervosa (Mandel & Kaynar, 1992; Metzger, Levine, McArdel, Wolfe, & Jimerson, 1999). Patients may complain of swollen "chipmunk-like" cheeks, further accentuating their fears of becoming overweight. The parotid hypertrophy is associated with elevations of serum amylase; measurement of amylase isoenzymes or lipase can distinguish between the parotids and the pancreas as the source of the hyperamylasemia. Return of the enlarged glands to a normal size is expected with successful treatment of the eating disorder but can take several months after resumption of normal eating behaviors.

Bulimic patients clearly have abnormal gastrointestinal motility. Delayed gastric emptying contributes to symptoms of bloating, early satiety, and abdominal pain. Prolonged whole gut transit times have been documented in bulimic individuals and presumably contribute to the abdominal discomfort and constipation experienced by these patients (Kamal et al., 1991). Frank ileus can develop, especially in patients with significant hypokalemia or other electrolyte abnormalities.

A variety of esophageal problems can complicate bulimia nervosa (Cuellar, Kaye, Hsu, & Van Thiel, 1988). Esophagitis can result from the recurrent vomiting and mucosal irritation by refluxed acid and gastric contents. Eventually, frank erosions, ulcerations, and strictures can develop. Barrett's esophagitis can occur in patients with chronic reflux and is associated with an increased risk of malignant transformation. Recurrent vomiting may also result in the formation of Mallory-Weiss tears in the esophagus with associated gastrointestinal bleeding. A feared consequence of recurrent vomiting is esophageal rupture with contamination and infection of the mediastinum. Known as Boerhaave's syndrome, this condition requires aggressive medical management with antibiotics and surgical drainage.

Bulimic patients are at risk of gastric dilatation and rupture after ingestion of large amounts of food during binges (Nakao et al., 2000). The risk may be increased if the patient attempts to induce vomiting. Nausea, vomiting, distention, and pain may herald gastric rupture and should prompt urgent medical evaluation. While cases of dilatation can be managed conservatively with nasogastric suction, gastric rupture requires surgical repair.

Small and large intestine dysfunction in bulimia is common. Prolonged gut transit times are well documented. Symptoms may be exacerbated in patients with hypokalemic ileus. Chronic use of laxatives can further disrupt intestinal peristalsis. Laxative abusers initially often complain of alternating diarrhea and constipation that can be difficult to distinguish from irritable bowel syndrome if the patient conceals the history of laxative use (Mitchell & Boutacoff, 1986). Eventually, these patients develop cathartic colon with loss of normal colonic function. Some even require colonic resection. Other complications of chronic laxative abuse include gastrointestinal bleeding, malabsorption, steatorrhea, and protein-losing gastroenteropathy. Colonoscopy may reveal black discoloration of the colon, termed *melanosis coli,* or evidence of low-grade inflammation.

Binge eating disorder complicated by obesity may also be complicated by gastrointestinal disorders (Crowell, Cheskin, & Musial, 1994). Obese patients are at increased risk of gallbladder disease, including formation of gallstones and bouts of cholecystitis. In addition, the use of very low-calorie diets has been associated with cholelithiasis (J. W. Anderson, Hamilton, & Brinkman-Kaplan, 1992). Obese patients are also prone to develop nonalcoholic steatohepatitis. This disease of uncertain etiology is characterized by abnormal liver enzymes indicative of chronic inflammation of the liver and in some patients can progress to cirrhosis and liver failure. Treatment is focused on weight loss.

Endocrine System and Metabolic Abnormalities

Endocrine and metabolic diseases are hallmark complications of the eating disorders (Levine, 2002; see Table 5.6). Abnormalities of the hypothalamic-pituitary axes characterize both anorexia and bulimia nervosa, generally being more severe in anorexic patients. Endocrine and metabolic perturbations have been the focus of much research, but it remains unclear for many of these abnormalities whether they result solely from the nutritional abnormalities or if they may play actual etiologic roles in the disordered eating (Laue, Gold, Richmond, & Chrousos, 1991; Mortola, Rasmussen, & Yen, 1989).

Anorexia nervosa is characterized by extensive abnormalities of the hypothalamic-pituitary-adrenal axis (Boyar et al., 1977; Gold et al., 1986). Sustained hypercortisolism is a prominent feature of the disease and is reflected in elevated levels of cortisol detectable in the serum and the cerebrospinal fluid. Patients have elevated levels of corticotropin-releasing hormone that stimulate increased cortisol production. Decreased metabolic clearance of cortisol appears to exacerbate the hypercortisolism. Nonsuppression of cortisol by dexamethasone, that is, nonsuppression on the dexamethasone suppression test, results from the sustained hypercortisolism.

Amenorrhea, one of the diagnostic criteria for anorexia nervosa, is the most obvious consequence of the abnormal hypothalamic-pituitary-gonadal axis in this illness (Devlin et al., 1989). Perturbations of the gonadotropin-releasing hormones result in a hypoestrogen state. Low levels of plasma estradiol, luteinizing hormone, and follicle-stimulating hormone that resemble the prepubescent state are observed in anorexics. An "immature" response (resembling that of premenarchal girls) of luteinizing hormone and follicle-stimulating hormone to gonadotropin-releasing hormones characterizes these patients.

Table 5.6   Major Endocrine and Metabolic Manifestations of Eating Disorders

Anorexia Nervosa	Bulimia Nervosa	Binge Eating Disorder
Abnormal HPA axis-sustained hypercortisolism.	Less severe HPA axis abnormalities.	Decreased fertility.
Non-suppression of DST.	Variable DST results.	Increased adverse perinatal outcomes.
Abnormal HPG axis–amenorrhea, estrogen deficiency.	HPG axis abnormalities—irregular menses.	Osteoarthritis.
Delayed onset of puberty.	Increased infertility, adverse perinatal outcomes.	Dyslipidemia, especially hypercholesterolemia.
Increased infertility, adverse perinatal outcomes.	Increased risk of hyperemesis gravidarum during pregnancy.	Diabetes mellitus-type II.
Abnormal HPT axis-euthyroid sick syndrome.	Abnormal/HPT axis function.	Gout.
Growth retardation.	Osteopneia/osteoporosis.	Decreased leptin levels.
Osteopenia, osteoporosis.	Abnormal leptin levels.	
Increased fracture risk.		
Trace mineral/vitamin deficiencies hypoglycemia.		
Diabetes insipidus.		
Elevated cholesterol.		
Abnormal leptin levels.		

Much controversy has arisen about whether the amenorrhea and low estrogen levels are solely secondary consequences of starvation or if they may reflect an etiologic defect in the hypothalamic-pituitary axis. A substantial portion of anorexics develop menstrual abnormalities before significant weight loss, and amenorrhea may persist for weeks to months despite weight restoration, suggesting the possibility of a primary hypothalamic-pituitary defect. Controversy also exists about the use of hormone replacement to ameliorate the hypoestrogen state. While the hormones may reverse some abnormalities, their efficacy in preventing osteoporosis is incomplete, and there is concern about long-term use of hormones—especially in adolescents. Furthermore, some experts have suggested that artificially induced resumption of menses may make both patients and health care providers more complacent about the importance of weight gain.

Abnormal function of the hypothalamic-pituitary-thyroid axis is also observed in individuals with anorexia nervosa. Thyroid function tests in most patients with significant anorexia nervosa are suggestive of a "low T3" or "euthyroid sick syndrome." In this case, the hypometabolic state of adaptation to starvation results in low to normal T4 levels, low T3 levels, and normal thyroid stimulating hormone (TSH) levels. Decreased peripheral conversion of T4 to T3 with preferential deiodination to the less active form of T3 known as reverse T3 explains the abnormal thyroid function test findings. Abnormalities in the response of TSH to stimulation by exogenous administration of thyrotropin-releasing hormone suggest additional abnormalities of the hypothalamic-pituitary axis. Although many anorexics complain of symptoms suggestive of true hypothyroidism such as fatigue, cold intolerance, hair loss, and slow heart rates, these usually represent an adaptive physiologic response to starvation. The appropriate treatment is weight gain. Thyroid hormone should be prescribed only for the patient with true hypothyroidism suggested by elevated TSH levels.

Patients with anorexia often have hypoglycemia (Gniuli, Liverani, Capristo, Greco, & Mingrone, 2001; Rich, Caine, Findling, & Shaker, 1990). Catabolism with depletion of glycogen stores is the most frequent etiology. Anorexics tend to have elevated growth hormone levels akin to those seen in other forms of starvation. Elevated basal levels of growth hormone reflect decreased somatomedin C. Recent studies have demonstrated marked reductions in insulin-like growth factor 1 (IGF-1), suggesting that therapeutic replacement might benefit these patients (Grinspoon, Miller, Herzog, Clemmons, & Klibanski, 2003). Anorexic patients also have impaired or erratic release of vasopressin that may result in a partial diabetes insipidus with resultant fluid and electrolyte abnormalities.

Patients with anorexia nervosa that develops at a young age may experience significant growth retardation (Levine, 2002). While some "catch-up" growth and improvement in height may accompany successful treatment, significant losses may be permanent, especially if weight is not restored until after closure of the epiphyseal growth plates.

One of the most worrisome medical manifestations of anorexia nervosa is loss of bone mineral density with the development of osteopenia and osteoporosis (Baker, Roberts, & Towell, 2000; Grinspoon et al., 1999, 2000; Jagielska et al., 2001; Rigotti, Nussbaum, Herzog, & Neer, 1984; Soyka, Grinspoon, Levitsky, Herzog, & Klibanski, 1999). Osteoporosis has been attributed both to decreased bone formation and increased bone resorption (Biller et al., 1989). Low estrogen states are associated predominantly with decreased bone formation. The increased bone resorption is likely linked to other factors, including hypercortisolism, poor dietary intake of calcium and/or vitamin D, elevated cytokine levels (especially interleukin-6), and possibly dysregulation of leptin (Lennkh et al., 1999; Newman & Halmi, 1989). The importance of these additional factors in the etiology of osteoporosis is substantiated by the fact that loss of bone mineral density appears to be greater in anorexia nervosa than in other states of estrogen deficiency and the observation that estrogen replacement is remarkably ineffective therapy for osteoporosis in anorexics (Golden et al., 2002; Robinson, Bachrach, & Katzman, 2000). The loss of bone density in anorexia nervosa is of great medical importance, including a markedly increased risk of fractures (Lucas, Melton, Crowson, & O'Fallon, 1999). Unfortunately, most studies suggest that much of the bone loss may be irreversible, especially in patients who developed the disease in adolescence and patients with long-standing symptoms before successful weight restoration (Hartman et al., 2000; Valla, Groenning, Syversen, & Hoeiseth, 2000; Ward, Brown, & Treasure, 1997).

The optimal management of osteoporosis in patients with anorexia nervosa remains undefined. All patients with anorexia nervosa should undergo bone densitometry testing to define the extent of bone mineral loss. Therapeutic interventions are controversial. While exercise is generally protective, clinicians should be cautious about recommending it to patients who may use this as an excuse for continuing excess exercise despite their energy-depleted state. Most experts do prescribe calcium and vitamin D supplementation, but their efficacy may be limited. While it may seem intuitive to prescribe estrogen replacement to these patients, studies provide little support for this approach (Bruni, Dei, Vicini, Beninato, & Magnani, 2000). Possibly because of the multifactorial etiology of osteoporosis in this patient population, estrogen does not appear to significantly alter the course of bone loss. Other approaches such as the use of biphosphonates, fluoride, or IGF-1 are being studied but cannot yet be routinely recommended. Currently, the best approach remains treatment of the underlying eating disorder to achieve weight gain.

Other endocrine and metabolic complications may be observed in anorexia nervosa. Despite their malnourished condition, anorexics tend to have elevated levels of serum cholesterol. Elevated serum carotene levels are frequent in anorexics and may be associated with clinically evident hypercarotenemia and a consequent yellow-orange discoloration of the skin, especially the palms. Vitamin deficiencies are uncommon, but cases of vitamin K deficiency, thiamine deficiency, pellagra, and scurvy have been anecdotally reported (Winston, Jamieson, Madira, Gatward, & Palmer, 2000). Trace mineral deficiencies may also occur. Some clinicians routinely test serum zinc levels and prescribe supplementation if deficiency is discovered.

Bulimia nervosa is also associated with endocrine and metabolic complications, but these tend to be less severe than those seen in anorexia nervosa (Pauporte & Walsh, 2001). Many of these complications may result from the intermittent caloric restriction that characterizes the disordered eating of some patients with bulimia nervosa. Most bulimic patients have normal cortisol levels, although some studies have suggested that a subset of these patients has hypothalamic-pituitary-adrenal axis abnormalities comparable but less severe than those of anorexics (Hudson et al., 1983; Mortola et al., 1989). Patients with bulimia nervosa often have abnormal dexamethasone suppression tests (Mitchell, Pyle, Hatsukami, & Eckert, 1984). Because most of these bulimics have normal serum cortisol levels, the cause of the nonsuppression is unclear. In some cases, this may represent erratic or delayed absorption of the dexamethasone in patients with abnormalities of gastric emptying or slowed gut transit times. In others, nonsuppression may reflect concomitant depression. Bulimic patients also have variable evidence of abnormal hypothalamic-pituitary-gonadal function (Devlin et al., 1989). Low or erratic estrogen and gonadotropin levels have been found in a portion of bulimic patients; many bulimics have irregular menses (Pirke et al., 1987). Occasionally, bulimic patients have evidence of abnormalities of the hypothalamic-pituitary-thyroid axis, including the low T3 syndrome (Kiriike, Nishiwaki, Izumiya, Maeda, & Kawakita, 1987). Overall, these endocrine abnormalities are less prominent than those seen in anorexia nervosa.

Binge eating disorder may also be associated with a variety of endocrine and metabolic abnormalities that reflect obesity. Obese patients often have dyslipidemia with hypercholesterolemia and hypertriglyceridemia. Testing of lipid levels is indicated in all obese patients, and if found to be elevated, lipid-lowering medications should be prescribed. Obese patients are also at increased risk of developing gout, and screening of serum uric acid levels is reasonable. Obese patients have an increased propensity to develop diabetes mellitus type 2, and screening fasting blood glucose testing is appropriate. Obese patients may also have abnormal dexamethasone tests. This usually does not reflect hypercortisolism and is more likely to be due to an inadequate test dose of dexamethasone for body weight. Repeat testing with a double dose of dexamethasone often indicates normal suppression. Finally, skeletal abnormalities also occur in obese patients, manifested most frequently as degenerative joint disease, especially of the weight-bearing joints such as the knees. The best management of these complications in the obese binge-eating patient is medically supervised weight loss. In the interim, careful screening and management of possible hyperlipidemia and hyperglycemia should be the focus of the clinician.

Renal System and Electrolyte Abnormalities

Electrolyte abnormalities are a major cause of morbidity and mortality in patients with eating disorders and represent an important area of focus for the medical physician caring for these individuals (see Table 5.7). Many of the deaths of patients with eating disorders can be attributed to electrolyte perturbations, especially hypokalemia. Extremely low-weight anorexics and bulimics actively engaging in purging behaviors are at the highest risk.

Hypokalemia can result from restricted intake in anorexics but most often reflects potassium losses due to purging behaviors such as vomiting and diuretic and laxative abuse. Purging causes losses of both fluid and electrolytes, resulting in a hypokalemic, hypochloremic metabolic "contraction" alkalosis. The dehydration results in stimulation of the renin-angiotensin-aldosterone system as the body tries in vain to retain fluids. The result is a pseudo-Bartter's syndrome (Mitchell, Pomeroy, Seppala, & Huber, 1988), which can cause excessive retention of fluid and accumulation of peripheral edema when normal intake is finally resumed. Correction of the hypokalemia and the alkalosis requires simultaneous replacement of potassium and fluids. Potassium supplements will prove ineffective if the contraction alkalosis is not reversed. Prolonged hypokalemia can cause serious organ dysfunction, including cardiac arrhythmias, muscle weakness, and hypokalemic nephropathy.

Other electrolyte abnormalities can complicate the eating disorders. Hypocalcemia, hypophosphatemia, and hypomagnesemia have all been reported in eating-disordered patients. Correction of low potassium and calcium may be ineffective until magnesium has been repleted. Metabolic acidosis can occur in patients who abuse laxatives and lose bicarbonate in their stools (Mitchell, Hatsukami, Pyle, Boutacoff, & Eckert, 1987). Electrolyte deficiencies, especially low phosphate levels, can be exacerbated during the refeeding syndrome in anorexics.

Elevated blood urea nitrogen and creatinine levels are frequently observed in patients with anorexia and bulimia nervosa (Boag, Weerakoon, Ginsburg, Havard, & Dandora, 1985). Most often, these reflect dehydration with prerenal kidney dysfunction. However, hypokalemic nephropathy can result in chronic renal failure. Reversible tubular dysfunction simulating Fanconi's syndrome has been described in anorexia nervosa (Alexandridis, Liamis, & Elisaf, 2001). Erratic vasopressin production has

Table 5.7   Major Renal/Electrolyte Manifestations of Eating Disorders

Anorexia Nervosa	Bulimia Nervosa	Binge Eating Disorder
Dehydration/volume depletion.	Dehydration/volume depletion.	—
Hypokalemia.	Hypokalemic "contraction" metabolic alkalosis.	
Refeeding hypophosphatemia.	Kaliopenic nephropathy.	

been linked to the development of partial diabetes insipidus that may be manifested with symptoms of polyuria.

Management of renal and electrolyte complications is critical to the treatment of eating disorders. Laboratory values should be monitored on an ongoing basis. Cessation of the restricting or purging behaviors is the most effective remedy. Oral potassium supplementation is appropriate for mild-moderate hypokalemia, with hospitalization and intravenous therapy reserved for the most severe or recalcitrant cases.

As discussed, reversal of associated metabolic alkalosis or concomitant hypomagnesemia may be necessary for potassium therapy to be effective. Treatment of pseudo-Bartter's syndrome relies on correction of the hypovolemic state. Reassurance and local therapy such as support stockings can ameliorate the symptoms of reflex edema formation.

Pulmonary System

Although complications of the pulmonary system are less frequent than those of other organ systems in the eating disorders, these illnesses can be life threatening and, as such, require vigilance for recognition (see Table 5.8). Pulmonary complications in anorexia nervosa occur predominantly during the refeeding syndrome. In bulimics, pulmonary complications usually occur secondary to recurrent vomiting; in binge eaters, obesity can compromise respiratory function.

Respiratory failure has been reported in anorexics with severe inanition (Ryan, Whittaker, & Road, 1992). In addition, the refeeding syndrome in anorexia nervosa can be complicated by respiratory failure if the patient develops significant hypophosphatemia. Therapy should be directed toward correction of the electrolyte abnormalities with ventilatory support as needed. In addition, rare cases of spontaneous pneumothorax have been reported in anorexia nervosa. These have been attributed to poor tissue integrity associated with malnutrition; however, it is difficult to exclude a contributory role of occult vomiting.

Pulmonary complications in bulimia nervosa usually occur secondary to vomiting. Aspiration of gastric contents can result in a bacterial pneumonia or chemical pneumonitis. Increased thoracic pressures during vomiting can result in spontaneous pneumothorax, pneumomediastinum, and/or subcutaneous emphysema. Complaints of shortness of breath in these patients should be investigated with careful physical examination and, if appropriate, chest roentgenogram.

Patients with binge eating disorder and obesity may develop sleep apnea. Patients note snoring, disrupted sleep, and daytime sleepiness. The diagnosis is confirmed by monitoring in a sleep-testing laboratory, and treatment is focused on weight loss and,

Table 5.8   Major Pulmonary Manifestations of Eating Disorders

Anorexia Nervosa	Bulimia Nervosa	Binge Eating Disorder
Respiratory failure complicating refeeding syndrome.	Subcutaneous emphysema. Pneumomediastinum. Aspiration pnneumonitis.	Sleep apnea. Obesity hypoventilation (Pickwickian syndrome).

if necessary, use of a face mask to deliver continuous positive airway pressure. Left untreated, the condition can be complicated by heart failure. In severe cases of obesity, patients may develop frank obesity hypoventilation syndrome, commonly referred to as *Pickwickian syndrome* after the literary character.

Other Organ Systems

Dermatologic conditions are common physical consequences of the eating disorders (Glorio et al., 2000; Gupta, Gupta, & Haberman, 1987; Strumia, Varotti, Manzato, & Gualandi, 2001; see Table 5.9). Anorexics tend to have dry skin and brittle hair and nails. Hair loss, especially on the scalp, is characteristic. Patients develop fine downy hair, called *lanugo hair,* especially on the face. Hypercarotenodermia manifests as a yellow-orange discoloration of the skin and is often most noticeable on the palms. Skin findings may also provide the initial suggestion of bulimia nervosa. Russell's sign is a classic finding in this disease. Bruising, abrasions, and/or callus formation on the dorsum of the hands results from damage to the skin by the teeth when the fingers are used to stimulate vomiting. In addition, purpura on the face or subconjunctival hemorrhages can be caused by the increased pressures generated during forceful vomiting. Fixed drug eruptions, such as photosensitivity reactions due to diuretics, can occur secondary to the abuse of drugs used for purging.

Dentists are often the first health care providers to detect physical signs of bulimia nervosa (Milosevic et al., 1997; Simmons et al., 1986; Studen-Pavlovich & Elliott, 2001; Table 5.9). Recurrent vomiting that bathes the teeth in gastric acid can cause significant damage and loss of dental enamel, termed *perimylolysis* (Roberts & Li, 1987; Simmons et al., 1986). Because amalgams are resistant to acid, the dental fillings appear increasingly prominent as enamel erosion progresses. This can result in

Table 5.9 Other Major Physical Manifestations of Eating Disorders

Anorexia Nervosa	Bulimia Nervosa	Binge Eating Disorder
Alopecia, especially on scalp.	Russell's sign.	Increased cancer risk.
Lanugo hair formation.	Dental enamel erosion.	Increased surgical risk.
Dry skin.	Abnormal cytokine levels.	Increased mortality due to complications of obesity.
Brittle hair, nails.	Skeletal muscle ipecac-associated myopathy.	
Anemia, thrombocytopenia, bone marrow failure.	Increased mortality—including cardiac arrhythmias.	
Leukopenia with relative lymphocytosis.		
Immune system perturbations.		
Abnormal cytokine levels.		
Enlarged brain ventricles, "pseudoatrophy."		
Other structural and functional brain abnormalities.		
Impaired thermoregulation.		
Increased mortality—especially suicide and cardiac events.		

the appearance of "floating amalgams." Dentists should advise patients of the potential long-term damage caused by this process. Careful rinsing of the mouth after vomiting and attention to good oral hygiene are critical to minimize dental damage (Studen-Pavlovich & Elliott, 2001).

Hematologic abnormalities are noted in many patients with anorexia nervosa (Devuyst, Lambert, Rodhain, Lefebvre, & Coche, 1993; Grinspoon et al., 1999; Howard, Leggat, & Chaudhry, 1992; see Table 5.9). Leukopenia with a relative lymphocytosis is common. In addition to the decreased numbers of neutrophils, several studies suggest that neutrophil function is also depressed. Decreased neutrophil chemotaxis and killing have been observed in some patients. Interestingly, most anorexics do not have an increased susceptibility to infection (Bowers & Eckert, 1978); the very lowest weight patients may be at some increased risk of bacterial infections. It also appears that anorexics may actually suffer from fewer viral illnesses. In extreme cases, frank bone marrow necrosis and failure can complicate starvation with the development of life-threatening pancytopenia (Bailly, Lambin, Garzon, & Parquet, 1994; Smith & Spivak, 1985).

A number of abnormalities of the immune system have been noted in patients with anorexia nervosa (Howard et al., 1992; see Table 5.9). Patients with severe weight loss have anergy to skin testing, suggesting depressed cell mediated immune responses. Various abnormalities of T-lymphocytes, including alterations in CD4+ and CD8+ T-cell numbers and ratios, have been reported, but further study is needed to resolve inconsistencies in these research findings (Fink, Eckert, Mitchell, Crosby, & Pomeroy, 1996). Significant reductions in complement, especially components of the alternative pathway, have been described (Pomeroy et al., 1997). Some reports of depressed immunoglobulin levels have appeared, but further studies are needed. Testing of immune parameters is not routinely indicated for anorexic patients at this time, but clinicians should be aware that understanding of these abnormalities may provide important future insights into disease mechanisms of anorexia nervosa.

Recent studies have provided potentially intriguing clues to the pathogenesis of eating disorders and associated medical complications. Cytokines are now recognized as important mediators of signaling between the brain and the immune system. These polypeptides are responsible for communication between the central nervous system and the endocrine and immune systems. Some studies have demonstrated elevated levels of interleukin-6 and other cytokines during starvation that tend to normalize with weight gain, while other studies have suggested decreases in serum concentrations of several of the pro-inflammatory cytokines (see Table 5.9). Further studies are needed to better define the role of cytokines in eating disorders (Corcos et al., 2003; Nagata, Tobitani, Kiriike, Iketani, & Yamagami, 1999; Pomeroy et al., 1994; Raymond et al., 2000).

Leptin is a recently identified hormone that acts to control appetite, food intake, and energy expenditure. Leptin is commonly known as the *satiety hormone*. Produced predominantly in adipocytes, increased leptin levels result in decreased appetite and energy expenditure. Leptin has also been closely linked to reproductive function, and mice with leptin deficiency have decreased fertility. Because leptin levels correlate closely with body weight, leptin is markedly decreased in low-weight anorexic patients. While some studies have shown that leptin regulation remains intact in anorexics, others have suggested that leptin levels (although decreased compared to normal weight controls) are actually elevated for body weight (Eckert et al., 1998; see Table 5.9). In the latter case, failure to completely downregulate leptin production during the starvation phase of anorexia nervosa could explain the perception of these patients that they are "full" even as they restrict calories. Studies of leptin in bulimia nervosa are more limited, but some research also suggests that there may be a relative excess of leptin or loss of normal responsiveness of leptin in these patients, possibly contributing to the binge-purge cycles (Frederich, Hu, Raymond, & Pomeroy, 2002). While not clinically useful at this time, hope remains that leptin or related hormones may eventually prove effective as therapeutic agents to control appetite and body weight (Mehler, Eckel, & Donahoo, 1999; Pauly, Lear, Hastings, & Birmingham, 2000).

Neurologic manifestations are common in patients with anorexia nervosa (see Table 5.9). Both structural and functional complications occur in anorexics. Imaging studies have clearly documented that there is loss of both gray and white matter in the brains of low-weight anorexics (Katzman, Christensen, Young, & Zipursky, 2001). Enlarged sulci and cerebrospinal fluid spaces result in a picture of "pseudo-atrophy" of the brain (Addolorato, Taronto, Capristo, & Gasbarrini, 1998; Krieg, Pirke, Lauer, & Backmund, 1988). While it has been thought that most of these structural abnormalities can reverse with weight gain, studies have suggested permanent loss of brain tissue in some patients. These structural abnormalities are accompanied by evidence of functional brain abnormalities as well (Katzman et al., 2001). Anorexics tend to perform poorly on several cognitive tasks, although general intelligence testing is intact. The most consistent findings are cognitive impairment of spatial testing. As with the structural abnormalities, it appears that some of these cognitive abnormalities persist even after successful treatment of the eating disorder. Therefore, speculation has arisen that these abnormalities may reflect evidence of a primary, etiologic central nervous disorder, as well as consequences of starvation.

Impaired thermoregulation is a common complaint of patients with anorexia nervosa, and acrocyanosis may be noted on physical exam (see Table 5.9). Indeed, anorexics do have aberrant autonomic responses when exposed to extremes of temperature. An increased prevalence of Raynaud's phenomenon has also been noted in these patients. Symptoms of disordered thermoregulation can be distressing to the patient, but no specific therapy other than anticipating the need for appropriate protective clothing is available.

Muscle weakness is a common complaint of patients with anorexia and bulimia nervosa (see Table 5.9). In anorexics, the weakness usually reflects lack of energy stores and loss of muscle mass. In bulimics, it is critical to consider the possibility of ipecac-induced skeletal muscle myopathy (Palmer & Guay, 1985). Patients who repeatedly abuse ipecac first note difficulty with climbing stairs that may progress to inability to walk even short distances. Treatment is supportive until drug levels decline.

Mortality is increased in each of the eating disorders (De Filippo, Signorini, Bracale, Pasanisi, & Contaldo, 2000; Emborg, 1999; Fichter & Quadflieg, 1999; Neumarker, 1997; Patton, 1988; Ratnasuriya, Eisler, Szmukler, & Russell, 1991; Strober, Freeman, & Morrell, 1997; Zipfel, Lowe, Reas, Deter, & Herzog, 2000; see Table 5.9). Anorexia nervosa has one of the highest mortality rates of any psychiatric disorder. Traditionally, mortality rates as high as 20% have been reported. More recent reports suggest that effective treatment can significantly reduce mortality. However, significant concern has been raised that financial pressures in the United States are limiting and delaying access to treatment, fueling fears that increased mortality may result. Deaths in anorexia nervosa are most commonly due to cardiac events and suicide (Isner, Roberts, Heymsfield, & Yager, 1985). Bulimia nervosa has a lower mortality rate than anorexia, but bulimic patients are also at significantly increased risk of death. The major concern is cardiac arrhythmias, especially those related to hypokalemia. Mortality rates have been less well studied in the more recently recognized binge eating disorder. Nevertheless, obese patients are clearly at increased risk of mortality. Increased rates of cancer, surgical complications, heart disease, and strokes are well defined in overweight individuals. Clinicians should recognize that, in addition to the psychological distress experienced by eating-disordered individuals, these patients are at significantly increased risk of death due to the physical manifestations of their illness.

DIFFERENTIAL DIAGNOSIS

A critical purpose of the medical assessment of patients with anorexia nervosa, bulimia nervosa, and binge eating is to eliminate the possibility of other medical etiologies of the disordered eating. A number of medical illnesses can mimic many of the symptoms of anorexia nervosa. Panypopituitarism due to tumors, infections, or hemorrhage can cause many of the same symptoms as anorexia nervosa. Similarly, patients with endocrine illnesses such as Addison's disease or hyperthyroidism may appear similar to the anorexic. Occult cancers can cause cachexia that may be difficult to distinguish from the weight loss that characterizes anorexia nervosa. Chronic infections such as tuberculosis and chronic inflammatory diseases such as inflammatory bowel disease can have weight loss and other evidence of debility similar to that observed in anorexia nervosa. Gastrointestinal disease with malabsorption can result in significant weight loss and mimic anorexia nervosa. Furthermore, many other psychiatric illnesses involve loss of appetite or food avoidance with consequent weight loss akin to that seen in patients with anorexia nervosa.

Bulimia nervosa can also be mimicked by a number of other illnesses. Diseases such as connective tissue disease with altered gastrointestinal peristalsis can cause recurrent vomiting. Inflammatory bowel diseases may result in many of the same symptoms as bulimia nervosa with altered gut function and abdominal discomfort. In addition, central nervous system tumors can cause recurrent vomiting.

Binge eating disorder must be differentiated from genetic or acquired central nervous system abnormalities that cause uncontrolled food craving. However, these are rare, and the genetic illnesses most commonly manifest during childhood.

In general, the best tool for ruling out these other diagnoses is a careful history and physical examination, augmented by directed screening laboratory assessment. Taking the time to perform a thorough and nonjudgmental history is more important and more fruitful than ordering long lists of expensive tests. For example, obtaining an accurate history of caloric restriction and fear of gaining weight can suggest the diagnosis of anorexia nervosa. Eliciting a history of self-induced vomiting will point the clinician to the identification of bulimia nervosa. Careful evaluation can correctly assess binge-eating patterns and excessive caloric intake in patients with binge eating syndrome. In addition, it is important to remember that most of the other illnesses in the differential diagnosis are accompanied by other pathologies that provide clues to the correct diagnosis.

ONGOING MEDICAL MANAGEMENT

Based on the initial medical evaluation, the medical clinician should define the requirements for ongoing medical management of the patient (Yager et al., 2000). Patients with identified medical complications may require frequent visits until the acute medical issue has resolved. In general, very low weight anorexic patients and bulimic patients with severe purging behaviors associated with electrolyte aberrations require the closest follow-up. These patients may need to have repeat evaluation on a weekly or monthly basis until stable. Other patients with less severe physical manifestations may require reassessment on a every six-month or annual basis. Patients and referring physicians should be advised that deterioration in the control of the eating disorder, plans to initiate new therapies, or new physical symptoms require reevaluation of the medical condition.

An important component of ongoing medical management is to counsel patients about the potential adverse physical consequences of the eating disorder and to reinforce the therapeutic recommendations of the eating disorders team. Careful explanations of the serious medical consequences of disordered eating can help motivate the patient to comply with the recommended psychiatric and behavioral treatment for the eating disorder.

The responsible medical clinician should be involved with decisions about nutritional management of eating-disordered patients (American Dietetic Association, 2001). This is particularly important in low-weight anorexic patients because of the risks associated with the refeeding syndrome (Swenne, 2000; Wada, Nagase, Koike, Kugai, & Nagata, 1992). Caloric replacement should be gradual and, for the lowest-weight patients, ideally occurs in an inpatient setting. Low-weight anorexic patients at risk for refeeding syndrome require cautious replacement of calories and fluid, careful monitoring of serum electrolytes, phosphorus, magnesium, and calcium levels. Medical evaluation focuses on detection of cardiac, respiratory, and neurologic complications during this high-risk period.

The medical physician should also be involved in the selection of weight loss methods recommended for obese patients with binge eating disorders. If very low-calorie diets are prescribed, close medical supervision is advised. Although the newer diet preparations appear to be safer than earlier versions, these patients still need to be monitored to ensure adequate fluid balance and to detect cardiac or liver complications of the diets (J. W. Anderson et al., 1992; Seim, Mitchell, Pomeroy, & de Zwaan, 1995). Some patients with morbid obesity may undergo bariatric surgery such as gastric bypass, gastroplasty, or banding. Medical management in these patients includes close attention to medical complications including gallstone formation and liver injury. In general, surgery should be reserved for patients with obesity associated with life-threatening medical conditions such as hypoventilation syndrome and who have failed nonsurgical attempts to lose weight.

Eating-disordered patients in whom hypokalemia or other electrolyte abnormalities are discovered during the medical assessment require careful medical management and monitoring until their condition has stabilized. Potassium replacement can usually be accomplished with oral supplements. Some patients with seriously low potassium levels that place them at significant risk of arrhythmias and other complications may require hospitalization and intravenous potassium repletion. It is critical to remember that metabolic contraction alkalosis may preclude the effectiveness of potassium supplements and that simultaneous correction of fluid status by cessation of purging behaviors must be emphasized. Attention should also be paid to correction of other electrolyte abnormalities, including hypomagnesemia and hypophosphatemia. Because relapse with resumption of purging is common, these patients should have laboratory testing on an ongoing basis.

Frequent dental evaluation is important for bulimic patients who are found to have significant enamel erosion (Milosevic et al., 1997). The use of bicarbonate rinses after vomiting has been advocated. Careful rinsing of the mouth to remove residual gastric acid before brushing the teeth can prevent further damage. Fluoride treatments in mouth rinses and applied by the dentist can also improve oral health. Careful dental evaluation on a regular basis is especially important for these patients.

Hormone replacement in hypogonadal patients with anorexia nervosa remains controversial (Bruni et al., 2000; Robinson et al., 2000). The use of replacement hormones, especially in adolescents and young women, may be associated with long-term adverse consequences, including increased risk of certain cancers. By extrapolation from recent studies of hormone replacement in postmenopausal women, combination hormonal therapy may actually increase risk of cardiac disease. Furthermore, the resumption of menses may allow complacency on the part of the patient, the family, and even the health care provider that the disease is "being treated" and facilitate failure to address the importance of weight gain. The decision of whether to prescribe hormone replacement for patients with anorexia nervosa must be individualized with careful counseling of patients about the risks and benefits. The medical clinician should ensure that the patient is scheduled for follow-up gynecologic examinations with Pap smears.

Treatment of osteoporosis remains an area of uncertainty in the management of anorexia nervosa (Golden et al., 2002; Valla et al., 2000; Ward et al., 1997). These patients are at significant risk of bone loss and fractures. Many experts had hoped that estrogen replacement would protect patients from developing osteoporosis as suggested in other estrogen-deficient populations. However, recent studies have highlighted the lack of efficacy of estrogen replacement for osteoporosis in anorexia nervosa, probably because of the multifactorial etiology of the disease. Supplementation with calcium and vitamin D is a reasonable approach until the results of studies on other approaches such as fluoride, biphosphonates, and IGF-1 are explored. The best therapy is successful treatment of the eating disorder with restoration of normal weight.

Eating-disordered patients should be counseled about the importance of discontinuing purging behaviors and the adverse effects associated with the abuse of diuretics, laxatives, diet pills, and ipecac. The use of bulk laxatives, controlled exercise, and dietary roughage can ameliorate the symptoms of poor gastrointestinal function that occur after cessation of use of stimulant laxatives. Patients should be reassured that the reflex edema associated with discontinuation of laxatives and diuretics due to secondary hyperaldosteronism will be transient. Mild fluid restriction and the use of support hose can minimize the accumulation of peripheral edema that occurs after discontinuing diuretics or laxatives. As the pseudo-Bartter's syndrome resolves, the fluid accumulation decreases and the symptomatic interventions become unnecessary.

Overall, recognition of the importance of the physical consequences of eating disorders is essential. Establishing a positive physician-patient relationship will facilitate early recognition and ease of medical management if the patient does develop new physical complications during the course of the illness. While the psychiatric aspects may dominate the clinical picture, the patient and all team members must remain alert to the possibility of secondary medical illnesses and understand that they can be life threatening. Medical follow-up should be part of the management plan for each patient with a serious eating disorder. While the plan is individualized for each patient on the basis of the severity of the eating disorder and the detection of medical complications during the initial assessment, all patients should be educated about the medical aspects of their illness and instructed on how to obtain needed medical evaluation if they develop physical symptoms or signs of illness. By incorporating careful medical assessment and management into the treatment plan, the health of the patient and chances of a successful outcome will be optimized.

INTERACTIONS WITH OTHER MEDICAL ILLNESSES

Patients with some other chronic medical illnesses, such as diabetes mellitus and cystic fibrosis, are at increased risk of developing an eating disorder and face additional challenges in the medical management of both illnesses. Illnesses that require careful dietary control such as renal failure, malabsorption, or hyperlipidemia may be particularly difficult to manage in the eating-disordered patient. Both patients and their health care providers must be cognizant of the interactions with these other medical illnesses and strive to avoid nutritional imbalances that compound the severity of both illnesses.

Patients with diabetes mellitus and eating disorders pose special challenges (Rodin & Daneman, 1992; Rydall, Rodin, Olmsted, Devenyi, & Daneman, 1997; Ward, Troop, Cachia, Watkins, & Treasure, 1995). Adolescents and young adults with type 1 insulin-dependent diabetes are at increased risk of developing an eating disorder. Diabetes is often associated with concerns about body image that may precipitate the development of an eating disorder. The importance of dietary regimentation in the management of diabetes can escalate food issues in these patients. Furthermore, the diabetic with an eating disorder can deliberately withhold insulin and induce hyperglycemia to accelerate weight loss. Food binges can make glucose control extremely difficult and place the patient at risk of diabetic ketoacidosis. Indeed, recent reports have emphasized that diabetic patients with an eating disorder have much poorer glucose control and a marked increase in the incidence of end-organ damage, including diabetic retinopathy and nephropathy. The clinician caring for patients with diabetes mellitus should be aware of the increased prevalence of eating disorders and be attentive to the special needs of this patient population.

Patients with cystic fibrosis and an eating disorder also require special attention. Like diabetes, cystic fibrosis may be associated with body image challenges. These patients develop malabsorption that can be exacerbated by the simultaneous presence of anorexia or bulimia nervosa. Cystic fibrosis patients often require special dietary management to maintain an adequate body weight, which may be resisted by the eating-disordered patient. In addition, cystic fibrosis patients are at risk of diabetes and the attendant risks previously discussed.

Many illnesses that require dietary management such as renal failure, malabsorption syndromes, inflammatory bowel disease, and pancreatitis may be more difficult to manage if the patient has an eating disorder. Medical providers should be aware of these interactions and work closely with the other members of the eating disorders team to help the patient deal with these special challenges.

PREGNANCY AND THE EATING DISORDERS

Reproductive function in women with eating disorders is frequently abnormal (Blais et al., 2000; Bulik et al., 1999; Deering, 2001; Katz & Vollenhaven, 2000; Kreipe & Mou, 2000; Morgan, 1999). Patients with eating disorders may have infertility and often experience more complications during pregnancy (Franko et al., 2001). Their children may suffer more adverse perinatal outcomes and may learn unhealthy attitudes toward eating. Conversely, some studies suggest that in some patients, the severity of the eating disorder is attenuated during pregnancy.

Infertility experts now recognize that patients may be unable to conceive because of an occult eating disorder. Screening for eating disorders is now recommended in many infertility practices. Accurate recognition of the diagnosis may prevent the need for expensive and uncomfortable evaluations for other causes of the infertility. Patients with anorexia nervosa have an increased risk of infertility (Bulik et al., 1999), presumably due to the well-documented abnormalities of the hypothalamic-pituitary-gonadotropin system. The best approach is to address the underlying eating disorder. This is particularly important because the weight gain associated with pregnancy may be particularly intolerable to the patient with anorexia nervosa, and she may respond by further restricting calories, thus placing the fetus at risk of inadequate nutrition. Women with active anorexia nervosa during pregnancy are at increased risk of requiring caesarian section and of having babies with low Apgar scores (Morgan, Lacey, & Sedgwick, 1999).

Bulimia nervosa also appears to be associated with an increased risk of infertility. In addition, some patients develop increased frequency of binge-purge episodes during pregnancy. In fact, bulimic patients appear to be at particular risk for hyperemesis gravidarum during their pregnancies.

Some studies also suggest that eating-disordered patients with anorexia and bulimia nervosa are at increased risk of postpartum depression (Morgan et al., 1999). Furthermore, these women may have increased difficulty with breast feeding. Concern has been raised about how well eating-disordered women can role-model healthy eating for their children, and it has been postulated that their offspring may be at risk for undernutrition and/or the development of an eating disorder.

Obese women, including those with binge eating disorder, also face problems with infertility. In addition, complications of pregnancy occur with increased frequency in overweight women. An increased incidence of adverse perinatal outcomes is seen in babies born to obese women.

Clinicians caring for women with infertility should include assessment for eating disorders in their evaluations. Screening for eating disorders has also been recommended for women with hyperemesis gravidarum during pregnancy and for women who fail to gain weight appropriately in pregnancy or who have small babies for gestational age. Successful treatment of underlying eating disorders before pregnancy may decrease the risk of complications. When a woman with an eating disorder does become pregnant, careful collaboration between the obstetrician and the eating disorders team will increase the likelihood of a successful outcome (Franko & Spurrell, 2000). Particular attention should be paid to monitoring for postpartum depression in this vulnerable population.

SUMMARY

The eating disorders are associated with myriad physical consequences and medical complications that threaten patients' health during their illness and even after recovery. Physical signs and symptoms can provide important clues to the presence of an eating disorder, and all clinicians should be aware of these manifestations to facilitate recognition and timely diagnosis of patients with eating disorders. Medical management of patients with known eating disorders should include an initial medical history and physical examination to assess the physical condition of the patient and detect somatic consequences. Complications related to each of the major organ systems have been described in patients with anorexia nervosa, bulimia nervosa, and binge eating syndrome. Ongoing medical management by a medical clinician experienced in the care of patients with eating disorders is recommended and should be tailored to the individual needs and physical condition of the patient. Particular challenges are posed by the presence of other chronic medical conditions such as diabetes mellitus or with pregnancy. Careful consideration of the physical manifestations of the eating disorders is an integral part of the treatment plan for each patient with an eating disorder.

REFERENCES

Addolorato, G., Taronto, C., Capristo, E., & Gasbarrini, G. (1998). A case of marked cerebellar atrophy in a women with anorexia nervosa and a review of the literature. *International Journal of Eating Disorders, 24,* 443–447.

Adson, D. E., Mitchell, J. E., & Trenkner, S. W. (1997). The superior mesenteric artery syndrome and acute gastric dilatation in eating disorders: A report of two cases and a review of the literature. *International Journal of Eating Disorders, 21,* 103–114.

Agras, W. S. (2001). The consequences and costs of the eating disorders. *Psychiatric Clinics of North America, 24,* 371–379.

Alexandridis, G., Liamis, G., & Elisaf, M. (2001). Reversible tubular dysfunction that mimicked Fanconi's syndrome in a patient with anorexia nervosa. *International Journal of Eating Disorders, 30,* 227–230.

American Academy of Pediatrics. (2003). Committee on adolescence: Identifying and treating eating disorders. *Pediatrics, 111,* 204–211.

American Dietetic Association. (2001). Position of the American Dietetic Association: Nutrition intervention in the treatment of anorexia nervosa, bulimia nervosa, and eating disorders not otherwise specified (EDNOS). *Journal of the American Dietetic Association, 101,* 810–819.

Anderson, J. W., Hamilton, C. C., & Brinkman-Kaplan, V. (1992). Benefits and risks of an intensive very-low-calorie diet program for severe obesity. *American Journal of Gastroenterology, 87,* 6–15.

Anderson, L., Shaw, J. M., & McCargar, L. (1997). Physiological effects of bulimia on the gastrointestinal tract. *Canadian Journal of Gastroenterology, 11,* 451–459.

Bailly, D., Lambin, I., Garzon, G., & Parquet, P. J. (1994). Bone marrow hypoplasia in anorexia nervosa: A case report. *International Journal of Eating Disorders, 16,* 97–100.

Baker, D., Roberts, R., & Towell, T. (2000). Factors predictive of bone mineral density in eating-disordered women: A longitudinal study. *International Journal of Eating Disorders, 27,* 29–35.

Becker, A. E., Grinspoon, S. K., Klibanski, A., & Herzog, D. B. (1999). Eating disorders. *New England Journal of Medicine, 340,* 1092–1098.

Biller, B. M., Saze, V., Herzog, D. B., Rosenthal, D. I., Holzman, S., & Klibonski, A. (1989). Mechanisms of osteoporosis in adult and adolescent women with anorexia nervosa. *Journal of Clinical Endocrinology and Metabolism, 68,* 548–554.

Blais, M. A., Becker, A. E., Burwell, R. A., Flores, A. T., Nussbaum, K. M., Greenwood, D. N., et al. (2000). Pregnancy: Outcome and impact on symptomatology in a cohort of eating disordered women. *International Journal of Eating Disorders, 27,* 140–149.

Boag, F., Weerakoon, J., Ginsburg, J., Havard, C. W., & Dandora, P. (1985). Diminished creatinine clearance in anorexia nervosa: Reversal with weight gain. *Journal of Clinical Pathology, 38,* 60–63.

Bowers, T. K., & Eckert, E. (1978). Leukopenia in anorexia nervosa: Lack of increased risk of infection. *Archives of Internal Medicine, 138,* 1520–1523.

Boyar, R. M., Hellman, K. L., Roffwarg, H. P., Katz, J., Zumoff, B., O'Connor, J., et al. (1977). Cortisol secretion and metabolism in anorexia nervosa. *New England Journal of Medicine, 296,* 190–193.

Brown, J. M., & Mehler, P. S. (2000). Medical complications occurring in adolescents with anorexia nervosa. *Western Journal of Medicine, 172,* 189–193.

Bruni, V., Dei, M., Vicini, I., Beninato, L., & Magnani, L. (2000). Estrogen replacement therapy in the management of osteopenia related to eating disorders. *Annals of the New York Academy of Sciences, 900,* 416–421.

Bulik, C. M., Sullivan, P. F., Fear, J. L., Pickering, A., Dawn, A., & McCullin, M. (1999). Fertility and reproduction in women with anorexia nervosa: A controlled study. *Journal of Clinical Psychiatry, 60,* 130–135.

Chiarioni, G., Bassotti, G., Monsignori, A., Menegotti, M., Salandini, L., DiMatteo, G., et al. (2000). Anorectal dysfunction in constipated women with anorexia nervosa. *Mayo Clinic Proceedings, 75,* 1015–1019.

Comerci, G. (1990). Medical complications of anorexia nervosa and bulimia. *Medical Clinics of North America, 74,* 1293–1310.

Cooke, R. A., & Chambers, J. B. (1995). Anorexia nervosa and the heart. *British Journal of Hospital Medicine, 54,* 313–317.

Corcos, M., Guilbaud, O., Paterniti, S., Moussa, M., Chambry, J., Chaouat, G., et al. (2003). Involvement of cytokines in eating disorders: A critical review of the human literature. *Psychoneuroendocrinology, 28,* 229–249.

Crow, S. J., Rosenberg, M. E., Mitchell, J. E., & Thuras, P. (2001). Urine electrolytes as markers of bulimia nervosa. *International Journal of Eating Disorders, 30,* 279–287.

Crowell, M. D., Cheskin, L. J., & Musial, F. (1994). Prevalence of gastrointestinal symptoms in obese and normal weight binge eaters. *American Journal of Gastroenterology, 89,* 387–391.

Cuellar, R. E., Kaye, W. H., Hsu, L. K., & Van Thiel, O. H. (1988). Upper gastrointestinal tract dysfunction in bulimia. *Digestive Diseases and Sciences, 33,* 1549–1553.

Cuellar, R. E., & Van Thiel, D. H. (1986). Gastrointestinal consequences of the eating disorders: Anorexia nervosa and bulimia. *American Journal of Gastroenterology, 81,* 1113–1124.

Deering, S. (2001). Eating disorders: Recognition, evaluation, and implications for obstetrician/gynecologists. *Primary Care Update Obstetrics and Gynecology, 8,* 31–35.

De Filippo, E., Signorini, A., Bracale, R., Pasanisi, F., & Contaldo, F. (2000). Hospital admission and mortality rates in anorexia nervosa: Experience from an integrated medical-psychiatric outpatient treatment. *Eating and Weight Disorders, 5,* 211–216.

Devlin, M. J., Walsh, B. T., Katz, J. L., Roose, S. P., Linkie, D. M., Wright, L., et al. (1989). Hypothalamic-pituitary-gonadal function in anorexia nervosa and bulimia. *Psychiatry Research, 28,* 11–24.

Devuyst, O., Lambert, M., Rodhain, J., Lefebvre, C., & Coche, E. (1993). Hematological changes and infectious complications in anorexia nervosa: A case study. *Quarterly Journal of Medicine, 86,* 791–799.

Dresser, L. P., Massey, E. W., Johnson, E. E., & Bossen, E. (1992). Ipecac myopathy and cardiomyopathy. *Journal of Neurology, Neurosurgery, and Psychiatry, 55,* 560–562.

Eckert, E. D., Pomeroy, C., Raymond, N., Kohler, P. F., Thuras, P., & Bowers, C. Y. (1998). Leptin in anorexia nervosa. *Journal of Clinical Endocrinology and Metabolism, 83,* 791–795.

Emborg, C. (1999). Mortality and causes of death in eating disorders in Denmark 1970–1993: A case register study. *International Journal of Eating Disorders, 25,* 243–251.

Fichter, M. M., & Quadflieg, N. (1999). Six-year course and outcome of anorexia nervosa. *International Journal of Eating Disorders, 26,* 359–385.

Fink, S., Eckert, E., Mitchell, J., Crosby, R., & Pomeroy, C. (1996). T-Lymphocyte subsets in patients with abnormal body weight: Longitudinal studies in anorexia nervosa and obesity. *International Journal of Eating Disorders, 20,* 295–305.

Fisher, M., Simpser, E., & Schneider, M. (2000). Hypophosphatemia secondary to oral refeeding in anorexia nervosa. *International Journal of Eating Disorders, 28,* 181–187.

Franko, D. L., Blais, M. A., Becker, A. E., Delinsky, S. S., Greenwood, O. N., Flores, A. T., et al. (2001). Pregnancy complications and neonatal outcomes in women with eating disorders. *American Journal of Psychiatry, 158,* 1461–1466.

Franko, D. L., & Spurrell, E. B. (2000). Detection and management of eating disorders during pregnancy. *Obstetrics and Gynecology, 95,* 942–946.

Frederich, R., Hu, S., Raymond, N., & Pomeroy, C. (2002). Leptin in anorexia nervosa and bulimia nervosa: Importance of assay technique and method of interpretation. *Journal of Laboratory and Clinical Medicine, 139,* 72–79.

Glorio, R., Allevato, M., De Pablo, A., Abbruzzese, M., Carmona, L., Savarin, M., et al. (2000). Prevalence of cutaneous manifestations in 200 patients with eating disorders. *International Journal of Dermatology, 39,* 348–353.

Gniuli, D., Liverani, E., Capristo, E., Greco, A. V., & Mingrone, G. (2001). Blunted glucose metabolism in anorexia nervosa. *Metabolism, 50,* 876–881.

Gold, P. W., Gwirtsman, H., Avgerinos, P. C., Nieman, L. K., Gallucci, W. T., Kaye, W., et al. (1986). Abnormal hypothalamic-pituitary-adrenal function in anorexia nervosa. *New England Journal of Medicine, 314,* 1335–1342.

Golden, N. H., Lanzkowsky, L., Schebendach, J., Palestro, C. J., Jacobson, M. S., & Shenker, I. R. (2002). The effect of estrogen-progestin treatment on bone mineral density in anorexia nervosa. *Journal of Pediatric Adolescent Gynecology, 15,* 135–143.

Grinspoon, S., Miller, K., Coyle, C., Krempin, J., Armstrong, C., Thomas, E., et al. (2000). Prevalence and predictive factors for regional osteopenia in women with anorexia nervosa. *Annals of Internal Medicine, 133,* 790–794.

Grinspoon, S., Miller, K., Coyle, C., Thomas, E., Pitts, S., Gross, E., et al. (1999). Severity of osteopenia in estrogen deficient women with anorexia nervosa and hypothalamic amenorrhea. *Journal of Clinical Endocrinology Metabolism, 84,* 2049–2055.

Grinspoon, S., Miller, K., Herzog, D., Clemmons, D., & Klibanski, A. (2003). Effects of recombinant human insulin-like growth factor (IGF)-I and estrogen administration on IGF-I, IGF binding protein (IGFBP)-2, and IGFBP-3 in anorexia nervosa: A randomized controlled study. *Journal of Clinical Endocrinology and Metabolism, 88,* 1142–1149.

Gupta, M. A., Gupta, A. K., & Haberman, H. F. (1987). Dermatologic signs in anorexia nervosa and bulimia nervosa. *Archives of Dermatology, 123,* 1386–1390.

Hartman, D., Crisp, A., Rooney, B., Rackow, C., Atkinson, R., & Patel, S. (2000). Bone density of women who have recovered from anorexia nervosa. *International Journal of Eating Disorders, 28,* 107–112.

Herzog, W., Deter, H. C., Fiehn, W., & Petzold, E. (1997). Medical findings and predictors of long-term physical outcome in anorexia nervosa. *Psychology Medicine, 27,* 269–279.

Howard, M. R., Leggat, H. M., & Chaudhry, S. (1992). Hematological and immunological abnormalities in eating disorders. *British Journal of Hospital Medicine, 48,* 234–239.

Hudson, J., Pope, H. G., Jr., Jonas, J. M., Laffer, P. S., Hudson, M. S., & Jelby, J. C. (1983). Hypothalamic-pituitary-adrenal axis hyperactivity in bulimia. *Psychiatry, 8,* 111–117.

Isner, J. M., Roberts, W. C., Heymsfield, S. B., & Yager, J. (1985). Anorexia nervosa and sudden death. *Annals of Internal Medicine, 102,* 49–52.

Jagielska, G., Wolanczyk, T., Komender, J., Tomaszewicz-Libudzic, C., Przedlacki, J., & Ostrowski, K. (2001). Bone mineral content and bone mineral density in adolescent girls with anorexia nervosa: A longitudinal study. *Acta Psychiatrica Scandinavica, 104,* 131–137.

Kamal, N., Chami, T., Andersen, A., Rosell, F. A., Schuster, M. M., & Whitehead, W. E. (1991). Delayed gastrointestinal transit times in anorexia nervosa and bulimia nervosa. *American Journal of Gastroenterology, 101,* 1320–1324.

Katz, M. G., & Vollenhaven, B. (2000). Productive consequences of anorexia nervosa. *British Journal of Obstetrics and Gynecology, 107,* 707–713.

Katzman, D. K., Christensen, B., Young, A. R., & Zipursky, R. B. (2001). Starving the brain: Structural abnormalities and cognitive impairment in adolescents with anorexia nervosa. *Seminars in Clinical Neuropsychiatry, 6,* 146–152.

Kiriike, N., Nishiwaki, S., Izumiya, Y., Maeda, Y., & Kawakita, Y. (1987). Thyrotropin, prolactin, and growth hormone responses to thyrotropin-releasing hormone in anorexia nervosa and bulimia. *Biological Psychiatry, 22,* 167–176.

Kreipe, R. E., & Harris, J. P. (1992). Myocardial impairment resulting from eating disorders. *Pediatric Annals, 21,* 760–768.

Kreipe, R. E., & Mou, S. M. (2000). Eating disorders in adolescents and young adults. *Obstetrics and Gynecology Clinics of North America, 27,* 101–124.

Krieg, J. C., Pirke, K. M., Lauer, C., & Backmund, H. (1988). Endocrine, metabolic, and cranial computed tomography findings in anorexia nervosa. *Biological Psychiatry, 23,* 377–387.

Laue, L., Gold, P. W., Richmond, A., & Chrousos, G. P. (1991). The hypothalamic-pituitary-adrenal axis in anorexia nervosa and bulimia nervosa: Pathophysiologic implications. *Advances in Pediatrics, 38,* 287–316.

Lennkh, C., de Zwaan, M., Bailer, U., Strnad, A., Nagy, C., El-Giamal, N., et al. (1999). Osteopenia in anorexia nervosa: Specific mechanism of bone loss. *Journal of Psychiatry Research, 33,* 349–356.

Levine, R. L. (2002). Endocrine aspects of eating disorders in adolescents. *Adolescent Medicine, 13,* 129–143.

Lucas, A. R., Melton, J., Crowson, C. S., O'Fallon, W. M. (1999). Long-term fracture risk among women with anorexia nervosa. *Mayo Clinic Proceedings, 74,* 972–977.

Mandel, L., & Kaynar, A. (1992). Bulimia and parotid swelling: A review and case report. *Journal of Oral Maxillofacial Surgery, 50,* 1122–1125.

McClain, C., Humphries, L. L., Hill, K. K., & Nickl, N. J. (1993). Gastrointestinal and nutritional aspects of eating disorders. *Journal of the American College of Nutrition, 12,* 466–474.

Mehler, P. S. (2001). Diagnosis and care of patients with anorexia nervosa in primary care settings. *Annals of Internal Medicine, 134,* 1048–1059.

Mehler, P. S., Eckel, R. H., & Donahoo, W. T. (1999). Leptin levels in restricting and purging anorexics. *International Journal of Eating Disorders, 26,* 186–194.

Metzger, E. D., Levine, J. M., McArdel, C. R., Wolfe, B. E., & Jimerson, D. C. (1999). Salivary gland enlargement and elevated serum amylase in bulimia nervosa. *Biological Psychiatry, 45,* 1520–1522.

Meyers, D. G., Starke, H., Pearson, P. H., Wilken, M. K., & Ferrell, J. R. (1987). Leaflet to left ventricular size disproportion and prolapse of a structurally normal mitral valve in anorexia nervosa. *American Journal of Cardiology, 60,* 911–914.

Milosevic, A., Brodie, D., & Slade, P. D. (1997). Dental erosion, oral hygiene, and nutrition in eating disorders. *International Journal of Eating Disorders, 21,* 195–199.

Mitchell, J. E., & Boutacoff, L. I. (1986). Laxative abuse complicating bulimia: Medical and treatment implications. *International Journal of Eating Disorders, 5,* 325–334.

Mitchell, J. E., Hatsukami, D., Pyle, R. L., Boutacoff, L. I., & Eckert, E. D. (1987). Metabolic acidosis as a marker for laxative abuse in patients with bulimia. *International Journal of Eating Disorders, 6,* 557–560.

Mitchell, J. E., Pomeroy, C., & Huber, M. (1988). A clinician's guide to the eating disorders medicine cabinet. *International Journal of Eating Disorders, 7,* 211–223.

Mitchell, J. E., Pomeroy, C., Seppala, M., & Huber, M. (1988). Pseudo-Bartter's syndrome, diuretic abuse, idiopathic edema and eating disorders. *International Journal of Eating Disorders, 7,* 225–237.

Mitchell, J. E., Pyle, R. L., Hatsukami, D., & Eckert, E. (1984). The dexamethasone suppression test in patients with bulimia. *Journal of Clinical Psychiatry, 45,* 508–511.

Mitchell, J. E., Pyle, R. L., Hatsukami, D., & Eckert, E. (1991). Enema abuse as a clinical feature of bulimia nervosa. *Psychosomatics, 32,* 102–104.

Mitchell, J. E., Seim, H. C., Colon, E., & Pomeroy, C. (1987). Medical complications and medical management of bulimia. *Annals of Internal Medicine, 107,* 71–77.

Morgan, J. F. (1999). Eating disorders and reproduction. *Australian and New Zealand Journal of Obstetrics and Gynecology, 39,* 167–173.

Morgan, J. F., Lacey, J. H., & Sedgwick, P. M. (1999). Impact of pregnancy on bulimia nervosa. *British Journal of Psychiatry, 174,* 135–140.

Mortola, J. F., Rasmussen, D. D., Yen, S. S. C. (1989). Alterations of the adrenocorticotropin-cortisol axis in normal weight bulimic women: Evidence for a central mechanism. *Journal of Clinical Endocrinology and Metabolism, 68,* 517–522.

Nagata, T., Tobitani, W., Kiriike, N., Iketani, T., & Yamagami, S. (1999). Capacity to produce cytokines during weight restoration in patients with anorexia nervosa. *Advances in Psychosomatic Medicine, 61,* 371–377.

Nakao, A., Isozaki, H., Iwagaki, H., Kanagawa, T., Takakura, N., & Tanaka, N. (2000). Gastric perforation caused by a bulimic attack in an anorexia nervosa patient: Report of a case. *Surgery Today, 30,* 435–437.

Neumarker, K.-J. (1997). Mortality and sudden death in anorexia nervosa. *International Journal of Eating Disorders, 21,* 205–212.

Newman, M. M., & Halmi, K. A. (1989). Relationship of bone density to estradiol and cortisol in anorexia nervosa and bulimia. *Psychiatry Research, 29,* 105–112.

Palla, B., & Litt, I. F. (1988). Medical complications of eating disorders in adolescents. *Pediatrics, 81,* 613–623.

Palmer, E. P., & Guay, A. T. (1985). Reversible myopathy secondary to abuse of ipecac in patients with major eating disorders. *New England Journal of Medicine, 313,* 1457–1459.

Patton, G. C. (1988). Mortality in eating disorders. *Psychological Medicine, 18,* 947–951.

Pauly, R. P., Lear, S. A., Hastings, F. C., & Birmingham, C. L. (2000). Resting energy expenditure and plasma leptin levels in anorexia nervosa during acute refeeding. *International Journal of Eating Disorders, 28,* 231–234.

Pauporte, J., & Walsh, B. T. (2001). Serum cholesterol in bulimia nervosa. *International Journal of Eating Disorders, 30,* 294–298.

Pirke, K. M., Fichter, M. M., Chlond, C., Schweiger, U., Laessle, R. G., Schwingenschloegel, M., et al. (1987). Disturbances of the menstrual cycle in bulimia nervosa. *Clinical Endocrinology, 27,* 245–251.

Pomeroy, C., Eckert, E., Hu, S., Eiken, B., Mentink, M., Crosby, R. D., et al. (1994). Role of interleukin-6 and transforming growth factor-ß in anorexia nervosa. *Biological Psychiatry, 36,* 836–839.

Pomeroy, C., & Mitchell, J. E. (1989). Medical complications and management of eating disorders. *Psychiatric Annals, 19,* 488–493.

Pomeroy, C., Mitchell, J. E., Eckert, E., Raymond, N., Crosby, R., & Dalmasso, A. P. (1997). Effect of body weight and caloric restriction on serum complement proteins, including factor D/adipsin: Studies in anorexia nervosa and obesity. *Clinical and Experimental Immunology, 108,* 507–515.

Pomeroy, D. C., & Santana, C. A. (2002). Eating disorders: A guide for the primary care physician. *Primary Care, 29,* 81–98.

Ratnasuriya, R. H., Eisler, I., Szmukler, G. I., & Russell, G. F. (1991). Anorexia nervosa: Outcome and prognostic factors after 20 years. *British Journal of Psychiatry, 158,* 495–502.

Raymond, N. C., Dysken, M., Bettin, K., Eckert, E. D., Crow, S. J., Markus, K., et al. (2000). Cytokine production in patients with anorexia nervosa, bulimia nervosa, and obesity. *International Journal of Eating Disorders, 28,* 293–302.

Rich, L. M., Caine, M. R., Findling, J. W., & Shaker, J. L. (1990). Hypoglycemic coma in anorexia nervosa: Case report and review of the literature. *Archives of Internal Medicine, 150,* 894–895.

Rigotti, N. A., Nussbaum, S. R., Herzog, D. B., & Neer, R. M. (1984). Osteoporosis in women with anorexia nervosa. *New England Journal of Medicine, 311,* 1601–1606.

Roberts, M. N., & Li, S.-H. (1987). Oral findings in anorexia nervosa and bulimia nervosa: A study of 47 cases. *Journal of the American Dental Association, 15,* 407–410.

Robinson, E., Bachrach, L. K., & Katzman, D. K. (2000). Use of hormone replacement therapy to reduce the risk of osteopenia in adolescent girls with anorexia nervosa. *Journal of Adolescent Health, 26,* 343–348.

Rodin, G. M., & Daneman, D. (1992). Eating disorders and IDDM. *Diabetes Care, 15,* 1402–1412.

Roerig, J. L., Mitchell, J. E., Myers, T. C., & Glass, J. B. (2002). Pharmacotherapy and medical complications of eating disorders in children and adolescents. *Child and Adolescent Psychiatric Clinics of North America, 11,* 365–385.

Ryan, C. F., Whittaker, J. S., & Road, J. D. (1992). Ventilatory dysfunction in severe anorexia nervosa. *Chest, 102,* 1286–1288.

Rydall, A. C., Rodin, G. M., Olmsted, M. P., Devenyi, R. G., & Daneman, D. (1997). Disordered eating behavior and microvascular complications in young women with insulin-dependent diabetes mellitus. *New England Journal of Medicine, 336,* 1849–1854.

Seim, H. C., Mitchell, J. E., Pomeroy, C., & de Zwaan, M. (1995). Electrocardiographic findings associated with very low calorie dieting. *International Journal of Obesity and Related Metabolic Disorders, 19,* 817–819.

Sharp, C. W., & Freeman, C. P. L. (1993). The medical complications of anorexia nervosa. *British Journal of Psychiatry, 162,* 452–462.

Simmons, M. S., Grayden, S. K., & Mitchell, J. E. (1986). The need for psychiatric-dental liaison in the treatment of bulimia. *American Journal of Psychiatry, 143,* 783–784.

Smith, R. R. L., & Spivak, J. L. (1985). Marrow cell necrosis in anorexia nervosa and involuntary starvation. *British Journal of Hematology, 60,* 525–530.

Soyka, L. A., Grinspoon, S., Levitsky, L. L., Herzog, D. B., & Klibanski, A. (1999). The effects of anorexia on bone metabolism in female adolescents. *Journal of Clinical Endocrinology and Metabolism, 84,* 4489–4496.

Strober, M., Freeman, R., & Morrell, W. (1997). The long-term course of severe anorexia nervosa in adolescents. *International Journal of Eating Disorders, 22,* 339–360.

Strumia, R., Varotti, E., Manzato, E., & Gualandi, M. (2001). Skin signs in anorexia nervosa. *Dermatology, 203,* 314–317.

Studen-Pavlovich, D., & Elliott, M. A. (2001). Eating disorders in women's oral health. *Dental Clinics of North America, 45,* 491–511.

Swenne, I. (2000). Heart risk associated with weight loss in anorexia nervosa and eating disorders: Electrocardiographic changes during the early phase of refeeding. *Acta Paediatrica, 89,* 447–452.

Turner, J., Batik, M., Palmer, L. J., Forbes, D., & McDermott, B. M. (2000). Detection and importance of laxative abuse in adolescents with anorexia nervosa. *Journal of American Academy of Child and Adolescent Psychiatry, 39,* 375–385.

Valla, A., Groenning, I. L., Syversen, U., & Hoeiseth, A. (2000). Anorexia nervosa: Slow regain of bone mass. *Osteoporosis International, 11,* 141–145.

Wada, S., Nagase, T., Koike, Y., Kugai, N., & Nagata, N. (1992). A case of anorexia nervosa with acute renal failure induced by rhabdomyolysis: Possible involvement of hypophosphatemia or phosphate depletion. *Internal Medicine, 31,* 478–482.

Walsh, J. M., Wheat, M. E., & Freund, K. (2000). Detection, evaluation and treatment of eating disorders: The role of the primary care physician. *Journal of General Internal Medicine, 15,* 577–590.

Ward, A., Brown, N., & Treasure, J. (1997). Persistent osteopenia after recovery from anorexia nervosa. *International Journal of Eating Disorders, 22,* 71–75.

Ward, A., Troop, N., Cachia, M., Watkins, P., & Treasure, J. (1995). Doubly disabled: Diabetes in combination with an eating disorder. *Postgraduate Medicine Journal, 71,* 546–550.

Winston, A. P., Jamieson, C. P., Madira, W., Gatward, N. M., & Palmer, R. L. (2000). Prevalence of thiamine deficiency in anorexia nervosa. *International Journal of Eating Disorders, 28,* 451–454.

Yager, J., Andersen, A., Devlin, M., Egger, H., Herzog, D., Mitchell, J., et al. (2000). Practice guidelines for the treatment of patients with eating disorders. *American Journal of Psychiatry, 157*(Suppl. 1), 1–39.

Zipfel, S., Lowe, B., Reas, D. L., Deter, H. C., & Herzog, W. (2000). Long term prognosis in anorexia nervosa. *Lancet, 355,* 721–722.

Chapter 6

PSYCHOLOGICAL ASSESSMENT OF EATING DISORDERS AND RELATED FEATURES

DREW A. ANDERSON AND CAROLINE A. PAULOSKY

This chapter provides a broad overview of the assessment of eating disorders. First, we review basic psychometric issues that should be considered when choosing assessment instruments. Next, we summarize common problems specific to the eating disorders that can complicate the assessment process. We then review and discuss a number of assessment measures, with a focus on psychometrically sound instruments that are actually used in the literature. Finally, we suggest some future directions for the assessment of eating disorders and eating pathology.

BASIC PSYCHOMETRIC ISSUES IN ASSESSMENT

Several psychometric issues need to be considered when choosing an assessment instrument. This brief overview can only begin to address these issues; more thorough discussions of psychometric standards are available (e.g., Joint Committee on Standards for Educational and Psychological Testing, 1999; Pedhazur & Schmelkin, 1991).

Reliability

The most basic of psychometric issues is reliability, which is commonly defined as the consistency of measurement when testing is repeated. While there are a number of types of reliability, test-retest, interrater, and internal consistency are the approaches most commonly seen in the literature.

Test-Retest Reliability

The simplest approach to determining reliability is the test-retest approach, in which a sample of people is given the same test on two separate occasions and the two sets of scores are correlated. Test-retest reliability measures the consistency of an examinee's responses over time, and, as such, is often called the *coefficient of stability*. While simple and easy to calculate, test-retest reliability does have shortcomings. In particular, shorter intervals between tests can lead to inflated reliability estimates because of carryover effects, while longer intervals can lead to lower reliability estimates because of real changes on the characteristic that is being assessed (Crocker & Algina, 1986; Pedhazur & Schmelkin, 1991). Thus, test-retest reliability should be used only with constructs that are thought to be stable.

Interrater Reliability

Interrater reliability is, in general, the extent to which two or more assessors agree on their ratings or codings of a behavior of interest. A number of formulas have been developed to determine interrater reliability, and some form of this metric is commonly reported in the assessment literature. It has been argued, however, that interrater reliability is not really a form of reliability at all; in fact, interrater reliability can be high even though reliability is low (Pedhazur & Schmelkin, 1991). Thus, this metric should be viewed with some caution.

Internal Consistency Reliability

Internal consistency reliability is most commonly measured by coefficient alpha, also called *coefficient $\forall$* or *Chronbach's alpha.* Coefficient alpha is calculated essentially by splitting a scale into as many parts as it has items and examining the relationship between those items. Because it can be calculated from only one administration of a test, internal consistency reliability addresses errors related to temporary fluctuations within a single occasion, such as fatigue (Pedhazur & Schmelkin, 1991). It is also related to the content of a scale or measure; thus, it is particularly useful when measuring constructs (Pedhazur & Schmelkin, 1991). However, while internal consistency is commonly thought to be a measure of the homogeneity or unidimensionality of a construct, this is not the case. Low internal consistency reliability can be interpreted that a measure is not homogeneous, but high internal consistency reliability does not necessarily mean that a measure is homogeneous (Crocker & Algina, 1986; Pedhazur & Schmelkin, 1991).

Finally, it should be noted that reliability is a necessary but not sufficient condition for validity. That is, even if a measure has acceptable levels of reliability, it may not be valid for the purposes for which it was designed.

Validity

The Joint Committee on Standards for Educational and Psychological Testing of the American Educational Research Association, the American Psychological Association, and the National Council on Measurement in Education defines *validity* most broadly as "the degree to which evidence and theory support the interpretations of test scores entailed by proposed uses of tests" (1999, p. 9). This evidence can be provided in a number of ways; some of the most common are described here.

Content Validity

Content validity consists of evidence provided by relating a test's content and the construct to which it is supposed to measure. One common way of determining content validity is to have a panel of experts judge how closely the items relate to the construct they are supposed to measure. A number of systems have been developed to assist in this task (e.g., Crocker & Algina, 1986).

Criterion Validity

Criterion validity consists of evidence provided by the ability to predict performance on another variable, or criterion, based on performance on the test in question. This other criterion may be measured at the same time as the test of interest (concurrent validity) or at some point in the future (predictive validity).

One problem with obtaining criterion validity is determining which criterion will be used as the comparison. Thorndike (1949) clearly defined the dilemma; as criteria become more important, they become more difficult to define and measure, and the most important criteria may even be conceptualized as constructs. Conversely, the easier a criteria is to obtain and measure, the less important it is likely to be. Thus, the choice of a criterion reflects a balance between ease of assessment and importance.

Criterion validity is commonly reported using the validity coefficient, which is simply the Pearson correlation between the test of interest and the criterion. In addition, regression analysis is often employed to derive a prediction equation from which an individual's performance on the criterion can be predicted given his or her score on the test of interest.

Construct Validity

Construct validity is commonly defined as the degree to which an assessment instrument actually measures the construct it is purported to measure. It is a complex process that has no definitive procedures; however, some approaches are commonly used to determine construct validation. In the multitrait-multimethod of determining construct validity (Campbell & Fiske, 1959), two or more methods of assessment of the same construct are identified, as are two or more other constructs that can be measured by similar methods to the construct of interest. Measurements are taken of each construct using each measure; correlations can then be calculated between all of the measure-construct combinations. A valid construct shows high correlations between measures of the same construct using different methods (convergent validity) and low correlations between measures of different constructs (discriminant validity). Factor analytic procedures are also commonly used to determine construct validity. In this approach, the match between an observed factor structure and the hypothesized construct is taken as evidence of construct validity.

SPECIAL ISSUES IN THE ASSESSMENT OF EATING DISORDERS

Diagnostic Dilemmas in the Eating Disorders

The most recent edition of the *Diagnostic and Statistical Manual of Mental Disorders* (*DSM-IV-TR*; American Psychiatric Association [APA], 2000) recognizes two specific eating disorder diagnoses: anorexia nervosa (AN) and bulimia nervosa (BN). Eating disorders that do not meet criteria for either AN or BN are given the diagnosis of eating disorder not otherwise specified (EDNOS). A third diagnosis, binge eating disorder (BED), has been proposed; it is included as a criteria set for further study in the *DSM-IV-TR* and is a specific example of EDNOS. The current *DSM-IV-TR* criteria have led to a number of diagnostic dilemmas; two of the most important are reviewed here.

High Rates of Eating Disorder Not Otherwise Specified (EDNOS)

A number of studies have found that the current diagnostic criteria for AN and BN exclude large numbers of individuals who have significant eating pathology but do not quite meet one or more of the diagnostic criteria for AN or BN (Bunnell, Shenker, Nussbaum, Jacobson, & Cooper, 1990; Heatherton, Nichols, Mahamedi, & Keel, 1995; Nicholls, Chater, & Lask, 2000; Ricca et al., 2001; Whitaker, 1992), resulting in a large proportion of those seeking treatment for eating disorders receiving a diagnosis of EDNOS.

This high proportion of EDNOS has important practical implications for the assessment and treatment of eating disorders. For example, Andersen and colleagues (Andersen, Bowers, & Watson, 2001) have argued that EDNOS is an overly broad diagnosis that is confusing to clinicians and sometimes denied for insurance payment. Also, NOS diagnoses often have the reputation of being "garbage can" diagnoses, which can give the impression that the problems of an individual with EDNOS are not as bad as those of an individual with the "real" disorders AN and BN.

One solution suggested is that altering current diagnostic criteria for AN and BN could decrease the proportion of cases receiving an EDNOS diagnosis (Andersen et al., 2001; Thaw, Williamson, & Martin, 2001). Thaw and colleagues found that two of the four *DSM-IV-TR* (2000) criteria for AN and three of the five criteria for BN have been challenged in the literature. They found that altering any one of these criteria had relatively little effect on the base rate of EDNOS diagnosis, but altering more than one simultaneously produced greater reductions in the base rate of EDNOS. The *DSM-IV-TR* does allow for professionals to use clinical judgment when using diagnostic criteria, so it is possible to give a diagnosis when symptoms fall just short of meeting the full criteria for a disorder. In fact, a substantial percentage of those with subclinical features of AN or BN go on to meet full diagnostic criteria at a later time (Herzog, Hopkins, & Burns, 1993). Judicious use of clinical judgment when considering an eating disorder diagnosis in a person who just fails to meet full criteria may be useful in cases where an EDNOS diagnosis would result in a lack of care.

Assessment of Binge Eating

One particular dilemma that assessors are likely to encounter during the diagnosis phase of assessment is determining whether a patient is engaging in binge eating. The binge eating debate has been reviewed thoroughly elsewhere (e.g., Anderson, Lundgren, Shapiro, & Paulosky, in press; Anderson & Maloney, 2001), but it is discussed briefly here. According to the *DSM-IV-TR* (2000), a binge episode must involve eating an amount of food that is definitely larger than most people would consider normal under the circumstances and be accompanied by a sense of lack of control over eating during the episode. However, a number of studies have shown that laypersons do not define a binge in these terms. Rather, they rely more on feelings of loss of control and violation of dietary standards to define an eating episode as a binge (Beglin & Fairburn, 1992; Johnson, Boutelle, Torgrud, Davig, & Turner, 2000; Telch, Pratt, & Niego, 1998). These studies suggest that simply asking an individual if they binge eat may lead to an inaccurate diagnosis.

The most common solution for overcoming this bias in assessing binge episodes involves letting a trained expert determine whether an eating episode meets *DSM-IV-TR*

(2000) criteria. For example, the Eating Disorders Examination (EDE; Fairburn & Cooper, 1993; see later discussion) was designed specifically to let the assessor evaluate each eating episode. Examination of self-monitoring has also been suggested as a way to obtain accurate information concerning binge episodes (Crowther & Sherwood, 1997; Williamson, 1990). However, these methods of assessment also have problems. Specifically, large errors in food estimation, particularly overestimation, are extremely common (Anderson, Williamson, Johnson, & Grieve, 1999; Hadigan, LaChaussee, Walsh, & Kissileff, 1992; Schoeller, 1995). Thus, even when patients describe an episode in which it seems that an objectively large amount of food has been eaten, their report may not be accurate.

Perhaps the only way to bypass the problems inherent in self-report of binge eating is to obtain a direct assessment of eating behavior via test meals (see later discussion). However, it may not be possible to administer a test meal for logistical reasons. In such cases, the EDE and food records represent the best options for obtaining accurate information because they allow for expert evaluation of eating episodes. It should be understood, however, that some degree of inaccuracy is inevitable with these methods. Furthermore, because of serious questions concerning accuracy, simple self-report of binge frequency should primarily be used only when accuracy of assessment is not critical.

Denial and Minimization of Eating Disorder Symptoms

Denial, minimization of symptoms, and treatment refusal are common among persons presenting for eating disorders, particularly those with AN (Goldner, Birmingham, & Smye, 1997; Hamburg, Herzog, Brotman, & Stasior, 1989; Harris, Wiseman, Wagner, & Halmi, 2001; Vitousek, Daly, & Heiser, 1991). In extreme cases, the patient completely denies that he or she has an eating disorder, even when there is objective evidence of the problem. This may be particularly true in patients with AN and adolescent patients with AN or BN who are brought to treatment by their parents or legal guardians against their wishes. For example, some patients with AN-like symptoms deny an eating disorder by reporting that they are losing weight because they "just don't feel hungry" or they are "just a picky eater." Similarly, even when caught purging by a friend or family member, some patients maintain that they were simply ill or had food poisoning. It has been suggested that persons with AN and BN deny their disorders for different reasons—those with AN, because they find dieting and thinness both positively and negatively reinforcing, and those with BN, because of a sense of shame concerning their behavior (Hamburg et al., 1989; Hayaki, Friedman, & Brownell, 2002; Vitousek et al., 1991).

Even if they do not completely deny having an eating disorder, patients may still minimize the severity of their problems. This minimization can take many forms. For example, a patient might underreport the frequency of binge-purge episodes or overreport food intake. Another common practice is to acknowledge problematic eating attitudes and behavior but minimize the disorder's impact on their lives or even emphasize the positive aspects of the disorder. Even many patients who are not particularly resistant to treatment can still identify positive aspects of their disorders (Serpell & Treasure, 2002; Serpell, Treasure, Teasdale, & Sullivan, 1999), and the past few years have seen the rise of the "pro-eating disorder" movement on the Internet, which considers eating disorders to be acceptable lifestyle choices (e.g., Graham, 2001).

Not all denial and minimization of symptoms are deliberate; patients may not be able to provide accurate information because of a variety of factors, including difficulty recognizing and expressing internal states and the secondary effects of starvation (Vitousek et al., 1991), as well as cognitive biases that affect information processing and memory (Williamson, Muller, Reas, & Thaw, 1999).

Denial and minimization affect all stages of the assessment process. For example, it may be difficult to identify eating disorder patients who are actively hiding their disorder in the screening or case identification phase of assessment. This is largely because, with the exception of severe weight loss, the central symptoms of AN and BN are covert. Even binge eating and purging, which are overt behavioral acts, are usually done in private. Unfortunately, eating disorder screening measures offer little help in cases of denial or resistance because they are face valid and are easy to "fake good." Thus, it is relatively easy for individuals with BN who do not desire treatment to hide their disorder. Because extreme thinness cannot easily be hidden, it is easier to identify individuals with AN once they have lost sufficient weight to meet the *DSM-IV-TR* (2000) criteria for the disorder (i.e., a loss of 15% or more of expected weight).

Similarly, denial and minimization can play an important role when evaluating treatment outcome. Because many eating disorder patients are at best ambivalent about treatment, there is a risk that they will portray their progress more favorably than may actually be the case to end treatment early. It is particularly difficult to obtain unbiased information from individuals with BN who receive treatment on an outpatient basis; the assessor must rely almost entirely on self-report to evaluate treatment progress. AN is more likely than BN to be treated on an inpatient basis, where it is easier to monitor changes in eating and weight gain. However, it is still extremely difficult to monitor other aspects of the disorder that are covert (e.g., fear of fatness). Not all phases of assessment are as vulnerable to denial and minimization, however; Vitousek and colleagues (1991) have suggested that denial and minimization do not hinder the diagnosis stage of assessment because eating disorder specialists are capable of eliciting accurate information from patients once an eating disorder is suspected.

Some strategies have been recommended in cases in which the assessor suspects denial or minimization. Williamson (1990) provides a number of suggestions, including obtaining collateral reports from significant others and using test meals. Vitousek and colleagues (1991) provide a number of suggestions for overcoming denial and distortion in a research context, including providing reinforcement for accurate self-report, separating research and therapy, and asking for behavioral responses rather than purely verbal ones.

COMMONLY USED MEASURES FOR ASSESSMENT OF EATING-RELATED PATHOLOGY

In this section, we review instruments designed to assess eating-related pathology. This list is by no means exhaustive; there is at least one entire book devoted to measures for eating disorders (Allison, 1995). This section is devoted to measures that are widely used in the literature and have good psychometric properties. As Crowther and Sherwood (1997) have noted, assessment of the eating disorders is best conceptualized as a process that occurs throughout treatment and accomplishes several purposes, including diagnosis, treatment planning, and evaluation of outcome. Accordingly, we have included suggestions for which phase(s) of treatment each measure is best suited.

Interviews

Semistructured: Eating Disorder Examination

The EDE (Fairburn & Cooper, 1993) was designed to assess symptoms of AN and BN and related psychopathology; it includes two behavioral indexes (Overeating and Methods of Extreme Weight Control) and four subscales (eating concern, restraint, shape concern, and weight concern). The EDE can be used to differentiate eating-disordered patients from controls (Cooper, Cooper, & Fairburn, 1989) as well as between persons with BN and restrained eaters (Cooper et al., 1989; Rosen, Vara, Wendt, & Leitenberg, 1990; Wilson & Smith, 1989). The overeating subscale is significantly positively correlated with daily caloric intake (Rosen et al., 1990).

Part of the reason for the EDE's acceptance has been its demonstrated reliability and validity. Interrater reliability for individual items and subscales has been found to be good (Cooper & Fairburn, 1987; Fairburn & Cooper, 1993). The test also has good test-retest reliability (Rizvi, Peterson, Crow, & Agras, 2000) and good internal consistency (Cooper et al., 1989). It has also demonstrated good discriminant and concurrent validity (Fairburn & Cooper, 1993). Another major strength of the EDE involves assessing binge eating. In the EDE, the interviewer, not the interviewee, decides whether a particular episode is a binge or not. This minimizes some, but not all, of the problems inherent in the assessment of binge eating (see previous discussion).

The EDE is not without its faults, however. First, it has been recommended that interviewers be trained to administer the EDE, and the interview can take more than an hour to complete (Wilson, 1993), which makes it impractical for clinical use. Second, one review found discrepancies between the EDE and other instruments in assessing the rate of binge eating, purgative episodes, and shape and weight concerns, which raises questions about the instrument's concurrent validity (Anderson & Maloney, 2001). Third, it is not clear whether the amounts of food reported by interviewees are accurate, which can influence the assessment of binge eating.

In conclusion, despite some shortcomings, the EDE is one of the most commonly used assessment methods in the outcome literature and is widely considered the gold standard for the assessment of eating disorders (Fairburn & Beglin, 1994). It is perhaps best used for diagnosis and assessment of treatment outcome in research studies, but it is probably too cumbersome to be used routinely in clinical practice.

Unstructured

Although their psychometric status is unknown, unstructured clinical interviews are an extremely common assessment tool. It is beyond the scope of this chapter to provide detailed guidelines for conducting an unstructured interview for eating-related pathology; Crowther and Sherwood (1997) provide such guidelines.

Self-Report Measures of General Eating Disorder Symptoms

Self-report measures have some advantages over interviews. In particular, they are easier to administer, and it has been suggested that patients admit eating-related problems more readily when they do not have to respond face-to-face with an interviewer (Keel, Crow, Davis, & Mitchell, 2002).

Eating Attitudes Test (EAT)

The EAT (Garner & Garfinkel, 1979) is a 40-item, self-report inventory originally intended to assess the symptoms of AN. A subsequent factor analysis found that 26 of the original 40 items accounted for most of the variance in total score; these items were termed the EAT-26 (Garner, Olmstead, Bohr, & Garfinkel, 1982). Many other versions of the EAT have been developed, including a computer-based version (Murrelle, Ainsworth, Bulger, Holliman, & Bulger, 1992), versions for children in grades three to six (Maloney, McGuire, & Daniels, 1988) and grades six to eight (Smolak & Levine, 1994), and several foreign language versions (Garfinkel & Newman, 2001).

The EAT, one of the first measures developed for the assessment of eating disorders, has been the subject of a number of psychometric studies (Garfinkel & Newman, 2001). While much of this research was done on the original version of the measure, the correlation between the EAT and EAT-26 is extremely high (r = .98; Garner et al., 1982). The EAT has been found to have good internal consistency and good test-retest reliability (Banasiak, Wertheim, Koerner, & Voudouris, 2001; Carter & Moss, 1984; Garner & Garfinkel, 1979). It also has good concurrent and discriminant validity with other eating disorder measures (Garner, 1997; Garfinkel & Newman, 2001; Williamson, Anderson, Jackman, & Jackson, 1995). The EAT is able to differentiate AN, BN, and BED from controls and can differentiate AN and BN from BED (Garfinkel & Newman, 2001; Williamson, Prather, McKenzie, & Blouin, 1990). It cannot, however, differentiate AN from BN (Garfinkel & Newman, 2001; Williamson et al., 1995).

The EAT has seven factors and the EAT-26 has three factors (Garfinkel & Newman, 2001); however, only the total score is commonly used in the literature. Norms are available for AN, BN, and BED, as well as for obese, female, and male controls (Garfinkel & Newman, 2001; Williamson et al., 1995). Scores of 30 on the EAT and 20 on the EAT-26 have been suggested as cutoff scores to identify individuals at risk for eating disorders (Garfinkel & Newman, 2001; Garner et al., 1982).

While the EAT (or EAT-26) cannot diagnose specific eating disorders, it may be used in research or clinical practice as a screening measure of general eating concerns. It is important to note, however, that high scores on the EAT do not provide definitive evidence of an eating disorder; further evaluation in such cases is necessary (Garfinkel & Newman, 2001). The EAT can also be used as a repeat assessment instrument to chart overall treatment progress (Garner, 1997).

Eating Disorders Inventory (EDI)

The original version of the EDI (Garner, Olmstead, & Polivy, 1983) was developed to assess the symptoms of AN and BN. It consists of eight scales: Bulimia, Body Dissatisfaction, Drive for Thinness, Ineffectiveness, Interoceptive Awareness, Interpersonal Distrust, Maturity Fears, and Perfectionism. The current version (EDI-2; Garner,

1991) includes three new scales: Asceticism, Impulse Regulation, and Social Insecurity, bringing the total number of items to 91.

Test-retest reliability for the original EDI is adequate (Crowther, Lilly, Crawford, & Shepard, 1992). For the EDI-2, better internal consistency for the original eight scales was found than for the three new scales (Eberenz & Gleaves, 1994). The EDI has been shown to discriminate between individuals with AN and controls (Garner et al., 1983), BN and controls (Schoemaker, Verbraak, Breteler, & van der Staak, 1997), and purging AN from nonpurging AN patients (Garner et al., 1983). Norms are available for adults (Garner, 1991) and adolescents (Rosen, Silberg, & Gross, 1988; Shore & Porter, 1990).

The Drive for Thinness, Bulimia, and Body Dissatisfaction scales appear to be most directly related to eating-disordered behavior and are most strongly correlated with eating-related pathology (Garner et al., 1983; Hurley, Palmer, & Stretch, 1990). However, scores on a number of the other scales have also been shown to be related to treatment outcome, and reductions in many of the EDI scores are seen in successfully treated patients with eating disorders (Anderson & Maloney, 2001; Bizeul, Sadowsky, & Rigaud, 2001; Thiel, Zueger, Jacoby, & Schuessler, 1998). In addition, scores on the Bulimia, Ineffectiveness, and Social Insecurity scales of the EDI have been found to be positively correlated with problematic eating behavior in nonbinge eating situations (Bourne, Bryant, Griffiths, Touyz, & Beumont, 1998).

The EDI is a commonly used assessment instrument in the treatment outcome literature. While not appropriate for diagnosis, the EDI can be extremely useful as both a screening measure and a measure for tracking progress throughout treatment.

Bulimia Test-Revised (BULIT-R)

The Bulimia Test (BULIT; Smith & Thelen, 1984) was developed as an inventory of the symptoms of BN. Its revision, the BULIT-R (Thelen, Farmer, Wonderlich, & Smith, 1991) updated the original test to conform to *DSM-III-R* criteria (APA, 1987). Correlation between the original BULIT and BULIT-R are extremely high ($r = .99$; Thelen et al., 1991), and the latest version contains 28 items.

Internal consistency reliability and test-retest reliability over a two-month interval for the BULIT-R were both good (Thelen et al., 1991). The measure has excellent concurrent, predictive, and discriminant validity (Williamson et al., 1995). It can discriminate between BN patients and those with AN and controls.

The authors of the BULIT-R recommended that a cutoff of 104 be used to differentiate individuals with BN from controls (Thelen et al., 1991), although lower cutoff scores have been recommended in cases where it is important to minimize false negatives (Welch, Thompson, & Hall, 1993).

The BULIT-R was designed specifically for detecting the symptoms of BN; it is not recommended for AN or BED populations. It is most useful as a screening measure in cases where BN is suspected, and it is also an excellent measure for tracking progress throughout treatment for BN.

Eating Disorder Diagnostic Scale (EDDS)

The EDDS (Stice, Telch, & Rizvi, 2000) is a 22-item, self-report inventory designed to diagnose BED, AN, and BN according to *DSM-IV* criteria (APA, 1994).

The EDDS has satisfactory test-retest reliability at a one-week interval, particularly for AN (Stice et al., 2000). Internal consistency reliability is also high, and the EDDS has demonstrated good content validity and convergent validity (Stice et al., 2000). One particular strength is that because of the controversy over the concept of a binge (see previous discussion), the term *binge* is not used in any of the questions on the scale.

The EDDS is a new measure, and it has not yet been widely used in the literature. However, it is a promising new assessment instrument for use in the diagnosis of eating disorders and deserves further study.

Self-Report Measures of Specific Eating-Related Domains

Several measures have been developed to assess specific constructs thought to be particularly important in the development and maintenance of the eating disorders. We briefly review some of these constructs and the measures developed for their assessment.

Restraint

Dietary restraint has long been thought to play a central role in the development and maintenance of eating disorders (Fairburn, 1997; Heatherton & Baumeister, 1991; Lowe, 1993; Polivy & Herman, 1993; Stice, Shaw, & Nemeroff, 1998). There has been a great deal of disagreement concerning how restraint should be assessed, however (Gorman & Allison, 1995; Heatherton, Herman, Polivy, King, & McGree, 1988; Lowe, 1993). We briefly review the most commonly used measures of restraint and discuss some differences between them.

The Restraint Scale (RS)   The RS (Herman & Polivy, 1980) is a 10-item, self-report questionnaire meant to identify chronic dieters. The RS appears to measure the consequences of chronic, unsuccessful dieting such as disinhibited eating and weight fluctuations (Gorman & Allison, 1995; Heatherton et al., 1988; Laessle, Tuschl, Kotthaus, & Pirke, 1989b; Lowe, 1993).

Several factor analyses of the RS have identified two subscales, termed Weight Fluctuation and Concern for Dieting, but the items loading on each factor have been inconsistent (van Strien, Breteler, & Ouwens, 2002). Some researchers have argued that the total score, not the factor scores, be used (Heatherton et al., 1988), while others have suggested the opposite (Van Strien et al., 2002). The use of the total score is more common in the literature.

Internal consistency is adequate for the overall RS and its two subscales (Allison, Kalinsky, & Gorman, 1992; Gorman & Allison, 1995; van Strien et al., 2002). Test-retest reliability has been found to be good (Gorman & Allison, 1995). The RS is able to predict obesity and weight change (Gorman & Allison, 1995), which shows support for construct validity of the scale.

Three-Factor Eating Questionnaire—Cognitive Restraint Scale (TFEQ-R)   The TFEQ (Stunkard & Messick, 1985) contains three factors: Cognitive Control of Eating, Disinhibition, and Susceptibility to Hunger. The TFEQ-R is the most commonly used of the three scales and contains 21 items. While the TFEQ-R was designed to expand on the RS, it appears to measure a slightly different aspect of restraint. Although it is commonly purported to measure short-term caloric restriction, it has been argued that individuals scoring high on the TFEQ-R may not actually be successfully reducing their intake to hypocaloric levels (Gorman & Allison, 1995; Heatherton et al., 1988; Laessle et al., 1989a, 1989b; Lowe, 1993; Tuschl, Laessle, Platte, & Pirke, 1990). Test-retest reliability of the TFEQ is good over two weeks (Allison et al., 1992) and one month (Stunkard & Messick, 1985). Convergent and divergent validity are also good (Gorman & Allison, 1995).

Dutch Eating Behavior Questionnaire (DEBQ)   The DEBQ (Van Strien, Frijters, Bergers, & Defares, 1986) is a 33-item inventory measuring three factors of eating behavior (restrained eating, emotional eating, and external eating). The emotional eating factor can be further broken down into eating in response to general emotions and eating in response to specific emotions. Of the three main scales, the restraint scale is the most reliable and valid and is a good measure of dieting behavior in its purest sense (Gorman & Allison, 1995).

The DEBQ has good test-retest reliability (Allison et al., 1992; Banasiak et al., 2001). The restraint scale of the DEBQ has high internal consistency (Gorman & Allison, 1995). The DEBQ in its entirety is able to differentiate between female patients with AN, BN, and women attending weight loss groups (Wardle, 1987). Other support for the validity of the DEBQ is questionable, and further research has been called for (Schlundt, 1995).

Body Image

Body image disturbance is thought to be an important factor contributing to eating disorders. Chapter 24 in this book covers the assessment of body image disturbance in detail.

Behavioral Assessment of Eating Disorder Pathology

Behavioral assessment procedures are designed to obtain a more direct measure of eating behavior than can be obtained via self-report questionnaires or interview. The two most common behavioral assessment procedures are reviewed here.

Self-Monitoring

Self-monitoring, broadly defined, is perhaps the most widely used assessment procedure in the assessment of eating pathology. It is particularly useful because it provides a fine-grained analysis of eating behavior and its surrounding context over time.

Many aspects of eating behavior can be monitored, including direct aspects of food intake and eating pathology (type and amount of food eaten, whether the amount eaten was a binge, whether the patient engaged in purgative behavior following the episode) as well as the larger context surrounding each eating episode (location, time of day, mood before and after eating, hunger before and after eating). Although there are no standardized procedures for self-monitoring, model forms are available (e.g., Schlundt, 1995; Williamson, 1990).

While self-monitoring can provide important data, this data is vulnerable to serious errors in accuracy. Some of the sources of error have already been discussed (e.g., deliberate minimization, inaccuracy in food estimation), but a host of other problems call the reliability and validity of self-monitoring data into question (Schlundt, 1995; Wolper, Heshka, & Heymsfield, 1995). In particular, estimation of exact caloric intake is elusive (Anderson et al., 1999; Schoeller, 1995; Wolper et al., 1995). Nevertheless, when viewed with appropriate caution, self-monitoring can provide useful information during all phases of the treatment process.

Test Meals

Test meals have been called "the quintessence of behavioral assessment of eating disorders" (Williamson, 1990, p. 43). They allow an assessor to bypass some of the problems inherent in self-report of eating by directly examining eating behavior. They also allow for the collection of information unobtainable by other means (e.g., rate of eating).

Test meals can be used in a number of ways in assessment. For example, during initial assessment, test meals can be extremely useful in cases where the assessor suspects denial or minimization of eating disorder symptoms. In such cases, the assessor asks that the patient come to the assessment session without having eaten for several hours. The patient is then asked to consume a food or foods that include typical "fear foods," such as a candy bar, potato chips, or fast food. Refusal to eat the test meal allows the assessor to confront the patient more directly about denial and minimization of symptoms.

Test meals can also be useful in assessing treatment progress (Williamson, 1990). In this case, a meal consisting of standard servings from each of the food groups is administered, and the amount of each food and overall calories consumed is calculated. The same meal is then administered periodically throughout treatment; the amount eaten can be used as an index of dietary restraint and change in the amount of food and calories consumed as an index of treatment progress.

Finally, a hierarchy of feared food can also be used as part of an exposure-type intervention, with test meals conceptualized as exposure sessions (e.g., Leitenberg, Rosen, Gross, Nudelman, & Vara, 1988; Williamson, 1990). Used in this way, progress along the hierarchy becomes an index of treatment progress.

In summary, test meals can provide direct information about eating behavior, progress in treatment, and dietary restraint beyond the information gathered via interview, questionnaire, or self-monitoring. Unfortunately, test meals do not appear to be used widely as an assessment tool (Andersen, 1995; Anderson & Maloney, 2001; Anderson, Williamson, Johnson, & Grieve, 2001), possibly because of practical concerns (e.g., preparing or obtaining food, time to administer the meal).

PATTERNS OF USE OF ASSESSMENT MEASURES

This chapter has reviewed only a few of the numerous assessment instruments developed for the assessment of eating disorder and eating-related pathology. A book of assessment measures for obesity and eating disorders published in the mid-1990s identified well over 60 measures in the literature at that time (Allison, 1995), and the number has increased since then. To determine which of the large number of these measures are commonly used in the research literature, 43 BN treatment studies were reviewed, including studies of both pharmacological and cognitive-behavioral interventions. The studies were obtained from previous reviews (Anderson & Maloney, 2001; Hartman, Hergoz, & Drinkmann, 1991; Keel & Mitchell, 1997; Walsh, 1991; Whittal, Agras, & Gould, 1999; Williamson, Anderson, & Gleaves, 1996) as well as a Psycinfo literature search using keywords "bulimia" and "treatment" and "outcome."

This review found that the eating disorders treatment outcome literature is dominated by relatively few assessment instruments. While a large number of instruments exist for the assessment of eating disordered thoughts, feelings, and behaviors, only 26 of these instruments were used in one or more treatment studies. Furthermore, of these 26, four instruments were clearly the most frequently used. Self-report of binge eating and purgative episodes were the most frequently used outcome measures overall (for binge eating: 34 studies, 79%; for purgative episodes: 33 studies, 77%). Three psychometrically validated measures (two self-report inventories and one interview) were also commonly used. The EAT was the most frequently used self-report inventory (21 studies, 49%), followed closely by the EDI and EDI-2, which together were used in 19 studies (44%). The EDE was used in eight studies (19%). The EDE was particularly common in more recent studies; many of the studies reviewed predated its development.

A similar literature review examining the AN treatment outcome literature was conducted with far fewer studies available for review. Results were similar to the review for BN, with the EAT and EDI also commonly used to assess AN. Additionally, the Morgan-Russell Outcome Assessment Schedule (Morgan & Hayward, 1988), a structured clinical interview, was frequently used.

In summary, the eating disorders treatment outcome literature indicates the use of relatively few assessment instruments, compared to the number of existing assessment measures. The implications of this finding are discussed in the next section.

FUTURE DIRECTIONS

A large number of assessment instruments devoted to the assessment of eating disorder pathology are available. However, relatively few of these measures appear to be used in the research literature. Viewed in one light, this is a strength, because most of these instruments have good psychometric properties and the use of a small number of instruments allows for direct comparisons of treatment effectiveness across research studies. However, the reliance on only a few measures has also led to shortcomings in the eating disorder literature. In particular, relatively few treatment studies assess all the domains thought to be central to the maintenance of eating disorders, and thus leave gaps in our understanding of effective treatments for these disorders (e.g., Anderson & Maloney, 2001). The use of additional assessment instruments will broaden our understanding of the critical factors associated with the development and treatment of eating disorders.

Another shortcoming in the eating disorder literature concerns the use of assessment instruments in actual clinical practice. To date, there has been no systematic evaluation of what assessment methods are used routinely in a clinical context. Issues of reliability and validity are no less important in clinical practice than in research, although the exact issues facing researchers and clinicians are not likely to be identical. Efforts should be undertaken to determine what problems of assessment routinely occur in a practice context and how to address those problems.

REFERENCES

Allison, D. B. (1995). *Handbook of assessment methods for eating behaviors and weight-related problems.* Newbury Park, CA: Sage.

Allison, D. B., Kalinsky, L. B., & Gorman, B. S. (1992). The comparative psychometric properties of three measures of dietary restraining. *Psychological Assessment, 4,* 391–398.

American Psychiatric Association. (1987). *Diagnostic and statistical manual of mental disorders* (3rd ed., rev.). Washington, DC: Author.

American Psychiatric Association. (1994). *Diagnostic and statistical manual of mental disorders* (4th ed.). Washington, DC: Author.

American Psychiatric Association. (2000). *Diagnostic and statistical manual of mental disorders* (4th ed., text rev.). Washington, DC: Author.

Andersen, A. E. (1995). A standard test meal to assess treatment response in anorexia nervosa patients. *Eating Disorders: Journal of Treatment and Prevention, 3,* 47–55.

Andersen, A. E., Bowers, W. A., & Watson, T. (2001). A slimming program for eating disorders not otherwise specified: Reconceptualizing a confusing, residual diagnostic category. *Psychiatric Clinics of North America, 24,* 271–280.

Anderson, D. A., Lundgren, J. D., Shapiro, J. R., & Paulosky, C. (in press). Clinical assessment of eating disorders: Review and recommendations. *Behavior Modification.*

Anderson, D. A., & Maloney, K. C. (2001). The efficacy of cognitive-behavioral therapy on the core symptoms of bulimia nervosa. *Clinical Psychology Review, 21,* 971–988.

Anderson, D. A., Williamson, D. A., Johnson, W. G., & Grieve, C. O. (1999). Estimation of food intake: Effects of the unit of estimation. *Eating and Weight Disorders, 4,* 6–9.

Anderson, D. A., Williamson, D. A., Johnson, W. G., & Grieve, C. O. (2001). Validity of test meals for determining binge eating. *Eating Behaviors, 2,* 105–112.

Banasiak, S. J., Wertheim, E. H., Koerner, J., & Voudouris, V. J. (2001). Test-retest reliability and internal consistency of a variety of measures of dietary restraint and body concerns in a sample of adolescent girls. *International Journal of Eating Disorders, 29,* 85–89.

Beglin, S. J., & Fairburn, C. G. (1992). What is meant by the term "binge"? *American Journal of Psychiatry, 149,* 123–124.

Bizeul, C., Sadowsky, N., & Rigaud, D. (2001). The prognostic value of initial EDI scores in anorexia nervosa patients: A prospective follow-up study of 5–10 years. *European Psychiatry, 16,* 232–238.

Bourne, S. K., Bryant, R. A., Griffiths, R. A., Touyz, S. W., & Beumont, P. J. V. (1998). Bulimia nervosa, restrained, and unrestrained eaters: A comparison of nonbinge eating behavior. *International Journal of Eating Disorders, 24,* 185–192.

Bunnell, D. W., Shenker, I. R., Nussbaum, M. P., Jacobson, M. S., & Cooper, P. (1990). Subclinical versus formal eating disorders: Differentiating psychological features. *International Journal of Eating Disorders, 9,* 357–362.

Campbell, D. T., & Fiske, D. W. (1959). Convergent and discriminant validation by the multitrait-multimethod matrix. *Psychological Bulletin, 56,* 81–105.

Carter, P. E., & Moss, R. A. (1984). Screening for anorexia and bulimia nervosa in a college population: Problems and limitations. *Addictive Behaviors, 9,* 17–31.

Cooper, Z., Cooper, P. J., & Fairburn, C. G. (1989). The validity of the Eating Disorder Examination and its subscales. *British Journal of Psychiatry, 154,* 807–812.

Cooper, Z., & Fairburn, C. G. (1987). The Eating Disorders Examination: A semistructured interview for the assessment of the specific psychopathology of eating disorders. *International Journal of Eating Disorders, 6,* 1–8.

Crocker, L., & Algina, J. (1986). *Introduction to classical and modern test theory.* Ft. Worth, TX: Harcourt, Brace and Jovanovich.

Crowther, J. H., Lilly, R. S., Crawford, P. A., & Shepard, K. L. (1992). The stability of the Eating Disorder Inventory. *International Journal of Eating Disorders, 12,* 97–101.

Crowther, J. H., & Sherwood, N. E. (1997). Assessment. In D. M. Garner & P. E. Garfinkel (Eds.), *Handbook of treatment for eating disorders* (2nd ed., pp. 34–49). New York: Guilford Press.

Eberenz, K. P., & Gleaves, D. H. (1994). An examination of the internal consistency and factor structure of the Eating Disorders Inventory-2 in a clinical sample. *International Journal of Eating Disorders, 16,* 371–379.

Fairburn, C. G. (1997). Eating disorders. In D. M. Clark & C. G. Fairburn (Eds.), *The science and practice of cognitive behavior therapy* (pp. 209–242). Oxford, England: Oxford University Press.

Fairburn, C. G., & Beglin, S. J. (1994). Assessment of eating disorders: Interview or self-report questionnaire? *International Journal of Eating Disorders, 16,* 363–370.

Fairburn, C. G., & Cooper, Z. (1993). The eating disorder examination. In C. G. Fairburn & G. T. Wilson (Eds.), *Binge eating: Nature, assessment, and treatment* (12th ed., pp. 317–360). New York: Guilford Press.

Garfinkel, P. E., & Newman, A. (2001). The Eating Attitudes Test: Twenty-five years later. *Eating and Weight Disorders, 6,* 1–24.

Garner, D. M. (1991). *Eating Disorder Inventory-2 manual.* Odessa, FL: Psychological Assessment Resources.

Garner, D. M. (1997). Psychoeducational principles in treatment. In D. M. Garner & P. E. Garfinkel (Eds.), *Handbook of treatment for eating disorders* (2nd ed., pp. 145–177). New York: Guilford Press.

Garner, D. M., & Garfinkel, P. E. (1979). The Eating Attitudes Test: An index of the symptoms of anorexia nervosa. *Psychological Medicine, 9,* 273–279.

Garner, D. M., Olmstead, M. P., Bohr, Y., & Garfinkel, P. E. (1982). The Eating Attitudes Test: Psychometric features and clinical correlates. *Psychological Medicine, 12,* 871–878.

Garner, D. M., Olmstead, M. P., & Polivy, J. (1983). Development and validation of a multidimensional eating disorder inventory for anorexia nervosa and bulimia. *International Journal of Eating Disorders, 2,* 15–34.

Goldner, E. M., Birmingham, C. L., & Smye, V. (1997). Addressing treatment refusal in anorexia nervosa: Clinical, ethical, and legal considerations. In D. M. Garner & P. E. Garfinkel (Eds.), *Handbook of treatment for eating disorders* (2nd ed., pp. 450–461). New York: Guilford Press.

Gorman, B. S., & Allison, D. B. (1995). Measures of restrained eating. In D. B. Allison (Ed.), *Handbook of assessment methods for eating behaviors and weight-related problems* (pp. 149–184). Newbury Park, CA: Sage.

Graham, J. (2001, August 5). Web sites offer "blueprint" for anorexia. *Seattle Times,* p. A11.

Hadigan, C. M., LaChaussee, J. L., Walsh, B. T., & Kissileff, H. R. (1992). 24-hour dietary recall in patients with bulimia nervosa. *International Journal of Eating Disorders, 12,* 107–111.

Hamburg, P., Herzog, D. B., Brotman, A. W., & Stasior, J. K. (1989). The treatment resistant eating disordered patient. *Psychiatric Annals, 19,* 494–499.

Harris, W. A., Wiseman, C. V., Wagner, S., & Halmi, K. A. (2001). The difficult-to-treat patient with eating disorder. In M. J. Dewan & R. W. Pies (Eds.), *The difficult-to-treat psychiatric patient* (pp. 243–271). Washington, DC: American Psychiatric Press.

Hartman, A., Hergoz, T., & Drinkman, A. (1991). Psychotherapy of bulimia nervosa: What is effective? A meta-analysis. *Journal of Psychosomatic Research, 36,* 159–167.

Hayaki, J., Friedman, M. A., & Brownell, K. D. (2002). Shame and severity of bulimic symptoms. *Eating Behaviors, 3,* 73–83.

Heatherton, T. F., & Baumeister, R. F. (1991). Binge-eating as an escape from awareness. *Psychological Bulletin, 110,* 86–108.

Heatherton, T. F., Herman, C. P., Polivy, J., King, G. A., & McGree, S. T. (1988). The (Mis)measurement of restraint: An analysis of conceptual and psychometric issues. *Journal of Abnormal Psychology, 97,* 19–28.

Heatherton, T. F., Nichols, P., Mahamedi, F., & Keel, P. (1995). Body weight, dieting, and eating disorder symptoms among college students, 1982 to 1992. *American Journal of Psychiatry, 152,* 1623–1629.

Herman, C. P., & Polivy, J. (1980). Restrained eating. In A. J. Stunkard (Ed.), *Obesity* (pp. 208–225). Philadelphia: Saunders.

Herzog, D. B., Hopkins, J. D., & Burns, C. D. (1993). A follow-up study of 33 subdiagnostic eating disordered women. *International Journal of Eating Disorders, 14,* 261–267.

Hurley, J. B., Palmer, R. L., & Stretch, D. (1990). The specificity of the Eating Disorders Inventory: A reappraisal. *International Journal of Eating Disorders, 9,* 419–424.

Johnson, W. G., Boutelle, K. N., Torgrud, L., Davig, J. P., & Turner, S. (2000). What is a binge? The influence of amount, duration, and loss of control criteria on judgments of binge eating. *International Journal of Eating Disorders, 27,* 471–479.

Joint Committee on Standards for Educational and Psychological Testing of the American Educational Research Association, American Psychological Association, & National Council on Measurement in Education. (1999). *Standards for educational and psychological testing.* Washington, DC: American Educational Research Association.

Keel, P. K., Crow, S., Davis, T. L., & Mitchell, J. E. (2002). Assessment of eating disorders: Comparison of interview and questionnaire data from a long-term follow-up study of bu limia nervosa. *Journal of Psychosomatic Research, 53,* 1043–1047.

Keel, P. K., & Mitchell, J. E. (1997). Outcome in bulimia nervosa. *American Journal of Psychiatry, 154,* 313–321.

Laessle, R. G., Tuschl, R. J., Kotthaus, B. C., & Pirke, K. M. (1989a). Behavioral and biological correlates of dietary restraint in everyday life. *Appetite, 12,* 83–94.

Laessle, R. G., Tuschl, R. J., Kotthaus, B. C., & Pirke, K. M. (1989b). A comparison of the validity of three scales for the assessment of dietary restraint. *Journal of Abnormal Psychology, 98,* 412–420.

Leitenberg, H., Rosen, J. C., Gross, J., Nudelman, S., & Vara, L. S. (1988). Exposure plus response prevention in treatment for bulimia nervosa. *Journal of Consulting and Clinical Psychology, 56,* 535–541.

Lowe, M. R. (1993). The effects of dieting on eating behavior: A three-factor model. *Psychological Bulletin, 114,* 100–121.

Maloney, M. J., McGuire, J. B., & Daniels, S. R. (1988). Reliability testing of a children's version of the Eating Attitudes Test. *Journal of the American Academy of Child and Adolescent Psychiatry, 24,* 541–543.

Morgan, H. G., & Hayward, A. E. (1988). Clinical assessment of anorexia nervosa: The Morgan-Russell Outcome Assessment Schedule. *British Journal of Psychiatry, 152,* 367–371.

Murrelle, L., Ainsworth, B. E., Bulger, J. D., Holliman, S. C., & Bulger, D. W. (1992). Computerized mental health risk appraisal for college students: User acceptability and correlation with standard paper-and-pencil questionnaires. *American Journal of Health Promotion, 7,* 90–92.

Nicholls, D., Chater, R., & Lask, B. (2000). Children into *DSM* don't go: A comparison of classification systems for eating disorders in childhood and early adolescence. *International Journal of Eating Disorders, 28,* 317–324.

Pedhazur, E. J., & Schmelkin, L. P. (1991). *Measurement, design, and analysis: An integrated approach.* Hillsdale, NJ: Erlbaum.

Polivy, J., & Herman, C. P. (1993). Etiology of binge eating: Psychological mechanisms. In C. G. Fairburn & G. T. Wilson (Eds.), *Binge eating: Nature, assessment, and treatment* (pp. 173–205). New York: Guilford Press.

128 Eating Disorders

Ricca, V., Mannucci, E., Mezzani, B., Di Bernardo, M., Zucchi, T., Paionni, A., et al. (2001). Psychopathological and clinical features of outpatients with an eating disorder not otherwise specified. *Eating and Weight Disorders, 6,* 157–165.

Rizvi, S. L., Peterson, C. B., Crow, J. C., & Agras, W. S. (2000). Test-retest reliability of the Eating Disorder Examination. *International Journal of Eating Disorders, 28,* 311–316.

Rosen, J. C., Silberg, N. T., & Gross, J. (1988). Eating Attitudes Test and Eating Disorders Inventory: Norms for adolescent girls and boys. *Journal of Consulting and Clinical Psychology, 56,* 305–308.

Rosen, J. C., Vara, L., Wendt, S., & Leitenberg, H. (1990). Validity studies of the Eating Disorder Examination. *International Journal of Eating Disorders, 9,* 519–528.

Schlundt, D. G. (1995). Assessment of specific eating behaviors and eating style. In D. B. Allison (Ed.), *Methods for the assessment of eating behaviors and weight related problems* (pp. 142–302). Newbury Park, CA: Sage.

Schoeller, D. A. (1995). Limitations in the assessment of dietary energy intake by self-report. *Metabolism, 44*(Suppl. 2), 18–22.

Schoemaker, E. J., Verbraak, M., Breteler, R., & van der Staak, C. (1997). The discriminant validity of the Eating Disorder Inventory-2. *British Journal of Clinical Psychology, 36,* 627–629.

Serpell, L., & Treasure, J. (2002). Bulimia nervosa: Friend or foe? The pros and cons of bulimia nervosa. *International Journal of Eating Disorders, 32,* 164–170.

Serpell, L., Treasure, J., Teasdale, J., & Sullivan, V. (1999). Anorexia nervosa: Friend or foe? *International Journal of Eating Disorders, 25,* 177–186.

Shore, R. A., & Porter, J. E. (1990). Normative and reliability data for 11 to 18 year olds on the Eating Disorders Inventory. *International Journal of Eating Disorders, 9,* 201–207.

Smith, M. C., & Thelen, M. H. (1984). Development and validation of a test for bulimia. *Journal of Consulting and Clinical Psychology, 52,* 863–872.

Smolak, L., & Levine, M. P. (1994). Psychometric properties of the Children's Eating Attitudes Test. *International Journal of Eating Disorders, 20,* 275–334.

Stice, E., Shaw, H., & Nemeroff, C. (1998). Dual pathway model of bulimia nervosa: Longitudinal support for dietary restraint and affect-regulation mechanisms. *Journal of Social and Clinical Psychology, 17,* 129–149.

Stice, E., Telch, C. F., & Rizvi, S. L. (2000). Development and validation of the Eating Disorder Diagnostic Scale: A brief self-report measure of anorexia, bulimia, and binge-eating disorder. *Psychological Assessment, 12*(2), 123–131.

Stunkard, A. J., & Messick, S. (1985). The Three Factor Eating Questionnaire to measure dietary restraining, disinhibition, and hunger. *Journal of Psychosomatic Research, 29,* 71–81.

Telch, C. F., Pratt, E. M., & Niego, S. H. (1998). Obese women with binge eating disorder define the term binge. *International Journal of Eating Disorders, 24,* 313–317.

Thaw, J. M., Williamson, D. A., & Martin, C. K. (2001). Impact of altering *DSM-IV* criteria for anorexia and bulimia nervosa on the base rates of eating disorder diagnoses. *Eating and Weight Disorders, 6,* 121–129.

Thelen, M. H., Farmer, J., Wonderlich, S., & Smith, M. (1991). A revision of the bulimia test: The BULIT-R. *Psychological Assessment, 3,* 119–124.

Thiel, A., Zueger, M., Jacoby, G. E., & Schuessler, G. (1998). Thirty-month outcome in patients with anorexia or bulimia nervosa and concomitant obsessive-compulsive disorder. *American Journal of Psychiatry, 155,* 244–249.

Thorndike, R. L. (1949). *Personnel selection: Test and measurement techniques.* New York: Wiley.

Tuschl, R. J., Laessle, R. G., Platte, P., & Pirke, K. M. (1990). Differences in food-choice frequencies between restrained and unrestrained eaters. *Appetite, 14,* 9–13.

Van Strien, T., Breteler, M. H. M., & Ouwens, M. A. (2002). Restraint scale, its subscales concern for dieting and weight fluctuation. *Personality and Individual Differences, 33,* 791–802.

Van Strien, T., Frijters, J. E. R., Bergers, G. P. A., & Defares, P. B. (1986). The Dutch Eating Behavior Questionnaire (DEBQ) for assessment of restrained, emotional, and external eating behavior. *International Journal of Eating Disorders, 5,* 295–315.

Vitousek, K. B., Daly, J., & Heiser, C. (1991). Reconstructing the internal world of the eating-disordered individual: Overcoming denial and distortion in self-report. *International Journal of Eating Disorders, 6,* 647–666.

Walsh, B. T. (1991). Psychopharmacologic treatment of bulimia nervosa. *Journal of Clinical Psychiatry, 52*(Suppl. 10), 34–38.

Wardle, J. (1987). Eating style: A validation study of the Dutch Eating Behavior Questionnaire in normal subjects and women with eating disorders. *Journal of Psychosomatic Research, 31*(2), 161–169.

Welch, G., Thompson, L., & Hall, A. (1993). The BULIT-R: Its reliability and clinical validity as a screening tool for *DSM-III-R* bulimia nervosa in a female tertiary education population. *International Journal of Eating Disorders, 14,* 95–105.

Whitaker, A. H. (1992). An epidemiological study of anorectic and bulimic symptoms in adolescent girls: Implications for pediatricians. *Pediatric Annals, 21,* 752–759.

Whittal, M. L., Agras, W. S., & Gould, R. A. (1999). Bulimia nervosa: A meta-analysis of psychosocial and pharmacological treatments. *Behavior Therapy, 30,* 117–135.

Williamson, D. A. (1990). *Assessment of eating disorders: Obesity, anorexia, and bulimia nervosa.* Elmsford, NY: Pergamon Press.

Williamson, D. A., Anderson, D. A., & Gleaves, D. H. (1996). Anorexia and bulimia: Structured interview methodologies and psychological assessment. In K. Thompson (Ed.), *Body image, eating disorders, and obesity: An integrative guide for assessment and treatment* (pp. 205–223). Washington, DC: American Psychological Association.

Williamson, D. A., Anderson, D. A., Jackman, L. P., & Jackson, S. R. (1995). Assessment of eating disordered thoughts, feelings, and behaviors. In D. B. Allison (Ed.), *Handbook of assessment methods for eating behaviors and weight-related problems* (pp. 347–386). Newbury Park, CA: Sage.

Williamson, D. A., Muller, S. L., Reas, D. L., & Thaw, J. M. (1999). Cognitive bias in eating disorders: Implications for theory and treatment. *Behavior Modification, 23,* 556–577.

Williamson, D. A., Prather, R. C., McKenzie, S. J., & Blouin, D. C. (1990). Behavioral assessment procedures can differentiate bulimia nervosa, compulsive overeater, obese, and normal subjects. *Behavioral Assessment, 12,* 239–352.

Wilson, G. T. (1993). Assessment of binge eating. In C. G. Fairburn & G. T. Wilson (Eds.), *Binge eating: Nature, assessment, and treatment* (pp. 227–249). New York: Guilford Press.

Wilson, G. T., & Smith, D. (1989). Assessment of bulimia nervosa: An evaluation of the Eating Disorder Examination. *International Journal of Eating Disorders, 8,* 173–179.

Wolper, C., Heshka, S., & Heymsfield, S. B. (1995). Measuring food intake: An overview. In D. B. Allison (Ed.), *Handbook of assessment methods for eating behaviors and weight-related problems* (pp. 215–240). Newbury Park, CA: Sage.

SECTION 3 TREATMENT

Chapter 7

COGNITIVE-BEHAVIORAL THERAPY IN THE TREATMENT OF ANOREXIA NERVOSA, BULIMIA NERVOSA, AND BINGE EATING DISORDER

KATHLEEN M. PIKE, MICHAEL J. DEVLIN, AND KATHARINE L. LOEB

Cognitive-Behavioral Therapy (CBT) is one of the *therapies of choice* when it comes to treatment for eating disorders. Originally developed by Aaron T. Beck for the treatment of depression (A. T. Beck, 1976; A. T. Beck, Freeman, & Associates, 1990; A. T. Beck, Rush, Shaw, & Emery, 1979), cognitive theory has grown to be one of the fundamental models used in mental health practice, and it continues to evolve in scope and application. As to eating disorders, CBT has been adapted, expanded, and evaluated in the treatment of anorexia nervosa (AN; Garner & Bemis, 1982, 1985; Garner, Vitousek, & Pike, 1997; Pike, Loeb, & Vitousek, 1996; Vitousek, 1996), bulimia nervosa (BN; Fairburn, 1985; Fairburn, Marcus, & Wilson, 1993), and binge eating disorder (BED; Marcus, 1997).

In the application of CBT to the treatment of the eating disorders, a common set of assumptions exists about the core features of the eating disorders, principles of therapy, and clinical interventions. There are also unique considerations and interventions involved in applying CBT to each of the eating disorders. The first part of this chapter articulates the fundamental assumptions and principles that define and describe CBT for the treatment of the eating disorders. The second part briefly reviews the empirical support of CBT in the treatment of AN, BN, and BED and highlights some of the specific issues associated with the application of CBT to each of these disorders. The third part moves beyond the "standard course of treatment" as described in the CBT manuals and discusses common issues that alter the nomothetic trajectory. Therapists providing treatment for eating disorders should be familiar with the empirically supported CBT treatment protocols; however, rarely does treatment for a unique individual proceed without requiring some changes from the manual in the actual delivery of treatment. This chapter highlights some common challenges and complications that arise in eating disorders treatment and provides case material in describing CBT approaches to addressing such issues.

COGNITIVE-BEHAVIORAL THERAPY FOR EATING DISORDERS

The Core Conceptualization of Cognitive-Behavioral Therapy

We do not attempt to review the enormous body of literature on cognitive theory and the practice of CBT within the parameters of this chapter but provide a brief outline of general principles of CBT. For a more complete discussion of the fundamental underpinnings of CBT, see A. T. Beck (1976), J. S. Beck (1995), Hawton, Salkovskis, Kirk, and Clark (1989), Hollon and Beck (1993), and Young (1990). Therapists providing CBT in the treatment of individuals with eating disorders should have knowledge of these works and a broad-based understanding of CBT through advanced training and supervision in addition to expertise in the treatment of eating disorders.

The fundamental tenets of the CBT model are that emotional and behavioral experiences are mediated by the way an individual cognitively processes information in a particular situation. Perceptions and cognitions mediate experience at multiple levels: Obvious and easily accessible thoughts operate at the surface; automatic thoughts run just beneath the surface and are often evaluative in nature; and ultimately more profound, often less accessible, core beliefs transcend single situations, serving as guiding principles or truths for an individual. According to CBT, life experiences inform and influence the development of core beliefs concerning self, others, and the world at large. Although these schemata are often so fundamental and assumed that they are not totally or immediately accessible, their impact on a given situation is apparent through intermediate rules, attitudes, and assumptions and immediate, automatic thoughts. This cognitive organization is necessary, normal, and healthy in managing the complexity of human experience. It becomes problematic when such cognitive constructs are overly rigid, faulty, or maladaptive, and it is the work of CBT to identify these problematic schemata and cognitions and promote healthier, more flexible, and adaptive cognitive and behavioral sets.

Overview of the Cognitive-Behavioral Therapy Model of Eating Disorders

The CBT model of eating disorders represents a specific application of the general CBT model. CBT conceptualizations of eating disorders have been articulated for BN (Fairburn, 1985; Fairburn, Marcus, et al., 1993; Wilson, Fairburn, & Agras, 1997), AN (Garner & Bemis, 1982, 1985; Garner et al., 1997; Pike et al., 1996; Vitousek, 1996), and BED (Marcus, 1997). According to these conceptualizations, eating disorders represent a confluence of cognitive disturbances overvaluing weight, shape, and appearance and behavioral disturbances in dietary regulation. According to this model, individuals with eating disorders overvalue weight and shape in an attempt to compensate for feelings of low self-esteem, believing that achieving a certain ideal will enhance their self-worth. However, individuals with eating disorders hold weight and shape ideals that are either out of reach or only attainable by engaging in behavioral disturbances, which can occur both in the form of extreme dietary restriction and in the form of extreme loss of control or overeating. In the case of restrictive AN, the extreme dietary restriction leads to a state of emaciation. In the case of BN, BED, and bulimic AN, binge eating bleeds through the attempts at dietary restriction. Additional dysregulation can occur in the form of compensatory behaviors such as vomiting, laxative, and diuretic abuse, all behavioral manifestations of an effort to commit to and achieve unrealistic, self-imposed weight and shape ideals. Additionally, the dysregulation of eating has been understood as an attempt to self-regulate and self-sooth, especially for those individuals whose eating disturbance is dominated by binge eating in the absence of extreme dietary restriction.

As illustrated in Figure 7.1, more than a decade ago, Fairburn and colleagues (Fairburn, 1985; Fairburn, Marcus, et al., 1993) provided a powerful and succinct diagram of the core features of the CBT model for BN. This model represents the focused conceptualization of a 20-session outpatient CBT treatment for BN. This model is elegant in its clarity of focus, it has therapeutic efficacy, and it has had formidable heuristic value across the entire spectrum of eating disorders. However, it does not fully articulate other important components of the eating disorders that are commonly addressed in the clinical practice of CBT, particularly in CBT for AN and BED. With the dual purpose of enhancing the extant CBT model for BN and articulating a model that can be more fully applied to a range of eating disorders, Fairburn, Cooper, and Safran (2002) have expanded the schematic representation of CBT. In this "transdiagnostic" schematic of CBT, Fairburn and colleagues have elaborated on the fundamental issues of low self-esteem and have incorporated the role of interpersonal issues, extreme perfectionism, and impairments in affect regulation into the more focused model of CBT for BN. It remains to be tested whether this expansion increases the efficacy of CBT for these disorders.

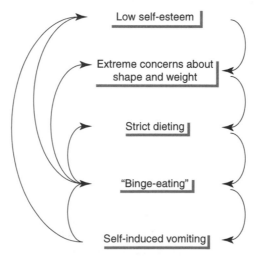

Cognitive-Behavioral Treatment Model

Low self-esteem

Extreme concerns about shape and weight

Strict dieting

"Binge-eating"

Self-induced vomiting

Figure 7.1 Cognitive Behavioral Model of Eating Disorders. *Source:* From "Cognitive-Behavioral Therapy for Binge Eating and Bulimia Nervosa: A Comprehensive Treatment Manual," pp. 361–404, by C. G. Fairburn, M. D. Marcus, and G. T. Wilson, in *Binge Eating: Nature, Assessment, and Treatment,* C. G. Fairburn and G. T. Wilson (Eds.), 1993, New York: Guilford Press. Reprinted with permission.

Core Principles of the Cognitive-Behavioral Therapy Model for Eating Disorders

The CBT model for eating disorders includes five principles:

1. *Self-worth of the individual with an eating disorder is overly determined by body weight, shape, and appearance.* One of the diagnostic criteria for AN and BN is a disturbance in body image (American Psychiatric Association [APA], 1994). Individuals with eating disorders imbue body weight, shape, and appearance with intense meaning and extreme importance and are acutely sensitive to minute changes in weight, shape, and appearance (Cooper & Fairburn, 1992; Geller et al., 1998). Weight fluctuations that would be imperceptible to others can dominate the experience of an individual with an eating disorder and can have a significant effect on self-worth and mood. The importance of weight and shape is negatively correlated with overall self-esteem and positively correlated with eating disorder symptomatology and internalization of societal values concerning appearance and weight (Geller, Johnston, & Madsen, 1997; Geller, Srikameswaran, Cockell, & Zaitsoff, 2000). Persistent overvaluation of weight and shape is associated with increased risk for relapse in individuals with BN (Fairburn, Peveler, Jones, Hope, & Doll, 1993).

2. *Individuals with eating disorders overvalue weight and shape to compensate for feelings of low self-esteem.* The CBT model for eating disorders posits that low self-esteem is at the core of the overvaluation of weight and shape. For an individual with an eating disorder, the pursuit of thinness is the pursuit of enhanced self-esteem. Thus, the values that make thinness a holy virtue and beauty a ticket to existential happiness are fundamental to the vulnerability for and maintenance of an eating disorder. Striegel-Moore, Silberstein, and Rodin (1986) eloquently describe how and why individuals with eating disorders believe that achieving certain physical beauty ideals will remediate deficits of self-esteem. Empirical data further document the inverse relationship between self-esteem and the importance of weight and shape (Geller et al., 2000). Nonetheless, for individuals with eating disorders, the belief that achievement of a physical ideal will enhance self-esteem is held with tenacity. The ironic result is that most individuals with eating disorders are not able to achieve their self-imposed weight and shape ideal, which results in ever-diminishing self-esteem rather than the intended effect of enhanced self-worth. As a result, the typical pattern is that individuals with eating disorders fall prey to increasingly extreme efforts to achieve their weight and shape ideals.

3. *Individuals with eating disorders attempt to self-regulate their emotional world and manage stressful interpersonal situations, at least in part, with food.* An important aspect of CBT for eating disorders that was not elaborated in the original focused model provided by Fairburn and colleagues is the role of the eating disorder in regulating affect. In the past decade, CBT has increasingly integrated interpersonal processes and issues while maintaining the fidelity of this therapeutic approach (e.g., Linehan, 1993; Liotti, 1993; Safran & Segal, 1990). Embedded in many CBT interventions is an understanding of the centrality of failures in affect regulation for individuals with eating disorders, and CBT formulations for AN and BED have always placed significant emphasis on interpersonal issues and understanding problems of

self-regulation, particularly affect regulation in eating disorders (Garner et al., 1997; Marcus, 1997; Pike et al., 1996). Accumulating data across the entire eating disorders spectrum indicates that the behavioral components of dietary restriction, binge eating, and compensatory efforts all play some role in managing emotional states that individuals with eating disorders have difficulty tolerating and managing. Thus, the behavioral components become routine coping strategies—restriction of intake manages anxiety, simplifies decision making, binge eating quells feelings of despair and distracts from feelings of depression, vomiting quiets feelings of self-loathing—albeit all of these strategies work only temporarily and at a high cost. They also fail to resolve the emotional issues that triggered the eating disordered behavior; therefore, inevitably, the unresolved issues and concomitant feelings return or may never really dissipate (Wegner et al., 2002), leading to the self-perpetuating cycle of the eating disorder.

In CBT, early interventions focus heavily on identifying the maintenance patterns of the eating disorder and thereby provide an opportunity for the client to increase his or her awareness of the failures in affect regulation and the ways in which the short-term coping strategies of the eating disorder interfere with achieving more complete and lasting resolutions. Building on this increased awareness, CBT strategies promote change that will result in healthier and more adaptive functioning. To the extent that individuals are not able to achieve such change despite increased awareness and commitment to change, more cognitive work in understanding underlying schemas may be warranted. Linehan's (1993) work aimed at enhancing emotional regulation and interpersonal effectiveness is based on sound cognitive-behavioral principles and may be effectively adapted for treatment of individuals with eating disorders.

4. *Eating disorders are multidetermined, and different factors can predispose, precipitate, and perpetuate an eating disorder.* Eating disorders are not only disorders of weight, shape, and eating. Eating disorders are multidetermined with genetic, biological, sociocultural, familial, and developmental factors, all contributing to an individual's degree of vulnerability for developing an eating disorder. Some risk factors for eating disorders are common across all disorders; others are specific to one disorder or another. The CBT model is particularly compatible with an understanding of eating disorders as multidetermined. Acknowledging that a range of factors may have contributed to the development of an eating disorder, CBT focuses on the proximal factors that precipitate and contribute to the maintenance of the disorder.

The distinction between etiological and maintenance factors is fundamental to CBT, and the CBT importance of focusing on perpetuating or maintenance issues in resolving eating disorders is supported by empirical data. For example, in the controlled trials for CBT for BN, where treatment stays focused on the issues linked to the maintenance of the disorder, a substantial percentage of clients achieve significant amelioration of symptoms and full remission (e.g., Agras, Walsh, Fairburn, Wilson, & Kraemer, 2000; Fairburn et al., 1991; Walsh et al., 1997). However, the data also lend credence to the importance in some cases of addressing more fundamental, long-standing issues associated with the risk for developing an eating disorder given that the briefer, maintenance-focused treatments leave a substantial percentage of individuals symptomatic. One of the challenges of future CBT initiatives is to determine empirically whether more expansive protocols actually enhance outcome.

5. *The symptoms of the eating disorder are not simply symbolic representations of underlying problems but are also significant in their own right and require focused attention.* This is a crucial and fundamental principle of CBT treatment conceptualization. It may be true that the eating disorder symptoms represent underlying problems at some symbolic level, but they are more than that. They directly affect emotional, behavioral, and cognitive processes in such a way that they infiltrate and contribute to global and fundamental aspects of psychological and physical health. CBT's focus on symptoms is not meant to be a superficial intervention that has no implications for what lies beneath. Instead, by beginning with the symptoms that are present and accessible, the therapy process has access to what is fundamental and significant in determining the emotional and psychological health of an individual and thereby has the potential to facilitate meaningful and profound change. If CBT were merely a superficial intervention, it would be like weeding a garden by snipping off the top leaves. Instead, CBT interventions begin with the top leaves and follow the organic connections until the roots of the problem have been identified and weeded out.

Cognitive-Behavioral Therapy Fundamentals Concerning the Therapeutic Relationship and the Structure of Treatment

Therapeutic relationship and the structure of treatment follow these 10 CBT fundamentals:

1. *CBT requires a sound therapeutic relationship between the client and therapist.* The potential of CBT lies in its ability to engage, challenge, and mobilize the client at multiple levels of cognitions, behaviors, and emotions; however, its success in achieving this aim will be greatly mediated by the client-therapist alliance (Garner et al., 1993; Orlinsky, Grawe, & Parks, 1994). Perhaps this is true for all good therapy, but it bears repeating. The nonspecific therapist qualities of warmth, empathy, respect, and openness are essential (Thompson & Williams, 1987; Truax & Mitchell, 1971). In addition, there are certain therapist qualities especially suited for CBT. As described by Young, Weinberger, and Beck (2001), effective CBT therapists are especially skilled at providing *accurate empathy* by seeing situations from their client's perspective and suspending their own assumptions and judgments. Skilled CBT therapists also think clearly, reasonably, and strategically, anticipating desired outcomes and challenging faulty reasoning and assumptions of clients at a therapeutically appropriate pace. Effective CBT therapists are comfortable being active in sessions, providing leadership, direction, and structure especially at the beginning of treatment. Certain client characteristics also shape the client-therapist relationship, the most central of which is the ability to engage in an honest and trusting therapeutic relationship. Although most BN and BED clients engage in treatment voluntarily, participation in treatment for individuals with AN is often pursued only under duress, and even among individuals with BN and BED, a significant subgroup of individuals has difficulty engaging in a constructive and trusting therapeutic alliance. When this is the case, greater attention needs to be focused on the therapeutic relationship to promote a good working alliance (Linehan, 1993; Young, 1990).

2. *The relationship between the therapist and client is collaborative.* Therapists and clients work together as partners in CBT. Each one brings his or her own expertise, and

neither can do the work alone. Right from the start, it is important to communicate to the client that one of the primary goals of therapy is for the client to become his or her "own therapist." In the initial phase of treatment, the therapist is generally more active in suggesting the focus and work in the session and between sessions; however, even from the start, the client and therapist set the goals and determine the agenda of a session together. Session priorities are set in accordance with how much distress is caused by a particular issue *and* the pragmatic concern of how amenable to change a particular issue is. In a similar way, work that the client does between sessions is decided collaboratively. As treatment progresses, the client assumes increasing responsibility and leadership in determining the focus of the work, both inside and in between sessions. Throughout the course of treatment, the essential importance of collaboration in therapy is emphasized.

3. *CBT begins with a focus on the present.* The starting point for CBT is on the proximal, perpetuating factors of the eating disorder. As articulated previously, CBT assumes that eating disorders are multidetermined and that different factors are involved in the development and maintenance of the disorders. So why not start at the beginning? According to CBT conceptualizations of treatment, addressing the current issues and bringing some resolution of symptoms is the most powerful starting point because it brings some immediate relief to the individual, increases a sense of self-efficacy, provides tangible effects that add credence to treatment, and brings clarity of vision in analyzing the more distal, developmental factors. From a CBT perspective, the current, perpetuating factors account for the divide between the desire to change and the inability to do so, and this is where the action of therapy begins. In clinical practice, moving between the here-and-now and the individual's developmental experience and long-standing cognitive schema requires extensive clinical judgment.

4. *CBT begins with a focus on the eating disorder symptoms.* Not only does CBT begin in the present but it begins by specifically targeting the current eating disorder pathology and its implication for functioning today. By the time individuals present for treatment, they have often been living with the eating disorder for an extended time, and the disorder has taken on a life of its own. CBT begins with focused and clear targets for change by focusing on the specific symptoms of the eating disorder on daily functioning, many of which are automatic and entrenched, perpetuated by fixed cognitions and schemas. CBT helps individuals alter their behavior by modifying dysfunctional beliefs and assumptions; CBT also helps individuals alter their cognitions by promoting behavior change. The behavioral disturbances of the eating disorder are readily apparent at the start of treatment, and behavioral changes provide real life experience to probe, challenge, and change faulty cognitions. Therefore, many of the initial CBT interventions target specific behavioral change with the assumption that interrupting the behavioral cycles will have a direct impact on daily functioning and that such impact will also force an individual to gain awareness of and change the dysfunctional cognitions that are core to the eating disorder as well.

5. *CBT therapy sessions have an explicit structure and duration.* Compared to many other therapeutic approaches, one of the most notable qualities of CBT is the explicit agenda setting and structuring of sessions (Fairburn, Marcus, et al., 1993; Garner et al., 1997). Before each session, therapists consider current issues and challenges of treatment and have potential issues to put on the agenda for treatment. Therapy sessions begin with collaborative agenda setting for the session by soliciting clients for their input and having the therapist provide his or her own recommendations for session

focus. Especially during the initial phase of treatment, CBT has a logical, stepwise sequence for introducing concepts, psychoeducational components, and strategies for achieving behavioral and cognitive change. Once an explicit agenda for the session is agreed on, the session proceeds with a discussion of identified issues. Time is allocated at the end of the session for a summary of the session and discussion of goals and objectives for work to be addressed between sessions.

In addition to structuring individual sessions, the structure of the course of therapy is typically explicitly stated in CBT. The empirically tested CBT protocol for BN is approximately 20 sessions (Fairburn, Marcus, et al., 1993), 22 sessions in 24 weeks for BED (Marcus, 1997), and 50 sessions in one year for AN relapse prevention (Pike, Vitousek, & Wilson, 1998). One reason that these protocols are time limited is that they were used in controlled clinical trials. Nonetheless, there is good clinical rationale for setting time limits on treatment at least with the intention of setting goals and evaluating treatment progress explicitly. In general clinical practice, there is more flexibility in structuring the duration of treatment. However, such flexibility should not forsake the opportunities accrued by clear goal setting, evaluation, and focus in treatment.

6. *Resolution of the eating disorder requires active work outside the therapy session.* As important as the therapy work done in sessions is the work that is done between sessions. Because the cognitive and behavioral components of the eating disorder are mostly activated outside psychotherapy sessions, much of the work of therapy actually takes place outside the sessions. It is important to emphasize the importance of work between sessions right from the start. The between-session work is designed to elucidate cognitions that contribute to maintenance of the eating disorder and promote experimentation with changes in behavior within the context of a supportive therapeutic environment. Between-session work includes self-monitoring of eating and related social, interpersonal experiences, as well as engagement in behavioral and cognitive exercises, the purpose of which is to help identify problematic patterns and experiment with change in a supportive, therapeutic environment. The investment that clients make in working on issues between sessions will be a function of the importance that therapists place on integrating and using this material in session.

7. *Psychoeducation is an important component of CBT.* Providing clients with accurate information about important aspects of eating disorder pathology is a core component of CBT. In the initial phase of therapy, CBT includes psychoeducational information about the naturalistic course of illness, nutritional education, the psychological and physiological effects of starvation, the ineffectiveness of dieting, the self-perpetuating cycle of binge eating and vomiting, and the ineffectiveness of vomiting and laxative abuse to promote weight loss as well as the deleterious medical consequences. Excellent references are available for therapists and clients (e.g., Becker, Grinspoon, Klibanski, & Herzog, 1999; Pomeroy & Mitchell, 2002). The hallmark study conducted by Keys and colleagues at the University of Minnesota during World War II (Keys, Brozek, Henschel, Mickelsen, & Taylor, 1950) provides a wealth of interesting and dramatic evidence of the profound impact that nutritional deprivation has on human functioning across a wide range of domains.

8. *Clarifying goals for treatment is crucial and sometimes complicated.* It is extremely important that treatment goals be explicitly stated in CBT. Although it might seem obvious that a client's goal is resolution of the eating disorder, this is often not the case. The incompatibility of certain goals and a lack of investment in recovery is a

common phenomenon. The lack of investment in recovery for individuals with AN is often publicly stated; the majority of individuals attend sessions only under duress. However, even in the cases of BN and BED, it is not unusual for individuals to be invested in resolution of some but not all the symptoms of the eating disorder. For example, many individuals with BN want to eliminate binge eating and purging; however, they do not want to relinquish investment in achieving a certain weight through dieting. Making apparent the incompatibility of these goals is a core piece of the work of CBT. In addition, individuals may have fears, concerns, and worries about treatment and recovery that will interfere with goal setting. If individuals fear that recovery from their eating disorder will leave them more vulnerable to interpersonal disappointment, it will be difficult for them to clearly commit to such goals. The work of CBT is to help individuals articulate such issues so that they can more clearly commit to their goals for treatment and help them make informed decisions concerning their life and recovery from the eating disorder.

9. *Issues of motivation will govern the focus and pace of treatment.* One of the essential first steps in treatment is cultivating and sustaining motivation for change; however, enlisting motivation for treatment can be difficult for all clients with eating disorders and is almost a universal issue in the treatment of individuals with AN. A significant amount of work has been devoted to understanding the role of motivation in treatment and articulating approaches for enhancing motivation (Miller & Rollnick, 1991; Prochaska & DiClemente, 1983; Prochaska, DiClemente, & Norcross, 1992). Specific applications for eating disorders treatment have been articulated by Vitousek and colleagues (Vitousek, Watson, & Wilson, 1998).

When clients have difficulty with motivation for treatment, it is essential to honestly explore the client's thinking about the advantages and disadvantages of symptoms. The Socratic method of engaging in honest exploration requires that therapists sincerely try to understand the client's perspective and personal values; otherwise, it is an exercise of rhetorical questioning masquerading as therapy. Once the therapist and client have a shared understanding of the client's thinking about the costs and benefits associated with change, cognitive and behavioral work that challenges assumptions and promotes experimentation will promote a reevaluation of fixed cognitive sets and behaviors that will include an exploration of issues of motivation and treatment goals.

10. *There are certain "nonnegotiables" in treatment.* Although not always explicit and articulated, rules or agreements among the individuals involved govern every relationship. CBT approaches to treatment make explicit from the onset of treatment the structure, goals, and core agreements that are required for the continuation of treatment. At the outset of treatment, it is important that the therapist and client establish, at a minimum, an oral agreement and, preferably, a written contract that stipulates the few but critical situations that would alter the therapy focus and process. This process provides documentation that each participant understands when treatment will be terminated and what procedures will be followed at that time. These nonnegotiable parameters represent an explicit agreement about how to manage imminent danger to self and others. Across all therapy situations, if a client is perceived to be in imminent danger of hurting himself or herself or someone else, the normative agreements concerning focus of treatment and client confidentiality change. In the case of eating disorders, specific points that should be explicitly addressed are:

- Procedures for managing weight monitoring and weight loss.
- When outpatient treatment will be terminated and inpatient treatment recommended.
- When involuntary inpatient admission would be pursued.

In the process of making this contract explicit, therapists and clients should discuss the particular issues and thresholds for when treatment would be terminated due to weight loss, extreme compensatory behaviors, substance use and abuse, and client deception.

SPECIFIC ADAPTATIONS OF COGNITIVE-BEHAVIORAL THERAPY AND EMPIRICAL RESEARCH SUPPORTING COGNITIVE-BEHAVIORAL THERAPY FOR BULIMIA NERVOSA, ANOREXIA NERVOSA, AND BINGE EATING DISORDER

Cognitive-Behavorial Therapy for Bulimia Nervosa

CBT for BN has been well described, and its efficacy is well documented. CBT for BN is the most thoroughly evaluated form of CBT, and it has consistently proved to be more effective than, or at least as effective as, any other psychotherapy to which it was compared (Agras, Telch, et al., 1994; Agras et al., 2000; Fairburn et al., 1991; Garner et al., 1993; Walsh et al., 1997). The findings from these studies of CBT report significant reductions in binge eating, purging, and dietary restraint. These studies also report that attitudes toward weight and shape improve, as does associated psychopathology such as depression, anxiety, and self-esteem. Furthermore, follow-up data indicate that gains achieved during the course of CBT tend to be maintained (Agras, Rossiter, et al., 1994; Agras, Telch, et al., 1994; Fairburn, Jones, Peveler, Hope, & O'Connor, 1993; Fairburn et al., 1995; Wilson et al., 1997).

Despite the strong empirical support for CBT in the treatment of BN, CBT is clearly not a panacea, and approximately 50% of individuals remain symptomatic at the end of treatment. Thus, as described previously, Fairburn and colleagues (2002) have expanded on the original Oxford model of CBT to include features that they believe may additionally mediate the efficacy of CBT. These four components are: clinical perfectionism, interpersonal factors, low self-esteem, and mood intolerance. Clinicians working in the field of eating disorders have long been aware of the relevance of these variables; however, Fairburn and colleagues (2002) have made a significant contribution to the field by thoughtfully articulating and integrating how to incorporate a broader focus in CBT treatment while maintaining the core CBT approach, which already has proven efficacy. The expanded form of CBT developed by Fairburn and colleagues has yet to be evaluated to ascertain whether the elaborations incorporated in the treatment will enhance the effects of CBT for BN or other eating disorders.

The original Oxford model for CBT treatment of BN has been well described (Fairburn, 1985; Fairburn, Marcus, et al., 1993), and the clinical application of the model has been thoroughly described elsewhere (e.g., Wilson & Pike, 2001). Therefore, only a brief overview is provided in this chapter. As described previously and illustrated in

Figure 7.1, the original Oxford model of CBT for BN focuses on the cognitive and behavioral factors that serve to maintain the BN. Efforts to achieve an unrealistic body weight, shape, or appearance (often all three) result in extreme forms of dietary restriction that then trigger episodes of binge eating. Compensatory behaviors such as vomiting, laxative abuse, and excessive exercise are enlisted to counteract the binge eating in a redoubling of efforts to achieve the perpetually elusive ideals of thinness and beauty.

The core components of the therapist-client relationship and the general structure of the therapy process as described in the first part of this chapter all apply to CBT for BN. The focused form of CBT for BN includes three stages of treatment. The initial phase of treatment (approximately eight sessions) addresses many of the core behavioral disturbances of BN. It introduces and uses self-monitoring, important psychoeducational material, the prescription of normalization of eating, weekly weighing, and the development of a range of strategies for reducing the risk for binge eating and purging episodes. In the second phase of treatment (approximately eight sessions), more emphasis is placed on the cognitive elements that are central to the eating disorder. Cognitive restructuring strategies and a range of problem-solving interventions are incorporated into the treatment to facilitate change. The final phase of treatment (approximately four sessions) focuses on relapse prevention.

Cognitive-Behavioral Therapy for Anorexia Nervosa

CBT for AN includes all of the core features described by Fairburn and colleagues in the Oxford model for BN. However, some important distinctions exist in the structure and formulation of CBT for AN (Garner et al., 1997; Pike et al., 1998), which reflect important differences in clinical presentation of the eating disorders. The most critical distinctions are:

1. CBT for AN generally requires a longer term approach and frequently includes inpatient treatment.
2. In general, CBT for AN focuses more heavily on issues of motivation and resistance given the characteristic, egosyntonic nature of AN.
3. CBT for AN generally requires greater attention to medical complications and effects of starvation on functioning.
4. CBT for AN has incorporated into treatment a broader focus on general maladaptive schemas in addition to the eating disorder self-schema (Garner & Bemis 1982, 1985; Guidano & Liotti, 1983; Pike et al., 1996; Vitousek & Ewald, 1993; Vitousek & Hollon, 1990).

Each of these points is elaborated briefly next.

The egosyntonic nature of AN makes it notorious among clinicians as one of the most recalcitrant conditions to treat (Vitousek et al., 1998). In contrast to almost any other disorder, rarely does the individual with AN seek treatment voluntarily, and if he or she does, it is generally for the relief from the food preoccupation and associated psychopathology but not because he or she desires weight gain and recovery (Hall,

1982; Vitousek et al., 1998). CBT for AN focuses to a great extent on the egosyntonic nature of the illness, the reinforcing and adaptive aspects of the disorder, and its role in protecting the individual from assuming appropriate developmental challenges such as increased independence and autonomy. CBT for AN also focuses to a great extent on the issues of motivation and combating the cognitive sets that support the secondary gains, such as the perceived advantages of illness and the idea that AN represents self-control and moral purity (Bemis, 1983; Vitousek & Ewald, 1993).

As compared to CBT for BN, CBT for AN has not benefited from the development of detailed treatment programs and empirical evaluation until recently. We are aware of three empirical investigations of CBT for AN. Pike and colleagues (Pike, Vitousek, & Wilson, 1998) developed a posthospitalization maintenance and follow-up CBT program for individuals with AN who had achieved weight restoration, whereas Serfaty and colleagues (Serfaty, Turkington, Heap, Ledsham, & Jolley, 1999) and McIntosh and colleagues (personal communication) conducted outpatient trials for nonhospitalized AN individuals. The posthospitalization program for AN developed by Pike and colleagues (Pike et al., 1998) is designed for individuals who have successfully completed inpatient treatment and consists of 50 individual sessions of 50-minute duration. Sessions are scheduled twice per week for the first 10 sessions and weekly thereafter, so the overall duration of treatment is one year as compared to four months for BN. The results from a randomized clinical trial indicate that CBT is effective in improving clinical outcome and preventing relapse in adult patients with AN (Pike, Walsh, Vitousek, Wilson, & Bauer, 2003).

The CBT protocol developed by Pike and colleagues is significantly longer than the standard intervention for BN because it includes a phase of treatment focused on identifying the broader general maladaptive schemas and eating disorder self-schema and includes treatment interventions that explicitly target the development of alternative bases for self-definition and self-evaluation. Given the issues of chronicity and high rates of relapse associated with AN, it is thought that such interventions may promote more lasting change and reduce relapse rates. However, given the lack of empirical studies examining the application of CBT to AN, we have yet to determine which components of treatment promote the most positive and lasting outcome.

The outpatient trials conducted by Serfaty and colleagues (1999) and McIntosh and colleagues (personal communication) report preliminary data concerning CBT for less severe AN. The study by Serfaty and colleagues suggests that CBT has good treatment retention compared to nutritional counseling; however, because of the attrition from the nutritional counseling condition, empirical assessment of efficacy of CBT was impossible. McIntosh and colleagues (personal communication) conducted a 20-session outpatient trial comparing CBT, interpersonal psychotherapy treatment (IPT), and nonspecific supportive clinical management (NSCM) for individuals with "spectrum" AN whose weight ranged from a body mass index (BMI) of 14.5 to 19 and whose duration of illness was less than five years. In this study, individuals in the NSCM faired better than the CBT group on global improvement, although the CBT group reported some significant symptom improvement in the secondary analyses. The findings from these studies are provocative but far from conclusive, and the utility of CBT in treating different AN subgroups and its efficacy at different stages of care need further study.

Cognitive-Behavioral Therapy for Binge Eating Disorder

Following closely on the initial descriptions of binge eating disorder (Spitzer et al., 1992, 1993) and based on adaptations of CBT for nonpurging BN (Telch, Agras, Rossiter, Wilfley, & Kenardy, 1990; Wilfley et al., 1993) and obese binge eaters (Smith, Marcus, & Kaye, 1992), the idea that CBT for BN could be adapted to treat obese patients with BED quickly came to the fore. Several studies have demonstrated that CBT is highly effective in suppressing binge eating in these patients at least in the short term (Agras, Telch, et al., 1994; Eldredge et al., 1999), with some evidence of long-term efficacy as well (Agras, Telch, Arnow, Eldredge, & Marnell, 1997; Marcus, Wing, & Fairburn, 1995; Wilfley et al., 2002).

What also became apparent in initial studies characterizing the new disorder was that obese patients with BED differed in important ways from patients with BN and that it would be important to take into account these differences in adapting CBT for BED. Although there is no published manual that outlines CBT for BED in detail, published manuals for CBT for binge eating (Fairburn, Marcus, et al., 1993) and descriptions of adaptations of CBT for BED (Marcus, 1997) are available to guide the clinician who wishes to tailor CBT to the special needs of obese patients with BED.

One important distinction between BED and BN is the role of dietary restraint in promoting binge eating. Clinical experience and systematic study suggest that the classic alternation between rigid dietary restraint and uncontrolled binge eating, which characterizes patients with BN, generally does not occur in obese patients with BED. Rather, these patients appear to have relatively low levels of dietary restraint even when not binge eating (Guss, Kissileff, Devlin, Zimmerli, & Walsh, 2002; Yanovski et al., 1992). However, dietary restraint may operate in a somewhat different way in these patients. Patients with BED often report periods of strict dieting and weight loss lasting for days, weeks, months, or even years, which ultimately prove to be unsustainable and give way to periods of surrender to binge eating and weight gain. It has been speculated that, in some patients, a kind of virtual restraint is operating, in which the patient has unrealistic ideas about acceptable eating, which the patient cannot even begin to actualize and feels defeated by his or her inability to do so. While this may be true for some, evidence suggests that most patients with BED have roughly the same idea of what constitutes a binge as comparable individuals without BED, but that their typical servings of foods are larger (Greeno, Wing, & Marcus, 1999). Thus, it is important in evaluating a patient with BED to determine the particular role and importance of dysregulated dietary restraint for that individual. Rather than simply helping the patient to lower level of restraint, the CBT therapist working with an obese BED patient may need to help the patient bolster his or her dietary restraint in many situations to achieve a system for regulating intake, which is realistic in the long term and balances consistency with flexibility. For obese patients with BED, the idea that binge eating may be less related to dysregulated dietary restraint and more related to the attempt to regulate affect and manage stress as described previously (core principle 3) is of particular importance.

Another important feature of obese patients with BED is that their weight is in a range that is at variance with cultural standards of beauty. Unlike patients with AN and most patients with BN, they are objectively overweight. Obese individuals in our society are truly the object of discrimination (Puhl & Brownell, 2001), and there are significant tangible costs and disadvantages associated with this body type. Obese patients with BED, like patients with AN and BN, evidence high levels of body shape and weight dissatisfaction (Wilfley, Schwartz, Spurrell, & Fairburn, 2000), but, for these individuals, this dissatisfaction is echoed by culturally sanctioned negative messages. Psychoeducation concerning the genetic and biological determinants of obesity (Devlin, Yanovski, & Wilson, 2000) can be extremely helpful in challenging patients' culturally reinforced beliefs that their obesity reflects a lack of willpower or an underlying character defect. Cognitive restructuring in this area may help patients to recognize that, despite the veracity of their perception of the cultural message ("I do not have the most popular body type"), their conclusions ("No one will ever be attracted to me") may be less well founded and clearly dysfunctional.

Finally, the goals of treatment for obese patients with BED may be somewhat different from those for patients with BN, particularly concerning weight. Although the goals of binge cessation and enhanced self-acceptance resemble those for BN, patients with BMI in the obese range (30 kg/m^2 or greater) are at increased risk for a range of medical comorbidities and would, therefore, benefit from even modest weight loss. However, based on the idea, well founded in clinical experience with BN, that normalization of eating and the attempt to lose weight are incompatible goals, the classic CBT approach for BED prioritizes binge cessation and self-acceptance and expressly defers weight loss (Marcus, 1997). In *obese* individuals with BED, however, it may be that these goals can be pursued simultaneously. In contrast to treatment packages that offer a sequence of CBT followed by weight loss treatment (Agras, Telch, et al., 1994), programs that combine treatment for binge eating with treatment for obesity have more recently been developed (Devlin, 2001). An important point is that weight loss and self-acceptance are compatible goals. Although patients entering treatment often believe that self-acceptance will hinder their efforts to change, clinical experience suggests that the opposite is more often true (Wilson, 1996).

CLINICAL ILLUSTRATIONS OF COGNITIVE-BEHAVIORAL THERAPY APPROACHES TO COMMON THERAPY ISSUES

In the first and second parts of this chapter, we reviewed the fundamental principles of CBT and application of CBT to the treatment of eating disorders. In this section, we present clinical case material to highlight a number of common therapeutic issues and challenges that arise in treatment. Although CBT manuals detail the standard CBT approaches to treating eating disorders, rarely does an individual's treatment follow the nomothetic course. The selected case material in this part of the chapter highlights ways in which actual treatment commonly veers from the course described in treatment manuals and discusses how to work within the CBT model to address these issues. The following examples are not meant to be exhaustive, nor is it suggested that there is a single, exclusive therapeutic intervention appropriate to each example. Rather, the following case material is meant to be illustrative of CBT in action.

Failure to Engage in Therapeutic Tasks between Sessions

As discussed in the first part of the chapter, an essential component of CBT is the work that is done between sessions. Between-session work continues throughout the course of treatment and varies depending on the stage of treatment and the issues at hand. Some interventions target cognitive restructuring; others focus on behavioral experimentation. When a client does not engage in the work between sessions, one of the agenda items in session should be an explicit exploration of why.

One of the first between-session pieces of work that is common across all CBT interventions is self-monitoring. Self-monitoring involves keeping track of eating behaviors and the associated interpersonal and emotional experiences. It is a powerful tool for helping a client reconnect to a process that has become automatic. Some of the primary questions for therapists in this situation are:

- Does the task seem useful to the client? To the therapist?
- Was the between-session work agreed to collaboratively?
- Is the task consistent with helping the client work toward treatment goals?
- What are the specific thoughts and feelings that make it difficult to follow through?
- Am I making use of between-session work in our sessions?
- Is the task in line with the client's level of motivation and commitment?

Case Example 1

One of the first between-session pieces of work that is common across all CBT interventions is self-monitoring, which involves keeping track of eating behaviors and associated interpersonal and emotional experiences throughout the day. It is a powerful tool for helping a client reconnect to a process that has become automatic. Jane, a 24-year-old woman with AN, agreed in session to self-monitor but claimed that she forgot to do so in one session and then in the subsequent session claimed that she didn't want to spend so much time thinking about food and, therefore, decided not to self-monitor. At the same time that she was not self-monitoring, she was losing weight and exercising more than an hour per day.

The therapist intervened by reviewing the rationale for self-monitoring and soliciting more fully Jane's thoughts and feelings about the process. In doing so, it became clear that Jane did not fully endorse the utility of self-monitoring, *and* she was not sure that she wanted to change her eating or exercise. Before addressing the specific utility of the self-monitoring, the therapist first addressed the issues of motivation and goal setting. The therapist worked with Jane to complete a cost-benefit analysis (see Table 7.1). By collaboratively articulating and acknowledging Jane's conflicting thoughts and feelings, the therapist demonstrated respect for Jane's struggle about recovery from her eating disorder. In addition, once articulated, it was much easier to address these issues and enlist Jane to engage in experimentation to determine whether her fears about changing her eating and exercise would be born out.

Once Jane agreed to suspend judgment long enough to experiment with change, the focus of treatment shifted to discussing how self-monitoring procedures could be made

Table 7.1   Decision Analysis Form

| If I . . . | Short-Term Consequences | | Long-Term Consequences | |
	Positive	Negative	Positive	Negative
Self-monitor my eating and exercise.	It puts me in "real control." Not pretending to be well when I'm not.	It will make me think about food more. Become more obsessed with my exercise and weight.	Don't know.	Not normal. Don't want to have an eating disorder forever.
Don't self-monitor my eating and exercise.	Feel normal. Won't feel so controlled. Can be spontaneous. Don't have to really know how much I am eating and exercising.	May keep losing weight. Can pretend I'm trying to recover but not really have to be totally honest.	Will be normal. Will be able to be more spontaneous.	Will not learn how to regulate and keep track of my eating and weight. May relapse more easily. Won't be in charge of my life if I keep on having this eating disorder.

useful and tolerable for Jane. Initially, Jane would commit only to filling out the self-monitoring in the morning and evening, making it an exercise in planning and review. Although eventually the goal was for her to self-monitor systematically throughout the course of the day, this was a first step that increased her connection to her eating and exercise. Having to write down her behaviors propelled her to engage in more self-reflection and rendered evident the fact that she was not eating as much as she had imagined before she started writing it down. With this new evidence in hand, she agreed to work on increasing her intake in systematic ways. Whereas previously she did not own this as a goal for treatment, the self-monitoring increased her ability to embrace this as a treatment goal. She recognized that she could increase positive actions of recovery by using self-monitoring to write about thoughts, feelings, and experiences linked to her eating disorder.

Case Example 2

Margaret, a 29-year-old woman with a seven-year history of BN, had difficulty working between sessions during the middle phase of treatment. She had made great strides in reducing her binge eating and purging; however, certain high-risk situations still triggered episodes approximately once per week. Margaret fully endorsed the CBT model for BN and reluctantly relinquished her goal of losing 15 pounds in the hope that it would help her overcome her BN. She had been eating three meals per day most of the time and only occasionally skipped meals. She reached a point of acceptance with her weight and shape that bodes well for long-term recovery, but the continuing binge eating and purging were a problem. Given Margaret's sincere investment in treatment and her clear commitment to recovery, Margaret's lingering episodes were addressed in a relatively straightforward manner.

Margaret and her therapist completed an inventory of the situations that continued to trigger binge-purge episodes (see Table 7.2). They identified some of the common features associated with these situations and then adopted a two-prong approach. At one level, Margaret and her therapist identified and challenged faulty cognitions and assumptions that rendered Margaret vulnerable to succumbing to the urge to binge and purge in these situations. Once these distortions were identified and challenged, Margaret was able to imagine other options and articulate several plans for averting a binge-purge episode. Having greater clarity as to the faulty cognitions that perpetuated the binge-purge cycles and having articulated coping strategies and alternatives in session, Margaret had more confidence about her ability to combat the urge to binge and purge between sessions. With increased confidence and practice, she was better able to make use of dysfunctional thought records to help her in the heat of the moment to avert an episode of binge eating and purging.

Table 7.2   Risk Hierarchy Form

Low-Risk Situations	When?	Why?
With my close friends.	All the time.	Will not binge-purge in public and usually I don't feel stressed when I am with them.
On vacation.	Almost all the time.	Easy and not stressed.
With my boyfriend.	Almost all the time.	I don't want him to know.
Medium-Risk Situations	When?	Why?
At work.	In the afternoon, especially if I skipped lunch.	Hungry, stressed, worried about performance.
Large parties.	Will binge but not purge in social situations because I lose control, eat forbidden foods.	Forbidden foods, can't control myself, get worried that no one really likes me, I'm not interesting.
High-Risk Situations	When?	Why?
At home alone.	Evenings, if work was hard, if I skipped meals.	Feel sorry for myself, feel like a loser, lonely, don't know what else to do when I'm feeling down.
After a fight with boyfriend.	Worry that he will leave me.	Get really nervous when he leaves me.
Late at night at home.	After going out, especially if I've been drinking.	Usually when I drink, I get out of control with my eating, too. Sometimes I drink because I'm depressed; sometimes I think I feel depressed because I've been drinking.

Issues of Motivation

It is universally agreed that motivation is the driving force for change. From a CBT perspective, problems with motivation in treatment are understood either as a misalignment of treatment goals and/or as a representation of cognitive distortions. Typically, it is not that a client is not motivated at all; the crux of the motivation issue is that the client is motivated to achieve goals that are inconsistent with the goals of recovery. Questions for the therapist in this situation are:

- What motivates my client in his or her daily life currently?
- What are my client's short-term and long-term goals?
- Do I understand my client's thinking about why he or she is invested in these goals?
- Do I share those goals for my client?
- If we have shared treatment goals but my client is not motivated to change certain thoughts or behaviors, have we discussed the incompatibility of certain cognitions or certain goals? Have we prioritized goals?
- Is my client not motivated because of problems with agency and self-doubt?

Case Example

Samantha is a 15-year-old girl with AN who has gained weight on an inpatient unit and sat sullenly throughout her initial outpatient CBT session of posthospital care. Her mother phoned the next day stating that Samantha was refusing to return for more treatment. Samantha's parents gave her the choice of continuing CBT or entering an intensive day treatment program, which would preclude school attendance. Samantha chose outpatient CBT and arrived at her second session proclaiming, "I don't want to be here."

For individuals with AN, the immediate advantages of the illness are vastly more salient than the long-term negative consequences. These advantages may include a sense of mastery at transcending basic somatic needs, reduced expectations from others, and the illusory belief that further weight loss will quiet excruciating shape and weight concerns. It is not unusual for a patient to say, "I don't want osteoporosis, but I just can't gain weight right now." The chronicity of AN does not reflect patients' ignorance of the risks associated with the disorder. Rather, other factors are simply more powerful influences of current motivation resulting in the decision to remain ill.

The "poor judgment" seen in AN—which, notably, is more understandable when viewed from the patient's perspective—is only potentiated by adolescence. Adolescence itself, in the absence of AN, is characterized by the developmental challenge of grasping the future implications of current behavior. Adolescents view themselves as immortal, immune from death. Therefore, therapists treating adolescents with AN are faced with a double-layered barrier to instilling motivation for change.

In the case of Samantha, the therapist chose to intervene by socratically inquiring about the client's motivation to remain anorexic. She asked the patient to articulate the positive aspects of AN and displayed interest in and respect for the pleasure Samantha derived from her disorder. The therapist's questions were designed to both engage the client and elicit information about Samantha's motivation to stay sick. This information was later incorporated into a decision analysis form (see Table 7.3). In conducting a decision analysis, the therapist asked Samantha what she knew about the long-term consequences of AN and added any missing facts in a calm tone. The therapist was careful not to attempt to mobilize Samantha's affect by being dramatic because a persuasive stance can often propel a client to adopt a more polarized viewpoint. The therapist focused primarily on the immediate negative consequences, which were more salient and meaningful for Samantha than the long-term implications of AN. For example, Samantha's soccer coach would not let her participate on the team if she didn't maintain a normal weight. In addition, Samantha's friends had been uncomfortable around her and no longer invited her to their houses on weekends. Samantha also expressed fear that another hospitalization would set her back a full year in school and delay entrance to college.

The therapist emphasized that Samantha's immediate future was in her own hands. Samantha's parents might be able to force her to attend treatment or to be rehospitalized should Samantha lose a significant amount of weight, but it was ultimately Samantha's choice to stay well or not. In reminding Samantha of her own agency, the therapist disarmed Samantha's defensive position and counteracted her expectation of the therapist as adversary. By feeling more in charge, Samantha was motivated to maintain her

Table 7.3   Decision Analysis Form

If I . . .	Short-Term Consequences		Long-Term Consequences	
	Positive	Negative	Positive	Negative
Keep losing weight	Easy, powerful, unique, special, no one else can do it.	No soccer. Friends are uncomfortable. Won't get invited to parties. Might get rehospitalized.	It is all I know, I'm good at it. Feel special (but also feels like a cop-out; weird, isn't it?).	No future. Will be seen as a loser. Is actually easy way out of dealing with life.
Stop losing weight	Can play sports. Better socially. Can stay connected to friends.	Will lose attention. Will stop being so special. Will have to deal with other problems.	Go to college on schedule. Can be "normal." Could have a real boyfriend, family, career, kids, life.	Have to change my ways. Have to figure out how to be special without the anorexia. Will not get so much attention. Will feel out of control. Will have a lot of pressure from my parents to be a doctor or something.

weight at a sufficient level to be able to continue to engage in activities with friends. During this time, the therapist encouraged Samantha to view treatment as an experiment. Using examples from the beginning of the session, the therapist clarified that she respected Samantha's needs (e.g., to be unique) and values (e.g., to never take the easy way out) and that therapy could be a collaborative process of experimenting with new, less costly ways of achieving those gains. Samantha returned for the third and subsequent sessions without protest but remained ambivalent about her illness throughout much of treatment. As she maintained her weight, however, her other symptoms lessened and she began to bring in other material to sessions.

Balancing between Promoting Change and Encouraging Acceptance

CBT emphasizes cognitive and behavioral change, and, in addition to motivation, therapeutic change hinges on a client's self-perception of agency. If clients believe that they are not able to achieve certain goals of recovery, they will not be able to engage in therapeutic experimentation to change cognitions or behaviors. Conversely, if they believe that they have "total control," they are bound to feel demoralized and demotivated when change does not come easily. A common challenge for CBT is achieving a balance between promoting a sense of agency and a sense of acceptance for clients. At each impasse in treatment, some questions a therapist might consider are:

- Where are we in terms of balancing the focus on change with the need to promote self-acceptance?
- Is my client realistic about what he or she can change and what is unchangeable?
- Have we made explicit my client's beliefs concerning self-perceived capacity to change a particular cognition or behavior?
- What does my client need to know to make an accurate assessment of his or her agency?

Case Example

One of the initial challenges in treating obese clients with BED is to orient the client to a treatment that is very different from treatments received in the past. In the first CBT session with Joanne, a 47-year-old woman with a history of obesity since childhood, the therapist explored the client's goals for treatment and discussed what Joanne could realistically achieve in treatment. While Joanne seemed enthusiastic about the philosophy of treatment—combining self-acceptance with healthy eating and healthy lifestyle change—she admitted that she was surprised that the therapist was not assigning her a diet. As she came in for session two, Joanne stated immediately that the program was not working for her. In the past, she had always lost at least five pounds in the first week, and she was extremely disappointed that, despite having kept self-monitoring records daily and having had no binge episodes, her weight remained the same.

The therapist empathized with Joanne's frustration but was somewhat puzzled because Joanne had seemed to agree that weight loss would not be an immediate goal of treatment. When this was pointed out, Joanne became tearful. She believed that, although the therapist had stated that weight loss was not a goal, he was actually disappointed in her for not losing weight. Although cognitive restructuring had not yet been introduced, the therapist took the opportunity to explore with Joanne the emotional and behavioral consequences of this thought and the degree to which it was based on past rather than current experience. Joanne had been criticized throughout her life for being overweight or for regaining weight after she had lost it, and doctors had, on several occasions, expressed frustration at her for not sticking to the diets they prescribed. Consequently, although Joanne believed she was successful in her career and her family life, she also believed that she was essentially a lazy and uncontrolled person because she could not stay on a diet. To begin to deconstruct Joanne's belief that her obesity was her fault, the therapist provided psychoeducational material and assigned reading on the biological, genetic, and environmental determinants of obesity. Although this was helpful, Joanne's beliefs about the causes of her obesity were an active area of cognitive restructuring throughout most of the rest of the treatment. Throughout the course of treatment, Joanne continued to work on trying to achieve a balance between behavior change and realistic self-acceptance.

Maladaptive Self-Schemas

According to the CBT model for eating disorders, low self-esteem renders an individual vulnerable to developing an eating disorder. However, for many individuals with eating disorders, the issues of low self-esteem extend to profound self-loathing. Such self-loathing is typically part of a constellation of cognitions that constitute maladaptive self-schemas (e.g., I binge eat to punish myself because that's what I deserve). Working at a schematic level to identify, articulate, and challenge such maladaptive schemas is often critical in getting clients mobilized. Focusing on cognitive interventions aimed at schema-based work is useful when clients seem "stuck" in therapy, report a desire to engage in the work of therapy but seem unable to do so, and employ fixed ideas about themselves to account for their failures to achieve their goals in treatment. Relevant questions for therapists in this situation include:

- What are the fundamental self-schemas that govern my client's approach to treatment?
- Does the client think he or she "deserves" to get well?
- Does the client think he or she is capable of functioning without the eating disorder?
- How does the self-schema serve my client?
- What does the client think he or she would lose by changing his or her self-perception?

Case Example

Although there is much about binge eating that is common across clients, variations of meaning and experience exist as well. Barbara, a 35-year-old obese woman with binge eating disorder, was the owner of a moderately successful small business and had many friends, although she often went through periods of depression and social isolation. Unlike many clients with BED, Barbara had great difficulty stopping binge eating, even in the short term. When exploring Barbara's thoughts and feelings while binge eating, the therapist learned that the experience was far from uniformly pleasant. Barbara explained that, after the initial excitement of ordering out for cheeseburgers, cake, and ice cream, the actual binge became an exercise in self-punishment. "I force myself to keep eating even after I'm full," she related, "and after a while I just feel sick, but I keep eating because that's what I deserve." Barbara's self-monitoring records reflected the range of self-denigrating labels she used to describe herself— lazy slob, fat cow, chubster, and so on—and the feelings of shame and self-directed anger that accompanied her binge episodes.

On becoming aware of this aspect of Barbara's binges, the therapist determined that cognitive work aimed at articulating and addressing maladaptive self-schemas was critical. She worked with Barbara to articulate the assumptions that underlay these thoughts. What were Barbara's beliefs about the degree to which she should be able to control her eating? What did it mean that she sometimes lost control? What values were reflected in Barbara's treatment of herself, and were these values that she embraced in other areas of her life? Decentering was particularly useful for Barbara as she realized that the standards she used to evaluate her own behavior were much stricter than those she would use to evaluate her friends. This implied that her standards were related to core beliefs about herself and paved the way for more in-depth schema-based work. Barbara gradually became aware of the degree to which her need to punish herself was based on core beliefs that she was selfish and unlovable, and she realized how her binge eating served to reinforce these beliefs.

Deception in Treatment

As with substance abuse and dependence, deception is often part of the fabric of the eating disorders. This deception can be self-directed (e.g., "I didn't eat dinner because I had the flu"), therapist-directed (e.g., water-loading to falsely inflate weight and avoid hospitalization), or, most commonly, a combination of the two. To the extent that the deception significantly interferes with treatment and rapport and/or puts a client at risk, it is essential that it be addressed. This results in the delicate task of confronting the client without compromising rapport. It is critical for therapists to remember that clients engage in deception for good reasons, and it is essential that therapists understand that deception serves to protect the eating disorder and is often employed when individuals feel most vulnerable. Asking the following questions may help ascertain when and how to address a client's deception:

- Why do I think my client is deceiving me?
- Have I asked the client directly and explained honestly why I don't understand or believe something that he or she has told me?
- What is my client afraid would happen if I knew the "truth?"
- Is my client deceiving me because he or she and I have different goals concerning treatment or different ideas about recovery?

- What does it say about the eating disorder that my client, an otherwise honest individual, will deceive me despite my efforts to work with him or her in treatment?

Case Example

Michelle is a 22-year-old with AN, binge-purge subtype, who had been in outpatient treatment for two months after successfully completing a three-month inpatient hospitalization. She denied having self-induced vomiting since before admission, although other patients on the unit had reported seeing her purge. In her initial CBT relapse prevention session, Michelle admitted that she had a tendency to deceive herself and others about her symptoms. At her 10th outpatient session, Michelle's laboratory test results indicated a low potassium level. The therapist discussed these results with Michelle, who immediately stated, "It must be a mistake because I'm not purging."

The therapist reminded Michelle of their earlier discussion and wondered aloud whether the electrolyte disturbance might indicate that Michelle was engaging in self-deception again. However, Michelle continued to vehemently deny purging. She indignantly insisted on being retested after the session but then left the office before the phlebotomist could draw blood. Michelle cancelled the next session. When Michelle returned to treatment the following week, the scale indicated that she had lost three pounds.

Rather than immediately confronting Michelle about her recent behavior, the therapist asked Michelle if she could remember a time from the past when she had deceived herself or others about her symptoms. Michelle quietly admitted that she had purged during her inpatient stay but denied doing so to the staff. The therapist decided to explore this situation using a dysfunctional thought record to understand better the connections between her thoughts, feelings, and behaviors on this point. By focusing on a recent, past event, the therapist was able to gather information relevant to the present situation and offer a context for Michelle to discuss these issues without having to explain or defend her current behavior. By choosing a less threatening focus, Michelle was able to be more open in discussing her automatic thoughts associated with purging on the unit and her corresponding emotions. As illustrated in Table 7.4, Michelle's automatic thoughts at the time included, "If I admit to purging, then nothing I've accomplished in the hospital will count," "The staff will be so disappointed in me if they know I purged," and "If I pretend it never happened, the urge to do it again will go away." Her associated emotions were anxiety and shame. Michelle and the therapist then challenged these thoughts by identifying cognitive distortions (e.g., mental filter), finding alternative viewpoints ("If I admit to purging, I can get the help I need to get fully well"), marshalling evidence for and against ("In the past, when I've pretended a symptom wasn't there, it just got worse"), and taking a scenario to its extreme and developing a vision of mastery ("The staff usually handles problems in a matter-of-fact way, but even if they were disappointed, I could handle that").

The therapist then expressed her concern that a similar process was taking place now in treatment. Because of the honest and Socratic posture of the therapist, Michelle experienced the discussion of the past situation as nonjudgmental and nonthreatening and, therefore, was more comfortable to disclose that she was, in fact, continuing to purge. The therapist and Michelle decided to do a decision analysis about deception and to collaboratively develop a contract for how to handle these

Table 7.4 Dysfunctional Thought Record

Situation	Emotions	Automatic Thoughts	Rational Responses/ Challenges	Outcome/Plan
Specific event or stream of thoughts, daydream or recollection leading up to emotional state.	Specific feelings (e.g., sad, anxious). Rate how strongly you feel each emotion (1 to 100).	Write automatic thoughts that preceded emotions; how much did you believe these thoughts?	Alternatives or challenges to automatic thoughts.	How much do you believe automatic thoughts now? What are you going to do now? What can you do differently in the future?
While on the inpatient unit, I purged several times but didn't tell anyone.	Anxiety (90) Shame (100)	If I admit to purging, then nothing I've accomplished in the hospital will count. If I pretend it never happened, the urge to do it again will go away. I am a total loser.	If I admit to purging, I can get the help I need to get fully well (challenging the mental filter and all or nothing thinking). In the past when I've pretended a symptom wasn't there, it just got worse. The staff usually handles problems in a matter-of-fact way, but even if they were disappointed, I could handle that (trying to engage in a positive way, envisioning mastery).	In the future, I need to trust my therapist; getting well is not going to be all or nothing; I am not a failure for not getting it all right; if I pretend I am well when I'm not, I'll never get well. Anxiety (20) Shame (10)

situations in the future. By anticipating and normalizing recurrences of denial and deception, Michelle's anxiety and shame were reduced.

Treatment Attendance without Engagement

Attending sessions is not the same as being engaged in treatment. When individuals continue to attend sessions but seem to be disengaged from the work of therapy, it is important to explicitly address the lack of investment and change. This requires that therapists remain vigilant to the goals of treatment and the work entailed. The following questions can help therapists monitor and address issues of engagement:

- Is my client not changing because he or she is not invested?
- If it is due to lack of investment, why would my client not be invested in treatment at this time?
- What is the self-schema that governs how the client thinks about himself or herself in relationship to the current work of therapy?

- What are the benefits of the status quo?
- What are the thoughts and fears associated with change?
- What is my client's general sense of agency?

Case Example

Frank was an obese 51-year-old married salesman with BED who appeared to be enthusiastic about beginning group CBT. Frank typically came early for group and enjoyed socializing in the waiting room with the other members of the group, most of whom were women. However, in contrast to most of the other group members who completed homework assignments, such as self-monitoring, Frank usually shrugged his shoulders and stated that he'd never been very good about getting his homework done. When other group members offered suggestions for increasing his commitment, for example, partnering with his 11-year-old daughter who was also obese, going on bicycle rides with his wife, telephoning another group member when tempted to binge, Frank always had a reason why it wouldn't work for him. Unlike another group member who felt upset that her progress was lagging behind that of the rest of the group, Frank didn't seem at all disturbed that his binge eating was not improved, although he paid lip service to being "bummed" that he was still binge eating. The group became somewhat frustrated with Frank, who assumed a "class clown" role, which often detracted from the emotional tone of the discussion. The group leaders contemplated recommending that Frank leave the group because his continued participation did not seem productive either for him or for the rest of the group. They intended to recommend that he consider reentering treatment when he felt more ready to take on the work that would be involved.

In week eight, Frank came to the group visibly disturbed. He had been to see his physician and was told that his serum cholesterol and triglycerides were extremely high and that he had borderline diabetes. He related that his father, also obese, had developed diabetes in his mid-50s and died of a heart attack at age 58. As the group explored this issue, they discovered that Frank believed that, no matter what he did at this point, it was probably too late for him. He described feeling hopeless about treatment because he thought it would be impossible for him to get down to a normal weight and adopt a healthy lifestyle. Yet, he was terrified that he would die before his daughter's high school graduation, as his father had died before his. Once this belief was articulated, the group worked with Frank to test it, to examine the similarities and differences between his and his father's situation, to examine the medical realities, and to reinforce the idea that even modest lifestyle changes could affect his overall health. The group leaders and members worked with Frank to begin self-monitoring in the evenings, his high-risk time. Frank was grateful for the group's suggestions and returned the next week having completed his homework assignment for the first time.

Not All Clients Make Use of All Aspects of Cognitive-Behavioral Therapy

CBT includes many components, and, for many individuals in treatment, some aspects of CBT are experienced as more relevant and useful than others. It is important to continuously monitor the efficacy of CBT and get input from clients about what seems to be most helpful. Not making use of certain CBT interventions is completely acceptable to the extent that clients and therapists understand and agree on what is being omitted and why. Pursuing the nomothetic course of CBT when it does not fit the needs of the particular individual is a failed application of CBT. In contrast, explicit discussion about the clinical utility of different aspects of CBT will promote investment and assist in prioritizing the focus of treatment and treatment goals. When a client is not making use of some component of CBT, some useful questions are:

- Does this lack of participation represent general disengagement from treatment?
- Is there something about my client's character or cognitive style that would make this aspect of CBT less useful?
- Is there some way to adapt the CBT intervention to make it useful?
- Is use of this CBT strategy needed for my client to achieve his or her therapy goals?
- Are there other CBT approaches that would address the therapeutic issue and be a better fit for my client?

Case Example

Hannah is a 16-year-old girl with BN. She responded well to the first stage of CBT for BN and stopped bingeing and purging two months into treatment. In the second stage, she successfully tackled dieting and easily learned problem-solving skills. However, she was unengaged in cognitive restructuring. Hannah reported that she understood the rationale for this technique but never seemed to be able to identify her distorted thoughts. At about session 10, she reported that she felt better and wanted to stop treatment, but her parents were forcing her to attend more sessions.

Not all patients are suited for cognitive restructuring, and adolescents in particular may not always relate well to the technique. This should not be misinterpreted as a lack of commitment to the therapy in general. However, because CBT appears to be superior to pure behavioral treatment, it is important that a therapist explore all options in engaging the patient in cognitive work. In Hannah's case, the therapist first inquired as to whether there was anything about cognitive restructuring that the patient found distasteful or uncomfortable. For instance, some patients find the process intrusive. When this was ruled out, the therapist tried assigning behavioral challenges to elicit easily identifiable automatic thoughts (e.g., trying on clothes in a communal dressing room), but Hannah still did not connect to the process. Finally, the therapist tried a more simplified version of cognitive restructuring often used with young children, but Hannah found this "silly."

The therapist and Hannah ultimately concluded that cognitive restructuring was not a useful technique in this case, and they proceeded to relapse prevention and the development of a maintenance plan. The therapist reframed the abbreviated course of treatment as reflective of Hannah's rapid progress and overall success in therapy. The therapist spoke to Hannah's parents and supported her decision to terminate before completing the contracted 20 visits. The therapist explained that she was available in the future if booster sessions were ever needed.

Issues of Relapse

The problem of relapse is real for all the eating disorders, and one of the fundamental components of all CBT interventions is relapse prevention. Relapse prevention entails reviewing gains that have been achieved, establishing plans for future maintenance, and devising strategies for addressing lapses in functioning to avert a full relapse. Some useful questions when addressing issues of relapse include:

- Does my client understand what the proximal triggers are for his or her eating disorder?
- Does my client understand the sequence of events that could lead to his or her own relapse?
- Does my client have a plan established to keep a lapse from escalating into a full relapse?
- Is my client realistic about his or her continued vulnerability?
- Is my client able to effectively implement what was learned during the course of CBT?

Case Example 1

Courtney is a 20-year-old patient with a one-year history of AN. Nine months ago, she tried outpatient treatment, but she did not gain weight; she entered the hospital, where she gained to 90% of normal body weight. Courtney was subsequently discharged to outpatient CBT for relapse prevention and immediately began losing weight. At each session, she stated, "I don't want to lose more weight but I don't want to gain either." The treatment contract was to terminate outpatient therapy and recommend rehospitalization if Courtney's weight dropped to 75% of normal.

The path to relapse in AN is a slippery slope. However, it is not uncommon for an individual with AN to deny that continued weight loss represents a trajectory of relapse, especially if he or she has never before experienced a relapse. Courtney entertained a fantasy of "controlled anorexia" in which she could stabilize at an underweight point without continuing to lose. Her wish was to lose enough weight to stop feeling fat, without losing so much that she would have to leave college and be rehospitalized. Courtney, therefore, had a dual distortion: first, that weight loss would improve—not heighten—body image distortions, and second, that she had exquisite control over the weight-loss process.

Rather than simply providing Courtney with the information that such control is elusive, the therapist used Socratic questioning to help Courtney openly explore the issue: "At each session, you have said you would like to maintain your weight, yet at the next session, you are unwilling to consider regaining even to the previous week's weight—can you help me understand that? You had predicted that you would be happy at 85% of normal body weight, yet when you got there, you decided to lose more weight. At what weight do you think you'll be satisfied? Were you satisfied there when you first developed the illness or did you keep losing? What will your life be like if you lose more weight? If you maintain? If you gain? Is it possible to sustain a subnormal weight?"

This exploration led to a constructive and elaborate decision analysis. Based on this work, Courtney concluded that if she continued restricting, she would likely be rehospitalized. Rather than taking a position or sounding alarmed about this outcome, the therapist graphed Courtney's weight loss with her and calculated that at the current rate, she would reach 75% of normal body weight within seven weeks. The therapist emphasized that Courtney had choice and control over how she spent those seven weeks but that if she did relapse, it should occur with her full awareness of the process, so that she could use what she learned in the future.

Courtney decided that because maintenance at a low weight was unlikely and she didn't want to be rehospitalized, she would choose weight gain. From that session forward, she increased her food intake and added drink supplements to her diet. She remained ambivalent about relinquishing the AN but constantly reminded herself of her life goals to become a lawyer, get married, and have children. Approximately once per month, Courtney would begin to fear her weight gain was uncontrollable and lapse into periods of dietary restriction. The consequent weight loss reminded her that subnormal weight maintenance was impossible.

Case Example 2

Given the likelihood of an initial positive treatment response for a client with BED, one situation that arises frequently is that of lapse or relapse. Alison was an attractive, well-groomed, moderately overweight woman in her mid-50s who responded quickly and enthusiastically to treatment. She was able to identify her high-risk situations, develop and use behavioral strategies to negotiate these situations, and stabilize her eating. She had a particular flair for coming up with beautifully prepared healthy dishes, and she took great pleasure in bringing the therapist a new flavorful and refreshing tea she'd found. One area on which she departed from the therapist's recommendation was that of weight monitoring. Although the therapist encouraged her to prioritize healthy lifestyle changes and self-acceptance over weight loss and to monitor trends rather than day-to-day fluctuations, Alison thought it was helpful to check her weight every day. That way, if her weight crept up a pound or two, she could react quickly and bring it back under control. Alison completed the initial 20-session course of treatment successfully, entirely stopped binge eating, and lost 25 pounds.

When Alison came in for her six-month follow-up visit, she was distressed. She had broken her leg in a skiing accident and, in contrast to her usual active schedule, was spending most of her time at home. She had begun snacking while watching TV and, for the past two weeks, had been binge eating most evenings after her husband went to bed. With her broken leg, she could not easily weigh herself, but she was sure she had gained weight, and her dress size had gone up two sizes. She tried to use the strategies that had been successful in the past but just couldn't seem to get started. When questioned about her binge eating, Alison revealed her belief that all the hard work she'd put in had been for nothing. She was angry that an accident had done this to her, and she believed that the self-control that she'd taken so much pride in was now no longer possible. Her attempts to take control and diet to quickly lose a dress size had led only to a return of her binge eating. Using Socratic questioning, the therapist helped her to identify that the key cognition was "Until I'm back down to a size 12, I'm fat and out of control." As a result of cognitive restructuring, Alison realized that the reason the techniques she'd learned were no longer working was that her standards had changed. Whereas when she'd started treatment, she was bolstered by small successes, now nothing short of an immediate 25-pound weight loss seemed good enough. While empathizing with Alison's anger at the consequences of the accident, the therapist helped her to reframe the situation as an opportunity to reevaluate her reliance on the scale and to examine what it would take for her to once again see herself as strong, controlled, and attractive. With this as a basis, Alison and the therapist developed realistic short-term goals and strategies for dealing with the current challenging circumstances, deferring weight loss until her eating had once again stabilized.

SUMMARY AND FUTURE DIRECTIONS

The application of CBT to the treatment of eating disorders has a long history, and, currently, CBT is often referred to as a "treatment of choice" for eating disorders. The efficacy of CBT in the treatment of BN is well supported by data from multiple clinical trials. However, even in the case of CBT for BN, a significant subgroup remains at least partially symptomatic at the end of treatment (Wilson, 1999). Moreover, the empirical database is less well established for BED, and only preliminary empirical data exist to support the application of CBT to AN (Pike et al., 2003; Vitousek, 2002). It is essential that continued efforts in clinical research refine, enhance, expand, and adapt current interventions with the goal of ultimately developing and documenting more efficacious treatments.

REFERENCES

Agras, W. S., Rossiter, E. M., Arnow, B., Telch, C. F., Raeburn, S. D., Bruce, B., et al. (1994). One-year follow-up of psychosocial and pharmacologic treatments for bulimia nervosa. *Journal of Clinical Psychiatry, 55,* 179–183.

Agras, W. S., Telch, C. F., Arnow, B., Eldredge, K., & Marnell, M. (1997). One-year follow-up of cognitive-behavioral therapy for obese individuals with binge eating disorder. *Journal of Consulting and Clinical Psychology, 65,* 343–347.

Agras, W. S., Telch, C. F., Arnow, B., Eldredge, K., Wilfley, D. E., Raeburn, S. D., et al. (1994). Weight loss, cognitive-behavioral and desipramine treatments in binge-eating disorder: An additive design. *Behavior Therapy, 25,* 225–238.

Agras, W. S., Walsh, B. T., Fairburn, C. G., Wilson, G. T., & Kraemer, H. C. (2000). A multicenter comparison of cognitive-behavioral therapy and interpersonal psychotherapy for bulimia nervosa. *Archives of General Psychiatry, 57,* 459–466.

American Psychiatric Association. (1994). *Diagnostic and statistical manual of mental disorders* (4th ed.). Washington, DC: Author.

Beck, A. T. (1976). *Cognitive therapy and the emotional disorders.* New York: International Universities Press.

Beck, A. T., Freeman, A., & Associates. (1990). *Cognitive therapy of personality disorders.* New York: Guilford Press.

Beck, A. T., Rush, A. H., Shaw, B. F., & Emery, G. (1979). *Cognitive therapy of depression.* New York: Guilford Press.

Beck, J. S. (1995). *Cognitive therapy: Basics and beyond.* New York: Guilford Press.

Becker, A. E., Grinspoon, S. K., Klibanski, A., & Herzog, D. B. (1999). Eating disorders. *New England Journal of Medicine, 340,* 1092–1098.

Bemis, K. M. (1983). A comparison of functional relationships in anorexia nervosa and phobia. In P. L. Darby, P. E. Garfinkel, D. M. Garner, & D. V. Coscina (Eds.), *Anorexia nervosa: Recent developments in research* (pp. 403–416). New York: Alan R. Liss.

Cooper, M. J., & Fairburn, C. G. (1992). Thoughts about eating, weight, and shape in anorexia nervosa and bulimia nervosa. *Behavior Research and Therapy, 30,* 501–511.

Devlin, M. J. (2001). Binge eating disorder and obesity: A combined treatment approach. *Psychiatric Clinics of North America, 24,* 325–335.

Devlin, M. J., Yanovski, S. Z., & Wilson, G. T. (2000). Obesity: What mental health professionals need to know. *American Journal of Psychiatry, 157,* 854–866.

Eldredge, K. L., Agras, W. S., Arnow, B., Telch, C. F., Bell, S., Castonguay, I., et al. (1999). The effects of extending cognitive-behavioral therapy for binge eating disorder among initial treatment nonresponders. *International Journal of Eating Disorders, 21,* 347–352.

Fairburn, C. G. (1985). Cognitive-behavioral treatment for bulimia. In D. M. Garner & P. E. Garfinkel (Eds.), *Handbook of psychotherapy for anorexia nervosa and bulimia* (pp. 160–192). New York: Guilford Press.

Fairburn, C. G., Cooper, Z., & Safran, R. (2002). Cognitive behavior therapy for eating disorders: A "transdiagnostic" theory and treatment. *Behavior Research and Therapy.*

Fairburn, C. G., Jones, R., Peveler, R. C., Carr, S. J., Solomon, R. A., O'Connor, M., et al. (1991). Three psychological treatments of bulimia nervosa. *Archives of General Psychiatry, 48,* 463–469.

Fairburn, C. G., Jones, R., Peveler, R. C., Hope, R. A., & O'Connor, M. (1993). Psychotherapy and bulimia nervosa: The longer-term effects of interpersonal psychotherapy, behavior therapy and cognitive behavior therapy. *Archives of General Psychiatry, 50,* 419–428.

Fairburn, C. G., Marcus, M. D., & Wilson, G. T. (1993). Cognitive-behavioral therapy for binge eating and bulimia nervosa: A comprehensive treatment manual. In C. G. Fairburn & G. T. Wilson (Eds.), *Binge eating: Nature, assessment, and treatment* (pp. 361–404). New York: Guilford Press.

Fairburn, C. G., Norman, P. A., Welch, S. L., O'Connor, M. E., Doll, H. A., & Peveler, R. C. (1995). A prospective study of outcome in bulimia nervosa and the long term effects of three psychological treatments. *Archives of General Psychiatry, 52,* 304–312.

Fairburn, C. G., Peveler, R. C., Jones, R., Hope, R. A., & Doll, H. (1993). Predictors of 12-month outcome in bulimia nervosa and the influence of attitudes to shape and weight. *Journal of Consulting and Clinical Psychology, 61,* 696–698.

Garner, D. M., & Bemis, K. M. (1982). Anorexia nervosa: A cognitive-behavioral approach to AN. *Cognitive Therapy and Research, 6,* 123–150.

Garner, D. M., & Bemis, K. M. (1985). Cognitive therapy for AN. In D. M. Garner & P. E. Garfinkel (Eds.), *Handbook of psychotherapy for anorexia nervosa and bulimia* (pp. 107–146). New York: Guilford Press.

Garner, D. M., Rockert, W., Garner, M. V., Davis, R., Olmsted, M. P., & Eagle, M. (1993). Comparison of cognitive-behavioral and supportive expressive therapy for bulimia nervosa. *American Journal of Psychiatry, 150,* 37–46.

Garner, D. M., Vitousek, K., & Pike, K. M. (1997). Cognitive behavioral therapy for anorexia nervosa. In D. M. Garner & P. E. Garfinkel (Eds.), *Handbook of treatment for eating disorders* (pp. 94–144). New York: Guilford Press.

Geller, J., Johnston, C., & Madsen, K. (1997). The role of shape and weight in self-concept: The shape and weight based self-esteem inventory. *Cognitive Therapy and Research, 21,* 5–24.

Geller, J., Johnston, C., Madsen, K., Goldner, E., Remick, R., & Birmingham, L. (1998). Shape and weight based self-esteem and the eating disorders. *International Journal of Eating Disorders, 24,* 285–298.

Geller, J., Srikameswaran, S., Cockell, S. J., & Zaitsoff, S. L. (2000). The assessment of shape and weight-based self-esteem in adolescents. *International Journal of Eating Disorders, 28,* 339–345.

Greeno, C. G., Wing, R. R., & Marcus, M. D. (1999). How many donuts is a "binge"? Women with BED eat more but do not have more restrictive standards than weight-matched non-BED women. *Addictive Behaviors, 24,* 299–303.

Guidano, V. F., & Liotti, G. (1983). *Cognitive processes and emotional disorders: A structural approach to psychotherapy.* New York: Guilford Press.

Guss, J. L., Kissileff, H. R., Devlin, M. J., Zimmerli, E., & Walsh, B. T. (2002, October). Binge size increases with body mass index in women with binge-eating disorder. *Obesity Research 10*(10), 1021–1029.

Hall, A. (1982). Deciding to stay an anorectic. *Postgraduate Medical Journal, 58,* 641–647.

Hawton, K., Salkovskis, P. M., Kirk, J., & Clark, D. M. (1989). *Cognitive behavior therapy for psychiatric problems: A practical guide.* Oxford, England: Oxford University Press.

Hollon, S. D., & Beck, A. T. (1993). Cognitive and cognitive-behavioral therapies. In A. E. Bergin & S. L. Garfield (Eds.), *Handbook of psychotherapy and behavior change: An empirical analysis* (4th ed., pp. 428–466). New York: Wiley.

Keys, A., Brozek, J., Henschel, A., Mickelsen, O., & Taylor, H. L. (1950). *The biology of human starvation* (Vols. 1 & 2). Minneapolis: University of Minnesota Press.

Linehan, M. M. (1993). *Cognitive-behavioral treatment of borderline personality disorder.* New York: Guilford Press.

Liotti, G. (1993). Disorganized attachment and dissociative experiences: An illustration of the developmental-ethological approach to cognitive therapy. In K. T. Kuehlwein & H. Rosen (Eds.), *Cognitive therapies in action: Evolving innovative practice* (pp. 213–239). San Francisco: Jossey-Bass.

Marcus, M. D. (1997). Adapting treatment for patients with binge-eating disorder. In D. M. Garner & P. E. Garfinkel (Eds.), *Handbook of treatment for eating disorders* (2nd ed., pp. 484–493). New York: Guilford Press.

Marcus, M. D., Wing, R. R., & Fairburn, C. G. (1995). Cognitive behavioral treatment of binge eating vs. behavioral weight control in the treatment of binge eating disorder. *Annals of Behavioral Medicine, 17*(Suppl.), S090.

Miller, W. R., & Rollnick, S. (1991). *Motivational interviewing.* New York: Guilford Press.

Orlinsky, D. E., Grawe, K., & Parks, B. K. (1994). Process and outcome in psychotherapy: *Noch einmal.* In A. E. Bergin & S. L Garfield (Eds.), *Handbook of psychotherapy and behavior change* (4th ed., pp. 270–376). New York: Wiley.

Pike, K. M., Loeb, K., & Vitousek, K. (1996). Cognitive behavioral treatment for anorexia nervosa and bulimia nervosa. In K. Thompson (Ed.), *Eating disorders, obesity and body image: A practical guide to assessment and treatment* (pp. 253–302). Washington, DC: American Psychological Association.

Pike, K. M., Vitousek, K. B., & Wilson, G. T. (1998). *Cognitive behavioral therapy treatment manual for posthospital treatment of anorexia nervosa.* Available upon request from the authors. Online requests may be directed to kpm2@columbia.edu.

Pike, K. M., Walsh, B. T., Vitousek, K. B., Wilson, G. T., & Bauer, J. (2003). *Cognitive behavioral treatment in the posthospital treatment of anorexia nervosa.* Manuscript submitted for publication.

Pomeroy, C., & Mitchell, J. (2002). Medical complications of anorexia nervosa and bulimia nervosa. In C. G. Fairburn & K. D. Brownell (Eds.), *Eating disorders and obesity* (2nd vol., pp. 278–285). New York: Guilford Press.

Prochaska, J. O., & DiClemente, C. C. (1983). Stages and processes of self-change in smoking: Toward an integrative model of change. *Journal of Consulting and Clinical Psychology, 5,* 390–395.

Prochaska, J. O., DiClemente, C. C., & Norcross, J. C. (1992). In search of how people change: Applications to addictive behavior. *American Psychologist, 47,* 1102–1114.

Puhl, R., & Brownell, K. D. (2001). Bias, discrimination, and obesity. *Obesity Research, 9,* 788–805.

Safran, J. D., & Segal, Z. V. (1990). *Interpersonal process in cognitive therapy.* New York: Basic Books.

Serfaty, M. A., Turkington, D., Heap, M., Ledsham, L., & Jolley, E. (1999). Cognitive therapy versus dietary counseling in the outpatient treatment of anorexia nervosa: Effects of the treatment phase. *European Eating Disorders Review, 7,* 334–350.

Smith, D. E., Marcus, M. D., & Kaye, W. (1992). Cognitive-behavioral treatment of obese binge eaters. *International Journal of Eating Disorders, 12,* 257–262.

Spitzer, R. L., Devlin, M. J., Walsh, B. T., Hasin, D., Wing, R. R., Marcus, M. D., et al. (1992). Binge eating disorder: A multisite field trial for the diagnostic criteria. *International Journal of Eating Disorders, 11,* 191–203.

Spitzer, R. L., Yanovski, S., Wadden, T., Wing, R., Marcus, M., Stunkard, A., et al. (1993). Binge eating disorder: Its further validation in a multisite study. *International Journal of Eating Disorders, 13,* 137–153.

Striegel-Moore, R. H., Silberstein, L. R., & Rodin, J. (1986). Toward an understanding of risk factors for bulimia. *American Psychologist, 41,* 146–163.

Telch, C. F., Agras, W. S., Rossiter, E. M., Wilfley, D., & Kenardy, J. (1990). Group cognitive-behavioral therapy for the nonpurging bulimic: An initial evaluation. *Journal of Consulting and Clinical Psychology, 58,* 629–635.

Thompson, J. K., & Williams, D. E. (1987). An interpersonally based cognitive behavioral psychotherapy. In M. Herson, R. M. Eisler, & P. M. Miller (Eds.), *Progress in behavior modification* (Vol. 21, pp. 230–258). New York: Sage.

Truax, C. B., & Mitchell, K. M. (1971). Research on certain therapist interpersonal skills in relation to process and outcome. In A. E. Bergin & S. L. Garfield (Eds.), *Handbook of psychotherapy and behavior change: An empirical analysis* (pp. 299–344). New York. Wiley.

Vitousek, K. B. (1996). The current status of cognitive-behavioral models of anorexia nervosa and bulimia nervosa. In P. M. Salkovskis (Ed.), *Frontiers of cognitive therapy* (pp. 383–418). New York: Guilford Press.

Vitousek, K. B. (2002). Cognitive-behavioral therapy for anorexia nervosa. In C. G. Fairburn & K. D. Brownell (Eds.), *Eating disorders and obesity* (2nd ed., pp. 308–313). New York: Guilford Press.

Vitousek, K. B., & Ewald, L. S. (1993). Self-representation in eating disorders: A cognitive perspective. In Z. Segal & S. Blatt (Eds.), *The self in emotional distress: Cognitive and psychodynamic perspectives* (pp. 221–257). New York: Guilford Press.

Vitousek, K. B., & Hollon, S. D. (1990). The investigation of schematic content and processing in eating disorders. *Cognitive Therapy and Research, 14*(2), 191–214.

Vitousek, K. B., Watson, S., & Wilson, G. T. (1998). Enhancing motivation in eating disorders. *Clinical Psychology Review, 18,* 476–498.

Walsh, B. T., Wilson, G. T., Loeb, K. L., Devlin, M. J., Pike, K. M., Roose, S. P., et al. (1997). Medication and psychotherapy in the treatment of bulimia nervosa. *American Journal of Psychiatry, 154,* 523–531.

Wegner, K. E., Smyth, J. M., Crosby, R. D., Wittrock, D., Wonderlich, S. A., & Mitchell, J. E. (2002). An evaluation of the relationship between mood and binge eating in the natural environment using ecological momentary assessment. *International Journal of Eating Disorders, 32,* 352–361.

Wilfley, D. E., Agras, W. S., Telch, C. F., Rossiter, E. M., Schneider, J. A., Cole, A. G., et al. (1993). Group cognitive-behavioral therapy and group interpersonal psychotherapy for the nonpurging bulimic individual: A controlled comparison. *Journal of Consulting and Clinical Psychology, 61,* 296–305.

Wilfley, D. E., Schwartz, M. B., Spurrell, E. B., & Fairburn, C. G. (2000). Using the Eating Disorder Examination to identify the specific psychopathology of binge eating disorder. *International Journal of Eating Disorders, 27,* 259–269.

Wilfley, D. E., Welch, R., Stein, R. I., Spurrell, E. B., Cohen, L. R., Saelens, B. E., et al. (2002). A randomized comparison of group cognitive-behavioral and group interpersonal psychotherapy for the treatment of overweight individuals with binge-eating disorder. *Archives of General Psychiatry, 59,* 713–721.

Wilson, G. T. (1996). Acceptance and change in the treatment of eating disorders. *Behavior Therapy, 27,* 417–439.

Wilson, G. T. (1999). Cognitive behavior therapy for eating disorders: Progress and problems. *Behavior Research and Therapy, 37,* 79–95.

Wilson, G. T., Fairburn, C. G., & Agras, W. S. (1997). Cognitive-behavioral therapy for bulimia nervosa. In D. M. Garner & P. Garfinkel (Eds.), *Handbook of treatment for eating disorders* (2nd ed., pp. 67–93). New York: Guilford Press.

Wilson, G. T., & Pike, K. M. (2001). Eating disorders. In D. H. Barlow (Ed.), *Clinical handbook of psychological disorders* (3rd ed., pp. 332–375). New York: Guilford Press.

Yanovski, S. Z., Leet, M., Yanovski, J. A., Flood, M., Gold, P. W., Kissileff, H. R., et al. (1992). Food selection and intake of obese women with binge-eating disorder. *American Journal of Clinical Nutrition, 56,* 975–980.

Young, J. E. (1990). Schema-focused cognitive therapy for personality disorders. In A. Beck & A. Freeman (Eds.), *Cognitive therapy for personality disorders.* New York: Guilford Press.

Young, J. E., Weinberger, A. D., & Beck, A. T. (2001). Cognitive therapy for depression. In D. H. Barlow (Ed.), *Clinical handbook of psychological disorders* (3rd ed., pp. 264–308) New York: Guilford Press.

Chapter 8

INTERPERSONAL PSYCHOTHERAPY FOR THE TREATMENT OF ANOREXIA NERVOSA, BULIMIA NERVOSA, AND BINGE EATING DISORDER

STACEY TANTLEFF-DUNN, JESSICA GOKEE-LaROSE, AND
RACHEL D. PETERSON

Interpersonal psychotherapy (IPT) is a present-oriented, short-term psychotherapy developed in the 1960s that has been empirically supported (Fairburn, 1997; Gillies, 2001; Klerman & Weissman, 1993; Swartz, 1999). Early IPT research was part of a study on relapse prevention for unipolar, nonpsychotic depressed outpatients that involved testing the efficacy of antidepressants and psychotherapy (Klerman & Weissman, 1993; Weissman, 1999). Klerman and colleagues merely intended to standardize therapy sessions among therapists for the research, not create a new form of psychotherapy. However, the manual created from their work is now known as *IPT* (Klerman, Weissman, Rounsaville, & Chevron, 1984; Weissman, 1999).

Several noteworthy theorists influenced the development of IPT. Harry Stack Sullivan, creator of the interpersonal school of psychiatry, maintained that to best understand people, their patterns of relationships and social functioning have to be taken into account. Adolph Meyer, whose biopsychosocial view of mental illness shaped IPT, theorized that an important component of psychopathology was that people's experiences in social interactions affected their ability to adjust to current surroundings (Klerman & Weissman, 1993). Finally, psychoanalyst John Bowlby's theories of attachment played a major role in the development of IPT (Klerman & Weissman, 1993). Bowlby's (1977) observation that a lack of bonding negatively affected mammals was generalized to humans because infants rely on social bonds to an even greater degree than other mammals.

Although the focus in IPT is clearly on interpersonal relationships, interpersonal difficulties are not presumed to "cause" mental illness; rather, they are conceptualized as playing an important role in the onset and maintenance of psychological disturbance (Frank & Spanier, 1995; Klerman & Weissman, 1993). IPT is based on the belief that mental illness is closely tied to impaired social functioning and, consequently, focuses on people within their social contexts (Frank & Spanier, 1995; Klerman & Weissman, 1993). Research supports the assumption that people with mental illness often experience difficulty in their interpersonal interactions (Gotlib & Schraedley, 2000). It is common, for example, for depressed people to associate the onset of their depression with an interpersonal antecedent (Swartz, 1999). Therefore, a major goal of IPT is to enhance interpersonal functioning and communication skills (Klerman & Weissman, 1993; Wilfley, Dounchis, & Welch, 2000).

In addition to enhancing interpersonal functioning, another objective of IPT is to reduce disorder symptomatology (Gotlib & Schraedley, 2000). While this is similar to other forms of psychotherapy, several features of IPT make it unique (Klerman & Weissman, 1993; Markowitz, Svartberg, & Swartz, 1998). Foremost, the hallmark of IPT is that the disorder and its symptoms are not the primary focus of the therapy sessions; they are all but purposely avoided (Gotlib & Schraedley, 2000; Klerman & Weissman, 1993; Weissman, 1999). Instead, IPT concentrates on interpersonal difficulties associated with the onset, maintenance, and relapse of mental illness (Klerman & Weissman, 1993). Exploration of past relationships is used to formulate this time line and more fully understand the client's current social functioning, but IPT maintains a focus on the present (Swartz, 1999; Wifely et al., 2000).

IPT is short-term, usually consisting of four to six months of 50-minute weekly sessions (Fairburn, 1998; Hinrichsen, 1999; Sole-Puig, 1997). Beginning with the first session, the time-limited aspect of treatment is stressed to the client because brevity of treatment can work to motivate both the therapist and client to use their time most effectively (Fairburn, 1997; Swartz, 1999). IPT subscribes to the medical model in which the client's "problem" is viewed as an illness and is, therefore, not the client's fault (Swartz, 1999). The therapist gives the appropriate diagnosis, and the client is then placed in the "sick role" (Gotlib & Schraedley, 2000). Allowing the client to understand and view his or her difficulties as a result of an illness and not a personal inadequacy helps to eliminate self-blame (Swartz, 1999). The therapist makes it clear, however, that this role is adverse and temporary (Swartz, 1999). The therapist then educates the client on the symptoms and the disorder itself so that the client may become an "expert" on the disorder (Swartz, 1999). As termination approaches, the client is educated on the possibility of relapse and how to manage if it does occur (Swartz, 1999).

The IPT therapist acts as a supportive, empathetic, warm "cheerleader" (Gillies, 2001; Klerman et al., 1984; Wifely et al., 2000). Similar to other psychotherapies, IPT uses rephrasing, genuine regard, and clarification to facilitate the therapeutic process (Wilfley et al., 2000). Unlike psychoanalysis, the IPT therapist is noninterpretive and active in the session (Fairburn, 1997; Klerman et al., 1984; Swartz, 1999; Wilfley et al., 2000). The therapist is nondirective, but keeps the session discussion on task, encouraging the client to direct the session whenever possible (Gillies, 2001; Wilfley et al., 2000).

Although IPT has been employed in some inpatient settings, it is not used for psychotic, suicidal, or severely mentally ill clients (Gillies, 2001). Regardless, Swartz (1999) and Sole-Puig (1997) view disorder-specific therapy, such as IPT, as progress in the field of mental health. IPT has been modified for various forms of depression (dysthymia, comorbid depression, bipolar disorder), adjustment disorders, borderline personality disorder, social phobia, bulimia, and for treatment with other specific populations (e.g., HIV, adolescents, elderly; Hinrichsen, 1999; Klerman & Weissman, 1993; Weissman & Markowitz, 1994).

THEORETICAL AND EMPIRICAL RATIONALE FOR INTERPERSONAL PSYCHOTHERAPY WITH EATING DISORDERS

Overall, empirical evidence supports the notion that interpersonal functioning may play a role in the development and/or maintenance of psychological disorders. Research has shown that individuals suffering from psychological disorders often have less supportive and smaller social support networks than control groups (Gotlib & Schraedley, 2000). Such findings have been reported among depressed individuals (e.g., Billings, Cronkite, & Moos, 1983; Billings & Moos, 1985), individuals diagnosed with substance abuse disorders (e.g., Hawkins & Fraser, 1985), as well as individuals with panic disorder (e.g., Markowitz, Weissman, Quellette, Lish, & Klerman, 1989). Similar findings exist for persons suffering from eating disorders (e.g., Tiller et al., 1997). In fact, Schmidt and colleagues (Schmidt, Tiller, Blanchard, Andrews, & Treasure, 1997) reported that the most serious life stressors experienced before the onset of an eating disorder involve relationships with friends and family. Further, researchers have estimated that 75% of individuals diagnosed with anorexia nervosa or bulimia nervosa experience a significant life stressor sometime during the year preceding the onset of the illness (Schmidt, Tiller, Blanchard, Andrew, & Treasure, 1997). Such findings are indicative of a link between interpersonal events and functioning and psychological disorders, particularly the development and/or maintenance of eating disorders. The directionality of this phenomenon is not yet clear. Nonetheless, whether individuals take a diathesis-stress view or adopt the perspective that eating-disordered individuals play a role in creating the stressful events in their lives, there is a strong interpersonal component in many disorders, including anorexia, bulimia, and binge eating disorder.

Researchers have suggested that IPT is a viable alternative to cognitive-behavioral therapy (CBT) in the treatment of bulimia and binge eating disorder (e.g., Apple, 1999; Birchall, 1999; Fairburn, 1997). Given that IPT does not focus directly on eating symptoms but on underlying problem areas, it is hypothesized that treatment may succeed in yielding changes in affect regulation, which in turn may impact the desire to binge (Apple, 1999). In fact, preliminary outcome studies (discussed in greater detail later in this chapter) have shown that IPT is successful in the reduction of eating disorder symptomatology at a rate nearly equal to that of CBT in some cases and often surpassing CBT at a one-year follow-up (Fairburn, Jones, Peveler, Hope, & O'Connor, 1993; Fairburn, Kirk, O'Connor, & Cooper, 1986; Wilfley et al., 1993). Apple (1999) suggests that the time necessary to make changes in relationships and interpersonal functioning may account for the fact that IPT appears to be somewhat slower acting when compared to CBT, although IPT may actually attain benefits that are equally lasting.

Much less empirical attention has been directed toward investigating the efficacy of IPT with anorexia. However, as McIntosh and colleagues (McIntosh, Bulik, McKenzie, Luty, & Jordan, 2000) suggest, anorexia nervosa is frequently conceptualized within a theoretical framework that is consistent with IPT. Etiological theories of anorexia often emphasize family as well as interpersonal dysfunction, and treatment consequently tends to focus on the family unit and communication patterns (McIntosh et al., 2000). Therefore, given the key role that interpersonal functioning plays in the conceptualization and treatment of anorexia, the preliminary success of IPT in treating bulimia nervosa, and the significant overlap between the two disorders, there is sufficient reason to advocate for the application of IPT to anorexia as well (McIntosh et al., 2000).

INTERPERSONAL INFLUENCES

Extant research provides evidence for the role of interpersonal influences on the development of body image and self-esteem, as well as for the role of body image disturbance in the development of eating disorders (see Tantleff-Dunn & Gokee, 2002; Thompson, Heinberg, Altabe, & Tantleff-Dunn, 1999). The influence of an individual's interpersonal environment may be direct, such as outright teasing or derogatory remarks and criticism, or some influences may be more indirect and subtle, such as ambiguous comments or nonverbal gestures. The negative consequences of receiving feedback, even when neutral in nature, have been well documented in the literature (Thompson et al., 1999).

Being teased by others is one of the most commonly reported factors that shape body satisfaction (Cash, 1995; Garner, 1997; Rieves & Cash, 1996). The experience of frequent teasing has been associated with higher levels of body dissatisfaction, eating disturbance, depression, and lower self-esteem (Fabian & Thompson, 1989); and a history of being teased is significantly associated with current levels of body image satisfaction (Cash, 1995; Thompson & Psaltis, 1988). In a longitudinal study, teasing predicted increases in body dissatisfaction (Cattarin & Thompson, 1994). Because peers and friends are among the most frequent and "worst" perpetrators of teasing, second only to brothers (Rieves & Cash, 1996), exploring responses to teasing and strengthening communication and assertiveness skills are potentially fruitful interpersonal focal points.

Another interpersonal factor that influences the development of body image and eating disturbance is the presence of appearance comparison tendencies (e.g., Cash, Cash, & Butters, 1983; Cattarin, Thompson, Thomas, & Williams, 2000; Heinberg & Thompson, 1992). The basic findings in this area of research suggest that women tend to become more dissatisfied with their own physical appearance when they compare themselves to attractive female models. From an interpersonal perspective, reducing comparison tendencies in general while addressing relationships that stimulate a great deal of comparison may be worthwhile therapeutic goals.

Research also suggests that perceptions as to peer acceptance may serve to elevate body image concerns and subsequent disturbance. The belief that thinness increases likeability is a predictor of weight and body image concerns (Oliver & Thelen, 1996). There is evidence of a modeling effect of peers as well. Adolescent females in friendship cliques exhibit similar levels of body image concern, dietary restraint, and extreme weight loss behaviors (Paxton, Schutz, Wertheim, & Muir, 1999). Similarly, college women who purge often know other women who purge, and women who have more friends who are dieting tend to exhibit more eating disorder symptomatology (Schwartz

& Thompson, 1981). Thus, in treating clients with eating disorders, it may be important to examine the prevalence and effect of eating disturbance in peers and significant others who may inadvertently be shaping the client's attitudes and behaviors as to weight and appearance. In a recent study of female adolescents, "Basing self-esteem on intimate relationships was associated with lower global and body self-esteem and higher levels of anorexic and bulimic eating disorder symptoms" (Geller, Zaitsoff, & Srikameswaran, 2002, p. 349). The authors of this study hypothesized that a focus on intimate relationships may result in inhibited self-expression, which previously has been linked with disordered eating (Zaitsoff, Geller, & Srikameswaran, 2002).

Understanding the role that parents play in shaping body image has been another focus of attention. Two main modes of parental influence have received empirical investigation:

1. A potential modeling effect based on parents' own body image and eating behavior.
2. Parents' attitudes toward their children's weight, shape, and diet (Thompson et al., 1999).

Research in this area generally has yielded mixed results. While some correlational studies have found a relationship between mothers' and daughters' dissatisfaction and disordered eating (Hill, Weaver, & Blundell, 1990; Pike & Rodin, 1991), others have failed to support such a link (Attie & Brooks-Gunn, 1989; Sanftner, Crowther, Crawford, & Watts, 1996; Thelen & Comier, 1995). The findings of Levine and colleagues suggest that weight- and shape-related teasing and criticism by family members may be related to drive for thinness and disturbed patterns of eating for girls (Levine, Smolak, & Hayden, 1994). Benedikt and colleagues found that, at the moderate level, mothers' influence was through direct encouragement of diet and weight loss, as opposed to modeling, whereas at more extreme levels, mothers' own dissatisfaction and use of extreme measures to lose weight predicted their daughters' behavior (Benedikt, Wertheim, & Love, 1998). Most recently, Vincent and McCabe (2000) found that direct influences of family, as opposed to the quality of the relationships, predicted body dissatisfaction and disordered eating in both boys and girls. They found that parental discussion and encouragement of weight loss predicted disordered eating behavior in girls and that maternal encouragement predicted binge eating and weight loss behaviors in boys. Overall, there is enough evidence to suggest that examining parent-child relationships and the impact of parental attitudes and behaviors related to weight and eating may prove to be a valuable therapeutic endeavor, particularly when eating disorder clients have close contact with their parents. This fits well within the framework of IPT.

Perhaps even more relevant to the discussion of IPT for eating disorders is the relationship among body image, eating disturbance, and romantic relationships. Murray, Touyz, and Beumont (1995) used open-ended interviews to compare interpersonal influences for females with eating disorders and both female and male controls and found that 48% of the total sample reported that members of the opposite sex affected their eating, exercise, and body satisfaction, with no significant differences between comparison groups. Mark and Crowther (1997) found that greater body dissatisfaction was associated with lower relationship satisfaction and that men's relationship satisfaction was significantly related to satisfaction with their partners' shape. More recently, marital discord was found to predict unhealthy dieting behaviors in women (Markey, Markey, & Birch, 2001). Another study found that ratings of marital satisfaction and intimacy were lower for eating disorder patients than their spouses, and those ratings improved significantly over the course of treatment for the eating disorder (Woodside, Lackstrom, & Shekter Wolfson, 2000). Dealing with interpersonal role disputes, including marital discord, is one of the primary focal points in IPT.

IMPLEMENTATION OF INTERPERSONAL PSYCHOTHERAPY FOR EATING DISORDERS

One aspect of the time-limited nature of IPT is the distinct phases of treatment, each containing specific responsibilities for both the client and therapist. Fairburn (1997) and Wilfley et al. (2002) have described the goals and strategies of each phase of IPT for eating disorders, outlined in the following sections.

Phase 1

During the first four to five therapy sessions, a complete diagnostic evaluation is conducted to assess symptoms and make the appropriate eating disorder diagnosis. On receiving the diagnosis, the client assumes the "sick role," which is particularly helpful in assisting eating-disordered clients to avoid their tendencies to please others and to refocus their energies on recovery. The therapist then helps the client understand that the symptoms are part of a treatable eating disorder. The prevalence of interpersonal difficulties among individuals with eating disorders is discussed, along with an explanation that some clients are not fully aware of their interpersonal stressors because they are distracted by their preoccupation with eating and body image concerns. The potential effectiveness of IPT is presented along with an explanation that the focus of this treatment is on interpersonal difficulties that may be contributing to the eating disorder, rather than on the eating problems themselves. The different phases of treatment are described, with an emphasis on the client's responsibility to identify current interpersonal challenges to be discussed once the initial assessment phase is completed. Underscoring the time-limited nature of the treatment is essential for encouraging the client to make the most of the relatively brief opportunity for progress. Generally in IPT, the need for medication is also discussed at this time. The decision as to whether to use medication concurrently with IPT depends on the client's history, illness severity, as well as his or her preferences (Hinrichsen, 1999; Klerman & Weissman, 1993; Swartz, 1999; Weissman, 1999).

An important part of the first phase is to establish the client's interpersonal history, with special attention to the interpersonal events associated with the onset and maintenance of the eating disorder. Establishing separate histories of eating problems, interpersonal relationships before and after their onset, significant life events, and history of problems with self-esteem and depression can help create a "life chart" that may facilitate drawing connections between the client's interpersonal functioning and eating disturbance.

From the interpersonal history and its themes, the therapist suggests one or two potential problem areas for the client to target in therapy. Four interpersonal problem areas are focal points in IPT: grief, role transitions, role disputes, and interpersonal deficits (Gillies, 2001; Swartz, 1999). If more than two areas require attention, researchers suggest that the therapist focus on the easier problem area first to enhance the client's motivation (Fairburn, 1997). Each of these problem areas is described here, along with an illustrative case example.

Grief

If the client has experienced the death of a loved one, the client and therapist may choose to concentrate on grief resulting from this loss (other types of losses are considered role transitions; Gillies, 2001). Although bereavement is a natural process for which most people do not require psychotherapy, in some cases, the reaction is beyond what is usual and healthy (Swartz, 1999). When the mourning process becomes extended and impairing, IPT may be beneficial (Gotlib & Schraedley, 2000). Not only could an intense emotional reaction be destructive, but also a person may have a delayed reaction to the passing or never have fully mourned a prior loss. Each of these situations may result in extreme and unexpected grief (Gotlib & Schraedley, 2000). When grieving is the focus, the therapist's role is to assist the client through the mourning process, to assess what has been lost, and to help the client find relationships and interests to replace the loss (Swartz, 1999). Fairburn reported that problems with grief were relatively uncommon among their patients with bulimia, but grief-related issues often are readily resolved and, therefore, may be worth addressing first (Fairburn, 1997).

Case Example

Mrs. S., a female client with binge eating disorder, shared that her third child was born with a serious heart defect that resulted in his death at the age of four years. Because of pressures of caring for their two young daughters, she and her husband had never fully grieved for their loss. Although they sought counseling, the treatment was very brief and focused on facilitating the siblings' mourning process. Thus, it was not until 10 years later when Mrs. S. began therapy with the goal of weight loss that she drew a connection between the onset of her binge eating and the tragic loss of her son. As a result of this insight, Mrs. S. was also able to identify the family's struggles with her son's illness and death as playing a role in her youngest daughter's eating problems. Family sessions later revealed that an unintended and unspoken code of silence about their loss had triggered a number of unhealthy emotional and behavioral consequences, including binge eating for Mrs. S. and restrictive dieting and body image disturbance for her daughter. Addressing their grief greatly improved communication within the family and facilitated the development of healthier coping mechanisms for Mrs. S. and her daughter.

Role Transitions

In IPT, any life-changing event is considered a role transition. This change can be a positive or negative event, such as new employment or divorce (Swartz, 1999). Both types of transitions can cause undue stress (Gotlib & Schraedley, 2000). Depressive symptoms and compromised self-esteem have been linked to major life changes that result in new and unfamiliar roles (Gillies, 2001; Gotlib & Schraedley, 2000). The goal in IPT is for the client to realistically assess both past and new roles, not idealizing the former and eventually embracing the new (Fairburn, 1997; Gillies, 2001; Weissman, 1999). The therapist also helps the client recognize possible barriers to successful role changes, determine how the new position can best be approached, and acquire new "coping strategies" (Apple, 1999; Gotlib & Schraedley, 2000; Swartz, 1999). Clients are encouraged to create "a sense of mastery" in their new role, while making necessary changes such as expanding social networks and developing current relationships (Gillies, 2001).

Case Example

Ms. G., an 18-year-old female with bulimia, graduated from a small high school and began attending a large university thousands of miles away from home. Ms. G. was an only child who was very close with her parents and part of a very close circle of childhood friends. Going away to college involved a sense of anonymity that both excited and frightened her. Within a few weeks, the pressures to impress others and win new friends was overwhelming. She described herself as having been "sheltered" and then "catapulted into adulthood." Early sessions in therapy focused on facilitating Ms. G.'s transition into college, independence, and adulthood. As Ms. G. created a new social support network at school and became increasingly confident that she could take care of herself, her purging decreased and her preoccupation with her physical appearance subsided.

Role Disputes

A role dispute occurs when people in a relationship have mismatched expectations. This may occur with any important figure (e.g., a spouse, parent, child, or coworker), thus a client could be experiencing more than one dispute (Gotlib & Schraedley, 2000; Swartz, 1999; Weissman, 1999). It is the therapist's task to help the client delve into the relationship and determine where the inconsistency lies (Weissman, 1999). When exploring role disputes, it is imperative to determine patterns in interactions. Klerman and colleagues (1984) noted that role disputes are often "repetitious" and related to depressive symptomatology (Gotlib & Schraedley, 2000). Understanding harmful patterns and preventing reoccurrences may thwart future difficulties and disorder relapse (Gotlib & Schraedley, 2000). A relationship that is made stronger, or the end of a damaging relationship through IPT, can be very beneficial to the client's recovery (Gotlib & Schraedley, 2000). Once the dispute has been identified, the therapist helps the client determine how to best approach the problem, alter expectations, and enhance communication. This involves encouraging the client to see the other person accurately and not glorify or denigrate him or her (Gillies, 2001; Gotlib & Schraedley, 2000; Swartz, 1999).

A role dispute can be in one of three stages: renegotiation, impasse, or dissolution. The therapist helps the client determine the stage of the relationship and create a plan to better the situation (Gillies, 2001; Weissman, 1999). Renegotiation occurs when people within the role dispute recognize the disparity between their expectations and plan to work together toward change. When experiencing a role dispute in this stage, the focus of IPT is teaching the client to communicate his or her needs and expectations to the other party in a positive manner (Gotlib & Schraedley, 2000; Weissman, 1999).

The second stage, impasse, starts when negotiation and communication have stopped (Weissman, 1999). By this stage, usually only resentment and "unspoken hostility" remain (Gotlib & Schraedley, 2000; Weissman, 1999). Therefore, the therapist's goal is to open lines of communication or help the client determine if the relationship can be salvaged (Gotlib & Schraedley, 2000; Weissman, 1999). The client ascertains options and if no solution is found, involved parties discuss appropriate ways to end the relationship (Weissman, 1999).

In the final stage, dissolution, disputes are irreconcilable and the parties work toward ending the relationship. The therapist helps the client to mourn the end of the relationship and find ways to replace what has been lost (Gotlib & Schraedley, 2000; Weissman, 1999).

Case Example

Mrs. L. was a 32-year-old stay-at-home mother who struggled with bulimia for more than 10 years. From the beginning of their relationship, Mr. L. was aware of his wife's struggles with her weight and negative body image. Although initially helpful, Mr. L.'s role as self-appointed nutritionist, weight monitor, workout coach, and therapist was becoming increasingly upsetting to Mrs. L., who perceived her husband's behavior as excessively controlling and critical. Whereas Mr. L. believed that his efforts were keeping his wife healthy, Mrs. L. recognized that her frustration with their deteriorating relationship triggered many of her binge-purge episodes. The couple was at an impasse, unable to negotiate a healthy way for Mr. L. to show concern for Mrs. L. without the level of overinvolvement and control that made her feel mistrusted and belittled. In therapy, the couple negotiated different boundaries for this aspect of their relationship, and Mrs. L. then felt more prepared to move forward with her recovery from bulimia with her husband's support rather than his supervision.

Interpersonal Deficits

In some less common cases, a client does not have an identifiable problem and the focus is on interpersonal deficits, although therapists should refrain from using the term *deficits* because it may hinder progress and negatively affect self-esteem (Gillies, 2001; Gotlib & Schraedley, 2000). In these instances, clients tend to have a history of negative relationships, a great deal of social isolation, and difficulty initiating and maintaining relationships (Fairburn, 1997; Swartz, 1999; Weissman, 1999). Therefore, the goal of therapy is to improve the number and quality of social interactions (Gillies, 2001; Swartz, 1999).

Although a fundamental characteristic of IPT is its "present-based" stance, when faced with interpersonal deficits, the therapist and client may have to focus on past relationships if there are no current close relationships (Gotlib & Schraedley, 2000). Past relationships as well as the client's new relationship with the therapist may serve as learning tools (Swartz, 1999). Sessions may include strategies for improving social functioning, such as communication analysis and role plays (Gotlib & Schraedley, 2000).

Case Example

D. was a 15-year-old female with anorexia who experienced great difficulty expressing her feelings. She was exceptionally shy, withdrawn, and generally felt alienated from both friends and family. She had a tendency to interpret most social interactions negatively, sensitive to any potential signs of rejection or criticism. As a result, she had only one close friend and strained relationships with family members. Developing a strong working alliance in therapy served as a springboard for increasing her sense of trust and practicing the interpersonal skills needed to forge new relationships with peers and improve communication with her parents. Through a series of interpersonal "experiments," D.'s efforts to reach out to others were reinforced. Although her parents had difficulty adjusting to their daughter's new assertive, direct expressions of emotion, D. was pleased with her increasing ability to voice rather than internalize her negative feelings.

Of the four interpersonal problems, interpersonal deficits pose the most trouble to clients and their therapists; thus, if possible, it is usually better for therapy to focus on one of the specific problem areas (Swartz, 1999). Because IPT is more successful for people with strong interpersonal relationships, working with clients who have interpersonal deficits requires realistic expectations. Progress made with this population is usually moderate (Gillies, 2001).

Phase 2

During the intermediate stage (approximately 8 to 10 sessions), each session begins with a question such as "How have you been since we last met?" or "Where shall we start today?" This opening question helps the client take the lead and stay focused on the present. While paying close attention to mood and events that have occurred since the last meeting, the therapist takes an active but nondirective role. Identifying themes and pointing out inconsistencies without making interpretations are the therapist main tasks during this stage. At the end of each session, the therapist reviews progress and, periodically, discusses changes made in each of the problem areas and the work that remains to be done. The therapist avoids making specific suggestions for change but collaboratively explores various options and reinforces the client's efforts to make improvements. The therapist-client relationship is generally not directly addressed except when feedback about how the client relates to the therapist would be helpful information for interpersonal growth.

Phase 3

In the last four to five sessions, the therapist ensures that the client understands that therapy is almost over and emotions as to the impending termination are processed (Swartz, 1999). This time is also used to review goals, summarize and acknowledge progress, and discuss stagnation and the possibility of relapse. Future difficulties are anticipated, and the recurrent nature of eating disturbance is discussed in the context of encouraging clients to be vigilant for signs or symptoms that warrant action to prevent further problems. The therapist must also remind clients that evidence suggests that it often takes months for the full benefits of IPT to be realized. Depending on the level of pathology and likelihood of relapse, a contract for further long-term therapy may need to be discussed (Gotlib & Schraedley, 2000).

HOW DOES INTERPERSONAL PSYCHOTHERAPY FOR EATING DISORDERS WORK?

In his chapter on IPT for bulimia, Fairburn (1997) described the mechanisms by which IPT may work. First, the client's ability to bring about changes in what have often been entrenched interpersonal problems may lead them to feel more capable of changing other aspects of their lives, including their eating problem. Second, the improvement in mood and self-esteem may result in a decrease in the severity of patients' concerns about appearance and weight, potentially decreasing their tendency to diet, which in turn may lessen their vulnerability to bingeing. Third, increased social activity may decrease the amount of unstructured time when clients may have been most vulnerable to binge eating. Finally, reduction in the frequency and severity of interpersonal stressors may lead directly to a decrease in the frequency of binge eating.

Case Example

Ms. B. was a 38-year-old obese female with binge eating disorder. She had been binge eating approximately three times per week for almost one year. Her binges typically consisted of going to a variety of ethnic restaurants for takeout on her way home from work or stopping at the grocery store for a large assortment of snack foods. She also routinely made impulsive lunchtime food selections that were high in calories, fat, and carbohydrates. She was unable to keep much food in her home because she usually ate everything available to her in the evening. Approximately 10 months before therapy began, Ms. B. attended a university-based obesity treatment program and successfully lost 50 pounds. Soon after returning home, however, Ms. B. was unable to maintain her new exercise and diet program and quickly regained the weight and lost much of the self-esteem she had developed because of the weight loss. On intake, Ms. B.'s chief complaints were obesity, binge eating, and depression. She underwent an evaluation with a psychiatrist, who prescribed antidepressants and referred her for psychotherapy.

Phase 1

After discussing Ms. B.'s presenting symptoms and the events leading to her referral, the therapist presented the IPT approach to treating eating disorders and described the different phases of treatment and typical course of therapy. Ms. B. was delighted with the novelty of the IPT approach because she felt that previous treatment taught her a great deal about nutrition and cognitive-behavioral strategies but did not result in any long-term success. The therapist led Ms. B. in a thorough review of her history, which included the completion of two life charts, one with major events in her life (e.g., her parents' divorce, her brother's death) and the other detailing her weight fluctuations and eating behaviors. Ms. B. indicated that she had been slightly overweight for most of her life and then experienced a steady increase in her weight over the previous eight years. A detailed discussion of her timelines led to Ms. B.'s realization that the weight gain coincided with the death of her only sibling and her marriage (soon after her loss) to a man she felt indebted to for his help during the difficult time of her sibling's illness. Although she liked the man she married very much, she did not feel a strong romantic connection with or physical attraction to him. Ms. B. reported that her husband drank too much and had difficulty maintaining employment. She supported him throughout several failed attempts to start new businesses, but eventually they grew apart. At the beginning of therapy, Ms. B. had initiated the process of divorcing her husband. Although sad that the marriage did not work out, Ms. B. felt certain about her decision and felt fortunate that she and her husband were maintaining their friendship and divorcing amicably.

In determining the focal problem areas, grief was clearly an issue for Ms. B. to address. In addition, interpersonal deficits emerged as an important theme. Ms. B. was very articulate, warm, and presented with a clear "need to please." Her ingratiating, unassertive interpersonal style turned out to be a lifelong pattern that greatly influenced her relationships and, as she and her therapist discovered, was linked to her binge eating. Ms. B. described having a "complete depletion of self-esteem," that often led her to behave passively with great self-deprecation and low expectations of herself and how others should treat her. She had only a few close friendships that often involved a great sense of obligation on her part, as did her relationship with her parents. She routinely agreed to things she later resented and rarely attempted to have her needs met in these relationships. Similarly, she recognized that she often felt angry about a variety of interpersonal issues at work but remained silent and dealt with her frustrations by indulging in her favorite foods afterwards. She had a history of brief employments, with interpersonal stressors factoring into her departure from several jobs. Recognizing the link among her low self-esteem, lack of assertiveness, unfulfilling relationships, and binge eating was a very powerful experience for Ms. B., who often worked hard to distract herself from her problems (usually with food) rather than confront them. Throughout the initial treatment phase, the therapist had to help Ms. B. overcome her tendency to respond, "I don't know" or "I don't remember" to probes. Her avoidance later subsided as she became more convinced that exploring interpersonal challenges was facilitating her goals to stop binge eating and eventually lose weight.

Phase 2

In first focusing on unresolved grief, Ms. B. was able to identify her tendency to nurture herself with food as an ineffective strategy that developed early in her grieving process. She expressed the many difficult emotions she "noticed" but did not allow herself to fully experience at the time of her brother's death. The family had several rituals surrounding his birthdays and the anniversary of his death, and those, along with exploring and expressing Ms. B's grief, facilitated greater acceptance of her loss and more awareness of its impact on her eating behavior.

The majority of the second phase of treatment was spent exploring her interpersonal communication patterns and recognizing the similarities in her familial, work, and social relationships that caused her difficulty. Ms. B. experimented with a variety of communication techniques to better express herself, improve her existing relationships, and begin to work toward increasing her social network. At the core of her difficulties was a lack of self-esteem that Ms. B. traced back to her parents' divorce and her subsequent struggle to fit into her stepfamilies. She associated a further decline in self-image with her more recent weight gain and subsequent fears about the negative evaluations of others.

After much thought about the impact of her weight gain on her marriage, Ms. B. realized that gaining the weight was a major turnoff to her husband, and the excess weight effectively warded off his sexual advances. She then not only saw how her relationships influenced her eating, but now understood her weight gain as, in some ways, communication behavior.

As Ms. B. began to understand the interpersonal patterns and triggers that typically precipitated her binges, she felt less inclined to eat, stating, "Now that I know what I'm doing, it's not working for me anymore. I'm no longer able to numb myself with eating like I used to." As a result, Ms. B. successfully stopped binge eating. Throughout the course of treatment, however, she continued to struggle with making poor food choices more often than preferred, but she felt much more in control of how much she ate and how much time she spent eating.

Phase 3

In the final stage of treatment, the therapist and Ms. B. reviewed her progress, including a better understanding of her relationship with food, cessation of binge eating, increased self-esteem, improved mood, and enhanced relationship skills. With her improved self-concept and restored self-efficacy, Ms. B.'s attention shifted to becoming more socially active and returning to her previous active, more adventuresome lifestyle. She joined a singles club, was making greater efforts to socialize with friends from work, and after feeling lost about her career for some time, Ms. B. updated her resume and constructed a clear, achievable set of career goals for improving her employment situation. She recognized that her obesity had become a protective factor, an excuse on which to blame the many interpersonal and professional disappointments in her life, and that she had been putting her desires and dreams on hold until she someday lost the weight. The therapist encouraged Ms. B. to return to previously enjoyed activities that might be reinforcing and fulfilling, thereby ceasing her self-imposed punishments for weight gain and potentially improving her mood.

As termination approached, the therapist emphasized ways to further enhance relationships with family and friends such that the support, openness, and empowerment she found so helpful in therapy could become part of her other relationships as well. Finally, the therapist reviewed the triggers to Ms. B.'s occasions of unhealthy eating, and Ms. B. devised a sound plan for choosing more adaptive alternatives (e.g., calling a friend, exercising, writing in her diary) when various stressors would make eating poorly very tempting.

EFFECTIVENESS OF INTERPERSONAL PSYCHOTHERAPY

Interpersonal therapy was originally developed for use with depressed individuals and has been well validated for use with this population (e.g., Elkin et al., 1989). Given the role that interpersonal factors are thought to play in many other disorders, the use of IPT has expanded far beyond its initial purpose. In fact, interpersonal therapy has received empirical support for the treatment of depressed adolescents (e.g., Mufson, Weissman,

Moreau, & Garfinkel, 1999), bipolar disorders (e.g., Ehlers, Frank, & Kupfer, 1988), as well as dysthymia (e.g., Markowitz, 1994, 1998). It is also receiving increasing empirical validation and mounting popularity for use in the treatment of eating disorders. Several IPT outcome studies are summarized in Table 8.1.

While CBT traditionally has been the treatment of choice for eating disorders, there has been increasing evidence of the efficacy of interpersonal therapy in treating this population. The effectiveness of IPT has been demonstrated for the treatment of bulimia nervosa (e.g., Fairburn et al., 1991, 1993, 1995) and binge eating disorder (e.g., Wilfley et al., 1993). Although the empirical evidence is still scant concerning use of IPT for the treatment of anorexia, researchers have presented a strong theoretical rationale for its use with this population and are calling for empirical studies to be conducted (e.g., McIntosh et al., 2000).

Fairburn and colleagues conducted the first study to examine the efficacy of interpersonal therapy for bulimia nervosa. They compared a form of CBT with a short-term focal therapy that emphasized interpersonal problems as opposed to the eating disorder itself. Patients in both treatment conditions improved, and changes were maintained over a 12-month follow-up. The findings favored CBT, but interpersonal therapy had a profound and sustained impact (Fairburn et al., 1986). Fairburn and colleagues published two additional studies in 1991 and 1993 that also provided support for the efficacy of interpersonal therapy. Patients with bulimia were randomly assigned to one of three treatment conditions: CBT, behavior therapy (BT), or IPT. Findings revealed substantial impacts of all three treatments during treatment, with CBT showing slightly more improvement. However, over time, those who received BT actually deteriorated, whereas those who received CBT and IPT continued to improve. In fact, those patients who participated in IPT actually surpassed those in the CBT condition over a 12-month follow-up period (Fairburn et al., 1993).

More recently, Fairburn and colleagues reassessed patients from their initial trials to determine if treatment effects had endured over time (Fairburn et al., 1995). The average length of follow-up was six years. Remarkably, given the time elapsed since the original studies, differential treatment effects were still evident. The results of this follow-up mirrored those of the 12-month follow-up, with BT faring the worst and both CBT and IPT continuing to do well.

Wilfley and her colleagues (1993) compared the effectiveness of group CBT and group IPT for binge eating. Participants were randomly assigned to one of three groups—group CBT, group IPT, or wait-list control group. Treatment was administered over 16 sessions. At posttreatment, both the CBT and IPT groups showed significant improvement, whereas the wait-list group did not. Binge eating remained significantly below baseline levels at both 6-month and 12-month follow-ups for both CBT and IPT. There were no significant differences between CBT and IPT at posttreatment or at either of the two follow-ups (Wilfley et al., 1993).

Wilfley and colleagues (2002) conducted another randomized trial comparing the effectiveness of group CBT and group IPT for the treatment of binge eating disorder. Treatment was administered over 20 weekly sessions, and assessments of binge eating and other eating psychopathology were taken before treatment, at posttreatment, and at 4-month and 12-month follow-up intervals. At posttreatment and at one-year follow-up, recovery rates were equivalent for the CBT and IPT groups, demonstrating the

Table 8.1   Outcome Studies of Interpersonal Psychotherapy for Eating Disorders

Study	Participants	Treatment	Findings
Agras et al., 1995	43 females and 7 males who met criteria for BED.	After 12 weeks of unsuccessful CBT, 12 weeks of 90-minute IPT group sessions were implemented.	There were no further improvements for CBT nonresponders after an additional 12 weeks of IPT.
Agras, Walsh, Fairburn, Wilson, & Kraemer, 2000	220 females who met criteria for BN.	IPT vs. CBT in an outpatient setting.	1. CBT was significantly more effective at end of treatment; however, there were no significant differences at follow-up. 2. At follow-up, IPT group showed continued improvement. CBT group either maintained or showed slight relapse.
Crafti, 2002	40 females who met criteria for AN, BN, BED, EDNOS, and subclinical eating disturbance.	WLC vs. combination of CBT and IPT (MEG) in an outpatient or hospital group setting.	1. Posttreatment, MEG led to abstinence of bingeing (56% to 58%) and purging (58% to 65%) for groups at both treatment locations as compared to the WLC group (5% and 33%, respectively). 2. MEG led to significant reductions in other symptomatology (e.g., body image dissatisfaction, drive for thinness, ineffectiveness) and increased self-esteem as compared to the WLC group. 3. At follow-up, cessation rates were maintained for both treatment locations and continued to be significantly higher than WLC.
Fairburn et al., 1991	75 females who met criteria for BN.	IPT vs. CBT vs. BT (with no overlap) in an outpatient setting.	1. All treatments improved frequency of binge eating, general psychiatric symptoms, and social adjustment. 2. CBT was superior to IPT and BT in its effects on dietary restriction, weight concerns, and EAT scores. 3. All treatments reduced the frequency of purging behaviors, but CBT and BT were significantly more effective than IPT at reducing vomiting. 4. CBT and IPT were more effective than BT in reducing shape concerns.

(continued)

Table 8.1   *(Continued)*

Study	Participants	Treatment	Findings
Fairburn et al., 1995	91 females who met criteria for BN.	CBT vs. FIT vs. BT long-term follow-up.	At a six-year follow-up, those who had received CBT or FIT were doing significantly better ⎡⎡⎡⎡ ⎡⎡⎡⎡ ⎡⎡⎡⎡⎡⎡⎡ ⎡⎡
Fairburn et al., 1993	75 females who met criteria for BN.	IPT vs. CBT vs. BT in an individual outpatient setting.	CBT and IPT were significantly better than BT in reducing bulimic symptomatology, dietary restraint, weight and shape concerns, EAT scores, general psychiatric and depressive symptoms, and social functioning. All gains were maintained at 12-month follow-up.
Fairburn et al., 1986	24 females who met criteria for BN.	CBT vs. STFP in an individual outpatient setting.	1. CBT was significantly more effective at reducing global clinical scales throughout a 12-month follow-up period. 2. Both treatments improved general psychopathology and depression, social adjustment, bulimic symptomatology, and increased weight. 3. CBT group maintained significantly lower scores on general pathology and depression than did STFP.
Jones et al., 1993	38 females who met criteria for BN.	IPT vs. CBT vs. BT in an individual outpatient setting.	1. All treatments reduced BE; however, BT and CBT showed a significantly faster rate of reduction as compared to IPT. 2. BT and CBT were significantly more effective in reducing purging behaviors. 3. There were significant changes in EAT scores for all treatment conditions, but BT and CBT showed continued improvement after week eight, whereas IPT did not. 4. Overall, treatment produced significant changes on depression and SE. However, no significant effects for condition were observed, although CBT had the quickest rate of change.
Mitchell et al., 2002	37 females who met criteria for BN.	After 12 weeks of unsuccessful CBT, IPT vs. medication management.	1. 24% of IPT participants achieved abstinence. 2. 19% of medication management achieved abstinence.

Table 8.1   *(Continued)*

Study	Participants	Treatment	Findings
Nevonen et al., 1999	29 females who met criteria for BN or EDNOS.	Sequenced CBT and IPT in a group setting (7 and 13 sessions, respectively).	1. Significant pre- and postdifferences on all measures and bulimic symptoms. 2. 72% of participants were in full or partial recovery at posttest. 3. Effects were sustained at one-year follow-up.
Wilfley et al., 1993	56 females who met criteria for non-purging BN.	IPT vs. CBT vs. WLC in an outpatient group setting.	1. Both CBT and IPT showed significant improvements in BE posttreatment. 2. Improvements were maintained at both 6-month and 12-month follow-ups.
Wilfley et al., 2002	162 overweight females who met criteria for BED.	IPT vs. CBT in a group setting.	1. Binge eating recovery rates were equivalent for CBT and IPT at posttreatment. 2. At one-year follow-up, both groups were still below pretreatment levels with no differences between groups
Wilson et al., 2002	154 participants who met criteria for BN.	IPT vs. CBT in an individual, outpatient setting.	1. CBT reduced vomiting and BE significantly more than IPT. 2. CBT and IPT both significantly reduced weight and shape concerns. 3. At follow-up, CBT and IPT resulted in similar reductions in BE (72% and 70%, respectively) and purging (61% and 62%, respectively).

Note: AN = Anorexia nervosa; BE = Binge eating; BED = Binge eating disorder; BN = Bulimia nervosa; BT = Behavior therapy; CBT = Cognitive-behavioral therapy; EAT = Eating Attitudes Test; EDNOS = Eating disorder not otherwise specified; FIT = Focal interpersonal therapy; IPT = interpersonal psychotherapy; MEG = Moderate eating group; SE = Self-esteem; STFP = Short-term focal psychotherapy; WLC = Waiting list control.

effectiveness of IPT for treating this population (Wilfley et al., 2002). Similarly, a multicenter comparison of CBT and IPT for bulimia nervosa (Agras, Walsh, Fairburn, Wilson, & Kraemer, 2000) demonstrated that CBT was superior to IPT at end of treatment, but there were no significant differences at follow-up on several outcome measures.

Given the previous research to suggest that CBT may have a quicker rate of change than IPT (e.g., Agras et al., 2000; Jones, Peveler, Hope, & Fairburn, 1993), Wilson, Fairburn, Agras, Walsh, and Kraemer (2002) recently completed another comparison focusing on time course and mechanisms of change of CBT. Consistent with previous work, CBT had a more rapid onset of symptom reduction and was significantly more effective than IPT in reducing both binge eating and vomiting following the 20-week treatment. However, at follow-up, CBT and IPT showed similar reductions in all bulimic symptoms.

Overall, particularly because it may work faster at ameliorating presenting symptoms (Agras et al., 2000; Wilson et al., 2002), CBT remains the current treatment of choice for bulimia, with IPT considered a secondary treatment to be considered when CBT fails. In their innovative study, Mitchell and his colleagues (2002) compared IPT with antidepressant medication as secondary treatments for clients who were treated unsuccessfully with CBT. There were no significant differences between the medication and IPT groups, with both approaches showing little effectiveness. However, because of unacceptably high attrition rates and the use of a single outcome criterion (abstinence), it is difficult to draw meaningful conclusions about the efficacy of the second-line treatments. The authors suggest that the most important implication of their findings is that the use of sequential treatments (i.e., clients undergo two complete treatment "packages") is not a viable approach, possibly because such treatment is unacceptably long for many clients. Identifying nonresponders in earlier phases of CBT may reduce total length of treatment and, therefore, reduce dropout rates.

An earlier study by Nevonen and colleagues (Nevonen, Broberg, Linstrom, & Levin, 1999), however, demonstrated the potential for success using a sequenced group CBT-IPT treatment for bulimia. Initially, cognitive-behavioral techniques were used and bulimic symptoms were targeted. After seven sessions, each participant received one individual transition session to evaluate the effectiveness of the CBT component and prepare for the IPT portion of treatment. The next 13 sessions focused on interpersonal problem areas and deliberately avoided focus on bulimic symptoms. At posttreatment, 70% of the sample was in either full or partial remission. Results were maintained at one-year follow-up, and significant changes in both depression and interpersonal sensitivity scores were attained as well (Nevonen et al., 1999).

In summary, although CBT continues to be the gold standard for the treatment of eating disorders, there is growing support that IPT is a valuable approach for a variety of problem areas, including bulimia and binge eating disorder. Based on the treatment outcome literature and theoretical fit with the conceptualization of eating disorders, IPT holds promise for the successful treatment of this population—not only as an alternative to CBT, but also as a comparable, first-line treatment option. Obviously, CBT has the advantage of stronger and more consistent empirical support, in addition to a potentially more rapid rate of change (e.g., Jones et al., 1993; Wilson et al., 2002). Additionally, Wilson and colleagues have recently argued that the disappearance of such treatment effects over time may be more a result of regression to the mean than the delayed treatment effects of IPT, as has been argued previously. Further, their findings suggest that the two treatment modalities appear to work through the same mechanism of change, contrary to previous hypotheses. However, numerous studies in the past decade have shown that IPT results not only in symptom reduction, but also in valuable, long-lasting changes in interpersonal functioning and cessation of eating disorder symptoms over periods of up to six years.

FUTURE DIRECTIONS

As with any new or innovative treatment, a great deal of research is still needed to fully assess the effectiveness of IPT in the treatment of eating disorders. Specifically, the notion of a combination treatment that merges the elements of CBT and IPT is intriguing. As Fairburn (1997) points out, such a fusion may prove to be difficult, but we would argue it is not impossible. Recently, Crafti (2002) conducted a seminal study in which she attempted to integrate CBT and IPT approaches for the treatment of various eating disorders. The combined treatment, described as "CBT with an increased focus on interpersonal issues" (p. 24), was delivered in a group format. Patients who received this form of treatment (both inpatient and outpatient) showed significantly higher levels of abstinence posttreatment when compared to a wait-list control group. Such results are an encouraging first step toward a successful integration of these two treatments. Further development and continued empirical validation of a hybrid CBT-IPT treatment is a worthwhile direction for future research. Prospective studies should seek to clearly delineate how both interpersonal and cognitive-behavioral components are used throughout each stage of treatment. Further, a more complex research design that compares the integrated treatment not only to a wait-list group, but also to groups that receive only CBT and IPT, is necessary.

In addition to research considering a union of CBT and IPT, there is also a clear need for more research on the use of IPT alone as a treatment for eating disorders. In particular, research exploring the use of IPT in the treatment of anorexia is scant. The family systems approach often taken in the treatment of anorexia would seem to lend itself well to an interpersonal focus in therapy. Because the lack of substantive dialogue concerning the patient's actual eating behaviors and weight may prove too problematic in treating anorexia, IPT would not be a viable option for some clients unless certain medical criteria are established before treatment. Further exploration of IPT for anorexia is warranted, especially in light of the limited success in treating this disorder with other types of therapy.

A potential benefit of using IPT, alone or as part of a combination treatment, surrounds the issue of treatment generalization. Recently, there has been a great deal of discussion as to whether the techniques that clients learn in CBT generalize to other areas of their lives. We would argue that IPT offers a broad focus of treatment that generalizes to other areas of a client's life in a way that CBT alone may not. Because IPT does not specifically focus on eating behavior but on interpersonal functioning in general, symptom reduction is only part of the benefit that the client receives. The client also learns ways of having more effective interpersonal interactions and healthier relationships, which can be extremely beneficial in reducing difficulties in various aspects of psychosocial functioning.

Ultimately, the decision whether to use CBT or IPT may best be made based on the etiology and presentation of the individual client and his or her symptoms. For example, we are currently treating a client with bulimia who has a history of severe sexual abuse by a family member and a variety of related interpersonal trust and betrayal issues. With such a client, an interpersonal approach to treatment seems a natural fit and has been successful to this point. Other clients, because of their history, personality, or some other variable, may respond better to a CBT approach. Perhaps we can best serve our clients by having knowledge and skill in both treatments and the awareness to judge when each might be most appropriate. Research designed to identify specific client variables that make success more probable with one approach than another would be extremely beneficial in this attempt to appropriately match clients to effective treatments.

REFERENCES

Agras, W. S., Telch, C. F., Arnow, B., Eldredge, K., Detzer, M., Henderson, J., et al. (1995). Does interpersonal therapy help patients with binge eating disorder who fail to respond to cognitive-behavioral therapy. *Journal of Consulting and Clinical Psychology, 63*(3), 356–360.

Agras, W. S., Walsh, B. T., Fairburn, C. G., Wilson, G. T., & Kraemer, C. H. (2000). A multicenter comparison of cognitive behavioral therapy and interpersonal psychotherapy for bulimia nervosa. *Archives of General Psychiatry, 57,* 459–466.

Apple, R. F. (1999). Interpersonal therapy for bulimia nervosa. *Journal of Clinical Psychology, 55*(6), 715–725.

Attie, I., & Brooks-Gunn, J. (1989). Development of eating problems in adolescent girls: A longitudinal study. *Developmental Psychology, 25*(1), 70–79.

Benedikt, R., Wertheim, E. H., & Love, A. (1998). Eating attitudes and weight-loss attempts in female adolescents and their mothers. *Journal of Youth and Adolescence, 27*(1), 43–57.

Billings, A. G., Cronkite, R. C., & Moos, R. H. (1983). Social-environmental factors in unipolar depression: Comparisons of depressed patients and nondepressed controls. *Journal of Abnormal Psychology, 92*(2), 119–133.

Billings, A. G., & Moos, R. H. (1985). Psychosocial processes of remission in unipolar depression: Comparing depressed patients with matched community controls. *Journal of Consulting and Clinical Psychology, 53*(3), 314–325.

Birchall, H. (1999). Interpersonal psychotherapy in the treatment of eating disorders. *European Eating Disorders Review, 7*(5), 315–320.

Bowlby, J. (1977). The making and breaking of affectional bonds. II: Some principles of psychotherapy. *British Journal of Psychiatry, 10,* 421–431.

Cash, T. F. (1995). Developmental teasing about physical appearance: Retrospective descriptions and relationships with body image. *Social Behavior and Personality, 23*(2), 123–129.

Cash, T. F., Cash, D. W., & Butters, J. W. (1983). "Mirror, mirror on the wall . . . ?": Contrast effects and self-evaluations of physical attractiveness. *Personality and Social Psychology, 9,* 359–364.

Cattarin, J. A., & Thompson, J. K. (1994). A three-year longitudinal study of body image and eating disturbance in adolescent females. *Eating Disorders: Journal of Treatment and Prevention, 2,* 114–125.

Cattarin, J. A., Thompson, J. K., Thomas, C., & Williams, R. (2000). Body image, mood, and televised images of attractiveness: The role of social comparison. *Journal of Social and Clinical Psychology, 19,* 220–239.

Crafti, N. (2002). Integrating cognitive-behavioral and interpersonal approaches in a group program for the eating disorders: Measuring effectiveness in a naturalistic setting. *Behavior Change, 19*(1), 22–38.

Ehlers, C. L., Frank, E., & Kupfer, D. J. (1988). Social zeitgebers and biological rhythms. *Archives of General Psychiatry, 45,* 948–952.

Elkin, I., Shea, M., Watkins, J. T., Imber, S. D., Sotsky, S. M., Collins, J. F., et al. (1989). National institute of mental health treatment of depression collaborative research program: General effectiveness of treatments. *Archives of General Psychiatry, 46,* 971–982.

Fabian, L. J., & Thompson, J. K. (1989). Body image and eating disturbance in young females. *International Journal of Eating Disorders, 8*(1), 63–74.

Fairburn, C. (1997). Interpersonal psychotherapy for bulimia nervosa. In D. M. Garner & P. E. Garfinkel (Eds.), *Handbook of treatment for eating disorders* (pp. 278–294). New York: Guilford Press.

Fairburn, C. (1998). Interpersonal psychotherapy for bulimia nervosa. In J. C. Markowitz (Ed.), *Interpersonal psychotherapy: Review of psychiatry series* (pp. 99–128). Washington, DC: American Psychiatric Press.

Fairburn, C., Jones, R., Peveler, R. C., Carr, S. J., Solomon, R. A., O'Connor, M. E., et al. (1991). Three psychological treatments for bulimia nervosa: A comparative trial. *Archives of General Psychiatry, 48,* 463–468.

Fairburn, C., Jones, R., Peveler, R. C., Hope, R. A., & O'Connor, M. (1993). Psychotherapy and bulimia nervosa. *Archives of General Psychiatry, 50,* 419–428.

Fairburn, C., Kirk, J., O'Connor, M., & Cooper, P. J. (1986). A comparison of two psychological treatments for bulimia nervosa. *Behavioral Research Therapy, 24*(6), 629–643.

Fairburn, C., Norman, P. A., Welch, S. L., O'Connor, E. M., Doll, A. H., & Peveler, R. C. (1995). A prospective study of outcome in bulimia nervosa and the long-term effects of three psychological treatments. *Archives of General Psychiatry, 52,* 304–312.

Frank, E., & Spanier, C. (1995). Interpersonal psychotherapy for depression: Overview, clinical efficacy, and future directions. *Clinical Psychology: Science and Practice, 2*(4), 349–369.

Garner, D. M. (1997). Psychoeducational principles in treatment. In D. M. Garner & P. E. Garfinkel (Eds.), *Handbook of treatment for eating disorders* (2nd ed., pp. 147–177). New York: Guilford Press.

Geller, J., Zaitsoff, S., & Srikameswaran, S. (2002). Beyond shape and weight: Exploring the relationship between nonbody determinants of self-esteem and eating disorder symptoms in adolescent females. *International Journal of Eating Disorders, 32*(3), 344–351.

Gillies, L. A. (2001). Interpersonal psychotherapy for depression and other disorders. In D. H. Barlow (Ed.), *Clinical handbook of psychological disorders: A step-by-step treatment manual* (pp. 309–331). New York: Guilford Press.

Gotlib, I. H., & Schraedley, P. K. (2000). Interpersonal psychotherapy. In C. R. Snyder & R. E. Ingram (Eds.), *Handbook of psychological change: Psychotherapy process and practices for the twenty-first century* (pp. 258–279). New York: Wiley.

Hawkins, J. D., & Fraser, M. W. (1985). Social networks of street drug users: A comparison of two theories. *Social Work Research and Abstracts, 21*(1), 3–12.

Heinberg, L. J., & Thompson, J. K. (1992). Social comparison: Gender, target importance ratings, and relation to body image disturbance. *Journal of Social Behavior and Personality, 7,* 335–344.

Hill, A. J., Weaver, C., & Blundell, J. E. (1990). Dieting concerns of 10-year old girls and their mothers. *British Journal of Clinical Psychology, 29*(3), 346–348.

Hinrichsen, G. A. (1999). Treating older adults with interpersonal psychotherapy for depression. *Journal of Clinical Psychology/In Session: Psychotherapy in Practice, 55*(8), 949–960.

Jones, R., Peveler, R. C., Hope, R. A., & Fairburn, C. G. (1993). Changes during treatment for bulimia nervosa: A comparison of three psychological treatments. *Behavior Research and Therapy, 31,* 479–485.

Klerman, G. L., & Weissman, M. M. (1993). Interpersonal psychotherapy for depression: Background and concepts. In G. L. Klerman & M. M. Weissman (Eds.), *New applications of interpersonal psychotherapy* (pp. 3–26). Washington, DC: American Psychiatric Press.

Klerman, G. L., Weissman, M. M., Rounsaville, B. J., & Chevron, E. S. (1984). *Interpersonal psychotherapy of depression.* New York: Basic Books.

Levine, M. P., Smolak, L., & Hayden, H. (1994). The relation of sociocultural factors to eating attitudes and behaviors among middle school girls. *Journal of Early Adolescence, 14*(4), 471–490.

Mark, S. K., & Crowther, J. H. (1997, August). *Body dissatisfaction and relationship satisfaction in dating couples.* Paper presented at the meeting of the American Psychological Association, Chicago.

Markey, C. N., Markey, P. M., & Birch, L. L. (2001). Interpersonal predictors of dieting practices among married couples. *Journal of Family Psychology, 15*(3), 464–475.

Markowitz, J. C. (1994). Psychotherapy of dysthymia. *American Journal of Psychiatry, 151*(8), 1114–1121.

Markowitz, J. C. (1998). *Interpersonal psychotherapy for dysthymic disorder.* Washington, DC: American Psychiatric Press.

Markowitz, J. C., Svartberg, M., & Swartz, H. A. (1998). Is IPT time-limited psychodynamic psychotherapy? *Journal of Psychotherapy Practice and Research, 7,* 185–195.

Markowitz, J. C., Weissman, M. M., Quellette, R., Lish, J. D., & Klerman, G. L. (1989). Quality of life in panic disorder. *Archives of General Psychiatry, 46*(11), 984–992.

McIntosh, V. V., Bulik, C. M., McKenzie, J. M., Luty, S. E., & Jordan, J. (2000). Interpersonal psychotherapy for anorexia nervosa. *International Journal of Eating Disorders, 27*(2), 125–139.

Mitchell, J., Halmi, K., Wilson, G. T., Agras, S., Kraemer, H., & Crow, S. (2002). A randomized secondary treatment study of women with bulimia nervosa nonresponsive to CBT. *International Journal of Eating Disorders, 32*(3), 271–281.

Mufson, L., Weissman, M. M., Moreau, D., & Garfinkel, R. (1999). Efficacy of interpersonal psychotherapy for depressed adolescents. *Archives of General Psychiatry, 56*(6), 573–579.

Murray, S. H., Touyz, S. W., & Beumont, P. J. V. (1995). The influence of personal relationships on women's eating behavior and body satisfaction. *Eating Disorders: The Journal of Treatment and Prevention, 3*(3), 243–252.

Nevonen, L., Broberg, A. G., Lindstrom, M., & Levin, B. (1999). A sequenced group psychotherapy model for bulimia nervosa patients: A pilot study. *European Eating Disorders Review, 7*(1), 17–27.

Oliver, K. K., & Thelen, M. H. (1996). Children's perceptions of peer influence on eating concerns. *Behavior Therapy, 27,* 25–39.

Paxton, S. J., Schutz, H. K., Wertheim, E. H., & Muir, S. L. (1999). Friendship clique and peer influences on body image concerns, dietary restraint, extreme weight-loss behaviors, and binge eating in adolescent girls. *Journal of Abnormal Psychology, 108*(2), 255–266.

Pike, K. M., & Rodin, J. (1991). Mothers, daughters, and disordered eating. *Journal of Abnormal Psychology, 100*(2), 198–204.

Rieves, L., & Cash, T. F. (1996). Social developmental factors and women's body-image attitudes. *Journal of Social Behavior and Personality, 11*(1), 63–78.

Sanftner, J. L., Crowther, J. H., Crawford, P. A., & Watts, D. D. (1996). Maternal influences (or lack thereof) on daughters' eating attitudes and behaviors. *Eating Disorders: Journal of Treatment and Prevention, 4*(2), 147–159.

Schmidt, U., Tiller, J., Blanchard, M., Andrews, B., & Treasure, J. (1997). Is there a specific trauma precipitating anorexia nervosa? *Psychological Medicine, 27*(3), 523–530.

Schwartz, D., & Thompson, M. (1981). Do anorexics get well? Current research and future needs. *American Journal of Psychiatry, 138*(3), 319–323.

Sole-Puig, J. (1997). The European launch of interpersonal psychotherapy in the Xth world congress of psychiatry. *European Psychiatry, 12,* 46–48.

Swartz, H. A. (1999). Interpersonal psychotherapy. In M. Hersen & A. S. Bellack (Eds.), *Handbook of comparative interventions for adult disorders* (pp. 139–155). New York: Wiley.

Tantleff-Dunn, S., & Gokee, J. L. (2002). Interpersonal influences on body image development. In T. F. Cash & T. Pruzinsky (Eds.), *Body image: A handbook of theory, research, and clinical practice* (pp. 108–116). New York: Guilford Press.

Thelen, M. H., & Comier, J. F. (1995). Desire to be thinner and weight control among children and their parents. *Behavior Therapy, 26,* 85–99.

Thompson, J. K., Heinberg, L. J., Altabe, M., & Tantleff-Dunn, S. (1999). *Exacting beauty: Theory, assessment and treatment of body image disturbance.* Washington, DC: American Psychological Association.

Thompson, J. K., & Psaltis, K. (1988). Multiple aspects and correlates of body figure ratings: A replication and extension of Fallon and Rozin. *International Journal of Eating Disorders, 7*(6), 813–817.

Tiller, J., Sloane, G., Schmidt, U., Troop, N., Power, M., & Treasure, J. L. (1997). Social support in patients with anorexia and bulimia nervosa. *International Journal of Eating Disorders, 21*(1), 31–38.

Vincent, M. A., & McCabe, M. P. (2000). Gender differences among adolescents in family, and peer influences on body dissatisfaction, weight loss, and binge eating behaviors. *Journal of Youth and Adolescence, 29*(2), 205–221.

Weissman, M. M. (1999). Interpersonal psychotherapy and the health care scene. In D. S. Janowsky (Ed.), *Psychotherapy indications and outcomes* (pp. 213–231). Washington, DC: American Psychiatric Press.

Weissman, M. M., & Markowitz, J. C. (1994). Interpersonal psychotherapy: Current status. *Archives of General Psychiatry, 51,* 599–606.

Wilfley, D. E., Agras, W. S., Telch, C. F., Rossiter, E. M., Schneider, J. A., Cole, A. G., et al. (1993). Group cognitive-behavioral therapy and group interpersonal psychotherapy for the nonpurging bulimic individual: A controlled comparison. *Journal of Consulting and Clinical Psychology, 61*(2), 296–305.

Wilfley, D. E., Dounchis, J. Z., & Welch, R. R. (2000). Interpersonal psychotherapy. In K. J. Miller & S. J. Mizes (Eds.), *Comparative treatments for eating disorders* (pp. 128–159). New York: Springer.

Wilfley, D. E., Welch, R. R., Stein, R. I., Spurrell, E. B., Cohen, L. R., Saelens, B. E., et al. (2002). A randomized comparison of group cognitive-behavioral therapy and group interpersonal psychotherapy for the treatment of overweight individuals with binge-eating disorder. *Archives of General Psychiatry, 59*(8), 713–721.

Wilson, G. T., Fairburn, C. G., Agras, W. S., Walsh, B. T., & Kraemer, H. (2002). Cognitive-behavioral therapy for bulimia nervosa: Time course and mechanisms of change. *Journal of Consulting and Clinical Psychology, 70*(2), 267–274.

Woodside, D. B., Lackstrom, J. B., & Shekter-Wolfson, L. (2000). Marriage in eating disorders: Comparisons between patients and spouses and changes over the course of treatment. *Journal of Psychosomatic Research, 49*(3), 165–168.

Zaitsoff, S. L., Geller, J., & Srikameswaran, S. (2002). Silencing the self and suppressed anger: Relationship to eating disorder symptoms in adolescent females. *European Eating Disorders Review, 10,* 50–51.

Chapter 9

PHARMACOLOGICAL TREATMENT OF ANOREXIA NERVOSA, BULIMIA NERVOSA, AND BINGE EATING DISORDER

MARTINA DE ZWAAN, JAMES L. ROERIG, AND JAMES E. MITCHELL

ANOREXIA NERVOSA

Anorexia nervosa (AN) is a potentially life-threatening illness characterized by a refusal to maintain normal body weight (at times to the point of emaciation), a fear of gaining weight, disordered perceptions including a disordered body image, and preoccupations with food (American Psychiatric Association [APA], 1994). Comorbid anxiety and depressive symptoms, as well as obsessive-compulsive symptoms, often are present. Considering this symptom complex, it is interesting to identify the target symptoms for which a practitioner may consider pharmacotherapy.

Food restriction and extreme weight loss would suggest trials with some type of agent that would increase appetite. However, in the acute phases of AN, the patient has substantial appetite and exhibits an ability to withstand the desire to eat. A clinician may consider the similarities between a disordered body image and the altered perceptions that are present in other psychiatric illnesses, such as schizophrenia, and entertain the use of an antipsychotic medication. Anxiety, depression, and obsessive-compulsive symptoms suggest conditions for which serotonergic antidepressants have been proven helpful in other diagnostic groups. Therefore, there is no lack of potential treatments that may be employed in the treatment of AN signs and symptoms. Unfortunately, the overwhelming outcome of much exploratory research is that few of these agents have been found helpful in rigorous placebo-controlled trials.

In reviewing the pharmacotherapy data, it is best to consider the treatment of AN in two phases: the acute phase or weight gain phase and the maintenance phase. The following reviews the data for a variety of pharmacological treatments for each phase of the illness.

The overwhelming objective for acute treatment of AN is the safe reestablishment of normal weight. This goal is often undertaken on an inpatient unit with intensive refeeding programs that are closely monitored medically. In addition, dietary counseling, individual and group psychotherapy, and family therapy are mainstays of rigorous programs. It is in this context that pharmacotherapy trials are often performed. The experimental treatment is added to the other treatment modalities. Thus, a potential "ceiling" effect may exist where the inpatient programs are producing maximum effect, which may overshadow any drug effect. Because of the life-threatening nature of this illness, it is difficult to consider any other treatment paradigm.

Antidepressants

A moderate number of case reports, case series, and non-placebo-controlled comparisons of various antidepressants are reported in the literature (Bergh, Eriksson, Lindberg, & Södersten, 1996; Brambilla, Draisci, Peirone, & Brunetta, 1995a, 1995b; Calandra, Gulino, Inserra, & Giuffrida, 1999; C. P. Ferguson, La Via, Crossan, & Kaye, 1999; J. Ferguson, 1987; Frank, Kaye, & Marcus, 2001; Gwirtsman, Guze, Yager, & Gainsley, 1990; Lyles, Sarkis, & Kemph, 1990; Pallanti, Quercioli, & Ramacciotti, 1997; Ricca et al., 1999; Santonastaso, Friederici, & Favaro, 2001; Strober, Pataki, Freeman, & DeAntonio, 1999). Often, the case reports and series are positive in reporting weight gain. The more recent trials that employ a more complicated design, usually comparing one drug to another or to cognitive-behavioral therapy (CBT), show mixed results. Depressive symptomatology, as well as obsessive and eating-related pathology, is often reported to improve regardless of improvement in weight.

Controlled trials of antidepressants in the treatment of AN are listed in Table 9.1. Three of four acute trials were negative. The dosage of the tricyclic agent was low in the trials of Lacey and Crisp (1980; clomipramine 50 mg/d) and Biederman et al. (1985; amitriptyline mean 115 mg/d). Halmi, Eckert, LaDu, and Cohen (1986) evaluated three outcome criteria (treatment efficiency, rate of weight gain, and number of days of treatment required to achieve target weight) in a four-week trial comparing amitriptyline, cyproheptadine, and placebo. The maximum doses were 160 mg/d for amitriptyline and 32 mg/d for cyproheptadine. Overall, no drug effect was found in relation to treatment efficiency. However, a significant improvement in time to reach target weight was found for the amitriptyline and cyproheptadine groups over placebo. The authors report that the subjects receiving active drug therapy attained their target weights an average of 10.5 days earlier than the subjects receiving placebo. Rate of weight gain was significantly different compared to placebo for those subjects taking cyproheptadine who had the greatest weight gain before drug initiation. Despite these findings, the authors indicate that the greater proportion of variance for both days to target weight and rate of weight gain was accounted for by the pretreatment weights on days one and seven.

Three maintenance trials are also listed in Table 9.1. Kaye, Weltzin, Hsu, and Bulik (1991) and Strober, Freeman, DeAntonio, Lampert, and Diamond (1997) are open trials, and Kaye et al. (2001) is a placebo-controlled trial. Strober et al.'s trial reported no difference between fluoxetine-treated subjects and historic controls. All patients were treated with a refeeding program and psychotherapy. Kaye et al. (1991) reported that fluoxetine prevented relapse in that 93.5% of the subjects maintained weight > 85% of average body weight for a mean of 11 ±6 months. These subjects were started on drug therapy after weight gain was achieved. The follow-up controlled study by Kaye et al. (2001) found that fluoxetine was significantly better than placebo in preventing relapse over one year of treatment (63% versus 16% remained well).

Table 9.1 Controlled Pharmacological Trials in Patients with Anorexia Nervosa

Study	N	Age (Years)	(%) Completers	Duration of Treatment	Agent/Dose	Outcome
Lacey & Crisp, 1980	CLO: 8 Plc.: 8 R.: 14 B/P: 2 inpatients	—	—	Variable	CLO: 50 mg	No difference in weight gain between CLO and Plc. All patients received behavior therapy. CLO dose low.
Biederman et al., 1985	AMI: 11 Plc.: 14 In- and out-patients	AMI: 18.4 ($SD = 4.9$) Plc.: 13.2 ($SD = 4.3$)	—	5 Wks.	AMI: $M = 115$ mg ($SD = 31$)	No difference between AMI and Plc. High refusal rate to enter study ($n = 18$). Side effects with AMI. All patients received psychotherapy. AMI-dose low.
Halmi et al., 1986	AMI: 23 CYP: 24 Plc.: 25 B/P: 33 inpatients	20.6 ($SD = 5.1$) Plc.: 13–36	AMI: 74 CYP: 83 Plc.: 64	4 Wks.	AMI: max.: 160 mg CYP: 32 mg	CYP, AMI > Plc. in reducing time to target weight. CYP only effective in restricting group. CYP had antidepressant effect. Side effects with AMI. All patients received psychotherapy and refeeding program.
Attia et al., 1998	FLX: 15 Plc.: 16 R.: 12 B/P: 19 inpatients	26.2 ($SD = 7.4$)	FLX: 73 Plc.: 75	7 Wks.	FLX: $M = 56$ mg	No difference in weight gain between FLX and Plc. All patients received psychotherapy.
Kaye et al., 2001	FLX: 16 Plc.: 19 all patients R: outpatients	FLX: 23 ($SD = 9$) Plc.: 22 ($SD = 6$)	FLX: 62.5 Plc.: 15.8	12 Mo. relapse prevention	FLX: 20 mg	FLX sig. > Plc. in preventing relapse (63% versus 16% completed 1 year without relapse). All patients received psychotherapy.

Note: AMI = Amitriptyline; B/P = Binge eating purging type; CBT = Cognitive-behavioral therapy; CLO = Clomipramine; CYP = Cyproheptadine; FLX = Fluoxetine; M = Mean; max. = Maximum; Mo. = Months; Plc. = Placebo; R = Restrictive type; SD = Standard deviation; Wks. = Weeks.

It has been proposed that acute treatment with antidepressants in the severe malnourished state may be ineffective because of the lack of important precursors to serotonin synthesis (Attia, Haiman, Walsh, & Flater, 1998; Kaye, Gendall, & Strober, 1998). Pharmacotherapy after reestablishment of appropriate weight may allow the antidepressant to exert its effects on serotonin and other neurotransmitters.

Cyproheptadine

Cyproheptadine has a variety of pharmacological effects. It is a serotonin-2a ($5HT_{2a}$) receptor antagonist, as well as a mild anticholinergic and antihistaminergic drug. As a result, the agent possesses appetite stimulating effects and may be sedating for some individuals. Three controlled trials have been published using cyproheptadine in the treatment of AN (Goldberg, Halmi, Eckert, Casper, & Davis, 1979; Halmi et al., 1986; Vigersky & Loriaux, 1977). Of the three, only the study by Halmi et al., discussed previously, was positive. In addition to the finding that, compared to placebo, it significantly decreased the number of days necessary to achieve normal weight, cyproheptadine was found to have a differential effect on the two subtypes of AN. Cyproheptadine significantly increased treatment efficiency in the nonbulimic AN subjects and decreased treatment efficiency in the bulimic subgroup. Cyproheptadine demonstrated a significant improvement in Hamilton Depression Rating Scale scores compared to placebo. However, the antidepressant effect was also associated with weight gain.

Antipsychotic Agents

Interest in the application of antipsychotic therapy in AN dates back to the mid-1960s. Target symptoms of weight and distorted body image provided the rationale for early trials. Typical antipsychotics are primarily prominent blockers at the dopamine-2 (D_2) receptors. They also possess antihistaminic effects; thus, most agents cause weight gain. Controlled trials with chlorpromazine (Dally & Sargant, 1966), pimozide (Vandereycken & Pierloot, 1982; Weizman, Tyano, Wijsenbeek, & Ben David, 1985), and sulpiride (Vandereycken, 1984) proved disappointing. No differences in weight gain were found compared to placebo. Furthermore, typical antipsychotics are difficult to tolerate. Reports of tardive dyskinesia, seizure activity, and increases in purging behavior (Condon, 1986; Dally & Sargant, 1966) have been published. In addition, pimozide has the potential for dose-related cardiac effects including QT prolongation, flattening, notching, and inversion of the T wave and U wave appearance in the EKG (Dulcan, Bregman, Weller, & Weller, 2001).

There are five new atypical agents on the market, including risperidone, olanzapine, quetiapine, ziprasidone, and aripiprazole with additional compounds in the drug industry pipeline. In general, these agents have little or no extrapyramidal effects (pseudoparkinsonism, dystonia, akathisia) and are felt to have a much reduced risk of tardive dyskinesia (Umbricht & Kane, 1996). In schizophrenia, they appear to be effective in refractory patients and to have efficacy in the area of negative symptoms and cognition (Beasley et al., 1996; Chouinard et al., 1993; Marder & Meibach, 1994; Meltzer & McGurk, 1999; Purdon et al., 2000; Tollefson & Sanger, 1997). Depressive and obsessional symptoms have also been found to be responsive in some patients (Ghaemi, Cherry, Katzow, & Goodwin, 2000; Konig et al., 2001; Mendelowitz & Liberman, 1995; Ramasubbu, Ravindran, & Lapierre, 2000; Stoll & Haura, 2000). Weight gain is associated with some of the atypicals as with the typical agents. Olanzapine is associated with prominent weight gain, risperidone and quetiapine are associated with weight gain somewhat less, and ziprasidone and aripiprazole have been reported to be weight neutral (Allison et al., 1999; Kane et al., 2002; Wirshing et al., 1999).

Atypical agents have been explored in the treatment of AN (see Table 9.2). Many of the cases represent difficult-to-treat patients who have not responded to other treatment modalities. All of the case reports for risperidone and olanzapine show a positive effect on weight gain. Symptoms that also responded included anxiety/agitation, obsessive thoughts, and core eating disorder symptoms, as well as paranoid ideation concerning body image or weight gain and preoccupation with food, compulsive hyperenergetic activity, and loss of realistic perceptions. Several patients stopped the atypical agent after weight regain and continued to do well.

An open, nonrandomized olanzapine series with comparison to nonpharmacotherapy controls did not show significant differences (Gaskill, Treat, McCabe, & Marcus, 2001). The olanzapine group had a greater number of previous hospitalizations, longer lengths of stay for the current hospitalizations, and more eating-related psychopathology. Both groups had their caloric intake maximized. A risperidone study was a retrospective, observational chart review currently in abstract form (Carver, Miller, Hagman, & Sigel, 2002). Details of the trial are not available; however, the authors reported trends toward positive results on a variety of parameters including weight gain, average calorie intake over the course of hospitalization, and length of stay.

Amisulpride is an "atypical" neuroleptic, which does not have effects at the $5HT_{2a}$ receptor but has a comparable clinical profile to the other atypical agents (Leucht, Pitschel-Walz, Engel, & Kissling, 2002). Ruggiero et al. (2001) performed an open-label comparison of clomipramine, fluoxetine, and amisulpride in AN patients. The pharmacotherapy was initiated at the beginning of the weight restoration phase of treatment for 35 AN restricting subtype patients. They were evaluated at baseline and after three months. The amisulpride and fluoxetine groups showed significant increases in mean weight from baseline to the end of the trial (38.4 ±8.3 kg to 42.6 ±10.1 kg [$p = .016$] and 40.9 ±6.9 kg to 42.7 ±7.5 kg [$p = .045$], respectively). The mean weight increase for the clomipramine group (3.3%) was not significant. However, in comparing the treatments, there was no significant difference for weight gain, weight phobia, body image, amenorrhea, or bulimic behavior. These findings are in contrast to other experiences with atypical agents. Further evaluation of atypical antipsychotics appears to be warranted. Many questions will arise if controlled trials support their efficacy, including exploration of what type of symptoms improve and by what mechanism, duration of treatment required, and pharmacoeconomic appraisals of the cost effectiveness of these pharmacotherapies.

Zinc

Common symptoms of AN, including weight loss, altered taste, amenorrhea, gastric distention, mood changes, and cutaneous findings, are also described in individuals with

Table 9.2 Uncontrolled Trials of Atypical Antipsychotics in the Treatment of Anorexia Nervosa

Study	N	Age (Years)	Duration of Treatment	Agent/Dose	Outcome
Fisman et al., 1996	1	13	12 Mo.	RIS: 1 mg	2.3 kg increase—maintained for one year. Comorbidity: autism, laxative use.
Hansen, 1999	1	49	7 Mo.	OLA: 5 mg	BMI: 12 to 19.9. Insight changed markedly, preoccupation with food and body image became less prominent, increased self-esteem. Comorbidity: OC symptoms, MDD.
Jensen & Mejlhede, 2000	3	50 30 34	2 Mo. 9 Mo. 2 Mo.	OLA: 5 mg	BMI: 13.8 to 21.5 BMI: 15.8 to 19 BMI: 18.5 to NA
La Via et al., 2000	B/P: 2	15 27	3.5 Mo. 22 Days	OLA: 10 mg	ABW: 46% to 92% Substantial reduction in core ED behaviors and agitation. ABW: 80% to 89%
Newman-Toker, 2000	R: 2	19 12	5 Mo. 9 Mo.	RIS: 1.5 mg	BMI: 14.6 to 19.8 Delusional thinking improved. QTc increased 400 to 421 ms. BMI: 15.9 to 19.7
Mehler et al., 2001	5	12-17	7.25 Wks.	OLA: 5–12.5 mg	BMI: 13.6 to 17 Reduction of delusional thinking, fear of weight gain, losing control, body image disturbances, compulsive activity. Rapid onset of effect (several days). One patient developed binge eating. Several patients stopped drug when normal weight was achieved and continued to do well.

(continued)

191

Table 9.2 (*Continued*)

Study	N	Age (Years)	Duration of Treatment	Agent/Dose	Outcome
Ruggiero et al., 2001	AMIS: 12 CLO: 13 FLX: 10 R: 35 inpatients	24.2	3 Mo.	AMIS: 50 mg CLO: 57.7 mg FLX: 28 mg	Weight increase not significantly different between groups: AMIS 11%, CLO 3.3%, FLX 4.5%. No significant differences in weight phobia, body image, amenorrhea. Refeeding program.
Gaskill et al., 2001	OLA: 23 Controls: 23 inpatients	NA	NA	OLA: M = 5.5 mg (1.25–15)	No difference in weight gain. OLA more chronic and symptomatic disease. Calorie intake was maximized for both groups.
Carver et al. 2002	RIS: 15 Controls: 15	NA	44.7 days	RIS: 0.5–1.5 mg	No significant difference, trend for shorter hospital stay with RIS. "Refractory" AN.

Note: AMIS = Amisulpride; B/P = Binge eating purging type; CLO = Clomipramine; DO = Dropouts; FLX = Fluoxetine; M = Mean; MDD = Major depressive disorder; Mo. = Months; NA = Not assessed; OC = Obsessive compulsive; OLA = Olanzapine; R = Restricting type; RIS = Risperidone; Wks. = Weeks.

zinc (Zn) deficiency (Bakan, 1979; Esca, Brenner, Mach, & Gschnait, 1979; Katz et al., 1987; McClain, Kasarskis, & Allen, 1985; Moynahan, 1976). McClain et al. (1992) suggested that zinc deficiency is a sustaining factor for abnormal eating in selected patients. These findings have led to the consideration of including Zn supplementation in the treatment regimen of AN.

A number of case reports and case series have appeared, suggesting the beneficial effects of zinc supplementation in AN patients (Bryce-Smith & Simpson, 1984; Esca et al., 1979; Safai-Kutti, 1990; Safai-Kutti & Kutti, 1984; Van Voorhees & Riba, 1992; Yamaguchi, Arita, Hara, Kimura, & Nawata, 1992). Reported benefits include increases in weight, improvement in taste acuity, normalization of mood, and return of menstruation. In an attempt to validate the case report literature, three randomized controlled trials have been performed (Birmingham, Goldner, & Bakan, 1994; Katz et al., 1987; Lask & Bryant-Waugh, 1993). Katz and colleagues investigated the use of 50 mg of elemental Zn compared to placebo in a parallel trial in 14 subjects with AN. A trend toward greater weight gain was observed in the supplemented group, but it did not reach significance. However, significantly lower depression and anxiety scores were found in the supplemented group compared to the placebo group. The second trial (Lask & Bryant-Waugh, 1993) was marred by a high dropout rate in the supplemented group related to the need for tube feedings that contained Zn. Thus, the tube feeding subjects were dropped from the protocol, leaving only three subjects receiving the Zn supplement. Birmingham et al. investigated the use of 28 mg of elemental Zn versus placebo in 35 subjects with AN. The rate of increase in BMI was twofold greater in the supplemented group compared to the control group, which was statistically significant ($p = .03$). Thus, considering the ease of use and tolerability of Zn preparations, there appears to be some benefit in ensuring that AN patients are supplemented with doses in the range of 28 to 50 mg of elemental Zn/day.

Miscellaneous Agents

A variety of other agents have been explored in the treatment of AN. Most of this exploration is in the form of case reports or small open-label trials. Lithium, with its mood-stabilizing properties and the ability to cause weight gain, was the subject of three case reports and one controlled trial (Barcai, 1977; Gross et al., 1981; Reilly, 1977; Stein, Hartshorn, Jones, & Steinberg, 1982). The case reports demonstrated weight gain and usually represented patients with diagnosed major depression or bipolar disorder. Unfortunately, Gross and colleagues could not confirm the effects seen in the case report literature. They compared lithium to placebo in a 16-subject, four-week randomized trial. All of the participants were in a refeeding program as well as behavioral treatment and individual and group psychotherapy. The lithium group weighed more and was eating a greater number of calories at baseline, making the study difficult to interpret. No differences were found between the active drug and placebo groups. In addition, pharmacokinetic difficulties would be expected with lithium in patients who are restricting their food intake. The kinetic profile of lithium is dependent on the patient's sodium and hydration status. Thus, the benefits of lithium use do not offset its risks.

Narcotic antagonists of various types have been explored in AN treatment (Luby, Marrazzi, & Kinzie, 1987; Marrazzi, Bacon, Kinzie, & Luby, 1995; Moore, Mills, &

Forster, 1981). In an attempt to demonstrate an antilipolytic effect of naloxone, Moore and colleagues administered naloxone by constant intravenous infusion in doses of 3.2 to 6.4 mg/d for approximately five weeks. The study population consisted of 12 female patients who were at least 25% below their ideal body weight. The patients also received psychotherapy and amitriptyline in doses of 50 to 200 mg/d. A target diet of 3,000 to 4,000 kcal/d was used. The naloxone infusion began approximately three weeks after admission. The patients demonstrated a significantly greater weight gain when receiving the infusion than one week before or one week postinfusion or four weeks postinfusion. However, it is difficult to determine if the weight gain was related to the infusion or to the other therapies. The lower weight gains at one and four weeks postinfusion may represent a plateau for weight gain. The weight gain after one week of infusion (four weeks of inpatient treatment) may have been due to the other therapies. The authors felt that an antilipolytic effect had occurred in light of a fall of plasma beta-hydroxybutyrate and nonesterified fatty acids associated with the naloxone infusion, which returned to preinfusion levels with the discontinuation of naloxone. Luby et al. reported weight gain in six of eight patients who received naltrexone, an orally active narcotic antagonist. However, the patients were receiving multiple other treatments, including total parenteral nutrition.

The only controlled trial of a narcotic antagonist was performed by Marrazzi, Bacon, et al. (1995), who were exploring their auto-addiction model of eating disorders. Six outpatient subjects diagnosed with AN, binge-purge subtype, who were also receiving weekly psychotherapy, were studied in a six-week crossover trial. They received naltrexone in a dose of 200 mg/d or placebo. Binge-purge frequency was significantly reduced during the naltrexone phase versus the placebo phase. The authors suggest that the effect of the naltrexone is to interrupt the addictive cycle rather than to change food intake. One concern in using higher doses of naltrexone is that of liver toxicity. In this six-week trial, no elevation of liver function tests was identified (Marrazzi, Wroblewski, Kinzie, & Luby, 1997). Confirmatory studies are needed to expand this data set in terms of diagnosis (AN—restrictor type), duration of treatment, and safety. Thus, it is interesting to consider the case report by Mendelson (2001) concerning tramadol, a mu opioid receptor agonist that also acts as a NE and 5-HT reuptake inhibitor (Raffa et al., 1992). A reduction of ritualistic eating behavior and a corresponding weight gain were observed. The patient had failed a prior course of fluoxetine treatment 60 mg/d over six months.

Other small studies have been reported, including a case of a patient diagnosed with AN and a seizure disorder who responded to a combination of valproate and clonazepam (Tachibana, Sugita, Teshima, & Hishikawa, 1989). Controlled trials have suggested no effect with tetrahydrocannabinol (Gross et al., 1983) and clonidine (Casper, Schlemmer, & Javaid, 1987).

AN patients have been reported to have elevated growth hormone (GH) levels when malnourished with low levels of insulin-like growth factor-1 (IGF-1; Counts, Gwirtsman, Carlsson, Lesem, & Cutler, 1992; Hill, Hill, McClain, Humphries, & McClain, 1993), a polypeptide that mediates the anabolic effects of GH (Hill, Bucuvalas, & McClain, 2000). Data in malnourished patients indicate that recombinant human growth hormone (rhGH) administration can promote nitrogen retention and increase IGF-1 levels (Clemmons & Underwood, 1992). Hill et al. (2000) reported a controlled trial of GH administration in 15 AN patients admitted for inpatient treatment. The subjects were randomized to receive rhGH (0.05 mg/kg subcutaneously each day) or placebo for 28 days. The results of the trial indicated that the rhGH group achieved cardiovascular stability (two consecutive mornings that the patient was no longer orthostatic by pulse) significantly faster than those on placebo (17 vs. 37 days, $p = .02$). Nonsignificant improvements were seen in weight gain and duration of hospitalization. This pilot study requires replication and extension.

Last, prokinetic agents have been used to stimulate the GI tract so as to relieve the bloating and early satiety symptoms that AN patients report with refeeding. Short-term studies of metoclopramide (Domstad, Shih, Humphries, DeLand, & Digenis, 1987), domperidone (Stacher et al., 1986), and cisapride (Stacher et al., 1986) have been shown to improve gastric emptying. However, differences in weight gain in controlled studies were not found among domperidone (Craigen, Kennedy, Garfinkel, & Jeejeebhoy, 1987), metoclopramide (Moldofsky, Jeuniewic, & Garfinkel, 1977), cisapride, and placebo (Stacher et al., 1993; Szmukler, Young, Miller, Lichtenstein, & Binns, 1995). Due to potential widening of the QTc interval, cisapride is no longer available.

BULIMIA NERVOSA

Treatment studies of bulimia nervosa (BN) have been easier to conduct and are more numerous because of its higher prevalence and because patients can usually be managed in an outpatient setting. In addition, compared to patients with AN, BN patients show a greater willingness to be treated.

Antidepressants

Most pharmacologic studies have focused on the use of antidepressants because of the observed frequent association of BN with depressive illness and in part because of the success of early antidepressant trials. To date, more than 20 controlled studies, summarized in Table 9.3, have been completed. Despite the fact that BN frequently has its onset during adolescence and early adulthood, the majority of the medication trials have been conducted with adults; thus, their results may not be applicable to children and adolescents. The drug that has been studied in the most patients is fluoxetine, which remains the only U.S. Food and Drug Administration (FDA)-approved drug for BN. It is of note that the number of pharmacological studies is declining with time.

The medication studies ranged in duration from 6 to 16 weeks, with most lasting about 8 weeks. Some studies excluded depressed subjects, and it appears that response to antidepressants is independent of mood status. Taken together, the trials show a definite effect of antidepressant drugs on improving characteristic symptoms of BN, such as binge eating, vomiting, and concerns about weight and shape. Most studies also demonstrated decreases in depressive and anxiety symptoms. However, there is little information on the extent to which dieting and fasting behaviors are replaced by normal meal patterns. Although the percentage reductions of binge eating and purging behavior are impressive in these studies, the percentage of subjects free of symptoms at the end of treatment is usually low. Abstinence rates at the end of treatment have ranged from 0%

Table 9.3 Antidepressants versus Placebo Randomized Trials in Bulimia Nervosa Subjects

Study	Max. Dosage (mg)	Duration (Weeks)	Medication vs. Placebo			
			N	% Completion	% BE	% Abstinent
Imipramine						
Pope et al., 1983	200 mg	6	11 vs. 11	82 vs. 91	70 vs. 2	—
Agras et al., 1987	300 mg	16	10 vs. 12	100 vs. 83	72 vs. 43	30 vs. 10
Mitchell et al., 1990	300 mg	10	54 vs. 31	57 vs. 84	49 vs. 2.5	10 vs. 16
Alger et al., 1991	200 mg Naltrexone 150 mg	8	Total: 28	Total: 79	22 vs. 30 vs. 30	—
Amitriptyline						
Mitchell & Groat, 1984	150 mg	8	21 vs. 17	76 vs. 94	72 vs. 52	—
Desipramine						
Hughes et al., 1986	200 mg	6	10 vs. 12	70 vs. 75	91 vs. +19	
Barlow et al., 1988	150 mg	6 Crossover	Total: 47	Total: 51	62 vs. 2.5	4 vs. —
Blouin et al., 1988	150 mg Fenfluram 60 mg	6 Crossover	Total: 36	Total: 61	—	—
Walsh et al., 1991	300 mg	6	40 vs. 38	77 vs. 84	47 vs. +7	13 vs. 8
Mianserin						
Sabine et al., 1983	60 mg	8	20 vs. 30	70 vs. 73	0 vs. 0	0 vs. 0
Bupropion						
Horne et al., 1988	450 mg	8 Early termination	55 vs. 26	Total: 88	60 vs. 23	30 vs. 0
Trazodone						
Pope et al., 1989	400 mg	6	23 vs. 23	74 vs. 87	31 vs. +21	10 vs. 0
Phenelzine						
Walsh et al., 1985	90 mg	8	20 vs. 18	50 vs. 72	65 vs. 6	43 vs. 0
Walsh et al., 1988	90 mg	8	31 vs. 31	58 vs. 68	64 vs. 5.5	35 vs. 4

Isocarboxazid						
Kennedy et al., 1988	60 mg	6 Crossover	Total: 29	Total: 62	—	33 vs. —
Brofaromine						
Kennedy et al., 1993	200 mg	8	19 vs. 17	79 vs. 76	62 vs. 50	19 vs. 13
Moclobemide						
Carruba et al., 2001	600 mg	6	38 vs. 39	74 vs. 61	22 vs. 44	—
Fluoxetine						
FBNCSG, 1992	60 mg	8	129 vs. 129 vs. 129	69 vs. 76 vs. 61	67 vs. 45 vs. 33	23 vs. 11 vs. 11
	20 mg					
Goldstein et al., 1995	60 mg	16	296 vs. 102	57 vs. 48	50 vs. 18	18 vs. 12

Note: BE = Binge eating.

to 68% with a mean of 24% (Mitchell, Peterson, Myers, & Wonderlich, 2001). Placebo responses are similarly variable but are generally less than half the size of the response for active drug treatment (Jimerson, Wolfe, Brotman, & Metzger, 1996). Only two of these trials (Mitchell & Groat, 1984; Sabine, Yonace, Farrington, Barratt, & Wakeling, 1983) have failed to support the efficacy of an antidepressant for eating symptoms in BN. As in other areas there appears to be a publication bias in medication treatment of BN. At least two unpublished reports of negative multicenter, multinational studies comparing fluvoxamine with placebo show a lack of greater efficacy of fluvoxamine compared to placebo (Corcos, Flament, Atger, & Jeammet, 1996; Freeman, 1998).

No differential effect concerning efficacy among the various classes of antidepressants could be demonstrated. The effects of selective serotonin reuptake inhibitors (SSRIs) other than fluoxetine, as well as newer antidepressants, still need to be studied in controlled trials. However, no studies directly compare two different classes of antidepressant medication. Because there is little evidence for superiority of response to a single class of antidepressants, differences in side effects may be a significant factor in the clinical choice of the antidepressant. A particular problem of treatment with tricyclic antidepressants (TCAs) is that of weight gain, whereas fluoxetine tends to produce a modest weight loss (Beumont et al., 1997; Fichter et al., 1991; Walsh et al., 1997) and even an increase in dietary restraint (Agras, Rossiter, et al., 1994). However, an increase in dietary restraint during treatment with fluoxetine or another appetite-reducing drug may prove countertherapeutic. It is generally agreed that patients with BN should learn to overcome their fear that normal eating will result in significant weight gain. Giving up restraint also helps to interrupt the cycle of fasting and binge eating. Discontinuation of fluoxetine may lead to increased appetite, subsequent weight regain, and the return of bulimic behavior (Beumont et al., 1997). Bupropion, even though effective when compared to placebo, is contraindicated in patients with BN because 5.7% of subjects in that study developed generalized tonic clonic seizures. Finally, the MAO inhibitor phenelzine is relatively rarely used in this patient population because of the necessity of dietary limitations to avoid tyramine reactions.

The time course of action of the medications appears to be similar to that found in major depression with a tendency for improvement to occur more quickly for BN than for depression, often as early as in the first week of treatment (Barlow, Blouin, Blouin, & Perez, 1998; Horne et al., 1988; Mitchell & Groat, 1984). It is generally recommended that treatment failure should be considered only if adequate doses have been administered for at least 8 to 12 weeks. In one study (Agras et al., 1992) involving desipramine, treatment for 24 weeks was more effective than treatment for 16 weeks, suggesting that longer periods are more appropriate. It is not clear if a time-limited course of medication will produce lasting improvement.

The recommended doses and blood levels are usually the same as those stated for the treatment of depression, with a tendency for higher dosages to be more effective. In a direct comparison of fluoxetine in a standard antidepressant dose of 20 mg versus 60 mg per day, the higher dose was more effective (Fluoxetine Bulimia Nervosa Collaborative Study Group [FBNCSG], 1992; Goldstein, Wilson, Thompson, Potvine, & Rampey, 1995).

For the bulimic patient whose response to a medication is unsatisfactory, switching to an alternative antidepressant might be useful. This option has been evaluated in only one controlled study. Walsh et al. (1997) used a sequence of desipramine for eight weeks, followed by fluoxetine for nonresponders. The rate of abstinence and reduction in binge eating (29% and 69%, respectively) tended to be higher than those seen in single drug trials, suggesting that sequential use may be a useful strategy. In addition, the use of sequential antidepressants was as effective as CBT (plus placebo). Two-thirds of the patients were switched from desipramine to fluoxetine during the course of the study.

Long-term benefits of short-term treatment protocols have been demonstrated only for psychotherapy but not for medication alone. In addition, there is, unfortunately, little evidence that continued treatment over an extended period with a single antidepressant is more effective than the use of a placebo. The therapeutic effect may be lost even when medication is maintained. Controlled studies reported a significant relapse rate (30% to 45%) while on maintenance medication in improved patients followed for four to six months (Pyle et al., 1990; Walsh, Hadigan, Devlin, Gladis, & Roose, 1991). The most recent placebo-controlled, double-blind study was conducted with fluoxetine over a one-year period after response to acute fluoxetine treatment (Romano, Halmi, Koke, & Lee, 2002). Responders to acute treatment with fluoxetine (at least 50% reduction of vomiting episodes) were randomly assigned to fluoxetine 60 mg or placebo for a one-year period. The total number of relapsers did not differ between groups (22.4% vs. 29.7%) and, in addition, the attrition rate not attributable to relapse was high (60.5% vs. 62.2%). Of the 150 patients who entered the maintenance phase and were randomized, only 19 remained in the study until the one-year follow-up. These findings raise the question: Would raising the dose, substituting a second antidepressant when relapse has occurred with the first medication, or adding a second drug improve outcome? Open-label studies suggest that the use of different antidepressants after relapse might be a useful approach (Mitchell et al., 1989; Pope, Hudson, Jonas, & Yurgelun-Todd, 1985; Pyle et al., 1990).

Alternative Medications

In addition to the antidepressants, a wide variety of medications have been investigated in placebo-controlled trials in patients with BN, including opiate antagonists (Alger, Schwalberg, Bigaouette, Michalek, & Howard, 1991; Igoin-Apfelbaum & Apfelbaum, 1987; Jonas & Gold, 1988; Marrazzi, Bacon, et al., 1995; Mitchell, Laine, Morley, & Levine, 1986; Mitchell et al., 1989), lithium (Hsu, Clement, Santhouse, & Ju, 1991), d-fenfluramine (Blouin et al., 1988; Russell, Checkley, Feldman, & Eisler, 1988), L-tryptophan (Krahn & Mitchell, 1985), anticonvulsants (Hoopes et al., 2002; Kaplan, Garfinkel, Darby, & Garner, 1983; Wermuth, Davis, Hollister, & Stunkard, 1977), and, most recently, ondansetron (Faris et al., 2000). In general, none of these drugs can be recommended for routine use without additional controlled studies. The fenfluramides have been withdrawn from the market worldwide because of a high incidence of valvular disease, and the use of tryptophan is limited by the reported association with eosinphilia-myalgia syndrome. Lithium did not demonstrate effectiveness; furthermore, there are obvious hazards in treating patients who may experience abnormalities in fluid and electrolyte regulation.

Treatment of "compulsive eating" with anticonvulsants such as phenytoin and carbamazapine was based on the theory that bulimia, given its episodic, uncontrollable nature, might be a variant of a seizure disorder. However, there is insufficient evidence as to the efficacy of these anticonvulsants in BN, and the rationale for their use now seems outdated. However, first results in abstract form are available for topiramate, a new antiepileptic agent (Hoopes et al., 2002). In a controlled trial with 68 patients receiving a median dose of 100 mg (25 mg to 400 mg), binge eating frequency decreased by 50% in the topiramate group and by 29% in the placebo group. The use of topiramate in eating disorders is problematic because of disturbing side effects such as paresthesias and hypoaesthesias, as well as cognitive impairments such as decreased concentration, attention, word fluency, and even confusion. When used, the drug has to be titrated very slowly, increasing the dosage by only 25 mg to 50 mg per week.

There is convincing evidence that endogenous opioid peptides are involved in the regulation of food intake. The controlled studies using naltrexone show contradictory results, with three studies finding no significant difference between naltrexone and placebo (Alger et al., 1991; Igoin-Apfelbaum & Apfelbaum, 1987; Mitchell et al., 1989). Higher dosages than used for detoxification or relapse prevention in drug and alcohol abuse seem to be more effective (e.g., 200 mg); however, higher dosages can be associated with potentially severe adverse effects including nausea, vomiting, and the elevation of liver enzymes. However, there are case reports describing treatment success with augmenting an existing antidepressant treatment by adding naltrexone (Neumeister, Winkler, & Woeber-Bingoel, 1999).

One study has suggested that the selective type 3 serotonin receptor antagonist and antiemetic ondansetron may be helpful in reducing binge eating and vomiting (Faris et al., 2000). After four weeks of treatment, patients receiving active drug exhibited a reduction of binge eating and vomiting of 50%. The drug (4 mg) was given 30 minutes before each meal and as needed when patients experienced an intense urge to binge eat (up to a maximum of 24 mg). The authors suggest that a perpetuating factor driving the abnormal eating behavior involves an increase in the basal tone of the vagus nerve because of repeated stimulation of the gastric branch of the vagus nerve by binge eating and vomiting. Increased afferent vagal activity contributes to the loss of satiety that bulimic patients frequently exhibit and might trigger the vomiting phase. Ondansetron acts to blunt this abnormal afferent activity via vagal inhibition and to support the resumption of normal hunger and satiation. However, this hypothesis is still highly speculative and needs further confirmation.

There is a large body of literature on open studies and case reports using newer antidepressants and other drugs in patients with BN that have not been followed by controlled clinical trials: reboxetine (El-Giamal et al., 2000), milnacipran (El-Giamal et al., 2001), methylphenidate (Sokol, Gray, Goldstein, & Kaye, 1999), flutamide (Bergman & Eriksson, 1996), ipsapirone (Geretsegger, Greimel, Roed, & Keppel Hesselink, 1995), sertraline (Roberts & Lydiard, 1993), paroxetine (Pigott, Sunderland, & Horn, 1986), pimozide (Faltus, 1993), sodium valproate (Herridge & Pope, 1985), nomifensine (Nassr, 1986), and methylamphetamine (Ong, Checkley, & Russell, 1983). However, the value of open studies is very limited.

Medication and Psychotherapy

Much work has supported the beneficial role for psychotherapy, particularly CBT in BN treatment. Six studies, summarized in Table 9.4, have systematically compared drugs to

Table 9.4   Antidepressant versus Psychotherapy Trials in Bulimia Nervosa Subjects

Study	N	% Completion	Treatment	Duration (Weeks)	% BE	% Abstinent
Involving CBT						
Mitchell et al.,	34	85	CBT + Placebo	10	89	45
1990	52	75	CBT + Imipramine		92	51
	54	57	Imipramine		49	16
	31	84	Placebo		2.5	—
Agras et al.,	12	Total: 83	CBT + Desipramine	16	57	—
1992	12		CBT + Desipramine	24	89	70
	12		Desipramine	16	+13	—
	12		Desipramine	24	44	42
	23		CBT	24	71	55
Leitenberg	7	86	CBT	20	—	71
et al., 1996	7	43	Desipramine			0
	7	71	CBT + Desipramine			57
Goldbloom	24	58	CBT	16	80	43
et al., 1997	23	52	Fluoxetine 60 mg		70	17
	29	41	CBT + Fluoxetine		87	25
Walsh et al.,	25	Total: 66	CBT + Placebo	16	65	24
1997	23		CBT + Medication*		87	52
	28		Medication*		69	29
	22		Supportive + Placebo		46	18
	22		Supportive + Medication*		55	18
Jacobi et al.,	19	58	CBT	16	42	26
2002	16	75	Fluoxetine 60 mg		46	13
	18	67	CBT + Fluoxetine		50	17
Not Involving CBT						
Fichter et al.,	20	100	Inpatient + Placebo	5	26	—
1991	19	100	Inpatient + Fluoxetine 60 mg		47	—
Beumont et al.,	33	79	NC + Placebo	8	80	62
1997	34	68	NC + Fluoxetine 60 mg		84	70
Mitchell et al.,	22	—	SH + Placebo	16	60	24
2001	21		SH + Fluoxetine 60 mg		67	26
	26		Fluoxetine 60 mg		50	16
	22		Placebo		32	9

Note: BE = Binge eating; CBT = Cognitive-behavioral therapy; NC = Nutritional counseling; SH = Self-help.

* Desipramine followed by fluoxetine.

psychotherapy with the combination treatment in BN outpatients. Although differing in many respects, these studies suggest that CBT is superior to drug therapy alone and the combination of the two is superior to medication alone. However, it is less clear how much benefit is derived from adding medication to effective psychological treatment. Some additional benefit was achieved by the addition of medication in some but not all studies; however, the cost-benefit ratio of additional pharmacotherapy is questionable. In addition, when antidepressants were combined with CBT, the acceptability of the psychological approach was significantly reduced, as indicated by a higher dropout rate (Bacaltchuk & Hay, 2002). Only one study clearly shows that medication added to CBT proved superior to CBT plus placebo in the reduction of binge eating and purging (Walsh et al., 1997). This study applied a two-stage medication intervention, in which a second antidepressant (fluoxetine) was employed if the first (desipramine) was either ineffective or poorly tolerated. However, there is evidence that, even if adding antidepressants to psychotherapy does not further reduce binge eating or purging, the combination does improve symptoms such as anxiety, depressed mood, and dietary restriction (Agras et al., 1992; Mitchell et al., 1990).

Three additional studies used combined treatment; however, they did not involve outpatient CBT (see Table 9.4). One study added fluoxetine to a comprehensive inpatient program (Fichter et al., 1991). Fluoxetine did not add to the effect of intensive inpatient treatment, which most likely demonstrates a ceiling effect. In another study, medication was added to eight weeks of nutritional counseling (NC; Beumont et al., 1997). No differences were found between NC with fluoxetine and NC with placebo; however, after discontinuation of the drug, patients on fluoxetine were more likely to have a recurrence of symptoms. The percentage of binge-free patients fell from almost 70% after eight weeks of treatment to 35.7% three months after fluoxetine was withdrawn. In addition, patients on fluoxetine lost weight during treatment and regained weight to 2.4 kg higher than baseline during the three-month follow-up. Finally, fluoxetine was added to a self-help condition (Mitchell et al., 2001). Fluoxetine alone was superior to placebo in reducing vomiting episodes, and a self-help manual was superior to no manual. The combination of the medication and the manual was superior to the use of the drug alone, suggesting a possible utility for such manuals in the treatment of women with BN who receive pharmacotherapy.

Sequential Treatment

Sequential treatment studies examine whether a second-level treatment would be effective for those who fail the first treatment (see Table 9.5). Mitchell et al. (2002) randomized 62 bulimic patients who remained symptomatic after 16 weeks of CBT either to 16 weeks of interpersonal psychotherapy treatment (IPT) or medication therapy (fluoxetine) initiated at a dose of 60 mg per day. Sequencing the treatment led to a high attrition rate with 32% during IPT and 48% during medication treatment. The rates of abstinence achieved during secondary treatment were low, with 16% for the subjects assigned to treatment with IPT and 10% for those assigned to medication. The authors conclude that sequencing treatment cannot be recommended because it appears to be of little clinical utility. More promising findings on the use of fluoxetine as a second-line treatment were reported in a small study by Walsh et al. (2000). They randomly assigned 22 patients with BN who had not responded to, or had relapsed following, CBT or IPT to receive placebo or fluoxetine 60 mg for eight weeks. Five (38%) of the 13 patients receiving fluoxetine were abstinent during the last 28 days of the study, compared to none of the patients receiving placebo. The frequency of binge eating and purging decreased in patients receiving fluoxetine but increased in placebo-treated patients. The authors conclude that pharmacotherapy may benefit some patients who do not satisfactorily respond to psychotherapy.

Table 9.5 Antidepressants as a Second Treatment in Patients with Bulimia

Study	Patients	N	% Completion	Treatment	Duration (Weeks)	% BE	% Abstinent
Fichter et al., 1996	After inpatient tx	37	49	Fluvoxamine 300 mg	15	+11	65
		35	86	Placebo		+170	35
Walsh et al., 2000	PT nonresponder	13	92	Fluoxetine 60 mg	8	82	38
		9	89	Placebo		+20	0
Mitchell et al., 2002	PT nonresponder	31	51	Medication*	16	—	10
		31	68	IPT		—	16

Note: BE = Binge eating; IPT = Interpersonal psychotherapy treatment; tx = Treatment.
*Fluoxetine 60 mg followed by desipramine.

Finally, one study examined the efficacy of fluvoxamine in patients with BN after intensive inpatient treatment (Fichter, Kruger, Rief, Holland, & Doehne, 1996). Seventy-two patients were randomized to fluvoxamine or placebo for 3 weeks in the hospital followed by 12 more weeks after discharge. At the end of inpatient treatment, roughly 60% of all patients were binge free. Dropout rates were high in the fluvoxamine-treated group (51%), with side effects (nausea, dizziness, and drowsiness) accounting for 22% of the dropouts. Twelve weeks after discharge, most patients showed some deterioration of symptoms; however, this was less pronounced in patients receiving fluvoxamine. About 65% of the patients receiving fluvoxamine were binge free compared to about 34% of the patients receiving placebo.

Another form of sequential treatment, called the *stepped care approach,* is currently under investigation. Such studies are based on the assumption that the use of highly specialized CBT treatment could be reserved for the group of patients who fail to respond to the less expensive and/or more available treatments such as self-help or medication. However, the role of medication within a stepped care framework remains to be established (Wilson, Vitousek, & Loeb, 2000).

BINGE EATING DISORDER

Binge eating disorder (BED) was included in the *DSM-IV* as a disorder for further study in the appendix and as an example of eating disorder not otherwise specified (EDNOS). The concept of a BED-like syndrome has appeared in the literature in various forms for some time. Various terms have been used—such as *binge eating* and *compulsive overeating,* although most of these terms have not been carefully defined. During the course of the deliberations of the *DSM-IV* Eating Disorder Work Group, the concept of BED began to coalesce and diagnostic criteria were developed. Since the *DSM-IV* was published, a rather substantial literature on BED has evolved; whether diagnostic criteria are in their final form or not, they do appear to identify a subgroup of individuals, most of whom are obese, who have high levels of psychopathology and who demonstrate marked distress as to their abnormal eating behavior.

Given the recency with which BED has become the object of intense study, this literature remains moderate and in transition; therefore, the most recently published studies should be consulted for information on the directions this field is taking. It is important to remember that most of these patients desire weight loss. The initial hope of researchers had been that if binge-eating behavior were targeted with success in treatment, many of these subjects would be able to lose weight, but this has not been the case. Interventions have been added in some protocols that target weight loss in addition to binge eating, and some of the more recent literature has focused on both areas.

Weight Loss Treatment

Two studies examined the efficacy of weight loss in binge eating versus nonbinge eating overweight subjects. The first protocol by Marcus et al. (1990) examined the relative efficacy of fluoxetine 60 mg and placebo when employed in combination with behavior therapy in overweight binge eating and nonbinge eating subjects. Of interest, subjects treated with fluoxetine attained greater weight loss than those treated with placebo, whether they were binge eaters or nonbinge eaters, although most subjects experienced a fairly rapid weight regain after fluoxetine was discontinued. A second study by de Zwaan, Nutzinger, and Schoenbeck (1992) examined the relative efficacy of fluvoxamine 100 mg or placebo when used in combination with either CBT or nutritional counseling (NC) in a double-blind randomized trial. In this protocol, the amount of weight loss achieved by binge eaters and nonbinge eaters was not significantly different. CBT and NC, as well as fluvoxamine and placebo, appeared to perform equally well, with no significant differences.

Eating Disorder Treatment

A number of double-blind, placebo-controlled randomized trials have been reported in subjects diagnosed with BED or its precursors, such as "atypical eating disorders," "nonpurging BN," or subjects scoring high on the Binge Eating Scale who are overweight. Many of these patients would meet criteria for BED by contemporary standards. These data are summarized in Table 9.6. In several of the studies, active medication has resulted in significant reductions in binge eating and, in some studies, in substantial rates of remission from binge eating symptoms. Weight loss results have been mixed, with some researchers finding evidence of substantial weight loss and others not. Thus, some studies have found that drug therapy resulted in reductions of binge eating but not significant weight loss (desipramine, imipramine, d-fenfluramine), while in some studies drug therapy appears to result in both reductions of binge eating and in greater loss than is seen with placebo (fluvoxamine, sertraline, topiramate). The sample sizes again have been small in many of these studies, and, given the heterogeneity of the diagnostic systems employed, the results are difficult to interpret. However, the two studies by Hudson et al. (1998, 2001), one involving fluvoxamine and one involving the antiepileptic drug topiramate, both with an "n" greater than 40 BED subjects, suggest that fluvoxamine and topiramate are of interest in terms of binge eating and weight reduction. These results indicate the need for larger, perhaps multicenter trials concerning the efficacy of these agents, perhaps coupled with other weight loss interventions, and when used on a more chronic basis. However, as mentioned in the BN section, topiramate has several central nervous system (CNS) side effects, limiting this drug's application in patients with BED.

Table 9.6 Controlled Pharmacological Trials in Patients with Binge Eating Disorder

Study	N	% Completion	Treatment	Duration (Weeks)	% BE	% Abstinent	Wt> Placebo
McCann & Agras, 1990	30	77	Desipramine	12	63	60	—
Alger et al., 1991	41	80	Imipramine	8	73	—	—
			Naltrexone		48	—	—
Stunkard et al., 1996	28	86	d-Fenfluramine	8	—	80	—
Hudson et al., 1998	85	79	Fluvoxamine	9	—	45	+
McElroy et al., 2000	34	76	Sertraline	6	85	54	+
Hudson et al., 2001	61	85	Topiramate	14	94	64	+

Note: BE = Binge eating.

Combined Treatment

A modest number of studies have used more complex designs employing combinations or sequential treatment paradigms. Agras, Telch, et al. (1994) employed a design involving 84 subjects, the design including behavioral weight loss treatment for all subjects with the addition of CBT and, in some cases, desipramine followed by behavioral weight loss treatment. The results suggested that CBT was preferable to behavioral weight loss treatment in reducing binge eating while behavioral weight loss treatment was better than CBT in inducing weight loss on a short-term basis. The addition of CBT to behavioral weight loss treatment resulted in an increased rate of remission from binge eating, and the addition of desipramine resulted in an increased weight loss compared to behavioral weight loss treatment alone.

Laederach-Hofman et al. (1999) examined the utility of imipramine and placebo when added to dietary counseling and psychological support. These authors found that imipramine was associated with greater reductions in binge eating frequency and weight loss in those receiving dietary counseling and psychological support, and this pattern still persisted at six-month follow-up. Most recently, Grilo, Masheb, Heninger, and Wilson (2002), using a four-cell design, examined the relative efficacy of fluoxetine 60 mg, placebo, CBT plus fluoxetine, and CBT plus placebo in 108 subjects assigned to 16 weeks of treatment. There were no differences in weight loss among the groups. However, the highest remission rates from binge eating were achieved in those who received CBT plus placebo (73%) or CBT plus fluoxetine (55%) versus those who received fluoxetine (29%) or placebo alone (30%). Devlin (2002) reported the results of an ongoing study using an almost identical design. In addition to CBT and fluoxetine, all patients received a 16-session group behavioral eating and weight management treatment (LEARN-BED). Again, fluoxetine did not add to the effects of individual CBT and did not differ from placebo.

The weight loss agent sibutramine, which may have an antidepressant effect given its serotonin and norepinephrine reuptake inhibition effects, would be hypothesized to be effective in binge eating as well as weight loss in those with BED and is currently being studied in a large multicenter trial. The results of this study should prove interesting, and the sample size involved should provide the power necessary for careful assessment of the drug's actions. Orlistat, the lipase inhibitor, is an agent that would be interesting to study in patients with BED, given the fact that use of this agent by necessity discourages the intake of high-fat foods, an intake pattern common among those with BED during binge eating episodes.

SUMMARY AND FUTURE DIRECTIONS

In the area of eating disorders, the role of drug treatment has less support compared to other psychiatric disorders such as schizophrenia or affective disorders. Unfortunately, most of the investigations of new therapies have occurred in adult patients. Considering that AN and BN present frequently in adolescents, there exists a need to verify efficacy and safety in this group.

Anorexia Nervosa

In considering the types of symptoms that a patient with AN presents, a number of potential drug therapy applications come readily to mind. As illustrated, these ideas usually have initially been investigated through case studies and small, uncontrolled trials. As with the publishing biases that exist, the reports that appear in the literature are almost invariably positive. In attempts to validate these new potential therapies, randomized controlled paradigms not uncommonly fail to confirm the results. This illustrates the need for confirmatory data before widespread application of a treatment. Applications of pharmacotherapy in the treatment of acute underweight AN is limited at this time. Only two agents, amitriptyline and cyproheptadine at higher doses, have been demonstrated to be helpful in improving weight gain. However, multiple studies also suggest a lack of efficacy for these compounds. It has been proposed that in the acute malnourished state, the dietary precursor is not available to enable the maximization of the reuptake effect of the antidepressant agents (Attia, Haiman, Walsh, & Flater, 1998; Kaye, Gendall, & Strober, 1998). In weight-restored AN patients, fluoxetine has been demonstrated to provide benefit as a maintenance treatment, reducing relapse in conjunction with psychological interventions. A therapeutic agent that assists patients in maintaining weight is an important addition to the AN therapeutic armamentarium. Traditional (typical) antipsychotics have not proven helpful in acute treatment of AN patients. In considering the atypical antipsychotics, the field is still at the case report stage. The reports appear to suggest that atypical agents such as risperidone and olanzapine should be investigated in randomized, placebo-controlled designs. With the reduction or absence of extrapyramidal side effects (EPS), the atypicals are substantially more tolerable than the older neuroleptics and may prove to have benefit.

Zinc supplementation, growth hormone (rhGH), and naltrexone have shown some promise in small controlled trials. While positive, these agents must be evaluated in larger studies to replicate and extend these preliminary findings.

There have been many dead ends in the search for helpful agents in the treatment of AN. With additional work, several of the potential trails now being investigated will result in useful additions to the treatment of these individuals.

Bulimia Nervosa

Antidepressants are one of the alternatives in the therapeutic armamentarium for the treatment of BN patients. However, their use as sole therapy does not seem sufficient to effectively treat most of these patients. For patients who have not been previously treated, it is generally appropriate to recommend a trial of an evidence-based psychotherapy before initiating medication. There is only little evidence that initiating therapy with a combination of CBT and treatment with fluoxetine is superior. Patients who are significantly depressed when entering treatment should be given an antidepressant for the mood-elevating effect of the drug, rather than specifically for the antibulimic effect. In addition, patients with very severe bulimic symptoms might profit from an antidepressant early in treatment because it can be difficult to engage and keep them in psychotherapy. Even though the results of controlled studies on drug treatment of psychotherapy nonresponders are equivocal, the addition of antidepressants might be helpful in patients who do not achieve an early significant reduction in bulimic episodes. Fluoxetine is the most systematically studied antidepressant agent. There is more evidence as to the beneficial effect of fluoxetine in a dosage of 60 mg/d than any other drug, and this, combined with its relatively favorable side effect profile, makes it the drug of first choice. If no or only partial response is noted, a reasonable alternative is to switch to an alternative SSRI or to desipramine hydrochloride. It would seem reasonable that the minimum duration of successful treatment should be six months. As for other psychiatric disorders, initiation of psychotropic medication for BN should be preceded by a comprehensive psychiatric assessment, a review of medical history, and baseline laboratory tests (APA, 2000).

More recently, the literature has evolved to include alternative treatment models such as the use of drugs in psychotherapy nonresponders (2 RCTs), as relapse prevention agent after successful in- or outpatient treatment (2 RCTs), and studies comparing the relative efficacy of psychotherapies, self-help, and pharmacotherapies and their combination (9 RCTs).

Additional studies are required to investigate the efficacy of SSRIs other than fluoxetine as well as of newer antidepressants and different classes of drugs in the treatment of BN. The issue of sequential medication trials has not been adequately studied, and there are no studies directly comparing two classes of antidepressants as to their efficacy, tolerability, and cost-effectiveness. The possible utility of drug augmentation strategies for patients with BN receiving antidepressant treatment has not been adequately addressed. In addition, emphasis should be placed on identifying nonresponders early during the course of a psychotherapy and evaluating pharmacotherapy at that point in treatment. Most studies were conducted in young adult bulimic patients without severe comorbidity, many of whom were volunteers responding to advertisements. Bulimic patients with personality disorders, substance abuse, and other relevant clinical conditions are usually excluded (Mitchell et al., 1997). Thus, some of the patients who are most difficult to treat may be excluded from controlled treatment trials, which might seriously impair the generalizability of results. Finally, the exploration of potential predictors of favorable outcome that might allow us to match patients to certain forms of pharmacotherapy is open to study.

Binge Eating Disorder

Because BED has only recently been incorporated in the *DSM,* treatment research on BED is at an early stage. As in BN, antidepressants should be considered an option in patients with BED. However, even though the reduction in binge eating frequency with antidepressants can be substantial, many patients improve without treatment and there is a risk for relapse after withdrawal of the drug. There is still a lack of long-term treatment studies. Because of evidence that BED is an unstable diagnosis with a tendency to remit over time, long-term studies need to be conducted comparing the natural course with long-term treatment outcome. In addition, the reduction in binge eating frequency does not necessarily lead to weight loss; however, complete abstinence from binge eating is positively related with weight reduction or weight maintenance. More research should be devoted to the development of new drugs for obesity.

REFERENCES

Agras, W. S., Dorian, B., Kirlkey, B. G., Arnow, B., & Bachman, J. (1987). Imipramine in the treatment of bulimia: A double blind controlled study. *International Journal of Eating Disorders, 6,* 29–38.

Agras, W. S., Rossiter, E. M., Arnow, B., Schneider, J., Telch, C. F., Raeburn, S. D., et al. (1992). Pharmacologic and cognitive-behavioral treatment for bulimia nervosa: A controlled comparison. *American Journal of Psychiatry, 149,* 82–87.

Agras, W. S., Rossiter, E. M., Arnow, B., Telch, C. F., Raeburn, S. D., Bruce, B., et al. (1994). One-year follow-up of psychosocial and pharmacologic treatment for bulimia nervosa. *Journal of Clinical Psychiatry, 55,* 179–183.

Agras, W. S., Telch, C. F., Arnow, B., Eldredge, K., Wilfley, D. E., Reaburn, S. D., et al. (1994). Weight loss, cognitive-behavioral, and desipramine treatments in binge-eating disorder: An additive design. *Behavior Therapy, 25,* 225–238.

Alger, S. A., Schwalberg, M. D., Bigaouette, J. M., Michalek, A. V., & Howard, L. J. (1991). Effect of a tricyclic antidepressant and opiate antagonist on binge-eating behavior in normoweight bulimic and obese, binge-eating subjects. *American Journal of Clinical Nutrition, 53,* 865–871.

Allison, D. B., Mentore, J. L., Heo, M., Chandler, L. P., Cappelleri, J. C., Infante, M. C., et al. (1999). Antipsychotic-induced weight gain: A comprehensive research synthesis. *American Journal of Psychiatry, 156,* 1686–1696.

American Psychiatric Association. (1994). *Diagnostic and statistical manual of mental disorders* (4th ed.). Washington, DC: Author.

American Psychiatric Association. (2000). Practice guideline for the treatment of patients with eating disorders (revision). *American Journal of Psychiatry, 157*(Suppl. 1), 1–39.

Attia, E., Haiman, C., Walsh, B. T., & Flater, S. R. (1998). Does fluoxetine augment the inpatient treatment of anorexia nervosa? *American Journal of Psychiatry, 155,* 548–551.

Bacaltchuk, J., & Hay, P. (2002). *Antidepressants versus placebo for people with bulimia nervosa* (Cochrane Review). In The Cochrane Library, Update Software, Oxford.

Bakan, R. (1979). The role of zinc in anorexia nervosa: Etiology and treatment. *Medical Hypothesis, 5,* 731–736.

Barcai, A. (1977). Lithium in adult anorexia nervosa, a pilot report on two patients. *Acta Psychiatrica Scandinavica, 55,* 97–101.

Barlow, J., Blouin, J., Blouin, A., & Perez, E. (1998). Treatment of bulimia with desipramine: A double-blind crossover study. *Canadian Journal of Psychiatry, 33,* 129–133.

Beasley, C. M., Jr., Tollefson, G., Tran, P., Satterlee, W., Sanger, T., & Hamilton, S. (1996). Olanzapine versus placebo and haloperidol: Acute phase results of the North American double-blind olanzapine trial. *Neuropsychopharmacology, 14,* 111–123.

Bergh, C., Eriksson, M., Lindberg, G., & Södersten, P. (1996). Selective serotonin reuptake inhibitors in anorexia (letter). *Lancet 348,* 1459–1460.

Bergman, L., & Eriksson, E. (1996). Marked symptom reduction in two women with bulimia nervosa treated with the testosterone receptor antagonist Flutamide. *Acta Psychiatrica Scandinavica, 94,* 137–139.

Beumont, P. J. V., Russell, J. D., Touyz, S. W., Buckley, C., Lowinger, K., Talbot, P., et al. (1997). Intensive nutritional counseling in bulimia nervosa: A role for supplementation with fluoxetine? *Australian New Zealand Journal of Psychiatry, 31,* 514–524.

Biederman, J., Herzog, D. B., Rivinus, T. M., Harper, G. P., Ferber, R. A., Rosenbaum, J. F., et al. (1985). Amitriptyline in the treatment of anorexia nervosa: A double-blind, placebo-controlled study. *Journal of Clinical Psychopharmacology, 5,* 10–16.

Birmingham, C. L., Goldner, E. M., & Bakan, R. (1994). Control trial of zinc supplementation and anorexia nervosa. *International Journal of Eating Disorders, 15,* 251–255.

Blouin, A. G., Blouin, J. H., Perez, E. L., Bushnik, T., Zuro, C., & Mulder, E. (1988). Treatment of bulimia with fenfluramine and desipramine. *Journal of Clinical Psychopharmacology, 8,* 261–269.

Brambilla, F., Draisci, A., Peirone, A., & Brunetta, M. (1995a). Combined cognitive-behavioral, psychopharmacological and nutritional therapy in eating disorders. I: Anorexia nervosa—restricted type. *Biological Psychiatry, 32,* 59–63.

Brambilla, F., Draisci, A., Peirone, A., & Brunetta, M. (1995b). Combined cognitive-behavioral, psychopharmacological and nutritional therapy in eating disorders. II: Anorexia nervosa—binge-eating/purging type. *Biological Psychiatry, 32,* 64–67.

Bryce-Smith, D., & Simpson, R. I. D. (1984). Case of anorexia nervosa responding to zinc sulphate. *Lancet, 11,* 350.

Calandra, C., Gulino, V., Inserra, L., & Giuffrida, A. (1999). The use of citalopram in an integrated approach to the treatment of eating disorders: An open trial. *Eating and Weight Disorders, 4,* 207–210.

Carruba, M. D., Cuzzolaro, M., Riva, L., Bosello, O., Liberty, S., Castra, R., et al. (2001). Efficacy and tolerability of moclobemide in bulimia nervosa: A placebo-controlled trial. *International Clinical Psychopharmacology, 16,* 27–32.

Carver, A. E., Miller, S., Hagman, J., & Sigel, E. (2002, April). *The use of risperidone for the treatment of anorexia nervosa.* Academy of Eating Disorders annual meeting, Boston.

Casper, R. C., Schlemmer, R. F., & Javaid, J. I. (1987). A placebo-controlled crossover study of oral clonidine in acute anorexia nervosa. *Psychiatry Research, 20,* 249–260.

Chouinard, G., Jones, B., Remington, G., Bloom, D., Addington, D., MacEwan, G. W., et al. (1993). A Canadian multicenter placebo-controlled study of fixed doses of risperidone and haloperidol in the treatment of chronic schizophrenic patients. *Journal of Clinical Psychopharmacology, 13,* 25–40.

Clemmons, D. R., & Underwood, L. E. (1992). Role of insulin-like growth factor I and growth hormone in reversing catabolic state. *Hormone Research, 38,* 37–40.

Condon, J. T. (1986). Long-term neuroleptic therapy and chronic anorexia nervosa complicated by tardive dyskinesia: A case report. *Acta Psychiatrica Scandinavica, 73,* 203–206.

Corcos, M., Flament, M., Atger, F., & Jeammet, P. (1996). Pharmacological treatment of bulimia nervosa. *L'Encephale, 12,* 133–142.

Counts, D. R., Gwirtsman, H., Carlsson, L. M., Lesem, M., & Cutler, G. B. (1992). The effects of anorexia nervosa and refeeding on growth hormone-binding protein, the insulin-like growth factors (IGFs) and the IGF-binding proteins. *Journal of Clinical Endocrinology and Metabolism, 75,* 762–767.

Craigen, D., Kennedy, S. H., Garfinkel, P. E., & Jeejeebhoy, K. (1987). Drugs that facilitate gastric emptying. In P. E. Garfinkel & D. M. Garner (Eds.), *The role of drug treatments for eating disorders* (pp. 161–176). New York: Brunnel/Mazel.

Dally, P., & Sargant, W. (1966). Treatment and outcome of anorexia nervosa. *British Medical Journal, 2,* 793–795.

Devlin, M. (2002, April 25–28). *Psychotherapy and medication for binge eating disorder.* Abstract Plenary session, International Conference on Eating Disorders, Boston.

de Zwaan, M., & Mitchell, J. E. (1992). Opiate antagonists and eating behavior in humans: A review. *Journal of Clinical Psychopharmacology, 32,* 1060–1072.

de Zwaan, M., Nutzinger, D. O., & Schoenbeck, G. (1992). Binge eating in overweight females. *Comprehensive Psychiatry, 33,* 256–261.

Domstad, P. A., Shih, W. J., Humphries, L., DeLand, F. H., & Digenis, G. A. (1987). Radionuclide gastric emptying studies in patients with anorexia nervosa. *Journal of Nuclear Medicine, 28,* 816–819.

Dulcan, M. K., Bregman, J., Weller, E. B., & Weller, R. (2001). Treatment of childhood and adolescent disorders. In A. F. Schatzberg & C. B. Nemeroff (Eds.), *Essentials of clinical psychopharmacology* (pp. 459–517). Washington, DC: American Psychiatric Press.

El-Giamal, N., de Zwaan, M., Bailer, U., Lennkh, C., Schüssler, P., Strnad, A., et al. (2000). Reboxetine in the treatment of bulimia nervosa: A report of seven cases. *International Clinical Psychopharmacology, 15,* 351–356.

El-Giamal, N., de Zwaan, M., Bailer, U., Strnad, A., Schüssler, P., & Kasper, S. (2001). Milnacipran in the treatment of bulimia nervosa: A report of 16 cases. *European Neuropsychopharmacology, 11,* S347–S348.

Esca, S. A., Brenner, W., Mach, K., & Gschnait, F. (1979). Kwashiorkor-like zinc deficiency syndrome in anorexia nervosa. *Acta Dermato-Venereologica, 59*, 361–364.

Fahy, T. A., Eisler, I., & Russell, G. F. (1993). A placebo-controlled trial of d-fenfluramine in bulimia nervosa. *British Journal of Psychiatry, 162*, 597–603.

Faltus, F. (1993). Pimozide in the therapy of eating disorders. *Cesko-Slovenska Psychiatrie, 1*, 24–26.

Faris, P. K., Kim, S. W., Meller, W. H., Goodale, R. L., Oakman, S. A., Hofbauer, R. D., et al. (2000). 5-HT$_3$ antagonist therapy of bulimia nervosa: A peripherally active agent for a central nervous system eating disorder? *Gastroenterology, 119*, 272–273.

Ferguson, C. P., La Via, M. C., Crossan, P. J., & Kaye, W. H. (1999). Are selective serotonin reuptake inhibitors effective in underweight anorexia nervosa? *International Journal of Eating Disorders, 25*, 11–27.

Ferguson, J. (1987). Treatment of an anorexia nervosa patient with fluoxetine. *American Journal of Psychiatry, 144*, 1239.

Fichter, M. M., Kruger, R., Rief, W., Holland, R., & Doehne, J. (1996). Fluvoxamine in prevention of relapse in bulimia nervosa: Effects on eating-specific psychopathology. *Journal of Clinical Psychopharmacology, 16*, 9–18.

Fichter, M. M., Leibl, K., Rief, W., Brunner, E., Schmidt-Auberger, S., & Engel, R. R. (1991). Fluoxetine vs placebo: A double-blind study with bulimic inpatients undergoing intensive psychotherapy. *Pharmacopsychiatry, 24*, 1–7.

Fisman, S., Steele, M., Short, J., Byrne, T., & Lavallee, C. (1996). Case study: Anorexia nervosa and autistic disorder in an adolescent girl. *Journal of the American Academy of Child and Adolescent Psychiatry, 35*, 937–940.

Fluoxetine Bulimia Nervosa Collaborative Study Group. (1992). Fluoxetine in the treatment of bulimia nervosa: A multicenter placebo-controlled double-blind trial. *Archives of General Psychiatry, 49*, 139–147.

Frank, G. K., Kaye, W. H., & Marcus, M. D. (2001). Sertraline in underweight binge eating/purging-type eating disorders: Five case reports. *International Journal of Eating Disorders, 29*, 495–498.

Freeman, C. (1998). Drug treatment for bulimia nervosa. *Biological Psychiatry, 37*, 72–79.

Gaskill, J. A., Treat, T. A., McCabe, E. B., & Marcus, M. D. (2001). Does olanzapine affect the rate of weight gain among inpatients with eating disorders? *Eating Disorders Review, 12*(6), 1–2.

Geretsegger, C., Greimel, K. V., Roed, I. S., & Keppel Hesselink, J. M. (1995). Ipsapirone in the treatment of bulimia nervosa: An open pilot study. *International Journal of Eating Disorders, 17*, 359–363.

Ghaemi, S. N., Cherry, E. L., Katzow, J. A., & Goodwin, F. K. (2000). Does olanzapine have antidepressant properties? A retrospective preliminary study. *Bipolar Disorder, 2*, 196–199.

Goldberg, S. C., Halmi, K. A., Eckert, E. D., Casper, R. C., & Davis, J. M. (1979). Cyproheptadine in anorexia nervosa. *British Journal of Psychiatry, 134*, 67–70.

Goldbloom, D. S., Olmsted, M., Davis, R., Clewes, J., Heinmaa, M., Rockert, W., et al. (1997). A randomized controlled trial of fluoxetine and cognitive behavioral therapy for bulimia nervosa: Short-term outcome. *Behavioural Research and Therapy, 35*(9), 803–811.

Goldstein, D. J., Wilson, M. G., Thompson, V. L., Potvin, J. H., & Rampey, A. H. (1995). The Fluoxetine Bulimia Nervosa Research Group: Long-term fluoxetine treatment of bulimia nervosa. *British Journal of Psychiatry, 166*, 660–666.

Grilo, C. M., Masheb, R. M., Heninger, G., & Wilson, G. T. (2002, April 25–28). *Controlled comparison of cognitive behavioral therapy and fluoxetine for binge eating disorder* [Abstract No. 95]. Academy of Eating Disorders, International Conference on Eating Disorders, Boston.

Gross, H. A., Ebert, M. H., Faden, V. B., Goldberg, S. C., Kaye, W. H., Caine, E. D., et al. (1981). A double-blind control trial of lithium carbonate primary anorexia nervosa. *Journal of Clinical Psychopharmacology, 6*, 376–381.

Gross, H. A., Evert, M. H., Faden, V. B., Goldberg, S. C., Kaye, W. H., Caine, E. D., et al. (1983). A double-blind trial of ^{9}-Tetrahydrocannabinol in primary anorexia nervosa. *Journal of Clinical Psychopharmacology, 3*, 165–171.

Gwirtsman, H. E., Guze, B. H., Yager, J., & Gainsley, B. (1990). Fluoxetine treatment of anorexia nervosa: An open clinical trial. *Journal of Clinical Psychiatry, 51,* 378–382.

Halmi, K. A., Eckert, E., LaDu, T. J., & Cohen, J. (1986). Anorexia nervosa: Treatment efficacy of cyproheptadine and amitriptyline. *Archives of General Psychiatry, 43,* 177–181.

Hansen, L. (1999). Olanzapine in the treatment of anorexia nervosa. *British Journal of Psychiatry, 175,* 592.

Herridge, P. L., & Pope, H. G. (1985). Treatment of bulimia and rapid cycling bipolar disorder with sodium valproate: A case report. *Journal of Clinical Psychopharmacology, 5,* 229–230.

Hill, K., Bucuvalas, J., & McClain, C. (2000). Pilot study of growth hormone administration during the refeeding malnourished anorexia nervosa patients. *Journal of Child and Adolescent Psychopharmacology, 10,* 3–8.

Hill, K. K., Hill, D. B., McClain, M., Humphries, L. L., & McClain, D. (1993). Serum insulin like growth factor I concentration in the recovery of patients with anorexia nervosa. *Journal of the American College of Nutrition, 12,* 475–478.

Hoopes, S. P., Reimherr, F. W., Kamin, M., Karvois, D., Rosenthal, N. E., & Karim, R. (2002, May 18–23). *Topiramate treatment of bulimia nervosa* [Abstract No. 7]. American Psychiatric Association 2002 annual meeting, Philadelphia.

Horne, R. L., Ferguson, J. M., Pope, H. G., Hudson, J. I., Lineberry, C. G., Ascher, J., et al. (1988). Treatment of bulimia with bupropion: A multicenter controlled trial. *Journal of Clinical Psychiatry, 49,* 262–266.

Hsu, L. K. G., Clement, L., Santhouse, R., & Ju, E. S. Y. (1991). Treatment of bulimia nervosa with lithium carbonate: A controlled study. *Journal of Nervous and Mental Diseases, 179,* 351–355.

Hudson, J. I., McElroy, S. L., Arnold, L. M., Shapira, N. A., Keck, P. E., & Rosenthal, N. (2001, November 28–December 1). *Topiramate in the treatment of binge eating disorder: A placebo-controlled trial* [Abstract No. 72]. Eating Disorders Research Society annual meeting, Bernalillo, NM.

Hudson, J. I., McElroy, S. L., Raymond, N. C., Crow, S., Keck, P. E., Carter, W. P., et al. (1998). Fluvoxamine in the treatment of binge-eating disorder. *American Journal of Psychiatry, 155,* 1756–1762.

Hughes, P. L., Wells, L. A., Cunningham, C. J., & Ilstrup, D. M. (1986). Treating bulimia with desipramine. *Archives of General Psychiatry, 43,* 182–186.

Igoin-Apfelbaum, L., & Apfelbaum, M. (1987). Naltrexone and bulimic symptoms. *Lancet, 7,* 1087–1088.

Jacobi, C., Dahme, B., & Dittmann, R. W. (2002). Cognitive-behavioral, fluoxetine and combined treatment for bulimia nervosa: Short-term and long-term results. *European Eating Disorders Review, 10,* 179–198.

Jensen, V. S., & Mejlhede, A. (2000). Anorexia nervosa: Treatment with olanzapine. *British Journal of Psychiatry, 177,* 187.

Jimerson, D. C., Wolfe, B. E., Brotman, A. W., & Metzger, E. D. (1996). Medications in the treatment of eating disorders. *Psychiatric Clinics of North America, 19,* 739–744.

Jonas, J. M., & Gold, M. S. (1988). The use of opiate antagonists in treating bulimia: A study of low-dose versus high-dose naltrexone. *Psychiatry Research, 24,* 195–199.

Kane, J. M., Carson, W. H., Saha, A. R., McQuade, R. D., Ingenito, G. G., Zimbroff, D. L., et al. (2002). Efficacy and safety of aripiprazole and haloperidol versus placebo in patients with schizophrenia and schizoaffective disorder. *Journal of Clinical Psychiatry, 63,* 763–771.

Kaplan, A. S., Garfinkel, P. E., Darby, P. L., & Garner, D. M. (1983). Carbamazepine in treatment of bulimia. *American Journal of Psychiatry, 140,* 1225–1226.

Katz, R. L., Keen, C. L., Litt, I. F., Hurley, L. S., Kellams-Harrison, K. M., & Glader, L. J. (1987). Zinc deficiency in anorexia nervosa. *Journal of Adolescent Health Care, 8,* 400–406.

Kaye, W., Gendall, K., & Strober, M. (1998). Serotonin neuronal function and selective serotonin reuptake inhibitor treatment in anorexia and bulimia nervosa. *Biological Psychiatry, 44,* 835–838.

Kaye, W. H., Nagata, T., Weltzin, T. E., Hsu, L. K., Sokol, M. S., McConaha, C., et al. (2001). Double-blind placebo-controlled administration of fluoxetine in restricting- and purging-type anorexia nervosa. *Biological Psychiatry, 49,* 644–652.

Kaye, W. H., Weltzin, T. E., Hsu, L. K. G., & Bulik, C. M. (1991). An open trial of fluoxetine in patients with anorexia nervosa. *Journal of Clinical Psychiatry, 52,* 464–471.

Kennedy, S. H., Goldbloom, D. S., Ralevski, E., Davis, C., D'Souza, J. D., & Lofchy, J. (1993). Is there a role for selective MAO-inhibitor therapy in bulimia nervosa? A placebo-controlled trial of brofaromine. *Journal of Clinical Psychopharmacology, 13,* 415–422.

Kennedy, S. H., Piran, N., Warsh, J. J., Prendergast, P., Mainprize, E., Whynot, C., et al. (1988). A trial of isocarboxazid in the treatment of bulimia nervosa. *Journal of Clinical Psychopharmacology, 8,* 391–396.

Konig, F., von Hippel, C., Petersdorff, T., Neuhoffer-Weiss, M., Wolfersdorf, M., & Kaschka, W. P. (2001). First experiences in combination therapy using olanzapine with SSRIs (citalopram, paroxetine) in delusional depression. *Neuropsychobiology, 43,* 170–174.

Krahn, D., & Mitchell, J. (1985). Use of L-tryptophan in treating bulimia. *American Journal of Psychiatry, 142,* 1130.

Lacey, J. H., & Crisp, A. H. (1980). Hunger, food intake and weight: The impact of clomipramine on a refeeding anorexia nervosa population. *Postgraduate Medicine Journal, 56*(Suppl. 1), 79–85.

Laederach-Hofman, K., Graf, C., Horber, F., Lippuner, K., Lederer, S., Michel, R., et al. (1999). Imipramine and diet counseling with psychological support in the treatment of obese binge eaters: A randomized, placebo-controlled double-blind study. *International Journal of Eating Disorders, 26,* 231–244.

Lask, B., & Bryant-Waugh, R. (1993). Zinc deficiency and childhood-onset anorexia nervosa. *Journal of Clinical Psychiatry, 54,* 63–66.

La Via, M. C., Gray, L., & Kaye, W. H. (2000). Case reports of olanzapine treatment of anorexia nervosa. *International Journal of Eating Disorders, 27,* 363–366.

Leitenberg, H., Rosen, J., Vara, L., Detzer, M., & Srebnik, D. (1994). Comparison of cognitive-behavior therapy and desipramine in the treatment of bulimia nervosa. *Behavioural Research and Therapy, 32,* 37–45.

Leucht, S., Pitschel-Walz, G., Engel, R. R., & Kissling, W. (2002). Amisulpride, an unusual "atypical" antipsychotic: A meta-analysis of randomized controlled trials. *American Journal of Psychiatry, 159,* 180–190.

Luby, E. D., Marrazzi, M. A., & Kinzie, J. (1987). Treatment of chronic anorexia nervosa with opiate blockade. *Journal of Clinical Psychopharmacology, 7,* 52–53.

Lyles, B., Sarkis, E., & Kemph, J. P. (1990). Fluoxetine and anorexia. *Journal of the American Academy of Child and Adolescent Psychiatry, 29,* 984–985.

Marcus, M. D., Wing, R. R., Ewing, L., Kern, E., McDermott, M., & Gooding, W. (1990). A double-blind, placebo-controlled trial of fluoxetine plus behavior modification in the treatment of obese binge-eaters and nonbinge-eaters. *American Journal of Psychiatry, 147,* 876–881.

Marder, S. R., & Meibach, R. C. (1994). Risperidone in the treatment of schizophrenia. *American Journal of Psychiatry, 151,* 825–835.

Marrazzi, M. A., Bacon, J. P., Kinzie, J., & Luby, E. D. (1995). Naltrexone use in the treatment of anorexia nervosa and bulimia nervosa. *International Clinical Psychopharmacology, 10,* 163–172.

Marrazzi, M. A., Markham, K. M., Kinzie, J., & Luby, E. D. (1995). Binge-eating disorder: Response to naltrexone. *International Journal of Obesity, 19,* 143–145.

Marrazzi, M. A., Wroblewski, J. M., Kinzie, J., & Luby, E. D. (1997). High-dose naltrexone and liver function safety. *American Journal of Addiction, 6,* 21–29.

McCann, U. D., & Agras, W. S. (1990). Successful treatment of nonpurging bulimia nervosa with desipramine: A double-blind, placebo-controlled study. *American Journal of Psychiatry, 147,* 1509–1513.

McClain, C. J., Kasarskis, E. J., & Allen, J. J. (1985). Functional consequences of zinc deficiency. *Progress in Food and Nutrition Science, 9,* 185–226.

McClain, C. J., Stuart, M. A., Vivian, B., McClain, M., Talwalker, R., Snelling, L., et al. (1992). Zn status before and after zinc supplementation of eating disorder patients. *Journal of the American College of Nutrition, 11,* 694–700.

McElroy, S. L., Casuto, L. S., Nelson, E. B., Lake, K. A., Soutullo, C. A., Keck, P. E., Jr., et al. (2000). Placebo controlled trial of sertraline in the treatment of binge eating disorder. *American Journal of Psychiatry, 157,* 1004–1006.

Mehler, C., Wewetzer, C., Schulze, U., Warnke, A., Theisen, F., & Dittmann, R. W. (2001). Olanzapine in children and adolescents with chronic anorexia nervosa. A study of five cases. *European Child and Adolescent Psychiatry, 10,* 151–157.

Meltzer, H. Y., & McGurk, S. R. (1999). The effects of fluoxetine, risperidone, and olanzapine on cognitive function and schizophrenia. *Schizophrenia Bulletin, 25,* 233–255.

Mendelowitz, A. J., & Liberman, S. A. (1995). New findings in the use of atypical antipsychotics: Focus on risperidone. *Journal of Clinical Psychiatry, 2,* 1–12.

Mendelson, S. D. (2001). Treatment of anorexia nervosa with tramadol. *American Journal of Psychiatry, 158,* 963–964.

Mitchell, J. E., Fletcher, L., Hanson, K., Pederson-Mussell, M., Seim, H., Crosby, R., et al. (1997). The relative efficacy of fluoxetine and manual-based self-help in the treatment of outpatients with bulimia nervosa. *Journal of Clinical Psychopharmacology, 21,* 298–304.

Mitchell, J. E., & Groat, R. (1984). A placebo-controlled double-blind trial of amitriptyline in bulimia. *Journal of Clinical Psychopharmacology, 4,* 186–193.

Mitchell, J. E., Halmi, K., Wilson, G. T., Agras, W. S., Kraemer, H., & Crow, S. (2002). A randomized secondary treatment study of women with bulimia nervosa who fail to respond to CBT. *International Journal of Eating Disorders, 32,* 271–281.

Mitchell, J. E., Laine, D. E., Morley, J. E., & Levine, A. S. (1986). Naloxone but not CCK-8 may attenuate binge-eating behavior in patients with the bulimia syndrome. *Biological Psychiatry, 21,* 1399–1406.

Mitchell, J. E., Peterson, C. B., Myers, T., & Wonderlich, S. (2001). Combining pharmacotherapy and psychotherapy in the treatment of patients with eating disorders. *Psychiatric Clinics of North America, 24,* 315–323.

Mitchell, J. E., Pyle, R. L., Eckert, E. D., Hatsukami, D., Pomeroy, C., & Zimmerman, R. (1989). Response to alternative antidepressants in imipramine nonresponders with bulimia nervosa. *Journal of Clinical Psychopharmacology, 9*(4), 291–293.

Mitchell, J. E., Pyle, R. L., Eckert, E. D., Hatsukami, D., Pomeroy, C., & Zimmerman, R. (1990). A comparison study of antidepressants and structured group therapy in the treatment of bulimia nervosa. *Archives of General Psychiatry, 47,* 149–157.

Moldofsky, H., Jeuniewic, N., & Garfinkel, P. E. (1977). Primary report of metoclopramide in anorexia nervosa. In R. A. Vigersky (Ed.), *Anorexia nervosa* (pp. 373–376). New York: Raven Press.

Moore, R., Mills, I. H., & Forster, A. (1981). Naloxone in the treatment of anorexia nervosa: Effect on weight gain and lipolysis. *Journal of the Royal Society of Medicine, 74,* 129–131.

Moynahan, E. J. (1976). Zinc deficiency and disturbances of mood and visual behavior. *Lancet, 1,* 91.

Nassr, D. G. (1986). Successful treatment of bulimia with nomifensine. *American Journal of Psychiatry, 143,* 373–374.

Neumeister, A., Winkler, A., & Woeber-Bingoel, C. (1999). Addition of naltrexone to fluoxetine in the treatment of binge-eating disorder. *American Journal of Psychiatry, 156,* 797.

Newman-Toker, J. (2000). Risperidone in anorexia nervosa. *Journal of the American Academy of Child and Adolescent Psychiatry, 39,* 941–942.

Ong, Y. L., Checkley, S. A., & Russell, G. F. M. (1983). Suppression of bulimic symptoms with methylamphetamine. *British Journal of Psychiatry, 143,* 288–293.

Pallanti, S., Quercioli, L., & Ramacciotti, A. (1997). Citalopram in anorexia nervosa. *Eating and Weight Disorders, 2,* 216–221.

Pigott, T. A., Sunderland, B. A., & Horn, L. (1986). *A pilot study of paroxetine in the treatment of bulimia nervosa* [Abstract No. 416, p. 312]. New Research Program and Abstracts of the 149th annual meeting of the American Psychiatric Association. Washington, DC: American Psychiatric Press.

Pope, H. G., Jr., Hudson, J. I., Jonas, J. M., & Yurgelun-Todd, D. (1983). Bulimia treated with imipramine: A placebo-controlled, double-blind study. *American Journal of Psychiatry, 140,* 554–558.

Pope, H. G., Jr., Hudson, J. I., Jonas, J. M., & Yurgelun-Todd, D. (1985). Antidepressant treatment of bulimia: A two-year follow-up study. *Journal of Clinical Psychopharmacology, 5,* 320–327.

Pope, H. G., Jr., Keck, P. E., Jr., McElroy, S. L., & Hudson, J. I. (1989). A placebo-controlled study of trazodone in bulimia nervosa. *Journal of Clinical Psychopharmacology, 9,* 254–259.

Purdon, S. E., Jones, B. D., Stip, E., Labelle, A., Addington, D., David, S. R., et al. (2000). Neuropsychological change in early phase schizophrenia during twelve months of treatment with olanzapine, risperidone, or haloperidol. The Canadian Collaborative Group for research and schizophrenia. *Archives of General Psychiatry, 57,* 249–258.

Pyle, R. L., Mitchell, J. E., Eckert, E. D., Hatsukami, D., Pomeroy, C., & Zimmerman, R. (1990). Maintenance treatment and 6-month outcome for bulimia patients who respond to initial treatment. *American Journal of Psychiatry, 147,* 871–875.

Raffa, R. B., Friderichs, E., Reiman, W., Shank, R. P., Codd, E. E., & Vaught, J. L. (1992). Opioid and nonopioid components independently contribute to the mechanism of action of tramadol, an "atypical" opioid analgesic. *Journal of Pharmacology and Experimental Therapeutics, 260,* 275–285.

Ramasubbu, R., Ravindran, A., & Lapierre, Y. (2000). Serotonin and dopamine antagonism in obsessive-compulsive disorder: Effective atypical antipsychotic drugs. *Pharmacology Psychiatry, 33,* 236–238.

Reilly, P. P. (1977). Anorexia nervosa. *Rhode Island Medical Journal, 60,* 419–422, 455–456.

Ricca, V., Mannucci, E., Paionni, A., DiBernardo, M., Cellini, M., Cabras, P. L., et al. (1999). Venlafaxine vs. fluoxetine in the treatment of atypical anorectic outpatients: A preliminary study. *Eating and Weight Disorders, 4,* 10–14.

Roberts, J. M., & Lydiard, R. B. (1993). Sertraline in the treatment of bulimia nervosa. *American Journal of Psychiatry, 150,* 1753.

Romano, S. J., Halmi, K. A., Koke, S. C., & Lee, J. S. (2002). A placebo-controlled study of fluoxetine in continued treatment of bulimia nervosa after successful acute fluoxetine treatment. *American Journal of Psychiatry, 159,* 96–102.

Ruggiero, G. M., Laini, V., Mauri, M. C., Ferrari, V., Clemente, A., Lugo, F., et al. (2001). A single blind comparison of amisulpride, fluoxetine and clomipramine in the treatment of restricting anorexics. *Progress in Neuro-Psychopharmacology and Biological Psychiatry, 25,* 1049–1059.

Russell, G. F. M., Checkley, S. A., Feldman, J., & Eisler, I. (1988). A controlled trial of d-fenfluramine in bulimia nervosa. *Clinical Neuropharmacology, 11*(Suppl. 1), S146–S159.

Sabine, E. J., Yonace, A., Farrington, A. J., Barratt, K. H., & Wakeling, A. (1983). Bulimia nervosa: A placebo-controlled, double-blind therapeutic trial of mianserin. *British Journal of Clinical Pharmacology, 15,* 195S–202S.

Safai-Kutti, S. (1990). Oral zinc supplementation in anorexia nervosa. *Acta Psychiatrica Scandinavica, 361* (Suppl.), S14–S17.

Safai-Kutti, S., & Kutti, J. (1984). Zinc and anorexia nervosa. *Annals of Internal Medicine, 100,* 317–318.

Santonastaso, P., Friederici, S., & Favaro, A. (2001). Sertraline in the treatment of restricting anorexia nervosa: An open controlled trial. *Journal of Child and Adolescent Psychopharmacology, 11,* 143–150.

Sokol, M. S., Gray, N. S., Goldstein, A., & Kaye, W. H. (1999). Methylphenidate treatment for bulimia nervosa associated with a cluster B personality disorder. *International Journal of Eating Disorders, 25,* 233–237.

Stacher, G., Abatzi-Wenzel, T. A., Wiesnagrotzki, S., Bergmann, H., Schneider, C., & Gaupmann, G. (1993). Gastric emptying, body weight and symptoms in primary anorexia nervosa. Long-term effects of cisapride. *British Journal of Psychiatry, 162,* 398–402.

Stacher, G., Kiss, A., Wiesnagrotzki, S., Bergmann, H., Hobart, J., & Schneider, C. (1986). Oesophageal and gastric motility disorders in patients categorized as having primary anorexia nervosa. *Gut, 27,* 1120–1126.

Stein, G. S., Hartshorn, S., Jones, J., & Steinberg, D. (1982). Lithium in a case of severe anorexia nervosa. *British Journal of Psychiatry, 140,* 526–528.

Stoll, A. L., & Haura, G. (2000). Tranylcypromine plus risperidone for treatment-refractory major depression. *Journal of Clinical Psychopharmacology, 20,* 495–496.

Strober, M., Freeman, R., DeAntonio, M., Lampert, C., & Diamond, J. (1997). Does adjunctive fluoxetine influence posthospital course of anorexia nervosa? A 24-month perspective, longitudinal follow-up and comparison with historical controls. *Psychopharmacology Bulletin, 33,* 425–431.

Strober, M., Pataki, C., Freeman, R., & DeAntonio, M. (1999). No effect of adjunctive fluoxetine on eating behavior or weight phobia during the inpatient treatment of anorexia nervosa: A historical case-control study. *Journal of Child and Adolescent Psychopharmacology, 9,* 195–201.

Stunkard, A., Berkowitz, R., Tanrikut, C., Reiss, E., & Young, L. (1996). d-Fenfluramine treatment of binge-eating disorder. *American Journal of Psychiatry, 153,* 1455–1459.

Szmukler, G. I., Young, G. P., Miller, G., Lichtenstein, M., & Binns, D. S. (1995). A controlled trial of cisapride in anorexia nervosa. *International Journal of Eating Disorders, 17,* 347–357.

Tachibana, N., Sugita, Y., Teshima, Y., & Hishikawa, Y. (1989). A case of anorexia nervosa with epileptic seizures showing favorable responses to sodium valproate and clonazepam. *Japanese Journal of Psychiatry and Neurology, 43,* 77–84.

Tollefson, G. D., & Sanger, T. M. (1997). Negative symptoms: A path analytic approach to a double-blind, placebo- and haloperidol-controlled clinical trial with olanzapine. *American Journal of Psychiatry, 154,* 466–474.

Umbricht, D., & Kane, J. M. (1996). Medical complications of new antipsychotic drugs. *Schizophrenia Bulletin, 22,* 475–483.

Vandereycken, W. (1984). Neuroleptics in the short-term treatment of anorexia nervosa: A double-blind placebo-controlled study with sulpiride. *British Journal of Psychiatry, 144,* 288–292.

Vandereycken, W., & Pierloot, R. (1982). Pimozide combined with behavior therapy in the short-term treatment of anorexia nervosa. *Acta Psychiatrica Scandinavica, 66,* 445–450.

Van Voorhees, A. S., & Riba, M. (1992). Acquired zinc deficiency in association with anorexia nervosa: Case report and review of the literature. *Pediatric Dermatology, 9,* 268–271.

Vigersky, R. A., & Loriaux, D. L. (1977). The effect of cyproheptadine in anorexia nervosa: A double-blind trial. In R. A. Vigersky (Ed.), *Anorexia nervosa* (pp. 349–356). New York: Raven Press.

Walsh, B. T., Agras, W. S., Devlin, M. J., Fairburn, C. G., Wilson, G. T., Kahn, C., et al. (2000). Fluoxetine for bulimia nervosa following poor response to psychotherapy. *American Journal of Psychiatry, 157,* 1332–1334.

Walsh, B. T., Gladis, M., Roose, S. P., Stewart, J. W., Stetner, F., & Glassman, A. H. (1988). Phenelzine vs placebo in 50 patients with bulimia. *Archives of General Psychiatry, 45,* 471–475.

Walsh, B. T., Hadigan, C., Devlin, M., Gladis, M., & Roose, S. (1991). Long-term outcome of antidepressant treatment for bulimia nervosa. *American Journal of Psychiatry, 148,* 1206–1212.

Walsh, B. T., Stewart, J. W., Roose, S. P., Gladis, M., & Glassman, A. (1985). A double-blind trial of phenelzine in bulimia. *Journal of Psychiatry Research, 19,* 485–489.

Walsh, B. T., Wilson, G. T., Loeb, K. L., Devlin, M. J., Pike, K. M., Roose, S. P., et al. (1997). Medication and psychotherapy in the treatment of bulimia nervosa. *American Journal of Psychiatry, 154,* 523–531.

Weizman, A., Tyano, S., Wijsenbeek, H., & Ben David, M. (1985). Behavior therapy, pimozide treatment and prolactin secretion in anorexia nervosa. *Psychotherapy and Psychosomatics, 43,* 136–140.

Wermuth, B. M., Davis, K. L., Hollister, L. E., & Stunkard, A. J. (1977). Phenytoin treatment of the binge-eating syndrome. *American Journal of Psychiatry, 134,* 1249–1253.

Wilson, G. T., Vitousek, K. M., & Loeb, K. L. (2000). Stepped care treatment for eating disorders. *Journal of Consulting and Clinical Psychology, 68,* 564–572.

Wirshing, D. A., Wirshing, W. C., Kysar, L., Berisford, M. A., Goldstein, D., Pashdag, J., et al. (1999). Novel antipsychotics: Comparison of weight gain liabilities. *Journal of Clinical Psychiatry, 60,* 358–363.

Yamaguchi, H., Arita, Y., Hara, Y., Kimura, T., & Nawata, H. (1992). Anorexia nervosa responding to zinc supplementation: A case report. *Gastroenterologia Japonica, 27,* 554–558.

Chapter 10

FAMILY APPROACHES FOR ANOREXIA NERVOSA AND BULIMIA NERVOSA

JAMES LOCK

Treatment for anorexia nervosa (AN) is understudied, despite the fact that AN is a serious psychological condition with a prevalence estimated at 0.48% among adolescent females between 15 and 19 years (Lucas, Beard, & O'Fallon, 1991). In addition, comorbid psychological conditions are common in AN, with up to 63% of all eating disorder patients reporting a lifetime affective disorder (Herzog, Keller, Sacks, Yeh, & Lavori, 1992). Over time, up to 35% of AN patients also suffer from obsessive-compulsive disorder, and there appears to be a moderate overlap of AN and avoidant personality disorder (Herzog, Keller, Sacks, et al., 1992; Herzog, Nussbaum, & Marmor, 1996). The mortality rates associated with this severely disabling condition are higher than for any other psychiatric disorder. Follow-up studies of varying lengths suggest that the aggregate mortality rate is approximately 5.6% per decade (Herzog et al., 2000). Overall, about half of these deaths are from suicide with the remainder due to the physical complications of AN. Follow-up studies suggest that recovery from AN is uncertain; approximately half have a good outcome, a quarter have intermediate outcomes, and about a quarter do poorly (Herzog, Keller, Lavori, Kenny, & Sacks, 1992).

Although AN was identified in the medical literature more than 125 years ago, research on the treatment of AN has been extremely circumscribed. There are only nine published outpatient controlled psychotherapy trials for AN (Channon, de Silva, Hemsley, & Perkins, 1989; Crisp et al., 1991; Dare, Eisler, Russell, Treasure, & Dodge, 2001; Eisler et al., 2000; Hall & Crisp, 1987; Le Grange, Eisler, Dare, & Russell, 1992; Robin et al., 1999; Russell, Szmukler, Dare, & Eisler, 1987; Treasure et al., 1995). These studies were conducted over a 20-year period and employed small sample sizes and variable outcome measures, so conclusions based on their results are problematic. Fewer than 600 subjects have been studied. Nonetheless, among the psychological studies, seven have explored some type of family approach to treatment of the disorder (Crisp et al., 1991; Dare et al., 2001; Eisler et al., 2000; Hall & Crisp, 1987; Le Grange et al., 1992; Robin et al., 1999; Russell et al., 1987). What data we have suggests that family therapy is important in the treatment of adolescents with AN.

BACKGROUND

Family approaches to AN treatment have long been controversial. When Sir William Gull and Charles Laseque independently described AN in the late nineteenth century, they took somewhat differing views of family involvement (Gull, 1874; Laseque, 1883). Gull proposed that families were "the worst attendants" while Lasegue viewed family treatment as necessary for recovery. Jean-Martin Charcot (Silverman, 1997) appeared to agree with Gull by recommending the suppression of friends and relationships for patients because their presence served to effectively check all progress. Thus, from the outset, a debate about involvement of family in the treatment of AN was established.

In the first half of the twentieth century, treatment of AN, like most psychiatric care, was dominated by psychoanalysis with its emphasis on individual treatment. Early psychoanalytic models developed by Waller, Kaufman, and Deutch focused on guilt and oral impregnation fantasies, with weight loss being seen as a defense mechanism (Waller, Kaufman, & Deutch, 1940). Thoma proposed that AN resulted from a regression to the oral stage and an abandonment of the genital stage (Thoma, 1967). Later, but still based in the psychoanalytic tradition, Hilda Bruch (1973) suggested that persons with AN are suffering from an inadequate sense of self (Bruch, 1973). To assist with this, treatment aims at helping to "find a voice" for this deficient self. This deficient self is putatively the result of a mother's failure to support the expression of and need for independence. Thus, treatment focuses on the therapeutic process of building this self, a kind of reparenting, which necessarily excludes the parents from the treatment process for the most part. Families are viewed as unnecessary or, worse, as interfering with this process.

An alternative model for the cause of AN was developed by Arthur Crisp, who speculated that AN was the result of phobic avoidance of adolescence (Crisp, 1980, 1997). In this developmental model, AN is an attempt to cope with anxieties and fears associated with pubertal change and psychosocial maturity. Thus, weight loss that results from excessive dieting and exercise leads to a body shape and hormonal status commensurate with preadolescence. In addition, because of medical and psychological sequelae of these behaviors and because of parental concerns about them, the patient's role in the family becomes more dependent and like that of a younger child. In these ways, the adolescent thus apparently accomplishes his or her end of avoiding adolescent struggles. The initial focus of psychotherapy is on restoration of normal weight so that the adolescent must confront the fears that precipitated the onset of AN. However, the ultimate focus of therapy is on helping the adolescent develop mastery over these anxieties through an increased understanding of why he or she is afraid of taking an adult role. In Crisp's model, treatment is highly focused on supporting the individual adolescent patient but often includes families as a crucial support for both the patient and the therapy itself.

In contradistinction from these individual approaches, family therapy for AN was pioneered by Salvador Minuchin and Mara Selvini Palazzoli in the 1970s. The family approach to treatment views the family as a system whose processes affect usual adolescent development. Although family systemic therapies have not been the subject of any randomized clinical trials, several noncontrolled trials of family therapy suggest that it is efficacious. First, Minuchin et al. (Minuchin, Rosman, & Baker, 1978) reported good outcomes in 86% of patients in a case series of 53 adolescents with AN treated with structural family therapy. Further, Stierlin and Weber in another case series of 42 patients treated with strategic family therapy reported that approximately two-thirds had recovered weight and menstruation at follow-up (Stierlin & Weber, 1989). The therapeutic approaches used in these two studies emphasize the family system as a potential solution for the dilemmas of AN in the adolescent patient; however, there is no emphasis on directly changing eating behaviors. Rather, the approach stresses family process, communication, and negotiation of adolescent developmental issues. Using structural and strategic interventions, these clinicians and their followers believe that the family's structure or style of management of problems needs to be corrected for patients to recover from AN. Family therapy for AN has been seen as a valuable treatment since the middle 1970s. Among clinicians, family therapy is often incorporated in the treatment of adolescents with AN. These types of treatments are specifically recommended for adolescents with AN by current American Psychiatric Association (APA) treatment guidelines (2000).

However, evidence is growing to suggest that adolescents with AN benefit from a specific form of family involvement in their treatment, called the *Maudsley approach*. This treatment was developed by Dare and Eisler at the Maudsley Hospital in London (Dare & Eisler, 1997) and was recently manualized (Lock, Le Grange, Agras, & Dare, 2001). Of the seven published controlled trials of family therapy for AN, a version of the Maudsley approach is included in four of them (Dare et al., 2001; Eisler et al., 2000; Le Grange et al., 1992; Russell et al., 1987). Dare credits many other clinicians and theoreticians with elements of his specific therapeutic approach. Family meals were used by Minuchin, while the agnostic view of the cause of the illness finds its origin in the work of Jay Haley. The process of empowering the family to find solutions to the problems that AN is causing is based on the nonauthoritarian stance of Milan systems therapy as well as feminist theory. The emphasis on separating the patient from the illness is based in part on narrative therapy techniques. However, Dare has crafted these interventions into a unique therapy for adolescents with AN. The treatment Dare and his colleagues devised starts from a premise that opposes the overall tradition of finding families pathological and blaming them directly or implicitly for the development of AN in their children. Instead, Dare takes an agnostic view of the cause of AN and considers the family to be the most important resource for recovery at the therapist's disposal.

ROLE OF FAMILY IN ADOLESCENT DEVELOPMENT

Much has been written about the conflicts between developing adolescents and their parents. For example, both Erikson and Blos portray adolescence as a period of conflict and struggle with parents to ensure that autonomy and independence are addressed—requirements for successful adulthood (Blos, 1967; Erikson, 1968). These authors coined terms such as *identity crisis* and *individuation,* which suggest a discomfort with the family and stress a need for the adolescent to separate from it. Because of these ideas, parents came to believe that adolescents should be expected to struggle with them; therefore, conflict was normal during adolescence and would eventually lead to a more healthy adulthood. However, these ideas were challenged by a number of empirical studies that suggested that, by far, the majority of adolescents had good relationships with their parents and for those with more difficulties, problems began well before the onset of adolescence. Moreover, it appeared that the best adolescent mental health was found among families characterized as close and having low conflict.

The evidence is clear that parenting does not stop at the end of childhood. A number of reports suggest that parents play a critical role in helping adolescents in mastering the tasks of this developmental period. In addition, a number of studies suggest that a particular style of parenting—authoritative parenting—is advantageous in supporting adolescents (Steinberg, Lamborn, & Dornbusch, 1994). This type of parenting is warm and involved (as opposed to either distant and hierarchical authoritarian parenting or neglectful/abusive parenting) as well as firm and consistent in establishing and enforcing guidelines, limits, and developmentally appropriate expectations. In addition, during adolescence in particular, authoritative parenting encourages and permits the adolescent to develop his or her own perspectives and opinions without unnecessary control or criticism. Studies of this type of parenting suggest that adolescents succeed better in school, report less depression and anxiety, are more self-reliant, and are less likely to engage in antisocial activities.

From these perspectives, parental involvement in helping an adolescent with an eating disorder would seem to be warranted. Without parental involvement, adolescents are potentially deprived of a resource to support their recovery and to assist them in moving forward in adolescent development. Few treatments of children and adolescents currently take as sharp a divide around the issue of parental involvement as do some advocates of individual treatment of adolescents with AN. In fact, among the empirically studied treatments for anxiety, depression, and conduct disorder, family involvement is seen as important to contributing to a good outcome (Brent et al., 1997; March, Mulle, & Herbel, 1994). However, based in part on theoretical ideas that adolescents with AN are expressing a need for control through their eating disorder resulting from parental excessive control and suppression of adolescent independence, parents being involved in treatment remains controversial.

FAMILY ASSESSMENT

If what Winnicott said is true—there's no such thing as a baby—then there's also no such thing as an adolescent, because like a baby, the adolescent is developmentally and emotionally best understood in the context of the family. To understand the family context, an assessment of family at the outset of treatment is necessary. There are a number of important principles in family assessment of eating disorders. The first principle to adhere to is to respect the adolescent as well as the parents in the assessment process. Therefore, we meet with the adolescent separately initially to gather information about his or her experience and perspective on what is happening. Following this, we meet with the parents without the adolescent present to gather their perspective on the eating problem independently.

In this chapter, we focus on the parental aspect of the assessment because assessment of the adolescent is covered elsewhere in this volume. It is optimal to see both parents for the interview. This alerts the parents at the outset to their importance and also provides an opportunity to provide important information about the illness and its treatment. Parents are asked to review the course of the development of the illness. How did the problem come to their attention? What efforts have they undertaken to assist with the problems they have perceived? Are there other psychiatric problems such as depression or anxiety or other new problematic behaviors? A careful review of the patient's eating problem is necessary because the patient's own account often overestimates intake and underestimates exercise and other weight loss behaviors. Parents may be able to provide a more accurate history. Certainly, the patient's version of events should be compared to that of the parents. In addition, a developmental history of the child and family should be conducted to assess the possible role of temperamental variables, family problems, and family weight and shape concerns in AN.

In the early meetings with the family, the therapist evaluates the family. Thus, family assessment is not a single event but an ongoing process. Among the specific characteristics the family therapist evaluates are cross-generation problems, poor parental alliances, and the degree of identity separation among family members. One important opportunity that is sometimes used in family therapy with AN is a therapeutic meal. Such a setting allows the therapist access to in vivo family processes around eating. Thus, patterns of communication, controlling behaviors, nurturing responses, ease of socialization, maintenance of personal and role boundaries, making alliances and coalitions, and solving problems can be seen during a meal.

At the conclusion of the evaluation period—which may take several family meetings—the therapist should have developed a formulation about how the family is structured and functions. There are a number of common examples of family structures found in families where a member has AN that may pose challenges to the therapist. For example, families with only one child can be challenging if the patient feels unsupported because he or she has no sibling allies. In addition, parents in these small families are usually able to focus more on their child and may be seen as being more involved with the child, which may challenge development in adolescence. On the other hand, families with a single parent may have a diverse set of concerns for a range of children and needs, making focus on the patient with AN more challenging. There is a tendency in such families to cross generational boundaries to assist with lack of parental resources in the family. Even when there are two parents, it is not uncommon to find that one of the parents has been removed from the parental role. Reasons for one parent removing himself or herself from the family include being angry with the spouse, patient, and/or illness; preoccupation with self or career; disorganization; other problems with the spouse; and feelings of incompetence in helping with the illness. Sometimes, even with intact marriages, a child may step into a parental role. When a sibling takes over the role of "parent," it potentially distorts the communication and roles of all other family members, making all of them less effective. Hence, when the therapist sees this configuration, it is important that the sibling ultimately be redirected to a more appropriate role. Also, not uncommonly, there are families where the patient has assumed such a dominant role in the family that he or she can be viewed as having taken on authority similar to a parent. This is sometimes the result of the intimidating influence of AN. In such cases, it can be said the AN is running the family. Parents are afraid of confronting their child because they fear they will make matters worse. Finally, in some families, there appears to be no one in a parental role. Parents in such families see their child as a "friend" or "collaborator," and the child has managed most personal decisions since early childhood.

The goal of the family assessment is to allow the therapist to understand both AN and its impact on the family as well as the potential impact of changes in the family or its approach to AN (depending on the school of family therapy to which the therapist belongs). This increased understanding guides the therapist, regardless of specific family therapy orientation.

MAJOR TYPES OF FAMILY TREATMENTS FOR ANOREXIA NERVOSA

As suggested previously, there are several major family approaches to AN treatment based on a range of schools of thought: structural family therapy, strategic family therapy, Milan family therapy, post-Milan family therapy, and Maudsley family therapy. An overview of each of these approaches, particularly as they apply to AN treatment, follows. Special emphasis is placed on the Maudsley model because it is the only treatment approach among these that has much empirical data support. However, because the Maudsley model is derived in part from these other approaches, it is helpful to better understand them.

Traditional family approaches see the patient as developing a problem in response to external factors such as traumas, poor parenting, genetic propensities, and cultural stresses. Family treatment employs the family to counteract the effects of these external causative factors. Thus, family intervention either modifies the problems in the family or, if this fails, separates the child from the family. Systemic family therapy approaches, in general, do not see the problem as belonging to the patient but to the family as a whole. Structural family therapy was devised based on observation of psychosomatic families (Liebman, Sargent, & Silver, 1983; Minuchin et al., 1978). Such families were observed as having characteristic transactional patterns that Minuchin described as enmeshed, overprotective, rigid, and conflict avoidant (Minuchin et al., 1978). Because the child played a critical role in the family's overall avoidance of conflict, symptoms were seen as powerfully supported by the family. Structural interventions are designed to alter the family organization by addressing these problematic transactional patterns through challenging alliances between parents and children, encouraging the development of stronger sibling subsystems, and promoting open communication. The result is that the child's emotional involvement with parents is reduced, while at the same time improving the effectiveness of the parental dyad. Therapeutic sessions are characterized by direct confrontation by the therapist of parental inadequacies, a strong authoritarian stance on the part of the therapist, and a relatively short focus on the symptoms of AN per se.

Strategic family therapy differs from structural family therapy in some important ways (Haley, 1973; Mandanes, 1981). First, the strategic family therapist holds an *agnostic* perspective as to the causes of psychological disorders. This makes strategic family therapy more circumscribed both in terms of aims and outcomes. Generally, strategic interventions are limited to addressing the impact of the symptoms of AN on the patient and family. Strategic family therapy is best known for its concepts related to promoting such changes. Specific strategic approaches to incite change include prescribing behaviors with paradoxical intentions, for example, asking a child to resist parental efforts to get her to eat to prevent premature compliance to parental authority; or suggesting the patient undertake behaviors that challenge the symptom, for example, recommending that a patient eat to have the strength to fight her parents.

Milan systems therapy shares characteristics with strategic and structural approaches, but families are differently conceived (Selvini-Palazzoli, 1974, 1988; Selvini-Palazzoli & Viaro, 1988). In the Milan school, families are seen as rigidly organized homeostatic mechanisms that are unusually resistant to change from the outside. Thus, the therapist must remain neutral to avoid provoking these homeostatic mechanisms that maintain the family system, thereby increasing resistance to change. The Milan family therapist does not make direct intervention, but by interviewing the family, encourages the family itself to become observers and challengers of their own process. Specifically, families are encouraged to find solutions that work for their family rather than rely on the outside authority of the therapist. In addition, based on their underlying view of families, therapists make a consistent effort to hold the family and its efforts in a positive, noncritical regard throughout therapy to prevent the family from withdrawing into older, less productive patterns.

Post-Milan approaches to family therapy focus more on the beliefs or meaning of symptoms to a family than on behaviors (Cecchin, 1987). Thus, the therapist addresses the narrative that the family as a whole has created. In this model, there is no ultimate truth belonging to either the family or the therapist; rather, reality is co-created. The goal of therapy is to help the family think about its own perspectives in line with usual Milan approaches but without the authority of an expert. In addition, the therapist is seen as joining the family and adopting a stance of curiosity and encouraging exploration, rather than directing behaviors either overtly (structural therapy) or covertly (Milan and strategic). One important outcome of these approaches is its special emphasis on allowing a separation of the illness from the patient because the illness narrative is not of his or her making (White, 1987).

A final approach to family therapy was devised specifically for AN by Dare and Eisler at the Maudsley hospital. This approach incorporates elements of the family therapy schools described previously. First, the approach takes an agnostic view of the cause of AN consistent with strategic family therapy. It also takes a nonauthoritarian stance while holding the family in positive regard and empowering the family as a resource consistent with Milan approaches to family therapy. It directs the therapist to facilitate parental alignment while forcing siblings into appropriate roles and employing a family meal consistent with structural family therapy. Finally, it places special emphasis on joining the family as a consultant and separating the illness of AN from the patient consistent with post-Milan narrative family approaches.

In general, the Maudsley approach views the AN patient as compromised primarily in terms of thoughts and preoccupations related to shape, weight, dieting, and exercise rather than symptoms being the result of family problems, inadequate psychological development, or traumatic injury. The principles of the approach are applied consistently regardless of the age of the patient. However, the approach does recognize variations in developmental aspects of the tasks of adolescents; for example, younger adolescents are likely more preoccupied by the physical changes associated with puberty, while older adolescents are working more on peer relationships and independence. As a result, the particular strategies used to refeed patients are explained to the adolescent and his or her family in accordance with developmental principles. For example, younger patients may find it less objectionable to have their parents take control of their eating than 18-year-olds. Whatever the age of the patient, parental control over eating is a temporary intervention with the aim that control over eating will be returned to the adolescent once weight has been restored and eating takes place without struggle.

The Maudsley approach broadly divides the treatment into three phases. The first phase is highly focused on the eating disorder. This extended focus on refeeding and weight gain sets the Maudsley approach apart from the other family therapy interventions that usually only briefly attend to these issues in deference to the exploration of family dynamics, structure, or communication. A family meal occurs early in the first phase and allows the therapist an opportunity to directly observe familial interaction patterns around eating. During this session, the therapist makes repeated and insistent requests for united parental action directed toward refeeding, despite the protests and anxieties associated with confronting these issues. The therapist sympathizes with the parents' difficulties and reiterates the need for action. The therapist endeavors to create and reinforce a strong parental alliance that is particularly focused on the need for joint efforts to defeat AN. At the same time, the therapist attempts to align the patient with the sibling subsystem. The therapist compliments the parents as much as possible on the positive aspects of their parenting skills. It is important that families not be directed to take a particular course of action but instead be encouraged to work out for themselves how best to refeed their anorexic child.

The second phase of treatment begins when the patient is gaining weight and eating takes place with minimal struggle. Often, the therapist notes that the family is relieved somewhat after having taken charge of the eating disorder. Although eating disorder symptoms are the main subject of sessions, the goal of the second phase is to assist the family in finding a way to return eating and weight control back to the patient. Often, this means that the family tests, in small ways initially, their child's ability to eat without monitoring and supervision. As the patient demonstrates continued independent mastery over eating, other issues that the family has had to postpone can now be brought forward for review.

The final phase of treatment begins when the patient achieves a healthy weight necessary for menstruation (in females). Therapy then turns to more general issues of adolescent development and the ways they have been affected by AN. Depending on the stage of adolescent development, this focus may include increased personal autonomy, parental boundaries, and parental focus on how their lives will change with the maturation of their child.

The Maudsley family treatment model is designed to take place over a period of a year, with initial sessions taking place weekly and tapering sessions down to biweekly in the second phase of treatment and monthly during the third phase. This schedule supports the idea that families need an intensively supportive period at the outset to get them started but that their capacities to take charge and manage the problem are encouraged with time and evidence of competence.

COMBINING INDIVIDUAL AND FAMILY TREATMENTS

In practice, family treatments are often combined with individual therapy. The main idea is that individual treatment potentially supports autonomy and independence, promotes self-development and confidence, and provides an opportunity for the adolescent to explore problems and issues without parental involvement (e.g., dating, substance experimentation, critical evaluations of the parents). In Robin et al., where family therapy was compared to an ego-oriented individual, psychotherapy (aimed at enhancing self-efficacy, self-esteem, and self-awareness) was compared to family therapy modeled after the Maudsley approach (though with some significant differences; Robin et al., 1999). It was postulated that those in individual therapy would demonstrate better outcomes on measures of psychological maturity and self-confidence. However, although family treatment restored weight and menses more quickly, there were no differences on outcomes on the psychological variables.

On the other hand, two studies using variants of the Maudsley approach suggest that seeing the patient independently of the parents may be warranted. Le Grange et al. and Eisler et al. found that, as with schizophrenia and major depression, familial *expressed emotion* (as expressed by high levels of parental criticism) may moderate treatment outcome in adolescents with AN (Eisler et al., 2000; Le Grange et al., 1992). Other studies suggested that higher levels of parental criticism are associated with higher treatment dropout and a poorer response to treatment (Szmukler, Eisler, Russell, & Dare, 1985). Specifically, Eisler et al. found that in families with higher levels of criticism, patients recovered better when the parents were seen separately. From this data, it appears that families who are not highly critical should be seen as a whole family (conjointly) to maximize the resources available to the patient. On the other hand, when families exhibit high criticism, it may be advisable to prevent the patient from experiencing this, and parents are seen separately from their child (separate family therapy). The injunctions and interventions of both conjoint and family therapy are identical, only the structure changes.

There is also good reason to consider that individual therapy may have a special role for older adolescents, who are more able to intellectually and emotionally use insight-oriented psychotherapy in conjunction with family work. In Russell et al., adolescents and adults over the age of 18 appeared to have done better with individual therapy (Russell et al., 1987). Developmentally, older adolescents are also more likely to have a need for more privacy because of dating, substance use experimentation, and choice of friends, which can be found in the individual therapy situation.

FAMILY TREATMENT AND BULIMIA NERVOSA

Although there are a large number of treatment studies for adult bulimia nervosa (BN), none has specifically included or investigated adolescents with BN. This finding is consistent with the overall paucity of clinical intervention research for adolescents in general and for eating disorders in particular. AN and BN are distinct syndromes, but there is considerable overlap in symptomatology. It is reasonable, then, to consider that treatments proved effective for adolescent AN might also help adolescent BN patients. The family context of patients with AN and BN differs (Attie & Brooks-Gunn, 1989; Humphrey, 1986, 1987). Family environments of AN patients have been described as being overprotective and overcontrolling (Minuchin et al., 1978). BN families, in contrast, appear to be more disengaged and chaotic; present with apparent hostility and conflict; and are perceived as neglectful, detached, and less competent (e.g., Strober & Humphrey, 1987). Some studies have shown that there may be a greater likelihood of conflict or criticism in families with a BN adolescent compared to their AN counterparts, but it is likely premature to talk about a "typical anorexic family" versus a "typical bulimic family." Notwithstanding the usual shameful secrecy of the bulimic behaviors and the usual difficulty in engaging adolescents in therapy, there appear to be good developmental reasons to consider family intervention for BN. From this perspective, it could be argued that adolescent BN and AN patients share similar challenges, for example, the negotiation of individuation, separation, sexuality, and so on. Therefore, it is clinically reasonable that adolescent BN patients still living with their families of origin would likely benefit from family involvement in their treatment.

Only scant scientific evidence supports family treatment of adolescents with BN. Eisler et al. found that binge and purge-type AN patients did just as well with family therapy as did purely restricting AN patients, suggesting that binge eating and purging could be managed with the support of parents (Eisler et al., 2000). In addition, in a preliminary report from the Maudsley group, Dodge et al., in a small case series of eight adolescent BN patients, found that family therapy was helpful for this group of patients and their families (Dodge, Hodes, Eisler, & Dare, 1995). Of particular help was the inclusion of education about the disorder and involvement of the parents in helping to stop the binge-purge cycle. Most patients responded positively and showed significant changes in bulimic symptoms from the start of treatment to one-year follow-up. These results are at best tentative because the study is small, follow-up was brief, and no control group was included.

In addition to these data, there are strong clinical reasons to involve the family in treatment of adolescents with BN (French et al., 2001; Holmbeck et al., 2000; Lock, Reisel, & Steiner, 2001). Involving the family provides an opportunity to explore pertinent family issues, such as behaviors and attitudes of parents and other family members that can contribute to heightened feelings of shame and guilt and thereby reinforce symptomatic behavior. Education about BN can be communicated to family members, and the impact of the eating disorder on family relationships can be addressed. Many adolescents respond well to parental involvement in meal planning and assisting with efforts to decrease binge eating and purging episodes once they understand that the therapist will ensure that parental involvement is supportive rather than critical (Lock, 2002). In fact, family involvement appears to help dilute feelings of shame and guilt that accompany BN by bringing the problem to light in the family context. At the same time, family involvement helps the therapist highlight to the parents the medical and psychological problems associated with BN and elicit their support in helping their child (Le Grange & Lock, 2002; Le Grange, Lock, & Dymek, in press). Such a perspective (Le Grange & Lock, 2002) can help to shift parental attitudes toward the patient and the illness from exasperation and anger to a more productive and sympathetic position.

As might be expected, patients who are less disturbed (less comorbid illness and personality problems) with healthier families (intact, consistent, and caring) appear to fare better with a family approach than those patients with significant complicating problems. These more disturbed adolescents and families require that therapists spend therapeutic time addressing these conflicts and difficulties as part of whatever approach is used. This likely requires additional therapeutic meetings (a more intensive treatment) than expected with usual treatment. Further, treatment focus is frequently disrupted by developments in the adolescents' lives unrelated directly to BN. Examples of these disruptions include breakups with friends and romantic partners, car accidents, school problems, drug or alcohol use, and conflicts with parents over independence. Parental problems can also complicate care. Some parents have severe marital problems, substance abuse problems, or vocational problems that prevent them from focusing appropriately on the well-being of their child. Therapists are able to continue work in most of these instances while briefly addressing these crisis situations and then returning to the work with BN. In some cases, however, these other problems become paramount and treatment for BN is discontinued—for example, suicidal behavior, running away from home, physical or sexual abuse, and serious substance abuse.

DIRECTIONS FOR RESEARCH

Family therapy research for eating disorders, particularly for AN, is somewhat more developed than other treatment approaches. As noted previously, seven of the nine published clinical trials involved some form of family therapy; in addition, several clinical case series support family interventions for AN. However, the need for larger scale clinical trials of family therapy, particularly the Maudsley approach, seems warranted given the promising outcomes that the small trials published to date suggest. In addition, it is important to understand better why some patients do not respond to family treatment and under what conditions the treatment is most likely to be helpful. The mechanisms for how the Maudsley approach works are also not well understood. Is it the empowerment of the parent to refeed the child, the supportive relationship with the family therapist, the involvement of the whole family to support the adolescent, or something else that underlies the treatment's success? The intensity of treatment (frequency of sessions and their intervals) and duration (length of overall treatment) of the Maudsley treatment are also not clearly understood. The initial studies suggested that 20 sessions in a year were needed (Russell et al., 1987); however, one study found that patients did well with fewer than 10 sessions over a six-month period (Le Grange et al., 1992). This is an important question because the costs to families and health care systems of AN is second only to schizophrenia (Striegel-Moore, Leslie, Petrill, Garvin, & Rosenheck, 2000). Finally, research for effective treatments for BN in adolescents is especially limited. Family therapy may be helpful with this age group and should be explored.

CONCLUSION

Family therapy is an important clinical intervention for adolescents with AN. Though data are limited, there is more research supporting its use and effectiveness than for any other current treatment for AN. This is particularly true for a specific form of family therapy, the Maudsley approach, which combines key elements from most of the major schools of family therapy into a unique approach to foster early weight gain under parental control, while in its latter phases, promoting adolescent independence and autonomy. Its application to adolescent BN patients is also promising.

REFERENCES

American Psychiatric Association. (2000, January). Practice guideline for the treatment of patients with eating disorders (Rev.). *American Journal of Psychiatry, 157*(Suppl.), 1–39.

Attie, I., & Brooks-Gunn, J. (1989). Development of eating problems in adolescent girls: A longitudinal study. *Developmental Psychology, 25,* 70–79.

Blos, P. (1967). The second individuation process of adolescence. *Psychoanalytic Studies of the Child, 2,* 162–177.

Brent, D., Holder, D., Kolko, D., Birmhaher, B., Baugher, M., Roth, C., et al. (1997). A clinical psychotherapy trial for adolescent depression comparing cognitive, family, and supportive therapy. *Archives of General Psychiatry, 54,* 877–885.

Bruch, H. (1973). *Eating disorders: Obesity, anorexia nervosa, and the person within.* New York: Basic Books.

Cecchin, G. (1987). Hypothesizing, circularity, and neutrality revisited: An invitation to curiosity. *Family Process, 26,* 405–414.

Channon, S., de Silva, P., Hemsley, D., & Perkins, R. (1989). A controlled trial of cognitive-behavioral and behavioral treatment of anorexia nervosa. *Behavioral Research and Therapy, 27*(5), 529–535.

Crisp, A. H. (1980). *Anorexia nervosa: Let me be.* London: Academic Press.

Crisp, A. H. (1997). Anorexia nervosa as flight from growth: Assessment and treatment based on the model. In D. M. Garner & P. Garfinkel (Eds.), *Handbook of treatment for eating disorders* (pp. 248–277). New York: Guilford Press.

Crisp, A. H., Norton, K., Gowers, S., Halek, C., Bowyer, C., Yeldham, D., et al. (1991). A controlled study of the effect of therapies aimed at adolescent and family psychopathology in anorexia nervosa. *British Journal of Psychiatry, 159,* 325–333.

Dare, C., & Eisler, I. (1997). Family therapy for anorexia nervosa. In D. M. Garner & P. Garfinkel (Eds.), *Handbook of treatment for eating disorders* (pp. 307–324). New York: Guilford Press.

Dare, C., Eisler, I., Russell, G., Treasure, J., & Dodge, E. (2001). Psychological therapies for adults with anorexia nervosa: Randomized controlled trial of outpatient treatments. *British Journal of Psychiatry, 178,* 216–221.

Dodge, E., Hodes, M., Eisler, I., & Dare, C. (1995). Family therapy for bulimia nervosa in adolescents: An exploratory study. *Journal of Family Therapy, 17,* 59–77.

Eisler, I., Dare, C., Hodes, M., Russell, G., Dodge, E., & Le Grange, D. (2000). Family therapy for adolescent anorexia nervosa: The results of a controlled comparison of two family interventions. *Journal of Child Psychology and Psychiatry, 41*(6), 727–736.

Erikson, E. (1968). *Identity: Youth and crisis.* New York: Norton.

French, S., Leffert, N., Story, M., Neumark-Sztainer, D., Hannan, P., & Benson, P. (2001). Adolescents binge/purge and weight loss behaviors: Associations with developmental assets. *Journal of Adolescent Health, 28,* 211–221.

Gull, W. (1874). Anorexia nervosa (apepsia hysterica, anorexia hysterica). *Transactions of the Clinical Society of London, 7,* 222–228.

Haley, J. (1973). *Uncommon therapy: The psychiatric techniques of Milton H. Erickson.* New York: Norton.

Hall, A., & Crisp, A. H. (1987). Brief psychotherapy in the treatment of anorexia nervosa: Outcome at one year. *British Journal of Psychiatry, 151,* 185–191.

Herzog, D. B., Greenwood, D. N., Dorer, D. J., Flores, A. T., Ekeblad, E. R., Richards, A., et al. (2000). Mortality in eating disorders: A descriptive study. *International Journal of Eating Disorders, 28,* 20–26.

Herzog, D. B., Keller, M. B., Lavori, P. W., Kenny, G. M., & Sacks, N. R. (1992). The prevalence of personality disorders in 210 women with eating disorders. *Journal of Clinical Psychiatry, 53*(5), 147–152.

Herzog, D. B., Keller, M. B., Sacks, N. R., Yeh, C. J., & Lavori, P. W. (1992). Psychiatric comorbidity in treatment-seeking anorexics and bulimics. *Journal of the American Academy of Child and Adolescent Psychiatry, 31*(5), 810–818.

Herzog, D. B., Nussbaum, K. M., & Marmor, A. K. (1996). Comorbidity and outcome in eating disorders. *Psychiatric Clinics of North America, 19*(4), 843–859.

Holmbeck, G., Colder, C., Shapera, W., Westhoven, V., Kenneally, L., & Updegrove, A. (2000). Working with adolescents: Guides from developmental psychology. In P. Kendall (Ed.), *Child and adolescent therapy* (pp. 334–385). New York: Guilford Press.

Humphrey, L. (1986). Structural analysis of parent-child relationships in eating disorders. *Journal of Abnormal Psychology, 95,* 395–402.

Humphrey, L. (1987). Comparison of bulimic-anorexic and nondistressed families using structural analysis of behavior. *Journal of the American Academy of Child and Adolescent Psychiatry, 26,* 248–255.

Lasegue, E. (1883). De l'anorexie hysterique [On hysterical anorexia]. *Archives Generales De Medecine, 21,* 384–403.

Le Grange, D., Eisler, I., Dare, C., & Russell, G. (1992). Evaluation of family treatments in adolescent anorexia nervosa: A pilot study. *International Journal of Eating Disorders, 12*(4), 347–357.

Le Grange, D., & Lock, J. (2002, August). Bulimia nervosa in adolescents: Treatment, eating pathology, and comorbidity. *South African Psychiatry Review,* 19–23.

Le Grange, D., Lock, J., & Dymek, M. (in press). Family-based therapy for adolescent with bulimia nervosa. *American Journal of Psychotherapy.*

Liebman, R., Sargent, J., & Silver, M. (1983). A family systems approach to the treatment of anorexia nervosa. *Journal of the American Academy of Child and Adolescent Psychiatry, 22,* 128–133.

Lock, J. (2002). Treating adolescents with eating disorders in the family context: Empirical and theoretical considerations. *Child and Adolescent Psychiatric Clinics of North America, 11,* 331–342.

Lock, J., Le Grange, D., Agras, W. S., & Dare, C. (2001). *Treatment manual for anorexia nervosa: A family-based approach.* New York: Guilford Press.

Lock, J., Reisel, B., & Steiner, H. (2001). Associated health risks of adolescents with disordered eating: How different are they from their peers? Results from a high school survey. *Child Psychiatry and Human Development, 31,* 249–265.

Lucas, A. R., Beard, C. M., & O'Fallon, W. M. (1991). 50-year trends in the incidence of anorexia nervosa in Rochester, Minn.: A population-based study. *American Journal of Psychiatry, 148,* 917–929.

Mandanes, C. (1981). *Strategic family therapy.* San Francisco: Jossey-Bass.

March, J., Mulle, K., & Herbel, B. (1994). Behavioral psychotherapy for children and adolescents with obsessive-compulsive disorder: An open trial of a new protocol driven treatment package. *Journal of the American Academy of Child and Adolescent Psychiatry, 33*(3), 333–341.

Minuchin, S., Rosman, B., & Baker, I. (1978). *Psychosomatic families: Anorexia nervosa in context.* Cambridge, MA: Harvard University Press.

Robin, A., Siegal, P., Moye, A., Gilroy, M., Dennis, A., & Sikand, A. (1999). A controlled comparison of family versus individual therapy for adolescents with anorexia nervosa. *Journal of the American Academy of Child and Adolescent Psychiatry, 38*(12), 1482–1489.

Russell, G. F., Szmukler, G. I., Dare, C., & Eisler, I. (1987). An evaluation of family therapy in anorexia nervosa and bulimia nervosa. *Archives of General Psychiatry, 44*(12), 1047–1056.

Selvini Palazzoli, M. (1974). *Self-starvation: From the intrapsychic to the transpersonal approach.* London: Chaucer.

Selvini-Palazzoli, M. S. (1988). *The work of Mara Selvini Palazzoli.* Northvale, NJ: Aronson.

Selvini-Palazzoli, M. S., & Viaro, M. (1988). The anorectic process in the family: A six-stage model as a guide for individual therapy. *Family Process, 27,* 129–148.

Silverman, J. (1997). Charcot's comments on the therapeutic role of isolation in the treatment of anorexia nervosa. *International Journal of Eating Disorders, 21,* 295–298.

Steinberg, L., Lamborn, S., & Dornbusch, S. (1994). Over-time changes in adjustment and competence among adolescents from authoritative, authoritarian, indulgent, and neglectful families. *Child Development, 30* 1266–1281.

Stierlin, H., & Weber, G. (1989). *Unlocking the family door: A systemic approach to the understanding and treatment of anorexia nervosa.* New York: Brunner/Mazel.

Striegel-Moore, R., Leslie, D., Petrill, S. A., Garvin, V., & Rosenheck, R. A. (2000). One-year use and cost of inpatient and outpatient services among female and male patients with an eating disorder: Evidence from a national database of health insurance claims. *International Journal of Eating Disorders, 27,* 381–389.

Strober, M., & Humphrey, L. (1987). Family contributions to the etiology and course of anorexia nervosa and bulimia nervosa. *Journal of Consulting Clinical Psychology, 55,* 654–659.

Szmukler, G. I., Eisler, I., Russell, G., & Dare, C. (1985). Anorexia nervosa, parental "expressed emotion" and dropping out of treatment. *British Journal of Psychiatry, 147,* 265–271.

Thoma, H. (1967). *Anorexia nervosa.* New York: International Universities Press.

Treasure, J., Todd, G., Brolly, M., Tiller, J., Nehmed, A., & Denman, F. (1995). A pilot study of a randomized trial of cognitive-behavioral analytical therapy vs educational behavioral therapy for adult anorexia nervosa. *Behavioral Research and Therapy, 33,* 363–367.

Waller, J., Kaufman, J., & Deutch, F. (1940). Anorexia nervosa: A psychosomatic entity. *Psychosomatic Medicine, 2,* 3–16.

White, M. (1987). Anorexia nervosa: A cybernetic perspective. *Family Therapy Collections, 20,* 117–129.

Chapter 11

DIALECTICAL BEHAVIOR THERAPY FOR EATING DISORDERS

ELIZABETH BLOCHER McCABE, MARIA C. LaVIA, AND
MARSHA D. MARCUS

This chapter provides an overview of dialectical behavior therapy (DBT) and presents a rationale for its use with eating disorder patients. The structure of treatment is described, and selected DBT concepts and strategies are highlighted because of their particular relevance and applicability to eating disorder patients. For a complete description of DBT, see Linehan's text (1993a) and accompanying skills manual (Linehan, 1993b).

WHAT IS DIALECTICAL BEHAVIOR THERAPY?

DBT was developed by Marsha Linehan for the treatment of patients with borderline personality disorder (BPD) and parasuicidal behaviors (suicidal and self-injurious behaviors). DBT uses a complete array of cognitive and behavioral techniques and, therefore, is a comprehensive cognitive-behavioral treatment. However, DBT extends traditional cognitive-behavioral treatments by incorporating acceptance-based philosophies and strategies, primarily Zen Buddhism practices, in the context of a dialectical philosophy.

Dialectics refers to an overarching worldview that emphasizes the interrelatedness and wholeness of reality. Dialectics assumes that reality is not static but comprises opposing forces, that is, thesis and antithesis. It is through synthesis of opposing forces that a new reality is developed and understood. Dialectics, therefore, can be understood as a systems perspective that characterizes reality as paradoxical and as being in continuous change and transition. One fundamental dialectic in the practice of DBT is the ongoing necessity of maintaining a balance between promoting change (behavior therapy) and acceptance (Zen). That is, only through acceptance of the current reality will patients be able to change. Moreover, acceptance of the current reality is, in fact, change. Other dialectics central to DBT are the balance between problem solving and validation, control and freedom, rationality and intuition, logic and paradox, and experiment and experience. In summary, a dialectical worldview is reflected in the philosophy and implementation of DBT and is a guiding principle in the conduct of the treatment.

WHY DIALECTICAL BEHAVIOR THERAPY FOR PATIENTS WITH EATING DISORDERS?

Because of DBT's demonstrated utility with other complex disorders, interest in DBT as a treatment approach for eating disorder patients is growing. Descriptions of DBT in the treatment of eating disorder patients are emerging in the literature and suggest potential benefit (McCabe & Marcus, 2002; Safer, Telch, & Agras, 2001; Telch, Agras, & Linehan, 2000). There are several reasons for interest in DBT as a treatment for disordered eating. Several are listed here, but this list is by no means exhaustive.

First, comorbid borderline personality disorder and parasuicidal behaviors are common among eating disorder patients. Suicide is one of the leading causes of death in anorexia nervosa (Steinhausen, 2002), indicating a need for effective strategies to manage the risk of suicidal behavior in eating disorder patients. Moreover, although not all eating disorder patients are acutely suicidal, they do engage in high-risk behaviors that may cause death and thus require effective behavior management. Next, there are substantial numbers of eating disorder patients who are refractory to front-line treatments and for whom adequate treatments have not been developed. We have found DBT to be a useful treatment for eating disorder patients who have failed to benefit sufficiently from a trial or trials of initial treatment.

We also have found that the biosocial model of BPD etiology proposed by Linehan is readily applicable to the etiology of severe eating disorders. Linehan (1993a) proposed a biosocial model of BPD that views symptoms as an effort to modulate overwhelming emotions that result from an ongoing transaction between biologic vulnerability of the affected individual and exposure to an invalidating environment. In the case of eating disorders, we posit that eating disorder behaviors also represent an effort on the part of patients to modulate or regulate emotion. That is, calorie or food restriction, binge eating and purging, and other eating disorder behaviors are effective methods for numbing, avoiding, or soothing negative or overwhelming affect. Mood dysregulation is a primary treatment target in DBT that is addressed in all treatment modes, which are described later.

Another reason for the utility of DBT with eating disorder patients is its emphasis on skill acquisition. Linehan (1993b) noted that the particular behavioral, intrapersonal and interpersonal difficulties common to borderline patients are a result of skills deficits. We have found that skills deficits are prominent in eating disorder patients as well. Particularly relevant is the DBT concept of *apparent competence*. Eating disorder patients, like BPD patients, are "apparently competent," in that despite a façade of accomplishment, eating disorder patients frequently lack basic skills necessary to be effective in many contexts, particularly those involving affectively charged interpersonal relationships. Consequently, the DBT emphasis on the acquisition of skills and skills practice has proven useful in the treatment of patients with chronic or refractory eating disorders.

Another reason that DBT principles are easily adapted for use with eating disorder patients is that eating disorder patients, like those with BPD, frequently elicit strong negative reactions from treaters that are often incorrectly attributed to the patient's character. These reactions negatively influence treatment. For example, eating disorder patients are often perceived as dishonest, vain, and manipulative, which engenders a negative response. Defining these difficulties as character flaws dampens hope for improvement. In contrast, understanding these behaviors as being related to a lack of skill in coping with unbearable anxiety or confusion engenders a more sympathetic and helpful response from treatment providers, friends, and family members.

The DBT emphasis on dialectics, specifically the need for therapists to balance pulling for change with acceptance of the difficulty of changing, is useful in addressing the treatment ambivalence so characteristic of eating disorder patients, especially those with anorexia nervosa. Eating disorder patients frequently resist and resent treatment interventions, which may be experienced as intrusive, controlling, and generally aversive. DBT therapists are trained to use emotional, behavioral, and cognitive validation strategies that are designed to acknowledge that symptom behaviors serve a meaningful function and represent a legitimate effort to deal with life circumstances (acceptance). However, DBT emphasizes the dialectic, which is that, although understandable, symptom behaviors also are associated with significant morbidity and mortality, and thus there is a need for behavior change.

Similarly, DBT emphasizes working with the tension between freedom and control. The DBT therapist is required to balance the exercise of control over the patient and the treatment and encouragement of his or her independence and autonomy. This dialectic is particularly salient to the management of patients with serious eating disorders. Eating disorder patients often struggle with issues related to control to an extent that seriously interferes with their ability to make appropriate treatment decisions. For example, for some patients, ambivalence about treatment is sometimes tied to a perceived (and reinforcing) sense of control achieved through the practice of eating disorder behaviors. Indeed, restoring a sense of mastery and control over the person's life without the use of maladaptive eating disorder behavior is an important treatment goal. For eating disorder therapists (and families of eating disorder patients), the balance between exercising control over the patient and encouraging patient independence and autonomy can be difficult to achieve. In addition to the utility of a dialectical worldview in dealing with ambivalence and need for control, DBT also explicates specific commitment strategies to help patients stay with treatment that are discussed in the context of the stages of treatment later in this chapter.

In summary, we have found DBT has utility for the treatment of chronic eating disorders because its philosophical underpinnings require a basic respect for the meaning of psychiatric symptoms in the context of patients' experiences and a matter-of-fact emphasis on the need for change. Moreover, DBT is a well-characterized methodology for working with difficult patients.

THEORETICAL UNDERPINNINGS

As noted previously, DBT is based on a biosocial theory of borderline personality disorder. Although originally formulated to explain the genesis and maintenance of borderline personality disorder, biosocial theory is applicable to other complex behavioral disorders, including eating disorders. Biosocial theory postulates that the transaction between a biological vulnerability to emotion dysregulation and an invalidating environment creates and maintains complex problem behaviors over time.

High sensitivity, high reactivity, and slow return to baseline characterize the biological vulnerability to emotion dysregulation. That is, reactions in individuals vulnerable to emotion dysregulation are easily and immediately aroused. Moreover, the reactions tend to be extreme and, once aroused, the emotional reaction is long lasting.

According to Linehan, "an invalidating environment is one in which communication of private experiences is met by erratic, inappropriate, and extreme responses" (Linehan 1993a, p. 49). The invalidating environment is characterized by a pervasive communication that the individual's responses and emotional reactions are incorrect, inappropriate, or faulty. Further, an invalidating environment fails to validate private experiences, oversimplifies the ease of problem solving, and punishes or intermittently reinforces emotional displays. Thus, in the DBT framework, it is the interaction between emotional vulnerability and an invalidating environment that promotes and maintains complex problem behavior.

The biosocial theory is consistent with etiological conceptualizations of eating disorders that postulate the combination of biological vulnerability and environmental factors as triggering and maintaining eating disorder symptoms. Failure to validate private experiences (e.g., "Stop crying or I'll give you something to cry about"), oversimplification of problem solving (e.g., "Just eat, what's so hard about that?"), and the variability and unpredictability of response from family members (eating disorder behavior is alternately reinforced, ignored, or punished) are characteristic themes that arise in therapy with eating disorder patients.

GOALS OF DIALECTICAL BEHAVIOR THERAPY

Linehan describes the overall goal of DBT as follows: "The overriding and pervasive target of DBT is to increase dialectical behavior patterns among borderline patients. Put simply, this means both enhancing dialectical patterns of thought and cognitive functioning, and also helping patients to change their typically extreme behaviors into more balanced, integrative responses to the moment" (Linehan 1993a, p. 120). Eating disorder patients tend to think in rigid and all-or-nothing terms. Moreover, they frequently exhibit extreme behaviors, for example, severely restricted intake followed by binge eating. Therefore, the DBT goal of balancing extremes in thinking and behavior is highly compatible with eating disorder treatment goals.

Achieving balance in thinking and behavior is integral to another DBT goal, that is, "to build a life worth living." For some eating disorder patients, like BPD patients, life is unending torment. For eating disorder patients, building a life worth living requires replacing the maladaptive thinking and behavior patterns that control their lives (obsessions about food and calories, fears of weight gain, and numerous behaviors designed to control weight and eating) and implementing more adaptive coping strategies.

In DBT, as in other cognitive-behavioral treatments, goals are described in terms of behaviors to increase or decrease. Because eating disorder patients have measurable behaviors that require modification, the establishment of specific behavioral goals is easily applied to the treatment of eating disorders. DBT organizes behavioral targets in terms of specific areas of functioning. The primary behavioral targets, listed in order of priority, are decreasing parasuicidal behaviors, decreasing therapy-interfering behaviors, decreasing behaviors that interfere with quality of life, and increasing behavioral skills. Within each of the behavioral targets, behavioral goals are defined based on continual behavioral assessment and are established in concert with the patient. These behavioral targets constitute the treatment hierarchy for outpatient individual therapy and are further described later.

DIALECTICAL BEHAVIOR THERAPY ASSUMPTIONS

DBT makes explicit assumptions about patients and therapy. These assumptions characterize the clinician stance toward patients and treatment and establish the tone of therapy and the context of treatment planning. They are worth noting because they are crucial to a philosophical understanding of DBT and because they are useful in the management of chronic eating disorder patients.

Two important DBT assumptions are that patients are doing the best they can do and want to improve. Eating disorder patients are difficult to treat. Their behavior seems irrational, exasperating, and sometimes frightening. Therapists and families may conclude that patients are not trying or do not want to improve. Moreover, it is sometimes difficult to discern subtle changes in behavior (increased food intake but no weight gain) or thinking (increased willingness to eat more but still not eating enough) that represent effort to change and a desire to improve. The magnitude of the change and the speed with which it occurs are not necessarily indicators of a person's motivation or desire to change. Many factors influence motivation; thus an understanding of motivation requires careful analysis and intervention. Maintaining the belief that patients are trying and want to improve keeps therapists alert to positive change, however minimal, and prompts them to acknowledge and reinforce the change.

Adoption of the assumption that patients are doing the best they can, however, must be balanced with another DBT assumption—that patients need to do better, try harder, and be more motivated to change. Simply having the desire to improve may not be sufficient to actually make and maintain the necessary changes. Therefore, therapists must assess the factors that negatively affect patients' efforts and motivation to improve and apply problem-solving strategies to help them increase their efforts and enhance their motivation.

The adoption of a clinical stance that incorporates the paradoxical assumptions that patients are doing the best they can do but need to try harder is particularly applicable to the treatment of individuals with severe eating disorders. For example, anorexia nervosa patients often feel unbearable anxiety at mealtimes. Therefore, any attempt to eat a meal is indication that they are doing the best they can. However, because of the implications of starving, and although patients are doing the best they can, it is clear that they must do better. Therapists help patients to do better and try harder by intervening with cognitive and behavioral strategies, skill instruction, and perhaps antianxiety medication to reduce the anxiety and enable the patient to implement the necessary changes.

Another DBT assumption is that patients must learn new behaviors in all relevant contexts. Eating disorder patients have learned to use eating disorder behaviors to help them cope with a variety of uncomfortable emotions and interpersonal situations. To effectively eliminate symptom behaviors, patients need to learn and generalize other, more adaptive behaviors to manage their continuing discomfort. For example, because DBT emphasizes that new behaviors must be learned and applied in all relevant contexts, hospitalization, which necessarily removes the patient from the usual environment, is discouraged. Instead, the DBT therapist treating anorexia nervosa patients would first apply cognitive strategies and behavioral contingencies, teach skills, and provide support and encouragement with the goal of having patients increase eating behavior at home, school, work, and other relevant settings. In summary, the DBT assumptions are readily applicable to the treatment of chronic eating disorder patients because they establish a nonjudgmental, supportive context for treatment in which the therapist can understand and validate symptom behavior while simultaneously expecting and prioritizing the emergence of new, more adaptive behaviors.

STAGES OF TREATMENT

DBT is broadly organized around four stages of therapy. The stages are not strictly chronological but can be understood as reflecting important areas that will be emphasized sequentially in the course of therapy. Pretreatment constitutes the first stage of treatment and is focused on preparations for therapy. These include orienting the patient to the treatment and eliciting commitment. The goals of this stage are for the patient and therapist to arrive at a mutual decision to work together to address areas that the patient wants to change. The second goal of this stage is for the therapist to identify and modify any beliefs or expectations held by the patient that will negatively affect the therapy process or influence a decision to prematurely terminate treatment. Commitment strategies typically are introduced during this stage of treatment, although they are used throughout the course of therapy to address and minimize ambivalence.

DBT commitment strategies are effective strategies for addressing the treatment ambivalence that is characteristic of chronic eating disorders patients. DBT explicitly recognizes the need to address commitment to change and commitment to treatment throughout the treatment process and specifies strategies for eliciting and maintaining commitment. For example, playing the devil's advocate by highlighting the difficulty of change (before the patient does) is designed to strengthen commitment and enhance the patient's sense of control. The therapist might indicate to patients that they may not possess the fortitude necessary to participate in DBT treatment. This strategy is designed to elicit from patients the counterargument that they are indeed capable of tolerating the vicissitudes of treatment.

The "foot in the door, door in the face" techniques are used to increase compliance with specific goals or behaviors. Foot in the door is an easy request followed by a more difficult request. Door in the face is the reverse of foot in the door; a difficult request is followed by an easier request. The combined strategy works by first obtaining a commitment to a relatively small change, then eliciting a commitment for a major change, then settling for a commitment to a moderate change. For example, the therapist elicits a commitment from a bulimia nervosa patient to not purge for one day. The therapist immediately follows this request with a request to not purge for one week. He or she then elicits from the patient a commitment to not purge for at least four out of the next seven days. The size of commitment requested (the amount of behavior change) is dependent on the degree of difficulty associated with keeping the commitment and the potential consequences of the target behavior. Ultimately, the agreed-on commitment should be achievable with increased effort from the patient.

Discussing the pros and cons of a commitment to change and connecting present commitments to prior commitments made by the patient are also effective strategies for eliciting, clarifying, and strengthening commitment from eating disorder patients. These strategies work by selling the very notion of commitment, by identifying and addressing the counterarguments that inevitably come up later in treatment, and by reminding patients of their prior commitments. Eating disorder patients typically are able to understand the value of commitment. They tend to have experience with making and honoring commitments in some areas of their lives. Moreover, "people-pleasing" tendencies that often characterize eating disorder patients may work to enhance motivation to honor commitments. Discussing the pros and cons of a commitment to change also helps to clarify the function of the eating disorder behavior for the patient and the therapist. Alternative behaviors that serve the same function can then be developed.

Finally, DBT therapists elicit commitment by stressing patients' freedom to make their own choices while simultaneously highlighting the absence of alternatives. Therapists obtain commitment using this strategy by acknowledging patients' right to practice eating disorder behaviors but clearly articulating the natural consequences of patients' choices (e.g., medical sequelae and increased debility). This is an especially relevant strategy for eating disorder patients who are acutely sensitive to control issues and for whom the consequences of eating disorder behavior can be devastating.

Stage One of DBT focuses on clearly identified behavioral targets (i.e., decreasing parasuicidal behavior, decreasing therapy-interfering behavior, decreasing quality-of-life-interfering behavior, and increasing behavioral skills) and has as its goals the attainment of basic capacities and the reduction of problematic symptom behaviors. Stage One is the primary focus of our work with eating disorder patients. This stage of treatment requires a one-year commitment from the patient and therapist to work together to reduce symptom behaviors and increase dialectical thinking and behavioral skill. Depending on progress made and the willingness of both patient and therapist, this phase of treatment may be extended beyond the initial commitment period of one year. It is generally expected that patients will have a working knowledge of the behavioral skills at the end of the first year but may not yet have integrated them into routine use.

Stage Two focuses on the reduction of posttraumatic stress and does not begin until there has been significant improvement in target behaviors and acquisition of behavioral skills. DBT does not specifically focus on reducing traumatic stress reactions until patients have achieved a level of behavioral skill competence and external supports to assist them in tolerating the distress created by exploration of the traumatic stress.

Stage Three occurs when patients have achieved a relative state of emotional and behavioral stability and are now focused on addressing issues related to self-respect and achieving personal goals. Patient goals in this stage include developing the ability to trust the self and to validate their own opinions, emotions, and actions. Achieving balance between dependence and independence is a focus of treatment during this stage.

TREATMENT MODES

DBT in its standard form is delivered through four treatment modes, individual out-patient psychotherapy, skills training group, telephone consultation, and case consultation meetings for therapists. Each mode has particular relevance for eating disorder treatment.

Individual Psychotherapy

Individual psychotherapy, which typically occurs weekly, is focused on current behavior. Individual therapy is organized and defined by a treatment hierarchy that specifies the behavioral targets and, thus, the agenda for each therapy session. Specifically, in each individual session, the DBT therapist is required to address parasuicidal behaviors first, treatment-interfering behaviors next, and only then addresses issues related to quality of life. The session treatment agenda is determined by reviewing the diary card. The diary card is used in DBT for self-monitoring and identifying the session agenda and target behaviors. We have modified the standard DBT diary card to reflect eating disorder behaviors and mood states. The diary cards are used to record the frequency and intensity of eating disorder and mood symptoms, DBT skills used, and weekly goals. The diary card is reviewed with the patient at the start of each individual session, and the recorded data are used to establish the session agenda. Completion of the diary card is required. If patients present to an individual session without the diary card, the session is spent analyzing why they do not have the card and recreating the content of the diary card from memory. Information gleaned from the diary card is addressed according to the treatment hierarchy. DBT's insistence on self-monitoring through use of a diary card effectively blocks characteristic attempts by eating disorder patients to avoid awareness of problem behaviors and affective states.

The DBT treatment hierarchy provides an effective framework for prioritizing and organizing the many problematic behaviors with which eating disorder patients present. As already noted, parasuicidal behavior is common among eating disorder patients. In the DBT framework, the elimination of parasuicidal behaviors is an explicit goal; consequently, the occurrence of parasuicidal ideation and behaviors are dealt with first in the individual therapy session. Any form of self-injury is fundamentally incompatible with the DBT goal of building a life worth living. Parasuicidal behavior is managed using a variety of cognitive and behavioral techniques, use of DBT skills, reliance on previous commitments, and overt reliance on the strength of the therapeutic relationship.

Behaviors that threaten the continuation of the therapy for either the patient or the therapist are considered therapy-interfering behaviors and are addressed next in the hierarchy. This category includes patient and therapist behaviors that interfere with the process of or decision to continue therapy. The attention given to therapy-interfering behavior in DBT serves to emphasize the necessity of a strong, positive interpersonal relationship between patient and therapist. DBT explicitly uses the relationship to achieve therapeutic goals. The relationship is conceptualized in two ways—the therapy itself and as the mechanism for effecting change. That is, a strong, positive relationship is, in and of itself, curative. The relationship also provides the context for learning the new behaviors that will result in a life worth living.

Thus, DBT defines, employs, and balances "the relationship as therapy" and "therapy through the relationship" (Linehan, 1993a, p. 515).

Patient therapy-interfering behaviors are behaviors that interfere with the patient's receiving therapy and include behavior that is nonattentive, noncollaborative, or noncompliant or behaviors that lead to therapist burnout. For example, missing sessions, lying, answering questions with "I don't know," and violating patient/therapist agreements are behaviors that prevent patients from receiving the therapy being offered and are thus therapy-interfering. For example, eating disorder patients and therapists often have agreements that specify a minimum weight necessary for outpatient therapy to continue. Falling below a minimally acceptable weight interferes with optimal cognitive functioning and jeopardizes outpatient status, and thus is an example of therapy-interfering behavior.

DBT also emphasizes the need for therapists to know and observe their personal limits. These limits are communicated to the patient with the intent of reducing the likelihood of therapist burnout, thereby maintaining the therapeutic relationship.

Behaviors that lead to therapist burnout are behaviors that push the therapist's or the organization's limits and decrease the therapist's willingness to work with the patient. For example, therapists working with eating disorder patients on an outpatient basis need to be aware of and arrange treatment for the medical risks associated with eating disorder behavior. Therapists must communicate to patients their expectation that patients will report physical symptoms and follow through with recommended medical interventions. Further, it must be communicated that failure to comply with these expectations cross the therapist's limits, damage the therapeutic relationship, and diminish willingness to continue outpatient work with the patient.

Therapy-interfering behaviors on the part of the therapist are also explicitly acknowledged and addressed in DBT. These behaviors generally fall into two categories: those that create therapeutic imbalance (e.g., too much emphasis on change and too little emphasis on validation) and those that demonstrate a lack of respect for the patient (e.g., judgmental attitude, canceling, or arriving late for sessions). Thus, in DBT both patient and therapist behaviors are subject to evaluation, discussion, and modification in the interest of promoting an effective therapeutic partnership that ensures continuity of the treatment and a context in which the therapy can continue and patients can learn, practice, and generalize new behavior.

Quality-of-life-interfering behaviors are next in the hierarchy and are defined as maladaptive behavior patterns that are inherently inconsistent with a life of reasonable quality. Most psychiatric symptoms, including symptoms of disordered eating, are examples of quality-of-life-interfering behaviors. Food and calorie restriction, binge eating, purge behaviors, overexercising, and other eating disorder behaviors are considered quality-of-life-interfering behaviors. However, when eating disorder behaviors violate therapist and patient agreements or when the behaviors interfere with the patient's ability to participate in sessions, they are elevated to the status of therapy-interfering behavior. For example, severely restricting food intake may negatively affect the patient's ability to focus during therapy sessions. In this context, ongoing restriction would be addressed as therapy interfering. Similarly, when eating disorder behaviors result in potentially life-threatening physical consequences (e.g., syrup of ipecac abuse, severe fluid restriction), the behavior is elevated to the status accorded in the hierarchy to parasuicidal behavior. Thus, life-threatening eating disorder behaviors become the exclusive focus of treatment until such time that they are no longer imminently life-threatening. Quality-of-life-interfering behavior, therefore, is managed using a variety of cognitive and behavioral techniques combined with the use of DBT skills and strategies designed to decrease problematic symptom behaviors.

The final treatment target in Stage One of DBT is increasing behavioral skills. An emphasis on skills acquisition is interwoven throughout the treatment hierarchy but also constitutes a distinct treatment target. The therapist's task is twofold: to teach behavioral skills and to elicit skillful behavior from the patient.

Dialectical Behavior Therapy Skills Training Group

Although use of skills is routinely addressed in individual therapy sessions, the primary mode for teaching and practicing behavioral skills is the DBT skills group. DBT behavioral skills training group is an essential mode of treatment and consists of four distinct skill modules: core mindfulness, emotion regulation, interpersonal effectiveness, and distress tolerance. The DBT skills reflect the fundamental dialectic in DBT: the balance between acceptance and change. Mindfulness and distress tolerance skills enhance acceptance. Emotion regulation and interpersonal effectiveness skills are strategies for promoting change. The skills are taught in a structured format, sequentially and repeatedly throughout the duration of the Stage One treatment contract. According to Linehan, the general goal of skills training in DBT is "To learn and refine skills in changing behavioral, emotional, and thinking patterns associated with problems in living that are causing misery and distress" (Linehan, 1993a, p. 144). DBT skills are described in great detail in Linehan's *DBT Skills Manual* (Linehan, 1993b); a brief summary of each and their applicability to eating disorders treatment is provided here.

Skills are essential for chronic or refractory eating disorder patients because, as already noted, despite the appearance of competence, eating disorder patients often lack the requisite skill to identify and regulate affective states, negotiate interpersonal conflict, and tolerate distress.

Core mindfulness skills are central to DBT and are based on psychological and behavioral versions of meditation practices from Eastern spiritual training, mostly Zen Buddhism. "Taking hold of one's mind" by implementing strategies designed to develop a lifestyle of participation with awareness is the primary objective. Also central to mindfulness is the concept of three primary states of mind—reasonable mind, emotion mind, and wise mind. These states of mind provide a framework for decision making. Reasonable mind is rational and emphasizes the use of logic and factual information to evaluate and plan. Reasonable mind is devoid of emotion. For example, the process of designing and building a bridge involves a series of reasonable mind decisions. In emotion mind, emotions override logical thought and control thinking. Running into a burning building to save a loved one is an example of an emotion mind decision. Practitioners of mindfulness recognize the necessity and usefulness of reasonable mind and emotion mind in particular situations but strive to balance these two states of mind to achieve wise mind. Wise mind is the integration of reasonable and emotion mind but goes beyond a mere synthesis of the two to create a state of intuitive knowing.

Mindfulness practice or "participation with awareness" is incompatible with the use of eating disorder behaviors to numb or avoid negative affect. An individual cannot be simultaneously mindful and engage in behaviors that effectively work to decrease awareness of affect. Mindfulness resembles exposure in that it involves increasing awareness of the mood states eating disorder patients typically seek to avoid. Eating disorder patients frequently are afraid or ashamed of their own thoughts and emotions. Consequently, mindfulness is a critical skill because it emphasizes nonjudgmental acceptance of all moods and encourages observation and labeling of emotions. Mindfulness is also useful for increasing awareness of and labeling of somatic cues (e.g., feelings of fullness, gastric distress) in eating disorder patients that may serve as triggers for aberrant behaviors. The "states of mind" conceptualization (i.e., emotion mind, reasonable mind, and wise mind) is also useful for targeting ambivalence in eating disorder patients because it promotes active and aware decision making. Finally, it provides a framework for evaluating decisions and is useful for teaching the difference between thoughts and emotions and the inherent value of each.

Emotion regulation skills focus on improving control over emotions and learning techniques for modulating emotions. The goals of this skill module are to understand emotions, reduce emotional vulnerability, and decrease emotional suffering. Emotion regulation skills are useful for educating eating disorder patients about the effects of eating disorder behaviors on mood. Hunger, malnutrition, and other physical symptoms are viewed as vulnerability factors for emotion dysregulation that can impede effective use of new skills. Like mindfulness, emotion regulation skills increase exposure to emotions by encouraging patients to experience their emotions without judging or attempting to inhibit or block them.

Developing assertiveness skills is a primary objective of the interpersonal effectiveness skills. These skills focus on teaching patients how to achieve objectives such as making requests and saying no to requests, while maintaining important interpersonal relationships and their self-respect. The inability to assertively communicate feelings and requests is not uncommon in eating disorder patients. Eating disorder patients often have uneven skill development, and the skills they do possess are often context specific. For example, an eating disorder patient may be able to successfully negotiate the demands and tasks associated with an academic curriculum but are often inept when negotiating interpersonal relationships in a social context. The interpersonal effectiveness skills address assertiveness deficits and challenge eating disorder patient tendencies to avoid conflict. These skills teach patients effective means to express thoughts and feelings and get needs met, thus decreasing reliance on a "people-pleasing" demeanor and symptoms to modulate negative moods.

Distress tolerance skills are crisis survival strategies. They are for use in situations that cannot be immediately changed. Skills taught in this module are distraction, self-soothing, strategies for improving the moment, and analysis of the pros and cons of tolerating the distressing situation. Because eating disorder behaviors such as restricting intake, binge eating, and purge behaviors enable eating disorder patients to avoid or tolerate uncomfortable, negative, or overwhelming affect, distress tolerance skills are critical to help eating disorder patients tolerate negative emotions.

There are situations specific to eating disorder patients for which distress tolerance skills are useful. Eating disorder patients often experience treatment as aversive. Weight gain in anorexia nervosa patients is emotionally distressing and often physically uncomfortable. Moreover, treatment is often foisted on unwilling, if not involuntary, patients, thus intensifying the perception of treatment as intrusive and unwarranted. Similarly, asking bulimia nervosa patients to stop binge eating and purging increases distress. The distress tolerance skills offer strategies for short-term use that enable patients to tolerate the distress caused by treatment until other adaptive strategies suitable for long-term use can be integrated into daily life. However, the following caveats apply to the use of distress tolerance skills with eating disorder patients.

First, the use of distraction, an effective distress tolerance skill, should be monitored for overuse. Eating disorder patients may choose to use distraction in situations that are not crisis situations and in instances when more change-oriented strategies may be indicated. For example, patients may tend to use distraction to avoid a conflictual interpersonal situation rather than address the conflict by applying interpersonal effectiveness skills. Attempts to use distraction to avoid noncrisis situations should be minimized.

One DBT distraction skill is the use of comparison as a technique for decreasing distress. Comparison is intended to decrease distress by focusing attention on the situations of others who are doing less well. Use of comparison is contraindicated for eating disorder patients for several reasons. First, anorexic patients often view their symptom behaviors as accomplishments and may "compete" to be the thinnest or eat the least. Therefore, comparison with other eating disorder patients may intensify, rather than decrease, symptom behaviors. Second, eating disorder patients' tendency to compare themselves to others is often targeted in treatment as a behavior to decrease. The comparisons generated by eating disorder patients tend to increase their distress and, as noted previously, increase symptom behavior ("She is thinner than I am so I must eat less"). Third, distortions and inaccuracies often characterize the comparisons made by eating disorder patients. For these reasons, we do not teach the use of comparison as a method for tolerating distress. Finally, distress tolerance skills include self-soothing through use of the five senses. For obvious reasons, we discourage eating disorder patients from using taste (or food) to distract from distressing emotions.

Telephone Consultation

The third treatment mode is telephone consultation. Guidelines for telephone consultation are explicitly defined in DBT. Telephone calls to individual therapists to obtain behavioral skills coaching are appropriate in the context of parasuicidal crises, when attempting to increase generalization of behavioral skills to everyday life, or to clarify or resolve interpersonal issues between the patient and therapist. In addition to its utility for preventing parasuicidal behaviors and resolving interpersonal conflict with the therapist, we find this mode of treatment to be especially useful for patients who need in-the-moment coaching to prevent or interrupt eating disorder behavior. It is often very difficult to implement behavior learned in session outside of session. The consultation call is an effective methodology for extending the session beyond the bounds of the therapist's office and into the patient's life. It effectively supports and reinforces the patient's behavior change efforts.

Case Consultation

The fourth treatment mode is case consultation. It is based on the DBT assumption that therapists treating borderline patients (and other difficult patients such as those with refractory eating disorders) need support. The consultation team provides support to the individual therapist and, consequently, promotes continuity of the therapeutic relationship. Moreover, the team helps the therapist to stay balanced in his or her interactions with the patient.

Like patients with BPD, eating disorder patients often elicit strong feelings from therapists and others who care for them. Moreover, they present with complex needs that require a team of professionals to address psychological, medical, and nutritional issues that may exceed the limits and skill of any single practitioner. The consultation team is an effective methodology for managing therapist reactions that may interfere with successful treatment and for coordinating care. The consultation team, which consists of at least one other DBT therapist, is charged with the responsibility of providing support and coaching to the therapists and skills trainers. As such, it is understood that the therapist treats the patient and the consultation team treats the therapist. The consultation team is designed to encourage open disclosure of therapists' interactions with patients and provide nonjudgmental, supportive case consultation.

CONCLUSION

We have found DBT to be an extremely useful treatment for managing refractory eating disorder patients. DBT offers systematic application of behavior change technology balanced with techniques that promote acceptance of the difficulties associated with recovery. DBT assumes a respectful stance toward patients and therapists and in so doing encourages patients and therapists to persist together in treatment until therapeutic objectives are realized. Because DBT is labor intensive and time consuming, we recommend its use only after front-line treatments have failed to achieve the desired outcomes. To learn more about DBT, see the Behavioral Technology Transfer Group web site, http://www.behavioraltech.com.

REFERENCES

Linehan, M. M. (1993a). *Cognitive behavioral treatment of borderline personality disorder.* New York: Guilford Press.

Linehan, M. M. (1993b). *Skills training for treating borderline personality disorder.* New York: Guilford Press.

McCabe, E. B., & Marcus, M. D. (2002). Question: Is dialectical behavior therapy useful in the management of anorexia nervosa? *Eating Disorders, 10,* 335–337.

Safer, D. L., Telch, C. F., & Agras, W. S. (2001). Dialectical behavior therapy for bulimia nervosa. *American Journal of Psychiatry, 4,* 632–634.

Steinhausen, H. C. (2002). The outcome of anorexia nervosa in the twentieth century. *American Journal of Psychiatry, 159,* 1284–1293.

Telch, C. F., Agras, W. S., & Linehan, M. M. (2000). Group dialectical behavior therapy for binge eating disorder a preliminary uncontrolled trial. *Behavior Therapy, 31,* 569–582.

Chapter 12

INTEGRATIVE COGNITIVE THERAPY FOR BULIMIA NERVOSA

CAROL B. PETERSON, STEPHEN A. WONDERLICH, JAMES E. MITCHELL, AND SCOTT J. CROW

Several manualized psychotherapies have been developed and tested for the treatment of bulimia nervosa (BN). Cognitive-behavioral therapy (CBT; Fairburn, Marcus, & Wilson, 1993; Mitchell et al., 1990, 1993), the most widely studied, has been evaluated in more than 20 randomized trials (see reviews by Mitchell & Peterson, 1997; Wilson & Fairburn, 1998). Interpersonal therapy (IPT; Fairburn, 1996) has also been investigated in several studies (Agras, Walsh, Fairburn, Wilson, & Kraemer, 2000; Fairburn et al., 1991; Fairburn, Jones, Peveler, Hope, & O'Connor, 1993). In general, both CBT and IPT have been found to be efficacious in reducing the frequency of binge eating and purging.

Although CBT and, to a lesser extent, IPT are well-established treatments for BN, the need for alternative treatment arises from the fact that a substantial subset of individuals with bulimic symptoms are not helped by these interventions (Mitchell, Hoberman, Peterson, Mussell, & Pyle, 1996). Although these types of treatments result in significant reductions in bulimic symptoms, abstinence rates for CBT are only about 50% (Craighead & Agras, 1991; Wilson, 1996), which is problematic because abstinence from binge eating and vomiting at the end of treatment appears to be one of the best predictors of long-term remission (Maddocks, Kaplan, Woodside, Langdon, & Piran, 1992). Recent data have indicated that most individuals who respond to CBT usually do so in the first month of therapy (Agras, Crow, Halmi, Mitchell, Wilson, & Kraemer, 2000); other participants may improve but are less likely to remit, and some decide to drop out because they perceive the treatment as unhelpful. Relapse rates are another problem in BN with approximately 30% of participants becoming symptomatic during follow-up, typically within the first few months after the completion of treatment (Mitchell, Davis, & Goff, 1985; Olmsted, Kaplan, & Rockert, 1994).

Integrative cognitive therapy (ICT) was developed as an alternative approach for the treatment of BN (Wonderlich, Mitchell, Peterson, & Crow, 2001; Wonderlich, Peterson, Mitchell, & Crow, 2000). The rationale for the development of ICT was to retain aspects of CBT that are thought to be highly therapeutic but to incorporate other techniques that may enhance the outcome of treatment. In particular, ICT includes interventions that have been used to treat other types of psychopathology: motivational enhancement, developed for the treatment of drug and alcohol problems (Miller & Rollnick, 1991) and used more recently for eating disorders (Geller, 2002; Vitousek, Watson, & Wilson, 1998); applications of self-discrepancy theory (Higgins, 1987), used to conceptualize and treat depression (Strauman, 1989); and interpersonal pattern analysis, used to treat personality disorders (Benjamin, 1993). In addition, ICT places a greater emphasis on self-oriented cognition as well as the role of affect in the context of cognitive treatment (Safran & Segal, 1996). Although developed specifically for the treatment of BN, ICT arose in the context of a larger movement toward expanding the scope of cognitive therapy (Clark, 1995) and integrating other psychotherapeutic techniques, including emphasizing emotion and interpersonal issues (Greenberg & Korman, 1993; Greenberg & Safran, 1987; Safran, 1990a, 1990b; Safran & Segal, 1996), developing an understanding of cognitive schemas (Safran, 1990a; Young, 1994), using the therapeutic relationship (Robins & Hayes, 1993; Safran & Segal, 1996), and focusing on developmental issues (Guidano, 1987). The aim of integrating techniques from other therapeutic approaches that target aspects of BN is to develop a treatment that will help a greater number of individuals with bulimic symptoms.

FEATURES OF INTEGRATIVE COGNITIVE THERAPY

ICT is a manual-based treatment that uses a clinician guide and a patient workbook. In addition, psychoeducational materials are provided using a handheld computer device (e.g., Palm Pilot). In contrast to other manualized approaches, a considerable amount of information is provided in the patient workbook and the handheld computer (e.g., model of symptoms, nutrition guidelines, description of interpersonal patterns, strategies for assertiveness). The patient workbook also contains numerous worksheets for participants to complete as they progress in treatment.

ICT is a time-limited treatment, usually consisting of 20 sessions. Sessions are held twice a week for the first month, then weekly for the remainder of treatment. Sessions are conducted individually. The length of sessions is 50 minutes. This treatment was developed for use with adults who are medically stable and can be treated on an outpatient basis. Although it contains an emphasis on nutritional rehabilitation in its second stage, ICT was not designed for individuals requiring significant weight restoration. In addition, it may not be an appropriate treatment for individuals with cognitive impairment or for those with very low motivation to change their eating disorder symptoms.

Consistent with CBT and in contrast to more traditional psychotherapies, the therapist takes an active role in ICT sessions. For example, the therapist provides the patient with detailed nutritional information early in treatment and works with the patient to facilitate the consumption of adequate meals and snacks. The therapist also provides feedback about interpersonal patterns and cognitive style. The therapist remains attuned to the patient's mood throughout treatment and elicits information about his or her affective experiences. Therapeutic style in ICT should be warm, engaging, nonauthoritarian, and collaborative.

COMPARISON OF INTEGRATIVE COGNITIVE THERAPY TO COGNITIVE-BEHAVIORAL THERAPY AND INTERPERSONAL THERAPY

ICT shares a number of common features with CBT and IPT. All three treatments are manual-based, time-limited, and present-focused. Table 12.1 summarizes the similarities and differences among ICT, CBT, and IPT. As shown in the table, ICT contains some of the same components as IPT, including an emphasis on emotional expression and a focus on current interpersonal functioning. ICT has the most in common with CBT, which is expected because behavioral and cognitive techniques were deliberately incorporated from CBT. ICT has a number of unique components, including motivational enhancement, modification of cognitive style, and the use of self-discrepancy to alter self-perception.

One of the unique aspects of ICT is the model that serves as its basis. CBT emphasizes the role of cognitions, behavioral, and biological factors that precipitate and maintain bulimic symptoms (Fairburn, Marcus, et al., 1993). According to the model of CBT, problematic cognitions about self, weight and shape, and eating result in extreme dietary restriction, which, in turn, results in binge eating and compensatory behaviors. In contrast, IPT assumes that interpersonal relationships influence the development and maintenance of bulimic symptoms (Fairburn, 1996). ICT is based on a model that emphasizes the interaction among temperament, environmental experiences, self-oriented cognition, interpersonal patterns, and biological factors.

Table 12.1   ICT versus CBT versus IPT: Clinical Approach and Techniques

	ICT	CBT	IPT
Motivational enhancement.	X		
Emphasis on consuming regular meals and snacks.	X	X	
Self-monitoring.	X	X	
Behavioral techniques, including alternative behaviors, stimulus control, exposure.	X	X	
Cognitive restructuring.	X	X	
Self-oriented cognition.	X	X	
Self-discrepancy.	X		
Self-regulatory cognitive style.	X		
Emphasis on affect.	X		X
Focus on current interpersonal relationships and patterns.	X		X
Identifying interpersonal schema.	X		
Relapse prevention.	X	X	
Psychoeducational emphasis.	X	X	
Homework.	X	X	

Note: ICT = Integrative cognitive therapy; CBT = Cognitive-behavioral therapy; IPT = Interpersonal psychotherapy.

INTEGRATIVE COGNITIVE MODEL OF BULIMIA NERVOSA

The model of the development and maintenance of symptoms of BN is shown in Figure 12.1 (Wonderlich et al., 2000, 2001). As illustrated, the model of ICT is multifactorial and includes biological, environmental, and psychological components. The model of BN that serves as the basis of ICT posits that environmental experiences interact with the individual's temperament, which elicits negative emotions that interfere with the development of secure interpersonal attachments and are maintained by problematic interpersonal behaviors and self-oriented cognition.

Temperament

Several studies have found that individuals with symptoms of BN report higher scores on measures of harm avoidance (Brewerton, Hand, & Bishop, 1993; Waller et al., 1993); this temperamental predisposition leads to an avoidance of situations that are harmful, including those that are threatening to self-esteem. Although stimulation-seeking may characterize a subset of individuals with BN (see Lilenfeld et al., 1997), the model posits that the temperament of the majority of patients can be characterized by a sensitivity to harm without a tendency toward novelty seeking (Berg, Crosby, Wonderlich, & Hawley, 2000).

Environment

Environmental experiences that interact with temperament to interfere with attachment include interpersonal rejection and criticism, which are especially powerful because individuals with bulimic symptoms have been found to reveal greater interpersonal sensitivity compared to individuals without eating disorder symptoms (Steiger, Gauvin, Jabalpurwala, Seguin, & Stotland, 1999). In addition, individuals with bulimic symptoms are more likely to have been adopted (Holden, 1991), experienced physical and sexual abuse during childhood (Welch & Fairburn, 1994, 1996; Wonderlich, Brewerton, Jocic, Dansky, & Abbott, 1997), and have a family history of substance use disorders and mood disorders (Fairburn, Welch, Doll, Davies, & O'Connor, 1997). Several studies have also found that individuals with bulimic symptoms describe their family environments as more disengaged, conflict-oriented, and nonnurturing, compared to individuals without bulimic symptoms (Strober & Humphrey, 1987; Wonderlich, 1992). These self-reported characteristics have been supported by observational investigations, which have found that families of individuals with bulimic symptoms are less effective in communicating to one another (Humphrey, 1989). Individuals with eating disorders have also been observed to exhibit unstable attachments (Cole-Detke & Kobak, 1996).

Self-Discrepancy and Mood

The ICT model posits that these childhood, adolescent, and adult interpersonal experiences interact with temperament and have a profound impact on the individual, including his or her self-concept and feelings of interpersonal security. In addition, the

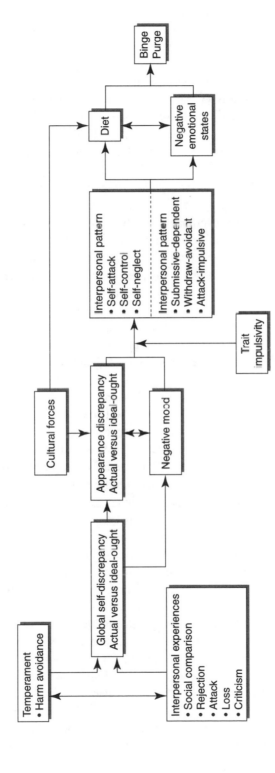

Figure 12.1 Model of the Development and Maintenance of Bulimia Nervosa Symptoms. *Source:* Modified from "Integrative Approaches to Treating Eating Disorders," p. 260, by S. A. Wonderlich, C. B. Peterson, J. E. Mitchell, and S. Crow, in *Comparative Treatments for Eating Disorders*, K. J. Miller and J. S. Mizes (Eds.), 2000, Copyright 2000 by New York: Springer. Used by permission.

individual develops cognitive schemas that organize and influence interpersonal behaviors and perceptions. The interaction between temperament and experience results in negative self-evaluation, which has been found to be a significant risk factor for BN (Fairburn et al., 1997). Based on self-discrepancy theory (Higgins, 1987; Higgins, Bond, Klein, & Strauman, 1986), the model posits that this negative self-evaluation is characterized by a discrepancy among different self constructs: actual self, ideal self, and ought self. The *actual self* refers to those attributes or features that the individual believes he or she actually possesses. The *ideal self* and the *ought self* refer to comparative standards to which the actual self may be compared. The ideal self refers to a representation of the attributes that the individual would ideally like to possess, while the ought self refers to attributes that the individual believes are his or her obligation or duty to possess. Given this configuration, it is possible to have both actual-ideal discrepancies and actual-ought discrepancies. For simplicity in the current treatment, we have consolidated these discrepancies into an actual-desired discrepancy, which becomes the fundamental self-discrepancy in ICT. This type of self-discrepancy has been observed in individuals with symptoms of depression (Strauman, 1989) and eating disorders (Strauman & Glenberg, 1994; Strauman, Vookles, Barenstein, Chaiken, & Higgins, 1991). Discrepancies between the individual's perceived actual and desired self create a sense of inadequacy (being flawed), which shapes the self-representation and is seen as a threat to interpersonal intimacy.

Due in large part to the influence of sociocultural factors that reinforce the ideal of thinness (Striegel-Moore, Silberstein, & Rodin, 1986), the discrepancy between the actual self and the desired self becomes focused on inadequacies in appearance (particularly weight and shape). The self-discrepancy elicits negative affect, including feelings of dysphoria and anxiety. In particular, Strauman and colleagues (Strauman & Glenberg, 1994; Strauman et al., 1991) found that self-ideal discrepancies were related to negative mood, body dissatisfaction, body size overestimation, and disturbances in eating. The discrepancy between the actual versus ideal appearance has also been found to function as a cognitive schema, which influences information processing and mood (Altabe & Thompson, 1996). The ICT model hypothesizes that self-discrepancies elicit both negative mood and body dissatisfaction, which exacerbate each other.

According to the ICT model of bulimic symptoms, self-discrepancy is important interpersonally because a failure to meet the desired standard is perceived as a threat to attachment. Specifically, the individual believes that the inadequacy that results from the discrepancy puts him or her at risk of criticism and rejection from others. For this reason, reducing the self-discrepancy is a strategy to increase interpersonal security. This process is reinforcing because the individual seeks to reduce negative mood states elicited by self-oriented discrepancy by reducing this discrepancy. The tendency to experience negative affect that has been observed in BN (Davis, Freeman, & Garner, 1988; Johnson & Larson, 1982; Ruderman & Grace, 1987) is thought to be the result of the discrepancies between the perceived self and how the individual believes that he or she wants to be or should be, which may also be a causal factor in the high levels of comorbid mood and anxiety disorders (Cooper & Fairburn, 1986; Wonderlich & Mitchell, 1997) and has been found to be a significant precipitant of binge eating (Meyer & Waller, 1999; Sherwood, Crowther, Wills, & Ben-Porath, 2000).

Interpersonal Relationships

The emphasis that the ICT model places on interpersonal patterns is based in part on the data indicating that individuals with BN exhibit problematic interpersonal relationships and social adjustment (Herzog, Norman, Rigotti, & Pepose, 1986; Norman & Herzog, 1984; Rorty, Yager, Buckwalter, & Rossotto, 1999). Individuals with symptoms of BN report having less supportive relationships, more social conflict, problems with social competence (Grisset & Norvell, 1992), more dependent relationships (Jacobson & Robbins, 1989), and problems with intimacy (Pruitt, Kappins, & Gorman, 1992).

The ICT model hypothesizes that individuals with BN engage in specific types of interpersonal patterns because of negative mood (Wonderlich & Swift, 1990), especially distress elicited by self-discrepancy, in an effort to avoid abandonment and interpersonal rejection (Benjamin, 1974, 1993). The main patterns are:

- Submission, in which the individual attempts to appease and gratify others.
- Withdrawal, in which the individual avoids engagement.
- Attack, which is hypothesized to be most common in the subtype of BN characterized by impulsivity and Axis II Cluster B traits and occurs when the individual perceives others as withdrawing from them.

The attack pattern is based on the hypothesis that individuals engage in hostile, controlling behaviors to prevent withdrawal (Benjamin, 1993). Submission and withdrawal patterns are thought to be associated with Bowlby's (1969) concepts of ambivalence and avoidance resulting from anxious attachment.

Self-Regulatory Style and Maintenance of Symptoms

Along with interpersonal styles, ICT emphasizes cognitive, self-regulatory styles as another strategy used in an attempt to modulate the distress triggered by self-discrepancy. According to the model, the three most common cognitive styles are:

1. Self-control, in which the individual attempts to control the self and achieve perfection to reduce discrepancy.
2. Self-attack, in which the individual blames himself or herself for the discrepancy.
3. Self-neglect, in which the individual attempts to avoid the discrepancy by engaging in reckless behaviors.

According to the ICT model, the individual with BN uses these cognitive styles to reduce negative mood associated with self-discrepancy. Although these interpersonal (e.g., submission, attack, withdrawal) and self-regulatory (e.g., self-control, self-attack, self-neglect) styles are used to lessen distress, they actually amplify negative affect and are ineffective in facilitating interpersonal intimacy. In addition, sociocultural factors reinforce the belief that the pursuit of an underweight body shape through excessive dietary restriction and exercise is an appropriate solution to improving a self that the individual views as flawed, and weight loss becomes negatively reinforcing by reducing the discrepancy. Nutritional deprivation resulting from excessive dieting and dichotomous rules about food selection leads to binge eating (Fairburn, Marcus, et al., 1993; Herman & Polivy, 1975; Keys, Brozek, Henschel, Mickelsen, & Taylor, 1950; Ruderman, 1986). Binge eating becomes reinforcing because it relieves hunger but also serves as a short-term strategy to avoid experiencing negative emotions (Heatherton & Baumeister, 1991; Sherwood et al., 2000). However, because of the strong emphasis placed on the pursuit of thinness as an ideal, purging or other compensatory behaviors are required to reduce the discrepancy between the perceived and the desired self. The binge eating and purging cycle is also maintained by physiological and neurochemical mechanisms (Blundell & Hill, 1993).

PHASES OF INTEGRATIVE COGNITIVE THERAPY

The four phases of ICT are summarized in Table 12.2. Phase One, consisting of sessions 1 to 3, includes introductory educational information and an emphasis on

Table 12.2　Outline of Integrative Cognitive Therapy (ICT)

Phase One: Enhancing Motivation and Psychoeducation (Sessions 1–3)
- Introduction.
- Education about bulimia nervosa (including model).
- Rationale for treatment.
- Motivational enhancement.
- Development of rapport.

Phase Two: Normalization of Eating and Coping Skills (Sessions 4–8)
- Education about risks of inadequate nutrition and role in causing and maintaining binge eating.
- Prescription of meal plan.
- Nutritional education.
- Behavioral techniques (e.g., stimulus control, exposure-response prevention).
- Cognitive restructuring.
- Education about sociocultural factors and body image.

Phase Three: Interpersonal Patterns and Cognitive Styles (Sessions 9–18)
- Self-regulatory style.
- Interpersonal pattern analysis.
- Strategies for assertive communication.
- Cognitive schemas.

Phase Four: Relapse Prevention and Lifestyle Management (Sessions 19–20)
- Education about relapse.
- Plan for lapse and relapse.
- Healthy lifestyle plan.
- Review of techniques and strategies that were helpful.
- Termination.

enhancing motivation. Phase Two, sessions 4 to 8, emphasizes nutritional rehabilitation and uses behavioral and cognitive techniques to facilitate consumption of appropriate food intake. Phase Three, sessions 9 to 18, focuses on interpersonal patterning and self-regulatory cognitive styles. Phase Four, sessions 19 and 20, includes relapse prevention techniques, lifestyle management, treatment consolidation, and termination.

Phase One: Enhancing Motivation and Psychoeducation (Sessions 1 to 3)

The primary goals of Phase One are to establish a therapeutic relationship, educate patients about BN and, especially, to increase their motivation in treatment and recovery. Many individuals with eating disorder symptoms express some hesitation about seeking treatment. Although this reluctance is often related to feelings of embarrassment or shame, feelings of ambivalence about changing symptoms are common (Vitousek et al., 1998). Facing similar ambivalence in treating individuals with chemical dependency, Miller and Rollnick (1991) developed a set of motivational interviewing techniques to improve treatment by enhancing motivation to change behaviors.

To conduct motivational interviewing, the therapist focuses on the patient's ambivalence and recognizes that the bulimic symptoms typically have several advantages (e.g., reducing fears about weight gain, reducing negative mood states) and many negative consequences (e.g., interpersonal problems, financial concerns, embarrassment). Miller and Rollnick (1991) emphasize the importance of expressing empathy through reflective listening. Instead of attempting to change the patient's perspective, the therapist listens without judgment and expresses an understanding of the patient's dilemma; for example, the bulimic symptoms are associated with positive consequences but he or she wants to change because of the negative consequences. Conveying a sense of understanding does not imply that the therapist must express approval or agreement (Miller & Rollnick, 1991).

Along with empathy, the therapist must avoid argumentation and roll with resistance when conducting motivational interviewing (Miller & Rollnick, 1991). This perspective contrasts significantly with the belief that the patient must be confronted and is based on the belief that arguing can increase the patient's conviction that he or she should not change. Similarly, resistance is viewed as expected and can be reframed by the therapist to provide a new perspective that the patient is able to consider but not forced to accept. In motivational interviewing, the relationship between the therapist and the patient should be collaborative, with the clinician taking a nonauthoritarian stance.

One of the most crucial strategies of motivational interviewing is to develop a discrepancy between how patients view their circumstances in contrast to how they would like them to be. The role of the therapist is to emphasize this discrepancy and to intensify it for patients. A clear understanding of the discrepancy allows patients to articulate their own motivation for making changes in their behaviors. In addition, the therapist should support the patient's self-efficacy and convey both that the behaviors can be changed and that the patient will be able to make these changes.

Miller and Rollnick (1991) discussed several aspects of motivational interviewing techniques, including the use of reflective listening, open-ended questions, and summary statements. In ICT, several sessions are used to enhance motivation using these principles and techniques. At the end of Phase One, the therapist and patient are typically in agreement about the discrepancy, including reasons for and against changing. In our experience with ICT, we have found that most patients are able to express a considerable amount of motivation to change their symptoms by the end of Phase One. However, both the therapist and the patient must recognize the likelihood of ongoing ambivalence and use motivational interviewing techniques whenever necessary throughout the remainder of treatment.

Psychoeducation is also important in Phase One of ICT. The patient is given the patient workbook and the handheld computer, which both contain introductory information about BN, including the model of how symptoms develop and are maintained, consequences and risks, clinical features, and an overview of and rationale for treatment. Although these materials are primarily delivered through homework with the emphasis in sessions on motivational interviewing, the therapist can supplement these educational materials through discussions in the therapy sessions.

Phase One also functions as a way of setting the stage for the remainder of psychotherapy. The therapist works to develop therapeutic rapport with the patient and emphasizes that ICT is highly collaborative. In addition, the therapist is attuned to the patient's emotional reactions during these initial sessions and uses questions and clarifying statements to highlight this emphasis.

Phase Two: Normalization of Eating and Coping Skills (Sessions 4 to 8)

The primary goal of Phase Two is to facilitate normal eating patterns by encouraging the consumption of regular meals and snacks and using behavioral and cognitive coping skills. Psychoeducation at the beginning of Phase Two emphasizes medical complications of BN and principles of healthy nutrition. The risks of nutritional deprivation, including symptoms of semistarvation (Keys et al., 1950), are presented, along with the risks of designating foods as good and bad with strict rules (Ruderman, 1986). The clinician emphasizes the biological and psychological risks of excessive dieting and explains to the patient the role of dieting in causing binge eating. In addition, the ineffectiveness of purging for weight control is explained (Fairburn, Marcus, et al., 1993).

Once the rationale for eating regular, nutritious meals and snacks is established, the clinician provides the patient with a detailed meal plan. Extensive explanations about nutrition and meal planning are provided in the patient workbook. In general, a meal plan with approximately 2,000 kcal/day is suggested. However, calorie counting is discouraged, and meal plans and self-monitoring use relatively standard food units or exchanges. Patients who are extremely restrictive in their eating patterns and/or fearful of increasing their food intake so dramatically are allowed to start at a meal plan with 1,500 kcal/day with the expectation that they will increase their overall intake as treatment progresses. Participants who are extremely active may be prescribed a meal plan that contains 2,500 kcal/day.

Meal planning and self-monitoring forms are critical to Phase Two. Patients are asked to note planned meals and snacks as well as those actually consumed. In addition, episodes of binge eating are written down, as well as associated stimuli that precede bulimic symptoms.

Because of the emphasis on emotional attunement in ICT, the therapist pays close attention to the patient's response to the meal plan and the suggestions for dramatic changes in eating patterns. Questions about feelings are frequent in this phase of treatment, and the therapist uses reflective listening techniques to validate the patient's fears and anxiety. Simultaneously, the therapist continues to review the rationale and evidence of why adequate nutritional intake is so essential in recovery. The therapist also sets the stage for Phase Three by emphasizing the importance of eating well as a foundation of self-care, in contrast to self-neglect or self-attack.

After the meal plan has been introduced, the therapist introduces skills that will enable the patient to eat regular meals and snacks. The therapist emphasizes the importance of changing eating patterns but also allows the patient to implement these changes gradually. The remainder of Phase Two emphasizes behavioral and cognitive techniques that can be used by the patient to normalize his or her eating. ICT assumes that reluctance on the part of the patient is usually the result of fear and anxiety; thus, techniques focus on identifying, expressing, and tolerating distress while developing new coping strategies. These techniques include gradual behavioral exposure to high-risk foods and situations, stimulus control (with an emphasis on identifying stimuli of restriction, binge eating, and purging), relaxation and breathing skills (Foa & Wilson, 1991), shaping, self-reinforcement, journaling, alternative behaviors, cognitive restructuring, and hypothesis testing. The therapist works with patients to identify techniques that are most helpful to them to develop a coping card that they can carry with them at all times. In addition, the workbook and handheld computer program contain parroting phrases that can be used during times of duress.

In-depth discussion of all of these behavioral and cognitive techniques in five sessions is obviously unrealistic. Instead, the therapist highlights those skills that appear to be most helpful to each patient. In addition, patients are encouraged to spend considerable time strengthening these skills on their own using the workbook and handheld computer, both of which contain these materials in self-help format. Throughout treatment, but especially in Phase Two, the therapist highlights the importance of homework in between sessions and emphasizes to patients that the more time they spend working on these skills, the better the outcome and likelihood of recovery. The efficacy of self-help techniques in the treatment of BN (e.g., Treasure et al., 1996) indicates the usefulness of delivering cognitive-behavioral techniques in written form.

Phase Two also includes information about the cultural influences on body image and encourages patients to:

- Change their unfair and unrealistic ideals about body size and shape.
- Begin to view their own bodies in a more accepting manner.

ICT emphasizes the powerful role of cultural factors in the development and maintenance of eating disorder symptoms (Garner, 1996). Changes in body image are facilitated by open-ended questioning in therapy sessions and in the workbook, psychoeducation about sociocultural standards and body size overestimation, and suggestions for facilitating acceptance—including avoiding certain types of clothes and situations (e.g., reading fashion magazines) and seeking out situations that support acceptance of current body size and shape. Behavioral exposure exercises and cognitive restructuring are also useful in improving acceptance of body size and shape.

Phase Three: Interpersonal Patterns and Cognitive Styles (Sessions 9 to 18)

Phase Three is the longest segment of ICT. The primary goals of Phase Three are to identify and modify problematic interpersonal patterns and cognitive styles that are thought to precipitate and maintain bulimic symptoms and reduce distress associated with self-oriented discrepancies. Although the primary focus of Phase Three is interpersonal and cognitive, the emphasis on the consumption of meals and snacks and cognitive-behavioral strategies to prevent bulimic symptoms is maintained. Patients are asked to continue self-monitoring as well as meal planning and to bring these forms to each session. Although the clinician typically spends less time in each session reviewing these materials during Phase Three, self-monitoring sheets are often useful in elucidating continuing problems and precipitants. In particular, the therapist pays attention to antecedents including negative mood, interpersonal patterns, self-regulatory style, and self-discrepancy, as well as stimuli emphasized in Phase Two, including nutritional deprivation and dichotomous rules about eating.

Education in the early part of Phase Three introduces the patient to self-discrepancy, referring to the difference between the patient's *actual self* (how the person perceives himself or herself) and *desired self* (how he or she would like to be). Although the therapist emphasizes the discrepancy between perceived and desired self in terms of appearance at first, discrepancies in other aspects of self-perception are also highlighted as they are revealed. The purpose of incorporating self-discrepancy into treatment at this point is to help patients understand that this discrepancy can be a considerable source of distress and to allow them to begin to modify their unrealistic standards for themselves as well as perceiving themselves more accurately. For example, patients can continue to challenge the unrealistic standards of beauty, as well as recognize their own tendency to overestimate their body size.

One of the most fundamental aspects of Phase Three is the use of interpersonal pattern analysis. Interpersonal pattern analysis is based on the circumplex model of interpersonal behavior developed by Benjamin (1974, 1993) that has been studied in individuals with eating disorder symptoms (Humphrey, 1989; Wonderlich, Klein, & Council, 1996; Wonderlich & Swift, 1990). The patient workbook contains a simplified version, including a summary of different interpersonal patterns. The patterns emphasized most often in ICT have been grouped by Benjamin into those that someone does to another person (e.g., control, affirm and accept, attack, ignore) and those patterns that an individual does in response to another person (e.g., separate, assert, submit, withdraw). Patients complete interpersonal logs and worksheets that allow them to become familiar with their own patterns. The clinician emphasizes conducting interpersonal analyses in situations that precede bulimic episodes, are associated with negative mood states, or are identified by the patient as significant. Patients bring specific examples of interpersonal transactions to each session to analyze them with the therapist, as well as working on their own to identify interpersonal patterns.

In addition to interpersonal patterns, Phase Three of ICT emphasizes identifying self-regulatory cognitive style. Specifically, examples of how an individual manages perceived flaws triggered by self-discrepancy include tendencies to self-control, self-attack, and self-neglect. The therapist helps patients recognize their own self-regulatory style, including the way that bulimic symptoms function within this pattern. For example, if a patient perceives that she is overweight (actual self) compared to her ideal, which is to be underweight (desired self), this discrepancy may lead her to diet excessively (self-control), which in turn triggers binge eating and purging followed by self-criticism (self-attack). When reviewing the patient's self-monitoring sheets, the clinician points out specific examples of self-control, self-neglect, and self-attack and discusses various strategies that the patient can use to develop self-acceptance.

Later sessions in this phase emphasize strategies of change on interpersonal and cognitive patterns. Patients are provided with specific suggestions about how to change these patterns in the workbook as well as in the sessions. The goal of ICT is to help the patient to develop relationships characterized by appropriate levels of differentiation and dependence (Benjamin, 1993). The therapist strongly emphasizes the use of assertive communication, in which patients express their thoughts and feelings directly and respectfully (rather than attacking or avoiding). Although psychoeducational information is provided to patients, the therapist also emphasizes the importance of hypothesis-testing and experimentation through exposure to make gradual changes in relationship patterns.

In Phase Three, the clinician also attempts to help patients identify interpersonal schemas that influence their interactions and cognitive style (Garner, Vitousek, & Pike, 1997; Guidano, 1987; Safran & Segal, 1996; Young, 1994). In this context, the treatment also focuses on clarifying the exact nature of the patient's self-discrepancies. At times, understanding the origins of these belief systems and schemas can be helpful in understanding them, especially when the patterns seem to be particularly entrenched. The therapist can also help the patient realize how the interpersonal behaviors, cognitive patterns, and eating disorder symptoms function as an attempt to reduce self-discrepancy, as well as helping the patient to realize how these approaches are ultimately unsuccessful.

Although emotions are emphasized throughout ICT, the therapist's attunement to the patient's emotions is especially important in Phase Three, during which discussions about self-perception and interpersonal relationships can elicit painful feelings. Throughout this phase, the therapist should work to clarify patients' feelings and encourage them to express those feelings during the sessions. Patients can also develop an understanding of the factors that trigger their negative emotions, especially self-discrepancy.

Phase Four: Relapse Prevention and Lifestyle Management (Sessions 19 and 20)

The primary goals of Phase Four are to introduce strategies to consolidate and solidify the progress made in treatment and to prevent relapse. Psychoeducation is provided in the workbook and by the clinician about the difference between a lapse and a relapse (Fairburn, Marcus, et al., 1993) to prevent the abstinence violation effect that can be caused by viewing success dichotomously (Marlatt & Gordon, 1985), which has been observed in individuals with eating disorders (Grilo & Shiffman, 1994). Patients are instructed to expect slips or lapses and are asked to prepare themselves for how they will manage problems when they occur. They consider what a potential lapse scenario might be like for them, as well as specific steps they can use to prevent a relapse from occurring.

Relapse prevention is also useful in helping patients identify strategies they have learned in treatment that have been effective for them. The clinician helps the patient recognize strategies that have been helpful in reducing and eliminating bulimic symptoms but also in promoting positive mood, improving self-regulatory style, and facilitating appropriate interpersonal relationships. Another aspect of relapse prevention is the *healthy lifestyle plan* in which patients designate time allotments for specific components of their schedule (e.g., hours per week to spend socializing, working). This process allows the patient and therapist to discuss ways that the patient would like to fill his or her time that was previously occupied by bulimic symptoms. Patients are also asked to review the progress they made in treatment. Because Phase Four includes termination, the final sessions include discussions about the patient's thoughts and feelings about finishing treatment.

PRELIMINARY OUTCOME DATA

ICT has been administered to nine pilot cases of women with bulimic symptoms at two university sites. Treatment was administered by doctoral-level psychologists. Weekly supervision sessions were held with several of the authors of the manual to discuss the implementation of ICT and difficulties that therapists encountered in working with specific patients. In addition, all sessions were audiotaped, and portions of these sessions were discussed in weekly supervision sessions.

At baseline, the average number of self-reported binge eating episodes per week was 4.3, and the average number of purging episodes per week was 6.7 on the Eating-Behaviors IV (Mitchell, Hatsukami, Eckert, & Pyle, 1985). At the final session (or the last session attended), the average number of self-reported binge eating episodes per week was 0.6, and the average number of purging episodes was 0.3. Among the nine participants, seven (78%) were abstinent from binge eating and eight (89%) were abstinent from purging at their final assessment. Although these data are from a very small sample in an uncontrolled study, the degree of improvement and percentage of abstinence from bulimic symptoms indicates that ICT is a promising treatment.

FUTURE DIRECTIONS AND RESEARCH

Although encouraging, the outcome data for ICT thus far are preliminary. The next step will be to establish the efficacy of ICT by comparing it to a wait-list control group, as well as CBT. Once the efficacy of ICT is established, it will be modified in future trials to tailor it to more specific comorbid conditions (e.g., Axis II pathology). ICT was specifically designed to be tested as a short-term intervention; however, it may be expanded for longer term treatment for individuals who are not helped by briefer psychotherapy. Future investigations will evaluate the optimal duration of treatment for individuals with various subtypes of bulimic symptoms.

CONCLUSION

ICT was developed as an alternative treatment for individuals with BN. Although it integrates aspects of CBT that have been found to be helpful to individuals with bulimic symptoms—including a prescription of regular meals and snacks, behavioral strategies, self-monitoring, cognitive restructuring, and relapse prevention—ICT incorporates additional treatment techniques—including motivational enhancement, interpersonal pattern analysis, and an emphasis on self-oriented cognition including self-discrepancy and self-regulatory style. ICT is still in an experimental phase, although the outcome data from pilot studies appear promising.

REFERENCES

Agras, W. S., Crow, S. J., Halmi, K. A., Mitchell, J. E., Wilson, G. T., & Kraemer, H. C. (2000). Outcome predictors for the cognitive behavior treatment of bulimia nervosa: Data from a multisite study. *American Journal of Psychiatry, 157,* 1302–1308.

Agras, W. S., Walsh, B. T., Fairburn, C. G., Wilson, G. T., & Kraemer, H. C. (2000). A multicenter comparison of cognitive-behavioral therapy and interpersonal psychotherapy for bulimia nervosa. *Archives of General Psychiatry, 57,* 459–466.

Altabe, M., & Thompson, K. (1996). Body image: A cognitive self-schema construct? *Cognitive Therapy and Research, 20,* 171–193.

Benjamin, L. S. (1974). Structural analysis of social behavior. *Psychological Review, 81,* 392–425.

Benjamin, L. S. (1993). *Interpersonal treatment of personality disorders.* New York: Guilford Press.

Berg, M. L., Crosby, R. D., Wonderlich, S. A., & Hawley, D. (2000). The relationship of temperament and perceptions of nonshared environment in bulimia nervosa. *International Journal of Eating Disorders, 28,* 148–154.

Blundell, J. E., & Hill, A. J. (1993). Binge eating: Psychobiological mechanisms. In C. G. Fairburn & G. T. Wilson (Eds.), *Binge eating: Nature, assessment, and treatment* (pp. 206–224). New York: Guilford Press.

Bowlby, J. (1969). *Attachment and loss. Volume I: Attachment.* New York: Basic Books.

Brewerton, T. D., Hand, L. D., & Bishop, E. R. (1993). The tridimensional personality questionnaire in eating disorder patients. *International Journal of Eating Disorders, 14,* 213–218.

Clark, D. A. (1995). Perceived limitations of standard cognitive therapy: A consideration of efforts to revise Beck's theory and therapy. *Journal of Cognitive Psychotherapy: An International Quarterly, 9,* 153–172.

Cole-Detke, H., & Kobak, R. (1996). Attachment processes in eating disorder and depression. *Journal of Consulting and Clinical Psychology, 64,* 282–290.

Cooper, P. J., & Fairburn, C. G. (1986). The depressive symptoms of bulimia nervosa. *British Journal of Psychiatry, 148,* 268–274.

Craighead, L. W., & Agras, W. S. (1991). Mechanisms of action in cognitive-behavioral and pharmacological interventions for obesity and bulimia nervosa. *Journal of Consulting and Clinical Psychology, 59,* 115–125.

Davis, R., Freeman, R. J., & Garner, D. M. (1988). A naturalistic investigation of eating behavior in bulimia nervosa. *Journal of Consulting and Clinical Psychology, 56,* 273–279.

Fairburn, C. G. (1996). Interpersonal psychotherapy for bulimia nervosa. In D. M. Garner & P. E. Garfinkel (Eds.), *Handbook of treatment for eating disorders* (2nd ed., pp. 278–294). New York: Guilford Press.

Fairburn, C. G., Jones, R., Peveler, R. C., Carr, S. J., Solomon, R. A., O'Connor, M. E., et al. (1991). Three psychological treatments for bulimia nervosa: A comparative trial. *Archives of General Psychiatry, 48,* 463–469.

Fairburn, C. G., Jones, R., Peveler, R. C., Hope, R. A., & O'Connor, M. (1993). Psychotherapy and bulimia nervosa: The longer-term effects of interpersonal psychotherapy, behavior therapy and cognitive behavior therapy. *Archives of General Psychiatry, 50,* 419–428.

Fairburn, C. G., Marcus, M., & Wilson, G. T. (1993). Cognitive-behavioral therapy for binge eating and bulimia nervosa: A comprehensive treatment manual. In C. G. Fairburn & G. T. Wilson (Eds.), *Binge eating: Nature, assessment, and treatment* (pp. 361–404). New York: Guilford Press.

Fairburn, C. G., Welch, S. L., Doll, H. A., Davies, B. A., & O'Connor, M. E. (1997). Risk factors for bulimia nervosa: A community based case control study. *Archives of General Psychiatry, 54,* 509–517.

Foa, E., & Wilson, R. (1991). *Stop obsessing: How to overcome your obsessions and compulsions.* New York: Bantam Books.

Garner, D. M. (1996). Psychoeducational principles in treatment. In D. M. Garner & P. E. Garfinkel (Eds.), *Handbook of treatment for eating disorders* (2nd ed., pp. 145–177). New York: Guilford Press.

Garner, D. M., Vitousek, K. M., & Pike, K. M. (1996). Cognitive-behavioral therapy for anorexia nervosa. In D. M. Garner & P. E. Garfinkel (Eds.), *Handbook of treatment for eating disorders* (2nd ed., pp. 94–144). New York: Guilford Press.

Geller, J. (2002). What a motivational approach is and what a motivational approach isn't: Reflections and responses. *European Eating Disorders Review, 10,* 155–160.

Greenberg, L. S., & Korman, L. (1993). Assimilating emotion into psychotherapy integration. *Journal of Psychotherapy Integration, 3,* 249–265.

Greenberg, L. S., & Safran, J. D. (1987). *Emotion in psychotherapy.* New York: Guilford Press.

Grilo, C. M., & Shiffman, S. (1994). Longitudinal investigation of the abstinence violation effect in binge eaters. *Journal of Consulting and Clinical Psychology, 62,* 611–619.

Grisset, N. I., & Norvell, N. K. (1992). Perceived social support, social skills, and quality of relationships in bulimic women. *Journal of Consulting and Clinical Psychology, 60,* 293–299.

Guidano, V. F. (1987). *Complexity of the self: A developmental approach to psychopathology and therapy.* New York: Guilford Press.

Heatherton, T. F., & Baumeister, R. F. (1991). Binge eating as escape from self awareness. *Psychological Bulletin, 110,* 86–108.

Herman, C. P., & Polivy, J. (1975). Anxiety, restraint, and eating behavior. *Journal of Abnormal Psychology, 84,* 666–672.

Herzog, D. B., Norman, D. K., Rigotti, N. A., & Pepose, M. (1986). Frequency of bulimic behaviors and associated social maladjustment in female graduate students. *Journal of Psychiatric Research, 20,* 355–361.

Higgins, E. T. (1987). Self-discrepancy: A theory relating self and affect. *Psychological Review, 94,* 319–340.

Higgins, E. T., Bond, R., Klein, R., & Strauman, T. J. (1986). Self-discrepancies and emotional vulnerability: How magnitude, accessibility and type of discrepancy influence affect. *Journal of Personality and Social Psychology, 51,* 5–15.

Holden, N. L. (1991). Adoption and eating disorders: A high risk group. *British Journal of Psychiatry, 158,* 829–833.

Humphrey, L. L. (1989). Observed family interactions among subtypes of eating disorders using structural analysis of social behavior. *Journal of Consulting and Clinical Psychology, 57,* 206–214.

Jacobson, R., & Robbins, C. J. (1989). Social dependency and social support in bulimic and nonbulimic women. *International Journal of Eating Disorders, 8,* 665–670.

Johnson, C., & Larson, R. (1982). An analysis of moods and behavior. *Psychosomatic Medicine, 44,* 341–351.

Keys, A., Brozek, J., Henschel, A., Mickelsen, O., & Taylor, H. L. (1950). *The biology of human starvation.* Minneapolis: University of Minnesota Press.

Lilenfeld, L. R., Kaye, W. H., Greeno, C. G., Merikangas, K. R., Plotnicov, K., Pollice, C., et al. (1997). Psychiatric disorders in women with bulimia nervosa and their first-degree relatives: Effects of comorbid substance dependence. *International Journal of Eating Disorders, 22,* 253–264.

Maddocks, S. E., Kaplan, A. S., Woodside, D. B., Langdon, L., & Piran, N. (1992). Two year follow-up of bulimia nervosa: The importance of abstinence as the criterion of outcome. *International Journal of Eating Disorders, 12,* 133–141.

Marlatt, G. A., & Gordon, J. R. (1985). *Relapse prevention: Maintenance strategies in the treatment of addictive behaviors.* New York: Guilford Press.

Meyer, C., & Waller, G. (1999). The impact of emotion upon eating behavior: The role of subliminal visual processing of threat cues. *International Journal of Eating Disorders, 25,* 319–326.

Miller, W. R., & Rollnick, S. (1991). *Motivational interviewing: Preparing people to change addictive behavior.* New York: Guilford Press.

Mitchell, J. E., Davis, L., & Goff, G. (1985). The process of relapse in patients with bulimia. *International Journal of Eating Disorders, 4,* 457–463.

Mitchell, J. E., Hatsukami, D., Eckert, E., & Pyle, R. (1985). Eating Disorders Questionnaire. *Psychopharmacology Bulletin, 21,* 1025–1043.

Mitchell, J. E., Hoberman, H. N., Peterson, C. B., Mussell, M., & Pyle, R. L. (1996). Research on the psychotherapy of bulimia nervosa: Half empty or half full. *International Journal of Eating Disorders, 20,* 219–229.

Mitchell, J. E., & Peterson, C. B. (1997). Cognitive-behavioral treatment of eating disorders. In L. J. Dickstein, M. B. Riba, & J. M. Oldham (Eds.), *Review of psychiatry* (Vol. 16, pp. 107–133). Washington, DC: American Psychiatric Press.

Mitchell, J. E., Pyle, R. L., Eckert, E. D., Hatsukami, D., Pomeroy, C., & Zimmerman, R. (1990). A comparison study of antidepressants and structured intensive group psychotherapy in the treatment of bulimia nervosa. *Archives of General Psychiatry, 47,* 149–157.

Mitchell, J. E., Pyle, R. L., Pomeroy, C., Zollman, M., Crosby, R., Seim, H., et al. (1993). Cognitive-behavioral group psychotherapy of bulimia nervosa: Importance of logistical variables. *International Journal of Eating Disorders, 14,* 277–287.

Norman, D. K., & Herzog, D. B. (1984). Persistent social maladjustment in bulimia: A one-year follow-up. *American Journal of Psychiatry, 143,* 444–446.

Olmsted, M. P., Kaplan, A., & Rockert, W. (1994). Rate and prediction of relapse in bulimia nervosa. *American Journal of Psychiatry, 151,* 738–743.

Pruitt, J. A., Kappins, R. E., & Gorman, P. W. (1992). Bulimia and fear of intimacy. *Journal of Clinical Psychology, 48,* 472–476.

Robins, C. J., & Hayes, A. M. (1993). An appraisal of cognitive therapy. *Journal of Consulting and Clinical Psychology, 61,* 205–214.

Rorty, M., Yager, J., Buckwalter, J. G., & Rossotto, E. (1999). Social support, social adjustment and recovery status in bulimia nervosa. *International Journal of Eating Disorders, 26,* 1–12.

Ruderman, A. J. (1986). Dietary restraint: A theoretical and empirical review. *Psychological Bulletin, 99,* 247–262.

Ruderman, A. J., & Grace, P. S. (1987). Bulimics and restrained eaters: A personality comparison. *Addictive Behaviors, 13,* 359–368.

Safran, J. D. (1990a). Toward a refinement of cognitive therapy in light of interpersonal theory. I: Theory. *Clinical Psychology Review, 10,* 87–105.

Safran, J. D. (1990b). Toward a refinement of cognitive therapy in light of interpersonal theory. II: Practice. *Clinical Psychology Review, 10,* 107–121.

Safran, J. D., & Segal, Z. V. (1996). *Interpersonal process in cognitive therapy.* Northvale, NJ: Aronson.

Sherwood, N. E., Crowther, J. H., Wills, L., & Ben-Porath, Y. S. (2000). The perceived function of eating for bulimic, subclinical bulimic, and noneating disordered women. *Behavior Therapy, 31,* 777–793.

Steiger, H., Gauvin, L., Jabalpurwala, S., Seguin, J. R., & Stotland, S. (1999). Hypersensitivity to social interactions in bulimic syndromes: Relationship to binge eating. *Journal of Consulting and Clinical Psychology, 67,* 765–775.

Strauman, T. J. (1989). Self-discrepancies in clinical depression and social phobia: Cognitive structures that underlie emotional disorders. *Journal of Abnormal Psychology, 98,* 5–14.

Strauman, T. J., & Glenberg, A. M. (1994). Self-concept and body-image disturbance: Which self-beliefs predict body size overestimation? *Cognitive Therapy and Research, 18,* 105–125.

Strauman, T. J., Vookles, J., Barenstein, V., Chaiken, S., & Higgins, E. T. (1991). Self-discrepancies and vulnerability to body dissatisfaction and disordered eating. *Journal of Personality and Social Psychology, 61,* 946–956.

Striegel-Moore, R. H., Silberstein, L. R., & Rodin, J. (1986). Toward an understanding of risk factors for bulimia. *American Psychologist, 41,* 246–263.

Strober, M., & Humphrey, L. L. (1987). Familial contributions to the etiology and course of anorexia nervosa and bulimia. *Journal of Consulting and Clinical Psychology, 55,* 654 659.

Treasure, J., Schmidt, U., Troop, N., Tiller, J., Todd, G., & Turnbull, S. (1996). Sequential treatment for bulimia nervosa incorporating a self-care manual. *British Journal of Psychiatry, 168,* 94–98.

Vitousek, K., Watson, S., & Wilson, G. T. (1998). Enhancing motivation for change in treatment resistant eating disorders. *Clinical Psychology Review, 18,* 391–420.

Waller, D. A., Petty, F., Hardy, B. W., Gullion, C. M., Murdock, M. V., & Rush, A. J. (1993). Tridimensional Personality Questionnaire and serotonin in bulimia nervosa. *Psychiatry Research, 48,* 9–15.

Welch, S. L., & Fairburn, C. G. (1994). Sexual abuse and bulimia nervosa: Three integrated case control comparisons. *American Journal of Psychiatry, 151,* 402–407.

Welch, S. L., & Fairburn, C. G. (1996). Childhood sexual and physical abuse as risk factors for the development of bulimia nervosa: A community-based case control study. *Child Abuse and Neglect, 20,* 633–642.

Wilson, G. T. (1996). Treatment of bulimia nervosa: When CBT fails. *Behavior Research and Therapy, 34,* 197–212.

Wilson, G. T., & Fairburn, C. G. (1998). Treatments for eating disorders. In P. E. Nathan & J. M. Gorman (Eds.), *Treatments that work* (pp. 501–530). New York: Oxford Press.

Wonderlich, S. A. (1992). Relationship of family and personality factors in bulimia nervosa. In J. H. Crowther, D. L. Tannenbaum, S. E. Hobfoll, & M. A. P. Stephens (Eds.), *The etiology of bulimia nervosa: The individual and family context* (pp. 170–196). Washington, DC: Hemisphere.

Wonderlich, S. A., Brewerton, T. D., Jocic, Z., Dansky, B. S., & Abbott, D. W. (1997). Relationship of childhood sexual abuse and eating disorders. *Journal of the American Academy of Child and Adolescent Psychiatry, 36,* 1107–1115.

Wonderlich, S. A., Klein, M., & Council, J. (1996). Relationship of social perceptions and self-concept in bulimia nervosa. *Journal of Consulting and Clinical Psychology, 64,* 1231–1238.

Wonderlich, S. A., & Mitchell, J. E. (1997). Eating disorders and comorbidity: Empirical, conceptual, and clinical implications. *Psychopharmacology Bulletin, 33,* 381–390.

Wonderlich, S. A., Mitchell, J. E., Peterson, C. B., & Crow, S. (2001). Integrative cognitive therapy for bulimic behavior. In R. H. Striegel-Moore & L. Smolak (Eds.), *Eating disorders: Innovative directions in research and practice* (pp. 173–195). Washington, DC: American Psychological Association.

Wonderlich, S. A., Peterson, C. B., Mitchell, J. E., & Crow, S. J. (2000). Integrative cognitive therapy for bulimic behavior. In K. J. Miller & J. S. Mizes (Eds.), *Comparative treatments for eating disorders* (pp. 258–282). New York: Springer.

Wonderlich, S. A., & Swift, W. J. (1990). Perception of parental relationships in eating disorder subtypes. *Journal of Abnormal Psychology, 99,* 353–360.

Young, J. E. (1994). *Cognitive therapy for personality disorders: A schema-focused approach* (2nd ed.). Sarasota, FL: Professional Resource Press.

Chapter 13

FEMINIST THERAPY AND EATING DISORDERS

NIVA PIRAN, KARIN JASPER, AND LEORA PINHAS

The feminist approach to therapy developed as a grassroots approach to addressing the prevalent social phenomena of violence against women and child sexual abuse (Enns, 1997). The practice of feminist therapy is, therefore, grounded in the socially critical study of oppression of diverse groups of women and in political advocacy aimed at social transformations (Enns, 1997). The provision of therapeutic spaces for women by feminist therapists aims not at minimizing the importance of social change but rather at concurrently creating healing relational spaces that counter adverse, widely sanctioned oppressive conditions. Within these alternative relational and dialogical spaces, shifts toward improved well-being can occur (L. S. Brown, 1994). The feminist approach to therapy, like all major therapeutic modalities, is in an ongoing process of scrutiny and further developments (Wyche & Rice, 1997). Nonetheless, it is possible to delineate several key dimensions that define therapy as feminist. Within these key dimensions that provide a feminist frame to therapy, therapists may use diverse approaches with varied emphases, such as dynamic, interpersonal, narrative, cognitive-behavioral, or psychoeducational (Wyche & Rice, 1997).

The chapter is organized around a set of key principles of feminist therapy and their particular applications to the treatment of body weight and shape preoccupation and eating disorders. Clinical examples follow a description of each key principle. The chapter is based on published feminist scholarship and on the authors' research and clinical experience in community-based counseling centers and hospital-based outpatient, day hospital, and inpatient settings for adolescents and adults with a spectrum of eating disorders.

KEY ELEMENT 1: CRITICAL EXAMINATION OF THE IMPACT OF SOCIAL CONTEXT AND SOCIALLY OPPRESSIVE SYSTEMS ON WOMEN'S PHYSICAL AND MENTAL WELL-BEING AND ON THEIR EXPERIENCE OF THEIR BODIES

Feminist theory, which seeks to conceptualize how gender operates in a culture and how it impacts on women's interpersonal, social, economic, political, and cultural interactions, provides the basis for feminist therapy (L. S. Brown, 1994). Feminists examine the impact of gender as it intersects with multiple other social variables such as social class, ethnocultural and racial heritage, immigration history, health status, and sexual orientation on women's well-being (C. Brown, 1994). Systems of oppression and discriminatory practices in the social, political, economic, and legal spheres are seen as underlying women's distress (Worell & Remer, 1992). In the practice of feminist therapy, therapists strive to examine, under the guidance of their clients, the clients' unique experiences in their respective social contexts and co-construct a critical analysis of these social forces as they shape their private lives. Validation of personal experiences through feminist scholarship, other women's stories, or self-disclosure by therapists helps weave the social context into personal stories.

Application to the Treatment of Eating Disorders

Social philosophers and critics such as Marx (1963) and Foucault (1979), including feminist social philosophers and critics such as Bordo (1993) and Rich (1986), have described the body as a social domain through which oppressive social structures inscribe, into individual citizens' bodies, systems of privilege, power, and control. For example, the high prevalence of sexual and physical violence perpetrated against girls and women is seen as a reflection, in the body domain, of gender inequity in power and privilege (Buchwald, Fletcher, & Roth, 1993). Further, social critics and philosophers contend that an examination of individuals' practices toward their own bodies reveals these cultural inscriptions and, hence, reflects social structures and systems of domination and oppression (Bordo, 1993). Women's disciplining of their own bodies in terms of size, shape, desires, or appetites is thus seen as grounded in dominant power structures and in widely sanctioned oppressive social values and prejudices and, hence, comprises a "crystallization of culture" (Bordo, 1993; for a review of relevant research, see Piran, 2001a). From a feminist perspective, different eating disorder patterns, as well as other behaviors such as having unprotected sexual contact, which may put girls and women at risk, occur on a continuum of risk and severity and are understandable outcomes of living in inequitable social circumstances. Further, they are seen as coping strategies to adverse contexts. While taking account of temperamental and individual factors, feminist therapists critically examine with their clients the cumulative impact of multiple social experiences that have disrupted and shaped these women's experiences, views, attitudes, and practices toward their bodies.

Clinical Examples

Gender and Space (Private Practice Counseling Client)

D. is a 40-year old woman who has lived, since the age of 14, with periods of anorexia and bulimia. D., the only daughter of a successful professional father and a work-at-home mother, has two younger brothers. D. described persistent feelings of discomfort in her body since her childhood, unless she was in selected "hiding spots" at home. D. recalled feeling this body discomfort for the first time when she was about 4 years old. She was carrying a large tray of food and drinks up the stairs for her mother, who had given birth two months prior to her second brother. To climb up the stairs with the heavy tray, she had to exceed and surpass what her body could naturally do, causing her to experience for the first time a state of disconnection from her body. Rewarded by her parents, D. continued this dutiful practice of nourishing others, while feeling deprived and burdened beyond her years. Her father carried ultimate power at home and was not involved in any caring capacity toward the children or his wife, who was powerless and relied on her daughter for nurturance. In addition, an aspect of the father's domineering status at home was his control of physical space in the house. He customarily "barged" into his daughter's room, regardless of her activities, insisting, for example, on his right to kiss her whenever he left for or returned from work. Consequently, unless D. was hiding, she never felt a sense of private physical space or freedom from duties associated with her body. These childhood experiences of deprivation, disrupted ownership of the body, and of "surpassing" her needs adversely affected the way she handled her appetites and desires throughout her life. In her different short-term partnering relationships with men, she kept a close lid on her own needs and found it challenging to negotiate a sense of physical safety.

In co-constructing the story in therapy, the feminist therapist included an invitation for D. to explore issues such as the distribution of power in the family, the gender inequity in power, the differing expectations for her as a girl compared with her brothers, myths about selfless caretaking and the gender inequity in caregiving in the family, her early experiences of anger and protest, and the relationship between social power and the experience of physical space at home (Bartky, 1988). The invitation to explore experiences critically was mainly achieved through validation of D.'s experiences by sharing the experiences of other women and feminist research and theory, hence, transforming personal stories to socially relevant knowledge (MacKinnon, 1989). The impact of these and other social nuances on the client's experiences of her body—such as her needs, appetites, desires, protests, or fears—comprised a focus in therapy. The experiences of physical and mental freedom (Piran, Carter, Thompson, & Pajouhandeh, 2002) and of protest and anger that D. "discovered" in her hiding spots during her childhood were invited in, reexperienced, and examined in the context of the therapy relationship. D. was encouraged on an ongoing basis to assert her needs, wishes, and goals in and out of therapy and examine how this expression affected her experience of herself, her body, and her sense of physical space. Her growing connection with herself and her body was associated with an increase in her self-caring activities, including her eating behavior. The assertive expression of needs and desires, including her need for a sense of control over her physical space, allowed for the development of more satisfying friendships as well as an intimate relationship. Further, D. has incorporated her critical understanding to enrich her field of work, which centers on social transformation.

This clinical example is used because it describes a relatively mundane familial circumstances of a privileged, White middle-to-high social class family in North America. The possibility of the occurrence of sexual abuse was explored with the client. A feminist antioppressive approach would tend to examine phenomena such as violations of personal boundaries and their impact on clients as continuous phenomena.

Considering the Context of Both Mother and Daughter (an Inpatient Client)

S., a 12-year-old girl, was admitted to a hospital for medical instability because of severe food and fluid restriction. This was her fourth admission to the hospital with a diagnosis of anorexia nervosa. She had been discharged about 10 days before read-mission. She lived with her parents and two younger brothers. On her return home, she refused to talk to her parents or have any real contact with them. She willingly went to school, but on return home, she would go to her room, lie in bed in the dark, and refuse to talk, eat, or drink. As a result, she rapidly deteriorated and her parents were distressed and at their limits, having tried everything they could think of to connect with her. They finally took her back to the hospital against her will—her father had physically carried her to the car. Once in the car, she settled down, and in the hospital, she was superficially compliant and would speak to staff about concrete issues but not about what she was feeling or thinking about her family, her life, or her eating disorder. Initially in the hospital, she became medically stable but remained psychologically and emotionally distant from both the staff and her family. Her parents, however, were very motivated and involved with her stay. The therapist began to work with the family to try to find a way for them to communicate with their daughter, who would leave the room whenever her parents entered it. As a result, the work began with the parents, and the therapist began to focus on understanding them as people and as a couple. She began to slowly develop an alliance with them, and they began to trust her. It was in the context of this relationship that the mother revealed a history of serious childhood sexual abuse. She had never told anyone about this—not even her husband. She did acknowledge that, as a result, she rejected everything "female," including a female body. She herself was an obligate exerciser and limited her eating to maintain an androgynous body type. Her husband also acknowledged that he had concerns about her eating, but they had never really discussed it. The mother began to do work on her own history, her own struggles with her femaleness, what it meant to have a daughter who was near the mother's age when the sexual abuse occurred, and what it meant to have a female child in light of her wish to reject all that was female. The couple also slowly began to talk with each other about these issues. This work had an important effect on their daughter, who slowly began to allow the parents back into her life. This was part of the work for S., who had individual and group therapy and spent some time in a residential program. However, the therapist's understanding of the social and family context of not only the child but also the parents, and helping them understand how it was interrelated, significantly affected her outcome. Helping S. and her mother negotiate their relationship in the context of what it means to be female in this culture and what it is to have a female offspring was an important turning point.

In summary, a feminist therapist extends an invitation to examine the social forces that shape the personal story in detail, mainly through a process of validation relying on collective feminist-based knowledge (MacKinnon, 1989). The analysis of context, power, and privilege helps form links between what may otherwise seem like disparate phenomena (such as gender role expectations and the sense of physical space in the family or a mother's history of sexual abuse and her daughter's anorexia).

KEY ELEMENT 2: EMPOWERMENT

Because feminist theory highlights the central role of social oppressions in adversely affecting the well-being of women from diverse backgrounds, empowerment of clients comprises another key element in feminist therapy (L. S. Brown, 1994; Enns, 1997; Worell & Remer, 1992). Feminist therapists examine in detail ways both to share power in therapy and empower the client in and outside therapy. As to the therapy relationship, feminist therapists are particularly aware of power differentials in the relationship related to their role as service providers and power differentials related to other social variables such as social class or race. To avoid reproducing adverse power imbalances encountered by women outside therapy, feminist therapists work toward balancing the power dynamics in therapy (Worell & Remer, 1992). Different techniques are used toward this goal, such as encouraging clients to select goals for therapy, evaluating its effectiveness and determining its process, establishing clients' own expertise over their life experiences and their meaning, demystifying the process of therapy, inviting discussions related to power differences in the therapy relationship, or using self-disclosure (L. S. Brown, 1994). In addition, through enhancement of clients' critical awareness, feminist therapy aims to empower women to make significant changes in their world (C. Brown, 1994; Enns, 1997). Feminist therapists encourage the development of other skills, such as assertiveness training, relaxation techniques, or new approaches to problem solving. In addition, feminist therapists encourage clients to use other resources to educate themselves, expand their understanding and expertise about their own and others' issues, and network with other women (Worell & Remer, 1992). Considering that oppression will always limit the well-being of women, feminist therapists who themselves work toward social transformation invite their clients to do the same (Enns, 1997).

Application to the Treatment of Eating Disorders

Gender-related experiences of social disempowerment are seen as centrally linked to the development of eating disorders. Hence, in the treatment of eating disorders, feminist therapists work toward the goal of empowering their clients in multiple ways. In the therapy relationship itself, feminist therapists use ongoing mutual negotiations in the setting of treatment goals, their nature, and their pace to allow clients to maintain control over their progress and to be successful in achieving their goals. When issues of medical safety arise, feminist therapists share their concerns openly with their clients as well as the decision process that may guide them to suggest alterations in ongoing behavioral contracts. Disempowerment in the therapy process is expected to lead to exacerbation in the behavioral symptoms.

It is particularly important to recognize that multiple developmental processes may precipitate experiences of great distress and of being out of control in adolescence. Adolescent girls may experience instability of identity related to body development (Brooks-Gunn & Reiter, 1990), exposure to weight and fat prejudice (Brooks-Gunn & Reiter, 1990) and to sexualization and objectification with puberty (Larkin, Rice, & Russell, 1999; Piran, 2001a, 2001b, 2002), increased pressure to "fit in" to larger social as well as peer-based norms while trying to become more autonomous from parents (Brooks-Gun & Reiter, 1990), challenges in dealing with sexual desire in the context of minimal adult support and contradictory social messages (Tolman, 1991), as well as increasing academic pressures.

Adults' behavior that may exacerbate this distress is an authoritarian approach that disallows the young people from developing autonomy through learning from their own experience (Dickerson, 1999). Young adolescents also do not have the power to arrest emotional, physical, or sexual abuse by adults. Alternatively, adults who do not exert authority when it is judicious to do so may also exacerbate adolescents' experience of being out of control, uncared for, and unsafe. Adolescents rebel against authority figures if they think the adults are being unfair, autocratic, controlling to satisfy their own needs, or making rules without really understanding their children and their situation. Treatment centers for eating disorders that deal specifically with adolescents are routinely faced with issues of power and control, especially because often a person troubled by anorexia or bulimia uses the restriction of food, control of weight, and bingeing and purging to manage the experience of being out of control. Because the eating disorder may become the focus of power struggles with the parent and treatment providers, the teen's actual development may be put on hold physically, socially, and academically, and the teen may become disconnected from her family members.

A feminist approach to therapy with hospitalized adolescents with eating disorders includes ongoing attention both to appropriate uses of power and the misuse of power, especially in light of widely sanctioned cultural biases such as adultism (Dickerson, 1999; Wipfler, 1995). *Adultism* is a bias that privileges adults to take control away from kids without seriously considering their experiences and without valuing their judgment or contribution, a devaluing experience that is internalized by adolescents. Another devaluing experience that may be exacerbated through the misuse of power is the cultural deprecation of the female body or of the importance of interpersonal connections in development. Awareness of cultural biases and concerns for fairness and justice guide decision making about the use of power in a feminist treatment setting. While it is not ethical treatment to let an adolescent with an eating disorder make choices when those choices are likely to result in cardiac problems, permanently decreased height, osteoporosis, infertility, or neuropsychological sequelae (Faith, Pinhas, Schmelefske, & Bryden, 2001), giving participants more choices in more areas, as their ability to think abstractly increases and their ability to consider themselves separately from their peers evolves, is an essential part of treatment. The regular questioning of the uses of power benefits staff members in helping them clarify where countertransference reactions lead them to take control in an angry way while justifying these actions through commonplace cultural biases. A collaborative process can, therefore, develop.

Clinical Examples

Multifamily Dinners in a Day Hospital Program

In an eating disorders day treatment program for adolescents, staff is committed to including the teens' "voices" in the running of the program, thereby encouraging development of autonomy and their experience of control in their lives, as long as implementing their ideas is consistent with the process of recovery. This approach is clearly outlined in the information package given to each family considering the program. Staff members have found that a consultative process with participants often produces ideas that are better suited to accomplishing program goals than the ideas of the staff alone.

For instance, the staff wanted to help the participants become able to eat with their families but did not want to isolate each family separately at a meal with a staff member "watching" them. Rather, their idea was to have a multifamily meal (e.g., Dare & Eisler, 2000) that would not isolate any individual family and would include staff providing support but also sharing the meal rather than just observing it. The first attempt involved teens sitting with their own families, each family at *its* own table, all in one room. Staff members sat at a table of their own and were visually available to all teens. This meal arrangement proved to be too difficult. None of the teens were able to complete the meal.

The staff's next idea, influenced by reading of the literature on multifamily meals, was for the teens to eat with an "adopted" family, again with each grouping at its own table. When staff communicated this idea at a parents' and teens' meeting, the teens asked for some time to meet privately to decide which of them would eat with which family. The staff agreed and the teens came back with a counterproposal to have two teens eat with two families. They each wanted to have the support of a peer and not be alone eating with a family they did not know well. The staff agreed. Shortly before the evening of this planned meal, one of the families was not able to attend. This left us with an odd number of families, so we could not follow the agreed-on plan. The staff gave the teens two options: a banquet style dinner with everyone at the same table or the original adopt-a-family idea. The teens chose the banquet style. They proposed a seating plan to which we gave input and a final plan was agreed on. The staff explained the roles of all: The teens' responsibility was to eat their meals, the parents' job was to make a pleasant conversational atmosphere, and the staff members were to keep time and give support to participants having difficulty. The meal went very well—all participants were able to complete their meals on time.

Holding on to Safety (a Private Practice in Counseling)

A., a 17-year-old White woman, a recent immigrant to Canada from the Middle East, and of modest financial means was discharged from her third hospitalization for the treatment of anorexia and bulimia nervosa. Like the two previous hospitalizations, this one was considered a failure because of insufficient weight gain and her "manipulative" and "dishonest" behavior as to bingeing and purging behavior. One of the issues in the initial consultation with the feminist therapist was the client's extensive use of laxatives, which had put her at medical risk before. During the first session, the client denied continued use of laxatives. The client's mother called the therapist before the second session to inform the therapist that she discovered a package of laxatives hidden in her daughter's handbag. In the beginning of the second session, the therapist talked about the phone call from the mother and shared that her concerns about the client's safety were affecting her ability to be fully present in listening to the issue the client was eager to discuss. The therapist discussed the risks associated with the laxative use and stated that, if the client still needed to use laxatives, they could decide together on a change in the amount of laxatives the client used, rather than cessation. The client explained that while she herself was "fed up" with the effect of laxatives, she definitely needed to carry an unopened package of laxatives on her "for safety" at all times. The therapist and client agreed that, should the client feel distressed enough to resort to using laxatives again, she would call the therapist first. The therapist emphasized the courage the client was exhibiting in attempting to change her use of laxatives and validated the client's understandable need for the experience of safety. The therapist also suggested that A. examine and let her know how safe she felt during the sessions and find out what makes A. feel safe in and outside therapy. A. continued to carry the package with her for the following three months. Once she felt safe talking in the sessions about the social rejection she experienced in her high school as a recent immigrant and her mother's illness with cancer, which was in remission, she discarded the package. One aspect of this client's recovery is that she has used the critical understanding and sense of empowerment developed in therapy not only to make changes in her own life but also to model for her mother the freedom to reach for new options.

Labeling an Abusive Relationship (Counseling Private Practice)

M., a 35-year-old professional White woman, who was making progress in her treatment for anorexia nervosa with a feminist therapist, experienced an increase in verbal, emotional, and threats of physical abuse by her husband in response to her growing confidence and assertiveness at home. While this client was extremely bright intellectually, the labeling of a behavior as abusive was challenging for her because she grew up in an abusive home. To avoid labeling the behavior for the client and to empower the client to assess her own situation, the therapist asked whether the client would be interested in reading a book chapter that described the experience of living in captivity in an abusive relationship (Herman, 1992, pp. 74–95). The therapist would then use that material to assess the quality of her partnership relationship. The client was curious to read the chapter. During the time between her weekly sessions, the client made a list of events that happened with her husband, as well as a list of her internal experiences while with him, and organized them according to the different key points outlined in the chapter. During the following therapy session, she educated the therapist about central aspects of her life with her husband and the labeling employed in the book to describe these experiences. This was a pivotal moment for her in feeling the power to start a process of separation from her husband. Exercising this power has been important not only for her, but also for her three growing daughters.

In summary, feminist therapists work to empower the eating disorder client using multiple strategies. Empowerment allows women to stay connected to their bodies, themselves, and others, while using these connections and their strengths to transform their social environment rather than discipline their own bodies.

KEY ELEMENT 3: CHANGE OCCURS IN THE CONTEXT OF RELATIONSHIPS

According to the self-in-relation model, women's positive connections to others validate their capacities as relational beings; provide the foundation for experiences of empowerment, competence, and self-esteem; and are central to their growth and well-being (Miller & Stiver, 1997). Feminist therapists honor the role of relationships for women in general and the power of relationships in facilitating processes of transformation and growth. Further, while being cognizant of differences in social contexts in terms of privilege and oppression, women therapists draw on their own social experiences as women to validate, amplify, and contextualize clients' telling of their own experiences (L. S. Brown, 1994).

Application to the Treatment of Eating Disorders

There are several reasons to highlight the therapy relationship in the treatment of eating disorders. The emphasis on autonomy, independence, and separation and the denigration of interdependence, symbolized by the idealization of the thin body shape and the rejection of the rounded female body, have been found in women who develop eating disorders (Steiner-Adair, 1991). Further, the silencing caused by trauma and despair that has led to the voiceless embodied expression of pain, struggle, and resistance found in eating disorders is impossible to reverse without the safety provided through the validation of pain, the acknowledged sharing of struggle by women, the respect for women's needs, as well as personal care and commitment (Steiner-Adair, 1991; Wooley, 1994). Learning through the therapy relationship to value women and their embodied and relational presence is an additional aspect of healing.

Clinical Example

An Interpersonal Experience of Acceptance and Mentoring (Hospital Outpatient Setting)

E., a 17-year-old, is the youngest of four girls. She lives in an upper middle-class neighborhood just outside a major city. Her parents are happily married, and both are successful professionally and financially. Her three older sisters have all excelled academically. All three are social and in committed relationships. E.'s family is Catholic but very liberal in their observance. In many ways, E.'s family is supportive, and her parents have raised daughters who are autonomous, empowered, and successful. E., however, is above average weight and has always been at least "plump" in a family where everyone else is naturally slender. In her attempt to diet and lose weight, she has developed binge eating disorder. E. has also chosen to be Wiccan, and her style of dress verges on Goth. Average in school, she is not sure that college is for her. She wants to travel and explore the world. She has not had a romantic relationship as an adolescent. She loves her family but feels like an outsider because of her obvious lack of success. She is the only one of her peers without a definite plan for college and professional success. She is not yet self-sufficient financially or personally and relies on her parents in developmentally appropriate ways. While there is no bad guy, it is clear that her family and social environment are disapproving of everything that makes E. unique and special; this has resulted in low self-esteem and frank self-dislike. Much of E.'s struggle could be corrected if she were older and could get out into the world and learn that her suburban experience is only one of an infinite variety of ways of living. However, she is not ready and, as yet, does not have the means to do this, as is true of most 17-year-old girls. Autonomy is a moot point when an individual, as part of normal development, is not ready to take it on.

The goal of therapy becomes how to value strengths and develop a counterculture appreciation of self in a relative vacuum. The most important function the therapist provided was to be supportive and admiring of E.'s struggles and thoughts as she moved toward self-knowledge. Having an adult woman to talk to, to admire, and to be admired by was the most useful part of treatment for E. The therapist played an important mentorship role. Part of the process included a judicious use of self-disclosure. The therapist let E. know that she herself had been considered weird as a teenager and had struggled with not fitting into her suburban culture. However, in growing up and leaving home, she was able to find a place where she fit in and had been able to create a life she was comfortable with. As well, deconstructing the cultural myth that high school years are supposed to be the best time of a person's life was also useful. E. came to the conclusion that it would be sad if that myth were true because that would mean that, at 18 years old, it would all be downhill for the next 70 years. E. was given permission to struggle through her adolescence as part of her route toward individuation and autonomy and to feel normal in that process, even in an environment that provided her with few real options. She was also able to see herself in her body and find it acceptable as she rejected some of the cultural demands for thinness that were oppressing her. Her eating symptoms slowly began to improve.

KEY ELEMENT 4: FEMINIST THERAPY FOCUSES ON STRENGTHS AND CREATIVE RESISTANCE

Feminist therapy emphasizes strengths and creativity in clients' responses to adverse circumstances. Rather than view behavioral responses to oppressive conditions as reflecting pathological deficits, feminist therapy frames these behavioral responses as understandable reactions to pathological conditions (Worell & Remer, 1992). The coping function of "symptoms" is, therefore, emphasized and respected in the process of therapy. It is also of value to recognize that in traditional mental health contexts, women's adaptations to cultural expectations (e.g., through behaving submissively or helplessly), as well as their resistance to such adaptations (e.g., through behaving assertively), may both be labeled as pathologies (Sturdivant, 1980).

Application to the Treatment of Eating Disorders

Viewing eating "symptomatology" as understandable coping strategies reflecting both adaptation and resistance to disruptive and oppressive contexts rather than framing them as reflecting intraindividual pathological deficits affects therapy in a most profound way. It legitimizes and validates the struggle expressed through the disordered eating patterns and, hence, encourages the challenging process of speaking what is initially unspeakable (Bordo, 1993; Steiner-Adair, 1991; Wooley, 1994). It implies that the energy and resourcefulness that have been invested in employing disordered eating patterns for the sake of survival can be gradually shifted toward longer term growth

(L. S. Brown, 1994). Further, it works toward balancing power inequities and control in the relationship, avoiding a sick versus healthy partnership (C. Brown, 1994). Last, it guides therapists to critically examine their own conceptualization of eating disorders as well as treatment and prevention practices (Bordo, 1993; Piran, 1999; Steiner-Adair, 1991; Wooley, 1994). For example, a client who is labeled *borderline* and *resistant* in a hospital setting where no safe forum is available to relate past experiences of trauma needs to continue and employ *survival* strategies, such as disordered eating patterns.

Clinical Example

Legitimizing the Search for Autonomy and Connection (Inpatient Setting)

R., a 15-year-old girl, was admitted to the hospital severely underweight. This was her 10th admission in three years; with each admission, she arrived weighing less and less and more and more severely medically compromised. R. could not keep herself healthy or safe and was seen as at serious risk of dying. She had spent most of the past three years either losing weight by severe restriction or getting renourished in the hospital. In both situations, she had little opportunity to engage in academic or social tasks that are normal to this age group. When at home, she lived with her mother and four younger siblings. She helped her mother with child care and housework and saw herself as her mother's assistant. The working hypothesis at the hospital, up to the last admission, was that this family had to become more motivated to recover, and the hospital's job was to keep the girl medically stable.

During this admission, R.'s care was transferred to a new psychiatrist, a woman who identified herself as a feminist. The new psychiatrist strongly recommended that R. stay in the hospital past the point of medical stabilization, to a weight that was closer to a healthy weight for her. She also recommended that instead of a discharge, a series of gradually longer passes be put into place to help R. integrate back to her home. A third recommendation was that R. not be discharged until there was a treatment program in place for her as an outpatient. With much support from the staff, R.'s mother was able to insist her daughter stay in the hospital and stick to the recommendations. The psychiatrist then spent time getting to know the patient and helping her think about what she wanted in her life and who she wanted to grow up to be. She also focused on whether the eating disorder was helping R. get what she wanted out of her life. R. felt she had a very positive and close relationship with her mother. She also felt that her mother had had a very difficult life raising five children on her own, and she wanted to help and support her mother. Being the oldest girl, R. worked hard throughout her childhood to be a good girl and to not give her mother any trouble. On reaching adolescence, however, experiencing and sharing her mother's burden, R. understandably struggled with her legitimate wish to grow and individuate in the context of maintaining her familial relationships. R. needed to rebel and be persistent with her wishes for individuation, while not disrupting her helping role at home. Her body then became her only domain of rebellion.

The treatment focused on supporting R. in steps to develop into an autonomous adult in the context of her relationships. Clearer limit setting gave her the emotional space to grow in tune with her own needs. R. was supported to individuate in more social and relational ways. Her mother worked to demonstrate a tolerance for individuation, and the patient was supported in seeing that she could be close to her mother and still get on with her own life. R.'s mother, for example, shifted from a long-term plan of having R. go to college in the city to a plan that affirmed R.'s wish to leave home while keeping connection with her mother. Affirming the validity of R.'s struggle for growth in relations was crucial to the gradual process of her recovery.

KEY ELEMENT 5: CREATING AN ALTERNATIVE RELATIONAL SUBVERSIVE SPACE

Feminist therapy aims to create a relational therapy space that counteracts adverse societal pressures. Creating more equitable dynamics and empowering the client in the therapy relationship is one such aspect. Feminist therapists aim to challenge beliefs about confining gender expectation, such as exclusive parenting by women, deference by women to authority figures, or only indirect expressions of anger toward others. Aspects of women's lives that have been both idealized and demeaned in the culture at large, such as mothering or women's relational capacities or interests, are being valued positively in the therapy. Voicing silenced aspects of women's lives, such as experiences of trauma, including the insidious trauma of facing daily expressions of prejudicial treatment, is another goal of feminist therapy (Wooley, 1994: Wyche & Rice, 1997). Feminist therapists are aware of the intersecting forms of oppression and do not privilege sexism over other forms of prejudice. Challenging constraining and oppressive social structures and prejudices allows for a process of rediscovery, empowering women to value and free multiple aspects of themselves (Worell & Remer, 1992). To facilitate the creation of such an alternative relational space, a feminist therapist has to examine the impact of her own social history on her internalization of oppression, privilege, constraining, and disruptive images of women (Bernandez, 1987).

Application to the Treatment of Body Weight and Shape Disorders

Women's and girls' problematic status in society has led to disruptive embodiment (Fine, 1992; Larkin et al., 1999; Piran, 2001b, 2002; Tolman, 1991). Feminist work of valuing women and women's lives and of supporting and cherishing new options of behavior and experience, such as owning appetites (Bordo, 1993); desires (Tolman, 1991); anger (Jack, 1991); power, talents, and ambition (Worell & Remer, 1992); and voice for the unspeakable (Wooley, 1994), are central in allowing women to be both powerful and embodied (Piran, 2002; Piran et al., 2002). Multiple widely sanctioned prejudices must be addressed to create an alternative and subversive relational space related not only to gender, but also, for example, to race, class, ethnic group membership, sexual orientation, or health status. The prejudice of adultism when working with adolescents has to be recognized as well (Dickerson, 1999). In providing an alternative relational space, the feminist therapist must be open to her own embodied oppressions and privileges (L. S. Brown, 1994: Steiner-Adair, 1991).

Case Example

Therapist Dealing with Internalized Oppression
(Outpatient Hospital Setting)

D., a 30-year-old woman, was treated in a hospital setting. In a session following the birth of a child to the therapist, the client stared at the therapist's stomach and said with great aversion, "You still have a big stomach." The therapist, who was cherishing having a child after years of wishing to have one and who felt accepting and even excited by the bodily changes that followed birth, unexpectedly felt shame about her stomach. This experience disallowed her to deal with the important material that came up right there and then in the therapy relationship. She, therefore, could also not convey or model to the client her positive experience of her body and its changes following pregnancy and birth. Following the session, the therapist reexamined her own shorter and longer term social history. In the shorter term, in the place of her work and because of her administrative role, her pregnancy was seen negatively as an "ill timed," "self-centered," "irresponsible" act. In the all-male administrative team meetings, her preoccupation with how her baby was doing at home seemed out of place and was kept "hidden." In her longer history, the therapist had absorbed multiple deprecating messages about mothers and motherhood. It was very important for the therapist to reexamine the impact of these internalized multiple oppressions following the birth of her first child and reconnect with her own sense of celebration of a full and fertile woman's body and her shifting roles and connections. This reflection allowed the therapist to be open to asking the client about her experience of the therapist's changed body shape and validate the ongoing challenges women face to body and self-acceptance, especially at times of meaningful transitions in their lives, such as puberty, pregnancy, or menopause. For this client, witnessing the therapist's acceptance of her rounder shape following pregnancy with no associated compromise in self-esteem was important.

KEY ELEMENT 6: FEMINIST THERAPY WORKS TOWARD SOCIAL TRANSFORMATION

Many feminist therapists work toward the goal of social transformation aimed at equitable social conditions for women and for other oppressed groups. This work can range from mobilizing women clients in therapy to make changes and educate significant people in their personal lives to, at the other end of the continuum, larger scale involvement in social action (Enns, 1997; Whalen, 1996). A large number of feminist therapists and researchers in the field of eating disorders have carried through work aimed at social and professional transformations. It is common to find feminist therapists in the field of eating disorders engage in larger educational and proactive preventative projects where they also clarify the political nature of their work. The ground-breaking volume *Feminist Perspectives on Eating Disorders* edited by Fallon, Katzman, and Wooley (1994) is one such example. Works such as C. Brown and Jasper (1993); Davis (1996); Friedman (1999); Irving (1999); Kearney-Cook and Striegel-Moore (1994); Larkin et al. (1999); Maine (2000); Orbach (1986); Piran, Levine, and Steiner-Adair (1999); Rabinor (1994); Root (1994); and Sigall and Pabst

(2002), among many other contributions, reflect the investment toward the cause of social and professional transformations.

CONCLUSION

The feminist approach to therapy with eating disorder clients has been applied to outpatient, day hospital, and inpatient settings. The application of a feminist frame to therapy, a frame defined by several key dimensions outlined in the chapter, allows for the use of different therapeutic techniques. In addition to being a therapeutic tool, feminist therapy contributes to the ongoing development of social etiological models for eating disorders because the process of therapy involves the critical examination of social experiences that disrupt women's experiences of their bodies and their selves (Piran, 2001a). The critical examination of living in a gendered body still needs to be incorporated into the wider professional literature. Feminist therapists, therefore, aim not only at therapeutic effectiveness but also at professional and social transformations.

REFERENCES

Bartky, S. L. (1988). Foucault, femininity, and the modernization of patriarchal power. In I. Diamond & L. Quinby (Eds.), *Feminism & Foucault: Reflections on resistance* (pp. 61–86). Boston: Northeastern University Press.

Bernandez, T. (1987). Gender based countertransference of female therapists in the psychotherapy of women. *Women and Therapy, 6*(2), 25–39.

Bordo, S. (1993). *Unbearable weight: Feminism, Western culture, and the body.* Berkeley: University of California Press.

Brooks-Gunn, J., & Reiter, E. O. (1990). The role of pubertal processes. In S. S. Feldman & G. R. Elliot (Eds.), *At the threshold* (pp. 17–53). Boston: Harvard Business School Press.

Brown, C., & Jasper, K. (1993). *Consuming passions.* Toronto, Ontario, Canada: Second Story Press.

Brown, L. S. (1994). *Subversive dialogues.* New York: HarperCollins.

Buchwald, E., Fletcher, P., & Roth, M. (1993). *Transforming a rape culture.* Minneapolis, MN: Milkweed Editions.

Dare, C., & Eisler, I. (2000). A multifamily group day treatment program for adolescent eating disorder. *European Eating Disorders Review, 8,* 4–18.

Davis, W. (1996). The last word. *Eating Disorders: Journal of Treatment and Prevention, 4,* 382–384.

Dickerson, V. (1999). *Narrative therapy with children, youth, and families.* Yaletown Narrative Therapy Training Program presentation, Toronto, Ontario, Canada.

Enns, C. Z. (1997). *Feminist theories and feminist psychotherapies: Origins, themes, and variations.* New York: Harrington Park Press.

Faith, K., Pinhas, L., Schmelefske, J., & Bryden, P. (2001). *Day treatment for adolescent eating disorders: Developing a feminist-informed model of care.* Southlake Regional Health Care Center, unpublished manuscript.

Fallon, P., Katzman, M. A., & Wooley, S. C. (Eds.). (1994). *Feminist perspectives on eating disorders* (pp. 171–211). New York: Guilford Press.

Fine, M. (1992). *Disruptive voices: The possibilities of feminist research.* Ann Arbor: University of Michigan Press.

Foucault, M. (1979). *Discipline and punish: The birth of the prison.* New York: Vintage Books.

Friedman, S. F. (1999). Discussion groups for girls: Decoding the language of fat. In N. Piran, M. P. Levine, & C. Steiner-Adair (Eds.), *Preventing eating disorders: A handbook of interventions and special challenges* (pp. 122–133). Philadelphia: Brunner/Mazel.

Herman, J. L. (1992). *Trauma and recovery.* New York: Basic Books.

Irving, L. M. (1999). A bolder model of prevention: Science, practice, and activism. In N. Piran, M. P. Levine, & C. Steiner-Adair (Eds.), *Preventing eating disorders: A handbook of interventions and special challenges* (pp. 63–83). Philadelphia: Brunner/Mazel.

Jack, D. C. (1991). *Silencing the self: Women and depression.* Cambridge, MA: Harvard University Press.

Kearney-Cooke, A., & Striegel-Moore, R. H. (1994). Treatment of childhood sexual abuse in anorexia nervosa and bulimia nervosa: A feminist psychodynamic approach. *International Journal of Eating Disorders, 15,* 305–319.

Larkin, J., Rice, C., & Russell, V. (1999). Sexual harassment and the prevention of eating disorders: Educating young women. In N. Piran, M. P. Levine, & C. Steiner-Adair (Eds.), *Preventing eating disorders: A handbook of interventions and special challenges* (pp. 194–206). Philadelphia: Brunner/Mazel.

MacKinnon, C. A. (1989). *Toward a feminist theory of the state.* Cambridge MA: Harvard University Press.

Mainc, M. (2000). *Body wars: Making peace with women's bodies (An activist's guide).* Carlsbad, CA: Gurze Books.

Marx, K. (1963). *The poverty of philosophy.* New York: International Universities Press.

Miller, J. B., & Stiver, I. P. (1997). *The healing connection.* Boston: Beacon Press.

Orbach, S. (1986). *Hunger strike.* New York: Norton.

Piran, N. (1999). The reduction of preoccupation with body weight and shape in schools: A feminist approach. In N. Piran, M. P. Levine, & C. Steiner-Adair (Eds.), *A handbook of interventions and special challenges* (pp. 148–159). Philadelphia: Brunner/Mazel.

Piran, N. (2001a). A gendered perspective on eating disorders and disordered eating. In J. Worell (Ed.), *Encyclopedia of gender* (pp. 369–378). San Diego, CA: Academic Press.

Piran, N. (2001b). Re-inhabiting the body from the inside out: Girls transform their school environment. In D. L. Tolman & M. Brydon-Miller (Eds.), *From subjects to subjectivities: A handbook of interpretive and participatory methods* (pp. 218–238). New York: New York University Press.

Piran, N. (2002). Embodiment: A mosaic of inquiries in the area of body weight and shape preoccupation. In S. Abbey (Ed.), *Ways of knowing in and through the body: Diverse perspectives on embodiment* (pp. 211–214). Welland, Ontario, Canada: Soleil.

Piran, N., Carter, W., Thompson, S., & Pajouhandeh, P. (2002). Powerful girls: A contradiction in terms? Young women speak about growing up in a girl's body. In S. Abbey (Ed.), *Ways of knowing in and through the body: Diverse perspectives on embodiment* (pp. 206–210). Welland, Ontario, Canada: Soleil.

Piran, N., Levine, M. P., & Steiner-Adair, C. (1999). *A handbook of interventions and special challenges.* Philadelphia: Brunner/Mazel.

Rabinor, J. R. (1994). Mothers, daughters, and eating disorders: Honoring the mother-daughter relationship. In P. Fallon, M. A. Katzman, & S. C. Wooley (Eds.), *Feminist perspectives on eating disorders* (pp. 272–286). New York: Guilford Press.

Rich, A. (1986). *Of woman born* (p. 285). New York: Norton.

Root, M. P. P. (1994). Mixed-race women. In L. Comas-Diaz & B. Greene (Eds.), *Women of color: Integrating ethnic and gender identities in psychotherapy* (pp. 455–478). New York: Guilford Press.

Sigall, B. A., & Pabst, M. S. (2002, April). *Gender literacy: Activities and interventions.* Paper presented at the Academy for Eating Disorders International Conference on Eating Disorders, Boston.

Steiner-Adair, C. (1991). When the body speaks: Girls, eating disorders and psychotherapy. In C. Gilligan, A. G. Rogers, & D. L. Tolman (Eds.), *Women, girls, & psychotherapy* (pp. 253–266). New York: Harrington Park Press.

Sturdivant, S. (1980). *Therapy with women: A feminist philosophy of treatment.* New York: Springer.

Tolman, D. L. (1991). Adolescent girls, women and sexuality: Discerning dilemmas of desire. In C. Gilligan, A. G. Rogers, & D. L. Tolman (Eds.), *Women, girls, & psychotherapy* (pp. 55–69). New York: Harrington Park Press.

Whalen, M. B. (1996). *Counseling to end violence against women.* Thousand Oaks, CA: Sage.

Wipfler, P. (1995). *Supporting adolescents.* Palo Alto, CA: Parents Leadership Institute.

Wooley, S. C. (1994). Sexual abuse and eating disorders: The concealed debate. In P. Fallon, M. A. Katzman, & S. C. Wooley (Eds.), *Feminist perspectives on eating disorders* (pp. 171–211). New York: Guilford Press.

Worell, J., & Remer, P. (1992). *Feminist perspectives in therapy.* New York: Wiley.

Wyche, K. F., & Rice, J. K. (1997). Feminist therapy: From dialogue to tenets. In J. Worell & N. G. Johnson (Eds.), *Shaping the future of feminist psychology: Education, research, and practice* (pp. 57–71). Washington, DC: American Psychological Association.

Chapter 14

INTERNET-BASED TREATMENT STRATEGIES

ANDREW J. WINZELBERG, KRISTINE H. LUCE, AND LIANA B. ABASCAL

With the introduction of low-cost computers and the rapid expansion of the Internet, health care providers are developing ways to use these tools to improve physical and mental health treatments. In this chapter, we first review advantages of Internet-delivered interventions; next, we look at recent developments in the use of technology for the treatment of eating disorders. Then, we consider potential future uses of this technology. Finally, we discuss many of the ethical issues concerning the use of Internet-based psychotherapeutic treatments.

A recent Pew Foundation survey (Rainie & Packel, 2001) on Internet use found that 104 million American adults reported having Internet access at the end of the year 2000. Although income disparities among individuals who have Internet access remain, the gap is narrowing. By the end of 2000, 38% of households who reported an annual income of less than $30,000 had Internet access, compared to 28% of like-ranked households in June 2000. Among households that reported having a $75,000 or greater annual income, 82% reported having Internet access.

In a more current Pew Foundation report (Fox & Rainie, 2002), the authors indicated that 62% of all Internet users and 72% of female Internet users reported seeking health information on the Internet. Slightly more than half of health seekers were between the ages of 18 and 29. On a typical day, six million Americans go online for health information, and a recent report by the Acting Director of the National Institute of Mental Health (NIMH) to the National Advisory Mental Health Council (2002) stated that the NIMH public information Web site received more than seven million "hits" in one month.

According to the Pew Foundation report (Fox & Rainie, 2002), 70% of those who sought health information reported that the information they received influenced their treatment decisions. Sixty-five percent of health seekers sought information on nutrition, exercise, or weight control; 39% sought mental health information; and 33% sought information about "a sensitive topic that is difficult to talk about." Nine percent of health seekers have participated in an Internet-delivered support group, and 14% of health seekers, who describe themselves as being in fair or poor health, have participated in an Internet-delivered support group. Despite the wide use of the Internet to solicit health information, the majority of users (86%) expressed concern about the reliability of the information they received. The Pew Foundation report (Fox & Rainie, 2002) found that anonymity and on-demand contact were the most frequently cited reasons for seeking online health information. Thus, it appears that Americans not only are interested in, but also actively seek out, information related to health and health care on the Internet despite being somewhat skeptical about the information they receive.

COMPONENTS

Internet-delivered interventions fall into two broad categories: the delivery of *information* and the delivery of *communication*. Information can be presented in the form of text, audio, pictures, video, and animation. As a communication vehicle, the Internet is used to connect two or more people. It can be private (e.g., electronic mail or e-mail) or public (e.g., a listserv). Messages can be delivered synchronously (i.e., real-time) in the form of chat rooms or instant messaging or asynchronously in the form of e-mail, newsgroups, and bulletin boards. Both synchronous and asynchronous communications are used to deliver support group and doctor-patient correspondence. Although we typically think of the communication that occurs on the Internet as text-based, it can also occur via audio and video.

Internet technology has the ability to solicit user input and tailor the output that is displayed based on individual input. This program feature is seen on many commercial Web sites. For example, a Web site that sells books may tailor the output content of the Web site based on the purchase history of the user. The next time the user who purchases health-related materials logs onto the Web site, similar related texts that reflect the individual purchasing pattern of the user appear on the screen. For mental health interventions, a program can be designed to selectively display information based on patient input and scoring on assessment instruments. Programs also can be designed to include role playing, simulations, and self-monitoring. For example, a self-monitoring log sheet can easily be adapted for this format to solicit information about a patient's thoughts, mood, social context, food intake, and physical activity. Because computer programs can be programmed to sort data by any number of variables (e.g., mood, social context), they are ideally suited to help patients identify patterns (e.g., engaging in binge eating when lonely). Once patterns are identified, they can be linked to specific suggestions for behavior modification (e.g., call a friend). Furthermore, programs can be designed to prompt patients to engage in contracted behaviors (e.g., e-mail or telephone reminder to eat regularly scheduled meals).

Further advances in microcomputers and cellular technology offer even more immediate connections to the Internet by use of handheld devices, such as cellular phones and personal digital assistants (e.g., Palm Pilot). This immediacy facilitates the real-time assessment of thoughts, feelings, and behavior and on-demand communication with others (e.g., seeking social support to prevent purging).

ADVANTAGES

Numerous advantages of using Internet-based interventions have been purported by providers and researchers. These potential advantages include, but are not limited to:

- Cost effectiveness.
- Availability and accessibility.
- Efficiency.
- Perceived anonymity, privacy, and confidentiality.
- Flexibility.

Although these advantages are frequently cited, research has yet to empirically demonstrate that Internet interventions actually provide the benefits that clinicians and researchers purport.

Cost Effectiveness

Compared to traditional face-to-face assessment and intervention, ones that are Internet-based have the potential to be more cost effective for four main reasons. First, after the initial design costs, maintenance of the system is relatively inexpensive and the marginal cost of treating additional patients is relatively low. For example, Houston and colleagues (2001) adapted the Center for Epidemiological Studies' depression scale (CES-D; Ogles, France, Lunnen, Bell, & Goldfarb, 1998) for the online assessment of depression. To assess more than 24,000 individuals, the authors reported that fixed costs totaled $9,000 and marginal costs for maintenance totaled $3,750, which is remarkably inexpensive compared to assessments requiring human interaction. Online assessment reduces labor and costs involved in photocopying and mailing questionnaires, a portion of which are never returned (Marks, 1999).

The second reason Internet-based assessments and interventions are more cost effective is that Internet-based psychoeducation material can be easily and economically updated and widely disseminated (Marks, 1999). Third, provider involvement can be reduced and, in the case of group interventions, groups can be moderated by a paraprofessional or peer (e.g., see www.something-fishy.org or http://boards.webmd.lycos.com/roundtable). The potential to reduce the economic burden of traditional interventions may give individuals who are economically disadvantaged the opportunity to obtain mental health services that they otherwise would not be able to afford. Finally, a quicker recovery may result from using the Internet as an adjunct to face-to-face psychotherapy because therapeutic work can occur beyond the standard 50-minute therapy session (Marks, 1999).

Availability and Accessibility

Provided that an individual has access to a computer and an active Internet connection, interventions delivered over the Internet can be made available continuously. Internet-delivered programs also have the potential to be accessed multiple times a week.

In comparison, face-to-face mental health interventions can be difficult to schedule because of constraints placed on personnel and physical resources. Consequently, many clinics (e.g., HMOs) and providers have long waiting lists requiring patients to wait months before an initial intake or assessment appointment. Internet interventions can reduce the time between initiating services and obtaining an appointment, thereby potentially minimizing or preventing exacerbation of symptoms. Face-to-face interventions also may be difficult to access because of patient limitations. Internet interventions may be particularly beneficial for individuals who work nonstandard hours, who travel (e.g., athletes, dancers), who are physically or psychiatrically disabled (e.g., agoraphobia), or who live in rural communities. In particular, adolescents and young adults with academic commitments and limited access to transportation may find the accessibility of Internet-delivered interventions appealing.

Efficiency

Internet-delivered interventions have the potential to reduce clinician burden with administrative tasks (Marks, 1999). For example, e-mail has been effectively used to recruit and assess potential participants for a treatment trial for bulimia nervosa (Robinson & Serfaty, 2001). Internet-based assessment may reduce measurement error (Marks, 1999). For example, computers can be programmed to direct respondents to answer only relevant questions, verify their responses, directly download data to a computer database, and score questionnaires immediately and precisely. If needed, data collected from automated questionnaires can be followed by a provider-directed interview that focuses on treatment-relevant concerns. As to use of the Internet for therapy-related tasks, Yager (2001) argues that using e-mail as an adjunct to psychotherapy is a time-efficient strategy that enhances treatment effectiveness. Standardized treatment protocols that are adapted for the Internet are less vulnerable to varying from an established treatment protocol because protocol adherence is hard-coded into the program. Electronic storage of medical records is also more easily automated with Internet-delivered interventions. For example, e-mail between provider and patient or documentation of participation in an Internet-delivered structured intervention could be automatically appended to a patient's medical record.

Anonymity, Privacy, and Confidentiality

Among the most attractive features of Internet interventions for patients is the perception of anonymity. Participants have the option of participating in psychotherapy from the privacy of their own homes and further concealing their identity by using aliases rather than real names or identifying information. Furthermore, the Internet format has the potential to equalize demographic variables such as age, ethnicity, and economic status (Winzelberg, 1997) and to reduce fears of stigmatization from patients concerned with their physical characteristics (e.g., obesity, physical disability). Internet interventions may be particularly attractive to mental health providers who wish to receive their own treatment, public figures, or residents of small communities who prefer to remain anonymous. Moreover, some participants may feel more comfortable disclosing sensitive personal information when they participate in Internet interventions because they perceive their communications to be anonymous and confidential (Newman, Consoli, & Taylor, 1997).

Flexibility

Internet technology is perhaps most appealing because of its flexibility. It is easy to combine psychoeducation programs with individual and group treatments. Internet-delivered group interventions can be moderated by a professional, paraprofessional, or layperson synchronously or asynchronously. The main advantages of synchronous groups are that they occur in real time and most closely resemble face-to-face support groups. The main advantages of asynchronous groups are that participants can review and respond to messages at their own convenience after thoughtful consideration and with the opportunity to edit their response (Childress, 2000). Winzelberg et al. (2003) reported that members of a Web-based asynchronous support group often spent more than one hour composing a message.

Internet-based interventions can be developed to allow participants to self-select content that is relevant to their unique situation. Self-directed programs allow participants to choose the pace at which they spend time reviewing or revisiting material. Alternately, a program can be designed in which the pace and session content are directed by the provider. Furthermore, computer algorithms based on participant responses to questionnaires and screening criteria can selectively direct the content so that patients who are participating in the same overall group intervention are simultaneously receiving individualized feedback and selective content.

CURRENT STATUS OF INTERNET-DELIVERED PROGRAMS

Despite the widespread interest in the Internet and the rapid expansion of mental health services provided through the Internet, it is somewhat surprising that no randomized clinical trials to evaluate Internet-delivered treatments for women with full syndrome eating disorders have been reported. Dozens of eating disorder support groups function on the World Wide Web and on commercial servers (e.g., see www.support-group.com). Most support groups have been initiated by patients and are either unmoderated or peer-moderated. Published reports of Internet-delivered eating disorder interventions fall into four categories:

1. Adjuncts to face-to-face treatments.
2. E-mail-delivered individual treatments.
3. Structured interventions designed for women who are selected for participation because they acknowledge having subthreshold symptomatology or they are determined to be at higher risk for developing eating disorders based on theoretically driven criteria.
4. Unstructured support groups.

All of the interventions that have been evaluated empirically included some type of human interaction. Participants interacted with a therapist, group moderator, or other group members. None of the interventions followed an entirely psychoeducational approach (e.g., workbook, video) whereby the participant was completely and independently self-guided through the material.

Three reports examined e-mail-based interventions. In the first, Yager (2001) used case examples to illustrate how e-mail can be used as an adjunct to standard face-to-face treatment for anorexia nervosa. Yager describes how e-mail, in addition to facilitating administrative tasks (e.g., scheduling appointments) and refilling of prescriptions, can be used to provide emotional support, monitor dietary intake, and maintain contact with patients during the referral process to ensure continuity of care. Yager further indicated that patients who had e-mail contact with him several times a week reported high levels of satisfaction and treatment adherence. To illustrate how emotional support is conveyed by a provider, an excerpt from an e-mail interaction with a 17-year-old female follows:

> Dr. Yager, Hi there sir. How are you? I'm ok. Not great. Yesterday in gym I was wearing an outfit that I haven't worn in a while . . . it felt different. I starting thinking about and noticing my body more. It sucked. . . . I feel awkward and a little sad about stuff, mostly my body and boys . . . I just feel kinda blahh last night and a little today too. Thanx for reading (listening sorta). I'll talk to you more on Thursday. Bye-bye. S
>
> His response: Hi S—I'm glad to be able to comfort you. You're really on the right track, and "slumps happen." See you tomorrow. JY (p. 127)

Second, Sansone (2001) similarly used case examples to illustrate how e-mail can be used as an adjunct to standard face-to-face psychotherapy. Sansone used e-mail to introduce patients with limited social support to one another. In contrast to Yager, Sansone did not report interacting with patients via e-mail or participating in the dialog between patients but used the electronic medium to help patients increase their social support network. Sansone used e-mail to introduce patients who were relatively well matched on level of social isolation, commitment to treatment, and the availability of a reasonable match with another patient.

Finally, in a small, uncontrolled study, Robinson and Serfaty (2001) evaluated the use of e-mail to recruit individuals with probable bulimia nervosa for an online psychotherapeutic intervention. In response to the authors' single e-mail to 20,000 staff and students at a London college, 52 women expressed interest in the study. Robinson and Serfaty estimated that one in three potential participants responded to the recruitment effort. Respondents were sent by e-mail an information sheet, consent form, and assessment questionnaires. Individuals who met the inclusion criteria for a probable diagnosis of bulimia nervosa were randomly assigned to one of two psychiatrists who provided either cognitive-behavioral or integrative-based treatment exclusively by e-mail. Although the intervention was not standardized or structured, participants were required, at a minimum, to maintain a food and symptom diary that they e-mailed to their psychiatrist twice a week. Weekly reminders were sent to participants who were noncompliant. The authors indicated that the skills required to provide treatment via e-mail were easily adapted from face-to-face treatment approaches. After three months of treatment, participants were found to have significantly reduced symptoms of depression and bulimia nervosa. Compliance, which was measured by the number of words sent in the e-mail, was significantly correlated with outcome. Participant satisfaction with the treatment modality was high, and retention was no different from what the authors observed in their face-to-face clinical work.

To our knowledge, the first Internet-delivered eating disorder intervention that was evaluated in a randomized trial targeted college-age women who were selected for participation because they acknowledged having subthreshold eating disorder symptomatology or high weight and shape concerns (Celio et al., 2000; Winzelberg et al., 1998, 2000). The goals of the program, *Student Bodies,* were to help women reduce their weight and shape concerns and develop healthier eating attitudes and practices. The design of *Student Bodies* incorporates content from the *Road to Recovery* psychoeducational intervention developed by Davis and colleagues (Davis et al., 1989), the binge eating intervention developed by Fairburn and colleagues (Fairburn & Carter, 1996; Fairburn et al., 1995), and the cognitive-behavioral body image interventions developed by Cash (1991).

Student Bodies had three central components and was divided into eight sessions. The components were psychoeducational readings, a Web-based body image journal, and a moderated asynchronous discussion group. The readings were selected to educate women about body image, healthy dietary and physical activity practices, and eating disorders. The body image journal allowed participants to monitor events that triggered body image dissatisfaction as well as ensuing thoughts and feelings about their body. The asynchronous discussion group gave participants a place to post their reactions to the group content and to receive from and provide to other group members emotional support. The discussion group was not designed to be a form of psychotherapy nor was it intended to replace psychotherapy, and this was clearly disclosed to participants at the onset. Rather, the primary role of the moderator was to encourage discussion. The moderator was responsible for identifying members who were disruptive to the group or who might be experiencing a psychiatric emergency. The following example illustrates how a participant used the discussion group to reflect on her own behavior and beliefs:

> My sister is 14, and she has been comparing herself to the girls in her class for about two years now. I know that she has learned to do this by watching me and my mother constantly criticize our own bodies and from being teased about her weight at school. Recently, she was feeling really depressed about her body, and my family wanted me to compliment my sister on her losing weight. I refused.
>
> My reasoning was this: I am happy to compliment my sister on something that she has control over, like school, or her acting, but when you base your self-worth on whether or not you lose weight, you are destined to feel bad, because you can always lose more. Unfortunately, as easy as it is for me to say this, I have trouble acting upon it. It feels like my future depends on whether or not I can lose those last five pounds . . . at least I can try not to perpetuate the cycle in my sister.

Since the creation of the *Student Bodies* program, six iterations have been developed and evaluated. Each new version of the program has been revised to incorporate research findings and feedback from participants. The first four versions of the program were evaluated with college-age women in controlled trials (Celio et al., 2000; Winzelberg et al., 1998, 2000; Zabinski, Pung, et al., 2001). Overall, although the effect sizes have been small to moderate, ranging from 0.23 to 0.54, the results demonstrate that participants report significant improvements in weight and shape concerns and healthier eating attitudes and behaviors.

More recently, *Student Bodies* was evaluated in a high school-age female sample (Abascal, 2001; Bruning-Brown, Winzelberg, Abascal, & Taylor, 2001). Bruning-Brown and colleagues (2001) examined students who completed the *Student Bodies* intervention as part of their required health course curriculum. To expand the scope of the treatment, Bruning-Brown et al. added a parent intervention to the *Student Bodies* program. Noting that previous literature demonstrated that familial factors contribute to the development of eating disorders (Levine, Smolak, & Hayden, 1994; Pike & Rodin, 1991; Smolak, Levine, & Schermer, 1998; Stice, Agras, & Hammer, 1998; Striegel-Moore & Kearney-Cooke, 1994; Taylor et al., 1998), Bruning-Brown and colleagues created an Internet-delivered intervention for parents whose daughters were concurrently completing the *Student Bodies* program. The goal of the intervention was to encourage parents to develop healthier attitudes about weight and shape concerns. The program challenged parents to examine whether they perpetuate unhealthy attitudes about weight and shape and to recognize the signs and symptoms of disordered eating. Compared to parents in the control group, parents who were assigned to complete the parent intervention reported significant decreases on measures that assessed critical attitudes about weight and shape. Effect sizes for the parent intervention were small to moderate, ranging from 0.48 to 0.61. Unfortunately, Bruning-Brown et al. found only small changes in students' eating behaviors and weight and shape concerns at postintervention, and these results were not maintained at follow-up.

In subsequent work with female high school students, Abascal and colleagues (Abascal, Bruning, Winzelberg, Dev, & Taylor, in press) used the flexibility that is inherent in Internet technology to simultaneously provide a universal and a targeted intervention in two studies with more than 250 students. Abascal stratified students by their level of risk for eating disorder psychopathology (i.e., higher and lower weight and shape concerns) and motivation to improve their body image (i.e., higher and lower motivation). Students in the same classroom were then assigned to universal (i.e., designed for the general population) and targeted (i.e., designed for a specific high-risk population) curriculums without the participants' awareness of being assigned to different groups. Students were assigned to one of three conditions: (1) higher risk and greater motivation, (2) lower risk and lesser motivation, or (3) combined. At the postintervention assessment, participants who were identified as being at higher risk reported significant improvements on measures of weight and shape concerns. Overall, Abascal found small to moderate effect sizes that ranged from 0.30 to 0.75.

In a later study (Abascal et al., in press), students in four classrooms were assigned to one of four groups: (1) higher risk and greater motivation, (2) higher risk and lesser motivation, (3) lower risk and lesser motivation, or (4) lower risk and greater motivation. Overall, groups with participants who acknowledged having greater motivation (i.e., groups 1 and 4) reported significant improvements on measures of weight and shape concerns. Participants in the other two groups (i.e., groups 2 and 3) reported no change. Students in the higher risk and greater motivation group (i.e., group 1) posted more positive and fewer negative comments in the group discussion than did participants in the other three groups (i.e., groups 2, 3, and 4). The following example illustrates how a student used the discussion group to acknowledge her own success:

This past weekend I overcame an incredible stumbling block in my life. I got up in the morning and went for a run. I put on my little shoes and went out into the cold and ran all alone for fifteen minutes. I am still so proud of myself. And today after school I think that I will do it again. I think that part of the reason I am doing it is because of Student Bodies. I am realizing that I need to keep my body healthy. So, yea for me!

Another innovative approach has been used to treat women with high weight and shape concerns and subclinical eating disorder symptoms (Zabinski, Pung, et al., 2001; Zabinski, Wilfley, et al., 2001). Zabinski, Wilfley, and colleagues (2001) designed a combined synchronous chat room, asynchronous newsgroup, and e-mail psychoeducational intervention. In the most recent study (Zabinski, Wilfley, et al., 2001), 60 college-age women who acknowledge having high weight and shape concerns were randomly assigned to either the intervention or to a wait-list control group. Ten participants were assigned to each group. Participants in the intervention group interacted in the synchronous chat room for one hour each week for eight weeks. In addition to participating in the synchronous group interaction, participants were expected to complete psychoeducational readings and cognitive-behavioral therapy exercises, and they were provided optional access to an asynchronous support group. Participants were sent, via e-mail, brief weekly summaries of the synchronous chat room discussions.

The content of the group sessions was structured and included themes about social comparisons, dietary restriction, negative self-talk and cognitive restructuring, social support, and coping with negative emotions. Participants in the intervention group reported significant reductions on eating disorder psychopathology measures (i.e., subscale scores on the Eating Disorder Examination Questionnaire—Self-Report Version [EDE-Q]; Fairburn & Beglin, 1994) and improvements in self-esteem. Effect sizes for the intervention were moderate and ranged from 0.51 to 0.74.

The pace and fluency of chat room interactions depend on the typing skills of the participants and the speed of the Internet connection. The following transcript illustrates not only how a typical chat room discussion on insight might unfold but also the potential complexity involved in tracking the discourse:

Zabinski: "keep an open mind . . . we'll go slowly J (participant's initial) first, I think it is important to realize where the pressures come from (media, friends, etc.) and just understand that the ideal is usually not realistic"

Member 1: "Sometimes I think I'm doing good and then all of a sudden it falls apart."

Member 2: "Exactly."

Zabinski: "So when you set yourself up for goals that are not very attainable—you are setting yourself up for failure!"

Member 3: "Yup."

Member 2: "I agree with Member 1."

Member 5: "Yes."

Member 2: "That's true."

Member 6: "Uhuh."

Member 4: "I think that I put a lot of pressure on myself to be thinner."

Member 1: "I'll have high self esteem one day and low the next. It's a toss of the coin . . . a rollercoaster."

Member 3: "I agree with Member 1."

Member 7: "Yes."

Member 8: "I'm the same way."

Two studies evaluated unmoderated, asynchronous support groups for eating disorder-related concerns (Gleason, 1995; Winzelberg, 1997). Both studies used qualitative analyses to examine ongoing groups. Gleason created an electronic bulletin board at Wellesley College to address concerns about body image, food, and eating. Participants were required to use their full names in the support group. Using a qualitative approach to examine the electronic bulletin board discourse, Gleason reported that women first discussed scholarly issues related to eating disorders and body image and later, as trust developed, shared their own concerns and issues. Gleason further reported that women who acknowledged having binge eating were more likely to use the newsgroup than were those who reported food restriction. Because behavioral and attitudinal outcome measures were not administered, it is unknown whether participation in the electronic bulletin board had any clinical effect.

Winzelberg (1997) evaluated an eating disorder support group created by participants on a commercial Internet service provider. Again, participants were required to use their full names. The majority of members identified themselves as having an active eating disorder (59%) or as being in remission from an eating disorder (14%). A discourse analysis of more than 300 messages that were posted during a three-month period was conducted. Results suggested that participants used the same assistance strategies that have been identified by participants in face-to-face support groups. The most common message content was self-disclosure (31%), followed by requests for information (23%) and direct provision of emotional support (16%). Group members most frequently provided support to one another through the use of self-disclosure and direct statements of support. Participants also commonly used the group to acquire information about eating disorders and related concerns. However, a significant portion (12%) of the information provided by other group members was inaccurate or outside the guidelines of conservative medical care. Winzelberg found that the majority of the group members participated in the group during evening and late night hours, at times when traditional sources of psychological support are either limited or unavailable. Like the Gleason (1995) study, no treatment outcome data were collected. The following dialog illustrates how members provide support to one another through self-disclosure, advice, and direct statements of support.

ORIGINAL POSTINGS

Self-Disclosure

"I am a scared 17 year old recovering from bulimia. All in all, things have been going okay, but I'm really confused tonight. I tried on an old pair of jeans that used to fit me so well. Needless to say, I should not have done that. Those jeans are so tight on me now. I wonder how they could have ever fit me. I can't believe that no one figured out what was going on with me last year—I was so skinny, but still felt so fat. I mean, I was so skinny, but I never even gave myself the chance to enjoy it. What a shame.

Anyway, I have to just keep reminding myself how much better I feel about myself this year in comparison to last. But I don't have anyone to talk to about how I feel sometimes. This group is my only hope. For a long time I really didn't think too much about my body as I put on weight. Although I haven't stepped on a scale in so long, tonight those jeans have put me over the edge. I get so confused sometimes. I'm not sure if, by paying more attention to losing weight, I will eventually lose control. It really scares me. Has anyone out there ever felt this way?"

Reply 1: Self-Disclosure, Advice, and Direct Support

"Hi. My name is Sue and I'm also 17. I feel I can relate to you because I'm a recovering anorexic/bulimic (2 years without bingeing or purging, but it feels like only yesterday that I quit). For 2 years I denied I had a problem until my parents sent me to a therapist. At first I was really pissed (therapy can be such a drag), but in the end it was worth it. I remember saving all of my 'skinny' clothes in the back of my closet (just to have an 'honest' way of knowing how much I really weigh). It really helped when I got rid of everything that didn't fit me anymore. (OK, so it was a painful and expensive change— but worth it!) Anyway, I hope you hang in there and e-mail me if you want to talk."

Reply 2: Self-Disclosure and Direct Support

"You and I have a lot in common. I can't stop thinking about my weight and how badly I want to be skinny. I used to weigh a lot less (I guess you could say I was underweight), but I've gained a lot of weight in order to get 'healthy.' Everyone says I look great, but if that's so, why don't I feel great? Why can't I stop wondering what it would be like to be the skinniest girl on the beach? The weirdest thing is that people (guys especially) seem to pay more attention to me now than when I was at my lower weight. I know that should make me feel better, but it doesn't. So far, I've avoided going back to my old habits (starving myself and purging), but I'm not sure how much longer I can hold out. This may sound sick, but it's nice to hear that there are other people there who are like me. I'm glad you told your story."

Reply 3: Advice, Self-Disclosure, Direct Support

"Get rid of all your clothes that don't fit. Maybe I should say that to myself. When I see my old tiny jeans I want to cry. I'm big-boned and muscular. I have to realize that I'm not meant to be all bones. Well, I'm sorry I'm such a bummer tonight. I will smile. There. Try real hard to have a good week at school. Smile."

Although mental health providers, researchers, patients, and family members of patients have begun to explore various uses of Internet technology for the treatment of eating disorders, the empirical study of these interventions remains in its infancy. The research to date is encouraging, but randomized clinical trials are needed to establish the effectiveness of these programs for the treatment of full syndrome eating disorders.

THE FUTURE OF INTERNET-DELIVERED PROGRAMS

To date, many of the components that are characteristic of Internet technology have not been incorporated into Internet-delivered eating disorder interventions. This section illustrates, using a stepped-care approach, how some of these features can be implemented for the treatment of eating disorders. We selected a stepped-care approach because it provides a conceptual framework to illustrate how varied and increasingly more complex intervention features can be added to provide a comprehensive and integrative treatment program.

In general, stepped-care approaches to the treatment of mental health disorders have predetermined stages or levels of therapeutic care that are based on severity criteria. The stage of treatment may include referrals for medical consultations (e.g., cardiology, psychiatry), inpatient hospitalization, and standard face-to-face individual or group psychotherapy. Assessment and feedback are integrated into the intervention. At each stage, patients are assessed to determine whether they are meeting the corresponding treatment goals, and feedback is provided to both patients and their providers. Satisfactory completion of treatment goals allows patients to progress to the next step (e.g., discharge from an inpatient unit to individual and group psychotherapy). Failure to meet the predetermined treatment goals allows patients to continue at the current level of treatment until the goals are met or to increase the level of therapeutic care (e.g., from group only to individual plus group).

Step 1: Online Assessment

The first step in a comprehensive treatment program for eating disorders is assessment. The assessment may be initiated either by referral from a health care provider or by a patient who logs onto a Web site that provides general information about eating disorders. An eating disorder assessment can be presented either as a stand-alone feature (e.g., a screening measure that lists the criteria for binge eating disorder) or as part of a comprehensive general mental health assessment (e.g., a measure that includes the criteria for eating disorders, depression, anxiety, and substance abuse). After completing the assessment, individuals who, based on predetermined algorithm-driven criteria, are classified as being low risk could be given individualized feedback about their assessment and directed to a general eating disorder, nutrition, and physical activity psychoeducational program. Moreover, they could be encouraged to independently complete or be directed by the program to complete the assessment in the future to evaluate possible change in symptoms.

In contrast, individuals who are identified as being higher risk could be advanced to the next step of care, which could include a similar psychoeducational program and an online support group. Individuals who acknowledge having criteria indicative of a probable eating disorder diagnosis could be directed to a more comprehensive online assessment or to seek further assessment and consultation from a mental health provider. Additional assessment could be offered in a variety of modalities including e-mail, instant text messaging, telephone, or face-to-face. Online screening instruments are now available on several eating disorder Web sites. For example, eating disorder symptoms can be assessed over the Internet at http://www.edreferral.com/assessment.htm using the Eating Attitudes Test (EAT-26; Garner, Olmsted, Bohr, & Garfinkel, 1982). Users who screen positive are referred to their physician or an eating disorders treatment specialist for further evaluation.

Similar Internet-delivered assessments have been used to screen for depression and alcohol use. Houston et al. (2001) found that a Web site that was designed to assess depression was widely used. More than 24,000 people completed the depression screening measure during an eight-month period. Fifty-eight percent of individuals who completed the screening instrument scored positive for depression. Houston et al. concluded that Internet-delivered screening instruments provided a useful, cost-effective vehicle for screening large numbers of individuals. Likewise, several Web sites provide anonymous assessment of alcohol use (see www.carebetter.com and www.camh.net). Cloud and Peacock (2001) reported that an Internet site that was designed to deliver an anonymous automated alcohol screening test and a brief intervention received more than 10,000 hits in six months. Individuals were directed to complete the Alcohol Use Disorders Identification Test (AUDIT; Saunders, Aasland, Babor, de la Puente, & Grant, 1993) and the Stages of Change Readiness and Treatment Eagerness Scale (SOCRATES; Miller & Tonigan, 1996).

Step 2. Self-Help

A self-help program that individuals complete independently could consist of structured psychoeducational and therapeutic components that are adapted for online delivery. The content could include information on the prevalence, symptoms, and etiology of eating disorders, strategies to develop or maintain healthy dietary and exercise practices, and suggestions for coping with negative thoughts and distressing emotions. This type of content is easily augmented and enhanced with interactive multimedia. For example, personal accounts recorded by patients who are in remission can be listened to or watched instead of passively read. Implementation of multimedia components may increase a participant's level of engagement and thereby motivate him or her to become more actively involved in the treatment process.

Structured self-monitoring, which is a standard component of cognitive-behavioral therapy, is easily incorporated in an Internet-delivered format. Participants can be cued to record eating disorder-related thoughts, feelings, and negative events. Moreover, content can be written that teaches participants how to restructure their negative thoughts to improve their mood. Furthermore, an interactive component can be developed to assist participants with meal planning to promote healthy eating practices (e.g., balanced meal plans) and to prevent binge eating (e.g., establishing a regular meal schedule). Finally, automated reminders that cue participants to eat, exercise, or complete a journal entry can be sent via e-mail, cellular phone message, or pop-up Web page window.

In addition to a self-guided intervention, a peer or unmoderated support group component could be designed and offered to patients. Patients could choose to interact with others via e-mail, bulletin board, chat room, or instant messaging. A group intervention gives patients the opportunity to talk with their peers, share success stories, or ask for support.

Because making a public statement or contract about changing a behavior is thought to increase the likelihood that the behavior will occur, a "virtual wall" could be provided for patients to publicly disclose behaviors that they would like to change and to vow to adopt healthy behavior. For example, a Web page could be created that is dedicated for patients to make public commitments to discontinue dieting, purging, or excessive checking of appearance.

An even more sophisticated program could include detailed animation environments (i.e., virtual worlds) that guide patients through skill acquisition exercises and systematic desensitization. Patients could select a personal avatar (i.e., a visual representation selected for use in the virtual world) to interact with other patients or preexisting characters. For example, patients could have the virtual experience of eating in public, exercising at a gym, or viewing themselves at different weights.

Less sophisticated Internet-delivered self-help programs have been developed for the treatment of depression. In an uncontrolled study, Christensen, Griffiths, and Korten (2002) found that participants who completed an Internet-delivered cognitive-behavioral program for the treatment of anxiety and depression (http://moodgym.anu.edu.au) significantly reduced their symptoms as they progressed through the modules in the program. During the first six-month period of operation, more than 80,000 hits from almost 3,000 users were counted, indicating significant interest in this delivery method.

Step 3. Guided Self-Help

A guided self-help program would include all the features that are available in a self-help program and minimal therapist contact. Therapist contact could be provided in many ways including:

- Therapist moderation of a support or therapy group.
- Brief contact by telephone, e-mail, or instant messaging for the purpose of setting goals, reviewing journal entries, exploring setbacks and obstacles, and reviewing progress made in the program.
- Therapist review of journal entries and assessment results to evaluate treatment progress and recommend the most appropriate level of therapeutic care.

This program closely resembles Zabinski, Pung, et al. (2001), and Zabinski, Wilfley, et al. (2001) as described previously.

Step 4. Therapist-Guided Treatments

Therapist-guided treatments could take many forms, from purely Internet-delivered programs to hybrid programs that combine Internet-delivered programs with traditional face-to-face treatments. All of the previously described psychoeducation components could be available to the patient, but the overall treatment would be directed by a therapist.

In Internet-only interventions, the communication between the patient and therapist could occur via e-mail, instant messaging, or in chat rooms. Both parties would agree, in advance, on specific guidelines to direct the treatment process. Internet-delivered group sessions could be structured much like traditional face-to-face groups, yet the group members could communicate with each other and the therapist either asynchronously or synchronously.

Step 5. Relapse Prevention

Whether psychological treatment is delivered face-to-face, via the Internet, or a combination of the two, patients could be directed to a relapse prevention module at the termination phase. Again, any of the self-help components that were described previously could remain available to the patients after termination of treatment. In addition, to increase the likelihood that therapeutic gains are maintained, periodic maintenance check-ins could be preprogrammed.

ETHICAL ISSUES

Before implementing any Internet-based intervention, there are several ethical issues that warrant careful consideration. Perhaps the most disconcerting among these concerns is the inability of providers to guarantee the anonymity of patients and the confidentiality of patients' Internet-based records. Security precautions are now mandated by the 1996 Health Insurance Portability and Accountability Act (HIPAA) and include securing computer systems, recommending that participants use alias logins, nonobvious passwords, and encrypted text, but patients need to be advised before joining a program that no guarantee can be made about protecting privacy.

The inability to verify the identity of an online user makes it difficult and potentially risky to enroll participants who have not been evaluated face-to-face. This is particularly important when treating minors. Minors are required by law to have consent from a parent or guardian to participate in therapeutic activities (Childress, 2000). Although identity cannot be guaranteed, providers can establish procedures that minimize the likelihood that a minor is participating in an intervention without parental consent (e.g., require physician referral, obtain written parental consent).

Because the Internet is theoretically free from geographical constraints, another ethical consideration is whether an online provider is practicing in a jurisdiction without a license (Fenichel et al., 2001). State laws vary in terms of determining where services are being received (i.e., location of provider or location of participant). Furthermore, if a provider is a considerable distance from a patient or does not have a risk management plan established (e.g., emergency contacts), the provider may not be able to respond prudently to emergency situations (Humphreys, Winzelberg, & Klaw, 2000).

Additional safety concerns related to the potential range of psychopathology with which participants may present also are important to consider before implementing an Internet-based intervention. For example, a provider may choose to limit the disclosure of particular details (e.g., detailed description of purging methods) that may exacerbate another participant's psychopathology (e.g., bulimia nervosa). Moreover, participants may experience an exacerbation of comorbid psychopathology (e.g., personality psychopathology, suicidal behavior, substance use, domestic violence) that not only may interfere with other participants' treatment, but also may be beyond the provider's expertise. To complicate matters, because the Internet is potentially continuously available to participants, a message indicating that a participant is in crisis and requires immediate action may not be read by the provider until much later (Taylor, Winzelberg, & Celio, 2001).

Several professional associations have developed ethical standards and recommendations to guide the practice of Internet-based research and clinical application. These organizations include, but are not limited to, the American Psychological Association, the American Psychiatric Association, the National Board for Certified Counselors, Inc., the Center for Credentialing and Education, Inc., and the International Society for Mental Health Online (also see Internet Healthcare Coalition, 2000, and Humphreys, Winzelberg, & Klaw, 2000; Kane & Sands, 1998).

In summary, mental health providers raise several ethical considerations about the provision of Internet-based interventions. Professional organizations have developed guidelines and standards but, to date, no legal standards have been established to guide the practice of Internet-based interventions.

CONCLUSION

Internet-delivered interventions for eating disorders have great promise. Technological advances offer a wide range of treatment components that can either replace or enhance traditional face-to-face treatments. Interventions can be used to screen patients and direct them into a stepped-care model of treatment. Ongoing patient assessments can provide information about treatment progress to both the patient and provider. To date, no randomized clinical trials have evaluated Internet-delivered treatments for full syndrome eating disorders. The limited amount of research that has been completed has sampled participants who acknowledge having subthreshold symptoms and who are classified as being at higher risk of developing an eating disorder. The results of these studies are promising. A number of case reports have highlighted the use of electronic communication as an adjunct to face-to-face treatments. In an ideal scenario, Internet-delivered interventions could be used in a comprehensive stepped-care approach to treating eating disorders.

Until researchers have the opportunity to fully evaluate Internet-delivered interventions, mental health providers and patients should be cautious about embracing this delivery mechanism. Early results are promising, but more research is needed. It is unknown what disorders and patient characteristics respond more effectively to this treatment modality. A number of ethical, legal, and practical issues (e.g., who will pay for Internet-delivered treatment) need to be resolved before these treatments can be fully implemented. Ultimately, we do not view the Internet or other advances in communication technologies as a panacea for the treatment of eating disorders, but rather, as a useful tool to aid in the identification and treatment of these disorders.

REFERENCES

Abascal, L. (2001). *An Internet-delivered intervention to enhance body image in high school students.* Unpublished master's thesis, San Francisco State University, San Francisco.

Abascal, L., Bruning, J., Winzelberg, A. J., Dev, P., & Taylor, C. B. (in press). Combining universal and targeted prevention for school based eating disorder programs. *International Journal of Eating Disorders.*

Bruning-Brown, J., Winzelberg, A., Abascal, L., & Taylor, C. B. (2001). *An evaluation of an Internet-delivered eating disorder prevention program for adolescents and their parents.* Manuscript submitted for publication.

Cash, T. F. (1991). *Body-image therapy: A program for self-directed change.* New York: Guilford Press.

Celio, A., Winzelberg, A. J., Wilfley, D., Eppstein-Herald, D., Springer, E., Dev, P., et al. (2000). Reducing risk factors for eating disorders: Comparison of an Internet- and a classroom-delivered psychoeducation program. *Journal of Clinical and Consulting Psychology, 68*(4), 650–657.

Childress, C. A. (2000). Ethical issues in providing online psychotherapeutic interventions. *Journal of Medical Internet Research, 2*(1), E5.

Christensen, H., Griffiths, K. M., & Korten, A. (2002). Web-based cognitive behavior therapy: Analysis of site usage and changes in depression and anxiety scores. *Journal of Medical Internet Research, 4,* E3.

Cloud, R. N., & Peacock, P. L. (2001). Internet screening and interventions for problem drinking: Results from the www.carebetter.com pilot study. *Alcoholism Treatment Quarterly, 19*(2), 23–44.

Davis, R., Dearing, S., Faulkner, J., Jasper, K., Olmsted, M., Rice, C., et al. (1989). *The road to recovery: A manual for participants in the psychoeducation group for bulimia nervosa.* Toronto, Ontario, Canada: Toronto Hospital, Toronto General Division.

Fairburn, C. G., & Beglin, S. J. (1994). Assessment of eating disorders: Interview or self-report questionnaire? *International Journal of Eating Disorders, 16*(4), 363–370.

Fairburn, C. G., & Carter, J. C. (1996). Self-help and guided self-help for binge eating problems. In D. M. Garner & P. E. Garfinkel (Eds.), *Handbook of treatment for eating disorders* (pp. 494–499). New York: Guilford Press.

Fairburn, C. G., Norman, P. A., Welch, S. L., O'Connor, M. E., Doll, H. A., & Peveler, R. C. (1995). A prospective study of outcome in bulimia nervosa and the long-tem effects of three psychological treatments. *Archives of General Psychiatry, 52,* 304–312.

Fenichel, M., Suler, J., Barak, A., Zelvin, E., Jones, G., Munro, K., et al. (2001). Myths and realities of online clinical work. Observations on the phenomena of online behavior, experience and therapeutic relationships. A 3rd-year report from ISMHO's Clinical Case Study Group. *International Society for Mental Health Online.* Retrieved July 24, 2002, from www.ismho.org/casestudy/myths.htm.

Fox, S., & Rainie, L. (2002, May 22). Vital decisions: How Internet users decide what information to trust when they or their loved ones are sick. *Pew Internet and American Life Project.* Retrieved June 25, 2002, from www.pewinternet.org.

Garner, D. M., Olmsted, M. P., Bohr, Y., & Garfinkel, P. E. (1982). The eating attitudes test: Psychometric features and clinical correlates. *Psychological Medicine, 12*(4), 871–878.

Gleason, N. A. (1995). A new approach to disordered eating: Using an electronic bulletin board to confront social pressure on body image. *Journal of American College Health, 44*(2), 78–80.

Houston, T. K., Cooper, L. A., Vu, H. T., Kahn, J., Toser, J., & Ford, D. E. (2001). Screening the public for depression through the Internet. *Psychiatric Services, 52*(3), 362–367.

Humphreys, K., Winzelberg, A., & Klaw, E. (2000). Psychologists' ethical responsibilities in Internet based groups: Issues, strategies, and a call for dialogue. *Professional Psychology: Research and Practice, 31*(5), 493–496.

Internet Healthcare Coalition. (2000, May 24). e-Health Code of Ethics. *Journal of Medical Internet Research, 2*(2), E9.

Kane, B., & Sands, D. Z. (1998). Guidelines for the clinical use of electronic mail with patients. The AMIA Internet Working Group, Task Force on Guidelines for the Use of Clinic-Patient Electronic Mail. *Journal of the American Medical Informatics Association, 5*(1), 104–111.

Levine, M. P., Smolak, L., & Hayden, H. (1994). The relation of sociocultural factors to eating attitudes and behaviors among middle school girls. *Journal of Early Adolescence, 14,* 471–490.

Marks, I. (1999). Computer aids to mental health care. *Canadian Journal of Psychiatry, 44,* 548–555.

Miller, W., & Tonigan, J. (1996). Assessing drinkers' motivation for change: The stages of change and readiness sale (SOCRATES). *Psychology of Addictive Behaviors, 10,* 81–89.

National Institute of Mental Health. (2002, January 25). *Acting director's report to the National Advisory Mental Health Council.* Retrieved July 17, 2002, from www.nimh.nih.gov/council/dir1_2002.cfm.

Newman, M. G., Consoli, A., & Taylor, C. B. (1997). Computers in assessment and cognitive behavioral treatment of clinical disorders: Anxiety as a case in point. *Behavior Therapy, 28,* 211–235.

Ogles, B. M., France, C. R., Lunnen, K. M., Bell, M. T., & Goldfarb, M. (1998). Computerized depression screening and awareness. *Community Mental Health Journal, 34*(1), 27–36.

Pike, K. M., & Rodin, J. (1991). Mothers, daughters and disordered eating. *Journal of Abnormal Psychology, 100,* 198–204.

Rainie, L., & Packel, D. (2001, February 18). More online, doing more: 16 million newcomers gain Internet access in the last half of 2000 as women, minorities, and families with modest incomes continue to surge online. *Pew Internet and American Life Project.* Retrieved June 25, 2002, from www.pewinternet.org.

Robinson, P. H., & Serfaty, M. A. (2001). The use of e-mail in the identification of bulimia nervosa and its treatment. *European Eating Disorders Review, 9*(3), 182–193.

Sansone, R. A. (2001). Patient-to-patient e-mail: Support for clinical practices. *Eating Disorders: Journal of Treatment and Prevention, 9*(4), 373–375.

Saunders, J. B., Aasland, O. G., Babor, T. F., de la Puente, J. R., & Grant, M. (1993). Development of the Alcohol Use Disorders Screening Test (AUDIT). WHO collaborative project on early detection of persons with harmful alcohol consumption—II. *Addiction, 88,* 791–804.

Smolak, L., Levine, M. P., & Schermer, F. (1998). Lessons from lessons: An evaluation of an elementary school prevention program. In G. Noordenbos & W. Vanderreycken (Eds.), *The prevention of eating disorders.* London: Athlone.

Stice, E., Agras, W. S., & Hammer, L. D. (1998). Risk factors for the emergence of childhood eating disturbances: A five-year prospective study. *International Journal of Eating Disorders, 25,* 375–387.

Striegel-Moore, R. H., & Kearney-Cooke, A. (1994). Exploring parents' attitudes and behaviors about their children's physical appearance. *International Journal of Eating Disorders, 15,* 377–385.

Taylor, C. B., Altman, T., Shisslak, C., Bryson, S., Estes, L. S., Gray, N., et al. (1998). Factors associated with weight concerns in adolescents. *International Journal of Eating Disorders, 24,* 31–42.

Taylor, C. B., Winzelberg, A. J., & Celio, A. (2001). Use of interactive media to prevent eating disorders. In R. Striegel-Moore & L. Smolak (Eds.), *Eating disorders: New directions for research and practice* (pp. 255–269). Washington, DC: American Psychological Association.

Winzelberg, A. J. (1997). The analysis of an electronic support group for individuals with eating disorders. *Computers in Human Behavior, 13*(3), 393–407.

Winzelberg, A. J., Classen, C., Roberts, H., Alpers, G., Dev, G., Koopman, C., et al. (2003). An evaluation of a web-based support group for women with primary breast cancer. *Cancer, 97*(5), 1164–1173.

Winzelberg, A. J., Epstein, D., Eldredge, K., Wilfley, D. E., Dasmahapatra, R., Dev, P., et al. (2000). Effectiveness of an Internet-based program for reducing risk factors for eating disorders. *Journal of Consulting and Clinical Psychology, 68*(2), 346–350.

Winzelberg, A. J., Taylor, C. B., Altman, T., Eldredge, K., Dev, P., & Constantinou, P. (1998). Evaluation of a computer-mediated eating disorder prevention program. *International Journal of Eating Disorders, 24,* 339–350.

Yager, J. (2001). E-mail as a therapeutic adjunct in the outpatient treatment of anorexia nervosa: Illustrative case material and discussion of the issues. *International Journal of Eating Disorders, 29*(2), 125–138.

Zabinski, M. F., Pung, M. P., Wilfley, D. E., Eppstein, D. L., Winzelberg, A. J., Celio, A., et al. (2001). Reducing risk factors for eating disorders: Targeting at-risk women with a computerized psychoeducational program. *International Journal of Eating Disorders, 29*(4), 401–408.

Zabinski, M. F., Wilfley, D. E., Pung, M. P., Winzelberg, A. J., Eldredge, K., & Taylor, C. B. (2001). *An interactive Internet-based intervention for women at risk of eating disorders: A pilot study.* Manuscript submitted for publication.

Chapter 15

INPATIENT AND PARTIAL HOSPITAL APPROACHES TO THE TREATMENT OF EATING DISORDERS

ANGELA S. GUARDA AND LESLIE J. HEINBERG

Given the significant morbidity and mortality of eating disorders (Harris & Barraclough, 1998; Sullivan, 1995), patients often require more intensive treatment than outpatient care can provide. This chapter reviews commonly used inpatient and partial hospital approaches to the treatment of eating disorders. Treatment guidelines rely largely on correlational studies and clinical experience. Surprisingly little controlled research informs this critical area of psychiatric intervention.

We begin with the phenomenology of anorexia nervosa and bulimia that presents unique problems in treating these patients. We then review evidence-based knowledge about inpatient and partial hospital treatment. Next, we describe a model integrated inpatient-partial hospital program with an outline of what we consider to be the ideal aspects of intensive eating disorders treatment. Data on weight restoration from a consecutive series of 150 underweight patients treated in such a program is presented. Finally, we discuss the need for increased empirical research aimed at elucidating components of effective treatment, matching patient characteristics to treatment setting, and sequencing of treatment options.

CHALLENGES IN TREATING EATING DISORDERS

Anorexia nervosa and bulimia are behavioral disorders in which overvalued fear of fatness drives a set of behaviors in the service of dieting. The problem may, therefore, be conceptualized as lying in what the patient "does." Control and choice are impaired in that the individual has great difficulty changing his or her behavior. Repeated engagement in disordered eating behavior, coupled with the physiological effects of starvation and/or the restrict-binge-purge cycle, sustains and exacerbates both preoccupation with food and weight and dissatisfaction with body shape. Successful treatment requires extinction of stimuli triggering habitual eating-disordered response patterns, such as conditioned emotional responses to high calorie foods. Behavioral inpatient treatment that focuses on normalizing eating behavior has consistently been shown to improve eating behavior in naturalistic studies (Andersen, Stoner, & Rolls, 1996; A. J. Wilson, Touyz, Dunn, & Beumont, 1989). Both anorectic and bulimic patients can be treated together on a specialty eating disorder unit. Research has not documented any need to provide separate therapy groups or treatments based on diagnosis.

Initial therapeutic goals should focus on behavioral change rather than emotional relief. Patients, however, usually present requesting the former and resisting the latter. This disparity between the aims of the patient and those of the treating team (McHugh & Slavney, 1998) makes progress difficult in the outpatient setting. Unlike the typical patient-provider dynamic, in which patient and clinician share the goal of full recovery and commitment to treatment, patients with eating disorders are typically ambivalent about changing their behavior because of intense fear of weight gain. They may enter treatment complaining of physical, cognitive, or emotional consequences of their eating disorder yet have little desire to give it up in its entirety; rather they hope to better control it. This presentation leads to far different challenges than does treatment of other psychiatric disorders (e.g., depression or anxiety). Sir William Gull, in some of the first clinical descriptions of anorexia nervosa, described caring for these patients as "a sparring match—she was most loquacious and obstinate, anxious to overdo herself both mentally and physically" (Gull, 1874). More recently, Russell (2002) has suggested that the diagnostic criteria for anorexia nervosa should be based on its most enduring aspect: denial of illness and resistance to treatment. Although severely underweight patients with anorexia nervosa may recognize a need to gain weight, they fear that if they relinquish control over their intake, they will gain too much weight. Similarly, bulimic patients may be motivated to stop bingeing and vomiting but are opposed to consuming binge foods in normal portions. However, because dieting behavior predicts onset of binge eating in longitudinal studies (Patton, Selzer, Coffey, & Wolfe, 1999; Stice, Presnell, & Spangler, 2002), successful treatment requires consumption of a regular balanced and varied diet including risk foods, despite body dissatisfaction or desire to lose weight. Calorie restriction dieting, even for overweight patients with bulimia, is best delayed at least six months beyond remission of symptoms. Although based on clinical experience and the research literature, this recommendation is often met with disagreement and counterattempts to lose weight that continue to trap the patient in the restraint-binge-purge cycle.

We propose that treatment requires a major cognitive shift most akin to a process of conversion. From viewing dieting as the answer to their problems, patients must come to recognize this behavior as a primary impairment to healthy function. In contrast, exploring hypothetical causes of the eating disorder or dieting behavior in psychotherapy, although helpful in resolving underlying difficulties and providing a meaningful narrative to patients in the long term, is not equivalent to, and often not likely to bring about, any significant behavioral change. Once established, disordered eating maintains itself and becomes a way of life. To recover, patients need to acknowledge their behavior, recognize its rewarding nature, and relinquish control over it. Given the polarity involved between the patient versus the team's goals, role induction and the building of a therapeutic alliance are of paramount importance for the newly admitted patient.

The impact of managed care presents another severe challenge to inpatient treatment of eating disorders. Sharply curtailed health benefits have drastically affected the availability of intensive treatment over the past decade (Kaye, Kaplan, & Zucker, 1996; Silber & Robb, 2002). The result has been an increased risk of short "revolving door admissions," which may contribute to chronicity of illness. Financial pressures have resulted in the closing of numerous treatment programs, and many states now lack specialized facilities for inpatient care of eating disorders. Clinicians are forced to treat patients in general medical or pediatric settings or to recommend that patients travel out of state for treatment. Insurance benefits are often inadequate to meet the needs of this population, especially in the case of severely underweight individuals who may require several months of intensive treatment for full weight restoration. High treatment costs, and pressures for discharge exerted by managed care erode patient motivation further impacting on care delivery. Ambivalent patients frequently avoid intensive treatment or rationalize prematurely leaving the hospital when continued weight gain becomes uncomfortable based on these economic factors.

EVIDENCE-BASED INPATIENT AND PARTIAL HOSPITAL TREATMENT FOR EATING DISORDERS: WHAT DO WE KNOW AND HOW DO WE KNOW IT?

Anorexia Nervosa

Multidisciplinary behavioral specialty units for anorexia nervosa are clinically well established as the most effective setting in which to achieve rapid weight restoration, generally on the order of 2 to 4 lbs gained/week (American Psychiatric Association [APA], 2000). Numerous published descriptions of such treatment exist (Andersen, Bowers, & Evans, 1997; Touyz & Beumont, 1997; Vandereycken, 1985; Van Furth, 1998). Less data is available describing partial hospitalization treatment, although economic pressure to shorten lengths of stay (Bremer & Herzog, 1997; Raw, 2000; Wiseman, Sunday, Klapper, Harris, & Halmi, 2001) has favored increased development of such programs (Kaye, Kaplan, et al., 1996). Partial hospitalization has been found effective in eventually achieving weight restoration in up to 50% of anorectic patients. However, partial hospital rates of weight gain are slower given the less supervised setting (Kaplan, Olmsted, Carter, & Woodside, 2001), with most programs averaging weekly weight gains of only 0.5 to 1.0 lbs/week (APA, 2000; Howard, Evans, Quintero-Howard, Bowers, & Andersen, 1999; Kaplan & Olmsted, 1997; Piran, Langdon, Kaplan, & Garfinkel, 1989). Despite increasing numbers of partial hospital programs for eating disorders, few clinical descriptions of such programs exist. Most programs employ a multidisciplinary team and focus on group therapy. However, intensity of care and admission criteria vary widely (Zipfel et al., 2002). When used in a step-up model of care where failure of outpatient, rather than progression from inpatient (step-down), is the entry point to partial hospital, this level of treatment requires significant patient motivation for success. In a correlational study of a step-down program by Howard et al., higher rates of treatment failure and need for readmission to inpatient were associated with a BMI of < 19 at transition to partial hospital, longer duration of illness, and amenorrhea.

No well-designed, long-term randomized controlled treatment studies (RCTs) of inpatient versus partial hospitalization or standard outpatient treatment have been completed. There remains significant debate over the ideal length of inpatient treatment and for whom it is necessary. A recent review of inpatient versus outpatient treatment trials was unable to draw any meaningful conclusions from the published literature because the one identified RCT and various case series comparing inpatient to outpatient care are plagued with methodological problems (Treasure & Schmidt, 2002). Similarly, little is known about how best to sequence inpatient and partial hospital or how to match patient characteristics to treatment intensity. High cost and dropout rates, difficulty with recruiting and randomizing patients to treatments of differing intensities, widely varying participant characteristics between groups, small sample sizes, brief treatment intervals, and low power to detect a clinical effect, as well as ethical issues surrounding randomization, have hampered such research.

Cross-sectional, correlational studies support the finding that inpatients who reach target weight are much less likely to relapse than those who do not (Baran, Weltzin, & Kaye, 1995; Commerford, Licinio, & Halmi, 1997). By contrast, there is no clinical evidence that partial weight restoration and brief hospital stays promote recovery in severely underweight patients (APA, 2000). Most experienced clinicians believe severely underweight patients are unlikely to be successfully weight restored in outpatient settings (APA, 2000; Kaplan et al., 2001), with the possible exceptions of adolescents treated in outpatient family therapy (Eisler et al., 2000; Le Grange, Eisler, Dare, & Russell, 1992; Robin et al., 1999) or recovery-motivated and behaviorally compliant patients in an intensive partial hospital program. Some clinicians, however, have argued that inpatient treatment is ineffective and may actually be harmful. A nonrandomized study comparing adolescents treated as inpatients to those treated solely on an outpatient basis reported worse outcome at two to seven years follow-up in hospitalized cases. However, most inpatients were treated on general psychiatric or pediatric units rather than specialized behavioral eating disorder services. Further, comorbid psychiatric illnesses, as well as illness severity, were not controlled for across treatment groups, nor was percent weight-restored reported for the inpatient cases (Gowers, Weetman, Shore, Hossain, & Elvins, 2000). The worse prognosis of the admitted patients may have reflected inadequate treatment setting or weight restoration, greater illness severity, poorer motivation for treatment, or comorbidity that necessitated inpatient treatment in the first place. A second correlational study by Ben-Tovim et al. (2001) similarly concluded that inpatient treatment does not affect long-term outcome but again failed to distinguish long-term outcome of patients discharged weight-restored from those who were only partially weight-restored. The authors divided their sample into those restored to a BMI of 16 or above versus less than 16 but did not separate out fully weight-restored cases, making their results difficult to interpret.

Most behavioral inpatient specialty units can successfully weight-restore essentially all patients to a normal BMI of 19 to 21 using a behavioral protocol involving nursing observation and nutritional rehabilitation with progressively increasing daily calorie intake. Importantly, strict operant conditioning programs involving negative reinforcers such as bed rest and isolation contingent on weight gain have been found no more effective than lenient behavioral programs (Touyz, Beumont, Glaun, Phillips, & Cowie, 1984). Treatment is typically implemented by a multidisciplinary team and includes nursing observation to block eating-disordered behaviors; behavior therapy; individual, family, and group therapy; nutritional and psycho-education; as well as life skills training. Psychotherapy generally employs elements of cognitive-behavioral

(Bowers, 2001; Garner, Vitousek, & Pike, 1997) and interpersonal therapy (McIntosh, Bulik, McKenzie, Luty, & Jordan, 2000) with a recent interest in dialectical behavior therapy (Fairburn, Cooper, & Shafran, 2002). Comparative studies of different therapies or treatment modalities (e.g., individual versus group) in inpatient or partial hospital settings have not been completed.

Due to the limited numbers of specialized eating disorder behavioral units, patients are often treated on medical or general psychiatric units. Controlled comparisons of these alternate inpatient settings to psychiatric behavioral specialty units are lacking. Similarly, nasogastric feeding and parenteral nutrition, often used on medical units, have not been adequately compared to oral refeeding. A recent nonrandomized study examined supplemental nocturnal nasogastric refeeding versus oral refeeding alone in adolescent inpatients and concluded that the former method resulted in more rapid weight gain (Robb et al., 2002). However, the nasogastric-feeding group received significantly more calories and, therefore, not surprisingly, gained weight faster. Furthermore, rates of weight gain in the group receiving oral refeeding averaged 1.7 lbs/week, well below those of several behavioral programs that employ oral refeeding alone (Guarda & Heinberg, 1999; Howard et al., 1999). As such, useful conclusions cannot be drawn on the comparative advantage of supplemental nasogastric tube feeding versus oral refeeding alone in a behavioral specialty unit setting. Although weight gain rates achieved with nasogastric or parenteral feeding can match those for oral refeeding, we assert that there are significant drawbacks to these refeeding methods in that they:

1. Do not desensitize individuals to fears of high calorie foods and expand food choice repertoire.
2. Do not normalize eating behavior.
3. Are not well-tolerated by patients.
4. Are more often associated with dangerous complications and the potentially life-threatening refeeding syndrome (Mehler & Weiner, 1993).

Even in the case of involuntarily committed patients, there is usually no need for nasogastric feeding in the presence of a specialized behavioral unit (Ramsay, Ward, Treasure, & Russell, 1999). A review of three studies of involuntarily committed inpatients reveals that these patients can be refed on a behavioral unit, confirming a clear short-term benefit to involuntary admission for life-threatening anorexia nervosa (Russell, 2001). What is more difficult to determine is the long-term outcome of involuntary inpatient treatment. Although mortality at a mean follow-up interval of 5.7 years was higher in involuntary patients than in voluntarily admitted controls (Ramsay et al. 1999), this most likely results from involuntarily committed individuals being less motivated for recovery rather than from involuntary treatment itself. Consistent with this hypothesis, two of the three studies reported higher rates of previous admissions in involuntary patients, suggesting greater illness severity and treatment resistance (Russell, 2001).

To date, no RCTs have concentrated on family therapy or counseling in inpatient or partial hospital treatment settings, although the effectiveness of outpatient family therapy in the treatment of adolescent anorexia nervosa is well established, suggesting that for this age group, integrating family work into inpatient and partial hospital settings may improve prognosis and speed recovery. Family therapy, both conjoint or separated, aimed at assisting parents to take appropriate control of their child's eating behavior, has been found superior to individual therapy in both relapse prevention after inpatient weight restoration and in the outpatient treatment of acute anorexia nervosa in adolescents with a less than three-year history of illness (Eisler et al., 1997, 2000; Le Grange, Eisler, Dare, & Russell, 1992; Russell, Szmukler, Dare, & Eisler, 1987). By contrast, the effect of outpatient family therapy on adult anorexia nervosa appears much more modest. Although one RCT found superior results for family versus comparison individual therapies over a one-year follow-up, the dropout rate was high and weight gains were poor, averaging 2.7 kg with recovery rates below 15% for each active treatment group (Dare, Eisler, Russell, Treasure, & Dodge, 2001), well below the 60% to 70% recovery rates observed in adolescent family therapy trials.

Conclusions drawn from inpatient trials are further limited by the fact that they usually involve the addition of a new treatment to standard care, which often differs between programs, making extrapolation of results difficult and minimizing differences with each new added intervention (Agras & Kraemer, 1984). Nonetheless, as pointed out recently by Hoek and Treasure (2002), the lack of RCT-based evidence should not be interpreted to mean that intensive treatment is of no value. Much is known about both treatment of the starvation state and its medical risks and complications (Keys, Brozek, Henschel, Mickelsen, & Taylor, 1950) that is applicable to anorexia nervosa. There is also evidence that targeted psychotherapy is probably more effective than supportive counseling alone (Dare et al., 2001). Finally, there is preliminary evidence that pharmacotherapy, although of little benefit with respect to weight restoration (Attia, Haiman, Walsh, & Flater, 1998), may be helpful in the relapse prevention stage of treatment (Kaye et al., 2001).

More relapse prevention studies following inpatient weight restoration are needed. Although short-term relapse rates for successfully treated inpatients are 30% to 50% within one year of discharge (Pike, 1998), the percentage of these relapses attributable to inadequate postdischarge outpatient care is unclear. Most clinicians agree that inpatient weight restoration needs to be followed by extended specialized outpatient care to prevent relapse. Long-term outcome studies indicate recovery rates of 40% to 70% following inpatient specialty care (Herpetz-Dahlmann, Muller, Herpetz, & Heussen, 2001; Lowe et al., 2001; Steinhausen, 1999); however, the recovery process tends to be protracted over several years and is characterized by a fluctuating course (Strober, Freeman, & Morrell, 1997). Analysis of the impact of a treatment intervention becomes complicated when patients are exposed to multiple treatment modalities over time, and the natural course of untreated anorexia nervosa remains unknown. Failure to control for response to inpatient treatment (e.g., degree of weight restoration) or to distinguish the course of first admissions from that of treatment-resistant patients further confuses interpretation of long-term outcome following inpatient treatment. Prognostic factors for treatment success in anorexia nervosa remain elusive. No factor has consistently been found to predict outcome across studies, although low admission and discharge weights, past treatment failures, long length of illness, comorbid psychiatric illness, extreme body image disturbance, and purging behaviors have all significantly predicted treatment failure in multiple studies.

Bulimia Nervosa

A significant body of evidence supports the efficacy of outpatient cognitive-behavioral therapy (CBT) and, to a lesser extent, interpersonal therapy (IPT) in decreasing binge-purge behavior in bulimia nervosa (Hay & Bacaltchuk, 2002; see Chapters 7 and 8 in this text); however, most studies have dropout rates as high as 20% to 35% (Agras et al., 2000; Mitchell, 1991; Walsh et al., 1997). Further, only 40% to 50% of treatment completers meet criteria for recovery, with early response to CBT being the best-known predictor of treatment outcome (Agras et al., 2000; G. T. Wilson et al., 1999). Focus on early abstinence and high-intensity treatment, characteristics which are generally built into inpatient behavioral treatment settings, has been shown to strengthen the effects of outpatient group CBT for bulimia (Mitchell, Pyle, et al., 1993). Although nearly all antidepressants studied are beneficial to some degree in decreasing bulimic symptoms in the short-term (Mitchell, Raymond, & Specker, 1993), abstinence rates with medication alone are lower than with CBT. Furthermore, generalizability is a concern given that RCTs have often been performed on carefully selected outpatients who are motivated for treatment, meet study criteria, and lack serious medical or psychiatric comorbidity. What then is the clinical treatment standard for the more than 50% of patients who either fail or drop out of a course of outpatient CBT or who have serious comorbidity that renders outpatient treatment unsafe or ineffective? Examples of such individuals include multi-impulsive bulimics who display multiple high-risk behaviors (e.g., self-injury and substance abuse, Lacey & Evans, 1986), patients with severe mood disorders, acutely suicidal patients, bulimic individuals with brittle diabetes, and those with comorbid personality disorders. Although such patients are often referred for inpatient or partial hospitalization, evidence-based knowledge concerning the effectiveness of hospital treatments on outcome of bulimia is even more limited than for anorexia nervosa.

Long-term outcome studies of individuals admitted for inpatient treatment reveal recovery rates of 40% to 60% (Fallon, Walsh, Sadik, Saoud, & Lukasik, 1991; Fichter & Quadflieg, 1997). As with anorexia nervosa, no randomized comparison of inpatient to outpatient treatment exists. A partial hospitalization study from the Toronto Eating Disorders Program with a minimum of six weeks of treatment (on average, five days per week, seven hours per day) found that more than 80% of patients reported either abstinence or bingeing and purging less than weekly during the last four weeks of treatment (Kaplan & Olmsted, 1997; Maddocks & Kaplan, 1991). As with outpatient CBT, rapid response to partial hospital treatment was predictive of lower relapse rates at two years postdischarge (Olmsted, Kaplan, Jacobsen, & Rockert, 1996). Furthermore, the same group found that patients who were totally abstinent at discharge (46%) were more likely to be abstinent and to lack significant psychopathology or functional impairment at follow-up (Maddocks, Kaplan, Woodside, Langdon, & Piran, 1992). In a small, short-term outcome study of eight-week inpatient treatment for bulimia, the duration of previous inpatient treatments and pretreatment level of depression were the best outcome predictors (Bossert, Schmolz, Wiegand, Junker, & Krieg, 1992). As with anorexia nervosa, relapses and remissions are very common, and recovery from bulimia is often a protracted process (Herzog, Nussbaum, & Marmor, 1996).

Relapse prevention techniques following inpatient or partial hospitalization for bulimia remain largely unexplored. Similar to the data on fluoxetine for relapse prevention in anorexia nervosa, preliminary evidence suggests that both fluoxetine (Romano, Halmi, Sarkar, Koke, & Lee, 2002) and fluvoxamine (Fichter, Kruger, Rief, Holland, & Dohne, 1996) may be helpful in preventing relapse following successful treatment of bulimia.

A MODEL INTEGRATED, STEP-DOWN, INPATIENT-PARTIAL HOSPITALIZATION PROGRAM FOR EATING DISORDERS

Given the paucity of evidence-based literature on inpatient and partial hospital treatment of anorexia nervosa and bulimia, limited guidance exists as to what aspects of inpatient and partial hospital treatment are ideal. Thus, we offer an outline of our program as a model for integrating inpatient and partial hospitalization for eating disorders. We provide a brief overview, followed by more detailed aspects of the behavioral protocol and data supporting its efficacy.

The Johns Hopkins Eating Disorders Program, started in 1976 by Arnold Andersen, MD, treats patients with anorexia nervosa, bulimia, eating disorder not otherwise specified (EDNOS), and atypical eating disorders. In 1992, as a result of managed care pressure, an integrated partial hospital program was created on the inpatient unit. Initially an eight hours per day, five days per week program, the partial hospital was expanded in 1995 and coverage was extended to 12 hours per day, 7 days per week. Supervised housing was added to improve partial hospital weight gain rates and allow for earlier transition to the partial program, without forfeiting the ability to assist patients in blocking their eating-disordered behaviors and maintaining healthier eating habits. The program admits both adolescents and adults, and approximately 25% of the population treated is between 12 and 18 years of age. Adolescents spend overnights with their parents once in the partial hospital. Despite controversy over whether adolescents should be treated on adult units, we have found that doing so results in equivalent weight gains, equivalent lowering of emotional distress (Heinberg, Guarda, Haug, Yacono-Freeman, & Ambrose, in press) and confers several unique advantages. Younger patients consistently comment that being exposed to chronic patients who have suffered long-term consequences of their eating disorder motivates them to recover and decreases eating-disordered competition among teenage peers. Older patients, in turn, tend to be protective of adolescents and to actively discourage younger patients from following in their footsteps. The concern that adolescents may be influenced by older peers to develop new eating-disordered behaviors appears unfounded because all behaviors are found in all age groups of eating-disordered patients and information on eating-disordered behavior is widely accessible to adolescents in the media and on the Web.

In the case of minors, family is actively involved in treatment, especially once in the partial program. Because individual psychotherapy does not appear to influence weight gain during acute inpatient refeeding (Danziger, Carel, Tyano, & Mimouni, 1989) and tends to dilute the effectiveness of group therapy, no scheduled individual therapy has been offered since 1996, although outpatient individual therapy is recommended after discharge. Group therapy is emphasized, obviating complications of individual therapy that arise on a ward milieu with a short length of stay, including refusal to talk in groups, staff splitting, and becoming overly attached to the individual therapist, creating termination issues at discharge.

Unit census for the combined inpatient and partial hospital is flexible, with an average of 13 patients daily and 120 admissions yearly since 1996. Length of stay is very variable with a mean inpatient length of stay of 23 days ($SD = 15.5$) and a mean partial hospital length of stay of 27 days ($SD = 17.8$) Combined average length of stay for the entire program is, therefore, seven weeks. Patients in partial hospital initially attend daily; however, their time in attendance is tapered contingent on clinical progress. On average, partial hospital patients spend 75% of days in the program. The integrated program is structured as a step-down treatment. Patients are rarely admitted directly to partial hospital. Instead, they spend a minimum of one to two days as inpatients to interrupt unhealthy behaviors, normalize eating, and become familiar with staff, peers, and the program structure. This initial period involves significant role induction and is focused on engaging the patient in treatment through psychoeducation, peer pressure, and formation of a therapeutic alliance with the treatment team. Staff maintains a supportive and empathic, yet firm, approach in interactions with patients, reinforcing the fact that treatment is difficult and may provoke anxiety but is indispensable to overcoming the eating disorder and its effects on physical, psychological, and social function. Repeated nonjudgmental confrontation is used throughout treatment to address evidence of eating-disordered cognitions or behaviors.

Criteria for inpatient admission are psychiatric or medical instability (e.g., suicidal, unstable electrolytes, BMI < 13, or severe bradycardia with HR < 40 bpm) or failure to progress following one month or more of specialized outpatient treatment. The majority of patients have a diagnosis of anorexia nervosa, often with severe medical or psychiatric comorbidity. Occasionally, patients are involuntarily committed at admission if their status is deemed life threatening and they refuse voluntary admission. There are no exclusionary criteria for admission as long as patients meet *Diagnostic and Statistical Manual of Mental Disorders,* Fourth Edition (*DSM-IV*), criteria for an eating disorder and their condition is severe enough to warrant inpatient treatment. Level of motivation for treatment is rarely considered an important factor in deciding whether a patient should be admitted since clinical observation indicates that motivation for recovery improves with successful treatment and behavioral change.

Treatment involves several components:

1. A uniformly applied behavioral protocol.
2. Daily multidisciplinary team rounds.
3. Nutritional rehabilitation, including weight restoration if underweight, and normalization of eating behavior.
4. Family involvement, mandatory in the case of adolescent patients.
5. A minimum of three hours of group therapy daily.
6. Relapse prevention and maintenance of healthy behaviors.

Integrating inpatient and partial hospital programs eliminates the need for communication between separate teams, avoids psychotherapeutic change and separation issues during transition between programs (Piran et al., 1989), facilitates adjusting patient attendance schedules in response to eating-disordered behavior or poor weight gain, and allows patients who are further along in recovery to serve as role models for newer admissions.

Behavioral Protocol

On admission, all patients are placed on the behavioral protocol, which involves nursing observation to block eating disorder behavior. Patients progress through a hierarchy of structured tasks aimed at normalizing food intake, broadening food repertoire, and developing increasing mastery of normal eating behavior. In the case of underweight patients, weight restoration to a BMI of 21, age-adjusted for individuals under 25 years of age, is a third goal. Underweight patients are initially placed on a 1,500 calories per day diet and advanced by 500 calories every two days to 3,500 to 4,000 calories per day by hospital day 10. Calories above 2,500 are provided as nutritional supplements to avoid mimicking binge-like food portioning. Patients admitted with a BMI < 13 are closely monitored medically, started at 1,200 calories per day on a low-fat, low-salt, low-lactose diet and advanced depending on medical status to minimize risk of refeeding syndrome. Calorie progression is slowed if there is significant evidence of peripheral edema, and labs are followed daily until medically stabilized. Bulimic patients, whether normal or overweight, are prescribed a weight maintenance, 2,000-calorie diet. Patients are weighed daily but do not see their weights unless they are on weight maintenance and close to discharge. Similarly, they are not informed of their target weight until they have maintained in this range for at least a week, preventing excessive focus on weight gain and behavioral reactions to such information on a daily basis (e.g., arguing, attempting to negotiate a lower goal weight). The information provided by daily weights helps the team recognize gaining or losing trends early and to adjust observation and calorie levels accordingly. For the first 10 days of treatment if underweight, and the first 5 days if on weight maintenance, patient meals are ordered by the dietician to expose patients to a wide range of foods they would otherwise be too anxious to sample. All foods are served in normal meal combinations and amounts. Exposure with response prevention and flooding techniques are used to extinguish anxiety over consuming risk foods and to broaden patients' food repertoires. Thereafter, patients start selecting their own meals and are taught to choose from all food groups using an adaptation of the diabetic exchange system (American Dietetic Association/American Diabetic Association, 1989). Patients must select balanced meals, including risk foods, and must demonstrate variety in food choice over time to maintain their selecting privileges. No dislikes are allowed, and patients are expected to complete their tray in 45 minutes. Vegetarianism is observed only if the family can corroborate that this pattern of eating preceded onset of dieting and fear of fatness symptoms by three years. Patients eat together and nursing staff monitors meals. If a patient fails to complete a meal on time, he or she is asked to sit in a quiet corner with a nurse and is encouraged to continue the meal until a group therapy session starts, at which point the patient leaves the meal temporarily to attend group. The group leader's task is to facilitate supportive confrontation of new patients or those who are less compliant by more senior, recovery-motivated patients. Generating such peer pressure is extremely effective in getting patients to complete their meals. More than 95% of patients are completing all three meals on time within days of admission. Nasogastric feeding is never necessary in this setting. Patients admitted with a PEG or TPN line are told they are expected to feed themselves and that their PEG or TPN line will be removed.

Between the hours of 8 A.M. and 10 P.M., patients are restricted to the day area in view of the nursing station, unless attending groups or at meals, to help block urges to exercise or purge. Bathroom use is supervised by nursing with regularly scheduled bathroom breaks every two hours. Nurses check the toilet before flushing. After 10 P.M. and before 8 A.M., patients are allowed to freely move around the unit, spend time in their rooms, and use the bathrooms unsupervised. Once compliant with the protocol, medically stable and gaining more than 3 lbs/week if underweight, patients are transitioned to partial hospital unless the team feels they cannot be treated safely and effectively in this less supervised setting.

Patients initially spend 12 hours a day in the partial hospitalization program and eat all meals on the unit. Supervision is gradually decreased, depending on progress with weight gain and behavioral compliance. Likewise, independence over meals and time off is gradually increased, starting with the task of going to the hospital cafeteria to select a meal independently and returning to the unit for a tray check by nursing. Next, patients are given leave at 4 P.M. to have a meal off campus alone or with family and, if they do well, earn a full day off from the program as attendance is tapered to three days per week before discharge to outpatient care. As patients practice normal eating behavior in progressively less supervised settings, relapse prevention is stressed, including methods of coping with:

- Dysphoric mood states and trigger situations.
- Independence over food selection.
- Return to the environment in which the patient was active in his or her eating disorder.

For patients on the weight gain protocol, calories are gradually reduced once at target weight, and exercise is introduced. Weight training rather than aerobic exercise is encouraged for patients with osteoporosis or osteopenia. Bulimic patients are permitted to exercise two to three hours a week in the hospital gym throughout their stay. All medically stable patients go on a daily 30-minute walk around campus with staff and participate in a daily stretch and relaxation or gentle yoga group.

For inpatients on weight gain with below-average weekly gains, the team may increase observation level and implement a stricter protocol, placing the patient on nursing observation at night or around the clock to interrupt exercise or clandestine purging behavior. Selecting privileges and the daily walk may also be revoked if poor weight gain or evidence of eating-disordered behavior persists. Bed rest is not used. Partial hospital patients who fail to gain more than 2 lbs/week in the partial program on a more lenient schedule are stepped back up to 12 hours per day, 7 days per week. Those who fail to gain adequately when attending full time may be temporarily readmitted to 24-hour inpatient care. Finally, in the case of partial hospital patients who are repeatedly disruptive of the unit milieu, for example, using substances or failing to maintain their weight once at target, suspension from the program for a week often proves to be a useful motivator to comply with treatment. Such patients are readmitted only if they have met the team's individualized treatment plan (e.g., gaining weight back to a predetermined target or having a clean urine).

At admission, patients often criticize the protocol as too controlling and paternalistic. However, once they reach the more independent partial hospital, the large majority report they are thankful that choice was initially taken away from them and are able to recognize how their eating disorder controlled their autonomy, preventing them from making rational behavioral choices.

Multidisciplinary Team

A multidisciplinary team comprising an attending and a resident psychiatrist, nursing and social work staff, an occupational therapist, and a dietician provide treatment. Medical consultants are involved in the treatment of patients with medical complications or significant medical comorbidity (e.g., diabetes). The treatment team meets daily, reviews progress, and speaks with each patient individually in rounds to plan treatment. Eating disorder patients can be exhausting to work with because of fluctuating motivation for treatment, a hallmark of the condition. Team rounds help manage and diffuse countertransference reactions to behaviorally difficult cases, maintain the team's cohesion, minimize opportunities for "staff splitting," and facilitate communication among staff. Decisions about patient privileges, time off in partial hospital, medication, and management of comorbidity are made in rounds. In patients with anorexia nervosa who present with a depressive syndrome, use of antidepressants is often delayed one to two weeks to see whether mood improves with refeeding alone.

Nutritional Rehabilitation and Weight Restoration

Normalizing eating behavior is a priority of treatment. Habit and conditioning are strong reinforcers of eating-disordered behavioral patterns. Patients experience compelling drives to restrict their food repertoire or engage in eating rituals such as dicing food, eating excessively slow or fast, hiding food, inappropriate mixing of food, and so on. Eating is a social activity for healthy individuals; however, those with an eating disorder often avoid social eating or food preparation. Teaching normal food preparation and social eating skills is, therefore, a critical focus of the program. Most newly admitted patients are too anxious about eating to prepare a normal meal; however, once in the partial hospital program, they are expected to have enough control over their eating behaviors to participate in a daily meal planning and preparation group. This activity rehearses skills necessary for relapse prevention and eventual success in maintaining behavioral change after discharge. Meal groups are run by nursing and occupational therapy staff and include menu planning, grocery shopping, cooking, and social eating activities (e.g., selecting food from a buffet, ordering carryout Chinese food or pizza, and attending restaurant outings).

Family Involvement

Adult Patients

Every effort is made to involve family in treatment. In the case of adult patients, a minimum of two family meetings is planned: (1) at admission, to orient the family to the protocol and to obtain a collateral history and (2) close to discharge, to facilitate discharge planning and, in some cases, draw up a family contract of expectations and consequences for both the patient's and parents' behavior. Such a plan may establish a minimum weight below which patients agree that their therapist may contact their parents or give permission for the family to contact their adult child's therapist if they are concerned about relapse. The focus of family meetings is on improving communication in the here and now and working together to maintain the patient's recovery and prevent relapse, rather than focus on past family conflicts. Parents are also invited to attend a weekly psychoeducational group together with their child.

Adolescent Patients

Parental involvement is seen as mandatory for successful treatment of adolescent patients. Role induction for parents is an important part of the admissions process. Staff takes a nonblaming stance, clarifying that parents are not responsible for their child's eating disorder but that it is crucial for them to participate in treatment as fully as possible if their child is to recover. The behavioral protocol and expectations for parental involvement are reviewed, and the importance of the family and team presenting a unified recovery-oriented position is stressed. Parents are told that ambivalence about treatment is a cardinal feature of eating disorders, especially anorexia nervosa, and that it is likely their child will initially balk at aspects of the treatment protocol and try to enlist family to negotiate for him or her in the service of the eating disorder. Parents are encouraged to address any questions they may have about the protocol to staff but not to let their child know should they disagree with the treatment in any way. They are reassured that over the course of the first week of treatment, their child is likely to engage with peers and the treatment team and that motivation to recover tends to improve with behavioral mastery of normal eating and with weight restoration.

Parents are expected to attend weekly family therapy meetings and a weekly psychoeducational group. Once their child is in the partial program, they meet with the dietician for instruction on the exchange system of food selection. They then shadow the nursing and occupational therapy staff in assisting their child to select and portion meals in the cafeteria, before having a family meal off the unit. Families requiring extra instruction due to potential problems such as conflict at home or a parent with restrictive eating behavior may be scheduled for a family meal prep with the occupational therapist. In the partial hospital, parents are also asked to attend team rounds approximately once a week to report on their child's progress or any problems at home. These meetings are important role-modeling opportunities, allowing parents to observe how the team interacts with their child and help to demystify treatment planning and the team's decision-making process.

Group Therapy

Group therapy is especially effective in behavioral disorders such as eating disorders (Fettes & Peters, 1992; McKisack & Waller, 1997), helping to both motivate patients and increase behavioral compliance with treatment. Group attendance is mandatory. Inpatients and partial patients share therapeutic groups, promoting healthy, recovery-focused competition, and group leaders take an active role. The need to stop all eating-disordered behavior is stressed. "Fat talk" and competitive eating-disordered comparisons are stigmatized. A combination of CBT, IPT, dialectical behavior therapy (DBT), and psychoeducational approaches is used. Group therapy (1) maintains motivation and a recovery-focused unit milieu, (2) engages ambivalent patients in treatment, and (3) helps newly admitted patients block their eating-disordered behavior and complete meals.

Patients participate in at least three psychotherapeutic groups daily. These include:

1. *Behavioral recovery group.* Aimed at discussion of daily progress in mastering healthy eating and combating cognitive distortions that sustain eating-disordered behavior. Group leaders actively encourage supportive confrontation in this group, thereby strengthening a recovery-focused group dynamic.

2. *Meal planning, preparation, and performance group.* Focuses on normalizing food selecting, preparation and portioning, and social eating skills.

3. *Body image group.* A cognitive-behavioral group based on exercises to correct irrational appraisals of body image, to promote critical media awareness, and to counter internalization of the thinness ideal and preoccupation with frequent comparisons of body shape to those of others.

4. *Self-esteem and skills training group.* Focuses on assertiveness training, coping, and communication skills.

5. *Family issues group.* Aimed at improving relationships with family and discussing ways to enlist relatives as supports in recovery.

6. *Psychoeducational group.* Covers information on symptoms, etiology, treatment, and medical and psychiatric complications of eating disorders.

7. *Nutrition group.* Includes information on risks of dieting, general nutritional information, and nondieting approaches to balanced eating.

8. *Discharge planning and relapse prevention group.* Focuses on recognizing environmental triggers, how to cope with returning to work or school, how to respond to questions by others, how to enlist support.

9. *Stretch and relaxation and yoga groups.* Include gentle exercises, body awareness, and relaxation skills.

Special Patient Populations

Patients with Other Behavioral Problems

The importance of not acting on feelings is stressed, as is the fact that behavior has consequences, whereas feelings tend to be transient responses to disappointment, frustration, or dysphoric mood states. Frequent comorbid behaviors found in the eating-disordered population, especially among purgers, include substance abuse and self-injurious behavior. Substance abuse includes illegal street drugs, alcohol, and laxative, diuretic, or diet pill abuse. For those patients abusing illegal drugs or alcohol, NA and AA attendance is prescribed once in the partial hospital. All laxatives, diuretics, or diet aids are discontinued at admission. A stool softener and psyllium supplement are prescribed for patients complaining of constipation. No regular laxatives are administered, although there may be occasional need for a laxative during refeeding in some patients. Regularization of bowel function usually occurs within a few weeks of admission with normalization of food intake.

Self-injurious behavior is stigmatized, and the reinforcing nature of repeatedly engaging in such behaviors is emphasized. Patients are taught alternative coping skills and methods of tolerating dysphoric feelings. This approach is very effective in interrupting and extinguishing such behavior.

Patients with a History of Sexual Abuse or Dissociative Symptoms

An effort is made to corroborate reports of sexual abuse or trauma by interviewing collateral informants, typically parents. Patients are encouraged to report credible histories of abuse to the legal authorities. An empathic and supportive approach is used. Stress is placed on changing eating behavior and countering eating-disordered thoughts as the initial goal of therapy. Patients who report dissociative symptoms are asked to actively stay in the here and now and avoid exploring past upsetting experiences until their eating behavior is under control. Group discussion of sexual or traumatic issues is discouraged. These are seen as topics best addressed after discharge in individual therapy and only once patients are able to tolerate discussing them without acting out on their eating disorder or other self-destructive behavior.

Atypical Eating Disorders

Occasionally, patients are admitted with atypical eating disorders, for example, psychogenic intractable vomiting or globus hystericus. These patients typically lack the cognitive body image disturbance or fear of fatness that characterizes anorexia nervosa or bulimia, yet they are fearful of eating for other reasons and may be very malnourished. Nonetheless, they can be successfully treated on a behavioral eating disorder unit. Response is often very rapid and, as with conversion disorders, may occur in a matter of days. Care is taken to clarify that the goal of admission is to help rehabilitate the digestive system and train patients to control their impulse to vomit or spit up food. Patients are reassured that although they feel they lack control of these responses, with enough practice and determination, they can learn to overcome them. Relaxation techniques are often useful. Although such patients' phenomenology differs in some ways from that of peers on the unit, focusing on commonalities such as feeling powerless to stop their behavior helps to integrate them with patient peers and thereby increases the effectiveness of group therapy.

EFFECTIVENESS OF THE PROGRAM IN ACHIEVING WEIGHT RESTORATION

We next present data on the effectiveness of the previously described program. Although ideally an RCT should be used to evaluate an intervention, the following naturalistic results suggest that this model of treatment leads to significant changes and can have an important clinical impact. The data focuses on patients placed on the weight gain protocol because of the clarity and simplicity of weight as a measurable outcome variable.

Consecutively admitted ($n = 150$) underweight patients in the Johns Hopkins inpatient-partial hospital eating disorders program who remained inpatient for at least seven days were assessed to evaluate the program's effectiveness in restoring weight and normalizing eating behavior. All had failed standard outpatient care, all had an eating disorder severe enough to warrant inpatient treatment, and 63% had had at least one prior admission to an eating disorder specialty unit.

Diagnosis was assigned by clinical interview using the Structured Clinical Interview for *DSM-IV* (First, Spitzer, Gibbon, & Williams, 1996). Patients who met partial criteria for anorexia nervosa or bulimia nervosa were classified as subthreshold anorexia nervosa, subthreshold bulimia, or atypical EDNOS. Diagnoses of participants were anorexia nervosa purging type (AN-P; 32%), anorexia nervosa restricting type (AN-R; 49%), underweight bulimia nervosa purging type (BN-P; 8%), subthreshold AN-R (4%), subthreshold AN-P (4%), underweight subthreshold BN-P (1%), and atypical EDNOS (2%). The majority of participants were female (97.2%), Caucasian (95.2%), never married (76.2%), and unemployed (57.7%). Average age was 25.6 years ($SD = 11.5$), and 31% were under age 18. All subjects were placed on the behavioral weight gain protocol.

Patients who dropped out of inpatient prematurely without transitioning to partial hospital (22%) were compared to the 78% who completed transition. Patient- or family-initiated discharges were more common in premature leavers ($X^2 = 25.99$; $p < .001$), and none were discharged for clinical improvement. Mean age was younger in patients who completed step-down ($M = 24.2$, $SD = 10.7$) versus early dropouts ($M = 31.0$; $SD = 13.0$; $t[1,148] = 2.87$; $p < .02$). No significant differences were found on Beck Depression Inventory scores (BDI; Beck, Rush, Shaw, & Emery, 1979), years of dieting before admission, number of prior eating disorder admissions, inpatient weight gain per week, or inpatient length of stay; and no overall multivariate effect for the Eating Disorders Inventory-2 (EDI-2; Garner, 1991) was found between groups. Because patients who left before transition to partial hospital were older and more likely to leave for patient or family-initiated reasons, they may represent a more chronic and less motivated population but otherwise appeared comparable to those who completed step-down.

The remaining results are based on the 117 (78%) patients who transitioned from inpatient to the partial hospitalization program. Mean BMI at inpatient admission was 16.1 ($SD = 2.1$), 18.3 ($SD = 2.0$) at step-down to partial hospital, and 19.6 ($SD = 1.9$) at discharge from partial hospital. A significant multivariate effect for time was found ($F [2,111] = 253.7$; $p < .001$), and all three time points differed from one another in post hoc comparisons (all p's $< .001$). Given that the age of 68% of the sample completing both inpatient and partial hospitalization was under 25, percent of age-adjusted target BMI at final discharge was calculated. Nearly half the sample (46%) was discharged at or above their age-adjusted target BMI, and 73% were within 5% of age-adjusted target BMI. Only 15% of patients who completed step-down to partial hospital had a final discharge BMI of less than 18.

Average inpatient and partial hospital weight gain rates were higher than those reported by most other programs (APA, 2000; Howard et al., 1999; Kaplan & Olmsted, 1997; Piran et al., 1989). Patients gained faster as inpatients ($F[1,115] = 52.14$; $p < .001$) with average weekly gains of 4.3 lbs/wk ($SD = 2.0$) versus mean partial hospital gains of 2.3 lbs/wk ($SD = 1.8$). Importantly, although occasional hypophosphatemia and mild to moderate peripheral edema occurred in very underweight inpatients, there were no cases of congestive heart failure in more than 350 patients treated between 1996 and 2001. Although fluid retention may occur during early refeeding, it cannot explain the observed partial hospital rate of gain because step-down occurred a mean of 19 days after admission when diuresis is more common than fluid retention. Furthermore, early transition of patients at high risk of edema was rare due to risk of medical instability. If fluid retention were playing a major role in inflating rates of gain, inpatient purgers would be expected to gain faster than restrictors (Neuberger, Rao, Weltzin, Greeno, & Kaye, 1995), yet no difference was found in inpatient weekly gains between anorexia subtypes. Restrictors gained significantly faster ($M = 2.8$; $SD = 1.5$) than purgers ($M = 1.8$; $SD = 2.0$) in the less supervised partial hospital setting ($t[1,108] = 2.97$; $p < .01$), however, possibly due to clandestine purging behavior in the latter group. In a preliminary follow-up study of the first 53 patients with anorexia nervosa in this sample, 52% of those who completed transition to partial hospital were successfully traced at three- to six-month follow-up by phone. Follow-up BMI was not significantly different from BMI at program discharge for this subsample. One of the strengths of this step-down model may be its contribution to relapse prevention. The gradual taper in attendance and increased autonomy over practice of healthy eating as patients move through the partial hospital program facilitate the application of skills learned in the highly structured inpatient setting to the real world environment facing the patient after discharge.

Several limitations of this study are worth noting. As previously mentioned, the design was naturalistic rather than a randomized controlled trial. Follow-up was by self-report and traced only half of the first 53 participants completing the program. The dropout rate, although relatively high, was typical of clinical practice and comparable to that reported by other partial hospital programs (Piran et al., 1989). While the majority of patients (73%) were within 5% of normal weight by discharge from the program, only 46% were fully weight-restored. Although nonideal, this percentage reflects the clinical reality of treating anorexia nervosa under the constraints of managed care and limited mental health benefits. Finally, as a tertiary referral, university hospital-based program, treatment-resistant patients were overrepresented.

Whether partial hospital alone is an effective alternative to this integrated step-down inpatient-partial hospital model and, if so, for whom remains unclear. Step-up treatment, relying on partial hospital admission as the entry point to inpatient, needs to be tested against step-down models of care because drive to diet often sabotages weight gain in outpatient settings, especially in the poorly motivated patient. Initial inpatient supervision interrupts unhealthy behaviors, helps engage the ambivalent patient, and may contribute to faster subsequent partial hospital weight gain.

Given the oftentimes egosyntonic nature of eating disorders, many patients are pressured or even coerced by important others to enter treatment. Researchers have examined the role of coercion in other psychiatric groups, but this has not been sufficiently explored in eating-disordered populations. Coerced or involuntary treatment is often supported by the argument that patients will likely change their views after receiving care. We recently examined eating disorder patients' perceptions about need for hospitalization and perceived coercion at admission, and after two weeks of treatment, we compared these to treatment response in 151 inpatients (Heinberg, Guarda, Marinilli, Haug, & Hussein, 2002). At admission, patients with Structured Clinical Interview for *DSM-IV* (SCID)-confirmed anorexia nervosa reported greater perceived coercion ($p < .001$) and pressure ($p < .03$), less procedural justice ($p < .001$), and were less likely to believe they needed hospitalization ($p < .05$) than did patients with bulimia. Diagnostic group differences however, were no longer significant two weeks postadmission.

Inpatients who did not believe they needed hospitalization (16%) and those who were ambivalent (20%) did not differ from those who thought they needed hospitalization on length of stay, admission, or discharge BMI or rate of weight gain. After two weeks, half of the 36% of patients who did not think they needed admission changed their minds. Although common, feelings of coercion do not appear to alter inpatient treatment success and are subject to change. This data calls into question whether assessment of motivation for treatment should determine timing of inpatient admission. Some patients may develop motivation for treatment only once they experience mastery over normal eating behavior and once positive effects of treatment outweigh weight phobia.

SUMMARY AND FUTURE DIRECTIONS FOR TREATMENT

Anorexia nervosa and bulimia are behavioral disorders characterized by a compelling drive to engage in dieting and ambivalence about changing this behavior. Initial treatment should be aimed at interrupting eating-disordered behavior and at weight restoration for underweight patients. Given the high readmission rates associated with incomplete weight restoration in anorexia nervosa, there is urgent need for RCTs comparing different treatment protocols and delineation of standards and treatment strategies for improving weight gains (Wiseman et al., 2001). For example, ideally, patients would be randomized to different levels of inpatient weight restoration. Unfortunately, such studies are all but impossible to conduct in clinical programs given the ethical implications and need to involve third-party payers in treatment.

At a minimum, however, clinical programs interested in research should regularly collect data at admission and discharge and examine aspects of treatment via component analysis to discern what program features are associated with better immediate outcome (e.g., adding a relapse prevention program). Currently, inpatient programs use an "everything but the kitchen sink" approach, including all aspects of treatment thought to be helpful. Instead, future research should help inpatient and partial hospital treatment refine their focus to include only those features determined to be most beneficial. Given the current health care climate and closing of many academic specialty centers for eating disorders, there is also a need to compare alternative treatment settings such as medical or general psychiatric units to care on a behavioral specialty unit. Randomizing patients to step-up versus step-down inpatient-partial hospital programs may help identify patient characteristics predictive of a good outcome in less intensive treatment settings.

Naturalistic studies can further examine the point in the course of treatment (e.g., at admission, during partial hospitalization, after discharge) that specific features are most helpful. When extreme symptoms of starvation and purging threaten life, most therapies are geared toward gaining immediate control over critical problem behaviors such as food avoidance, self-induced vomiting, laxative abuse, and so on. Whether patients can participate in and benefit from psychotherapy such as CBT during this acute phase of medical stabilization has not been tested. Similarly, whether CBT after medical stabilization or goal weight has been obtained is most beneficial is also untested. More work is needed on CBT approaches to addressing body dissatisfaction in this population. It may be that the timing, setting, and intensity of treatment all play a role in ensuring successful outcomes. In the case of adolescent patients, outpatient RCT data suggest that involvement of family in inpatient and partial hospital treatment may speed recovery. The issue of whether adolescents should be treated separate from adult patients remains controversial and important to examine because of the paucity of dedicated behavioral adolescent eating disorders units.

Researchers have shown interest in tailoring treatment to patient characteristics such as readiness for change (Levy, 1997; Vitousek, Watson, & Wilson, 1998) and illness severity (Bulik, Sullivan, Carter, McIntosh, & Joyce, 1999; Turnbull et al., 1997). Because ambivalence toward treatment is a cardinal feature of these disorders, the effect of perceived coercion to seek treatment (e.g., pressure by family, peers, school, or employers) on prognosis should be analyzed further, both from a practical and ethical standpoint and in relationship to assessment of readiness for change.

The high cost of inpatient treatment for eating disorders and the limited evidence of long-term positive effect are often cited in support of the current trend toward less intensive treatment settings. However, cost analysis should bear in mind treatment objectives. Because weight restoration is thought to be crucial to full recovery from anorexia nervosa, cost analysis should compare the cost per pound of weight gained in different treatment settings, rather than the cost per day or unit of service. In fact, preliminary data on cost per pound of weight gained suggests that the average cost of partial hospitalization may be no less expensive than inpatient specialty care (Guarda & Heinberg, 2002). If so, partial hospitalization may be cost effective only for behaviorally compliant patients able to gain weight in less supervised clinical settings. We have found that, when compared to behaviorally compliant patients, poorly compliant patients who exhibit multiple problem behaviors (e.g., exercising, restricting, vomiting, bingeing) as inpatients have worse partial hospital, but equivalent inpatient, rates of weight gain (Guarda, Heinberg, Haug, & Ambrose, 2000). Keeping these patients in a highly structured inpatient setting for a longer period may help convert them and decrease their ambivalence toward treatment, thereby improving prognosis. Although this is untested, we do know that the decreases in average lengths of stay over the past 15 years have been accompanied by increases in readmission and have paralleled a decrease in discharge BMI over time (Wiseman et al., 2001). Research on cost-effectiveness of treatment for anorexia nervosa and bulimia should be incorporated in future RCTs because cost of treatment increasingly restricts its availability in this era of managed care (Agras, 2001).

Finally, although there is ample evidence that inpatient treatment is effective in restoring weight and normalizing eating behavior, relapse rates remain high even after successful inpatient or partial hospital treatment of both anorexia nervosa and bulimia. In the case of anorexia nervosa, refeeding alone, although necessary for recovery, is often not sufficient in the absence of longer term relapse prevention measures. RCTs comparing different postdischarge relapse prevention care for successfully treated patients are essential to draw firm conclusions on the efficacy of inpatient and partial hospital treatment of these behavioral conditions.

REFERENCES

Agras, W. S. (2001). The consequences and costs of eating disorders. *Psychiatric Clinics of North America, 24,* 371–379.

Agras, W. S., Crow, S. J., Halmi, K. A., Mitchell, J. E., Wilson, G. T., & Kraemer, H. C. (2000). Outcome predictors for the cognitive behavior treatment of bulimia nervosa: Data from a multisite study. *American Journal of Psychiatry, 157*(8), 1302–1308.

Agras, W. S., & Kraemer, H. C. (1984). The treatment of anorexia nervosa: Do different treatments have different outcomes? In A. J. Stunkard & E. Stellar (Eds.), *Eating and its disorders* (pp. 193–207). New York: Raven Press.

American Dietetic Association/American Diabetic Association. (1989). *Exchange lists for weight management.* Chicago: Author.

American Psychiatric Association. (2000, January). Practice guidelines for the treatment of patients with eating disorders (Rev.). *American Journal of Psychiatry, 157*(Suppl.), 1–39.

Andersen, A. E., Bowers, W. A., & Evans, K. (1997). Inpatient treatment of anorexia nervosa. In D. M. Garner & P. F. Garfinkel (Eds.), *Handbook of treatment for eating disorders* (pp. 327–353). New York: Guilford Press.

Andersen, A. E., Stoner, S. A., & Rolls, B. J. (1996). Improved eating behavior in eating-disordered inpatients after treatment: Documentation in a naturalistic setting. *International Journal of Eating Disorders, 20,* 397–403.

Attia, E., Haiman, C., Walsh, B. T., & Flater, S. R. (1998). Does fluoxetine augment the inpatient treatment of anorexia nervosa? *American Journal of Psychiatry, 155,* 548–551.

Baran, S. A., Weltzin, T. E., & Kaye, W. H. (1995). Low discharge weight and outcome in anorexia nervosa. *American Journal of Psychiatry, 152*(7), 1070–1072.

Beck, A. T., Rush, A. J., Shaw, B. F., & Emery, G. (1979). *Cognitive therapy for depression.* New York: Guilford Press.

Ben-Tovim, D. I., Walker, K., Gilchrist, P., Freeman, R., Kalucy, R., & Esterman, A. (2001). Outcome in patients with eating disorders: A 5-year study. *Lancet, 357,* 1254–1257.

Bossert, S., Schmolz, U., Wiegand, M., Junker, M., & Krieg, J. C. (1992). Predictors of short-term treatment outcome in bulimia nervosa inpatients. *Behavior Research and Therapy, 30,* 193–199.

Bowers, W. A. (2001). Basic principles for applying cognitive-behavioral therapy to anorexia nervosa. *Psychiatric Clinics of North America, 24,* 293–303.

Bremer, J., & Herzog, D. (1997). Are insurance agencies making treatment decisions? *Journal of the American Academy of Child and Adolescent Psychiatry, 36*(11), 1488–1489.

Bulik, C. M., Sullivan, P. F., Carter, F. A., McIntosh, V. V., & Joyce, P. R. (1999). Predictors of rapid and sustained response to cognitive-behavioral therapy for bulimia nervosa. *International Journal of Eating Disorders, 26,* 137–144.

Commerford, M. C., Licinio, J., & Halmi, K. A. (1997). Guidelines for discharging eating disordered inpatients. *Eating Disorders, 5,* 69–74.

Danziger, Y., Carel, C. A., Tyano, S., & Mimouni, M. (1989). Is psychotherapy mandatory during the acute refeeding period in the treatment of anorexia nervosa? *Journal of Adolescent Health Care, 10,* 328–331.

Dare, C., Eisler, I., Russell, G., Treasure, J., & Dodge, L. (2001). Psychological therapies for adults with anorexia nervosa: Randomized controlled trial of out-patient treatments. *British Journal of Psychiatry, 178,* 216–221.

Eisler, I., Dare, C., Hodes, M., Dodge, E., Russell, G., & Le Grange, D. (2000). Family therapy for anorexia nervosa in adolescents: The results of a controlled comparison of two family interventions. *Journal of Child Psychology and Psychiatry, 41,* 727–736.

Eisler, I., Dare, C., Russell, G. F. M., Szmukler, G., Le Grange, D., & Dodge, E. (1997). Family and individual therapy in AN: A 5-year follow-up. *Archives of General Psychiatry, 54,* 1025–1030.

Fairburn, C., Cooper, Z., & Shafran, R. (2002). *A new "transdiagnostic" cognitive behavioral treatment for eating disorders.* Workshop presented at the 2002 International Conference on Eating Disorders, Boston.

Fallon, B. A., Walsh, B. T., Sadik, C., Saoud, J. B., & Lukasik, V. (1991). Outcome and clinical course in inpatient bulimic women. A 2- to 9-year follow up study. *Journal of Clinical Psychiatry, 52,* 272–278.

Fettes, P. A., & Peters, J. M. (1992). A meta-analysis of group treatments for bulimia nervosa. *International Journal of Eating Disorders, 11,* 97–110.

Fichter, M. M., Kruger, R., Rief, W., Holland, R., & Dohne, J. (1996). Fluvoxamine in prevention of relapse in bulimia nervosa: Effects on eating-specific psychopathology. *Journal of Clinical Psychopharmacology, 16,* 9–18.

Fichter, M. M., & Quadflieg, N. (1997). Six-year course of bulimia nervosa. *International Journal of Eating Disorders, 22,* 361–384.

First, M. B., Spitzer, R. L., Gibbon, M., & Williams, J. B. W. (1996). *Structured clinical interview for DSM-IV Axis I disorders.* New York: Biometrics Research.

Garner, D. M. (1991). *Eating Disorder Inventory-2.* Odessa, FL: Psychological Assessment Resources.

Garner, D. M., Vitousek, K. M., & Pike, K. M. (1997). Cognitive-behavioral therapy of anorexia nervosa. In D. M. Garner & P. E. Garfinkel (Eds.), *Handbook of treatment for eating disorders* (pp. 67–93). New York: Guilford Press.

Gowers, S. G., Weetman, J., Shore, A., Hossain, F., & Elvins, R. (2000). Impact of hospitalization on the outcome of adolescent anorexia nervosa. *British Journal of Psychiatry, 176,* 138–141.

Guarda, A. S., & Heinberg, L. J. (1999). *Effective weight gain in a step down partial hospitalization program for eating disorders.* Poster presented at the Academy of Eating Disorders 1999 Annual Meeting, San Diego, CA.

Guarda, A. S., & Heinberg, L. J. (2002). *Partial hospitalization for anorexia nervosa: Who gains, how and at what cost?* Paper presented at the American Psychiatric Association 2002 annual meeting, Philadelphia.

Guarda, A. S., Heinberg, L. J., Haug, N., & Ambrose, D. (2000). *Behavioral predictors of short term anorexia nervosa outcome in an inpatient/partial hospitalization program.* Paper presented at the Academy for Eating Disorders' 9th International Conference on Eating Disorders, New York.

Gull, W. W. (1874). Anorexia nervosa (apepsia hysterica, anorexia hysterica). *Transactions of the Clinical Society of London, 7,* 22–28.

Harris, E. C. H., & Barraclough, B. (1998). Excess mortality of mental disorder. *British Journal of Psychiatry, 173,* 11–53.

Hay, P., & Bacaltchuk, J. (2002). Bulimia nervosa. In S. Barton (Ed.), *Clinical evidence* (7th ed., pp. 21–31). London: BMJ Publishing Group.

Heinberg, L. J., Guarda, A. S., Haug, N. A., Yacono-Freeman, L. M., & Ambrose, D. (in press). Clinical course and short-term outcome of hospitalized adolescents with eating disorders: Can success be achieved on an adult eating disorders unit? *Eating and Weight Disorders: Studies on Anorexia, Bulimia and Obesity.*

Heinberg, L. J., Guarda, A. S., Marinilli, A. S., Haug, N., & Hussain, S. (2002). *Perceived coercion among hospitalized patients with anorexia nervosa.* Poster presented at the annual meeting of the Eating Disorders Research Society, Charleston, SC.

Herpetz-Dahlmann, B. H., Muller, B., Herpetz, S., & Heussen, N. (2001). Prospective 10-year follow-up in adolescent anorexia nervosa: Course, outcome, psychiatric comorbidity and psychosocial adaptation. *Journal of Child Psychology and Psychiatry, 42,* 603–612.

Herzog, D. B., Nussbaum, K. M., & Marmor, A. K. (1996). Comorbidity and outcome in eating disorders. *Psychiatric Clinics of North America, 19,* 843–859.

Hoek, H. W., & Treasure, J. (2002). Evidence based treatments for anorexia nervosa. *European Psychiatry, 17*(Suppl. 1), 17.

Howard, W. T., Evans, K. K., Quintero-Howard, C. V., Bowers, W. A., & Andersen, A. E. (1999). Predictors of success or failure of transition to day hospital treatment for inpatients with anorexia nervosa. *American Journal of Psychiatry, 156,* 1697–1702.

Kaplan, A. S., & Olmsted, M. P. (1997). Partial hospitalization. In D. M. Garner & P. E. Garfinkel (Eds.), *Handbook of treatment for eating disorders* (2nd ed., pp. 354–360). New York: Guilford Press.

Kaplan, A. S., Olmsted, M. P., Carter, J. C., & Woodside, B. (2001). Matching patient variables to treatment intensity. *Psychiatric Clinics of North America, 24,* 281–292.

Kaye, W. H., Kaplan, A. S., & Zucker, M. L. (1996). Treating eating-disorder patients in a managed care environment: Contemporary American issues and a Canadian response. *Eating Disorders, 19*(4), 793–810.

Kaye, W. H., Nagata, T., Weltzin, T. E., Hsu, L. K. G., Sokol, M. S., McConaba, C., et al. (2001). Double-blind controlled administration of fluoxetine in restricting- and purging-type anorexia nervosa. *Biological Psychiatry, 10,* 151–157.

Keys, A., Brozek, K., Henschel, A., Mickelsen, O., & Taylor, H. L. (1950). *The biology of human starvation.* Minneapolis: University of Minnesota Press.

Lacey, J. H., & Evans, C. D. H. (1986). The impulsivist: A multiimpulsive personality disorder. *British Journal of Addiction, 81,* 641–649.

Le Grange, D., Eisler, I., Dare, C., & Russell, G. F. M. (1992). Evaluation of family treatments in adolescent anorexia nervosa: A pilot study. *International Journal of Eating Disorders, 12,* 347–357.

Levy, R. K. (1997). The transtheoretical model of change: An application to bulimia nervosa. *Psychotherapy, 34,* 278–285.

Lowe, B., Zipfel, S., Buchholz, C., Dupont, Y., Reas, D. L., & Herzog, W. (2001). Long-term outcome of anorexia nervosa in a prospective 21-year follow-up study. *Psychological Medicine, 21,* 881–890.

Maddocks, S. E., & Kaplan, A. S. (1991). The prediction of treatment response in bulimia nervosa: A study of patient variables. *British Journal of Psychiatry, 159,* 846–849.

Maddocks, S. E., Kaplan, A. S., Woodside, D. B., Langdon, L., & Piran, N. (1992). Two year follow-up of bulimia nervosa: The importance of abstinence as the criterion of outcome. *International Journal of Eating Disorders, 12,* 133–141.

McHugh, P. R., & Slavney, P. R. (1998). *The perspectives of psychiatry* (2nd ed.). Baltimore: Johns Hopkins University Press.

McIntosh, V. V., Bulik, C. M., McKenzie, J. M., Luty, S. E., & Jordan, J. (2000). Interpersonal psychotherapy for anorexia nervosa. *International Journal of Eating Disorders, 27,* 125–139.

McKisack, C., & Waller, G. (1997). Factors influencing the outcome of group psychotherapy for bulimia nervosa. *International Journal of Eating Disorders, 22,* 1–13.

Mehler, P. S., & Weiner, K. L. (1993). Anorexia nervosa and total parenteral nutrition. *International Journal of Eating Disorders, 14,* 297–304.

Mitchell, J. E. (1991). A review of controlled trials of psychotherapy for bulimia nervosa. *Journal of Psychosomatic Research, 35*(Suppl. 1), 23–31.

Mitchell, J. E., Pyle, R. L., Pomeroy, C., Zollman, M., Crosby, R., Seim, H., et al. (1993). Cognitive-behavioral group psychotherapy or bulimia nervosa: Importance of logistical variables. *International Journal of Eating Disorders, 14,* 277–287.

Mitchell, J. E., Raymond, N., & Specker, S. (1993). A review of the controlled trials of pharmacotherapy and psychotherapy in the treatment of bulimia nervosa. *International Journal of Eating Disorders, 14*(3), 229–247.

Neuberger, S. K., Rao, R., Weltzin, T. E., Greeno, C., & Kaye, W. H. (1995). Differences in weight gain between restrictor and bulimic anorectics. *International Journal of Eating Disorders, 17,* 331–335.

Olmsted, M. P., Kaplan, A. S., Jacobsen, M., & Rockert, W. (1996). Rapid responders to treatment of bulimia nervosa. *International Journal of Eating Disorders, 19,* 279–285.

Patton, G. C., Selzer, R., Coffey, J. B., & Wolfe, R. (1999). Onset of adolescent eating disorders: A population based cohort study over 3 years. *British Medical Journal, 318,* 765–768.

Pike, K. M. (1998). Long-term course of anorexia nervosa: Response, relapse, remission and recovery. *Clinical Psychology Review, 18,* 447–475.

Piran, N., Langdon, L., Kaplan, A., & Garfinkel, P. E. (1989). Evaluation of a day hospital program for eating disorders. *International Journal of Eating Disorders, 8*(5), 523–532.

Ramsay, R., Ward, A., Treasure, J., & Russell, G. F. M. (1999). Compulsory treatment in anorexia nervosa. *British Journal of Psychiatry, 175,* 147–153.

Raw, S. D. (2000). Anorexic patients face difficulties in obtaining insurance reimbursement. *Behavior Therapist,* 16–17.

Robb, A. S., Silber, T. J., Orrell-Valente, J. K., Valadez-Meltszer, A., Ellis, N., Dadson, M. J., et al. (2002). Supplemental nocturnal nasogastric refeeding for better short-term outcome in hospitalized adolescent girls with anorexia nervosa. *American Journal of Psychiatry, 159,* 1347–1353.

Robin, A. L., Siegel, P. T., Moye, A. W., Gilroy, M., Baker, D. A., & Sikand, A. (1999). A controlled comparison of family versus individual therapy for adolescents with anorexia nervosa. *Journal of the Academy of Child and Adolescent Psychiatry, 38,* 1482–1489.

Romano, S., Halmi, K. A., Sarkar, N. P., Koke, S. C., & Lee, J. S. (2002). A placebo-controlled study of fluoxetine in continued treatment of bulimia nervosa after successful fluoxetine treatment. *American Journal of Psychiatry, 159,* 96–102.

Russell, G. F. M. (2001). Involuntary treatment in anorexia nervosa. *Psychiatric Clinics of North America, 24,* 337–349.

Russell, G. F. M. (2002). *Is it time to rethink the diagnostic criteria of anorexia nervosa?* Paper presented at the annual meeting of the Eating Disorders Research Society, Charleston, SC.

Russell, G. F. M., Szmukler, G. I., Dare, C., & Eisler, I. (1987). An evaluation of family therapy in anorexia nervosa and bulimia nervosa. *Archives of General Psychiatry, 44,* 1047–1056.

Silber, T. J., & Robb, A. S. (2002). Eating disorders and health insurance: Understanding and overcoming obstacles to treatment. *Child and Adolescent Psychiatric Clinics of North America, 11,* 419–428.

Steinhausen, H. C. (1999). Eating disorders. In H. C. Steinhausen & F. C. Verhulst (Eds.), *Risk and outcomes in developmental psychopathology* (pp. 210–230). Oxford, England: Oxford University Press.

Stice, E., Presnell, K., & Spangler, D. (2002). Risk factors for binge eating onset in adolescent girls: A 2-year prospective investigation. *Health-Psychology, 21*(2), 131–138.

Strober, M., Freeman, R., & Morrell, W. (1997). The long-term course of severe anorexia nervosa in adolescents: Survival analysis of recovery, relapse and outcome predictors over 10–15 years in a prospective study. *International Journal of Eating Disorders, 22,* 339–360.

Sullivan, P. F. (1995). Mortality in anorexia nervosa. *American Journal of Psychiatry, 152*(7), 1073–1074.

Touyz, S. W., & Beumont, P. J. V. (1997). Behavioral treatment to promote weight gain in anorexia nervosa. In D. M. Garner & P. F. Garfinkel (Eds.), *Handbook of treatment for eating disorders* (pp. 361–371). New York: Guilford Press.

Touyz, S. W., Beumont, P. J. V., Glaun, D., Phillips, T., & Cowie, I. (1984). A comparison of lenient and strict operant conditioning programs in refeeding patients with anorexia nervosa. *British Journal of Psychiatry, 144,* 517–520.

Treasure, J., & Schmidt, U. (2002). Anorexia nervosa. In S. Barton (Ed.), *Clinical evidence* (7th ed., pp. 1–10). London: BMJ Publishing Group.

Turnbull, S. J., Schmidt, U., Troop, N. A., Tiller, J., Todd, G., & Treasure, J. (1997). Predictors of outcome for two treatments for bulimia nervosa: Short and long term. *International Journal of Eating Disorders, 21,* 17–22.

Vandereycken, W. (1985). Inpatient treatment of anorexia nervosa: Some research-guided changes. *Journal of Psychiatric Research, 19,* 413–422.

Van Furth, E. F. (1998). The treatment of anorexia nervosa. In H. W. Hoek, J. Treasure, & M. A. Katzman (Eds.), *Neurobiology in the treatment of eating disorders* (pp. 315–330). New York: Wiley.

Vitousek, K., Watson, S., & Wilson, T. G. (1998). Enhancing motivation for change in treatment-resistant eating disorders. *Clinical Psychology Review, 18,* 391–420.

Walsh, B. T., Wilson, G. T., Loeb, K. L., Devlin, M. J., Pike, K. M., Roose, S. P., et al. (1997). Medication and psychotherapy in the treatment of bulimia nervosa. *American Journal of Psychiatry, 154*(4), 523–531.

Wilson, A. J., Touyz, S. W., Dunn, S. M., & Beumont, P. J. V. (1989). The Eating Behavior Rating Scale (EBRS): A measure of eating pathology in anorexia nervosa. *International Journal of Eating Disorders, 8,* 583–592.

Wilson, G. T., Loeb, K. L., Walsh, B. T., Labouvie, E., Petkova, E., Liu, X., et al. (1999). Psychological versus pharmacological treatments of bulimia nervosa: Predictors and processes of change. *Journal of Consulting and Clinical Psychology, 67*(4), 451–459.

Wiseman, C. V., Sunday, S. R., Klapper, F., Harris, W. A., & Halmi, K. A. (2001). Changing patterns of hospitalization in eating disorder patients. *International Journal of Eating Disorders, 30*, 69–74.

Zipfel, S., Reas, D. L., Thornton, C., Olmsted, M. P., Williamson, D. A., Gerlinghoff, M., et al. (2002). Day hospitalization for eating disorders: A systematic review of the literature. *International Journal of Eating Disorders, 31*, 105–117.

PART II

Obesity

Chapter 16 ————————————————————————

GENETIC AND BIOLOGICAL RISK FACTORS

MARK B. COPE, JOSÉ R. FERNÁNDEZ, AND DAVID B. ALLISON

Obesity is a complex condition where energy intake exceeds energy expenditure. Genetic and environmental influences have been identified as causes for this condition, and researchers in the field of obesity are trying to elucidate the specific genetic and environmental components responsible for its genesis.

Hundreds of DNA sequences have been putatively associated with this disorder (Rankinen et al., 2002), and many of these have been identified in animal models and/or among humans. Table 16.1 shows the number of identified single-gene mutation disorders, Mendelian disorders, quantitative trait loci (QTLs) from animal models, associations with candidate genes, and loci from linkage studies reported in the 2001 "obesity map" (Rankinen et al., 2002). These numbers highlight the complexity of obesity genetics. With the advent of specialized molecular screening techniques such as microarrays (Allison, 2002; Duggan, Bittner, Chen, Meltzer, & Trent, 1999; Lipshutz, Fodor, Gingeras, & Lockhart, 1999) and the sequencing of the human genome (McPherson et al., 2001; Venter et al., 2001), the field of obesity genetics continues to expand tremendously.

Determining specific genes that regulate energy balance has been challenging for researchers because of the environmental influences present and the epigenetic effect on these complex phenotypes. As pictured in Figure 16.1, separating clearly defined

Table 16.1   Mendelian Disorders, QTLs, Associations, and Linkage Studies Have Revealed Possible Genes Involved with the Etiology of Obesity

Category of Obesity	Number of Genes/ Loci Mapped
Single-gene disorders	6
Mendelian disorders	25
QTLs from animal models	165
Associations	58
Linkages	59

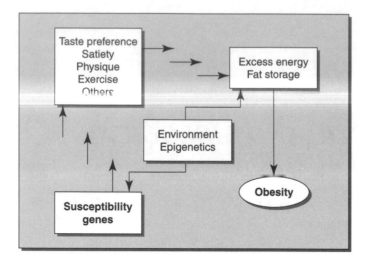

Figure 16.1   Interplay of Susceptibility Genes and Environmental Factors That Lead to Obesity.

genetic susceptibility and environmental influences that lead to weight gain is a challenge that continues to be a matter of investigation.

Knowing which genes control the energy homeostatic pathways, including the behavioral ones, will be valuable for predicting future risk of obesity and for developing therapeutics to treat obesity. Although many pieces of the obesity genetics puzzle have been discovered, many more are likely to be discovered and fitting of all these pieces together remains to be done.

Solving the overall puzzle of coordinating obesity genes into a functional model that can be used to fully understand the ontogeny of obesity is the ultimate goal for researchers. Armed with such knowledge, we will be better positioned to develop therapeutic and preventive approaches, including the development of novel pharmacologic agents. Some companies computer-simulate human disorders such as obesity and then develop effective new treatments for the disorder. This type of technological advancement will dramatically reduce the time and cost needed to develop pharmacotherapy in the future.

In this chapter, we present an overview of basic genetic concepts, followed by a description of adult obesity, childhood obesity, and types of studies used to discover obesity genes in populations. A discussion of nutrition (energy intake) and exercise (energy expenditure) in the context of obesity genetics is also presented. We also review methods for identifying genetic influences in the population and discuss specific genetic sequences that may contribute to obesity-related traits.

GENETICS

A gene can be described as a unit factor of biological inheritance. It is a physical structure of deoxyribonucleic acid (DNA) containing information that is passed from generation to generation. DNA is composed of nitrogenous bases attached to a sugar-phosphate backbone and paired by hydrogen bonds in a helical structure. Genes are located on physical structures named chromosomes, and the position of each gene in a particular chromosome is referred to as a *locus*. Although each gene codes for a specific protein that responds to a specific function, different forms of the same protein can exist, coded by different forms of the same gene. Different forms of the same gene are named *alleles*. These alleles play a pivotal role in genetic analysis because they account in part for the observed variation in a trait (phenotypic variation). Variants in sequences of DNA are named *polymorphisms*. Single nucleotide polymorphisms (SNPs) result from a single base mutation substituting one nucleotide for another and are particularly important in obesity research because they may be the genetic factors that account for the majority of obesity-related conditions (Kagawa et al., 2002).

It is important for geneticists to assess the part of the phenotypic variation that is due to genes. *Heritability* (h^2) refers to the degree to which observed phenotypic differences for a trait are due to genetic variability and is calculated by the formula $h^2 = V_G/V_P$, where V_G represents the genetic variation and V_P represents the phenotypic variation. Heritability is calculated using analysis of variance among individuals of a known genetic relationship (Klug & Cummings, 2002).

EPIGENETICS

Phenotypic variation results from both genetic and environmental components. In 1942, Waddington referred to *epigenetics* as the study of processes by which genotype gives rise to phenotype and, in 1994, Holliday defined epigenetics as the study of changes in gene function that do not entail a change in DNA sequence (Wu & Morris, 2001). For example, in a rat experiment investigating the possible effects of overnourishment during sensitive periods of development, Diaz and Taylor found that excess nourishment changed the metabolic phenotype of one generation in such a way that the two subsequent generations were also affected (Diaz & Taylor, 1998). First-generation (F_1) female rats were divided into three groups with one group being naturally reared (NR) by their mothers, the second group (MF; match fed) was fed enough formula through gastric fistulas to have growth equivalent to the first group, and the third group (ON; over nourished) being fed excessive formula so that their growth was accelerated compared to the other two groups. At 123 days of age, all groups were put into breeding pairs with normal male rats. The second-generation (F_2) females were weaned normally (not given excess nourishment) and at 114 days of age put into breeding pairs with normal males. A third generation (F_3) of female rats was weaned normally. F_1 ON rats were significantly larger than the control groups, F_2 ON offspring were significantly smaller than the control group, and F_3 animals from ON grandmothers were heavier at weaning than the other groups. How did the overnourishment of the first group of rats cause the phenotypes of the two subsequent generations to be different? This could be the result of not only the genetic influence, but also an environmental developmental influence (Diaz & Taylor, 1998). The environment may work, in part, through inherited mechanisms in a kind of "neo-Lamarckism" (Jablonka & Lamb, 1989).

OBESITY AMONG US—PREVALENCE AND DEFINITION

Obesity is the state of a body resulting from energy intake exceeding energy expenditure for prolonged periods resulting in excessive body fat gain, and this excess body fat increases morbidity and mortality rates (Visscher & Seidell, 2001). Adults with a body mass index (BMI) greater than 30 kg/m^2 are considered obese (NIH, 1998). Several factors including appetite or food preferences, fuel metabolism, physical activity, and muscle fiber type and function contribute to body weight and fat, and each of these factors is influenced by genetics (Martinez, 2000).

OBESITY IN CHILDREN

Obesity rates among children are growing steadily (Ebbeling, Pawlak, & Ludwig, 2002). According to the American Dietetic Association (ADA), while the health status of children in the United States has generally improved over the past three decades, the number of children who are overweight has more than doubled (Cummings, Parham, & Strain, 2002). Approximately 4.7 million American children now meet the criteria for overweight (Cummings et al., 2002). Between 1976 and 2000, the percent of American children (6 to 11 years old) that were overweight increased from 4% to 15.3%, and in adolescents (12 to 19 years old), the rate rose from 5% to 15.5% (Ogden, Flegal, Carroll, & Johnson, 2002). This problem is not isolated within the United States. Societies throughout the world have reported increases in childhood obesity, and higher rates of childhood obesity presage widespread adult obesity in the future, considering approximately 40% of overweight children will become overweight adults (Maffeis et al., 2002).

Discovering genes regulating early childhood obesity is complicated because of the lack of universal criteria for determining accurate rates of childhood obesity and overweight. Different societies have adopted separate obesity indicators, and to make accurate comparisons between populations, epidemiological studies would need to use the same indicator, the same cut-off, and, whenever possible, recent reference curves suitable for the particular population surveyed (Luciano, Bressan, Bolognani, Castellarin, & Zoppi, 2001). Finding a genetic link to early etiology of obesity in children may be an important step in alleviating adult obesity and its associated morbidities.

TYPES OF STUDIES USED TO DISCOVER OBESITY GENES

Studies of BMI correlations in monozygotic twins and dizygotic twins suggest an estimated heritability of obesity around 70% (Allison et al., 1996; Barsh, Farooqi, & O'Rahilly, 2000; Comuzzie & Allison, 1998; Segal & Allison, 2002), while in biological/adoptive siblings, this estimate is much lower—around 20% to 60% (Maes, Neale, & Eaves, 1997). Considering all factors, from available information, it seems that heritability estimates above 50% and somewhere around 70% are most reasonable given current knowledge (Allison et al., 2003).

Because of the genetic control obtained through breeding experiments and the environmental control in laboratories, animal models have also become popular methods for studying obesity genetics. Obesity-related genes have been "knocked out" or overexpressed in animal models (Arch, 2002; Butler & Cone, 2001, 2002; Tschop & Heiman, 2001), providing some information about the possible molecular causes of this condition.

NUTRITION

Genes that regulate food intake are not well documented, and the genetics of eating encompass an immense range of topics, ranging from taste preference to the palatability of food to the molecular and chemical controls of eating. Each of these topics is important and is described here, followed by a detailed review of some of the more familiar obesity genes.

Taste Preference

There is some evidence that taste preference is controlled by a number of genes, and a family of candidate taste receptors (the TRBs) has been identified with diverse protein sequences. The diversity among these receptors is consistent with the ability for humans to detect a variety of taste; however, it appears that these TRBs control bitter transduction pathways rather than sweet (Matsunami, Montmayeur, & Buck, 2000).

Saccharin, an artificial sweetener, was used to discover a locus on mouse chromosome 4 called *Sac* and is responsible for phenotypic variations among inbred mouse strains (Capeless & Whitney, 1995) for sweet taste. Some mice are tasters while others are nontasters of saccharin. In mice, Tas1r3 gene maps to within 20,000 base pairs of *Sac* and is expressed in taste receptor cells (Li et al., 2001). The product of the Tas1r3 gene is T1r3 protein, a member of the family of G-protein coupled receptors.

The human TAS1R3 gene has been mapped and is expressed as T1R3 protein in taste receptor cells, but most importantly, it is likely a sweet-liganded taste receptor (binds sweet compounds; Max et al., 2001). Two other T1r genes, T1r1 and T1r2, which code for receptors T1R1 and T1R2, may allow for the diversity among sweet taste within a single taste bud (Lewcock & Reed, 2001). Nelson et al. reported that T1R1 and T1R3 combine to function as an amino acid sensor that responds to L-amino acids, but not their D-enantiomers or other compounds (Nelson et al., 2002).

These examples do not detail the complete picture for taste preference. Continuing progress will ultimately allow for a better molecular understanding of how sweet and bitter taste are involved with what each person eats, which could lead to an understanding of why some people prefer the taste of chocolate rather than lemon icebox pie. These discoveries may aid in the understanding of obesity genetics by identifying individuals who prefer and are sensitive to sweet or high-calorie, dense foods.

Palatability of Food

Palatability of food also seems to be influenced by genes. In a study to assess genetic and environmental effects on palatability, twins (identical and fraternal) living independently were asked to record palatability of meals, meal sizes, and relationships between palatability and intake. De Castro and Plunkett found that inheritance accounted for 23% of the variance in the before-meal palatability ratings while familial environment was not a significant effect (de Castro & Plunkett, 2001). These findings suggest that while free-living (natural environment, i.e., not in a calorimetry chamber) humans have choices of what to eat, there appears to be an inherit tendency to eat highly palatable foods. Genes, in a number of ways, influence ingestive behavior, and genetic preferences for high-fat, palatable foods, readily available in today's environment, are a concern.

Molecular and Chemical Control of Eating

In humans, when energy stores are depleted, circulating levels of the hormone leptin decrease and hypothalamic neurotransmitters are produced, signaling an increase in energy intake. Briefly, leptin binds the leptin receptor in the hypothalamus, stimulating a specific signaling cascade that results in the inhibition of several orexigenic neuropeptides, NPY (neuropeptide Y), MCH (melanin-concentrating hormone), orexins, and AgRP (agouti-related peptide), while stimulating several anorexigenic peptides, a-MSH (a-melanocyte-stimulating hormone), which acts on MC4R (melanocortin-4 receptor); CART (cocaine and amphetamine-regulated transcript); and CRH (corticotropin-releasing-hormone; Jequier, 2002). In the opposite direction, melanocyte-stimulating hormone (MSH), which is a precursor of pro-opiomelanocortin (POMC), signals for a decrease in appetite and possibly signals for increased energy expenditure (Michaud, 2001). Any gene involved with this array of signaling cascades in either direction could be associated with the obesity phenotype.

The orexigenic peptide, NPY, in coordination with leptin, controls nutrient intake and energy expenditure (Wilding, 2002). There are five functional NPY receptors (Y1, Y2, Y3, Y4, Y5) with the Y1 and Y5 subtypes expressed in the paraventricular hypothalamus and adipose tissue (Herzog et al., 1997; Serradeil-Le Gal et al., 2000). NPY containing neurons are targeted by leptin and may explain increased energy intake and decreased expenditure that occurs with leptin signaling defects (Schwartz, Seeley, Campfield, Burn, & Baskin, 1996). Administration of NPY to animals causes a sustained increase of food intake (Stanley, Kyrkouli, Lampert, & Leibowitz, 1986). However, NPY knockout mice have normal body weight with only slight responses to food deprivation (Wilding, 2002). This indicates that our genes may be programmed to preserve body mass in the face of starvation, and NPY in coordination with leptin keeps body mass in homeostasis. Any defect in NPY gene or NPY receptor(s) could lead to potential energy imbalance, leading to an obese phenotype.

AgRP, produced by NPY neurons, promotes energy intake and decreases energy expenditure by antagonizing a-melanocortin-stimulating hormone (a-MSH) through the melanocyte receptor 4 (MC4R; Marsh et al., 1999). AgRP injections cause increased food intake in rats (Hagan, Rushing, Benoit, Woods, & Seeley, 2001), and transgenic mice overexpressing AgRP are obese (Ollmann et al., 1997). Dubern et al. (2001) found that 1 in 63 severely obese children had a heterozygous missense mutation in the AgRP gene; however, normal phenotypes had similar frequency. The role of AgRP in the etiology of human obesity is not clear, but it is likely a minor gene involved with body weight regulation.

OBESITY GENES

Monogenic forms of human obesity have been identified as a result of mutations in the following genes: leptin, leptin receptor, POMC, MC4R, and peroxisome-proliferator-activated receptor gamma 2 (PPAR-gamma 2; Arner, 2000). However, common obesities are polygenic, and there is very little evidence that any one or two specific genes cause the more common forms of obesity. These monogenic forms of obesity are described.

Leptin and Leptin Receptor

The *ob* gene or leptin gene was first discovered in obese mice in the 1950s, and it was sequenced and cloned in the 1990s (Zhang et al., 1994). Leptin is the encoded protein product of the *ob* gene (Halaas et al., 1995), and it is produced primarily in adipocytes. Mice that are homozygous for an inactivating mutation in the *ob* gene (ob/ob) develop obesity (Ingalls, Dickie, & Snell, 1996) and Type II diabetes—a syndrome similar to that found in many morbidly obese humans (Kahn & Flier, 2000).

Our understanding how leptin and its receptor regulate appetite and energy expenditure is rapidly developing. Leptin may not be a critical satiety factor in humans in developed societies because changes in food intake do not induce short-term increases in plasma leptin levels (Considine et al., 1996). However, leptin levels do reflect the amount of energy stored in adipose tissue. Obese humans have high plasma leptin concentrations related to the size of adipose tissue (Hamilton, Paglia, Kwan, & Deitel, 1995), but this elevated leptin signal does not induce the expected responses (i.e., a reduction in food intake and an increase in energy expenditure; Jequier, 2002) and is sometimes referred to as *leptin resistance.*

In rodents as well as in humans, homozygous mutations in genes encoding leptin (Ingalls et al., 1996; Montague et al., 1997) or the leptin receptor (Chua et al., 1996; Clement et al., 1998) cause early-onset morbid obesity, hyperphagia, and reduced energy expenditure. Studies have demonstrated that *ob* gene expression is increased in human obesity (Montague et al., 1997). Allison and Heo (1998) found a linkage of BMI to the genome region containing the human *ob* gene. However, mutations of *ob* gene present in the mouse are rare in the human population (Strosberg & Issad, 1999), and common polymorphisms of the human leptin receptor are not associated with BMI or waist circumference (Heo et al., 2002).

In just over a decade, leptin and its receptor have become targets for obesity genetics research. Rodent models and the rare human cases of monogenetic mutations lend support to the hypothesis that these genes are involved in the etiology of obesity—to what extent is unknown. Further work will be required to detail the precise mechanisms, but through these discoveries with leptin, the roles of other genes have been identified.

MC4R

There is equivocal evidence that mutations in the MC4R gene are involved with human obesity (Mergen, Mergen, Ozata, Oner, & Oner, 2001). MC4R is expressed in the hypothalamus and has high affinity for a-MSH, a product of the pro-opiomelanocortin

(POMC) gene (Fan, Boston, Kesterson, Hruby, & Cone, 1997). Homozygous mice for a MC4R-null allele have late-onset obesity with increased food intake, which suggests that a-MSH signaling through MC4R binding must be involved with appetite and satiety control (Huszar et al., 1997). An association with percent body fat and MC4R mutation was found in 124 Quebec families (Chagnon et al., 1997). Heterozygous missense mutations of MC4R were reported in 11 of 446 subjects, which correlated with early-onset obesity (Farooqi et al., 2000). Four of 63 severely obese had heterozygous missense mutations in MC4R while 283 nonobese lacked the mutations (Dubern et al., 2001). These studies show some association between MC4R and obesity; however, another study revealed that MC4R sequence variations were not significantly associated with severe obesity (Jacobson et al., 2002). Gu et al. found that MC4R variants are unlikely to be a common cause of obesity because of the low frequency of functional mutations (Gu et al., 1999). The precise involvement of MC4R in the progression of obesity is not completely understood, and further analysis will be required before its role is determined.

POMC

A loss of POMC function causes obesity in mice (Yaswen, Diehl, Brennan, & Hochgeschwender, 1999) and humans (Krude et al., 1998). While complete POMC deletions are rare, four studies have found QTLs determining obesity-related traits in chromosome 2, which encompasses the POMC gene (Comuzzie et al., 1997; Hager et al., 1998; Hixson et al., 1999; Rotimi et al., 1999). An amino acid missense substitution in the POMC gene, R236G, produces an aberrant fusion protein that can interfere with signaling through MC4R (Challis et al., 2002). The fusion of this protein to the MC4R receptor acts as an agonist, reducing the normal effect of a-MSH, leading to a predisposition to obesity through hyperphagia.

PPAR-Gamma 2

PPAR-gamma 2 is a transcription factor, which plays a role in adipocyte differentiation, and, therefore, gene mutations for this factor might predispose people to obesity. A study evaluating the PPAR-gamma 2 gene for mutations at or near a site of serine phosphorylation at position 114 that negatively regulates the transcriptional activity of the protein was accomplished (Ristow, Muller-Wieland, Pfeiffer, Krone, & Kahn, 1998). Four of the 121 obese subjects had a missense mutation in the gene for PPAR-gamma 2, while none of the 237 normal weight subjects had this mutation (Ristow et al., 1998). The four obese subjects with the mutation were morbidly obese with BMIs ranging from 37.9 to 47.3, while the other obese subjects had a mean BMI of 33.6 (Ristow et al., 1998). This mutation in the gene coding for the PPAR-gamma 2 transcription factor may accelerate adipocyte differentiation, resulting in an obese phenotype (Ristow et al., 1998).

Monogenetic forms of human obesity are rare; however, fully understanding these forms of obesity will be advantageous for researchers attempting to solve the obesity genetics puzzle. Leptin, leptin receptor, MC4R, and POMC genes help researchers understand the complexity of obesity, but in no way do these few genes reveal the underlying causes of the more common polygenetic forms of the condition. Not only do the pieces of the eating genetics puzzle need to be fitted together precisely, but also an enhanced understanding of energy expenditure genetics will be required to develop the complete obesity genetics map.

GENES INFLUENCING ENERGY EXPENDITURE

Do genes actually determine an individual's level of physical activity and, on the other hand, can physical activity alter gene expressions in a manner to protect against obesity? There are, at this point, no concrete answers to these questions, but some evidence supports that there are genes responsible for an individual's activity level, especially genes involved with muscle development and type. Most people can lose weight by increasing their physical activity levels; however, discovering alterations in specific genes caused by increased physical activity is difficult because of the biological interactions of both genes and the environment. Some evidence has indicated that muscle type may predispose individuals to be active or inactive.

Muscle

Muscle biology has revealed a number of possible genetic links related to how much and to what extent a person will exercise. The amount of energy expended during a bout with exercise depends on five factors: type, energy economy, intensity of activity, muscle groups used during activity, and range of motion during activity (Weinsier, Hunter, Heini, Goran, & Sell, 1998). People may not be equally predisposed to engage in physical activity as a result of genes encoding for muscle fiber types (Weinsier et al., 1998). Obese individuals have increased fast-twitch muscle fibers (Howard et al., 1991; Wade, Marbut, & Round, 1990), which have decreased oxidative capacity (i.e., have less endurance to continue exercising) while world-class athletes and leaner individuals have more prominent slow-twitch muscle fibers.

Angiotensin I converting enzyme (ACE) is a candidate gene for exercise-related phenotypes and may play a role in skeletal muscle growth (Bray, 2000). With one or two insertion alleles in the ACE gene, a greater duration in repetitive arm flexion time after exercise training was found compared to deletion/deletion homozygotes for ACE gene (Montgomery et al., 1998).

Skeletal muscle mitochondrial proton leak is thought to control a large proportion of resting metabolic rate (Rolfe, Newman, Buckingham, Clark, & Brand, 1999). The uncoupling protein 3, UCP3, is involved with disposal of excess energy within the skeletal muscle (Boss et al., 1998; Vidal-Puig, Solanes, Grujic, Flier, & Lowell, 1997), and any abnormality in the gene coding for UCP3 may predispose an individual to obesity. Harper et al. performed muscle biopsies on obese diet-resistant and diet-responsive women to investigate proton leak respiration and UCP3 mRNA expression (Harper et al., 2002). Proton leak respiration was 51% higher, and expression of UCP3 mRNA was 25% greater in diet-responsive than in diet-resistant women (Harper et al., 2002). In other words, women who lost weight by changing their diet had increased energy expenditure in their muscles because of proton leakage, which appears to be regulated by UCP3.

A UCP3 gene splice mutation in the intron between exons 6 and 7 results in an inability to synthesize mRNA for the long isoform of UCP3 (Chung et al., 1999). This mutation was detected in African American subjects, but linkage (sib pair), association, and transmission disequilibrium testing studies did not support a significant role for UCP3 in determining body composition of the subjects (Chung et al., 1999). The current understanding of UCP3 in the etiology of human obesity is not conclusive, and additional studies will be required to ascertain its final association to obesity.

Over and Underfeeding

Twelve pairs of male identical twins, who consumed 4.18 MegaJoules a day surplus for six days per week over a 100-day period, experienced significant gains in body weight and fat (Bouchard et al., 1990). Each man's body adapted differently to the excess calories, and a definite pattern was seen with at least three times more variance in response between pairs of twins than within the pairs (Bouchard et al., 1990). Twins were more likely to respond to overfeeding in similar ways than when one brother from two different sets of twins was compared. The response between identical twin pairs suggests that fat storage is likely influenced by genotype (Bouchard et al., 1990).

In a negative energy balance experiment, seven pairs of young adult male identical twins exercised on cycle ergometers twice a day for nine out of 10 days over 93 days and were kept on a constant daily energy and nutrient intake (Bouchard & Tremblay, 1997). Average body weight loss was five kilograms and was entirely accounted for by fat loss (Bouchard & Tremblay, 1997). Large individual differences in response to the exercise were noted; however, identical twins were more alike in responses than control subjects with different genes, particularly for body fat loss and energy use (Bouchard & Tremblay, 1997).

During a 40-day therapeutic weight loss experiment, 14 pairs of premenopausal female obese identical twins had body composition, intra-abdominal fat, and resting metabolic rate measurements taken before and after the weight loss regimen. There was a high correlation among members of twin pairs for losses in body weight ($r = 0.85$; $p < 0.001$) and losses in body fat ($r = 0.88$; $p < 0.0001$), but no resemblances were found for decreases in RMR and RQ (Hainer et al., 2000); however, metabolic efficiency was correlated within twin pairs ($r = 0.77$; $p < 0.001$; Hainer et al., 2001). These intrapair correlations in very low calorie, diet-induced weight and fat losses, along with the high correlation in metabolic efficiency among female obese identical twin pairs, suggest a possible important role of genetic factors in response to this weight reduction regimen (Hainer et al., 2000, 2001).

The family of adrenoceptors may be involved with fat accumulation although the mechanism(s) for this effect are unknown. Excess body fat accumulation, as well as low energy expenditure and impaired fat oxidation, has been documented for a Trp64Arg polymorphism in the ß₃-adrenoceptor (Garcia-Rubi et al., 1998; Shuldiner, Silver, Roth, & Walston, 1996; Walston et al., 1995; Widen et al., 1995). There is a Gln27Glu polymorphism in the ß₂-adrenoceptor, and homozygotes for the Glu allele display a greater fat mass than Gln homozygotes or heterozygotes (Large et al., 1997).

A common genetic variant of the human ß₁-adrenoceptor gene, Gly389Arg, has been identified in a cohort of normal individuals (Mason, Moore, Green, & Liggett, 1999).

Dionne et al. (2002) investigated this polymorphism in a population of Caucasian women between ages 19 and 87. The women ($n = 931$) were genotyped for the Gly389Arg polymorphism, and the association of the variant with body weight and BMI was examined (Dionne et al., 2002). In a subsample of 214 of these women, the variant's association with direct measures of body fat and energy balance phenotypes (energy expenditure, physical activity, energy intake, etc.) were examined (Dionne et al., 2002). Results indicated that the Arg allele was significantly associated with a greater body weight and BMI in both heterozygous and homozygous states and that this association is likely attributable to greater fat mass as measured by dual x-ray absorptiometry.

SUMMARY AND FUTURE DIRECTIONS

This chapter gives a background and overview of the complexity associated with obesity genetics. As discussed, a number of genes have been investigated for eating and energy intake, but like the genes studied for energy expenditure and fat accumulation, there is very little evidence showing specific associations to the common forms of obesity found throughout the world. More detailed genetic mapping will be required to pinpoint the genes responsible for increased calorie intake and decreased physical activity. It is important to remember that obesity is a complex phenotype, which in turn means there are a number of genes responsible for its etiology, and those genes are highly dependent on the environment. Although progress has been made, the puzzle remains unsolved. Researchers in the future will discover more genes and, perhaps, someday put all the pieces of the obesity puzzle together so that future generations do not have to suffer from this condition and its associated morbidities.

REFERENCES

Allison, D. B. (2002). Statistical methods for microarray research for drug target identification. *2002 Proceedings of the American Statistical Association, Biopharmaceutical Section* [CD-ROM], 1–8.

Allison, D. B., & Heo, M. (1998). Meta-analysis of linkage data under worst-case conditions: A demonstration using the human OB region. *Genetics, 148,* 859–865.

Allison, D. B., Kaprio, J., Korkeila, M., Koskenvuo, M., Neale, M. C., & Hayakawa, K. (1996). The heritability of body mass index among an international sample of monozygotic twins reared apart. *International Journal of Obesity and Related Metabolic Disorders, 20,* 501–506.

Allison, D. B., Pietrobelli, A., Faith, M. S., Fontaine, K. R., Gropp, E., & Fernández, J. R. (2003). Genetic influences on obesity. In R. Eckel (Ed.), *Obesity: Mechanisms and clinical management* (pp. 31–74). New York: Elsevier.

Arch, J. R. (2002). Lessons in obesity from transgenic animals. *Journal of Endocrinological Investigation, 25,* 867–875.

Arner, P. (2000). Obesity: A genetic disease of adipose tissue? *British Journal of Nutrition, 83*(Suppl. 1), S9–S16.

Barsh, G. S., Farooqi, I. S., & O'Rahilly, S. (2000). Genetics of body-weight regulation. *Nature, 404,* 644–651.

Boss, O., Samec, S., Kuhne, F., Bijlenga, P., Assimacopoulos-Jeannet, F., Seydoux, J., et al. (1998). Uncoupling protein-3 expression in rodent skeletal muscle is modulated by food intake but not by changes in environmental temperature. *Journal of Biological Chemistry, 273,* 5–8.

Bouchard, C., & Tremblay, A. (1997). Genetic influences on the response of body fat and fat distribution to positive and negative energy balances in human identical twins. *Journal of Nutrition, 127,* 943S–947S.

Bouchard, C., Tremblay, A., Despres, J. P., Nadeau, A., Lupien, P. J., Theriault, G., et al. (1990). The response to long-term overfeeding in identical twins. *New England Journal of Medicine, 322,* 1477–1482.

Bray, M. S. (2000). Genomics, genes, and environmental interaction: The role of exercise. *Journal of Applied Physiology, 88,* 788–792.

Butler, A. A., & Cone, R. D. (2001). Knockout models resulting in the development of obesity. *Trends in Genetics, 17,* S50 S54.

Butler, A. A., & Cone, R. D. (2002). The melanocortin receptors: Lessons from knockout models. *Neuropeptides, 36,* 77.

Capeless, C. G., & Whitney, G. (1995). The genetic basis of preference for sweet substances among inbred strains of mice: Preference ratio phenotypes and the alleles of the *Sac* and dpa loci. *Chemical Senses, 20,* 291–298.

Chagnon, Y. C., Chen, W. J., Perusse, L., Chagnon, M., Nadeau, A., Wilkison, W. O., et al. (1997). Linkage and association studies between the melanocortin receptors 4 and 5 genes and obesity-related phenotypes in the Quebec Family Study. *Molecular Medicine, 3,* 663–673.

Challis, B. G., Pritchard, L. E., Creemers, J. W., Delplanque, J., Keogh, J. M., Luan, J., et al. (2002). A missense mutation disrupting a dibasic prohormone processing site in pro-opiomelanocortin (POMC) increases susceptibility to early-onset obesity through a novel molecular mechanism. *Human Molecular Genetics, 11,* 1997–2004.

Chua, S. C., Jr., Chung, W. K., Wu-Peng, X. S., Zhang, Y., Liu, S. M., Tartaglia, L., et al. (1996). Phenotypes of mouse diabetes and rat fatty due to mutations in the OB (leptin) receptor. *Science, 271,* 994–996.

Chung, W. K., Luke, A., Cooper, R. S., Rotini, C., Vidal-Puig, A., Rosenbaum, M., et al. (1999). Genetic and physiologic analysis of the role of uncoupling protein 3 in human energy homeostasis. *Diabetes, 48,* 1890–1895.

Clement, K., Vaisse, C., Lahlou, N., Cabrol, S., Pelloux, V., Cassuto, D., et al. (1998). A mutation in the human leptin receptor gene causes obesity and pituitary dysfunction. *Nature, 392,* 398–401.

Comuzzie, A. G., & Allison, D. B. (1998). The search for human obesity genes. *Science, 280,* 1374–1377.

Comuzzie, A. G., Hixson, J. E., Almasy, L., Mitchell, B. D., Mahaney, M. C., Dyer, T. D., et al. (1997). A major quantitative trait locus determining serum leptin levels and fat mass is located on human chromosome 2. *Nature Genetics, 15,* 273–276.

Considine, R. V., Sinha, M. K., Heiman, M. L., Kriauciunas, A., Stephens, T. W., Nyce, M. R., et al. (1996). Serum immunoreactive-leptin concentrations in normal-weight and obese humans. *New England Journal of Medicine, 334,* 292–295.

Cummings, S., Parham, E. S., & Strain, G. W. (2002). Weight management: Position of the American Dietetics Association. *Journal of the American Dietetics Association, 102,* 1145–1155.

de Castro, J. M., & Plunkett, S. S. (2001). How genes control real world intake: Palatability—intake relationships. *Nutrition, 17,* 266–268.

Diaz, J., & Taylor, E. M. (1998). Abnormally high nourishment during sensitive periods results in body weight changes across generations. *Obesity Research, 6,* 368–374.

Dionne, I. J., Garant, M. J., Nolan, A. A., Pollin, T. I., Lewis, D. G., Shuldiner, A. R., et al. (2002). Association between obesity and a polymorphism in the beta(1)-adrenoceptor gene (Gly389Arg ADRB1) in Caucasian women. *International Journal of Obesity and Related Metabolic Disorders, 26,* 633–639.

Dubern, B., Clement, K., Pelloux, V., Froguel, P., Girardet, J. P., Guy-Grand, B., et al. (2001). Mutational analysis of melanocortin-4 receptor, agouti-related protein, and alpha-melanocyte-stimulating hormone genes in severely obese children. *Journal of Pediatrics, 139,* 204–209.

Duggan, D. J., Bittner, M., Chen, Y., Meltzer, P., & Trent, J. M. (1999). Expression profiling using cDNA microarrays. *Nature Genetics, 21,* 10–14.

Ebbeling, C. B., Pawlak, D. B., & Ludwig, D. S. (2002). Childhood obesity: Public-health crisis, common sense cure. *Lancet, 360,* 473–482.

Fan, W., Boston, B. A., Kesterson, R. A., Hruby, V. J., & Cone, R. D. (1997). Role of melanocortinergic neurons in feeding and the agouti obesity syndrome. *Nature, 385,* 165–168.

Farooqi, I. S., Yeo, G. S., Keogh, J. M., Aminian, S., Jebb, S. A., Butler, G., et al. (2000). Dominant and recessive inheritance of morbid obesity associated with melanocortin 4 receptor deficiency. *Journal of Clinical Investigation, 106,* 271–279.

Garcia-Rubi, E., Starling, R. D., Tchernof, A., Matthews, D. E., Walston, J. D., Shuldiner, A. R., et al. (1998). Trp64Arg variant of the beta3-adrenoceptor and insulin resistance in obese postmenopausal women. *Journal of Clinical Endocrinology Metabolism, 83,* 4002–4005.

Gu, W., Tu, Z., Kleyn, P. W., Kissebah, A., Duprat, L., Lee, J., et al. (1999). Identification and functional analysis of novel human melanocortin-4 receptor variants. *Diabetes, 48,* 635–639.

Hagan, M. M., Rushing, P. A., Benoit, S. C., Woods, S. C., & Seeley, R. J. (2001). Opioid receptor involvement in the effect of AgRP-(83–132) on food intake and food selection. *American Journal of Physiology Regulatory Integrative & Comparative Physiology, 280,* R814–R821.

Hager, J., Dina, C., Francke, S., Dubois, S., Houari, M., Vatin, V., et al. (1998). A genome-wide scan for human obesity genes reveals a major susceptibility locus on chromosome 10. *Nature Genetics, 20,* 304–308.

Hainer, V., Stunkard, A. J., Kunesova, M., Parizkova, J., Stich, V., & Allison, D. B. (2000). Intrapair resemblance in very low calorie diet-induced weight loss in female obese identical twins. *International Journal of Obesity and Related Metabolic Disorders, 24,* 1051–1057.

Hainer, V., Stunkard, A. J., Kunesova, M., Parizkova, J., Stich, V., & Allison, D. B. (2001). A twin study of weight loss and metabolic efficiency. *International Journal of Obesity and Related Metabolic Disorders, 25,* 533–537.

Halaas, J. L., Gajiwala, K. S., Maffei, M., Cohen, S. L., Chait, B. T., Rabinowitz, D., et al. (1995). Weight-reducing effects of the plasma protein encoded by the obese gene. *Science, 269,* 543–546.

Hamilton, B. S., Paglia, D., Kwan, A. Y., & Deitel, M. (1995). Increased obese mRNA expression in omental fat cells from massively obese humans. *Nature Medicine, 1,* 953–956.

Harper, M. E., Dent, R., Monemdjou, S., Bezaire, V., Van Wyck, L., Wells, G., et al. (2002). Decreased mitochondrial proton leak and reduced expression of uncoupling protein 3 in skeletal muscle of obese diet-resistant women. *Diabetes, 51,* 2459–2466.

Heo, M., Leibel, R. L., Fontaine, K. R., Boyer, B. B., Chung, W. K., Koulu, M., et al. (2002). A meta-analytic investigation of linkage and association of common leptin receptor (LEPR) polymorphisms with body mass index and waist circumference. *International Journal of Obesity and Related Metabolic Disorders, 26,* 640–646.

Herzog, H., Darby, K., Ball, H., Hort, Y., Beck-Sickinger, A., & Shine, J. (1997). Overlapping gene structure of the human neuropeptide Y receptor subtypes Y1 and Y5 suggests coordinate transcriptional regulation. *Genomics, 41,* 315–319.

Hixson, J. E., Almasy, L., Cole, S., Birnbaum, S., Mitchell, B. D., Mahaney, M. C., et al. (1999). Normal variation in leptin levels in associated with polymorphisms in the proopiomelanocortin gene, POMC. *Journal of Clinical Endocrinology and Metabolism, 84,* 3187–3191.

Holliday, R., (1994). Epigenetics: An overview. *Developmental Genetics, 15,* 453–457.

Howard, B. V., Bogardus, C., Ravussin, E., Foley, J. E., Lillioja, S., Mott, D. M., et al. (1991). Studies of the etiology of obesity in Pima Indians. *American Journal of Clinical Nutrition, 53,* 1577S–1585S.

Huszar, D., Lynch, C. A., Fairchild-Huntress, V., Dunmore, J. H., Fang, Q., Berkemeier, L. R., et al. (1997). Targeted disruption of the melanocortin-4 receptor results in obesity in mice. *Cell, 88,* 131–141.

Ingalls, A. M., Dickie, M. M., & Snell, G. D. (1996). Obese, a new mutation in the house mouse. *Obesity Research, 4,* 101.

Jablonka, E., & Lamb, M. J. (1989). The inheritance of acquired epigenetic variations. *Journal of Theoretical Biology, 139,* 69–83.

Jacobson, P., Ukkola, O., Rankinen, T., Snyder, E. E., Leon, A. S., Rao, D. C., et al. (2002). Melanocortin 4 receptor sequence variations are seldom a cause of human obesity: The Swedish Obese Subjects, the HERITAGE Family Study, and a Memphis cohort. *Journal of Clinical Endocrinology and Metabolism, 87,* 4442–4446.

Jequier, E. (2002). Leptin signaling, adiposity, and energy balance. *Annals of the New York Academy of Sciences, 967,* 379–388.

Kagawa, Y., Yanagisawa, Y., Hasegawa, K., Suzuki, H., Yasuda, K., Kudo, H., et al. (2002). Single nucleotide polymorphisms of thrifty genes for energy metabolism: Evolutionary origins and prospects for intervention to prevent obesity-related diseases. *Biochemical and Biophysical Research Communications, 295,* 207–222.

Kahn, B. B., & Flier, J. S. (2000). Obesity and insulin resistance. *Journal of Clinical Investigation, 106,* 473–481.

Klug, W. S., & Cummings, S. (2002). *Essentials of genetics* (4th ed.). Upper Saddle River, NJ: Prentice-Hall.

Krude, H., Biebermann, H., Luck, W., Horn, R., Brabant, G., & Gruters, A. (1998). Severe early-onset obesity, adrenal insufficiency and red hair pigmentation caused by POMC mutations in humans. *Nature Genetics, 19,* 155–157.

Large, V., Hellstrom, L., Reynisdottir, S., Lonnqvist, F., Eriksson, P., Lannfelt, L., et al. (1997). Human beta-2 adrenoceptor gene polymorphisms are highly frequent in obesity and associate with altered adipocyte beta-2 adrenoceptor function. *Journal of Clinical Investigation, 100,* 3005–3013.

Lewcock, J. W., & Reed, R. R. (2001). Sweet successes. *Neuron, 31,* 515–517.

Li, X., Inoue, M., Reed, D. R., Huque, T., Puchalski, R. B., Tordoff, M. G., et al. (2001). High-resolution genetic mapping of the saccharin preference locus *(Sac)* and the putative sweet taste receptor (T1R1) gene (Gpr70) to mouse distal Chromosome 4. *Mammalian Genome, 12,* 13–16.

Lipshutz, R. J., Fodor, S. P., Gingeras, T. R., & Lockhart, D. J. (1999). High density synthetic oligonucleotide arrays. *Nature Genetics, 21,* 20–24.

Luciano, A., Bressan, F., Bolognani, M., Castellarin, A., & Zoppi, G. (2001). Childhood obesity: Different definition criteria, different prevalence rate. *Minerva Pediatrica, 53,* 537–541.

Maes, H. H., Neale, M. C., & Eaves, L. J. (1997). Genetic and environmental factors in relative body weight and human adiposity. *Behavior Genetics, 27,* 325–351.

Maffeis, C., Moghetti, P., Grezzani, A., Clementi, M., Gaudino, R., & Tato, L. (2002). Insulin resistance and the persistence of obesity from childhood into adulthood. *Journal of Clinical Endocrinology and Metabolism, 87,* 71–76.

Marsh, D. J., Hollopeter, G., Huszar, D., Laufer, R., Yagaloff, K. A., Fisher, S. L., et al. (1999). Response of melanocortin-4 receptor-deficient mice to anorectic and orexigenic peptides. *Nature Genetics, 21,* 119–122.

Martinez, J. A. (2000). Body-weight regulation: Causes of obesity. *Proceeding of the Nutrition Society, 59,* 337–345.

Mason, D. A., Moore, J. D., Green, S. A., & Liggett, S. B. (1999). A gain-of-function polymorphism in a G-protein coupling domain of the human beta1-adrenergic receptor. *Journal of Biological Chemistry, 274,* 12670–12674.

Matsunami, H., Montmayeur, J. P., & Buck, L. B. (2000). A family of candidate taste receptors in human and mouse. *Nature, 404,* 601–604.

Max, M., Shanker, Y. G., Huang, L., Rong, M., Liu, Z., Campagne, F., et al. (2001). Tas1r3, encoding a new candidate taste receptor, is allelic to the sweet responsiveness locus *Sac. Nature Genetics, 28,* 58–63.

McPherson, J. D., Marra, M., Hillier, L., Waterston, R. H., Chinwalla, A., Wallis, J., et al. (2001). A physical map of the human genome. *Nature, 409,* 934–941.

Mergen, M., Mergen, H., Ozata, M., Oner, R., & Oner, C. (2001). A novel melanocortin 4 receptor (MC4R) gene mutation associated with morbid obesity. *Journal of Clinical Endocrinology and Metabolism, 86,* 3448.

Michaud, J. L. (2001). The developmental program of the hypothalamus and its disorders. *Clinical Genetics, 60,* 255–263.

Montague, C. T., Farooqi, I. S., Whitehead, J. P., Soos, M. A., Rau, H., Wareham, N. J., et al. (1997). Congenital leptin deficiency is associated with severe early-onset obesity in humans. *Nature, 387,* 903–908.

Montgomery, H. E., Marshall, R., Hemingway, H., Myerson, S., Clarkson, P., Dollery, C., et al. (1998). Human gene for physical performance. *Nature, 393,* 221–222.

National Heart, Lung, and Blood Institute Obesity Education Initiative. (1998, June). The practical guide: Identification, evaluation, and treatment of overweight and obesity in adults. Retrieved from http://www.nhlbi.nih.gov/guidelines/obesity/prctgd_b.pdf.

Nelson, G., Chandrashekar, J., Hoon, M. A., Feng, L., Zhao, G., Ryba, N. J., et al. (2002). An amino-acid taste receptor. *Nature, 416,* 199–202.

Ogden, C. L., Flegal, K. M., Carroll, M. D., & Johnson, C. L. (2002). Prevalence and trends in overweight among, U.S. children and adolescents, 1999–2000. *Journal of the American Medical Association, 288,* 1728–1732.

Ollmann, M. M., Wilson, B. D., Yang, Y. K., Kerns, J. A., Chen, Y., Gantz, I., et al. (1997). Antagonism of central melanocortin receptors in vitro and in vivo by agouti-related protein. *Science, 278,* 135–138.

Rankinen, T., Perusse, L., Weisnagel, S. J., Snyder, E. E., Chagnon, Y. C., & Bouchard, C. (2002). The human obesity gene map: The 2001 update. *Obesity Research, 10,* 196–243.

Ristow, M., Muller-Wieland, D., Pfeiffer, A., Krone, W., & Kahn, C. R. (1998). Obesity associated with a mutation in a genetic regulator of adipocyte differentiation. *New England Journal of Medicine, 339,* 953–959.

Rolfe, D. F., Newman, J. M., Buckingham, J. A., Clark, M. G., & Brand, M. D. (1999). Contribution of mitochondrial proton leak to respiration rate in working skeletal muscle and liver and to SMR. *American Journal of Physiology, 276,* C692–C699.

Rotimi, C. N., Comuzzie, A. G., Lowe, W. L., Luke, A., Blangero, J., & Cooper, R. S. (1999). The quantitative trait locus on chromosome 2 for serum leptin levels is confirmed in African Americans. *Diabetes, 48,* 643–644.

Schwartz, M. W., Seeley, R. J., Campfield, L. A., Burn, P., & Baskin, D. G. (1996). Identification of targets of leptin action in rat hypothalamus. *Journal of Clinical Investigation, 98,* 1101–1106.

Segal, N. L., & Allison, D. B. (2002). Twins and virtual twins: Bases of relative body weight revisited. *International Journal of Obesity and Related Metabolic Disorders, 26,* 437–441.

Serradeil-Le Gal, C., Lafontan, M., Raufaste, D., Marchand, J., Pouzet, B., Casellas, P., et al. (2000). Characterization of NPY receptors controlling lipolysis and leptin secretion in human adipocytes. *FEBS Letters, 475,* 150–156.

Shuldiner, A. R., Silver, K., Roth, J., & Walston, J. (1996). Beta 3-adrenoceptor gene variant in obesity and insulin resistance. *Lancet, 348,* 1584–1585.

Stanley, B. G., Kyrkouli, S. E., Lampert, S., & Leibowitz, S. F. (1986). Neuropeptide Y chronically injected into the hypothalamus: A powerful neurochemical inducer of hyperphagia and obesity. *Peptides, 7,* 1189–1192.

Strosberg, A. D., & Issad, T. (1999). The involvement of leptin in humans revealed by mutations in leptin and leptin receptor genes. *Trends in Pharmacological Sciences, 20,* 227–230.

Tschop, M., & Heiman, M. L. (2001). Rodent obesity models: An overview. *Experimental and Clinical Endocrinology and Diabetes, 109,* 307–319.

Venter, J. C., Adams, M. D., Myers, E. W., Li, P. W., Mural, R. J., Sutton, G. G., et al. (2001). The sequence of the human genome. *Science, 291,* 1304–1351.

Vidal-Puig, A., Solanes, G., Grujic, D., Flier, J. S., & Lowell, B. B. (1997). UCP3: An uncoupling protein homologue expressed preferentially and abundantly in skeletal muscle and brown adipose tissue. *Biochemical and Biophysical Research Communications, 235,* 79–82.

Visscher, T. L., & Seidell, J. C. (2001). The public health impact of obesity. *Annual Review of Public Health, 22,* 355–375.

Waddington, C. H. (1942). Untitled. *Endeavor, 1,* 18.

Wade, A. J., Marbut, M. M., & Round, J. M. (1990). Muscle fibre type and aetiology of obesity. *Lancet, 335,* 805–808.

Walston, J., Silver, K., Bogardus, C., Knowler, W. C., Celi, F. S., Austin, S., et al. (1995). Time of onset of noninsulin-dependent diabetes mellitus and genetic variation in the beta 3-adrenergic-receptor gene. *New England Journal of Medicine, 333,* 343–347.

Weinsier, R. L., Hunter, G. R., Heini, A. F., Goran, M. I., & Sell, S. M. (1998). The etiology of obesity: Relative contribution of metabolic factors, diet, and physical activity. *American Journal of Medicine, 105,* 145–150.

Widen, E., Lehto, M., Kanninen, T., Walston, J., Shuldiner, A. R., & Groop, L. C. (1995). Association of a polymorphism in the beta 3-adrenergic-receptor gene with features of the insulin resistance syndrome in Finns. *New England Journal of Medicine, 333,* 348–351.

Wilding, J. P. (2002). Neuropeptides and appetite control. *Diabetic Medicine, 19,* 619–627.

Wu, C., & Morris, J. R. (2001). Genes, genetics, and epigenetics: A correspondence. *Science, 293,* 1103–1105.

Yaswen, L., Diehl, N., Brennan, M. B., & Hochgeschwender, U. (1999). Obesity in the mouse model of pro-opiomelanocortin deficiency responds to peripheral melanocortin. *Nature Medicine, 5,* 1066–1070.

Zhang, Y., Proenca, R., Maffei, M., Barone, M., Leopold, L., & Friedman, J. M. (1994). Positional cloning of the mouse obese gene and its human homologue. *Nature, 372,* 425–432.

Chapter 17

THE TOXIC ENVIRONMENT AND OBESITY: CONTRIBUTION AND CURE

KATHRYN E. HENDERSON AND KELLY D. BROWNELL

We are amidst a global health crisis that affects 54 million Americans and more than 300 million people worldwide. Obesity has serious health and economic consequences and resists treatment. Most striking is that the key contributor to increasing prevalence—the environment—and the best hope for control—prevention—have been virtually ignored.

PREVALENCE AND COSTS OF OBESITY

By 1999, rates of obesity (BMI $\geq$ 30) in the United States reached 30%, with an additional 34% of individuals meeting criteria for overweight (BMI of 25 to 29.9; National Center for Health Statistics, 1999). These figures translate to 54 million obese adults in the United States today (Thompson & Wolf, 2001) and 300 million obese individuals worldwide (James, Leach, Kalamara, & Shayeghi, 2001). These figures also represent a dramatic increase over the previous decade, with the curve particularly steep in rates for children and adolescents (Flegal, Carroll, Kuczmarski, & Johnson, 1998; World Health Organization [WHO], 1998).

The costs of obesity are staggering. Obesity increases risk for cardiovascular disease, diabetes, hypertension, stroke, gallbladder disease, respiratory disease, musculoskeletal problems, and hormone-related cancers (Must et al., 1999). Approximately 325,000 deaths per year are attributable to obesity-related causes (Allison, Fontaine, Manson, Stevens, & VanItallie, 1999); for 25- to 35-year-olds, for example, severe obesity is associated with a 12-fold increase in mortality. Risk is determined in part by the distribution of fat on the body, with intra-abdominal adiposity putting individuals at greatest risk (WHO, 1998).

Risk for increased mental health difficulties does not appear to increase with BMI. As a group, the obese do not experience greater psychiatric symptoms than their nonobese counterparts (Telch & Agras, 1994); but in the presence of risk factors such as binge eating and body image disturbance, obesity can have serious effects. The stigma associated with obesity can have dramatic effects on the quality of life of obese persons. Obese women are less likely to complete high school, less likely to marry, and have lower household incomes. Overweight individuals are subjected to prejudice and discrimination when seeking college admissions, employment, and housing (Puhl & Brownell, 2001).

This combination of serious sequelae and rapidly increasing prevalence means that obesity has become the single most expensive health problem in the United States, surpassing smoking and alcohol in its medical and financial impact. Sturm (2002) analyzed U.S. national health data to demonstrate that obesity is associated with a 36% increase in both inpatient and outpatient spending and a 77% increase in medications, compared to increases of 21% and 28%, respectively, for those same services for smokers. Alcohol use is associated with effects smaller than that for smokers. Thompson and Wolf (2001) reviewed the literature on the medical-care cost of obesity. Their distillation of modeling and database studies demonstrates that obesity accounts for an estimated 5.5% to 7.0% of U.S. health expenditures and 2.0% to 3.5% of health expenditures for other nations for which data are currently available. In the United States, this amounts to $118 billion. Thompson and Wolf were forced to reach "the inescapable conclusion that obesity exacts an immense economic toll in various countries throughout the world" (p. 189).

OBESITY: A GLOBAL EPIDEMIC

In 1998, the World Health Organization (WHO) declared obesity a global epidemic. The staggering U.S. figures are accompanied by similarly worrying reports of increasing rates of obesity around the world. Western Europe sports rates of 15% to 20%, while some Eastern European nations have observed rates of up to 40% to 50% (Bjorntorp, 1997). While prevalence tends to be highest in North America, the Middle East, and Central and Eastern Europe (James et al., 2001), the problem is no longer limited to developed nations. We are now seeing climbing rates of obesity in Mexico, Malaysia, and South Africa (Popkin & Doak, 1998). In the more urbanized Cape Town, rates of obesity are 12% for girls and 16% for boys, while in Klein Karoo, a poorer and much less developed rural town only 300 km away, rates are 1% for boys and 2% for girls.

Ulijaszek (2001) studied inhabitants of the island of Rarotonga of the Pacific Region. In the Pacific, obesity has long been regarded a sign of social status and thus is not a new phenomenon. However, prevalence has increased dramatically. In 1966, obesity rates on Rarotonga were 14% for men and 44% for women. Twenty years later, these figures had jumped to a startling 52% for men and 57% for women. Ulijaszek's analyses confirm that this trend is a function of the greater degree of modernization on Rarotonga relative to other Cook Islands. In Japan, obesity in men has doubled since 1982; in young women, it has nearly doubled since that time. China has seen similar increases in obesity in women in recent years (WHO, 1998).

FATTENING OUR CHILDREN

Bellizzi (2002) presented the most recent international data on childhood obesity at the 2002 World Health Assembly. Obesity in children is increasing at rates greater than that of adults—in Egypt, for example, obesity in 4-year-olds exceeds 25%. An estimated 22 million children under the age of 5 are overweight worldwide. In Mexico, Peru, and Chile, the rate of overweight in 4- to 10-year-olds exceeds 25%. In Malta, more than 40% of 10-year-olds are overweight. Paradoxically, in developing nations, obesity is observed to occur simultaneously with malnutrition. Further, populations in developing nations appear to have a tendency to develop greater abdominal obesity, which, as noted earlier, is associated with greater risk for cardiovascular disease and other health problems. Thus, these populations are doubly hit by the obesity pandemic.

Bellizi also presented data from the U.S. National Longitudinal Survey of Youth. The prevalence of overweight in 4-to 12-year-old Latino children nearly doubled between 1986 and 1998, from 20% to 40%. Increases were similar in African American children. Bogin and Loucky (1997) have studied the Mayan children who have migrated from Guatemala to Los Angeles and rural central Florida. These children were heavier and carried more fat than children who remained in Guatemala. Rates of obesity in the children living in the United States reached an alarming 42%. While earlier data suggested that, in developing nations, obesity was occurring in wealthier segments of society (Bjorntorp, 1997), that trend appears to be changing such that obesity is now becoming universally associated with poverty, even in developing countries (James et al., 2001).

This collection of figures highlights two important points. First, the obesity epidemic is a worldwide phenomenon. Second—and most relevant to the present discussion—the spread of the problem is clearly associated with the spread of modernization. As we advance technologically, we are getting fatter.

PERSPECTIVES ON OBESITY: PUBLIC HEALTH VERSUS MEDICAL MODELS

Until recently, a traditional medical model has prevailed in both explaining obesity and in attempts to deal with it as a problem. Traditional models drive the search for individual causes and focus on treatment rather than prevention. Those working within these models seek to help people once they have a problem and measure success not in effects on prevalence but in the ability to help individuals in controlled trials lose weight.

The public health perspective looks for causes of a problem in the population and for methods for reducing the public health burden a problem creates. Treatment and prevention efforts are implemented at the population level and may take into account variables outside the individual that may be contributing to the problem, such as environmental factors.

In theory, the public health model implies incorporation of environmental interventions to prevent obesity, perhaps with a special focus on children, but, in fact, almost nothing has been done in this arena. It is perhaps the greatest oversight in the obesity field. The public has been informed about the health consequences of obesity and, to some extent, nutrition and exercise information has been disseminated in schools, communities, work sites, and through the media. What is missing is the systematic study and analysis of the environmental causes of obesity and the design of prevention programs from this knowledge base.

OBESITY TREATMENTS: TOUGH GOING WITH A TOUGH PROBLEM

Billions of dollars in research funds have gone to the development and implementation of obesity treatments, especially drugs. Treatments include commercial weight loss programs, professionally directed behavioral treatments, pharmacological treatments, and surgical treatments. There exist little data on the success of commercial weight loss programs. Professionally directed behavioral treatments typically produce initial weight loss, with stricter regimens producing quicker and more dramatic results, but regain is a major issue (Douketis, Feightner, Attia, & Feldman, 1999). The exception is behavioral treatments for obesity in children, for which longer term maintenance has been demonstrated, but only in a few studies (Epstein, Valoski, Wing, & McCurley, 1994). The two primary pharmacologic agents in use currently are a serotonin-norepinephrine reuptake inhibitor (Sibutramine) that appears to act on receptors in the hypothalamus that control satiety and a lipase inhibitor (Orlistat) that produces weight loss by blocking the absorption of fat. These medications produce initial weight loss of 7% to 15% of body weight; it is not known whether these losses are maintained over time without continued medication (Bray & Greenway, 1999). Additionally, side effects of the medications render them intolerable for some individuals.

Surgical treatments are recommended typically only for those who meet criteria for Class 3 obesity (i.e., BMI > 40) or for those with a BMI > 35 *and* comorbid health risk factors. Gastric restriction and malabsorption procedures produce drastic weight loss, often 100 pounds or more. Follow-up data indicate that these losses are well maintained in studies as long as 14 years. Significant health improvements are associated with these large weight losses (Pories & Beshay, 2002). Surgery can be life saving but is reserved for the heaviest people and is expensive.

Obesity treatment overall has been disappointing. Further, even if these treatments were effective, the large-scale dissemination of such labor-intensive interventions to the ever-growing population of obese individuals is neither logistically nor economically feasible. Treatment simply will not affect prevalence and, therefore, is not currently a public health intervention.

ETIOLOGY OF OBESITY

The etiology of obesity is simple—a person gains weight when taking in more calories than are expended. How this imbalance comes about, however, represents the confluence of complex biological, psychological, and environmental factors. Between 25% and 40% of population body weight is genetically determined through the mechanisms of fat cell number, basal metabolic rate, weight gain in response to overfeeding, and other factors (Bouchard, 2002). The remainder is accounted for by an individual's behavior and interactions with biology and the environment.

Almost all obesity intervention efforts to date have targeted the individual, either via biology (e.g., pharmacological interventions) or behavior. Given that the problem continues to grow, these avenues would appear less than fruitful. It seems unlikely that stepping up the pace of individually aimed interventions would yield greater success.

Indeed, we live in a society in which thinness is highly idealized and individuals are under constant pressure to conform to that ideal; it is questionable whether pressure *could* be stepped up.

IMPACT OF THE ENVIRONMENT

The International Obesity Task Force (IOTF) has proclaimed "The current obesity pandemic reflects the profound changes to society over the past 20 to 30 years that have created an environment that promotes a sedentary lifestyle and the consumption of a high fat, energy dense diet" (IOTF, 2002). Exactly what specific environmental factors have contributed to the problem and how we might address them is not clear, for data are sparse. Here we briefly present the existing data, then offer our speculation on other possible factors.

Both cross-sectional and longitudinal data have demonstrated the power of modernization in promoting obesity. As nations become more "Americanized," their obesity problem grows. Further, individuals who move from less modernized to more modernized countries gain weight. A number of researchers have studied the health of immigrants. Some of the relevant child studies are detailed earlier in this chapter. Other examples include Wandel's (1993) research, in which immigrants who moved from developing nations to European countries increased their risk for coronary heart disease and Type II diabetes.

Work by Ravussin, Valencia, Esparza, Bennett, and Schulz (1994) provides probably the most well-known example of this phenomenon. This group studied the Pima Indians, who are originally from Mexico but some of whom have migrated to Arizona. The average Arizona Pima woman weighed 44 pounds more than the average Pima woman in Mexico. The clear genetic similarity between these two groups forces the conclusion that the environment must be responsible for these differences.

What makes a modernized, Americanized environment so damaging? Individuals in today's society are constantly exposed to heavily advertised, inexpensive, energy-dense foods of low nutritional value, and an increasingly sedentary lifestyle is supported by technological advances. We refer to this set of circumstances as the *toxic environment* (Brownell, 2002; Horgen & Brownell, 1998, 2002).

Fast, convenient, readily available food has become the meal of choice for many. Such food is generally cheap, quick, tasty, and available everywhere and at any time—this is decidedly not the case for more nutritious foods, which can be pricier, take time to prepare, and are not available on every street corner. Further, fat and sugar make food taste good, thus more nutritious choices simply cannot compete.

As if this were not enough, fast food is made to be "fun," and popular characters tout the products worldwide. Toys of movie and television characters are offered with the meals to make them more enticing to children. Portion sizes also play a big role in our increasing girth. We live in the age of the "supersized" meal: Bigger must be better, and we feel cheated if we do not receive gargantuan portions. The food industry is happy to comply because greater profit margins come from selling larger portions.

Television may act as a "triple hit," particularly for children. While watching TV, children are exposed to myriad food advertisements, the bulk of which are for soft drinks, candy, fast food, sugary cereals, and high-fat or high-sugar snack foods (Dibb, 1996). Further, the more hours they are sedentary before a television, the fewer hours they can be active (Horgen, Choate, & Brownell, 2001). Finally, they are likely to be snacking while viewing; having been encouraged during the viewing to consume high-fat, sugary snack foods, they are not likely to be choosing healthy foods.

If home is not a safe haven for children, school hardly presents a welcome alternative. Unhealthy snack food products are advertised to children via school "news" programs (Brand & Greenberg, 1994). Snack foods, candy, and soft drinks are readily available in vending machines in the schools, and fast food is served in many school cafeterias (Hager, 1998). The very institutions that should be inoculating our children against poor health practices are promoting them.

Levitsky (2002) has summarized fascinating data on human feeding. When individuals are overfed, they do not subsequently reduce their food intake. When snacks are added to their daily regimen, people do not alter their consumption at meals. Finally, consumption increases proportionally to the amount of food served, the variety of foods offered, and the number of other people eating with that individual. When we consider these data in the context of our current environment, the obesity pandemic is hardly surprising.

In many ways, the environment is the precise opposite of what it should be to prevent obesity. Unhealthy food has everything going for it, except that it is unhealthy. For a decreasing number of people, health concerns prevail over the environmental inducements, but it is not a battle easily won for individuals. The battle at the national level is going very badly indeed.

IGNORING THE PROBLEM

Obesity treatment is clearly not the solution. People with the problem deserve help but, as we mentioned earlier, approaching obesity as a public health issue places prevention as a much higher priority than treatment, given limitations of existing treatments. The current focus on treatment has far-reaching implications. Resources are limited, so funds devoted to research or the implementation of individually focused treatment draws money from work on prevention. This conceptual bias is reflected in research funding priorities, underrepresentation of this topic at academic conferences, and even this book. This chapter was invited after the book contents were nearly fixed, and the attention in its contents to treatment over prevention reflects the general stance of the field.

In September 2002, the Food and Nutrition Board of the Institute of Medicine released a 1,000-page report compiled by 21 experts recommending that individuals exercise for one hour per day and follow certain nutrition guidelines. Government agencies have been fine-tuning such recommendations for decades, yet obesity continues to rise at shocking rates. No equivalent report has been done on preventing obesity. At the National Institutes of Health, prevention is the focus of a tiny amount of the research funded on obesity.

Why has the environmental contribution to obesity been ignored so long, thus preventing progress on prevention? Why do we continue to rely on individual treatments for obesity or, when thinking prevention at all, on approaches that require the individual to engage in Herculean efforts to withstand the pressure of an overwhelming environment?

The strong presence of the medical model appears part of the explanation. Obesity has been considered an individual rather than collective responsibility. British obesity researcher Philip James was quoted recently identifying the strong history of American "individualist" philosophy as the major barrier to addressing the environmental contributors to obesity (Hellmich, 2002). In addition, the stigma associated with obesity (Puhl & Brownell, 2001) deflects attention away from causes of the problem outside the individual.

PREVENTION OF OBESITY—POLICY INITIATIVES

Given the difficulty in treating obesity, prevention is the obvious alternative. Given the clear contribution of the environment to promoting weight gain and the challenge in changing individual behavior within this environment, inventions targeted at modifying the environment would seem appropriate. And given the pervasiveness of the toxic environment and the degree to which it has become culturally supported, broader levels of intervention are essential.

There exist little data on large-scale environmentally based prevention efforts. However, a heart disease prevention program in Finland provides some evidence that such efforts can be effective in producing meaningful change. Some areas of the country saw a more than 75% reduction in premature deaths related to heart disease and stroke over a 20-year period following combined efforts of government and professionals at the policy level. Policy initiatives included setting and enforcing nutritional standards for food served in schools and at public catering outlets without a consequent increase in meal prices, as well as initiatives aimed at increasing physical activity (Puska, Vartiainen, Tuomilehto, Salomaa, & Nissinen, 1998).

Thus, prevention efforts must include not only encouragement of the individual to make personal change but also an environment that supports that change.

Jeffrey (2002) has joined us (Brownell, 2002; Horgen & Brownell, 1998, 2002) in suggesting a number of policy initiatives. To date, these initiatives have not been taken up. We thus present them again, and we again exhort others to join our cause:

- *Regulate the caloric density of foods and portion sizes of high-calorie foods.* Such an initiative would treat high-calorie/low-nutrient foods as an environmental toxin. Many chemicals are regulated with respect to concentration for our protection; this proposal is along those lines.

- *Regulate advertising of unhealthy food items.* Advertising of tobacco products is restricted, and both alcohol and tobacco products are required to sport warning labels. Similarly, the public should be warned of the dangers of high-calorie/low-nutrient foods and should not be exposed to an endless parading of dangerous products. It is of particular importance to restrict advertising aimed at children, who do not have the knowledge and capacity to make healthy choices. Thus, advertising during certain types of television programming or preceding certain kinds of movies would be off-limits.

- *Tax food advertising.* The promotion of unhealthy foods would become increasingly expensive. The extension of this proposal would have the revenue earmarked for the promotion of more nutritious foods.

- *Eliminate the availability of soft drinks, fast foods, and unhealthy snack foods in schools.* Children do not need to consume soft drinks, candy bars, and chips at school, nor do they need fast food in school cafeterias. In fact, schools are the very place in which some positive control might be exercised over their diets. Health education is a legitimate and important part of children's education; supporting the fast-food industry within their educational base communicates, at best, a contradictory message.

- *Eliminate food advertising in schools.* Schools should not act as conduits to the exploitation of children through advertising.

- *Tax unhealthy foods.* This particular initiative has actually been enacted in three states in the United States, targeting "nonessential foods," "nonnutritious foods," and "snack foods." The taxes were unpopular because what was taxed was arbitrary, the food industry fought the taxes with heavy lobbying efforts, and in no case was the revenue earmarked for programs related to health. The taxes had been enacted to repair a state's budget deficit, not to affect food intake. The logic behind a food tax is that it will raise revenue (a small tax) or raise revenue and render the taxed food less affordable (larger taxes), thus steering people toward healthier foods. Because unhealthy foods tend to be less expensive than their healthier counterparts, such a tax could make food generally less affordable for poorer segments of the population. A food tax makes the most sense if revenue generated is used to subsidize the healthier foods.

- *Subsidize healthier food choices.* This initiative is the logical corollary of taxing unhealthy foods. Better food needs to be more accessible. The relationship between poverty and obesity underlines the importance of such an initiative.

- *Increase availability of and ease of participation in exercise.* Certainly, providing readier access to exercise for all populations during all seasons is critical. However, those who currently have access often fail to make use of facilities. Thus, incentive programs may be the key. For example, insurance rates might be lowered for those who are physically active. It is imperative that schools also make exercise a priority. Children should be active daily, and schools are in a position to see that this happens.

- *Improve public health education.* What we are proposing would differ from the current educational practices of exhorting individuals to change their behavior. Possible targets include destigmatizing obesity and increasing parental awareness of the food-related dangers to which their children are exposed.

Recently, some members of the food industry appear to be taking an interest in their potential contribution to the problem and the role they may play in the solution. McDonald's™, for example, recently announced its intention to adopt a "healthier" fat (lower in saturated fats and transfatty acids while higher in polyunsaturated fats) in which to fry its products (Barboza, 2002). While such a move has been recognized as a positive step toward reducing cholesterol levels, products remain as high in fat and calories as ever. One concern is that individuals may view the use of healthier fats as license to consume even more of these products, thereby consuming even greater numbers of calories.

CONCLUSIONS AND FUTURE DIRECTIONS

Obesity has become the leading health problem of the United States and one of the leading health problems worldwide. Children are particularly affected. Treatment efforts that target the individual are laudable but have proven ineffective in reversing this dangerous problem. Prevention initiatives that target the environment are the logical next step. The problem is overwhelming, thus initiatives must be bold and creative. We urge researchers in the field to rise to the challenge and think creatively with respect to prevention.

REFERENCES

Allison, D. B., Fontaine, K. R., Manson, J. E., Stevens, J., & VanItallie, T. B. (1999). Annual deaths attributable to obesity in the United States. *Journal of the American Medical Association, 282,* 1530–1538.

Barboza, D. (2002, September 4). McDonald's new recipe lowers goo for arteries. *New York Times,* p. A16.

Bellizzi, M. (2002, May). *Childhood obesity: The emerging global epidemic.* Paper presented at the 2002 convention of the World Health Assembly, Geneva, Switzerland.

Bjorntorp, P. (1997). Obesity. *Lancet, 350,* 423–426.

Bogin, B., & Loucky, J. (1997). Plasticity, political economy, and physical growth status of Guatemala Mayan children living in the United States. *American Journal of Physical Anthropology, 102,* 17–32.

Bouchard, C. (2002). Genetic influences on body weight and shape. In C. G. Fairburn & K. D. Brownell (Eds.), *Eating disorders and obesity* (2nd ed., pp. 16–21). New York: Guilford Press.

Brand, J., & Greenberg, B. (1994). Commercials in the classroom: The impact of Channel One advertising. *Journal of Advertising Research, 34,* 18–23.

Bray, G. A., & Greenway, F. L. (1999). Current and potential drugs for treatment of obesity. *Endocrine Reviews, 20,* 805–875.

Brownell, K. D. (2002). Public policy and the prevention of obesity. In C. G. Fairburn & K. D. Brownell (Eds.), *Eating disorders and obesity* (pp. 619–623). New York: Guilford Press.

Dibb, S. (1996). *A spoonful of sugar: Television food advertising aimed at children: An international comparative survey.* London: Consumers International.

Douketis, J. D., Feightner, J. W., Attia, J., & Feldman, W. F. (1999). Periodic health examination, 1999 update: Detection, prevention, and treatment of obesity. *Canadian Medical Association Journal, 160,* 513–524.

Epstein, L. H., Valoski, A. M., Wing, R. R., & McCurley, J. (1994). Ten year outcomes of behavioral family-based treatment for childhood obesity. *Health Psychology, 13,* 373–383.

Flegal, K. M., Carroll, M. D., Kuczmarski, R. J., & Johnson, C. L. (1998). Overweight and obesity in the United States: Prevalence and trends, 1960–1994. *International Journal of Obesity, 22,* 39–47.

Food and Nutrition Board, Institute of Medicine. (2002, September). *Dietary reference intakes for energy, carbohydrates, fiber, fat, protein and amino acids (macronutrients).* Retrieved November 22, 2002, from www.nap.edu/books/0309085373/html.

Hager, D. L. (1998). Fast food or fast fat-Part I. *Weight Control Digest, 8,* 758–761.

Hellmich, N. (2002, August 21). United States wallowing in unhealthy ways: Obesity expert points finger at fat-city society. *USA Today.* Retrieved November 23, 2002, from www.usatoday.com/news/health/2002-08-21-james_x.htm.

Horgen, K. B., & Brownell, K. D. (1998). Policy change as a means for reducing the prevalence and impact of alcoholism, smoking, and obesity. In W. R. Miller & N. Heather (Eds.), *Treating addictive behaviors* (2nd ed., pp. 105–118). New York: Plenum Press.

Horgen, K. B., & Brownell, K. D. (2002). Confronting the toxic environment: Environmental and public health actions in a world crisis. In T. A. Wadden & A. J. Stunkard (Eds.), *Handbook of obesity treatment* (pp. 95–106). New York: Guilford Press.

Horgen, K. B., Choate, M., & Brownell, K. D. (2001). Television food advertising: Targeting kids in the toxic environment. In D. Singer & J. Singer (Eds.), *Handbook of children and the media* (pp. 447–461). Thousand Oaks, CA: Sage.

International Obesity Task Force. (2002). *About obesity.* Retrieved November 15, 2002, from www.iotf.org.

James, P. T., Leach, R., Kalamara, E., & Shayeghi, M. (2001). The worldwide obesity epidemic. *Obesity Research, 9*(Suppl. 4), 228S–233S.

Jeffrey, R. W. (2002). Public health approaches to the management of obesity. In C. G. Fairburn & K. D. Brownell (Eds.), *Eating disorders and obesity* (2nd ed., pp. 613–618). New York: Guilford Press.

Levitsky, D. A. (2002). Putting behavior back into feeding behavior: A tribute to George Collier. *Appetite, 38,* 143–148.

Must, A., Spadano, J., Coakley, E. H., Field, A. E., Colditz, G., & Dietz, W. H. (1999). The disease burden associated with overweight and obesity. *Journal of the American Medical Association, 282,* 1523–1529.

National Center for Health Statistics. (1999). *Prevalence of overweight and obesity among adults: United States, 1999.* Retrieved April 27, 2003, from http://www.cdc.gov/nchs/products/pubs /pubd/hestats/obese/obse99tab1.htm.

Popkin, B. M., & Doak, C. M. (1998). The obesity epidemic is a worldwide phenomenon. *Nutrition Reviews, 56*(4), 106–114.

Pories, W. J., & Beshay, J. E. (2002). Surgery for obesity: Procedures and weight loss. In C. G. Fairburn & K. D. Brownell (Eds.), *Eating disorders and obesity* (2nd ed., pp. 562–567). New York: Guilford Press.

Puhl, R., & Brownell, K. D. (2001). Bias, discrimination, and obesity. *Obesity Research, 9,* 788–805.

Puska, P., Vartiainen, E., Tuomilehto, J., Salomaa, V., & Nissinen, A. (1998). Changes in premature deaths in Finland: Successful long-term prevention of cardiovascular diseases. *Bulletin of the World Health Organization, 76,* 419–425.

Ravussin, E., Valencia, M. E., Esparza, J., Bennett, P. H., & Schulz, L. O. (1994). Effects of a traditional lifestyle on obesity in Pima Indians. *Diabetes Care, 17,* 1067–1074.

Sturm, R. (2002). The effects of obesity, smoking, and drinking on medical problems and costs: Obesity outranks both smoking and drinking in its deleterious effects on health and health costs. *Health Affairs, 21*(2), 245–253.

Telch, C. F., & Agras, W. S. (1994). Obesity, binge eating and psychopathology: Are they related? *International Journal of Eating Disorders, 15,* 53–61.

Thompson, D., & Wolf, A. M. (2001). The medical-care cost burden of obesity. *Obesity Reviews, 2,* 189–197.

Ulijaszek, S. J. (2001). Socioeconomic status, body size and physical activity of adults on Rarotonga, the Cook Islands. *Annals of Human Biology, 28,* 554–563.

Wandel, M. (1993). Nutrition-related diseases and dietary change among Third World immigrants in northern Europe. *Nutrition and Health, 9,* 117–133.

World Health Organization. (1998). *Obesity: Preventing and managing the global epidemic.* Geneva, Switzerland: Author.

Chapter 18

PSYCHOSOCIAL AND BEHAVIORAL CONSEQUENCES OF OBESITY

DIANNE NEUMARK-SZTAINER AND JESS HAINES

Obesity is associated with an array of adverse physical consequences that point to a need for interventions aimed at the prevention and treatment of obesity (U.S. Department of Health and Human Services, 2001). Obesity is also associated with harmful psychosocial and behavioral consequences that arise from culture-bound values emphasizing the importance of thinness (World Health Organization [WHO], 1997). This suggests a need for interventions aimed at decreasing the various forms of weight-related stigmatization that occur in our society. To develop such interventions, a clear understanding of the associations among obesity, weight-related stigmatization, and adverse psychosocial and behavioral consequences is needed.

Much of the work of our research team has been aimed at trying to better understand the experience of being fat in a thin-oriented society. More specifically, our work has aimed to increase our understanding of the psychosocial and behavioral consequences associated with obesity to guide the development of interventions aimed at preventing obesity and other weight-related disorders. Our work has focused primarily on adolescents, among whom weight-related concerns tend to be strong, body and more global self-esteem issues tend to be intertwined, and sensitivity to negative weight-related comments made by others can be high. We have used both quantitative and qualitative research methodologies to explore weight-related stigmatization, psychosocial concerns, and health-compromising behaviors among overweight individuals. Quantitative surveys of large population-based samples have been useful in examining associations between obesity and its psychosocial and behavioral consequences (Neumark-Sztainer et al., 1997; Neumark-Sztainer, Story, Hannan, Perry, & Irving, 2002). In-depth interviews with smaller samples of overweight youth have provided additional information about the experiences that they face within their families, at schools, and in other situations (Neumark-Sztainer, Story, & Faibisch, 1998; Neumark-Sztainer, Story, Faibisch, Ohlson, & Adamiak, 1999).

In this chapter, we examine the psychosocial and behavioral consequences of obesity identified in our own research and in the work of others. We first present some of the key research findings examining the social and economic consequences of being overweight in a society in which thinness is valued. We then examine the potential implications of being overweight and of being exposed to weight-related stigmatization on psychological well-being and health-compromising behaviors. Implications for working toward the prevention of obesity and its associated psychosocial and behavioral consequences are discussed.

SOCIAL CONSEQUENCES OF OBESITY

Negative attitudes about body fat have led to various forms of weight-related stigmatization. As described in the following section, studies have found that overweight children, adolescents, and adults are negatively stereotyped, treated differently, and face discrimination in many facets of life.

Social Consequences Faced by Overweight Children

Studies have found that children tend to attribute negative characteristics that are unrelated to weight or appearance to overweight children (Brylinsky, 1994; DeJong & Kleck, 1986; Hill & Silver, 1995; Richardson, Goodman, Hastorf, & Dornbusch, 1961; Staffieri, 1967). In a landmark study conducted in 1967, 6- to 10-year-old boys assigned various adjectives to silhouette drawings of a thin, muscular, and obese body shape (Staffieri, 1967). A range of negative attributes, such as "lazy," "dirty," "stupid," "ugly," "liar," and "cheat," were attributed more often to the silhouette of the obese child than to the drawings of the other body shape. Using pictures of children with a range of physical characteristics, including disabilities, Richardson et al. found that the picture representing the overweight child was the one least liked and least likely to be considered a potential playmate by the children in the study. It is unclear how these hypothetical scenarios reflect the real-life experiences of obese children. One study has suggested that attitudes may be less negative in real-life situations than in these more abstract or hypothetical situations; Lawson (1980) found no relationship between the stereotypes attached to drawings and same-item judgments of overweight peers among a sample of 84 children in grades 2 to 6. Thus, the desirable norms relating to body shape did not appear to be used to evaluate their fellow classmates. On the other hand, Strauss, Smith, Frame, and Forehand (1984) found that overweight elementary school children were rejected more often and liked less by peers compared to average-weight children of the same age. Further research is needed to elucidate the relationship between children's beliefs about obese peers and their behavior toward them.

Social Consequences Faced by Overweight Adolescents

Negative attitudes concerning obesity and weight-related stigmatization continue into adolescence (Crandall, 1995; Sobal, Nicolopoulos, & Lee, 1995). A number of studies have suggested that overweight adolescents, particularly overweight girls, may be perceived as less desirable partners for romantic relationships. In a study of 786 high school students, Sobal et al. found that adolescents, in particular boys, expressed low comfort levels in dating overweight peers, and comfort levels were lowest for dating a very overweight individual. Pearce, Boergers, and Prinstein (2002) also looked at romantic relationships of an ethnically diverse group of 416 adolescents and found that obese girls were less likely to date than their peers. Obese boys, on the other hand, did not report dating less than their peers. Pearce et al. speculate that this may be because boys may not be judged by potential romantic partners according to their weight to the same extent as girls.

Our own work has clearly demonstrated that overweight adolescents perceive that they are treated differently because of their weight. In a qualitative study in which 50 overweight African American and Caucasian adolescent girls were interviewed about their weight-related experiences, all but two of the girls described stigmatizing experiences, such as name calling and teasing (Neumark-Sztainer et al., 1998). The girls also described hurtful comments and behaviors by family members and peers that appeared to be less intentional. For example, one girl described growing up with a father who constantly criticized her for being lazy and told her that she needed to "get up and go walk around." One girl described how people make assumptions about personal hygiene and attractiveness as to being overweight:

> I'm trying to think of how I'm treated differently because I'm big. Um, there's an assumption that all big people stink. . . . That's the worst one I don't like, because I know I don't stink. I mean you know that's an assumption that everybody has, they automatically think that I'm going to smell like something . . . because you're bigger and you can't clean as well. Hey, I get in the tub every day.

In Project EAT, a population-based study of eating patterns and weight concerns among 4,746 teens, nearly one-quarter of the youths reported being teased about their weight in the past year (Neumark-Sztainer, Falkner, et al., 2002). Overweight youth were at greatest risk for being teased; 63% of very overweight girls and 58% of very overweight boys reported being teased about their weight by their peers. The potential impact of weight teasing on disordered eating behaviors and on overall psychological well-being among Project EAT participants was significant, as is discussed in a later section of this chapter.

Measuring only overt forms of weight stigmatization, such as teasing, may not provide a complete account of the impact of weight stigmatization. Research has shown that girls are more likely to use their friendship status as a way of victimizing a peer (e.g., excluding a peer from social activities) versus overt victimization (Crick, 1997; Galen & Underwood, 1997). Pearce et al. (2002) measured both types of victimization and found that obese boys reported more overt victimization than their overweight and average-weight peers, but no significant difference in relational victimization. Obese girls reported experiencing more relational victimization than their average-weight peers. There was no significant difference between the weight groups for overt victimization among the girls. Because relationships have been shown to be central to the formation of the personal and group identity of girls, even more than they are for boys, this type of victimization may put obese girls at particular risk for experiencing psychological and social difficulties (Fabian & Thompson, 1989). Further inquiry is necessary to determine how best to assess the different experiences of stigmatization across gender and the potential impact of these experiences on psychosocial well-being.

Social Consequences Faced by Overweight Adults

Studies have indicated that weight-related stigmatization also exists in adult populations. One study examined weight stigmatization in adult members of a fat acceptance group. Obese participants of the group were significantly more likely than other members of the group to report victimization, such as negative nicknames and exclusion from sports or social gatherings. Obese participants also reported attempting to conceal their weight by choosing jobs where weight would not be an issue (e.g., telephone sales) to avoid public harassment and employment discrimination (Rothblum, Brand, Miller, & Oetjen, 1990). A second study assessed the prevalence of perceived weight-related mistreatment due to weight in a general community-based sample of 187 men and 800 women (Falkner, French, Jeffery, & Neumark-Sztainer, 1999). Twenty-two percent of women and 17% of men reported weight-related mistreatment. The most commonly reported sources of mistreatment among women were strangers (13%) and a spouse or loved one (12%). Men were most likely to report mistreatment by a spouse or loved one (10%) and friends (8%). Perceived weight-related mistreatment was positively associated with BMI. Reported mistreatment was much more prevalent among individuals in the highest quartile of the BMI distribution (43%) than among those in the lowest BMI quartile (6%; Falkner et al., 1999).

As with adolescents, obesity may negatively impact romantic relationships and marriage opportunities, particularly for women. This was found in a prospective study that followed 10,039 adolescents and young adults over an eight-year period (Gortmaker, Must, Perrin, Sobol, & Dietz, 1993). At follow-up, women who had been overweight (BMI > 95th percentile) at the start of the study were 20% less likely to be married than women who had not been overweight. Men who began the study overweight were 11% less likely to be married at follow-up (Gortmaker et al., 1993). In contrast, people with other chronic physical conditions did not differ from the nonoverweight subjects as to marital status.

Economic Consequences Associated with Obesity

Obesity may also be associated with adverse economic consequences (Gortmaker et al., 1993; Pagan & Davila, 1997; Register & Williams, 1997). An analysis from the National Longitudinal Survey Youth Cohort examined earnings in more than 8,000 men and women 18 to 25 years old and reported that obese women earned 12% less than nonobese women (Register & Williams, 1997). Similar to studies that followed, this study indicated that the economic penalty of obesity seems to be specific to women (Pagan & Davila, 1997; Register & Williams, 1997). Another longitudinal study following young adults over eight years found that obese women earned more than $6,000 less than nonobese women (Gortmaker et al., 1993). Research suggests that obese men do not face the same wage penalty but are underrepresented and paid less than nonobese men in managerial and professional occupations and are overrepresented in transportation occupations (Gortmaker et al., 1993; Register & Williams, 1997).

Adverse economic consequences faced by overweight individuals may be due to discriminatory employment practices and educational opportunities. Puhl and Brownell (2001) reviewed numerous experimental studies investigating hiring decisions by manipulating perceptions of employee weight, either through written description, photograph, or video (Decker, 1987; Larkin & Pines, 1979; Pingitore, Dugoni, Tindale, & Spring, 1994; Rothblum, Miller, & Garbutt, 1988). Participants in these studies were randomly assigned to a condition in which a fictional job applicant was described or pictured as overweight or average weight, and participants were asked to evaluate the applicant (Decker, 1987; Larkin & Pines, 1979; Pingitore et al., 1994; Rothblum et al., 1988). Despite having identical resumes, the overweight applicants were consistently judged more negatively and were less often recommended for jobs. Experimental research has also suggested that obese employees may have lower promotion prospects than average-weight employees. In a study of 168 managers and supervisors who were asked to evaluate the promotion potential of a hypothetical employee, the obese candidate received lower promotion recommendations versus a normal weight peer, despite identical qualifications (Brink, 1988).

A primary means to improving socioeconomic status is obtaining a college education. Research suggests that obese students may have a more difficult time obtaining a college degree because of overt weight stigmatization, including poor evaluations, low college acceptance rates, and dismissal because of their weight (Solovay, 2000; Weiler & Helms, 1993). An early study conducted in 1966 found that obese students were significantly less likely to be accepted to college, despite having equivalent application rates and academic performance to nonobese peers (Canning & Mayer, 1966). Obese women were accepted less frequently (31%) than were obese men (42%). Replication of this study is needed to determine the extent to which discriminatory practices presently occur.

An additional and related obstacle is that parents may be less likely to pay for their obese children's college expenses. In a study of how undergraduates pay for their education expenses, Crandall (1995) found that average-weight students received more family financial support than overweight students, who depend more on financial aid and jobs. This effect was larger and more reliable for daughters than for sons. This difference in family financial support remained even after controlling for parents' education level and income, race, family size, and number of children attending college (Crandall, 1995).

Limitations in these studies need to be taken into account in drawing conclusions about associations between weight status and socioeconomic status, employment practices, and educational opportunities. These limitations include the use of hypothetical situations (e.g., in examining discrimination in hiring practices) and the lack of adequate controlling for possible confounders such as age, race, and gender. In spite of these limitations, this body of literature suggests adverse economic consequences associated with being overweight in our society.

Weight-Related Stigmatization in Educational and Health Care Settings

Overweight individuals facing weight-related stigmatization should be able to seek guidance and comfort in educational and health care settings. Because of the important role of educators and health care providers and their ongoing contact with students and patients, both have the potential to have a large impact on overweight youth and adults. However, studies have suggested that some educators and health care providers may have negative attitudes about obesity that have the potential for interfering with their ability to provide overweight students and patients with the help that they may need.

We explored weight-related attitudes among 115 middle school and high school teachers and school health workers (Neumark-Sztainer, Harris, & Story, 1999). Approximately one-fifth of the school staff expressed the view that obese persons are more emotional, less tidy, less likely to succeed at work, and have personalities different from nonobese persons. About one-quarter of the respondents viewed obese persons as having more family problems than nonobese persons and agreed with the statement, "One of the worst things that could happen to a person would be for him or her to become obese." We found it encouraging that the vast majority of the school staff did not associate obesity with characteristics unrelated to weight. School staff members have many formal and informal opportunities for interactions with overweight students and their peers. Their own attitudes may translate into behaviors that can help or hinder overweight students and the environment in which weight stigmatization by other students may occur.

Studies have similarly revealed that some health care providers may hold negative attitudes toward obese individuals. In one study, medical students rated morbidly obese people more negatively than moderately obese and nonobese persons as to a number of humanistic qualities (e.g., good/bad), personality traits (e.g., pleasant/unpleasant), and body image (e.g., beautiful/ugly; Blumberg & Mellis, 1980). In another study, two-thirds of family physicians claimed that their obese patients lacked self-control, and 39% claimed they were lazy (Price, Desmond, Krol, Snyder, & O'Connell, 1987). Health care providers have opportunities for interacting on a one-to-one basis with overweight persons and their significant others. Sensitivity to weight-related concerns is important because some studies have suggested that obese persons hesitate in seeking health care (Adams, Smith, Wilbur, & Grady, 1993; Fontaine, Faith, Allison, & Cheskin, 1998; Olson, Schumaker, & Yawn, 1994). Obese women have been found to be more likely than nonobese women to delay or cancel appointments, particularly for important preventive services such as breast examinations and gynecologic examinations (Fontaine et al., 1998). A study that surveyed women as to why they cancel or delay visits found that 32% of women with a BMI > 27 and 55% of those with a BMI > 35 delayed or cancelled visits because they knew they would be weighed; the most common response for delaying appointments was embarrassment about weight (Olson et al., 1994).

Further study is needed to assess how negative attitudes in the health professions affect practice. Changes to improve obese patients' health care experience must also be investigated. Some suggested changes for those who treat obese patients include recognizing obesity as a chronic medical condition, improving knowledge of nutrition and multidisciplinary treatments, becoming familiar with community resources, creating more accessible environments for obese persons by providing armless chairs and larger examination gowns, and treating patients with respect and support (Frank, 1993).

Weight-Related Stigmatization Summary

This body of literature demonstrates that obese individuals deal with various forms of weight-related stigmatization. Overweight individuals report hurtful weight-related experiences, including being directly teased about their weight and being the object of less direct weight-related comments. Overweight adolescents and adults may have fewer opportunities for romantic relationships and marriage. Furthermore, obesity may be associated with negative economic consequences. Negative stereotypes associated with obesity reported by employers, educators, and health care providers can have a deleterious effect on the lives of obese individuals. Changes in the ways in which overweight people are viewed and treated in our society are needed.

PSYCHOSOCIAL AND BEHAVIORAL CONSEQUENCES OF OBESITY AND WEIGHT-RELATED STIGMATIZATION

In light of the pervasive weight-related stigmatization faced by many overweight individuals, differences in global and weight-specific psychological concerns and behaviors might be anticipated. In this section, we describe associations between obesity and global psychological concerns, such as self-esteem and depression, weight-specific concerns and behaviors, and behaviors with implications for weight gain (i.e., binge eating) and healthy weight management (i.e., physical activity). In addition, we review some of the research that has examined associations between weight stigmatization and psychological and behavioral consequences.

Global Psychosocial Concerns

Self-esteem is influenced by our perceptions as to how others regard us and treat us. The previous discussion indicates that many overweight individuals perceive that others make negative assumptions about them and treat them differently because of their weight. Thus, we might expect to find large differences in self-esteem between overweight and nonoverweight individuals. Further, we might expect to find stronger associations among children and adolescents than among adults because of developmental and social processes, with the strongest associations among adolescents for whom appearance, fitting in with the norm, and social interactions tend to be key issues. Indeed, assumptions are often made about overweight children and adolescents having low self-esteem. These assumptions are partially supported by research findings. In a review of the literature examining associations between obesity and self-esteem among children and adolescents, French, Story, and Perry (1995) found stronger associations among adolescents than among children. However, findings were not consistent across studies. About one-half of the cross-sectional studies (13 out of 25) showed lower self-esteem in obese children and adolescents than in their nonobese counterparts. No studies reported higher levels of self-esteem in obese youth than in nonobese youth. In adolescents, cross-sectional studies were consistent in finding associations between obesity and both global- and body-esteem. Results from the few prospective studies that were reviewed were inconsistent. Results from treatment programs showed improvements in self-esteem, but in most cases, changes in self-esteem were not related to weight loss. Thus, findings suggest that obesity tends to be associated with a lower self-esteem, particularly in adolescents, but associations tend to be modest and are not consistent across studies.

In addition to examining issues of self-esteem, studies have also examined associations between obesity and other psychological concerns among children and adolescents. Findings from population-based studies on children indicate that overweight children do not stand out from their normal weight peers as to level of emotional problems, such as depression and anxiety (Friedman & Brownell, 1995). A study by Wadden et al. found no significant differences between obese and nonobese subjects in measures of depression (Wadden, Foster, Stunkard, & Linowitz, 1989). Sallade (1973) similarly observed that obese and nonobese children did not differ significantly on measures of personality function. Some studies comparing clinical and nonclinical populations of obese children did find a higher incidence of emotional problems in the clinical group (Banis et al., 1988; Israel & Shapiro, 1985; Kimm, Sweeney, Janosky, & MacMillan, 1991). However, clinical populations may be more overweight or may have more psychological disturbances than population-based samples; thus, these results may not be generalizable to the population as a whole. More studies that use appropriate control groups are needed to uncover the comorbidity of psychopathology and obesity in clinical and population-based samples.

As seen with the research into the relation between weight and emotional problems among children, studies investigating this topic among adolescent populations have produced inconsistent findings (Friedman & Brownell, 1995). Striking differences appear in the literature between early reports on clinical populations in which overweight adolescents are portrayed as being at greater risk for depression and anxiety and more recent population-based studies in which differences between overweight and nonoverweight populations have been found to be minimal and inconsistent (Friedman & Brownell, 1995). For example, in a study of more than 30,000 adolescents, emotional well-being and suicidal ideation were not strongly associated with weight status (Neumark-Sztainer et al., 1997). These inconsistencies may be due to the different samples studied (i.e., clinical or population-based). There also may have been a shift in the etiology of obesity over time; in earlier times, psychological factors may have played a larger role in the etiology of obesity, whereas in more modern times, socioenvironmental factors may be playing a larger etiological role.

In contrast to the research conducted among children and adolescents, the focus with adults has tended to be more on emotional problems, such as anxiety and depression, with only limited research on self- and body-esteem. Based on their meta-analysis of studies investigating psychological correlates of obesity, Friedman and Brownell (1995) concluded that, compared to obese adolescent girls who tend to exhibit both body dissatisfaction and low levels of self- and body-esteem, obese women appear only to exhibit body dissatisfaction. This difference among these age groups may indicate that pressures to be thin are higher during adolescent years or that adult women have developed higher self-esteem from other aspects of life rather than focusing on physical appearance.

As to emotional problems, population studies have generally failed to find significant differences between obese and nonobese adults (Friedman & Brownell, 1995). These results are similar to those seen in studies involving adolescent and child populations. Moore et al. examined a representative sample of 1,660 urban residents and found that obese and nonobese individuals did not show differences on anxiety and depression levels (Moore, Stunkard, & Srole, 1962). Stewart and Brook (1983) similarly observed only small differences between obese and nonobese subjects in their study of 5,817 adults. In this investigation, however, obese individuals were found to be significantly less depressed and anxious than were their nonobese counterparts. Results from numerous other studies confirm the impression that there are few significant differences in psychological status between obese and nonobese in the general population (Faubel, 1989; Hallstrom & Noppa, 1981; Moore, Stunkard, & Srole, 1997; Stewart & Brook, 1983; Wadden et al., 1989).

In contrast to population data, studies of overweight persons seeking treatment for weight reduction suggest that emotional disturbance is more common among the obese (Friedman & Brownell, 1995). Numerous studies that used the Minnesota Multiphasic Personality Inventory to assess psychological status found at least mild levels of depression among clinical populations. Many of these studies failed to include appropriate control groups (Friedman & Brownell, 1995), which is critical because most people seeking treatment, regardless of the particular disorder, report psychological distress (Fitzgibbon, Stolley, & Kirschenbaum, 1993).

Friedman and Brownell (1995) suggest that weak and inconsistent findings in comparisons between overweight and nonoverweight populations may be because overweight individuals are treated as one homogeneous group, when in fact they are heterogeneous. They propose studying obese populations in an attempt to identify factors that place certain overweight individuals at risk for psychological concerns. For example, they suggest that studying obesity and its psychosocial consequences among various ethnic groups may reveal that sociocultural norms for acceptable body size may influence which individuals experience adverse psychological consequences of obesity. Other factors that may place certain overweight individuals at risk for psychosocial consequences include the way in which others treat them, that is, if they have been teased about their weight or have experienced other forms of weight-related stigmatization.

A recent study by our research team demonstrates the potential for weight teasing to strongly affect the psychological well-being of adolescents (Eisenberg, Neumark-Sztainer, & Story, in press). Being teased about body weight by family members and/or peers was consistently associated with poorer scores in body satisfaction, self-esteem, depressive symptoms, and higher percentages of youth reporting suicide ideation and suicide attempts. These associations held for both boys and girls, across racial and ethnic groups and weight groups. Weight teasing by peers was reported by 30% of girls and 25% of boys. Weight teasing by family members was reported by 29% of girls and 16% of boys. Approximately 15% of girls and 10% of boys indicated that both peers and family members had teased them about their weight. Youth who were teased by both sources had greater risk on all five outcome measures than teasing from either a single source or no teasing. For example, suicide ideation was reported by 51% of girls teased by both sources, 39% of girls teased by one source, and 25% of girls who were not teased. Although numbers were lower among boys, a similar pattern was found; suicide ideation was reported by 34% of boys teased by both sources, 24% of boys teased by one source, and 14% of youth who were not teased. BMI was not significantly associated with most outcome measures after teasing was entered into multivariate models, indicating that the experience of being teased about weight, rather than actual body weight, appears to be the relevant factor for self-esteem, depressive symptoms, and suicidal ideation and attempts (Eisenberg et al., in press). However, it is important to note that overweight youth were at much greater risk of being teased about their weight than nonoverweight youth (Neumark-Sztainer, Falkner, et al., 2002). Thus, overweight youth are at increased risk for being teased about their weight, and being teased places youth at high risk for an array of global psychological concerns.

Body Image and Unhealthy Weight Control Behaviors

Associations between obesity and measures of body image have consistently been found to be strong. As previously discussed, in the review by French et al. (1995) on the associations between obesity and self-esteem, associations between obesity and body-esteem were consistently found, particularly among adolescents. We also found strong associations between weight status and a variety of body image variables among adolescents in Project EAT (Neumark-Sztainer, Falkner, et al., 2002). For example, among adolescent girls, low body satisfaction was reported by 32%, 38%, 59%, and 66% of underweight, average-weight, moderately overweight, and very overweight girls, respectively. Among adolescent boys, low body satisfaction was reported by 29%, 19%, 27%, and 48% of underweight, average-weight, moderately overweight, and very overweight boys, respectively. In adult populations, research suggests that 41% of men and 55% of women in the United States are dissatisfied with their weight (Cash, Winstead, & Janda, 1986). This discontent has been shown to be greater at higher levels of adiposity (Smith, Thompson, Raczynski, & Hilner, 1999).

Research findings also indicate that overweight individuals are more likely to report the use of unhealthy weight control behaviors than nonoverweight individuals. For example, in a study of 9,118 adolescents, we found that very unhealthy weight control behaviors (i.e., diet pills, laxatives, diuretics, or self-induced vomiting) in the past seven days were reported by 14% of the very overweight girls (BMI ≥ 95th percentile for age and gender) as compared to 7% of the average-weight girls (BMI: 15th to 85th percentile; Neumark-Sztainer, Story, Falkner, Beuhring, & Resnick, 1999). Among boys, these behaviors were reported by 5% of the very overweight boys and 3% of the average-weight boys. More recently, we found similar patterns of association in Project EAT using more detailed measures of weight control behaviors and measured BMI values (Neumark-Sztainer, Story, et al., 2002).

Studies have also found associations between weight teasing and both body dissatisfaction and the use of unhealthy weight control behaviors. Most of this work has been done with adolescents and young adults. In a study of 121 adolescent girls, Fabian and Thompson (1989) found that both teasing frequency and teasing effect (how much the teasing upset the subjects) were significantly associated with body dissatisfaction, eating disturbances, and depression. Stormer and Thompson (1996) studied 162 female college students and found that a history of being teased about appearance contributed to explaining the variance in body dissatisfaction and eating disturbance, albeit the contribution was small after controlling for factors such as self-esteem, level of obesity, and internalization of cultural norms concerning beauty and thinness. In Project EAT, we found strong associations between weight teasing and unhealthy weight control behaviors in overweight and nonoverweight adolescents (Neumark-Sztainer, Faulkner, et al., 2002). Unhealthy weight control behaviors were reported by 80% of the overweight girls who perceived that they were teased frequently about their weight and 68% of the overweight girls who were not teased. Among overweight boys, the association was stronger; unhealthy weight control behaviors were reported by 62% of the boys who were teased about their weight and 42% of those who were not teased. Associations remained statistically significant after adjusting for BMI and sociodemographic characteristics, suggesting that the teasing was responsible for the higher rates of unhealthy weight control. In a study of adult women seeking treatment for obesity, the frequency of being teased about weight and size while growing up was negatively correlated with evaluation of appearance and positively correlated with body dissatisfaction (Grilo, Wilfley, Brownell, & Rodin, 1994). Subjects with early-onset obesity reported greater body dissatisfaction than did subjects with adult-onset obesity, suggesting that weight teasing while growing up may represent a risk factor of negative body image. Also of note is the lack of association between general appearance teasing and body image among this sample of adult women (Grilo et al., 1994). These findings suggest that being teased specifically about an individual's weight has a more adverse effect on body image than more general teasing.

Binge Eating

Overweight individuals are more likely to engage in binge eating than their nonoverweight counterparts (Marcus, 1993). In Project EAT, binge eating behaviors were reported by 9% of underweight girls, 16% of average-weight girls, 19% of moderately overweight girls, and 21% of very overweight girls. Binge eating was reported by 6% of underweight and average-weight boys, 10% of moderately overweight boys, and 12% of very overweight boys (Neumark-Sztainer, Story, et al., 2002). In a nonclinical sample of adult women enrolled in a weight gain prevention program, binge eating was reported by 9% of nonoverweight women and 21% of overweight women (French, Jeffery, Sherwood, & Neumark-Sztainer, 1999). Binge eating tends to be more prevalent among overweight individuals seeking treatment for weight loss. Devlin, Walsh, Spitzer, and Hasin (1992) reviewed the relevant literature and estimated that between 25% and 50% of overweight people seeking treatment for weight loss engage in binge eating.

A number of factors may be contributing to the high rates of binge eating among overweight individuals, including physiological factors (increased appetite), behavioral factors (e.g., as a response to dietary restraint), psychological factors (e.g., response to depressive mood), and social factors (e.g., increased exposure to stressful situations such as weight-related stigmatization). Concerning the latter point, we have found that overweight adolescents who report being teased frequently about their weight are at increased risk for binge eating as compared to overweight adolescents who are not teased about their weight. Among overweight adolescents, binge eating was reported by 29% of girls and 18% of boys who reported frequent weight teasing and by 16% of girls and 7% of overweight boys who were not teased. These associations remained statistically significant after controlling for differences in BMI and sociodemographic characteristics. Brown, Cash, and Lewis (1989) compared a sample of adolescent female binge-purgers ($n = 114$) to a matched group of female controls using data from a nationwide survey on body image. They found that binge-purgers were more likely than controls to report that during childhood, peers made fun of them or rejected them because of their appearance.

Physical Activity

Numerous cross-sectional studies have shown that overweight children and adolescents are less likely to engage in physical activity and are more likely to engage in sedentary leisure time activities than their nonoverweight counterparts (Deheeger, Rolland-Cachera, & Fontvielle, 1997; Fontvielle, Kriska, & Ravussin, 1997; Gordon-Larsen, 2001; Gortmaker, Dietz, & Cheung, 1990; Guillaume, Lapidus, Bjontorp, & Lambert, 1997; Moussa, Skaik, Selwanes, Yaghy, & Bin-Othman, 1994; Ross & Pate, 1987; U.S. Department of Health and Human Services, 1996). Reasons for these lower levels of physical activity may include discomfort engaging in physical activity, lack of physically active overweight role models, and embarrassment (Neumark-Sztainer & Story, 1997; Taylor et al., 1999). These barriers to physical activity may lead to reciprocal causality in which less active children and youth become more overweight, which may, in turn, lead to further declines in physical activity.

Compared to research with adolescents and children, the evidence concerning the association of physical activity and weight among adults is not as strong. While some studies have suggested that higher levels of physical activity are associated with lower body weight (Ball, Owen, Salmon, Bauman, & Gore, 2001; Dipietro, 1995; Grilo, 1995; Kromhout, Saris, & Horst, 1988; Westerterp, 1998), others show no relation between these factors or associations in one gender group but not in the other (Folsom et al., 1985; Westerterp, 1999a, 1999b; Westerterp & Goran, 1997; Williamson et al., 1993). Williamson et al. (1993) examined both cross-sectional and prospective relations between leisure-time physical activity and BMI in a representative population sample of 9,325 men and women. Both the cross-sectional and prospective analysis revealed that the associations between these factors were significantly stronger for women than men. In contrast, other studies have reported stronger inverse associations between physical activity and BMI or body fat in men than in women (Westerterp & Goran, 1997; Westerterp, Mejer, Kester, Wouters, & Ten Hoor, 1992).

Our review of the literature investigating barriers to physical activity in adults uncovered only one study that examined weight-related impediments to physical activity. The findings of this study, conducted among 2,298 Australian adults, show that the perception of being too fat to exercise is a barrier to physical activity among some overweight individuals (Ball, Crawford, & Owen, 2000). Women were more likely than men to report that being too fat was a barrier to increasing their physical activity.

Programs that include activities to improve self-esteem and body image in addition to encouraging easily achievable, noncompetitive, low- to moderate-intensity physical activity may be useful in overcoming barriers to physical activity and increasing self-efficacy to be active among overweight populations.

Psychological and Behavioral Consequences Summary

Studies do not consistently show differences in global psychosocial concerns between overweight and nonoverweight individuals. In contrast, large differences in weight-specific psychosocial concerns and behaviors are consistently found between overweight and nonoverweight individuals. Furthermore, overweight individuals are at increased risk for a number of behaviors such as unhealthy dieting, binge eating, and physical inactivity that may negatively impact their dietary intake and overall health and, ironically, may place them at risk for further weight gain. Fewer studies have examined associations between weight-related stigmatization and both global and weight-specific psychosocial concerns and behaviors. The studies that have been done in this area indicate that

Table 18.1   Summary of Psychosocial and Behavioral Consequences of Obesity

Psychosocial and Behavioral Consequence	Key Research Findings
Weight stigmatization	Overweight children, adolescents, and adults are at increased risk for various forms of stigmatization including teasing and discriminatory employment practices. Overweight women also have decreased opportunities for romantic relationships and marriage.
Global psychological consequences	Evidence for global psychosocial consequences, such as self-esteem, anxiety, and depression, is weak and inconsistent in population-based studies of overweight individuals. Evidence among clinical populations shows a stronger positive association between BMI and global psychosocial consequences. A few studies have found strong associations between weight stigmatization and global psychosocial consequences among adolescents.
Weight-specific psychological consequences	There is strong evidence for the positive association between obesity and body dissatisfaction. An association between weight stigmatization and body dissatisfaction has also been found in a few studies.
Behavioral consequences	Evidence for association between obesity and unhealthy weight control practices and binge eating is strong. Obesity is inversely associated with physical activity, especially in children and adolescents. Weight stigmatization has been linked to unhealthy weight control behaviors and binge eating in adolescents.

weight-related stigmatization can have adverse consequences for both global and weight-specific psychological concerns and behaviors. An overview of the key psychosocial and behavioral consequences of obesity is provided in Table 18.1.

IMPLICATIONS FOR INTERVENTIONS

The high prevalence of weight-related stigmatization and its strong associations with adverse psychological and behavioral consequences point to a strong need for interventions aimed at: (1) decreasing weight stigmatization by others, (2) increasing skills for coping with weight stigmatization among overweight individuals, and (3) providing support for overweight individuals facing weight stigmatization by significant others.

Decreasing Weight-Related Stigmatization

Educational and policy interventions are needed to address and decrease weight stigmatization facing students in school settings, employees in work settings, patients in health care settings, and, more broadly, individuals living in societies in which thinness is valued for reasons other than health.

One potential method for decreasing weight stigmatization and ensuing discriminatory practices is to alter the negative manner in which people view obesity. Only a few studies have attempted to reduce peoples' negative attitudes about obesity (Anesbury & Tiggemann, 2000; Bell & Morgan, 2000; Crandall, 1994; Robinson, Bacon, & O'Reilly, 1993; Weise, Wilson, Jobes, & Neises, 1992). One intervention attempted to change the negative attitudes among medical students (Weise et al., 1992). Before randomization to a control condition or to an educational intervention that included videos, written materials, and role playing exercises, the majority of medical students characterized obese individuals as lazy, sloppy, and lacking in self-control. After the educational course, students demonstrated significantly improved attitudes and beliefs about obesity compared to the control group. The effectiveness of the intervention was still supported one year later (Weise et al., 1992).

We are currently in the early stages of developing an elementary school program aimed at the prevention of weight-related disorders that will include the development of a school-wide teasing policy. Students will be involved in the development of a plan for addressing weight teasing. They will be involved in deciding what they want the standards to be and in establishing consequences if there is an infraction of the standards (i.e., a student teases another student about his or her weight). Results of key informant interviews with school staff have indicated the importance of addressing weight teasing in a broader prevention program. School staff members support the development of appropriate policies for addressing weight teasing, similar to those that have been developed for other areas of bullying and teasing.

At present, no federal laws exist to prohibit discrimination based on weight at the state level, and few locations have implemented weight-specific legislation. The District of Columbia forbids discrimination on the basis of appearance including weight; and Santa Cruz and San Francisco, California, include weight in their definition of unlawful discrimination (Puhl & Brownell, 2001). Antidiscrimination policies at the state or institutional level may be required to alleviate the adverse social and economic consequences of obesity.

Increasing Coping Skills for Dealing with Weight-Related Stigmatization

In an ideal world, overweight individuals would not need to learn how to cope with weight-related stigmatization due to effective interventions aimed at its prevention. Because overweight individuals will likely continue to be exposed to stigmatization, they need to be provided with skills for recognizing, coping, and adequately reacting to different types of stigmatization to decrease its occurrence and minimize its impact on their psychosocial well-being. In a study of health care providers working with adolescents, we found that less than one-half of the dietitians and the pediatricians who deal with weight-related issues with overweight youth report discussing weight-related stigmatization (Neumark-Sztainer, Story, Evans, & Ireland, 1999). In contrast, these issues were discussed by more than 90% of the psychologists and social workers, who may feel more confident of their ability to ask appropriate questions and to engage in a helpful discussion with an adolescent who has experienced weight stigmatization. Sobal (1990) describes a four-component model for coping with stigmatization that may help health care providers, educators, and others working with overweight individuals who have been stigmatized:

1. *Recognition:* awareness that obesity is stigmatized and understanding about stigma.
2. *Readiness:* anticipation, preparation, and prevention of stigmatizing acts.
3. *Reaction:* immediate and long-term coping with stigmatizing acts.
4. *Repair:* recovery from problems resulting from stigmatization and reform of actions and values of others.

Thus, using this model as a guide, health care providers or educators could ask about weight-stigmatizing experiences in a manner that lets the individual know that these types of experiences are fairly common, that they may occur in direct or indirect manners, and that they should not be tolerated. The next steps would be to develop a plan for addressing future instances of weight stigmatization if they should occur. It is important to discuss the impact that being teased may have had on the individual. In severe cases, it may be appropriate to engage the assistance of a mental health care provider, but the primary care health provider or school educator is often in the best position to have initial discussions on weight stigmatization.

Providing Support for Overweight Individuals

Family members of overweight individuals and other significant others (e.g., educators, health care providers, spouses, peers) can provide support in coping with weight-related stigmatization to decrease its potential impact on psychosocial well-being.

A study by Mellin, Neumark-Sztainer, Story, Ireland, and Resnick (2001) found that overweight adolescents who had supportive families were more resilient and fared better than overweight adolescents whose families were less supportive. Families need guidance in helping their overweight children to make healthy lifestyle choices to prevent excessive weight gain (e.g., get involved with various physical activities, reduce television viewing), avoid unhealthy weight control behaviors, and adopt an overall sense of self-acceptance and self-worth. Overweight children reared in supportive families will feel better about themselves and will be less likely to suffer the psychosocial consequences associated with being overweight. At the same time, families of overweight children need to provide opportunities and gentle encouragement for healthy eating and physical activity. The balance between these messages may present challenges for parents, and discussing different options with an informed and sensitive health care provider may be of help. Satter (1996) has proposed a model based on "trust," which some parents may find helpful in fostering healthy eating patterns in their overweight children. She suggests that parents should take responsibility for providing wholesome and appealing food at predictable and pleasant times. However, once they have done their part, parents must trust children to pick and choose from the available foods.

As previously discussed, some health care providers and educators hold negative attitudes about obesity that have the potential to interfere with their ability to act in a supportive manner toward overweight patients and students. However, the majority of health care providers and educators do not hold negative attitudes and are very interested in learning how they can be more supportive. In a survey of school staff, we found that the majority of school-based health care providers and teachers were interested in attending a staff training on the prevention of weight-related disturbances (Neumark-Sztainer, Harris, et al., 1999). Material on how to prevent weight stigmatization and how to promote the psychosocial well-being of overweight youth could be incorporated into such sessions. Suggested activities include self examination of their own weight-related attitudes and experiences growing up, dissemination of accurate facts about the harmful consequences of weight teasing among youth, and role playing different scenarios to address the victim and perpetrator of weight teasing.

Prevention of Obesity and Weight Stigmatization: Is It Possible?

How can we best work toward preventing adverse psychosocial and behavioral consequences associated with obesity? Some might argue that to prevent these adverse consequences, we need to place our efforts on preventing and treating obesity. If effective, this type of approach would have the added benefit of preventing adverse physical

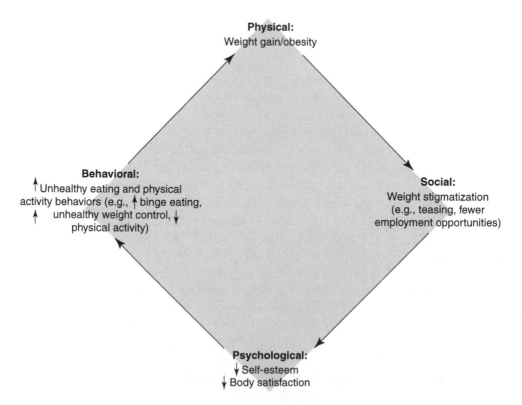

Figure 18.1   Obesity, Weight Stigmatization, and Adverse Psychological and Behavioral Consequences: An Ongoing Cycle.

consequences associated with obesity. Others might argue that weight-related stigmatization is so unfair and its associated psychological and behavioral consequences are so severe that actions directed toward the prevention of any type of weight stigmatization need to take precedence over actions aimed at obesity prevention. Because there will always be diversity in size and shape in individuals in our society, this type of approach could be viewed as more humane and realistic. We believe that the truth lies somewhere in the middle and that it is possible and necessary to simultaneously work toward the prevention of obesity *and* its adverse psychosocial and behavioral consequences.

Two possible scenarios are presented in Figures 18.1 and 18.2. The first scenario (Figure 18.1) represents a simplified version of the current situation. Weight gain and obesity are often met with weight-related stigmatization, such as derogatory remarks, outright weight teasing, fewer dating opportunities, and difficulties in obtaining a job or being promoted. Weight-related stigmatization may negatively impact an individual's self-esteem and, in particular, body image, which may lead to behaviors such as unhealthy dieting, binge eating, and decreased physical activity. Ironically, these behaviors are likely to lead to further weight gain; thus, the cycle continues.

An alternative scenario, which could guide the development of interventions aimed at preventing both obesity and its psychosocial and behavioral consequences,

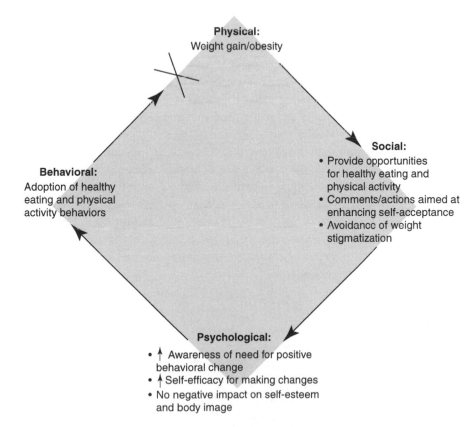

Figure 18.2 A Proposed Alternative Cycle to Guide the Development of Interventions Aimed at Preventing Obesity *and* Its Adverse Psychosocial and Behavioral Consequences: Breaking the Cycle.

is portrayed in Figure 18.2. In this scenario, weight gain and obesity are not met with derogatory comments, but rather with comments and actions aimed at enhancing self-acceptance and opportunities and gentle encouragement to engage in health-promoting behaviors.

For example, in health care settings, health care providers would take the time to discuss issues of concern to individuals who are disturbed about their weight and/or have experienced weight stigmatization, within a nonjudgmental and unhurried atmosphere, and jointly consider possibilities for addressing these concerns. This type of approach is hypothesized to lead to an awareness of the need for change without leading to adverse effects on self-esteem, body image, and other measures of psychological well-being. This approach is further hypothesized to lead to the adoption of healthy eating and physical activity patterns. Thus, the chain of events leading to increased weight gain can be halted.

The scenario proposed in Figure 18.2 guided the development of "New Moves," a school-based program for overweight girls or girls at risk for becoming overweight because of low levels of physical activity. "New Moves" is an alternative physical education class for high school girls that aims to provide a comfortable and supportive environment for physical activity, guidance in adopting healthy eating patterns and avoiding unhealthy dieting and binge eating, and social support for improved self-image and body image (Neumark-Sztainer, Story, Hannan, & Rex, in press). The program was enthusiastically received by participants and school staff and appeared to fill a niche in high school physical education programs.

In summary, obesity is associated with an array of adverse psychosocial and behavioral consequences. Research suggests that some of these consequences may be more strongly related to weight stigmatization than to obesity in and of itself. Additional research is needed to further elucidate these associations. However, interventions aimed at preventing obesity and its psychosocial and behavioral consequences are sorely needed now. Interventions need to include strong and comprehensive evaluation designs to assess program impact and to ensure that there are no unintentional harmful effects on outcomes. Ideas for the development of suitable messages and effective interventions to address these complex and multifaceted issues will not be easy. It is important to avoid becoming discouraged with less than optimal results. It is essential to honestly communicate and share ideas about successful and unsuccessful intervention components with our colleagues and those individuals that we are trying to serve to develop the best possible interventions aimed at preventing obesity and its adverse psychosocial and behavioral consequences.

REFERENCES

Adams, C. H., Smith, N. J., Wilbur, D. C., & Grady, K. E. (1993). The relationship of obesity to the frequency of pelvic examinations: Do physicians and patient attitudes make a difference? *Women and Health, 20,* 45–57.

Anesbury, T., & Tiggemann, M. (2000). An attempt to reduce negative stereotyping of obesity in children by changing controllability beliefs. *Health Education Research, 15,* 145–152.

Ball, K., Crawford, D., & Owen, N. (2000). Too fat to exercise? Obesity as a barrier to physical activity. *Australian and New Zealand Journal of Public Health, 24*(3), 331–333.

Ball, K., Owen, N., Salmon, J., Bauman, A., & Gore, C. J. (2001). Associations of physical activity with body weight and fat in men and women. *International Journal of Obesity and Related Metabolic Disorders, 25,* 914–919.

Banis, H. T., Varni, J. W., Wallander, J. L., Korsch, B. M., Jay, S. M., Adler, R., et al. (1988). Psychological and social adjustment of obese children and their families. *Child Care Health Development, 14*(3), 157–173.

Bell, S. K., & Morgan, S. B. (2000). Children's attitudes and behavioral intentions toward a peer presented as obese: Does medical explanation for the obesity make a difference? *Journal of Pediatric Psychology, 25,* 137–145.

Blumberg, P., & Mellis, L. (1980). Medical students' attitudes toward the obese and the morbidly obese. *International Journal of Eating Disorders, 4,* 169–175.

Brink, T. (1988). Obesity and job discrimination: Mediation via personality stereotypes? *Perceptual and Motor Skills, 66,* 494.

Brown, T. A., Cash, T. F., & Lewis, R. J. (1989). Body-image disturbances in adolescent female binge-purgers: A brief report of the results of a national survey in the United States. *Journal of Child Psychology and Psychiatry, 30*(4), 605–613.

Brylinsky, J. A. (1994). The identification of body build stereotypes in young children. *Journal of Research in Personality, 28,* 170–181.

Canning, H., & Mayer, J. (1966). Obesity: Its possible effects on college admission. *New England Journal of Medicine, 275,* 1172–1174.

Cash, T. F., Winstead, B. W., & Janda, L. H. (1986). The great American shape-up. *Psychology Today, 20*(4), 30–37.

Crandall, C. S. (1994). Prejudice against fat people: Ideology and self-interest. *Journal of Personality and Social Psychology, 66*(5), 882–894.

Crandall, C. S. (1995). Do parents discriminate against their heavyweight daughters? *Personality and Social Psychology Bulletin, 21*(7), 724–735.

Crick, N. R. (1997). Engagement in gender normative versus nonnormative forms of aggression: Links to social-psychological adjustment. *Developmental Psychology, 33,* 610–617.

Decker, W. H. (1987). Attributions based on managers' self-presentation, sex, and weight. *Psychological Reports, 61,* 175–181.

Deheeger, M., Rolland-Cachera, M. F., & Fontvielle, A. M. (1997). Physical activity and body composition in 10 year old French children: Linkages with nutritional intake? *International Journal of Obesity and Related Metabolic Disorders, 21,* 372–379.

DeJong, W., & Kleck, R. E. (1986). The social psychological effects of overweight. In C. P. Herman, M. P. Zanna, & E. T. Higgins (Eds.), *Physical appearance, stigma and social behavior: The Ontario symposium* (Vol. 3, p. 322). Hillsdale, NJ: Erlbaum.

Devlin, M., Walsh, B. T., Spitzer, R., & Hasin, D. (1992). Is there another binge eating disorder? A review of the literature on overeating in the absence of bulimia nervosa. *International Journal of Eating Disorders, 11*(4), 333–340.

Dipietro, L. (1995). Physical activity, body weight, and adiposity: An epidemiologic perspective. *Exercise Sport Science Review, 23,* 275–303.

Eisenberg, M. E., Neumark-Sztainer, D., & Story, M. (in press). Associations of weight-based teasing and emotional well-being among adolescents. *Archives of Pediatrics and Adolescent Medicine.*

Fabian, L. J., & Thompson, J. K. (1989). Body image and eating disturbance in young females. *International Journal of Eating Disorders, 8*(1), 63–74.

Falkner, N., French, S., Jeffery, R., & Neumark-Sztainer, D. (1999). Mistreatment due to weight prevalence and sources of perceived mistreatment in women and men. *Obesity Research, 7*(6), 572–576.

Faubel, M. (1989). Body image and depression in women with early and late onset obesity. *Journal of Psychology, 123*(4), 385–395.

Fitzgibbon, M. L., Stolley, M. R., & Kirschenbaum, D. S. (1993). Obese people who seek treatment have different characteristics than those who do not seek treatment. *Health Psychology, 12*(5), 342–345.

Folsom, A. R., Caspersen, C. J., Taylor, H. L., Jacobs, D. R., Luepker, R. V., Gomez-Marin, O., et al. (1985). Leisure time physical activity and its relationship to coronary risk factors in a population-based sample. *American Journal of Epidemiology, 121*, 570–579.

Fontaine, K. R., Faith, M. S., Allison, D. B., & Cheskin, L. J. (1998, July/August). Body weight and health care among women in the general population. *Archives of Family Medicine, 7*, 381–384.

Fontvielle, A. M., Kriska, A., & Ravussin, E. (1997). Decreased physical activity in Pima Indian compared with Caucasian children. *International Journal of Obesity and Related Metabolic Disorders, 17*, 445–452.

Frank, A. (1993). Futility and avoidance: Medical professionals in the treatment of obesity. *Journal of the American Medical Association, 269*(16), 2132–2133.

French, S. A., Jeffery, R. W., Sherwood, N. E., & Neumark-Sztainer, D. (1999). Prevalence and correlates of binge eating in a nonclinical sample of women enrolled in a weight gain prevention program. *International Journal of Obesity and Related Metabolic Disorders, 23*(6), 576–585.

French, S. A., Story, M., & Perry, C. L. (1995). Self-esteem and obesity in children and adolescents: A literature review. *Obesity Research, 3*(5), 479–490.

Friedman, M. A., & Brownell, K. D. (1995). Psychological correlates of obesity: Moving to the next research generation. *Psychological Bulletin, 117*(1), 3–20.

Galen, B. R., & Underwood, M. K. (1997). A developmental investigation of social aggression among children. *Developmental Psychology, 33*, 589–600.

Gordon-Larsen, P. (2001). Obesity-related knowledge, attitudes, and behaviors in obese and nonobese urban Philadelphia female adolescents. *Obesity Research, 9*(2), 112–118.

Gortmaker, S. L., Dietz, W. H., & Cheung, L. W. Y. (1990). Inactivity, diet, and the fattening of America. *Journal of the American Dietetic Association, 90*, 1247–1255.

Gortmaker, S. L., Must, A., Perrin, J. M., Sobol, A., & Dietz, W. H. (1993). Social and economic consequences of overweight in adolescence and young adulthood. *New England Journal of Medicine, 329*(14), 1008–1012.

Grilo, C. M. (1995). The role of physical activity in weight loss and weight loss management. *Medical Exercise and Nutritional Health, 4*, 60–76.

Grilo, C. M., Wilfley, D. E., Brownell, K. D., & Rodin, J. (1994). Teasing, body image, and self-esteem in a clinical sample of obese women. *Addictive Behaviors, 19*(4), 443–450.

Guillaume, M., Lapidus, L., Bjontorp, P., & Lambert, A. (1997). Physical activity, and obesity and cardiovascular risk factors in children: The Belgian Luxembourg Child Study. *Obesity Research, 5*, 549–556.

Hallstrom, T., & Noppa, H. (1981). Obesity in women in relation to mental illness, social factors, and personality traits. *Journal of Psychosomatic Research, 25*(2), 75–82.

Hill, A. J., & Silver, E. K. (1995). Fat, friendless and unhealthy: 9-year old children's perception of body shape stereotypes. *International Journal of Obesity, 19*, 423–430.

Israel, A. C., & Shapiro, L. S. (1985). Behavior problems of obese children enrolling in a weight reduction program. *Journal of Pediatric Psychology, 10*(4), 449–460.

Kimm, S. Y. S., Sweeney, C. G., Janosky, J. E., & MacMillan, J. P. (1991). Self-concept measures and childhood obesity: A descriptive analysis. *Developmental and Behavioral Pediatrics, 12*(1), 19–24.

Kromhout, D., Saris, W. H., & Horst, C. H. (1988). Energy intake, energy expenditure, and smoking in relation to body fatness: The Zutphen Study. *American Journal of Clinical Nutrition, 47*, 668–674.

Larkin, J., & Pines, H. (1979). No fat persons need apply. *Sociology of Work and Occupations, 6*(3), 312–327.

Lawson, M. C. (1980). Development of body build stereotypes, peer ratings, and self-esteem in Australian children. *Journal of Psychology, 104*, 111–118.

Marcus, M. (1993). Binge eating in obesity. In C. G. Fairburn & G. T. Wilson (Eds.), *Binge eating: Nature, assessment, and treatment* (pp. 77–96). New York: Guilford Press.

Mellin, A. E., Neumark-Sztainer, D., Story, M., Ireland, M., & Resnick, M. D. (2001). Unhealthy behaviors and psychosocial difficulties among overweight youth: The potential impact of familial factors. *Journal of Adolescent Health, 31,* 145–153.

Moore, M. E., Stunkard, A. J., & Srole, L. (1962). Obesity, social class and mental illness. *Journal of the American Medical Association, 181,* 962–966.

Moore, M. E., Stunkard, A. J., & Srole, L. (1997). Obesity, social class, and mental illness. *Obesity Research, 5*(5), 503–508.

Moussa, M. A. A., Skaik, M. B., Selwanes, S. B., Yaghy, O. Y., & Bin-Othman, S. A. (1994). Factors associated with obesity in school children. *International Journal of Obesity and Related Metabolic Disorders, 18,* 513–515.

Neumark-Sztainer, D., Falkner, N., Story, M., Perry, C., Hannan, P. J., & Mulert, S. (2002). Weight-teasing among adolescents: Correlations with weight status and disordered eating behaviors. *International Journal of Obesity and Related Metabolic Disorders, 26*(1), 123–131.

Neumark-Sztainer, D., Harris, T., & Story, M. (1999). Beliefs and attitudes about obesity among teachers and school health care providers working with adolescents. *Journal of Nutrition Education, 31,* 3–9.

Neumark-Sztainer, D., & Story, M. (1997). Recommendations from overweight youth regarding school-based weight control programs. *Journal of School Health, 67*(10), 428–433.

Neumark-Sztainer, D., Story, M., Evans, T., & Ireland, M. (1999). Weight-related issues among overweight adolescents: What are health care providers doing? *Topics in Clinical Nutrition, 14*(3), 62–68.

Neumark-Sztainer, D., Story, M., & Faibisch, L. (1998). Perceived stigmatization among overweight African American and Caucasian adolescent girls. *Journal of Adolescent Health, 23*(5), 264–270.

Neumark-Sztainer, D., Story, M., Faibisch, L., Ohlson, J., & Adamiak, M. (1999). Issues of self-image among overweight African American and Caucasian adolescent girls: A qualitative study. *Journal of Nutrition Education, 31*(6), 311–320.

Neumark-Sztainer, D., Story, M., Falkner, N. H., Beuhring, T., & Resnick, M. D. (1999). Sociodemographic and personal characteristics of adolescents engaged in weight loss and weight/muscle gain behaviors: Who is doing what? *Preventive Medicine, 28*(1), 40–50.

Neumark-Sztainer, D., Story, M., French, S., Hannan, P., Resnick, M., & Blum, R. W. (1997). Psychosocial concerns and health compromising behaviors among overweight and nonoverweight adolescents. *Obesity Research, 5*(3), 237–249.

Neumark-Sztainer, D., Story, M., Hannan, P. J., Perry, C. L., & Irving, L. M. (2002). Weight-related concerns and behaviors among overweight and nonoverweight adolescents: Implications for preventing weight-related disorders. *Archives of Pediatrics and Adolescent Medicine, 156,* 171–178.

Neumark-Sztainer, D., Story, M., Hannan, P. J., & Rex, J. (in press). New moves: A school-based obesity prevention program for adolescent girls. *Preventive Medicine.*

Olson, C. L., Schumaker, H. D., & Yawn, B. P. (1994). Overweight women delay medical care. *Archives of Family Medicine, 3,* 888–892.

Pagan, J. A., & Davila, A. (1997). Obesity, occupational attainment, and earnings. *Social Science Quarterly, 78*(3), 756–770.

Pearce, M. J., Boergers, J., & Prinstein, M. J. (2002). Adolescent obesity, overt and relational peer victimization, and romantic relationships. *Obesity Research, 10*(5), 386–393.

Pingitore, R., Dugoni, B. L., Tindale, R. S., & Spring, B. (1994). Bias against overweight job applicants in a simulated employment interview. *Journal of Applied Psychology, 79*(6), 909–917.

Price, J., Desmond, S., Krol, R., Snyder, F., & O'Connell, J. (1987). Family practice physicians' beliefs, attitudes, and practices regarding obesity. *American Journal of Preventive Medicine, 3*(6), 339–345.

Puhl, R., & Brownell, K. D. (2001). Bias, discrimination, and obesity. *Obesity Research, 9*(12), 788–804.

Register, C. A., & Williams, D. R. (1997). Wage effects of obesity among young workers. *Social Science Quarterly, 71,* 130–141.

Richardson, S. A., Goodman, N., Hastorf, A. H., & Dornbusch, S. M. (1961). Cultural uniformity in reaction to physical disabilities. *American Sociological Review, 26,* 241–247.

Robinson, B. B. E., Bacon, J. G., & O'Reilly, J. (1993). Fat phobia: Measuring, understanding, and changing anti-fat attitudes. *International Journal of Eating Disorders, 14*(4), 467–480.

Ross, J. G., & Pate, R. R. (1987). The National Children and Youth Fitness Study II. *Journal of Physical Education and Recreational Dance, 58,* 51–56.

Rothblum, E. D., Brand, P., Miller, C., & Oetjen, H. (1990). The relationship between obesity, employment discrimination and employment-related victimization. *Journal of Vocational Behavior, 37,* 251–266.

Rothblum, E. D., Miller, C. T., & Garbutt, B. (1988). Stereotypes of obese female job applicants. *International Journal of Eating Disorders, 7*(2), 277–283.

Sallade, J. (1973). A comparison of the psychological adjustment of obese vs. nonobese children. *Journal of Psychosomatic Research, 17,* 89–96.

Satter, E. M. (1996). Internal regulation and the evolution of normal growth as the basis for prevention of obesity in children. *Journal of the American Dietetic Association, 96*(9), 860–864.

Smith, D. E., Thompson, J. K., Raczynski, J. M., & Hilner, J. E. (1999). Body image among men and women in a biracial cohort: The CARDIA Study. *International Journal of Eating Disorders, 25*(1), 71–82.

Sobal, J. (1990). Obesity and nutritional sociology: A model for coping with the stigma of obesity. *Obesity and Nutritional Sociology, 9,* 125–141.

Sobal, J., Nicolopoulos, V., & Lee, J. (1995). Attitudes about overweight and dating among secondary students. *International Journal of Obesity, 19,* 376–381.

Solovay, S. (2000). *Tipping the scales of injustice: Fighting weight-based discrimination.* Amherst, NY: Prometheus Books.

Staffieri, J. R. (1967). A study of social stereotype in children. *Journal of Perspectives in Social Psychology, 7,* 101–107.

Stewart, A. L., & Brook, R. H. (1983). Effects of being overweight. *American Journal of Public Health, 73*(2), 171–178.

Stormer, S., & Thompson, J. (1996). Explanations of body image disturbance: A test of maturational status, negative verbal commentary, social comparison, and sociocultural hypotheses. *International Journal of Eating Disorders, 19,* 193–202.

Strauss, C. C., Smith, K., Frame, C., & Forehand, R. (1984). Personal and interpersonal characteristics associated with childhood obesity. *Journal of Pediatric Psychology, 10,* 337–343.

Taylor, W. C., Yancey, A. K., Leslie, J., Murray, N. G., Cummings, S. S., Sharkey, S. A., et al. (1999). Physical activity among African American and Latino middle school girls: Consistent beliefs, expectations, and experiences across two sites. *Women and Health, 30*(2), 67–82.

U.S. Department of Health and Human Services. (1996). *Physical activity and health: A report of the Surgeon General-Executive Summary.* Washington, DC: Centers for Disease Control and Prevention, National Center for Chronic Disease Prevention and Health Promotion, The President's Council on Physical Fitness and Sports.

U.S. Department of Health and Human Services. (2001). *The Surgeon General's call to action to prevent and decrease overweight and obesity.* Rockville, MD: Office of Disease Prevention and Health Promotion; Centers for Disease Control and Prevention, National Institutes of Health.

Wadden, T. A., Foster, G. D., Stunkard, A. J., & Linowitz, J. R. (1989). Dissatisfaction with weight and figure in obese girls: Discontent but not depression. *International Journal of Obesity and Related Metabolic Disorders, 13,* 89–97.

Weiler, K., & Helms, L. B. (1993). Responsibilities of nursing education: The lessons of *Russell v. Salve Regina. Journal of Professional Nurses, 9,* 131–138.

Weise, H. J. C., Wilson, J. F., Jobes, R. A., & Neises, M. (1992). Obesity stigma reduction in medical students. *International Journal of Obesity and Related Metabolic Disorders, 16,* 859–868.

Westerterp, K. R. (1998). Alterations in energy balance with exercise. *American Journal of Clinical Nutrition, 68*(4), 970S–974S.

Westerterp, K. R. (1999a). Assessment of physical activity level in relation to obesity: Current evidence and research issues. *Medicine and Science in Sports and Exercise, 31*(Suppl. 11), S522–S525.

Westerterp, K. R. (1999b). Obesity and physical activity. *International Journal of Obesity and Related Metabolic Disorders, 23*(Suppl. 1), 59–64.

Westerterp, K. R., & Goran, M. I. (1997). Relationship between physical activity related energy expenditure and body composition: A gender difference. *International Journal of Obesity and Related Metabolic Disorders, 21,* 184–188.

Westerterp, K. R., Mejer, G. A. L., Kester, A. D. M., Wouters, L., & Ten Hoor, F. (1992). Fat-free mass as a function of fat mass and habitual activity level. *International Journal of Sports Medicine, 13,* 163–166.

Williamson, D. F., Madans, J., Anda, R. F., Kleinman, J. C., Kahn, H. S., & Byers, T. (1993). Recreational physical activity and ten-year weight change in a U.S. national cohort. *International Journal of Obesity and Related Metabolic Disorders, 17,* 279–286.

World Health Organization. (1997). *Obesity: Preventing and managing the global epidemic.* Geneva, Switzerland: Author, Division of Noncommunicable Diseases.

Chapter 19 ───────────────────────────────

ASSESSMENT OF MEDICAL STATUS AND PHYSICAL FACTORS

M. AMMAR HATAHET AND NIKHIL V. DHURANDHAR

Unique social, psychological, environmental, and medical conditions associated with obesity require a distinctive approach to its medical assessment. Many obese individuals have low self-esteem because of the social stigma associated with obesity. Repeated unsuccessful attempts at managing body weight add to the frustration and anger of many overweight people. A typical patient seeking obesity treatment has tried several weight loss programs, may have lost (and regained) hundreds of pounds repeatedly, and may be very skeptical about yet another weight management program. Medical assessment of obese patients is often complicated and time consuming. These complications include aspects of the history as well as the physical examination itself. Often, patients present with obesity of long standing, and it is hard for them to remember the chronological sequence of the onset and progression of the disease.

The clinical exam is often limited by several factors ranging from facilities—such as the availability of appropriate examination tables, room space, scales, chairs, and gowns to accommodate the grossly obese patients—to the physical appearance of the patient. Many parts of the examination are limited by the amount of fat that presents a barrier between the doctor and the organs to be examined. Obesity is often associated with multiple comorbid conditions, which may be influenced by weight reduction. Such comorbidities need to be detected and addressed. In addition, the role of education about all aspects of obesity cannot be overemphasized. Providing factual information to the patient about the program and gradually building up the patient's confidence and trust in the program are imperative.

Thus, history taking, medical assessment, and treatment of obesity provide special challenges. This chapter does not discuss detailed and routine medical techniques required to examine a patient but provides distinctive considerations involved in assessing a patient for weight management. Only the salient aspects of medical assessment are discussed. It should be noted that this chapter is intended to serve as a guideline only, and it is not a substitute for a physician's preferred approach to patient examinations.

EVALUATION OF AN OBESE PATIENT

The following five aspects should be considered when evaluating an obese patient:

1. Clinic setting.
2. History.
3. Physical examination.
4. Investigations.
5. Health risk assessment.

Clinic Setting

For physicians as well as patients, obesity is a difficult disease to manage. A clinic setting that clearly conveys empathy and compassion to patients is the first step toward evaluating obese patients. Special needs of a clinic that offers obesity treatment are discussed in the following paragraphs.

Despite attempts to educate patients, most people prefer to maintain confidentiality about their weight and weight loss because of the stigma attached to obesity. It is important to respect the sensitivity of patients about such issues. Clinics that offer care for obese patients should provide for the special needs of obese patients. Easy wheelchair access and, if possible, a location on the first floor with a separate entrance are desirable. Comfortable, sturdy, wide, and armless chairs should be provided. The reading material available to patients in the waiting area should be carefully chosen and may include information about obesity, nutrition, and even articles about appropriate weight loss programs. Wall posterboards may be used to share information about research or new useful products in the field. The boards can be used as a patient forum for exchange of ideas and solutions related to weight loss. Editorial control of such bulletin boards is required to prevent misinformation from being posted.

The scale for weighing the patient should be located in a place that provides privacy to patients and should have a capacity of at least 600 lb. Small blood pressure cuffs may be inaccurate in obese patients, and small gowns for physical examination are inadequate and embarrassing; therefore, large cuffs and gowns should be used.

Obesity treatment is influenced in a major way by interaction among the clinic staff and patients. The staff must be supportive and empathetic with obese patients and their health conditions. Body weight is a sensitive issue for obese people, who are held to a higher standard of willpower than the general populace, and "fat jokes" and cartoons have no place in an obesity clinic. Nutrition education and behavior modification are important components of a good weight loss program, and the staff should be knowledgeable in these areas. Body weights of the staff may be important to some patients, and patient response may be varied. Lean staff members may be viewed as either role models or as those who would not understand the plight of an obese person. On the other hand, patients may sympathize with an overweight staff member or may doubt the ability of the overweight staff member to help them. Confronting these paradoxical feelings with clear explanations of the etiology and pathogenesis of obesity is necessary to clear these biases.

History

Taking the history and conducting a clinical examination can be challenging in obese patients. A systematic approach is critical. In addition to the regular aspects of history taking, questions should include inquiry about the onset, duration, and progress of obesity. Such a history taking should include the following.

Onset of Obesity

Although an accurate answer is difficult to obtain (and verify), response to a question such as "When did you first become obese or even chubby?" indicates how chronic the problem has been. A weight gain since age 18 increases associated health risk (Willett et al., 1995).

Duration

Childhood and adolescent weight status is reported to predict health risks in adult life (Must, Jacques, Dallal, Bajema, & Dietz, 1992). In our experience, obesity of longer duration is more refractory than that of relatively recent onset. Obesity of long standing may be associated with a certain degree of frustration experienced by the patient after several weight loss attempts. It is also possible that the obesity-associated comorbidities have had more time to develop if the obesity is of long standing.

Recent Weight Changes

An obese person seeking medical treatment of obesity may be weight stable or gaining or losing weight at baseline, which may differentially influence the treatment outcome. Merely arresting or attenuating weight gain could be considered an achievement in someone gaining weight rapidly. An obese person already losing weight before initiating the treatment may be near the plateau and should be cautioned about such a possibility. Such a patient may have a reduced total energy requirement, which may influence the diet prescription.

Family History

Presence of a family history of obesity may indicate genetic involvement, underlying familial conditions such as hypothyroidism, or simply a shared environment conducive to weight gain. A strong history of obesity in the immediate family of an obese child warrants strong weight loss recommendations and education to the family members.

Dietary History

A patient's cooperation and adherence to a dietary regimen depend on the patient's comfort level with the prescribed dietary regimen. It is important to prescribe a diet that suits the lifestyle of the patients and that considers likes and dislikes; food cravings; eating patterns; religious, cultural, and other special dietary preferences; as well as food allergies. An attempt should be made to accommodate patients' special requests and to be considerate of their usual lifestyles. To achieve the goal, relevant dietary information should be obtained from the patient. If patients are not comfortable with interventions concerning diet or exercise, the compliance will be poor.

Exercise History

A detailed history of exercise and physical activity is the cornerstone of an assessment aimed at providing exercise recommendations. One of the objectives is to assess how much activity a patient is capable of currently without developing symptoms of cardiac or respiratory compromise. Although not as reliable as stress testing, history does help in considering stress test recommendations. If a patient is already engaged in a regular exercise regimen, determine the type, duration, intensity, and frequency of exercise and if there are symptoms or complaints associated with it. Symptomatic patients will need further evaluation, dependent on their area of symptomatology, and their exercise should be decreased until such studies are done.

History of Associated Conditions

A number of medical conditions associated with obesity may influence dietary, exercise, or drug prescriptions for weight management. A comprehensive weight management treatment warrants that such conditions be considered and addressed appropriately.

Coronary Artery Disease   The presence of coronary artery disease (CAD), including history of bypass surgery, does not necessarily preclude exercise or dietary changes. Careful evaluation of exercise capability with stress testing followed by a gradual buildup of exercise is recommended. CAD also has an impact on drug use.

Coronary Artery Disease Risk Factors   The presence of major CAD risk factors such as hypertension, diabetes, dyslipidemia, smoking, and homocysteinemia should be noted and appropriately assessed, which may lead to uncovering of underlying CAD. In addition, diabetes, smoking-induced emphysema, or hypertension may influence exercise prescription. Presence of diabetes has a significant effect on dietary prescription. Caution is needed while prescribing certain antiobesity agents (sibutramine) to hypertensive patients (Ryan, Kaiser, & Bray, 1995).

Congestive Heart Failure   Left ventricular dysfunction is a significant limiting factor for exercise. Patients in classes II and III of the New York Heart Failure Classification, when maximally treated, can exercise. Such an exercise program, however, needs to be very carefully monitored. Frequent but shorter bouts of exercise may be tolerated based on symptoms.

Respiratory Disease   A number of factors may determine prescription and the ability of a patient to exercise. An adequately treated and controlled asthma or pulmonary insufficiency should not prohibit exercise but will require close monitoring and possibly referral. An organized pulmonary rehabilitation program should be the cornerstone of an exercise program in the presence of dyspnea at rest.

Neuromuscular   Compromise secondary to musculoskeletal or neurological conditions needs evaluation to determine the optimal modes of exercise. A previous history of stroke, muscle weakness, or abnormal gait should be carefully evaluated. A risk for fall or injury due to instability or weakness should be addressed and appropriately handled. Such considerations are important for determining the type of exercise (aerobic versus anaerobic and upper versus lower extremities).

Hematological A history of easy bruising or bleeding abnormality affects the type of exercise prescribed. High impact exercises should be avoided in the presence of such a history. Because acute sickle cell attacks may also be precipitated by dehydration, it is extremely important to ensure adequate hydration for both aerobic and anaerobic exercise. In fact, adequate hydration is important for all exercisers.

Psychiatric Many psychiatric illnesses could have a direct effect on patient motivation as well as compliance with dietary or exercise regimen. Patients with obsessive-compulsive disorder may be prone to episodes of overexercise. A history of eating disorders is particularly important. Binge eating disorder or bulimia may influence the diet prescription and require counseling. Obesity drugs are not recommended for those with a history of anorexia nervosa.

Other Systemic Diseases Other severe systemic conditions such as hepatic or renal malfunction need to be noted and addressed. In addition to affecting dietary choices and degree of caloric restriction, extreme caution is required in using obesity drugs in these conditions.

Medication

It is important to obtain a complete list of current medications taken by the patient including over-the-counter (OTC) medications. Many medications may increase appetite and weight by affecting neurotransmitters in the brain—particularly acetylcholine and dopamine, the latter being part of the "reward system" (Baumann et al., 2000), whereas some medications may worsen or limit ability to exercise. Table 19.1 lists drugs associated with weight gain. Phenothiazines (chlorpromazine) and butyrophenones (haloperidol) are associated with weight gain to varying degrees. Of the newer atypical antipsychotics such as clozapine, risperidone, olanzapine, quetiapine, and ziprasidone, only the latter seems to have a favorable effect on weight, while the

Table 19.1 Drugs Associated with Weight Gain

Cyproheptadine
Glucocortocoids
Insulin
Lithium
Phenothiazines
Progestagens
Sulfonylureas
Tricyclic antidepressants
Valproate

rest are associated with weight gain (Allison & Casey, 2001; Bailey, 2002; Sachs & Guille, 1999). Tricyclic antidepressants (TCAs) and tetracyclic antidepressants—as well as monoamine oxidase inhibitors (MAOs) and several of the selective serotonin reuptake inhibitors (SSRIs) such as paroxetine, citalopram, and luvoxamine—are associated with weight gain; sertraline and venlafaxine seem to have a neutral effect, whereas fluoxetine and wellbutrin seem to enhance weight loss (Darga, Carroll-Michals, Botsford, & Lucas, 1991; Gadde et al., 2001; Goldstein et al., 1994; Hatahet & Dhurandhar, 2002).

Although insulin sensitizers, thioglitazones, are used for reducing insulin resistance to improve diabetes mellitus type 2 control, unfortunately, they are associated with weight gain. Similarly, sulfonylureas are associated with weight gain. The antidiabetic medication metformin appears to produce some weight loss (Brown & Brillon, 1999; Charles & Eschwege, 1999; Day, 1999; Hauner, 1999).

Dosage for some drugs needs monitoring and adjusting as the weight loss ensues. Sulfonylurea and insulin may potentiate the action of exercise and increase the risk of hypoglycemia. Weight loss improves glucose disposal by the body, and it is important to appropriately adjust the dose of diabetic medications with weight loss. Similarly, a monitoring of hypertension medication is warranted. Blood pressure tends to decrease and normalize with weight loss, and a gradual reduction of the dosage may be necessary to prevent the blood pressure from dropping below the safe limits.

When used excessively, short-acting inhaled bronchodilators, such as ß-adrenergics, may cause hypokalemia, tachycardia, and increased cardiac output. When combined with the exercise-induced increased cardiac demand, this may lead to cardiac ischemia, which may not have been detected before. Hence, caution should be exercised, and close monitoring of heart rate and blood pressure during exercise may be necessary in such cases.

It is important to know and record any OTC obesity medications that a patient may be taking. Many of the cold preparations contain sympathetomimetic agents such as pseudoephedrine or caffeine that may lead to tachycardia and worsening of hypertension. Patients may intentionally or otherwise not disclose OTCs, or they may not consider laxative use or abuse worth reporting. While some may not be harmful, patients should be educated about useless and possibly harmful medications. In addition, recording such medications has medico-legal significance, should they cause any adverse reaction when the patient is under your care.

Finally, a careful history of previously prescribed antiobesity agents may yield important information. For instance, previous use of fenfluramine and dexfenfluramine should prompt a careful cardiac and pulmonary exam to rule out valvular heart lesions and the very rare pulmonary hypertension.

Physical Examination

A standard physical examination needs to be modified for an obese patient to address the unique challenges of obesity treatment. The following sections describe suggested modifications to a standard physical exam and the rationale for recommending the modifications.

Medical Examination

A general assessment begins with the overall status of the patient: grooming, cleanliness, and posture. Abdominal girth (waist circumference), an indicator of obesity-related risk, is measured at the level of anterior iliac crests while the patient is standing up. This should be done at every visit. Height should be measured without shoes. Weight should be measured in an examination gown. To minimize variability, these anthropometric measurements should be taken under similar conditions (clothing, equipment, and staff). For assessing the degree of obesity, body mass index (BMI) is preferred over ideal body weight charts. BMI is calculated by the following formula: body weight (kg)/(height in meters)^2. Regardless of age and gender, BMI correlates well with body fat content and with health risks of obesity. It should be noted that BMI does overestimate body fat in very muscular subjects or in presence of edema and underestimates fat in muscle wasting (e.g., elderly). Definition of obesity and health risk categories based on BMI are discussed in the following sections.

Vital Signs   An extra large sphygmomanometer cuff is needed to obtain accurate blood pressure reading in patients with large arms.

Constitutional   Check for evidence of snoring or apnea events by asking the patient as well as the spouse and other family members. The disruption of normal nocturnal sleep and recurrent episodes of hypoxia and awakening of obstructive sleep apnea (OSA) may lead to intellectual impairment, memory loss, personality disturbance, and impotence (O'Brien & Gozal, 2002). OSA is also a risk factor for motor vehicle accidents, and patients should be warned about driving or operating heavy machinery. Increased daytime sleepiness is an important clue. Decreased energy level may suggest sleep apnea. Obstructive sleep apnea and hypoventilation syndrome may lead to hypoxemia, hypercapnea, and, rarely, cardiac arrhythmia. The patient may need appropriate workup.

Skin   Acanthosis nigricans, a condition with increased pigmentation in the folds of the neck, axilla, and over the knuckles may be present in obesity. This may signify insulin resistance but could also be seen in acromegaly and gastrointestinal cancers and should be evaluated accordingly.

Fragilitas cutis inguinalis is a dermatological phenomenon associated with obesity (Ganor & Even-Paz, 1967). Skin in the groin region ruptures in a linear fashion at right angles to the applied force. In addition, skin irritation caused by the thighs rubbing together may be present and may make walking very uncomfortable. Purple striation on the abdomen may suggest Cushing's syndrome. Varicose veins are also common among obese patients, with a propensity for venous thrombosis.

Head and Neck   Neck size should be recorded. A thick neck may be present with polycystic ovary disease. Thyroid gland size and texture should be assessed. Careful auscultation of the carotid arteries may reveal bruits suggestive of atherosclerosis. Fundoscopic exam may reveal pappiledema in the rare young obese female with increased intracranial pressure.

Chest   Although it may be difficult, point of maximum cardiac impulse should be noted. A lateral or downward deviation may suggest the presence of ventricular hypertrophy. A loud P2 may suggest pulmonary hypertension. Hearing extra heart sounds as well as valvular lesions may warrant an echocardiogram.

Inspection of the chest in severely obese patients invariably shows decreased lung expansion. Decreased breath sounds in the bases are also common in severely obese patients, which may indicate restrictive pulmonary disease. Presence of wheezing may suggest asthma, although the degree of small airway obstructions does not usually correlate with the amount of wheezing. Bilateral basal crackles are suggestive of left ventricular heart failure.

Postmenopausal breast cancer is significantly increased with obesity, so a careful breast exam is extremely important. In addition, patients should be encouraged to do a monthly self-exam at home and arrange for yearly mammograms after menopause.

Abdomen   In addition to measuring abdominal girth, ruling out organomegaly and ascites, albeit difficult, is crucial. Abnormal masses, positive fluid wave, or shifting dullness should prompt further evaluation with an ultrasound or a CAT scan.

Neurological   Any ataxia or neurological deficit should prompt an extensive neurological exam. Gait abnormalities, neuropathies, and weakness should be accounted for when designing the exercise program. Headaches may suggest pseudo tumor cerebri.

Musculoskeletal   Pain in the knees secondary to osteoarthritis may be the most bothersome symptom of obesity. Worsening pain after physical activity with or without swelling may be suggestive of the diagnosis. Morning stiffness usually lasts less than half an hour. The presence of erythema, significant swelling, or tenderness of the joints suggests other etiologies of arthritis. Current physical activity as well as limitations should be recorded. Any pain or swelling, deformity, or muscle weakness should prompt more extensive evaluation. Stability and range of motion of every joint should be assessed. All muscle groups should be examined for tone and strength.

Additional Review of the Systems

Cardiovascular   Even in the absence of angina, obese patients are at high risk for having significant coronary artery disease, increased risk for heart failure (Crisostomo et al., 1999; Grandi et al., 2000; Kenchaiah et al., 2002), and left ventricular hypertrophy (Crisotomoto et al., 2001), which may be reversible with weight loss (Karason, Wallentin, Larsson, & Sjostrom, 1998). A careful history of exercise-induced chest pain and/or dyspnea is extremely important. On examination, carotid or femoral artery bruits, as well as a fourth heart sound (S4) that is indicative of decreased compliance of the ventricles may be present. Like S3, S4 is a soft sound that is best heard along the left sternal border and the apex using the bell of the stethoscope with the patient slightly leaning forward. It is very difficult to elicit an S4 in morbidly obese patients because of the chest wall barrier.

Symptoms of heart failure such as orthopnea and paroxysmal nocturnal dyspnea should be noted. Similarly, recent history of claudication and discoloration of extremities should be reviewed. History of intermittent claudication of the legs that occurs at the same amount of walking or exercise is suggestive of peripheral vascular disease.

Fundoscopic findings, auscultated bruits in the carotids or the femoral arteries, and poor peripheral pulses are all suggestive of significant atherosclerotic and peripheral vascular disease.

Respiratory   Check for wheezing and dyspnea. Review history of smoking and acute and chronic respiratory symptoms.

Gastrointestinal   Signs and symptoms suggestive of a gallbladder disease or a liver disease should be considered during an examination. The risk of gallbladder disease increases with age, body weight, and parity (Bernstein, Giefer, Vieira, Werner, & Rimm, 1977). Obese women between 20 and 30 years of age had a sixfold increase in the risk of developing gallbladder disease compared to nonobese women of the same age (Bernstein et al., 1977). In addition, obese patients are at risk for gallstones during periods of rapid weight reduction.

Abnormalities of liver function are common in obesity. Bray (1986) has stated that the frequency of steatosis is 68% to 94% in obese individuals. Rarely, fatty livers may progress to cirrhosis. Fatty liver in obese patients is usually asymptomatic, but the liver enzymes (ALT, AST) may be mildly elevated (Youssef & McCullough, 2002; Yu & Keefe, 2002) and may improve with weight loss. An occasional worsening of liver function studies during weight loss is seen in patients with a prior history of hepatitis.

Hiatal and abdominal hernias are more common in the obese and should be looked for. A history of constipation favors a diagnosis of hypothyroidism in the presence of other suggestive symptoms. History of irritable bowel syndrome may preclude the use of the antiobesity drug orlistat. Persistent diarrhea in an obese patient may suggest laxative abuse.

Genitourinary   History of menstrual disturbance as well as infertility should be reviewed. Menstrual irregularities are common in obesity, which may revert to normal on weight loss (Glass, Burman, Dahms, & Boehm, 1981). It should be remembered that in pregnant, obese women, frequency of toxemia, hypertension, diabetes mellitus, difficult labor, and Caesarean sections is greater and the duration of labor is longer (Gross, Sokol, & King, 1980; Hodgkinson & Husain, 1980; Peckham & Christianson, 1971). In addition, an obese woman considering pregnancy should be adequately informed and guided appropriately.

Urinary frequency, nephromegaly, microalbuminuria, and renal damage are associated with obesity even in the absence of diabetes, hypertension, and arteriosclerosis (De Jong, Verhave, Pinto-Sietsma, & Hillege, 2002).

Endocrine   Because of the high prevalence of type II diabetes mellitus among obese patients, signs and symptoms of diabetes and its complications should be looked for. Likewise, hypothyroidism is relatively common especially around menopause. Obesity with an enlarged tongue, hypotension, bradycardia, hyporeflexia, hypotonia, cold intolerance, constipation, fatigue, hair loss, dry skin, brittle nails, puffy eyelids, menorrhagia, and leg cramps may suggest hypothyroidism.

Other endocrine involvements are relatively rare but may need attention in occasional cases. Symptoms suggestive of these conditions should prompt further workup.

Polycystic ovarian disease (PCOD) is characterized by infertility, hirsutism, insulin resistance, obesity, and amenorrhea. Abdominal obesity and a thick neck may be present. The primary defect may be at the hypothalamic-pituitary axis. Weight loss is a major component of its treatment, along with insulin sensitizers such as metformin (Bongain, Isnard, & Gillet, 1998; R. J. Norman & Clark, 1998; Pasquali, Casimirri, & Vicennati, 1997). Cushing's syndrome is another abnormality resulting from hyperplasia, adenoma, or carcinoma of the adrenal glands secreting excess corticosteroids. The syndrome includes obesity, hypertension, glucose intolerance, amenorrhea, hirsutism, and fullness of face. Pinkish-purple striae, particularly on the abdomen, are classic signs of adrenocortical excess, whereas light-colored or silver striae are stretch marks consistent with previous weight loss. Fat accumulation is characteristically seen in the supraclavicular fossa and over the dorsal posterior cervical region. Overnight dexamethasone suppression test is considered a reliable and valid test for screening Cushing's syndrome in obese patients (Ness-Abramof et al., 2002). Hypothalamic disorders such as Froehlich's syndrome, Laurence-Moon-Biedl syndrome (retinitis pigmentosa, skull deformity, polydactyly), and Prader-Willi syndrome (hypotonia, predilection for diabetes mellitus) occur in childhood and are associated with hypogonadism and mental retardation.

Low growth hormone levels, low testosterone in males, and high testosterone in females are associated with abdominal obesity. In addition, insulinomas are frequently present with obesity. Because of the direct or indirect involvement of all the endocrine glands in adipose tissue metabolism and obesity, the endocrine system appears to function like a close-knit little family with a great deal of interaction influencing the body fat stores.

Investigations

Body Fat Determination

Body fat determination offers several benefits in addition to body weight measurements. Obesity is characterized by excess fat accumulation, and, therefore, measurement of body fat is relevant for diagnosis and for monitoring progress. Body fat changes in response to weight loss treatment help in determining the composition of the weight lost (water versus fat or muscle) as well as in assessing progress particularly during the periods when body weight may not show much reduction (e.g., water retention or exercise-induced increase in lean body mass).

Several techniques are available for determining body fat content. Generally, complexity of these techniques is proportional to the accuracy and reproducibility of the measurement. Although underwater weighing is considered the gold standard for body composition determination, the required setup is too elaborate for an outpatient obesity program in a private practice. Air displacement plethysmography (BOD-POD) is a more patient-friendly but expensive technique. On the other hand, skin fold measurements is the simplest of techniques but suffers from low accuracy and reproducibility. Body impedance analysis could be considered for body fat determination in a clinical setting. It is recommended that body fat be determined at baseline and at predetermined intervals to monitor progress. A respirometer may be employed to determine the resting or exercise energy expenditure in specific situations.

Blood Testing

Complete blood count, thyroid, kidney and liver functions, fasting lipid profile, and blood glucose are probably the minimum tests needed. Low thyroxin T_4 and elevated thyroid stimulating hormone (TSH) are the hallmarks of primary hypothyroidism (Guha, Krishnaswamy, & Peiris, 2002; Krotkiewski, 2002; Osman, Gammage, & Franklyn, 2001). Plasma creatinine value as an indicator of kidney function may be misleading in obese patients because higher than normal levels may reflect the increased weight rather than actual kidney disease. Therefore, in such cases, creatinine clearance may be determined.

Erythrocytosis and hypercapnea may be present because of alveolar hypoventilation in very obese individuals. Slightly elevated ALT and AST are common findings in obesity, especially in the presence of steatosis and are usually rectified on weight loss. Significantly elevated ALT and AST levels may suggest the presence of active liver disease.

Elevated triglycerides, high levels of low-density lipoproteins (LDL), and low levels of high-density lipoproteins (HDL) are common findings in obese patients. Significant dyslipidemia suggests the need for more extensive evaluation for the presence of atherosclerosis.

Glucose intolerance is more common in obese individuals than frank diabetes, but many of these individuals eventually become diabetics. If diabetes is suspected, documenting fasting blood sugar above 126 mg/dL, random blood sugar over 200 mg/dL, or elevated glycosylated hemoglobin on three separate occasions illustrates the diagnosis (Takiya & Chawla, 2002).

A baseline blood glucose and fasting lipid profile is also useful in determining improvement in hyperglycemia and dyslipidemia with weight loss. Patients with abnormal fasting lipid or glucose profile should be advised to keep a lifelong vigil even after weight reduction.

Resting Electrocardiogram

Resting electrocardiogram (EKG) is mandatory in all patients. Obesity is associated with the presence of left ventricular hypertrophy (LVH) and decreased sensitivity of the EKG due to attenuating effects of the adipose tissue on QRS amplitudes. To correct for these effects, the Framingham-adjusted Cornell voltage tool, which takes into account age, sex, and BMI, may be used. Sokolow-Lyon voltage seems to have a much poorer sensitivity (Abergel, Tase, Menard, & Chatellier, 1996; J. E. Norman & Levy, 1996; Okin, Roman, Devereux, & Kligfield, 1996). Bradycardia and low voltage may suggest the presence of hypothyroidism. Axis deviation may be secondary to obesity but could also be the result of ventricular hypertrophy. It is important to assess any ischemic changes or clues of previous myocardial infarction. Any ischemic abnormality on resting EKG should prompt additional cardiac testing. Abdominal obesity may also be responsible for a prolonged QTC interval in premenopausal women (Park & Swan, 1997).

For an obese individual with an unremarkable history and physical examination, a complete blood count, thyroid function tests, glucose, lipid profile, liver and kidney function tests, in addition to a resting EKG may be adequate to initiate a treatment plan.

Significant abnormalities of these baseline tests or abnormal findings in history or physical examination will require further investigations.

Additional Investigations

The following tests are not necessarily a part of routine investigations for obesity treatment but may be indicated in some individuals requiring further evaluation.

Exercise Stress Testing   The reduced work tolerance in obese patients seems to be linked to a reduced oxygen supply to the muscles during activity (Salvadori et al., 1999). Exercise stress testing (EST) assesses the cardiopulmonary fitness, work capacity, and the cardiopulmonary performance using different measurements of oxygen uptake (VO_2) and heart rate to estimate cardiac output. In postmenopausal women, age-adjusted maximal heart rate, respiratory exchange ratio, and plateau in oxygen uptake may be used for the measurement of maximal oxygen consumption (Misquita et al., 2001). Excess body fat, however, does not influence maximal aerobic capacity as measured by VO_2max. In adolescents, a 12-minute walk/run test could be used to measure physical performance (Drinkard et al., 2001). It is noted that distraction of severely obese adolescents during a treadmill stress test may have a positive effect on running time (De Bourdeaudhuji et al., 2002). When prescribing an exercise program, a 70% VO_2max seems to provide the necessary stimulus for obese patients to improve exercise tolerance and body composition. If not tolerated, it will not be done and, therefore, a lesser level of exercise may be in order. In patients with CAD, rehabilitation programs have used the goal of 70% to 85% of the maximal heart rate or 10 to 15 heartbeats below the level of any exercise-induced symptomatic or silent ischemia (Lavie & Milani, 1996).

Echocardiography and Stress Echocardiography   Echocardiography can assess left ventricular mass, left ventricular systolic function, and diastolic filling (Alpert et al., 1997; Benjamin & Levy, 1999). Echocardiography can also detect cardiomyopathy as well as valvular lesions that may have been caused by the use of fenfluramine or dexfenfluramine (Connolly et al., 1997; Davidoff et al., 2001; Kasper, Hruban, & Baughman, 1992; Pallasch, 1999), although such fenfluramine-associated lesions have been reported to be nonprogressive or reversible (Gardin et al., 2001; Vagelos, Jacobs, Popp, & Liang, 2002). Stress echocardiography in expert hands could replace nucleotide stress studies. Ventricular hypertrophy and pulmonary hypertension are also easily demonstrable by echocardiography. Echocardiography, however, may be limited in severely obese patients because of increased thickness of chest wall.

Pulmonary Function Tests   Pulmonary function tests (PFTs) not only differentiate restrictive pulmonary disease from asthma and chronic obstructive pulmonary disease but also may be used to monitor improvement in the disease after treatment and weight loss. The degree of respiratory restrictions may also influence the exercise prescription (Sahebjami, 1998).

Sleep Studies   A history of snoring, increased daytime sleepiness, and witnessed apnea events is highly suggestive of obstructive sleep apnea. Obstructive sleep apnea is also associated with pulmonary hypertension and leg edema (Blankfield & Zyzanski, 2002; Malhotra & White, 2002). Examination may reveal findings suggestive of right ventricular hypertrophy and pulmonary hypertension such as right ventricular heave and a loud pulmonic component of the second heart sound P_2 outside the pulmonic auscultatory area.

Polysomnography is the gold standard for the diagnosis of obstructive sleep apnea. The presence of snoring, increased daytime sleepiness, and a large neck size, along with previously mentioned signs and symptoms, should prompt such an exam (Chung, Jairam, Hussain, & Shapiro, 2002; Malhotra & White, 2002; Nixon & Brouillette, 2002).

Ultrasound of the Abdomen and Pelvis   This test may aid in differentiating between fat mass and other abdominal or pelvic masses. The test may also be useful in detecting gallstones and steatosis, common occurrences in obesity. The test is safe, well tolerated, and relatively inexpensive. It is, however, incapable of measuring visceral fat, a major determinant of CAD risk.

Computerized Axial Tomography (CAT Scan) and Magnetic Resonance Imaging (MRI) Both tests are very useful for ruling out intra-abdominal and pelvic masses. In addition, they give a better measurement of visceral fat than the ultrasound. Both are expensive, uncomfortable for the patient, and time consuming, and they should be used prudently. A single slice CAT scan may, however, provide valuable information about visceral fat with a reasonable cost. Increase in visceral fat has been associated with insulin resistance, which in turn predisposes to atherosclerosis and cardiovascular disease (Trovato et al., 2001). However, methods to determine visceral fat content are not routinely employed in an outpatient clinic setting and are generally reserved for research studies.

Health Risk Assessment

In 1998, the National Heart, Lung, and Blood Institute (NHLBI), in collaboration with the North American Association for the Study of Obesity, published an evidence report to guide the assessment and management of obesity (NHLBI, 1998). The guidelines recommend classification of obesity to determine relative risk of the disease. The process of medical assessment of a patient for obesity treatment is incomplete without risk stratification. Such a determination provides the basis for treatment goals and strategies. For instance, pharmacotherapy and surgery have shown great promise in obesity treatment, but both approaches have several potential adverse effects. Risk stratification helps in weighing potential merits versus the drawbacks of a particular treatment approach. Pharmacotherapy is not recommended for patients without risk factors and BMI < 30 kg/M^2, and surgery is not recommended for patients with BMI < 35 kg/M^2.

The risk status assessment includes the determination of the following:

1. Degree of overweight or obesity using BMI (see Table 19.2).
2. Presence of abdominal obesity as determined by the waist circumference measurements (see Table 19.2).
3. Presence of concomitant CVD risk factors or other comorbidities.

Table 19.2   Stratification of the Degree of Obesity

	BMI (kg/m²)	Disease Risk Relative to Normal Weight and Waist Circumference	
		Men: ≤ 40 in. Women: ≤ 35 in.	> 40 in. > 35 in.
Underweight	< 18.5	—	—
Normal weight	18.5–24.9	—	—
Overweight	25.0–29.9	Increased	High
Obese Class I	30.0–34.9	High	Very high
Obese Class II	35.0–39.9	Very high	Very high
Obese Class III	> 40.0	Extremely high	Extremely high

Note: Adapted from "Clinical Guidelines on the Identification, Evaluation, and Treatment of Overweight and Obesity in Adults: The Evidence Report," by National Heart, Lung, and Blood Institute, 1998, *Obesity Research* 6(Suppl. 2), pp. 51S–183S.

The NHLBI evidence report (1998) states that risk could be relative or absolute. Relative risk relates to the need to reduce weight but not directly to the required intensity of risk factor modification, whereas absolute risk is based on the presence of associated diseases or risk factors.

Relative Risk of Obesity

The relative risk categories are based on BMI and waist circumference (see Table 19.2). A BMI of 18.5 to 24.9 is considered normal. The risk increases with increasing BMI classes. Furthermore, abdominal obesity, as determined by a waist circumference ≥ 35 inches in females and ≥ 40 inches in males confers an additional increased risk.

It should be noted that the relationship of BMI and body fat varies with ethnicity and susceptibility of an individual to the risk factors at a given BMI. The classification gives broad guidelines, and clinical judgment should be exercised in individual cases.

Absolute Risk of Obesity

Table 19.3 lists factors that increase the absolute risk of obesity. Patients with established coronary heart disease (CHD), as evidenced by a history of myocardial infarction or angina, atherosclerotic diseases, such as peripheral arterial disease or embolic stroke, type 2 diabetes, or sleep apnea have a very high absolute risk that triggers the need for intense risk-factor modification and management of the diseases present.

In addition, cardiovascular risk factors also confer a high absolute risk when three or more are present. Cigarette smoking, hypertension, dyslipidemia, impaired glucose handling, a strong family history of premature CHD, gender, and age contribute to the absolute cardiovascular risk due to obesity.

Table 19.3 Factors That Increase the Absolute Risk of Obesity

1. Established coronary heart disease.
2. History of:
   • Myocardial infarction.
   • Coronary artery surgery.
   • Stable or unstable angina pectoris.
   • Coronary artery procedures (angioplasty).
3. Presence of other atherosclerotic diseases.
   • Peripheral arterial disease.
   • Symptomatic carotid artery disease.
   • Abnormal aoric aneurysm.
4. Type 2 diabetes.
5. Sleep apnea.
6. Lack of physical activity.
7. Cardiovascular risk factors (high absolute risk if > three risk factors are present).
   • Cigarette smoking.
   • Hypertension.
     −≥140 mm Hg systolic or ≥ 90 mm Hg diastolic or on antihypertensive medications.
   • LDL-cholesterol ≥ 160 mg/dL.
   • Borderline LDL (130–159 mg/dL) with two risk factors.
   • HDL-cholesterol ≤ 35 mg/dL.
   • Triglycerides ≥ 400 mg/dL.
   • Impaired fasting glucose.
     −Diabetic: Fasting glucose ≥ 126 mg/dL.
     −2-h post prandial glucose ≥ 200 mg/dL.
     −Impaired fasting glucose 110–125 mg/dL.
   • Family history of premature of CHD.
   • Age: Male ≥ 45; Female ≥ 55.

Adapted from "Clinical Guidelines on the Identification, Evaluation, and Treatment of Overweight and Obesity in Adults: The Evidence Report," by National Heart, Lung, and Blood Institute, 1998, *Obesity Resource 6*(Suppl. 2), pp. 51S–183S.

EVALUATION AND FOLLOW-UP FORMS

In addition to the information routinely collected during a standard medical examination, obesity treatment requires specific information. Therefore, the standard case history and physical exam forms need some modification for obesity treatment. Tables 19.4 and 19.5 illustrate forms that may be used for the initial and follow-up visits, respectively, in addition to the standard forms. Some of the information is collected to obtain baseline data (see Table 19.4). Several factors such as the marital status, presence of children in the house, and dietary likes and dislikes may influence the prescription for dietary and lifestyle modification and, therefore, are noteworthy. A follow-up visit form (see Table 19.5) is designed to note progress in weight and fat loss as well as to monitor any adverse effects. Several possible adverse effects are listed, and patients should be encouraged to check all that apply. The practice perhaps

Table 19.4 Patient Questionnaire for the Initial Visit

INITIAL VISIT

PT NUMBER: _____ NAME: _____ DATE: _____

Therapist: _____ MD/NP

Sex: _____ Age: _____ Date of birth: _____

Marital status: _____

Children (in the household): _____ Children (not in the same household): _____

Weight: _____ Height: _____

BMI: _____ % Body fat: _____ Waist: _____ Hip: _____

Blood pressure: _____ Pulse: _____

History of obesity:

      Duration: _____

      Onset: _____

      Progress: _____

Please check the appropriate spaces:

Family History	Obesity	Diabetes	Hypertension	CHD
Father				
Mother				
Brothers				
Sisters				
Grandfather				
Grandmother				

Exercise:

Type: _____ Times exercised this past week? _____ Minutes per week? _____

Diet: Strong likes: _____ Strong dislikes: _____

      Cravings: _____ Food allergies: _____

Table 19.5   Patient Questionnaire for Follow-Up Visits

FOLLOW-UP VISIT

PT NUMBER: _____   NAME: _____   DATE: _____

Type of visit (circle):   Individual / Group / Weigh in / Special

Therapist: _____   MD/NP

Weight: _____   Blood pressure: _____   Pulse: _____

Waist: _____   Hip: _____

SINCE THE LAST VISIT:

1. Following diet (circle): Perfectly   Good   Fair   Poor   Not at all
2. Exercise: Type: _____   Times exercised this past week? _____
   Minutes per week? _____
3. Daily activity (circle):   Extreme   Moderate   Fair   Poor   Minimal
4. Any illness: Yes _____   No _____   Describe: _____
5. Any Clinic/Hospital visit: Yes _____   No _____   Describe: _____
6. Cigarettes smoked: _____   Packs per day_____   or Cigarettes per day _____
7. Medications (circle): Usual / Changed (list): _____
8. Days off obesity medications since last visit: _____
9. Reason for not taking drug: _____

ANY PROBLEMS SINCE LAST VISIT:

1. Abdominal pain	2. Abnormal heart beats	6. Binge eating
4. Altered sense of time	5. Anxiety	9. Depression
	8. Constipation	C. Drowsiness
7. Blurred vision	B. Dizziness	F. Gallbladder disease
A. Diarrhea	E. Fatigue	I. High sex drive
D. Dry mouth	H. Headache	L. Loss of concentration
G. Hair loss	K. Leg cramps	O. Nausea
J. Insomnia	N. Memory loss	R. Tremor
M. Low sex drive	Q. Skin rash	U. Skin bruising
P. Nervousness	T. Vomiting	X. Irritability/Anger
S. Vivid/weird dreams	W. Mood elevation	Y. Other/Comments
V. Sweating	3. Abnormal menses	

Obesity Medications:

1. _____ mg _____/day   2. _____ mg _____/day

Comments:

_____

_____

Note: Modified from "Drug Treatment of Obesity: Guidelines for an Outpatient Program," by N. V. Dhurandhar and R. L. Atkinson, Summer, 1997, *American Journal of Bariatric Medicine,* pp. 18–23.

overestimates adverse effects, which may be preferable to missing adverse effects related to dieting or antiobesity medications.

CONCLUSION

Multifactorial etiology, complex interactions of several organs and systems, psychological and behavioral factors involvement, and the refractory nature of obesity, coupled with the social stigma and bias against the obese, have made evaluation and treatment of the obese uniquely different. Assessment and treatment of obesity begins with showing empathy for the condition through clinic setting and staff attitude. During a medical examination, effort should be made to identify the causes of obesity. Ongoing research will expand our knowledge in this area. Such determinations may help in targeting the treatment to the causes instead of a generic approach for weight loss. Obesity-associated comorbidities should be detected and treated. Comorbidities such as impaired glucose handling and hypertension respond to weight loss, and baseline information should be collected to closely monitor the progress in response to treatment. Finally, the relative and absolute risk factor determinations associated with obesity should help in determining the nature and intensity of the intervention. Such a comprehensive medical evaluation of an obese patient forms the basis for an effective treatment plan.

REFERENCES

Abergel, E., Tase, M., Menard, J., & Chatellier, G. (1996). Influence of obesity on the diagnostic value of electrocardiographic criteria for detecting left ventricular hypertrophy. *American Journal of Cardiology, 77*, 739–744.

Allison, D. B., & Casey, D. E. (2001). Antipsychotic-induced weight gain: A review of the literature. *Journal of Clinical Psychiatry, 62*(Suppl. 7), 22–31.

Alpert, M. A., Terry, B. E., Mulekar, M., Cohen, M. V., Massey, C. V., Fan, T. M., et al. (1997). Cardiac morphology and left ventricular function in normotensive morbidly obese patients with and without congestive heart failure, and effect of weight loss. *American Journal of Cardiology, 80*, 736–740.

Bailey, K. P. (2002). Weight gain associated with antipsychotic agents. *Journal of Psychosocial Nursing and Mental Health Services, 40*, 15–19.

Baumann, M. H., Ayestas, M. A., Dersch, C. M., Brockington, A., Rice, K. C., & Rothman, R. B. (2000). Effects of phentermine and fenfluramine on extracellular dopamine and serotonin in rat nucleus accumbens: Therapeutic implications. *Synapse, 36*, 102–113.

Benjamin, E. J., & Levy, D. (1999). Why is left ventricular hypertrophy so predictive of morbidity and mortality? *American Journal of the Medical Sciences, 317*, 168–175.

Bernstein, R. A., Giefer, E. E., Vieira, J. J., Werner, L. H., & Rimm, A. A. (1977). Gall bladder disease. II: Utilization of the life table method in obtaining clinically useful information. TOPS. *Journal of Chronic Diseases, 30*, 529–541.

Blankfield, R. P., & Zyzanski, S. J. (2002). Bilateral leg edema, pulmonary hypertension, and obstructive sleep apnea: A cross-sectional study. *Journal of Family Practice, 51*, 561–564.

Bongain, A., Isnard, V., & Gillet, J. Y. (1998). Obesity in obstetrics and gynaecology. *European Journal of Obstetrics, Gynecology, and Reproductive Biology, 77*, 217–228.

Bray, G. A. (1986). Effects of obesity on health and happiness. In K. D. Brownell & J. P. Foreyt (Eds.), *Handbook of eating disorders* (pp. 3–45). New York: Basic Books.

Brown, D. L., & Brillon, D. (1999). New directions in type 2 diabetes mellitus: An update of current oral antidiabetic therapy [Review]. *Journal of the National Medical Association, 91,* 389–395.

Charles, M. A., & Eschwege, E. (1999). Prevention of type 2 diabetes: Role of metformin. *Drugs, 58*(Suppl. 1), 71–73.

Chung, S. A., Jairam, S., Hussain, M. R., & Shapiro, C. M. (2002). How, what, and why of sleep apnea: Perspectives for primary care physicians. *Canadian Family Physician, 48,* 1073–1080.

Connolly, H. M., Crary, J. L., McGoon, M. D., Hensrud, D. D., Edwards, B. S., Edwards, W. D., et al. (1997). Valvular heart disease associated with fenfluramine-phentermine. *New England Journal of Medicine, 337,* 581–588.

Crisostomo, L. L., Araujo, L. M., Camara, E., Carvalho, C., Silva, F. A., Vieira, M., et al. (1999). Comparison of left ventricular mass and function in obese versus nonobese women < 40 years of age. *American Journal of Cardiology, 84,* 1127–1129.

Crisostomo, L. L., Araujo, L. M., Camara, E., Carvalho, C., Silva, F. A., Vieira, M., et al. (2001). Left ventricular mass and function in young obese women. *International Journal of Obesity and Related Metabolic Disorders, 25,* 233–238.

Darga, L. L., Carroll-Michals, L., Botsford, S. J., & Lucas, C. P. (1991). Fluoxetine's effect on weight loss in obese subjects. *American Journal of Clinical Nutrition, 54,* 321–325.

Davidoff, R., McTiernan, A., Constantine, G., Davis, K. D., Balady, G. J., Mendes, L. A., et al. (2001). Echocardiographic examination of women previously treated with fenfluramine: Long-term follow-up of a randomized, double-blind, placebo-controlled trial. *Archives of Internal Medicine, 161,* 1429–1436.

Day, C. (1999). Thiazolidinediones: A new class of antidiabetic drugs. *Diabetic Medicine, 16,* 179–192.

De Bourdeaudhuji, I., Crombez, G., Deforche, B., Vinaimont, F., Debode, P., & Bouckaert, J. (2002). Effects of distraction on treadmill running time in severely obese children and adolescents. *International Journal of Obesity and Related Metabolic Disorders, 26,* 1023–1029.

De Jong, P. E., Verhave, J. C., Pinto-Sietsma, S. J., & Hillege, H. L. (2002, December 26). Obesity and target organ damage: The kidney [For the PREVEND study group]. *International Journal of Obesity and Related Metabolic Disorders, 26*(Suppl. 4), S21–S24.

Drinkard, B., McDuffie, J., McCann, S., Uwaifo, G. I., Nicholson, J., & Yanovski, J. A. (2001). Relationships between walk/run performance and cardiorespiratory fitness in adolescents who are overweight. *Physical Therapy, 81,* 1889–1896.

Gadde, K. M., Parker, C. B., Maner, L. G., Wagner, H. R., Logue, E. J., Drezner, M. K., et al. (2001). Bupropion for weight loss: An investigation of efficacy and tolerability in overweight and obese women. *Obesity Research, 9,* 544–551.

Ganor, S., & Even-Paz, Z. (1967). Fragilitas cutis inguinalis: A phenomenon associated with obesity. *Dermatologia, 134,* 113–124.

Gardin, J. M., Weissman, N. J., Leung, C., Panza, J. A., Fernicola, D., Davis, K. D., et al. (2001, October 24–31). Clinical and echocardiographic follow-up of patients previously treated with dexfenfluramine or phentermine/fenfluramine. *Journal of the American Medical Association, 286*(16), 2011–2014.

Glass, A. R., Burman, K. D., Dahms, W. T., & Boehm, T. M. (1981). Endocrine function in human obesity. *Metabolism, 30,* 89–103.

Goldstein, D. J., Rampey, A. H., Jr., Enas, G. G., Potvin, J. H., Fludzinski, L. A., & Levine, L. R. (1994). Fluoxetine: A randomized clinical trial in the treatment of obesity. *International Journal of Obesity and Related Metabolic Disorders, 18,* 129–135.

Grandi, A. M., Zanzi, P., Piantanida, E., Gaudio, G., Bertolini, A., Guasti, L., et al. (2000). Obesity and left ventricular diastolic function: Noninvasive study in normotensives and newly diagnosed never-treated hypertensives. *International Journal of Obesity and Related Metabolic Disorders, 24,* 954–958.

Gross, T., Sokol, R. J., & King, K. C. (1980). Obesity in pregnancy: Risks and outcome. *Obstetrics Gynecology, 56,* 446–450.

Guha, B., Krishnaswamy, G., & Peiris, A. (2002). The diagnosis and management of hypothyroidism. *Southern Medical Association Journal, 95,* 475–480.

Hatahet, M. A., & Dhurandhar, N. V. (2002). Antiobesity drugs: Current and future issues. *Current Diabetes Reports, 2,* 409–415.

Hauner, H. (1999). The impact of pharmacotherapy on weight management in type 2 diabetes. *International Journal of Obesity and Related Metabolic Disorders, 23*(Suppl. 7), S12–S17.

Hodgkinson, R., & Husain, F. J. (1980). Caesarean section associated with gross obesity. *British Journal of Anaesthesia, 52,* 919–923.

Karason, K., Wallentin, I., Larsson, B., & Sjostrom, L. (1998). Effects of obesity and weight loss on cardiac function and valvular performance. *Obesity Research, 6,* 422–429.

Kasper, E. K., Hruban, R. H., & Baughman, K. L. (1992). Cardiomyopathy of obesity: A clinicopathologic evaluation of 43 obese patients with heart failure. *American Journal of Cardiology, 70,* 921–924.

Kenchaiah, S., Evans, J. C., Levy, D., Wilson, P. W., Benjamin, E. J., Larson, M. G., et al. (2002). Obesity and the risk of heart failure. *New England Journal of Medicine, 347,* 305–313.

Krotkiewski, M. (2002). Thyroid hormones in the pathogenesis and treatment of obesity. *European Journal of Pharmacology, 440,* 85–98.

Lavie, C. J., & Milani, R. V. (1996). Effects of cardiac rehabilitation and exercise training in obese patients with coronary artery disease. *Chest, 109,* 52–56.

Malhotra, A., & White, D. P. (2002). Obstructive sleep apnoea. *Lancet, 360,* 237–245.

Misquita, N. A., Davis, D. C., Dobrovolny, C. L., Ryan, A. S., Dennis, K. E., & Nicklas, B. J. (2001). Applicability of maximal oxygen consumption criteria in obese, postmenopausal women. *Journal of Women's Health and Gender-Based Medicine, 10,* 879–885.

Must, A., Jacques, P. E., Dallal, G. E., Bajema, C. J., & Dietz, W. H. (1992). Long-term morbidity and mortality of overweight adolescents. A follow-up of the Harvard Growth Study of 1922 to 1935. *New England Journal of Medicine, 327,* 1350–1355.

National Heart, Lung, and Blood Institute (NHLBI). (1998). Clinical guidelines on the identification, evaluation, and treatment of overweight and obesity in adults: The evidence report. *Obesity Research, 6*(Suppl. 2), 51S–183S.

Ness-Abramof, R., Nabriski, D., Apovian, C. M., Niven, M., Weiss, E., Shapiro, M. S., et al. (2002). Overnight dexamethasone suppression test: A reliable screen for Cushing's syndrome in the obese. *Obesity Research, 10,* 1217–1221.

Nixon, G. M., & Brouillette, R. T. (2002). Diagnostic techniques for obstructive sleep apnoea: Is polysomnography necessary? *Pediatric Respiratory Reviews, 3,* 18–24.

Norman, J. E., Jr., & Levy, D. (1996). Adjustment of ECG left ventricular hypertrophy criteria for body mass index and age improves classification accuracy: The effects of hypertension and obesity. *Journal of Electrocardiology, 29*(Suppl.), 241–247.

Norman, R. J., & Clark, A. M. (1998). Obesity and reproductive disorders: A review. *Reproduction, Fertility, and Development, 10,* 55–63.

O'Brien, L. M., & Gozal, D. (2002). Behavioral and neurocognitive implications of snoring and obstructive sleep apnoea in children: Facts and theory. *Pediatric Respiratory Reviews, 3,* 3–9.

Okin, P. M., Roman, M. J., Devereux, R. B., & Kligfield, P. (1996). ECG identification of left ventricular hypertrophy: Relationship of test performance to body habitus. *Journal of Electrocardiology, 29*(Suppl.), 256–261.

Osman, F., Gammage, M. D., & Franklyn, J. A. (2001). Thyroid disease and its treatment: Short-term and long-term cardiovascular consequences. *Current Opinion in Pharmacology, 1,* 626–631.

Pallasch, T. J. (1999). Current status of fenfluramine/dexfenfluramine-induced cardiac valvulopathy. *Journal of the California Dental Association, 27,* 400–404.

Park, J. J., & Swan, P. D. (1997). Effect of obesity and regional adiposity on the QTc interval in women. *International Journal of Obesity and Related Metabolic Disorders, 21,* 1104–1110.

Pasquali, R., Casimirri, F., & Vicennati, V. (1997). Weight control and its beneficial effect on fertility in women with obesity and polycystic ovary syndrome. *Human Reproduction, 12*(Suppl. 1), 82–87.

Peckham, C. H., & Christianson, R. E. (1971). The relationship between prepregnancy weight and certain obstetric factors. *American Journal of Obstetrics Gynecology, 111,* 1–7.

Ryan, D. H., Kaiser, P., & Bray, G. A. (1995). Sibutramine: A novel new agent for obesity treatment. *Obesity Research, 3*(Suppl. 4), 553S–559S.

Sachs, G. S., & Guille, C. (1999). Weight gain associated with use of psychotropic medications. *Journal of Clinical Psychiatry, 60*(Suppl. 21), 16–19.

Sahebjami, H. (1998). Dyspnea in obese healthy men. *Chest, 114,* 1373–1377.

Salvadori, A., Fanari, P., Fontana, M., Buontempi, L., Saezza, A., Baudo, S., et al. (1999). Oxygen uptake and cardiac performance in obese and normal subjects during exercise. *Respiration, 66,* 25–33.

Takiya, L., & Chawla, S. (2002). Therapeutic options for the management of Type 2 diabetes mellitus *American Journal of Managed Care, 8,* 1009–1023.

Trovato, G. M., Catalano, D., Caruso, G., Squatrito, R., Venturino, M., Degano, C., et al. (2001). Relationship between cardiac function and insulin resistance in obese patients. *Diabetes, Nutrition and Metabolism: Clinical and Experimental, 14,* 325–328.

Vagelos, R., Jacobs, M., Popp, R. L., & Liang, D. (2002). Reversal of Phen-Fen associated valvular regurgitation documented by serial echocardiography. *Journal of the American Society of Echocardiography, 15*(6), 653–657.

Willett, W. C., Manson, J. E., Stampfer, M. J., Colditz, G. A., Rosner, B., Speizer, F. E., et al. (1995). Weight, weight change and coronary heart disease in women: Risk within the normal weight range. *Journal of the American Medical Association, 273,* 461–465.

Youssef, W., & McCullough, A. J. (2002). Diabetes mellitus, obesity, and hepatic steatosis. *Seminars in Gastrointestinal Disease, 13,* 17–30.

Yu, A. S., & Keeffe, E. B. (2002). Nonalcoholic fatty liver disease. *Reviews in Gastroenterological Disorders, 2,* 11–19.

Chapter 20

BEHAVIORAL ASSESSMENT OF OBESITY

SUZANNE PHELAN AND THOMAS A. WADDEN

One of the difficulties associated with selecting an appropriate treatment for obese individuals is adequate assessment. Behavioral assessment consists of a set of techniques as well as a way of thinking about the cause and functions of behaviors such as eating and exercise. The core assumption of behavioral assessment is that problem behaviors are most effectively understood by focusing on the specific events that surround them. Thus, the typical assessment includes measures of behavior as well as its antecedents (both internal and external) and consequences. One of the advantages of this approach is that it is directly tied to how these behaviors can be changed. The behaviors and psychosocial variables evaluated at the time of the assessment will help determine treatment targets and also provide a clear accountability during treatment of how the patient is doing, beyond the measurement of weight.

An extremely diverse number of approaches and assessment techniques can be used, including self-report, naturalistic observation, interviewing, and self-monitoring. The assessment described in this chapter expands on a previous model proposed by Wadden and Foster (1992) and Wadden and Phelan (2002). This approach relies primarily on interviewing in conjunction with self-report inventories and self-monitoring to evaluate four domains: physical/biological factors, environmental factors, social/psychological factors, and timing for weight control.

Ultimately, the practitioner's goal is not only to identify possible treatment targets but also to place each aspect of the information derived from a behavioral interview into a wider context, which ultimately gives patients an understanding of their obesity and their struggles with it.

BEGINNING THE ASSESSMENT

Objective Measures

Before the interview, we ask patients to complete the Beck Depression Inventory-II (BDI-II; Beck, Steer, & Brown, 1996) and the Weight and Lifestyle Inventory (WALI; Wadden & Foster, 2001), which is reprinted in a chapter by Wadden and Phelan (2002).

The BDI-II is a 21-item questionnaire that measures specific symptoms of depression. It takes approximately five minutes to complete and is easy to score and interpret. The internal consistency, test-retest reliability, and validity of the BDI-II are well-established (Beck et al., 1996). The WALI is a paper and pencil questionnaire that assesses biological, environmental, and social/psychological factors, as well as the timing for weight control. The items on the WALI have acceptable reliability (Wadden, Bartlett, et al., 1992); however, the predictive validity of this inventory is unknown. We typically send the WALI to patients before the interview and ask them to bring the completed questionnaire with them to their scheduled appointment. The BDI-II is completed on arrival for the assessment.

Reviewing these questionnaires before the interview allows the practitioner to identify key areas on which to focus during the evaluation, such as binge eating or depressive symptoms. The completion of these questionnaires may also provide a proxy for future patient adherence. Patients who fail to complete or bring the WALI to the assessment, for example, may have difficulties completing other paper and pen activities required during treatment (e.g., food records). The promptness of patients' arrival for their scheduled appointment or the number of times they may have needed to reschedule may also be noted as possible indicators of future promptness and attendance, although this hypothesis has not been empirically evaluated.

Before initiating the interview, we also obtain a measure of the patient's weight. It is important that the office contain a scale that can weigh patients of very high weights (> 300 lb). The patient's weight is used to calculate the body mass index (BMI) and informs treatment decisions made during the evaluation. Occasionally, a patient may refuse to be weighed. In such cases, the practitioner may discuss the reasons the patient is avoiding the scale and then weigh the patient after the interview, if possible. Some patients feel more comfortable being weighed without knowing the number on the scale. Such persons will need to revisit this issue during treatment.

Initiating the Interview

We typically initiate the interview by focusing on a nonthreatening topic, such as patients' occupations, where they live, or their leisure activities. Addressing these topics may seem unnecessary but ultimately helps in developing rapport with patients and in identifying their interpersonal style, including their sense of humor, shyness, and so on. Factors that would clearly interfere with patients' involvement in group may be observed. For example, patients who are unfocused or demand a lot of clinical attention may be burdensome or difficult to manage in a group setting and more adequately treated on an individual basis. After this 5- to 10-minute discussion, the practitioner should provide a brief overview of the topics to be discussed. In addition, any initial questions the patient might have about the assessment can be addressed.

ASSESSMENT COMPONENTS

The focus area of the assessment is guided, in part, by patients' responses to the questionnaires reviewed by the practitioner before the assessment. In addition, the order in which the practitioner assesses the various factors (e.g., physical, environmental, psychological, and timing) may be altered to fit the needs of an individual patient (e.g., if a patient is eager to discuss a particular topic at the outset of the interview).

Physical Characteristics

A comprehensive discussion of the evaluation of physical and medical factors of obesity has been provided in Chapter 18. In the context of the behavioral assessment, the primary goal is to obtain an estimate of the degree to which an individual's obesity may be due to physical/biological factors that could limit the amount of weight lost in behavioral or other interventions. An estimate can be garnered by assessing the patient's body weight, waist circumference, fat cell size and number, and genetic influences. Furthermore, obtaining an assessment of the patient's current medical status and obesity-related comorbidities may provide a means of enhancing a patient's motivation to lose weight during challenging times of treatment.

Body Weight

As noted earlier, a key piece of information obtained in the behavioral assessment is the patient's weight. With this information and the patient's height, BMI can be calculated. BMI correlates highly with total body fat and is calculated as body weight in kilograms divided by height in meters, squared. The National Heart, Lung, and Blood Institute (NHLBI, 1998) recommends classifying obesity based on categories of BMI (see Table 20.1). These classifications are made based on the point at which the risk of developing obesity-related comorbidities is clearly apparent.

A patient's level of obesity may be the most consistent predictor of treatment outcome. Greater baseline level of body weight is associated with greater short- and long-term weight losses (Foreyt et al., 1982; Wadden, Foster, & Letizia, 1994). Some studies suggest greater attrition in heavier patients (Clark, Guise, & Niaura, 1995), but other studies contradict these findings (Ek, Andersson, Barkeling, & Rossner, 1996). Practitioners may caution leaner patients considering a weight loss group that the absolute amount of weight they lose during treatment may be less than that of

Table 20.1   Classification of Overweight and Obesity by BMI

	BMI kg/m2	Obesity Class
Underweight	< 18.5	
Normal+	18.5–24.9	
Overweight	25.0–29.9	
Obesity	30.0–34.9	I
	35.0–39.9	II
Extreme obesity	≥ 40	III

Adapted from "Clinical Guidelines on the Identification, Evaluation, and Treatment of Overweight and Obesity in Adults: The Evidence Report," by National Heart, Lung, and Blood Institute, 1998, *Obesity Resource* 6(Suppl. 2), pp. 51S–210S.

heavier patients in the group. Heavier patients may be encouraged to learn that they are likely to experience significant weight loss during treatment, although realistic expectations should be promoted.

Waist Circumference

A second measure that can be obtained is the waist circumference (WC), which may be used to assess body fat distribution (van der Kooy & Seidell, 1993). Upper body fat distribution is associated with an increased risk of cardiovascular disease, insulin resistance, type 2 diabetes, and stroke, even after controlling for BMI (Bjorntorp, 1998; Despres et al., 1990; Pouliot et al., 1994). Research is mixed on the effect of WC on weight loss and maintenance (Carmichael, Swinburn, & Wilson, 1998; Wadden & Letizia, 1992). However, a reduction in WC is associated with significant improvements in health (Wirth & Steinmetz, 1998).

Fat Cell Size and Number

Patients' body weight may be used to characterize whether their obesity represents an increase in fat cell size (hypertrophic obesity) or fat cell number (hyperplastic obesity). Individuals characterized only by an increase in fat cell size have a reasonable chance of achieving "normal" weight because cell hypertrophy appears to be reversible (Krotkiewski et al., 1977). However, excess cell number (i.e., hyperplasia) is not reversible (Naslun, Hallgren, & Sjostrom, 1988). Thus, even with weight loss, patients with severe, hyperplastic obesity are likely to have two to three times the average number of fat cells and fat mass, which may limit their weight loss.

Fat cell size and number may be estimated by determining the total amount of body fat (e.g., through underwater weighing) and evaluating fat cells microscopically. However, less expensive and more practical estimations may be derived based on the patient's body weight (see Figure 20.1).

Patients who are approximately 50 kg or more above their ideal body weight may be encouraged to set realistic weight loss goals given the probably of their having hyperplastic obesity.

Genetic Factors

Studies of twins, adoptees, and families suggest that genetic factors account for an estimated 20% to 40% of the variance in body weight. Heritability estimates from some twin studies are even higher (up to 90%; Bouchard, 1994). Chapter 16 provides a detailed discussion of the genetics of obesity. Although there are no sufficient methods available for assessing an individual's genetic predisposition to obesity, several factors may be reviewed in the behavioral assessment to identify an increased role of biological, as compared to environmental, influences in the etiology of obesity. These include the age of onset of obesity, family history of obesity, and the patient's weight loss history.

Age of Onset of Obesity   Childhood onset of obesity increases the likelihood of an increased number of fat cells and is generally related to greater body weight as an adult (Bjorntorp et al., 1975; Guo, Roche, Chumlea, Gardner, & Siervogel, 1994; Serdula et al., 1993; Sjostrom, 1980; Whitaker, Wright, Pepe, Seidel, & Dietz, 1997). Persons with child or adolescent onset of their obesity can lose a significant amount of weight but are

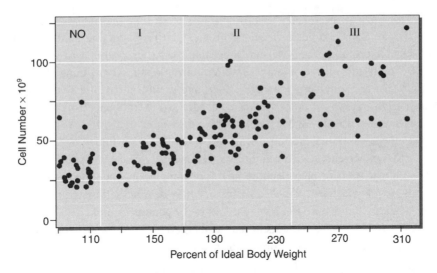

Figure 20.1   The Relationship between Fat Cell Number (in Billions) and Percent of Ideal Body Weight (as determined by the 1959 Metropolitan Life Insurance Co. Height and Weight Tables). I, II, and III refer to three groups of subjects with increasing severity of obesity. NO refers to nonobese subjects. *Source:* From "Biochemistry and Development of Adipose Tissue in Man," pp. 21–48, by R. L. Leibel, E. M. Berry, and J. Hirsch, in *Health and Obesity,* H. L. Conn, E. A. DeFelice, and P. Kuo (Eds.), 1983, New York: Raven. Copyright 1983 by Raven Press. Reprinted with permission from Raven Press.

unlikely to reach "average" weight due, in part, to the irreversibility of increased fat cell number (discussed previously).

The age of onset of obesity during adulthood (i.e., after age 18) does not appear to significantly affect treatment outcome. In studies of adults, no differences in weight loss as a function of age are generally found (Crawford, Jeffery, & French, 2000; Wadden, Vogt, Foster, & Anderson, 1998; Wing, Shoemaker, Marcus, McDermott, & Gooding, 1990), although one study found that attrition was higher in younger adults (Clark, Niaura, King, & Pera, 1996). Age of onset can be evaluated by assessing the patient's weight history, including the patient's highest weight at various age intervals (i.e., ages 5 to 10, 11 to 15), their lowest lifetime weight, and the age when they were first overweight by 10 pounds or more (Wadden & Phelan, 2002).

Family History   Obesity runs in family and is due, in part, to shared genetic characteristics (Lake, Power, & Cole, 1997; Stunkard et al., 1986; Whitaker et al., 1997). Maternal obesity appears to be a stronger risk factor than paternal obesity (Hashimoto, Kawasaki, Kikuchi, Takahashi, & Uchivama, 1995; Mafeis, Talamini, & Tato, 1998). Assessment of family history may be conducted by inquiring about the weights and heights of patients' mother, father, brothers, and sisters. Weights of maternal and paternal grandparents may also be obtained.

Weight Loss History   It has been hypothesized that patients with an extensive history of weight loss and regain may be genetically predisposed to maintain a higher body weight (Keesey, 1986). Although a history of weight loss and regain is often considered a risk factor for poor performance in weight loss programs, the literature on this topic is inconsistent. Some studies have found greater dieting history related to diminished weight loss (Kiernan, King, Kraemer, Stefanick, & Killen, 1998) and weight maintenance (Gormally, Rardin, & Black, 1980; McGuire, Wing, Klem, Lang, & Hill, 1999; Pasman, Saris, & Westerterp-Plantega, 1999) and greater attrition (Yass-Reed, Barry, & Dacey, 1993). However, other studies contradict these findings (Hoie & Bruusgaard, 1999; Pekkarinen, Takala, & Mustajoki, 1996; Yass-Reed et al., 1993).

Nonetheless, assessing dieting history provides the opportunity to learn about the patient's past experiences with weight loss treatments. Negative past experiences with very low calorie diets or pharmacotherapy, for example, may need to be discussed and erroneous beliefs clarified. Weight loss history may be assessed by inquiring about the number of diets that resulted in a weight loss of 10 pounds or more (Wadden, Bartlett, et al., 1992) and by asking patients to list the method used to lose weight, the age at the time of the diet, and the number of pounds lost for each diet (Wadden & Phelan, 2002).

Medical Comorbidities

Preliminary research suggests that medical status, in addition to the diagnosis of obesity, may negatively affect weight loss outcomes in behavioral treatment (Clark et al., 1996; Karlsson et al., 1994). For example, one study found that higher baseline systolic blood pressure and untreated hypertension were related to lower attendance at treatment sessions (Clark et al., 1996). Other studies have found that the maintenance of weight loss may be poorer in diabetic compared to no diabetic individuals (Guar, Wing, & Grant, 1995; Khan, St. Peter, Breen, Hartley, & Vessel, 1999).

While the impact of health status on treatment outcome awaits further investigation, reviewing a patient's medical comorbidities can provide a useful means of assessing change during treatment. Medication reductions or decreases in blood pressure during weight loss provide observable and positive outcomes and potential incentives for continued efforts at weight control. Assessment of medical comorbidities may be done informally during the behavioral assessment by reviewing the presence of several health problems (e.g., sleep apnea, high blood pressure, diabetes). However, assessment should ultimately be done in the context of a broader assessment of medical and physical status of the patient, as discussed in Chapter 18.

Summarizing Physical Characteristics

Practitioners who identify a probable biological predisposition to obesity should be careful to communicate this information in a way that will benefit the patient. Some patients find relief in learning that their predisposition could explain, in part, why they have had to struggle in their attempts at weight control. Other patients may react by saying, "What's the use of trying; it's all in the genes!" We typically reassure patients that although genes influence body weight and that it may seem unfair that some people have a genetic tendency to gain weight, these facts do not mean that patients cannot control their weight. The practitioner may explain that obesity is not a trait like eye color, which is determined at the moment of conception and does not change. A tendency for obesity is inherited and this tendency needs to have an environment that will nurture its development before it becomes a reality. Modifying the environment to decrease high calorie foods and to increase physical activity will lower the chance that a genetic tendency will become a reality. Furthermore, such behavior changes will likely result in significant improvements in obesity-related comorbidities and longevity (Blackburn, 1995; Kanders & Blackburn, 1992; Lee & Paffenbarger, 1992).

ENVIRONMENTAL FACTORS

Environmental factors play a clear role in the development of obesity. This is suggested by research showing that people of the same genetic makeup who move to industrialized cultures from less industrialized cultures have a corresponding increase in body weight (Bhatnagar et al., 1995). Similarly, changes in the gene pool could not possibly account for the significant increase in obesity that has occurred since 1980 in both adults and children (Flegal, Carroll, Kuczmarski, & Johnson, 1998; Troiano, Flegal, Kuczmarski, Campbell, & Johnson, 1995; World Health Organization [WHO], 1998). Indeed, the environment of industrialized countries has been viewed as so severely promoting of obesity that it has been labeled "toxic" (Battle & Brownell, 1996). Food intake, problem eating, environmental cues, and physical activity must be examined to better understand the environmental influences on obesity.

Food Intake

Several aspects of food intake should be evaluated, including the number of eating episodes per day, caloric intake, and dietary composition. Ideally, information about food intake is obtained from food records completed the week or two before the behavioral assessment (mailed to patients at the time when the appointment was scheduled). If the dietary records were not obtained before assessment, patients may be asked to report what they typically eat, including the time, type, and amount of food consumed on a typical weekday and a typical weekend day (see Table 20.2).

Alternatively, dietary composition can be assessed by the use of a food frequency questionnaire, such as the Block Food Frequency Questionnaire (Block, Woods, Potosky, & Clifford, 1990). The Block Questionnaire is a well-validated and easily administered measure that takes approximately 15 to 20 minutes to complete (Block et al., 1990).

In reviewing any assessment of food intake, however, the practitioner should note that obese individuals typically underestimate their intake by 30% to 50% (Lichtman et al., 1992; Schoeller, 1988, 1995; Schoeller & Fjeld, 1991). Other, more accurate means for assessing energy requirements exist (i.e., the doubly labeled water method) but are expensive and impractical in the context of behavioral assessment. Given the limitations in assessing food intake, the behavioral assessment serves only to provide an impression of the patient's food intake that can be further refined during treatment.

Number of Meals and Snacks Per Day

Evaluating the frequency and timing of meals and snacks and the consistency of the meal pattern will inform treatment decisions in relation to meal structure. Studies indicate that obese individuals tend to shift the timing of meals to later in the day (Berteus Forslund, Lindroos, Sjostrom, & Lissner, 2002) and often skip breakfast (Ortega et al.,

Table 20.2   Food Intake Recall

Meal	Time	Location	Food and Beverages Consumed	Amount
Breakfast				
Morning snack				
Lunch				
Afternoon snack				
Dinner				
Evening snack				

Source: From "Behavioral Assessment of the Obese Patient," pp. 186–226, by T. A. Wadden and S. Phelan, in *Handbook of Obesity Treatment,* T. A. Wadden and A. J. Stunkard (Eds.), 2002, New York: Guilford Press. Copyright 2002 by Guilford Press.

1998). Individuals who skip meals (Schlundt, Hill, Sbrocco, Pope-Cordle, & Kasser, 1990) or have highly variable eating patterns (Roger, 1999) tend to have greater hunger and disinhibition, which could ultimately undermine weight control efforts. Some short-term studies have shown that skipping breakfast is associated with eating higher calorie-dense foods later in the day (Morgan, Zabik, & Stampley, 1986; Schlundt, Sbrocco, & Bell, 1989). Skipping breakfast also appears uncommon in individuals who are success-ful at weight loss maintenance (Kayman, Bruvold, & Stern, 1990; Wyatt et al., 2002). Thus, a principal goal of treatment is to establish a structured meal plan, which includes breakfast.

Calorie Intake

To induce weight loss, practitioners typically prescribe a fixed calorie diet (e.g., 1,500 to 1,800 kcal/day for men and 1,200 to 1,500 kcal/day for women) that results in a loss of about one pound per week. Fixed calorie diets are based on a rough estimate of en-ergy intake. More precise estimates can be obtained by measuring resting energy ex-penditure by indirect calorimetry. However, a self-reported estimate of caloric intake is useful in determining whether patients believe their obesity is from overeating or other factors. This can be evaluated by asking patients whether they eat the same amount as people of average weight, more than such people, or less than people of average weight. For patients who report consuming more than average, the practitioner can emphasize that this is actually good news because it means there is a clear area to focus on during treatment. Individuals who report eating an unexpectedly low energy intake are most likely unaware of the amount of food that they consume. The practitioner may emphasize the difficulty in counting portion sizes and keeping track of calories, further discussed in treatment.

Dietary Composition

Dietary composition may be examined from at least two vantage points. First, the fat content of the patient's diet should be estimated. Of all the macronutrients, fat is the most energy dense, providing nine calories per gram compared to seven for alcohol and four for protein and carbohydrate. Because fat is the most calorically dense, its consumption is likely to increase the risk of subsequent weight gain (Golay & Bobbioni, 1997; Lissner, Levitsky, Strupp, Kalkwarf, & Roe, 1987; Stubbs, Harbron, & Murgatroyd, 1995). Reducing fat intake alone has been found to promote modest weight loss (NHLBI, 1998). In addition, reducing fat is helpful from the standpoint of improving cardiac health, independent of weight loss (Renaud & Lanzmann-Petithory, 2001).

Practitioners may also want to evaluate the variety of the patient's diet. Diets that contain a variety of foods may contribute to the development and maintenance of obesity (Raynor & Epstein, 2001). In addition, animal and human studies have shown that food consumption increases when there is more variety in a meal and that greater dietary variety is associated with increased body weight (Raynor & Epstein, 2001). Patients who report consuming a lot of variety in their diets, particularly in high fat or sweet foods, may benefit from the use of meal replacements or structured meal plans (Ditschuneit, Flechtner-Mors, & Adler, 1999; Raynor & Epstein, 2001).

Problem Eating

Binge Eating

Approximately 20% to 30% of obese individuals who seek weight loss report problems with binge eating (Marcus, Wing, & Hopkins, 1988). As reviewed in Chapter 4, binge eating disorder (BED) is characterized by the consumption of a large amount of food in a discrete period of time and by the patient's report of loss of control during the eating episode. The overeating is not followed by compensatory behaviors (such as vomiting or laxative abuse). Marked distress must occur in at least three areas, including eating very rapidly, eating until uncomfortably full, eating when not hungry, eating alone, or feeling guilty after a binge (American Psychiatric Association [APA], 1994; Spitzer et al., 1992). Individuals with BED are more likely to report symptoms of depression, anxiety, and other psychopathology (Marcus et al., 1988; Sherwood, Jeffery, & Wing, 1999; Spitzer et al., 1992, 1993; Telch & Agras, 1994; Wadden, Foster, Letizia, & Wilk, 1993).

Binge eaters are commonly thought to fare worse in treatment compared to nonbinge eaters (Yanovski, 1993). Disinhibition and binge eating scores have been related to increasing risk of weight regain (Fogelholm, Kukkonen-Harjula, & Oja, 1999; Karlsson et al., 1994; McGuire et al., 1999; Pasman et al., 1999). However, several studies have found no differences in weight loss between obese binge eaters and nonbinge eaters (Gladis et al., 1998; Sherwood et al., 1999; Wadden, Foster, & Letizia, 1992). For example, in one study (Sherwood et al., 1999), baseline binge status was not associated with 6-month weight loss and was only a weak predictor of diminished weight loss at

18 months. The weak relationship between binge status and weight change was reduced when depressive symptomatology scores were added to the analyses, suggesting that depression may moderate the relationship between binge eating and weight loss. However, the directionality of the relationships among depression, binge eating, and weight loss could not be determined in this study. Binge eaters may be at greater risk of dropping out of treatment (Marcus et al., 1988; Sherwood et al., 1999), which might explain the inconsistent findings reviewed previously.

Patients with BED appear to benefit from traditional behavioral weight control programs; they lose weight and experience a reduction in binge episodes. Practitioners, however, may want to monitor eating behavior, particularly during weight maintenance. Furthermore, simply recognizing the problem of binge eating at the time of the behavioral assessment can provide a sense of relief for patients who struggle with this disorder, often in private.

Binge eating can be assessed by the Questionnaire on Eating and Weight Patterns-Revised (QEWP-R; Spitzer et al., 1992; Yanovski, 1993). This 28-item instrument provides decision rules for diagnosing BED and has been found to have adequate validity and reliability (Spitzer et al., 1992). The practitioner should confirm whether an objectively large amount of food was eaten by having patients describe a recent binge episode during the interview.

Night Eating

Night-eating syndrome occurs in approximately 1.5% of the general population (Rand, MacGregor, & Stunkard, 1997) and in 8.9% to 27% of obese individuals seeking weight loss treatment (Rand et al., 1997; Stunkard, 1959). Night-eating syndrome has not yet been formally defined as an eating disorder in the *Diagnostic and Statistical Manual for Mental Disorders, (DSM-IV*; APA, 1994). However, provisional criteria developed by Birketvedt and colleagues (1999) are provided in Table 20.3.

As shown in Table 20.3, night-eating syndrome is characterized by a lack of appetite for breakfast, the consumption of more than 50% of daily calories after the evening meal, and waking up at least once per night to consume high-carbohydrate

Table 20.3 Diagnostic Criteria for Night-Eating Disorder

Provisional Criteria for Night-Eating Disorder
Morning anorexia, even if the subject eats breakfast.
Evening hyperphagia. At least 50% of the daily caloric intake is consumed in snacks after the last evening meal.
Awakening at least once a night at least three nights per week.
Consumption of high calorie snacks during the awakening on frequent occasions.
The pattern occurs for a period of at least three months.
Subject does not meet criteria for any other eating disorders.

Source: Material adapted from "Behavioral and Neuroendocrine Characteristics of the Night-Eating Syndrome," by G. Birketvedt, J. Florholmen, J. Sundsfjord, B. Osterud, D. Dinges, W. Bilker, et al., 1999, *Journal of the American Medical Association, 282,* pp. 657–663.

snacks. Identifying patients with this disorder provides information that may be useful in planning treatment. Studies are currently being conducted to better understand the principal characteristics, prevalence, etiology, and treatment of night-eating syndrome.

Environmental Cues

As noted earlier, one of the defining characteristics of behavioral assessment is the evaluation of the factors that surround eating and inactivity. The Antecedent-Behavior-Consequence (ABC) model is typically used in the assessment of environmental contributors to obesity (Brownell, 1998; see Figure 20.2).

Antecedent refers to the environmental events that elicit or evoke overeating. Antecedents to eating and activity may include people, places, activities, times, and emotions. Places may include the patient's desk, kitchen, living room, or car and are likely to contain two additional triggers to eat—the sight and smell of food. Activities such as watching television, talking on the phone, studying, or reading may also trigger eating. Television viewing, in particular, is significantly related to overeating and has been linked to an increased prevalence of obesity (Dietz & Gortmaker, 1985; Gortmaker et al., 1996). Internal factors, including emotions (e.g., dysphoria, stress, boredom, or anger) or distorted thoughts (e.g., I'll never succeed at this), may also precede eating. In treatment, patients will be encouraged to break the link between the triggers and the problem behavior.

Behavior refers to the specific factors that define the eating problem. Typically, the problem behavior represents an immediate reaction to the trigger and arises without much thought. The behavior is defined in very specific and observable terms (e.g., the amount and types of food consumed, the rate of eating). Treatment will aim to reduce the problem behaviors by increasing awareness, primarily through self-monitoring.

Consequence refers to the events that follow the problem behavior. Positive consequences of eating are usually immediate and definite. Commonly, patients report that they eat because it "tastes good." However, overeating may also be a reaction to feeling awkward in social situations, or it may provide a sense of escape or relief from stress. In treatment, patients will be encouraged to replace eating with positive behaviors that have similar effects (e.g., exercising rather than eating to relieve stress).

The practitioner's goal in conducting an ABC analysis is to assess cues that contribute to overeating, which can then be addressed in treatment. Patients who have few triggers associated with eating at the outset of treatment appear to do better in treatment (Carmody, Brunner, & St. Jeor, 1995; French, Jeffery, & Wing, 1994). Triggers and consequences may be assessed by asking about events perceived to contribute to weight gain, as illustrated in the Eating Habits section of the WALI (see Table 20.4). Assessment of eating behavior (i.e., meal pattern, calorie intake, dietary composition, problem eating) was reviewed in the previous section.

Figure 20.2   Functional Analysis Behavioral Chain (ABC Analysis).

Table 20.4   The Eating Habits Section of the WALI Questionnaire

Eating Habits

Please indicate the degree to which each of the following behaviors causes you to gain weight. In answering these questions, please use the five-point scale below. Pick the one number that best describes how much of the behavior contributes to your increased weight:

1. Does not contribute at all.
2. Contributes a small amount.
3. Contributes a moderate amount.
4. Contributes a large amount.
5. Contributes the greatest amount.

_____ A. Eating too much food.

_____ B. Overeating at breakfast.

_____ C. Overeating at lunch.

_____ D. Overeating at dinner.

_____ E. Snacking between meals.

_____ F. Snacking after dinner.

_____ G. Eating because I feel physically hungry.

_____ H. Eating because I crave certain foods.

_____ I. Eating because I don't feel full.

_____ J. Eating because I can't stop once I've begun.

_____ K. Eating because of the good taste of foods.

_____ L. Eating in response to the sight or smell of food.

_____ M. Eating while cooking or preparing food.

_____ N. Eating when anxious.

_____ O. Eating when tired.

_____ P. Eating when bored.

_____ Q. Eating when stressed.

_____ R. Eating when angry.

_____ S. Eating when depressed/upset.

_____ T. Eating when socializing/celebrating.

_____ U. Eating when happy.

_____ V. Eating when alone.

_____ W. Eating with family/friends.

_____ X. Eating at business functions.

Please indicate any other factors that contribute a moderate or large amount to your weight gain.

_____

Source: From "Behavioral Assessment of the Obese Patient," pp. 186–226, by T. A. Wadden and S. Phelan, in *Handbook of Obesity Treatment,* T. A. Wadden and A. J. Stunkard (Eds.), 2002, New York: Guilford Press. Copyright 2002 by Guilford Press.

Physical Activity

The ABC model may be used to understand not only eating but also inactivity. It is generally accepted that with the modernization of society, energy expenditure has decreased and is at least partly responsible for the increasing prevalence of obesity (Hill, Wyatt, & Melanson, 2000; Prentice & Jebb, 1995; Weinsier, Hunter, Heini, Goran, & Sell, 1998). The decrease in energy expenditure is most likely due to changes in activities of daily living (Weinsier et al., 1998) promoted by a proliferation of energy-saving devices (see Table 20.5).

Sedentary behavior is significantly related to increased weight (Brownell, 1995) and is a recognized risk factor for cardiovascular disease (Ravussin et al., 1997). Increased physical activity is the single best predictor of the maintenance of weight loss (Pronk & Wing, 1994) and appears to decrease the risk of morbidity and mortality, independent of weight loss (Blair & Leermakers, 2002).

A few simple questions may provide a practical and efficient means of assessing physical activity, for example, "How many minutes do you spend each week in planned physical activity, such as brisk walking or swimming? Approximately how many city blocks to you walk each day? How many flights of stairs do you climb each day?" Sedentary behavior, such as television viewing, computer and videogame use, and driving time, may also be evaluated by weekly number of minutes for each activity.

If a more formal assessment is desired, the Physical Activity Recall (PAR; Blair, 1984) or the Paffenbarger (Paffenbarger, Wing, & Hyde, 1978) questionnaires may be used. The PAR is available in interviewer and self-administered versions and categorizes

Table 20.5 Energy-Saving Devices

Personal computers.

Telecommuting.

Cellular phones.

E-mail/Internet.

Intercoms.

Moving sidewalks.

Remote controls.

Garage door openers.

Shopping by phone.

Food delivery services.

Phone extensions.

Dishwashers.

Escalators/elevators.

Cable movies.

Drive-thru windows.

Computer games.

activities by their intensity; the Paffenbarger questionnaire is a one-page inventory that evaluates habitual daily and weekly activity. Measures of sedentary behaviors, such as television viewing and computer use, are only beginning to be used and validated.

In addition to assessing current physical activity, we typically inquire as to a patient's exercise preferences. This includes the type of activity (i.e., walking, swimming, aerobics), as well as whether the individual prefers to exercise alone or with others. Perceived barriers to physical activity may also be reviewed. The most common barriers cited by patients include lack of time, lack of social support, inclement weather, disruption in routine, lack of access to facilities, and dislike of vigorous exercise (Dishman & Sallis, 1994). Patients who are most active before treatment may have better success in long-term weight loss (Weinsier et al., 2002). However, patients who report several barriers and/or very little in the way of physical activity may be encouraged that modifying these behaviors need not be done all at once, but progressively. Furthermore, their lack of activity affords the practitioner a clear area that can be worked on to promote weight loss.

Summarizing the Role of Environmental Factors

Summarizing behavioral factors for patients provides the practitioner with the opportunity to emphasize that, even if a patient has inherited a tendency to be overweight, modifying the environment to include low calorie, low fat foods and to increase physical activity can counteract a genetic predisposition. The more environmental "trouble spots" identified, the more room there is for behavior change and successful weight loss. The practitioner should review the most salient triggers reported by the patient (e.g., emotional eating, pressures to eat from others) and reinforce that these may be modified in treatment.

Cases in which an individual reports consuming a low calorie diet and exercising regularly may be more problematic. The practitioner should emphasize the importance of patients' keeping very accurate food records to decrease the underestimation of calorie intake. Patients may also be able to increase the intensity or duration of their physical activity.

SOCIAL/PSYCHOLOGICAL FACTORS

This component of the assessment inquires about the patient's social relationships, including their living arrangements, satisfaction with personal relationships, and expected social support during weight loss. Furthermore, the patient's mood and psychosocial status are evaluated. The overall goal is to understand the role that eating, inactivity, and obesity play in a patient's social and emotional lives.

Social Context of Weight Loss

Social factors can have a powerful influence on obese individuals' treatment response (Wing & Jeffery, 1999). Patients with greater social support have larger short- and long-term weight losses (Foreyt & Goodrick, 1991) and are more likely to complete treatment (Yass-Reed et al., 1993). There are many different types of social support (see Table 20.6).

Tangible assistance may include receiving rides to and from treatment or having someone to help with cooking, grocery shopping, and food preparation. Support may also be provided in the form of information by answering questions, talking through the various options for treatment, or looking up information on the Internet. Still other people may offer emotional support by bolstering the patient's sense of self-worth or assisting with weight loss efforts.

For patients who have an active social life, the practitioner may inquire about how their social network will respond to their changing eating and activity habits. We frequently ask, "What did your partner (or friends) do that helped you lose weight the last time you tried? What did your partner (or friends) do that hindered your weight control efforts?" The practitioner and patient may want to invite family members to a session if they are identified as a significant barrier to weight control.

A lack of social support may also need to be addressed. Preliminary research suggests that a lack of social support can undermine treat outcome (Foreyt & Goodrick, 1991). Research also indicates that the social support provided by other group members in behavioral treatment programs may be helpful to those who lack other sources of support (Wing & Jeffery, 1999). Practitioners may foster the development of relationships outside treatment, which has the potential to ultimately build social support and thereby aid in weight control efforts. Social support can be assessed by asking patients about their marital status, whether they have children and/or an intimate partner, and the number of persons they consider friends. Whether the significant people in the patient's life strongly support, support, feel neutral, oppose, or strongly oppose the patient's efforts to lose weight can also be assessed.

Psychological Status

Obesity is a highly stigmatized condition in the United States and most industrialized countries (Friedman & Brownell, 1995; Wadden, Womble, Stunkard, & Anderson, 2002). Obese individuals must contend with social discrimination in employment, salary levels, education, and social relationships (Rand & MacGregor, 1990; Roehling, 1999; Rothblum, Brand, Miller, & Oetjen, 1989). Health professionals (including doctors, medical student, nutritionists, and nurses) may even hold negative stereotypes and attitudes toward obesity (Price, Desmond, Krol, Snyder, & O'Connell, 1987).

Table 20.6   Social Support for Weight Loss

Types of Social Support	Examples
Tangible	Giving a ride to treatment, buying low calorie foods for patient, walking with patient.
Informational	Reading treatment materials with patient, researching weight loss strategies, researching calorie-counting books.
Emotional	Providing support and encouragement through high-risk situations.

Whether there are any psychological ramifications of social stigma and discrimination is surprisingly unclear. Research in this area has revealed that scores on standard psychological tests differ little, if at all, between obese and nonobese individuals in the general population (Friedman & Brownell, 1995). Nonetheless, increased levels of depression and other psychopathology are common in obese men and women who seek weight loss treatment (Fitzgibbon, Stolley, & Kirschenbaum, 1993; McReynolds, 1983). In addition, many obese individuals may suffer from body image disturbances, impaired quality of life, or reduced self-efficacy.

Coexisting Mood Disorders

Fewer than 10% of obese individuals who present for weight loss treatment are likely to meet the diagnostic criteria for major depressive episode (APA, 1994). More patients report symptoms of depression that are consistent with dysthymic disorder (Wadden et al., 2000), which is a milder, chronic form of depression. Dysthymia is frequently accompanied by binge eating and reports of distress with work or personal relationships.

Weight loss is unlikely to improve major depression and could make it worse (Wadden & Bartlett, 1992). Furthermore, individuals with high levels of depression may be at greater risk of dropping out of treatment (Clark et al., 1996; Marcus et al., 1988). We typically advise patients with significant depression to seek treatment of their mood disorder before undertaking weight loss. We indicate that weight loss requires substantial time, effort, and concentration, which participants will struggle to find when they are depressed.

Dysthymic disorder is not a contraindication for weight loss treatment. Patients with mild depressive symptoms appear as likely to lose weight in treatment and experience improvements in mood as patients with few to no symptoms of depression (Gladis et al., 1998; Karlsson et al., 1994; Marcus et al., 1988; Pekkarinen et al., 1996; Wadden & Letizia, 1992). This may be due, in part, to the mood-enhancing effects of exercise (Brosse, Sheets, Lett, & Blumenthal, 2002), which is included in all behavioral weight loss programs.

Both formal and informal assessments can be used to evaluate the presence of co-occurring mood disorders. Informally, patients may be asked to describe, for the past month, their mood, sleep, energy level, and satisfaction with work, leisure activities, and personal relationships. Depression may be more formally evaluated by assessing for specific symptoms of depression (e.g., depressed mood most of the day, nearly every day; markedly diminished interest or pleasure in almost all activities; feelings of worthlessness). We recommend routinely administering the BDI-II (Beck et al., 1996), as described previously. Patients with scores under 17 are generally not of clinical concern, unless suicidal ideation is reported (Beck et al., 1996). Patients with scores over 17 should be assessed more fully in terms of their affect, behavior, and cognition. Scores over 29 indicate severe depression that definitely requires professional attention. It may be useful to contact the patient's therapist (if the patient has one) and determine whether the elevation represents the patient's chronic state or, in fact, an episode of depression.

History of Sexual Abuse

The relationship between history of sexual abuse and obesity is unclear. Some studies have suggested that severely obese individuals have higher than expected rates of abuse (Brewerton, O'Neil, Dansky, & Kilpatrick, 1999; Felitti, 1993), but other research has contradicted these findings (Sansone, Sansone, & Fine, 1995; Wiederman, Sansone, & Sansone, 1999). In assessing history of sexual abuse, we typically provide a rationale for the assessment that acknowledges the possibility that some women with a history of sexual abuse may feel anxious or vulnerable because of weight loss.

In patients who report a history of abuse, the practitioner may inquire whether they have received counseling or other help with this issue. With patients who have received treatment, we ask the extent to which they feel that they have recovered from the abuse. For patients who report that they have not recovered or have never received counseling, we always encourage them to do so. Some decline, stating that they do not think it will help or is too expensive. We acknowledge these concerns but emphasize how helpful professional assistance can be.

Physical or sexual abuse is not a contraindication to weight reduction. We have found that these patients usually lose weight satisfactorily. Practitioners, however, should be alert to possible adverse experiences that occur as patients lose weight and attract more attention from members of the opposite sex.

Body Image

Many obese individuals presenting for treatment report significant distress about body image. A minority of patients may present with a condition called *body image disparagement* (Stunkard & Mendelson, 1967). Individuals with body image disparagement believe their bodies are "ugly and despicable and that others view them with hostility and contempt." Stewart and Williamson have described body image disparagement and methods of assessing it in this volume (Chapter 24). These include the Multidimensional Body-Self Relations Questionnaire (Cash, 1994), as well as the Body Dysmorphic Disorder, Self-Report Scale (Rosen & Reiter, 1996). Specific treatments have been developed for patients suffering from body image problems (see Chapter 24). Body image tends to improve with weight loss (Foster, Wadden, & Vogt, 1997; Wadden et al., 1994) but can be improved independent of weight loss (Ramirez & Rosen, 2001).

Quality of Life

Quality of life is a loosely defined construct but generally refers to impairments in physical and psychosocial functioning. The impact of obesity on quality of life is substantial, mostly in relation to physical functioning (Barofsky, Fontaine, & Cheskin, 1998; Le Pen, Levy, Loos, Banzet, & Basdevant, 1998). Impairments in work and social activities have also been reported (Kolotkin, Head, Hamilton, & Tse, 1995). These impairments clearly improve with weight loss (Choban, Onyejekwe, Burge, & Flancbaum, 1999; Fontaine et al., 1999). Several instruments are available to assess quality of life (Kolotkin, Meter, & Williams, 2001). The most widely used instrument is the Short Form (SF-36) Health Survey, which includes eight scales that measure mental health, energy level, and role and social functioning (Ware, 1993; Ware & Sherbourne, 1992). The SF-36 is easily scored and has excellent validity and reliability.

Self-Efficacy

Self-efficacy is defined as confidence in one's ability to perform a behavior required to produce a desired outcome (Bandura, 1977). As applied to weight control, self-efficacy has been defined as a person's judgment of his or her ability to cope effectively in high-risk situations (Clark, Abrams, Niaura, Eaton, & Rossi, 1991). Several studies have reported that reduced levels of self-efficacy before treatment are significantly related to poorer weight loss (Edell, Edington, Herd, O'Brien, & Witkin, 1987; Forster & Jeffery, 1986; Glynn & Ruderman, 1986; Oettingen & Wadden, 1991). Thus, patients who report little confidence in their ability to adhere to treatment tend to lose less weight than those who are more confident.

The practitioner may informally assess patients' self-efficacy concerning a variety of weight control skills, such as reducing calories, increasing exercise, or self-monitoring. Alternatively, scales such as the Weight Efficacy Life-Style Questionnaire (WEL) may be used. On the WEL, respondents are asked to rate their confidence in resisting eating in 20 tempting situations. Items are rated using a 10-point Likert-type scale in which higher scores indicate greater confidence in resisting overeating in the specified situation. Internal consistency of the WEL is good (Clark et al., 1991). The patient and practitioner should explore the reasons for low efficacy ratings that may be addressed during treatment.

Summarizing Psychosocial Factors

Most obese individuals present to treatment with normal psychological functioning (Friedman & Brownell, 1995; Wadden et al., 2002; see Chapter 17). For patients reporting significant depressive symptoms, the practitioner should acknowledge that patient's mood disorder and review the relevant symptoms (e.g., feeling sad, having trouble concentrating, feeling like things aren't going to get better). Patients' desire to lose weight should be commended and their chances of success promoted by having their mood disturbance treated first. After an appropriate referral is made and the patient's depression is treated, the patient should be encouraged to recontact the provider to further discuss weight control.

Patients who report experiencing mild to moderate depressive symptoms and/or problem eating may be informed that weight reduction can produce significant improvement in these domains. Similarly, body image, quality of life, and self-efficacy are often enhanced with weight loss.

TIMING FOR WEIGHT CONTROL

This section of the assessment inquires about the timing of the planned weight loss effort and patients' motivations for seeking weight loss treatment. Barriers that might interfere with successful weight control are also reviewed.

Reasons for Seeking Weight Loss

Assessing patients' initial reasons for pursuing weight loss can enhance motivation during treatment. Patients present for treatment for a variety of reasons including a medical event (e.g., sleep apnea, lower back pain, fatigue), emotional trigger (e.g., "My husband left me and my lawyer told me it was because I was fat"), or lifestyle change (e.g., getting a new job; Klem, Wing, McGuire, Seagle, & Hill, 1997). In evaluating the reasons the patient is presenting for treatment, the practitioner should consider whether the triggering event is a temporary motivator (e.g., losing weight for a wedding or reunion) or one that can sustain the patient's efforts in the long term. We typically assess a patient's reasons for pursuing treatment informally with the questions, "Why do you want to lose weight now, as compared to one year ago?" and, "What has prompted you to lose weight now?"

Stressful Life Events

Epidemiological studies have shown that stress precedes significant weight gains (Korkeila, Kaprio, Rissanen, Koskenvuo, & Sorensen, 1998). Few treatment studies have evaluated the role of stress in treatment success, and available research is mixed. One study reported no relationship between stress and subsequent weight loss (Pekkarinen et al., 1996). By contrast, another found that patients who discontinued treatment during the first two months endorsed more stressors at baseline than persons who remained in treatment. The distinguishing stressors were "relationship with significant other," "events related to parents," and "financial or legal difficulties" (Wadden & Letizia, 1992).

Until further research is conducted, we generally recommend that persons who report that they are experiencing high stress, as compared to their usual levels, consider delaying weight reduction until the stressor has passed. As noted previously, weight loss requires a significant amount of time and effort, which a patient may not have under times of significant stress. Treatment during this time may serve primarily to prevent weight gain.

There are both formal and informal ways of assessing stress. We typically ask patients whether they are experiencing stress in relation to several domains (e.g., work, health, spouse or significant other, children, parents, financial or legal trouble, school moving, or other areas). We also ask patients to anticipate how stressful their life will be in the next six months and how much time per week they will be able to devote to weight control efforts. A formal assessment can also be conducted using the 10-item version of Cohen's Perceived Stress Scale (Cohen, Kamarck, & Mermelstein, 1983; Cohen & Williamson, 1988). This brief scale assesses perceptions of stress over the past month. It has been found to have adequate reliability and validity (Cohen et al., 1983; Cohen & Williamson, 1988).

Other Barriers

In evaluating the timing for weight loss, another factor that should be considered is the patient's travel or vacation schedule. If a behavioral intervention is to be used, the individual should be able to attend clinic at least every other week or on a weekly basis. It is critical that patients get off to a successful start, which may be facilitated by continuity of care during the first few months. Initial weight loss is associated with long-term success (Jeffery, Wing, & Mayer, 1998; Wadden & Letizia, 1992).

Summarizing Temporal Factors

In a minority of people presenting for treatment, the timing for weight control may be inappropriate. Patients who are experiencing significant stress should be commended for seeking weight loss treatment but advised that they may be more successful if they wait until the stressor has passed. If there are few life stressors present and the patient appears motivated, the timing is likely favorable.

TREATMENT GOALS

Before discussing treatment options, the practitioner should review patients' expectations for treatment. Research has found that patients expect to lose approximately 30% of their initial body weight (Foster, Wadden, Phelan, Sarwer, & Sanderson, 2001; Foster, Wadden, Vogt, & Brewer, 1997). However, losses of this size are consistently produced only by surgical interventions. Standard behavioral programs induce about a 10% weight loss (Wadden, Sarwer, & Berkowitz, 1999; Wing, 1998).

The difference between patients' expectations and probable treatment outcome need not be completely reconciled. It is important not to extinguish motivation for change by overemphasizing the unlikelihood of meeting large weight loss goals (Phelan & Foster, 2001). Rather, the clinician should assess the degree to which the patient would be willing to accept smaller outcomes as successful and discuss how maintaining the patient's desired amount of weight loss could be difficult. The practitioner can stress that losing 10% of initial body weight is related to significant physical and psychosocial improvement (NHLBI, 1998). A modest weight loss goal should be considered as a first step, after which additional weight loss can be considered.

SELECTING THE BEST TREATMENT

Following discussion of the patient's weight loss goals, treatment options may be discussed. A variety of interventions are available, as reviewed by Sarwer, Foster, and Wadden in Chapter 21. As a general rule, more intensive therapy is recommended for individuals with higher BMIs who are at greater risk of health problems (NHLBI, 1998). Thus, the practitioner may discuss bariatric surgery with persons with a BMI > 40 kg/m^2, who have lost and regained weight repeatedly and who have adverse physical consequences of their obesity. A portion-controlled diet, followed by pharmacotherapy for weight maintenance, would be recommended for patients who are uncomfortable with bariatric surgery. At the other end of the continuum, patients with a BMI < 30 kg/m^2 might be advised to participate in a behavioral weight loss program.

There is little evidence that matching patients' preference for individual or group treatment affects their treatment outcome (Renjilian et al., 2001). Nonetheless, patients' preferences will likely play a role in the type of treatment they ultimately decide to pursue. Once a recommendation is made, patients should be given time to consider the recommendation before committing to it. If necessary, a second meeting can be set to discuss the treatment options and answer any questions.

After a treatment is selected, the practitioner should provide an overview of the course of treatment. This includes discussing the duration and frequency of treatment visits, the "homework" that patients will be asked to complete (e.g., keeping food records), and the expected results of therapy, including weight loss and improvements in physical and psychological functioning. Patients should be encouraged to ask questions about the proposed course of treatment.

In concluding the assessment, the practitioner should again provide the patient with the opportunity to ask any questions. Patients should leave the initial assessment having learned something new about their weight problem and with a good understanding of the course of treatment and what to expect next.

CONCLUSION

Characteristically, behavioral assessment is said to emphasize objective measurement, the reliability and validity of measures, and the Antecedent-Behavior-Consequence analysis of an individual patient's behavior. However, in practice, the assessment and treatment selection are based on a mixture of both objective and subjective assessments. As discussed, there are still unresolved questions about the relationship to weight loss of both biological and behavioral factors. More prospective research into the causes and correlates of obesity and how these relate to treatment outcome will yield better assessment conceptualization to facilitate clinical work with this population.

REFERENCES

American Psychiatric Association. (1994). *Diagnostic and statistical manual of mental disorders* (4th ed.). Washington, DC: Author.

Bandura, A. (1977). Self-efficacy: Toward a unifying theory of behavior change. *Psychological Review, 84,* 191–215.

Barofsky, I., Fontaine, K. R., & Cheskin, L. J. (1998). Pain in the obese: Impact on health-related quality of life. *Annals of Behavioral Medicine, 19,* 408–410.

Battle, K. E., & Brownell, K. D. (1996). Confronting a rising tide of eating disorders and obesity: Treatment vs. prevention and policy. *Addictive Behaviors, 21*(6), 755–765.

Beck, A. T., Steer, R. A., & Brown, G. K. (1996). *Manual for Beck Depression Inventory-II.* San Antonio, TX: Psychological Corporation.

Berteus Forslund, H., Lindroos, A. K., Sjostrom, L., & Lissner, L. (2002). Meal patterns and obesity in Swedish women: A simple instrument describing usual meal types, frequency and temporal distribution. *European Journal of Clinical Nutrition, 56*(8), 740–747.

Bhatnagar, D., Anand, I. S., Durrington, P. N., Patel, D. J., Wander, G. S., Mackness, M. J., et al. (1995). Coronary risk factors in people from Indian subcontinent living in west London and their siblings in India. *Lancet, 345*(8947), 405–409.

Birketvedt, G., Florholmen, J., Sundsfjord, J., Osterud, B., Dinges, D., Bilker, W., et al. (1999). Behavioral and neuroendocrine characteristics of the night-eating syndrome. *Journal of the American Medical Association, 282,* 657–663.

Bjorntorp, P. (1998). Etiology of the metabolic syndrome. In G. A. Bray, C. Bouchard, & W. P. T. James (Eds.), *Handbook of obesity* (pp. 573–600). New York: Marcel Dekker.

Bjorntorp, P., Calgren, G., Isaksson, B., Krotkiewski, M., Larsson, B., & Sjostrom, L. (1975). Effect of an energy reduced dietary regimen in relation to adipose tissue cellularity. *American Journal of Clinical Nutrition, 28,* 445–452.

Blackburn, G. L. (1995). Effects of weight loss on weight-related risk factors. In K. D. Brownell & C. G. Fairburn (Eds.), *Eating disorders and obesity: A comprehensive handbook* (pp. 406–410). New York: Guilford Press.

Blair, S. N. (1984). How to assess exercise habits and physical fitness. In J. D. Matarazzo, S. M. Weiss, J. A. Herd, & N. E. Miller (Eds.), *Behavioral health: A handbook of health enhancement and disease prevention* (pp. 424–427). New York: Wiley.

Blair, S. N., & Leermakers, E. A. (2002). Exercise and weight management. In T. A. Wadden & A. J. Stunkard (Eds.), *Handbook of obesity treatment* (pp. 283–300). New York: Guilford Press.

Block, G., Woods, M., Potosky, A., & Clifford, C. (1990). Validation of a self-administered diet history questionnaire using multiple diet records. *Journal of Clinical Epidemiology, 43,* 1327–1335.

Bouchard, C. (1994). Genetics of obesity: Overview and research direction. In C. Bouchard (Ed.), *The genetics of obesity* (pp. 223–233). Boca Raton, FL: CRC Press.

Brewerton, T. D., O'Neil, P. M., Dansky, B. S., & Kilpatrick, D. G. (1999). Links between morbid obesity, victimization, PTSD, major depression, and bulimia in a national sample of women. *Obesity Research, 7*(Suppl.), 56S.

Brosse, A. L., Sheets, E. S., Lett, H. S., & Blumenthal, J. A. (2002). Exercise and the treatment of clinical depression in adults: Recent findings and future directions. *Sports Medicine, 32*(12), 741–760.

Brownell, K. D. (1995). Exercise in the treatment of obesity. In K. D. Brownell & C. G. Fairburn (Eds.), *Eating disorders and obesity: A comprehensive handbook* (pp. 437–438). New York: Guilford Press.

Brownell, K. D. (1998). *The LEARN Program for weight control* (7th ed.). Dallas, TX: American Health.

Carmichael, H. E., Swinburn, B. A., & Wilson, M. R. (1998). Lower fat intake as a predictor of initial and sustained weight loss in obese subjects consuming an otherwise ad libitum diet. *Journal of American Dietetic Association, 98*(1), 35–39.

Carmody, T. P., Brunner, R. L., & St. Jeor, S. T. (1995). Dietary helplessness and disinhibition in weight cyclers and maintainers. *International Journal of Eating Disorders, 18*(3), 247–256.

Cash, T. F. (1994). *The Multidimensional Body-Self Relations Questionnaire users' manual.* Norfolk, VA: Old Dominion University.

Choban, P. S., Onyejekwe, J., Burge, J. C., & Flancbaum, L. (1999). A health status assessment of the impact of weight loss following Roux-en-Y gastric bypass for clinically severe obesity. *Journal of the American College of Surgeons, 188*(5), 491–497.

Clark, M. M., Abrams, D. B., Niaura, R. S., Eaton, C. A., & Rossi, J. S. (1991). Self-efficacy in weight management. *Journal of Consulting and Clinical Psychology, 59,* 739–744.

Clark, M. M., Guise, B. J., & Niaura, R. S. (1995). Obesity level and attrition: Support for patient-treatment matching in obesity treatment. *Obesity Research, 3*(1), 63–64.

Clark, M. M., Niaura, R., King, T. K., & Pera, V. (1996). Depression, smoking, activity level, and health status: Pretreatment predictors of attrition in obesity treatment. *Addictive Behaviors, 21*(4), 509–513.

Cohen, S., Kamarck, T., & Mermelstein, R. (1983). A global measure of perceived stress. *Journal of Health and Social Behavior, 24,* 385–396.

Cohen, S., & Williamson, G. (1988). Perceived stress in a probability sample of the United States. In S. Spacapam & S. Oskamp (Eds.), *The social psychology of health: Claremont Symposium on applied social psychology.* Newbury Park, CA: Sage.

Crawford, D., Jeffery, R. W., & French, S. A. (2000). Can anyone successfully control their weight? Findings of a three year community-based study of men and women. *International Journal of Obesity and Related Metabolic Disorders, 24,* 1107–1110.

Despres, J., Moorjani, S., Lupien, P. J., Tremblay, A., Nadeau, A., & Bouchard, C. (1990). Regional distribution of body fat, plasma lipoproteins, and cardiovascular disease. *Arteriosclerosis, 10*(4), 497–511.

Dietz, W. H., & Gortmaker, S. L. (1985). Do we fatten our children at the television set? Obesity and television viewing in children and adolescents. *Pediatrics, 75,* 807–812.

Dishman, R. K., & Sallis, J. F. (1994). Determinants and interventions for physical activity and exercise. In C. Bouchard, R. J. Shephard, & T. Stephens (Eds.), *Physical activity, fitness, and health* (pp. 214–238). Champaign, IL: Human Kinetics.

Ditschuneit, H. H., Flechtner-Mors, M., & Adler, G. (1999). Metabolic and weight loss effects of long-term dietary intervention in obese subjects. *American Journal of Clinical Nutrition, 69,* 198–204.

Edell, B. H., Edington, S., Herd, B., O'Brien, R. M., & Witkin, G. (1987). Self-efficacy and self-motivation as predictors of weight loss. *Addictive Behaviors, 12,* 63–66.

Ek, A., Andersson, I., Barkeling, B., & Rossner, S. (1996). Obesity treatment and attrition: No relationship to obesity level. *Obesity Research, 4*(3), 295–296.

Felitti, V. J. (1993). Childhood sexual abuse, depression, and family dysfunction in obese persons. *Southern Medical Journal, 86,* 732–736.

Fitzgibbon, M. L., Stolley, M. R., & Kirschenbaum, D. S. (1993). Obese people who seek treatment have different characteristics than those who do not seek treatment. *Health Psychology, 12*(5), 342–345.

Flegal, K. M., Carroll, M. D., Kuczmarski, R. J., & Johnson, C. L. (1998). Overweight and obesity in the United States: Prevalence and trends, 1960–1994. *International Journal of Obesity and Related Metabolic Disorders, 22*(1), 39–47.

Fogelholm, M., Kukkonen-Harjula, K., & Oja, P. (1999). Eating control and physical activity as determinants of short-term weight maintenance after a very-low-calorie diet among obese women. *International Journal of Obesity and Related Metabolic Disorders, 23,* 203–210.

Fontaine, K. R., Barofsky, I., Anderson, R. E., Bartlett, S. J., Wiersema, L., Cheskin, L. J., et al. (1999). Impact of weight loss on health-related quality of life. *Quality of Life Research, 8*(3), 275–277.

Foreyt, J. P., & Goodrick, K. G. (1991). Factors common to successful therapy for the obese patient. *Medicine and Science in Sports and Exercise, 23*(3), 292–297.

Foreyt, J. P., Mitchell, R. E., Garner, K. T., Gee, M., Scott, L. W., & Gotto, A. M. (1982). Behavioral treatment of obesity: Results and limitations. *Behavioral Therapy, 13,* 153–161.

Forster, J. L., & Jeffery, R. W. (1986). Gender differences related to weight history, eating patterns, efficacy expectations, self-esteem, and weight loss among participants in a weight reduction program. *Addictive Behaviors, 11,* 141–147.

Foster, G. D., Wadden, T. A., Phelan, S., Sarwer, D. B., & Sanderson, R. S. (2001). Obese patients' perceptions of treatment outcomes and the factors that influence them. *Archives of Internal Medicine, 161*(17), 2133–2139.

Foster, G. D., Wadden, T. A., & Vogt, R. A. (1997). Body image in obese women before, during, and after weight loss treatment. *Health Psychology, 16*(3), 226–229.

Foster, G. D., Wadden, T. A., Vogt, R. A., & Brewer, G. (1997). What is a reasonable weight loss? Patients' expectations and evaluations of obesity treatment outcomes. *Journal of Consulting and Clinical Psychology, 65*(1), 79–85.

French, S. A., Jeffery, R. W., & Wing, R. R. (1994). Sex differences among participants in a weight-control program. *Addictive Behaviors, 19*(2), 147–158.

Friedman, M. A., & Brownell, K. D. (1995). Psychological correlates of obesity: Moving to the next research generation. *Psychological Bulletin, 117,* 3–20.

Gladis, N. M., Wadden, T. A., Vogt, R., Foster, G., Kuehnel, R. H., & Bartlett, S. J. (1998). Behavioral treatment of obese binge eaters: Do they need different care? *Journal of Psychosomatic Research, 44,* 375–384.

Glynn, S. M., & Ruderman, A. J. (1986). The development and validation of an eating self-efficacy scale. *Cognitive Therapy and Research, 10,* 403–420.

Golay, A., & Bobbioni, E. (1997). The role of dietary fat in obesity. *International Journal of Obesity and Related Metabolic Disorders, 21*(S3), S2–S11.

Gormally, J., Rardin, D., & Black, S. (1980). Correlates of successful response to a behavioral weight control clinic. *Journal of Counseling Psychology, 27,* 179–191.

Gortmaker, S. L., Must, A., Sobol, A. M., Peterson, K., Colditz, G. A., & Dietz, W. H. (1996). Television viewing as a cause of increasing obesity among children in the United States, 1986–1990. *Archives of Pediatrics and Adolescent Medicine, 150*(4), 356–362.

Guare, J. C., Wing, R. R., & Grant, A. (1995). Comparison of obese NIDDM and nondiabetic women: Short- and long-term weight loss. *Obesity Research, 3*(4), 329–335.

Guo, S. S., Roche, A. F., Chumlea, W. C., Gardner, J. C., & Siervogel, R. M. (1994). The predictive value of childhood body mass index values for overweight at age 35. *American Journal of Clinical Nutrition, 59,* 810–819.

Hashimoto, N., Kawasaki, T., Kikuchi, T., Takahashi, H., & Uchivama, M. (1995). Influence of parental obesity on the physical constitution of preschool children in Japan. *Acta Paediatrica Japonica, 37*(2), 150–153.

Hill, J. O., Wyatt, H. R., & Melanson, E. L. (2000). Genetic and environmental contributions to obesity. *Medical Clinics of North America, 84*(2), 333–346.

Hoie, L. H., & Bruusgaard, D. (1999). Predictors of long-term weight reduction in obese patients after initial very-low-calorie diet. *Advances in Therapy, 16*(6), 285–289.

Jeffery, R. W., Wing, R. R., & Mayer, R. R. (1998). Are smaller weight losses or more achievable weight loss goals better in the long term for obese patients? *Journal of Consulting and Clinical Psychology, 66*(4), 641–645.

Kanders, B., & Blackburn, G. L. (1992). Reducing primary risk factors by therapeutic weight loss. In T. A. Wadden & T. B. VanItallie (Eds.), *Treatment of the seriously obese patient* (pp. 213–230). New York: Guilford Press.

Karlsson, J., Hallgren, P., Kral, J. G., Lindroos, A. K., Sjostrom, L., & Sullivan, M. (1994). Predictors and effects of long-term dieting on mental well-being and weight loss in obese women. *Appetite, 23,* 15–26.

Kayman, S., Bruvold, W., & Stern, J. S. (1990). Maintenance and relapse after weight loss in women: Behavioral aspects. *American Journal of Clinical Nutrition, 52,* 800–807.

Keesey, R. E. (1986). A set-point theory of obesity. In K. D. Brownell & J. P. Foreyt (Eds.), *Handbook of eating disorders* (pp. 63–87). New York: Basic Books.

Khan, M., St. Peter, J., Breen, G., Hartley, G., & Vessey, J. (1999). Diabetes disease stage predicts weight loss outcomes with long term appetite suppressants. *Diabetes, 48*(Suppl. 1), A308.

Kiernan, M., King, A. C., Kraemer, H. C., Stefanick, M., & Killen, J. D. (1998). Characteristics of successful and unsuccessful dieters: An application of signal detection methodology. *Annals of Behavioral Medicine, 20*(1), 1–6.

Klem, M. L., Wing, R. R., McGuire, M. T., Seagle, H. M., & Hill, J. O. (1997). A descriptive study of individuals successful at long-term maintenance of substantial weight loss. *American Journal of Clinical Nutrition, 66,* 239–246.

Kolotkin, R. L., Head, S., Hamilton, M., & Tse, C. J. (1995). Assessing the impact of weight on quality of life. *Obesity Research, 3,* 49–56.

Kolotkin, R. L., Meter, K., & Williams, G. R. (2001). Quality of life and obesity. *Obesity Reviews, 2,* 219–229.

Korkeila, M., Kaprio, J., Rissanen, A., Koskenvuo, M., & Sorensen, T. I. (1998). Predictors of major weight gain in adult Finns: Stress, life satisfaction and personality traits. *International Journal of Obesity and Related Metabolic Disorders, 22*(10), 949–957.

Krotkiewski, M., Sjostrom, L., Bjorntorp, P., Carlgren, G., Garellick, G., & Smith, U. (1977). Adipose tissue cellularity in relation to prognosis for weight reduction. *International Journal of Obesity and Related Metabolic Disorders, 1*(4), 395–416.

Lake, J. K., Power, C., & Cole, T. J. (1997). Child to adult body mass index in the 1958 British birth cohort: Associations with parental obesity. *Archives of Disease in Childhood, 77*(5), 376–381.

Lee, I.-M., & Paffenbarger, R. S. (1992). Change in body weight and longevity. *Journal of the American Medical Association, 268,* 2045–2049.

Le Pen, C., Levy, E., Loos, F., Banzet, M. N., & Basdevant, A. (1998). "Specific" scale compared with "generic" scale: A double measurement of the quality of life in a French community sample of obese subjects. *Journal of Epidemiology and Community Health,* *52*(7), 445–450.

Lichtman, S. W., Pisarska, K., Berman, E. R., Pestone, M., Dowling, H., Offenbacher, E., et al. (1992). Discrepancy between self-reported and actual caloric intake and exercise in obese subjects. *New England Journal of Medicine, 327*(27), 1893–1898.

Lissner, L., Levitsky, D. A., Strupp, B. J., Kalkwarf, H. J., & Roe, D. A. (1987). Dietary fat and the regulation of energy intake in human subjects. *American Journal of Clinical Nutrition, 46,* 886–892.

Mafeis, C., Talamini, G., & Tato, L. (1998). Influence of diet, physical activity, and parents' obesity on children's adiposity: A four-year longitudinal study. *International Journal of Obesity and Related Metabolic Disorders, 22*(8), 758–764.

Marcus, M. D., Wing, R. R., & Hopkins, J. (1988). Obese binge eaters: Affect, cognitions, and response to behavioral weight control. *Journal of Consulting and Clinical Psychology, 56,* 433–439.

McGuire, M. T., Wing, R. R., Klem, M. L., Lang, W., & Hill, J. O. (1999). What predicts weight regain in a group of successful weight losers? *Journal of Consulting and Clinical Psychology, 67*(2), 177–185.

McReynolds, W. T. (1983). Toward a psychology of obesity: Review of research on the role of personality and level of adjustment. *International Journal of Eating Disorders, 2,* 37–58.

Morgan, K. J., Zabik, M. E., & Stampley, G. L. (1986). The role of breakfast in the diet adequacy of the U.S. population. *Journal of the American College of Nutrition, 5,* 551–563.

Naslun, I., Hallgren, P., & Sjostrom, L. (1988). Fat-cell weight and number before and after gastric surgery for morbid obesity in women. *International Journal of Obesity, 12,* 191–197.

National Heart, Lung, and Blood Institute. (1998). Clinical guidelines on the identification, evaluation, and treatment of overweight and obesity in adults: The evidence report. *Obesity Research, 6,* 51S–210S.

Oettingen, G., & Wadden, T. A. (1991). Expectation, fantasy, and weight loss: Is the impact of positive thinking always positive? *Cognitive Therapy and Research, 15,* 167–175.

Ortega, R. M., Requejo, A. M., Lopez-Sobaler, A. M., Quintas, M. E., Andres, P., Redondo, M. R., et al. (1998). Difference in the breakfast habits of overweight/obese and normal weight schoolchildren. *International Journal of Vitamin and Nutrition Research, 68*(2), 125–132.

Paffenbarger, R. S., Wing, A. L., & Hyde, R. T. (1978). Physical activity as an index of heart attack risk in college alumni. *American Journal of Epidemiology, 108,* 161–175.

Pasman, W. J., Saris, W. H., & Westerterp-Plantega, M. S. (1999). Predictors of weight maintenance. *Obesity Research, 7*(1), 43–50.

Pekkarinen, T., Takala, I., & Mustajoki, P. (1996). Two year maintenance of weight loss after VLCD and behavioral therapy for obesity: Correlation to the scores of questionnaires measuring eating behavior. *International Journal of Obesity and Related Metabolic Disorders, 20,* 332–337.

Phelan, S., & Foster, G. (2001, March). *Improving body image and self-esteem in obese women.* Paper presented at the Society of Behavioral Medicine, Seattle, WA.

Pouliot, M. C., Despres, J., Lemieux, S., Moorjani, S., Bouchard, C., Tremblay, A., et al. (1994). Waist circumference and abdominal sagittal diameter: Best simple anthropometric indexes of abdominal visceral adipose tissue accumulation and related cardiovascular risk in men and women. *American Journal of Cardiology, 73,* 460–468.

Prentice, A. M., & Jebb, S. A. (1995). Obesity in Britain: Gluttony or sloth? *British Medical Journal, 311,* 437–439.

Price, J. H., Desmond, S. M., Krol, R. A., Snyder, F. F., & O'Connell, J. K. (1987). Family practice physicians' beliefs, attitudes and practices regarding obesity. *American Journal of Preventive Medicine, 3*(6), 215–220.

Pronk, N. P., & Wing, R. R. (1994). Physical activity and long-term maintenance of weight loss. *Obesity Research, 2*(6), 587–599.

Ramirez, E. M., & Rosen, J. C. (2001). A comparison of weight control and weight control plus body image therapy for obese men and women. *Journal of Consulting and Clinical Psychology, 69*(3), 440–446.

Rand, C. S. W., & MacGregor, A. M. C. (1990). Morbidly obese patients' perceptions of social discrimination before and after surgery for obesity. *Southern Medical Journal, 83,* 1390–1395.

Rand, C. S. W., MacGregor, A. M. C., & Stunkard, A. J. (1997). The night eating syndrome in the general population and among postoperative obesity surgery patients. *International Journal of Eating Disorders, 22,* 65–69.

Ravussin, E., Pratley, R. W., Maffei, M., Wang, H., Friedman, J. M., Bennett, P. H., et al. (1997). Relatively low plasma leptin concentrations precede weight gain in Pima Indians. *National Medicine, 3*(S2), 238–240.

Raynor, H. A., & Epstein, L. H. (2001). Dietary variety, energy regulation, and obesity. *Psychological Bulletin, 127*(3), 325–341.

Renaud, S., & Lanzmann-Petithory, D. (2001). Coronary heart disease: Dietary links and pathogenesis. *Public Health and Nutrition, 4*(2B), 459–474.

Renjilian, D. A., Perri, M. G., Nezu, A. M., McKelvey, W. F., Shermer, R. L., & Anton, S. D. (2001). Individual versus group therapy for obesity: Effects of matching participants to their treatment preferences. *Journal of Consulting and Clinical Psychology, 69*(4), 717–721.

Roehling, M. V. (1999). Weight-based discrimination in employment: Psychological and legal aspects. *Personnel Psychology, 52*(4), 969–1016.

Roger, P. (1999). Eating habits and appetite control: A psychobiological perspective. *Proceedings of the Nutrition Society, 58*(1), 59–67.

Rosen, J. C., & Reiter, J. (1996). Development of the Body Dysmorphic Disorder Examination. *Behavior Research and Therapy, 34,* 755–766.

Rothblum, E. D., Brand, P. A., Miller, C., & Oetjen, H. (1989). Results of the NAAFA survey on employment discrimination: Part II. *NAAFA Newsletter, 17,* 4–6.

Sansone, R. A., Sansone, L. A., & Fine, M. A. (1995). The relationship of obesity to borderline personality symptomology, self-harm behaviors, and sexual abuse in female subjects in a primary-care medical setting. *Journal of Personality Disorders, 9*(3), 254–265.

Schlundt, D. G., Hill, J. O., Sbrocco, T., Pope-Cordle, J., & Kasser, T. (1990). Obesity: A biogenetic or biobehavioral problem. *International Journal of Obesity, 14*(9), 815–828.

Schlundt, D. G., Sbrocco, T., & Bell, C. (1989). Identification of high-risk situations in a behavioral weight loss program: Application of the relapse prevention model. *International Journal of Obesity and Related Metabolic Disorders, 13,* 223–234.

Schoeller, D. A. (1988). Measurement of energy expenditure in free-living humans by using doubly labeled water. *Journal of Nutrition, 118,* 1278–1289.

Schoeller, D. A. (1995). Limitations in the assessment of dietary energy intake by self-report. *Metabolism, 44*(2), 18–22.

Schoeller, D. A., & Fjeld, C. R. (1991). Human energy metabolism: What have we learned from the doubly labeled water method? *Annual Review in Nutrition, 11,* 355–373.

Serdula, M. K., Ivery, D., Coates, R. J., Freedman, D. S., Williamson, D. F., & Byers, T. (1993). Do obese children become obese adults? A review of the literature. *Preventive Medicine, 22,* 167–177.

Sherwood, N. E., Jeffery, R. W., & Wing, R. R. (1999). Binge status as a predictor of weight loss treatment outcome. *International Journal of Obesity, 23,* 485–493.

Sjostrom, L. (1980). Fat cells and body weight. In A. J. Stunkard (Ed.), *Obesity* (pp. 72–100). Philadelphia: Saunders.

Spitzer, R. L., Devlin, M., Walsh, B. T., Hasin, D., Wing, R., Marcus, M., et al. (1992). Binge eating disorder: A multisite field trial of the diagnostic criteria. *International Journal of Eating Disorders, 11,* 191–203.

Spitzer, R. L., Yanovski, S. Z., Wadden, T. A., Marcus, M. D., Stunkard, A. J., Devlin, M., et al. (1993). Binge eating disorder: Its further validation in a multisite study. *International Journal of Eating Disorders, 13,* 137–153.

Stubbs, R. J., Harbron, C. G., & Murgatroyd, P. R. (1995). Covert manipulation of dietary fat and energy density: Effect of substrate flux and food intake in men eating ad libitum. *American Journal of Clinical Nutrition, 62,* 316–329.

Stunkard, A. J. (1959). Eating patterns and obesity. *Psychiatric Quarterly, 33,* 284–294.

Stunkard, A. J., & Mendelson, M. (1967). Obesity and the body image: Characteristics of disturbances in the body image of some obese persons. *American Journal of Psychiatry, 123,* 1296–1300.

Stunkard, A. J., Sorenson, T. I. A., Hanis, C., Teasdale, T. W., Chakraborty, R., Schull, W. J., et al. (1986). An adoption study of human obesity. *New England Journal of Medicine, 314,* 193–198.

Telch, C. F., & Agras, W. S. (1994). Obesity, binge eating and psychopathology: Are they related? *International Journal of Eating Disorders, 15*(1), 53–61.

Troiano, R. P., Flegal, K. M., Kuczmarski, R. J., Campbell, S. M., & Johnson, C. L. (1995, October). Overweight prevalence and trends for children and adolescents. *Archives of Pediatric and Adolescent Medicine, 149,* 1085–1091.

van der Kooy, K., & Seidell, J. (1993). Techniques for the measurement of visceral fat: A practical guide. *International Journal of Obesity, 17,* 187–196.

Wadden, T. A., Anderson, D. A., Foster, G. D., Bennett, A., Steinberg, C., & Sarwer, D. B. (2000). Obese women's perceptions of their physician's weight management attitudes and practices. *Archives of Family Medicine, 9,* 854–860.

Wadden, T. A., & Bartlett, S. J. (1992). Very-low-calorie diets: An overview and appraisal. In T. A. Wadden & T. B. VanItallie (Eds.), *Treatment of the seriously obese patient* (pp. 44–79). New York: Guilford Press.

Wadden, T. A., Bartlett, S. J., Letizia, K. A., Foster, G. D., Stunkard, A. J., & Conill, A. (1992). Relationship of dieting history to resting metabolic rate, body composition, eating behavior and subsequent weight loss. *American Journal of Clinical Nutrition, 56,* 2065–2115.

Wadden, T. A., & Foster, G. D. (1992). Behavioral assessment and treatment of markedly obese patients. In T. A. Wadden & T. B. VanItallie (Eds.), *Treatment of the seriously obese patient* (pp. 290–330). New York: Guilford Press.

Wadden, T. A., & Foster, G. D. (2001). *Weight and Lifestyle Inventory.* Philadelphia: University of Pennsylvania.

Wadden, T. A., Foster, G. D., & Letizia, K. A. (1992). Response of obese binge eaters to treatment by behavior therapy combined with very low calorie diet. *Journal of Consulting and Clinical Psychology, 60*(5), 808–811.

Wadden, T. A., Foster, G. D., & Letizia, K. A. (1994). One-year behavioral treatment of obesity: Comparison of moderate and severe caloric restrictions and the effects of weight maintenance therapy. *Journal of Consulting and Clinical Psychology, 62*(1), 165–171.

Wadden, T. A., Foster, G. D., Letizia, K. A., & Wilk, J. E. (1993). Metabolic and psychological characteristics of obese binge eaters. *International Journal of Eating Disorders, 14,* 17–25.

Wadden, T. A., & Letizia, K. A. (1992). Predictors of attrition and weight loss in persons treated by moderate and severe caloric restriction. In T. A. Wadden & T. B. VanItallie (Eds.), *Treatment of the seriously obese patient* (pp. 383–410). New York: Guilford Press.

Wadden, T. A., & Phelan, S. (2002). Behavioral assessment of the obese patient. In T. A. Wadden & A. J. Stunkard (Eds.), *Handbook of obesity treatment* (pp. 186–226). New York: Guilford Press.

Wadden, T. A., Sarwer, D. B., & Berkowitz, R. I. (1999). Behavioral treatment of the overweight patient. *Baillière's Clinical Endocrinology and Metabolism, 13,* 93–107.

Wadden, T. A., Vogt, R. A., Foster, G. D., & Anderson, D. A. (1998). Exercise and the maintenance of weight loss: 1-year follow-up of a controlled clinical trial. *Journal of Consulting and Clinical Psychology, 66*(2), 429–433.

Wadden, T. A., Womble, L. G., Stunkard, A. J., & Anderson, D. A. (2002). Psychosocial consequences of obesity and weight loss. In T. A. Wadden & A. J. Stunkard (Eds.), *Handbook of obesity treatment* (pp. 144–172). New York: Guilford Press.

Ware, J. E. (1993). *SF-36 Health Survey: Manual and Interpretation Guide.* Boston: Nimrod Press.

Ware, J. E., & Sherbourne, C. D. (1992). The MOS 36-item short-form health survey (SF-36). I: Conceptual framework and item selection. *Medical Care, 30*(6), 473–483.

Weinsier, R. L., Hunter, G. R., Desmond, R. A., Byrne, N. M., Zuckerman, P. A., & Darnel, B. E. (2002). Free-living activity energy expenditure in women successful and unsuccessful at maintaining a normal body weight. *American Journal of Clinical Nutrition, 75*(3), 499–504.

Weinsier, R. L., Hunter, G. R., Heini, A. F., Goran, M., & Sell, S. (1998). The etiology of obesity: Relative contribution of metabolic factors, diet, and physical activity. *American Journal of Medicine, 105*(2), 145–150.

Whitaker, R. C., Wright, J. A., Pepe, M. S., Seidel, K. D., & Dietz, W. H. (1997). Predicting obesity in young adulthood from childhood and parental obesity. *New England Journal of Medicine, 25,* 869–873.

Wiederman, M. W., Sansone, R. A., & Sansone, L. A. (1999). Obesity among sexually abused women: An adaptive function for some? *Women and Health, 29*(1), 29–100.

Wing, R. R. (1998). Behavioral approaches to the treatment of obesity. In G. A. Bray, C. Bouchard, & W. P. T. James (Eds.), *Handbook of obesity* (pp. 855–873). New York: Marcel Dekker.

Wing, R. R., & Jeffery, R. W. (1999). Benefits of recruiting participants with friends and increasing social support for weight loss and maintenance. *Journal of Consulting and Clinical Psychology, 67*(1), 132–138.

Wing, R. R., Shoemaker, M., Marcus, M. D., McDermott, M., & Gooding, W. (1990). Variables associated with weight loss and improvements in glycemic control in type II diabetic patients in behavioral weight control programs. *International Journal of Obesity and Related Metabolic Disorders, 14*(495), 503.

Wirth, A., & Steinmetz, B. (1998). Gender differences in changes in subcutaneous and intraabdominal fat during weight reduction: An ultrasound study. *Obesity Research, 6*(6), 393–399.

World Health Organization. (1998). *Obesity: Preventing and managing the global epidemic.* Geneva, Switzerland: Author.

Wyatt, H. R., Grunwald, G. K., Mosca, C. L., Klem, M., Wing, R. R., & Hill, J. O. (2002). Long-term weight loss and breakfast in subjects in the National Weight Control Registry. *Obesity Research, 10*(2), 78–82.

Yanovski, S. Z. (1993). Binge eating disorder: Current knowledge and future directions. *Obesity Research, 1,* 306–324.

Yass-Reed, E. M., Barry, N. J., & Dacey, C. M. (1993). Examination of pretreatment predictors of attrition in a VLCD and behavior therapy weight-loss program. *Addictive Behaviors, 18*(4), 431–435.

Chapter 21 ———————————————————————————

TREATMENT OF OBESITY I: ADULT OBESITY

DAVID B. SARWER, GARY D. FOSTER, AND THOMAS A. WADDEN

In the past decade, obesity has become a health epidemic in the United States. *Obesity* refers to an excess of body fat and is best categorized by the body mass index (BMI). BMI, the ratio of an individual's weight to height, is calculated by dividing weight in kilograms by height in meters squared (see Table 21.1). The National Heart, Lung, and Blood Institute of the National Institutes of Health (NHLBI, 1998) and the World Health Organization (WHO, 1998) define obesity as a BMI > 30.0 kg/m². (Individuals with a BMI between 25.0 and 29.9 kg/m² are considered overweight. Those with a BMI between 18.5 and 24.9 kg/m² are classified as normal weight.) The most recent statistics suggest that 65% of Americans are overweight and 31% are obese (Flegal, Carroll, Ogden, & Johnson, 2002). Adding additional concern to the problem of adult obesity is the likelihood that most of the 10% to 15% of children and adolescents who are now obese will remain obese in adulthood (Flegal, Carroll, Kuczmarski, & Johnson, 1998).

The prevalence of obesity is higher among women (34%) than men (28%; Flegal et al., 2002). Minority groups, particularly minority women, are disproportionately affected. Approximately 50% of African American women are obese, as compared to 40% of Hispanic American women and 30% of Caucasian women (Flegal et al., 2002). The differences among racial groups are smaller among men. Twenty-nine percent of Hispanic American men, 28% of African American men, and 27% of Caucasian men are obese (Flegal et al., 2002). Higher prevalence of obesity as compared to Caucasians has also been found in other minority groups in the United States, including Puerto Rican, Cuban American, American Indian, Alaskan Native, and Western Samoan (Kumanyika, 1994). Obesity is reaching epidemic proportions in other Westernized countries and is now spreading to less affluent countries in Central and South America (Popkin, 1994). There is little to suggest that the spread of obesity both within and outside the United States will slow in the future.

In our mass media, appearance-driven culture, excess body weight is frequently seen as an aesthetic issue. There is little doubt that body weight is related to body image. More significantly, however, obesity is strongly related to increased risk of morbidity and mortality (NHLBI, 1998). Obese individuals are at increased risk for, and frequently suffer from, a variety of significant health problems including cardiovascular disease (heart disease and hypertension), type 2 diabetes, osteoarthritis, sleep apnea,

Table 21.1 Body Mass Index

BMI Table

Weight (lb)

Height (ft/in)	120	130	140	150	160	170	180	190	200	210	220	230	240	250	260	270	280	290	300	310	320	330
4'5"	30	33	35	38	40	43	45	48	50	53	55	58	60	63	65	68	70	73	75	78	80	83
4'6"	29	31	34	36	39	41	43	46	48	51	53	56	58	60	63	65	68	70	72	75	77	80
4'7"	28	30	33	35	37	40	42	44	47	49	51	54	56	58	61	63	65	68	70	72	75	77
4'8"	27	29	31	34	36	38	40	43	45	47	49	52	54	56	58	61	63	65	67	70	72	74
4'9"	26	28	30	33	35	37	39	41	43	46	48	50	52	54	56	59	61	63	65	67	69	72
4'10"	25	27	29	31	34	36	38	40	42	44	46	48	50	52	54	57	59	61	63	65	67	69
4'11"	24	26	28	30	32	34	36	38	40	43	45	47	49	51	53	55	57	59	61	63	65	67
5'0"	24	25	27	29	31	33	35	37	39	41	43	45	47	49	51	53	55	57	59	61	63	65
5'1"	23	25	26	28	30	32	34	36	38	40	42	44	45	47	49	51	53	55	57	59	61	62
5'2"	22	24	25	27	29	31	33	35	37	38	40	42	44	46	48	49	51	53	55	57	59	60
5'3"	21	23	25	27	28	30	32	34	36	37	39	41	43	44	46	48	50	51	53	55	57	59
5'4"	21	22	24	26	28	29	31	33	34	36	38	40	41	43	45	46	48	50	52	53	55	57
5'5"	20	22	23	25	27	28	30	32	33	35	37	38	40	42	43	45	47	48	50	52	53	55
5'6"	19	21	23	24	26	27	29	31	32	34	36	37	39	40	42	44	45	47	48	50	52	53
5'7"	19	20	22	24	25	27	28	30	31	33	35	36	38	39	41	42	44	46	47	49	50	52
5'8"	18	20	21	23	24	26	27	29	30	32	34	35	37	38	40	41	43	44	46	47	49	50
5'9"	18	19	21	22	24	25	27	28	30	31	33	34	36	37	38	40	41	43	44	46	47	49
5'10"	17	19	20	22	23	24	26	27	29	30	32	33	35	36	37	39	40	42	43	45	46	47
5'11"	17	18	20	21	22	24	25	27	28	29	31	32	34	35	36	38	39	41	42	43	45	46
6'0"	16	18	19	20	22	23	24	26	27	29	30	31	33	34	36	37	38	39	41	42	43	45
6'1"	16	17	19	20	21	22	24	25	26	28	29	30	32	33	34	36	37	38	40	41	42	44
6'2"	15	17	18	19	21	22	23	24	26	27	28	30	31	32	33	35	36	37	39	40	41	42
6'3"	15	16	18	19	20	21	23	24	25	26	28	29	30	31	33	34	35	36	38	39	40	41
6'4"	15	16	17	18	20	21	22	23	24	26	27	28	29	31	32	33	34	35	37	38	39	40
6'5"	14	15	17	18	19	20	21	23	24	25	26	27	29	30	31	32	33	34	36	37	38	39
6'6"	14	15	16	17	19	20	21	22	23	24	25	26	27	29	30	31	32	33	35	36	37	38
6'7"	14	15	16	17	18	19	20	21	23	24	25	26	27	28	29	30	31	32	34	35	36	37
6'8"	13	14	15	17	18	19	20	21	22	23	24	25	26	28	29	30	31	32	33	34	35	36
6'9"	13	14	15	16	17	18	19	20	21	23	25	25	26	27	28	29	30	31	32	33	34	35
6'10"	13	14	15	16	17	18	19	20	21	22	24	24	25	26	27	28	29	30	31	32	34	35

Less risk → More risk

422

and certain cancers. Obese individuals also are at increased risk for death. Among nonsmokers between the ages of 45 and 75, the risk of death increases linearly with BMI; the risk is even greater among smokers (Stevens et al., 1998). Individuals with a BMI of 30 kg/m^2, as compared to those with a normal BMI, have a 30% greater risk of death. For those with a BMI > 40 kg/m^2, the risk of premature death is approximately 100% greater (Manson et al., 1995).

This chapter reviews the treatment of excess body weight and obesity in adults. We begin with a discussion of goals for treatment, which are typically established following a comprehensive assessment (Phelan & Wadden, Chapter 20, this volume; Wadden & Phelan, 2002). We outline treatment algorithms that have been developed to assist providers in recommending appropriate treatments based on a patient's BMI and weight-related health problems. We detail treatments for individuals who are overweight, those who are obese, and those who are severely obese and may warrant surgical treatment. The chapter concludes with a discussion of the treatment of additional weight-related issues, such as binge eating disorder and body image dissatisfaction.

WEIGHT LOSS TREATMENT GOALS

Before the onset of any weight loss effort, overweight or obese individuals should establish goals for treatment. Ideally, these goals are developed in consultation with a health care provider (e.g., physician, psychologist, or dietitian) following a thorough physical and psychological assessment (Phelan & Wadden, Chapter 20, this volume). The NHLBI guidelines, developed by an expert panel, recommend two specific goals for treatment (NHLBI, 1998). The first is for overweight or obese individuals to lose 10% of their initial body weight within a six-month period. The second goal involves the prevention of weight regain, with the goal of maintaining a 5% reduction in weight at least six months after treatment.

A 10% weight loss is attainable for many obese individuals through a variety of treatment methods, as detailed later. Although considered a successful weight loss by many health professionals, this goal is frequently considered "disappointing" by many obese persons (Foster, Wadden, Vogt, & Brewer, 1997). Several studies have found that obese individuals frequently enter a weight loss program with the goal of losing 20% to 35% of their current weight (Foster, Wadden, Phelan, Sarwer, & Swain-Sanderson, 2001; Foster et al., 1997; Jeffery, Wing, & Mayer, 1998; O'Neil, Smith, Foster, & Anderson, 2000). Patients cling to this goal after being told repeatedly that they will likely lose only 10% to 15% of their weight (Wadden et al., in press). Patients' expectations of losing one-fifth to one-third of their body weight are wildly unrealistic for most treatment approaches short of bariatric surgery. Thus, one of the first, and perhaps greatest, challenges in working with obese patients is to help them develop realistic weight loss goals.

Encouragingly, weight losses of as little as 10% can frequently improve obesity-related comorbidities (e.g., hypertension, abnormal glucose tolerance, abnormal lipid concentrations; Agricultural Research Service, 1995; Blackburn, 1995; Institute of Medicine, 1995; NHLBI, 1998; WHO, 1998). The health benefits of these more realistic losses should be emphasized to patients before the onset of treatment. Patients who successfully lose 10% of their weight can attempt to lose additional weight. Patients should be cautioned, however, about striving to reach their ideal body weight—the former, traditional goal of weight reduction. Ideal body weights, and even body weights associated with significant events such as weddings and graduations, are often unattainable for the majority of obese patients (Sarwer, Allison, & Berkowitz, in press). Thus, patients should be reminded frequently that a 10% weight loss is considered successful. Failure to accept this as a satisfactory treatment outcome may lead to frustration and disappointment, which ultimately may be related to weigh regain. A 10% weight loss, however, may not improve psychosocial functioning of some patients to the desired extent. If further improvements in body image and self-esteem are desired, a referral for psychotherapy may be appropriate.

AN OBESITY TREATMENT ALGORITHM

The NHLBI guidelines provide specific recommendations for obesity treatment (NHLBI, 1998). Treatment options are considered based on the patient's BMI and the presence of significant comorbid medical conditions or risk factors. The patient's waist to hip ratio and fitness level also should be considered (NHLBI, 1998). Similar to these guidelines, Wadden, Brownell, and Foster (2002) have proposed an algorithm for selecting a weight loss intervention that is based on a patient's BMI and risk of obesity-related health problems (see Figure 21.1). It provides not only a suggested treatment but also more and less intensive treatment options based on other related factors. We use this scheme to organize our discussion of obesity treatments.

TREATMENTS FOR OVERWEIGHT PERSONS WITH A BODY MASS INDEX BETWEEN 25.0 AND 30.0 KG/M²

Overweight men and women have a variety of treatment options. These include diet and exercise programs that are self-directed or accompanied by physician counseling. Many overweight individuals enroll in commercial or other self-help programs. Others participate in behavior modification programs, typically in hospital-based settings.

Self-Directed Diet and Exercise Programs

Self-directed weight loss programs are likely the most frequently used treatment approach for overweight and obese individuals. Men and women who wish to lose weight encounter these programs from an endless number of sources—books, popular magazines, friends, family members, coworkers, and the Internet. Such popular diets recommend a range of caloric intake, from total fasts, very low-calorie diets (less than 800 kcal per day), low-calorie diets (between 800 and 1,200 kcal per day), to balanced-deficit diets (1,200 or more kcal per day). Total fasts are associated with significant health risks and are not recommended for weigh reduction (Melanson & Dwyer, 2002). Low- and very low-calorie diets are most appropriate for persons with BMIs > 30 kg/m², as discussed in detail later.

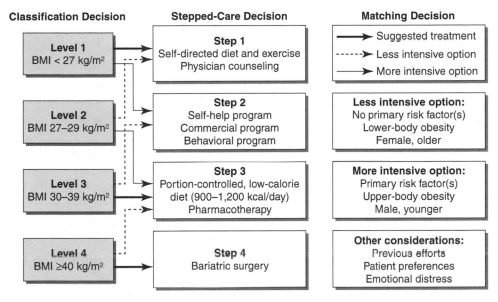

Figure 21.1   A Conceptual Scheme Showing a Three-Stage Process for Selecting a Treatment Approach. The first step, the Classification Decision, divides people into four levels based on body mass index (BMI). This level dictates which of four steps would be appropriate in the second stage, the Stepped-Care Decision. This indicates that the least intensive, costly, and risky approach will be used from among the treatment alternatives. The heavy solid arrow between the two boxes identifies the treatment most likely to be appropriate. The third stage, the Matching Decision, is used to make a final treatment selection, based on the assessment of the patient's need for weight reduction, as judged by the actual presence of comorbid conditions or other risk factors. The arrow (between boxes) with broken lines indicates a reduced need for weight reduction because of the absence of risk factors. The arrow with thin, solid lines shows the more intensive treatment option, appropriate for persons with a significant comorbid condition. For example, many patients with a BMI of 27 to 29 kg/m^2 do not have health complications. The appropriate treatment for such individuals would include a commercial program or a behavioral or self-help approach. By contrast, the practitioner may wish to consider pharmacotherapy for an individual with a BMI of 29 kg/m^2 who also has type II diabetes. Patients with significant psychiatric problems, or who want more support in changing diet and exercise habits, can be referred for adjunct care. Reprinted with permission of Thomas A. Wadden, PhD, Kelly Brownell, PhD, and Gary D. Foster, PhD.

Popular diet books promote a wide range of theories on the best approach to weight loss. These include high- and low-protein diets, high- and low-carbohydrate regimens, high-fat approaches, and meal plans based on the glycemic index. Some diet books, such as *Dr. Atkins' New Diet Revolution* (Atkins, 2002), cut across several categories. Such diets often wax and wane in popularity, often in the face of little, if any, empirical support for their efficacy (Freedman, King, & Kennedy, 2001). While they may help some individuals lose weight in the short term, few teach proper lifelong eating habits. Nevertheless, one or more weight loss books can usually be found on the bestseller list.

Balanced-deficit diets may be the most popular of the self-directed weight loss approaches. These approaches are referred to as "balanced" because the nutritional composition is similar to that recommended for nondieters. They are relatively low in fat (< 30% calories), moderate in protein (10% to 15% calories), and high in complex carbohydrates (> 55% calories) and fiber (25 to 30 g per day; Melanson & Dwyer, 2002). These approaches can be found in a variety of books and are frequently recommended by nutritionists and dietitians. Balanced-deficit diets are a cornerstone of many commercial and behavioral programs discussed later.

Some overweight individuals also increase their level of exercise in an attempt to lose weight, either alone or in combination with a reduction in food intake. Many overweight individuals erroneously believe that an increase in activity level in and of itself will produce significant weight loss. In fact, most studies suggest that increasing physical activity without a reduction in caloric intake produces only modest weight losses (Blair & Leermakers, 2002). The addition of a modest amount of exercise (30 to 60 minutes per day, three times per week) to a balanced-deficit diet increases weight loss by approximately 2 kg (NHLBI, 1998). Although statistics suggest little change in the level of physical activity among Americans over the past several decades (U.S. Department of Health and Human Services, 1996), many investigators believe that we have developed increasing sedentary habits (e.g., television, the Internet, video and computer games) that have contributed to our obesity epidemic (Blair & Leermakers, 2002).

The *LEARN Program for Weight Management 2000,* developed by Brownell (2000), is a self-help manual that includes both a balanced-deficit diet and physical activity recommendations for a 16-week period. It also provides specific suggestions to identify and alter maladaptive weight-related behaviors. Readers of the manual enrolled in a weekly group behavioral modification program have lost approximately 7 to 10 kgs (Brownell, Heckerman, Westlake, Hayes, & Monti, 1978; Brownell & Stunkard, 1981; Wadden, Foster, & Letizia, 1994). Unfortunately, the program appears to be less effective when used without behavioral modification classes and weekly weigh-ins (Wing, Venditti, Jakicic, Polley, & Lang, 1998).

Given the lack of research on most self-directed diet and exercise programs, it is impossible to reach conclusions about their effectiveness. While these approaches may produce a weight loss initially, patients likely fail to maintain these losses over the long term. Our collective clinical experience supports this. Most obese patients who present for more intensive behavioral, pharmacologic, or surgical treatment typically report a long history of failed self-directed weight loss efforts.

Physician Counseling

Primary care physicians, as well as obstetrician/gynecologists and internal medicine physicians, would appear to be valuable resources for overweight individuals who wish to lose weight. In reality, the vast majority of primary care physicians do not assist patients with weight loss (Aronne, 2002). Doctors may encourage patients to lose weight or make treatment recommendations, but they rarely provide counseling. This is likely the result of a variety of factors (Aronne, 2002). Many physicians lack specific training in weight loss; others see treatment as ineffective and time-consuming. Weight loss treatment is typically not a reimbursable charge to health insurance, further decreasing the motivation for physicians to offer treatment.

Moreover, several studies have suggested that many physicians hold negative attitudes about their overweight and obese patients (for a detailed review, see Puhl & Brownell, 2001). Some practitioners believe that patients have caused their weight problems by not eating a healthy diet. Others hold the more stigmatizing view that obesity is the result of a moral failing or patients' inability to control their impulses (e.g., Harris, Hamaday, & Mochan, 1999; Price, Desmond, Krol, Snyder, & O'Connell, 1987). While physicians may not overtly share these attitudes with their patients, they likely are communicated in some fashion. Overweight and obese patients are typically dissatisfied with the weight loss care they receive from their physicians (Wadden et al., 2000). Others likely do not turn to their physicians for weight loss treatment (Rand & MacGregor, 1990; Wadden et al., 2000).

Despite these barriers, physicians can play a central role in the treatment of the obesity epidemic (Aronne, 2002; Sarwer, Womble, & Berkowitz, 2001; Wadden et al., 2000). At a minimum, physicians should be able to provide a comprehensive assessment of the health problems associated with excess body weight. In addition, they should be prepared to assess the biological, environmental, and social/psychological factors that influence a patient's body weight (Phelan & Wadden, Chapter 20, this volume; Sarwer et al., 2001; Wadden & Phelan, 2002). Ideally, physicians will be actively involved in helping patients develop realistic treatment goals and counseling patients on their eating and exercise habits (Sarwer et al., 2001). The efficacy of physician counseling for weight loss, however, is unknown. Physicians not interested in providing active treatment can play a role in weight reduction by providing specific treatment recommendations, including referrals to professionals such as nutritionists, dietitians, and mental health professionals.

Commercial and Self-Help Programs

Like self-directed weight loss approaches, commercial and self-help programs are very popular treatment options for overweight and obese persons. These programs, often designed by medical professionals, typically focus on diet and lifestyle modification. Treatment, however, is typically provided by laypersons (Womble, Wang, & Wadden, 2002). Therefore, these programs are most appropriate for overweight individuals without significant health problems.

Commercial Programs

Examples of popular commercial programs include Weight Watchers, Jenny Craig, and L.A. Weight Loss. While similar, these programs vary in recommended diet (some require the purchase of the company's food; others do not), structure of counseling, and cost (Womble et al., 2002). Of these programs, Weight Watchers is the largest, reportedly having enrolled more than 25 million people throughout the world in the past 40 years (Weight Watchers International, 2000). It is also the only commercial program we are aware of with published data supporting the efficacy of the program. As compared to persons enrolled in a self-help program, Weight Watchers' participants lost significantly more weight after one year of treatment (5.0 kg v. 1.7 kg; Heshka et al., 2000). Two studies of "lifetime members," who maintained their goal weight for at least six weeks after completing the program, indicated that 19% to 37% were within five pounds of their goal weight at least five years after treatment (Christakis & Miller-Kovach, 1996; Lowe, Miller-Kovach, Frye, & Phelan, 1999).

Self-Help Programs

Similar to commercial programs, self-help programs offer treatment by laypersons, many of whom also struggle with their weight and are "graduates" of the program. These programs are based on the belief that persons with the same conditions can provide understanding in a way that those without the condition cannot. Overeaters Anonymous (OA) may be the most widely known self-help program. The 12-step treatment is modeled after Alcoholics Anonymous; the goal of OA is abstinence from compulsive overeating. Empirical support for the approach is limited.

Another popular self-help program is Take Off Pounds Sensibly (TOPS). Unlike OA, TOPS participants are encouraged to obtain a diet and exercise plan from their physicians. TOPS endorses the American Dietetic Association exchange program and has incorporated behavioral treatment components into its program. Although in existence for more than 50 years, only a few studies demonstrate the efficacy of the program.

Supermarket Self-Help

Overweight individuals also can find assistance with their weight loss efforts at the supermarket. A variety of portion-controlled, low calorie/low fat foods from a wide range of manufacturers are available, including lunch and dinner entrees, pantry foods, and even desserts (Womble et al., 2002). These products can help overweight individuals adhere to a reduced calorie goal and assist in weight loss (Metz et al., 1997).

Another increasingly popular option is the use of meal replacement drinks or bars. These products typically contain approximately 200 to 250 kcal per serving and include no stimulants or appetite suppressants. The SlimFast Plan, for example, encourages consumers to use SlimFast for breakfast or lunch and to eat a sensible dinner. Recommended total caloric intake is 1,200 kcal per day, an amount that can produce a weight loss of 1 to 2 lbs per week. Several studies suggest the potential effectiveness of this approach (Ditschuneit, Flechtner-Mors, Johnson, & Adler, 1999; Flechtner-Mors, Ditschuneit, Johnson, Suchard, & Adler, 2000; Heber, Ashley, Wang, & Elashoff, 1994), although further research is needed.

Web-Based Programs

Just as the Internet has invaded many areas of daily life, it also has found a place in weight loss. Nutri/Systems Inc., once a popular commercial weight loss program, reorganized in 1999 as www.nutrisystem.com and is now an entirely online company (Womble et al., 2002). Another popular Internet-based program is www.eDiets.com. The Web site has many features. It provides subscribers with customized diets, shopping lists, and a virtual visit with a dietitian. The site also gives weekly recommendations for a walking program. It has a variety of other interactive features, including online chats, newsletters, and a help desk. Programs such as these potentially show great promise, and their efficacy is currently being investigated.

Behavioral Treatment

Behavior modification strategies play a central role in most successful weight loss programs. Behaviorally based treatment is one of the most widely researched interventions, the focus of hundreds of clinical trials over the past several decades. These programs include well-known treatment components, including self-monitoring, problem solving, stimulus control, and social support. In addition, cognitive interventions are often used to address issues such as emotional eating. These programs often incorporate treatment manuals, such as the *LEARN Program for Weight Control* (Brownell, 2000). The primary goal of treatment is to help individuals identify and modify inappropriate eating, exercise, and thinking habits that contribute to their weight problem (Sarwer & Wadden, 1999).

Behavioral treatment can be provided individually or in a group format. Both approaches have pros and cons. Individual treatment provides patients with more one-on-one time. It also provides patients with a forum in which they can comfortably discuss other related issues with the treatment provider. Group treatment provides patients with a sense that they are not alone in their struggles with their weight. Treatment groups often develop a sense of camaraderie that may positively impact adherence to treatment. The most definitive study of this issue found that group treatment was superior to individual treatment (Renjilian et al., 2001).

There are several elements to behavioral treatment. Our discussion here focuses on three central components—self-monitoring, nutrition counseling, and physical activity.

Self-Monitoring

Self-monitoring of daily food and beverage intake is likely the cornerstone of behavioral treatment for weight loss (Sarwer et al., in press; Sarwer & Wadden, 1999). In addition to recording what and how much they eat and drink each day, patients indicate the time, place, activity, and emotions experienced while eating. This more detailed monitoring allows patients to identify maladaptive eating patterns. Problem-solving and stimulus control techniques can be taught to interrupt these patterns. Stimulus control is used to modify the precursors of eating to create a more restricted set of environmental events that trigger eating. More intensive cognitive-behavioral interventions may be required for those patients who resist keeping food records or for those who demonstrate more complex eating patterns triggered by frequent, strong emotional experiences (Sarwer et al., in press).

Nutrition Education

Most behavioral weight loss programs provide nutrition education to patients. Many behavioral programs provide patients with general information, often in the form of a balanced-deficit diet, rather than prescribe a rigid, low-calorie diet. The Food Guide Pyramid (National Livestock and Meat Board, 1993) is frequently used to provide guidelines for daily food intake. It instructs persons to consume 6 to 11 servings of bread, cereal, rice, and pasta; 3 to 5 servings of vegetables; 2 to 4 servings of fruit; 2 to 3 servings of milk, yogurt, and cheese; and 2 to 3 servings of meat, poultry, fish, and eggs each day. In September 2002, the National Academy of Sciences released new nutritional recommendations for the consumption of carbohydrates, fiber, and fat

(National Academy of Sciences, 2002). They recommend that adults consume at least 130 g per day of carbohydrates, 38 to 25 g per day of fiber, and limit fat intake to 20% to 35% of daily caloric intake.

Following these guidelines, dieting women and men usually limit their calories to 1,200 and 1,500 kcal, respectively (Nondieting women and men typically consume 1,800 and 2,500 kcal per day, respectively). In reducing caloric intake, dieters are encouraged to consume foods that they enjoy without avoiding "forbidden foods." Forbidden foods are typically high in fat and sugar content and include items such as chocolate, cookies, and ice cream, as well as other calorically dense products such as fast-food meals. Patients are encouraged to eat these foods in moderation and smaller portions.

Physical Activity

While the self-monitoring and nutritional components help patients reduce energy intake, physical activity increases energy expenditure. The physical and psychological benefits of regular exercise are well established; however, exercise may only modestly contribute to weight loss (NHLBI, 1998). Nevertheless, regular exercise appears to be an important part of long-term weight maintenance. Several studies suggest that patients who lose weight and keep it off exercise regularly (Ballor & Poehlman, 1994; Klem, Wing, McGuire, Seagle, & Hill, 1997; Saris, 1998).

Physical activity can be divided into two broad categories—programmed activity and lifestyle activity (Brownell, 2000). Programmed activity is the "traditional" form of exercise and involves regularly planned periods (i.e., 20 to 40 minutes) of physical exertion at a high intensity level (i.e., 60% to 80% maximum heart rate) such as running, swimming, and cycling. Lifestyle activity involves increasing activity throughout the day by practices such as taking the stairs and parking far from building entrances. The main goal of this form of activity is to increase energy expenditure without worrying about level of intensity. Increasing lifestyle activity may be particularly useful for overweight and obese individuals who do not enjoy programmed activity because of physical discomfort or psychological upset (Sarwer et al., in press).

Behavioral programs typically encourage patients to increase both forms of activity (Fox, 1992). Walking can be considered both a programmed and lifestyle activity and may be an ideal form of exercise for obese individuals. At least one study has found that a program of diet and increased lifestyle activity (30 minutes per day) may be just as beneficial to a person's health as a program consisting of diet plus vigorous activity (three step-aerobic classes per week; Andersen et al., 1999).

Treatment Outcomes

Most of the research on the efficacy of behavioral treatment has taken place in clinical trials conducted in university-based hospital settings. Reviews of controlled randomized trials have shown that participants lose an average of 9% of their starting body weight in 20 weeks of treatment (Sarwer & Wadden, 1999; Wadden, Sarwer, & Berkowitz, 1999; Wing, 2002). Unfortunately, patients typically regain about 30% to 35% of their weight in the year after treatment and frequently regain 100% of the weight lost within five years (Wadden, Sternberg, Letizia, Stunkard, & Foster, 1990). Several studies, however, have demonstrated the benefits of long-term behavioral treatment (Perri et al., 1988; Viegener et al., 1990; Wadden et al., 1994; Wing, Blair, Marcus, Epstein, & Harvey, 1994). For example, patients who attended group maintenance sessions every other week for one year following weight reduction maintained 13.0 kg of their 13.2 kg end-of-treatment weight loss. While extended treatment is beneficial, it does not increase weight loss beyond that achieved in the first 20 to 26 weeks. Moreover, long-term treatment appears to only delay, rather than prevent, weight regain (Perri et al., 1988; Wing et al., 1994). Participants in the study described previously regained 3 kg in the six months following termination of the weight maintenance program.

TREATMENTS FOR OBESE PERSONS WITH A BODY MASS INDEX BETWEEN 30.0 AND 40.0 KG/M^2

Individuals with a BMI between 30.0 and 40.0 kg/m^2 are defined clinically as obese. In addition to the less intensive treatment options described previously, two other treatments are appropriate: low- and very low-calorie diets and pharmacologic treatment.

Low- and Very Low-Calorie Diets

Low- (800 to 1,200 kcal per day) or very low- (800 kcal per day) calorie diets frequently use liquid meal replacement products (e.g., Optifast) to help patients reduce their caloric intake in a nutritious, safe manner. These programs are usually hospital-based and physician supervised. Patients typically use a liquid diet for 12 to 16 weeks, consuming four to six "shakes" a day. This provides patients with the recommended daily allowance of vitamins and minerals. During treatment, patients typically receive medical monitoring and nutritional counseling. Some programs restrict the consumption of regular food, while others encourage patients to have reduced calorie entrée and cup of salad for dinner. At the end of the treatment period, patients are returned to a 1,500 kcal per day diet.

Low- and very low-calorie diets are appealing to patients because they often produce a rapid initial weight loss. Several studies have found that patients on a very low-calorie diet lost approximately 15% to 20% of their weight after 8 to 12 weeks (Wadden et al., 1994; Wadden & Stunkard, 1986; Wing et al., 1991, 1994). Unfortunately, patients regain approximately 35% to 50% of their weight loss in the year following treatment (Wadden & Osei, 2002). Nonetheless, because of their large initial loss, participants may maintain a clinically significant weight loss for several years (Womble et al., 2002). Three years following treatment with the Optifast Core Program, 73% of men and 55% of women maintained a weight loss of 5% (Wadden & Frey, 1997). Similarly, a study of the Health Management Resources low-calorie diet program found 50% of participants three years after treatment and 35% of participants seven years after treatment maintained a 5% weight loss (Anderson, Vichitbandra, Qian, & Kryscio, 1999). Although these weight losses appear modest, they meet the criterion of successful weight maintenance proposed by the Institute of Medicine (1995).

Phamacologic Treatment

The pharmacologic treatment of obesity has a long and checkered past. Countless agents have been tried as potential weight loss drugs, often with disastrous results (Bray, 2002). Presently, the Food and Drug Administration has approved two medications for the long-term treatment of obesity. Sibutramine (Meridia) is a serotonin and norepi-nephrine reuptake inhibitor that increases feelings of fullness (i.e., satiation), ultimately resulting in a decrease in appetite (Lean, 1997). Orlistat (Xenical) is a gastrointestinal lipase inhibitor that prevents the absorption of fat in the digestive system (Sjostrom et al., 1998). (See Bray, 2002, for a detailed discussion of these medications, as well as other medications used for short-term weight loss.) Despite the very different mecha-nisms of action of these medications, studies have found that both produce weight losses of approximately 7% to 10% (i.e., Bray et al., 1996, 1999; Hill et al., 1999; James et al., 2000; Sjostrom et al., 1998).

These weight losses are similar to those seen with behavioral treatment. This is sur-prising to many individuals because weight loss medications are frequently touted by the mass media as the "magic bullet" for weight control (Sarwer & Wadden, 1999). Both medications, however, may be more effective than behavioral treatment in the long-term management of obesity. Patients who remain on medication beyond one year have been found to maintain losses of 7% to 8% of initial weight (Davidson et al., 1999; Jones, Smith, Kelly, & Gray, 1995; Sjostrom et al., 1998). This kind of weight mainte-nance is also possible for patients receiving behavioral care; however, it seems to take much more time and effort to sustain these losses. Thus, the greatest strength of phar-macotherapy may lie in its ability to help patients maintain weight loss (Wadden & Osei, 2002).

Recently, the efficacy of a combined pharmacologic and behavioral approach has been investigated. This combination makes intuitive sense. Phamacologic agents induce weight loss by modifying *internal* signals associated with eating. In contrast, behavioral modification induces weight loss by helping patients with their *external* environment (Wadden & Phelan, 2002). As the two treatments differ in their mechanisms of action, they may serve to augment each other and produce larger weight losses. A study of sibu-tramine (Wadden, Berkowitz, Sarwer, Prus-Wisniewski, & Steinberg, 2001) suggests that a combined approach to treatment may maximize patients' weight losses. This ap-proach may be particularly useful in a primary care setting, where physicians typically do not have the time and resources to provide intensive behavioral treatment (Wadden et al., 1997).

TREATMENT FOR OBESE PERSONS WITH A BODY MASS INDEX ABOVE 40.0 KG/M²

Bariatric surgery ("stomach stapling") is an increasingly popular option for individuals with severe obesity. Eligible patients must have a BMI ≥ 40 kg/m² or > 35 kg/m² with the presence of one or more obesity-related comorbidities (i.e., heart disease, hyperten-sion, type 2 diabetes, sleep apnea). Patients typically receive one of two basic surgical procedures. The vertical banded gastroplasty (VBG) involves the creation of a small stomach pouch at the base of the esophagus (approximately 30 to 50 ml in size), which severely limits food intake. The gastric bypass procedure also involves the creation of a small stomach pouch. However, the remaining area of the stomach and part of the intes-tine (duodenum) are bypassed by attaching the small pouch to the jejunum. The bypass works by not only limiting food intake but also creating malabsorption of calories. The typical weight losses associated with both procedures are between 25% and 35% of the patient's preoperative body weight (Albrecht & Pories, 1999; Kral, 1998). Several studies, however, have suggested that the bypass procedure results in significantly larger weight losses as compared to the VBG (e.g., Sugarman, Starkey, & Birkenhauer, 1987). Ten percent to 15% of patients who receive both procedures are thought to regain their lost weight or fail to reach an acceptable weight loss (Latifi, Kellum, DeMaria, & Sugarman, 2002). Cosmetic procedures such as liposuction are not a treatment for obesity because liposuction typically results in very modest weight losses.

Although these are surgical treatments, mental health professionals can play a significant role in the treatment of these patients pre- and postoperatively (Sarwer et al., in press). Many surgeons require patients to undergo a psychological evaluation before surgery. These evaluations are similar to the basic behavioral assessment described by Phelan and Wadden (see Chapter 20, this volume; Wadden et al., 2001). In the evaluation, several additional questions should be addressed:

- Has the patient exhausted more conservative treatment options?
- Is the patient free of psychopathology (most typically major depression) that may impact his or her ability to learn and adhere to the rigorous demands of the postoperative diet?
- Does the patient have an appreciation of the significant behavioral changes required to achieve a successful postoperative result?

If the answer to any of these questions is no, further education or psychological treatment should be recommended. Psychologists also may encounter bariatric surgery patients postoperatively, typically to address difficulties with the postoperative diet or other issues, such as depression or body image dissatisfaction (Sarwer et al., in press).

ADDITIONAL TREATMENT APPROACHES

The focus of obesity treatment is traditionally weight loss. Several issues related to an individual's obesity may warrant treatment in conjunction with weight reduction. Obese individuals who struggle with binge eating, night eating, and body image dissatisfaction can often receive treatment for these conditions as they are losing weight. Alternatively, nondieting approaches to treatment can help individuals improve their eating habits and enhance their self-esteem without losing weight.

Binge Eating Disorder

Obese persons may suffer from binge eating disorder (BED), which is currently a provisional diagnosis under additional research in the *Diagnostic and Statistical Manual of Mental Disorders* (*DSM-IV-TR*; American Psychiatric Association [APA], 2000). BED is defined as eating a very large amount of food in a discrete period of time (two hours), while feeling out of control. These episodes are accompanied by at least three of the following symptoms: eating much more rapidly than usual, eating until feeling uncomfortably full, eating large amounts of food when not physically hungry, eating alone because of embarrassment, and feeling disgusted with self, depressed, or very guilty after eating. These episodes are not accompanied by purging behaviors (i.e., vomiting, laxative abuse, or excessive exercise), distinguishing BED from bulimia nervosa. The diagnosis requires an average of two binges per week for a period of six months (APA, 2000).

Initial estimates suggested that approximately 30% of obese individuals presenting for weight loss treatment had BED (Spitzer et al., 1992). More recent studies that have used interview-based assessments of the diagnosis have found occurrence rates between 7% and 19% (Basdevant, Pouillon, & Lahlon, 1995; Brody, Walsh, & Devlin, 1994; Stunkard et al., 1996). Community-based studies suggest a prevalence rate of approximately 2% (Bruce & Agras, 1992; Spitzer et al., 1992). Some of the discrepancy in the rates of occurrence across the various studies may be a function of a lack of consensus on what constitutes an amount of food "definitely larger than what most people would eat during a similar period of time or under similar circumstances" (APA, 2000).

Cognitive-behavioral therapy, administered in individual, group, and self-help formats, is effective in the treatment of BED (Agras, Telch, Arnow, Eldredge, & Marnell, 1997; Carter & Fairburn, 1998; Fairburn, 1995; Marcus, Wing, & Fairburn, 1995; Wilfley et al., 1993). Interpersonal treatment approaches also have shown significant reductions in bingeing (Wilfley et al., 1993; Wilfley & Cohen, 1997). None of these interventions, however, typically produce significant weight loss. Pharmacotherapy, usually with antidepressants, may be effective in the short term, but once it is discontinued, the bingeing predictably returns (Alger, Schwalberg, Bigaouette, Michalek, & Howard, 1991; Hudson et al., 1998; Stunkard et al., 1996). Psychiatric comorbidity is common in persons with BED. If the comorbid conditions are severe enough, they should take priority in treatment because binge eating often decreases in response to treatment of other disorders (Stunkard & Allison, in press).

Night Eating Syndrome

Stunkard first described the night eating syndrome (NES) in 1955 (Stunkard, Grace, & Wolff, 1955). After almost a half century of little research, there has been renewed interest in the disorder. NES consists of several core symptoms, including morning anorexia, evening hyperphagia, and initial insomnia and/or inability to maintain sleep throughout the night. NES is often accompanied by a depressed mood, especially later in the day. While NES occurs in both normal weight and overweight individuals, the syndrome is thought to promote obesity (Stunkard, 2002). It is estimated to occur in approximately 1.5% of the general population (Rand, MacGregor, & Stunkard, 1997) but has been found in 15% of obese persons seeking weight loss treatment (Stunkard et al., 1996).

Evidence suggests a potential relationship between stress and NES. Cortisol, a stress-related hormone, is characteristically elevated (Allison et al., in press; Birketvedt et al., 1999). Melatonin and leptin, which typically rise at night to help maintain sleep and suppress appetite, respectively, do not increase as expected in persons with NES (Birketvedt et al., 1999). While melatonin is available as an over-the-counter treatment, anecdotal reports do not support its effectiveness.

Over-the-counter sleeping pills and hypnotics also do not appear to be effective. Formal treatments for NES are still in the developmental stage. Initial reports suggest that sertraline (Zoloft) may be effective in reducing NES (O'Reardon, Stunkard, & Allison, in press).

Body Image Dissatisfaction

Overweight and obese women frequently report heightened body image dissatisfaction (e.g., Foster et al., 1997; Sarwer, Wadden, & Foster, 1998). This dissatisfaction often has a detrimental impact on behavior. Overweight individuals frequently report extreme self-consciousness, excessive camouflaging, and avoidance of activity as a result of concerns about their weight and shape (Rosen, Orosan, & Reiter, 1995; Sarwer et al., 1998). For many individuals, this dissatisfaction is related to decreased self-esteem and increased depressive symptoms (Foster et al., 1997; Grilo, Wilfley, Brownell, & Rodin, 1994; Sarwer et al., 1998).

Body image dissatisfaction appears to play a significant role in motivating weight loss efforts (Sarwer & Thompson, 2002). Several studies have found that body image improves following weight reduction (Adami et al., 1994; Cash, 1994; Foster et al., 1997; Halmi, Long, Stunkard, & Mason, 1980). In contrast, other studies have suggested that cognitive-behavioral treatments that focus on self-esteem and body image can lead to improvements in body image in the absence of weight loss (Polivy & Herman, 1992; Rosen et al., 1995; Roughan, Seddon, & Vernon-Roberts, 1990). Ramirez and Rosen (2001) combined a behavioral weight control program with a cognitive-behavioral body image program that resulted in both a 10% weight loss and improvement in body image and self-esteem. This combined approach holds great promise in helping overweight and obese individuals effectively address the physical and psychological effects of obesity (Sarwer & Thompson, 2002).

Nondieting Approaches

Some have proposed that dieting should not be used in the treatment of obesity itself (Garner & Wooley, 1991; Polivy & Herman, 1992). This argument is based on the generally poor long-term results of weight loss efforts, as well as concerns that dieting may be associated with adverse physical or psychological effects, in addition to binge eating (Polivy & Herman, 1985). Few studies of obese dieters support the latter concerns (National Task Force on the Prevention and Treatment of Obesity, 2000). Nonetheless, several nondieting or undieting approaches have been proposed that, although differing in their specific methods, generally seek to:

1. Increase awareness about dieting's ill effects.
2. Provide education about the biological basis of body weight.
3. Help patients stop restricting their caloric intake and avoiding prohibited foods.
4. Encourage the use of internal cues such as hunger and fullness to guide eating rather than external cues such as calories or fat grams.

5. Improve self-esteem and body image through self-acceptance rather than through weight loss.

6. Increase physical activity (Foreyt & Goodrick, 1992; Foster & McGuckin, 2002; Hirschmann & Munter, 1988; Polivy & Herman, 1992).

The few available studies suggest that nondieting approaches produce significant psychosocial changes but have little effect on weight (see Foster & McGuckin, 2002, for a review). Physiological variables (e.g., lipids, fitness) are rarely studied. Nondieting approaches merit further investigation in randomized controlled trials. Such trials will need to clearly define what is meant by "dieting" and "nondieting" because the nondieting approaches and standard behavioral interventions for weight loss have more in common than might be thought (e.g., eating a variety of foods in moderation, using stimulus control, increasing physical activity).

SUMMARY

The rate of adult obesity in the United States has increased dramatically and has now reached epidemic proportions. Obesity is associated with increased rates of morbidity and mortality. Individuals seeking weight reduction have a variety of treatment options depending on their BMI, weight-related health problems, and previous weight loss experience. Self-directed, commercial, and self-help programs are likely the most widely used approaches but have little evidence to support their efficacy. Numerous studies of behavior modification have demonstrated its short-term efficacy, but it frequently fails to help patients maintain their weight losses over several years. Low- and very low-calorie diets, as well as pharmacologic treatment, are appropriate for some obese individuals. These approaches are also successful in the short term, but little evidence currently supports their effectiveness in long-term weight control. Bariatric surgery is an increasingly popular treatment for severely obese individuals who have failed with more conservative treatments. Patients lose approximately 30% of their body weight postoperatively and are frequently successful in maintaining these losses over many years. Obese individuals often suffer from related problems, including binge eating, night eating, and body image dissatisfaction, which may need treatment in conjunction with weight loss. Additional research on almost all weight loss treatments is warranted in an effort to stem the rapidly rising tide of adult obesity.

REFERENCES

Adami, G. F., Gandolfo, P., Campostano, A., Bauer, B., Cocchi, F., & Scopinaro, N. (1994). Eating Disorder Inventory in the assessment of psychosocial status in the obese patient prior to and at long-term following biliopancreatic diversion for obesity. *International Journal of Eating Disorders, 15,* 265–274.

Agras, W. S., Telch, C. F., Arnow, B., Eldredge, K., & Marnell, M. (1997). One-year follow-up of cognitive-behavioral therapy for obese individuals with binge eating disorder. *Journal of Consulting and Clinical Psychology, 65*(2), 343–347.

Agricultural Research Service. (1995). *Report of the Dietary Guidelines Advisory Committee on the Dietary Guidelines for Americans.*

Albrecht, R. J., & Pories, W. J. (1999). Surgical intervention for the severely obese. *Baillière's Clinical Endocrinology and Metabolism, 13,* 149–172.

Alger, S. A., Schwalberg, M. D., Bigaouette, J. M., Michalek, A. V., & Howard, I. J. (1991). Effect of a tricyclic antidepressant and opiate antagonist on binge-eating behavior: A double-blind, placebo-controlled study. *American Journal of Clinical Nutrition, 53,* 865–871.

Allison, K. C., O'Reardon, J. P., Dinges, D. S., & Stunkard, A. J. (in press). *Behavioral, psychosocial and neuroendocrine aspects of the Night Eating syndrome.* Manuscript submitted for publication.

American Psychiatric Association. (2000). *Diagnostic and statistical manual of mental disorders* (4th ed., text rev.). Washington, DC: Author.

Andersen, R. E., Wadden, T. A., Bartlett, S. J., Zemel, B. S., Verde, T. J., & Franckowiak, S. C. (1999). Effects of lifestyle activity vs. structured aerobic exercise in obese women: A randomized trial. *Journal of the American Medical Association, 281,* 335–340.

Anderson, J. W., Vichitbandra, S., Qian, W., & Kryscio, R. J. (1999). Long-term weight maintenance after an intensive weight-loss program. *Journal of the American College of Nutrition, 18,* 620–627.

Aronne, L. J. (2002). Treatment of obesity in the primary care setting. In T. A. Wadden & A. J. Stunkard (Eds.), *Handbook of obesity treatment* (pp. 383–394). New York: Guilford Press.

Atkins, R. C. (2002). *Dr. Atkins' new diet revolution* (3rd ed.). New York: Avon Books.

Ballor, D. L., & Poehlman, E. T. (1994). Exercise training enhances fat-free mass preservation during diet-induced weight loss: A meta-analytical finding. *International Journal of Eating Disorders, 18,* 35–40.

Basdevant, A., Pouillon, M., & Lahlon, W. (1995). Prevalence of binge eating disorder in different populations of French women. *International Journal of Eating Disorders, 18,* 309–315.

Birketvedt, G., Florholmen, J., Sundsfjord, J., Osterud, B., Dinges, D., Bilker, W., et al. (1999). Behavioral and neuroendocrine characteristics of the night-eating syndrome. *Journal of the American Medical Association, 282,* 657–663.

Blackburn, G. L. (1995). Effect of degree of weight loss on health benefits. *Obesity Research, 3,* 211S-216S.

Blair, S. N., & Leermakers, E. A. (2002). Exercise and weight management. In T. A. Wadden & A. J. Stunkard (Eds.), *Handbook of obesity treatment* (pp. 283–300). New York: Guilford Press.

Bray, G. A. (2002). Drug treatment of obesity. In T. A. Wadden & A. J. Stunkard (Eds.), *Handbook of obesity treatment* (pp. 317–338). New York: Guilford Press.

Bray, G. A., Blackburn, G. L., Ferguson, J. M., Greenway, F. L., Jain, A. K., Mendel, C. M., et al. (1999). Sibutramine produces dose-related weight loss. *Obesity Research, 7,* 189–198.

Bray, G. A., Ryan, D. H., Gordon, D., Heidingsfelder, H., Cerise, F., & Wilson, K. (1996). A double-blind randomized placebo-controlled trial of sibutramine. *Obesity Research, 4,* 263–270.

Brody, M. L., Walsh, B. T., & Devlin, M. J. (1994). Binge eating disorder: Reliability and validity of a new diagnostic category. *Journal of Consulting and Clinical Psychology, 62,* 381–386.

Brownell, K. D. (2000). *The LEARN Program for weight control.* Dallas, TX: American Health.

Brownell, K. D., Heckerman, C. L., Westlake, R. J., Hayes, S. C., & Monti, P. M. (1978). The effect of couples training and partner cooperativeness in the behavioral treatment of obesity. *Behavior Research and Therapy, 16,* 323–333.

Brownell, K. D., & Stunkard, A. J. (1981). Couples training, pharmacotherapy, and behavior therapy in the treatment of obesity. *Archives of General Psychiatry, 38,* 1224–1232.

Bruce, B., & Agras, W. S. (1992). Binge eating in females: A population-based investigation. *International Journal of Eating Disorders, 12,* 365–373.

Carter, J. C., & Fairburn, C. G. (1998). Cognitive behavioral self-help for binge eating disorder: A controlled effectiveness study. *Journal of Consulting and Clinical Psychology, 66,* 616–623.

Cash, T. F. (1994). Body image and weight changes in a multisite comprehensive very-low-calorie diet program. *Behavior Therapy, 25,* 239–254.

Christakis, G., & Miller-Kovach, K. (1996). Maintenance of weight goal among Weight Watchers lifetime members. *Nutrition Today, 31(1),* 29–31.

Davidson, M. H., Hauptman, J., DiGirolamo, M., Foreyt, J. P., Halsted, C. H., Heber, D., et al. (1999). Weight control and risk factor reduction in obese subjects treated for 2 years with orlistat: A randomized controlled trial. *Journal of American Medicine, 281,* 235–242.

Ditschuneit, H. H., Flechtner-Mors, M., Johnson, T. D., & Adler, G. (1999). Metabolic and weight loss effects of long-term dietary intervention in obese subjects. *American Journal of Clinical Nutrition, 69,* 198–204.

Fairburn, C. G. (1995). *Overcoming binge eating.* New York: Guilford Press.

Flechtner-Mors, M., Ditschuneit, H. H., Johnson, T. D., Suchard, M. A., & Adler, G. (2000). Metabolic and weight loss effects of long-term dietary intervention in obese patients: Four-year results. *Obesity Research, 8,* 399–402.

Flegal, K. M., Carroll, M. D., Kuczmarski, R. J., & Johnson, C. L. (1998). Overweight and obesity in the United States: Prevalence and trends, 1960–1994. *International Journal of Obesity, 22,* 39–47.

Flegal, K. M., Carroll, M. D., Odgen, C. L., & Johnson, C. L. (2002). Prevalence and trends in obesity among U.S. adults, 1999–2000. *Journal of the American Medical Association, 288,* 1723–1727.

Foreyt, J. P., & Goodrick, G. K. (1992). *Living without dieting.* Houston, TX: Harrison.

Foster, G. D., & McGuckin, B. (2002). Nondieting approaches: Principles, practices, and evidence. In T. A. Wadden & A. J. Stunkard (Eds.), *Handbook of obesity treatment* (pp. 494–512). New York: Guilford Press.

Foster, G. D., Wadden, T. A., Phelan, S., Sarwer, D. B., & Swain-Sanderson, R. (2001). Obese patients' perceptions of treatment outcomes and the factors that influence them. *Archives of Internal Medicine, 161,* 2133–2139.

Foster, G. D., Wadden, T. A., Vogt, R. A., & Brewer, G. (1997). What is a reasonable weight loss? Patients' expectations and evaluations of obesity treatment outcomes. *Journal of Consulting and Clinical Psychology, 65,* 79–85.

Fox, K. R. (1992). A clinical approach to exercise in the markedly obese. In T. A. Wadden & T. B. VanItallie (Eds.), *Treatment of the seriously obese patient* (pp. 354–382). New York: Guilford Press.

Freedman, M. R., King, J., & Kennedy, E. (2001). Popular diets: A scientific review. *Obesity Research, 9*(Suppl. 1), 1S–40S.

Garner, D. M., & Wooley, S. C. (1991). Confronting the failure of behavioral and dietary treatments for obesity. *Clinical Psychology Review, 11,* 729–780.

Grilo, C. M., Wilfley, D. E., Brownell, K. D., & Rodin, J. (1994). Teasing, body image, and self-esteem in a clinical sample of obese women. *Addictive Behaviors, 19,* 443–450.

Halmi, K. A., Long, M., Stunkard, A. J., & Mason, E. (1980). Psychiatric diagnosis of morbidly obese gastric bypass patients. *American Journal of Psychiatry, 137,* 470–472.

Harris, J. E., Hamaday, V., & Mochan, E. (1999). Osteopathic family physicians' attitudes, knowledge, and self-reported practices regarding obesity. *Journal of the American Osteopathic Association, 99,* 358–365.

Heber, D., Ashley, J. M., Wang, H. J., & Elashoff, R. M. (1994). Clinical evaluation of a minimal intervention meal replacement regimen for weight reduction. *Journal of the American College of Nutrition, 6,* 608–614.

Heshka, S., Anderson, J. W., Atkinson, R. L., Phinney, S. D., Greenway, F., Hill, J. D., et al. (2000). Self-help weight loss versus a structured commercial program after 1 year: A randomized controlled study [Addendum]. *FASEB Journal, 14,* 37.

Hill, J. O., Hauptman, J., Anderson, J. W., Fujioka, K., O'Neil, P. M., Smith, D. K., et al. (1999). Orlistat, a lipase inhibitor, for weight maintenance after conventional dieting: A 1-y study. *American Journal of Clinical Nutrition, 69,* 1108–1116.

Hirschmann, J. R., & Munter, C. H. (1988). *Overcoming overeating: Living free in the world of food.* Reading, MA: Addison-Wesley.

Hudson, J. I., McElroy, S. L., Raymond, N. C., Crow, S., Keck, P. E., Carter, W. P., et al. (1998). Fluvoxamine in the treatment of being eating disorder: A multicenter placebo-controlled, double-blind trial. *American Journal of Psychiatry, 155,* 1756–1762.

Institute of Medicine. (1995). *Weighing the options: Criteria for evaluating weight management programs.* Washington, DC: Government Printing Office.

James, W. P. T., Astrup, A., Finer, N., Hilsted, J., Kopelman, P., Rossner, S., et al. (2000). Effect of sibutramine on weight maintenance after weight loss: A randomised trial. *Lancet, 356,* 2119–2126.

Jeffery, R. W., Wing, R. R., & Mayer, R. R. (1998). Are smaller weight losses or more achievable weight loss goals better in the long term for obese patients? *Journal of Consulting and Clinical Psychology, 66,* 641–645.

Jones, S. P., Smith, I. G., Kelly, F., & Gray, J. A. (1995). Long-term weight loss with sibutramine. *International Journal of Obesity, 19*(Suppl.), 41.

Klem, M. L., Wing, R. R., McGuire, M. T., Seagle, H. M., & Hill, J. O. (1997). A descriptive study of individuals successful at long-term maintenance of substantial weight loss. *American Journal of Clinical Nutrition, 66,* 239–246.

Kral, J. G. (1998). Surgical treatment of obesity. In G. A. Bray, C. Bouchard, & W. P. T. James (Eds.), *Handbook of obesity* (pp. 977–993). New York: Marcel Dekker.

Kumanyika, S. K. (1994). Obesity in minority populations: An epidemiological assessment. *Obesity Research, 2,* 166–182.

Latifi, R., Kellum, J. M., DeMaria, E. J., & Sugerman, H. J. (2002). Surgical treatment of obesity. In T. A. Wadden & A. J. Stunkard (Eds.), *Handbook of obesity treatment* (pp. 339–356). New York: Guilford Press.

Lean, M. E. J. (1997). Sibutramine: A review of clinical efficacy. *International Journal of Obesity, 21,* 30S–36S.

Lowe, M. R., Miller-Kovach, K., Frye, N., & Phelan, S. P. (1999). An initial evaluation of a commercial weight loss program: Short-term effects on weight, eating behavior, and mood. *Obesity Research, 7*(1), 51–59.

Manson, J. E., Willett, W. C., Stampfer, M. J., Colditz, G. A., Hunter, D. J., Hankinson, S. E., et al. (1995). Body weight and mortality among women. *New England Journal of Medicine, 333,* 677–685.

Marcus, M. D., Wing, R. R., & Fairburn, C. G. (1995). Cognitive behavioral treatment of binge eating vs. behavioral weight control on the treatment of binge eating disorder. *Annals of Behavioral Medicine, 17,* S090.

Melanson, K., & Dwyer, J. (2002). Popular diets for treatment of overweight and obesity. In T. A. Wadden & A. J. Stunkard (Eds.), *Handbook of obesity treatment* (pp. 249–282). New York: Guilford Press.

Metz, J. A., Kris-Etherton, P. M., Morris, C. D., Mustad, V. A., Stern, J. S., Oparil, S., et al. (1997). Dietary compliance and cardiovascular risk reduction with a prepared meal plan compared with a self-selected diet. *American Journal of Clinical Nutrition, 66,* 373–385.

National Academy of Sciences. (2002). *Dietary reference intakes for energy, carbohydrates, fiber, fat, protein and amino acids (macronutrients).* Food and Nutrition Board.

National Heart, Lung, and Blood Institute Obesity Education Initiative Expert Panel. (1998). Clinical guidelines on the identification, evaluation, and treatment of overweight and obesity in adults: The evidence report. *Obesity Research, 6,* 51S–209S.

National Livestock and Meat Board. (1993). *Food Guide Pyramid.* Chicago: Author.

National Task Force on the Prevention and Treatment of Obesity. (2000). Dieting and the development of eating disorders in overweight and obese adults. *Archives of Internal Medicine, 160,* 2581–2589.

O'Neil, P. M., Smith, C. F., Foster, G. D., & Anderson, D. A. (2000). The perceived relative worth of reaching and maintaining goal weight. *International Journal of Obesity and Related Metabolic Disorders, 24*(8), 1069–1076.

O'Reardon, J. P., Stunkard, A. J., & Allison, K. C. (in press). *A clinical trial of sertraline in the treatment of the night eating syndrome.* Manuscript submitted for publication.

Perri, M. G., McAllister, D. A., Gange, J. J., Jordan, R. C., McAdoo, W. G., & Nezu, A. M. (1988). Effects of four maintenance programs on the long-term management of obesity. *Journal of Consulting and Clinical Psychology, 56,* 529–534.

Polivy, J., & Herman, C. P. (1985). Dieting and bingeing: A causal analysis. *American Psychologist, 40,* 193–201.

Polivy, J., & Herman, C. P. (1992). Undieting: A program to help people stop dieting. *International Journal of Eating Disorders, 11,* 261–268.

Popkin, B. M. (1994). The nutrition transition in low-income countries: An emerging crisis. *Nutrition Review, 52,* 285–298.

Price, R. A., Desmond, S. M., Krol, R. A., Snyder, F. F., & O'Connell, J. K. (1987). Family practice physicians' beliefs, attitudes, and practices regarding obesity. *American Journal of Clinical Nutrition, 66,* 551–556.

Puhl, R., & Brownell, K. D. (2001). Bias, discrimination, and obesity. *Obesity Research, 9*(12), 788–805.

Ramirez, E. M., & Rosen, J. C. (2001). A comparison of weight control and body image therapy for obese men and women. *Journal of Consulting and Clinical Psychology, 69,* 440–446.

Rand, C. S. W., & MacGregor, A. M. C. (1990). Morbidly obese patients' perceptions of social discrimination before and after surgery for obesity. *Southern Medical Journal, 83,* 1390–1395.

Rand, C. S. W., MacGregor, A. M. C., & Stunkard, A. (1997). The night eating syndrome in the general population and among the postoperative obesity surgery patients. *International Journal of Eating Disorders, 22,* 65–69.

Renjilian, D. A., Perri, M. G., Nezu, A. M., McKelvey, W. F., Shermer, R. L., & Anton, S. D. (2001). Individual vs. group therapy for obesity: Effects of matching participants to their treatment preferences. *Journal of Consulting and Clinical Psychology, 69,* 717–721.

Rosen, J. C., Orosan, P., & Reiter, J. (1995). Cognitive behavior therapy for negative body image in obese women. *Behavior Therapy, 26,* 25–42.

Roughan, P., Seddon, E., & Vernon-Roberts, J. (1990). Long-term effects of a psychologically based group program for women preoccupied with body weight and eating behavior. *International Journal of Obesity, 14,* 135–147.

Saris, W. H. M. (1998). Fit, fat, and fat-free: The metabolic aspects of weight control. *International Journal of Obesity, 22,* S15–S21.

Sarwer, D. B., Allison, K. C., & Berkowitz, R. I. (in press). Assessment and treatment of obesity in a primary care setting. In L. J. Haas (Ed.), *Handbook of primary-care psychology.* New York: Oxford University Press.

Sarwer, D. B., & Thompson, J. K. (2002). Obesity and body image disturbance. In T. A. Wadden & A. J. Stunkard (Eds.), *Handbook of obesity treatment* (pp. 447–464). New York: Guilford Press.

Sarwer, D. B., & Wadden, T. A. (1999). The treatment of obesity: What's new, what's recommended. *Journal of Women's Health and Gender Based Medicine, 8,* 483–492.

Sarwer, D. B., Wadden, T. A., & Foster, G. D. (1998). Assessment of body image dissatisfaction in obese women: Specificity, severity, and clinical significance. *Journal of Consulting and Clinical Psychology, 66,* 651–654.

Sarwer, D. B., Womble, L. G., & Berkowitz, R. I. (2001). Behavioral treatment of obesity in the primary care setting. In B. Gumbiner (Ed.), *Obesity* (pp. 202–221). Philadelphia: American College of Physicians Press.

Sjostrom, L., Rissanen, A., Andersen, T., Boldrin, M., Golay, A., Koppeschaar, H. P. F., et al. (1998). Randomized placebo-controlled trial of orlistat for weight loss and prevention of weight regain in obese patients. *Lancet, 352,* 167–172.

Spitzer, R. L., Devlin, M., Walsh, T. B., Hasin, D., Marcus, M. D., Stunkard, A. J., et al. (1992). Binge eating disorder: A multisite field trial of the diagnostic criteria. *International Journal of Eating Disorders, 11,* 191–203.

Stevens, J., Cai, J., Pamuk, E. R., Williamson, D. F., Thun, M. J., & Wood, J. L. (1998). The effect of age on the association between body-mass index and mortality. *New England Journal of Medicine, 338,* 1–7.

Stunkard, A. J. (2002). Binge-eating disorder and night-eating syndrome. In T. A. Wadden & A. J. Stunkard (Eds.), *Handbook of obesity treatment* (pp. 107–124). New York: Guilford Press.

Stunkard, A. J., & Allison, K. C. (in press). Two forms of disordered eating in obesity: Binge eating and night eating. *International Journal of Obesity.*

Stunkard, A. J., Berkowitz, R. I., Wadden, T. A., Tanrikut, C., Reiss, E., & Young, L. (1996). Binge eating disorder and the night eating syndrome. *International Journal of Obesity, 20,* 1–6.

Stunkard, A. J., Grace, W. J., & Wolff, H. G. (1955). The night-eating syndrome: A pattern of food intake among certain obese patients. *American Journal of Medicine, 19,* 78–86.

Sugarman, H. J., Starkey, J. V., & Birkenhauer, R. A. (1987). A randomized prospective trial of gastric bypass versus vertical banded gastroplasty for morbid obesity and their effects on sweets versus nonsweet eaters. *Annals of Surgery, 205,* 613–624.

U.S. Department of Health and Human Services. (1996). *Physical activity and health: A report of the Surgeon General.* Atlanta, GA: Centers for Disease Control and Prevention.

Viegener, B. J., Perri, M. G., Nezu, A. M., Renjilian, D. A., McKelvey, W. F., & Schein, R. L. (1990). Effect of an intermittent, low-fat, low-calorie diet in the behavioral treatment of obesity. *Behavior Therapy, 21,* 499–509.

Wadden, T. A., Anderson, D. A., Foster, G. D., Bennett, A., Steinberg, C., & Sarwer, D. B. (2000). Obese women's perceptions of their doctors' weight management attitudes and behaviors. *Archives of Family Medicine, 9,* 854–860.

Wadden, T. A., Berkowitz, R. I., Sarwer, D. B., Prus-Wisniewski, R., & Steinberg, C. M. (2001). Benefits of lifestyle modification in the pharmacologic treatment of obesity: A randomized trial. *Archives of Internal Medicine, 161,* 218–227.

Wadden, T. A., Berkowitz, R. I., Vogt, R. A., Steen, S. N., Stunkard, A. J., & Foster, G. D. (1997). Lifestyle modification in the pharmacologic treatment of obesity: A pilot investigation of a potential primary care approach. *Obesity Research, 6,* 278–284.

Wadden, T. A., Brownell, K. D., & Foster, G. D. (2002). Obesity: Responding to the global epidemic. *Journal of Consulting and Clinical Psychology, 70*(3), 510–525.

Wadden, T. A., Foster, G. D., & Letizia, K. A. (1994). One-year behavioral treatment of obesity: Comparison of moderate and severe caloric restriction and the effects of weight maintenance therapy. *Journal of Consulting and Clinical Psychology, 62,* 165–171.

Wadden, T. A., & Frey, D. L. (1997). A multicenter evaluation of a proprietary program for the treatment of marked obesity: A five-year follow-up. *International Journal of Eating Disorders, 22,* 203–212.

Wadden, T. A., & Osei, S. (2002). The treatment of obesity: An overview. In T. A. Wadden & A. J. Stunkard (Eds.), *Handbook of obesity treatment* (pp. 229–248). New York: Guilford Press.

Wadden, T. A., & Phelan, S. (2002). Behavioral assessment of the obese patient. In T. A. Wadden & A. J. Stunkard (Eds.), *Handbook of obesity treatment* (pp. 229–248). New York: Guilford Press.

Wadden, T. A., Sarwer, D. B., & Berkowitz, R. I. (1999). Behavioral treatment of the overweight patient. *Baillière's Clinical Endocrinology and Metabolism, 13,* 93–107.

Wadden, T. A., Sternberg, J. A., Letizia, K. A., Stunkard, A. J., & Foster, G. D. (1990). Treatment of obesity by very-low-calorie diet, behavior therapy and their combination: A Five-year perspective. *International Journal of Obesity, 51,* 167–172.

Wadden, T. A., & Stunkard, A. J. (1986). A controlled trial of very-low-calorie diet, behavior therapy, and their combination in the treatment of obesity. *Journal of Consulting and Clinical Psychology, 4,* 482–488.

Wadden, T. A., Womble, L. G., Sarwer, D. B., Berkowitz, R. I., Clark, V. L., & Foster, G. D. (in press). *Great expectations: "I'm losing 25% of my weight no matter what you say."* Manuscript submitted for publication.

Weight Watchers International. (2000, April 5). *About Weight Watchers.* Available from www.weightwatchers.com/wwx.

Wilfley, D. E., Agras, W. S., Telch, C. F., Rossiter, E. M., Schneider, J. A., Cole, A. G., et al. (1993). Group cognitive-behavioral therapy and group interpersonal psychotherapy for the nonpurging bulimic individual: A controlled comparison. *Journal of Consulting and Clinical Psychology, 61,* 296–305.

Wilfley, D. E., & Cohen, L. R. (1997). Psychological treatment of bulimia nervosa and binge eating disorder. *Psychopharmacology Bulletin, 33,* 437–454.

Wing, R. R. (2002). Behavioral weight control. In T. A. Wadden & A. J. Stunkard (Eds.), *Handbook of obesity treatment* (pp. 301–316). New York: Guilford Press.

Wing, R. R., Blair, E. H., Marcus, M. D., Epstein, L. H., & Harvey, J. (1994). Year-long weight loss treatment for obese patients with type 2 diabetes: Does including an intermittent very-low-calorie diet improve outcome? *American Journal of Medicine, 97,* 354–362.

Wing, R. R., Marcus, M. D., Salata, R., Epstein, L. H., Miaskiewicz, S., & Blair, E. H. (1991). Effects of a very-low-calorie diet on long-term glycemic control in obese Type 2 diabetic subjects. *Archives of Internal Medicine, 151,* 1334–1340.

Wing, R. R., Venditti, E. M., Jakicic, J. M., Polley, B. A., & Lang, W. (1998). Lifestyle intervention in overweight individuals with a family history of diabetes. *Diabetes Care, 21*(3), 350–359.

Womble, L. G., Wang, S. S., & Wadden, T. A. (2002). Commercial and self-help weight loss programs. In T. A. Wadden & A. J. Stunkard (Eds.), *Handbook of obesity treatment* (pp. 395–415). New York: Guilford Press.

World Health Organization. (1998). *Obesity: Preventing and managing the global epidemic.* Geneva, Switzerland: World Health Organization.

Chapter 22 ————————————————————————

TREATMENT OF OBESITY II: CHILDHOOD AND ADOLESCENT OBESITY

JORDANA COOPERBERG AND MYLES S. FAITH

Childhood obesity is one of the most increasingly prevalent and concerning public health disorders facing society (Odgen, Flegal, Carroll, & Johnson, 2002). Whereas pediatric obesity was once seen as a disorder that children would grow out of or less important than adulthood obesity, this is no longer the case. As this chapter shows, pediatric obesity is associated with medical health complications and, if left untreated, will likely track into adulthood. In recognition of these facts, expert consensus panels have developed guidelines to determine what criteria should be considered when determining which children should be treated, as well as appropriate treatment goals. As reviewed herein, assessment of health-related complications such as elevated blood pressure and cholesterol have become important considerations given the apparent rise in Type 2 diabetes in youth.

This chapter reviews current treatment guidelines and recommendations for pediatric obesity, while emphasizing the importance of monitoring comorbidities. We review the health complications of obesity, followed by a review of expert panel recommendations for identifying those children who are the most appropriate candidates for treatment. As indicated in the review, the presence of concurrent health complications plays an important role in this process. We then review the critical treatment components for pediatric obesity (including diet, physical activity, and parent involvement), followed by data indicating that treatment can yield improvements in obesity-related comorbidities. We end by discussing emerging themes concerning childhood obesity treatment.

ASSOCIATED HEALTH RISKS OF CHILDHOOD OBESITY

Childhood obesity and adolescent obesity are associated with various health risks, both physical and psychosocial. The increasing presence and severity of childhood obesity is reflected by increasing hospital costs associated with obesity. Based on a 2001 constant U.S. dollar value, obesity-associated annual hospital costs increased more than threefold—from $35 million between 1979 and 1981 to $127 million between

1997 and 1999. Among all hospital discharges, the proportion of discharges with obesity-associated diseases has increased dramatically among youth 6 to 17 years old in the past 20 years (Dietz, 1998). These statistics are of concern because childhood obesity is likely to carry on into adulthood, with 80% of obese adolescents becoming obese adults (Goran, 2001).

Adult obesity is associated with cardiovascular disease, hypertension, Type 2 diabetes, and increased risk of certain cancers (e.g., colon, rectum, prostate, perhaps breast; Faith & Allison, 1996). Although researchers are only beginning to understand the long-term effects of childhood obesity on adulthood metabolic complications, there is little question that being obese during childhood is associated with alarming health complications during youth. Childhood obesity is associated with several health complications that are known precursors to non-insulin-dependent diabetes mellitus (or Type 2 diabetes; Dietz, 2001). Most notably, studies have linked pediatric obesity to glucose intolerance and insulin resistance.

Glucose intolerance is a condition that is indicated by elevated blood sugar levels, but not to levels high enough for a diagnosis of Type 2 diabetes. A recent clinic-based study found that 25% of obese children 4 to 11 years old and 21% of obese children 11 to 18 years old had glucose intolerance (Sinha et al., 2002). Moreover, 14 girls in the sample had polycystic ovary syndrome (POS), a disorder that is associated with menstrual irregularities, hirsutism due to high androgen levels, infertility, and cysts on their ovaries. Compared to obese girls without POS, obese girls with POS are more likely to have metabolic derangements that include insulin resistance (Lewy et al., 2001).

Insulin resistance, another precursor to Type 2 diabetes, refers to a condition in which the body's cells are resistant to insulin secreted by the pancreas. Because insulin enables the cells to take up glucose for energy utilization, insulin resistance prevents the glucose from entering the cells as easily. Consequently, the glucose remains in the blood, which raises blood sugar levels. Many studies confirm that childhood obesity is associated with insulin resistance (Dietz, 1998). For example, a recent school-based study of more than 12,000 fifth- to eighth-grade boys and girls found significant associations between insulin resistance and body fat (Sinaiko et al., 2001). Moreover, the authors found evidence for the clustering of increased body fat, elevated triglycerides and low-density lipoprotein (LDL) cholesterol ("bad cholesterol"), reduced high-density lipoprotein (HDL) cholesterol ("good cholesterol"), and elevated high blood pressure among the most insulin-resistant children. This suggests potential emergence of a "metabolic syndrome" during childhood.

Still, the relationship among these risk factors is not simple. Interesting results come from a 14-year prospective study of children who were 10 years old on average and obese at baseline but had normal blood glucose levels (Maffeis et al., 2002). Results indicated that, among girls, childhood obesity was a risk factor for adulthood obesity whereas low insulin resistance levels were actually *protective* against adulthood obesity. In boys, childhood insulin resistance levels did not predict their weight as adults. These data illustrate the complex relations among obesity and metabolic disease during childhood and their long-term effects on adult health (Freedman, Khan, Dietz, Srinivasan, & Berenson, 2001).

Elevated blood pressure is also associated with pediatric obesity. One study found that elevated blood pressure occurred approximately nine times more frequently among obese than nonobese children. (Lauer, Connor, & Leaverton, 1975). Recently, Daniels, Witt, Glascock, Khoury, and Kimball (2002) examined the predictors of left atrial enlargement in children and adolescents with essential hypertension. This condition is especially of concern given its association with cardiovascular disease and stroke in adults. In a sample of 112 adolescents, body mass index (BMI) was significantly elevated among participants with left atrial enlargement.

Hyperlipidemia can occur among obese children and adolescents, with a profile that typically includes elevated LDL cholesterol and triglycerides and lowered HDL cholesterol levels (Freedman, Srinivasan, & Burke, 1987). This pattern has been documented in numerous studies (e.g., Arslanian & Suprasongsin, 1996; Sinaiko, Donahue, Jacobs, & Prineas, 1999; Steinberger, Moorehead, Katch, & Rocchini, 1995).

With respect to Type 2 diabetes per se, data suggest that the prevalence is increasing in pediatric samples. Among teenagers, the prevalence was reported to be 50.9% for Pima Indians (a Native American tribe genetically predisposed to obesity and related metabolic complications), 4.5% for other American Indian populations, and 2.3% for Canadian First Nation people from Manitoba (Fagot-Campagna et al., 2000). Among Pima Indian children, the prevalence of Type 2 diabetes increased from 0% (1967 to 1976) to 1.4% (1987 to 1996) among 10- to 14-year-old boys and from 2.43% to 3.78% among 15- to 19-year-old boys. The prevalence increased from 0.72% (1967 to 1976) to 2.88% (1987 to 1996) in 10- to 14-year-old girls and from 2.73% to 5.31% for 15- to 19-year-old girls during the same period (Dabelea et al., 1998). Pinhas-Hamiel, Dolan, and Daniels (1996) observed a dramatic increase in newly diagnosed Type 2 diabetes cases, which accounted for one-third of all new cases of diabetes in Cincinnati in 1994. This trend coincided with the concurrent increases in pediatric obesity.

Although sleep apnea appears in approximately fewer than 7% of obese children, one-third of the children whose body weight was 150% over ideal body weight with a history of breathing difficulties during sleep were found to have apnea (Mallory, Fiser, & Jackson, 1989). In a recent study of obese children who snored, de la Eva, Baur, Donaghue, and Waters (2002) found that obstructive sleep apnea had significant and independent associations with child BMI and insulin levels. These results further underscore the potential interplay among obesity-related complications.

The psychosocial effects of pediatric obesity are equally alarming. Discrimination and prejudice against overweight children begin during childhood (Gortmaker, Must, Perrin, Sobol, & Dietz, 1993). Society attributes various negative character traits to obesity, such as laziness and carelessness (Crandall & Schiffhauer, 1998). Children may be excluded from friendships solely based on their physical size. Faith, Leone, Ayers, Heo, and Pietrobelli (2002) showed that weight teasing during sports and physical activity is associated with poorer attitudes toward sports and perhaps reduced participation in certain physical activities. Gortmaker et al. (1993) showed that women who had been obese as adolescents earned less money, were less educated, and were less likely to be married during early adulthood than women who were not obese as teenagers. There are limited data to suggest an association between weight status and global self-esteem in children (Kaplan & Wadden, 1986), although obese children tend to have poorer body images than their nonobese counterparts (Striegel-Moore et al., 2000).

In summary, the medical and psychological health complications of childhood obesity are well documented. Of most concern may be recent data on the apparent increasing prevalence of Type 2 diabetes in pediatric samples and the clustering of obesity and metabolic symptoms. Fortunately, as reviewed later in this chapter, a small but mounting literature suggests that weight loss can improve children's metabolic profile in addition to their weight.

WHICH CHILDREN SHOULD RECEIVE TREATMENT?

Because pediatric obesity is a complicated disorder that may be associated with medical complications, a critical issue is which children should receive treatment? The following guidelines, based on an expert-panel consensus report, are recommended for evaluating children as appropriate candidates for treatment (Barlow & Dietz, 1998). Figures 22.1 and 22.2 present an overview of these guidelines, which include a two-stage screening process. The initial screen focuses on the child's or adolescent's BMI (kg/m^2). For those children whose BMI is equal to or exceeds the 95th percentile (age- and sex-specific), an

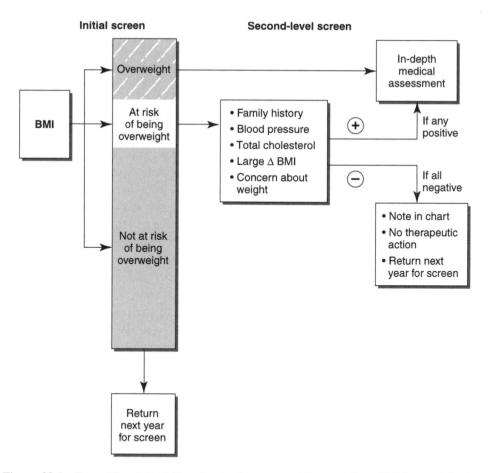

Figure 22.1   Expert Panel Guidelines for the Screening of Overweight in Children and Adolescents. *Source:* From "Obesity Evaluation and Treatment: Expert Committee Recommendations," by S. E. Barlow and W. H. Dietz, 1998, *Pediatrics, 102,* p. e.29. Reprinted with permission from the American Academy of Pediatrics.

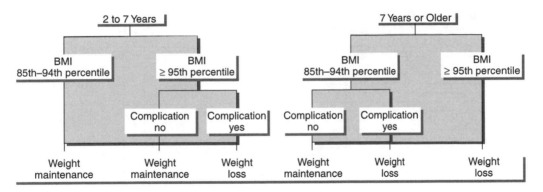

Figure 22.2 Expert Panel Treatment Guidelines for Children Who Are At-Risk for Overweight or Overweight. *Source:* From "Obesity Evaluation and Treatment: Expert Committee Recommendations," by S. E. Barlow and W. H. Dietz, 1998, *Pediatrics, 102,* p. e.29. Reprinted with permission from the American Academy of Pediatrics.

in-depth medical assessment is recommended. These children are technically referred to as "overweight." For any child whose BMI falls between the 85th and 94th percentiles (i.e., "at risk for overweight"), a second-level screen determines if an in-depth medical assessment is warranted. This second-level screen should focus on the following five domains, with further medical assessment recommended for those children showing any of these characteristics:

- Family history of cardiovascular disease, parental hypercholesterolemia, unknown family history (see American Academy of Pediatrics, 1992), and/or family history of diabetes mellitus or parental obesity.
- High blood pressure (see Second Task Force on Blood Pressure Control in Children, 1987).
- Elevated total cholesterol, that is, ≥ 5.2 mmol/L or ≥ 200 mg/dL (see National Cholesterol Education Program, 1991).
- A large recent increase in BMI (e.g., an annual increase of 3 to 4 BMI units).
- Child/adolescent concerns about weight or display of any emotional or psychological manifestations possibly related to overweight or perceptions of overweight.

Expert guidelines indicate an in-depth medical examination for any child who is at risk for overweight and scores positive on *any* of these criteria. By contrast, medical examination is not indicated for children who are at risk for overweight but score negative on *all* of these criteria.

Health practitioners can access updated BMI growth charts from the Centers for Disease Control (www.cdc.gov/growthcharts). These charts include BMI-for-age percentile curves, which offer age- and gender-specific charts for specifying a child's BMI percentile. Figure 22.3 illustrates the BMI-for-age growth charts for boys and girls, respectively.

Recently, an international set of guidelines for defining overweight and obesity in children and adolescents was proposed (Cole, Bellizzi, Flegal, & Dietz, 2000). Using

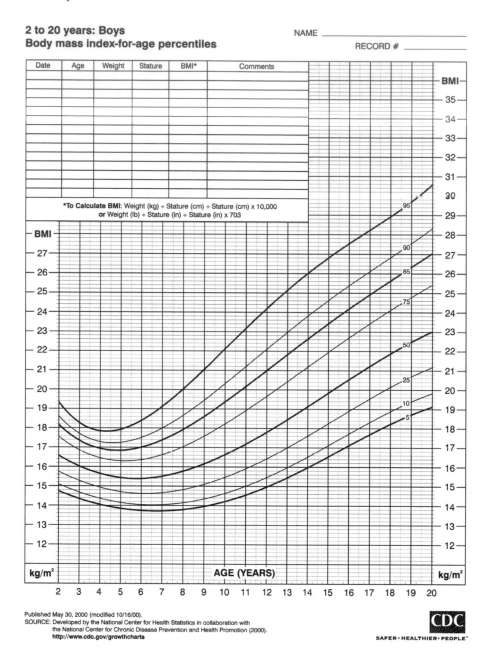

2 to 20 years: Boys
Body mass index-for-age percentiles

NAME _____

RECORD # _____

*To Calculate BMI: Weight (kg) ÷ Stature (cm) ÷ Stature (cm) x 10,000
or Weight (lb) ÷ Stature (in) ÷ Stature (in) x 703

Published May 30, 2000 (modified 10/16/00).
SOURCE: Developed by the National Center for Health Statistics in collaboration with
the National Center for Chronic Disease Prevention and Health Promotion (2000).
http://www.cdc.gov/growthcharts

Figure 22.3   BMI-for-Age Growth Charts for 2 to 20 Year-Old Boys and Girls. Reprinted with permission from the American Academy of Pediatrics.

data from Brazil, Great Britain, Hong Kong, the Netherlands, Singapore, and the United States, growth curves were constructed for each age group to identify those BMI scores that would "project" to a BMI of 25 (i.e., overweight) or 30 (i.e., obese) at 18 years of age. Thus, they provide BMI cutoffs for overweight and obesity from ages 2 to 18 by half years for males and females. Table 22.1 illustrates some of the overweight and obesity cutoffs, per the suggested international criteria.

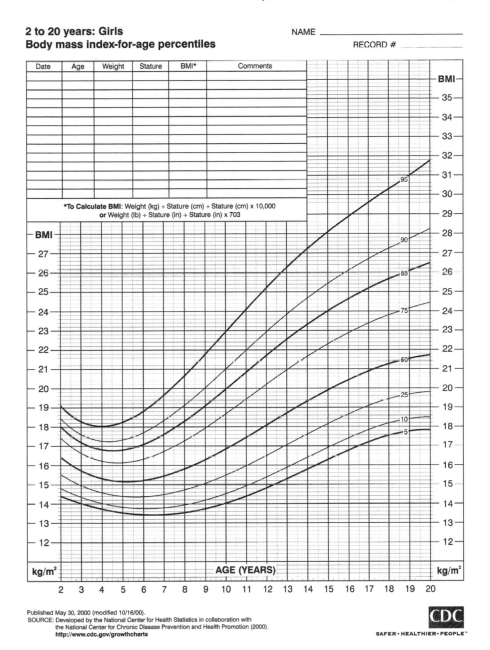

2 to 20 years: Girls
Body mass index-for-age percentiles

NAME _____

RECORD # _____

*To Calculate BMI: Weight (kg) ÷ Stature (cm) ÷ Stature (cm) x 10,000
or Weight (lb) ÷ Stature (in) ÷ Stature (in) x 703

Published May 30, 2000 (modified 10/16/00).
SOURCE: Developed by the National Center for Health Statistics in collaboration with
the National Center for Chronic Disease Prevention and Health Promotion (2000).
http://www.cdc.gov/growthcharts

CDC
SAFER·HEALTHIER·PEOPLE™

Figure 22.3   *(Continued)*

TREATMENT COMPONENTS

A more detailed review of the pediatric obesity treatment literature is provided
elsewhere (Epstein, Myers, Raynor, & Saelens, 1998; Jelalian & Saelens, 1999). Family-
based behavioral treatment programs have been the most extensively studied interventions to date and have reliably produced the best short- and long-term results.

Table 22.1   International BMI Cutoffs for Defining Overweight
and Obesity in Children and Adolescents

Age	Males Overweight	Females Obesity	Overweight	Obesity
5	17.4	19.3	17.1	19.2
6	17.6	19.8	17.3	19.7
7	17.9	20.6	17.8	20.5
8	18.4	21.6	18.3	21.6
9	19.1	22.8	19.1	22.8
10	19.8	24.0	19.9	24.1
11	20.6	25.1	20.7	25.4
12	21.2	26.0	21.7	26.7
13	21.9	26.8	22.6	27.8

Source: From "Establishing a Standard Definition for Child Overweight and
Obesity Worldwide: International Survey," by T. J. Cole, M. C. Bellizzi, K. M.
Flegal, and W. H. Dietz, 2000, *British Medical Journal, 320,* pp. 1240–1243.

Family-based behavioral treatments stem from the philosophical foundation that obesity results in large part from maladaptive behaviors that have been learned, reinforced, and sustained by environmental contingencies. To that end, treatment strives
to teach the family members the behavioral skills necessary to establish and sustain
healthier eating and physical activity patterns. Nutrition information and education
alone are believed to have minimal impact on behavior change.

Behavior modification strategies such as behavioral contracting, stimulus control,
and positive reinforcement, therefore, set the foundation to help children lose
weight (Coates, Jeffery, et al., 1982; Epstein, Wing, Steranchak, Dickson, & Michelson, 1980; Johnson et al., 1997). *Behavioral contracting* refers to an explicit contract
among family members that stipulates the behavioral goals that family members will
attempt to reach and the reinforcements they will receive for attaining such goals. Rewards other than food and money are used. Family-based and interpersonal rewards
are used instead (e.g., praise, family trips, sports equipment). *Stimulus control* refers
to practical restructuring of the physical home environment such that healthier foods
become more readily accessible whereas high-fat, high-sugar foods are less accessible. Positive reinforcement strategies for families form the foundation for treatment
as parents are trained to move away from punitive parenting strategies to more positive parenting strategies. Table 22.2 summarizes suggested parenting strategies for
behavioral treatment.

Research suggests that dietary modification is a powerful and necessary component for
child weight loss. Treatments focusing solely on dietary modification have achieved short-
(Epstein, Wing, Penner, & Kress, 1985; Rocchini et al., 1988) and long-term weight losses
(Epstein, Valoski, Wing, & McCurley, 1994). Short-term interventions lacking a dietary
component achieved mixed results (Blomquist, Borjeson, Larsson, Persson, & Sterky,
1965; Epstein, Wing, Koeske, Ossip, & Beck, 1982), but there is no evidence for long-term
efficacy of treatments lacking a dietary component.

Table 22.2   Suggested Parenting Guidelines for Pediatric Obesity Treatment

Find reasons to praise the child's behavior.

Never use food as a reward.

Parents can ask for "rewards" for children in exchange for the changes in their own behavior.

Establish daily family meal and snack times.

Parents or caregivers should determine what food is offered and when, and the child should decide whether to eat.

Offer only healthy options.

Remove temptations.

Be a role model.

Be consistent.

Source: From "Obesity Evaluation and Treatment: Expert Committee Recommendations," by S. E. Barlow and W. H. Dietz, 1998, *Pediatrics, 102* p. e.29, available from http://www .pediatrics.org /cgi/content/full/102/3/e29.

Many programs have used Epstein's Traffic Light Diet (Epstein & Squires, 1988) or a variant for dietary prescriptions. Using the USDA's Food Guide Pyramid as its foundation (see Figure 22.4), children are encouraged to increase intake of low-fat, nutrient-rich green foods (e.g., fruits and vegetables), to consume moderate-calorie yellow foods in moderation (e.g., certain grain foods), and minimize, if not eliminate, high-fat, high-sugar red foods (e.g., candies). Detailed lists of food alternatives and their corresponding calories are provided to families, who are encouraged to try new and varied green and yellow foods. Most behavioral programs initially strive to reduce children's total daily caloric intake while maintaining adequate nutrition for development and growth. A recommended first step is increasing children's awareness of eating habits through self-monitoring, with parental help. With appropriate reductions of total calories and fat intake, children can meet their nutritional needs through increasing the nutrient density of foods eaten, shift toward negative energy balance, and gradually substitute for unhealthy food choices. There is no evidence to date that carefully controlled behavioral programs promote disordered eating or formal eating disorders among child participants (Epstein, Valoski, et al., 1994). Few studies have evaluated different nutrition plans or tested particular aspects of the overall dietary component (Epstein et al., 1998).

Physical activity is a central component of pediatric obesity treatment. The most successful pediatric obesity programs have included a physical activity component (e.g., Epstein, Wing, Koeske, & Valoski, 1985; Epstein, Valoski, et al., 1994), but physical activity components have not always augmented the effects of dietary modification (Hills & Parker, 1988; Rocchini, Katch, Schork, & Kelch, 1987). There appear to be consistent short-term effects of physical activity interventions on both children's weight status and cardiorespiratory fitness (e.g., Epstein, Valoski, Vara, et al., 1995) and other cardiovascular health benefits (Rocchini et al., 1988; Sasaki, Shindo, Tanaka, Ando, & Arakawa, 1987).

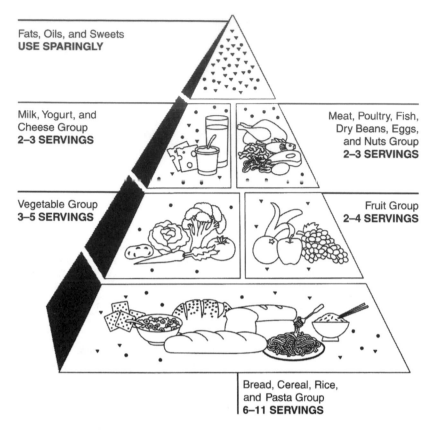

Figure 22.4   USDA Food Pyramid Guidelines.

Exercise programs that stress planned aerobic sessions seem to be more beneficial for children's weight loss than lower energy expenditure calisthenics programs (Epstein, Wing, Koeske, et al., 1985; Epstein, Valoski, et al., 1994). However, for long-term weight maintenance, data suggest that the best results are achieved through lifestyle approaches that attempt to weave physical activity into day-in, day-out, every-day living (Epstein et al., 1982; Epstein, Wing, Koeske, et al., 1985; Epstein, Valoski, et al., 1994). Lifestyle interventions work to integrate more physical activity into daily activities (e.g., climbing stairs instead of taking the elevator, parking the car at a distance from a supermarket, walking to the grocery store).

Research suggests that weight loss can also be achieved by targeting reductions in sedentary activities (e.g., TV viewing) rather than targeting increased physical activity per se (Epstein, Paluch, Gordy, & Dorn, 2000; Epstein, Valoski, Vara, et al., 1995). These studies show that children who discontinue sedentary activities will naturally redistribute some of their time to physical activity. Although children who reduce targeted sedentary activities redistribute some of their time to other sedentary activities, data indicate that children do, nonetheless, allocate enough time to increased physical activities to facilitate weight management. Hence, targeting reduced sedentary activity (e.g., TV viewing, video games, computers) has become a vital treatment strategy.

The American College of Sports Medicine and Centers for Disease Control recommendations for physical activity are similar for children and adults (U.S. Department of Health and Human Services, 1996). Children 2 years of age and older are encouraged to engage in moderate- to vigorous-intensity physical activity for at least one-half hour on most days. However, this recommendation is for the goal of long-term health promotion and not for pediatric weight loss per se. In fact, others have recommended higher levels of physical activity for youth and the inclusion of physical activity focusing on maintaining or increasing strength as well as cardiorespiratory fitness, particularly among adolescents (Pate, Trost, & Williams, 1998). It is reasonable to assume that most overweight children's level of physical activity is initially inadequate for weight loss and that approaches to increase duration, frequency, and, ultimately, intensity of physical activity are warranted. More research is needed to clarify the long-term effects of physical activity interventions to determine physical activity programs that maximize outcomes (Epstein & Goldfield, 1999).

Parental participation in childhood and adolescent weight loss programs has received considerable attention. Some treatments have targeted parents exclusively (Golan, Weizman, Apter, & Fainaru, 1998), the child or adolescent exclusively (e.g., Brownell, Kelman, & Stunkard, 1983; Kirschenbaum, Harris, & Tomarken, 1984), the parent and the child or adolescent seen primarily together (e.g., Wadden et al., 1990), or, most commonly, the parent and child or adolescent participating separately for at least part of the treatment session (e.g., Epstein, Valoski, Vara, et al., 1995). Some research indicates significant increases in treatment associated with parental involvement, while Haddock et al.'s meta-analytic review revealed that parental involvement did not necessarily yield more effective outcomes. This contradiction may be explained by the varying ages of the children in the studies, with younger children requiring greater parental involvement. The most robust weight control programs for prepubertal children have included at least some separate, but simultaneous, participation by parents (Epstein, Valoski, Wing, & McCurley, 1990). Among obese adolescents, there is some evidence that parents' separate but concurrent participation is valuable (Brownell et al., 1983), but not all studies support this conclusion (Coates, Killen, & Slinkard, 1982; Wadden et al., 1990). Clinic experience suggests that weight loss in the absence of parental involvement is very challenging.

In summary, expert consensus suggests that a lifestyle approach to changing overweight children's eating habits has the potential to gradually decrease overall caloric intake, to minimize the risk of youths' failing to meet recommended nutrient intake, and to maximize long-term weight control (Barlow & Dietz, 1998). This may be especially true for children who are mildly to moderately obese. More restrictive approaches, such as protein-sparing modified fasts and very low calorie diets have been less frequently investigated. Those studies conducted suggest long-term outcomes similar to those induced by moderate caloric restrictive diets among moderately overweight adolescents (Figueroa-Colon, von Almen, Franklin, Schuftan, & Suskind, 1993). These more restrictive dietary plans have been recommended in combination with careful physician monitoring for severely obese adolescents or less overweight adolescents with major health complications secondary to obesity (Stallings, Archibald, Pencharz, Harrison, & Bell, 1988). Table 22.3 lists expert panel recommendations for general treatment guidelines for pediatric obesity (Barlow & Dietz, 1998). Table 22.4 lists several practical resources for families, including Web sites and books.

Table 22.3   General Guidelines for Pediatric Obesity Treatment

Intervention should begin early.

The family must be ready for change.

Clinicians should educate families about medical complications of obesity.

Clinicians should involve the family and all caregivers in the treatment program.

Treatment programs should institute permanent changes, not short-term diets or exercise programs aimed at rapid weight loss.

As part of the treatment program, a family should learn to monitor eating and activity.

The treatment program should help the family make small, gradual changes.

Clinicians should encourage and empathize and not criticize.

A variety of experienced professionals can accomplish many aspects of a weight management program.

Source: From "Obesity Evaluation and Treatment: Expert Committee Recommendations," by S. E. Barlow and W. H. Dietz, 1998. *Pediatrics, 102* p. e.29, available from http://www .pediatrics.org /cgi/content/full/102/3/e29.

THE EFFICACY OF BEHAVIORAL TREATMENT FOR CHILDHOOD OBESITY

Compared to the treatment of adult obesity, the treatment of pediatric obesity has achieved much better outcomes over short- and long-term periods (Epstein, Valoski, Kalarchian, et al., 1995; Wilson, 1994). Reviews of the literature (Epstein et al., 1998; Haddock, Shadish, Klesges, & Stein, 1994; Jelalian & Saelens, 1999) identified 14 published studies that evaluated changes in percent overweight for at least one year and included some follow-up evaluation. Of these studies, three studies reported poor maintenance (i.e., subjects maintained less than a 10% decrease in percent overweight), eight studies reported moderate maintenance (i.e., subjects maintained a 10% to 20% decrease in percent overweight), and only three studies reported good maintenance (i.e., subjects maintained a 20% or greater decrease in percent overweight). Among those achieving good maintenance, one treatment study by Brownell et al. (1983) achieved an average of 20.5% change in percent overweight in the most effective treatment group for the 12 of 14 adolescents who were still available for follow-up. Another study (Epstein, Wing, Koeske, et al., 1985) reported an average 20% decrease in children's percent overweight that was even maintained at 10-year follow-up (Epstein, Valoski, et al., 1994). These long-term outcomes are particularly encouraging relative to the poor long-term outcomes obtained by adult weight control programs (Jeffery et al., 2000).

Several reasons have been suggested for the apparent superiority of childhood obesity treatment. First, children may require less self-motivation than adults to maintain behavior change because the primary agent of change is external (typically the parent). Second, children may have less ingrained and, therefore, more malleable dietary and physical activity habits than adults. Children are generally more physically active than adults (U.S. Department of Health and Human Services, 1996), which may be beneficial for their long-term weight maintenance. Finally, children often have the benefit of incurring percent overweight changes while maintaining their weight because of increases in height.

Although behavioral treatment has been shown to be the most effective strategy for dealing with childhood obesity, it is often difficult for practitioners to take advantage of

Table 22.4   Web Sites and Books Concerning Pediatric Obesity

Web Sites	Source	Subject
http://www.cdc.gov/nccdphp/dnpa/bmi/bmi-for-age.htm	Centers for Disease Control.	Measurements of BMI for children.
http://www.eatright.org/nfs/#Kid's%20Nutrition%20Needs	American Dietetic Association.	Links to nutritional tips for children.
http://www.diabetes.org/main/community/forecast/page79.jsp	American Diabetes Association.	Facts about Type 2 diabetes and the rise in children.
http://www.diabetes.org/main/community/forecast/page79.jsp	ivillage.com.	Tips on weight loss for children.
http://www.aboutourkids.org/articles/eatingtips.html	About Our Kids.	Developing healthy eating habits in children.

Books	Authors	Publisher
Treating Childhood and Adolescent Obesity	D. S. Kirschenbaum, W. G. Johnson, and P. M. Stalonas Jr., 1987.	New York: Pergamon Press.
Overweight Teenagers	M. D. LeBow, 1995.	New York: Plenum Press.
Fat-Proof Your Child	J. C. Piscatella, 1997.	New York: Workman Publishing.
The American Academy of Pediatrics Guide to Your Child's Nutrition: Making Peace at the Table and Building Healthy Eating Habits for Life	W. H. Dietz and L. Stern, 1999.	New York: Villard.
Trim Kids	M. Sothern, 2001.	New York: HarperResource.
The Traffic Light Diet	L. H. Epstein and S. Squires, 1978.	Boston: Little Brown & Co.

the available information. Barlow and Dietz (1998) found that health care providers reported difficulty with using such treatment for various reasons. Behavior and eating modification requires a significant time commitment by the patient, the family, and the practitioner and is difficult to achieve.

EMERGING AREAS

An important emerging area of research is assessment of obesity-related comorbidities and treatment innovations that will more effectively alleviate these conditions. Of most concern are the cardiovascular disease and metabolic derangements discussed in this chapter. Fortunately, data indicate that behavioral interventions can improve these comorbidities. For example, Figueroa-Colon et al. (1993) found that serum cholesterol values decreased significantly after 10 weeks of treatment in a sample of obese children. Gutin, Cucuzzo, Islam, Smith, and Stachura (1996) reported improvements in various cholesterol measures and triglycerides following a fitness training intervention in obese girls. Knip and Nuutinen (1993) also reported improvements in lipid profile among obese children who lost weight and found that these improvements persisted over five years. Other studies have reported improvements in insulin sensitivity (Hoffman, Stumbo, Janz, & Nielsen, 1995; Rocchini et al., 1987) and blood pressure (Brownell et al., 1983; Coates, Jeffery, et al., 1982). Although this literature is limited, these studies illustrate that important metabolic improvements may be obtainable from most weight loss attainment in children. This is expected to be an active area of clinical research.

The greatest increments in childhood obesity, on a population level, are occurring among the heaviest children (Troiano & Flegal, 1998). For serious cases of adolescent obesity, gastric surgery and pharmaceuticals may become options in the future. Dietz (1983) advises that weight loss medications be considered only for teenagers who are significantly obese and have limited treatment options. Currently, Sibutramine (a serotonin and noreprinephrine inhibitor) and Orlistat (a gastric lipase inhibitor) are the only FDA-approved weight control agents for individuals 16 years of age and older. Sufficient research is still lacking on the safety of weight loss medications for children and adolescents, but this area is expected to be one of increasing interest in the upcoming years (Berkowitz, Lyke, & Wadden, 2001).

Bariatric surgery is considered a potentially viable therapy only for adult patients who are morbidly obese, with a BMI greater than 40 kg/m^2, when more conservative approaches have been chronically unsuccessful. The two most common procedures currently performed are gastric bypass and vertical banded gastroplasty. Rand et al. described the experiences of 34 adolescents who went through a gastric surgery. Results appeared to be relatively successful, with a preoperative average BMI of 47 that was reduced to 32 after surgery. While self-esteem and psychosocial adjustments were improved, compliance with behavioral adjustments was low. Until further research is conducted, surgical options should be considered in an experimental stage and, even then, only when other nonsurgical options have been fully explored.

CONCLUSION

Family-based behavioral interventions are currently the treatment of choice for childhood and adolescent obesity. These methods, when introduced with consistency and in a positive milieu, can achieve short- and long-term weight changes that surpass the sorts of improvements that most obese adults seem able to achieve. Still, improvements are extremely difficult without the backing of the entire family system. Parents often fail to see a problem or are unwilling to make the personal changes that are pivotal to the child's success. It is hoped that mounting evidence for the serious health complication of childhood obesity and the fact that these disorders can be better managed by weight loss will capture the attention of and result in an enhanced commitment to change by parents.

REFERENCES

American Academy of Pediatrics. (1992). Statement on cholesterol. *Pediatrics, 90,* 469–473.
Arslanian, S., & Suprasongsin, C. (1996). Insulin sensitivity, lipids, and body composition in childhood: Is "syndrome X" present? *Journal of Clinical Endocrinology Metabolism, 81,* 1058–1062.

Barlow, S. E., & Dietz, W. H. (1998). Obesity evaluation and treatment: Expert committee recommendations. *Pediatrics, 102,* e.29. Available from www.pediatrics.org /cgi/content/full /102/3/e29.

Berkowitz, R. I., Lyke, J., & Wadden, T. A. (2001). Treatment of child and adolescent obesity. In F. Johnston & G. Foster (Eds.), *Obesity, growth and development* (pp. 169–184). London: Smith-Gordon.

Blomquist, B., Borjeson, M., Larsson, Y., Persson, B., & Sterky, G. (1965). The effect of physical activity on the body measurements and work capacity of overweight boys. *Acta Paediatrica Scandinavica, 54,* 566–572.

Brownell, K. D., Kelman, J. H., & Stunkard, A. J. (1983). Treatment of obese children with and without their mothers: Changes in weight and blood pressure. *Pediatrics, 71,* 515–523.

Coates, T. J., Jeffery, R. W., Slinkard, L. A., Killen, J. D., & Danaher, B. G. (1982). Frequency of contact and monetary reward in weight loss, lipid change, and blood pressure reduction with adolescents. *Behavior Therapy, 13*(2), 175–185.

Coates, T. J., Killen, J. D., & Slinkard, L. A. (1982). Parent participation in a treatment program for overweight adolescents. *International Journal of Eating Disorders, 1,* 37–48.

Cole, T. J., Bellizzi, M. C., Flegal, K. M., & Dietz, W. H. (2000). Establishing a standard definition for child overweight and obesity worldwide: International survey. *British Medical Journal, 320,* 1240–1243.

Crandall, C. S., & Schiffhauer, K. L. (1998). Anti-fat prejudice: Beliefs, values, and American culture. *Obesity Research, 6,* 458–460.

Dabelea, D., Hanson, R. L., Bennett, P. H., Roumain, J., Knowler, W. C., & Pettitt, D. J. (1998). Increasing prevalence of Type II diabetes in American Indian children. *Diabetologia, 11,* 904–910.

Daniels, S. R., Witt, S. A., Glascock, B., Khoury, P. R., & Kimball, T. R. (2002). Left atrial size in children with hypertension: The influence of obesity, blood pressure, and left ventricular mass. *Journal of Pediatrics, 141,* 186–190.

de la Eva, R. C., Baur, L. A., Donaghue, K. C., & Waters, K. A. (2002). Metabolic correlates with obstructive sleep apnea in obese subjects. *Journal of Pediatrics, 140,* 654–659.

Dietz, W. H. (1983). Childhood obesity: Susceptibility, cause, and management. *Journal of Pediatrics, 103,* 676–686.

Dietz, W. H. (1998). Health consequences of obesity in youth: Childhood predictors of adult disease. *Pediatrics, 101,* 518–525.

Dietz, W. H. (2001). Overweight and precursors of type 2 diabetes mellitus in children and adolescents. *Journal of Pediatrics, 138,* 453–454.

Dietz, W. H., & Mei, Z. (2002). Is failure to thrive a greater concern than obesity? *Journal of Pediatrics, 141,* 6–7.

Epstein, L. H., & Goldfield, G. S. (1999). Physical activity in the treatment of childhood overweight and obesity: Current evidence and research issues. *Medicine and Science in Sports and Exercise, 31,* S553–S559.

Epstein, L. H., Myers, M. D., Raynor, H. A., & Saelens, B. E. (1998). Treatment of pediatric obesity. *Pediatrics, 101,* 554–570.

Epstein, L. H., Paluch, R. A., Gordy, C. C., & Dorn, J. (2000). Decreasing sedentary behaviors in treating pediatric obesity. *Archives of Pediatric and Adolescent Medicine, 154,* 220–226.

Epstein, L. H., & Squires, S. (1988). *The Stoplight Diet for children: An eight-week program for parents and children.* Boston: Little, Brown.

Epstein, L. H., Valoski, A. M., Kalarchian, M. A., & McCurley, J. (1995). Do children lose and maintain weight easier than adults: A comparison of child and parent weight changes from six months to ten years. *Obesity Research, 3,* 411–417.

Epstein, L. H., Valoski, A. M., Vara, L. S., McCurley, J., Wisniewski, L., Kalarchian, M. A., et al. (1995). Effects of decreasing sedentary behavior and increasing activity on weight change in obese children. *Health Psychology, 14,* 109–115.

Epstein, L. H., Valoski, A. M., Wing, R. R., & McCurley, J. (1990). Ten-year follow-up of behavioral, family-based treatment for obese children. *Journal of the American Medical Association, 264,* 2519–2523.

Epstein, L. H., Valoski, A. M., Wing, R. R., & McCurley, J. (1994). Ten-year outcomes of behavioral family-based treatment for childhood obesity. *Health Psychology, 13,* 373–383.

Epstein, L. H., Wing, R. R., Koeske, R., Ossip, D., & Beck, S. (1982). A comparison of lifestyle change and programmed aerobic exercise on weight and fitness changes in obese children. *Behavior Therapy, 13,* 651–665.

Epstein, L. H., Wing, R. R., Koeske, R., & Valoski, A. (1985). A comparison of lifestyle exercise, aerobic exercise, and calisthenics on weight loss in obese children. *Behavior Therapy, 16,* 345–356.

Epstein, L. H., Wing, R. R., Penner, B. C., & Kress, M. J. (1985). Effect of diet and controlled exercise on weight loss in obese children. *Journal of Pediatrics, 107,* 358–361.

Epstein, L. H., Wing, R. R., Steranchak, L., Dickson, B., & Michelson, J. (1980). Comparison of family-based behavior modification and nutrition education for childhood obesity. *Journal of Pediatric Psychology, 5*(1), 25–36.

Epstein, L. H., Wisniewski, L., & Wing, R. (1994). Child and parent psychological problems influence child weight control. *Obesity Research, 2,* 509–515.

Fagot-Campagna, A., Pettitt, D. J., Engelgau, M. M., Burrows, N. R., Geiss, L. S., Valdez, R., et al. (2000). Type 2 diabetes among North American children and adolescents: An epidemiologic review and a public health perspective. *Journal of Pediatrics, 136,* 664–672.

Faith, M. S., & Allison, D. B. (1996). Obesity and physical health: Looking for shades of gray. *Weight Control Digest, 6,* 539–540.

Faith, M. S., Leone, M. A., Ayers, T. S., Heo, M., & Pietrobelli A. (2002) Weight criticism during physical activity, coping skills, and reported physical activity in children. *Pediatrics, 110,* e23.

Favaro, A., & Santonastaso, P. (1995). Effects of parents' psychological characteristics and eating behavior on childhood obesity and dietary compliance. *Journal of Psychosomatic Research, 39,* 145–151.

Figueroa-Colon, R., von Almen, T. K., Franklin, F. A., Schuftan, C., & Suskind, R. M. (1993). Comparison of two hypocaloric diets in obese children. *American Journal of Diseases of Children, 147,* 160–166.

Freedman, D. S., Khan, L. K., Dietz, W. H., Srinivasan, S. R., & Berenson, G. S. (2001). Relationship of childhood obesity to coronary heart disease risk factors in adulthood: The Bogalusa Heart Study. *Pediatrics, 108,* 712–718.

Freedman, D. S., Srinivasan, S. R., & Burke, G. L. (1987). Relation of body fat distribution to hyperinsulinemia in children and adolescents: The Bogalusa Heart Study. *American Journal of Clinical Nutrition, 46,* 403–410.

Golan, M., Weizman, A., Apter, A., & Fainaru, M. (1998). Parents as the exclusive agents of change in the treatment of childhood obesity. *American Journal of Clinical Nutrition, 67,* 1130–1135.

Goran, M. I. (2001). Metabolic precursors and effects of obesity in children: A decade of progress, 1990–1999. *American Journal of Clinical Nutrition, 73,* 158–171.

Gortmaker, S. L., Must, A., Perrin, J. M., Sobol, A. M., & Dietz, W. H. (1993). Social and economic consequences of overweight in adolescence and young adulthood. *New England Journal of Medicine, 329,* 1008–1012.

Gutin, B., Cucuzzo, N., Islam, S., Smith, C., & Stachura, M. E. (1996). Physical training, lifestyle education, and coronary risk factors in obese girls. *Medicine and Science in Sports and Exercise, 28*(1), 19–23.

Haddock, C. K., Shadish, W. R., Klesges, R. C., & Stein, R. J. (1994). Treatments for childhood and adolescent obesity. *Annals of Behavioral Medicine, 16,* 235–244.

Hills, A. P., & Parker, A. W. (1988). Obesity management via diet and exercise intervention. *Child: Care, Health, and Development, 14,* 409–416.

Hoffman, R. P., Stumbo, P. J., Janz, K. F., & Nielsen, D. H. (1995). Altered insulin resistance is associated with increased dietary weight loss in obese children. *Hormone Research, 44,* 17–22.

Jeffery, R. W., Drewnowski, A., Epstein, L. H., Stunkard, A. J., Wilson, G. T., Wing, R. R., et al. (2000). Long-term maintenance of weight loss: Current status. *Health Psychology, 19*(Suppl. 1), 5–16.

Jelalian, E., & Saelens, B. E. (1999). Intervention for pediatric obesity: Treatments that work. *Journal of Pediatric Psychology, 24,* 223–248.

Johnson, W. G., Hinkel, L. K., Carr, R. E., Anderson, D. A., Lemmon, C. R., Engler, L. B., et al. (1997). Dietary and exercise interventions for juvenile obesity: Long-term effects of behavioral and public health models. *Obesity Research, 5,* 257–261.

Kaplan, K. M., & Wadden, T. A. (1986). Childhood obesity and self-esteem. *Journal of Pediatrics, 109,* 367–370.

Kirschenbaum, D. S., Harris, E. S., & Tomarken, A. J. (1984). Effects of parental involvement in behavioral weight loss therapy for preadolescents. *Behavior Therapy, 15,* 485–500.

Knip, M., & Nuutinen, O. (1993). Long-term effects of weight reduction on serum lipids and plasma insulin in obese children. *American Journal of Clinical Nutrition, 57,* 490–493.

Lauer, R. M., Connor, W. E., & Leaverton, P. E. (1975). Coronary heart disease risk factors in school children: The Muscatine study. *Journal of Pediatrics, 86,* 697–706.

Lewy, V. D., Danadian, K., Witchel, S. F., & Arslanian, S. (2001). Early metabolic abnormalities in adolescent girls with polycystic ovarian syndrome. *Journal of Pediatrics, 138,* 38–44.

Maffeis, P., Moghetti, A., Grezzani, A., Clementi, M., Gaudino, R., & Tato, L. (2002). Insulin resistance and the persistence of obesity from childhood into adulthood. *Journal of Clinical Endocrinology and Metabolism, 87,* 171–176.

National Cholesterol Education Program. (1991). *Report of the expert panel on blood cholesterol levels in children and adolescents* (No. 91 2732). Washington, DC: U.S. Government Printing Office.

Ogden, C. L., Flegal, K. M., Carroll, M. D., & Johnson, C. L. (2002). Prevalence and trends in overweight among US children and adolescents, 1999–2000. *Journal of the American Medical Association, 288*(14), 1728–1732.

Pate, R., Trost, S., & Williams, C. (1998). Critique of existing guidelines for physical activity in young people. In S. Biddle, J. Sallis, & N. Cavill (Eds.), *Young and active? Young people and health-enhancing physical activity: Evidence and implications* (pp. 162–176). London: Health Education Authority.

Pinhas-Hamiel, O., Dolan, L. M., & Daniels, S. R. (1996). Increased incidence of non-insulin-dependent diabetes mellitus among adolescents. *Journal of Pediatrics, 128,* 608–615.

Rocchini, A. P., Katch, V., Anderson, J., Hinderliter, J., Becque, D., Martin, M., et al. (1988). Blood pressure in obese adolescents: Effect of weight loss. *Pediatrics, 82,* 16–23.

Rocchini, A. P., Katch, V., Schork, A., & Kelch, R. P. (1987). Insulin and blood pressure during weight loss in obese adolescents. *Hypertension, 10,* 267–273.

Sasaki, J., Shindo, M., Tanaka, H., Ando, M., & Arakawa, K. (1987). A long-term aerobic exercise program decreases the obesity index and increases the high density lipoprotein cholesterol concentration in obese children. *International Journal of Obesity, 11,* 339–345.

Second Task Force on Blood Pressure Control in Children. (1987). Report on the second Task Force on Blood Pressure Control in Children—1987. *Pediatrics, 79,* 1–25.

Sinaiko, A. R., Donahue, R. P., Jacobs, D. R., Jr., & Prineas, R. J. (1999). Relation of weight and rate of increase in weight during childhood and adolescence to body size, blood pressure, fasting insulin, and lipids in young adults: The Minneapolis Children's Blood Pressure Study. *Circulation, 11,* 1471–1476.

Sinaiko, A. R., Jacobs, D. R., Jr., Steinberger, J., Moran, A., Luepker, R., Rocchini, A. P., et al. (2001). Insulin resistance syndrome in childhood: Associations of the euglycemic insulin clamp and fasting insulin with fatness and other risk factors. *Journal of Pediatrics, 139,* 700–707.

Sinha, R., Fisch, G., Teague, B., Tamborlane, W. V., Banyas, B., Allen, K., et al. (2002). Prevalence of impaired glucose tolerance among children and adolescents with marked obesity. *New England Journal of Medicine, 346,* 802–810.

Stallings, V. A., Archibald, E. H., Pencharz, P. B., Harrison, J. E., & Bell, J. E. (1988). One-year follow-up of weight, total body potassium, and total body nitrogen in obese adolescents treated with the protein-sparing modified fast. *American Journal of Clinical Nutrition, 48,* 91–94.

Steinberger, J., Moorehead, C., Katch, V., & Rocchini, A. P. (1995). Relationship between insulin resistance and abnormal lipid profile in obese adolescents. *Journal of Pediatrics, 127,* 1009.

Striegel-Moore, R. H., Schreiber, G. B., Lo, A., Crawford, P., Obarzanek, E., & Rodin, J. (2000). Eating disorder symptoms in a cohort of 11- to 16-year-old black and white girls: The NHLBI growth and health study. *International Journal of Eating Disorders, 27,* 49–66.

Troiano, R. P., & Flegal, K. M. (1998). Overweight children and adolescents: Description, epidemiology, and demographics. *Pediatrics, 101,* 491–504.

U.S. Department of Health and Human Services. (1996). *Physical activity and health: A report of the Surgeon General.* Atlanta, GA: U.S. Department of Health and Human Services.

Wadden, T. A., Stunkard, A. J., Rich, L., Rubin, C. J., Sweidel, G., & McKinney, S. (1990). Obesity in black adolescent girls: A controlled clinical trial of treatment by diet, behavior modification, and parental support. *Pediatrics, 85,* 345–352.

Wilson, G. T. (1994). Behavioral treatment of obesity: Thirty years and counting. *Advances in Behavior Research and Therapy, 16*(1), 31–75.

PART III

Body Image Disturbances and Body Dysmorphic Disorder

Chapter 23

RISK FACTORS FOR THE DEVELOPMENT OF BODY IMAGE DISTURBANCES

ELEANOR H. WERTHEIM, SUSAN J. PAXTON, AND SIMONE BLANEY

This chapter addresses risk factors for the development of body image disturbances. Generally, researchers propose that multiple risk factors exist, covering biological, social, and psychological domains. Each of these domains is discussed, including descriptions of the hypothesized risk factors, possible mechanisms that link them to body image disturbance, and the sorts of evidence that are the basis for proposing them to be risk factors. In addition, a separate section includes a review of those studies that have used a prospective design. While body image concerns are often associated with eating disorders, this chapter reviews only predictors of body image variables, although at times dieting behaviors are referred to because they are associated with some types of body image concerns.

The context of risk factor research has been well described previously by Shisslak and Crago (2001; based on Kazdin, Kraemer, Kessler, Kupfer, & Offord, 1997), the aim of such research being to develop etiological models, to identify individuals most at risk, and to guide prevention and intervention. Both *risk* factors (antecedent conditions predicting undesirable outcomes) and *protective* factors (antecedent conditions predicting more positive or less undesirable outcomes) are of interest, although the bulk of research has focused on the former type.

AN OVERVIEW OF PROPOSED RISK FACTORS

Biological Factors

To a greater extent, body features are determined by biological and genetic factors. Biological characteristics may play an important role in the development of body image disturbances through several channels. First, neurobiological disorders or biological characteristics can directly influence individuals' perception of their bodies. Extreme examples of this process include gross misperception of body features such as perceptual "neglect" of a body part in some neuropsychological disorders or the phantom limb phenomenon in which individuals perceive a surgically removed limb as still present (Cummings, 1988). Parietal lobe-related epilepsy or migraines can be associated with a variety of types of body misperception, including right-left orientation deficits and hallucinations or delusions that the body is much larger or smaller than it actually is (Braun & Chouinard, 1992). A more moderate example of a biological factor in body perception is an overestimation of waist size during the premenstrual phase of the cycle (Altabe & Thompson, 1990). A second manner in which biological factors may operate is through particular body features causing discomfort or inconvenience, which directly leads to body concerns or disturbances, as in the case of very large breasts (Glatt et al., 1999), a pregnant body, menstruation (Altabe & Thompson, 1990; Carr-Nangle, Johnson, Bergeron, & Nangle, 1994), or specific physical disabilities.

Finally, certain biologically determined characteristics become risk factors only when they depart from socially determined norms of attractiveness or individual ideals and are considered both undesirable and important. A variety of such socially evaluated features exist, including male pattern hair loss (Cash, 1990), height, skin characteristics, breast size, facial features, and disfigurement (Thompson, Heinberg, Altabe, & Tantleff-Dunn, 1999). The most commonly discussed body features have been body size (overweight or underweight) and shape (relative proportions of waist, hips, etc.). In Western cultures, body size and shape are often associated with body dissatisfaction and weight concerns. Individuals with the highest body mass index (BMI) are more likely to report body dissatisfaction than those in the normal- or low-weight range; among females, even normal-weight individuals are often overconcerned about their bodies (Afifi-Soweid, Najem Kteily, & Shediac-Rizkallah, 2002; Kennett & Nisbet, 1998; Maude, Wertheim, Paxton, Gibbons, & Szmukler, 1993; Paxton et al., 1991). The moderating effects of sociocultural influences are discussed more fully later.

Actual body size appears to influence both individuals' body ideals and body perception. For example, in correlational studies in which individuals rate a series of figures to indicate which figure represents how they currently look and which is closest to their perception of their ideal size, the two ratings are highly correlated (Dunkley, Wertheim, & Paxton, 2001), even in women with eating disorders (Wertheim & Weiss, 1989); increases in weight in women have been shown to be paralleled by increases in ideal weight (Cooley & Toray, 2001). These findings suggest that individuals' body ideals are, at least partially, influenced by their actual body size; however, where large discrepancies remain or if this process leads to an ideal that is a "moving target" that can never be reached, body disturbance could result. In relation to body size influencing body perception, smaller individuals are more likely to overestimate their body size (Thompson, Penner, & Altabe, 1990). Thus, actual body size and shape can form a setting condition, which influences a variety of other factors that can potentially lead to body image disturbance.

Sociocultural Influences

Sociocultural models of the development of body image disturbance propose that standards of beauty within society in general or in the more proximal environments in which individuals live (e.g., in schools, families, neighborhoods) influence individuals' opinions about and feelings toward their own bodies. When these social standards or ideals are both difficult to achieve and portrayed as highly important, they may set the stage for body disturbances in those who perceive that they do not meet the socially prescribed ideals. Evidence for sociocultural risk factors comes from a variety of sources, which are discussed in turn.

Differences in the Beauty Ideals and Body Concerns across Cultures

The sociocultural hypothesis can be tested at a basic level by examining whether differences in beauty ideals and body concerns exist among cultures, such as in separate regions of the world or in ethnic groups in a particular country. Research suggests that such ethnic and cultural differences do exist in preferred body features such as weight and shape (Neumark-Sztainer et al., 2002) or skin toning and breast size (Altabe, 1998). For example, numerous studies have found that, despite higher rates of obesity, Black women in Western cultures are more satisfied with their weight and appearance than White women, and they accept a wider range of body weights including a larger body size as ideal (Franko & Striegel-Moore, 2002; Lovejoy, 2001; Neumark-Sztainer et al., 2002). Similarly, in the non-Western society of Ghana, male and female university students of U.S. origin chose thinner ideal figure sizes than those of Ghanaian origin, and U.S.-origin women (as opposed to women from Ghana or men) were the most likely to be dissatisfied with their bodies (Cogan, Bhalla, Sefa-Dedeh, & Rothblum, 1996).

Further evidence of the cultural origins of these ethnic differences comes from studies including measures of cultural identity or acculturation. For example, stronger African American cultural identity within an African American sample has been associated with less susceptibility to certain types of body dissatisfaction (Makkar & Strube, 1995; Pumariega, Gustavson, Gustavson, Motes, & Ayers, 1994). Similarly, immigrating to a Western culture at an earlier age has been found to predict thinness ideals in Hispanic American females (Lopez, Blix, & Blix, 1995).

In summary, there is some descriptive evidence that beauty ideals and body concerns vary among cultures. While these studies are consistent with culture as a possible risk factor, further causal evidence is necessary for strong conclusions to be made. Cultural issues implicated in eating disorders are discussed in more depth in Chapter 24.

Changes in the Ideal Image of Beauty over Time

Not only does the ideal image of beauty vary among cultures, but it also changes over time in an individual culture. Current societal ideals are likely to establish certain body types as more at risk. Probably because of widespread research concern about eating disorders, most research on this topic has documented changing societal patterns in relation to the female body shape.

Ideals of beauty as portrayed through art have suggested that in some earlier centuries, voluptuous female forms, at times pregnant-like, at other times generally curvaceous or hourglass-shaped, have been favored (Fallon, 1990; O'Dea, 1995; Thompson, Heinberg, et al., 1999). Over the course of the twentieth century, ideals of female beauty varied, becoming progressively more slim or less curvaceous in the latter half of the century, as demonstrated by the decreased size of *Playboy* magazine models, Miss America beauty pageant contestants, *London* magazine models, ballet dancers, and fashion shop mannequins (Abraham, Beumont, Fraser, & Llewellyn-Jones, 1982; Garner, Garfinkel, Schwartz, & Thompson, 1980; Morris, Cooper, & Cooper, 1989; Rintala & Mustajoki,

1992; Wiseman, Gray, Mosimann, & Ahrens, 1992). These icons of beauty are generally considered underweight when compared to healthy or standard weight norms (Garner et al., 1980), as are other models of beauty, such as children's Barbie and Ken dolls (Norton, Olds, Olive, & Dank, 1996). In the latter part of the twentieth century, changes have also been documented in preferences about male body shapes, particularly related to increases in musculature (e.g., Pope, Phillips, & Olivardia, 2000; Silverstein, Perdue, Peterson, & Kelly, 1986).

Paralleling movement toward a thinner ideal of female beauty have been increases in media articles encouraging weight loss through dieting or, more recently, exercise (Garner et al., 1980; Silverstein et al., 1986; Wiseman et al., 1992). While this sort of evidence that cultural ideals influence body concerns is only correlational, it does suggest that societal ideals of beauty can form *setting conditions* in which individuals are likely to develop body concerns when they depart from those standards.

Parent Influences

While within a culture, body-related ideals may exist, immediate subcultural influences are likely to be important in transmitting these values directly. A major proximal risk factor for children is thought to be parental influence. Both mothers and fathers play a role in communicating values about weight, shape, and body attributes (Striegel-Moore & Kearney-Cooke, 1994; Wertheim, Martin, Prior, Sanson, & Smart, 2002; Wertheim, Mee, & Paxton, 1999). Research to date has focused on two main types of parental influence:

1. *Parental modeling* of behaviors related to weight concerns involving parents having body concerns of their own or attempting to lose weight through various methods.

2. *Direct communications* that either evaluate the child's body or encourage the child to change his or her body weight or shape.

Parent influence studies are generally cross-sectional. While perceptions of children are likely to be important predictors of body image concerns, they do not directly address the question of actual environmental influence, so the studies reviewed here all include parent as well as child reports.

In general, there is consistent evidence that children who have body concerns and diet are more likely to have parents who encourage them to lose weight or who make negative comments about the child's body (Keel, Heatherton, Harnden, & Hornig, 1997; Moreno & Thelen, 1993; Pike & Rodin, 1991; Thelen & Cormier, 1995; Wertheim et al., 1999). Parents who suggest a child lose weight often do have heavier children; however, even when BMI is controlled for, a significant (though reduced) relationship is often found between parent encouragement of a child to lose weight and children's own dieting or weight concerns (Benedikt, Wertheim, & Love, 1998; Thelen & Cormier, 1995; Wertheim et al., 2002).

Evidence is less clear about modeling effects, with some studies finding similarities between parent and child (Pike & Rodin, 1991; Ruther & Richman, 1993); others finding no relationship (Attie & Brooks-Gunn, 1989; Byely, Archibald, Graber, &

Brooks-Gunn, 2000; Kanakis & Thelen, 1995; Keel et al., 1997; Moreno & Thelen, 1993; Thelen & Cormier, 1995); and still others finding a relationship on one measure but not another (Benedikt et al., 1998; Hill & Franklin, 1998; Hill, Weaver, & Blundell, 1990; Wertheim et al., 2002). In addition, in girls around puberty, menstrual status may be a moderator, with mother-child similarities in drive for thinness found only in menstrual girls (Sanftner, Crowther, Crawford, & Watts, 1996; Usmiani & Daniluk, 1997; Wertheim et al., 2002).

Overall, these studies suggest that moderate parental concerns about their own bodies are not always influential on the child, unless they translate into direct communications about the child's body or the parent models obvious weight loss behaviors, such as crash dieting and skipping meals, in which case those specific behaviors are more likely to be reported by the child as well (Benedikt et al., 1998; Wertheim et al., 1999). Parental commentary about children's bodies appears to be a stronger risk factor for the development of body concerns in children, although the mostly cross-sectional nature of research to date limits causal conclusions.

Peer Environment

Peers provide another important proximal social environment, and they may affect an individual's body satisfaction in several ways. As with parents, peers may play a role in setting and communicating values about weight and desirable body image, thereby dictating appearance norms and ideals. In addition, peers may actively reward or punish adherence to body appearance norms, reinforcing satisfaction in a body conforming to the prevailing ideal or dissatisfaction in a body that does not conform. Cross-sectional associations support each of these possibilities, though the extent to which these associations reflect causal mechanisms is not yet clear.

Adolescent females within friendship groups have been shown to have similar levels of body dissatisfaction, at least partially independent of BMI, depression, and self-esteem (Paxton, Schutz, Wertheim, & Muir, 1999). While it is not clear whether girls become more like their peers over time, join friendship groups with similar attitudes to their own, or do both, this finding of friendship group similarities does support the existence of peer and friendship group norms in relation to body concerns. Friendship groups exhibiting relatively high body dissatisfaction were also more likely to talk about weight, shape, and dieting. This style of talk, especially "I'm so fat," "No, you're not" conversations, has been described as "fat talk" (Nichter, 2000; Nichter & Vuckovic, 1994). One of the consequences of "fat talk" may be to set norms about acceptable body shape and size, the importance of body shape, and appropriate behaviors to maintain or achieve the ideal.

An individual's perception that peers consider weight and shape to be important has also been found to be a strong correlate of weight concerns and body dissatisfaction in individual girls (Barr Taylor et al., 1998; Paxton et al., 1999). "Fat talk" may communicate the importance of weight and shape and the initiator's anxiety. Qualitative research suggests that "fat talk" may provide reassurance to the initiator and affirmation from friends for the initiator but may also result in insecurity and body image concerns in the recipient (Nichter, 2000; Nichter & Vuckovic, 1994; Wertheim, Paxton, Schutz, & Muir, 1997). In an ingenious experimental manipulation of "fat talk" in which a slim confederate either complained about her weight or conversed about neutral topics, young women exposed to the "fat talk" condition reported lower body satisfaction following exposure (Stice, Maxfield, & Wells, in press). When weight and shape are regarded as particularly important to peers, anxiety about conforming to ideals and attention to perceived deviations from the ideals in self are likely to be higher.

One way for an individual to determine the extent to which he or she conforms to peer group weight and shape norms is to engage in body comparison with peers. Thus, peers may serve as points of comparison so that individuals may determine their "place" within their own most relevant social environment. Research supports peers as being major targets of body comparison (Heinberg & Thompson, 1992; Schutz, Paxton, & Wertheim, 2002; Wertheim et al., 1997).

Peers may actively reinforce body image attitudes. In adolescents, the reward of popularity is frequently viewed as dependent on conforming to the thin body image ideal (Nichter & Vuckovic, 1994; Wertheim et al., 1997). On the other hand, a powerful reinforcer of negative body image is likely to be teasing, though not necessarily from peers exclusively. In cross-sectional studies, weight and shape teasing is a strong correlate of body dissatisfaction independent of actual BMI (Barr Taylor et al., 1998; Lunner et al., 2000; Paxton et al., 1999; Thompson & Heinberg, 1993; Wertheim, Koerner, & Paxton, 2001; Wertheim et al., 1997), and in a retrospective study, Cash (1995) implicated teasing as a potential causal factor for body dissatisfaction. One prospective study has shown weight-related teasing to be a predictor of later general body dissatisfaction after initial body dissatisfaction had been controlled for (Cattarin & Thompson, 1994). Further longitudinal and experimental research is required to confirm weight and shape teasing as causally related to body dissatisfaction.

The potential for peers to play a protective role and support the development of positive body image also needs to be considered. Just as peer body dissatisfaction is associated with self body dissatisfaction, peer satisfaction and low peer shape and weight concern is associated with lower self-dissatisfaction (Paxton et al., 1999). Positive peer influence has been described more specifically in relation to deterring extreme weight loss behaviors than determining body image (Wertheim et al., 1997). However, indirect support for a positive role of peers is gained from the success of a school-based peer support group intervention in improving weight and appearance esteem over a three-month period (McVey, Lieberman, Voorberg, Wardrope, & Blackmore, 2001).

Media Influence

Visual presentations of slim, idealized women and athletic men are inescapable in the Western world. These idealized body shapes are portrayed as associated with happiness and social success; and while presented as the images to which we should aspire, they are unobtainable for the vast majority by virtue of the rare body shape and image manipulation (Pope et al., 2000; Thompson, Heinberg, et al., 1999). The rift between the ideal presented in the media and the reality for most individuals is assumed to be one source of body dissatisfaction. But, as excellent reviews highlight (e.g., Levine & Smolak, 1996; Levine, Piran, & Stoddard, 1999), individuals engage with media in many complex ways, and the consequences of exposure to idealized images are not consistent across individuals. Researchers have looked for support for a role of media in the development of body dissatisfaction by examining the relationship between the amount of media exposure and body image. However, findings have been inconsistent;

some studies have observed associations between high media exposure and poor body image or disturbed eating, while others have not or have found associations with only some forms of media (e.g., Becker, Burwell, Gilman, Herzog, & Hamburg, 2002; Botta, 1999; Cusumano & Thompson, 1997; Harrison & Cantor, 1997; Leit, Gray, & Pope, 2002; Stice, Schupak-Neuberg, Shaw, & Stein, 1994; Stice, Spangler, & Agras, 2001; Tiggemann & Pickering, 1996).

Experimental designs have been used to examine the short-term impact on body image in women of exposure to slim, idealized female images. Again, findings from individual studies have been somewhat mixed. However, a meta-analysis of 25 controlled experimental studies found that body image was significantly more negative after viewing thin media images than after control conditions (Groesz, Levine, & Murnen, 2002). This effect was stronger in studies of women under 19 years old. Recent research indicates that individual differences are likely to influence the effect of image exposure. Internalization of the thin ideal, appearance comparison, and initial body dissatisfaction have been found to predict a more negative impact of idealized image exposure in adolescent girls (Durkin & Paxton, 2002). If thinness is highly valued and frequent comparisons are made between self and idealized images, typically, the observations made will have negative implications for self-evaluation. A mechanism of action in the relationship between body image and media image exposure is proposed by Hargreaves and Tiggemann (2002). They observed that the effect of appearance-related television commercials on body image was moderated by level of appearance schema and suggest that exposure to appearance-related commercials act by priming appearance-related schema.

While experimental studies generally indicate short-term negative effects on body image of exposure to idealized media images, it is not clear how long these effects are sustained nor whether there is a relationship between short-term impact and long-term, stable body dissatisfaction. It is plausible that repeated exposure in vulnerable individuals could have a cumulative impact, resulting in body dissatisfaction although further prospective research is required to explore this issue.

Additive Effects of Multiple Sociocultural "Agents"

Theoretically, it would be expected that individuals who are at greatest risk of developing body concerns would live in a total environment that includes a greater endorsement of unhealthy body-related norms. While cross-cultural studies and studies of special high-risk environments, such as ballet schools (Piran, 1999; Szmukler, Eisler, Gillies, & Hayward, 1985), shed light on this issue, another approach is to determine—in individuals in the same culture—which types of sociocultural agents are seen as providing most pressure to be thin and whether the effects of these different types of agents is additive.

Several self-report studies have examined the relationships of media, family, and peers simultaneously in children and adolescents and have found that the effects are indeed additive, with reports of multiple agents pressuring individuals to be thin being associated with smaller thinness ideals and more body concerns (Dunkley et al., 2001; Levine, Smolak, & Hayden, 1994; Taylor et al., 1998). These findings offer further support for the idea that body concerns are most likely to emerge in the context of a general subculture of weight and shape consciousness in which multiple agents apply (or at least are perceived to apply) influence. The findings have implications for prevention work, in which total social environments may need to be changed for the interventions to be most effective.

Developmental Factors

Developmental transitions may be important factors in triggering psychological disturbances, including those associated with the body. The most discussed developmental period is puberty, although other times of developmental transition may be important as well, such as early childhood when body ideals and concerns are likely to start (Ricciardelli & McCabe, 2001; Truby & Paxton, 2002), pregnancy, and mid- or later life.

Puberty

During puberty, both boys and girls find themselves going through large changes in their bodies, to which they must adjust in a relatively short period of time. In addition, children develop during this period at different rates and may become concerned if they compare their own bodies to that of their peers. Concerns could potentially develop either if individuals are very early maturing or very late maturing because, in either case, they do not match the norm, during a time when "fitting in" is seen as highly important.

As discussed later, while longitudinal studies of pubertal development as a risk factor have had mixed findings, there is some evidence that early menstrual onset predicts greater body dissatisfaction. However, this relationship may be mediated by associated increases in body size. For girls, in particular, pubertal development and associated milestones such as pubic hair distribution or breast maturation are associated with higher adiposity and greater body size (Brown, Koenig, Demorales, McGuire, & Mersia, 1996; Kimm, Barton, Obarzanek, & Crawford, 1997; Richards, Boxer, Petersen, & Albrecht, 1990; Wertheim et al., 2002). Thus, during puberty, girls in current Western societies find themselves moving farther from the current societally preferred thinness ideal of beauty, the slim tubular body, which can then place them at risk of body concerns.

Pregnancy

During pregnancy, women experience substantial body changes that result in inconvenience and discomfort (e.g., morning sickness, difficulty bending down; Moore, 1978) as well as a departure from current Western ideals of beauty (weight gain, stretch marks). As a result, this life stage for women is potentially a risk period for the development of body image disturbances. For example, if women retain their normal prepregnant expectations of how they should look, they may be at risk of increased body concerns during the pregnancy. Alternatively, women may temporarily relax their normal body standards, knowing that the phase is temporary and has other benefits (Davies & Wardle, 1994; Richardson, 1990). In this latter case, the postpartum phase is potentially one of greater risk, when women find themselves with residual weight gain or semipregnant appearance after the birth of the baby.

While most women appear to adjust well to body changes during pregnancy, the last trimester appears to be the time of most risk, and a subgroup of women report distress about weight gain (Boscaglia, Skouteris, & Wertheim, 2003; Fairburn & Welch, 1990;

Goodwin, Astbury, & McMeeken, 2000; Mercer, 1981; Richardson, 1990; Strang & Sullivan, 1985). During the postpartum, persisting alterations in body shape have been found to surprise and/or distress many women, leading to decreased body satisfaction compared to prepregnancy (Leifer, 1977; Stein & Fairburn, 1996; Strang & Sullivan, 1985). Women who appear to be at greatest risk during the postpartum are those who fail to lose weight gained during pregnancy (Stein & Fairburn, 1996) and those who already had body concerns before the pregnancy (Devine, Bove, & Olson, 2000; Fairburn & Welch, 1990; Leifer, 1977). Thus, pregnancy and the postpartum are likely to be risk periods in the context of greater weight gain and a predisposing vulnerability to body concerns.

Menopause and Older Age

Most developmental body image research has examined transitions at younger ages. However, several studies have examined body image in relation to menopause in women and to aging in both genders in cross-sectional designs, with the underlying assumption that in Western societies in which a youth-centered body image ideal prevails, body image dissatisfaction increases with aging. In a study of women ages 35 to 65 years, Deeks and McCabe (2001) observed that the effects of age and menopausal stage could not be separated and that, in general, younger women had more positive ratings of appearance satisfaction than older women. Other cross-sectional studies, however, have found body dissatisfaction to be similar in women across middle and older age groups, suggesting stability of body image in adulthood (Lewis & Cachelin, 2001; Paxton & Phythian, 1999; Tiggemann & Lynch, 2001). Further studies suggest that appearance anxiety and importance of appearance may be less in older women (Pliner, Chaiken, & Flett, 1990; Tiggemann & Lynch, 2001). Only a few studies have examined body image in relation to age in adult men. Paxton and Phythian observed less appearance evaluation (satisfaction) in older-age men compared to middle-age men. However, in older men, less value is placed on appearance (Paxton & Phythian, 1999; Pliner et al., 1990). These findings related to aging in both women and men suggest that the impact of body dissatisfaction later in life may be moderated by a lower importance placed on appearance. However, interpretation of studies of menopause, aging, and body image is severely limited by the absence of longitudinal studies because differences or stability across age groups may well reflect cohort effects rather than developmental changes.

Life Events

Sexual Abuse

Particular life events or experiences have the potential to increase the risk of body image concerns. One of the most researched experiences is sexual abuse. Several hypotheses have been offered for how sexual abuse could lead to body disturbances, including through altering the meaning of the body, through an increase in bodily shame, and through attempts to control the body and make it less vulnerable (Andrews, 1995; Beckman & Burns, 1990; Connors, 2001; Kearney-Cooke & Striegel-Moore, 1994). A review of studies of sexual abuse as a risk factor (Connors, 2001) indicated evidence for increased body self-consciousness in young children who have been sexually abused and for more weight concerns, body dissatisfaction, and dieting in adolescents and older individuals with a history of sexual abuse. However, findings are not always consistent in relation to the form that body concerns take or whether they are indeed increased in sexually abused groups (particularly in older samples). Furthermore, the specific pathways are just beginning to be examined (e.g., Trent & Petrie, 2001), although numerous mediator and moderator variables have been discussed, such as general distress and psychopathology, family support, general family dysfunction, early puberty, and how negatively the abuse was experienced at the time it occurred (Connors, 2001). In addition, effects on body image might vary depending on the nature of abuse, for example, whether it involves overt sexual contact or more covert forms such as unwanted sexual attention (Weiner & Thompson, 1997; Whealin & Jackson, 2002). More research is needed to clarify sexual abuse as a potential risk factor.

Individual Factors

Gender

Gender is an important moderator variable in understanding the risk factors related to body disturbances. While it is likely that the general types of biopsychosocial risk factors and processes are similar across genders, the specific nature of these influences may differ for males and females. For example, both males and females are likely to be at risk if they live in an environment that devalues their particular body type. However, the specific nature of the ideal body and the relative importance placed on that ideal are likely to differ between genders in various social contexts.

As an example, studies that have examined body figure ideals and considered differences between individuals' ratings of their current versus their ideal body size indicate that, when dissatisfied with their current shape, the vast majority of females desire to be thinner. In contrast, when males are dissatisfied with their weight, about half (or more) wish to gain weight (Anderson, Huston, Schmitt, Linbarger, & Wright, 2001; Maude et al., 1993), and males tend to prefer a more muscular body (Cohane & Pope, 2001). These gender differences are likely to derive from sociocultural ideals stressing different preferred body shapes for males and females.

Sexual Orientation

Sexual orientation can be considered an individual risk factor related to specific subcultural norms about appearance. Specifically, it has been suggested that a greater emphasis on physical attractiveness in homosexual males places them at greater risk of body concerns than heterosexual males. Conversely, lesbian women have been proposed to be at less risk due to a decreased emphasis on appearance (French, Story, Remafedi, Resnick, & Blum, 1996). Studies have largely supported these conjectures in men, with homosexual men reporting greater body and weight dissatisfaction (Beren, Hayden, Wilfley, & Grilo, 1996; French et al., 1996; Siever, 1994). Findings related to lesbian versus heterosexual women have been more mixed, with some results indicating no differences and others indicating lesbian women to be more accepting of higher weights or less concerned about body size (Beren et al., 1996; Brand, Rothblum, & Solomon, 1992; French et al., 1996; Gettelman & Thompson, 1993; Siever, 1994; Striegel-Moore, Tucker, & Hsu, 1990).

Individual Psychological Factors

A range of potential psychological risk factors for body dissatisfaction has been examined, including depression, anxiety, low self-esteem, and negative emotionality. It may be proposed that these characteristics result in negative self-evaluations, including poor body image. However, while negative affect and low self-esteem have been consistently found to be correlates of body dissatisfaction (Grilo, Wilfley, Brownell, & Rodin, 1994; Ohring, Graber, & Brooks-Gunn, 2002; Paxton et al., 1999; Stormer & Thompson, 1996; Thompson & Psaltis, 1988), evidence for a causal link is not so strong. Poorer Time 1 emotional tone was associated with body dissatisfaction at two-year follow-up in adolescent girls in one study (Ohring et al., 2002). But in the majority of longitudinal studies exploring this issue, as described further later, there is little evidence of a causal relationship (e.g., Button, Sonuga-Barke, Davies, & Thompson, 1996; Holsen, Kraft, & Roysamb, 2001; G. C. Martin et al., 2000). There is growing evidence to suggest that rather than depression causing body dissatisfaction, body dissatisfaction may precede the development of depression (e.g., Stice & Bearman, 2001; Stice, Hayward, Cameron, Killen, & Taylor, 2000).

Evidence is emerging for potential causal roles in the development of body dissatisfaction for two individual psychological characteristics that are more specifically body focused—internalization of the thin ideal and body comparison. Internalization of the thin ideal, reflecting the desire to emulate the thin ideal and perception of the importance placed on thinness for success and attractiveness, has been proposed to mediate the relationship between social influences and body dissatisfaction (Stice, 1994; Thompson, Heinberg, et al., 1999), such that social pressures from peers, parents, and the media are said to exert their influence on body dissatisfaction by increasing individuals' internalization of societal thinness ideals. A relationship between internalization of the thin ideal and body dissatisfaction is supported by cross-sectional research (Stormer & Thompson, 1996), and two longitudinal studies have found internalization of the thin ideal to predict later body dissatisfaction (Stice, 2001; Stice & Whitenton, 2002). In addition, experimental studies have observed that internalization of the thin ideal is associated with short-term increases in appearance dissatisfaction following exposure to thin female media images in adolescent girls and college women (Cattarin, Thompson, Thomas, & Williams, 2000; Durkin & Paxton, 2002; Heinberg & Thompson, 1995).

Derived from Festinger's (1954) social comparison theory, the individual attribute of body comparison is the degree to which a person compares his or her own body with those of others. A negative body evaluation may develop when body comparison results in a person's becoming more aware of his or her own perceived physical failings (Thompson, Heinberg, et al., 1999), especially when the motive for comparison is self-evaluation (M. C. Martin & Gentry, 1997). Fisher, Dunn, and Thompson (in press) have identified two primary comparison dimensions in adolescents: weight/nonweight and muscle/nonmuscle, with females emphasizing body sites along the former dimension while males emphasize body areas along the latter dimension. Individuals vary in the extent to which they report comparing their bodies with others, and there is a strong correlation between body comparison tendency and body dissatisfaction (e.g., Paxton et al., 1999; Schutz et al., 2002; Striegel-Moore, McAvay, & Rodin, 1986). While, theoretically, the effect of a body comparison could be a positive evaluation of the self

(Festinger, 1954), this seems rarely to be the outcome (Schutz et al., 2002) While a causal relationship has yet to be confirmed, as described later in relation to multifactorial models, structural equation modeling (SEM) of cross-sectional data sets indicates that body comparison precedes body dissatisfaction (van den Berg, Thompson, Brandon, & Coovert, 2002). Further support for a role for body comparison in the development of body dissatisfaction emerges from experimental research. While specifically investigating short-term changes in body dissatisfaction, studies have found body comparison tendency to predict the negative impact on body image of viewing idealized female media images in adolescent and college-age women (Cattarin et al., 2000; Durkin & Paxton, 2002). Thus, a variety of methods have suggested that a person's internalization of the thin ideal and tendency to compare his or her body to others can be a risk factor for body dissatisfaction.

MULTIFACTORIAL MODELS OF THE DEVELOPMENT OF BODY DISSATISFACTION

A number of authors have developed multifactorial, integrative models for the development of body image concerns (e.g., Cash, 1996; Stice, 1994; Thompson et al., 1999; van den Berg, Wertheim, Thompson, & Paxton, 2002), change in body image satisfaction following exposure to idealized female images (Durkin & Paxton, 2002), overvalued ideas about the personal implications of body shape and weight (Wade & Lowes, 2002), and drive for thinness (Lunner et al., 2000; Wertheim et al., 2001). The models demonstrate a recognition of the complex interaction among individual attributes and sociocultural factors and suggest potential linking mechanisms.

Cash (1996, 2002) proposed that the causes of dysfunctional body experiences are historical, developmental, and proximal influences that govern day-to-day body experiences (see Figure 23.1). The historical influences include cultural socialization, interpersonal experiences (e.g., teasing history), physical characteristics (e.g., BMI), and personality attributes (e.g., social confidence and self-esteem). These influences affect the development of body image schema that may be activated by everyday events such as social scrutiny, social comparisons, and wearing certain clothes. These everyday experiences are associated with internal dialogues (thoughts, interpretations, and conclusions) that potentiate body image emotions and provide the motivation for behaviors that help lessen their impact—such as avoiding situations, seeking social reinforcement, and compensatory actions. These behaviors are further reinforced by their emotion-regulating role. Cash's model is a very valuable one because it provides suggestions of not only causal pathways, but also psychological mechanisms that act to maintain body image dysphoria.

A particularly influential model of the development of body dissatisfaction was articulated by Stice (1994) in the context of a model of the development of bulimia nervosa (see Figure 23.2). Importantly, in this model, Stice described the role of interactions between sociocultural influences and individual attributes in the development of body dissatisfaction. He proposed that family, peer, and media influences act as transmitters of cultural norms that emphasize the importance of appearance and thinness to attractiveness, femininity, and success. These factors contribute to the internalization of beliefs

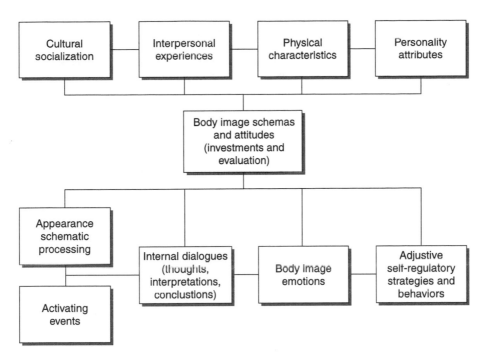

Figure 23.1 A Cognitive-Behavioural Model of Body Image Development and Experiences. Reproduced from "Cognitive Behavioral Perspectives on Body Image," pp. 38–46, by T. F. Cash, in *Body Image: A Handbook of Theory, Research, and Clinical Practice*, T. F. Cash and T. Pruzinsky (Eds.), 2002, New York: Guilford Press.

about the importance of thinness, but their impact is moderated by the individual attributes of self-esteem and identity confusion. The greater the internalization of the thin ideal, usually a very difficult ideal to attain, the greater the likelihood of body dissatisfaction. This relationship is moderated by weight; the greater a person's size, the more likely the person will have difficulty in meeting the pressures to be thin. The role of the internalization of the thin ideal as a mediator between sociocultural pressures and body dissatisfaction has been widely supported by empirical research (e.g., Stice et al., 1994; Stice, Shaw, & Nemeroff, 1998).

Thompson, Heinberg, et al. (1999) have proposed hypothetical integrative models for the development of body image disturbance, describing relationships among sociocultural pressures, internalization of the thin ideal, body comparison, and global psychological functioning. In a partial test of these models, in college students using SEM, van den Berg et al. (2002) found body comparison mediated the impact of perfectionism and perceived family and media influences on body dissatisfaction, while BMI and global psychological functioning had direct effects on body dissatisfaction. Perceived peer influences had a direct effect on dietary restriction but not on body dissatisfaction (see Figure 23.3). This model suggests that perception of environmental pressures to be thin increases body comparison behavior, which has a negative impact on body dissatisfaction.

Durkin, Paxton, and Sorbello (2002) have examined an integrative model of characteristics that contribute to more negative impact on body satisfaction of viewing idealized female media images in two samples of Australian and one sample of Italian grade

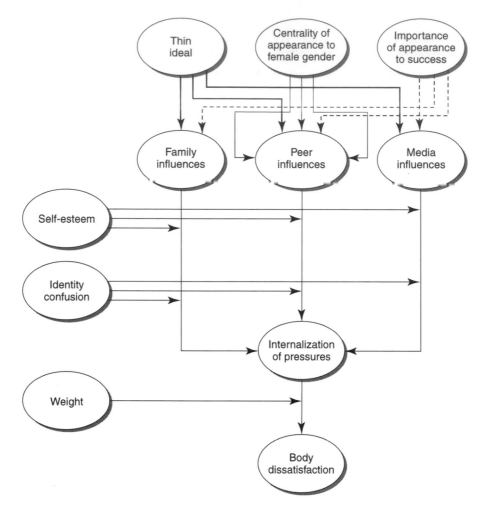

Figure 23.2 Influences on the Development of Body Dissatisfaction. *Source:* Proposed in "Review of the Evidence for a Sociocultural Model of Bulimia Nervosa and an Exploration of the Mechanisms of Action," by E. Stice, 1994, *Clinical Psychology Review, 14,* pp. 633–661. Reprinted with permission from Elsevier.

10 girls using SEM techniques. Change in body satisfaction after viewing idealized female images was predicted by body comparison tendency. Psychological functioning and internalization of the thin ideal directly predicted body comparisons tendency. In addition, the impact of psychological functioning on body comparisons tendency was mediated by internalization of the thin ideal.

Wade and Lowes' (2002) examination of predictors of overvalued ideas about the personal implications of body shape and weight (potentially a precursor of body dissatisfaction) is somewhat consistent with these models of pathways to body dissatisfaction. They observed that perfectionism, conflict between parents, and comments about weight and shape negatively predicted self-esteem, which negatively predicted overvalued ideas.

Finally, numerous studies investigating the interrelationship of factors that contribute to body dissatisfaction have particularly explored the role of weight and shape teasing. One SEM analysis in college women explored the relationship among maturational

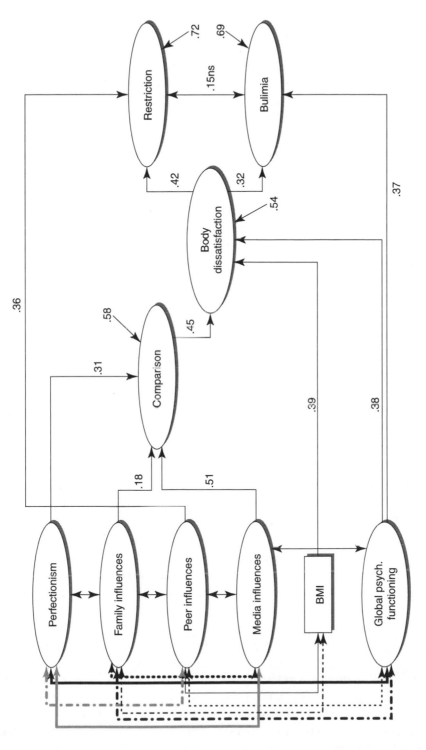

Figure 23.3 Multifactorial Model of the Development of Body Dissatisfaction and Disordered Eating. From "The Tripartite Influence Model of Body Image and Eating Disturbance: a Covariance Structure Modelling Investigation Testing the Mediational Role of Appearance Comparison," by P. van den Berg, J. K. Thompson, K. Brandon, and M. Coovert, 2002, Journal of Psychosomatic Research. pp. 1007–1020. Reprinted with permission from Elsevier.

timing, teasing, body comparison, body image, eating disturbance, and self-esteem (Thompson, Coovert, & Stormer, 1999). The model of best fit indicated that the relationship between teasing and body dissatisfaction was partially mediated by body comparison. Research has also examined the relationships among BMI, teasing history, and body dissatisfaction. With some differences among samples, the impact of larger BMI on body dissatisfaction is typically at least partially mediated by teasing history (Lunner et al., 2000; van den Berg, Wertheim, et al., 2002; Wertheim et al., 2001).

While each of the multifactorial studies has examined the potential impact of somewhat different variables on the development of body dissatisfaction, there are some important consistencies. Both historical and proximal influences play important roles. Global psychological functioning, perceptions of family and media influences, teasing history, and importance of thinness/internalization of thin ideal appear to affect body comparisons, contributing to the experience of body image dysphoria. While these pathways need further confirmation in longitudinal studies, one particular advantage of integrated models is that they point to both distal and proximal influences that may be valuable target points for body image prevention interventions. In addition, they assist in elucidating mechanisms that may account for variation in body dissatisfaction despite the ubiquitous nature of cultural endorsement of the thin ideal in the Western world.

FINDINGS OF LONGITUDINAL RESEARCH

Although cross-sectional studies can assist in understanding the relationship between risk factors and body image concerns, they do not indicate whether predictor variables actually precede body concerns, a necessary condition for them to be considered true risk factors. In contrast, prospective studies enable these temporal relations to be determined. The 19 published longitudinal studies predicting body concerns are reviewed next (see Table 23.1).

Most longitudinal studies predicting body image concerns have included girls 10 to 17 years old at baseline; seven studies included participants under 10 years old, and three included participants greater than 18 years at baseline. Study durations have ranged from 25 weeks to 13 years, with most assessing participants twice over a one- or two-year period. Only four studies have included boys, and most studies included mainly White girls (with one study including mainly Black girls). Most studies controlled for baseline levels of body image concerns; hence, the focus was on influences related to changes in body image concerns over time, rather than the initial development of body concerns.

Biological Factors

Eleven longitudinal studies have examined the role of BMI, levels of obesity, and body fat in predicting weight dissatisfaction and body image concerns. The results indicate that in childhood and adolescence, increases in body size are often predictive of weight dissatisfaction reflecting wanting to be thinner; such studies have included prepubertal and postpubertal girls and boys (Field et al., 2001; Gardner, Friedman, & Jackson, 1999), 10- to 15-year-old girls (Cattarin & Thompson, 1994; Stice & Whitenton, 2002),

Table 23.1 Longitudinal Studies of Predictors of Body Image Concerns

Author(s)	Sample and Location	Time 1 Age/Grade (range)	Measurement Occasions/ Length of Study	Outcome Variable (Measure)	Significant Baseline Predictor Variables	Nonsignificant Baseline Predictor Variables	Control for Time 1 Body Image
Archibald, Graber, & Brooks-Gunn (1999)	127 girls[a, b] and their mothers from U.S.	10–14 years	2/1 year	Body image (SIQYA-BI).	Body image.	Age, breast development, BMI, family relationships.	Yes
Button, Sonuga-Barke, Davies, & Thompson (1996)	397 girls[a, b] from U.K.	11–12 years	2/4 years	Feelings of fatness (single item). Weight dissatisfaction (current—ideal weight).	Fatness concern. Fatness concern.	Self-esteem, social class perceived health status, family relationships, school problems, general worrying, nervousness.	No
Byely, Archibald, Graber, & Brooks-Gunn (2000)	77 girls and their mothers[a, b] from U.S.	13–17 years	2/1 year	Body image (nine-item version of SIQYA-BI).	Body image.	BMI, age, family relations, maternal modeling factors (mother's BMI, EAT-26, and body image), social influences (friends' dieting behavior, told to diet, mother's perception of daughter's weight).	Yes
Cattarin & Thompson (1994)	87 girls[a, c] from U.S.	10–15 years	2/3 years	Body image (SIQYA-BI). Body dissatisfaction (EDI-BD).	Body image. Teasing. Body dissatisfaction. Level of obesity.	Age, maturational status, level of obesity. Age, maturational status, teasing.	Yes
Field, Camargo, Taylor, Berkey, Roberts, & Colditz (2001)	6,770 girls and 5,287 boys[e] from U.S.	9–14 years	2/1 year	Weight concerns (McKnight Risk Factor Survey, Shisslak et al. 1999).	Higher BMI, thinness important to either parent (for girls), mother trying to lose weight (for boys), making efforts to look like same-sex figures in the media.	Not becoming fat important to either parent (for boys), mother trying to lose weight (for girls), thinness important to peers.	Yes

(continued)

Table 23.1 *(Continued)*

Author(s)	Sample and Location	Time 1 Age/Grade (range)	Measurement Occasions/ Length of Study	Outcome Variable (Measure)	Significant Baseline Predictor Variables	Nonsignificant Baseline Predictor Variables	Control for Time 1 Body Image
Gardner, Friedman, & Jackson (1999)	204 boys and girls[a, d, f] from U.S.	6–12 years	2/1 year	Body satisfaction (ideal-perceived body size).	Decreases in weight. Increases in height. Increases in BMI.	Changes in self-esteem. Changes in body esteem.	No
Halpern, Udry, Campbell, & Suchindran (1999)	200 Black and White girls[d] from U.S.	7th–8th grade	5/2 years	Weight dissatisfaction (single item "How happy are you with how much you weigh now?").	Pubertal development (when body fat was not predictor), body fat, race (being White), and body fat (being White and having more body fat).	Pubertal development (when body fat was a predictor), obesity, age at menarche, mother's education, dating (in past six months), sexual activity (petting/coital).	Yes
Holsen, Kraft, & Roysamb (2001)	326 boys, 319 girls[e] from Norway	13 years	3/5 years	Body image (general satisfaction with appearance and body [Alsaker, 1992]).		Depressed mood.	Yes
M. C. Martin, Wertheim, Prior, Smart, Sanson, & Oberklaid (2000)	1,206 boys and girls[a] from Australia	4–8 months	5/13 years	Body dissatisfaction (EDI-BD).	Negative emotionality at 7 to 8 years only (when size was and was not a covariate) for boys.	Persistence, approach-withdrawal, food fussiness, and activity (for boys and girls). Negative emotionality (for girls).	No
Meyer & Waller (2001)	41 women[e] from U.K.	18–21 years	3/25 weeks	Convergence of body dissatisfaction (based on EDI-BD scores).	Shared living environments.		No
Ohring, Graber, & Brooks-Gunn (2002)	120 girls[a, b] from U.S.	7th–10th grade	3/8 years	Body image (SIQYA-BI).	Higher BMIs, higher EAT total, higher EAT diet and bulimia, poorer emotional tone, earlier age at menarche.	Oral control.	Yes

480

Study	Sample	Age	Waves/interval	Body image measure			Longitudinal
Slap, Khalid, Paikoff, Brooks-Gunn, & Warren (1994)	54 girls[a,b] from U.S.	10–14 years	2/1 year	Enhanced body image (SIQYA-BI).	Body image. Increases in breast stage.	Changes in menarcheal status, BMI, pubic hair stage, and timing, various pubertal hormones, breast timing.	Yes
Smolak, Levine, & Gralen (1994)	79 girls[a,c] from U.S.	6th grade	2/2 years	Body dissatisfaction (current—ideal shape visual rating scale [Cohn et al., 1987]). Body satisfaction (single item "…how satisfied are you with your body shape?").	Synchrony of dating and menarche.	Dating status. Menarcheal status. Dating status. Menarcheal status. Synchrony of dating and menarche.	Yes
Spangler (2002)	231 girls[a,d] from U.S.	13–17 years	3/20 months	Body dissatisfaction (Body Parts Scale [Berscheid et al., 1973]).	Dysfunctional beliefs about appearance.		Yes
Stice (2001)	231 girls[a,d] from U.S.	13–17 years	3/20 months	Body dissatisfaction (Body Parts Scale [Berscheid et al., 1973]).	Pressure to be thin. Thin-ideal internalization.		Yes
Stice & Whitenton (2002)	496 girls[a,d] from U.S.	11–15 years	2/1 year	Body dissatisfaction (satisfaction and dissatisfaction with Body Parts Scale [Berscheid et al., 1973]).	Higher BMI. Perceived pressure to be thin. Thin-ideal internalization. Deficits in perceived social support.	Early menarche. Weight-related teasing. Depressive symptoms.	Yes
Thompson, Coovert, Richards, Johnson, & Cattarin (1995)	87 girls[a,c] from U.S.	10–15 years	2/3 years	Body image (SIQYA-BI). Body dissatisfaction (EDI-BD).	Overweight. Teasing. Overweight. Teasing.		No

(continued)

Table 23.1 *(Continued)*

Author(s)	Sample and Location	Time 1 Age/Grade (range)	Measurement Occasions/ Length of Study	Outcome Variable (Measure)	Significant Baseline Predictor Variables	Nonsignificant Baseline Predictor Variables	Control for Time 1 Body Image
Vogeltanz-Holm, Wonderlich, Lewis, Wilsnack, Harris, Wilsnack, & Kristjanson (2000)	709 women[a, d] from U.S.	21 years +	2/5 years	Weight concerns (single item measuring self-perception of importance of weight and shape).	Weight concerns. Younger age. Lower BMI.	Mother's and father's education, drinking, and level of affiliation; growing up without both biological parents. Intercourse before age 15, childhood sexual abuse, frequency/quantity/problems with drinking, dependence symptoms, illicit drug use, current smoker, anxiety, lifetime major depression, ethnicity, marital status, education.	Yes
Vohs, Heatherton, & Herrin (2001)	342 women[a, d] from U.S.	16–24 years	2/1 year	Decreased body satisfaction (single item).	Increase in BMI.		Yes

Notes: [a] = Mostly White.
    [b] = Mostly middle to upper class.
    [c] = Mostly working to middle class.
    [d] = SES information not presented
    [e] = Race or SES information not presented.

EDI-BD = Body Dissatisfaction subscale of the Eating Disorder Inventory (Garner et al., 1983; Garner, 1991); SIQYA-BI = Body Image subscale of the Self-Image Questionnaire for Young Adolescents (Petersen et al., 1984).

and young women entering college (Vohs, Heatherton, & Herrin, 2001). In seventh- and eighth-grade girls, higher body fat measured on a continuous scale, but not presence of obesity measured categorically, has also been found to predict weight dissatisfaction (Halpern, Udry, Campbell, & Suchindran, 1999).

Of three studies that examined body size as a predictor of more general body image concerns (not specifically weight related), two studies found no relationship (Archibald, Graber, & Brooks-Gunn, 1999; Slap, Khalid, Paikoff, Brooks-Gunn, & Warren, 1994), and one indicated higher BMI was predictive after baseline body image was controlled for (Ohring et al., 2002). A final study of general body image concerns indicated that in the same cohort, level of obesity predicted body image concerns only when baseline body image levels were not controlled for (Cattarin & Thompson, 1994; Thompson, Coovert, Richards, Johnson, & Cattarin, 1995). A final study examining importance placed on weight and shape found in adult women that *lower* baseline BMI predicted greater importance placed on weight and shape five years later (Vogeltanz-Holm et al., 2000).

In summary, several studies of children and adolescents have indicated that level of obesity/BMI predicted increases in weight dissatisfaction (distress over a too-large body). However, evidence that body size predicts more general body image concerns or changes (e.g., those related to general appearance, health, or strength) is less strong.

Seven longitudinal studies have examined the role of pubertal factors. In younger girls, increases in breast stage predicted enhanced body image (Slap et al., 1994); however, in older adolescent girls, level of breast development (Archibald et al., 1999) and timing of breast development, pubic hair stage or timing, and pubertal hormones (Slap et al., 1994) did not predict body image. Studies of *onset of* menarche have been mixed. In three studies, age of menarche did not predict either body image (Slap et al., 1994) or weight dissatisfaction (Halpern et al., 1999), and early onset of menarche did not predict body dissatisfaction (Stice & Whitenton, 2002). Two further studies did find earlier pubertal development predicted body concerns, with early onset of menarche predicting body image concerns in one (Ohring et al., 2002) and pubertal development predicting weight dissatisfaction in another (Halpern et al., 1999). However, in the latter study, when body size was partialled out, pubertal development no longer predicted weight dissatisfaction; similarly, in another study where body size was controlled for (Cattarin & Thompson, 1994), maturational status failed to predict body image concerns or weight dissatisfaction. Thus, the effects of early pubertal development may be mediated by increased body size.

Psychological Factors

Nine longitudinal studies have examined psychological, emotional, cognitive, and behavioral factors as possible risk factors. As to factors related to eating, in adolescent girls, disordered eating, dieting, and bulimia, but not oral control, have predicted body image concerns (Byely et al., 2000; Ohring et al., 2002), while in another study, early childhood food fussiness did not predict body dissatisfaction at 13 years old (G. C. Martin et al., 2000). In three studies, beliefs about appearance have yielded significant results, with dysfunctional beliefs about appearance (Spangler, 2002) and internalization of the thin ideal (Stice, 2001; Stice & Whitenton, 2002) predicting increases in weight dissatisfaction.

Affective and general psychopathology-related characteristics have usually failed to be predictive in prospective studies; these studies have examined depressed mood (Holsen et al., 2001; Stice & Whitenton, 2002), a history of major depressive episode (Vogeltanz-Holm et al., 2000), self-esteem (Button et al., 1996; Gardner et al., 1999), general nervousness or anxiety (Button et al., 1996; Vogeltanz-Holm et al., 2000), and substance and alcohol abuse and dependence (Vogeltanz-Holm et al., 2000). In a study of temperament, persistence, approach-withdrawal, and activity failed to predict body dissatisfaction; and negative emotionality in late childhood (but not early childhood or adolescence) predicted body dissatisfaction in boys only (G. C. Martin et al., 2000). A final study of 7th- to 10th-grade girls grouped according to trajectory did find that poorer emotional tone predicted both recurrent and transient body image concerns over a two-year period (Ohring et al., 2002). Thus, while most studies have failed to find psychopathology and personality-related variables to be predictive of later body concerns, there are occasional exceptions.

Sociocultural Factors

Twelve longitudinal studies have examined the role of sociocultural factors with five studies reporting some factors that predicted body image concerns or weight dissatisfaction, but most not finding a significant relationship. In adolescents, perceived pressure to be thin predicted greater weight dissatisfaction (Stice, 2001; Stice & Whitenton, 2002), and teasing related to a person's appearance predicted increases in general body image concerns (Cattarin & Thompson, 1994) but not weight dissatisfaction when Time 1 measures were not controlled for (Stice & Whitenton, 2002; Thompson et al., 1995). Certain peer influences (e.g., friend's dieting behavior, importance of thinness to peers) did not predict body image concerns or weight concerns in girls and boys (Byely et al., 2000; Field et al., 2001). In contrast, making attempts to look like same-sex media figures predicted increases in weight concerns in girls and boys (Field et al., 2001). For girls, perceived parental importance of thinness predicted increases in weight concerns (Field et al., 2001), although maternal modeling factors (e.g., mother's dieting behavior and body image) did not predict body image or weight concerns (Byely et al., 2000; Field et al., 2001). For boys, perceived parental importance of becoming fat did not predict increases in weight concerns, although mother's dieting behavior did (Field et al., 2001).

In two studies, general family and parental relationships (Archibald et al., 1999; Button et al., 1996) did not predict body image concerns or weight dissatisfaction although in a third study, deficits in perceived social support (from either peers or parents) predicted increases in body dissatisfaction in adolescent girls (Stice & Whitenton, 2002). In adult women, occurrence of sexual intercourse before age 15 years and sexual abuse did not predict increases in weight and shape concerns (Vogeltanz-Holm et al., 2000). Furthermore, dating and sexual experiences did not predict either weight or shape dissatisfaction as independent variables (Halpern et al., 1999; Smolak, Levine, & Gralen, 1993) although in an interaction, synchronous onset of dating and menarche did predict weight dissatisfaction (Smolak et al., 1993). In young adult women, sharing the same living environments led to a temporary convergence in body dissatisfaction (Meyer & Waller, 2001).

Summary, Limitations, and Directions for Future Longitudinal Research

The longitudinal studies that examined predictors of body image concerns and weight dissatisfaction indicate that a relatively small number of the putative biopsychosocial risk factors have been shown to be predictive longitudinally. The strongest findings relate to a role of higher BMI/level of obesity in predicting weight dissatisfaction; and while early pubertal development in girls has been predictive in some studies, it may be accounted for by higher body size. Two studies have supported the role of internalization of the thinness ideal and perceived pressures to be thin; one study has supported the role of having dysfunctional beliefs about appearance in predicting weight dissatisfaction. Individual studies have found that in adolescent girls, poorer emotional tone, being teased about weight, and eating pathology have predicted increases in general body image concerns. However, other variables have failed to predict later body concerns.

Several possible reasons may explain why many risk factors identified in cross-sectional and retrospective studies were not longitudinally predictive of increases in body image concerns. Some factors may have concurrent associations with body image concerns only, be consequences of body image concerns, or lead to the initial development of body concerns, yet have a limited role in predicting change in body image over time. Furthermore, most studies report moderate to high levels of stability of body concerns ranging from $r = .39$ to $.80$ (Byely et al., 2000; Cooley & Toray, 2001; Rauste-Von Wright, 1989; Slap et al., 1994; Smolak et al., 1993; Wichstrom, 2000), so there may be limited variance left to explain after body concerns become established. A final issue involves ensuring that the timing between pre- and postassessments is appropriate to detect the pattern of change. For example, if 8 months elapse between pre- and postassessments, but a causal sequence took only 1 month to complete or took 12 months, the prospective design will miss such transitions. Similarly, if the causal sequence takes different amounts of times for different girls, it may be missed. Ideally, more frequent assessments would need to be made, although this approach, too, has methodological difficulties associated with repeated assessments and possible individual variation in the timing of pathways.

A limitation of the longitudinal studies to date includes their relatively homogeneous samples of White North American girls from middle- to upper-class socioeconomic backgrounds, which limits their generalizability. In addition, with the exception of body size, pubertal development, and internalization of the thinness ideal, few risk factors have been examined in more than one study; hence, results have not been replicated. Further, other risk factors or the interaction between risk factors may be important in influencing change in body image concerns. For example, in one study, dating and onset of menarche did not independently predict weight dissatisfaction; however, the interaction between the two predictors did (Smolak et al., 1993).

CONCLUDING COMMENTS AND FUTURE DIRECTIONS

In this review, a variety of putative risk factors for body image disturbances have been described, including biological, developmental, sociocultural, and individual psychological variables. While much of the research is self-report and cross-sectional in nature, limiting conclusions that can be reached, more sophisticated methods have been emerging in the literature to assess the actual risk status of these factors. These methods have included multiple raters, randomized intervention studies, structural equation modeling, and longitudinal designs. Multifactorial models of risk factors that more clearly point to mediating and moderating relationships are also promising trends in the literature.

While much of the discussion in this chapter has focused on general body dissatisfaction and weight concerns as an outcome, it should be noted that body image disturbances can take many forms. Body image is generally agreed to be multidimensional covering multiple aspects, so risk factors may operate on different aspects of body image—such as drive to be thinner; general body size dissatisfaction (nondirectional in terms of size); general appearance dissatisfaction; fitness, health, and strength; body ideal; salience or importance of appearance; and perceptual accuracy. Therefore, it is important to differentiate which aspect of body image is being examined and preferably include multiple measures of body image disturbance to ascertain which risk factors influence specific types of outcomes.

To further inform about factors that predict initial development and increases in body image concerns, further prospective and intervention studies are needed. Future longitudinal studies would ideally take baseline assessments when participants have not yet developed such concerns (e.g., in early years of life) and follow these participants into young adulthood. This research could also examine risk factors that have not yet been examined prospectively (e.g., media exposure) as well as interactions among risk factors in predicting body image concerns. Replication, including heterogeneous samples, is also needed. In addition, because prospective studies clarify temporal order but not causality, intervention studies of various sorts are needed. Research efforts, such as randomized prevention trials (e.g., Stice, Mazotti, Weibel, & Agras, 2000), that endeavor to target and attenuate risk factors and determine whether subsequent decreases in body image concerns are observed will provide further evidence of the causal role of specific risk factors.

REFERENCES

Abraham, S., Beumont, P. J. V., Fraser, I., & Llewellyn-Jones, D. (1982). Body weight, exercise and menstrual status among ballet dancers in training. *British Journal of Obstetrics and Gynaecology, 89,* 507–510.

Afifi-Soweid, R. A., Najem Kteily, M. B., & Shediac-Rizkallah, M. C. (2002). Preoccupation with weight and disordered eating behaviors of students at a university in Lebanon. *International Journal of Eating Disorders, 32,* 52–57.

Altabe, M. (1998). Ethnicity and body image: Quantitative and qualitative analysis. *International Journal of Eating Disorders, 23,* 153–159.

Altabe, M., & Thompson, J. K. (1990). Menstrual cycle, body image, and eating disturbance. *International Journal of Eating Disorders, 9,* 395–402.

Anderson, D. R., Huston, A. C., Schmitt, K. L., Linbarger, D. L., & Wright, J. C. (2001). Early childhood television viewing and adolescent behavior: The recontact study. *Monographs of the Society for Research in Child Development, 66*(Serial No. 264), 1–156.

Andrews, B. (1995). Bodily shame as a mediator between abusive experiences and depression. *Journal of Abnormal Psychology, 9*, 487–492.

Archibald, A. B., Graber, J. A., & Brooks-Gunn, J. (1999). Associations among parent-adolescent relationships, pubertal growth, dieting, and body image in young adolescent girls: A short-term longitudinal study. *Journal of Research on Adolescence, 9*, 395–415.

Attie, I., & Brooks-Gunn, J. B. (1989). Development of eating problems in adolescent girls: A longitudinal study. *Developmental Psychology, 25*, 70–79.

Barr Taylor, C., Sharpe, T., Shisslak, C., Bryson, S., Estes, L. S., Gray, N., et al. (1998). Factors associated with weight concerns in adolescent girls. *International Journal of Eating Disorders, 24*, 31–42.

Becker, A. E., Burwell, R. A., Gilman, S. E., Herzog, D. B., & Hamburg, P. (2002). Eating behaviors and attitudes following prolonged exposure to television among ethnic Fijian adolescent girls. *British Journal of Psychiatry, 180*, 509–514.

Beckman, K., & Burns, G. (1990). Relation of sexual abuse and bulimia in college women. *International Journal of Eating Disorders, 9*, 487–492.

Benedikt, R., Wertheim, E. H., & Love, A. (1998). Eating attitudes and weight loss attempts in female adolescents and their mothers. *Journal of Youth and Adolescence, 27*, 43–57.

Beren, S. E., Hayden, H. A., Wilfley, D. E., & Grilo, C. M. (1996). The influence of sexual orientation on body dissatisfaction in adult men and women. *International Journal of Eating Disorders, 20*, 135–141.

Boscaglia, N., Skouteris, H., & Wertheim, E. H. (2003). Changes in body image satisfaction during pregnancy: A comparison of high exercising and low exercising women. *Australian and New Zealand Journal of Obstetrics and Gynaecology, 43*, 41–45.

Botta, R. A. (1999). Television images and adolescent girls' body image disturbance. *Journal of Communication, 49*, 22–41.

Brand, P. A., Rothblum, E. D., & Solomon, L. J. (1992). A comparison of lesbians, gay men and heterosexuals on weight and restrained eating. *International Journal of Eating Disorders, 11*, 253–259.

Braun, C. M. J., & Chouinard, M. (1992). Is anorexia nervosa a neurological disease? *Neuropsychology Review, 3*, 171–212.

Brown, D., Koenig, T., Demorales, A., McGuire, K., & Mersia, C. (1996). Menarche age, fatness, and fat distribution in Hawaiian adolescents. *American Journal of Physical Anthropology, 99*, 239–247.

Button, E. J., Sonuga-Barke, E. J., Davies, J., & Thompson, M. (1996). A prospective study of self-esteem in the prediction of eating problems in adolescent schoolgirls: Questionnaire findings. *British Journal of Clinical Psychology, 35*, 193–203.

Byely, L., Archibald, A. B., Graber, J., & Brooks-Gunn, J. (2000). A prospective study of familial and social influences on girls' body image and dieting. *International Journal of Eating Disorders, 28*, 155–164.

Carr-Nangle, R. E., Johnson, W. G., Bergeron, K. C., & Nangle, D. W. (1994). Body image changes over the menstrual cycle in normal women. *International Journal of Eating Disorders, 16*, 267–273.

Cash, T. F. (1990). Losing hair, losing points? The effects of male pattern baldness on social impression formation. *Journal of Applied Social Psychology, 20*, 154–167.

Cash, T. F. (1995). Developmental teasing about physical appearance: Retrospective descriptions and relationships with body image. *Social Behavior and Personality, 23*, 123–130.

Cash, T. F. (1996). The treatment of body image disturbance. In J. K. Thompson (Ed.), *Body image, eating disorders, and obesity: An integrative guide for assessment and treatment.* Washington, DC: American Psychological Association.

Cash, T. F. (2002). Cognitive-behavioral perspectives on body image. In T. F. Cash & T. Pruzinsky (Eds.), *Body image: A handbook of theory, research and clinical practice* (pp. 38–46). New York: Guilford Press.

Cattarin, J. A., & Thompson, J. K. (1994). A three-year longitudinal study of body image, eating concerns, and general psychological functioning in adolescent females. *Eating Disorders: Journal of Treatment and Prevention, 2,* 114–125.

Cattarin, J. A., Thompson, J. K., Thomas, C., & Williams, R. (2000). Body image, mood, and televised images of attractiveness: The role of social comparison. *Journal of Social and Clinical Psychology, 19,* 220–239.

Cogan, J. C., Bhalla, S. K., Sefa-Dedeh, A., & Rothblum, E. D. (1996). A comparison study of United States and African students on perceptions of obesity and thinness. *Journal of Cross-Cultural Psychology, 27,* 98–113.

Cohane, G. H., & Pope, H. G. (2001). Body image in boys: A review of the literature. *International Journal of Eating Disorders, 29,* 373–379.

Connors, M. E. (2001). Relationship of sexual abuse to body image and eating problems. In J. K. Thompson & L. Smolak (Eds.), *Body image, eating disorders, and obesity in youth: Assessment, prevention and treatment* (pp. 149–168). Washington, DC: American Psychological Association.

Cooley, E., & Toray, T. (2001). Body image and personality predictors of eating disorder symptoms during the college years. *International Journal of Eating Disorders, 30,* 28–36.

Cummings, W. J. K. (1988). The neurobiology of the body schema. *British Journal of Psychiatry, 153*(Suppl. 2), 7–11.

Cusumano, D., & Thompson, J. (1997). Body image and body shape ideals in magazines: Exposure, awareness, and internalization. *Sex Roles, 37,* 701–721.

Davies, K., & Wardle, J. (1994). Body image and dieting in pregnancy. *Journal of Psychosomatic Research, 38,* 787–799.

Deeks, A. A., & McCabe, M. P. (2001). Menopausal stage and age and perceptions of body image. *Psychology and Health, 16,* 367–379.

Devine, C. M., Bove, C. F., & Olson, C. M. (2000). Continuity and change in women's weight orientations and lifestyle practices through pregnancy and the postpartum period: The influence of life course trajectories and transitional events. *Social Science and Medicine, 50,* 567–582.

Dunkley, T., Wertheim, E. H., & Paxton, S. J. (2001). Examination of a model of multiple sociocultural influences on adolescent girls' body dissatisfaction and dietary restraint. *Adolescence, 36,* 265–279.

Durkin, S. J., & Paxton, S. J. (2002). Predictors of vulnerability to reduced body image satisfaction and psychological well-being in response to exposure to idealized female media images in adolescent girls. *Journal of Psychosomatic Research, 53,* 995–1005.

Durkin, S. J., Paxton, S. J., & Sorbello, M. (2002, April). *Mediational influence of internalisation and comparison tendency on the impact of media exposure on adolescent girls' body satisfaction.* Paper presented to the Academy for Eating Disorders 2002 International Conference on Eating Disorders, New York.

Fairburn, C. G., & Welch, S. L. (1990). The impact of pregnancy on eating habits and attitudes to shape and weight. *International Journal of Eating Disorders, 9,* 153–160.

Fallon, A. E. (1990). Culture in the mirror: Sociocultural determinants of body image. In T. F. Cash & T. Pruzinsky (Eds.), *Body images: Development, deviance and change* (pp. 80–109). New York: Guilford Press.

Festinger, L. (1954). A theory of social comparison processes. *Human Relations, 7,* 117–140.

Field, A. E., Camargo, C. A., Taylor, C. B., Berkey, C. S., Roberts, S. B., & Colditz, G. A. (2001). Peer, parent, and media influences on the development of weight concerns and frequent dieting among preadolescent and adolescent girls and boys. *Pediatrics, 107,* 55–60.

Fisher, E., Dunn, M., & Thompson, J. K. (in press). Social comparison and body image: An investigation of body comparison processes using multidimensional scaling. *Journal of Social and Clinical Psychology.*

Franko, D., & Striegel-Moore, R. H. (2002). The role of body dissatisfaction as a risk factor for depression in adolescent girls: Are the differences black and white? *Journal of Psychosomatic Research, 53,* 975–983.

French, S. A., Story, M., Remafedi, G., Resnick, M. D., & Blum, R. W. (1996). Sexual orientation and prevalence of body dissatisfaction and eating disordered behaviors: A population-based study of adolescents. *International Journal of Eating Disorders, 19,* 119–126.

Gardner, R. M., Friedman, B. N., & Jackson, N. A. (1999). Body size estimations, body dissatisfaction, and ideal size preferences in children six through thirteen. *Journal of Youth and Adolescence, 28,* 603–618.

Garner, D. M. (1991). *Manual for the Eating Disorders Inventory-2 (EDI-2).* Odessa, FL: Psychological Assessment Resources.

Garner, D. M., Garfinkel, P. E., Schwartz, D., & Thompson, M. (1980). Cultural expectations of thinness among women. *Psychological Reports, 47,* 483–491.

Garner, D. M., Olmsted, M. A., & Polivy, J. (1983). Development of a multidimensional eating disorder inventory for anorexia nervosa and bulimia. *International Journal of Eating Disorders, 2,* 15–34.

Gettelman, T. E., & Thompson, J. K. (1993). Actual differences and stereotypical perceptions in body image and eating disturbance: A comparison of male and female heterosexual and homosexual samples. *Sex Roles, 29,* 545–562.

Glatt, B. S., Sarwer, D. B., O'Hara, D. E., Hamori, C., Bucky, L. P., & La Rossa, D. (1999). A retrospective study of changes in physical symptoms and body image after reduction mammaplasty. *Plastic and Reconstructive Surgery, 65,* 76–82.

Goodwin, A., Astbury, J., & McMeeken, J. (2000). Body image and psychological well-being in pregnancy: A comparison of high exercisers and nonhigh exercisers. *Australian and New Zealand Journal of Obstetrics and Gynaecology, 40,* 442–447.

Grilo, C. M., Wilfley, D. E., Brownell, K. D., & Rodin, J. (1994). Teasing, body image, and self-esteem in a clinical sample of obese women. *Addictive Behaviors, 19,* 443–450.

Groesz, L. M., Levine, M. P., & Murnen, S. K. (2002). The effect of experimental presentation of thin media images on body satisfaction: A meta-analytic review. *International Journal of Eating Disorders, 31,* 1–16.

Halpern, C. T., Udry, J. R., Campbell, B., & Suchindran, C. (1999). Effects of body fat on weight concerns, dating, and sexual activity: A longitudinal analysis of black and white adolescent girls. *Developmental Psychology, 35,* 721–736.

Hargreaves, D., & Tiggemann, M. (2002). The effect of television commercials on mood and body dissatisfaction: The role of appearance-schema activation. *Journal of Social and Clinical Psychology, 21,* 287–308.

Harrison, K., & Cantor, J. (1997). The relationship between media consumption and eating disorders. *Journal of Communication, 47,* 40–67.

Heinberg, L. J., & Thompson, J. K. (1992). Social comparison: Gender, target importance ratings and relation to body image disturbance. *Journal of Social Behavior and Personality, 7,* 335–344.

Heinberg, L. J., & Thompson, J. K. (1995). Body image and televised images of thinness and attractiveness: A controlled laboratory investigation. *Journal of Social and Clinical Psychology, 14,* 325–338.

Hill, A. J., & Franklin, J. A. (1998). Mothers, daughters and dieting: Investigating the transmission of weight control. *British Journal of Clinical Psychology, 37,* 3–13.

Hill, A. J., Weaver, C., & Blundell, J. E. (1990). Dieting concerns of 10-year-old girls and their mothers. *British Journal of Clinical Psychology, 29,* 346–348.

Holsen, I., Kraft, P., & Roysamb, E. (2001). The relationship between body image and depressed mood in adolescence: A 5-year longitudinal panel study. *Journal of Health Psychology, 6,* 613–627.

Kanakis, D. M., & Thelen, M. H. (1995). Parental variables associated with bulimia nervosa. *Addictive Behaviors, 20,* 491–500.

Kazdin, A. E., Kraemer, H. C., Kessler, R. C., Kupfer, D. J., & Offord, D. R. (1997). Contributions of risk factor research to developmental psychopathology. *Clinical Psychology Review, 17,* 375–406.

Kearney-Cooke, A., & Striegel-Moore, R. H. (1994). Treatment of childhood sexual abuse in anorexia nervosa and bulimia nervosa: A feminist psychodynamic approach. *International Journal of Eating Disorders, 15,* 305–319.

Keel, P. K., Heatherton, T. F., Harnden, J. L., & Hornig, C. D. (1997). *Eating Disorders: Journal of Treatment and Prevention, 5,* 216–228.

Kennett, D. J., & Nisbet, C. (1998). The influence of body mass index and learned resourcefulness skills on body image and lifestyle practices. *Patient Education and Counseling, 33,* 1–12.

Kimm, S. Y., Barton, B. A., Obarzanek, E., & Crawford, P. (1997). Changes in adiposity in a biracial cohort during puberty: NHLBI Growth and Health Study (NGHS) *Canadian Journal of Cardiology, 13*(Suppl. B), 218B.

Leifer, M. (1977). Psychological changes accompanying pregnancy and motherhood. *Genetic Psychological Monographs, 95,* 55–96.

Leit, R. A., Gray, J. J., & Pope, H. G. (2002). The media's representation of the ideal male body: A cause for muscle dysmorphia? *International Journal of Eating Disorders, 31,* 334–338.

Levine, M. P., Piran, N., & Stoddard, C. (1999). Mission more possible: Media literacy, activism, and advocacy as primary prevention. In N. Piran, M. P. Levine, & C. Steiner-Adair (Eds.), *Preventing eating disorders: A handbook of interventions and special challenges.* Philadelphia: Brunner/Mazel.

Levine, M. P., & Smolak, L. (1996). Media as a context for the development of disordered eating. In L. Smolak, M. Levine, & R. Striegel-Moore (Eds.), *The developmental psychopathology of eating disorders: Implications for research, prevention, and treatment* (pp. 235–257). Mahwah, NJ: Erlbaum.

Levine, M. P., Smolak, L., & Hayden, H. (1994). The relation of sociocultural factors to eating attitudes and behaviors among middle school girls. *Journal of Early Adolescence, 14,* 471–490.

Lewis, D. M., & Cachelin, F. M. (2001). Body image, body dissatisfaction, and eating attitudes in midlife and elderly women. *Eating Disorders: Journal of Treatment and Prevention, 9,* 29–39.

Lopez, E., Blix, G., & Blix, A. (1995). Body image of Latinas compared to body image of non-Latina White women. *Health Values: Journal of Health Behavior, Education, and Promotion, 19,* 3–10.

Lovejoy, M. (2001). Disturbances in the social body: Differences in body image and eating problems among African American and White women. *Gender and Society, 15,* 239–261.

Lunner, K., Wertheim, E. H., Thompson, J. K., Paxton, S. J., McDonald, F., & Halvarsson, R. (2000). A cross-cultural investigation of the role of teasing, and weight and dieting concerns in adolescent girls from Sweden and Australia. *International Journal of Eating Disorders, 48,* 430–435.

Makkar, J. K., & Strube, M. J. (1995). Black women's self-perceptions of attractiveness following exposure to White versus Black beauty standards: The moderating role of racial identity and self-esteem. *Journal of Applied Social Psychology, 25,* 1547–1566.

Martin, G. C., Wertheim, E. H., Prior, M., Smart, D., Sanson, A., & Oberklaid, F. (2000). A longitudinal study of the role of childhood temperament in the later development of eating concerns. *International Journal of Eating Disorders, 27,* 150–162.

Martin, M. C., & Gentry, J. W. (1997). Stuck in the model trap: The effects of beautiful models in ads on female preadolescents and adolescents. *Journal of Advertising, 26,* 19–33.

Maude, D., Wertheim, E. H., Paxton, S., Gibbons, K., & Szmukler, G. I. (1993). Body dissatisfaction, weight loss behaviors, and bulimic tendencies in Australian adolescents with an estimate of data representativeness. *Australian Psychologist, 28,* 118–127.

McVey, G. L., Lieberman, M., Voorberg, N., Wardrope, D., & Blackmore, E. (2001). *School-based peer support groups: A new approach to the prevention of disordered eating.* Unpublished manuscript.

Mercer, R. T. (1981). The nurse and maternal tasks of early postpartum. *American Journal of Maternal Child Nursing, 6,* 341–345.

Meyer, C., & Waller, G. (2001). Social convergence of disturbed eating attitudes in young adult women. *Journal of Nervous and Mental Diseases, 189,* 114–119.

Moore, D. S. (1978). The body image in pregnancy. *Journal of Nurse Midwifery, 28,* 17–26.

Moreno, A., & Thelen, H. (1993). Parental factors related to bulimia nervosa. *Addictive Behaviors, 18,* 681–689.

Morris, A., Cooper, T., & Cooper, P. J. (1989). The changing shape of female fashion models. *International Journal of Eating Disorders, 8,* 593–596.

Neumark-Sztainer, D., Croll, J., Story, M., Hannan, P. J., French, S., & Perry, C. (2002). Ethnic/racial differences in weight related concerns and behaviors among adolescent girls and boys: Findings from Project EAT. *Journal of Psychosomatic Research, 53,* 963–974.

Nichter, M. (2000). *Fat talk: What girls and their parents say about dieting.* Cambridge, MA: Harvard University Press.

Nichter, M., & Vuckovic, N. (1994). Fat talk: Body image among adolescent females. In N. Sault (Ed.), *Many mirrors: Body image and social relations* (pp. 109–131). New Brunswick, NJ: Rutgers University Press.

Norton, K. I., Olds, T. S., Olive, S., & Dank, S. (1996). Ken and Barbie at life size. *Sex Roles, 34,* 287–295.

O'Dea, J. (1995). Body image and nutritional status among adolescents and adults: A review of the literature. *Australian Journal of Nutrition and Dietetics, 52,* 56–67.

Ohring, R., Graber, J. A., & Brooks-Gunn, J. (2002). Girls' recurrent and concurrent body dissatisfaction: Correlates and Consequences over 8 years. *International Journal of Eating Disorders, 31,* 404–415.

Paxton, S. J., & Phythian, K. (1999). Body image, self-esteem, and health status in middle and later adulthood. *Australian Psychologist, 34,* 116–121.

Paxton, S. J., Schutz, H. K., Wertheim, E. H., & Muir, S. L. (1999). Friendship clique and peer influences on body image concerns, dietary restraint, extreme weight-loss behaviors, and binge eating in adolescent girls. *Journal of Abnormal Psychology, 108,* 255–266.

Paxton, S. J., Wertheim, E. H., Gibbons, K., Szmukler, G. I., Hillier, L., & Petrovich, J. L. (1991). Body image satisfaction, dieting beliefs and weight loss behaviors in adolescent girls and boys. *Journal of Youth and Adolescence, 20,* 361–379.

Pike, K. M., & Rodin, J. (1991). Mother, daughters, and disordered eating. *Journal of Abnormal Psychology, 100,* 198–204.

Piran, N. (1999). On the move from tertiary to secondary and primary prevention: Working with an elite dance school. In N. Piran, M. P. Levine, & C. Steiner-Adair (Eds.), *Preventing eating disorders: A handbook of interventions and special challenges* (pp. 256–269). New York: Brunner/Mazel.

Pliner, P., Chaiken, S., & Flett, G. L. (1990). Gender differences in concern with body weight and physical appearance over the lifespan. *Personality and Social Psychology Bulletin, 16,* 263–273.

Pope, H. G., Jr., Phillips, K. A., & Olivardia, R. (2000). *The Adonis complex: The secret crisis of male body obsession.* New York: Free Press.

Pumariega, A. J., Gustavson, C. R., Gustavson, J. C., Motes, P. S., & Ayers, S. (1994). Eating attitudes in African American women: The Essence Eating Disorders Survey. *Eating Disorders: Journal of Treatment and Prevention, 2,* 5–16.

Rauste-Von Wright, M. (1989). Body image satisfaction in adolescent girls and boys: A longitudinal study. *Journal of Youth and Adolescence, 18,* 71–83.

Ricciardelli, L. A., & McCabe, M. P. (2001). Children's body image concerns and eating disturbance: A review of the literature. *Clinical Psychology Review, 21,* 325–344.

Richards, M. H., Boxer, A. M., Petersen, A. C., & Albrecht, R. (1990). Relation of weight to body image in pubertal girls and boys from two communities. *Developmental Psychology, 26,* 313–321.

Richardson, P. (1990). Women's experiences of body change during normal pregnancy. *Maternal Child Nursing Journal, 19,* 93–111.

Rintala, M., & Mustajoki, P. (1992). Could mannequins menstruate? *British Medical Journal, 305,* 1575–1576.

Ruther, N. M., & Richman, C. L. (1993). The relationship between mothers' eating restraint and their children's attitudes and behaviors. *Bulletin of the Psychosonomic Society, 31,* 217–220.

Sanftner, J. L., Crowther, J. H., Crawford, P. A., & Watts, D. D. (1996). Maternal influences (or lack thereof) on daughters' eating attitudes and behaviors. *Eating Disorders: Journal of Treatment and Prevention, 4,* 147–159.

Schutz, H. J., Paxton, S. J., & Wertheim, E. H. (2002). Investigations of body comparison among adolescent girls. *Journal of Applied Social Psychology, 32,* 1906–1937.

Shisslak, C. M., & Crago, M. (2001). Risk and protective factors in the development of eating disorders. In J. K. Thompson & L. Smolak (Eds.), *Body image, eating disorders, and obesity in youth: Assessment, prevention and treatment* (pp. 103–126). Washington, DC: American Psychological Association.

Siever, M. D. (1994). Sexual orientation and gender as factors in socioculturally acquired vulnerability to body dissatisfaction and eating disorders. *Journal of Consulting and Clinical Psychology, 62,* 252–260.

Silverstein, B., Perdue, L., Peterson, B., & Kelly, E. (1986). The role of the mass media in promoting a thin standard of bodily attractiveness for women. *Sex Roles, 14,* 519–532.

Slap, G. B., Khalid, N., Paikoff, R. L., Brooks-Gunn, J., & Warren, M. P. (1994). Evolving self-image, pubertal manifestations, and pubertal hormones: Preliminary findings in young adolescent girls. *Journal of Adolescent Health, 15,* 327–335.

Smolak, L., Levine, M. P., & Gralen, S. (1993). The impact of puberty and dating on eating problems among middle school girls. *Journal of Youth and Adolescence, 22,* 355–368.

Spangler, D. L. (2002). Testing the cognitive model of eating disorders: The role of dysfunctional beliefs about appearance. *Behavior Therapy, 33,* 87–105.

Stein, A., & Fairburn, C. G. (1996). Eating habits and attitudes in the postpartum period. *Psychosomatic Medicine, 54,* 321–325.

Stice, E. (1994). Review of the evidence for a sociocultural model of bulimia nervosa and an exploration of the mechanisms of action. *Clinical Psychology Review, 14,* 633–661.

Stice, E. (2001). A prospective test of the dual-pathway model of bulimic pathology: Mediating effects of dieting and negative affect. *Journal of Abnormal Psychology, 110,* 124–135.

Stice, E., & Bearman, S. K. (2001). Body image and eating disturbances prospectively predict growth in depressive symptoms in adolescent girls: A growth curve analysis. *Developmental Psychology, 37,* 597–607.

Stice, E., Hayward, C., Cameron, R., Killen, J. D., & Taylor, C. B. (2000). Body image and eating related factors predict onset of depression in female adolescents: A longitudinal study. *Journal of Abnormal Psychology, 109,* 438–444.

Stice, E., Maxfield, J., & Wells, T. (in press). Adverse effects of social pressure to be thin on young women: An experimental investigation of the effect of "fat talk." *International Journal of Eating Disorders.*

Stice, E., Mazotti, L., Weibel, D., & Agras, W. S. (2000). Dissonance prevention program decreases thin-ideal internalization, body dissatisfaction, dieting, negative affect, and bulimic symptoms: A preliminary experiment. *International Journal of Eating Disorders, 27,* 206–217.

Stice, E., Schupak-Neuberg, E., Shaw, H. E., & Stein, R. I. (1994). Relation of media exposure to eating disorder symptomatology: An examination of mediating mechanisms. *Journal of Abnormal Psychology, 103,* 836–840.

Stice, E., Shaw, H., & Nemeroff, C. (1998). Dual pathway model of bulimia nervosa: Longitudinal support for dietary restraint and affect regulation mechanisms. *Journal of Social and Clinical Psychology, 17,* 129–149.

Stice, E., Spangler, D., & Agras, W. S. (2001). Exposure to media-portrayed thin-ideal images adversely affects vulnerable girls: A longitudinal study. *Journal of Social and Clinical Psychology, 20,* 270–288.

Stice, E., & Whitenton, K. (2002). Risk factors for body dissatisfaction in adolescent girls: A longitudinal investigation. *Developmental Psychology, 38,* 669–678.

Stormer, S. M., & Thompson, J. K. (1996). Explanations of body image disturbance: A test of maturational status, negative verbal commentary, social comparison, and sociocultural hypotheses. *International Journal of Eating Disorders, 19,* 193–202.

Strang, V. R., & Sullivan, P. L. (1985). Body image attitudes in pregnancy and the postpartum. *Journal of Obstetric, Gynecologic, and Neonatal Nursing, 14,* 332–337.

Striegel-Moore, R. H., & Kearney-Cooke, A. (1993). Exploring parents' attitudes and behaviors about their children's physical appearance. *International Journal of Eating Disorders, 15,* 377–385.

Striegel-Moore, R. H., McAvay, G., & Rodin, J. (1986). Psychological and behavioral correlates of feeling fat in women. *International Journal of Eating Disorders, 5,* 935–947.

Striegel-Moore, R. H., Tucker, N., & Hsu, J. (1990). Body image dissatisfaction and disordered eating in lesbian college students. *International Journal of Eating Disorders, 9,* 493–500.

Szmukler, G. I., Eisler, I., Gillies, C., & Hayward, M. E. (1985). The implications of anorexia nervosa in a ballet school. *Journal of Psychiatric Research, 19,* 177–181.

Taylor, C. B., Sharpe, T., Shisslak, C., Bryson, S., Estes, L. S., Gray, N., et al. (1998). Factors associated with weight concerns in adolescent girls. *International Journal of Eating Disorders, 24,* 31–42.

Thelen, M. H., & Cormier, J. F. (1995). Desire to be thinner and weight control among children and their parents. *Behavior Therapy, 26,* 85–99.

Thompson, J. K., Coovert, M. D., Richards, K. J., Johnson, S., & Cattarin, J. (1995). Development of body image, eating concerns, and general psychological functioning in female adolescents: Covariance structure modeling and longitudinal investigations. *International Journal of Eating Disorders, 18,* 221–236.

Thompson, J. K., Coovert, M. D., & Stormer, S. M. (1999). Body image, social comparison, and eating disturbance: A covariance structure modeling investigation. *International Journal of Eating Disorders, 26,* 43–51.

Thompson, J. K., & Heinberg, L. J. (1993). Preliminary test of two hypotheses of body image disturbance. *International Journal of Eating Disorders, 14,* 59–63.

Thompson, J. K., Heinberg, L. J., Altabe, M., & Tantleff-Dunn, S. (1999). *Exacting beauty: Theory, assessment, and treatment of body image disturbance.* Washington, DC: American Psychological Association.

Thompson, J. K., Penner, L. A., & Altabe, M. N. (1990). Procedures, problems and progress in the assessment of body images. In T. F. Cash & T. Pruzinsky (Eds.), *Body images: Development, deviance and change* (pp. 21–50). New York: Guilford Press.

Thompson, J. K., & Psaltis, K. (1988). Multiple aspects and correlates of body figure ratings: A replication and extension of Fallon and Rozin (1985). *International Journal of Eating Disorders, 7,* 813–817.

Tiggemann, M., & Lynch, J. E. (2001). Body image across the lifespan in adult women: The role of self-objectification. *Developmental Psychology, 37,* 243–253.

Tiggemann, M., & Pickering, A. S. (1996). Role of television in adolescent women's body dissatisfaction and drive for thinness. *International Journal of Eating Disorders, 20,* 199–203.

Trent, T. A., & Petrie, M. M. (2001). Sexual abuse and eating disorders: A test of a conceptual model. *Sex Roles, 44,* 17–32.

Truby, H., & Paxton, S. J. (2002). Development of the Children's Body Image Scale [British]. *Journal of Clinical Psychology, 41,* 185–203.

Usmiani, S., & Daniluk, J. (1997). Mothers and their adolescent daughters: Relationship between self-esteem, gender role identity, and body image. *Journal of Youth and Adolescence, 26,* 45–62.

van den Berg, P., Thompson, J. K., Brandon, K., & Coovert, M. (2002). The tripartite influence model of body image and eating disturbance: A covariance structure modelling investigation testing the mediational role of appearance comparison. *Journal of Psychosomatic Research*, 1007–1020.

van den Berg, P., Wertheim, E. H., Thompson, J. K., & Paxton, S. J. (2002). Development of body image, eating disturbance and general psychological functioning in adolescent females: A replication using covariance structure modeling in an Australian sample. *International Journal of Eating Disorders, 32*, 46–51.

Vogeltanz-Holm, N. D., Wonderlich, S. A., Lewis, B. A., Wilsnack, S. C., Harris, T. R., Wilsnack, R. W., et al. (2000). Longitudinal predictors of binge eating, intense dieting, and weight concerns in a national sample of women. *Behavior Therapy, 31*, 221–235.

Vohs, K. D., Heatherton, T. F., & Herrin, M. (2001). Disordered eating and the transition to college: A prospective study. *International Journal of Eating Disorders, 29*, 280–288.

Wade, T. D., & Lowes, J. (2002). Variables associated with disturbed eating habits and overvalued ideas about personal implications of body shape and weight in a female adolescent population. *International Journal of Eating Disorders, 32*, 39–45.

Weiner, K. E., & Thompson, J. K. (1997). Overt and covert sexual abuse: Relationship to body image and eating disturbance. *International Journal of Eating Disorders, 22*, 273–284.

Wertheim, E. H., Koerner, J., & Paxton, S. J. (2001). Longitudinal predictors of restrictive eating and bulimic tendencies in three different age groups of adolescent girls. *Journal of Youth and Adolescents, 30*, 69–81.

Wertheim, E. H., Martin, G., Prior, M., Sanson, A., & Smart, D. (2002). Parent influences in the transmission of eating and weight related values and behaviors. *Eating Disorders: Journal of Treatment and Prevention, 10*, 329–342.

Wertheim, E. H., Mee, V., & Paxton, S. J. (1999). Relationships among adolescent girls' eating behaviors and their parents' weight related attitudes and behaviors. *Sex Roles, 41*, 169–187.

Wertheim, E. H., Paxton, S. J., Schutz, H. K., & Muir, S. L. (1997). Why do adolescent girls watch their weight? An interview study examining sociocultural pressures to be thin. *Journal of Psychosomatic Research, 42*, 345–355.

Wertheim, E. H., & Weiss, K. (1989). A description of 144 bulimic women who contacted a research program for help. *Australian Psychologist, 24*, 187–201.

Whealin, J. M., & Jackson, J. L. (2002). Childhood unwanted sexual attention and young women's present self-concept. *Journal of Interpersonal Violence, 17*, 854–871.

Wichstrom, L. (2000). Psychological and behavioral factors unpredictive of disordered eating: A prospective study of the general adolescent population in Norway. *International Journal of Eating Disorders, 28*, 33–42.

Wiseman, C. V., Gray, J. J., Mosimann, J. E., & Ahrens, A. H. (1992). Cultural expectations of thinness in women: An update. *International Journal of Eating Disorders, 11*, 85–89.

Chapter 24

ASSESSMENT OF BODY IMAGE DISTURBANCES

TIFFANY M. STEWART AND DONALD A. WILLIAMSON

BODY IMAGE ASSESSMENT: THE ALLIANCE BETWEEN CONCEPTUAL FOUNDATIONS AND METHODS

Two implicit assumptions of modern scientific philosophy are:

1. You cannot objectively study any phenomenon unless you can reliably and validly measure the phenomenon of interest.
2. You must have a theoretical framework to specifically test hypotheses using a reliable and valid method (Beck & Holmes, 1968).

As noted by Cash and Pruzinsky (2002), research on body image has exploded over the past 10 years. Yet, despite the phenomenal growth of interest in this topic, interest in the theoretical foundations of this research has lagged considerably. Many different body image assessment procedures have been developed, and the types of approaches are very diverse. In most measurement approaches, it is not readily apparent if there is one conceptual framework for the approach. We describe three theoretical frameworks that have stimulated the development of the methods. For the categories of procedures, we specify the conceptual foundations that appear to be most relevant for those particular methods. This chapter emphasizes the assessment of disturbances of body image, not just the measurement of body image, per se.

Perceptual Theories

The earliest theories of body image can be traced to Schilder's (1935) definition of body image as the "picture of our own body which we form in our own mind" (p. 11). Early theories of body image considered body image primarily the consequence of so-matosensory, for example, feelings of movement, interoceptive cues, visual cues, and awareness (Kinsbourne, 2002). Therefore, psychophysical models of perception were viewed as highly relevant. Many of the earlier body size estimation methods were based on this conceptual foundation. In this context, the term *body image disturbance* reflects either over- or underestimation of body size (sometimes called *body image distortion*). The disturbance may be measured as a function of the whole body or specific body areas, for example, hips, abdomen, or thighs.

Sociocultural Theories

For the past 20 years, understanding the basis of physical attractiveness has been a strong focus of social psychology. Much of this research has focused on facial attractiveness, with some body image researchers who have expanded this research to the study of physical attractiveness of the entire body, including body size and shape (e.g., Cash, 2002a). Sociocultural theories of body image are primarily derived from three social psychology theories: social expectancy theory, implicit personality theory, and status generalization theory (Jackson, 2002). These theories postulate that cultural values strongly influence:

1. Individual values, for example, the selection of an ideal body size/shape or the primary characteristics of beauty.
2. Behavior, for example, drive for thinness, use of compensatory behavior to control body weight, and dieting.

This theoretical perspective is compatible with the feminist perspective that objectified body consciousness is a product of social influences (McKinley, 2002). While most of this research has focused on physical attractiveness that is not specific to body size/shape, a number of body image measures have been developed to assess sociocultural influences on attitudes, beliefs, expectancies, and behavior that are relevant to eating disorders and obesity. Most measures of general satisfaction with appearance and measures of satisfaction with body size/shape are highly correlated. Yet, there is some evidence that, for eating disorders, a clear distinction should be made between concerns about general physical appearance and concerns about body size/shape (Strong, Williamson, Netemeyer, & Geer, 2000). In the context of sociocultural theory, disturbances of body image involve negative attitudes, expectancies, or experience related to cultural aspects of the body experience.

Cognitive-Behavioral Theories

Cognitive-behavioral (Cash, 2002a; Williamson, 1990) and, more recently, purely cognitive theories (Williamson, 1996; Williamson, Stewart, White, & York-Crowe, 2002) have provided a conceptual framework that incorporates: (1) the sociocultural perspective, (2) research related to biased information processing, (3) emotional/behavioral reactions, and (4) influences of body-related stimuli on behavior. Many of the recent body image assessment procedures appear to have emerged from these theories. Cognitive-behavioral theories postulate that body-related stimuli activate the body schema, a memory store that is developed through life experiences relevant to a person's body size, appearance, and so on; and to the values, expectancies, and so on, related to cultural values/messages to body image. Therefore, from the perspective of the cognitive-behavioral theory, disturbances of body image involve negative cognitive emotions and behavioral reactions to body-related information. In this regard, body image assessment procedures have been developed to measure subjective attitudes about bodily attributes, perceptions of actual or current body size, ideal body size, and behaviors related to body image (e.g., body checking, avoidance of feared situations, and restrictive eating). This theory has direct relevance to eating disorders (Williamson et al., 2002) and to obesity (Sarwer & Thompson, 2002; Williamson, 1990).

ORGANIZATION OF THE CHAPTER

In this chapter, measures are reviewed as they relate to the perceptual, sociocultural, and cognitive-behavioral theories of body image. The body image assessment measures are divided into four groups:

1. Size estimation procedures, that is, figural stimuli and perceptual measures.
2. Body size/shape dissatisfaction procedures.
3. Sociocultural procedures, for example, risk factors and internalization of the thin ideal.
4. Behavioral measures, that is, body checking and avoidance.

Size estimation procedures include figural stimuli and perceptual measures and are derived primarily from perceptual theory. Body size/shape dissatisfaction measures and behavioral measures are generally derived from the cognitive-behavioral perspective. Sociocultural measures (derived from the sociocultural perspective) include measures related to psychosocial risk factors for eating disorders, media influence, and internalization of the thin ideal. For each type of body image assessment that is presented in the text, a comprehensive description for the use of the measure and information concerning evidence for the reliability and validity of the method is provided. In addition, tables are provided to present summary information about additional measures.

CLARIFICATION OF CONSTRUCTS AND DEFINITIONS

Over the past three decades, many constructs related to body image have been described. Researchers have used different terms interchangeably, which often makes the comparison of different studies difficult. In this section, key concepts in the body image literature are defined for use in this chapter. We believe that the term *body image* represents a multifaceted construct pertaining to an individual's perception, self, attitudes about that perception, as well as associated behaviors. The term *body image disturbance* represents some type of maladaptive response related to the body image construct. Table 24.1 summarizes some of the important terms used in reference to body image and body image disturbance. For example, terms such as *body dissatisfaction, negative body image, body dysphoria,* and *overconcern with body size and shape* are often used interchangeably in the body image literature and represent an attitudinal aspect of body image. Likewise, the terms *body distortion, current body size, ideal body size,* and *acceptable/reasonable*

Table 24.1   Clarification of Body Image Terms

Terms Used in This Chapter	Definition	Similar To
Body image.	A person's mental image and evaluation of his or her physical appearance and the influence of these perceptions and attitudes on his or her behaviors (Rosen, 1995).	Size perception accuracy. Body size estimation.
Body image disturbance.	Any form of affective, cognitive, perceptual, or behavioral disturbance that is directly related to concerns about body size or shape (Thompson, 1995). Disturbance in the way in which an individual's body weight or shape is experienced; undue influence of body weight or shape on self-evaluation (DSM, 1994).	Body image distortion. Body size/shape dissatisfaction. Body size overestimation.
Body image distortion/ size overestimation.	The degree to which an individual misperceives current body size, particularly in the way that is larger than actual current body size (Williamson, 1990).	Body image disturbance. Body image distortion.
Body image/size dissatisfaction.	The discrepancy between an individual's perceived current body size and perceived ideal body size (Williamson, 1990). Discomfort with some aspect of the appearance of body size/shape (Cash, 2002).	Weight satisfaction. Appearance satisfaction. Body esteem. Body image disturbance. Negative body image.
Overconcern with body size and shape.	Excessive worry about body size/shape in people that are normal or underweight.	Body concern.
Body dysphoria.	Extreme concern about body size/shape in individuals who are normal weight or underweight.	Body distress. Overconcern with body size/shape. Weight/shape preoccupation.
Current/actual body size estimate.	An individual's actual body size as defined by height and weight or body mass index.	Self-estimate.
Ideal body size/preference for thinness.	A body size or shape that an individual would prefer if he or she could have any body size desired. A standard used as an ideal standard for judging satisfaction with current body size (Williamson, 1990).	Drive for thinness.
Acceptable/reasonable body size.	A body size or shape that an individual perceives may be maintained over a long period of time (Stewart et al., 2002).	Weight/shape goal.
Drive for thinness.	Efforts made by an individual (e.g., thoughts, emotions, behaviors) to decrease size and shape (Williamson, 1990).	Preference for thinness. Ideal body size.

Note: Refer to *Exacting Beauty,* by J. K. Thompson, L. J. Heinberg, M. Altabe, and S. Tantleff-Dunn, 1999, Washington, DC: American Psychological Association, for more general definitions and a greater variety of terms.

body size represent the perceptual conceptualization of body size, expressing an over- or underestimation of body size. The term *drive for thinness* represents the cognitive-behavioral conceptualization in that it is the expression of thoughts and behaviors that motivate the achievement of a thin body size.

For the purpose of this chapter, we use the terms listed in Table 24.1 throughout the chapter and provide definitions for them. We also indicate terms that are similar to the terms used in this chapter. By using a few well-defined terms, we hope that the information in this chapter is presented with greater clarity. For a more detailed discussion of the definition of terms related to body image, see Thompson, Heinberg, Altabe, and Tantleff-Dunn (1999).

REVIEW OF ASSESSMENT METHODS

Over the past 30 years, the total number of body image assessment procedures has expanded beyond the scope of a relatively brief review of the literature. For a comprehensive review of the earlier literature, see Thompson (1990), Thompson et al. (1999), and Thompson and van den Berg (2002). In this chapter, we present some of the measures that have been used extensively or report very new methods from recent publications. These methods are summarized in Tables 24.2 to 24.6. The tables are organized to reflect the participant characteristics (sex, age, and race) of the validation sample, method (questionnaires, computer, other), labor intensity (high, low), and psychometrics (valid, reliable) of each method. Because of space limitation, only a few of these methods are reviewed extensively in the text.

Body Size Estimation Measures—Figural Stimuli

Williamson (1996) observed that most figural stimuli methods for assessing body image can be conceptualized as a measure of cognitive bias. These procedures are summarized in Table 24.2. Silhouette measures consist of sets of schematic figures (male and/or female), which range from underweight to overweight. Subjects are asked to select figures based on the perception of their current body size and their perception of their ideal body size. The difference between subjects' perception of their current body and their ideal body size yields the discrepancy that is considered to represent the individual's level of dissatisfaction with his or her own body.

These methods have been found to be reliable, valid, and easily administered procedures (e.g., Stewart, Williamson, Smeets, & Greenway, 2000; Stunkard, Sorenson, & Schulsinger, 1983; Thompson & Altabe, 1991; Williamson, Davis, Bennett, Goreczny, & Gleaves, 1989). Some of these methods present the stimuli in a fixed order (e.g., Stunkard et al., 1983), and others present the stimuli in a random order (e.g., Williamson et al., 1989).

Figure Rating Scale (FRS)

Stunkard et al. (1983) created the first set of silhouette scales that was applicable to males and females. The FRS is a frequently used measure that consists of nine schematic figures in a fixed order varying from a small size to a larger size for males

Table 24.2 Size Estimation Procedures: Figural Stimuli

Measure	Authors	Sex M	Sex F	Age Child/Adolescent	Age Adult	Race White	Race Minority	Method Paper and Pencil	Method Computer	Method Other	Labor L	Labor H	Psychometrics Valid	Psychometrics Reliable
Figure Rating Scale (FRS)	Stunkard et al. (1983)	X	X		X	X				X	X	X	X	X
Body Image Assessment (BIA)	Williamson, Davis, Bennett, Goreczny, & Gleaves (1989)		X		X	X	X			X	X	X	X	X
Body Image Assessment for Obesity (BIA-O)	Williamson, Womble, Zucker, Reas, White, Blouin, & Greenway (2000)	X	X		X	X	X			X	X	X	X	X
Body Morph Assessment (BMA)	Stewart, Williamson, Smeets, & Greenway (2000)		X		X	X			X		X		X	
Body Morph Assessment 2.0 (BMA 2.0)	Stewart, Williamson, & Allen (2002)	X	X		X	X	X		X		X		X	
Body Image Assessment Child (BIA-C) and Pre-adolescent (BIA-P)	Veron-Guidry & Williamson (1996)	X	X	X		X	X			X	X		X	X
Body Image Testing System (BITS)	Schlundt & Bell (1993)	X	X		X	X	X		X		X		X	X
Body Build	Dickerson-Parnell, Jones, Braddy, & Parnell (1987)	X	X		X	X	X		X				X	
Contour Drawing Rating Scale	Thompson & Gray (1995)	X	X		X	X	X			X	X	X	X	X
Body Rating Scales for Adolescent Females (BRS)	Sherman, Iacono, & Donnelly (1995)		X	X		X				X	X		X	X
Body Image Silhouette Scale	Powers & Erickson (1986)		X		X	X	X			X	X			
Breast/Chest Rating Scale (BCRS)	Thompson & Tantleff (1992)	X	X		X	X				X	X			X

Note: H = High; L = Low.

and females. This measure was shown to have good test-retest reliability and moderate convergent validity with other measures of body dissatisfaction (Thompson & Altabe, 1991).

Body Image Assessment (BIA)

The BIA (Williamson et al., 1989) uses nine silhouettes of only female body shapes. The silhouettes range from very thin to overweight body sizes and are presented in a random order. Test-retest reliability and convergent validity was shown to be good for the BIA. Normative data were established as a function of actual body size so that raw scores could be interpreted in terms of standardized scores.

Body Image Assessment for Obesity (BIA-O)

The BIA-O (Williamson et al., 2000) is an extension of the BIA to obese body sizes and to men and women. The BIA-O uses 18 silhouettes of female and male body shapes. The silhouettes range from very thin to obese body sizes. Participants are asked to select their current, ideal, and reasonable body sizes. The discrepancy between the participant's current body size score and the participant's ideal body size score is derived as an index of body size dissatisfaction. Test-retest reliability and validity were shown to be good for the BIA-O. Normative data for current, ideal body, and reasonable size were established as a function of actual body size so that raw scores could be interpreted in terms of standardized scores.

Body Morph Assessment 2.0 (BMA 2.0)

The BMA 2.0 (Stewart, Williamson, & Allen, 2002), an extension of the original BMA, is designed to serve as a realistic, valid, and precise measure of body image. A prototype of the new BMA 2.0 was found to be valid and reliable (Stewart et al., 2000). The BMA 2.0 measures body image in individuals ranging from very thin to very obese. The BMA 2.0 uses a computer "morph" movie of a human body. Figural stimuli are presented one at a time on a computer screen, in an order that moves from thin to fat, or fat to thin. The battery consists of several morph movies. These morph movies are distinguished between sex and race. The image of the human body that is used with each subject is an image that matches the subject's race and sex. The morph demonstrates the transformation of an exceptionally thin body into an obese body or vice versa. There are a total of 100 increments between the two endpoints of the thin and obese bodies. Test-retest reliability was demonstrated for the selections of current body size (CBS), ideal body size (IBS), and acceptable body size (ABS). Content, convergent, and discriminant were also demonstrated. Norms were established for men and women (Stewart et al., 2002).

Although there has been concern about the figural stimuli measures (Gardner, Friedman, & Jackson, 1998), recent measures have addressed and resolved difficulties of scale coarseness, restriction of scale range, method of presentation, and adequate validity and reliability (e.g., Body Morph Assessment 2.0).

Body Image Assessment for Preadolescents and Children (BIA-C, BIA-P)

The BIA-C and the BIA-P (Veron-Guidry & Williamson, 1996) are modifications of the BIA procedure developed by Williamson et al. (1989). The procedures involve sets of body image silhouettes that correspond to male and female children and preadolescents. Each set of silhouettes (a total of four sets) has nine body sizes ranging from very thin to very large. Convergent validity was demonstrated on these measures by comparison to measures of body dysphoria and eating disorder symptoms. Test-retest reliability was demonstrated and norms were established.

Other Measures

Other measures in this category consist of the Body Image Silhouette Scale, Breast/Chest Rating Scale, Contour Drawing Scale, Body Rating Scale for Adolescent Females, Body Image Testing System, and Body Build (see Table 24.2 for details).

Body Size Estimation: Perceptual

Early (pre-1990) measures of body size estimation were based on a perceptual theory of body image (Kinsbourne, 2002). With few exceptions (e.g., Shafran & Fairburn, 2002), this approach has fallen into disfavor over the past decade. Perceptual measures assess primarily a pictorial representation of the body. These measures are summarized in Table 24.3. The single-site measures provide for the assessment of size perception accuracy at individual body sites. With the single-site measurement procedures, the subject's actual size is measured with body calipers. The percentage over- or underestimation of size may be estimated from the formula: estimated size divided by actual size (for a specific body site x 100). With the whole-image procedures, the individual views a whole-body image. These images may consist of mirror images, pictorial, or video presentation of the image. The images may be altered to represent an image larger or smaller than actual size. The subjects' task with this type of measure is to match the perception of their actual size to an image. An index of underestimation or overestimation is computed by this matching process.

In general, single-site measures have been shown to be reliable and internally consistent (e.g., Ben-Tovim, Walker, Murray, & Chin, 1990; Ruff & Barrios, 1986; Slade, 1985). The whole-body measures have been shown to be generally reliable and internally consistent (e.g., Bowden, Touyz, Rodriques, Hensley, & Beumont, 1989; Brodie, Slade, & Rose, 1989; Gardner, Martinez, & Sandoval, 1987; Garfinkel, Moldofsky, & Garner, 1979; Touyz, Beumont, Collins, & Cowie, 1985).

Body Image Detection Device (BIDD)

The BIDD (Ruff & Barrios, 1986) is a single-site measure. It involves adjusting the width of a light beam projected on a wall to match perceived size of a specific body site. This measure was designed to determine individuals' accuracy in estimating the size of body parts. Typically, the estimation of face, chest, waist, hips, and thighs is employed. The original studies of the BIDD demonstrated good interrater reliability, internal consistency, and temporal stability, but later studies questioned the validity of this method (Mizes, 1991).

Adjustable Light Beam (ALBA)

The ALBA (Thompson & Spana, 1988) is a single-site measure. It involves the adjustment of four light beams projected on a wall to match perceived size of cheeks, waist,

Table 24.3 Size Estimation Procedures: Perceptual

Measure	Authors	Sex		Age		Race		Method			Labor		Psychometrics	
		M	F	Child/ Adolescent	Adult	White	Minority	Paper and Pencil	Computer	Other	C	I	Valid	Reliable
Body Image Detection Device (BIDD)	Ruff & Barrios (1986)	X	X		X	X	X			X		X	X	X
Adjustable Light Beam (ALBA)	Thompson & Spana (1988)		X		X	X				X		X	X	X
Digital Photography	Shafran & Fairburn (2002)		X		X	X				X		X	X	
Distorting Video Camera	Freeman et al. (1984)	X	X	X	X	X	X			X		X	X	X
Image Marking Procedure (IMP)	Askevold (1975)		X		X	X	X			X		X	X	X
Movable Caliper Technique (MCT): Visual Size Estimation (VSE)	Slade & Russell (1973)	X	X	X	X					X	X		X	X

Note: C = Convenient; I = Inconvenient.

hips, and thighs. Test-retest reliability for this measure was established. Convergent validity was demonstrated with a comparison of the ALBA to other measures of size estimation, including body-part and adjusting-image procedures.

Digital Photography

The digital photography whole-body method of body image assessment was designed to assess the perception of body size under real-life situations, for example, viewing self in the mirror (Shafran & Fairburn, 2002). This measure uses a mirror, a screen, and a digital photography system to project a photograph of the individual onto an adjacent screen to compare the individual's actual reflection in the mirror to the projected image (photograph) on the screen. This procedure was used to derive an estimation of the accuracy of an individual's perceived body size and was designed to assess perception of body size as opposed to a memory for body size.

Distorting Video Camera

The distorting video camera method (Freeman, Thomas, Solyom, & Hunter, 1984) is a whole-body method. It involves using a video camera to produce images, which appear 20% thinner to 40% fatter than the current size of an individual. Reliability and convergent validity were demonstrated by comparison with a similar measure (i.e., distorting photograph technique).

Other Measures

Other measures included in this category are the image marking procedure, movable caliper technique, distorting mirror, distorting photograph technique, distorting television method, distorting video technique, and the TV-video method. See Table 24.3 for details. Most of these procedures have been regarded as "high labor intensity" because of the equipment setup and procedures and/or requirements of participants (e.g., putting on a leotard) for the administration of the procedure.

Body Dissatisfaction Measures

The dissatisfaction with body size or appearance has been assessed using numerous measures. These measures primarily assess nonpictorial representation of body image, consisting of a measurement of the dispositional element of body image, such as feelings, attitudes, or beliefs concerning body image. The theoretical basis for most of these measures is cognitive-behavioral theory. These measures are summarized in Table 24.4.

Overall, measures used to assess the dissatisfaction component have been found to be reliable, valid, and are easily administered (e.g., Brown, Cash, & Mikulka, 1990; Cooper, Taylor, Cooper, & Fairburn, 1987; Franzoi & Shields, 1984; Garner, Olmsted, & Polivy, 1983).

Body Shape Questionnaire (BSQ)

The BSQ (Cooper et al., 1987) is a 34-item self-report measure used to measure concerns with body shape, in particular the experience of "feeling fat" (Cooper et al., 1987). Participants indicate the frequency with which they experience specific body-related events. The BSQ has been validated as a measure of concern with body size

Table 24.4 Body Dissatisfaction Measures

Measure	Authors	Sex M	Sex F	Age Child/ Adolescent	Age Adult	Race White	Race Minority	Method Paper and Pencil	Method Computer	Method Other	Labor L	Labor H	Valid	Reliable
Body Shape Questionnaire (BSQ)	Cooper et al. (1987)	X	X		X	X	X	X			X		X	X
Multidimensional Body-Self Relations Questionnaire: Body Areas Satisfaction Scale (MBSRQ)	Cash, Winstead, & Janda (1986)	X	X	X	X	X	X	X			X		X	X
Eating Disorder Inventory-2: Body Dissatisfaction Scale (EDI-2)	Garner, 1991		X	X	X	X	X	X			X		X	X
Physical Appearance State and Trait Anxiety Scale (PASTAS)	Reed et al. (1991)		X		X	X	X	X			X		X	X
Body Image States Scale	Cash, Fleming, Alindogan, Steadman, & Whitehead (2002)	X	X		X	X	X	X			X			X
Body Esteem Scale (BES)	Franzoi & Shields (1984)	X	X	X	X	X	X	X			X		X	X
Body Satisfaction Scale (BSS)	Slade, Dewey, Newton, Brodie, & Kiemle (1990)		X		X	X	X	X			X		X	X
Color-A-Person Dissatisfaction Test	Wooley & Roll (1991)	X	X		X	X	X	X			X		X	X
Body Attitudes Questionnaire (BAQ)	Coppenolle, Probst, Vandereycken, Goris & Goris & Meerman (1990)		X		X	X	X	X			X		X	X

Note: H = High; L = Low.

and shape. The BSQ has been demonstrated to be a valid indicator of eating disorder symptoms with women and with gay men (Strong et al., 2000). Concurrent validity of the measure has been found to be satisfactory. Good test-retest reliability and criterion validity have also been reported (Rosen, Jones, Ramirez, & Waxman, 1996). Shortened versions of the BSQ (8 and 16 items) have also been reported (Evans & Dolan, 1993).

Multidimensional Body-Self Relations Questionnaire (MBSRQ)

The MBSRQ (Brown et al., 1990) is a self-report attitudinal assessment of evaluation and orientation related to appearance. Using a five-point response format (1 = definitely disagree to 5 = definitely agree), individuals respond to 69 items related to their attitudes in three domains: physical appearance, physical fitness, and health/illness. Within each of these domains, two subscales are measured: evaluation (satisfaction, liking, and attainment) and orientation (degree of importance, attention given to, and related behaviors). Factor analysis of the MBSRQ yielded seven scales (Brown et al., 1990): appearance evaluation, appearance orientation, fitness evaluation, fitness orientation, health evaluation, health orientation, and illness orientation. The MBSRQ has been found to have adequate validity and reliability. In addition, there are three other MBSRQ scales with relevance to body image assessment: body areas satisfaction scale, overweight preoccupation scale, and self-classified weight scale.

Eating Disorder Inventory 2: Body Dissatisfaction Scale (EDI-2)

The EDI-2 body dissatisfaction scale (Garner, 1991) is part (includes nine items) of the 91-item EDI-2. The EDI-2 was developed from an earlier version of the Eating Disorder Inventory (EDI; Garner et al., 1983). The body dissatisfaction scale assesses attitudes related to body shape. Specifically, this scale measures the construct of body dissatisfaction. This scale was constructed to measure dissatisfaction through representation that specific body parts are too large, especially those parts associated with increased fatness at puberty. Construct validity has been demonstrated. Convergent and discriminant validity were also established.

Other Measures

Additional measures in this category consist of the Body Esteem Scale, Body Satisfaction Scale, Color-A-Person Dissatisfaction Test, Body Attitudes Questionnaire, Physical Appearance State and Trait Anxiety Scale, and the Body Image States Scale. See Table 24.4 for details.

Sociocultural Measures

The sociocultural perspective of body image includes measures that assess aspects of sociocultural influences on body image, for example, psychosocial risk factors, media influences, and the internalization of the thin ideal. Sociocultural theories (Jackson, 2002) form the basis for most of these measures. Overall, methods used to assess the sociocultural aspects of body image have been found to be valid and reliable. These measures are summarized in Table 24.5.

Table 24.5 Sociocultural Measures

Measure	Authors	Sex M	Sex F	Age Child/ Adolescent	Age Adult	Race White	Race Minority	Method Paper and Pencil	Method Computer	Method Other	Labor L	Labor H	Psychometrics Valid	Psychometrics Reliable
Sociocultural Attitudes Toward Appearance Questionnaire (SATAQ)	Heinberg, Thompson, & Stormer (1995)		X		X	X	X	X			X		X	X
Situational Inventory of Body Image Dysphoria (SIBID)	Cash (1994)	X	X		X	X	X	X			X		X	X
Perception of Teasing Scale (PTS)	Thompson, Cattarin, Fowler, & Fisher (1995)		X		X	X	X	X			X		X	X
Sociocultural Internalization of Appearance Questionnaire-Adolescents	Keery, Shroff, Thompson, Wertheim, & Smolak (in press)	X	X	X		X	X	X			X		X	X
Body Image Quality of Life Inventory	Cash & Fleming (2002)		X		X	X	X	X			X		X	X
Body Image Ideals Questionnaire	Cash & Szymanski (1995)	X	X		X	X	X	X			X		X	X
Appearance Schemas Inventory	Cash & Labarge (1996)	X	X		X	X	X	X			X		X	X

Note: H = High; L = Low.

Sociocultural Attitudes toward Appearance Questionnaire (SATAQ)

The 14-item SATAQ (Heinberg, Thompson, & Stormer, 1995), a self-report measure, is designed to assess women's recognition and acceptance of standards sanctioned by society as to appearance. Individuals are asked to rate statements on a five-point Likert format (1 = completely disagree to 5 = completely agree) that best reflects their agreement with the statement. Statements are related to personal attitudes toward sociocultural standards of appearance (e.g., "I believe clothes look better on thin models," "I tend to compare my body to people in magazines and on TV"). This measure was shown to have good convergent validity. The SATAQ was later refined and is currently in its third version (Thompson, van den Berg, Roehrig, Guarda, & Heinberg, in press). This measure has also been found to be valid and reliable.

Situational Inventory of Body Image Dysphoria (SIBID)

The SIBID (Cash, 1994) is a 48-item self-report questionnaire designed to assess an individual's negative body image emotions in everyday life situations. Internal consistency was demonstrated for both men and women. Moderate convergent validity was found with other measures of body image (e.g., body image evaluation, behavioral avoidance, and dysfunctional investment in physical appearance). Normative data was generated for both men and women. Cash (2002b) reported a short form (20 items) of the SIBID that yielded psychometric data similar to those reported for the longer version.

Other Measures

Additional measures include the Body Image Quality of Life Inventory, Body Image Ideals Questionnaire, Appearance Schemas Inventory, and the Sociocultural Internalization of Appearance Questionnaire—Adolescents. See Table 24.5 for details.

Behavioral Measures

The behavioral aspect of body image has primarily targeted body-checking behaviors and avoided situations pertaining to fears or anxiety related to body image disturbance. These measures are summarized in Table 24.6. They have been found to be valid and reliable.

Body Checking Questionnaire (BCQ)

Behavioral symptoms as related to body image consists of compulsive checking of various body areas, for example, stomach or hips or the entire body, for example, observation using a mirror or compulsive weighing, to detect minute changes in fatness. The BCQ (Reas, Whisenhunt, Netemeyer, & Williamson, 2002) measures the severity of this behavioral symptom. Reliability and validity of this brief self-report inventory was established by Reas et al. (2002). The BCQ was also found to differentiate normal controls and eating disorder patients.

Body Image Avoidance Questionnaire

The Body Image Avoidance Questionnaire (Rosen, Srebnik, Saltzberg, & Wendt, 1991) is a self-report measure that assesses behavioral tendencies that frequently

Table 24.6 Behavioral Measures

Measure	Authors	Sex		Age		Race		Method			Labor		Psychometrics	
		M	F	Child/ Adolescent	Adult	White	Minority	Paper and Pencil	Computer	Other	L	H	Valid	Reliable
Body Checking Questionnaire (BCQ)	Reas, Whisenhunt, Netemeyer, & Williamson (2002)	X	X	X	X	X	X	X			X		X	X
Body Image Avoidance Questionnaire	Rosen, Srebnik, Saltzberg, & Wendt (1991)	X	X		X	X	X	X			X		X	X
Muscle Appearance Satisfaction Scale (MASS)	Mayville, Williamson, White, Netemeyer, & Drab (2002)	X			X	X	X	X			X		X	X

Note: H = High; L = Low.

accompany body image disturbance. The questionnaire has 19 items and a particular focus on the avoidance of situations that promote anxiety and concern about physical appearance (e.g., "I avoid going clothes shopping," "I do not go out socially if it involves eating," "I weigh myself"). This measure demonstrated adequate internal consistency and test-retest reliability. Norms were provided on a sample of 353 female psychology students.

Muscle Appearance Satisfaction Scale (MASS)

Body image concerns in men is a problem that only recently has been the focus of study. The MASS (Mayville, Williamson, White, Netemeyer, & Drab, 2002) is a brief 19-item self-report measure that assesses excessive concern with the appearance of muscularity. Men who are obsessed with body size often perceive their bodies to be too thin and insufficiently muscular. This "reverse body image distortion" is associated with compulsive weight lifting and use of steroids to correct this "appearance defect." The MASS includes five stable factors: bodybuilding dependence, muscle checking, substance use, injury, and muscle satisfaction. The MASS was found to be valid and reliable (Mayville et al., 2002).

SUMMARY AND CONCLUSIONS

Great care and selection should be initiated when choosing an appropriate body image measure. Whether for research or clinical purposes, we feel that it is important to select a measure appropriate for the conceptual foundation and construct of interest. It is useful for the researcher or clinician to recognize the theoretical foundation of the research or clinical assessment question (e.g., sociocultural question, perceptual, cognitive-behavioral) and the exact construct that should be measured (e.g., body size estimation, dissatisfaction, behavioral).

Studies of eating disorders and obesity have generally focused on the measurement of body size/shape dissatisfaction and have discussed these tests as "body image" measures. It is important to note that body image assessment spans many dimensions other than body dissatisfaction. For example, figural stimuli measures (e.g., BIA, BIA-O, BMA 2.0) allow for not only an index of body dissatisfaction, but also overestimation of body size and the selection of ideal or acceptable body size, which (in the context of norms) measures drive for thinness. Some of these measures (e.g., BIA-O, BMA 2.0) measure body image in thin, normal-weight, and obese individuals.

Consideration of the psychometric properties of the measures is also important when assessing the construct of interest. It is important to evaluate and choose an appropriate measure based on the standardization sample in relation to the population or individual in which a measure will be used. For example, some measures are appropriate only for women, others should not be used with obese people, and other measures are designed only for use with children. Most of the methods have established good reliability and validity. However, there are some exceptions. Tables 24.2 to 24.6 summarize these and other aspects (i.e., race of validation sample, type of method, and labor intensity). It is our hope that these tables and the information provided in this chapter provide a convenient reference source for clinicians and researchers who need to make informed decisions about the selection of body image measures.

REFERENCES

Askevold, R. (1975). Measuring body image: Preliminary report on a new method. *Psychotherapy and Psychosomatics, 26,* 71–77.

Beck, L. W., & Holmes, R. L. (1968). *Philosophic Inquiry: An introduction to philosophy* (2nd ed.). Upper Saddle River, NJ: Prentice-Hall.

Ben-Tovim, D. I., Walker, M. K., Murray, H., & Chin, G. (1990). Body size estimates: Body image or body attitude measures? *International Journal of Eating Disorders, 9,* 57–68.

Bowden, P. K., Touyz, S. W., Rodriques, P. J., Hensley, R., & Beumont, P. J. V. (1989). Distorting patient or distorting instrument? Body shape disturbance in patients with anorexia nervosa and bulimia. *British Journal of Psychiatry, 155,* 196–201.

Brodie, D. A., & Slade, P. D. (1988). The relationship between body image and body-fat in adult women. *Psychological Medicine, 18,* 623–631.

Brodie, D. A., Slade, P. D., & Rose, H. (1989). Reliability measures in distorting body image. *Perceptual and Motor Skills, 69*(3, Pt. 1), 723–732.

Brown, T. A., Cash, T. F., & Mikulka, P. J. (1990). Attitudinal body-image assessment: Factor analysis of the Body Self Relations Questionnaire. *Journal of Personality Assessment, 55,* 135–144.

Cash, T. F. (1994). The situational inventory of body image dysphoria: Contextual assessment of body image. *Behavior Therapist, 17,* 133–134.

Cash, T. F. (2002a). Cognitive-behavioral perspectives on body image. In T. F. Cash & T. Pruzinsky (Eds.), *Body image: A handbook of theory, research, and clinical practice* (pp. 38–46). New York: Guilford Press.

Cash, T. F. (2002b). The situational inventory of body image dysphoria: Psychometric evidence and development of a short form. *International Journal of Eating Disorders, 32*(3), 362–366.

Cash, T. F., & Fleming, E. C. (2002). The impact of body-image experiences: Development of the body image quality of life inventory. *International Journal of Eating Disorders, 31,* 455–460.

Cash, T. F., Fleming, E. C., Alindogan, J., Steadman, L., & Whitehead, A. (2002). Beyond body image as a trait: The development and validation of the body image states scale. *Eating Disorders: Journal of Treatment and Prevention, 10,* 103–113.

Cash, T. F., & Labarge, A. S. (1996). Development of the appearance schemas inventory: A new cognitive body-image assessment. *Cognitive Therapy and Research, 20,* 37–50.

Cash, T. F., & Pruzinsky, T. (2002). *Body image: A handbook of theory, research, and clinical practice.* New York: Guilford Press.

Cash, T. F., Winstead, B. A., & Janda, L. H. (1986). Body image survey report: The great American shape-up. *Psychology Today, 24,* 30–37.

Cooper, P. J., Taylor, M. J., Cooper, Z., & Fairburn, C. G. (1987). The development and validation of the body shape questionnaire. *International Journal of Eating Disorders, 6,* 485–494.

Coppenolle, H. V., Probst, M., Vandereycken, W., Goris, M., & Meermann, R. (1990). Construction of a questionnaire on the body experience of anorexia nervosa. In H. Remschmidt & M. H. Schmidt (Eds.), *Anorexia nervosa* (pp. 103–113). Stuttgart, Germany: Hogrefe & Huber.

Dickerson-Parnell, B., Jones, M., Braddy, D., & Parnell, C. P. (1987). Assessment of body image perceptions using a computer program. *Behavior Research Methods, Instruments, and Computers, 19,* 353–354.

Evans, C., & Dolan, B. (1993). Body shape questionnaire: Derivation of shortened "alternate forms." *International Journal of Eating Disorders, 13*(3), 315–321.

Franzoi, S. L., & Shields, S. A. (1984). The body esteem scale: Multidimensional structure and sex differences in a college population. *Journal of Personality Assessment, 48,* 173–178.

Freeman, R. F., Thomas, C. D., Solyom, L., & Hunter, M. A. (1984). A modified video camera for measuring body image distortion: Technical description and reliability. *Psychological Medicine, 14,* 411–416.

Gardner, R. M., Friedman, B. N., & Jackson, N. A. (1998). Methodological concerns when using silhouettes to measure body image. *Perceptual and Motor Skills, 86,* 387–395.

Gardner, R. M., Martinez, R., & Sandoval, Y. (1987). Obesity and body image: An evaluation of sensory and nonsensory components. *Psychological Medicine, 17,* 927–932.

Garfinkel, P. E., Moldofsky, H., & Garner, D. M. (1979). The stability of perceptual disturbances in anorexia nervosa. *Psychological Medicine, 9,* 703–708.

Garner, D. M. (1991). *Eating Disorder Inventory-2 manual.* Odessa, FL: Psychological Assessment Resources.

Garner, D. M., Olmstead, M. A., & Polivy, J. (1983). Development and validation of a multidimensional eating disorder inventory for anorexia nervosa and bulimia. *International Journal of Eating Disorders, 2,* 15–34.

Glucksman, M., & Hirsch, J. (1969). The response of obese patients to weight reduction. III: The perception of body size. *Psychosomatic Medicine, 31,* 1–17.

Heinberg, L. J., Thompson, J. K., & Stormer, S. (1995). Development and validation of the sociocultural attitudes toward appearance questionnaire (SATAQ). *International Journal of Eating Disorders, 17,* 81–89.

Jackson, L. A. (2002). Physical attractiveness: A sociocultural perspective. In T. F. Cash & T. Pruzinsky (Eds.), *Body image: A handbook of theory, research, and clinical practice* (pp. 13–21). New York: Guilford Press.

Kerry, H., Shroff, H., Thompson, J. K., Wertheim, E., & Smolak, L. (in press). The Sociocultural Internalization of Appearance Questionnaire—Adolescents. *Eating and Weight Disorders: Studies on Anorexia, Bulimia, and Obesity.*

Kinsbourne, M. (2002). The brain and body awareness. In T. F. Cash & T. Pruzinsky (Eds.), *Body image: A handbook of theory, research, and clinical practice* (pp. 22–29). New York: Guilford Press.

Mayville, S. B., Williamson, D. A., White, M. A., Netemeyer, R., & Drab, D. L. (2002). Development of the muscle appearance satisfaction scale: A self-report measure for the assessment of muscle dysmorphia symptoms. *Assessment, 9,* 351–360.

McKinley, N. M. (2002). Feminist perspectives and objectified body consciousness. In T. F. Cash & T. Pruzinsky (Eds.), *Body image: A handbook of theory, research, and clinical practice* (pp. 55–64). New York: Guilford Press.

Mizes, J. S. (1991). Validity of the body image detection device. *Addictive Behaviors, 16,* 411–417.

Powers, P. D., & Erickson, M. T. (1986). Body image in women and its relationship to self-image and body satisfaction. *Journal of Obesity and Weight Regulation, 5,* 37–50.

Reas, D. L., Whisenhunt, B. L., Netemeyer, R., & Williamson, D. A. (2002). Development of the Body Checking Questionnaire: A self-report measure of body checking behavior. *International Journal of Eating Disorders, 31,* 324–333.

Reed, D., Thompson, J. K., Brannick, M. T., & Sacco, W. P. (1991). Development and validation of the physical appearance state and trait anxiety scale (PASTAS). *Journal of Anxiety Disorders, 5,* 323–332.

Rosen, J. C., Jones, A., Ramirez, E., & Waxman, S. (1996). Body shape questionnaire: Studies of validity and reliability. *International Journal of Eating Disorders, 20*(3), 315–319.

Rosen, J. C., Srebnik, D., Saltzberg, E., & Wendt, S. (1991). Development of a body image avoidance questionnaire. *Psychological Assessment, 3*(1), 32–37.

Ruff, G. A., & Barrios, B. A. (1986). Realistic assessment of body image. *Behavioral Assessment, 8,* 237–252.

Sarwer, D. B., & Thompson, J. K. (2002). Obesity and body image disturbance. In T. A. Wadden & A. J. Stunkard (Eds.), *Handbook of obesity treatment* (pp. 447–464). New York: Guilford Press.

Schilder, P. (1935). *The image and appearance of the human body*. New York: International Universities Press.

Schlundt, D. G., & Bell, C. (1993). Body image testing system: A microcomputer program for assessing body image. *Journal of Psychopathology and Behavioral Assessment, 15,* 267–285.

Shafran, R., & Fairburn, C. G. (2002). A new ecologically valid method to assess body size estimation and body size dissatisfaction. *International Journal of Eating Disorders, 32*(4), 458–465.

Sherman, D. K., Iacono, W. G., & Donnelly, J. M. (1995). Development and validation of body rating scales for adolescent females. *International Journal of Eating Disorders, 18*(4), 327–333.

Slade, P. D. (1985). A review of body-image studies in anorexia nervosa and bulimia nervosa. *Journal of Psychiatric Research, 19,* 255–265.

Slade, P. D., Dewey, M. E., Newton, T., Brodie, D., & Kiemle, G. (1990). Development and preliminary validation of the body satisfaction scale (BSS). *Psychology and Health, 4,* 213–220.

Slade, P. D., & Russell, G. F. M. (1973). Awareness of body dimensions in anorexia nervosa: Cross-sectional and longitudinal studies. *Psychological Medicine, 3,* 188–199.

Stewart, T. M., Williamson, D. A., & Allen, R. (2002). *The body morph assessment 2.0 (BMA 2.0): A psychometric study*. Paper presented at the meeting of the Association for the Advancement of Behavior Therapy, Reno, NV.

Stewart, T. M., Williamson, D. A., Smeets, M. A. M., & Greenway, F. L. (2000). A computerized assessment of body image: A psychometric study. *Obesity Research, 9*(1), 43–50.

Strong, S. M., Williamson, D. A., Netemeyer, R. G., & Geer, J. H. (2000). Eating disorder symptoms and concerns about body differ as a function of gender and sexual orientation. *Journal of Clinical and Consulting Psychology, 19*(2), 240–255.

Stunkard, A., Sorensen, T., & Schulsinger, F. (1983). Use of the Danish adoption register for the study of obesity and thinness. In S. Kety, L. P. Rowland, R. L. Sidman, & S. W. Matthysse (Eds.), *The genetics of neurological and psychiatric disorders* (pp. 115–120). New York: Raven Press.

Thompson, J. K. (1990). *Body image disturbance: Assessment and treatment*. Elmsford, NY: Pergamon Press.

Thompson, J. K. (1995). Assessment of body image. In D. Allison (Ed.), *Handbook of assessment methods for eating behavior, and weight-related problems* (pp. 49–81). Thousand Oaks, CA: Sage.

Thompson, J. K., & Altabe, M. N. (1991). Psychometric qualities of the figure rating scale. *International Journal of Eating Disorders, 10,* 615–619.

Thompson, J. K., Cattarin, J., Fowler, B., & Fisher, E. (1995). The Perception of Teasing Scale (POTS): A revision and extension of the Physical Appearance Related Teasing Scale (PARTS). *Journal of Personality Assessment, 65,* 146–157.

Thompson, J. K., Heinberg, L. J., Altabe, M., & Tantleff-Dunn, S. (1999). *Exacting beauty: Theory, assessment and treatment of body image disturbance*. Washington, DC: American Psychological Association.

Thompson, J. K., & Spana, R. E. (1988). The adjustable light beam method for the assessment of size estimation accuracy: Description, psychometrics, and normative data. *International Journal of Eating Disorders, 7,* 521–526.

Thompson, J. K., & Tantleff, S. (1992). Female and make ratings of upper torso: Actual, ideal, and stereotypical conceptions. *Journal of Social Behavior and Personality, 7,* 345–354.

Thompson, J. K., & van den Berg, P. (2002). Measuring body image attitudes among adolescents and adults. In T. Cash & J. Pruzinsky (Eds.), *Body image: A handbook of theory, research, and clinical practice* (pp. 142–153). New York: Guilford Press.

Thompson, J. K., van den Berg, P., Roehrig, M., Guarda, A. S., Heinberg, L. J., (in press). The Sociocultural Attitudes Toward Appearance Questionnaire-3. *International Journal of Eating Disorders*.

Thompson, M. A., & Gray, J. J. (1995). Development and validation of a new body image assessment scale. *Journal of Personality Assessment, 64,* 258–269.

Touyz, S. W., Beumont, P. J. V., Collins, J. K., & Cowie, I. (1985). Body shape perception in bulimia and anorexia nervosa. *International Journal of Eating Disorders, 4,* 261–265.

Veron-Guidry, S., & Williamson, D. A. (1996). Development of a body image assessment procedure for children and preadolescents. *International Journal of Eating Disorders, 20(3).* 287–293.

Williamson, D. A. (1990). *Assessment of eating disorders: Obesity, anorexia, and bulimia nervosa.* New York: Pergamon Press.

Williamson, D. A. (1996). Body image disturbances in eating disorders: A form of cognitive bias? *Eating Disorders: Journal of Treatment and Prevention, 4,* 47–58.

Williamson, D. A., Davis, C. J., Bennett, S. M., Goreczny, A. J., & Gleaves, D. H. (1989). Development of a simple procedure for assessing body image disturbances. *Behavioral Assessment, 11,* 433–446.

Williamson, D. A., Stewart, T. M., White, M. A., & York-Crowe, E. (2002). An information-processing perspective on body image. In T. F. Cash & T. Pruzinsky (Eds.), *Body image: A handbook of theory, research, and clinical practice* (pp. 47–54). New York: Guilford Press.

Williamson, D. A., Womble, L. G., Zucker, N. L., Reas, D. L., White, M. A., Blouin, D. C., et al. (2000). Body image assessment for obesity (BIA-O): Development of a new procedure. *International Journal of Obesity, 24,* 1326–1332.

Wooley, O. W., & Roll, S. (1991). The Color-A-Person body dissatisfaction test: Stability, internal consistency, validity, and factor structure. *Journal of Personality Assessment, 56,* 395–413.

Chapter 25

TREATMENT OF
BODY IMAGE DISTURBANCES

THOMAS F. CASH AND JOSHUA I. HRABOSKY

Body image refers to individuals' attitudes toward their body, especially its appearance, which can have a significant impact on psychosocial functioning (Cash, 2002c; Cash & Pruzinsky, 2002). Body image attitudes include an *evaluation/affect* component, including individuals' body satisfaction/dissatisfaction as well as evaluative beliefs about their looks. These evaluations substantially stem from the extent of congruence or discrepancy between self-perceived and idealized physical attributes. These evaluations also entail body image affective experiences in everyday life situations. A second facet of body image attitudes is an *investment* dimension—the cognitive, behavioral, and emotional importance of appearance to the person and his or her sense of self (Cash, 2002b).

Body image problems can be placed on a continuum of severity, ranging from relatively negligible discontent with certain physical characteristics resulting in casual grooming behaviors (e.g., using makeup to cover up a blemish) to anxious, obsessive fixation on appearance resulting in extreme coping or compensatory behaviors (e.g., restrictive dieting, social avoidance, or compulsive exercising). Because a more severe negative body image can impair psychosocial well-being and quality of life, treatments of body image disturbances are receiving more clinical and scientific attention. As other contributors to this volume discuss, eating disorders are among the most maladaptive manifestations of body image dysfunction. According to the *Diagnostic and Statistical Manual of Mental Disorders* (*DSM-IV-TR;* American Psychiatric Association [APA], 2000), body image disturbance is a primary defining feature of anorexia nervosa and bulimia nervosa. Body dysmorphic disorder (BDD) is also primarily characterized by severe body image preoccupation and distress (APA, 2000). Furthermore, body image disturbances may also be associated with gender-identity disorder and certain somatic delusional disorders (APA, 2000). Finally, a negative body image can have deleterious psychosocial consequences such as depression (Noles, Cash, & Winstead, 1985), social anxiety (Cash & Fleming, 2002a), impaired sexual functioning (Wiederman, 2002), and poor self-esteem (Powell & Hendricks, 1999).

The principal purpose of this chapter is to provide a contemporary conceptualization of body image and its treatment. We first briefly discuss the epidemiology of body image problems, followed by a cognitive-behavioral perspective on their development.

Next, we examine in detail the empirical support for body image therapy, especially cognitive-behavioral treatment (CBT), which has received the greatest scientific scrutiny. Our review considers the specific role of body image CBT in the treatment of eating disorders, as well as the impact of eating disorder treatments in general on body image functioning. We then examine studies of body image CBT for BDD and obesity, followed by the investigations with subclinical, body-dissatisfied persons. Finally, we delineate the body image CBT program for the treatment of body image difficulties and disorders (Cash, 1991, 1995, 1996, 1997; Cash & Grant, 1995; Cash & Strachan, 2002).

PREVALENCE OF BODY IMAGE DISTURBANCES

Prevalence rates of *negative body image* or *body image disturbance* are difficult to quantify, largely because of considerable inconsistency in their definitions. Researchers often equate these terms with "body (or body image) dissatisfaction," including any discontent with one or more aspects of an individual's body. Most prevalence data on such dissatisfaction have come from a series of large-sample surveys conducted in 1972, 1985, and 1996 by *Psychology Today* magazine (Berscheid, Walster, & Bohrnstedt, 1973; Cash, Winstead, & Janda, 1986; Garner, 1997). Despite possible self-selection biases that might overrepresent persons with greater body image concerns, these surveys are often cited as supporting two main conclusions (Cash, 2002d). First, significant gender differences exist in body image discontent, with females reporting greater dissatisfaction with most physical characteristics than do males. Second, the data suggest that the prevalence of body image dissatisfaction has worsened for *both* sexes over the span of 25 years. For example, the percentage of men dissatisfied with their overall appearance substantially increased between each period—15% in 1972, 34% in 1985, and 43% in 1996. The prevalence of women reporting overall appearance dissatisfaction also increased considerably over this period—23% in 1972, 38% in 1985, and 56% in 1996.

A meta-analysis of body image research spanning the pre-1970s to 1995 (Feingold & Mazzella, 1998) found a widening gender difference over the period, indicating either that women's but not men's body images have worsened or that women's dissatisfaction increased more precipitously than men's. However, as Cash (2002d) has reviewed, other longitudinal and cross-sectional survey studies point to possible improvements in women's body images in the past decade (see Cash, Morrow, Hrabosky, & Perry, 2003; Heatherton, Mahamedi, Striepe, Field, & Keel, 1997; Heatherton, Nichols, Mahamedi, & Keel, 1995).

We believe that body image dissatisfaction alone is an inadequate criterion of body image disturbance (Cash, 2002d). Discontent with some physical attribute or even with a person's overall appearance does not necessarily produce significant emotional distress nor does it always impair psychosocial functioning. For example, in a recent database of more than 600 college students (Cash, 2002f), 14% of the men and 33% of the women reported dissatisfaction with their overall physical appearance. In addition, respondents rated how often they felt significant distress about their appearance and how often their body image interfered with aspects of their life (e.g., feelings about self, relationships with others, or functioning at school or work). Using a conjunctive definition of body image disturbance (i.e., dissatisfaction plus the occurrence of significant distress somewhat or more often plus the experience of impairment somewhat or more often), the data indicated that only 6% of men and 19% of women met the criteria for body image disturbance. Thus, about half of persons reporting overall body image discontent indicated that this negative evaluation produced significant distress and impairment in their life.

BODY IMAGE DEVELOPMENT AND PROCESSES

Body image, whether healthy or dysfunctional, is shaped by historical, developmental factors and proximal, concurrent influences. Figure 25.1 summarizes these variables. Although we present this heuristic model without causal arrows, we believe that there is a reciprocally interactive causal loop vis-à-vis environmental events, internal personal processes, and the individual's behaviors (Cash, 2002b). Historical factors refer to past events, attributes, and experiences as well as developmental processes that affect how people come to think, feel, and behave as to their body. Powerful historical influences include cultural socialization, interpersonal experiences (including both peer and familial influences), actual physical characteristics (and their impact on an individual's development), and personality attributes that affect how the individual construes his or her body. For the sake of this chapter's brevity, we do not review the extensive literature on these historical determinants of body image development. We refer the reader to other elucidating works (Cash, 2002g; Cash & Pruzinsky, 2002; Thompson, Heinberg, Altabe, & Tantleff-Dunn, 1999; Thompson & Smolak, 2001).

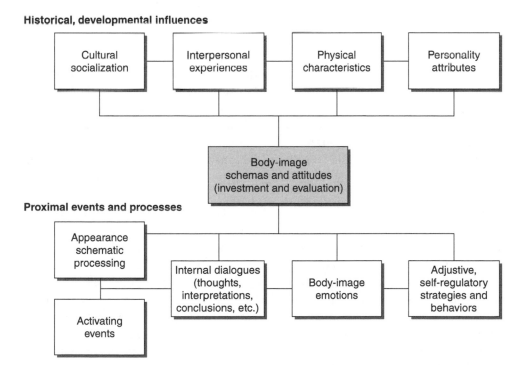

Figure 25.1 A Cognitive Behavioral Model of Body Image Development and Processes. Reproduced from "Cognitive Behavioral Perspectives on Body Image," pp. 38–46, by T. F. Cash, in *Body Image: A Handbook of Theory, Research, and Clinical Practice,* T. F. Cash and T. Pruzinsky (Eds.), 2002, New York: Guilford Press.

Because of their special relevance to body image CBT and disturbance, we discuss proximal factors at greater length. *Proximal factors* refer to current life events and how they are perceived, processed, and reacted to emotionally and behaviorally (Cash, 2002b). Proximal events include any precipitating or maintaining factors vis-à-vis and individual's body image experiences in everyday life. As explained previously, two core attitudinal elements of body image are cognitive-behavioral investment in and affective evaluation of the individual's physical appearance. An important integrative construct of attitudinal body image is the developed *self-schema* as it relates to appearance. Markus (1977) defined self-schemas as "cognitive generalizations about the self, derived from past experiences, that organize and guide the processing of self-related information contained in an individual's social experience" (p. 64). The individual who is schematic toward a specific self-dimension (e.g., physical appearance) will likely process information related to that dimension differently than an individual who is not. For example, Smolak and Levine (1996) argue that a person with a *thinness schema* is most likely to selectively process information that is relevant to and supportive of self-conceptions of thinness and attractiveness. Body image schemas reflect the individual's core assumptions and beliefs about the salience of appearance in his or her life, including its centrality to sense of self (Cash & Labarge, 1996; Cash, Melnyk, & Hrabosky, in press).

A situation or event can serve as an activator of schematic information processing as to an individual's appearance (Williamson, Stewart, White, & York-Crowe, 2002). Thus, contextual cues play a major role in the individual's body image experiences at any particular moment. Appearance-schematic persons place more importance on, pay more attention to, and preferentially process information relevant to their appearance. Many events can provoke body image thoughts and emotions—events such as social scrutiny, exposure to certain media images, weighing, exercising, mirror exposure, a specific mood, and changes in appearance. The cognitive effects of these triggers may include automatic thoughts, inferences, interpretations, and conclusions about appearance. For appearance-schematic individuals with a negative evaluative body image, these inner dialogues are habitual, flawed, and dysfunctional. These processes give rise to body image dysphoria, such as feelings of anxiety (including self-consciousness), shame, dejection, jealousy, or anger.

Individuals use various adjustive strategies to manage or cope with these distressing body image thoughts and emotions (Cash, 2002b). For example, avoidant strategies include behavioral avoidance of certain situations or people, wearing certain body-concealing attire, or efforts to deny or ignore their distress. Appearance-correcting strategies include rituals to alter the perceived "offending" characteristic (e.g., dieting or exercise behavior). Seeking social feedback is another approach, whereby individuals solicit reassurance from others to invalidate or discount concerns. Compensatory strategies entail attempts to enhance other self-evaluative attributes (physical or otherwise), such as improving hairstyle to compensate for weight-related concerns. It is important to recognize that negative reinforcement processes often govern these well-engrained efforts, as individuals seek to avoid or escape negative body image thoughts and emotions. These processes differ conceptually and consequentially from self-regulatory actions in pursuit of positive self-reinforcement, such as grooming behaviors to engender thoughts and feelings of body satisfaction or exercise behaviors to promote experiences of competence.

There is a surprising dearth of knowledge on coping processes in relation to body image functioning. Cash and his colleagues (Cash, Santos, & Williams, 2003), developed the Body Image Coping Strategies Inventory to assess how individuals deal with situations or events that threaten their body image. For both sexes, dysfunctional body image schemas were significantly related to the strategy of avoiding the threat or thoughts about it (avoidance coping) and attempts at changing their appearance (appearance fixing). Moreover, these two coping strategies, unlike the third strategy of rational coping focusing on positive self-care and use of social support, were strongly correlated with body image dysphoria.

BODY IMAGE TREATMENT OUTCOME STUDIES

Despite the growth in quantity and quality of body image treatment research, it remains surprisingly limited in light of the increasing recognition of the psychosocial importance of body image. This section of the chapter examines empirical trials of body image therapy. We review the research on the efficacy and effectiveness of cognitive-behavioral body image therapies (i.e., body image CBT) for individuals with clinical disorders as well as those with "subclinical" body image disturbances.

Body Image Treatment for Eating Disorders

Despite body image disturbance being a primary defining feature of anorexia nervosa (AN) and bulimia nervosa (BN; APA, 2000), reducing body image disturbance is underemphasized in the treatments of these disorders. Furthermore, although the *DSM-IV-TR* does not include body image disturbances as a criterion for binge-eating disorder (BED), researchers argue that significantly elevated level of dysfunctional body image attitudes about weight and shape is a major characteristic of the disorder (Grilo, 2002). For example, Cargill and colleagues (Cargill, Clark, Pera, Niaura, & Abrams, 1999) found that obese individuals suffering with BED are more likely to report heightened body image disturbances than non-binge-eating obese individuals. In their review, Schwartz and Brownell (2002) concluded that greater body image dissatisfaction occurs among persons with BED regardless of their actual weight.

Cognitive-behavioral therapy for BN has received much empirical attention, mainly due to the manual-based treatment approach developed by Fairburn and his colleagues (Fairburn, Marcus, & Wilson, 1993; Wilson, Fairburn, & Agras, 1997). Accepted as a treatment of choice, manual-based CBT has been highly efficacious in treating bulimic symptoms (see Fairburn, 2002). Yet, how much emphasis does this treatment place on body image concerns? In their description of the program, Wilson et al. concentrate primarily on the modification of problematic and habitual eating behaviors and cognitions; however, very little treatment focuses on changing attitudes toward body weight and shape.

CBT has also increasingly become a treatment of choice for AN, despite less empirical research (Vitousek, 2002). Unlike CBT for BN, CBT for AN seems to devote more attention to the client's attitudes and perception of weight and weight gain (Garner, Vitousek, & Pike, 1997). Garner and his colleagues (1997; Garner, 2002) argue that the topic of physical appearance is unavoidable in the treatment of AN because clients will be gaining weight while undergoing therapy. Body image, in this case, affects the motivation of the individual to gain weight, forcing the issue to be addressed while the individual is "becoming 'fatter'" (Garner et al., 1997, p. 95).

One recent study specifically examined the effects of body image treatment on AN patients. Key et al. (2002) assigned 15 anorexic inpatient females to a standard and a modified body image treatment group. Both conditions received psychoeducation on the development of body image, completed homework and group work on maladaptive cognitions and underlying assumptions, exposure exercises via type of clothing worn, and discussions on the relationship between sexual intercourse and body image. Patients in the modified treatment condition also received progressive mirror exposure. Women stood before a full-length mirror and looked at their clothed body for increasing periods of time each week. Key et al. found that mirror confrontation enhanced body image treatment. All else being equal, the modified treatment group reported significant and sustained improvements in body dissatisfaction at six months after conclusion of treatment while the standard treatment condition did not result in any significant changes in body satisfaction.

Vandereycken and his colleagues have acknowledged body image change as a central aim of their treatment of AN. In 1987, Vandereycken, Depreitere, and Probst introduced a body-oriented form of therapy focusing on patients' body experiences instead of solely on eating behaviors to aid the reinterpretation of their body as a "potentially pleasant instrument" (1987, p. 255). The intervention involves video confrontation, which is exposure and response to a videotape of the patient placed in a vulnerable, body-accentuating situation (e.g., wearing a bathing suit). Such video confrontation in conjunction with cognitive restructuring has received some empirical support in alleviating disordered eating behaviors (Probst, Van Coppenolle, & Vandereycken, 1995; Probst, Vandereycken, Van Coppenolle, & Pieters, 1999).

To the best of our knowledge, no study has ever compared CBT with and without a body image treatment component with patients suffering from either BN or AN. Most randomized, controlled trials of CBT have examined a manual-based program for BN (e.g., Agras, Walsh, Fairburn, Wilson, & Kraemer, 2000) in comparison with another form of treatment (e.g., pharmacological treatment or interpersonal psychotherapy). Very few controlled studies of CBT for AN have been conducted, and results are mixed from those studies (Vitousek, 2002). Rosen (1996) argues that weight restoration and reduction in eating pathology for the anorexic or bulimic patient do not guarantee improvements in body image dissatisfaction or dysphoria. In fact, the persistence of body image dissatisfaction, after treatment of eating disturbances, is a reliable predictor of relapse in BN (e.g., Fairburn, Peveler, Jones, Hope, & Doll, 1993).

Consequently, it is essential to examine body image CBT as a therapeutic contribution to changes in eating behaviors and body image, as well as to prevent relapse of AN and BN. Some researchers argue, however, that body image is a secondary factor in the etiology of AN. Fairburn, Shafran, and Cooper (1999), in an updated cognitive-behavioral perspective on the maintaining factors of anorexia, view the individual's need to control eating as the primary impetus for disordered eating behaviors rather than shape and weight concerns. They argue that although body image is a central feature of AN in Westernized societies, it is not an essential characteristic of the disorder in general (Fairburn et al., 1999). Pike, Devlin, and Loeb thoroughly discuss CBT for AN and BN in Chapter 7 of this volume.

Body Image Outcomes in the Treatment of Eating Disorders

Historically, few studies of psychotherapeutic outcomes for eating disorder treatments included body image measures or interventions. More recent studies have begun examining body image outcomes, despite no or minimal inclusion of focal body image treatment procedures, and have substantiated significant albeit modest reductions in body image dissatisfaction (see Rosen, 1996, for review). For example, in an early study comparing the efficacy of CBT and pharmacological treatment in decreasing bulimic symptoms, Mitchell and his colleagues (1990) randomly assigned 171 BN outpatients to receive: (1) imipramine only, (2) CBT and imipramine, (3) CBT and placebo, and (4) placebo only. Despite no intervention for patients' body weight and shape concerns, the CBT program produced significant improvements in body dissatisfaction, whereas pharmacological treatment alone did not. Including imipramine with CBT did not augment CBT's improvement of body image (Mitchell et al., 1990). Leitenberg and his colleagues (1994) found similar results with BN individuals who were randomly assigned to: (1) CBT alone, (2) CBT and desipramine, or (3) desipramine alone. Despite a high dropout rate, participants' body shape and weight concerns significantly improved with CBT. An addition of desipramine did not enhance these changes, and desipramine alone did not alter body image.

Fairburn and his colleagues (Fairburn, Jones, Peveler, Hope, & O'Connor, 1993; Fairburn et al., 1991) found that, by including brief cognitive restructuring for patients' body weight and shape concerns, body image dissatisfaction improved immediately after treatment in comparison to interpersonal and behavior therapies that did not attend to body attitudes and concerns. However, Fairburn, Jones, et al. found in a sample of 75 BN outpatients that interpersonal psychotherapy (IPT) resulted in a significant and comparable reduction in weight and shape concerns relative to CBT at a one-year follow-up. These findings suggest that although CBT may be more effective in short-term body image outcomes, IPT may be as effective in the long term.

Agras, Walsh, et al. (2000) similarly found that CBT initially resulted in superior improvements in general psychopathology and bulimic symptoms compared to IPT, but at one-year follow-up, the two treatments were comparable on outcomes for body weight and shape concerns. However, as discussed earlier, Fairburn, Peveler, et al. (1993) found that patients with the greatest enduring body image discontent were most prone to relapse of bulimic symptoms. Thus, Fairburn and his colleagues have stressed the "need to reduce the degree of [body image] attitudinal disturbance to minimize the risk of relapse" (p. 698). Moreover, body image dissatisfaction may have implications for treatment compliance. Coker, Vize, Wade, and Cooper (1993) found that BN patients who were unable to engage in CBT had significantly more dissatisfaction with their body weight. Agras, Crow, et al. (2000) concurred, finding that out of 194 BN outpatients, the 48 patients who prematurely dropped out of CBT had significantly greater weight and shape concerns.

Psychoeducation, a traditional component of CBT, has been evaluated for its efficacy in improving bulimic symptoms. Davis and his colleagues have done much of this research and initially found that, when administered to 50 females in a group format in five 90-minute sessions over a four-week period, the program resulted in significant changes in eating disturbance but not in body dissatisfaction (Davis, Olmsted, & Rockert, 1990). Olmsted et al. (1991) administered a similar psychoeducational protocol and compared its effects on bulimic symptoms to those of a longer course of individual CBT, both of which included a body image component. Although CBT was the more effective treatment in reducing binge-purge behaviors, both treatments resulted in an equivalent and significant improvement in body dissatisfaction (Olmsted et al., 1991). Finally, Davis, McVey, Heinmaa, Rockert, and Kennedy (1999) compared the effects of psychoeducation alone with those of psychoeducation and CBT combined. The researchers found that the combined treatment led to significantly greater reductions in bulimic symptoms, including weight and shape concerns, relative to psychoeducation alone, as well as significantly higher remission rates after 16 months.

In the treatment of binge-eating disorder (BED), CBT has begun to gain empirical support in its effectiveness in reducing binge eating and body dissatisfaction. In fact, data suggest that treatment in self-help (e.g., Carter & Fairburn, 1998) and in therapist-guided (e.g., Wolff & Clark, 2001) formats are both effective in reducing weight and shape concerns in BED patients. Carter and Fairburn (1998) administered a CBT self-help program to 72 community-based participants in a pure self-help format and a therapist-guided self-help format. Along with significant reductions in binge eating, both groups reported significantly greater reductions in weight and shape concerns than those in a waitlist control condition. These reductions were maintained after six months. Peterson and her colleagues (1998) found that when group CBT is administered in a therapist-led format, a videotape format, or a pure self-help format, body dissatisfaction improved significantly at posttreatment, as well as at one-month, six-month, and one-year follow-ups (Peterson et al., 2001).

Despite repeated findings that manual-based CBT has positive effects on body image evaluations in eating disorders, researchers argue that it has been less effective in reducing patients' excessive weight and shape concerns than in reducing or eliminating behavioral symptoms, such as binge-purge behaviors and restrictive dieting (Wilson, 1999). Given the modesty of the body image interventions in these protocols, this conclusion is not surprising. Furthermore, the *clinical* significance of body image improvements vis-à-vis CBT is just beginning to be explored. Because a statistically significant change in body image does not necessarily entail restoration of normal or adaptive body image functioning (Grant & Cash, 1995), it is important to determine participants' functional recovery rates. In a study of the efficacy of manualized CBT for bulimic symptoms, Tuschen-Caffier, Pook, and Frank (2001) reported *both* statistically and clinically significant improvements in body dissatisfaction at posttreatment and one-year follow-up as the result of CBT with 66 bulimic outpatients.

Finally, when body image outcomes are assessed in the treatment of eating disorders, they are almost always limited to a single measure of evaluative body image, such as weight and shape discontent. This ignores the multidimensional nature of the body image construct (Cash & Pruzinsky, 2002) and neglects an important defining feature of AN and BN—the undue influence of body image as a source of self-evaluation (APA, 2000). This latter dimension pertains to an individual's psychological investment in appearance or "appearance schematicity" (Cash, 2002b; Cash & Deagle, 1997; Cash &

Labarge, 1996). We believe that this dimension is as important as body image dissatisfaction in indexing the outcomes of body image and other interventions in the treatment of eating disorders.

Treatment of Body Dysmorphic Disorder

The essential diagnostic feature of body dysmorphic disorder (BDD) is a preoccupation with an imagined or exaggerated defect in appearance (APA, 2000). Olivardia's Chapter 26 in this volume offers further information on this disorder. CBT therapy has received growing empirical support in the treatment of BDD (Phillips, 2002; Veale, 2002). The purpose of this section is to examine efficacy findings from randomized, controlled trials of CBT for BDD.

Rosen, Reiter, and Orosan (1995) conducted the first controlled treatment-outcome study of body image CBT's effectiveness in treating BDD. The authors assigned 54 BDD patients to waitlist control and treatment conditions. Body image CBT consisted of eight 2-hour group sessions to modify intrusive and dysfunctional thoughts about appearance, reduce distressing self-consciousness through exposure to avoided or feared body image contexts, and decrease excessive appearance-checking behaviors. Based on body image assessments at pretreatment, posttreatment, and four-month follow-up, findings indicated a significant reduction of BDD symptoms, including improvement in body image evaluation, for recipients of body image CBT relative to controls. Changes were sustained at the follow-up.

Veale and his colleagues (1996) randomly assigned 19 BDD patients (17 females) without weight and shape concerns to either 12 weeks of CBT or a waitlist condition. Based on pre- and posttest data from the Yale-Brown Obsessive-Compulsive Scale for Body Dysmorphic Disorder, CBT led to a significant reduction in BDD symptoms and improvement in mood relative to the control condition.

Finally, Neziroglu, McKay, Todaro, and Yaryura-Tobias (1996) administered a similar body image CBT to 17 BDD patients. It included exposure and response prevention and cognitive restructuring. Patients reported significant improvements in BDD symptoms, with less than 30% of the patients reporting clinically significant scores on the Yale-Brown measure after treatment. While body image CBT appears to hold great promise for treating BDD, there is still a dearth of randomized, controlled trials with good follow-up evaluations.

Body Image Treatment with Obese Persons

The treatment of body image for overweight and obese individuals has only recently emerged. Sarwer and Thompson (2002) state that because body image is considered a psychological issue, while obesity is considered a physical condition with some psychological elements, it is not surprising that through 1990, no obesity treatment study included a body image intervention. This disregard is troubling given that this population is much more likely to report body image dissatisfaction and distress than are average-weight individuals (Cash & Roy, 1999; Schwartz & Brownell, 2002). One justification is that many clinicians and researchers perceive weight loss as the best way to improve body image experiences of obese persons. Most weight-management programs understandably emphasize eating and exercise behaviors, while minimizing or ignoring body image issues. However, in their recent review, Foster and Matz (2002) conclude that body image change may result from weight loss for many but not all obese individuals and that these changes may endure only if the weight loss is sustained, which is rare. Thus, body image treatments for obese or overweight persons are worthy of consideration, whether as an alternative or an adjunct to weight-loss interventions.

Body image CBT for obese individuals has been found to be promising (Cash & Roy, 1999; Foster & Matz, 2002). Rosen, Orosan, and Reiter (1995) adapted and administered a body image CBT program to this population. Fifty-one body-dissatisfied, obese women were randomly assigned to a waitlist control condition or to a treatment consisting of one 2-hour meeting per week over eight weeks. Despite no significant weight loss, CBT-treated participants, in comparison to controls, reported significantly improved weight and shape satisfaction, reduced size overestimation, fewer body dysmorphic symptoms, enhanced global self-esteem, and less dysfunctional eating patterns immediately after treatment and at a four-month follow-up. Furthermore, individual body image changes were independent of weight changes.

Ramirez and Rosen (2001) examined the effects of body image CBT and a weight-control program in comparison to the 16-week weight-control program alone. They randomly assigned 88 obese women and men to receive one of the two programs; 74% completed treatment and the combined condition had a significantly lower attrition rate. At posttreatment, participants receiving only weight control lost 10.5% of their initial weight, while those receiving combined treatment lost 8.7%. Both groups reported significant and comparable improvements in body image, self-esteem, and eating concerns, which were maintained at three months. However, at a one-year follow-up, there was significant partial regain of weight by both groups, with weight-control-alone participants regaining more weight. No group differences occurred on any of the psychological scales. Ramirez and Rosen suggest that adding a weight-control program to a body image treatment may have undermined the effectiveness of the body image intervention. Foster and Matz (2002) suggest that this "trumping" effect might be alleviated by different sequences of body image and weight-control interventions.

Z. Cooper and Fairburn (2002), in fact, argue that body image therapy may be more useful when offered after weight-control treatment is successfully completed as a means of improving long-term weight-loss maintenance by addressing the cognitive processes that mediate patients' outcome expectations. The practicality of body image treatment for obese individuals exists because of the growing prevalence of obesity in our culture (Mokdad et al., 1999), the social prejudice and adversities associated with obesity (Cash & Roy, 1999), and the potential difficulty for individuals to lose weight and sustain their losses (Brownell & Rodin, 1994). Any combined treatment must ultimately enable individuals to distinguish their goals of body acceptance and healthy weight loss. In our culture, this is by no means an easy task.

Body Image Treatment with Body-Dissatisfied, Subclinical Populations

While body image disturbances are characteristic of persons with eating disorders and BDD, they also exist in the general population, especially among "normal" female adults and adolescents (Striegel-Moore & Franko, 2002). Therefore, it is not surprising that most body image treatment studies have focused on body-dissatisfied women who also present various associated symptoms, including low self-esteem, social anxiety, depressive symptoms, and problematic eating behaviors. We now review the body of evidence on these studies—both randomized, controlled trials and comparative treatment studies.

Butters and Cash (1987) pioneered the examination of the efficacy of a manualized body image CBT program. They enlisted 31 highly body-dissatisfied women, who were within 25% of desirable weight, and randomly assigned them to a six-week CBT program or a waitlist control condition. Treatment consisted of one-hour weekly structured, individual-treatment sessions of body image education, relaxation training, desensitization, identification and restructuring of negative body image thoughts, enhancement of positive body image activities, generalization training, relapse prevention, and stress inoculation. Butters and Cash found that, relative to controls who did not change, CBT participants reported significantly greater improvements in body image evaluations, reduced appearance investment, fewer dysfunctional body image cognitions, and less mirror-exposure distress. They maintained these gains at a seven-week follow-up. Immediate treatment outcomes were replicated for the control participants who subsequently received an abbreviated three-week program consisting largely of cognitive interventions.

Dworkin and Kerr (1987) concurrently evaluated the efficacy of cognitive, cognitive-behavioral, and reflective therapies for body image relative to a waitlist control condition. They randomly assigned 79 college women to one of the four groups. Treatments consisted of three 30-minute student-administered counseling sessions. Cognitive therapy included administration of a self-report inventory of body image beliefs, cognitive restructuring of automatic thoughts, homework assignments, and generalization strategies. Cognitive-behavioral therapy was similar but also included self-reinforcement and imagery exercises. Finally, reflective therapy facilitated participants' exploration of body image experiences during specific developmental periods of their lives and assigned a journal for homework. All conditions resulted in improved body satisfaction and self-concept; however, the three treatment conditions were superior to the waitlist condition. Cognitive therapy resulted in the largest gains, while CBT and reflective treatment resulted in comparable effects. The major limitations of Dworkin and Kerr's research are the minimal treatment participants received in terms of the number and duration of sessions and the lack of a follow-up assessment.

Seeking to improve on earlier studies, Rosen, Saltzberg, and Srebnik (1989) randomly assigned 23 average-weight, body-dissatisfied college women to either body image CBT or a control treatment. To control for demand characteristics and nonspecific treatment elements, the latter condition consisted of minimal treatment focusing on the discovery and discussion of their body image experiences. Treatment for both conditions consisted of six weekly two-hour small-group sessions. Body image CBT included education, homework exercises, identification and restructuring of maladaptive body image cognitions and behaviors, and body-size and weight-estimation exercises aimed to correct perceptual distortions. The minimal treatment did not include structured exercises aimed to correct maladaptive cognitions, behaviors, and perceptions.

Rosen et al. (1989) found body image CBT to be superior to minimal treatment. Despite reporting substantial perceptual body-size distortions at pretreatment, participants receiving body image CBT reported significantly more accurate estimates that fell within the normal range both at posttest and at a two-month follow-up. In contrast, minimal treatment did not result in changes in body-size perceptual estimates over time. Although both groups reported improved body satisfaction at posttreatment, only CBT participants sustained this change at follow-up and scored within the normal range both at posttreatment and at follow-up. Finally, only CBT participants reported significant decreases in body image avoidance.

Rosen, Cado, Silberg, Srebnik, and Wendt (1990) subsequently performed a dismantling study of the efficacy of this body image CBT intervention with and without size perception training. They randomly assigned 24 average-weight, body-dissatisfied college women (without current or previous eating disorders) to receive body image CBT for six weekly two-hour sessions with or without training in accurate body-size perception. The researchers assessed body image, as well as eating attitudes and behaviors at pretreatment, posttreatment, and three-month follow-up.

Rosen et al. (1990) found the two conditions did not differ at any of the three assessment periods. Both treatments resulted in significant improvements of body image, psychological adjustment, and disturbed eating patterns. Gains were maintained at follow-up, except that the reported frequency of binge eating episodes returned to baseline. These findings reconfirm the efficacy of body image CBT. Because perceptual training did not produce better outcomes, even on perceptual size estimation, the authors concluded that body-size estimates may become more accurate because of changes in cognitive evaluation. This study was the first to find that body image CBT improved eating attitudes even if not addressed in treatment.

Using a variation of Butters and Cash's (1987) program, Fisher and Thompson (1994) examined the comparative effectiveness of body image CBT and a physical exercise program. Fifty-four body-dissatisfied college females, who weighed within 12.5% of an actuarial norm and denied any eating disturbances, were randomly assigned to one of the treatment groups or to a no-treatment control condition. Both treatment groups received six weekly one-hour sessions. Exercise therapy included body image and exercise education, low-impact aerobics, weight-lifting, and homework consisting of an exercise regimen.

Fisher and Thompson (1994) found that both treatments significantly decreased body image anxiety and dissatisfaction, while the control condition did not. Significant decreases in body image avoidance behaviors and body-size overestimation were found in all groups. The attrition rate between posttreatment and follow-up (over 50%) precluded conclusions about the maintenance of outcomes. Despite the observed changes, Fisher and Thompson (1994) questioned the clinical significance of their results and cautioned that although exercise training may reduce body dissatisfaction (as other recent studies have shown; Martin & Lichtenberger, 2002), it may also risk reinforcing beliefs that body acceptance requires changing an individual's body.

Grant and Cash (1995) performed the first efficacy study of body image CBT in both a group therapy modality and a largely self-directed format with modest therapist contact. The authors used Cash's (1991) audiocassette program, *Body Image Therapy: A Program for Self-Directed Change,* which expanded the program of Butters and Cash (1987). Participants were 23 college women who reported significant negative body image, with no current or previous eating disorder, a weight within 25% of the norm, and no concurrent psychological treatment. Both groups were assessed before treatment, after treatment, and at a two-month follow-up period.

Although both randomly assigned groups completed the audiocassette program, the modest-contact group met for 15 to 20 minutes weekly with a research assistant who explained and reviewed homework, reinforced compliance, and facilitated solving of any problems with the program. Group therapy participants completed 11 weekly 90-minute sessions over four months. Treatment entailed self-assessment of body image development; self-monitoring; relaxation training; systematic body-desensitization; identifying, monitoring, and correcting inaccurate body image assumptions; altering dysfunctional thoughts; self-assessment of self-defeating body image behaviors; exposure, response prevention, and body image stress inoculation; review of cognitive-behavioral skills; and relapse prevention strategies.

Treatment outcomes for the two modalities were equivalent, with all changes maintained at the two-month follow-up. Changes included significant improvements in body image satisfaction and evaluation, reductions in negative body image affect across situational contexts, less overweight preoccupation, and more congruence between self and ideal body size. Other changes included reductions in schematic investment in appearance, fewer cognitive body image errors and negative body image thoughts, and less focus on and avoidance of appearance during sexual relations. Grant and Cash (1995) also found improvements in self-esteem, social-evaluative anxiety, sexual self-consciousness, depression, and disordered eating. Improvements in body image for both conditions were clinically significant.

Cash and Lavallee (1997) subsequently compared Grant and Cash's (1995) data with those of an equally body-dissatisfied sample that received Cash's body image self-help book (1995) *What Do You See When You Look in the Mirror?* administered without face-to-face professional contact. These 16 participants received assignments via postal mail, and contact consisted of 5- to 10-minute scheduled weekly telephone conversations with a research assistant to discuss compliance with assigned reading and homework activities. Cash's (1995) self-help book consisted of eight steps with cognitive-behavioral procedures detailed subsequently in this chapter. Compared to the combined treatment conditions of Grant and Cash, this minimal-contact treatment resulted in equivalent body image and psychosocial outcomes, with equivalent compliance. Intent-to-treat analyses, which included dropouts with the assumption of no change, confirmed these reliable improvements. Grant and Cash observed a functional recovery rate of 57% of participants in the modest-contact CBT condition; the rate for the minimal-contact CBT from Cash and Lavallee's study was 75%.

Lavallee and Cash (1997) further empirically studied Cash's (1995) body image self-help book, in comparison with McKay and Fanning's (1992) self-help CBT text for self-esteem improvement. Thirty-seven body-dissatisfied college women were randomly assigned one of the two books at an initial face-to-face meeting with a research assistant and received a schedule for the completion of the sections of each book over a nine-week period. There was no contact with participants beyond the pre- and post-treatment assessments.

Each bibliotherapeutic program produced statistically and clinically significant improvements in body image evaluation, investment, and affect. While neither intervention enhanced global self-esteem, only body image CBT lowered social anxiety, and only self-esteem CBT reduced depressive symptoms. After controlling for pretest levels, body image CBT was superior to self-esteem CBT in reducing eating pathology and in producing body image outcomes that reflected less problem severity. For both treatments, greater procedural compliance was significantly related to better body image outcomes.

Smith, Wolfe, and Laframboise (2001) administered body image CBT, modeled after Cash's (1995) program, to body-dissatisfied obligatory (or compulsive) and nonobligatory exercisers. Obligatory exercisers exercise often and feel unable to control their impulse to exercise despite a physical injury or social demands. The sample of 94 average-weight women were 17 or older, with no eating disorder in the past five years, and were not receiving psychotherapy or psychotropic medication. They were randomly assigned to either body image CBT or a waitlist condition. Treatment consisted of eight weekly 1.5-hour group sessions (6 to 10 participants in each group). Body image, obsessive-compulsive characteristics, and exercise status were assessed at pretreatment, posttreatment, and two-month follow-up.

As hypothesized, at pretreatment, obligatory exercisers reported significantly greater obsessive-compulsive checking behaviors, fat anxiety, and overall hip and thigh dissatisfaction than nonobligatory exercisers. Treatment resulted in significant improvements in body image affect, evaluation, cognitive-behavioral investment in appearance, and weight perception. These changes differed significantly from the control condition and were maintained at follow-up. Relative to controls, body image CBT also reduced the self-ideal discrepancy vis-à-vis participants' views of their hips and thighs, although obligatory exercisers receiving CBT remained significantly more discrepant than nonobligatory exercisers. Nonetheless, the two groups experienced relatively equivalent improvements in body image and in obsessive-compulsive tendencies, suggesting that compulsive exercising tendencies do not preclude positive responses to body image CBT.

In 1997, Cash published a refinement of his program as *The Body Image Workbook: An 8-Step Program for Learning to Like Your Looks.* Two recent dismantling studies examined the effectiveness of selected components of this program for improving body image and associated psychosocial functioning. First, Strachan and Cash (2002) enlisted 86 women and 3 men who experienced significantly distressing or impairing body dissatisfaction and were interested in improving their body image via self-help. There was no face-to-face contact with participants. Direct contact was limited to an initial phone conversation. All assessments and self-help materials were distributed and returned by postal mail. Participants randomly received either a combination of psychoeducation and systematic self-monitoring or a combination of these components plus techniques for identifying and altering dysfunctional body image cognitions. Both groups were required to complete their respective programs in six weeks. Reassessment occurred two weeks after treatment. Body image evaluation and dysphoria, schematic appearance investment, dysfunctional body image behaviors, and overweight preoccupation were assessed, as well as social self-esteem, social-evaluative anxiety, depression, and eating attitudes.

Strachan and Cash (2002) found that both conditions resulted in statistically significant improvements on all measures of body image, except for the behavioral inventory. Clinical significance analyses indicated moderate functional recovery rates. In addition, participants in both conditions reported better social self-esteem, reduced social-evaluative anxiety, and fewer depressive symptoms; changes in eating pathology were not significant. The lack of outcome differences between the two treatment conditions may have been due to minimal compliance with the added cognitive-change techniques in the second condition. Despite a high attrition rate (53%) observed in this self-help study, intent-to-treat analyses confirmed the observed changes. Strachan and Cash argued that such attrition and waning procedural compliance might result from the lack of contact between participants and program assistants or researchers.

Given Strachan and Cash's (2002) findings, Cash and Hrabosky (in press) investigated the combined treatment of psychoeducation and systematic self-monitoring under more supervised circumstances. They enlisted 25 college students (22 women, 3 men) who, as in the Strachan and Cash study (2002), reported significantly distressing or impairing body dissatisfaction and a desire to improve their body image through self-help. However, unlike Strachan and Cash, the protocol involved more contact with participants—namely, weekly face-to-face meetings for instructions, pre- and posttreatment assessments, and exchanging of materials, as well as some e-mail and telephone communications. Treatment consisted of a three-week program with one week of psychoeducation followed by two weeks of daily body image self-monitoring. Body image dissatisfaction and preoccupation, situational body image distress, and schematic investment in appearance were assessed at pre- and posttreatment. Furthermore, global self-esteem, social-evaluative anxiety, and eating attitudes were assessed.

Following the program, participants reported significantly enhanced body image evaluations, including reductions in self-perceived severity of their body image problems. They experienced significantly less overweight preoccupation, less cross-situational body image dysphoria, and reduced investment in appearance as a source of self-evaluation. Finally, these changes generalized to improvements in eating attitudes, which Strachan and Cash (2002) did not find, as well as increased global self-esteem and less social-evaluative anxiety. In addition, only 13.8% of enrollees in Cash and Hrabosky's study dropped out, and all did so immediately after the initial orientation/pretest session. This contrasts with the 53% attrition rate found by Strachan and Cash. Although the difference may be due to Cash and Hrabosky's face-to-face contact with participants who were expected to turn in completed assignments weekly, the fact that the program lasted three weeks instead of six weeks may also have contributed to the lower attrition rate.

In summary, the collective findings of these controlled or comparison studies consistently support evidence for the efficacy of cognitive-behavioral techniques, whether in a therapist-delivered or monitored modality or in a more purely self-help approach. These investigations confirm the amelioration of body image problems among individuals (mostly women) who do not necessarily present with a clinical disorder. Body image CBT appears to be effective in clinically improving body image evaluation and investment, as well as body image dysphoria and perceptual distortion. Moreover, these gains often generalize to other areas of psychosocial functioning associated with negative body image, including self-esteem, eating attitudes, social anxiety, and depression. Although most studies to date examined fairly comprehensive programs (e.g., Cash's 8-step program), recent research indicates the effectiveness of certain components of manualized, body image CBT in a relatively brief period of time. Although favorable changes may result from a largely self-administered modality of body image CBT, procedural compliance and outcomes may be compromised in the absence of some regular external oversight. Further controlled research must be performed on each of the components to determine how effective they can be when used in isolation. Finally, while most body image improvements have been found to be sustained for at least two or three months posttreatment in studies that evaluate maintenance, longer follow-ups are a priority in future investigations.

COGNITIVE-BEHAVIORAL THERAPY FOR BODY IMAGE: A COMPREHENSIVE PROGRAM

In the remainder of this chapter, we summarize the elements of a body image CBT program (Cash, 1997). This summary is not meant to represent a treatment manual, and clinicians should consult *The Body Image Workbook* for procedural details as well as for extensive materials that are assigned and discussed during therapy. As implied previously, however, we do not believe that any or all interventions are necessary for change. Based on a thorough assessment of individuals, clinical practitioners should administer (or assign) and monitor those therapeutic components that match clients' needs. It is crucial that the practitioner ascertain the functional relationship between the client's particular body image strengths and vulnerabilities and his or her other presenting psychological difficulties or disorders. For example, while body image may be a primary issue for persons with eating disorders or BDD, its salience may vary considerably among individuals with social phobia, mood disorders, or sexual dysfunction. Thus, there is no substitute for well-conceived assessment and case formulation.

Step 1: Body Image Assessment and Goal Setting

The first step of body image CBT is a thorough body image assessment, which serves as (1) baseline indicators of multiple facets of an individual's body image experiences, (2) information for feedback to educate the client about specific strengths and difficulties and as evidence of the causal processes in the client's body image experiences, and (3) pivotal information for treatment planning. *The Body Image Workbook* includes many of these measures and instructions for scoring and interpretation. Thompson and van den Berg (2002) also provide a useful compendium of body image assessments. Elsewhere in this volume, contributors review potentially useful instruments. We highlight several psychometrically sound measures:

- The Multidimensional Body-Self Relations Questionnaire (MBSRQ) is an omnibus attitudinal body image assessment (Brown, Cash, & Mikulka, 1990; Cash, 2000a). Its multiple subscales include Appearance Evaluation, the Body Areas Satisfaction Scale, Appearance Orientation, Self-Classified Weight, and Overweight Preoccupation. A more extensive version of the MBSRQ has scales to assess fitness/health evaluation and investment.
- The Body Image Ideals Questionnaire assesses the strength of and perceived discrepancy from personal ideals of physical attributes, such as weight, muscularity, complexion, and so on (Cash, 2000a; Cash & Szymanski, 1995; Szymanski & Cash, 1995).
- The Body-Shape Questionnaire (BSQ) is a popular measure of concerns about body weight and shape (P. J. Cooper, Taylor, Cooper, & Fairburn, 1987).

- The Situational Inventory of Body Image Dysphoria (SIBID; Cash, 2000a, 2002f) assesses negative body image emotions in various situational contexts.

- The Appearance Schemas Inventory (Cash & Labarge, 1996) measures attitudes that reflect dysfunctional investment in an individual's appearance. A recent revision of this inventory (Cash et al., in press) assesses the self-evaluative salience and motivational salience of appearance.

- The Body Image Quality of Life Inventory (Cash & Fleming, 2002b) is a brief measure of the extent to which a person's body image positively or negatively affects aspects of his or her life (e.g., self-esteem, social functioning, eating, sexuality, moods).

- Rosen and Reiter's (1996) Body Dysmorphic Disorder Examination (BDDE) is a validated structured clinical interview, also available as a self-report questionnaire, to facilitate the diagnosis of BDD.

After assessment, the clinician works collaboratively with clients in setting goals for change. Such goals may include improving body image thoughts and evaluations, controlling body image emotions, altering physical ideals, a change in appearance-invested behaviors, and so on.

Step 2: Body Image Psychoeducation and Self-Discoveries

It is crucial for the clinician to articulate to the client the principles of cognitive-behavioral therapy, explaining the rationale behind learning, unlearning, and relearning patterns of cognitions, emotions, and behavior. Therapy is collaborative, with the client playing an active role in the development of specific competencies and in changing her or his own behavior.

Clients must develop a framework for understanding the origins and components of their own body image experiences. They receive information to "normalize" their body image concerns vis-à-vis epidemiological evidence and the determinants of body image experiences. The clinician also promotes rational knowledge through discussing the truths and myths about the effects of objective physical appearance on people's lives, as well as the stronger and potentially damaging effects of subjective body image. Clients are provided a framework and specific exercises to understand the components and causes of negative body image, including historical and concurrent, personal and cultural influences. Clients document critical events and experiences, from early childhood to the present, that were significant in their own body image development. As therapy progresses, the clinician and the client work together to apply this knowledge to the client's life, examining both predisposing developmental determinants and proximal influences on current body image experiences.

The client and clinician begin to elucidate proximal influences, working together to identify the "Activators" (precipitating events and situations), "Beliefs" (thoughts, assumptions, perceptions, and interpretations), and "Consequences" (resultant emotions and adjustive behaviors). The client is taught how to self-monitor these experiences and systematically keeps a "body image diary" to capture these A-B-C sequences. These diaries and the themes that they evince are an important focus of in-session discussions and interventions.

Step 3: Relaxation and Body Image Desensitization

The goal of this facet of treatment is to facilitate clients' exposure to the foci and contexts of their bodily discontent and dysphoria. Clients are encouraged to develop self-control over their reactions. Mind-and-body relaxation training includes progressive muscle relaxation, diaphragmatic breathing, mental imagery exercises, and self-instructional and autogenic techniques. After a week of practice (ideally using a tape), the client begins to apply the relaxation techniques directly to body image distress. The clinician collaborates with the client in constructing two body image hierarchies: (1) body areas or attributes associated with varying degrees of discontent and (2) situations or events that trigger body image distress. The items on each hierarchy are ranked from those resulting in least to greatest distress.

Clients apply the acquired relaxation skills in body image desensitization to manage discomfort as they progressively picture body areas and contexts, from least to most distressing, with the goals of controlling and reducing discomfort. Each item is imagined for increasingly more time as the client moves up the hierarchy with reasonable control of distress. The client begins this work initially in sessions with the clinician and continues it as daily homework, noting progress and difficulties. Mirror desensitization is carried out privately at home while the client is entirely or mostly undressed. For obvious professional and ethical reasons, the latter is never completed in the presence of the clinician. Despite total privacy, many individuals experience great distress and resist this procedure, and the clinician should use judgment in determining if and when this should be done. Even if the clinician opts to postpone or omit body image desensitization, the relaxation skills still may be valuable to clients' coping efforts.

Step 4: Identifying and Challenging Appearance Assumptions

Most individuals with body image problems are highly appearance schematic, having implicit beliefs or assumptions that associate perceived appearance with their sense of self, their past, and their future, particularly with respect to how others view and accept them. For example, an individual may come to believe that "the first thing that people will notice about me is what's wrong with my appearance," or that "it is my duty to always look my best." This aspect of treatment targets the assumptions clients endorse (e.g., on the Appearance Schemas Inventory). The goal is to discover the impact core assumptions have in guiding dysfunctional body image thoughts, feelings, and behaviors and to reveal how such beliefs are extreme, overgeneralized, or unsubstantiated.

In tackling appearance assumptions, the clinician must first describe and emphasize the impact these core beliefs can have on the development and maintenance of maladaptive body image. As clients are asked to expand on their personal beliefs about these "schemas," the clinician draws on specific episodes of body image distress to illustrate connections between the underlying assumptions and their influences on thoughts, feelings, and behaviors. The clinician engages clients in a Socratic dialogue exploring the evidence of the veracity or inaccuracy of the belief. As homework, clients write about each assumption: "When I assume _____, then I focus on _____, and I think _____, and I feel _____." Clients then write out any possible exceptions, contradictions, and flaws with each assumption. The clinician reinforces and elaborates on (1) evidence of the body image implications of clients' assumptions, and (2) instances of effective challenging of the assumptions. It is important, however, to determine the function of the assumption. That is, the clinician should not attack the perceived absurdity of an assumption, for it may have some essence of truth to it. Instead, he or she should explore the need for and consequences of the assumption, determining the potential outcome of its contradiction and elimination. They then collaborate in developing new, rational, and balanced perspectives, which the client writes down and rehearses.

Step 5: Identifying and Correcting Cognitive Errors

This step logically follows the previous one. The clinician first helps clients learn how to correctly identify specific body image errors or distortions in thinking and then develops strategies to alter them. The clinician provides the client with a description and examples of eight common body image errors (e.g., "Beauty or Beast," "Blame Game," "Mind Misreading"). Together they review the client's body image diaries for A-B-C sequences that exemplify each distortion. It is helpful for the clinician to coach and model corrective thinking strategies for typically maladaptive "Private Body Talk." The client is also urged to link these distortions with previously identified appearance assumptions. Before performing an in vivo correction of identified cognitive distortions, the client identifies them in representative episodes found in diary homework sequences. For each cognitive distortion, the client identifies the faulty private body talk, identifies what distortions it contains, and disputes each distortion with corrective thinking by writing what his or her "new inner voice" would say.

The client and clinician collaboratively elaborate and rehearse these counterarguments. The new inner voice includes the "stop, look, and listen" technique, which refers to (1) *stopping* the negative self-talk, (2) *looking* at activating events and maladaptive private body talk to detect cognitive errors that are producing negative body image emotional reactions, and (3) *listening* to more rational and accurate self-statements that correct the cognitive errors. One means of facilitating achievement of accurate, rational thinking is by audiotaping corrective thinking dialogues and listening to them daily. Corrective thinking can also be identified and documented in the continued completion of body image diaries, which now add daily entries for in vivo *disputations* and their emotional *effects,* which creates an A-B-C-D-E sequence.

Step 6: Changing Self-Defeating Body Image Behaviors

The goal of this facet of treatment is to modify maladaptive behaviors associated with a negative body image. Body-dissatisfied clients, who typically attempt to avoid or escape negative body image experiences, are taught that while these behaviors may offer some temporary emotional relief, they perpetuate body image dissatisfaction and dysphoria. These behaviors include the avoidance of practices, people, poses, or places that accentuate their disliked physical features. Other behaviors include certain compulsive checking and grooming rituals.

During this phase of treatment, the clinician first educates the client on the function and maladaptivity of these self-defeating behaviors. They then work collaboratively in identifying the client's current behaviors, as the client monitors and records them in everyday life. The client constructs hierarchies of each type of behavioral pattern. Two hierarchies for avoidant behavior—one for practices, persons, poses, and places avoided, and a second for grooming-to-hide behaviors—are ordered in terms of the client's efficacy expectations for being able to alter behavior. A third hierarchy is used to arrange compulsive patterns in order of expected ability to refrain from performing the designated ritual.

Clients are taught Cash's (1997) PACE strategy, a stress inoculation technique with four steps: (1) *prepare* and rehearse an exact plan to confront avoidant behaviors or refraining from rituals; (2) *act* on the plan; (3) *cope,* using relaxation, imagery, or corrective thinking to manage any distress; and (4) *enjoy,* using any predetermined self-rewards for a successful outcome. The client develops and carries out a detailed PACE strategy for each self-defeating pattern, from easiest to most difficult activities. After each attempt, the client records results in a diary and makes any strategic changes as needed. Finally, a similar procedure for graduated exposure and response prevention is developed and executed to alter appearance-preoccupied, compulsive patterns. The client relies on acquired skills in corrective thinking and coping.

Step 7: Enhancing Positive Body Image

Therapeutic change has thus far targeted negative cognitive and behavioral aspects of body image. The purpose of this stage of treatment is to increase positive body experiences, with a goal of expanding on the client's mastery and pleasure in "treating the body right." This aspect of treatment also applies the metaphor that body image reflects a relationship of the individual with his or her body, akin to a friendship or marriage.

The clinician initially has the client take "affirmative actions" to enhance body image through a series of experiential assignments in the context of this metaphor. Next, the client identifies various body-related activities over the past year and the level of mastery and the pleasure derived from each. The client selects activities from each of three categories—appearance, health and fitness, and sensate experiences—and then carries out one or two daily, recording the mastery and pleasure experiences of each. Perhaps the most important of these activities is regular physical exercise to enhance fitness rather than alter appearance (e.g., weight loss). The clinician reviews and reinforces clients' self-regulatory abilities to promote their positive body-related experiences.

Other enhancement exercises include brief mirror affirmations and an activity in which the client anticipates how she or he would think, feel, and act differently if body image ideals were actually attained. The clinician then has the client enact this experience.

Step 8: Relapse Prevention and Maintaining
Body Image Changes

In this final phase of body image treatment, the client and clinician explicitly evaluate changes and identify goals for future work. They develop specific strategies to prevent setbacks, cope with high-risk situations, and maintain body image changes. Often clients report that troublesome interactions with certain individuals precipitate body image distress. If these issues have not been dealt with previously, the clinician models and the client rehearses interpersonal problem-solving skills to manage such challenging situations. The clinician helps the client use the PACE strategy in anticipating difficulties as well as developing plans to manage them. The client and clinician work collaboratively in preparing for high-risk situations by drawing on previously learned cognitive and behavioral strategies. The clinician normalizes temporary setbacks as signals to implement skills learned in the program.

CONCLUSIONS AND FUTURE DIRECTIONS

Conceptual and empirical advances have facilitated our understanding and improvement of body image and its dysfunctions (Cash & Pruzinsky, 2002). Cognitive-behavioral body image therapy has empirical support for reducing body disturbances in subclinical samples and in body dysmorphic disorder. Controlled studies of other interventions, such as psychodynamic, interpersonal, and experiential therapies, are largely unavailable (Cash & Pruzinsky, 2002). Although body image therapy is also crucial in the extant treatments for eating disorders and obesity, its relative contribution to the outcomes of their treatments remains largely unstudied and unknown. Most empirical trials of body image CBT have been conducted with women, yet it warrants evaluation with men and with body image disturbances such as "muscle dysmorphia" (Olivardia, 2002; Pope, Phillips, & Olivardia, 2000; Westmoreland Corson & Andersen, 2002). Similarly neglected are body image intervention studies with people receiving medical or surgical treatments for appearance-altering conditions (Cash & Pruzinsky, 2002). Finally, the examination of the effectiveness of purely psychoeducational body image interventions in the prevention and change of body image and associated problems, such as eating disorders, falls beyond this chapter's scope. This is the topic of Stice's informative chapter (Chapter 3) in this volume, as well as a review elsewhere by Winzelberg, Abascal, and Taylor (2002).

Of utmost importance is the clinical practitioner's ability to apply a treatment protocol, such as the one described in this chapter, to clients with body image disturbances that are functionally related to their principal presenting disorders. With the constraints of today's financially managed mental health care system, it is unlikely that clinicians will implement the entire program outlined in this chapter, especially if body image disturbance is not the primary presenting psychopathology. Consequently, as the aforementioned dismantling studies attest, efficient and effective body image interventions must be investigated. In addition to the continued conduct of controlled experiments on treatment efficacy, clinical research in "usual care" settings in the science-based practice of body image therapy is greatly needed.

REFERENCES

Agras, W. S., Crow, S. J., Halmi, K. A., Mitchell, J. E., Wilson, G. T., & Kraemer, H. C. (2000). Outcome predictors for the cognitive behavior treatment of bulimia nervosa: Data from a multisite study. *American Journal of Psychiatry, 157,* 1302–1308.

Agras, W. S., Walsh, B. T., Fairburn, C. G., Wilson, G. T., & Kraemer, H. C. (2000). A multicenter comparison of cognitive-behavioral therapy and interpersonal psychotherapy for bulimia nervosa. *Archives of General Psychiatry, 57,* 459–466.

American Psychiatric Association. (2000). *Diagnostic and statistical manual of mental disorders* (4th ed., text rev.). Washington, DC: Author.

Berscheid, E., Walster, E., & Bohrnstedt, G. (1973, November). The happy American body: A survey report. *Psychology Today, 7,* 119–131.

Brown, T. A., Cash, T. F., & Mikulka, P. J. (1990). Attitudinal body image assessment: Factor analysis of the Body-Self Relations Questionnaire. *Journal of Personality Assessment, 55,* 135–144.

Brownell, K. D., & Rodin, J. (1994). The dieting maelstrom: Is it possible and advisable to lose weight? *American Psychologist, 49,* 781–791.

Butters, J. W., & Cash, T. F. (1987). Cognitive-behavioral treatment of women's body image dissatisfaction. *Journal of Counseling and Clinical Psychology, 55,* 889–897.

Cargill, B. R., Clark, M. M., Pera, V., Niaura, R. S., & Abrams, D. A. (1999). Binge eating, body image and depression and self-efficacy in an obese clinical population. *Obesity Research, 7,* 379–386.

Carter, J. C., & Fairburn, C. G. (1998). Cognitive-behavioral self-help for binge eating disorder: A controlled effectiveness study. *Journal of Consulting and Clinical Psychology, 66,* 616–623.

Cash, T. F. (1991). *Body image therapy: A program for self-directed change.* New York: Guilford Press.

Cash, T. F. (1995). *What do you see when you look in the mirror? Helping yourself to a positive body image.* New York: Bantam Books.

Cash, T. F. (1996). The treatment of body image disturbances. In J. K. Thompson (Ed.), *Body image, eating disorders, and obesity: An integrative guide for assessment and treatment* (pp. 83–107). Washington, DC: American Psychological Association.

Cash, T. F. (1997). *The Body Image Workbook: An 8-step program for learning to like your looks.* Oakland, CA: New Harbinger.

Cash, T. F. (2000a). *Body image assessments: Manuals and questionnaires.* Available from www.body images.com.

Cash, T. F. (2002b). Body image: Cognitive behavioral perspectives. In T. F. Cash & T. Pruzinsky (Eds.), *Body image: A handbook of theory, research, and clinical practice* (pp. 38–46). New York: Guilford Press.

Cash, T. F. (2002c). The management of body image problems. In C. G. Fairburn & K. D. Brownell (Eds.), *Eating disorders and obesity: A comprehensive handbook* (2nd ed., pp. 599–603). New York: Guilford Press.

Cash, T. F. (2002d). A "negative body image": Evaluating epidemiological evidence. In T. F. Cash & T. Pruzinsky (Eds.), *Body image: A handbook of theory, research, and clinical practice* (pp. 269–276). New York: Guilford Press.

Cash, T. F. (2002e). [Research on college students' body images.] Unpublished raw data.

Cash, T. F. (2002f). The Situational Inventory of Body Image Dysphoria: Psychometric evidence and development of a short form. *International Journal of Eating Disorders, 32,* 362–366.

Cash, T. F. (2002g). Women's body images. In G. Wingood & R. DiClemente (Eds.), *Handbook of women's sexual and reproductive health* (pp. 175–194). New York: Plenum Press.

Cash, T. F., & Deagle, E. A., III. (1997). The nature and extent of body image disturbances in anorexia nervosa and bulimia nervosa: A meta-analysis. *International Journal of Eating Disorders, 22,* 107–125.

Cash, T. F., & Fleming, E. C. (2002a). Body images and social relations. In T. F. Cash & T. Pruzinsky (Eds.), *Body image: A handbook of theory, research, and clinical practice* (pp. 277–286). New York: Guilford Press.

Cash, T. F., & Fleming, E. C. (2002b). The impact of body image experiences: Development of the Body Image Quality of Life Inventory. *International Journal of Eating Disorders, 31,* 455–460.

Cash, T. F., & Grant, J. R. (1995). Cognitive-behavioral treatment of body image disturbances. In V. B. van Hasselt & M. Hersen (Eds.), *Sourcebook of psychological treatment manuals for adult disorders* (pp. 567–614). New York: Plenum Press.

Cash, T. F., & Hrabosky, J. I. (in press). The effects of psychoeducation and self-monitoring in a cognitive-behavioral program for body image improvement. *Eating Disorders: Journal of Treatment and Prevention.*

Cash, T. F., & Labarge, A. S. (1996). Development of the Appearance Schemas Inventory: A new cognitive body image assessment. *Cognitive Therapy and Research, 20,* 37–50.

Cash, T. F., & Lavallee, D. M. (1997). Cognitive-behavioral body image therapy: Extended evidence of the efficacy of a self-directed program. *Journal of Rational-Emotive and Cognitive-Behavior Therapy, 15,* 281–294.

Cash, T. F., Melnyk, S., & Hrabosky, J. I. (in press). The assessment of body image investment: An extensive revision of the Appearance Schemas Inventory. *International Journal of Eating Disorders.*

Cash, T. F., Morrow, J. A., Hrabosky, J. I., & Perry, A. A. (2003). *How has body image changed? A cross-sectional study of college women and men from 1983 to 2001.* Manuscript submitted for publication.

Cash, T. F., & Pruzinsky, T. (Eds.). (2002). *Body image: A handbook of theory, research, and clinical practice.* New York: Guilford Press.

Cash, T. F., & Roy, R. E. (1999). Pounds of flesh: Weight, gender, and body images. In J. Sobal & D. Maurer (Eds.), *Interpreting weight: The social management of fatness and thinness* (pp. 209–228). Hawthorne, NY: Aldine de Gruyter.

Cash, T. F., Santos, M. T., & Williams, E. F. (2003). *Dealing with body image challenges: Development of the Body Image Coping Strategies Inventory.* Manuscript submitted for publication.

Cash, T. F., & Strachan, M. D. (2002). Cognitive behavioral approaches to changing body image. In T. F. Cash & T. Pruzinsky (Eds.), *Body image: A handbook of theory, research, and clinical practice* (pp. 478–486). New York: Guilford Press.

Cash, T. F., & Szymanski, M. (1995). Development and validation of the Body Image Ideals Questionnaire. *Journal of Personality Assessment, 64,* 466–477.

Cash, T. F., Winstead, B. A., & Janda, L. H. (1986, April). The great American shape-up: Body image survey report. *Psychology Today, 20,* 30–37.

Coker, S., Vize, C., Wade, T., & Cooper, P. J. (1993). Patients with bulimia nervosa who fail to engage in cognitive behavior therapy. *International Journal of Eating Disorders, 13,* 35–40.

Cooper, P. J., Taylor, M. J., Cooper, Z., & Fairburn, C. G. (1987). The development and validation of the Body Shape Questionnaire. *International Journal of Eating Disorders, 6,* 486–494.

Cooper, Z., & Fairburn, C. G. (2002). Cognitive-behavioral treatment of obesity. In T. A. Wadden & A. J. Stunkard (Eds.), *Handbook of obesity treatment* (pp. 465–479). New York: Guilford Press.

Davis, R., McVey, G., Heinmaa, M., Rockert, W., & Kennedy, S. (1999). Sequencing of cognitive-behavioral treatments for bulimia nervosa. *International Journal of Eating Disorders, 25,* 361–374.

Davis, R., Olmsted, M. P., & Rockert, W. (1990). Brief group psychoeducation for bulimia nervosa: Assessing the clinical significance of change. *Journal of Consulting and Clinical Psychology, 58,* 882–885.

Dworkin, S. H., & Kerr, B. A. (1987). Comparison of interventions for women experiencing body image problems. *Journal of Counseling Psychology, 34,* 136–140.

Fairburn, C. G. (2002). Cognitive-behavioral therapy for bulimia nervosa. In C. G. Fairburn & K. D. Brownell (Eds.), *Eating disorders and obesity: A comprehensive handbook* (2nd ed., pp. 233–237). New York: Guilford Press.

Fairburn, C. G., Jones, R., Peveler, R. C., Carr, S. J., Solomon, R. A., O'Connor, M. E., et al. (1991). Three psychological treatments for bulimia nervosa: A comparative trial. *Archives of General Psychiatry, 48,* 463–469.

Fairburn, C. G., Jones, R., Peveler, R. C., Hope, R. A., & O'Connor, M. (1993). Psychotherapy and bulimia nervosa: Longer-term effects of interpersonal psychotherapy, behavior therapy, and cognitive behavior therapy. *Archives of General Psychiatry, 50,* 419–428.

Fairburn, C. G., Marcus, M. D., & Wilson, G. T. (1993). Cognitive-behavioral therapy for binge eating and bulimia nervosa: A comprehensive treatment manual. In G. G. Fairburn & G. T. Wilson (Eds.), *Binge eating: Nature, assessment, and treatment* (pp. 361–404). New York: Guilford Press.

Fairburn, C. G., Peveler, R. C., Jones, R., Hope, R. A., & Doll, H. A. (1993). Predictors of 12-month outcome in bulimia nervosa and the influence of attitudes to shape and weight. *Journal of Consulting and Clinical Psychology, 61,* 696–698.

Fairburn, C. G., Shafran, R., & Cooper, Z. (1999). A cognitive behavioral theory of anorexia nervosa. *Behavior Research and Therapy, 37,* 1–13.

Feingold, A., & Mazzella, R. (1998). Gender differences in body image are increasing. *Psychological Science, 9,* 190–195.

Fisher, E., & Thompson, J. K. (1994). A comparative evaluation of cognitive-behavioral therapy (CBT) versus exercise therapy (ET) for the treatment of body image disturbance: Preliminary findings. *Behavior Modification, 18,* 171–185.

Foster, G. D., & Matz, P. E. (2002). Weight loss and changes in body image. In T. F. Cash & T. Pruzinsky (Eds.), *Body image: A handbook of theory, research, and clinical practice* (pp. 405–413). New York: Guilford Press.

Garner, D. M. (1997, January/February). The 1997 body image survey results. *Psychology Today, 30,* 30–44, 75–80, 84.

Garner, D. M. (2002). Body image and anorexia nervosa. In T. F. Cash & T. Pruzinsky (Eds.), *Body image: A handbook of theory, research, and clinical practice* (pp. 295–303). New York: Guilford Press.

Garner, D. M., Vitousek, K. M., & Pike, K. M. (1997). Cognitive-behavioral therapy for anorexia nervosa. In D. M. Garner & P. E. Garfinkel (Eds.), *Handbook of treatment for eating disorders* (2nd ed., pp. 94–144). New York: Guilford Press.

Grant, J. R., & Cash, T. F. (1995). Cognitive-behavioral body image therapy: Comparative efficacy of group and modest-contact treatments. *Behavior Therapy, 26,* 69–84.

Grilo, C. M. (2002). Binge eating disorder. In C. G. Fairburn & K. D. Brownell (Eds.), *Eating disorders and obesity: A comprehensive handbook* (2nd ed., pp. 178–182). New York: Guilford Press.

Heatherton, T. F., Mahamedi, F., Striepe, M., Field, A. E., & Keel, P. (1997). A 10-year longitudinal study of body weight, dieting, and eating disorder symptoms. *Journal of Abnormal Psychology, 106,* 117–125.

Heatherton, T. F., Nichols, P., Mahamedi, F., & Keel, P. (1995). Body weight, dieting, and eating disorder symptoms among college students, 1982 to 1992. *American Journal of Psychiatry, 152,* 1623–1629.

Key, A., George, C. L., Beattie, D., Stammers, K., Lacey, H., & Waller, G. (2002). Body image treatment within an inpatient program for anorexia nervosa: The role of mirror exposure in the desensitization process. *International Journal of Eating Disorders, 31,* 85–190.

Lavallee, D. M., & Cash, T. F. (1997, November). *The comparative efficacy of two cognitive-behavioral self-help programs for a negative body image.* Poster presented at the meeting of the Association for Advancement of Behavior Therapy, Miami Beach, FL.

Leitenberg, H., Rosen, J. C., Wolf, J., Vara, L. S., Detzer, M. J., & Srebnik, D. (1994). Comparison of cognitive-behavior therapy and desipramine in the treatment of bulimia nervosa. *Behavior Research and Therapy, 32,* 37–45.

Markus, H. (1977). Self-schemata and processing information about the self. *Journal of Personality and Social Psychology, 35,* 63–78.

Martin, K. A., & Lichtenberger, C. M. (2002). Fitness enhancement and changes in body image. In T. F. Cash & T. Pruzinsky (Eds.), *Body image: A handbook of theory, research, and clinical practice* (pp. 414–421). New York: Guilford Press.

McKay, M., & Fanning, P. (1992). *Self-esteem: A proven program of cognitive techniques for assessing, improving, and maintaining your self-esteem.* Oakland, CA: New Harbinger.

Mitchell, J. E., Pyle, R. L., Eckert, E. D., Hatsukami, D. H., Pomeroy, C., & Zimmerman, R. (1990). A comparison study of antidepressants and structured intensive group psychotherapy in the treatment of bulimia nervosa. *Archives of General Psychiatry, 47,* 149–157.

Mokdad, A. H., Serdula, M. K., Dietz, W. H., Bowman, B. A., Marks, J. S., & Kaplan, J. P. (1999). The spread of the obesity epidemic in the United States, 1991–1998. *Journal of the American Medical Association, 282,* 1519–1532.

Neziroglu, F., McKay, D., Todaro, J., & Yaryura-Tobias, J. A. (1996). Effect of cognitive behavior therapy on persons with body dysmorphic disorder and comorbid Axis II diagnoses. *Behavior Therapy, 27,* 67–77.

Noles, S. W., Cash, T. F., & Winstead, B. A. (1985). Body image, physical attractiveness, and depression. *Journal of Consulting and Clinical Psychology, 53,* 88–94.

Olivardia, R. (2002). Body image and muscularity. In T. F. Cash & T. Pruzinsky (Eds.), *Body image: A handbook of theory, research, and clinical practice* (pp. 210–218). New York: Guilford Press.

Olmsted, M. P., Davis, R., Rockert, W., Irvine, M. J., Eagle, M., & Garner, D. M. (1991). Efficacy of a brief group psychoeducational intervention for bulimia nervosa. *Behavior Research and Therapy, 29,* 71–83.

Peterson, C. B., Mitchell, J. E., Engbloom, S., Nugent, S., Mussell, M. P., Crow, S. J., et al. (2001). Self-help versus therapist-led group cognitive-behavioral treatment of binge eating disorder at follow-up. *International Journal of Eating Disorders, 30,* 363–374.

Peterson, C. B., Mitchell, J. E., Engbloom, S., Nugent, S., Mussell, M. P., & Miller, J. P. (1998). Group cognitive-behavioral treatment of binge eating disorder: A comparison of therapist-led versus self-help formats. *International Journal of Eating Disorders, 24,* 125–136.

Phillips, K. A. (2002). Body image and body dysmorphic disorder. In T. F. Cash & T. Pruzinsky (Eds.), *Body image: A handbook of theory, research, and clinical practice* (pp. 312–321). New York: Guilford Press.

Pope, H. G., Jr., Phillips, K. A., & Olivardia, R. (2000). *The Adonis Complex: The secret crisis of male body obsession.* New York: Free Press.

Powell, M. R., & Hendricks, B. (1999). Body schema, gender, and other correlates in nonclinical populations. *Genetic, Social, and General Psychology Monographs, 125*(4), 333–412.

Probst, M., Van Coppenolle, H., & Vandereycken, W. (1995). Body experience in anorexia nervosa patients: An overview of therapeutic approaches. *Eating Disorders: Journal of Treatment and Prevention, 3,* 145–157.

Probst, M., Vandereycken, W., Van Coppenolle, H., & Pieters, G. (1999). Body experience in eating disorders before and after treatment: A follow-up study. *European Psychiatry, 14,* 333–340.

Ramirez, E. M., & Rosen, J. C. (2001). A comparison of weight control and weight control plus body image therapy for obese men and women. *Journal of Consulting and Clinical Psychology, 69,* 440–446.

Rosen, J. C. (1996). Body image assessment and treatment in controlled studies of eating disorders. *International Journal of Eating Disorders, 20,* 331–343.

Rosen, J. C., Cado, S., Silberg, N. T., Srebnik, D., & Wendt, S. (1990). Cognitive behavior therapy with and without size perception training for women with body image disturbance. *Behavior Therapy, 21,* 481–498.

Rosen, J. C., Orosan, P., & Reiter, J. (1995). Cognitive behavior therapy for negative body image in obese women. *Behavior Therapy, 26,* 25–42.

Rosen, J. C., & Reiter, J. (1996). Development of the Body Dysmorphic Disorder Examination. *Behavior Research and Therapy, 34,* 755–766.

Rosen, J. C., Reiter, J., & Orosan, P. (1995). Cognitive-behavioral body image therapy for body dysmorphic disorder. *Journal of Consulting and Clinical Psychology, 63,* 263–269.

Rosen, J. C., Saltzberg, E., & Srebnik, D. (1989). Cognitive behavior therapy for negative body image. *Behavior Therapy, 20,* 394–404.

Sarwer, D. B., & Thompson, J. K. (2002). Obesity and body image disturbance. In T. A. Wadden & A. J. Stunkard (Eds.), *Handbook of obesity treatment* (pp. 447–464). New York: Guilford Press.

Schwartz, M. B., & Brownell, K. D. (2002). Obesity and body image. In T. F. Cash & T. Pruzinsky (Eds.), *Body image: A handbook of theory, research, and clinical practice* (pp. 200–209). New York: Guilford Press.

Smith, J. E., Wolfe, B. L., & Laframboise, D. E. (2001). Body image treatment for a community sample of obligatory and nonobligatory exercisers. *International Journal of Eating Disorders, 30,* 375–388.

Smolak, L., & Levine, M. P. (1996). Adolescent transitions and the development of eating problems. In L. Smolak, M. P. Levine, & R. Striegel-Moore (Eds.), *The developmental psychopathology of eating disorders: Implications for research, prevention, and treatment* (pp. 207–233). Mahwah, NJ: Erlbaum.

Strachan, M. D., & Cash, T. F. (2002). Self-help for a negative body image: A comparison of components of a cognitive-behavioral program. *Behavior Therapy, 33,* 235–251.

Striegel-Moore, R. H., & Franko, D. L. (2002). Body image issues among girls and women. In T. F. Cash & T. Pruzinsky (Eds.), *Body image: A handbook of theory, research, and clinical practice* (pp. 183–191). New York: Guilford Press.

Szymanski, M., & Cash, T. F. (1995). Body image disturbances and self-discrepancy theory: Expansion of the Body Image Ideals Questionnaire. *Journal of Social and Clinical Psychology, 14,* 134–146.

Thompson, J. K., Heinberg, L. J., Altabe, M., & Tantleff-Dunn, S. (1999). *Exacting beauty: Theory, assessment, and treatment of body image disturbance.* Washington, DC: American Psychological Association.

Thompson, J. K., & Smolak, L. (Eds.). (2001). *Body image, eating disorders, and obesity in youth: Assessment, prevention, and treatment.* Washington, DC: American Psychological Association.

Thompson, J. K., & van den Berg, P. (2002). Measuring body image attitudes among adolescents and adults. In T. F. Cash & T. Pruzinsky (Eds.), *Body image: A handbook of theory, research, and clinical practice* (pp. 142–154). New York: Guilford Press.

Tuschen-Caffier, B., Pook, M., & Frank, M. (2001). Evaluation of manual-based cognitive-behavioral therapy for bulimia nervosa in a service setting. *Behavior Research and Therapy, 39,* 299–308.

Vandereycken, W., Depreitere, L., & Probst, M. (1987). Body-oriented therapy for anorexia nervosa patients. *American Journal of Psychotherapy, 41,* 252–259.

Veale, D. (2002). Cognitive-behavioral therapy for body dysmorphic disorder. In D. J. Castle & K. A. Phillips (Eds.), *Disorders of body image* (pp. 121–138). Petersfield, England: Wrightson Biomedical.

Veale, D., Gournay, K., Dryden, W., Boocock, A., Shah, F., Wilson, R., et al. (1996). Body dysmorphic disorder: A cognitive behavioral model and pilot randomised controlled trial. *Behavior Research and Therapy, 34,* 717–729.

Vitousek, K. B. (2002). Cognitive-behavioral therapy for anorexia nervosa. In C. G. Fairburn & K. D. Brownell (Eds.), *Eating disorders and obesity: A comprehensive handbook* (2nd ed., pp. 308–313). New York: Guilford Press.

Westmoreland-Corson, P., & Andersen, A. E. (2002). Body image issues among boys and men. In T. F. Cash & T. Pruzinsky (Eds.), *Body image: A handbook of theory, research, and clinical practice* (pp. 192–199). New York: Guilford Press.

Wiederman, M. W. (2002). Body image and sexual functioning. In T. F. Cash & T. Pruzinsky (Eds.), *Body image: A handbook of theory, research, and clinical practice* (pp. 287–294). New York: Guilford Press.

Williamson, D. A., Stewart, T. M., White, M. A., & York-Crowe, E. (2002). An information-processing perspective on body image. In T. F. Cash & T. Pruzinsky (Eds.), *Body image: A handbook of theory, research, and clinical practice* (pp. 47–54). New York: Guilford Press.

Wilson, G. T. (1999). Cognitive behavior therapy for eating disorders: Progress and problems. *Behavior Research and Therapy, 37,* S79–S95.

Wilson, G. T., Fairburn, C. G., & Agras, W. S. (1997). Cognitive-behavioral therapy for bulimia nervosa. In D. M. Garner & P. E. Garfinkel (Eds.), *Handbook of treatment for eating disorders* (2nd ed., pp. 67–93). New York: Guilford Press.

Winzelberg, A. J., Abascal, L., & Taylor, C. B. (2002). Psychoeducational approaches to the prevention and change of negative body image. In T. F. Cash & T. Pruzinsky (Eds.), *Body image: A handbook of theory, research, and clinical practice* (pp. 487–496). New York: Guilford Press.

Wolff, G. E., & Clark, M. M. (2001). Changes in eating self-efficacy and body image following cognitive-behavioral group therapy for binge eating disorder: A clinical study. *Eating Behaviors, 2,* 97–104.

Chapter 26

BODY DYSMORPHIC DISORDER

RODERTO OLIVARDIA

Body dysmorphic disorder (BDD) is known as the disorder of imagined ugliness (Phillips, McElroy, Keck, Pope, & Hudson, 1993) and represents one of the most misunderstood diagnoses in the *Diagnostic and Statistical Manual of Mental Disorders, fourth edition (DSM-IV)*. Although BDD is conceived by many to be a new clinical phenomenon, it was first described by Morselli (1891) more than 100 years ago and named *dysmorphophobia.* The term *dysmorphia* comes from the Greek term for ugliness. Morselli described almost 80 patients who displayed symptoms that are remarkably similar to what modern-day sufferers of BDD experience. He described patients who were engaging in behavioral rituals and whose social lives were highly compromised by their appearance concerns. Even with this history, BDD was not present in the American scientific literature until 1987, when it was granted its diagnostic status in the *DSM-III-R* (Phillips, 1996b).

Currently, BDD is relegated to the diagnostic category of the somatoform disorders (American Psychiatric Association [APA], 1994). Experts agree that BDD does not seem to fit into this category and should be considered in the category of anxiety disorders, where obsessive-compulsive disorder (OCD) lies. Research suggests that BDD represents a part of the OCD spectrum disorders (McElroy, Phillips, & Keck, 1994; Phillips, McElroy, Hudson, & Pope, 1995; Phillips, Price, Greenberg, & Rasmussen, 2001).

According to the *DSM-IV,* the symptoms are:

1. A preoccupation with an imagined defect in appearance. If a slight physical anomaly is present, the person's concern is markedly excessive.

2. The preoccupation causes clinically significant distress or impairment in social, occupational, or other important areas of functioning.

3. The preoccupation is not better accounted for by another mental disorder (APA, 1994).

Compared to the diagnostic criteria for a major depressive episode or Posttraumatic Stress Disorder (PTSD), the limited criteria for BDD leave much room for misinterpretation by clinicians and laypersons alike (Phillips, 1996b). As to the first criteria, individuals with BDD are constantly preoccupied with a part of their appearance that is not seen by others in the same way it is seen by them. For example (all example names are fictitious), Paul, 32, sees his nose as "gigantic," when in fact he has an ordinarily shaped nose. Betty, 54, views her legs as "chicken-like," while her friends think she is crazy because they see nothing unusual about her legs. Trey, 18, looks in the mirror and sees "ugly, deep wrinkles" in his face, when in fact his face is completely free of wrinkles. All of these individuals are consumed with thoughts that others are noticing their "flaws." Clients assume that their clinicians can automatically spot the area of preoccupation because to the sufferer, the appearance defect is obvious. Most of the time, the clinician cannot determine what the area of concern is because the body part looks normal.

BODY IMAGE IN BODY DYSMORPHIC DISORDER

It is not entirely clear as to whether the person with BDD actually *sees* the body part differently (sensory difference) or may see it accurately but *thinks or feels* about it differently than others (cognitive and evaluative difference). If an individual sees the part differently, it may suggest a delusional or psychotic disorder. There is a question as to whether there is a delusional or psychotic subtype to BDD for those individuals who are 100% convinced that their perceived defect is real or whether the individual solely carries a psychotic disorder diagnosis. One study compared 48 patients with nondelusional BDD with 52 patients with delusional BDD (Phillips, Nierenberg, Brendel, & Fava, 1996). The two groups did not differ significantly in demographic, phenomenological, course of illness, associated features, comorbidity, and treatment response variables. Thus, the delusional aspect of BDD seems to represent a more extreme end in the continuum of severity of BDD. In fact, delusional subjects had higher scores on BDD assessments, suggesting that the BDD was more severe.

Emerging research also suggests that people with BDD may see their body parts accurately but have their perception colored by negative cognitions and emotions (Veale, 2002). Phillips (1996b) discusses how individuals with BDD tend to overfocus or selectively attend to various appearance details and become fixated on them. Robert, 33, would look in the mirror and stare at his nose for hours at a time. He explored every pore, curve, and millimeter of skin on his nose. When asked what he thinks others perceive when they see him, he replied, "I know this sounds crazy, but I truly think they are totally neglecting my body, seeing a small head and this monstrosity of a nose. All they really see is the huge nose." It is hardly surprising that Robert would make this assumption. The manner in which we construct our body image comes from a combination of visual and cognitive/attitudinal cues (Cash & Pruzinsky, 1990). If all Robert saw when he viewed himself was his nose and every minute detail of it, the mental representation or picture he would have of his complete body image would then become selectively focused and overrepresented by his nose. He assumes that others are paying as close attention to his nose as he is. Thomas and Goldberg (1995) found that people with BDD were actually better than normal controls at assessing facial proportions. This would suggest that their sensory-visual processing may not be particularly impaired. Deckersbach and colleagues (2000) found that individuals with BDD focus on isolated details rather than on the overall schematic when completing the Rey-Osterrieth

Complex Figure Test, which assesses copy performance. They assessed 17 BDD patients with 17 healthy controls and found that patients with BDD displayed organizational and executive functioning deficits. They concluded that BDD patients demonstrate impairment in verbal and nonverbal memory. This seems to lend more support to the theory that many BDD patients are highly affected by their cognitive processing in viewing their appearance and may simply place higher emphasis on aesthetics than people without BDD. Veale and colleagues (Veale, Ennis, & Lambrou, 2002) tested this notion and found that 20% of BDD patients ($n = 100$) were more likely to have had an occupation or education in art or design, compared to only 4% of patients with depression, 3% of patients with OCD, and none of the PTSD patients. The authors entertain two conclusions about this result: Either the art education influenced and may contribute to the development of BDD, or people with BDD may simply gravitate to art because they are invested in aesthetics and visual detail.

The first criterion for BDD also notes that if there is a slight anomaly, the person's concern is markedly excessive. Freda, 40, was extremely anxious about being seen in public because of facial wrinkles. Gregory, 16, was depressed because he had slight acne. Unlike flaws that are not perceived by others, slight defects in appearance may be perceived congruently by the BDD patient and others. Individuals could still be diagnosed with BDD if their reaction to this flaw is exaggerated. For example, while many teenagers who have acne may be very dissatisfied with their appearance, most continue to function normally. They still go to school, have friends, and think well of themselves, while the functioning of people with BDD deteriorates because of their appearance. They may be in bed for days, refusing to go to school for fear that others will call them "ugly," and struggle with suicidal thoughts.

BODY AREAS OF CONCERN

Men and women with BDD may worry about any aspect of their appearance; however, the dominant appearance concerns are focused on head and facial features (Phillips, 1996b). In one study of 30 men and women with BDD, 63% were preoccupied with their hair, 50% with their nose, and 50% were concerned about their skin, while 27% were obsessed with their eyes, and 20% were concerned with their overall face or head. Other areas of concern included the chin (17%), teeth (13%), ears (7%), buttocks (7%), and arms (7%). An individual may simultaneously be preoccupied with several body parts. The nature of the concern can vary among individuals. Frank, 41, was obsessed with having too much body hair, while Lionel, 37, was preoccupied with having too little hair on his chest. Margot, 29, hated the way her eyes were shaped, referring to them as "alien eyes," while Jane, 48, thought her eyes looked "too masculine." Kendra, 16, was preoccupied by her perception that her teeth were excessively yellow, while Mitch, 39, felt his teeth were crooked. People with BDD describe their dissatisfied body part in harsh, critical terms.

There is an emerging concern about men who are excessively preoccupied with their physiques (Pope, Gruber, Choi, Olivardia, & Phillips, 1997; Pope, Phillips, & Olivardia, 2000). This subcategory of BDD, known as *muscle dysmorphia,* affects men nearly exclusively. Men with this form of BDD believe that their body build is too small or inadequately muscular, although they are usually very muscular and in good shape (Olivardia, 2001; Olivardia, Pope, & Hudson, 2000). This was first described as *reverse anorexia* or *bigorexia* (Pope, Katz, & Hudson, 1993). Justin, 24, was told by his friends that he looked very muscular and strong, but Justin believed that he looked like a "scrawny, prepubescent freak."

INSIGHT

The level of insight that people with BDD display toward their perceived defect varies (Phillips, 1996b). *Insight* refers to the recognition that the distorted image is, in fact, inaccurate or skewed. Phillips and colleagues (1993) found that 53% of their sample of BDD patients were not entirely convinced that their defects were real, but they also struggled with strong thoughts that their perceptions were real. Anita, 23, would state, "Sometimes no matter what you tell me, I know my skin is horrific. Other times, I question that and think my mind must be playing tricks on me." Forty percent of the patients were delusional in that they were completely convinced that their defects were real, despite any contradicting evidence. Ken, 44, was absolutely convinced that his head was triple the size of the average head. This perception was not changed even when his head was measured and found to be exactly the size of an average adult head. Only 7% of the patients had good insight into the fact that their defects were imagined rather than real. Karen, 36, would say, "I know I am making a bigger deal out of my cheeks than I should. It is so irrational, but I just can't shake the idea that they are too chubby." Clinicians who treat BDD note that many patients may display poor insight at the initiation of treatment only to have it shift to a higher level of insight with treatment (Phillips & McElroy, 1993). Levels of insight can also be affected by environmental triggers, such as stress or socially anxious situations.

COGNITIVE ASPECTS OF BODY DYSMORPHIC DISORDER

Individuals with BDD are constantly obsessing about their perceived defect. Phillips and colleagues (1993) noted that patients used terms such as *obsessed, fixated,* and *tormented* when describing their preoccupation. Some claimed that every waking hour was spent thinking about their preoccupation. Approximately 25% of BDD sufferers think about their "flaw" for one to three hours a day, 25% spend three to eight hours per day, while more than 40% report thinking about their perceived defect for more than eight hours per day (Phillips, 1996b). Less than 10% spend less than an hour obsessing about their body part(s). Despite many attempts to not think about their appearance, people with BDD find themselves trapped in a constant state of obsession. Even when appearing as if they are not thinking about their "flaw," patients with BDD can be consumed with thoughts of ugliness. William, 27, was a telemarketing representative who reported that he would often not remember what he just said to someone because he would get "mentally lost in thoughts" around his hair. Some patients are never free of their mental torment, sometimes dreaming of their "defect." Karessa, 26, would dream that her skin was so ugly that she would be denied access to public buildings, restaurants, her place of work, and even her own home: "No one wanted me because I was so despicably ugly."

Individuals with BDD find it very difficult to resist these thoughts. They may attempt to distract themselves from the thoughts, trying to avert their attention but are often unsuccessful. Because they failed in the past to successfully resist the preoccupations, more than 40% make little to no effort to resist their thoughts (Phillips, 1996b). People with BDD do not feel that they have complete control over their cognitions. The majority (46%) feel they exhibit little control, while 18% report having no control whatsoever over their preoccupying thoughts.

In addition to the nagging obsessions, individuals with BDD often display cognitive distortions in their thinking and make faulty assumptions about environmental and interpersonal cues (Geremia & Neziroglu, 2001; Pope et al., 2000; Veale, 2002). Patients with BDD often filter information in a manner that leaves them attending to the negative and discounting the positive (Pope et al., 2000). Tomasso, 30, would think about how much he dislikes his height, without considering the many aspects of his appearance he may be satisfied with. The focus on the negative leaves people with BDD feeling as if there is nothing positive about their appearance. Patients with BDD also display all-or-nothing thinking around their appearance (Pope et al., 2000). If they see one slight imperfection, it means they are ugly. There is no gray area. Because perfection is virtually impossible to attain, these people are setting themselves up for failure and disappointment. Another cognitive distortion is personalization (Veale, 2002). This is the faulty assumption that external cues and occurrences are confirmation of their "defect" and the idea that others are taking special notice of these people and their preoccupation. This is also known as *referential thinking* (Phillips, 1996b). Anytime Oliver, 55, heard people laughing nearby, he concluded that they were poking fun at his thinning hair. He would assume this even when evidence suggested that they weren't laughing at him. Many BDD patients have reported an extreme catch-22 personalization thought: "If people look at me, it is because I am so ugly and repulsive. If people do not look at me or look at me and then turn away, it is because I am clearly too ugly to be looked at." This statement exemplifies the state of mental confinement many BDD sufferers endure. Men and women with BDD also suffer from the "shoulds" (Pope et al., 2000), rigid rules of how they should look and act. Any slight violation of the rules constitutes a major infraction. James, 40, felt he should have thick, black hair that raised 4 inches off his head. Kelly, 17, felt that her eyes should be blue and her skin should be "baby skin" to be pretty. Many of the standards they set for themselves are often unrealistic. While some people with BDD feel they should look a certain way to be acceptable, many victims of this illness are struggling to perceive themselves as normal, average, and human. Michael, 22, felt that he looked like a cross between an extraterrestrial and the Elephant Man: "I don't need to look perfect. I just want to look human, so that people can just look right past me. I don't want to be noticed."

Even when faced with disconfirming evidence, the cognitive beliefs held by people with BDD are often rigid and inflexible. Much of this may simply have to do with the need for congruence. Because individuals may see or perceive a body part as "ugly" or "defected," they find it very difficult to imagine that what they are seeing is inaccurate or imagined. Therefore, when evidence to the contrary of their perception presents itself (such as a compliment), these people are faced with a dilemma. If they accept the contrary evidence, their original perception was wrong, which may leave them feeling "crazy," "vain," or "dumb." If they deny the evidence and develop a theory for the evidence (such as "They are just complimenting me because they obviously know how pathetic I look"), their original perception is intact, along with the feeling that their internal reality matches their external one. This theory of congruence deserves empirical attention. However, clinical data has lent evidence to this notion. One patient remarked, "I'd rather think I'm ugly than think I was crazy and ugly."

Even more important than the initial thought an individual may have is the underlying assumption that is derived from that thought (Veale, 2002; Veale et al., 1996). Even if these individuals were to assume that their cognition was accurate, such as that they have an ugly nose, what would that truly mean? People with BDD often feel that this defect makes them unlovable or inferior. Marcus, 36, who had muscle dysmorphia, felt that anything less than a large, muscular physique made him a "wimp" and a "sissy" and that no one would want to be with him, whereas Darlene, 19, felt that having small breasts made her powerless as a person. Patients commonly remark that they need to look good externally to compensate for how bad they feel internally.

BEHAVIORAL ASPECTS OF BODY DYSMORPHIC DISORDER

Almost all sufferers with BDD engage in repetitive, compulsive behaviors that are designed to relieve anxiety (Phillips, 1996b). The average number of behaviors performed is four (Phillips, 1996b). The intent may be to engage in the behavior for a short period of time or only once. However, the temporary relief of anxiety strongly reinforces the behavior, creating a system where the individual must engage in these repetitive behaviors on a constant basis.

Mirror Checking/Avoidance

One of the most common compulsive behaviors is mirror checking (Phillips, 1996a; Veale & Riley, 2001). One study found that 73% of BDD patients excessively checked mirrors and other reflecting surfaces, such as CDs, store windows, car window reflections, cutlery, toasters, and spoons for up to four hours daily. Another investigation compared 55 controls with 52 BDD patients in terms of mirror gazing (Veale & Riley, 2001). Before looking in the mirror, BDD patients, as compared to controls, were more likely to hope that they would look different and felt they would feel worse if they did not look in the mirror. They were driven by the need to assess their exact appearance and were more likely to attend to internal feelings about their appearance rather than on the specific body parts. Another interesting phenomena is that people with BDD were more likely to practice their "best face" in front of the mirror and fantasized what their appearance would be like if they could change it, something the authors term "mental cosmetic surgery" (Veale & Riley, 2001). Although one of the motivating factors in checking mirrors is to inevitably feel better about themselves and their appearance, the opposite happens. Part of the reason lies in the high expectations before looking in the mirror. The hope when they look in the mirror is that the body part has miraculously changed, when in reality, their perception has stayed the same.

Cheryl, 38, would fit in four hours of mirror checking time in the morning before work. She had to wake up at 4 A.M. to accommodate her compulsion. "I had to check for at least four hours before work to make sure that I wouldn't look gross when I went into work. It starts with checking my hair, then checking my skin, then my teeth. I used to be late for work every day, so I wake up at 4 to prevent being late for work." Damon, 31, would feel the urge to look in any reflection he passed: "Malls are awful for me. There are too many store windows that reflect . . . too many mirrors. I have to do everything in my power to not look in every reflection. I still end up probably spending a total of 30 minutes out of the two hours I am at the mall looking at myself. I hate it. People think I am so vain."

Up to 35% of patients with BDD completely avoid mirrors in an attempt to rid themselves of the urge to check (Phillips, 1996a). Some go to great lengths to make sure they will never be "stuck" in front of a mirror. Patients may throw out home mirrors, cover them up, remove rearview mirrors in their car (which is obviously unsafe), or walk in a strange way in public so that they will not see mirrors. "My life is so much easier without mirrors. I still struggle with the urge to check, but if I don't have access to a mirror, my urge decreases," remarked 34-year-old Charlotte. Avoiding mirrors completely is not necessarily the solution to this problem, although it may seem to be the only resolve for BDD sufferers. A complete avoidance of mirrors only makes it more difficult when they are eventually presented with their reflection. Serena, 22, avoided mirrors for almost two years. She never looked in any reflection, put makeup on in the dark, and tried on clothes without the mirror. One day she was in a department store and caught a glimpse of herself in one of the store mirrors accidentally. She spent the next *six hours* examining her skin. "I felt possessed by some force. It was as if I was in my home, unaware that anyone was around me. Meanwhile, I am staring at my face for the whole day. I didn't realize how long I was there until the security guards came to escort me out of the store. I was even resisting them, asking if I could just look for 10 more minutes. It was definitely the lowest point for me. My feet also hurt that night, because I was standing in the same spot for the whole day." Serena realized that avoiding mirrors may have helped her in the short term but failed to help her in the long term. She is now learning to use the mirror appropriately, rather than as an all-or-nothing behavior.

Camouflaging

Up to 85% of patients with BDD camouflage their preoccupation in an attempt to hide it from the outside world (Phillips, 1996b). They may use makeup, dark glasses, or a hat. Elizabeth, 25, would apply an excessive amount of makeup to her face because she felt her skin was "atrocious." Ed, 42, always wore his baseball cap because he did not want others to see his "thinning" hair. Phillips (1996a) reports that 16% of BDD patients camouflage with their hand.

Grooming/Beautification Techniques

Approximately 35% of BDD patients engage in excessive grooming behaviors (Phillips, 1996a). This can include compulsively brushing their hair, applying skin lotions or moisturizers on their faces, excessive shaving, tanning the skin, removing body hair, excessive brushing of the teeth, or putting on makeup. The routines people with BDD subject themselves to are literally exhausting. Mary, 39, describes her routine:

> Before I go to bed, I spend about two and a half hours on trying to improve my appearance. I wash my face about six or seven times to strip it of all oils. I don't want to subject my coworkers to my greasy, shiny face the next day. After washing my face, I apply the first of seven different facial products. They deal with different problems like wrinkles, oily skin, bags under the eyes, redness in the face, dryness, blackheads, and circles under the eyes. While the products are working their way into my skin, I get really close to the mirror and inspect it under my bathroom's florescent lighting, which is always the best lighting to point out your flaws. I see every pore, every inch of skin, and hope that it will look better the next morning. I then get very depressed that I am so ugly and that no one will ever really love me. I wouldn't blame them. I look like a freak. The next morning I then wash my face three or four more times and then take a shower and then repeat the nightly ritual again. I then apply my makeup, which takes about an hour or so, and go to work. The funny thing is I still feel awful and ugly and anxious, even after doing all of those things. I guess I do them because I would feel worse if I didn't do them, although I can't imagine feeling worse than I do now.

Men and women often report that they don't necessarily set out to groom for hours. They feel they need to do it, until it feels "just right." What constitutes "just right" varies among individuals. Researchers note that this is similar to how people with OCD describe their time in performing their compulsions, such as handwashing (Simeon, Hollander, Stein, Cohen, & Aronowitz, 1995). Accompanying this behavior is the excessive buying of beauty and cosmetic products (Phillips, 1996b). Patients sometimes spend hundreds of dollars a month to accommodate their BDD rituals.

Skin Picking

Approximately 27% of patients with BDD pick their skin compulsively in attempts to rid their skin of imperfections (Phillips & Taub, 1995). They use tweezers, their fingers, and even razor blades. Patients describe the rush involved in getting something, such as a pimple, out of their skin. Ellen, 18, would remark, "I like to see stuff fly. That way I know it is out of my skin, and my skin is cleaner as a result." Skin picking also serves the purpose of reducing anxiety in individuals. This practice can sometimes result in major damage to the skin, including lesions, scarring, and blood loss (O'Sullivan, Phillips, Keuthen, & Wilhelm, 1999). There is a documented case of a female who was picking at her neck with tweezers so viciously that she exposed her carotid artery and required emergency surgery (O'Sullivan et al., 1999).

Reassurance Seeking

Close to half of all individuals with BDD seek and ask for reassurance from others about their "flaw" (Phillips, 1996b). This can become very frustrating to those close to the person with BDD. Fred, 25, who had muscle dysmorphia, would ask his father up to 100 times in an hour if he was muscular and whether he looked smaller than he did an hour ago. Ileana, 28, would ask her husband about whether her eyes looked "normal" at least 50 times a day. He found it very difficult to deal with her constant asking. Once Adam, 29, exhausted the patience of his friends and family, he turned to strangers for reassurance. "I would do it with subtlety. I'd be on the train and casually ask someone if my nose looked strange. Most of the time, no one thought I was crazy, until I asked 'Are you sure?' " The trap of reassurance seeking is that persons with BDD are never satisfied by the answer they receive. If people respond by saying the body part looks fine, the patient assumes that the person is "just saying it to be nice," or isn't looking carefully enough. If the person confirms the patient's view of the body part, the patient then feels bad that others can notice the "defect." Either way, reassurance seeking leads to the same destination

Scrutinizing Others' Appearance

Over 90% of patients with BDD scrutinize others' appearance and make comparisons against their own appearance (Phillips, 1996b). Because persons with BDD think so negatively about their appearance, they often see the other person's appearance as positive. People with BDD often place higher standards and are more critical when it comes to their own appearance than others. Carlos, 36, would stare at other men's biceps and compare them against his. "You can imagine what people must have thought about that. I couldn't help it. I would look at details of the biceps and compare them to mine to see who had a bigger bicep. Even when a guy's bicep was clearly smaller than mine, it somehow looked better on him than it would on me. I really could never win. I always came out looking worse." The irrationality of this compulsion is demonstrated best with Janine, 32, who would constantly scrutinize her sister's appearance, always feeling her sister looked prettier, although they were identical twins who were virtually indistinguishable in their appearance.

Exercise

Many individuals with BDD may excessively exercise to correct their "flaw." This is especially true for men with muscle dysmorphia (Olivardia, 2001; Olivardia et al., 2000; Pope et al., 2000). Some men with muscle dysmorphia lift weights for more than three hours per day to build their physiques. They may resort to intense, unhealthy exercise routines to prevent themselves from getting smaller. Steroid use is also common among men with muscle dysmorphia (Olivardia, 2001). Rick, 27, would lift weights for two hours, perform 1,000 sit-ups, 1,000 push-ups, and use an exercise machine for an hour every day. Anything less than that would result in great anxiety on his part. "I would be too nervous that my muscle would waste away if I missed a routine, let alone a whole day of exercising."

The majority of BDD patients (37%) spend anywhere from one to three hours per day performing any of these behaviors (Phillips, 1996b). Twenty-seven percent spend anywhere from three to eight hours daily. Only 8% spend less than one hour per day and 5% spend more than eight hours per day. Almost 40% of individuals with BDD try to resist performing the behavior most or some of the time, while 54% rarely or never try to resist (Phillips, 1996b). Scott, 29, remarked, "Why bother to resist? I know sooner or later I will be sucked into doing it. It's like a vacuum cleaner that stands on the same spot. Eventually it will get the dust that's clinging to the bottom of the rug." While 15%

of individuals feel much or complete control over these behaviors, 59% report having little or no control. One of the primary reinforcers in performing the behaviors is the reduction in anxiety. More than 50% of BDD patients reported that they would feel severe or extreme, disabling distress if they could not perform the behavior, 25% would experience moderate distress, while 26% reported mild or no distress if they could not perform the behavior (Phillips, 1996b).

Cosmetic Surgery

Many patients seek cosmetic surgeons or dermatologists before they seek treatment for the BDD (Phillips, 1996a). One study found that 77% of BDD patients had sought out cosmetic procedures as a solution for their BDD (Phillips, Grant, Siniscalchi, & Albertini, 2001). Dermatologic treatment was most often received (45%). Another report found that almost 50% of BDD patients had sought dermatological treatment (Phillips & Diaz, 1997). A study of 268 dermatology patients found that 12% fulfilled the diagnostic criteria for BDD (Phillips, Dufresne, Wilkel, & Vittorio, 2000), while another study found a 7% rate of BDD in a sample of cosmetic surgery patients (Sarwer, Wadden, Pertschuk, & Whitaker, 1998).

Cosmetic surgery is contraindicated for BDD patients because their perception is distorted to begin with (Phillips, 1996b). People with BDD have unrealistic expectations as to what surgery will do for their appearance and for their lives as a whole. They may think that their lives will "finally fall into place" and that "everyone will finally like them and accept them" or that they "will be free of anxiety" once they change the supposed defect. They are unable to cope if it does not come out exactly as if they imagined it would. Some may become so unhappy with the changed body part that they resort to another procedure for the same part (Ishigooka et al., 1998). Debra, 30, subjected herself to four rhinoplasties, until they "got it right." Researchers have termed this compulsion to undergo multiple cosmetic procedures as *polysurgery addiction* (Ishigooka et al., 1998). Even if they eventually become satisfied with the "new" body part, they may then become dissatisfied with other parts of their appearance and seek more cosmetic surgeries. For example, Alexa, 42, had a facelift because she felt her face was "too saggy," despite her family and friends thinking her face looked very youthful and discouraging the surgery. Although Alexa liked her facelift, she was increasingly preoccupied with how her other facial features looked on her new face. "My cheekbones now don't look right. My eyes look alien now. My lips are too thin." She felt the only solution to these newfound problems was more cosmetic surgery. Studies support the contraindication of surgery for BDD patients. Veale (2000) found that 76% of patients were dissatisfied with the outcome after receiving surgery. One study of 109 research subjects with BDD found that 83% had no change or an exacerbation of their BDD symptoms (Phillips & Diaz, 1997). Some reports also describe patients who resorted to performing cosmetic procedures on themselves in an effort to improve their appearance (Phillips, 1996a; Veale, 2000). One case involved a man who cut his own nose open and replaced his own cartilage with the cartilage of a chicken (Phillips, 1996b). In some cases, despite an objectively acceptable outcome, the patient may sue or even become violent toward the treating physician (Phillips, 1991).

It is important for nonpsychiatric physicians to be aware of BDD, to educate patients about the disorder, and to attempt to refer them for treatment to a qualified mental health professional or physician who can prescribe appropriate treatment. More efforts are being made to alert cosmetic surgeons of BDD (Sarwer & Didie, 2002).

The irony of many of these behaviors is that it may actually create a defect or spectacle of the person's appearance. The scalp of Eleanor, 15, would become lacerated because she would brush it more than 100 times with a coarse brush, thus actually creating a problem that needed attention and would most likely warrant looks from others—the very thing she meant to avoid by constantly brushing her hair. Candace, 35, would pick her skin so that it would be free of any "bumps." Meanwhile, an hour of picking would result in noticeable flaring, bleeding, and red bumps all over her face. Don, 18, would wash his face so often that it would become raw and irritated—the very look he was trying to rid himself of. Sheila, 31, put on enormous amounts of makeup to hide her "scars" and "not be noticed by anyone." Meanwhile, her family and friends reported that she looked like "a clown" and was bringing more attention to her face. Patients are often confused when confronted by these instances. Some report that people are noticing them because they did not do an adequate job in covering up or preventing the "flaw." Others understand that their compulsive behavior and its results are what warrant looks from others, versus their appearance per se. Even when they recognize that they may be exacerbating their "flaw" and drawing unwanted attention to themselves, they still feel the need to do it for several reasons. Some simply can't resist the urge to perform the behavior. Others note that they would rather be stared at and called a freak for wearing too much makeup than being seen as ugly without makeup. "At least I can say to myself that they think I'm ugly because of something I did to myself versus something I am," remarked one patient. Finally, many patients have remarked that even though they are unhappy with exacerbating (or creating) their "flaw," there exists some comfort when others perceive the defect in the same way the patient does, leading to validation and empathy for the patient. As mentioned earlier, the need for congruence in a person's internal and external reality may sometimes drive him or her to behaviors that may have egodystonic elements. Leonard, 30, remarked: "I know that constantly wearing my hat is causing my hair to become thinner, limper, and more unhealthy. I have to wear the hat, though, to cover my baldness (Leonard had a thick, full head of hair). I have to say, though, as weird as this sounds, but having my wife tell me that she is beginning to notice my hair looking bad is somewhat of a relief to me. It confirms that I haven't been imagining this and that I'm sane."

IMPAIRMENT IN FUNCTIONING

Obsessive thoughts and compulsive behaviors present a difficult challenge in the lives of individuals with BDD (Phillips, 1991). The effect of BDD on patient's lives is profound. When compared to individuals from the general population, as well as depressed patients, BDD patients scored worse on a quality of life scale (Phillips, 2000b). An individual's self-esteem becomes eroded because of the illness (Phillips, 1996b). Patients feel an enormous amount of stress dealing with their BDD symptoms (DeMarco, Li, Phillips, & McElroy, 1998). They feel anxious constantly because they are always in their skin. This stress manifests itself in occupational and social interference. Almost all (97%) of the patients avoided usual activities, such as work and social situations, for fear of embarrassment, while 30% had been housebound for a period of time due to the BDD (Phillips, 1996b). Barry, 34, would go out only at night, for fear that people might comment on his "puny" body build, while Jan, 21, would often skip social outings with her friends because she was concerned that she looked ugly. Interpersonal relationships can be destroyed by this illness (Phillips, 1996b; Pope et al., 2000). Couples have discussed how this illness can affect their sexual lives if one partner has BDD. Martin discussed how his wife's BDD affected their relationship: "I think she's beautiful, but she doesn't believe me. She said that she doesn't want to subject me to her ugly body." Another research subject discussed that he did not kiss his girlfriend for fear that she might transmit calories through her saliva, resulting in a loss of muscle mass (Olivardia, 2001). Many sufferers discuss how they lose friends because of the illness. "My friends think I am being arrogant by ditching them at the last minute. It is the opposite. I look in the mirror before I go out and forget it. I'm in for the night. This has totally destroyed my social life," remarks Bruce, 23. Patients have been fired or suspended from jobs because they are always late or missing days because of BDD symptoms (Phillips, 1996b). In a study of 33 children and adolescents with BDD, 18% had dropped out of school because of their BDD symptoms (Albertini & Phillips, 1999).

Suicidal ideation and behavior present a serious problem in individuals with BDD. One report stated that 30% of adults and more than 20% of adolescents with BDD have attempted suicide (Phillips, McElroy, Keck, Pope, & Hudson, 1993). Phillips (1996a) found that suicidal ideation was present in 23% of the patients, while 17% attempted suicide. Altamura and colleagues (Altamura, Paluello, Mundo, Medda, & Mannu, 2001) found that 50% of BDD patients displayed suicidal ideation. Christopher, 48, felt that the struggle of dealing with this illness was too painful and burdensome for his family. He ended his life and remarked in his suicide note that he did not want an open casket wake for fear that people might ridicule his appearance in the coffin.

Family members of BDD sufferers also endure an enormous amount of stress dealing with this illness (Phillips, 1996b). Parents, siblings, friends, and spouses have all described how the constant reassurance seeking and other compulsive behaviors displayed by their loved ones with BDD have been, at best, frustrating to deal with. Sometimes the loved one may lash out in anger to the person with BDD. David, 50, recalled how he once yelled at his son with BDD. "I just had it. After the 100th time of being asked how his face looked, I couldn't take it. He wasn't listening to me telling him that he looked fine. So I thought I should say something different to have him stop. I yelled 'YOUR FACE LOOKS LIKE A WRECK!!! IS THAT WHAT YOU WANT TO HEAR? IT LOOKS AWFUL!!' My son believed that, even though I could spend an entire day telling him otherwise. I felt like such a bad parent yelling that. His face doesn't look ugly. He is such a handsome kid. I said that out of anger." David's response is not uncommon. Family members are often at wit's end in dealing with an illness that is difficult to grasp.

PREVALENCE OF BODY DYSMORPHIC DISORDER

Although BDD is misunderstood, it is, unfortunately, common. According to Phillips (1996b), approximately 1% to 2% of the population has BDD. That translates into anywhere from 2.5 million to 5 million individuals in the United States alone. BDD is common in psychiatric settings (Phillips, 1996b). Other studies have found a 0.7% rate of BDD in women between ages 36 and 44 (Otto, Wilhelm, Cohen, & Harlow, 2001), 2.2% in a sample of adolescents (Mayville, Katz, Gipson, & Cabral, 1999), a 4% rate in American college students (Bohne et al., 2002), and 1.1% in a sample of adults (Bienvenu et al., 2000). There are many factors that lead to the theory that rates of BDD may be even higher than what has been shown empirically. Patients with BDD may never present themselves in clinical or research settings because of embarrassment, shame, or being housebound. They fear being called "vain" or "narcissistic" by others. They may be misdiagnosed as having another illness or seek treatment in a nonpsychiatric setting.

DEMOGRAPHICS

The mean age of onset for BDD seems to be between 14 and 16 years of age (Phillips & Diaz, 1997; Phillips et al., 1993), although patients as young as 4 years and as old as 80 have been identified (Phillips, 1996b). The majority of patients in clinical series have never been married, and many are unemployed (Phillips & Diaz, 1997). Another study found that 83% had never been married and 57% were unemployed. Fifty-four percent of the patients were living with either their parents or in a supervised setting (Phillips et al., 1993). Contrary to popular belief, BDD is just as common in men as it is in women (Phillips, 1996b; Pope et al., 2000). A study of 188 patients with BDD reported that 51% of the sample was male (Phillips & Diaz, 1997). Other studies have also shown a higher rate of men (Phillips et al., 1993; Veale et al., 1996). Although BDD is phenomenologically similar in both sexes, men and women may have different areas of concern. One study found that women tend to focus more on their hips, pick their skin, and camouflage with makeup more often than men, while men are more likely to be preoccupied with their muscularity (muscle dysmorphia), genitals, and hair. Women were more likely to have a comorbid diagnosis of bulimia nervosa, while men were more likely to abuse alcohol (Phillips & Diaz, 1997). Another study found that men were more concerned with their genitals, body hair, and height, while women were preoccupied with breasts and legs (Perugi et al., 1997).

COURSE OF ILLNESS

Prospective studies have not been conducted yet, but clinical data and case studies suggest that the illness can persist for many years (Phillips, 1996b). Phillips et al. (1993) found that the course of illness had a mean duration of 18.3 years. Whether early detection and intervention may decrease the course of the illness is currently unknown.

ETIOLOGICAL FACTORS

Biological

Researchers have hypothesized that BDD is part of the OCD spectrum disorders, which share a common genetic or biological predisposition (Hollander, 1993; Phillips, 1996b; Phillips et al., 1993). Family history studies have demonstrated that BDD may run in families, along with OCD (Bienvenu et al., 2000). The favorable response to selective serotonin reuptake inhibitors (SSRIs) suggests that BDD involves serotonin (Hollander et al., 1999; Hollander, Liebowitz, Winchel, Klumker, & Klein, 1989; Phillips, 2000a; Phillips, Albertini, & Rasmussen, 2002; Phillips, Dwight, & McElroy, 1998). However, it is unclear whether the dysregulation of serotonin serves as a causal factor in BDD, a result of BDD, or neither. Deckersbach and colleagues (2000) found that BDD patients had impairment in executive functioning, based on neuropsychological tests.

Psychological

Few studies have assessed psychological factors as possible etiological factors in BDD. One study discovered that BDD patients reported lower scores on the Parental Bonding Instrument than published norms (Phillips, Steketee, & Shapiro, 1996). Other psychological predisposing factors may include history of being teased, early rejection or neglect, history of trauma or sexual abuse, sense of perfectionism, and low self-esteem (Phillips, 1996b). More studies must be conducted to ascertain whether these factors are exclusive to BDD versus other psychiatric diagnoses and whether they represent causal factors or associated features of BDD.

Sociocultural

There is no doubt that cultural images of beauty influence the way men and women think and perceive their bodies (Pope et al., 2000; Wolf, 1991). Women are bombarded by a steady diet of images of thin women with large breasts and perfect skin, hair, and teeth. Advertisements, television, film, and music videos all promote images that women aspire to (Wolf, 1991). Men are also fed images of muscular, masculine men with full heads of hair and large genital bulges. Anything less than that ideal leave many men feeling inadequate about their masculinity (Pope et al., 2000). There is no doubt that these images affect those living with BDD, but whether they serve as an etiological factor is a question that deserves empirical attention.

It seems that there is not one singular etiological category that explains BDD. Its cause is most likely a combination of all of the previously discussed factors (Phillips, 1996b).

Comorbid Diagnoses

Depression is the most common comorbid disorder with BDD (Phillips, 1996b). Sixty percent of BDD patients are currently depressed, and more than 80% have a lifetime prevalence of depression (Phillips & Diaz, 1997; Phillips, Nierenberg, et al., 1996). BDD was found in 14% of patients with atypical major depression, which almost matched the rate of eating disorders in the same sample (16%; Phillips, Nierenberg, et al., 1996).

OCD is also common in BDD patients. They share the experience of intrusive thoughts and repetitive behaviors. Twelve percent of patients with OCD in one study were also diagnosed as having BDD. Insight was more impaired in the BDD/OCD group than the OCD group (Simeon et al., 1995). Brawman-Mintzer and colleagues (1995) found that BDD was diagnosed in 8% of OCD patients in their sample. Phillips and Diaz

(1997) reported a 30% comorbidity of OCD in their sample of BDD patients. Other studies support the comorbidity of OCD and BDD (Hollander, Cohen, & Simeon, 1993; Hollander & Wong, 1995; Phillips et al., 1993).

Social phobia is also highly comorbid with BDD. Both groups are highly anxious in social situations, although in the case of social phobia, the anxiety does not necessarily revolve around appearance concerns and compulsive behaviors aren't present. Brawman-Mintzer and colleagues (1995) found that 11% of patients with social phobia also had BDD. Another study reported that 38% of patients with BDD were also diagnosed with social phobia (Phillips & Diaz, 1997), while another found that 43% of BDD patients had social phobia (Phillips et al., 1993).

Eating disorders are not uncommon in BDD patients. They share the phenomena of a disturbed body image, although in the case of eating disorders, the focus is on the body shape or weight. One study found that 39% of a sample of female anorexics were found to also have BDD around concerns not related to their weight (Grant, Kim, & Eckert, 2002). Phillips and colleagues (1993) found that 10% of their BDD sample had a lifetime prevalence of an eating disorder.

ASSESSMENT

Assessment of BDD is usually from self-report or semistructured measures. One measure is the BDD Diagnostic Module of the Structured Clinical Interview for the *DSM-IV* Axis I Disorders (SCID-IV; First, Spitzer, Gibbon, & Williams, 1995). An interviewer would ask an individual whether he or she has been very worried about an aspect of their appearance. If the person answers affirmatively, the interviewer proceeds with questions related to how it affects their lives. This instrument has excellent interrater reliability (Phillips, 1996b).

Another measure is the BDD-Yale Brown Obsessive-Compulsive Scale (Y-BOCS). This semistructured interview assesses BDD symptoms in the past week. It is made up of 12 items that ask to rate the severity, on a scale of 1 to 5, of time occupied by, interference due to, distress associated with, resistance against thoughts of, and degree of control over thoughts about the body defect. The severity of time spent, interference, distress, resistance, and degree of control over compulsive behaviors related to body defect, as well as insight level and avoidance activities are also assessed. Phillips (1996b) found an average score of 28.5 ±7.8 for BDD patients. It is reported to have acceptable psychometric properties (Phillips, 1996b).

The Body Dysmorphic Disorder Examination is another useful assessment measure (Rosen & Reiter, 1996). This measure assesses frequencies of various interfering behaviors of BDD, such as camouflaging, checking, and reassurance seeking. Other items are related to self-consciousness in public situations, negative self-evaluation, and avoidance behavior. It is reported to have good psychometric properties.

TREATMENT

Although treatment studies are still somewhat preliminary, certain medications and psychological treatments appear effective for BDD. Case series, open-label studies, and controlled treatment trials indicate that the serotonin reuptake inhibitors (SRIs; fluoxe-tine, citalopram, fluvoxamine, sertraline, paroxetine, and clomipramine) are effective for a majority of patients with BDD (Hollander et al., 1989, 1994, 1999; Phillips, 2000b; Phillips et al., 1993, 1998, 2002). It appears that higher doses and longer treat-ment trials than are usually required for depression are often needed to treat BDD.

Cognitive-behavioral techniques, similar to what might be used for obsessive-compulsive disorder—such as restructuring distorted thoughts, exposure, and response prevention therapy—also appear effective for many patients (McKay, 1999; Neziroglu, McKay, Todaro, & Yaryura Tobias, 1996; Neziroglu & Yaryura-Tobias, 1993; Rosen, Reiter, & Orosan, 1995; Veale, 2001, 2002; Veale et al., 1996; Wilhelm, Otto, Lohr, & Deckersbach, 1999).

There are many elements to cognitive-behavioral therapy (CBT). Patients with BDD should first get an education on the diagnosis. This includes knowledge of the symp-toms and treatment. This knowledge helps in reducing the feelings of shame and isola-tion many people with this illness feel. I often recommend reading *The Broken Mirror* by Katharine Phillips (1996b) or providing them with some case vignettes.

After psychoeducation, cognitive therapy techniques may be employed. Cognitive therapy is aimed at restructuring distorted thought patterns and attempting to reframe them with accurate evidence. For example, Fred would employ the cognitive distortion known as mind reading. He would think that everyone is noticing and evaluating his teeth. This thought would then lead to certain behaviors and feelings. He would think that anytime he heard someone laughing, they were laughing because his teeth were so yellow and crooked. Fred was instructed to fill out mood monitoring sheets, which jour-nal his thoughts and feelings related to a triggering situation. Then he was instructed to challenge his thoughts and generate a list of alternative explanations for the situation. In this case, he came up with several other reasons why someone might be laughing that have nothing to do with his teeth. One explanation was simply that "maybe they told each other a funny joke that had nothing to do with me." Practicing this can aid in even-tually helping the person realize that their thoughts are more reflective of their feelings and self-consciousness than what is accurately going on around them. Preliminary stud-ies show that cognitive therapy can significantly improve BDD symptoms (Veale et al., 1996). As one challenges their distorted thought patterns, core beliefs about themselves may emerge. Such beliefs include, "I have to look perfect in order to be loved." It makes sense that anyone would be desperate to look perfect if they truly believed this thought. These core beliefs can also be challenged.

Behavioral therapy is aimed at reducing certain behaviors, such as mirror checking, excessive grooming, and reassurance seeking, while increasing other behaviors, such as social exposure. Exposure therapy is quite helpful with these patients (Neziroglu & Yaryura-Tobias, 1993). Exposure is immersing the patient in a situation that increases their anxiety. The goal is to increase their anxiety so that the person eventually habit-uates to it. For this, a clinician may create a hierarchy of stressful situations with the patient and move through the hierarchy. Richard felt going out without his hat on a sunny day was the most stressful situation for him. His hierarchy included going out on a cloudy day without his hat, walking around the mall without his hat, and so on until eventually he was walking outside on a sunny day without his hat. Response prevention is coupled with exposure therapy to aid the patient in not performing their typical com-pulsion. This might include looking in the mirror without skin picking or limiting the amount of time spent at the mirror. It is also helpful to develop a list of techniques that one can do instead of performing the compulsion, such as squeezing a ball, listening to music, or doing a crossword puzzle. Other behavioral techniques include having the patient write notes to themselves to help them out of the "automatic" nature of their compulsions. Mary, a skin picker, would post index cards on her bathroom door that read, "If you do not have to pee, you do not need to go into the bathroom." If her urge was too strong and she still went inside the bathroom, she had another reminder on her mirror that read "PICKING CAUSES SCARS." This would often help her reduce or prevent the skin-picking episode. A combination of CBT with medications appears to be the most effective treatment for BDD (Phillips, 1996b). Although no systematic studies of supportive or psychodynamic therapies have been done in BDD, these treatments when used alone appear ineffective for BDD symptoms (Phillips et al., 1993). Such treatment may, however, help patients in dealing with some of the interpersonal experiences or issues related to BDD or with other problems they may have. Many men feel that their masculinity is compromised by having BDD—an issue that may potentially be helped by therapy (Pope, Phillips, & Olivardia, 2000).

Future studies are needed to investigate these and other treatment interventions. In the meantime, it is recommended that men and women with BDD seek help from a professional who has experience treating BDD or other disorders in the obsessive-compulsive spectrum.

SUMMARY/FUTURE DIRECTIONS

Body dysmorphic disorder is a psychiatric illness characterized by a preoccupation with a part of the body. An individual perceives the part of the body as "defected" or "ugly," when, in reality, the body part looks fine. These negative thoughts, along with compulsive behaviors, significantly affect and impair the lives of the millions of men and women who struggle with BDD. Many individuals suffer in silence with this illness because they are ashamed and embarrassed. It appears that biological, psychological, and social factors contribute to the development of BDD. Treatment approaches, such as SSRIs and cognitive-behavioral therapy, appear to be effective for the treatment of BDD.

BDD officially appeared in the *DSM-III-R* as an independent diagnostic entity in 1987, thus research is still needed in this area. The comorbidity of personality disorders needs further development, as well as psychosocial contributors (such as trauma, peer relations, media images) to the development of BDD. Cases of BDD are expected to continue to increase. Research on the prevention and treatment of this illness is essential to enhance our scientific and clinical understanding of this phenomenon. Increased awareness will also aid sufferers to come forward and seek the treatment they desperately need.

REFERENCES

Albertini, R. S., & Phillips, K. A. (1999). 33 cases of body dysmorphic disorder in children and adolescents. *Journal of American Academy of Child and Adolescence Psychiatry, 38,* 453–459.

Altamura, C., Paluello, M. M., Mundo, E., Medda, S., & Mannu, P. (2001). Clinical and subclinical body dysmorphic disorder. *European Archives of Psychiatry and Clinical Neuroscience, 251*(3), 105–108.

American Psychiatric Association. (1994). *Diagnostic and statistical manual of mental disorders* (4th ed.). Washington, DC: Author.

Bienvenu, O. J., Samuels, J. F., Riddle, M. A., Hoehn-Saric, R., Liang, K., Cullen, B., et al. (2000). The relationship of obsessive-compulsive disorder to possible spectrum disorders: Results from a family study. *Biological Psychiatry, 48,* 287–293.

Bohne, A., Wilhelm, S., Keuthen, N. J., Florin, I., Baer, L., & Jenike, M. A. (2002). Prevalence of body dysmorphic disorder in a German college student sample. *Psychiatry Research, 109*(1), 101–104.

Brawman-Mintzer, O., Lydiard, R. B., Phillips, K. A., Morton, A., Czepowicz, V., Emmanuel, N., et al. (1995). Body dysmorphic disorder in patients with anxiety disorders and major depression: A comorbidity study. *American Journal of Psychiatry, 152*(11), 1665–1667.

Cash, T. F., & Pruzinsky, T. (1990). *Body image: Development deviance and change.* New York: Guilford Press.

Deckersbach, T., Savage, C. R., Phillips, K. A., Wilhelm, S., Buhlmann, U., Rauch, S. L., et al. (2000). Characteristics of memory dysfunction in body dysmorphic disorder. *Journal of the International Neuropsychological Society, 6*(6), 673–681.

DeMarco, L. M., Li, L. C., Phillips, K. A., & McElroy, S. L. (1998). Perceived stress in body dysmorphic disorder. *Journal of Nervous and Mental Diseases, 186,* 724–726.

First, M. B., Spitzer, R. L., Gibbon, M., & Williams, J. B. W. (1995). *Structured Clinical Interview for* DSM-IV *Axis I Disorders* (patient ed). New York: State Psychiatric Institute, Biometrics Research.

Geremia, G., & Neziroglu, F. (2001). Cognitive therapy in the treatment of body dysmorphic disorder. *Clinical Psychology and Psychotherapy, 8,* 243–251.

Grant, J. E., Kim, S. W., & Eckert, E. D. (2002). Body dysmorphic disorder in patients with anorexia nervosa: Prevalence, clinical features and delusionality of body image. *International Journal of Eating Disorders, 32*(3), 291–300.

Hollander, E. (Ed.). (1993). *Obsessive-compulsive related disorders.* Washington, DC: American Psychiatric Press.

Hollander, E., Allen, A., Kwon, J., Aronowitz, B., Schmeidler, J., Wong, C., et al. (1999). Clomipramine vs. desipramine crossover trial in body dysmorphic disorder: Selective efficacy of a serotonin reuptake inhibitor in imagined ugliness. *Archives of General Psychiatry, 56,* 1033–1039.

Hollander, E., Cohen, L. J., & Simeon, D. (1993). Body dysmorphic disorder. *Psychiatric Annals, 23,* 359–364.

Hollander, E., Cohen, L. J., & Simeon, D., et al. (1994). Fluvoxamine treatment of body dysmorphic disorder (letter). *Journal of Clinical Psychopharmacology, 14,* 75–77.

Hollander, E., Liebowitz, M. R., Winchel, R., Klumker, A., & Klein, D. F. (1989). Treatment of body dysmorphic disorder with serotonin reuptake blockers. *American Journal of Psychiatry, 146,* 768–770.

Hollander, E., & Wong, C. (1995). Introduction: Obsessive-compulsive spectrum disorders. *Journal of Clinical Psychiatry, 56*(4), 3–6.

Ishigooka, J., Iwao, M., Suzuki, M., Fukuyama, Y., Murasaki, M., & Miura, S. (1998). Demographic features of patients seeking cosmetic surgery. *Psychiatry of Clinical Neuroscience, 52,* 283–287.

Mayville, S., Katz, R. C., Gipson, M. T., & Cabral, K. (1999). Assessing the prevalence of body dysmorphic disorder in an ethnically diverse group of adolescents. *Journal of Child and Family Studies, 8,* 357–362.

McElroy, S. L., Phillips, K. A., & Keck, P. E., Jr. (1994). Obsessive-compulsive spectrum disorders. *Journal of Clinical Psychiatry, 55,* 33–51.

McKay, D. (1999). Two-year follow-up of behavioral treatment and maintenance for body dysmorphic disorder. *Behavioral Modification, 23,* 620–629.

Morselli, E. (1891). Sulla dismorfofobia e sulla tafefobia. *Bolletinno della R accademia di Genova, 6,* 110–119.

Neziroglu, F., McKay, D., Todaro, J., & Yaryura-Tobias, J. A. (1996). Effects of cognitive behavior therapy on persons with body dysmorphic disorder and comorbid Axis II diagnoses. *Behavior Therapy, 27,* 67–77.

Neziroglu, F., & Yaryura-Tobias, J. A. (1993). Exposure, response prevention, and cognitive therapy in the treatment of body dysmorphic disorder. *Behavior Therapy, 24,* 431–438.

Olivardia, R. (2001). Mirror, mirror on the wall, who's the largest of them all? *Harvard Review of Psychiatry, 9,* 254–259.

Olivardia, R., Pope, H. G., & Hudson, J. I. (2000). Muscle dysmorphia in male weightlifters: A case-control study. *American Journal of Psychiatry, 157,* 1291–1296.

O'Sullivan, R. L., Phillips, K. A., Keuthen, N. J., & Wilhelm, S. (1999). Near fatal skin picking from delusional body dysmorphic disorder responsive to fluvoxamine. *Psychosomatics, 40,* 79–81.

Otto, M. W., Wilhelm, S., Cohen, L. S., & Harlow, B. L. (2001). Prevalence of body dysmorphic disorder in a community sample of women. *American Journal of Psychiatry, 158*(12), 2061–2063.

Perugi, G., Akiskal, H. S., Giannotti, D., Frare, F., Divaio, S., & Cassano, G. B. (1997). Gender-related differences in body dysmorphic disorder (dysmorphophobia). *Journal of Nervous and Mental Diseases, 185,* 578–582.

Phillips, K. A. (1991). Body dysmorphic disorder: The distress of imagined ugliness. *American Journal of Psychiatry, 148,* 1138–1149.

Phillips, K. A. (1996a). Body dysmorphic disorder: Diagnosis and treatment of imagined ugliness. *Journal of Clinical Psychiatry, 57*(8), 61–64.

Phillips, K. A. (1996b). *The Broken mirror: Understanding and treating body dysmorphic disorder.* New York: Oxford University Press.

Phillips, K. A. (2000a). Quality of life for patients with body dysmorphic disorder. *Journal of Nervous and Mental Diseases, 188,* 170–175.

Phillips, K. A. (2000b). Pharmacologic treatment of body dysmorphic disorder: A review of empirical data and a proposed treatment algorithm. *Psychiatry Clinical North America, 7,* 59–82.

Phillips, K. A., Albertini, R. S., & Rasmussen, S. A. (2002). A randomized placebo-controlled trial of fluoxetine in body dysmorphic disorder. *Archives of General Psychiatry, 59*(4), 381–388.

Phillips, K. A., & Diaz, S. F. (1997). Gender differences in body dysmorphic disorder. *Journal of Nervous and Mental Diseases, 185,* 570–577.

Phillips, K. A., Dufresne, R. G., Jr., Wilkel, C. S., & Vittorio, C. (2000). Rate of body dysmorphic disorder in dermatology patients. *Journal of the American Academy of Dermatology, 42,* 436–444.

Phillips, K. A., Dwight, M. M., & McElroy, S. L. (1998). Efficacy and safety of fluvoxamine in body dysmorphic disorder. *Journal of Clinical Psychiatry, 59,* 165–171.

Phillips, K. A., Grant, J., Siniscalchi, J., & Albertini, R. S. (2001). Surgical and nonpsychiatric medical treatment of patients with body dysmorphic disorder. *Psychosomatics, 42*(6), 504–510.

Phillips, K. A., & McElroy, S. L. (1993). Insight, overvalued ideation, and delusional thinking in body dysmorphic disorder: Theoretical and treatment implications. *Journal of Nervous and Mental Diseases, 181,* 699–702.

Phillips, K. A., McElroy, S. L., Hudson, J. I., & Pope, H. G., Jr. (1995). Body dysmorphic disorder: An obsessive compulsive spectrum disorder, a form of affective spectrum disorder, or both? *Journal of Clinical Psychiatry, 56,* 41–51.

Phillips, K. A., McElroy, S. L., Keck, P. E., Jr., Pope, H. G., Jr., & Hudson, J. I. (1993). Body dysmorphic disorder: 30 cases of imagined ugliness. *American Journal of Psychiatry, 150,* 302–308.

Phillips, K. A., Nierenberg, A. A., Brendel, G., & Fava, M. (1996). Prevalence and clinical features of body dysmorphic disorder in atypical major depression. *Journal of Nervous and Mental Diseases, 184,* 125–129.

Phillips, K. A., Price, L. H., Greenberg, B. D., & Rasmussen, S. A. (2001). Should *DSM*'s diagnostic groupings be changed? In K. A. Phillips, M. B. First, & H. Pincus (Eds.), *Advancing DSM: Dilemmas in psychiatric diagnosis.* Washington, DC: American Psychiatric Press.

Phillips, K. A., Steketee, G., & Shapiro, L. (1996). *Parental bonding in OCD and body dysmorphic disorder.* New Research Program and Abstracts, American Psychiatric Association 149th annual meeting, New York.

Phillips, K. A., & Taub, S. L. (1995). Skin picking as a symptom of body dysmorphic disorder. *Psychopharmacology Bulletin, 31,* 279–288.

Pope, H. G., Jr., Gruber, A. J., Choi, P., Olivardia, R., & Phillips, K. A. (1997). Muscle dysmorphia: An underrecognized form of body dysmorphic disorder. *Psychosomatics, 38,* 548–557.

Pope, H. G., Jr., Katz, D. L., & Hudson, J. I. (1993). Anorexia nervosa and "reverse anorexia" among 108 male bodybuilders. *Comprehensive Psychiatry, 34*(6), 406–409.

Pope, H. G., Jr., Phillips, K. A., & Olivardia, R. (2000). *The Adonis complex: The secret crisis of male body obsession.* New York: Free Press.

Rosen, J. C., & Reiter, J. (1996). Development of the Body Dysmorphic Disorder Examination. *Behavior Research and Therapy, 34*(9), 755–766.

Rosen, J. C., Reiter, J., & Orosan, P. (1995). Cognitive-behavioral body image therapy for body dysmorphic disorder. *Journal of Consulting and Clinical Psychology, 63,* 263–269.

Sarwer, D. B., & Didie, E. R. (2002). Body image in cosmetic surgical and dermatological practice. In D. J. Castle & K. A. Phillips (Eds.), *Disorders of body image* (pp. 37–54). Hampshire, United Kingdom: Wrightson Biomedical Publishing Ltd.

Sarwer, D. B., Wadden, T. A., Pertschuk, M. J., & Whitaker, L. A. (1998). Body image dissatisfaction and body dysmorphic disorder in 100 cosmetic surgery patients. *Plastic Reconstructive Surgery, 101,* 1644–1649.

Simeon, D., Hollander, E., Stein, D. J., Cohen, L., & Aronowitz, B. (1995). Body dysmorphic disorder in the *DSM-IV* field trial for obsessive-compulsive disorder. *American Journal of Psychiatry, 152*(8), 1207–1209.

Thomas, C. S., & Goldberg, D. P. (1995). Appearance, body image and distress in facial dysmorphophobia. *Acta Psychiatrica Scandinavica, 92,* 231–236.

Veale, D. (2000). Outcome of cosmetic surgery and "DIY" surgery in patients with body dysmorphic disorder. *Psychiatric Bulletin, 24*(6), 218–221.

Veale, D. (2001). Cognitive behavior therapy for body dysmorphic disorder. *Advances in Psychiatric Treatment, 7,* 125–132.

Veale, D. (2002). Cognitive behavior therapy for body dysmorphic disorder. In D. J. Castle & K. A. Phillips (Eds.), *Disorders of body image* (pp. 121–138). Hampshire, England: Wrightson Biomedical.

Veale, D., Ennis, M., & Lambrou, C. (2002). Possible association of body dysmorphic disorder with an occupation or education in art and design. *American Journal of Psychiatry, 159,* 1788–1790.

Veale, D., Gournay, K., Dryden, W., Boocock, A., Shah, F., Willson, R., et al. (1996). Body dysmorphic disorder: A cognitive behavioral model and pilot randomized controlled trial. *Behavior Research and Therapy, 34,* 717–729.

Veale, D., & Riley, S. (2001). Mirror, mirror on the wall, who is the ugliest of them all? The psychopathology of mirror gazing in body dysmorphic disorder. *Behavior Research and Therapy, 39*(12), 1381–1393.

Wilhelm, S., Otto, M. W., Lohr, B., & Deckersbach, T. (1999). Cognitive behavior group therapy for body dysmorphic disorder: A case series. *Behavior Research and Therapy, 37,* 71–75.

Wolf, N. (1991). *The beauty myth.* New York: Doubleday.

PART IV

Special Topics

Chapter 27

SOCIOCULTURAL ASPECTS OF EATING DISORDERS

EILEEN P. ANDERSON-FYE AND ANNE E. BECKER

Sociocultural contributions to etiology for eating disorders are suggested by observational data (i.e., clinical, historical, and anthropological) associating specific features of social and cultural context with the presence of eating disorders or disordered eating and population data demonstrating cross-cultural and cross-ethnic variation in prevalence. In addition, a growing number of experimental and epidemiologic studies link suspected social and cultural risk factors with the increased prevalence of eating disorders. Finally, cross-cultural variation in the phenomenologic manifestations of anorexia nervosa has been reported, further suggesting cultural contributions to the pathogenesis of eating disorders. Despite these multiple lines of evidence supporting the role of sociocultural contributions to both prevalence and phenomenology of eating disorders, the specific mechanisms by which social and cultural contexts exert this influence remain incompletely understood.

Because prevention programs to date have drawn heavily on assumptions of the role of cultural context in shaping disordered eating attitudes and behaviors, an enhanced understanding of the ways in which cultural context contributes to risk among diverse populations is likely to strategically inform prevention efforts for eating disorders. Moreover, such advances will facilitate the development of culturally specific and sensitive therapeutic interventions. In this chapter, we review the observational, epidemiologic, and experimental data supporting the contributions of sociocultural factors to the etiology of eating disorders and suggest future directions for research in this area.

HISTORICAL PERSPECTIVE

Historical data suggest that the emergence of eating disorders as diagnostic entities was closely tied to cultural and social contexts. Moreover, a longitudinal perspective on prevalence supports that these disorders have become increasingly common over the past few decades. Notwithstanding the strong evidence of a genetic component to the etiology of eating disorders (Kendler et al., 1991; Strober, Freeman, Lampert, Diamond, & Kaye, 2000), these longitudinal data provide clear evidence of the importance of sociocultural contributions for risk for eating disorders given the rapid increase in prevalence over a short span of time. Anorexia nervosa was only first alluded to in the medical literature in 1689 by Morton in a description of two cases of "nervous consumption" (Silverman, 1997). A clinical syndrome consistent with anorexia nervosa was not described until the nineteenth century descriptions by Gull (1997), Lasegue (1997), and Marcé (Silverman, 1989). Clinical cases with clear bulimic symptoms were not described until 1903 (Pope, Hudson, & Mialet, 1985), and bulimia nervosa was not formally described as a syndrome until the late 1970s when Boskind-Lodhal reported on the "binge" component of "bulimarexia" (Boskind-Lodhal, 1976) and Russell then described bulimia nervosa (G. Russell, 1979). Since being established as diagnostic categories, eating disorders have appeared to become increasingly prevalent in Western nations among females of all ethnicities, class backgrounds, and age groups and among males.

Historical scholarship also links specific sociocultural contexts with disordered eating. For instance, references to self-starvation appear to have increased in the historical record after the spread of Christianity in Europe (Bemporad, 1996). Religious or ascetic fasting in the West has been recognized since the Middle Ages, though self-starvation linked to pursuit of thinness did not appear in the literature until the turn of the twentieth century (Brumberg, 1988). Before this time, anorexic behavior among females appears to have been linked with the achievement of specific goals such as freedom from restrictive social roles for women (Bell, 1985) or pursuit of spiritual purity (Yates, 1989). Religious or cultural emphasis on self-control has been linked with eating disorders in both historical (Bell, 1985; Bynum, 1988) and contemporary studies (Bruch, 1966; Rowland, 1970; Sykes, Leuser, Melia, & Gross, 1988), with Judeo-Christianity particularly implicated in both records. Psychological explanations for anorexia nervosa appeared in Freud's and Janet's work around the turn of the twentieth century (Bemporad, 1996). Social and familial context emerged as central to the pathogenesis of anorexia nervosa in Bruch's work (1966). Indeed, Bruch's clinical observations led to the (subsequently refuted) conventional wisdom that anorexia nervosa is an illness that specifically afflicts affluent White, high-achieving women. This clinical stereotype persisted until recently (Gard & Freeman, 1996) and may have been perpetuated by variations in help-seeking patterns, clinician bias (Becker, Franko, Speck, & Herzog, 2003), and other factors related to ethnic, racial, and class-based disparities in access to care.

EATING DISORDERS AMONG WORLD POPULATIONS

Although eating disorders appear to have global distribution—having been reported in Asia (Tsai, 2000), Africa (Hooper & Garner, 1986; Szabo & Hollands, 1997), the Middle East (Nasser, 1988), Latin America (Pumarino & Vivanco, 1982), the Caribbean (Hoek, van Harten, van Hoeken, & Susser, 1998), Pacific Island societies (Becker, Burwell, Gilman, Herzog, & Hamburg, 2002), and Eastern Europe (Steinhausen, 1984), in addition to North America and Western Europe—prevalence studies have found that they are less common in preindustrialized, non-Western societies than postindustrialized and Western societies. This cross-cultural variation in the prevalence of eating disorders further supports the role of sociocultural factors in their development. As noted previously, eating disorders were first reported in Western Europe and the United

States, and these societies have comparatively similar rates of anorexia and bulimia nervosa and binge eating disorder (Pike & Walsh, 1996). In addition, industrialized non-Western nations that participate in the global economy, such as Japan and Eastern European nations, have also been reported to have similar rates of eating disorders (Kuboki, Nomura, Ide, Suematsu, & Araki, 1996; Steinhausen, 1984).

CROSS-CULTURAL VARIATION IN PHENOMENOLOGY OF EATING DISORDERS

The cross-cultural comparison of eating disorders prevalence is complicated by evidence that the phenomenologic manifestations of anorexia nervosa vary with cultural context. Lee's seminal work in a Hong Kong Chinese population suggests that the "fat phobia" essential to establishing a diagnosis of anorexia nervosa in the *Diagnostic and Statistical Manual of Mental Disorders,* fourth edition *(DSM-IV)*, may be present in only a minority of subjects there (Lee, Ho, & Hsu, 1993). Likewise, Lee and colleagues found an absence of a uniform "drive for thinness" among Chinese clinical and nonclinical samples in Hong Kong in contrast to Western reports (Lee, 1991, 1995; Lee, Lee, Leung, & Yu, 1997). In addition, Lee (1994) identified cases of anorexia nervosa without the diagnostic criterion of "fat phobia" that otherwise exhibit the full-syndrome disorder in Hong Kong, India, Malaysia, Singapore, and Japan. Similarly, five cases of anorexia nervosa reported in India did not manifest the body image disturbance characteristic of Western anorexia nervosa (Khandelwal, Sharan, & Saxena, 1995). Moreover, in a comparison study between Indian and Canadian young women, though there were no differences between the groups on core features of eating disorders, the body image construct reported by both groups was found to be significantly different (Gupta, Chaturvedi, Chandarana, & Johnson, 2001).

Whereas some patients in Hong Kong and mainland China (Chun, Mitchell, Li, & Yu, 1992) do endorse the weight concerns that typify anorexia nervosa in the West, Lee posits that fat-phobic anorexia nervosa in Asia may reflect an assimilation of Western ideas rather than an indigenous symptom. With high levels of transnational migration of ideas, images, and peoples around the world (Appadurai, 1996), distinguishing between symptoms that are indigenous versus assimilated is sometimes difficult yet also central to culturally relevant clinical intervention. The apparent phenomenologic variation of anorexia nervosa strongly suggests that caution be exercised in investigating prevalence of eating disorders with screening instruments developed for Western populations. For example, a prevalence study using the Eating Attitudes Test (EAT) in a sample of 580 North Indian girls found that the subjects misinterpreted the questions (King & Bhugra, 1989).

In addition to concerns about cross-cultural and cross-linguistic validity of standard eating disorders assessment instruments, the *DSM-IV* diagnostic criteria specifying "excessive" concern with weight and body shape required for both anorexia and bulimia nervosa introduce a critical degree of cultural relativity into the diagnostic process. Finally, much of the cross-cultural work reports prevalence of disordered eating rather than of full-syndrome eating disorders. Although etiologic continuity is supported across a spectrum of eating disturbances in Western populations (Kendler et al., 1991; Walters & Kendler, 1995), the same relationship between symptoms and eating disorders cannot necessarily be assumed in other cultural contexts, particularly as to food and body-related attitudes and behaviors that are deeply culturally embedded. Future research investigating cultural salience, distress, and impairment associated with disordered eating will be critical to establishing their local clinical significance.

Asia

In East and Southeast Asia, eating disorders have been identified in China, Japan, Korea, Malaysia, Singapore, and Taiwan (Tsai, 2000). Notwithstanding reports about the difference in clinical presentation of anorexia nervosa in some areas of East and Southeast Asia (Kuboki et al., 1996), the phenomenology of anorexia nervosa in Japan (Tanaka, Kiriike, Nagata, & Riku, 2001) and Singapore (Ung, Lee, & Kua, 1997) appears similar to that reported in Western nations.

Anorexia and bulimia nervosa are reported in China, though the rates of both disorders appear to be lower than in Western nations (Lee, Chiu, & Chen, 1989; Lee, Hsu, & Wing, 1992). South Korea has been found to have similar rates of eating pathology as the United States (Lippincott & Hwang, 1999), though Korean Americans were found to have comparatively lower rates (Ko & Cohen, 1998). In addition, Kope and Sack (1987) reported on three cases of anorexia nervosa in Southeast Asian refugees. No studies we are aware of report rates of binge eating disorder (BED) in East or Southeast Asia. However, an illness predating reports of bulimia and BED that is characterized by binge eating, *Kibarashi-gui,* has been described in Japan (Nogami & Yabana, 1977). Finally, eating disorders have been reported in both India and Pakistan as well as in emigrant groups from both countries (Khandelwal et al., 1995; Mumford, Whitehouse, & Choudry, 1992; Mumford, Whitehouse, & Platts, 1991; Sjostedt, Schumaker, & Nathawat, 1998). Taken as a whole, the Asian data indicate the need for not only additional prevalence studies, but also continued rigorous qualitative, meaning-centered investigation into the pathogenesis of eating disorders.

Africa and the Middle East

Generally, with the exception of South Africa, there are few reports of eating disorders in Africa. Case reports combined with isolated student studies comprise much of the data concerning eating disorders in sub-Saharan Africa. In Nigeria, a 22-year-old woman was reported with anorexia nervosa in 1981 (Nwaefuna, 1981). A decade later, a study of female secondary and university students in Nigeria found that binge eating, vomiting, and laxative abuse are common, though the prevalence of full-syndrome bulimia nervosa was not assessed (Oyewumi & Kazarian, 1992). Laxative usage was found to be common in an ethnic Yoruba rural community in Nigeria, though the exact connection between this finding and disordered eating is unknown (Lewis & Kale, 1979). Also in the early 1980s, an upwardly mobile Black Zimbabwean woman reared in England was described with anorexia nervosa (Buchan & Gregory, 1984). Shortly afterwards, Hooper and Garner (1986) reported on a study of anorectic and bulimic behavior among White, Black, and mixed-race schoolgirls in Zimbabwe.

South Africa appears to have the highest prevalence of eating disorders in sub-Saharan Africa. Moreover, eating disorders there appear to be equally, if not more, common among non-Caucasian females than Caucasians. In a community-based prevalence study of secondary school-age girls, Szabo and Hollands (1997) found relatively high prevalence rates of abnormal eating attitudes among the entire sample. Black students reported a significantly higher prevalence figure (37.5%) when compared with their White counterparts (20.67%). Caradas and colleagues (Caradas, Lambert, & Charlton, 2001) found the prevalence of abnormal eating attitudes among schoolgirls to be high as well, though this study found equal occurrence among girls of varied ethnic backgrounds. In a study of 1,435 South African university students, Le Grange, Telch, and Tibbs (1998) found that Black students reported more disordered eating attitudes and bulimia than White, mixed-race, or Asian students. Further, this study found a comparable percentage of Black and Caucasian students who scored within a clinical range on test measures. Why Black students in South Africa appear to report relatively high levels of disordered eating is not clear, nor are there study distinctions drawn among Black ethnic subgroups.

In the Middle East, eating disorders or disordered eating have been reported in Egypt (Nasser, 1988, 1994), Iran (Nobakht & Dezhkam, 2000), Oman (Al-Adawi et al., 2002), and Israel (Mitrany, Lubin, Chetrit, & Modan, 1995). In Egypt, the prevalence of bulimia nervosa among high school girls is comparable to that in Western societies at 1.2% (Nasser, 1994). Similarly, in Tehran, Iran, schoolgirls were found to report eating disorders in rates equivalent to Western societies and more frequently than in other non-Western societies (Nobakht & Dezhkam, 2000). A recent study in Oman demonstrated that Omani teenagers scored significantly higher than non-Omani teenage subjects (i.e., British, Western European, and North American) on the EAT (Al-Adawi et al., 2002).

Full-syndrome eating disorders (Mitrany et al., 1995), partial-syndrome eating disorders (Stein, Meged, & Bar-Hanin, 1997), and disordered eating symptoms (Halevy & Halevy, 2000) also appear to be common in Israel. Anorexia and bulimia nervosa were assessed and found among female Israeli defense force recruits (Scheinberg et al., 1992). In addition, one study of a community sample of 534 female high school students in Israel reported a very high prevalence of partial syndrome eating disorders (using *DSM-III-R* criteria), identifying it in 20% of those surveyed (Stein et al., 1997). In a study of younger girls in Jerusalem, subjects were also found to have relatively high levels of disordered eating, with a significant increase between the sixth and seventh grades (Halevy & Halevy, 2000).

Latin America and the Caribbean

In Latin America and the Caribbean, formal epidemiologic data are missing for much of the region, though clinical and observational data indicate that the prevalence of eating disorders may be increasing. In Chile, 30 cases of eating disorders were reported in 1982 by Pumarino and Vivanco (1982). In 1987, the same authors concluded that eating disorders were increasingly prevalent in Chile (Pumarino & Vivanco, 1987). In Argentina, 10% to 30% of university women in one study reported dieting behaviors and 1.5% to 4% reported bingeing (Zuckerfeld, Fuchs, & Cormillot, 1988). Argentinean cultural values have emphasized a strong preference for slender women, and it appears that overweight women may be socially and economically penalized in Argentina, creating strong social pressure for thinness (Gordon, 2001), though these effects have not been empirically tested. Phenomenologically, 20 cases of anorexia nervosa reported on in Brazil looked similar to the Western presentation of the disorder (Negrao & Cordas, 1996). In Mexico, eating disorders are thought to be common and increasing, especially among urban, upwardly mobile, and university populations, though more data are needed to assess prevalence (Barriguette, 2002).

In the Caribbean, obesity has been identified as a public health problem for women (Scott, 1997), though anorexia and bulimia nervosa have not been much studied. In Belize, both a Central American and Caribbean nation, eating-disordered attitudes have been reported to span a range that includes pathology, though eating-disordered behaviors are as yet considered rare (Anderson-Fye, 2000). In a study of Belizean high school girls, eating attitudes and behaviors were found to be only moderately correlated, with disordered attitudes and behaviors not necessarily predictive of each other (Anderson-Fye, 2000). Those showing the most behavioral pathology were considered upwardly mobile and involved in the Western-focused tourism industry (Anderson-Fye, 2002). In the most sophisticated incidence study in the region, Hoek and colleagues (1998) found an annual incidence of anorexia nervosa of 2.6 per 100,000 women in Curaçao. Though this rate is comparable to Western rates, the disorders were found only among Creole, upwardly mobile women, not among Black women (Hoek, 2002). In Santo Domingo, Dominican Republic, a survey of health care providers concerning their patients indicated that eating disorders are present with possibly increasing prevalence, though the wealthiest patients traveled to the United States or Europe for treatment (Vasquez, 2002). Binge eating disorder has not been studied in the Caribbean, though ethnographic accounts suggest that it may be present (Anderson-Fye, 2002).

Small-Scale, Indigenous Populations

The occurrence of eating disorders in small-scale societies relatively isolated from Western influence are of interest in understanding the relationship between Western cultural contexts and disordered eating. In the Azores, a small Atlantic volcanic island group belonging to Portugal, low prevalence of eating disorders was found despite higher rates on mainland Portugal (DeAzevedo & Ferriera, 1992). Its relative isolation was credited as a protective factor. Similarly, before the introduction of television and concomitant rapid modernization in Fiji, eating disorders were reported to be rare or nonexistent among Fijians, a small-scale indigenous population in Melanesia (Becker, 1995). On the other hand, binge eating and binge eating disorder occur in Fijian women at rates comparable to Western populations (Becker et al., 2002). Although there is some evidence that the occurrence of binge eating in Fiji may be related to acculturated attitudes toward body shape there, the correlates of binge eating are similar to those reported in Western populations (Becker et al., 2002).

EATING DISORDERS AMONG ETHNIC MINORITY POPULATIONS

Contrary to initial reports that eating disorders predominantly occur among Caucasian populations (Bruch, 1966), ethnic minority groups in Western nations appear to have approximately equivalent rates of eating disorders and disordered eating. In fact, some groups, including Native American girls (J. E. Smith & Krejci, 1991), Latinas (Robinson et al., 1996), and Afro-Caribbean (Reiss, 1996) and Asian (Dolan, Lacey, & Evans, 1990) women in Britain, have been reported to have even higher rates of eating pathology than non-Latino Whites in the same regions. One major limitation of much of the research on ethnic minorities and eating concerns is the conflation of multiple distinct subgroups into a unitary category such as "Asian American" or "Hispanic." Such homogeneous categories may miss important distinctions between groups that might better identify eating disorder patterns and risk factors.

Though the data on Native Americans are scarce, they suggest that this group may have the highest risk for eating disorders of any U.S. ethnic minority group. Crago and colleagues found eating disturbances to be more common among Native Americans than among Caucasians, African Americans, Latinos, or Asian Americans (Crago, Shisslak, & Estes, 1996). J. E. Smith and Krejci (1991) also found comparatively high rates of eating pathology among Native American youth. Among Native Americans, Yates (1989) found eating pathology to be more common in those who left the reservation than those who remained; this finding resonates with other data suggesting that social transition may contribute to risk for disordered eating.

Latina adolescent and adult populations have been found to have prevalence rates of bulimia nervosa and anorexia nervosa comparable to or greater than non-Latina White rates (Pemberton, Vernon, & Lee, 1996; Pumariega, 1986; Rhea, 1999; Rosen & Gross, 1987). Similarly, rates of BED are reported to be as high or higher among Latinas than African American or non-Latino White women (Bruce & Agras, 1992; Fitzgibbon et al., 1998). Despite the similar rates of eating disorders, Latina girls and women have also been found to report preferences for larger body size (Winkleby, Gardner, & Taylor, 1996) and indicate less concern about weight than non-Latino White women (Crago et al., 1996). This paradoxical finding raises interesting questions about the relationship between body size ideals and behavioral eating pathology, suggesting that eating disorders may develop despite a range of body size preferences and concerns about weight.

When compared with non-Latino White samples, anorexia nervosa is reported to be less common among African American girls and women (Andersen & Hay, 1985; Crago et al., 1996; Root, 1990). By contrast, comparative data concerning the prevalence of eating disorders and disordered eating attitudes and behaviors among African American women are mixed. Though some studies have reported that African American women are less likely than Caucasian women to exhibit bulimic symptoms or develop bulimia (Gray, Ford, & Kelly, 1987), others report equivalent rates of the disorder (Field, Colditz, & Peterson, 1997; Le Grange, Telch, & Tibbs, 1998; B. Thompson, 1992). Laxative and diuretic abuse appear to be higher in African American samples than in Whites (Emmons, 1992; Field et al., 1997; Pumariega, Gustavson, Gustavson, Stone Motes, & Ayers, 1994), though the data on self-induced vomiting are mixed with some studies reporting lower rates (Emmons, 1992) and some higher (Field et al., 1997). One study reported drive for thinness to also be higher among preadolescent Black girls when compared with non-Latino White girls (Striegel-Moore, Schreiber, Pike, Wilfley, & Rodin, 1995). BED appears to be at least as prevalent among African American as White women in both clinical and community samples (D. E. Smith, Marcus, Lewis, Fitzgibbon, & Schreiner, 1998; Spitzer et al., 1993; Striegel-Moore, Wilfley, Pike, Dohm, & Fairburn,

2000; Yanovski, Gormally, Leser, Gwirtsman, & Yanovski, 1994; Yanovski, Nelson, Dubbert, & Spitzer, 1993).

Eating disorders among Asian Americans are not well studied, but generally suggest that disordered eating behaviors and attitudes are less prevalent in this population than others. Data are limited by the tendency to collapse distinctive ethnic subgroupings together for analysis. Lucero and colleagues found that Caucasian college women were more than five times as likely than Asian American college women to report disordered eating attitudes (Lucero, Hicks, Bramlette, Brassington, & Welter, 1992). Similarly, Crago and colleagues (1996) found Asian American girls to be less likely to report eating disturbances than African Americans, non-Latino Whites, Latinas, or Native Americans. Another study found a low prevalence of eating disorders among Korean Americans (Ko & Cohen, 1998). On the other hand, a study of 969 non-Latino White, Latina, and Asian American middle school students found Asian American girls to have higher body dissatisfaction than White girls but lower body dissatisfaction than Latinas (Robinson et al., 1996). In both Britain (Dolan, Lacey, & Evans, 1990) and Australia (Sjostedt et al., 1998), East Indian girls have been found to be at greater risk for disordered eating than their Caucasian counterparts, though this group has not been studied in the United States.

Studies investigating cross-ethnic rates of dieting have shown mixed results. Several demonstrate that those of ethnic minority backgrounds—African American, Latina, Russian, Ghanaian, Asian—were less likely to report restrained eating than their non ethnic minority White counterparts (Cogan, Bhalla, Sefa-Dedeh, & Rothblum, 1996; Neff, Sargent, McKeown, Jackson, & Valois, 1997; Neumark-Sztainer, Story, Falkner, Beuhring, & Resnick, 1999; Rucker & Cash, 1992; Stevens et al., 1997; Tsai, 2000). Moreover, African American and Latino high school students were not only less likely than non-Latino Whites to diet and exercise but also more likely to report weight gain behavior (Stevens et al., 1997). In the same vein, Asian women reported restrained eating and body dissatisfaction half as often as Caucasians (Khandelwal et al., 1995). On the other hand, others demonstrate high levels of weight loss behaviors among ethnic minority groups. For example, a cross-sectional descriptive study of Navajo Indians found that one-half of the women were trying to lose weight (White et al., 1997). A cross-sectional comparison of African American and White girls found that after adjusting for BMI, there were no significant racial differences in attempts to lose weight or the practice of chronic dieting. More African American girls were, however, trying to gain weight (Schreiber et al., 1996). A prospective, longitudinal study of African American and White girls found that the African American subjects were more than twice as likely to engage frequently in the targeted weight-related eating practices (McNutt et al., 1997). Though dieting and weight loss behaviors do not necessarily lead to eating disorders, they appear to increase risk of developing the disorders (Daee et al., 2002).

Additional research investigating the prevalence and phenomenology of eating disorders among ethnic minorities is needed. There have not been large-scale community studies in the United States with enough ethnic minority participants to assess risk for anorexia nervosa. Moreover, studies indicate that clinician bias against referring those who belong to ethnic minority groups for eating disorder treatment may in fact contribute to an underreporting of the disorders in clinical populations (Becker et al., 2003). Finally, differences in help-seeking patterns and pathways to care among ethnic minority populations (Good, James, Good, & Becker, 2002) may continue to contribute to the stereotype that eating disorders are more common among non-Latino Whites.

There has not been empirical support for the hypothesis that ethnic minorities are relatively protected from developing eating disorders because they belong to cultures that do not overvalue thinness and may in fact value more robust body shapes. The impact of ethnicity on eating disorders pathogenesis and risk remains understudied. In particular, because individuals often negotiate multiple overlapping cultural contexts with conflicting values and goals, cultural factors enhancing risk for disordered eating are challenging to identify.

SOCIOECONOMIC INFLUENCES ON EATING DISORDERS AND DISORDERED EATING

Individual socioeconomic status (SES) within a nation has been thought to be related to preference for thinness and eating disorder prevalence, though the empirical data are varied as to how. Much research has claimed a link between higher SES and increased risk of disordered eating across ethnicity (Andersen & Hay, 1985; Bruch, 1966; Drewnowski, Kurth, & Krahn, 1994; Hart & Ollendick, 1985; Silber, 1986). In contrast, some data show no association between higher SES and increased eating disorders (Gard & Freeman, 1996; Gray et al., 1987), and yet other data display an inverse relationship where females of lower SES exhibit more disordered eating (Pope, Champoux, & Hudson, 1987; B. Thompson, 1992). Bulimia nervosa may be associated with a wider variety of SES backgrounds than anorexia (Gard & Freeman, 1996; Pike & Walsh, 1996). Rogers and colleagues (Rogers, Resnick, Mitchell, & Blum, 1997) found a positive association between SES and dieting behaviors in community samples, but no SES association to clinically significant eating disorders. Similarly, Story and colleagues (1991) found a positive association between SES and dieting behaviors among 36,000 adolescents in schools but also less pathological eating behaviors among higher SES students. Such studies raise questions about clinical versus nonclinical samples and SES. Review of the research confirms that eating disorders are found in all SES groups, with no group being exempt (Davis & Yager, 1992).

EATING DISORDERS IN OCCUPATIONAL, ATHLETIC, AND GAY SUBCULTURES

Certain subcultures have been found to have higher rates of eating disorders than the general population. For example, a higher prevalence of eating disorders has been found among ballet dancers, models, skaters, gymnasts, rowers, jockeys, and wrestlers (Braisted, Mellin, Gong, & Irwin, 1985; Garfinkel & Garner, 1982; Garner, Rosen, & Barry, 1998; Green, 2001; King & Mezey, 1987; Le Grange et al., 1994; Rucinski, 1989; Sundgot-Borgen, 1999; Thiel, Gottfried, & Hesse, 1993). These data strongly suggest that social pressures for thinness or weight control enhance risk for eating disorders in multiple ways. Occupational rituals such as weigh-ins and strict weight classes overtly aim to manage weight (Thiel et al., 1993). More subtly, preferences for thinner bodies and tight competition may influence drive for thinness (Ryan, 2000). In addition, several of these athletic subcultural groups recruit young people before the pubescent growth spurt. The conflict between adolescents experiencing the physical maturation processes of puberty and strict sport requirements is thought to increase risk of eating disorders (Braisted et al., 1985; Garner et al., 1998).

Likewise, gay men have been found to have higher rates of disordered eating than heterosexual men (Carlat, Camargo, & Herzog, 1997; C. J. Russell & Keel, 2002). In a clinic-based study, 42% of men treated for bulimia nervosa in a fifteen-year period were gay, suggesting a particular link between bulimia and homosexuality among men (Siever, 1994). In a population-based study of adolescents, gay males were more likely to report poor body image, frequent dieting, binge eating, and purging behaviors compared with heterosexual males. The exact mechanisms that raise risk in this subculture across age groups are unknown, though some have speculated that emphasis on appearance (Siever, 1994; Silberstein, Mishkind, Striegel-Moore, Timko, & Rodin, 1989), increased feminine characteristics (Meyer, Blissett, & Oldfield, 2001), and increased stress from sexual minority status (Stronski Huwiler & Remafedi, 1998) may contribute to risk. The fact that subcultures with a particular emphasis on control of body shape and weight report higher prevalence of eating disorders than the general population provides additional evidence for the central role of sociocultural factors in eating disorder etiology.

CULTURAL DYNAMICS, WESTERN CULTURE, AND EATING DISORDERS

The historical, cross-cultural, cross-ethnic, and subcultural differences in the prevalence of eating disorders and disordered eating attitudes and behaviors provide incontrovertible evidence that social and cultural contexts contribute to risk for eating disorders. However, an understanding of mechanisms by which social and cultural contexts may directly pose risk or moderate other risk factors is incomplete. For example, although there is a rich social science literature speculating on how Western culture may contribute to risk for disordered eating (Bordo, 1990; Turner, 1984), many of these theories remain empirically unevaluated. However, some compelling epidemiological and experimental data suggest channels by which cultural factors may contribute to risk. Of these, cultural body ideals that favor thinness, exposure to print and televised media, cultural and social transition, and modernization (Becker et al., 2002; Stice, Maxfield, & Wells, in press) have emerged as leading cultural factors, which will require further investigation to establish their role.

Much of the literature and theory on how cultural context promotes risk for disordered eating is based on an early model, which presumes the internalization of a cultural valuation of thinness and subsequent body dissatisfaction that, in turn, may lead to disordered eating (Garner & Garfinkel, 1980; Stice, Schupak-Neuberg, Shaw, & Stein, 1994; Striegel-Moore, Silberstein, & Rodin, 1986). Thinness likely gained popularity as a North American cultural ideal in the early twentieth century after the romanticization of tuberculosis (Sontag, 1979), the institutionalization of American beauty culture through commercial products and motion pictures, and ready-to-wear clothing—which standardized sizes—and advertising, both of which encouraged women to compare themselves with one another (Bordo, 1990; Brumberg, 1988; Lasch, 1978); and actual fear of fatness emerged as a rationale for food refusal associated with anorexia nervosa after 1930 (Lee, 1995; Selvini-Palazzoli, 1985). This preoccupation with fatness versus thinness has arguably been linked with aesthetic body ideals for women in the United States over the ensuing century. In a now classic study, Garner and colleagues (1980) showed that Miss America contestants and *Playboy* centerfolds gradually became thinner over time—perhaps both mirroring and propagating a value of slenderness among women—and paralleled an increase in prevalence of eating disorders in the United States. Other experimental research has documented that social pressure to be thin indeed increases body dissatisfaction (Stice et al., in press). Such data have been the basis of intervention programs in the United States with varying degrees of success (Austin, 2000, 2001).

Conversely, several investigators have proposed that culture-specific body aesthetic ideals that favor larger body size may be protective against eating disorders (El-Sarrag, 1968; Furnham & Baguma, 1994). For example, in a comparative study between Ugandan and British subjects, the Ugandans preferred heavier bodies (Furnham & Baguma, 1994). Similarly, British Kenyans rated larger body shapes more favorably and smaller body shapes less favorably when compared with Asian British and Anglo-British (Furnham & Alibhai, 1983). In Northern Sudan, where chronic undernourishment is a problem, large bodies are considered attractive, and anorexia nervosa is rare (El-Sarrag, 1968). From a psychocultural view historically and contemporaneously, it is thought that the individual rejection of food exists mainly in context of abundance of food, and conversely, that scarcity of food would protect against the choice of food restriction as a psychopathological mechanism of control. However, because the relationship among body ideals, body satisfaction, and disordered eating appears to vary with ethnicity, it does not appear that disparities in body shape ideals can necessarily explain differences in prevalence of disordered eating. For instance, whereas Latina girls and women have been found to report larger aesthetic body ideals (Winkleby et al., 1996) and less concern about weight than non-Latino Whites (Crago et al., 1996), research suggests equivalent rates of disordered eating among non-Latino White and Latino youth (Crago et al., 1996; J. E. Smith & Krejci, 1991). On the other hand, the lower likelihood of dieting at each developmental milestone noted in African American women when compared with Caucasian women was found to be less because of less social pressure about their weight (Striegel-Moore, Wilfley, Caldwell, Needham, & Brownell, 1996). Similarly, another study reported that African Americans demonstrated less strict criteria for perceiving fatness than Whites, who reported more eating restraint and disordered eating (Rucker & Cash, 1992).

ADDITIONAL CULTURAL FACTORS RELEVANT TO DISORDERED EATING

Although much of the early research in sociocultural influences on disordered eating has focused on cross-cultural and cross-ethnic differences in body aesthetic ideals as a primary means by which cultural difference contributes to risk, pathways to disordered eating may stem from other culturally embedded attitudes and practices concerning dietary patterns, body image, and body ethics. For example, the motivation to reshape the body as a means of representing personal qualities may be uniquely characteristic of mainstream North American culture (Becker, 1994). In other cultures, relatively more emphasis is placed on *care* of the body (i.e., attention to nurturing, grooming, or style) rather than on its appearance (Becker, 1995; Rubin, Fitts, & Becker, in press).

Numerous observational and experimental studies have demonstrated an association between reported media exposure and changes in body image (Becker et al., 2002; Field, Camargo, Taylor, Berkey, & Colditz, 1999; Harrison & Cantor, 1997; Irving, 1990; Richins, 1991; Stice et al., 1994; Tiggemann & Pickering, 1996). Because of the difficulty of isolating the effects of media exposure on young women in Western societies in which individuals have been chronically exposed, mechanisms by which media exposure may contribute to risk for disordered eating have not been well understood. Much of this research has been based on the theoretical premise that exposure to idealized images of beauty in the media stimulates social comparison (Festinger, 1954) and potential body image disturbance or dissatisfaction (J. K. Thompson & Heinberg, 1993). However, data from a study investigating effects of the introduction of television to Fiji have also suggested alternative plausible hypotheses. For example, narrative data from Fijian teenage study subjects indicated that girls wished to lose weight to enhance social and economic opportunities that they perceived accompanied a thin body (Becker et al., 2002). Although extrapolation from this study population requires caution, an association between upward mobility and disordered eating has been demonstrated in other study populations. For example, studies have demonstrated an association between upward mobility and eating disorders among African Americans, Latinos (Silber, 1986), Native Americans (Yates, 1989), and Asians in the United States (Soomro, Crisp, Lynch, Tran, & Joughin, 1995). Likewise, efforts to attain a higher socioeconomic status were associated with eating disorders among Afro-Caribbean women in Britain (Soomro, Crisp, Lynch, Tran, & Joughin, 1995). Moreover, in other non-Western societies— Zimbabwe (Buchan & Gregory, 1984) and Belize (Anderson-Fye, 2000)—upward mobility has also been associated with disordered eating. To the extent that girls and young women perceive that social status is enhanced by positioning themselves competitively through the informed use of cultural symbols—for example, by bodily appearance and thinness (Becker & Hamburg, 1996)—adolescent girls and young women may model their appearance on media images. This is particularly problematic for children in immigrant families for whom the usual parental "map of experience" is lacking and who may substitute alternative "cultural guides" from the media as resources for negotiating successful social strategies in a new environment (Suárez-Orozco & Suárez-Orozco, 2001). These studies further support the hypothesis that disordered eating may stem from efforts to enhance social status in some girls and women.

CULTURAL TRANSITION: GLOBALIZATION, ACCULTURATION, AND ASSIMILATION

A growing number of studies have documented the association of cultural and social transition with disordered eating attitudes and behaviors and eating disorders. Societies experiencing globalizing cultural change as well as individuals undergoing emigration from developing or non-Western nations to developed, Western nations appear to be particularly vulnerable to heightened risk for eating disorders. Several sophisticated studies have compared rates of disordered eating among adolescents and young women residing in their country of origin with those who have immigrated to a Western society. Immigration to a Western society has been shown to enhance risk for eating disorders. For example, female South Asian immigrants to Britain were found to have more disordered eating attitudes than their counterparts who did not immigrate (Mumford et al., 1991, 1992). Among the Pakistani immigrant girls, the girls classified as more traditional had a greater risk of eating-disordered behavior (Mumford et al., 1991), in contrast to other studies that demonstrate a higher prevalence of disordered eating associated with increasing Westernization. The stress associated with simultaneous negotiation of multiple cultures and presumably gender role expectations might be related to increased risk of body image and eating disturbance as it seems to be in the historical record. In a comparative study of matched samples of Arab undergraduate students in London and Cairo, Nasser (1986) found higher prevalence of disordered eating attitudes and six cases of bulimia nervosa in the British sample compared with lower prevalence and no cases of bulimia in the Egyptian sample. On the other hand, one comparative study between traditional women in Iran with little exposure to Western cultures and those who had immigrated to the United States (Los Angeles) found no differences in prevalence of disordered eating, indicating that exposure to Western culture did not appear to affect disordered eating attitudes and behaviors in this population (Abdollahi & Mann, 2001). Qualitative examination of the disordered eating within the two groups may provide additional information as to whether Western cultural exposure may influence disordered eating in ways other than its prevalence, for example, its phenomenologic manifestations.

Significant exposure to Western cultural ideas, values, and images appears to increase risk for eating disorders and disordered eating, at least among young females, in most places where this has been studied. Westernization has been associated with reported increases in eating disorders and disordered eating in Egypt (Nasser, 1994), Hong Kong (Lee, 1996), India (King & Bhugra, 1989), Japan (Suematsu, Ishikawa, Kuboki, & Ito, 1985), Malaysia (Buchrich, 1981), Pakistan (Choudry & Mumford, 1992), Fiji (Becker et al., 2002), and Zimbabwe (Hooper & Garner, 1986), along with other nations. *Western culture* here is defined as those core cultural values, morés, and ideas attributable to Western Europe and the United States and characterizing mainstream dominant North American culture. The aforementioned Fijian data speak dramatically to the profound impact of assimilation on disordered eating behaviors and attitudes. Among the schoolgirls in this study, narrative data showed their behaviors and attitudes to be not only a pursuit of aesthetic ideals but also an emulation of the television characters' dramatized lives and attainments via achievement of similar body types (Becker et al., 2002). The illusion that television characters accessed glamorous lifestyles through having a particular appearance appears to have been enough to undermine longstanding and deeply held cultural values supporting robust body size and appetites. Indeed, data from this study demonstrate that in addition to the impact of imported Western media images, cultural values that can moderate risk for eating disorders may be assimilated, such as positive regard for youth and beauty, an emphasis on "work" on the body as a legitimate and important pursuit, and the very belief that bodies *can* be reshaped (Becker, 1995).

In Curaçao, Hoek and colleagues (1998) found that the incidence of eating disorders among the upwardly mobile Creole population was comparable to that of Western populations. It is interesting that anorexia nervosa was absent in the Black population of the same locale (Hoek, 2002). In contrast, multiple studies in South Africa have found the Black population to be at greatest risk, though arguably, this population is undergoing social transition and is struggling for upward mobility and societal assimilation (Caradas et al., 2001; Le Grange et al., 1998; Szabo & Hollands, 1997). In a rapidly developing area of Belize, Anderson-Fye (2002) found the most upwardly mobile schoolgirls with direct economic ties to the burgeoning tourism industry to report the most eating-disordered behaviors in the sample, though the attitudes of these same girls were not considered disordered. This finding was in contrast to the bulk of the population of high school girls in which attitudes were significantly more disordered than behaviors, suggesting that cases of behavior associated with a full-syndrome eating disorder may look different from a normative shift in eating attitudes among a population undergoing social transition. In an interesting immigration comparison, Fichter and colleagues (Fichter, Weyerer, Sourdi, & Sourdi, 1983) found Greek women in their homeland to idealize dieting and slenderness more than their counterparts who immigrated to Munich, Germany. However, the prevalence of anorexia nervosa was higher in the Munich sample, which the authors felt was attributable to stresses of immigration and cultural change.

In a recent study in the United States, stress associated with acculturation superimposed on body dissatisfaction was found to place U.S. minority women at greater risk for bulimic symptoms (Perez, Voelz, Pettit, & Joiner, 2002). On the other hand, the lack of acculturative stress was a potential buffer to bulimic symptoms for Black and Latina women, even with the presence of body dissatisfaction. Only one study reported more disordered eating attitudes among women in the country of origin, South Korea, when compared with Korean American immigrants (Ko & Cohen, 1998). These studies point to the convincing role of cultural change and immigration in increasing risk of eating disorders and also implicate at least some aspects of Westernization specifically. Moreover, because technological advances are helping to perpetuate cultural transmission and change globally at an increasing rate (Appadurai, 1996), eating disorders in these situations are likely to remain a growing problem and need to be studied more closely. Finally, though many argue that Westernization is a key component of widespread eating disorders (Boyadjieva & Steinhausen, 1996; Brumberg, 1988; Bryant-Waugh & Lask, 1991; Garner & Garfinkel, 1980), the extent to which the introduction specifically of Western cultural values, lifestyles, and epistemologies in the processes of development affects the pathogenesis of eating disorders remains unclear.

It can be difficult to tease out industrialization as distinct from cultural Westernization, and others have argued that *modernization,* not simply Westernization, contributes to the development of eating disorders in a society. Specifically, food abundance, changing weight norms, material affluence, and transitioning social roles for women have been suggested as social factors contributing to risk for eating disorders in East Asia (Lee, 1996). Partially consistent with this view, Appels (1986) suggests that it is cultural conflict created in postindustrial societies that underlies the genesis of anorexia in a given culture. The almost uniformly higher prevalence of eating disorders in urban areas compared with rural areas—with a more pronounced urban-rural difference in developing nations—supports this hypothesis (Gordon, 2001; Hoek et al., 1995; Kuboki et al.,

1996; Rathner & Messner, 1993; Sjostedt et al., 1988; Story et al., 1991). In developed, Western nations, the differences tend to be less pronounced (Rathner & Messner, 1993; Story et al., 1991). Only one comparative study reviewed reported significantly more disordered eating attitudes among rural than urban college women in India (Sjostedt et al., 1998). However, migration into urban areas likely poses additional complex social stressors that potentially contribute to disordered eating and require further evaluation.

GENDER AND FEMINIST PERSPECTIVES

Girls and women account for 90% to 95% of those with anorexia and bulimia nervosa, indicating the gendered nature of the disorders (Andersen & Holman, 1997). Several theoretical accounts have been offered to account for this empirical finding. One widely embraced hypothesis suggests that anorexic behavior may represent the negotiation of personal and bodily control in a social context that otherwise relatively restricts opportunities for autonomy among young women. This struggle is ultimately expressed through extreme efforts to control an individual's body, a restraint that ironically escalates out of control into disorder (Bruch, 1966; Orbach, 1979). Therefore, it follows that eating disorders commonly begin in the developmental period of adolescence, when girls encounter the weight of social limitations of gender socialization and sexism in Western nations just as their bodies are changing with sexual maturation (Gilligan, Lyons, & Hamner, 1992; B. Thompson, 1994).

Increased risk of eating disorders in some contexts seems to be associated with gender role conflict for girls and women, especially in the midst of multiple and sometimes contradictory demands (Bruch, 1966; Perlick & Silverstein, 1994; Raphael & Lacey, 1992). Girls who strive for perfection, particularly in the midst of irreconcilable demands such as aggressive achievement and feminine demureness, are thought to be at greatest risk (Steiner-Adair, 1992). This hypothesis is further supported by data from numerous studies demonstrating that risk for disordered eating is increased in situations in which alternatives to traditional female role activities are introduced through media or migration (Anderson-Fye, 2002; Mumford et al., 1991, 1992). Slenderness among girls and women across many societies arguably provides resolution of the dilemma between a wish to be successful in both traditionally and nontraditionally feminine arenas.

Moreover, on a societal level, feminist scholars have examined a link between women's increasing public and economic power in the United States and thinner, less curvaceous ideals of beauty as portrayed in the media (Bordo, 1993). For example, a causal relationship has been posited between women's increasing success outside the home and more restrictive standards of beauty. Women must then expend more effort to meet the tighter ideals, just as they have less flexibility in time to do so (Orbach, 1979; Steiner-Adair, 1992). In one empirical study looking at the relationship between women's success and thin ideals, a negative correlation was found between the proportion of women in the United States with higher education and the curvaceousness of women's bodies in *Vogue* and *Playboy* magazines (Barber, 1998). The ideal woman then becomes one who can erase much of her femininity via extreme thinness but then is ironically preoccupied with this bodily pursuit of reducing herself in a show of hyperfemininity (Bordo, 1993; Seid, 1989). Some have even suggested that the ultimate resolution to these dilemmas of femininity through manipulation and discipline of the "docile body" is death due to starvation (Bordo, 1990).

The "tyranny of slenderness" (Chernin, 1981) and the industries of diet, exercise, drugs, and surgery built around it (Bordo, 1990) have been argued to trap women in an ever-escalating expenditure of money, time, and effort ultimately gaining them little but ill health. More restrictive and insidious than their predecessors such as corsets, these contemporary industries of bodily manipulation and control are paired with an intense cultural fear of fatness (Orbach, 1979). Thinness and fatness have become imbued with moral overtones where many women would do anything to avoid becoming fat, with its concomitant associations of ugliness, laziness, and even moral ineptitude (Orbach, 1979). From this perspective, eating disorders are not solely a patient's problem but also require alteration of sociocultural context to provide an environment in which healthy bodies—not thin bodies necessarily—are valued. Feminist perspectives have been instrumental in shifting the focus on thinness as an aesthetic ideal from an individual to a social preoccupation (Orbach, 1979). This reframe relocates the pathology in a social context and suggests that social remedies must be used alongside individual therapies to address the sociocultural roots of the disorders.

CONCLUSION

Cross-cultural, cross-ethnic, and historical differences in the prevalence of eating disorders and disordered eating support the significant role of sociocultural context in contributing to and moderating risk. Epidemiologic studies demonstrating the association of immigration into a Western society and conflict between Western and traditional cultural ideas and values with disordered eating also provide compelling evidence of the impact of cultural context on the development of disordered eating attitudes and behaviors. In addition, experimental studies investigating the effects of social pressure to be thin and of exposure to media images that provoke social comparison suggest some mechanisms by which social and cultural context may contribute to risk.

Notwithstanding the substantial epidemiologic evidence linking cultural and social contexts to eating disorders and disordered eating, the specific mechanisms by which these contexts contribute risk for eating disorders remain incompletely understood. Moreover, despite the theoretically appealing social science and feminist literature on putative cultural mechanisms leading to body image and eating disorders, the hypotheses suggested in this literature remain largely unevaluated by empirical studies. Future research will need to bridge the gap between epidemiologic data and social science-based theory by integrating perspectives from epidemiology, psychology, psychiatry, and anthropology, and by using both epidemiologic and qualitative approaches. Such research will undoubtedly contribute to a more nuanced and empirically supported understanding of how social and cultural context contribute to risk for eating disorders. This enhanced understanding of the etiology of eating disorders can strategically inform therapeutic interventions and prevention efforts. Especially in light of increasingly rapid transnational movement of ideas, images, and people, understanding both the incidence and risk factors for the development of eating disorders is crucial to rendering intervention and prevention efforts more culturally sensitive, appropriate, and effective in the United States and abroad. Finally, contributions to risk that are based in social context may require social policy remedies rather than the individually based approach most often taken with prevention and treatment efforts.

REFERENCES

Abdollahi, P., & Mann, T. (2001). Eating disorder symptoms and body image concerns in Iran: Comparisons between Iranian women in Iran and in America. *International Journal of Eating Disorders, 30*(3), 259–268.

Al-Adawi, S., Dorvlo, A. S., Burke, D. T., Al-Bahlani, S., Martin, R. G., & Al-Ismaily, S. (2002). Presence and severity of anorexia and bulimia among male and female Omani and non-Omani adolescents. *Journal of the American Academy of Child and Adolescent Psychiatry, 41*(9), 1124–1130.

Andersen, A. E., & Hay, A. (1985). Racial and socioeconomic influences in anorexia nervosa and bulimia. *International Journal of Eating Disorders, 4*(4), 479–487.

Andersen, A. E., & Holman, J. E. (1997). Males with eating disorders: Challenges for treatment and research. *Psychopharmacology Bulletin, 33*(3), 391–397.

Anderson-Fye, E. P. (2000). *Self-reported eating attitudes among high school girls in Belize: A quantitative survey.* Unpublished qualifying paper, Harvard University, Cambridge, MA.

Anderson-Fye, E. P. (2002). *Never leave yourself: Belizean schoolgirls' psychological development in cultural context.* Unpublished doctoral dissertation, Harvard University, Cambridge, MA.

Appadurai, A. (1996). *Modernity at large: Cultural dimensions of globalization.* Minneapolis: University of Minnesota.

Appels, A. (1986). Culture and disease. *Social Science and Medicine, 23,* 477–483.

Austin, S. B. (2000). Prevention research in eating disorders: Theory and new directions. *Psychological Medicine, 30*(6), 1249–1262.

Austin, S. B. (2001). Population-based prevention of eating disorders: An application of the Rose prevention model. *Preventive Medicine, 32*(3), 268–283.

Barber, N. (1998). The slender ideal and eating disorders: An interdisciplinary "telescope" model. *International Journal of Eating Disorders, 23,* 295–307.

Barriguette, M. J. A. (2002). Culturas distintas: Modelo Inter-Cultural para la observación de conductas, prevención y tratamiento de los trastornos de la alimentación [Different cultures: Intercultural model for the observation of behavior, prevention and treatment of eating disorders]. In L. Rojo (Ed.), *Anorexia nervosa desde sus orígenes a su tratamiento* [Anorexia nervosa from its origins to its treatment]. Madrid, Spain: Planeta.

Becker, A. E. (1994). Nurturing and negligence: Working on others' bodies in Fiji. In T. J. Csordas (Ed.), *Embodiment and experience* (pp. 100–115). Cambridge, MA: Cambridge University.

Becker, A. E. (1995). *Body, self, and society: The view from Fiji.* Philadelphia: University of Pennsylvania.

Becker, A. E., Burwell, R., Gilman, S. E., Herzog, D., & Hamburg, P. (2002). Eating behaviors and attitudes following prolonged exposure to television among ethnic Fijian adolescent girls. *British Journal of Psychiatry, 180,* 509–514.

Becker, A. E., Franko, D., Speck, A., & Herzog, D. B. (2003). Ethnicity and differential access to care for eating disorder symptoms. *International Journal of Eating Disorders, 33,* 205–212.

Becker, A. E., & Hamburg, P. (1996). Culture, the media, and eating disorders. *Harvard Review of Psychiatry, 4*(3), 163–167.

Bell, W. (1985). *Holy anorexia.* Chicago: University of Chicago Press.

Bemporad, J. R. (1996). Self-starvation through the ages: Reflections on the prehistory of anorexia nervosa. *International Journal of Eating Disorders, 19*(3), 217–237.

Bordo, S. (1990). Reading the slender body. In M. Jacobus, E. F. Keller, & S. Shuttleworth (Eds.), *Body/politics: Women and the discourses of science* (pp. 83–112). New York: Routledge.

Bordo, S. (1993). *Unbearable weight: Feminism, Western culture, and the body.* Berkeley: University of California.

Boskind-Lodhal, M. (1976). Cinderella's stepsisters: A feminist perspective on anorexia nervosa and bulimia. *Signs, 2,* 342–356.

Boyadjieva, S., & Steinhausen, H. C. (1996). The eating attitudes test and the eating disorders inventory in four Bulgarian clinical and nonclinical samples. *International Journal of Eating Disorders, 19*(1), 93–98.

Braisted, J. R., Mellin, L., Gong, E. J., & Irwin, C. E., Jr. (1985). The adolescent ballet dancer: Nutritional practices and characteristics associated with anorexia nervosa. *Journal of Adolescent Health Care, 6*(5), 365–371.

Bruce, B., & Agras, W. S. (1992). Binge eating in females: A population-based investigation. *International Journal of Eating Disorders, 12,* 365–373.

Bruch, H. (1966). Anorexia nervosa and its differential diagnosis. *Journal of Nervous and Mental Disorders, 141,* 555–566.

Brumberg, J. (1988). *Fasting girls: The history of anorexia nervosa.* New York: Penguin Books.

Bryant-Waugh, R., & Lask, B. (1991). Anorexia nervosa in a group of Asian children living in Britain. *British Journal of Psychiatry, 158,* 229–233.

Buchan, T., & Gregory, L. D. (1984). Anorexia nervosa in a Black Zimbabwean. *British Journal of Psychiatry, 145,* 326–330.

Buchrich, N. (1981). Frequency of presentation of anorexia nervosa in Malaysia, Australia, and New Zealand. *Journal of Psychiatry, 15,* 153–155.

Bynum, C. (1988). *Holy feast and holy fast: The religious significance of food to Medieval women.* Berkeley: University of California.

Caradas, A. A., Lambert, E. V., & Charlton, K. E. (2001). An ethnic comparison of eating attitudes and associated body image concerns in adolescent South African schoolgirls. *Journal of Human Nutrition and Dietetics, 14*(2), 111–120.

Carlat, D. J., Camargo, C. A., Jr., & Herzog, D. B. (1997). Eating disorders in males: A report on 135 patients. *American Journal of Psychiatry, 154*(8), 1127–1132.

Chernin, K. (1981). *The obsession: Reflections on the tyranny of slenderness.* New York: Harper & Row.

Choudry, I., & Mumford, D. (1992). A pilot study of eating disorders in Mirpur (Pakistan) using an Urdu version of the Eating Attitudes Test. *International Journal of Eating Disorders, 11,* 243–251.

Chun, Z. F., Mitchell, J. E., Li, K., & Yu, W. M. (1992). The prevalence of anorexia nervosa and bulimia nervosa among freshman medical college students in China. *International Journal of Eating Disorders, 12,* 209–214.

Cogan, J. C., Bhalla, S. K., Sefa-Dedeh, A., & Rothblum, E. D. (1996). A comparison study of, U.S., & African students on perceptions of obesity and thinness. *Journal of Cross Cultural Psychology, 27,* 98–113.

Crago, M., Shisslak, C. M., & Estes, L. S. (1996). Eating disturbances among American minority groups: A review. *International Journal of Eating Disorders, 19*(3), 239–248.

Daee, A., Robinson, P., Lawson, M., Turpin, J. A., Gregory, B., & Tobias, J. D. (2002). Psychologic and physiologic effects of dieting in adolescents. *Southern Medical Journal, 95*(9), 1032–1041.

Davis, C., & Yager, J. (1992). Transcultural aspects of eating disorders: A critical literature review. *Culture, Medicine and Psychiatry, 16*(3), 377–394.

DeAzevedo, M. H. P., & Ferriera, C. P. (1992). Anorexia nervosa and bulimia: A prevalence study. *Acta Psychiatrica Scandinavica, 86,* 432–436.

Dolan, B., Lacey, J. H., & Evans, C. (1990). Eating behavior and attitudes to weight and shape in British women from three ethnic groups. *British Journal of Psychiatry, 157,* 523–528.

Drewnowski, A., Kurth, C., & Krahn, D. (1994). Body weight and dieting in adolescence: Impact of socioeconomic status. *International Journal of Eating Disorders, 16*(1), 61–65.

El-Sarrag, M. E. (1968). Psychiatry in the Northern Sudan: A study in comparative psychiatry. *British Journal of Psychiatry, 11*(4), 946–948.

Emmons, L. (1992). Dieting and purging behavior in Black and White high school students. *Journal of the American Dietetic Association, 92*(3), 306–312.

Festinger, L. (1954). A theory of social comparison processes. *Human Relations, 7,* 117–140.

Fichter, M. W., Weyerer, S., Sourdi, L., & Sourdi, Z. (1983). The epidemiology of anorexia nervosa: A comparison of Greek adolescents living in Germany and Greek adolescents living in Greece. In P. L. Darby, P. E. Garfinkel, D. M. Garner, & D. V. Coscina (Eds.), *Anorexia nervosa: Recent developments in research* (pp. 95–105). New York: Alan R. Liss.

Field, A. E., Camargo, C. A., Jr., Taylor, C. B., Berkey, C. S., & Colditz, G. A. (1999). Relation of peer and media influences to the development of purging behaviors among preadolescent and adolescent girls. *Archives of Pediatrics and Adolescent Medicine, 153*(11), 1184–1189.

Field, A. E., Colditz, G. A., & Peterson, K. E. (1997). Racial/ethnic and gender differences in concern with weight and in bulimic behaviors among adolescents. *Obesity Research, 5*(5), 447–454.

Fitzgibbon, M. L., Spring, B., Avellone, M. E., Blackman, L. R., Pinitore, R., & Stolley, M. R. (1998). Correlates of binge eating in Hispanic, Black, and White women. *International Journal of Eating Disorders, 24*(1), 43–52.

Furnham, A., & Alibhai, N. (1983). Cross-cultural differences in the perception of female body shapes. *Psychological Medicine, 13*(4), 829–837.

Furnham, A., & Baguma, P. (1994). Cross-cultural differences in the evaluation of male and female body shapes. *International Journal of Eating Disorders, 15,* 81–89.

Gard, M., & Freeman, C. (1996). The dismantling of a myth: A review of eating disorders and socioeconomic status. *International Journal of Eating Disorders, 20*(1), 1–12.

Garfinkel, P. E., & Garner, D. M. (1982). *Anorexia nervosa: A multidimensional perspective.* New York: Brunner/Mazel.

Garner, D. M., & Garfinkel, P. E. (1980). Sociocultural factors in the development of anorexia nervosa. *Psychological Medicine, 10*(4), 647–656.

Garner, D. M., Rosen, L. W., & Barry, D. (1998). Eating disorders among athletes: Research and recommendations. *Child and Adolescent Psychiatric Clinics of North America, 7*(4), 839–857.

Gilligan, C., Lyons, N., & Hamner, T. (Eds.). (1992). *Making connections: The relational worlds of adolescent girls at Emma Willard school.* Cambridge, MA: Harvard University Press.

Good, M. J. D., James, C., Good, B. J., & Becker, A. E. (2002). The culture of medicine and racial, ethnic and class disparities in health care. In B. Smedley, A. Y. Stith, & A. R. Nelson (Eds.), *Unequal treatment: Confronting racial and ethnic disparities in health care.* Report to Institute of Medicine Committee on Understanding and Eliminating Racial and Ethnic Disparities in Health Care. Washington, DC: National Academy Press.

Gordon, R. A. (1990). *Anorexia and bulimia: Anatomy of a social epidemic.* Cambridge, MA: Blackwell.

Gordon, R. A. (2001). Eating disorders East and West: A culture-bound syndrome unbound. In M. Nasser, M. Katzman, & R. Gordon (Eds.), *Eating disorders and cultures in transition* (pp. 1–16). East Sussex, England: Brunner-Routledge.

Gray, J., Ford, K., & Kelly, L. (1987). The prevalence of bulimia in a Black college population. *International Journal of Eating Disorders, 6*(6), 733–740.

Green, E. L. (2001). Cognitive occupational hazards and psychopathology of the artist. *Occupational Medicine, 16*(4), 679–687.

Gull, W. W. (1997). Anorexia nervosa (1868 historical reprint). *Obesity Research, 5*(5), 498–502.

Gupta, M. A., Chaturvedi, S. K., Chandarana, P. C., & Johnson, A. M. (2001). Weight-related body image concerns among 18–24 year-old women in Canada and India: An empirical comparative study. *Journal of Psychosomatic Research, 50,* 193–198.

Halevy, N., & Halevy, A. (2000). Eating disorders in early adolescence: Study from the section on young adolescent nutrition in Jerusalem. *Harefuah, 138*(7), 523–531, 616.

Harrison, K., & Cantor, J. (1997). The relationship between media consumption and eating disorders. *Journal of Communication, 47,* 40–67.

Hart, K. J., & Ollendick, T. H. (1985). Prevalence of bulimia in working and university women. *American Journal of Psychiatry, 142*(7), 851–854.

Hoek, H. W. (2002). *The occurrence of eating disorders at Curacao.* Boston: Academy for Eating Disorders International Conference on Eating Disorders.

Hoek, H. W., Bartelds, A. I., Bosveld, J. J., van der Graaf, Y., Limpens, V. E., Maiwald, M., et al. (1995). Impact of urbanization on detection rates of eating disorders. *American Journal of Psychiatry, 152*(9), 1272–1278.

Hoek, H. W., van Harten, P. N., van Hoeken, D., & Susser, E. (1998). Lack of relation between culture and anorexia nervosa: Results of an incidence study on Curaçao. *New England Journal of Medicine, 338*(17), 1231–1232.

Hooper, M., & Garner, D. (1986). Application of the Eating Disorders Inventory to a sample of Black, White, and mixed race schoolgirls in Zimbabwe. *International Journal of Eating Disorders, 5,* 161–168.

Irving, L. M. (1990). Mirror images: Effects of the standard of beauty on the self- and body-esteem of women exhibiting varying levels of bulimic symptoms. *Journal of Social and Clinical Psychology, 9,* 230–242.

Kendler, K. S., MacLean, C., Neale, M., Kessler, R., Heath, A., & Eaves, L. (1991). The genetic epidemiology of bulimia nervosa. *American Journal of Psychiatry, 148*(12), 1627–1637.

Khandelwal, S. K., Sharan, P., & Saxena, S. (1995). Eating disorders: An Indian perspective. *International Journal of Social Psychiatry, 41,* 132–146.

King, M. B., & Bhugra, D. (1989). Eating disorders: Lessons from a cross-cultural study. *Psychological Medicine, 19,* 955–958.

King, M. B., & Mezey, G. (1987). Eating behavior of male racing jockeys. *Psychological Medicine, 17*(1), 249–253.

Ko, C., & Cohen, H. (1998). Intraethnic comparison of eating attitudes in native Koreans and Korean Americans using a Korean translation of the eating attitudes test. *Journal of Nervous and Mental Diseases, 186*(10), 631–636.

Kope, T. M., & Sack, W. H. (1987). Anorexia nervosa in Southeast Asian refugees: A report on three cases. *Journal of the American Academy of Child and Adolescent Psychiatry, 26*(5), 795–797.

Kuboki, T., Nomura, S., Ide, M., Suematsu, H., & Araki, S. (1996). Epidemiological data on anorexia nervosa in Japan. *Psychiatry Research, 62,* 11–16.

Lasch, C. (1978). *The culture of narcissism: American life in an age of diminishing expectations.* New York: Norton.

Lasegue, E. (1997). On hysterical anorexia (1873 historical reprint). *Obesity Research, 5*(5), 492–497.

Lee, S. (1991). Anorexia nervosa in Hong Kong: A Chinese perspective. *Psychological Medicine, 21*(3), 703–711.

Lee, S. (1994). The Diagnostic Interview Schedule and anorexia nervosa in Hong Kong. *Archives of General Psychiatry, 51,* 251–252.

Lee, S. (1995). Self-starvation in context: Toward a culturally sensitive understanding of anorexia nervosa. *Social Science and Medicine, 41*(1), 25–36.

Lee, S. (1996). Reconsidering the status of anorexia nervosa as a Western culture-bound syndrome. *Social Science Medicine, 42*(1), 21–34.

Lee, S., Chiu, H. F., & Chen, C. N. (1989). Anorexia nervosa in Hong Kong: Why not more in Chinese? *British Journal of Psychiatry, 154,* 683–688.

Lee, S., Ho, T. P., & Hsu, L. K. (1993). Fat phobic and nonfat phobic anorexia nervosa: A comparative study of 70 Chinese patients in Hong Kong. *Psychological Medicine, 23,* 999–1017.

Lee, S., Hsu, L. K., & Wing, Y. K. (1992). Bulimia nervosa in Hong Kong Chinese patients. *British Journal of Psychiatry, 161,* 545–551.

Lee, S., Lee, A. M., Leung, T., & Yu, H. (1997). Psychometric properties of the Eating Disorders Inventory (EDI-1) in a nonclinical Chinese population in Hong Kong. *International Journal of Eating Disorders, 21*(2), 187–194.

Le Grange, D., Telch, C. F., & Tibbs, J. (1998). Eating attitudes and behaviors in 1,435 South African Caucasian and non-Caucasian college students. *American Journal of Psychiatry, 155*(2), 250–254.

Le Grange, D., Tibbs, J., & Noakes, T. D. (1994). Implications of a diagnosis of anorexia nervosa in a ballet school. *International Journal of Eating Disorders, 15*(4), 369–376.

Lewis, E. A., & Kale, O. O. (1979). Laxative usage in a Yoruba rural community. *Nigerian Medical Journal, 9*(4), 449–452.

Lippincott, J. A., & Hwang, H. S. (1999). On cultural attitudes toward eating of women students in Pennsylvania and South Korea. *Psychological Reports, 85,* 701–702.

Lucero, K., Hicks, R. A., Bramlette, J., Brassington, G. S., & Welter, M. G. (1992). Frequency of eating problems among Asian and Caucasian college women. *Psychological Reports, 71*(1), 255–258.

McNutt, S. W., Hu, Y., Schreiber, G. B., Crawford, P. B., Obarzanek, E., & Mellin, L. (1997). A longitudinal study of the dietary practices of Black and White girls 9 and 10 years old at enrollment: The NHLBI Growth and Health Study. *Journal of Adolescent Health, 20*(1), 27–37.

Meyer, C., Blissett, J., & Oldfield, C. (2001). Sexual orientation and eating psychopathology: The role of masculinity and femininity. *International Journal of Eating Disorders, 29*(3), 314–318.

Mitrany, E., Lubin, F., Chetrit, A., & Modan, B. (1995). Eating disorders among Jewish female adolescents in Israel: A 5-year study. *Journal of Adolescent Health, 16*(6), 454–457.

Mumford, D. B., Whitehouse, A. M., & Choudry, I. (1992). Survey of eating disorders in English-medium schools in Lahore, Pakistan. *International Journal of Eating Disorders, 11,* 173–184.

Mumford, D. B., Whitehouse, A. M., & Platts, M. (1991). Sociocultural correlates of eating disorders among Asian schoolgirls in Bradford. *British Journal of Psychiatry, 158,* 222–228.

Nasser, M. (1986). Comparative study of the prevalence of abnormal eating attitudes among Arab female students of both London and Cairo universities. *Psychological Medicine, 16*(3), 621–625.

Nasser, M. (1988). Eating disorders: The cultural dimension. *Social Psychiatry and Psychiatric Epidemiology, 23*(3), 184–187.

Nasser, M. (1994). Screening for abnormal eating attitudes in a population of Egyptian secondary school girls. *Social Psychiatry and Psychiatric Epidemiology, 29*(1), 25–30.

Neff, L. J., Sargent, R. G., McKeown, R. E., Jackson, K. L., & Valois, R. F. (1997). Black and white differences in body size perceptions and weight management practices among adolescent females. *Journal of Adolescent Health, 20,* 459–465.

Negrao, A. B., & Cordas, T. A. (1996). Clinical characteristics and course of anorexia nervosa in Latin America, a Brazilian sample. *Psychiatry Research, 62*(1), 17–21.

Neumark-Sztainer, D., Story, M., Falkner, N. H., Beuhring, T., & Resnick, M. D. (1999). Sociodemographic and personal characteristics of adolescents engaged in weight loss and weight/muscle gain behaviors: Who is doing what? *Preventive Medicine, 28*(1), 40–50.

Nobakht, M., & Dezhkam, M. (2000). An epidemiological study of eating disorders in Iran. *International Journal of Eating Disorders, 28*(3), 265–271.

Nogami, Y., & Yabana, F. (1977). On Kibarashi-gui. *Japanese Journal of Psychiatry and Neurology, 31,* 159–166.

Nwaefuna, A. (1981). Anorexia nervosa in a developing country. *British Journal of Psychiatry, 138,* 270–271.

Orbach, S. (1979). *Fat is a feminist issue.* New York: Berkeley Books.

Oyewumi, L. K., & Kazarian, S. S. (1992). Abnormal eating attitudes among a group of Nigerian youths. I: Bulimic behavior. *East African Medical Journal, 69,* 663–666.

Pemberton, A., Vernon, S., & Lee, E. S. (1996). Prevalence and correlates of bulimia nervosa and bulimic behaviors in a racially diverse sample of undergraduate students in two universities in Southeast Texas. *American Journal of Epidemiology, 144*(5), 450–455.

Perez, M., Voelz, Z. R., Pettit, J. W., & Joiner, T. E., Jr. (2002). The role of acculturative stress and body dissatisfaction in predicting bulimic symptomatology across ethnic groups. *International Journal of Eating Disorders, 31*(4), 442–454.

Perlick, D., & Silverstein, B. (1994). Faces of female discontent: Depression, disordered eating, and changing gender roles. In P. Fallon, M. Katzman, & S. Wooley (Eds.), *Feminist perspectives on eating disorders* (pp. 77–93). New York: Guilford Press.

Pike, K. M., & Walsh, B. T. (1996). Ethnicity and eating disorders: Implications for incidence and treatment. *Psychopharmacology Bulletin, 32*(2), 265–274.

Pope, H. G., Jr., Champoux, R. F., & Hudson, J. I. (1987). Eating disorder and socioeconomic class: Anorexia nervosa and bulimia in nine communities. *Journal of Nervous and Mental Diseases, 175*(10), 620–623.

Pope, H. G., Jr., Hudson, J. I., & Mialet, J. P. (1985). Bulimia in the late nineteenth century: The observations of Pierre Janet. *Psychological Medicine, 15*(4), 739–743.

Pumariega, A. J. (1986). Acculturation and eating attitudes in adolescent girls: A comparative and correlational study. *Journal of the American Academy of Child Psychiatry, 25*(2), 276–279.

Pumariega, A. J., Gustavson, C. R., Gustavson, J. C., Stone Motes, P. S., & Ayers, S. (1994). Eating attitudes in African American women: The Essence eating disorders survey. *Eating Disorders, 2*, 5–16.

Pumarino, H., & Vivanco, N. (1982). Anorexia nervosa: Medical and psychiatric characteristics of 30 cases. *Revista Medica de Chile, 110*(11), 1081–1092.

Pumarino, H., & Vivanco, N. (1987). Appetite and eating disorders: An increasing pathology? *Revista Medica de Chile, 115*(8), 785–787.

Raphael, F. J., & Lacey, J. H. (1992). Sociocultural aspects of eating disorders. *Annals of Medicine, 24*, 293–296.

Rathner, F., & Messner, K. (1993). Detection of eating disorders in a small rural town: An epidemiological study. *Psychological Medicine, 23*, 175–184.

Reiss, D. (1996). Abnormal eating attitudes and behaviors in two ethnic groups from a female British urban population. *Psychological Medicine, 26*, 289–299.

Rhea, D. J. (1999). Eating disorder behaviors of ethnically diverse urban female adolescent athletes and nonathletes. *Journal of Adolescence, 22*(3), 379–388.

Richins, M. L. (1991). Social comparison and the idealized images of advertising. *Journal of Consumer Research, 18*, 71–83.

Robinson, T. N., Killen, J. D., Litt, I. F., Hammer, L. D., Wilson, D. M., Haydel, K. F., et al. (1996). Ethnicity and body dissatisfaction: Are Hispanic and Asian girls at increased risk for eating disorders? *Journal of Adolescent Health, 19*(6), 384–393.

Rogers, L., Resnick, M., Mitchell, J., & Blum, R. (1997). The relationship between socioeconomic status and eating-disordered behaviors in a community sample of adolescent girls. *International Journal of Eating Disorders, 22*, 15–23.

Root, M. P. P. (1990). Disordered eating in women of color. *Sex Roles, 22*(7/8), 525–536.

Rosen, J. C., & Gross, J. (1987). Prevalence of weight reducing and weight gaining in adolescent girls and boys. *Health Psychology, 6*(2), 131–147.

Rowland, C. (1970). Anorexia nervosa: A survey of the literature and review of 30 cases. *International Psychiatry Clinics, 7*(1), 37–137.

Rubin, L., Fitts, M., & Becker, A. E. (in press). Whatever feels good in my soul: Body ethics and aesthetics among African American and Latina women. *Culture, Medicine and Psychiatry, 27*(1), 49–75.

Rucinski, A. (1989). Relationship of body image and dietary intake of competitive ice skaters. *Journal of the American Dietetic Association, 89*(1), 98–100.

Rucker, C. E., & Cash, T. F. (1992). Body images, body-size perceptions, and eating behaviors among African American and White college women. *International Journal of Eating Disorders, 3*, 291–299.

Russell, C. J., & Keel, P. K. (2002). Homosexuality as a specific risk factor for eating disorders in men. *International Journal of Eating Disorders, 31*(3), 300–306.

Russell, G. (1979). Bulimia nervosa: An ominous variant of anorexia nervosa. *Psychological Medicine, 9*(3), 429–448.

Ryan, J. (2000). *Little girls in pretty boxes: The making and breaking of elite gymnasts and figure skaters.* New York: Warner Books.

Scheinberg, Z., Bleich, A., Koslovsky, M., Apter, A., Mark, M., Kotler, B. M., et al. (1992). Prevalence of eating disorders among female Israel defense force recruits. *Harefuah, 123*(3/4), 73–78, 156.

Schreiber, G. B., Robins, M., Striegel-Moore, R., Obarzanek, E., Morrison, J. A., & Wright, D. J. (1996). Weight modification efforts reported by Black and White preadolescent girls: National Heart, Lung, and Blood Institute Growth and Health Study. *Pediatrics, 98*(1), 63–70.

Scott, G. (1997). Health needs of Caribbean women: Challenges for the nineties. In E. Leo-Rhynie, B. Bailey, & C. Barrow (Eds.), *Gender: A Caribbean multi-disciplinary perspective* (pp. 243–251). Kingston, Jamaica: Ian Randle.

Seid, R. P. (1989). *Never too thin: Why women are at war with their bodies.* New York: Prentice-Hall.

Selvini-Palazzoli, M. S. (1985). Anorexia nervosa: A syndrome of the affluent society. *Transcultural Psychiatric Research Review, 22,* 199–204.

Siever, M. D. (1994). Sexual orientation and gender as factors in socioculturally acquired vulnerability to body dissatisfaction and eating disorders. *Journal of Consulting and Clinical Psychology, 62*(2), 252–260.

Silber, T. J. (1986). Anorexia nervosa in Blacks and Hispanics. *International Journal of Eating Disorders, 5*(1), 121–128.

Silberstein, L. R., Mishkind, M. E., Striegel-Moore, R. H., Timko, C., & Rodin, J. (1989). Men and their bodies: A comparison of homosexual and heterosexual men. *Psychosomatic Medicine, 51*(3), 337–346.

Silverman, J. A. (1989). Louis-Victor Marcé, 1828–1864: Anorexia nervosa's forgotten man. *Psychological Medicine, 19*(4), 833–835.

Silverman, J. A. (1997). Charcot's comments on the therapeutic role of isolation in the treatment of anorexia nervosa. *International Journal of Eating Disorders, 21*(3), 295–298.

Sjostedt, J. P., Schumaker, J. F., & Nathawat, S. S. (1998). Eating disorders among Indian and Australian university students. *Journal of Social Psychology, 138*(3), 351–357.

Smith, D. E., Marcus, M. D., Lewis, C., Fitzgibbon, M., & Schreiner, P. (1998). Prevalence of binge eating disorder, obesity, and depression in a biracial cohort of young adults. *Annals of Behavioral Medicine, 20,* 227–232.

Smith, J. E., & Krejci, J. (1991). Minorities join the majority: Eating disturbances among Hispanic and Native American youth. *International Journal of Eating Disorders, 10*(2), 179–186.

Sontag, S. (1979). *Illness as metaphor.* New York: Vintage Books.

Soomro, G. M., Crisp, A. H., Lynch, D., Tran, D., & Joughin, N. (1995). Anorexia nervosa in "non-White" populations. *British Journal of Psychiatry, 167,* 385–389.

Spitzer, R. L., Yanovski, S., Wadden, T., Wing, R., Marcus, M. D., Stunkard, A., et al. (1993). Binge eating disorder: Its further validation in a multisite study. *International Journal of Eating Disorders, 13,* 137–153.

Stein, D., Meged, S., & Bar-Hanin, T. (1997). Partial eating disorders in a community sample of female adolescents. *Journal of the American Academy of Child and Adolescent Psychiatry, 36*(8), 1116–1123.

Steiner-Adair, C. (1992). The body politic: Normal female adolescent development and the development of eating disorders. In C. Gilligan, N. Lyons, & T. Hamner (Eds.), *Making connections: The relational worlds of adolescent girls at Emma Willard school* (pp. 162–182). Cambridge, MA: Harvard University Press.

Steinhausen, H. C. (1984). Transcultural comparison of eating attitudes in young females and anorectic patients. *Archiv für Psychiatrie und Nervenkrankheiten, 234*(3), 198–201.

Stevens, J., Alexandrov, A. A., Smimova, S. G., Deev, A. D., Gershunskaya, Y. B., David, C. E., et al. (1997). Comparison of attitudes and behaviors related to nutrition, body size, dieting, and hunger in Russian, Black Americans, and White American adolescents. *Obesity Research, 5,* 227–236.

Stice, E., Maxfield, J., & Wells, T. (in press). Adverse effects of social pressure to be thin on young women: An experimental investigation of the effects of "fat talk." *International Journal of Eating Disorders.*

Stice, E., Schupak-Neuberg, E., Shaw, H. E., & Stein, R. I. (1994). Relation of media exposure to eating disorder symptomatology: An examination of mediating mechanisms. *Journal of Abnormal Psychology, 103*(4), 836–840.

Story, M., Rosenwinkel, K., Himes, J., Resnick, M., Harris, L. J., & Blum, R. W. (1991). Demographic and risk factors associated with chronic dieting in adolescents. *American Journal of Diseases in Children, 145,* 994–998.

Striegel-Moore, R. H., Schreiber, G. B., Pike, K. M., Wilfley, D. E., & Rodin, J. (1995). Drive for thinness in Black and White preadolescent girls. *International Journal of Eating Disorders, 18*(1), 59–69.

Striegel-Moore, R. H., Silberstein, L. R., & Rodin, J. (1986). Toward an understanding of risk factors for bulimia. *American Psychologist, 41,* 246–263.

Striegel-Moore, R. H., Wilfley, D. E., Caldwell, M. B., Needham, M. L., & Brownell, K. D. (1996). Weight-related attitudes and behaviors of women who diet to lose weight: A comparison of Black dieters and White dieters. *Obesity Research, 4*(2), 109–116.

Striegel-Moore, R. H., Wilfley, D. E., Pike, K. M., Dohm, F. A., & Fairburn, C. G. (2000). Recurrent binge eating in Black American women. *Archives of Family Medicine, 9*(1), 83–87.

Strober, M., Freeman, R., Lampert, C., Diamond, J., & Kaye, W. (2000). Controlled family study of anorexia nervosa and bulimia nervosa: Evidence of shared liability and transmission of partial syndromes. *American Journal of Psychiatry, 157*(3), 393–401.

Stronski Huwiler, S. M., & Remafedi, G. (1998). Adolescent homosexuality. *Advances in Pediatrics, 45,* 107–144.

Suárez-Orozco, C., & Suárez-Orozco, M. (2001). *Children of immigration.* Cambridge, MA: Harvard University Press.

Suematsu, H., Ishikawa, H., Kuboki, T., & Ito, T. (1985). Statistical studies on anorexia nervosa in Japan: Detailed clinical data on 1,011 patients. *Psychotherapy and Psychosomatics, 43,* 96–103.

Sundgot-Borgen, J. (1999). Eating disorders among male and female elite athletes. *British Journal of Sports Medicine, 33*(6), 434.

Sykes, D. K., Jr., Leuser, B., Melia, M., & Gross, M. (1988). A demographic analysis of 252 patients with anorexia nervosa and bulimia. *International Journal of Psychosomatics, 35*(1/4), 5–9.

Szabo, C. P., & Hollands, C. (1997). Abnormal eating attitudes in secondary-school girls in South Africa: A preliminary study. *South African Medical Journal, 87*(Suppl. 4), 524–526, 528–530.

Tanaka, H., Kiriike, N., Nagata, T., & Riku, K. (2001). Outcome of severe anorexia nervosa patients receiving inpatient treatment in Japan: An 8-year follow-up study. *Psychiatry and Clinical Neuroscience, 55,* 389–396.

Thiel, A., Gottfried, H., & Hesse, F. W. (1993). Subclinical eating disorders in male athletes. A study of the low weight category in rowers and wrestlers. *Acta Psychiatrica Scandinavica, 88*(4), 259–265.

Thompson, B. (1992). "A way outa no way": Eating problems among African American, Latina, and White women. *Gender and Society, 6*(4), 546–561.

Thompson, B. (1994). Food, bodies, and growing up female: Childhood lessons about culture, race, and class. In P. Fallon, M. Katzman, & S. Wooley (Eds.), *Feminist perspectives on eating disorders* (pp. 355–378). New York: Guilford Press.

Thompson, J. K., & Heinberg, L. J. (1993). Preliminary test of two hypotheses of body image disturbance. *International Journal of Eating Disorders, 14*(1), 59–63.

Tiggemann, M., & Pickering, A. S. (1996). The role of television in adolescent women's body dissatisfaction and drive for thinness. *International Journal of Eating Disorders, 20,* 199–203.

Tsai, G. (2000). Eating disorders in the Far East. *Eating and Weight Disorders, 5,* 183–197.

Turner, B. (1984). *The body and society: Explorations in social theory.* Oxford, England: Blackwell.

Ung, E. K., Lee, S., & Kua, E. H. (1997). Anorexia and bulimia: A Singapore perspective. *Singapore Medical Journal, 38,* 332–335.

Vasquez, J. P. (2002). *Informe sobre los trastornos de la conducta alimenatia en Republica Dominicana* [Report on the eating disordered behavior in the Dominican Republic]. In Annual Report of Hispanoamerica Special Interest Group, Academy of Eating Disorders, McLean, VA.

Walters, E. E., & Kendler, K. S. (1995). Anorexia nervosa and anorexic-like syndromes in a population-based female twin sample. *American Journal of Psychiatry, 152*(1), 64–71.

White, L. L., Ballew, C., Gilbert, T. J., Mendlein, J. M., Mokdad, A. H., & Strauss, K. F. (1997). Weight, body image, and weight control practices of Navajo Indians: Findings from the Navajo Health and Nutrition Survey. *Journal of Nutrition.127*(Suppl. 10), 2094S–2098S.

Winkleby, M. A., Gardner, C. D., & Taylor, C. B. (1996). The influence of gender and socioeconomic factors on Hispanic/White differences in body mass index. *Preventive Medicine, 25*(2), 203–211.

Yanovski, S. Z., Gormally, J. F., Leser, M. S., Gwirtsman, H. E., & Yanovski, J. A. (1994). Binge eating disorder affects outcome of comprehensive very-low-caloric diet treatment. *Obesity Research, 2,* 205–212.

Yanovski, S. Z., Nelson, J. E., Dubbert, B. K., & Spitzer, R. L. (1993). Association of binge eating disorder and psychiatric comorbidity in obese subjects. *American Journal of Psychiatry, 150,* 1472–1479.

Yates, A. (1989). Current perspectives on the eating disorders. I: History, psychological and biological aspects. *Journal of the American Academy of Child and Adolescent Psychiatry, 28*(6), 813–828.

Zuckerfeld, R., Fuchs, A., & Cormillot, A. (1988). Characterization and detection of bulimia in the city of Buenos Aires. *Acta Psiquiatrica y Psicologica de America Latina, 34* [Latina American Journal of Psychiatry and Psychology](4), 298–302.

Chapter 28

A FEMINIST APPROACH TO EATING DISORDERS

LINDA SMOLAK AND SARAH K. MURNEN

Eating disorders are the most gendered categories described in the *Diagnostic and Statistical Manual of Mental Disorders,* fourth edition (*DSM-IV),* with eight to nine times more women than men suffering from anorexia nervosa (AN) and bulimia nervosa (BN; American Psychiatric Association [APA], 1994). In addition, girls and women are much more likely than boys and men to report attitudes and behaviors, such as weight and shape concern or dieting, that predict the development of AN and BN. The gender differences emerge in elementary school and are found in every American ethnic group that has been studied (Smolak & Levine, 2001; Smolak & Murnen, 2001).

These data should not be interpreted as indicating that boys and men have no body image problems. Some men do suffer from AN or BN. Gay men seem to be more likely to have eating disorders than are heterosexual men (Andersen, 2002). In addition, a notable minority of boys and men want to be larger, both in height and muscle mass (see Cohane & Pope, 2001; Labre, 2002 for reviews). Some of these boys and men are willing to take extreme, health-endangering steps to try to achieve a more muscular body, including using anabolic steroids or food supplements. Furthermore, men are more likely than women to use steroids or food supplements to build bulk. For example, one study of adolescents found that five times as many boys as girls reported using steroids in the past week (2.5% vs. 0.5%; Neumark-Sztainer, Story, Falkner, Beuhring, & Resnick, 1999). Thus, body image and eating problems among males also show the effects of gender.

Both eating disorders and steroid/food supplement abuse carry substantial short-term and long-term physical and psychological risks (Hill & Pomeroy, 2001; Labre, 2002). There is little evidence that direct, inherent biological differences between men and women are instrumental in the gender differences in the *initiation* of negative body image or body shape management (Smolak & Murnen, 2001). Certainly, neurochemical and other changes that accompany starvation and purging play a role in the intensification and maintenance of AN and BN (Kaye, 2002; Kaye & Strober, 1999). Indeed, dieting may cause neurochemical changes that lead to eating disorders (Walsh, Oldman, Franklin, Fairburn, & Cowen, 1995). But, at some point, the retrospective path from AN and BN leads back to sociocultural factors. For example, sociocultural factors, including media, peers, and parents, have been found to play a role in the initiation of dieting

(Huon & Strong, 1998) and the internalization of the thin ideal (J. K. Thompson & Stice, 2001), both of which are risk factors for the development of eating disorders.

Similarly, although the data are significantly more sparse, sociocultural factors have been implicated in the initiation of food supplement abuse. This may, in turn, lead to steroid abuse, which may lead to the use of other drugs (Labre, 2002). Thus, while biochemical processes may be instrumental in the intensification and maintenance of food supplement or steroid abuse, the root causes of initiation appear to be primarily sociocultural.

The combination of gender differences and evidence of sociocultural origin in body image problems, weight and shape control, eating disorders, and steroid abuse demand a close examination of how gender contributes to these problems. Analyses of gender roles as measured by traditional sex role inventories are likely to be insufficient given the conceptual limitations of such measures (Murnen & Smolak, 1998; Smolak & Murnen, 2001). Instead, we need theories that examine the "lived experiences" of women and men to understand how body comes to have such different meaning for each gender. Feminist theory provides a framework for such analysis.

In this chapter, we focus on women and their lived experiences, though we sometimes use men's experiences as a counterpoint, because we are focusing on eating disorders, which are more common in women than in men. Additionally, considerably more data are available on girls and women than on boys and men. At present, it is not self-evident that theories and findings concerning women and body issues can be directly applied to men.

RELEVANCE OF FEMINIST THEORY

Even in the twenty-first century, it is often difficult to find substantial attention given to feminist theory. Feminist theory is often seen as "blaming men" or ignoring physiological differences and causes. The animosity toward feminism has been evident in eating disorders theory and research (e.g., Wooley, 1994). However, the indifference (or worse) of many researchers toward feminist theory appears to be based on a fundamental misunderstanding of the approach.

Feminists begin by arguing that gender roles are socially constructed. As such, gender roles serve a function in society. In modern American society, for example, gender roles tell us that men are rational rather than emotional and, hence, are well equipped to be leaders. Women, on the other hand, are socially connected and emotional and so are better able to raise children or otherwise provide nurturance to people. The gap is so widely endorsed and enacted that some theorists have argued that it must have evolutionary roots (Buss, 1987; Gutmann, 1975). Nonetheless, changes in the roles over time and across cultures as well as evidence showing more similarity than difference between the genders on many fundamental characteristics have led feminists to reject this argument.

For example, social role theory (Eagly, 1987, 1997) suggests that the distribution of women and men into different social roles leads to gender differences in social behavior. Although the distribution of women and men into social roles is viewed as the underlying cause of gender differences in behavior, the impact of roles on behavior is mediated by psychological and social processes such as traditional gender roles, stereotyping, and processes related to stereotyping (Eagly, Wood, & Diekman, 2000). Women are more likely to be placed in caretaker roles, so they develop psychological characteristics consistent with these roles such as nurturance, while men are more likely to be placed in roles that require instrumental traits. The fact that men are more likely to be in instrumental roles means that they spend more time in paid employment in industrial societies, which translates into more power for men relative to women. This greater male power leads to androcentrism so that cultural values and products are defined in terms of men's needs, values, strengths, and interests. Women are defined in relation to men in androcentric cultures; women's value is seen in relation to what they can provide for men. This means that greater objectification of women is possible because women don't define themselves; rather, a primary value of women is that they can be sexual partners to men.

Gender roles are pervasive in society. Even toddlers can identify what tasks and clothing belong to mommy and which belong to daddy. Gender roles are enacted on not only an individual level but also institutional levels. The different gender distributions in elementary school teachers versus college professors, for example, reminds us (or shows us) that women are better with small children who need nurturance while men can better introduce mature minds to complex, abstract thought. One consequence of adopting a feminist perspective, then, is that the individual is no longer the sole focus of analysis as in most of psychology. Instead, feminism leads us toward a more ecological approach, one that examines the society that constructed and maintains the gender roles. The conclusion is likely to be that we need to alter society and culture if we wish to reduce body and eating problems.

It is beyond the scope of this chapter to explore all aspects of the gender roles assigned to women and men. We provide brief descriptions of each role, placing it within societal levels, that will generally capture the differences. There are sharply defined gender roles that represent a masculinist, androcentric perspective. American society currently tends to devalue and pathologize what is female. Examples include the low pay for preschool workers, the limited availability of child care, treating menstruation and menopause as disease states that require medication, resisting the development of a normal female body by labeling it as fat, and arguing that women want to be raped or cry "rape" when it suits their purpose. The ironies, for example, of extolling motherhood while failing to give it meaningful financial status (Bergmann, 1981; Orenstein, 2000) or marketing revealing clothing to adolescent girls and then arguing that such clothing invites rape further underscore the societally encoded disadvantages of being female.

Maleness, on the other hand, is glorified and exaggerated. "Playing like a girl" is an insult but "being a man about it" or "taking it like a man" is evidence of maturity and even courage. This is not to say that the glorification of maleness always works out well for men. For example, the importance of rationality over emotion has certainly cost men in terms of their relationships to their children. The stereotype that men are always aggressive or are hypersexual has contributed to more than one boy's injury or illness. Arguably, it is the emphasis on *physical* power and strength, an element of manliness, that contributes to steroid use.

Thus, gender roles carry costs to both men and women. Feminist analysis is valuable in understanding those costs and their effects. Relative powerlessness and lack of control over aspects of their daily lives are part of the role assigned to girls and women that has contributed to poor body image and eating problems.

CONTROL AND POWER

Clinicians and theorists have long suggested that AN is rooted in a sense of a chaotic, out-of-control life. Adolescent girls, facing new social, familial, academic, and physical challenges may feel overwhelmed and unable to get a handle on their daily lives. They can, however, control their eating. They believe that no one can force them to eat; more importantly, perhaps, they are proud of their iron-willed determination not to eat. They are proud of their self-control (e.g., Bruch, 1973).

Women suffering from BN have been characterized as impulsive, as unable to control their eating. Binges have been characterized as "impulsive." They have also been described as "dissociative" (Heatherton & Baumeister, 1991), permitting the woman to escape from feelings of anger, sadness, guilt, or powerlessness (B. Thompson, 1994). But, a concern about weight and shape and the dependence of a woman's self-worth on controlling body shape are also part of BN. Once the woman realizes she has been "out-of-control" and has overeaten, she will attempt to reassert control by compensating for the binge.

Thus, both AN and BN are intricately related to control issues. What are the control issues? In what ways do women feel out of control? Most importantly, why are their bodies the sites that girls and women choose to play out their control conflicts?

LOSING CONTROL

AN and, particularly, BN are rare among children younger than 13. During this period, AN is apparently more common among girls than boys. However, perhaps as many as a quarter of the children presenting with AN are boys, a rate about double that of adults (Bryant-Waugh & Lask, 2002). Some childhood eating disorders, such as selective eating, may actually be more common in boys than girls (Bryant-Waugh & Lask, 2002). It is during adolescence that most cases of AN and BN develop. The developmental transitions during adolescence seem to be particularly vulnerable periods (Smolak & Levine, 1996). This suggests that adolescent transitions may, at least for some girls, feel so chaotic that eating disorders develop as a coping mechanism.

There is an increase in the percentage of girls who are concerned with their weight and shape as well as increases in calorie-restrictive dieting and other weight control methods during the middle school years (ages 11 to 14). Puberty is commonly cited as the cause of this increase. Many studies have looked at the relationship of puberty to eating problems (see Smolak & Levine, 1996, for a review). In general, it does appear that there is an increase in weight concerns and weight control at the time of puberty (e.g., Gralen, Levine, Smolak, & Murnen, 1990). This may reflect the social implications of the weight and fat gain that girls experience during puberty. Girls routinely gain 40 or more pounds during puberty. Furthermore, the fat to muscle ratio shifts so that girls now have relatively more fat than they did when they were younger and relatively more fat than boys do. The media ideal of long legs and a thin, low percentage fat body is closer to the first stages of puberty than to the shape girls have at the end of puberty. Normal, healthy development, then, is moving girls away from the cultural ideal of beauty. This may be one way in which girls feel a lack of control. Boys may feel a lack of control temporarily also; after all, they feel gawky, too, as their arms and legs grow rapidly and they are embarrassed by breaking voices and facial fuzz (or lack thereof). The difference is that by the end of puberty, most boys are closer to the culturally sanctioned ideal body shape for men.

In addition, puberty represents sexual maturity and, in the United States, an increase in the socially acceptable sexualization of the female body. Increases in both dating and sexual harassment underscore this. Indeed, it now becomes acceptable, or at least expected, that strangers feel entitled to comment on a girl's body (Bryant, 1993; Larkin, Rice, & Russell, 1999). This may serve to heighten the girl's focus on her body at a time when rapid changes may already make her self-conscious. Sexual harassment may make girls feel as if their bodies are no longer their own. Rather, they are increasingly treated as commodities to be looked at and evaluated by others, particularly by boys and men.

The timing of puberty has often been found to be a predictor of psychopathology. More specifically, early maturing girls appear to be at greater risk for a variety of behavioral and psychological problems (Hayward et al., 1997). However, research now suggests that early maturation is not a direct, long-term risk factor for the development of eating disorders (e.g., Graber, Brooks-Gunn, Paikoff, & Warren, 1994; McKnight Investigators, 2003) although if early maturation results in a relatively high BMI (Graber et al., 1994) or co-occurs with other stressors (Smolak, Levine, & Gralen, 1993), early puberty may appear to be a risk factor.

The idea of increased risk with simultaneous stressors is an important one because it emphasizes the context within which puberty occurs. Many girls, for example, start middle school and begin dating within a year of menarche. Such multiple stressors are associated with lowered self-esteem (Simmons, Burgeson, Carlton-Ford, & Blyth, 1987) as well as with the later development of eating problems (Smolak et al., 1993). While the stressors listed here (school transitions, dating, puberty) are all normative, it is possible that some girls experience nonnormative stressors, including parental divorce or, perhaps, dating violence (Silverman, Raj, Mucci, & Hathaway, 2001).

Sexual harassment, sexual abuse, and dating violence deserve special attention. All three have been at least correlated with body image and eating problems (Connors, 2001; Harned, 2000; Murnen & Smolak, 2000; Silverman et al., 2001; Smolak & Murnen, 2001). And all three show girls that their bodies can be used in frightening, degrading, violent ways without their consent. As Susan Brownmiller (1975) noted three decades ago, the purpose of rape and less violent forms of sexual degradation (Sheffield, 1995) is to keep girls in their place, to remind them that men can, if they so desire, be in charge of women's bodies. This represents what may be the most extreme loss of control that girls and women face.

Furthermore, girls may find their social support system going through important changes as they face the early adolescence transition. Their relationships with their parents may be marked by increased distance and conflict, though the parent-child bonds are not fractured. New schools may separate friends, and increased social competition among girls may result in relationship aggression (Simmons, 2002; White, 2002) such that girls may not be able to rely on their elementary school friends. Once again, then, the girls feel a loss of control, even powerlessness.

This sense of powerlessness may be heightened by the socialized requirement that girls are responsible for the maintenance of relationships (Brown & Gilligan, 1992;

Taylor, Gilligan, & Sullivan, 1995). Their responsibility for their relationships often results in putting the relationship before their own needs. Girls may tolerate inconsiderate or even abusive treatment to keep the relationship alive. This may result in a "loss of voice," silencing the self so completely that girls no longer understand or know their own needs and desires. Among adult women, loss of voice has been related to dietary restraint, binge eating, and emotional eating. These relationships were much smaller or, in the case of emotional eating, nonexistent among men (Smolak & Munsterteiger, 2002). Smolak and Munsterteiger claim that although there are measures of loss of voice available for use with adult women, there are problems with the interpretation of such measures. There is also a measure of loss of voice for use with adolescents (Tolman & Porche, 2000), though it has not yet been widely used. The measurement and, indeed, the development of voice are important topics for future research.

Similar issues during the late adolescence transition (Smolak & Levine, 1996), a peak time for the onset of BN, can be outlined. There are social transitions in friendships and family relationships, increased risk of rape, academic or work changes, and perhaps even increases in weight associated with college food, a lack of time for exercise, or pregnancy.

During transitions, existing social, personality, and cognitive structures are broken down and replaced with new ones. This implies that coping mechanisms may be less strong, making these vulnerable periods (Smolak & Levine, 1996). Nonetheless, there is some continuity in functioning. One possibility is that weight concerns (Killen, 1996) or thinness schema (Smolak & Levine, 1996) may be strengthened as the girls face new stressors or challenges. The belief in and importance of becoming or staying thin enough may extend into new realms, such as career success or popularity with boys. Furthermore, girls may see few avenues for achievement that do not involve attractiveness. Thus, weight concerns may become the girl's dominant coping style, a way of asserting control over *something*. This is consistent with research suggesting that girls who are troubled before puberty are more troubled by the challenges of puberty (Caspi & Moffitt, 1991). It is also consistent with objectification theory's model of girls' development.

OBJECTIFICATION THEORY

Objectification theory (Fredrickson & Roberts, 1997) rests on the premise that the meanings of the male body and of the female body are socially constructed and, as such, are different. This argument has also been popular among postmodern philosophers (e.g., Bordo, 1993; Foucault, 1979). The core idea is that physiological differences between males and females are not nearly extensive enough to account for differences in social roles. Instead, social roles have been developed that determine gendered behavioral differences (see also Eagly, 1987, 1997). There is, for example, no physiological difference that accounts for the fact that all U.S. presidents have been men or that the vast majority of secretaries are women. There is no physiological reason why women wear dresses and men don't. And there is no physiological reason why men looking for a partner judge women's appearance as their most important criterion while women are more concerned about personality and financial status.

According to objectification theory, the critical difference between men and women is that society defines men's bodies as things that act or perform tasks while women's bodies are things to be looked at and evaluated (Fredrickson & Roberts, 1997). Women's bodies are supposed to be aesthetically pleasing. Hence, women spend more money (and time) on hair care, makeup, fashionable clothing, plastic surgery, and other beauty products than men do. Women want to look good to attract a man who will provide them with financial and emotional security as well as protect them from physical harm. Financial security and protection from harm are difficult for women to obtain without help from a man. It is still the case, for example, that women make significantly less money than men do in every job category and at every educational level that the federal government tracks (United States Department of Labor, 2002). And adolescent girls are as likely to be sexually assaulted as boys are to be robbed (Wordes & Nunez, 2002).

So girls and young women recognize three things:

1. An excellent, socially sanctioned way to achieve social status, financial security, and physical protection is to attract a man.
2. Men look at and evaluate women's bodies; even elementary school girls appear to be aware of this (Murnen & Smolak, 2000).
3. Many men prefer women who look like the cultural ideal.

Even preschool age children attribute more negative characteristics to fat women than to fat men (Turnbull, Heaslip, & McLeod, 2000). So, they come to the not unreasonable conclusion that beauty, including thinness, is the best path to a successful adulthood. They increase their self-monitoring of their appearance, including their weight and shape, to achieve this goal. In the terms of objectification theory, girls "internalize the gaze" of the other. The girls now engage in self-objectification and treat themselves as a commodity to be viewed and evaluated.

It is worth emphasizing that we are talking about girls, not women. While prepubescent boys are not expected to be muscular, young girls are expected to try to be thin and attractive. Indeed, even preschool girls play with makeup and dress up in gowns and high heels. Elementary school girls are often worried about getting or being fat; some even engage in exercise or dieting to control their "shapes" (Smolak & Levine, 2001). The internalization of the gaze of the other and the thin ideal begins early.

Several mechanisms influence this internalization. Girls receive messages from the media, their parents, and peers. This message, which is more consistent and comes more frequently from multiple sources than is true for boys, convinces girls of the importance of appearance (Smolak & Levine, 2001). This is one of the factors that contributes to the internalization of the thin ideal, an important risk factor for the development of eating problems (J. K. Thompson & Stice, 2001). The internalization of the thin ideal might be considered an outcome of the internalization of the objectifying gaze (see Figure 28.1). There is already some research suggesting that the internalization of objectification is related to body shame, negative body image, and disordered eating (Fredrickson, Roberts, Noll, Quinn, & Twenge, 1998; McKinley, 1998, 1999; McKinley & Hyde, 1996; Tiggemann & Lynch, 2001).

Occupations, such as ballet dancing, provide another indication of the potential link between internalization of the objectifying gaze and eating problems. Ballet dancers have additional objectification pressures because of professional requirements to look graceful

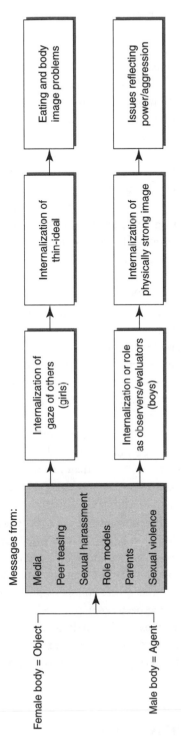

Figure 28.1 Objectification and Eating Problems.

and lithe on stage. These requirements have, at least since Balanchine, meant that women who are ballet dancers need to be very thin; indeed, research has found these girls and women have elevated body dissatisfaction and disordered eating (e.g., Hamilton, Brooks-Gunn, & Warren, 1986). Tiggemann and Slater (2001) reported that former ballet dancers score higher on self-objectification and disturbed eating than undergraduate women. More importantly, the differences between the two groups' disturbed eating scores were heavily influenced by the differences in self-objectification.

Indeed, in any situation in which the sense of "being on display" is intensified, women's body shame and dieting increases (Fredrickson et al., 1998). Fredrickson et al., in an ingenious experiment, had women try on bathing suits or sweaters. Those who tried on bathing suits reported greater body shame and higher levels of dietary restraint. Furthermore, when women and men in this situation were compared, only the women showed the increases in body shame and dietary restraint.

Age trends in objectification, body dissatisfaction, dieting, and disordered eating provide another interesting example (McKinley, 1999; Tiggemann & Lynch, 2001). Disordered eating seems to decline with age, at least after the early adult transition (Heatherton, Mahamedi, Striepe, Field, & Keel, 1997). But, body dissatisfaction does not decline. Body dissatisfaction is a predictor of the development of disordered eating in girls and young women (Stice, 2001). There must either be a breakdown in the relationship between body dissatisfaction and disordered eating in older women, or there must be a mediating variable that links body dissatisfaction to eating problems. This mediator may be more common in younger women than older women. Data from Tiggemann and Lynch's (2001) study suggest that self-objectification is this mediator. Self-objectification appears to be more common in young women, whose attractiveness is considered important for marriageability, than in older women, whose sexuality and attractiveness are ignored and devalued by society (Fredrickson & Roberts, 1997; Tiggemann & Lynch, 2001). For example, McKinley (1999) reported that middle-age women report lower surveillance and body shame than do their college-age daughters. This does not mean, however, that older women are immune to the evaluative gaze of others. McKinley also found that partner approval of looks was significantly related to body esteem in both college- and middle-age women.

Evidence also suggests that college women have higher surveillance and body shame scores than do college men (McKinley, 1998). McKinley reported that the Objectified Body Consciousness (OBC) Scale scores and actual versus ideal body weight fully mediated the gender difference in body esteem. In other words, the gender difference in body esteem that McKinley found in this college sample became nonsignificant once objectification and the difference between actual and desired weight were considered.

Objectification theory may substantially help to explain the gendered nature of eating problems and body dissatisfaction. The differential objectification of male versus female bodies and how culture serves to enforce this difference are important avenues for future research.

MEASURING OBJECTIFICATION

Concepts that try to capture cultural influences are notoriously difficult to operationalize. This may be one reason that it has been difficult to assess the effects of racism or sexism on individual development and behavior. If we consider objectification to be part of women's "lived experience" dictated by cultural standards, it becomes important to consider how we might measure objectification.

There have been two general approaches to the conceptualization and measurement of self-objectification. The OBC Scale, developed by Nita McKinley and Janet Hyde (1996), has been used in several studies; and the Self-Objectification Scale (SO), developed by Noll and Fredrickson (1998), has been used by researchers working within the objectification theory outlined by Fredrickson and Roberts (1997). Both of these research programs recognize that the objectification of women is prevalent in our culture and that this objectification is linked with women's body image and eating problems through internalizing processes. Both groups point out that commonly used measures of body dissatisfaction are limited because they don't examine the influence of sociocultural factors; such scales focus on individual variables such as how a person feels about her body or thinks about her body and compares it to an ideal but do not incorporate a cultural perspective. In other words, most existing body dissatisfaction measures do not reflect feminist theory.

McKinley and Hyde (1996) developed the OBC Scale from a social construction perspective. They argued that we live in a culture that objectifies women, and the OBC measures the extent to which women adopt beliefs that support this experience of objectification. Persistent objectification can lead to the internalization of objectification, which has proposed consequences for body issues, much as the internalization of the thin ideal has ramifications for body image. An item from each of the three subscales of the OBC is listed in Table 28.1. The *body surveillance* subscale measures the extent to which women think about how others see them. The internalization of these cultural standards is theorized to result in *body shame*, which is measured by the second subscale. Finally, *control beliefs* can develop that emphasize that women are responsible for how their bodies look and that they can control their appearance with some effort. Feeling a sense of control can be positive in that a woman can gain a sense of competence in a socially acceptable way, but it can be negative in that it can encourage behaviors such as restricted eating (McKinley & Hyde, 1996).

In terms of validity and reliability of the OBC, McKinley and Hyde (1996) tested 121 undergraduate women in their initial study and determined the initial subscale items through factor analysis. They found that the alpha coefficients of internal consistency were .89 for surveillance, .75 for body shame, and .72 for control beliefs. The subscale scores were significantly correlated with one another. McKinley and Hyde found that control beliefs correlated with restricted eating, dieting, exercising to control weight, and wearing clothes to look thinner. The surveillance subscale scores correlated with public self-consciousness. They examined the subscales in middle-age women, too, and found high alpha coefficients indicating good internal consistency.

McKinley (1999) found in a study comparing mothers and daughters on the OBC that there were both similarities and differences in scale responses and in how scale responses were correlated with other measures. For example, middle-age women had lower levels of body surveillance and body shame compared to younger women, and surveillance was related to body esteem in young women but not in middle-age women. Body shame was negatively correlated with body esteem and physical well-being in both groups of women. McKinley (1999) interpreted the data as indicating that it is important to examine cultural, developmental, and familial contexts in understanding

Table 28.1   Two major approaches to the measurement of objectification issues
in women

Objectified Body Consciousness Scale[a]

Sample items are listed below for the three subscales. Participants are asked to indicate
the extent to which they agree or disagree with each item using a 5-point Likert scale.

Surveillance Subscale

During the day, I think about how I look many times.

Body Shame Scale

When I can't control my weight, I feel like something must be wrong with me.

Control Scale

I can weigh what I'm supposed to when I try hard enough.

Self-Objectification Questionnaire[b]

Attributes on the scale are listed below. People are asked to rank order all 12 attributes
(randomly ordered) in terms of their importance with 1 being most important. Scores
for appearance and competence attributes are summed separately; then a difference
score is computed with higher scores indicating more emphasis on appearance.

Appearance-Based Attributes

Physical attractiveness, coloring, weight, sex appeal, measurements, muscle tone.

Importance of Competence-Based Attributes

Muscular strength, physical coordination, stamina, health, physical fitness, physical
energy level.

[a]From "The Objectified Body Consciousness Scale: Development and Validation," by
N. M. McKinley and J. S. Hyde, 1996, *Psychology of Women Quarterly, 20,* pp. 181–215.
[b]From "A Mediational Model Linking Self-Objectification, Body Shame, and Disordered Eating,"
by S. M. Noll and B. L. Fredrickson, 1998, *Psychology of Women Quarterly, 22,* pp. 623–636.

women's body experiences. In another study, McKinley (1998) found that although the
OBC subscales were internally consistent for male college students, relationships between the subscale scores and scores on a body esteem inventory were stronger among
women than among men. In addition, gender differences in body esteem were no longer
significant when OBC was entered into regression equations, supporting the idea that it
is the effects of cultural experiences associated with being a woman that predict body
problems in women.

The other major conceptualization of objectification issues comes from the work of
Barbara Fredrickson and colleagues (1998). As explained previously, it is argued that
the objectification of women can lead to many circumstances when women's attention
is called to their body, leading to self-objectification. Although there are some benefits

to self-objectification (women improve their appearance, which influences their social and economic life outcomes), there are some costs proposed in terms of increased opportunities to experience shame and anxiety, decreased opportunities to experience peak motivational states, and diminished awareness of internal bodily states (Fredrickson & Roberts, 1997).

Self-objectification can be conceptualized as a state (i.e., situationally induced) as well as a more enduring trait. The more a woman internalizes the dehumanizing cultural messages of sexual objectification, the more likely she is to self-objectify and the more likely she is then to experience the affective consequences of self-objectification such as body shame and depression. In terms of state self-objectification, Fredrickson et al. (1998) found that when women tried on swimwear, they became more aware of their bodies, which, in turn, led to body shame, restrained eating, and diminished cognitive performance.

In terms of trait self-objectification, Noll and Fredrickson (1998) developed the Self-Objectification Scale (SO). They argued that individuals vary in the degree to which they self-objectify and that these individual differences can be quantified by having individuals rank the importance they give to a set of body attributes that include both observable, appearance-based attributes and nonobservable, competence-based attributes. On the SO, respondents are asked to rank a list of body attributes in ascending order of how important each is to their physical self-concept with the highest impact a rank of 1 and the lowest a rank of 12. The six appearance-based attributes (e.g., physical attractiveness) and the six competence-based attributes (e.g., muscular strength) are listed in Table 28.1. It is argued that people who are high in self-objectification think more about what their body looks like than what it can do. Scores are computed by summing ranks for the appearance and competence attributes separately, then computing a difference score. Scores range from -36 to 37 with higher scores reflecting a greater emphasis on appearance, which indicates greater self-objectification. Note that it is the concern with physical appearance that is an issue in objectification theory and not the amount of satisfaction with appearance that is commonly measured by other scales such as body esteem inventories (e.g., Franzoi & Shields, 1984).

A couple of studies have addressed the reliability and validity of the SO scale. Noll and Fredrickson (1998) found that scores on the scale had high test-retest reliability ($r = .92$, $p < .001$) and that women had higher scores than men. Scores on the scale were positively correlated with appearance anxiety, body satisfaction, and scores on an eating disorders inventory as well. In another study (Miner-Rubino, Twenge, & Fredrickson, 2002), it was found that women who scored higher on trait self-objectification scored higher on measures of body shame, neuroticism/anxiety, and depression. In addition, intellect was negatively correlated with scores. The authors suggested that women who spend a lot of time thinking about their bodies have less cognitive energy left to think clearly and creatively.

SUMMARY AND CONCLUSIONS

Body image and eating problems are clearly gendered. Indeed, the gender differences for AN and BN are among the largest of all of the psychological disorders classified in the *DSM-IV*. Yet, traditional measures of masculinity and femininity have yielded little information about the development of these problems. On the other hand, several aspects of women's lived experiences, such as sexual harassment and sexual assault, do appear to be related to eating problems. In this chapter, we have presented a feminist perspective, emphasizing objectification theory, as a potential tool for understanding the etiology of body image and eating problems among girls and women.

Research conducted using the OBC and SO scales suggests that the internalizing of objectification is indeed related to women's body issues. The limited developmental and cross-situational research conducted shows us that a cultural perspective on understanding women's body issues is important. At least one study has demonstrated that gender differences in body esteem disappear once objectification is taken into account. More research as to how the "lived experiences" of women contribute to women's problems with body dissatisfaction is desperately needed. We need to understand more thoroughly how elements of the proximal and distal contexts of development influence body image and eating issues for both genders.

Such research may well lead to new models of intervention emphasizing changing the context over simply changing the individual. Niva Piran's (1999) prevention work with an elite ballet school exemplifies this approach. It may also lead to new forms of therapy that, again, recognize that the environment is involved in the initiation and maintenance of eating problems. Trying to change only the individual runs the risk of putting her right back into a toxic environment. Future research must address the effects of this medical model approach compared to a more feminist contextual approach.

REFERENCES

American Psychiatric Association. (1994). *Diagnostic and statistical manual of mental disorders* (4th ed.). Washington, DC: Author.

Andersen, A. (2002). Eating disorders in males. In C. Fairburn & K. Brownell (Eds.), *Eating disorders and obesity* (2nd ed., pp. 188–192). New York: Guilford Press.

Bergmann, B. (1981). The economic risks of being a housewife. *American Economic Review, 71,* 81–86.

Bordo, S. (1993). *Unbearable weight: Feminism, Western culture, and the body.* Berkeley: University of California Press.

Brown, L., & Gilligan, C. (1992). *Meeting at the crossroads.* Cambridge, MA: Harvard University Press.

Brownmiller, S. (1975). *Against our will: Men, women and rape.* Toronto, Ontario, Canada: Bantam Books.

Bruch, H. (1973). *Eating disorders: Obesity, anorexia nervosa, and the person within.* New York: Basic Books.

Bryant, A. (1993). Hostile hallways: The AAUW Survey on Sexual Harassment in American's schools. *Journal of School Health, 63,* 355–357.

Bryant-Waugh, R., & Lask, B. (2002). Childhood-onset eating disorders. In C. Fairburn & K. Brownell (Eds.), *Eating disorders and obesity: A comprehensive handbook* (2nd ed., pp. 210–214). New York: Guilford Press.

Buss, D. (1987). Sex differences in human mate selection criteria: An evolutionary perspective. In C. Crawford, M. Smith, & D. Krebs (Eds.), *Sociobiology and psychology: Ideas, issues, and applications.* Hillsdale, NJ: Erlbaum.

Caspi, A., & Moffitt, T. (1991). Individual differences are accentuated during periods of social change: The sample case of girls at puberty. *Journal of Personality and Social Psychology, 61,* 157–168.

Cohane, G. H., & Pope, H. G. (2001). Body image in boys: A review of the literature. *International Journal of Eating Disorders, 29,* 373–379.

Connors, M. (2001). Relationship of sexual abuse to body image and eating problems. In J. K. Thompson & L. Smolak (Eds.), *Body image, eating disorders, and obesity in youth: Assessment, prevention, and treatment* (pp. 149–168). Washington, DC: American Psychological Association.

Eagly, A. H. (1987). *Sex differences in social behavior: A social role interpretation.* Hillsdale, NJ: Erlbaum.

Eagly, A. H. (1997). Sex differences in social behavior: Comparing social role theory and evolutionary psychology. *American Psychologist, 52,* 1380–1383.

Eagly, A. H., Wood, W., & Dickman, A. B. (2000). Social role theory of sex differences and similarities: A current appraisal. In T. Eckes & H. M. Trautner (Eds.), *The developmental social psychology of gender* (pp. 123–174). Mahwah, NJ: Erlbaum.

Foucault, M. (1979). *Discipline and punish.* New York: Vintage.

Franzoi, S. L., & Shields, S. A. (1984). The Body Esteem Scale: Multidimensional structure and sex differences in a college population. *Journal of Personality Assessment, 48,* 173–178.

Fredrickson, B., & Roberts, T. (1997). Objectification theory: Toward understanding women's lived experiences and mental health risks. *Psychology of Women Quarterly, 21,* 173–206.

Fredrickson, B., Roberts, T., Noll, S., Quinn, D., & Twenge, J. (1998). That swimsuit becomes you: Sex differences in self-objectification, restrained eating, and math performance. *Journal of Personality and Social Psychology, 75,* 269–284.

Graber, J., Brooks-Gunn, J., Paikoff, R., & Warren, M. (1997). Prediction of eating problems: An 8-year study of adolescent girls. *Developmental Psychology, 30,* 823–834.

Gralen, S., Levine, M., Smolak, L., & Murnen, S. (1990). Dieting and disordered eating during early and middle adolescence. *International Journal of Eating Disorders, 9,* 501–512.

Gutmann, D. (1975). Parenthood: A key to comparative study of the life cycle. In N. Datan & L. Ginsberg (Eds.), *Life-span developmental psychology: Normative life crises* (pp. 167–184). New York: Academic Press.

Hamilton, L., Brooks-Gunn, J., & Warren, M. (1986). Nutritional intake of female dancers: A reflection of eating problems. *International Journal of Eating Disorders, 5,* 369–376.

Harned, M. (2000). Harassed bodies: An examination of the relationships among women's experiences of sexual harassment, body image, and eating disturbances. *Psychology of Women Quarterly, 24,* 336–348.

Hayward, C., Killen, J., Wilson, D., Hammer, L., Litt, I., Kraemer, H., et al. (1997). Psychiatric risk associated with early puberty in adolescent girls. *Journal of the American Academy of Child and Adolescent Psychiatry, 36,* 255–262.

Heatherton, T., & Baumeister, R. (1991). Binge eating as an escape from self awareness. *Psychological Bulletin, 110,* 86–108.

Heatherton, T., Mahamedi, F., Striepe, M., Field, A., & Keel, P. (1997). A 10-year longitudinal study of body weight, dieting, and eating disorder symptoms. *Journal of Abnormal Psychology, 106,* 117–125.

Hill, K., & Pomeroy, C. (2001). Assessment of physical status of children and adolescents with eating disorders and obesity. In J. K. Thompson & L. Smolak (Ed.), *Body image, eating disorders, and obesity in youth* (pp. 171–192). Washington, DC: American Psychological Association.

Huon, G., & Strong, K. (1998). The initiation and the maintenance of dieting: Structural models for large-scale longitudinal investigations. *International Journal of Eating Disorders, 23,* 361–370.

Kaye, W. (2002). Central nervous system neurotransmitter activity in anorexia nervosa and bulimia nervosa. In C. Fairburn & K. Brownell (Eds.), *Eating disorders and obesity* (2nd ed., pp. 272–277). New York: Guilford Press.

Kaye, W., & Strober, M. (1999). Neurobiology of eating disorders. In D. Charney, E. Nestler, & W. Bunney (Eds.), *Neurobiological foundations of mental illness* (pp. 891–906). New York: Oxford University Press.

Killen, J. (1996). Development and evaluation of a school-based eating disorders symptoms prevention program. In L. Smolak, M. P. Levine, & R. Striegel-Moore (Eds.), *The developmental psychopathology of eathing disorders* (pp. 313–340). Mahwah, NJ: Erlbaum.

Labre, M. (2002). Adolescent boys and the muscular male body ideal. *Journal of Adolescent Health, 30,* 233–242.

Larkin, J., Rice, C., & Russell, V. (1999). Sexual harassment and the prevention of eating disorders: Educating young women. In N. Piran, M. Levine, & C. Steiner-Adair (Eds.), *Preventing eating disorders: A handbook of interventions and special challenges* (pp. 194–207). Philadelphia: Brunner/Mazel.

McKinley, N. M. (1998). Gender differences in undergraduates' body esteem: The mediating effect of objectified body consciousness and actual/ideal weight discrepancy. *Sex Roles, 39,* 113–123.

McKinley, N. M. (1999). Women and objectified body consciousness: Mothers' and daughters' body experience in cultural, developmental, and familial context. *Developmental Psychology, 35,* 760–769.

McKinley, N. M., & Hyde, J. S. (1996). The objectified body consciousness scale: Development and validation. *Psychology of Women Quarterly, 20,* 181–215.

McKnight Investigators. (2003). Risk factors for the onset of eating disorders in adolescent girls: Results of the McKnight Longitudinal Risk Factor Study. *American Journal of Psychiatry, 160,* 248–254.

Miner-Rubino, K., Twenge, J. M., & Fredrickson, B. L. (2002). Trait self-objectification in women: Affective and personality correlates. *Journal of Research in Personality, 36,* 147–172.

Murnen, S., & Smolak, L. (1998). Femininity, masculinity, and disordered eating: A meta-analytic approach. *International Journal of Eating Disorders, 22,* 231–242.

Murnen, S., & Smolak, L. (2000). The experience of sexual harassment among grade-school students: Early socialization of female subordination? *Sex Roles, 43,* 1–17.

Neumark-Sztainer, D., Story, M., Falkner, N. H., Beuhring, T., & Resnick, M. D. (1999). Sociodemographic and personal characteristics of adolescents engaged in weight loss and weight/muscle gain behaviors: Who is doing what? *Preventive Medicine, 28*(1), 40–50.

Noll, S. M., & Fredrickson, B. L. (1998). A mediational model linking self-objectification, body shame, and disordered eating. *Psychology of Women Quarterly, 22,* 623–636.

Orenstein, P. (2000). *Flux: Women on sex, work, love, kids, and life in a half-changed world.* New York: Doubleday.

Piran, N. (1999). Eating disorders: A trial of prevention in a high risk school setting. *Journal of Primary Prevention, 20,* 75–90.

Sheffield, C. (1995). Sexual terrorism. In J. Freeman (Ed.), *Women: A feminist perspective* (pp. 1–21). Mountain View, CA: Mayfield.

Silverman, J., Raj, A., Mucci, L., & Hathaway, J. (2001). Dating violence against adolescent girls and associated substance use, unhealthy weight control, sexual risk behavior, pregnancy, and suicidality. *Journal of the American Medical Association, 286,* 572–579.

Simmons, R. (2002). *Odd girl out: The hidden culture of aggression in girls.* New York: Harcourt.

Simmons, R., Burgeson, R., Carlton-Ford, S., & Blyth, D. (1987). The impact of cumulative change in early adolescence. *Child Development, 58,* 1220–1234.

Smolak, L., & Levine, M. P. (1996). Adolescent transitions and the development of eating problems. In L. Smolak, M. P. Levine, & R. Striegel-Moore (Eds.), *The developmental psychopathology of eating disorders: Implications for research, prevention, and treatment* (pp. 207–234). Mahwah, NJ: Erlbaum.

Smolak, L., & Levine, M. P. (2001). Body image in children. In J. K. Thompson & L. Smolak (Eds.), *Body image, eating disorders, and obesity in youth* (pp. 41–66). Washington, DC: American Psychological Association.

Smolak, L., Levine, M. P., & Gralen, S. (1993). The impact of puberty and dating on eating problems among middle school girls. *Journal of Youth and Adolescence, 22,* 355–368.

Smolak, L., & Munsterteiger, B. (2002). The relationship of gender and voice to depression and eating disorders. *Psychology of Women Quarterly, 26,* 234–241.

Smolak, L., & Murnen, S. (2001). Gender and eating problems. In R. Striegel-Moore & L. Smolak (Eds.), *Eating disorders: Innovative directions in research and practice* (pp. 91–110). Washington, DC: American Psychological Association.

Stice, E. (2001). Risk factors for eating pathology: Recent advances and future directions. In R. Striegel-Moore & L. Smolak (Eds.), *Eating disorders: Innovative directions in research and practice* (pp. 51–74). Washington, DC: American Psychological Association.

Taylor, J., Gilligan, C., & Sullivan, A. (1995). *Between voice and silence: Women and girls, race and relationship.* Cambridge, MA: Harvard University Press.

Thompson, B. (1994). *A hunger so wide and so deep: American women speak out on eating problems.* Minneapolis: University of Minnesota Press.

Thompson, J. K., & Stice, E. (2001). Thin-ideal internalization: Mounting evidence for a new risk factor for body-image disturbance and eating pathology. *Current Directions in Psychological Science, 10,* 181–183.

Tiggemann, M., & Lynch, J. (2001). Body image across the life span in adult women: The role of self-objectification. *Developmental Psychology, 37,* 243–253.

Tiggemann, M., & Slater, A. (2001). A test of objectification theory in former dancers and nondancers. *Psychology of Women Quarterly, 25,* 57–64.

Tolman, D., & Porche, M. (2000). The Adolescent Femininity Ideology Scale: Development and validation of a new measure for girls. *Psychology of Women Quarterly, 24,* 365–376.

Turnbull, J., Heaslip, S., & McLeod, H. (2000). Preschool children's attitudes to fat and normal male and female stimulus figures. *International Journal of Obesity, 24,* 1705–1706.

United States Department of Labor. (2002, September 2). *Usual earnings of wage and salary workers: Second quarter 2002.* Available from bls.gov/news.release/pdf/wkyeng.pdf.

Walsh, A., Oldman, A., Franklin, M., Fairburn, C., & Cowen, P. (1995). Dieting decreases plasma tryptophan and increases prolactin response to d-fenfluramine in women but not in men. *Journal of Affective Disorders, 33,* 89–97.

White, E. (2002). *Fast girls: Teenage tribes and the myth of the slut.* New York: Scribner.

Wooley, S. (1994). Sexual abuse and eating disorders: The concealed debate. In P. Fallon, M. Katzman, & S. Wooley (Eds.), *Feminist perspectives on eating disorders* (pp. 171–211). New York: Guilford Press.

Wordes, M., & Nunez, M. (2002, May). *Our vulnerable teenagers: Their victimization, its consequences, and directions for prevention and intervention.* Oakland CA: National Council on Crime and Delinquency. Available from www.nccd-crc.org.

Chapter 29

WEIGHT AND SHAPE CONCERNS OF BOYS AND MEN

MARITA P. McCABE AND LINA A. RICCIARDELLI

It is widely accepted among researchers that body dissatisfaction and other weight and shape concerns have become more prevalent among adolescent boys and adult males in recent years (e.g., Abell & Richards, 1996; Furnham & Calnan, 1998; McCabe & Ricciardelli, 2001a; Neumark-Sztainer, Story, Falkner, Beuhring, & Resnick, 1999; Pope, Phillips, & Olivardia, 2000). Overall, it is estimated that about a third of males desire a thinner body size while another third desire a larger and more muscular body (e.g., Drewnowski, Kurth, & Krahn, 1995; Furnham & Calnan, 1998; McCabe & Ricciardelli, 2001c; Raudenbush & Zellner, 1997; Ricciardelli & McCabe, 2001a). Although there has been a growing interest in men's body image concerns in the past decade, a significant number of adolescent boys and adult males were shown to demonstrate concerns about their bodies more than 30 years ago (Huenemann, Shapiro, Hampton, & Mitchell, 1966). For example, Huenemann et al. found that approximately half of adolescent boys surveyed desired larger biceps, shoulders, and chests.

The renewed interest in men's weight and shape concerns has been attributed to the growing trend for male bodies to be featured in popular male magazines and the greater number of muscular male images depicted in films (Andersen & Di Domenico, 1992; Nemeroff, Stein, Diehl, & Smilack, 1994; Pope, Phillips, et al., 2000; Spitzer, Henderson, & Zivian, 1999). Both film stars and contestants for Mr. Universe have become increasingly more muscular (Connan, 1998). Male icons have also become increasingly muscular over the past 50 years (Wroblewska, 1997), and the depiction of male models in magazines has become more muscular since the 1950s (Leit, Pope, & Gray, 2001; Spitzer et al., 1999). For example, Spitzer et al. found that the body sizes of male *Playgirl* models had increased from the 1950s to 1997. Likewise, Leit et al. found that the body sizes of *Playgirl* models had become more dense and muscular from 1973 to 1997. The same trend is also reflected in action figure heroes, such as GI Joe, who have become more muscular, with physiques comparable to advanced bodybuilders and some exceeding the muscularity of even the largest human bodybuilders (Pope, Olivardia, Gruber, & Borowiecki, 1999). In addition, with the advent of steroids, bodybuilders have become more muscular (Pope et al., 1999), and weight training has become more prevalent and is even viewed as a normative behavior among many men (Connan, 1998).

This research suggests that body image has become more central in contemporary male culture than in previous decades (Connan, 1998; Pope, Gruber, et al., 2000). While appearance and weight concerns have always been viewed as closely related to women's self-esteem (e.g., Fox, Page, Armstrong, & Kirby, 1994; Lerner, Orlos, & Knapp, 1976; Striegel-Moore, McAvay, & Rodin, 1986), appearance and weight concerns are now also viewed as important for perceived and probably actual success for men (Connan, 1998; Pope, Gruber, et al., 2000). This chapter first considers health risk behaviors associated with body dissatisfaction among males. It then considers weight and shape concerns among preadolescent boys, adolescent boys, and adult men and the impact of both biological and sociocultural factors on these concerns. Finally, programs that are relevant for boys and men directed at altering weight and shape concerns are evaluated.

DEVELOPMENT OF HEALTH RISK BEHAVIORS

Weight and shape concerns for a significant number of males may lead to disturbing behavioral problems such as extreme weight loss behaviors, binge eating, eating disorders, exercise dependence, and steroid use. The majority of studies conducted on these topics have focused on adolescents and college students. However, an increasing number of studies have also found evidence for weight loss behaviors and food preoccupation among children, which may be risk factors for developing disordered eating and related behaviors in adolescence and adulthood (Ricciardelli & McCabe, 2001a).

Because it is estimated that about a third of males desire a leaner body (Furnham & Calnan, 1998; McCabe & Ricciardelli, 2001a; Raudenbush & Zellner, 1997; Ricciardelli & McCabe, 2001a), it is not surprising that dieting and exercising to lose weight appear to be relatively common in males. Studies have shown that between 15% and 52% of males compared to 44% to 68% of females are trying to lose weight by dieting and exercise (e.g., Drewnowski et al., 1995; Garfinkel et al., 1995; Krowchuck, Kreiter, Woods, Sinal, & DuRant, 1998; Neumark-Sztainer & Hannan, 2000; Nowak, Speare, & Crawford, 1996; Serdula et al., 1993; Zuckerman, Colby, Ware, & Lazerson, 1986). Other more extreme weight loss strategies such as diet pill usage, laxatives, and purging are used less frequently by both males and females. Estimates for these strategies range between 1% and 6% for males and 1% and 8% for females (e.g., Maude, Wertheim, Paxton, Gibbons, & Szmukler, 1993; Moore, 1990; Neumark-Sztainer et al., 1999; Ross & Ivis, 1999).

One of the difficulties associated with assessing binge eating in males is that it is often interpreted and experienced differently by males and females. For example, males are more likely than females to report large binges and recurrent binge eating, while females are more likely to experience negative affect associated with their binge eating (Whitaker et al., 1989). Because different definitions and criteria have been used to define binge eating, it is not surprising that estimates of the prevalence of this aspect of disordered eating vary from 14% to 49% for males and from 17% to 79% for females (Katzman, Wolchik, & Braver, 1984; Maude et al., 1993; Moore, 1990; Neumark-Sztainer & Hannan, 2000; Olivardia, Pope, Mangweth, & Hudson, 1995; Whitaker et al., 1989; Zuckerman et al., 1986).

The overall prevalence of eating disorders and disordered eating among males is lower than that found among women (American Psychiatric Association [APA], 1994; Moore, 1990). In the general population, anorexia nervosa is extremely rare among males, while it affects about 1% of women. However, of individuals with bulimia nervosa, approximately 10% are males (APA, 1994). It has been estimated that bulimia nervosa affects between 0.1% and 0.7% of males (Carlat & Camargo, 1991; Garfinkel et al., 1995), while the prevalence of bulimia nervosa among females varies between 1.1% and 3.5% (APA, 1994; Garfinkel et al., 1995).

Although fewer males develop eating disorders and disordered eating symptoms, an overall examination of the correlates and risk factors associated with disordered eating symptoms in clinical, community, college, and adolescent samples of males has revealed many similarities and few differences from those found in females (e.g., Carlat & Camargo, 1991; Field et al., 2001; Keel, Klump, Leon, & Fulkerson, 1998; Lock, Reisel, & Steiner, 2001; Olivardia et al., 1995; Wichstrom, 2000).

Males who have significant weight and shape concerns are also more likely to use exercise as a body change strategy than females (McCabe & Ricciardelli, 2001a). As a result, many males may develop exercise dependence. *Exercise dependence* has been defined as a process that compels an individual to exercise in spite of obstacles and results in physical and psychological symptoms of depression and guilt when exercise is withdrawn (Baekeland, 1970; Bamber, Cockerill, Rodgers, & Carroll, 2000; Brehm & Steffen, 1998). Using these criteria, it has been found that 5% of adolescent boys can be classified as being exercise dependent, with a further 15% being classified as "at risk" of exercise dependence (McCabe & Ricciardelli, 2001b).

Because it is estimated that between a fifth and a third of males would like a larger and/or more muscular body, it is not surprising that many adolescents and adult men engage in weight- and muscle-building strategies (Drewnowski et al., 1995; Furnham & Calnan, 1998; McCabe & Ricciardelli, 2001a; Ricciardelli & McCabe, 2001c; Rosen, Gross, & Vara, 1987). One of the major problems associated with males wanting to become more muscular, gain body size and weight, and increase body strength is the increased likelihood of using anabolic steroids to achieve quick results (Brower, Blow, & Hill, 1994; Wang, Yesalis, Fitzhugh, Buckely, & Smiciklas-Wright, 1994; Wichstrom & Pedersen, 2001). Estimates for the number of American males using steroids range from 1% to 12%, as compared to 0.5% to 2.5% for females (e.g., Drewnowski et al., 1995; Middleman & DuRant, 1996; Neumark-Sztainer et al., 1999; Stilger & Yesalis, 1999; Wang et al., 1994; Yesalis, Barsukiewicz, Kopstein, & Bahrke, 1997). Estimates for the number of males using steroids in other countries—which include Australia, Britain, Norway, South Africa, and Sweden—tend to be lower than U.S. estimates and range between 1% and 3.2% (Bahrke, Yesalis, Kopstein, & Stephens, 2000; Beel, Maycock, & McLean, 1998; Kindlundh, Hagekull, Isacson, & Nyberg, 2001; McCabe & Ricciardelli, 2002; Wichstrom & Pedersen, 2001). The different level of steroid use between the United States and other countries may be due to the greater difficulty of obtaining steroids outside the United States. However, whether estimates of steroid use are based on the levels found within or outside the United States, the data clearly suggest that the problem of steroid use is as high or even higher than the estimated incidence of anorexia nervosa and bulimia nervosa among females (Spitzer et al., 1999).

These findings indicate that additional health risk behaviors are adopted by males other than those adopted by females. Because these behaviors are primarily designed to alter body size and shape, these findings are not surprising given the differences in the ideal body form for males and females promoted by our society (Leit et al., 2001; Mishkind, Rodin, Silberstein, & Striegel-Moore, 1986).

WEIGHT AND SHAPE CONCERNS AND SOCIOCULTURAL INFLUENCES

To examine how weight and shape concerns change throughout the lifespan, the remainder of this chapter separately evaluates the literature relating to weight and shape concerns and the role of sociocultural influences on these concerns. Within each section, research findings related to these factors for boys in childhood, adolescence, and adulthood are evaluated. Body mass index (BMI) is one of the major factors shown to contribute to body image concerns in each age group and is included as a subheading in the relevant sections. Methodological factors that limit the interpretation of the findings are also considered.

Weight and Shape Concerns

Children

Most of the research on weight and shape concerns during childhood has focused on girls and has primarily evaluated the desire to be thinner (see Ricciardelli & McCabe, 2001a, for a review of the literature on body dissatisfaction among children). The following discussion focuses on the findings among male respondents in both studies that have included boys and girls, as well as those that sampled only boys. Polce-Lynch, Myers, Kilmartin, Forssmann-Falck, and Kliewer (1998) found that 10- to 11-year-old girls were more likely to indicate that they experienced negative feelings about their bodies, whereas boys of the same age were more likely to indicate a positive body image. Cusumano and Thompson (1997) found similar gender differences in the levels of body dissatisfaction among 8- to 11-year-old children.

These data seem to suggest that boys are more satisfied with their bodies than girls. However, there are still high levels of body dissatisfaction among boys. Schur, Sanders, and Steiner (2000) evaluated body dissatisfaction among children in grades 3 to 6. There was no age breakdown for the results, but the data indicated that 48.3% of boys wanted to lose weight, 13.8% of boys desired no change, and 37.9% of boys wanted to gain weight. These results indicate that even at this young age, there is a high level of body dissatisfaction among boys, who are fairly evenly split between wanting to lose weight and wanting to gain weight. However, it is difficult to generalize these findings to other children because of the small number of boys ($n = 31$) who participated in the study.

Parkinson, Tovée, and Cohen-Tovée (1998) found that younger boys desired a smaller body than their current shape, whereas older boys desired a leaner shape than their perceived current body shape. This may indicate that as boys get older, they become more aware of the sociocultural ideal for males and recognize that there is pressure to strive for not only a larger body, but also a body that demonstrates muscular strength and tone. It also appears that boys become more dissatisfied as they get older. Folk, Pedersen, and Cullari (1993) found that boys in grade 6 were more dissatisfied with body weight than boys in grade 3, and there was a strong association between body dissatisfaction and a negative self-concept, particularly for boys in grade 6.

Because of children's stage of cognitive development, figure-rating scales are frequently used to evaluate their levels of body dissatisfaction. These studies consistently demonstrate that girls rate their ideal figure as substantially smaller than their current figure, whereas for boys there is no difference in the ratings. These findings applied for boys and girls from ages 6 to 12 years (Collins, 1991; Tiggemann & Pennington, 1990; Tiggemann & Wilson-Barrett, 1998; S. Williamson & Delin, 2001). Wood, Becker, and Thompson (1996) also found that for girls and boys ages 8 to 10 years, girls wanted to be thinner, and boys wanted, on average, to be the same size. Consistent with these findings, Gardner, Friedman, Stark, and Jackson (1999) used a video image of the child's body and found high levels of body dissatisfaction that increased with age for girls 6 to 12 years, whereas body dissatisfaction among boys was lower for all ages. These results need to be treated with caution because although there may be no average difference between boys' current figure and their ideal, this may result from equal numbers of boys wanting to be bigger and smaller. Therefore, these preferences cancel each other out, which may result in a finding of no apparent discrepancy for boys between their current and ideal bodies.

In contrast to these findings, Cullari, Rohrer, and Bahn (1998) used figure drawings and found that for boys and girls ages 10 to 11 years, 36% of girls and 35% of boys wanted to be thinner, 12% of girls and 8% of boys wanted to be larger, and 52% of girls and 57% of boys wanted to remain the same weight. Consistent with these findings, Rand and Wright (2001) also found that both boys and girls ages 9 to 10 years selected the same ideal size for boys and girls and did not show a preference for a thinner ideal for girls. These findings would seem to suggest that obtaining average ratings for body dissatisfaction may mask the direction of desired body image changes.

Schur et al. (2000) used interviews to evaluate levels of body dissatisfaction among children ages 8 to 13 years. Although girls wanted to lose more weight than boys on average, there were no substantial differences in the direction of body change for boys and girls. Schur et al. found that among the girls, 41.9% wanted to look thinner, 51.6% did not want any change, and 6.5% wanted to look heavier. For the boys, 35.5% wanted to look thinner, 45.2% wanted no change, and 19.4% wanted to look heavier. McCabe and Ricciardelli (2003a) found that 39% of 8- to 11-year-old boys had dieted, whereas 50% of 8- to 11-year-old girls had engaged in dieting. Interestingly, about 58% of both boys and girls had exercised to lose weight. There were no gender differences in levels of body dissatisfaction, but boys were more likely to focus on increasing their muscle size.

Body Mass Index   It is possible that these findings may relate to the BMI of the respondents. Sands, Tricker, Sherman, Armatas, and Maschette (1997) examined the body image of boys and girls ages 10 and 11 years. They found that twice as many girls as boys indicated a preference to be thinner, and this preference was more likely to apply to children with a larger BMI. In fact, most studies have found a strong relationship between BMI and body dissatisfaction among children. For example, Vander Wal and Thelen (2000) found that obese children ages 9 to 11.5 years were more likely to be dissatisfied with their weight than normal weight children, and girls indicated greater concerns than boys. McCabe and Ricciardelli (2003a) also found that respondents with a higher BMI were more focused on weight loss, but there were no gender differences in these findings.

Conclusion   Few studies have examined weight and shape concerns among young boys. Available data suggest that boys are primarily satisfied with their bodies, with a substantial minority wanting a thinner body and only a small proportion indicating that they wanted to be larger. However, it is not clear whether these boys want more body mass or more muscles. As boys move closer to adolescence, they appear to be more attuned to the sociocultural ideal for males because older boys wanted a larger body shape.

These findings need to be treated with caution. Often, the terms *smaller body, lose weight,* and *thinner* (as well as *larger body, gain weight, fatter*) are used interchangeably, as if they have the same meaning. However, some boys may want to change their body weight but not the shape of their bodies. They may also want to become leaner but maintain their current weight. The use of different words that are sometimes used to imply the same meanings, and sometimes different meanings, confuses the nature of the findings from past research. This is particularly problematic with children, who may experience difficulties in understanding the differences between the various terms used to describe their bodies and answer questions in relation to one term as if it had the same meaning as another (e.g., confusing body weight and shape).

A further difficulty with studying children is that the use of different techniques to evaluate body dissatisfaction may produce different findings. For example, figure drawings are focused on the whole body, whereas many questionnaire measures examine body image on a part-by-part basis. Because few scales have been developed specifically for children, they may have difficulties interpreting Likert scales, as well as understanding what the question is asking. Interviews allow body image to be explored in a manner relevant to the particular child, but there may be difficulties with acquiescence in these situations and difficulties in comparing the responses between different children, as well as to findings from the use of questionnaires.

Adolescent Boys

Most studies of male body image have been conducted on adolescent boys. There have been mixed findings in relation to levels of weight and shape concerns, with the majority of these studies indicating that levels of body dissatisfaction among adolescent boys are lower then among adolescent girls. For example, Rosenblum and Lewis (1999) suggested that sex differences in body dissatisfaction emerge between 13 and 15 years of age, with girls showing an increase and boys showing a decrease in body dissatisfaction over this age period. However, the different levels of body concerns may be due to some adolescent boys' wanting larger bodies, whereas others want to lose weight; therefore, the overall level of body concerns may be similar for boys and girls.

Nowak et al. (1996) found that more than half of the adolescent girls in their sample wanted to lose weight, whereas only 27% of the adolescent boys wanted to lose weight. This finding suggests that levels of body dissatisfaction are lower for adolescent boys than for adolescent girls, but participants were not asked about whether they wanted to gain weight or increase muscle size or tone. In a review of the literature on body image, Moore (1993) proposed that about one-third of adolescent boys are dissatisfied with their weight, whereas two-thirds of adolescent girls experience body dissatisfaction.

However, Moore focused only on the desire of males to gain weight. Both Nowak et al. and Moore appeared to be addressing only one aspect of body image among adolescent boys (desire to be smaller or larger); therefore, they do not provide a complete picture of body dissatisfaction among adolescent boys. In fact, most of the questionnaire measures that address body image concerns are designed for girls and fail to evaluate a desire for increased bulk, muscle size, or tone (Ricciardelli & McCabe, 2002).

However, Furnham and Calnan (1998) found that adolescent boys were about equally divided between those who wanted to gain weight and those who wanted to lose weight, and, similar to females, about two-thirds of adolescent boys indicated that they were dissatisfied with their bodies. Middleman, Vazquez, and Durant (1998) also found that although 61.5% of girls wanted to lose weight, only 21.5% of boys wanted to lose weight, whereas 6.8% of girls and 36.3% of adolescent boys wanted to gain weight. The complexities of studying weight and shape concerns have also been highlighted by two more recent studies. Ricciardelli and McCabe (2001b) found that among young adolescent boys, 29.6% of the boys wanted to be thinner, 16.6% were at their desired body size, whereas 53.8% wanted to be bigger. McCabe and Ricciardelli (2001a) also found that 75% of young adolescent boys wanted to change the shape of their bodies. These authors found that 55% of adolescent boys wanted to increase their muscles, and 65% wanted to change the size and strength of their muscles, particularly their chest and stomach muscles.

In an older study, Maude et al. (1993) found that twice as many adolescent girls were dissatisfied with their bodies compared to adolescent boys. The authors found that 25.5% of girls and 6.1% of boys perceived that they were overweight, whereas 4.1% of girls and 14.2% of boys perceived that they were underweight. A surprisingly high percentage of respondents (70.4% of girls and 79.7% of boys) perceived that they were normal weight. However, respondents were not asked whether they were dissatisfied with their bodies, only whether their weight was appropriate. This different type of question may explain the differences in findings between this study and other studies.

As for the research reported earlier with children, obtaining average results in terms of body dissatisfaction may lead to a loss of information in relation to the absolute levels of body dissatisfaction. For example, Phelps et al. (1993) found that adolescent boys were generally pleased with their body proportions, whereas adolescent girls demonstrated higher levels of body dissatisfaction. However, average scores were calculated on the figure preference test, and given that some boys may have indicated a smaller figure and some a larger figure as an ideal, this may have resulted in the overall finding of low levels of body dissatisfaction.

In contrast to these findings, other data suggest that adolescent boys experience higher levels of body satisfaction than adolescent girls (Koff, Rierdan, & Stubbs, 1990; McCabe & Ricciardelli 2001a, 2003b; Rierdan, Koff, & Stubbs, 1988). These findings may be due to the stage of adolescence at which the data were obtained. For example, both Siegel, Yancey, Aneshensel, and Schuler (1999) and Alsaker (1992) found that late-maturing boys were most likely to experience higher levels of body dissatisfaction. Thus, data collected at mid-adolescence may demonstrate high levels of body dissatisfaction among male respondents if they are late maturers. Puberty results in increased height and muscular size for many adolescent boys. Boys who have already experienced puberty are, therefore, more likely to approach the sociocultural ideal body form for boys of a V-shaped muscular build (Raudenbush & Zellner, 1997). Late-maturing boys are less likely to have this physique and thus may experience higher levels of body dissatisfaction. The role of pubertal timing on body image concerns is considered in more detail later in this chapter.

A variable that has received little attention in the research literature is the importance attached to body image. Even if there are few gender differences in the levels of body dissatisfaction between adolescent boys and girls, the importance placed on body image appears to be much greater for adolescent girls than it is for adolescent boys. This difference may result from the increased pressure on adolescent girls to achieve the ideal body portrayed by the media (Thompson & Heinberg, 1999). However, boys who place higher levels of importance on their body size are more likely to be dissatisfied with their bodies (Ricciardelli & McCabe, in press).

Body Mass Index   The role of BMI in weight and shape concerns among adolescent boys also needs to be considered. Higher BMI has been found to be associated with more body dissatisfaction in adolescent boys (Blyth et al., 1981; Leon, Fulkerson, Perry, & Early-Zald, 1995; Paxton et al., 1991; Vincent & McCabe, 2000). However, a curvilinear relationship was first noted by Blyth et al., who found that both obese and thinner than average adolescent boys were more dissatisfied with their weight. More recently, Falkner et al. (2001) have also found that the greatest prevalence of negative social, educational, and psychological effects was experienced by obese and underweight boys. More specifically, obese boys were more likely than average-weight boys to report feeling that their friends cared little about them, to experience serious emotional problems, and to leave school early (Falkner et al., 2001). Compared with average-weight males, underweight boys were more likely to report feeling their father and friends cared little about them, to dislike school, and to be expected not to finish school (Falkner et al., 2001). Finally, both obese and underweight boys were less likely to hang out with their friends in the past week and thought of themselves as below-average students (Falkner et al., 2001).

The complex relationship between BMI and body image concerns for males is further demonstrated in the results of Rosenblum and Lewis' (1999) longitudinal study. Being underweight at 13 and 15 years of age unexpectedly predicted better body image in males at 18 years. This shows the importance of examining longer term effects and suggests that the pressures for a slim physique with extremely low levels of body fat are experienced by boys as well as girls (Rosenblum & Lewis, 1999).

Pubertal Timing   Another important biological factor that needs to be considered when examining adolescents boys' body image concerns is pubertal timing. The timing of pubertal development is considered one of the most salient factors for determining whether puberty is associated with any adjustment difficulties (Graber, Lewinsohn, Seeley, & Brooks-Gunn, 1997). It has been predicted that both early- and late-maturing adolescents manifest more social, emotional, and behavioral problems than their on-time age mates (Ge, Conger, Elder, 1996; Williams & Currie, 2000).

There is increasing evidence that early-maturing girls and late-maturing boys show more psychological problems than other adolescents. Research has shown that girls who are early maturers tend to be less popular with their peers, they have poorer self-esteem, they are more likely to be depressed, they tend to exhibit more delinquent and substance abuse problems as well as other general behavioral problems, and they perform poorer on school achievement (e.g., Blyth, Simmons, & Zakin, 1985; Dubas, Graber, & Petersen, 1991; Ge et al., 1996; Graber et al., 1997; Petersen, Sarigiani, & Kennedy, 1991; Rierdan & Koff, 1991; Siegel et al., 1999; Simmons & Blyth, 1987; Stice, Presnell, & Bearman, 2001; Williams & Currie, 2000). Although fewer studies have examined the impact of pubertal timing on social, emotional, and behavioral development in males, several studies have linked late maturation in boys with less social competence, low peer popularity, more conflict with parents, more internalizing tendencies, more drinking problems, and lower school achievement (Andersson & Magnusson, 1990; Blyth et al., 1985; Dubas et al., 1991; Freedman, 1990; Graber et al., 1997; Jones, 1965; Siegel et al., 1999). On the other hand, these same studies have linked early maturation in boys with higher levels of physical attractiveness, superior physique and athletic abilities, more advanced social skills, greater self-confidence, higher levels of self-esteem, a more overactive and gregarious style of personality, and greater popularity with their peers.

The overall social disadvantages of early-maturing girls and late-maturing boys have also been found in the case of body dissatisfaction. Early-maturing girls have been found to be at the greatest risk of body dissatisfaction (e.g., see Blyth et al., 1985, for a review of earlier studies; McCabe & Ricciardelli, 2002; Siegel et al., 1999; Simmons & Blyth, 1987; Williams & Currie, 2000). In contrast, late-maturing males have been found more likely to experience higher levels of body dissatisfaction (Alsaker, 1992; Blyth et al., 1981, 1985; Freedman, 1990; McCabe & Ricciardelli, 2002; Siegel et al., 1999). The overall different effects of pubertal timing on body dissatisfaction and its impact on BMI for boys and girls are consistent with the different cultural ideals of attractiveness for men and women. With pubertal development, girls experience a normative increase in body fat and their hips broaden. As a result, physical changes move girls further away from society's ideal body shape for a woman, so after the onset of puberty many girls report heightened levels of body dissatisfaction and poorer self-image (e.g., Attie & Brooks-Gunn, 1989). However, the onset of puberty moves the majority of boys closer to the societal ideal shape for a man. Boys add muscle and their shoulder width increases, which are physical characteristics that fit the ideal cultural messages for men's body shape and size. Therefore, it is not surprising that early-maturing boys seem to develop more favorable attitudes toward their bodies. In addition, their greater size and strength may make adolescent boys more capable athletes, and athletic prowess brings them social recognition. These maturational differences between girls and boys also help explain why overall girls' body image worsens while boys' improves between the ages of 13 and 18 years (Rosenblum & Lewis, 1999).

Conclusion   The discrepancy in gender differences in levels of weight and shape concerns among adolescent boys and girls may relate to different questions being asked in different studies. For example, studies in which it is found that adolescent girls experience higher levels of dissatisfaction than adolescent boys primarily focus on the desire to be smaller and strategies to lose weight (e.g., Richards, Casper, & Larson, 1990). Questions about gaining weight or increasing muscles have not been examined in the majority of past studies (Ricciardelli & McCabe, 2002). Because losing weight would generally take adolescent males away from the sociocultural ideal body form for boys, it is not surprising that these studies demonstrate that girls are more dissatisfied than boys. If questions related to wanting to be larger and more muscular, as well as being smaller, were included as options, there might be fewer differences between adolescent boys and girls in their levels of body dissatisfaction. One new scale has been constructed to evaluate perceived pressures to lose weight, gain weight, and increase muscles (McCabe & Ricciardelli, 2001d). However, these dimensions are not yet reflected in current instruments that assess body dissatisfaction.

Adult Men

Although most research on the weight and shape concerns of adults has focused on women, some studies have examined this issue among adult men. Studies seem to indicate that weight and shape concerns among adult men are not as straightforward as they are among adult women. The literature has fairly consistently indicated that men are about evenly split between wanting to lose weight and wanting to gain weight. For example, as early as the late 1980s, Drewnowski and Yee (1987) found that 40% of college students wanted to lose weight and 45% wanted to gain weight. Silberstein, Striegel-Moore, Timko, and Rodin (1988) obtained similar results, with college males indicating that they were as likely to want to be larger as they wanted to be thinner. Consistent with these findings, Drewnowski et al. (1995) found that 46% of 18-year-old men wanted to gain weight and 32% wanted to lose weight. In contrast to the findings, Abell and Richards (1996) found that college men were more dissatisfied with their weight than college women, and these males showed a predominant desire to be heavier. Although these findings are different from most studies that indicate that women are more dissatisfied with their bodies than men, the sample size in the study was small (41 men, 43 women); therefore, the results should be treated with caution.

Rozin and Fallon (1988) found that although both adult men and women expressed a desire to lose weight, women showed a greater concern about weight and eating. Further, Gupta and Schork (1993) found that although both adult men and women demonstrated a correlation between aging-related concerns about appearance and "drive for thinness," women also demonstrated correlations between body dissatisfaction and "drive for thinness," as well as the belief that weight loss is associated with youthful looks. Oberg and Tornstam (1999) found that at all ages, adult women attached higher levels of importance to the attractiveness of their bodies than men. In a meta-analysis of gender differences in attractiveness, Feingold and Mazzella (1998) found that men were more satisfied with their bodies than women and considered themselves more attractive. This gender difference was smaller in adulthood than during adolescence, although women showed greater variability in their levels of body dissatisfaction in adulthood than men.

However, the relationship between body image and gender may not be as simple as these studies would suggest. For example, Jackson, Sullivan, and Rostker (1988) found that although college women were engaged in more appearance-directed behaviors than men, gender role was an important predictor of body image among both men and women. In fact, feminine men were found to have a poor body image in a number of domains, whereas masculine women had a more favorable body image. These results may indicate that gender does not shape the body image of adult men but that men are more likely to adopt a masculine sex role and strive toward the stereotyped ideal male body.

A further factor to consider in drawing conclusions about weight and shape concerns is the role played by sexual orientation. For example, the literature consistently indicates that gay men demonstrate higher levels of body dissatisfaction than heterosexual men (Beren, Hayden, Wilfley, & Grilo, 1996; French, Story, Remafedi, Resnick, & Blum, 1996; Lakkis, Ricciardelli, & Williams, 1999; Siever, 1994; Strong, Singh, & Randall, 2000; I. Williamson & Hartley, 1998). However, as also indicated by Jackson et al.'s (1988) study, it appears that level of femininity, rather than actual sexual orientation, explains these higher levels of body dissatisfaction (Lakkis et al., 1999; Meyer, Blissett, & Oldfield, 2001; Strong et al., 2000). Because these studies have primarily focused on desire for weight loss, it is important to further explore the extent to which both sexual orientation and sex role affect desire for the muscular ideal and levels of body dissatisfaction. In fact, Boroughs and Thompson (2002) found that gay men did not show a greater preference for muscularity than heterosexual men, although they did perceive their upper torsos as smaller than that of heterosexual men.

These findings on weight and shape concerns are limited by a number of factors. Most results were obtained on college men, whose mean ages ranged from 18 to 21 years; therefore, the extent to which the findings can be generalized to middle-age and older men is limited. In fact, given that older men are likely to be heavier than respondents in these studies, they may indicate a greater desire than a male college population to lose weight (Heatherton, Mahamedi, Striepe, Field, & Keel, 1997).

It is also unclear from these studies whether adult men who want to gain weight want to actually increase their weight or increase the size and tone of their muscles. Because respondents are frequently not asked about increasing muscle tone, adult men who indicate that they want to increase their weight may actually want an increase in the size of their muscles, not increased adipose tissue. This suggestion is in line with the sociocultural ideal for men, which is a muscular body build, rather than a large body build per se. Little research has targeted adult males' body dissatisfaction with different body parts (i.e., chest, shoulders, biceps) despite the fact that this dissatisfaction was highlighted as early as 1954 by Jourard and Secord.

Interestingly, the goal for a larger muscular body is common across a range of cultural groups. Pope, Gruber, et al. (2000) found that men from France, Austria, and America indicated on average that their ideal body was 13 kg more muscular than their current body. In fact, it appears that men who show the greatest drive for an increased build also show the highest levels of body dissatisfaction. These findings would be expected to apply to men who are more involved in active exercise. However, McDonald and Thompson (1992) found that college men who were physically active were less likely than physically active college women to demonstrate high levels of body dissatisfaction. Perhaps the finding in relation to body dissatisfaction relates to the nature of the physical activity, that is, whether the person engages in activities that require a large body build, as opposed to a more athletic body build.

Blouin and Goldfield (1995) found that bodybuilders reported higher levels of body dissatisfaction and higher drive for bulk and drive for thinness than runners. Similar results were obtained by Pasman and Thompson (1988) in their study of runners and weightlifters. In contrast, Boroughs and Thompson (2002) found that bodybuilders expressed lower overall body dissatisfaction but a larger ideal upper torso than runners. Nudelman, Rosen, and Leitenberg (1988) found that male runners were no different in their levels of body dissatisfaction (as assessed by being intent on losing weight and negatively preoccupied with weight) than nonactive men. This is despite the fact that male runners have been proposed to resemble women with anorexia nervosa and bulimia nervosa as to their body attributes and eating behaviors. Huddy and Cash (1997) found that male marathon runners were more invested in their physical fitness and their appearance. The findings from these different studies suggest that the nature of the questions asked influences the levels of body dissatisfaction obtained and determines the level of differences in body dissatisfaction between different groups.

The previous findings are consistent with the findings related to the muscular sociocultural ideal for males. Men are generally striving for this ideal body form, which is reflected in the nature of the dissatisfaction that they experience with their bodies. Further, those males who are most removed from achieving this body build, or those who place most importance on achieving this body build, are the ones who are most likely to experience higher levels of body dissatisfaction.

Body Mass Index   Women of all age groups generally strive for a slimmer body regardless of their BMI, and this finding has been consistent among adult women. In contrast, some adult men seem to strive for a slimmer body, whereas others want a larger, more muscular body. The extent to which these different findings relate to the BMI of adult men has not been fully explored. One further study by Pingitore, Spring, and Garfield (1997) with college-age men and women found that as BMI increased for both men and women, respondents experienced increasing levels of body dissatisfaction, although this increase was substantially higher for women than it was for men.

The relationship between BMI and weight and shape concerns in males has been found to be more complex than females. Although many women with low BMIs desire to be thinner than their current body sizes, the trend is reversed for males, because many men with average BMIs perceive themselves as underweight (Betz, Mintz, & Speakmon, 1994) and desire to be larger and/or more muscular (Raudenbush & Zellner, 1997; Rosenblum & Lewis, 1999). Moreover, body image and self-image concerns, more generally, among males who are below average weight for their height or view themselves as underweight are very negative (Harmatz, Gronendyke, & Thomas, 1985; Tata, Fox, & Cooper, 2001). Underweight adult males have been found to demonstrate an extremely negative self-image and poor social adjustment equal to and often more negative than overweight females. More specifically, underweight adult males viewed themselves as less handsome, less good natured, and having less sex appeal than other males and females. Their extremely negative body image impeded their social adjustment, which presented even more problems for these men than those presented by women who were overweight. These results would be best interpreted within the sociocultural framework of ideal body forms for men and women.

As with the literature on children and adolescents, a substantial amount of the research that examines body image among adults focuses on a desire to be thinner. For example, Tiggemann (1994) found that being overweight was associated with body dissatisfaction among adult women but not men. Likewise, Muth and Cash (1997) found that among college-age men and women, women expressed higher levels of body dissatisfaction than men. Levels were highest for women with higher BMI, whereas men demonstrated a curvilinear relationship between body dissatisfaction and weight, with those with a high or low BMI demonstrating the highest levels of body dissatisfaction. These gender differences appear to apply across all age groups (Paxton & Phythian, 1999), although the measures employed by Paxton and Phythian were primarily directed at feeling fat and a desire to lose weight. In contrast to these findings, Smith, Handley, and Eldredge (1998) found no gender differences between male and female undergraduate students in their levels of body dissatisfaction. However, the sample size for this study was small ($n = 178$), so the volunteers for the study may not have been representative of the broader population of college men and women.

Conclusion   One of the major problems with this literature is that it has largely used samples of college youth to draw conclusions about weight and shape concerns among adult men. Whereas adolescent boys are primarily focused on increasing muscle size, adult men appear more focused on losing weight and increasing muscle tone—particularly true as men get older. Men also appear to attribute less importance to the appearance of their bodies than women.

It is not clear if the size and shape of their bodies become more or less important over the lifespan for men. Although body appearance remains important throughout the lifespan for women, no data are available on the importance of appearance for older men. Importance of appearance may not be a straightforward question for adult men and women because it relates not only to what they look like, but also to their health, fitness, and general well-being. All of these aspects of body image need to be examined to determine if it is the adult man's appearance that is causing him to be dissatisfied or if the dissatisfaction relates more to the functioning and capacity of his body.

Sociocultural Influences

Children

Limited research has examined the role of sociocultural influences on body image among children. It has primarily evaluated the influence of parents (particularly mothers) and has largely focused on girls. Less research has examined the role of peers and the media.

Smolak, Levine, and Schermer (1999) evaluated the influence of both the direct comments and modeling of weight concerns of both mother and father on boys and girls ages 9 to 11 years. The results demonstrated that boys were generally not affected by parental messages and that the direct parental comments, particularly by mothers, were more influential than modeling of weight and shape concerns. However, these concerns were primarily focused on weight loss; therefore, the impact of feedback related to either messages to gain weight or increase muscle were not evaluated. Consistent with these findings, Schur et al. (2000) found that parents were the main source of information on dieting among children ages 8 to 13 years, but the impact of this information on body image was not evaluated. Thelen and Cormier (1995) also found that although the associations between weight and shape concerns and parental messages were stronger for girls, encouragement from both mothers and fathers to lose weight was associated with a desire to be thinner for boys. If desire and pressures to be bigger and more muscular were also evaluated, the perceived pressures may have been greater for boys.

Oliver and Thelen (1996) examined the influence of peers on body image concerns among boys and girls ages 9 to 11 years. Girls were more likely than boys to believe that being thin would increase peer likeability. However, the question of whether they would be more likeable if they had larger bodies was not raised. These results suggest that children, particularly girls, seem to believe that they need to adhere to the sociocultural ideal body form to be popular. The extent to which these messages are also detected by boys is not clear because studies with children have not focused on the perceived pressures to have a large, muscular body build.

A recent adaptation of the Sociocultural Attitudes Toward Appearance Questionnaire for children has been developed by Smolak, Levine, and Thompson (2001). An analysis of this questionnaire for boys identified three factors: internalization of the muscular ideal (e.g., "I wish I looked like a bodybuilder"), awareness of the ideal body (e.g., "In today's society, it is important to always look attractive"), and the being muscular and looking good (e.g., "People think that the more muscular you are, the better you look in clothes"). The main factor associated with body dissatisfaction and both weight loss and muscle-building strategies for boys was internalization of the muscular ideal.

The role of the media on children's weight and shape concerns has received little attention in the literature. One measure developed for children is the multidimensional Media Influence Scale by Cusumano and Thompson (2001). An analysis of this scale identified three factors for both boys and girls: internalization of the thin ideal (e.g., "I try to look like the models in magazines"), awareness of the thin ideal (e.g., "Clothes look better on people who are thin"), and perceived pressure from the media to achieve thinness (e.g., "Watching TV or reading magazines makes me want to diet or lose weight"). However, the subscales were found only weakly associated with body dissatisfaction in boys—probably because it did not assess internalization, awareness, and perceived media pressure to achieve muscularity, which may be more relevant to males of all ages.

The data related to sociocultural influences on young boys are extremely limited. The limited research has focused on perceived pressures to lose weight. Because this strategy may take many boys away from their sociocultural ideal, it is not surprising that young boys are generally not influenced by these pressures. Research on sociocultural pressures also needs to focus on perceived pressure to be larger or to have increased muscles.

Adolescent Boys

Males are being exposed through television, movies, magazines, and other sources to an idealized male body image that is far more muscular than an average man, but relatively little research has examined whether males internalize these messages and whether these messages are having any impact on their body image concerns and related behaviors.

It has been suggested that adolescent boys may be less influenced by sociocultural pressures than adolescent girls (Andersen & Holman, 1997; Steen, Wadden, Foster, & Andersen, 1996). For example, one study found that attempts to lose weight were fairly rare even among obese boys and that boys were not influenced by their parents' encouragement to lose weight (Steen et al., 1996). However, other studies have shown that parents and peers play an important role in shaping body image concerns and body change strategies for both adolescent boys and girls (McCabe & Ricciardelli, 2003c; McCabe, Ricciardelli, & Finemore, 2002; Ricciardelli & McCabe, 2002a; Vincent & McCabe, 2000). For example, in a recent longitudinal study, we found that weight loss strategies in adolescent boys over an eight-month period were predicted by perceived parental and peer pressure to lose weight (McCabe & Ricciardelli, in 2003b). Similarly, weight-gain strategies in adolescent boys were predicted by perceived parental and peer pressure to gain weight (McCabe & Ricciardelli, in 2003b). Levinson, Powell, and Steelman (1986) found that parental feedback was less negative for boys than for girls; therefore, gender differences in levels of body dissatisfaction may be at least partly due to perceived pressure from parents.

O'Koon (1997) examined the impact of parental and peer attachment on self-image. He found that although attachment to parents was important to adolescent boys, even among late adolescent boys, the level of peer attachment was most likely to have an effect on body image. Ricciardelli, McCabe, and Banfield (2000) found that both peers and the media played a more significant role on body dissatisfaction among adolescent boys than parents. Vincent and McCabe (2000) also found that poor peer relationships and negative comments from peers predicted body dissatisfaction among adolescent boys, and negative comments from mothers also had an impact. This impact was smaller than it was for adolescent girls. Likewise, Wertheim et al. (1992) found that although parental relationships impacted both body image and disordered eating among adolescent girls, these relationships played a much smaller role in the body image of adolescent boys. The authors suggested that factors other than parents shape body image among adolescent boys.

However, it is possible that parents play a stronger role than this past research would suggest because these studies focused on weight loss strategies. Parents may play a more significant role in shaping body dissatisfaction among adolescent boys if the impact of messages related to weight gain and increased muscles is also evaluated. In fact, McCabe and Ricciardelli (2003c) conducted a study with 1,266 adolescents (622 boys, 644 girls) that investigated the role of parents, peers, and the media on a range of body change strategies. They found that parents (both mother and father) played a significant role on weight gain and strategies to increase muscle, as well as weight loss, among adolescent boys. Because adolescent boys have been found to have a higher self-esteem than adolescent girls (Hoare & Cosgrove, 1998), the messages may not be having an impact on the body dissatisfaction of adolescent boys, or they may just ignore the messages. Consistent with this proposal, McCabe and Ricciardelli (2001c) found that sociocultural influences on weight control and muscle building were not as strong for boys as weight control techniques were for girls. However, McCabe and Ricciardelli did not explore whether the messages were being detected but just not having an influence on behavior.

Additional studies have examined the perceived role of the media on adolescent boys' body image concerns (Field et al., 2001; McCabe & Ricciardelli, 2003c; Ricciardelli et al., 2000). In one cross-sectional survey, media influences to lose weight were found associated with weight loss strategies, media influences to gain weight were associated with weight gain strategies, and media influences to increase muscles were associated with both body dissatisfaction and the importance boys placed on their body image (McCabe & Ricciardelli; 2003c). Similarly, in another study, adolescent boys who reported making substantial efforts to look like same-sex figures in the media were more likely to become concerned with their weight (Field et al., 2001). However, in a more in-depth interview study, several boys viewed the media as having a positive effect on their body image, while for many boys, the media was viewed as having no effect on body image (Ricciardelli et al., 2000). This is a striking difference to research on girls because girls perceive the media to be a major force that leads to body dissatisfaction (Wertheim, Paxton, Schultz, & Muir, 1997). Two other findings also differed from those frequently reported for girls. It has been found that several adolescent boys reported receiving positive comments about their bodies from their mothers and female friends (Ricciardelli et al., 2000). In contrast to boys, girls do not report receiving positive messages from family members or their female or male friends (Wertheim et al., 1997). A further study found that social comparisons were used infrequently by boys and that for some boys, the use of social comparisons was associated with a more positive body image (Ricciardelli et al., 2000). On the other hand, it has been found that girls frequently engage in social comparisons, and such social comparisons are linked to body dissatisfaction and dieting (Stormer & Thompson, 1996).

Two factors that may explain why some adolescent boys may be less influenced by sociocultural factors and why some of these influences may lead to more positive outcomes are self-esteem and negative affect. In comparison to girls, boys have higher levels of self-esteem and lower levels of negative affect (e.g., Hoare & Cosgrove, 1998; Keel, Fulkerson, & Leon, 1997; Nolen-Hoeksema & Girgus, 1994). If these gender differences in levels of self-esteem and negative affect are correct, boys may be better equipped to ignore sociocultural messages from family, friends, and the media. Evidence consistent with this view was found in a recent study by Ricciardelli and McCabe (2001c). Although perceived media messages were not an important influence in directly predicting boys' body dissatisfaction and body change strategies, a closer examination of the results for adolescent boys indicated that self-esteem moderated perceived media influences (Ricciardelli & McCabe, 2001c). That is, higher levels of perceived pressure from the media to lose weight predicted body dissatisfaction, and perceived pressure from the media to increase muscles predicted strategies to increase muscle size but only when boys reported low levels of self-esteem. Self-esteem was also found to moderate perceived pressure from female friends in predicting weight loss strategies and perceived pressure from fathers in predicting strategies to increase muscle size. As for the perceived influence of the media, the results showed that higher levels of perceived pressure from female friends to lose weight and perceived pressure from fathers to gain muscles were found to be influential only in determining body change strategies when levels of self-esteem were low among the adolescent boys.

These results suggest that primarily adolescent boys with lower levels of self-esteem were more likely to be affected by higher levels of perceived sociocultural pressures. However, additional findings indicated that lower levels of self-esteem predicted body dissatisfaction among boys but only if perceived sociocultural pressures were low; if sociocultural pressures were high, self-esteem had no effect on body dissatisfaction (Ricciardelli & McCabe, 2001c). The specific sociocultural influences that moderated the effects of self-esteem on body dissatisfaction were perceived pressure from fathers and male friends to lose weight and perceived pressure from the media to gain muscles. These results indicated that although boys with low self-esteem may be more susceptible to sociocultural pressures, these pressures do not overall impact negatively on boys' body dissatisfaction. Rather, it seems as if boys are able to use the information received from their fathers, male friends, and the media to compensate for their low self-esteem. However, longitudinal and more in-depth interview studies are needed to more fully understand how perceived and actual sociocultural pressures may moderate adolescent boys' self-esteem and body dissatisfaction.

Males are still subjected to a wider range of acceptable body shapes and sizes in the media and relatively fewer media messages in comparison to females (Andersen & Di Domenico, 1992; Andersen & Holman, 1997; Nemeroff et al., 1994). Adolescent boys who read more magazines and watch more television programs with muscular male images may be more affected by the influence of the media. However, actual exposure to specific types of media messages has not been examined in many past studies, and none of these studies have examined actual exposure to muscular male images.

Longitudinal studies that evaluate the temporal relationships between perceived sociocultural pressures and weight and shape concerns still need to be conducted. These studies will lead to a more comprehensive understanding of the areas of weight and shape concerns for adolescent boys, as well as a better understanding of the sociocultural pressures that are operating to influence their levels of weight and shape concerns.

Adult Men

There has been limited research on the sociocultural influences that impact on weight and shape concerns among adult men. A number of studies have found that men perceive that the ideal body form for men held by both other men and women is bulkier than their current body form (Cohn & Adler, 1992; Demarest & Allen, 2000). In fact, Pope, Gruber, et al. (2000), in a study that included men from three cultural groups (Austria, France, America), found that all men perceived that women preferred a larger body than they were themselves.

Mishkind et al. (1986) indicated that men experience significant pressure from a range of factors within the society to achieve the muscular ideal; therefore, men consistently experienced body dissatisfaction, particularly with their chest, stomach, and shoulders. These authors claimed that this pressure is further strengthened by the association between muscularity and masculinity and emphasized the importance of the association between the male's body image and his sense of self. Gillett and White (1992) also suggested that sociocultural pressures for the muscular ideal for men come from multiple sources within the broader cultural environment. These pressures are related to the male body form as a sign of masculinity and power; therefore, any man who fails to achieve this body form is vulnerable and experiences anxieties associated with this vulnerability. The authors claimed that there is a strong force in our society for men to adhere to this ideal, with high levels of body dissatisfaction experienced among the men who fail to do so.

The impact of the feedback from parents on body image seems to be stronger for college women than college men. A study by Schwartz, Phares, Tantleff-Dunn, and Thompson (1999) demonstrated that parental feedback about appearance affected body dissatisfaction for college women, but there was no relationship between parental feedback and body dissatisfaction for college men. These findings may indicate that the nature of the feedback is more negative for women or that there is stronger pressure on women from parents to adhere to the societal ideal for body size and shape. Another explanation is that the feedback from parents is not as important for men as it is for women or the level of self-esteem among men protects them from the feedback and, therefore, does not have the same impact on levels of body dissatisfaction among men.

These results suggest that it is not simply exposure or awareness of societal messages that affects body image. This is consistent with studies among adolescent men that suggest that their higher levels of self-esteem may protect them from these societal messages. Although there have been no studies to empirically evaluate the different aspects of media influence among men, Cusumano and Thompson (1997) found that among college women, simple exposure to messages from the media did not predict body dissatisfaction. Awareness of societal pressures was a significant predictor, but the strongest predictor of body dissatisfaction was internalization of social standards of appearance. Research is now needed to determine whether this is the case for males.

Powerful images have also been presented in the media concerning the ideal male body. Trujillo (1995) examined the images of male bodies on television, in particular on football programs. He found that the three images portrayed of the male body were tool, weapon, and object of gaze. These three aspects of male bodies are consistent with the sociocultural view of men's bodies as adhering to a lean mesomorphic muscular ideal. However, for these images to affect body dissatisfaction among men, the forms that they represent need to be internalized. For sociocultural pressures to affect body image, it may not be enough that men are exposed to messages about the ideal body form from the various sociocultural influences. They may also need to be aware of these messages and internalize them so that they shape what is considered ideal for a male body form and influence their levels of body dissatisfaction.

Ogden and Mundray (1996) examined the effects of brief magazine exposure to either thin-ideal figures or fat and unattractive figures on body dissatisfaction and other body image concerns for both adult males and females. Similar effects were found for both males and females, although the effects were overall stronger for females. Both adult males and females felt less satisfied with their bodies—their chests/busts, waists, and hips—after viewing the thin pictures but more satisfied with their overall bodies and the specific body parts after viewing the fat pictures. Both males and females also rated themselves as feeling less sexy, less attractive, and less fit after exposure to the thin images, while they felt more sexy, more attractive, and more fit after exposure to the fat images. However, there were no effects for the males for feeling fat and feeling toned. Only the females reported feeling more fat and less toned after viewing the thin pictures and feeling less fat and less toned after viewing the fat images.

In contrast, Kalodner (1997), in another study with male adults, found that exposure to thin male models had no effect on body dissatisfaction for males. Whether results would be stronger for muscular images needs to be examined. It is also important to determine if media images transmitted with video as opposed to magazines would produce stronger effects. It is possible that the effects of the media may be moderated by other factors, such as past exposure to these images and other individual factors.

In a more recent study, Leit, Gray, and Pope (2002) conducted an experimental study that involved a group of college men briefly viewing advertisements of muscular men. The results demonstrated higher levels of body dissatisfaction after exposure to these advertisements. It is difficult to draw conclusions about the long-term effect of media exposure from this study. Further research is needed to determine the role of the media in predicting body image concerns among men.

Sociocultural messages concerning the ideal male body have become more prevalent over the past 20 years. The impact of these messages on levels of body dissatisfaction and other weight and shape concerns has largely not been investigated. More research is needed to determine the nature of these messages, the principal sources that are relevant for adult males, the extent to which these messages are internalized, as well as their impact on body dissatisfaction and other aspects of weight and shape concerns.

PREVENTION PROGRAMS TO ADDRESS WEIGHT AND SHAPE CONCERNS AMONG MALES

Numerous prevention and intervention programs for body image concerns have been developed and implemented. The primary goals of these programs are to prevent the development of negative body image, improve body image, as well as prevent and reduce its impact on well-being. Because these programs aim to prevent the onset of problems, they would be more usefully implemented at an earlier age than intervention programs, which predominantly focus on people already experiencing problems.

As with the research into body image, the large majority of these programs have been targeted at females and address concerns found to be of greater relevance to females. Some programs have included males, although these programs have still focused on the factors found relevant for females. Most of these programs have been developed for adolescents, although a few have been modified for children. None have been developed specifically for males, although some assess variables that are also relevant for males.

Different combinations of strategies have been used in body image programs, including education, discussion, activities, and therapy. A brief discussion of these different types of programs follows.

Education, Discussion, and Activities

Kater, Rohwer, and Levine (2000) developed a program that presented information about healthy living and biological factors that was designed to shape what people look like. While the program included education, the lessons used more active and experiential learning than some programs and aimed to teach critical thinking, as well as develop the children's identity based on competency and interests rather than their body image. The results indicated positive changes in knowledge, attitudes, and behavioral intentions for boys and girls.

A program developed by Neumark-Sztainer, Butler, and Palti (1995), also based on education, discussion, and activities, assisted the development of student assertiveness to resist the pressures from society. The results indicated moderate effects on knowledge and behaviors, as well as preventing the onset of unhealthy eating practices, such as unhealthy dieting and binge eating. Carter, Stewart, Dunn, and Fairburn (1997) also developed a program that focused on sociocultural pressures and addressed dieting, body esteem, and self-esteem. The program involved education, role plays, and discussion. The results of this program indicated a decrease in the negative attitudes and behaviors related to eating disorders among females.

Rather than including information about healthy and unhealthy eating and exercise practices, O'Dea and Abraham (2000) focused their program on self-esteem. The

"Everybody's Different" program aimed to develop individuals' self-esteem by looking at areas such as stereotypes and learning to accept and value differences and involving others outside the class, such as family, to learn to receive positive feedback. The program resulted in improvements in body satisfaction and self-concept among female participants, with the importance of social acceptance decreasing following the program. The issues outlined in these programs, although not specifically developed for males, included information and strategies relevant for males as well as females.

Discussion and Activities

Stice, Mazotti, Weibel, and Agras (2000) used discussion and activities in their preventative program for eating disorders. Young adult female participants voluntarily argued and critically evaluated the thin ideal. The program addressed the development of the thin ideal and its impact on individuals and society. The results indicated a decrease in thin-ideal internalization, body dissatisfaction, dieting, negative affect, and bulimic symptomatology. This approach is suited to small groups and may be applicable to males. For this type of approach to be successful, participants need an understanding about the cultural thin ideal, the skills to take different perspectives from their own, and the ability to argue successfully. The knowledge, understanding, and perspective-taking skills required may be unavailable to young adolescent boys; therefore, this type of program may not be successful with these respondents, even if modified to incorporate issues more relevant to adolescent boys.

Therapy

Rosen, Saltzberg, and Srebnik (1989) used cognitive-behavioral therapy, in which participants discussed body image, size perception, thoughts and attitudes about appearance, and avoidance of body-related behaviors, such as eating food in public. In comparison to the controls, those who participated in the program indicated an improvement in size perception, body dissatisfaction, and behavioral avoidance. Changes were evident in current behaviors rather than in the prevention of onset of unhealthy behaviors.

Summary

From the studies evaluated, the program strategy does not appear to be the critical factor in determining the success of the program. While all of the different strategies were found to improve knowledge, they had relatively little impact on attitudes and behaviors. These programs have primarily been developed for and implemented with female participants. Further programs need to specifically address areas of concerns for males.

CONCLUSION

This chapter has evaluated the literature that relates to levels of body dissatisfaction and weight and shape concerns among males across the lifespan and the sociocultural pressures that determine these concerns. The literature in this area is not as extensive as the literature that relates to female body image concerns. It has also frequently focused on issues that are relevant to females (i.e., obtaining a smaller body, losing weight); therefore, it has not provided a comprehensive picture of levels of body dissatisfaction in males. This has probably resulted in an underestimation of the level of male problems in this area.

This chapter has demonstrated the importance of evaluating the different aspects of body dissatisfaction, ensuring that the assessment tools are relevant to male problems, as well as the need to be sensitive to how the meaning of body dissatisfaction may change throughout the lifespan. By understanding these issues more clearly, it will be possible to obtain a more accurate idea of body dissatisfaction in males and determine the impact of body dissatisfaction on health risk behaviors (e.g., dieting, bingeing, exercise dependence, use of food supplements and steroids) adopted by males at different developmental stages.

Body image concerns are a significant problem for males as young as 6 years of age. Given the association between body dissatisfaction and disordered eating, as well as other health risk behaviors, this is of concern for professionals working with males. There is a need to highlight the nature of body dissatisfaction in males so that body dissatisfaction and disordered eating are not simply seen as female problems. It is then important to develop preventative and intervention programs so that body dissatisfaction can be addressed before it leads to behaviors that require clinical interventions.

REFERENCES

Abell, S. C., & Richards, M. H. (1996). The relationship between body shape satisfaction and self-esteem: An investigation of gender and class differences. *Journal of Youth and Adolescence, 25,* 691–703.

Alsaker, F. D. (1992). Pubertal timing, overweight, and psychological adjustment. *Journal of Early Adolescence, 12,* 396–419.

American Psychiatric Association. (1994). *Diagnostic and statistical manual of mental disorders* (4th ed.). Washington, DC: Author.

Andersen, A. E., & Di Domenico, L. (1992). Diet vs. shape content of popular male and female magazines: A dose-response relationship to the incidence of eating disorders? *International Journal of Eating Disorders, 11,* 283–287.

Andersen, A. E., & Holman, J. E. (1997). Males with eating disorders: Challenges for treatment and research. *Psychopharmacology Bulletin, 33,* 391–397.

Andersson, T., & Magnusson, D. (1990). Biological maturation in adolescence and the development of drinking habits and alcohol abuse among young males: A prospective longitudinal study. *Journal of Youth and Adolescence, 19,* 33–41.

Attie, I., & Brooks-Gunn, J. (1989). Developing of eating problems in adolescent girls: A longitudinal study. *Developmental Psychology, 25,* 70–79.

Baekeland, F. (1970). Exercise deprivation: Sleep and psychological reactions. *Archives of General Psychiatry, 22,* 365–369.

Bahrke, M. S., Yesalis, C. E., Kopstein, A. N., & Stephens, J. A. (2000). Risk factors associated with anabolic-androgenic steroid use among adolescents. *Sports Medicine, 29,* 397–405.

Bamber, D., Cockerill, I. M., Rodgers, S., & Carroll, D. (2000). "It's exercise or nothing": A qualitative analysis of exercise dependence. *British Journal of Sports Medicine, 34,* 423–430.

Beel, A., Maycock, B., & McLean, N. (1998). Current perspectives on anabolic steroids. *Drug and Alcohol Review, 17,* 87–103.

Beren, S. E., Hayden, H. A., Wilfley, D. E., & Grilo, C. M. (1996). The influence of sexual orientation on body dissatisfaction in adult men and women. *International Journal of Eating Disorders, 20,* 135–141.

Betz, N. E., Mintz, L., & Speakmon, G. (1994). Gender differences in the accuracy of self-reported weight. *Sex Roles, 30,* 543–552.

Blouin, A. G., & Goldfield, G. S. (1995). Body image and steroid use in male bodybuilders. *International Journal of Eating Disorders, 18,* 159–165.

Blyth, D. A., Simmons, R. G., Bulcroft, R., Felt, D., Van Cleave, E. F., & Bush, D. M. (1981). The effects of physical development in self-image and satisfaction with body image for early adolescent males. *Research in the Community and Mental Health, 2,* 43–73.

Blyth, D. A., Simmons, R. G., & Zakin, D. F. (1985). Satisfaction with body image for early adolescent females: The impact of pubertal timing within different school environments. *Journal of Youth and Adolescence, 14,* 207–225.

Boroughs, M., & Thompson, J. K. (2002). Exercise status and sexual body image disturbance and eating disorders in males. *International Journal of Eating Disorders, 31,* 307–311.

Brehm, B. J., & Steffen, J. J. (1998). Relation between obligatory exercise and eating disorders. *American Journal of Health Behavior, 22,* 108–119.

Brower, K. J., Blow, F. C., & Hill, E. M. (1994). Risk factors for anabolic-androgenic steroid use in men. *Journal of Psychiatric Research, 28,* 369–380.

Carlat, D. J., & Camargo, C. A. (1991). Review of bulimia nervosa in males. *American Journal of Psychiatry, 148,* 831–843.

Carter, J. C., Stewart, D. A., Dunn, V. J., & Fairburn, C. G. (1997). Primary prevention of eating disorders: Might do more harm than good? *International Journal of Eating Disorders, 22,* 167–172.

Cohn, L. D., & Adler, N. E. (1992). Female and male perceptions of ideal body shapes: Distorted views among Caucasian college students. *Psychology of Women Quarterly, 16,* 69–79.

Collins, M. E. (1991). Body figure perceptions and preferences among preadolescent children. *International Journal of Eating Disorders, 10,* 199–208.

Connan, F. (1998). Machismo nervosa: An ominous variant of bulimia nervosa? *European Eating Disorders Review, 6,* 154–159.

Cullari, S., Rohrer, J. M., & Bahn, C. (1998). Body-image perceptions across sex and age groups. *Perceptual and Motor Skills, 87,* 839–847.

Cusumano, D. L., & Thompson, J. K. (1997). Body image and body shape ideals in magazines: Exposure, awareness, and internalization. *Sex Roles, 37,* 701–721.

Cusumano, D. L., & Thompson, J. K. (2001). Media influence and body image in 8–11 year-old boys and girls: A preliminary report on the Multidimensional Media Influence Scale. *International Journal of Eating Disorders, 29,* 37–44.

Demarest, J., & Allen, R. (2000). Body image: Gender, ethics, and age differences. *Journal of Social Psychology, 140,* 465–472.

Drewnowski, A., Kurth, C. L., & Krahn, D. D. (1995). Effects of body image on dieting, exercise, and anabolic steroid use in adolescent males. *International Journal of Eating Disorders, 17,* 381–386.

Drewnowski, A., & Yee, D. K. (1987). Men and body image: Are males satisfied with their body weight? *Psychosomatic Medicine, 49,* 626–634.

Dubas, J. S., Graber, J. A., & Petersen, A. C. (1991). The effects of pubertal development on achievement during adolescence. *American Journal of Education, 99,* 444–460.

Falkner, N. H., Neumark-Sztainer, D., Story, M., Jeffery, R. W., Beuhring, T., & Resnick, M. D. (2001). Social, educational, and psychological correlated of weight status in adolescents. *Obesity Research, 9,* 32–42.

Feingold, A., & Mazzella, R. (1998). Gender differences in body image are increasing. *Psychological Science, 9,* 190–195.

Field, A. E., Camargo, C. A., Taylor, C. B., Berkey, C. S., Roberts, S. B., & Colditz, G. A. (2001). Peer, parent, and media influences on the development of weight concerns and frequent dieting among preadolescent and adolescent girls and boys. *Pediatrics, 107,* 54–60.

Folk, L., Pedersen, J., & Cullari, S. (1993). Body satisfaction and self-concept of third- and sixth-grade students. *Perceptual and Motor Skills, 76,* 547–553.

Fox, K., Page, A., Armstrong, N., & Kirby, B. (1994). Dietary restraint and self-perceptions in early adolescence. *Personality and Individual Differences, 17,* 87–96.

Freedman, R. (1990). Cognitive-behavioral perspectives on body image change. In T. F. Cash & T. Pruzinsky (Eds.), *Body image: Development, deviance, and change* (pp. 273–295). New York: Guilford Press.

French, S. A., Story, M., Remafedi, G., Resnick, M. D., & Blum, R. W. (1996). Sexual orientation and prevalence of body dissatisfaction and eating disordered behaviors: A population-based study of adolescents. *International Journal of Eating Disorders, 19,* 119–126.

Furnham, A., & Calnan, A. (1998). Eating disturbance, self-esteem, reasons for exercising and body weight dissatisfaction in adolescent males. *European Eating Disorders Review, 6,* 58–72.

Gardner, R. M., Friedman, B. N., Stark, K., & Jackson, N. A. (1999). Body-size estimations in children six through fourteen: A longitudinal study. *Perceptual and Motor Skills, 88,* 541–555.

Garfinkel, P. E., Kin, E., Goering, P., Spegg, C., Goldbloom, D. S., Kennedy, S., et al. (1995). Bulimia nervosa in a Canadian community sample: Prevalence and comparison of subgroups. *American Journal of Psychiatry, 152,* 1052–1058.

Ge, X., Conger, R. D., & Elder, G. H. (1996). Coming of age too early: Pubertal influences on girls' vulnerability to psychological distress. *Child Development, 67,* 3386–3400.

Gillett, J., & White, P. G. (1992). Male bodybuilding and the reassertion of hegemonic masculinity: A critical feminist perspective. *Play and Culture, 5,* 358–369.

Graber, J. A., Lewinsohn, P. M., Seeley, M. S., & Brooks-Gunn, J. (1997). Is psychopathology associated with the timing of pubertal development? *Journal of the American Academy of Child and Adolescent Psychiatry, 36,* 1768–1776.

Gupta, M. A., & Schork, N. J. (1993). Aging-related concerns and body image: Possible future implications for eating disorders. *International Journal of Eating Disorders, 14,* 481–486.

Harmatz, M. G., Gronendyke, J., & Thomas, T. (1985). The underweight male: The unrecognized problem group of body image research. *Journal of Obesity and Weight Regulation, 4,* 258–267.

Heatherton, T. F., Mahamedi, F., Striepe, M., Field, A. E., & Keel, P. (1997). A 10-year longitudinal study of body weight, dieting, and eating disorder symptoms. *Journal of Abnormal Psychology, 106,* 117–125.

Hoare, P., & Cosgrove, L. (1998). Eating habits, body-esteem and self-esteem in Scottish children and adolescents. *Journal of Psychosomatic Research, 45,* 425–431.

Huddy, D. C., & Cash, T. F. (1997). Body-image attitudes among male marathon runners: A controlled comparative study. *International Journal of Sport Psychology, 28,* 227–236.

Huenemann, R. L., Shapiro, L. R., Hampton, M. D., & Mitchell, B. W. (1966). A longitudinal study of gross body composition and body conformation and association with food and activity in teenage population: Views of teenage subjects on body conformation, food and activity. *American Journal of Clinical Nutrition, 18,* 323–338.

Jackson, L. A., Sullivan, L. A., & Rostker, R. (1988). Gender, gender role, and body image. *Sex Roles, 19,* 429–443.

Jones, M. C. (1965). Psychological correlates of somatic development. *Child Development, 56,* 899–911.

Jourard, S. M., & Secord, P. F. (1954). Body size and body-cathexis. *Journal of Counseling Psychology, 18,* 1984.

Kalodner, C. R. (1997). Media influences on male and female noneating disordered college students: A significant issue. *Eating Disorders, 5,* 47–57.

Kater, K. J., Rohwer, J., & Levine, M. P. (2000). An elementary school project for developing healthy body image and reducing risk factors for unhealthy and disordered eating. *Eating Disorders, 8,* 3–16.

Katzman, M. A., Wolchik, S. A., & Braver, S. L. (1984). The prevalence of frequent binge eating and bulimia in a nonclinical college sample. *International Journal of Eating Disorders, 3,* 53–62.

Keel, P. K., Fulkerson, J. A., & Leon, G. R. (1997). Disordered eating precursors in pre- and early adolescent girls and boys. *Journal of Youth and Adolescence, 26,* 203–216.

Keel, P. K., Klump, K. L., Leon, G. R., & Fulkerson, J. A. (1998). Disordered eating in adolescent males from a school-based sample. *International Journal of Eating Disorders, 23,* 125–132.

Kindlundh, A. M. S., Hagekull, B., Isacson, D. G. L., & Nyberg, F. (2001). Adolescent use of anabolic-androgenic steroids and relations to self-reports of social, personality and health aspects. *European Journal of Health, 11,* 322–328.

Koff, E., Rierdan, J., & Stubbs, M. L. (1990). Gender, body image, and self-concept in early adolescence. *Journal of Early Adolescence, 10,* 56–68.

Krowchuck, D. P., Kreiter, S. R., Woods, C. R., Sinal, S. H., & DuRant, R. H. (1998). Problem dieting behaviors among young adolescents. *Archives of Pediatrics and Adolescent Medicine, 152,* 884–889.

Lakkis, J., Ricciardelli, L. A., & Williams, R. J. (1999). Role of sexual orientation and gender-related traits in disordered eating. *Sex Roles, 41,* 1–16.

Leit, R. A., Gray, J. J., & Pope, H. G. (2002). The media's representation of the ideal male body: A cause for muscle dysmorphia? *International Journal of Eating Disorders, 31,* 334–338.

Leit, R. A., Pope, H. G., & Gray, J. J. (2001). Cultural expectations of muscularity in men: The evolution of playgirl centerfolds. *International Journal of Eating Disorders, 29,* 90–93.

Leon, G. R., Fulkerson, J. A., Perry, C. L., & Early-Zald, M. B. (1995). Prospective analysis of personality and behavioral vulnerabilities and gender influences in the later development of disordered eating. *Journal of Abnormal Psychology, 104,* 140–149.

Lerner, R. M., Orlos, J. B., & Knapp, J. R. (1976). Physical attractiveness, physical ineffectiveness and self-concept in late adolescents. *Adolescence, 43,* 313–326.

Levinson, R., Powell, B., & Steelman, L. C. (1986). Social location, significant others and body image among adolescents. *Social Psychology Quarterly, 49,* 330–337.

Lock, J., Reisel, B., & Steiner, H. (2001). Associated health risks of adolescents with disordered eating: How different are they from their peers? Results from a high school survey. *Child Psychiatry and Human Development, 31,* 249–265.

Maude, D., Wertheim, E. H., Paxton, S., Gibbons, K., & Szmukler, G. (1993). Body dissatisfaction, weight loss behaviors, and bulimic tendencies in Australian adolescents with an estimate of female data representativeness. *Australian Psychologist, 28,* 128–132.

McCabe, M. P., & Ricciardelli, L. A. (2001a). Body image and body change techniques among young adolescent males. *European Eating Disorders Review, 9,* 1–13.

McCabe, M. P., & Ricciardelli, L. A. (2001b). Parents, peers and media influence on body image and strategies to body increase and decrease body size among adolescent boys and girls. *Adolescence, 36,* 225–240.

McCabe, M. P., & Ricciardelli, L. A. (2001c). The structure of the Perceived Sociocultural Influences on Body Image and Body Change Questionnaire. *International Journal of Behavioral Medicine, 8,* 19–41.

McCabe, M. P., & Ricciardelli, L. A. (2001d). [Exercise dependence scores in adolescent males.] Unpublished raw data.

McCabe, M. P., & Ricciardelli, L. A. (2002). *A longitudinal study of pubertal timing and health risk behaviors among adolescent boys and girls.* Manuscript submitted for publication.

McCabe, M. P., & Ricciardelli, L. A. (2003a). Body image and strategies to lose weight and increase muscle among boys and girls. *Health Psychology, 22,* 39–46.

McCabe, M. P., & Ricciardelli, L. A. (2003b). A longitudinal study of body change strategies among adolescent males. *Journal of Youth and Adolescence, 32,* 105–113.

McCabe, M. P., & Ricciardelli, L. A. (2003c). Sociocultural influences on body image and body change strategies among adolescent boys and girls. *Journal of Social Psychology, 143,* 5–26.

McCabe, M. P., Ricciardelli, L. A., & Finemore, J. (2002). The role of puberty, media, and popularity with peers as strategies to increase weight, decrease weight and increase muscle tone among adolescent boys and girls. *Journal of Psychosomatic Research, 52,* 145–153.

McDonald, K., & Thompson, J. K. (1992). Eating disturbance, body image dissatisfaction, and reasons for exercising: Gender differences and correlational findings. *International Journal of Eating Disorders, 11,* 298–292.

Meyer, C., Blissett, J., & Oldfield, C. (2001). Sexual orientation and eating psychopathology: The role of masculinity and femininity. *International Journal of Eating Disorders, 29,* 314–318.

Middleman, A. B., & DuRant, R. H. (1996). Anabolic steroid use and associated health risk behaviors. *Sports Medicine, 21,* 251–255.

Middleman, A. B., Vazquez, I., & DuRant, R. H. (1998). Eating patterns, physical activity, and attempts to change weight among adolescents. *Journal of Adolescent Health, 22,* 37–42.

Mishkind, M. E., Rodin, J., Silberstein, L. R., & Striegel-Moore, R. H. (1986). The embodiment of masculinity. *American Behavioral Scientist, 29,* 545–562.

Moore, D. C. (1990). Body image and eating behavior in adolescent boys. *American Journal of Diseases in Children, 144,* 475–479.

Moore, D. C. (1993). Body image and eating behavior in adolescents. *Journal of the American College of Nutrition, 12,* 505–510.

Muth, J. L., & Cash, T. F. (1997). Body-image attitudes: What difference does gender make? *Journal of Applied Social Psychology, 27,* 1438–1452.

Nemeroff, C. J., Stein, R. I., Diehl, N. S., & Smilack, K. M. (1994). From the Cleavers to the Clintons: Role choices and body orientation as reflected in magazine article content. *International Journal Eating Disorders, 16,* 167–176.

Neumark-Sztainer, D., Butler, R., & Palti, H. (1995). Eating disturbance among adolescent girls: Evaluation of a school based primary prevention program. *Society for Nutrition Education, 27,* 24–31.

Neumark-Sztainer, D., & Hannan, P. J. (2000). Weight-related behaviors among adolescent girls and boys: Results from a national survey. *Archives of Pediatrics and Adolescent Medicine, 154,* 569–577.

Neumark-Sztainer, D., Story, M., Falkner, N. H., Beuhreng, T., & Resnick, M. D. (1999). Sociodemographic and personal characteristics of adolescents engaged in weight loss and weight/muscles gain behaviors: Who is doing what? *Preventative Medicine, 28,* 40–50.

Nolen-Hoeksema, S., & Girgus, J. S. (1994). The emergence of gender differences in depression during adolescence. *Psychological Bulletin, 115,* 424–443.

Nowak, M., Speare, R., & Crawford, D. (1996). Gender differences in adolescent weight and shape-related beliefs and behaviors. *Journal of Pediatric and Child Health, 32,* 148–152.

Nudelman, S., Rosen, J. C., & Leitenberg, H. (1988). Dissimilarities in eating attitudes, body image distortion, depression, and self-esteem between high-intensity male runners and women with bulimia nervosa. *International Journal of Eating Disorders, 7,* 625–634.

Oberg, P., & Tornstam, L. (1999). Body images among men and women of different ages. *Aging and Society, 19,* 629–644.

O'Dea, J. A., & Abraham, S. (2000). Improving body image, eating attitudes, and behaviors of young male and female adolescents: A new educational approach that focuses on self esteem. *International Journal of Eating Disorders, 28,* 43–57.

Ogden, J., & Mundray, K. (1996). The effect of the media on body satisfaction: The role of gender and size. *European Eating Disorders Review, 4,* 171–182.

O'Koon, J. (1997). Attachment to parents and peers in late adolescence and their relationship with self-image. *Adolescence, 32,* 471–482.

Olivardia, R., Pope, H. G., Mangweth, B., & Hudson, J. I. (1995). Eating disorders in college men. *American Journal of Psychiatry, 152,* 1279–1285.

Oliver, K. K., & Thelen, M. H. (1996). Children's perceptions of peer influence on eating concerns. *Behavior Therapy, 27,* 25–39.

Parkinson, K. N., Tovée, M. J., & Cohen-Tovée, E. M. (1998). Body shape perceptions of preadolescent and young adolescent children. *European Eating Disorder Review, 6,* 126–135.

Pasman, L., & Thompson, J. K. (1988). Body image and eating disturbance in obligatory runners, obligatory weightlifters, and sedentary individuals. *International Journal of Eating Disorders, 7,* 759–769.

Paxton, S. J., & Phythian, K. (1999). Body image, self-esteem, and health status in middle and later adulthood. *Australian Psychologist, 34,* 116–121.

Paxton, S. J., Wertheim, E. H., Gibbons, K., Szmukler, G. I., Hillier, L., & Petrovich, J. L. (1991). Body image satisfaction, dieting beliefs, and weight loss behaviors in adolescent girls and boys. *Journal of Youth and Adolescence, 20,* 361–379.

Petersen, A. C., Sarigiani, P. A., & Kennedy, R. E. (1991). Adolescent depression: Why more girls? *Journal of Youth and Adolescence, 20,* 247–271.

Phelps, L., Swift Johnston, L., Jimenez, D. P., Wilczenski, F. L., Andrea, R. K., & Healy, R. W. (1993). Figure preference, body dissatisfaction, and body distortion in adolescence. *Journal of Adolescent Research, 8,* 297–310.

Pingitore, R., Spring, B., & Garfield, D. (1997). Gender differences in body satisfaction. *Obesity Research, 5,* 402–409.

Polce-Lynch, M., Myers, B. J., Kilmartin, C. T., Forssmann-Falck, R., & Kliewer, W. (1998). Gender and age patterns in emotional expression, body image, and self-esteem: A qualitative analysis. *Sex Roles, 38,* 1025–1041.

Pope, H. G., Gruber, A. J., Mangweth, B., Bureau, B., deCol, C., Jouvent, R., et al. (2000). Body image perception among men in three countries. *American Journal of Psychiatry, 157,* 1297–1301.

Pope, H. G., Jr., Olivardia, R., Gruber, A., & Borowiecki, J. (1999). Evolving ideals of male body image as seen through action toys. *International Journal of Eating Disorders, 26,* 65–72.

Pope, H. G., Jr., Phillips, K. A., & Olivardia, R. (2000). *The Adonis complex: The secret crisis of male body obsession.* New York: Free Press.

Rand, C. S. W., & Wright, B. A. (2001). Thinner females and heavier males: Who says? A comparison of female to male ideal body sizes across a wide age span. *International Journal of Eating Disorders, 29,* 45–50.

Raudenbush, B., & Zellner, D. A. (1997). Nobody's satisfied: Effect of abnormal eating behaviors and perceived and actual weight status on body image satisfaction in males and females. *Journal of Social and Clinical Psychology, 16,* 95–110.

Ricciardelli, L. A., & McCabe, M. P. (2001a). Children's body image concerns and eating disturbance: A review of the literature. *Clinical Psychology Review, 21,* 325–344.

Ricciardelli, L. A., & McCabe, M. P. (2001b). Dietary restraint and negative affect as mediators of body dissatisfaction and bulimic behaviors in adolescent girls and boys. *Behavior Research and Therapy, 39,* 1317–1328.

Ricciardelli, L. A., & McCabe, M. P. (2001c). Self-esteem and negative affect as moderators of sociocultural influences on body dissatisfaction, strategies to decrease weight and strategies to increase muscle tone among adolescent boys and girls. *Sex Roles, 44,* 189–207.

Ricciardelli, L. A., & McCabe, M. P. (2002). Psychometric evaluation of the Body Change Inventory: An assessment instrument for adolescent boys and girls. *Eating Behaviors, 3,* 45–59.

Ricciardelli, L. A., & McCabe, M. P. (2003). A longitudinal analysis of the role of biopsychosocial factors in predicting body change strategies among adolescent boys. *Sex Roles, 45,* 349–360.

Ricciardelli, L. A., & McCabe, M. P. (in press). Sociocultural and individual influences on muscle gain and weight loss strategies among adolescent boys and girls. *Psychology in the Schools.*

Ricciardelli, L. A., McCabe, M. P., & Banfield, S. (2000). Body image and body change methods in adolescent boys: Role of parents, friends and the media. *Journal of Psychosomatic Research, 49,* 189–197.

Richards, M. H., Casper, R. C., & Larson, R. (1990). Weight and eating concerns among pre- and young adolescent boys and girls. *Journal of Adolescent Health Care, 11,* 203–209.

Rierdan, J., & Koff, E. (1991). Depressive symptomatology among very early maturing girls. *Journal of Youth and Adolescence, 20,* 415–425.

Rierdan, J., Koff, E., & Stubbs, M. L. (1988). Gender, depression, and body image in early adolescents. *Journal of Early Adolescence, 8,* 109–117.

Rosen, J. C., Gross, J., & Vara, L. (1987). Psychological adjustment of adolescents attempting to lose or gain weight. *Journal of Consulting and Clinical Psychology, 55,* 742–747.

Rosen, J. C., Saltzberg, E., & Srebnik, D. (1989). Cognitive behavior therapy for negative body image. *Behavior Therapy, 20,* 393–404.

Rosenblum, G. D., & Lewis, M. (1999). The relations among body image, physical attractiveness and body mass in adolescence. *Child Development, 70,* 50–64.

Ross, H. E., & Ivis, F. (1999). Binge eating and substance use among male and female adolescents. *International Journal of Eating Disorders, 26,* 245–260.

Rozin, P., & Fallon, A. (1988). Body image, attitudes to weight, and misperceptions of figure preferences of the opposite sex: A comparison of men and women in two generations. *Journal of Abnormal Psychology, 97,* 342–345.

Sands, R., Tricker, J., Sherman, C., Armatas, C., & Maschette, W. (1997). Disordered eating patterns, body image, self-esteem, and physical activity in preadolescent school children. *International Journal of Eating Disorders, 21,* 159–166.

Schur, E. A., Sanders, M., & Steiner, H. (2000). Body dissatisfaction and dieting in young children. *International Journal of Eating Disorders, 27,* 74–82.

Schwartz, D. J., Phares, V., Tantleff-Dunn, S., & Thompson, J. K. (1999). Body image, psychological functioning, and parental feedback regarding physical appearance. *International Journal of Eating Disorders, 25,* 339–343.

Serdula, M. K., Collins, M. E., Williamson, D. F., Anda, R. F., Pamuk, E., & Byers, T. E. (1993). Weight control practices of U.S. adolescents and adults. *Annals of Internal Medicine, 119,* 667–671.

Siegel, J. M., Yancey, A. K., Aneshensel, C. S., & Schuler, R. (1999). Body image, perceived pubertal timing, and adolescent mental health. *Journal of Adolescent Health, 25,* 155–165.

Siever, M. D. (1994). Sexual orientation and gender as factors in socioculturally acquired vulnerability to body dissatisfaction and eating disorders. *Journal of Consulting and Clinical Psychology, 62,* 252–260.

Silberstein, L. R., Striegel-Moore, R. H., Timko, C., & Rodin, J. (1988). Behavioral and psychological implications of body dissatisfaction: Do men and women differ? *Sex Roles, 19,* 219–231.

Simmons, R. G., & Blyth, D. A. (1987). Moving into adolescence: *The impact of pubertal change and school context.* Hawthorne, NJ: Aldine de Gruyter.

Smith, B. L., Handley, P., & Eldredge, D. (1998). Sex differences in exercise motivation and body-image satisfaction among college students. *Perceptual and Motor Skills, 86,* 723–732.

Smolak, L., Levine, M. P., & Schermer, F. (1999). Parental input and weight concerns among elementary school children. *International Journal of Eating Disorders, 25,* 263–271.

Smolak, L., Levine, M. P., & Thompson, J. K. (2001). The use of the Sociocultural Attitudes toward Appearance Questionnaire with middle school boys and girls. *International Journal of Eating Disorders, 29,* 216–223.

Spitzer, B. L., Henderson, K. A., & Zivian, M. T. (1999). Gender differences in population versus media body sizes: A comparison over four decades. *Sex Roles, 40,* 545–565.

Steen, S. N., Wadden, T. A., Foster, G. D., & Andersen, R. E. (1996). Are obese adolescent boys ignoring an important health risk. *International Journal of Eating Disorders, 20,* 281–286.

Stice, E., Mazotti, L., Weibel, D., & Agras, W. S. (2000). Dissonance prevention program decreases thin-ideal internalisation, body dissatisfaction, dieting, negative affect, and bulimic symptoms: A preliminary experiment. *International Journal of Eating Disorders, 27,* 206–217.

Stice, E., Presnell, K., & Bearman, S. K. (2001). Relation of early menarche to depression, eating disorders, substance abuse, and comorbid psychopathology among adolescent girls. *Developmental Psychology, 37,* 608–619.

Stilger, V. G., & Yesalis, C. E. (1999). Anabolic-androgenic steroid use among high school football players. *Journal of Community Health, 24,* 131–145.

Stormer, S. M., & Thompson, J. K. (1996). Explanations of body image disturbance: A test of maturational status, negative verbal commentary, social comparison, and sociocultural hypotheses. *International Journal of Eating Disorders, 19,* 193–202.

Striegel-Moore, R. H., McAvay, G., & Rodin, J. (1986). Psychological and behavioral correlates of feeling fat in women. *International Journal of Eating Disorders, 5,* 935–947.

Strong, S. M., Singh, D., & Randall, P. K. (2000). Childhood gender nonconformity and body dissatisfaction in gay and heterosexual men. *Sex Roles, 43,* 427–439.

Tata, P., Fox, J., & Cooper, J. (2001). An investigation into the influence of gender and parenting styles on excessive exercise and disordered eating. *European Eating Disorders Review, 9,* 194–206.

Thelen, M. H., & Cormier, J. F. (1995). Desire to be thinner and weight control among children and their parents. *Behavior Therapy, 26,* 85–99.

Thompson, J. K., & Heinberg, L. J. (1999). The media's influence on body image disturbance and eating disorders: We've reviled them, now can we rehabilitate them? *Journal of Social Issues, 55,* 339–353.

Tiggemann, M. (1994). Gender differences in the interrelationships between weight dissatisfaction, restraint, and self-esteem. *Sex Roles, 30,* 319–330.

Tiggemann, M., & Pennington, B. (1990). The development of gender differences in body-size dissatisfaction. *Australian Psychologist, 25,* 306–313.

Tiggemann, M., & Wilson-Barrett, E. (1998). Children's figure ratings: Relationship to self-esteem and negative stereotyping. *International Journal of Eating Disorders, 23,* 83–88.

Trujillo, N. (1995). Machines, missiles, and men: Images of the male body on ABC's Monday Night Football. *Sociology of Sport Journal, 12,* 403–423.

Vander Wal, J. S., & Thelen, M. H. (2000). Eating and body image concerns among obese and average-weight children. *Addictive Behaviors, 25,* 775–778.

Vincent, M. A., & McCabe, M. P. (2000). Gender differences among adolescents in family and peer influences on body dissatisfaction, weight loss and binge eating behaviors. *Journal of Youth and Adolescence, 29,* 205–211.

Wang, M. Q., Yesalis, C. E., Fitzhugh, E. C., Buckely, W. E., & Smiciklas-Wright, H. (1994). Desire for weight gain and potential risk of adolescent males using anabolic steroids. *Perceptual and Motor Skills, 78,* 267–274.

Wertheim, E. H., Paxton, S. J., Maude, D., Szmukler, G. I., Gibbons, K., & Hiller, L. (1992). Psychosocial predictors of weight loss behaviors and binge eating in adolescent girls and boys. *International Journal of Eating Disorders, 12,* 151–160.

Wertheim, E. H., Paxton, S. J., Schultz, H. K., & Muir, S. L. (1997). Why do adolescent girls watch their weight? An interview study examining sociocultural pressures to be thin. *Journal of Psychosomatic Research, 42,* 345–355.

Whitaker, A., Davies, M., Shaffer, D., Johnson, J., Abrama, S., Walsh, B. T., et al. (1989). The struggle to be thin: A survey of anorexic and bulimic symptoms in a nonreferred adolescent population. *Psychological Medicine, 19,* 143–163.

Wichstrom, L. (2000). Psychological and behavioral factors unpredictive of disordered eating: A prospective study of the general adolescent population in Norway. *International Journal of Eating Disorders, 28,* 33–42.

Wichstrom, L., & Pedersen, W. (2001). Use of anabolic-androgenic steroids in adolescence: Winning, looking good or being bad? *Journal of Studies on Alcohol, 62,* 5–13.

Williams, J. M., & Currie, C. (2000). Self-esteem and physical development in early adolescence: Pubertal timing and body image. *Journal of Early Adolescence, 20,* 139–149.

Williamson, I., & Hartley, P. (1998). British research into the increased vulnerability of young gay men to eating disturbance and body dissatisfaction. *European Eating Disorders Review, 6,* 160–170.

Williamson, S., & Delin, C. (2001). Young children's figural selections: Accuracy of reporting and body size dissatisfaction. *International Journal of Eating Disorders, 29,* 80–84.

Wood, K. C., Becker, J. A., & Thompson, J. K. (1996). Body image dissatisfaction in preadolescent children. *Journal of Applied Developmental Psychology, 17,* 85–100.

Wroblewska, A. (1997). Androgenic–anabolic steroids and body dysmorphia in young men. *Journal of Psychosomatic Research, 42,* 225–234.

Yesalis, C. E., Barsukiewicz, C. K., Kopstein, A. N., & Bahrke, M. S. (1997). Trends in anabolic-androgenic steroid use among adolescents. *Archives of Pediatrics and Adolescent Medicine, 151,* 1197–1206.

Zuckerman, D. M., Colby, A., Ware, N. C., & Lazerson, J. S. (1986). The prevalence of bulimia among college students. *American Journal of Public Health, 76,* 1135–1137.

Chapter 30

EATING PROBLEMS IN CHILDHOOD AND ADOLESCENCE

DASHA NICHOLLS

This chapter examines the range of feeding and eating problems from birth to early adolescence. Textbooks, clinicians, and diagnostic manuals traditionally separate feeding problems from eating problems with relatively limited examination of the relationship and continuities between the two. In particular, the term *feeding disorders* implies an interactional component between caregiver and child, while *eating disorders* implies autonomy of self-regulation and care. In developmental terms, however, the transition from feeding to eating is far less clear. This is true for typically developing children, who vary enormously in the degree of dependence they exhibit around food. It becomes particularly emphasized in the context of illness or disability, when the capacity of the child to follow normal trajectories toward self-regulation is delayed or deviated. Thus, functional preschool children may be described as "eating" if they exhibit the capacity to select food, regulate energy needs, and exhibit socially adaptive eating behavior. By contrast, a 12-year-old girl with anorexia nervosa may, in the context of her illness, become fully dependent on her parents to select appropriate food, determine her nutritional needs, and even feed her.

Understanding the transition from feeding to eating requires an understanding of how control and responsibility around food intake are determined and negotiated in both a developmental and a systemic context within relationships and within cultures. This process of transfer of responsibility for eating from caregiver to child is a careful balance of timing and encouragement—too much parental regulation and the child may rebel; too much autonomy for the child and he or she may not be able to cope. As such, the transition from feeding to eating is highly susceptible to tension and conflict, particularly over issues of autonomy and control. It is also a point of communication between a child and his or her parent, and it can be a means for communicating distress or anxiety. The role of beliefs and cognitions about food intake in relation to gender may also be important (Jacobi, Agras, & Hammer, 2001) in terms of the development of problem eating in the early years. The emphasis in this chapter is on understanding emotional, psychological, and behavioral aspects of feeding and eating problems and not on the medical and developmental disorders that such feeding difficulties may often accompany. For a review of diagnosis and treatment of feeding difficulties in children with developmental difficulties, see Rebert, Stanton, and Schwarz (1991); and for feeding difficulties associated with illness, see Harris, Blissett, and Johnson (2000). Although underresearched, there is some evidence that the nature of feeding problems found in children with and without medical conditions does not differ significantly in type but only in frequency or intensity (Crist & Napier-Phillips, 2001; Stark et al., 2000).

RECOGNITION AND CLASSIFICATION

Feeding Problems

The *Diagnostic and Statistical Manual of Mental Disorders* (*DSM-IV*), and The International Classification of Diseases (ICD 10) distinguish two specific subtypes of feeding problems: pica and rumination.

Pica

Pica describes the persistent eating of nonnutritive substances over an extended period of time (more than a month). The type of substance eaten tends to vary with age and developmental capacity. For example, younger children may eat paint, string, or hair; older children, leaves and pebbles; and adolescents, clay or soil. Pica is associated with developmental disorders, including learning disability and pervasive developmental disorders, where its severity is related to the degree of disability. It is usually diagnosed separately only if of particular severity such that specific intervention is required, for example, when medical complications occur as a result of toxicity. Poverty, neglect, and lack of supervision increase the risk for pica in vulnerable individuals. Epidemiological data on pica are limited, and the ingestion of nonnutritive substances may be common in preschool children and should not be considered abnormal unless persistent and severe. In a sample of 472 children attending pediatric clinics, Stein et al. found that pica was associated with parasomnias such as sleep walking, nightmares, night terrors, and banging head or rocking in sleep (M. A. Stein, Mendelsohn, Obermeyer, Amromin, & Benca, 2001). Case reports have suggested a role for selective serotonin reuptake inhibitors in the treatment of pica (D. J. Stein, Bouwer, & Van Heerden, 1996).

Rumination

Rumination is a syndrome characterized by the effortless regurgitation of recently ingested food. It has been linked to severe medical and psychosocial conditions including malnutrition, aspiration pneumonia, and complete social withdrawal and is seen in three distinct populations: infants; individuals with psychiatric and neurologic disorders, particularly developmental disabilities; and adults who do not have overt psychiatric or neurologic disorders (Olden, 2001). The hallmark of rumination, which separates it from other disorders of the upper gastrointestinal tract (such as gastroesophageal reflux disease), is that in rumination, the stomach contents appear in the mouth without retching or nausea. Rather, the subject appears to make a conscious decision on how to handle the regurgitated material after it presents into the oropharynx. It usually occurs very soon after a meal and tends to last for one to two hours.

Rumination is relatively rare, but potentially fatal when it occurs in infants. It is thought to be a form of self-stimulation in this age group. Observation of rumination is all that is needed to make the diagnosis, although often rumination ceases as soon as the infant notices the observer. Parents may not report the symptom spontaneously but may recognize it when described. The infant who ruminates may not retain enough nutrients and may develop potentially lethal malnutrition, a complication that seldom, if ever, occurs in older ruminators. Sensory and/or emotional deprivation are both associated with rumination in children, which may explain the increased incidence of rumination in institutionalized children, infants in intensive care units, and in normal infants with attachment disorders.

The management of patients with rumination needs to be individualized and is best delivered by a multidisciplinary team. In infant rumination, the aim of treatment is to provide a nurturing environment and comforting care to the infant and to help the mother improve her ability to recognize and respond sensitively to her infant's physical and emotional needs. In mentally handicapped children, providing a nurturing caregiver may not be sufficient and behavioral therapy may be necessary.

In adolescents, rumination can be associated with weight loss and vomiting (Khan, Hyman, Cocjin, & Di Lorenzo, 2000), and treatment includes nutritional support in combination with medication, cognitive and relaxation techniques, and pain management. Rumination may present to gastroenterologists rather than to mental health practitioners when a collaborative approach can be very effective, for example, combining the use of medication to decrease acid damage to the esophagus with psychological therapy aimed at identifying situations and emotions that trigger the symptoms. A multidisciplinary team approach is associated with satisfactory recovery in most patients.

Feeding Disorder of Infancy and Early Childhood.

These two specific feeding disorders aside, there remain a number of feeding and eating behaviors in childhood and early adolescence that are currently classified under the generic diagnosis of "feeding disorders of infancy and early childhood." The classification of feeding disorders has been hampered by a lack of knowledge about feeding behaviors in healthy, typically developing children. For example, information about typical length of mealtimes in infants and toddlers has only recently been established, from which a definition of slow eating can be derived (Reau, Senturia, Lebailly, & Christoffel, 1996). In this study, more than 30 minutes was considered slow. In addition, many studies have found that feeding issues are a common concern of parents in community samples. More than 50% of parents report one problem feeding behavior, and more than 20% report multiple problems (Crist & Napier-Phillips, 2001) in children between 9 months and 7 years old. Trying to get children to eat food during structured mealtimes appears to provide the most tension for parents. Findings do not suggest that psychosocial variables such as marital status, socioeconomic status, or the child's birth order are significantly associated with reported frequency and number of feeding problems. Problem feeding is more likely among the children of parents who report using strategies such as coaxing, threats, making multiple meals, and force feeding (Crist & Napier-Phillips, 2001).

A number of different approaches have been taken to attempt to classify feeding disorders based on children presenting to clinical services. There is no international consensus on how to name these behaviors or how they should be classified. Furthermore, although there is extensive literature relating to feeding problems of infancy and early childhood (usually preschool), there is very little published work about feeding and eating problems presenting in middle childhood. The way feeding disorders are categorized tends to depend on the profession to which they have presented and use terms that have been found to be meaningful in a clinical context. For example, from a medical perspective, Burklow, Phelps, Schultz, McConnell, and Rudolph (1998) proposed a coding system for complex feeding disorders based on combinations of five categories: structural abnormalities, neurological conditions, behavioral issues, cardiorespiratory problems, and metabolic dysfunction. In this scheme, behavioral issues were defined very broadly to include feeding difficulties arising from psychosocial difficulties, negative feeding behavior shaped and maintained by reinforcement, and/or emotional difficulties (e.g., phobias, depression). Using this system, 85% of cases were classified in the behavioral category, suggesting that a biobehavioral conceptualization may be more appropriate.

Speech and language therapists tend to consider the presence or absence of oromotor dysfunction a key factor (Wickendon, 2000), grouping feeding problems according to dysfunctional or disorganized feeding (Palmer, Crawley, & Blanco, 1993). Dysfunctional feeding patterns tend not to resolve over time and are associated with other neurological diagnoses and motor difficulties. Disorganized feeding either resolves over time or is related to later sensory problems. It can be helpful to think separately about motor and sensory problems, although inevitably the two interact.

There are a number of psychological classifications, and these depend on particular approaches and whether the child, the parent, or child/parent interaction is the basis for defining the problem. A symptom-based approach to classification may be helpful in behavioral management, for example, problems with texture, problems with quantity, and problems with range (Douglas, 2000). Harris et al. (1992) take an even more pragmatic approach, simply identifying two types of food refusal that may occur separately or together: refusal to take in sufficient calories and refusal to take a sufficient range of foods. Chatoor and colleagues have described a number of feeding problems based on attachment-separation theory, the best characterized of which are infantile anorexia (Chatoor, Hirsch, Ganiban, Persinger, & Hamburger, 1998) and posttraumatic feeding disorder of infancy (Chatoor, Ganiban, Harrison, & Hirsch, 2001). Finally, attempts have been made to classify parental responses to feeding, in recognition of the role that managing the "balance of power" (Birch & Fisher, 1995) has on feeding problems. These authors identified three types of parenting styles applicable to feeding: highly controlling, laissez-faire, and responsive. Highly controlling and laissez-faire parenting may interfere with self-regulation of children's feeding behaviors. Perhaps most importantly in this context is the association between highly controlling parenting and maternal eating disorders (A. Stein et al., 2001) and the link to feeding problems in their offspring (Whelan & Cooper, 2000). Maternal feeding practices and perceptions of their child's eating have also been linked to later overweight (Birch & Fisher, 2000).

One study is of particular note in terms of its research methodology. Crist and Napier-Phillips (2001) used a feeding screening questionnaire, the Behavioral Pediatrics Feeding Assessment Scale (BPFAS), to empirically derive subtypes of feeding problems from a sample of 96 control and 249 clinically referred subjects. Using a principal components analysis, they identified the following factors, which accounted for 55% of the total variance for the combined clinical and normative groups.

Picky Eaters   This factor essentially represents the willingness of children to try new foods and the variety of food groups that the child accepts. This continuum of feeding problems runs from the "picky eating" pattern, common during the toddler years, to the more severe end of the continuum where children have narrowed their food selection to the extent that they are consuming insufficient amounts of key vitamins and minerals. This type of feeding pattern has also been termed *selective eating* (Bryant-Waugh, 2000) or *preservative feeding disorder* (Harris & Booth, 1992), both of which convey the extreme selectivity in preferred foods and resistance to trying new foods (food neophobia). Overall caloric intake is often adequate for these children, and growth and development are usually normal (Nicholls, Christie, Randall, & Lask, 2001). Reau et al. (1996) found an association between picky eating and length of mealtimes and speculated that lengthened mealtimes might reflect underlying oral motor dysfunction in some cases. Jacobi et al. (2001) aimed to clarify and validate the nature of picky eating by examining the relationship between parental report of picky eating and objective behavioral measures and also looked at both parent and child precursors of picky eating. Of 29 cases classified as "picky" on the basis of parent report, objective measures confirmed a lower number and variety of foods consumed, predominantly the avoidance of vegetables. These authors found no association between picky eating and slow eating. Picky eating, sometimes to an extreme degree, is commonly found in children with autistic spectrum disorders.

Toddler Refusal-General   The behaviors identified with this factor included whining or crying, tantrums, and spitting out food. This refusal pattern was associated with younger children and appeared to be more general in nature as opposed to food specific, and it may be linked to other types of oppositional behavior. Parent training approaches may be most fruitful.

Toddler Refusal-Textured Foods   The behaviors that loaded on this factor included problems chewing food; eating only ground, soft food; letting food sit in the mouth without swallowing it; and choking or gagging. This type of refusal behavior appeared to relate closely to making the transition from soft to chewy foods and appeared to reflect the individual child's difficulty in handling textured foods or the selective refusal of textured foods, rather than a general disruption of mealtime behavior. Clinical experience suggests some overlap between this factor and picky eating, and where the two co-occur, the picky eating may be more persistent. Problems with textured food are also found in children with neurodevelopmental disorders such as autism.

Older Children Refusal-General   This factor included behaviors associated with older children such as delaying eating by talking, trying to negotiate what food the child will eat, getting up from the table during meals, and refusing to eat much at a meal but requesting food immediately after the meal. Much of the nutritional intake of these children was gained through snacking between meals. Although these behaviors lengthen the mealtime, they seem to reflect general disruptive behavior, rather than possible oral motor difficulties.

Stallers   This factor was not as well defined as the others. The authors labeled it *stallers* because the feature of "letting food sit in the mouth without swallowing it" was common to all cases. It was associated with a preference for fluids over food (e.g., would rather drink than eat, drinks milk). This feeding pattern may be similar to *restrictive eating*, a term that Bryant-Waugh and Lask (1995) have used to describe children with a constitutionally small appetite, who show limited interest in food, have small appetites, and who grow and develop normally in the lower percentiles for weight and height. This type of feeding pattern could, therefore, be considered a normal variant. Clinical presentation is often due to anxiety about growth, and there may be a long history of attempts to feed the child more than he or she is able to manage. Indeed, feeding practices such as coercion to eat, excessive anxiety about weight gain, and conflict over food can precipitate food refusal, vomiting, and failure to thrive.

None of the five groups outlined previously would seem to identify a single factor reflecting the more serious condition of failure to thrive, which describes a pattern of faltering development because of poor weight gain. It may be that failure to thrive can result through any of the feeding problems described previously if sufficiently severe and/or other factors contribute to exacerbation of feeding problems, such as the use of coercion or other negative parent-child interactions. Although malnutrition is the end point, disentangling the complex contributions of child, parent, and their interactions is not always straightforward. Failure to thrive can be, but is not always, associated with other evidence of neglect and deprivation.

This way of grouping feeding problems is not dissimilar to other attempts at classification but has the advantage of being empirically derived. There are a number of limitations, however. First, only 45% of the variance was accounted for by these factors. Second, larger sample sizes are needed to determine whether any of these patterns of feeding behavior are more common for specific medical conditions than for others. Nevertheless, the avoidance of a false psychological/medical dichotomy seems helpful.

Perhaps surprisingly, only one prospective study has examined the role of early feeding problems in the development of subsequent onset of eating disorders (Marchi & Cohen, 1990), although feeding problems have been identified as a risk factor from retrospective studies (Jacobs & Isaacs, 1986; Rastam, 1992). In a sample of 659 children and their mothers interviewed three times between 1 and 21 years of age, picky eating in early childhood was found to predict symptoms of anorexia nervosa in later adolescence (Marchi & Cohen, 1990). Marchi and Cohen defined *picky eating* by the presence of three of the following (maternally reported) behaviors of the child: "does not eat enough," "is often or very often choosy about food," "usually eats slowly," and "is usually not interested in food." Thus, the concept of picky eating is broader than that defined previously, in which only choosiness is a feature.

Eating Disorders

True eating disorders have been described in children as young as 7 years old. True eating disorders can be understood as disorders characterized by grossly disordered or chaotic eating behavior associated with morbid preoccupation with body weight and shape. For these disorders, anorexia nervosa (AN) and bulimia nervosa (BN), the overall clinical presentation is similar to that in adults, with some important differences that reflect developmental and gender-based differences in expression rather than differences in the disorder per se.

In children with AN, common weight control behaviors include restricted food intake, eating restraint, excessive exercising, and self-induced vomiting. It is particularly common for children to restrict fluid as well as food, which has been argued is a result of problems with abstract thinking. Fluid restriction can cause considerable medical concern. Compensatory behaviors such as laxative or diuretic misuse are less common in younger children, although other features of AN found in older patients can be identified in young children, including preoccupation with food, eating, and calories; a distorted view of "normal" amount of food; guilt associated with eating; increased interest in food preparation and recipes; concern about eating in front of others; and low self-esteem. How these features are manifest depend, among other things, on the child's degree of psychological and emotional maturity, including the capacity for self-awareness and autonomy. Younger patients almost all live at home and commonly come from intact families (Gowers, Crisp, Joughin, & Bhat, 1991). The suggestion that early-onset AN is a less serious illness is not supported by some studies (Arnow, Sanders, & Steiner, 1999; Gowers et al., 1991). For example, Jacobs and Isaacs identified greater premorbid feeding problems and more behavioral problems before becoming ill in prepubertal children with AN, while the illness was very similar in the pre- and postpubertal children in terms of sexual anxiety and self-injury rates (Jacobs & Isaacs, 1986). An increased association with low mood has been variously described in early-onset populations, as have difficulties with expression and emotional language. Recently, Cooper et al. have attempted to specifically address some of the nosological issues in early-onset anorexia nervosa (Cooper, Watkins, Bryant-Waugh, & Lask, 2002). First, is the psychopathological profile of premenarcheal onset AN the same as that of postmenarcheal onset? Second, is the psychopathology of early-onset AN clearly differentiated from that of other eating disturbances presenting in a similar age group? Using the childhood version of the eating disorders examination (EDE; Bryant-Waugh, Cooper, Taylor, & Lask, 1996; Fairburn & Cooper, 1993), early-onset patients with AN had scores comparable to later onset patients on all subscales apart from eating concern, but both AN groups were clearly distinguishable from those with other types of eating problem. Rates of depression were also comparable between the two AN groups and higher than with other types of eating problems.

Presentation in Boys

A number of studies suggest that boys are overrepresented in the younger age group presenting with severe eating disorders (Fosson, Knibbs, Bryant-Waugh, & Lask, 1987; Jacobs & Isaacs, 1986). AN in boys may be characterized by concern around fitness and health, dietary restriction related to "healthy" diet (e.g., related to worries about heart disease). Shape is often more important than weight in self-evaluation. Excessive exercising is very common, and there is a strong association with obsessive-compulsive disorder (Shafran, Bryant-Waugh, Lask, & Arscott, 1995). Bryant-Waugh (1993) has argued that boys with AN may be particularly vulnerable in terms of predisposing factors, given the relative lack of pubertal and sociocultural triggers that have been suggested in etiological models of AN in young girls. Thus, characteristics such as increased sensitivity to food smells and textures, picky eating, and intense attachments and separation anxiety are not uncommon findings in boys with restrictive eating patterns.

Bulimia Nervosa

Bulimia nervosa (BN) remains rare in the preadolescent population, with very few case reports in the literature (Kent, Lacey, & McCluskey, 1992). Clinical presentation is similar to that in adults, and weight control behaviors are similar to those seen in

AN, although with more laxative abuse. Most bulimic children engage in bingeing with compensatory vomiting. While perfectionism and low body weight predict the onset of AN, negative emotion and family history of overweight predict onset of BN (Tyrka, Waldron, Graber, & Brooks-Gunn, 2002). BN is often associated with "teenage" problems, such as underage drinking, smoking, sexual activity, and so on. Depression and self-harm are often features. Chaotic and disordered eating in conjunction with vomiting when found in early-onset AN suggests later bulimic behavior, but the full syndrome is rarely seen in childhood.

Eating Disorders Not Presently Classifiable

As stated previously, there are a number of ways of classifying feeding and eating problems, and these have largely focused on feeding problems in young children and on the eating disorders of AN and BN. There is growing interest in "eating disorders not otherwise specified" (EDNOS), which account for around 50% of cases presenting to adult clinics. Broadly speaking, these cases do feature a preoccupation with weight and shape and have been conceptualized as part of the continuum of "dieting disorders" (Beumont, Garner, & Touyz, 1994). In the younger onset population (school age to early adolescence), in a number of patients who present clinically who do not fit into any of the current classification systems (Nicholls, Chater, & Lask, 2000), food avoidance is the primary presenting feature. Food avoidance emotional disorder (FAED; Higgs, Goodyer, & Birch, 1989), psychogenic vomiting, food phobias, and functional dysphagia are just some of the terms that have been used to describe problem eating behaviors in this age group (Nicholls & Bryant-Waugh, 2003). These children may have other medically unexplained symptoms, and their parents may attribute weight loss to an undiagnosed physical disorder. If this is the case, the physical concerns should be addressed with a comprehensive physical assessment and an open mind. Inevitably, some cases will have previously unidentified organic pathology, the most common being inflammatory bowel diseases, food allergies, and intracranial pathology (De Vile, Sufraz, Lask, & Stanhope, 1995). Some children develop specific circumscribed fears in relation to food, which are associated with specific cognitions. Fears that are common include a fear of vomiting and a fear of contamination or poisoning. Generalized anxiety unrelated to food may also be present; in these cases, anxiety management techniques in combination with family work can be effective once nutritional intake has been reestablished. This heterogeneous group of patients needs further systematic investigation. Direct continuity with later eating disorders has not been demonstrated.

ASSESSMENT

Assessment is one of the most important aspects of any approach to management and can in itself be a powerful intervention. It should ideally be based on a theoretical or conceptual model for the development of eating difficulties in children; encompass biological, psychological, behavioral, and social components; and be based on a developmental and systemic understanding. Any assessment protocol will need to be comprehensive enough to gather relevant information to address the range of feeding and eating problems thus far described and is likely to require the skills of a multi-disciplinary team.

Medical Aspects

In addition to aiding diagnosis and management decisions, information obtained from physical assessments can be powerful information for both sufferers and parents/care-givers, which can influence motivation to change. Furthermore, medical concerns are often the main cause for concern or the reason that the problem has been taken seriously, and medical assessment and ongoing evaluation are, therefore, crucial to a biopsychosocial approach to feeding and eating problems. Medical aspects of feeding and eating problems that are unique to younger patients are growth retardation (and related failure to thrive), pubertal delay or arrest, and reduction of peak bone mass (Kreipe et al., 1995). Certain age-related differences in feeding and eating behavior can also influence likely medical concerns. For example, children may avoid all foods containing certain vitamins or minerals or may restrict fluid as well as food. Most of the medical complications in adolescents with an eating disorder improve with nutritional rehabilitation and recovery from the eating disorder, but some are potentially irreversible. Because of the potentially irreversible effects of malnutrition on physical, psychological, and emotional growth and development in children and adolescents, it has been suggested that the threshold for intervention should be lower than in adults. Monitoring of growth and development should continue until the young person has returned to both medical and psychological health.

A number of publications outline medical complications in the younger patient (Fisher et al., 1995; Katzman & Zipursky, 1997; Kreipe et al., 1995; Nicholls & Stanhope, 2000). Significant gaps in knowledge remain, however. There is no internationally agreed cutoff for malnutrition in children comparable to that for obesity (Cole, Bellizzi, Flegal, & Dietz, 2000), no weight and height adjusted for pubertal maturation, and no standards for expected catch-up after a period of growth failure. The concept of *target weight* in early-onset populations remains one of controversy, with the need for clinical precision at odds with the complexity and heterogeneity of adolescence. As such, a wide variation in clinical practice exists.

Assessing Malnutrition

Assessment of the degree of malnutrition is useful both as a guide to management and as a predictor of outcome. Measures such as percent body mass index (BMI; Cole, Freeman, & Preece, 1995) can be valuable pointers and screening instruments but may be a poor reflection of a child's fat reserves. Independent assessment of fat mass and fat free mass gives a better idea of nutritional status, but care must be given to measurement techniques and adjustment for growth (Nicholls, Wells, Singhal, & Stanhope, 2002). Increasingly complex measures of body composition are being validated in childhood; while these are invaluable in research, they should still be interpreted with caution in children and adolescents (Trocki & Shepherd, 2000). Clinical judgment, together with vital signs (pulse, blood pressure, temperature, and circulation), may be the best indicator of nutritional status in the acute stages, while motoring of growth and development—including bone age, pubertal development, and bone density—are the best indicators of adequate nutrition in the longer term. Weight and height charts are of more value for monitoring change than for assessing the significance of a single measurement. More importantly, growth charts emphasize the rate of expected weight gain for a child. Over the past few years, many countries have published BMI percentiles for children (e.g., Cole et al., 1995; Luciano, Bressan, & Zoppi, 1997; Williams, 2000), which enables nutritional status to be more conveniently and routinely assessed. Amenorrhea is less helpful as a physical sign than in adults because adolescents often miss three or more cycles in the first one to two years or may have primary amenorrhea.

Puberty and Menstruation

Endocrine function is intimately related to nutritional status. The impact of endocrine activity can be seen in pubertal development and on serial pelvic ultrasound scans (Key, Mason, Allan, & Lask, 2002; Lai, de Bruyn, Lask, Bryant-Waugh, & Hankins, 1994), which are of particular value when healthy weight is in dispute. There is no equivalent technique to pelvic ultrasound for assessing progress in boys, other than observing pubertal development by Tanner staging (Tanner & Whitehouse, 1966). The percentage BMI at which menses occurs is normally distributed within ± 2 BMI SDS (i.e., 2nd to 98th percentile BMI, mean 50th percentile) but is age dependent, with taller, slimmer girls menstruating later (Nicholls, 2002). There was no significant difference in the range of percentage BMI for eating disorders patients from those of normal adolescents once age is taken into account.

Impact on Bone Density

Eating disorders, particularly AN, occur at a time of peak bone mass formation; and osteopenia has been reported in adolescent girls with AN, together with evidence of low bone formation markers. Over 12 months, bone density has been shown to rise, most closely correlated with increase in lean body mass (Soyka et al., 2002) and with increased markers of bone turnover. However, more than one year may be necessary before deficits due to malnutrition are fully seen (Nicholls, 2002). The extent to which "catch-up" in bone formation is possible is not yet known for children and young adolescents, but it is likely that in children who have not completed growth and puberty, bone loss can be at least partially compensated for.

Assessment of Psychological, Behavioral, and Social Aspects

A good starting point is usually a discussion with the child and parents about the history and development of the eating difficulty, starting from the time when someone first became aware that there might be a problem. We have found it helpful to draw a time line that includes changes in eating, weight, and related concerns. At presentation, it is also necessary to conduct a mental state examination to contribute to a risk assessment, which includes assessment of comorbid disorders; this is often best conducted with the child alone. Specific eating behavior and psychopathology are useful to assess, for example, using the child version of the EDE (child report; Bryant-Waugh et al., 1996) or one of a number of feeding questionnaires that have been derived for clinical use (parent report) such as the Dutch Eating Behavior Questionnaire (Braet &

Van Strien, 1997). In younger children, it may be useful to observe the feeding difficulty, and video material can be used therapeutically to demonstrate specific behaviors, interactions, and, later, to show change. Finally, the child's current general functioning should also be assessed (including school and social functioning).

Assessment of Developmental Issues

We have found it useful to take a personal history, including important events in the child's life. This can be drawn on a time line, which can then be placed next to the one with weight and eating history, enabling potential links to be explored more easily. The personal history should also include a developmental history, including early feeding, milestones, and so on; the child's medical history; and any history of emotional and/or behavioral problems.

Assessment of Systemic Context

Assessment of systemic context involves gathering information about the family, its wider context, and the family's past contact with health professionals. In addition to gathering information about family history of weight and shape issues as well as family medical and psychiatric history, the aim is to identify strengths, resources, and sources of support. This can be done through drawing a family tree involving any members of the family who live at home. It is important to gain some impression of the family's social context, their ethnic background, and any relevant associated beliefs and practices.

As to the eating difficulty, we routinely ask each member of the family how they understand it and how it affects them. Finally, we ask parents what they have tried in terms of managing the problem and who or what they have found helpful in the past. This will also allow a picture of help-seeking and professional networks to be identified.

A final part of the assessment process is to ascertain where the child and the parents are in terms of their wish to change, to assess their perception of their own ability to achieve change, and to assess their understanding of the process by which change can be achieved.

The assessment process allows more than a diagnosis to be established. It encompasses a risk assessment in terms of physical compromise, suicide/self harm, vulnerability to abuse/neglect, and risk of aggression/violence to others. It enables the impact of the eating difficulty on the child's development and general functioning and also on the family to be determined. Expectations of treatment are ascertained, together with some provisional information about level of motivation and readiness to change. A formulation can be made within a developmental/systemic framework, and this formulation can be shared with the family as a starting point for a collaborative approach to the problem.

MANAGEMENT

Whatever the feeding or eating problem, the child's needs are to be able to eat enough to grow and develop normally and to ensure that food is not the means through which feelings (including conflict and anger) are communicated and emotional needs met. The aim is to restore the child to his or her appropriate developmental track in terms of physical, social, and psychological well-being and functioning. At this time, there is no separate body of evidence-based treatments for children with feeding and eating disorders, including AN. The following ideas have been developed through clinical practice.

The type of treatment offered or appropriate depends on the context of the service. This reflects the fact that children with eating difficulties are seen by a variety of professionals in a variety of settings, including pediatric or mental health settings; generic and specialist services; outpatient, inpatient, and day patient services; and across a wide range in terms of age and types of eating problems seen. Whatever the context, certain important aspects differ from adult patients. First, the patient/client is not a single individual. Issues about engagement in treatment, motivation to change, consent, and confidentiality all need to take into account the fact that children are brought for treatment. Medical concerns may be more urgent and necessitate prompt action. Related is the need for awareness of statutory responsibilities concerning child protection and duty of care.

In the younger age group, it is our expectation that intervention will involve those with parental responsibility. The initial management plan depends on findings from the assessment, which have established the nature of the problem, any immediate risks, and an understanding of the problem and what might be maintaining it. It will also have established the child's and family's stances to treatment and formed the basis for a therapeutic alliance. Because these features are unique and differ across the types of disorder, with the age of the child, across cultures, and within individual families, prescriptive plans for intervention are inappropriate. The following principles may be useful.

First, successful intervention involves understanding, not just identifying or recognizing a problem. In this age group in particular, understanding the eating problem includes a consideration of developmental and systemic issues. A second principle of intervention in the younger population is that change is best achieved through enhancing and supporting the child's and parents' problem-solving and communication skills. In this model, the role of the therapist is to elicit, enhance, encourage, and even suggest. Finally, treatment of choice is to treat the eating disorder, not the complication. This does not mean the aim is to "get to the cause of the problem" because it may be easier to influence factors maintaining the problem than those that started it. It does mean that an understanding of the problem beyond its nutritional and behavioral manifestation will be required for successful resolution.

Intervention begins with feedback from the assessment process and establishing a mutually acceptable formulation of the problem. It may be useful to look at the gains and losses involved in changing the problem (a risk/benefit analysis). Learning to engage all those who have come for treatment is a core skill in the management of younger patients and their families and one that requires particular time and attention. The purpose and practice of therapy should be overt and understandable, whatever its nature. This includes agreeing on a format, identifying shared (and nonshared) aims and expectations, and identifying how progress in treatment can be reviewed. Early in the treatment process, lines of communication need to be clarified. What information will be shared with whom, which professionals need to be informed, and how issues of confidentiality for the young person will be managed should be specified. It is our practice to routinely copy correspondence to parents.

Children and parents are involved in the decision-making process, which requires the provision of information—information about onset, course, prognosis, and outcome and information about physical aspects, behavioral aspects, and emotional aspects. We provide contact addresses and a reading list and encourage questions. Information sharing demystifies the problem and allows parents and young people to make informed decisions in a way that attempts to minimize the escalation of issues around power and control.

Family Work

While a few advocate a medical/illness model (Bergh & Södersten, 1998), most adopt an approach that includes close family involvement. The nature of family work has changed considerably over the years, as have assumptions about the role of the family in etiology. Family work is the first-line treatment for AN (with or without binge-purges) in younger patients. Controlled treatment trials in AN have shown that for patients under the age of 18 with an illness of less than three years duration, family work was more effective at one year (Russell, Szmukler, Dare, & Eisler, 1987) and five years (Eisler et al., 1997) than individual therapy alone. The treatment developed for these treatment trials has been published in manual form (Lock, Le Grange, Agras, & Dare, 2000), and further studies using this family-based approach are underway. This will enable specific questions about the efficacy of the approach in different patient subpopulations to be addressed. The model of family therapy used in the approach emphasizes parental responsibility and authority in response to their child's crisis and conceptualizes the family as a resource, not the problem. The other key concept in this form of therapy is "externalization" of the illness (White, 1989), which enables detachment from the problem and allows the family to join against the problem (anorexia), rather than focusing on exploration of family functioning. Alternatives to family therapy should be considered if parents are highly critical of their child, if intrafamilial abuse is suspected, or if parents have their own difficulties that may be impinging on treatment or are severely burdened with guilt. Parental counseling uses the same principles as family work but without the young person present, and it has been shown to be equally effective as conjoint family therapy in the treatment of adolescent AN (Eisler et al., 2000).

Mistrust of professionals and self-blame are common for parents. They may have been told explicitly that they are to blame, or they may have developed a sense of failure while attempting to overcome their child's difficulties. Sometimes, parents may have developed a rejecting stance to their child or see the eating behavior as a personal attack (and their child may see it in that way, too). Helping parents to bear the illness and the rejection that goes with it, without rejecting their child, is essential. Engaging parents means agreeing on understanding and frame of reference. Within this, the parents' needs must be addressed in a way that does not enhance their sense of guilt but does reinforce their responsibility. Groups for parents (Nicholls & Magagna, 1997) or for families (Scholz & Asen, 2001) can be very effective, and treatment trials of multifamily therapy are underway. Connecting parents to other parents also helps to overcome isolation.

For feeding problems and atypical eating problems, there are no published trials of specific family-based therapies, although the principles for collaborative working apply equally. Behavioral techniques have a role in changing concrete, measurable aspects of behavior but have little impact on thoughts, beliefs, and feelings.

Individual Work

Parental support for any individual work is crucial and will be enhanced by agreeing with the child and parent(s) on the process by which progress and feedback from the work can be shared. Individual therapy can have many formats, for example, cognitive-behavioral therapy (CBT), psychodynamic, or play therapy. Children can find individual "talking" therapies intrusive, particularly those who have difficulties with emotional aspects of communication. This may be influenced not only by the age and developmental stage of the child but also by his or her nutritional status. The therapist may, therefore, need to be flexible about how he or she finds a way to communicate with the child. The focus of work may be to help the child to find new ways of communicating or to enable the child to explore new ideas. Specific techniques such as messy play can be useful for children who are fearful of messes, smells, and textures. Other specific indications for individual work include treatment for concurrent depression, obsessive-compulsive disorder, or specific anxieties such as fear of swallowing or choking, where age-appropriate CBT is the treatment of choice. For a more detailed account of some of the therapeutic techniques for use in children with eating disorders, see Christie (2000) and Magagna (2000). Ideas include age-appropriate diaries, the use of games, and "worry bags" (Binnay & Wright, 1997).

Physical Interventions

Children and young adolescents with established feeding and eating disorders warrant medical monitoring and treatment to limit or reverse the impact of known physical complications. Nutritional disturbances are common and are related to the severity and duration of disordered eating behavior. Abnormalities of minerals, vitamins, and trace elements can occur, although generally are not clinically significant and are reversible with nutritional rehabilitation. Inadequate intake of energy, protein, and calcium, on the other hand, is crucial to growth and attainment of peak bone mass. At present, there are no randomized trials of nutritional supplementation. The use of hormonal treatments has not been systematically evaluated but may be worth considering in severe chronic AN in consultation with appropriate specialists, the young person, and his or her family. Thresholds for hospitalization may be somewhat lower in younger patients. Arrested growth and development would suggest the need for specialized care from both a physical and therapeutic point of view.

Significant advances have been made in recent years in pharmacological treatments for eating disorders in adults. Multiple double-blind, placebo-controlled studies have documented the short-term efficacy of antidepressant medications in BN. While the usefulness of pharmacological treatments for the acute treatment of AN is less clear, recent evidence suggests a role for medication in the relapse-prevention stage of the illness. The majority of the medication trials for the eating disorders have been conducted with adults, and the literature on the pharmacological treatment of children and adolescents with these disorders is very limited (see Kotler & Walsh, 2000, for review). Nevertheless, medication is used in clinical practice for management of specific symptoms such as low mood, obsessional behaviors, and extreme agitation. The most widely prescribed medications are selective serotonin uptake inhibitors and the newer major tranquilizers such as risperidone (Newman-Toker, 2000). Medication can be considered an adjunct to other therapies, particularly when they could enhance the capacity of the child to make use of other therapy. For example, alprazolam may be a useful adjunct in the treatment of functional dysphagia (Atkins, Lundy, & Pumariega, 1994).

On occasions when nasogastric feeding or other forms of enteral feeding are necessary, appropriate dietetic advice and a feeding rate suited to the age and nutritional status of the child are sought. Thresholds for feeding depend on the clinical situation and the treatment context. The most important aspect of treatment interventions of this kind is the careful consideration of issues relating to consent for both the child and parents. Manley, Smye, and Srikameswaran (2001) offer a framework for considering ethical decision making in the care of young people with eating disorders, intended as guidance when difficult decisions about care such as tube feeding need to be addressed. Neiderman, Farley, Richardson, and Lask (2001) used subjective information from adolescents and their parents in the development of clinical guidelines for nasogastric tube use. Diverse views were expressed by both patients and parents, with reactions more positive than anticipated.

Schooling

The assessment process will establish the level of the child's functioning in school and any areas of unmet need. These may be important to identify and bring to the attention of relevant professionals because they may be important in the maintenance of feeding problems. For example, in a child with unrecognized developmental difficulties, a more infantile feeding pattern may enable the child to receive a higher level of support than other children of the same age and, as such, may serve a very important function. Unless the child's needs for support can be met in other areas, the feeding problem may prove difficult to influence. Where possible, parents should be encouraged to address issues directly with the school on behalf of their child.

Patients with AN have often managed to sustain academic excellence at school despite severe malnourishment. This is often at the expense of long additional hours of work and compromise of friendships. The interruption that treatment will present to schoolwork is a cause for concern to the child, parent, and school. Unrealistic expectations can come from parents but often come from the child's attempts to maintain approval and self-esteem. Close liaison with school professionals and assessment of special educational needs are particularly important for children returning to school after inpatient admission.

Hospitalization

Inpatient, day hospital, and outpatient treatment should be available to young people with feeding and eating disorders in a way that allows the whole family to be involved, if necessary. Inpatient admission for medical/nutritional concerns can be usefully differentiated from mental health issues necessitating admission (e.g., severe depression, failure of outpatient therapy) in terms of the aims of admission and the appropriate treatment context. Up to 80% of children and adolescents are hospitalized at some point during their illness (Nussbaum, Shenker, Baird, & Saravay, 1985), although it is not yet established whether this improves outcome (Gowers, Weetman, Shore, Hossain, & Elvins, 2000). The optimal duration of hospitalization for young people has not been established, nor has optimal rate of weight gain. Relapse rates may be higher for patients who are discharged at very low body weight. In adolescents who relapse after discharge, however, rate of weight gain during hospitalization correlates with rate of weight loss on discharge (Lay, Jennen-Steinmetz, Reinhard, & Schmidt, 2002), and nutritional rehabilitation is only one aspect of care that needs consideration.

Working with the Wider System

Points for consideration in working with a complex network of professionals, as is often the case for complex and severe cases, include agreement about communication, both written and verbal, within the network and within the family. The potential for disagreement and misunderstanding is high, and views can easily become polarized if communication breaks down. It can be helpful to consider how those involved will respond to crises, clarify policies and procedures, and identify statutory roles and responsibilities.

The issue of consent to treatment for the young person and his or her parents is complex and is most likely to require consideration in the treatment of AN. The precise legal issues differ from country to country, although the general framework outlined by Manley and colleagues (2001) is useful. Some specific issues merit highlighting. The first is the difference between giving and withholding consent. Young people may not have the capacity, either on the basis of age or mental state, to give consent, while being within their rights to withhold consent (refuse). A related issue is that consent and competence are specific to a particular decision. Each decision for which consent is required needs to be considered from the young person's point of view, and his or her opinion should be sought. On occasions where agreement cannot be reached, local policies concerning child protection and legal responsibilities are important to clarify so that accurate information can be given to caregivers and young people and agreed on among professionals.

Although treatment is specific to the problem and to the child and family, a number of elements are essential. Treatment of young people with feeding and eating disorders works best when it is collaborative and based on a comprehensive, multidisciplinary assessment. Treatment should be appropriate to the level of complexity. Not all patients need intensive or assertive intervention. Treatment should be responsive to the developmental stage, physically and psychologically, of the child and take into account both the degree of independence the child has in the family and the resources in the family to support him or her. In other words, treatment should fit the patient. The treating team needs clear policies and guidelines, enabling them to respond to medical and psychiatric urgency when needed. Finally, assessment and treatment approaches need to be reviewed, developed, and evaluated.

OUTCOME

Remarkably little is known of the outcome of feeding disorders in the Western world, although the effects of malnutrition are well documented from studies in developing countries. In one of very few studies, the developmental sequelae of infant failure to thrive

(FTT) were examined in 42 unreferred 6-year-olds with a history of severe FTT at age 1 year. At 6 years, children with a history of FTT were considerably smaller than matched comparisons in terms of BMI and height and weight percentiles. FTT cases had more limited quantitative and memory skills than controls, but there were no significant differences in general cognitive functioning when maternal IQ was taken into consideration. In this small series, therefore, there was little evidence of adverse effects of early malnutrition on cognitive functioning by school age.

For AN, only a few studies have reported long-term follow-up in younger patients only, although many studies include some young patients (Steinhausen, 1997). Overall, outcome in childhood onset AN is roughly equivalent to later onset disorders.

For selective (picky) eating that has persisted into late childhood or adolescence, in our sample of 20 children, only those who had had specific intervention improved their range of foods (Nicholls et al., 2001). These were selected cases referred to a specialist service, and the generalizability of these findings is unclear.

CONCLUSIONS AND FUTURE DIRECTIONS

Feeding and eating disorders with onset during childhood, while sharing many common features with later onset disorders, need to be considered separately from the point of view of recognition, consequences, and management. The principle of care is a comprehensive, multidisciplinary approach, with close collaboration with parents. The consequences of failing to treat at an early stage, particularly in terms of physical sequelae, must be emphasized. There are still many areas where knowledge is lacking, both in terms of theoretical understanding and treatment approaches—particularly so for feeding problems, where issues of classification remain far from resolved and treatment and outcome studies are lacking. A developmental framework encompassing the range of feeding and eating problems from childhood through adulthood is needed as increasing evidence of continuities between feeding and eating problems are found.

REFERENCES

Arnow, B., Sanders, M. J., & Steiner, H. (1999). Premenarcheal versus postmenarcheal anorexia nervosa: A comparative study. *Clinical Child Psychology and Psychiatry, 4*(3), 403–414.

Atkins, D. L., Lundy, M. S., & Pumariega, A. J. (1994). A multimodal approach to functional dysphagia. *Journal of the American Academy of Child and Adolescent Psychiatry, 33*(7), 1012–1016.

Bergh, C., & Södersten, P. (1998). Anorexia nervosa: Rediscovery of a disorder. *Lancet, 351*(9113), 1427–1429.

Beumont, P. J. V., Garner, D. M., & Touyz, S. W. (1994). Diagnoses of eating or dieting disorders: What may we learn from past mistakes? *International Journal of Eating Disorders, 16*(4), 349–362.

Binnay, V., & Wright, J. C. (1997). The bag of feelings: An ideographic technique for the assessment and exploration of feelings in children and adolescents. *Clinical Child Psychology and Psychiatry, 2*, 449–462.

Birch, L. L., & Fisher, J. O. (1995). Appetite and eating behavior in children. *Pediatric Clinics of North America, 42*(4), 931–953.

Birch, L. L., & Fisher, J. O. (2000). Mothers' child-feeding practices influence daughters' eating and weight. *American Journal of Clinical Nutrition, 71*(5), 1054–1061.

Braet, C., & Van Strien, T. (1997). Assessment of emotional, externally induced and restrained eating behavior in nine to twelve-year-old obese and nonobese children. *Behavioural Research and Therapy, 35*(9), 863–873.

Bryant-Waugh, R. (1993). Anorexia nervosa in young boys. *Neuropsychiatrie de l'Enfance, 41*(5/6), 287–290.

Bryant-Waugh, R. (2000). Overview of the eating disorders. In B. Lask & R. Bryant-Waugh (Eds.), *Anorexia nervosa and related eating disorders in childhood and adolescence* (pp. 27–40). Hove, England: Psychology Press.

Bryant-Waugh, R., Cooper, P., Taylor, C., & Lask, B. (1996). The use of the Eating Disorder Examination with children: A pilot study. *International Journal of Eating Disorders, 19*(4), 391–397.

Bryant-Waugh, R., & Lask, B. (1995). Eating disorders in children. *Journal of Child Psychology and Psychiatry, 36*(2), 191–202.

Burklow, K. A., Phelps, A. N., Schultz, J. R., McConnell, K., & Rudolph, C. (1998). Classifying complex pediatric feeding disorders. *Journal of Pediatric Gastroenterology Nutrition, 27*(2), 143–147.

Chatoor, I., Ganiban, J., Harrison, J., & Hirsch, R. (2001). Observation of feeding in the diagnosis of posttraumatic feeding disorder of infancy. *Journal of the American Academy of Child and Adolescent Psychiatry, 40*(5), 595–602.

Chatoor, I., Hirsch, R., Ganiban, J., Persinger, M., & Hamburger, E. (1998). Diagnosing infantile anorexia: The observation of mother-infant interactions. *Journal of the American Academy of Child and Adolescent Psychiatry, 37*(9), 959–967.

Christie, D. (2000). Cognitive-behavioral techniques for children with eating disorders. In B. Lask & R. Bryant-Waugh (Eds.), *Anorexia nervosa and related eating disorders in childhood and adolescence* (pp. 205–226). Hove, England: Psychology Press.

Cole, T. J., Bellizzi, M. C., Flegal, K. M., & Dietz, W. H. (2000). Establishing a standard definition for child overweight and obesity worldwide: International survey. *British Medical Journal, 320*(7244), 1240–1243.

Cole, T. J., Freeman, J. V., & Preece, M. A. (1995). Body Mass Index reference curves for the UK 1990. *Archives of Disease in Childhood, 73*(1), 25–29.

Cooper, P. J., Watkins, B., Bryant-Waugh, R., & Lask, B. (2002). The nosological status of early onset anorexia nervosa. *Psychological Medicine, 32*(5), 873–880.

Crist, W., & Napier-Phillips, A. (2001). Mealtime behaviors of young children: A comparison of normative and clinical data. *Journal of Developmental and Behavioral Pediatrics, 22*(5), 279–286.

De Vile, C. J., Sufraz, R., Lask, B., & Stanhope, R. (1995). Occult intracranial tumours masquerading as early onset anorexia nervosa. *British Medical Journal, 311,* 1359–1360.

Douglas, J. (2000). Behavioral approaches to the assessment and management of feeding problems in young children. In A. Southall & A. Schwartz (Eds.), *Feeding problems in children: A practical guide* (pp. 42–57). Abingdon, Oxon, England: Radcliffe Medical Press.

Eisler, I., Dare, C., Hodes, M., Russell, G., Dodge, E., & Le Grange, D. (2000). Family therapy for adolescent anorexia nervosa: The results of a controlled comparison of two family interventions. *Journal of Child Psychology and Psychiatry, 41*(6), 727–736.

Eisler, I., Dare, C., Russell, G. F., Szmukler, G., Le Grange, D., & Dodge, E. (1997). Family and individual therapy in anorexia nervosa: A 5-year follow-up. *Archives of General Psychiatry, 54*(11), 1025–1030.

Fairburn, C. G., & Cooper, Z. (1993). The Eating Disorders Examination (12th ed.). In C. G. Fairburn & G. T. Wilson (Eds.), *Binge eating: Nature, assessment and treatment* (pp. 317–332). New York: Guilford Press.

Fisher, M., Golden, N. H., Katzman, D. K., Kreipe, R. E., Rees, J., Schebendach, J., et al. (1995). Eating disorders in adolescents: A background paper. *Journal of Adolescent Health, 16,* 420–437.

Fosson, A., Knibbs, J., Bryant-Waugh, R., & Lask, B. (1987). Early onset anorexia nervosa. *Archives of Disease in Childhood, 62,* 114–118.

Gowers, S. G., Crisp, A. H., Joughin, N., & Bhat, A. (1991). Premenarcheal anorexia nervosa. *Journal of Child Psychology and Psychiatry, 32*(3), 515–524.

Gowers, S. G., Weetman, J., Shore, A., Hossain, F., & Elvins, R. (2000). Impact of hospitalisation on the outcome of adolescent anorexia nervosa. *British Journal of Psychiatry, 176,* 138–141.

Harris, G., Blissett, J., & Johnson, R. (2000). Food refusal associated with illness. *Child Psychology and Psychiatry Review, 5*(4), 148–156.

Harris, G., & Booth, I. W. (1992). The nature and management of eating problems in preschool children. In P. J. Cooper & A. Stein (Eds.), *Feeding problems and eating disorders in children and adolescents* (Monographs in Clinical Pediatrics No. 5, pp. 61–85). Chur, Switzerland: Harwood Academic.

Higgs, J. F., Goodyer, I. M., & Birch, J. (1989). Anorexia nervosa and food avoidance emotional disorder. *Archives of Disease in Childhood, 64,* 346–351.

Jacobi, C., Agras, W. S., & Hammer, L. (2001). Predicting children's reported eating disturbances at 8 years of age. *Journal of the American Academy of Child and Adolescent Psychiatry, 40*(3), 364–372.

Jacobs, B. W., & Isaacs, S. (1986). Prepubertal anorexia nervosa: A retrospective controlled study. *Journal of Child Psychology and Psychiatry, 27*(2), 237–250.

Katzman, D. K., & Zipursky, R. B. (1997). Adolescents with anorexia nervosa: The impact of the disorder on bones and brains. *Annals of the New York Academy of Sciences, 817,* 127–137.

Kent, A., Lacey, J. H., & McCluskey, S. E. (1992). Premenarchal bulimia nervosa. *Journal of Psychosomatic Research, 36*(3), 205–210.

Key, A., Mason, H., Allan, R., & Lask, B. (2002). Restoration of ovarian and uterine maturity in adolescents with anorexia nervosa. *International Journal of Eating Disorders, 32*(3), 319–325.

Khan, S., Hyman, P. E., Cocjin, J., & Di Lorenzo, C. (2000). Rumination syndrome in adolescents. *Journal of Pediatrics, 136*(4), 528–531.

Kotler, L. A., & Walsh, B. T. (2000). Eating disorders in children and adolescents: Pharmacological therapies. *European Child Adolescent Psychiatry, 9*(Suppl. 1), I108–I116.

Kreipe, R. E., Golden, N. H., Katzman, D. K., Fisher, M., Rees, J., Tonkin, R. S., et al. (1995). Eating disorders in adolescents. A position paper of the Society for Adolescent Medicine [see comments]. *Journal of Adolescent Health, 16*(6), 476–479.

Lai, K. Y., de Bruyn, R., Lask, B., Bryant-Waugh, R., & Hankins, M. (1994). Use of pelvic ultrasound to monitor ovarian and uterine maturity in childhood onset anorexia nervosa. *Archives of Disease in Childhood, 71*(3), 228–231.

Lay, B., Jennen-Steinmetz, C., Reinhard, I., & Schmidt, M. H. (2002). Characteristics of inpatient weight gain in adolescent anorexia nervosa: Relation to speed of relapse and readmission. *European Eating Disorders Review, 10*(1), 22–40.

Lock, J., Le Grange, D., Agras, S., & Dare, C. (2000). *Treatment manual for anorexia nervosa.* New York: Guilford Press.

Luciano, A., Bressan, F., & Zoppi, G. (1997). Body Mass Index reference curves for children aged 3–19 years from Verona, Italy. *European Journal of Clinical Nutrition, 51*(1), 6–10.

Magagna, J. (2000). Psychodynamic therapy. In B. Lask & R. Bryant-Waugh (Eds.), *Anorexia nervosa and related eating disorders in childhood and adolescence.* Hove, England: Psychology Press.

Manley, R., Smye, V., & Srikameswaran, S. (2001). Addressing complex ethical issues in the treatment of children and adolescents with eating disorders: Application of a framework for ethical decision making. *European Eating Disorders Review, 9*(3), 144–166.

Marchi, M., & Cohen, P. (1990). Early childhood eating behaviors and adolescent eating disorders. *Journal of the American Academy of Child and Adolescent Psychiatry, 29*(1), 112–117.

Neiderman, M., Farley, A., Richardson, J., & Lask, B. (2001). Nasogastric feeding in children and adolescents with eating disorders: Toward good practice. *International Journal of Eating Disorders, 29*(4), 441–448.

Newman-Toker, J. (2000). Risperidone in anorexia nervosa. *Journal of the American Academy of Child and Adolescent Psychiatry, 39*(8), 941–942.

Nicholls, D. (2002). *The growth and development of children with prepubertal and pubertal eating disorders: Cross sectional and longitudinal findings and their interpretation.* London: Institute of Child Health.

Nicholls, D., & Bryant-Waugh, R. (2003). Children and young adolescents. In J. Treasure, U. Schmidt, & E. van Furth (Eds.), *Handbook of eating disorders* (pp. 415–433). Chichester, England: Wiley.

Nicholls, D., Chater, R., & Lask, B. (2000). Children into *DSM-IV* don't go: A comparison of classification systems for eating disorders in childhood and early adolescence. *International Journal of Eating Disorders, 28*(3), 317–324.

Nicholls, D., Christie, D., Randall, L., & Lask, B. (2001). Selective eating: Symptom, disorder or normal variant? *Clinical Child Psychology and Psychiatry, 6*(2), 257–270.

Nicholls, D., & Magagna, J. (1997). A Group for the Parents of Children with Eating Disorders. *Clinical Child Psychology and Psychiatry, 2*(4), 565–578.

Nicholls, D., & Stanhope, R. (2000). Medical complications of anorexia nervosa in children and young adults. *European Eating Disorders Review, 8*(2), 170–180.

Nicholls, D., Wells, J. C., Singhal, A., & Stanhope, R. (2002). Body composition in early onset eating disorders. *European Journal of Clinical Nutrition, 56*(9), 857–865.

Nussbaum, M., Shenker, I. R., Baird, D., & Saravay, S. (1985). Follow-up investigation in patients with anorexia nervosa. *Journal of Pediatrics, 106*(5), 835–840.

Olden, K. W. (2001). Rumination. *Current Treatment Options in Gastroenterology, 4*(4), 351–358.

Palmer, M. M., Crawley, K., & Blanco, I. A. (1993). Neonatal Oral-Motor Assessment scale: A reliability study. *Journal of Perinatology, 13*(1), 28–35.

Rastam, M. (1992). Anorexia nervosa in 51 Swedish adolescents: Premorbid problems and comorbidity. *Journal of the American Academy of Child and Adolescent Psychiatry, 31*(5), 819–829.

Reau, N. R., Senturia, Y. D., Lebailly, S. A., & Christoffel, K. K. (1996). Infant and toddler feeding patterns and problems: Normative data and a new direction. Pediatric Practice Research Group. *Journal of Developmental and Behavioral Pediatrics, 17*(3), 149–153.

Rebert, W. M., Stanton, A. L., & Schwarz, R. M. (1991). Influence of personality attributes and daily moods on bulimic eating patterns. *Addictive Behaviors, 16*(6), 497–505.

Russell, G. F., Szmukler, G. I., Dare, C., & Eisler, I. (1987). An evaluation of family therapy in anorexia nervosa and bulimia nervosa. *Archives of General Psychiatry, 44*(12), 1047–1056.

Scholz, M., & Asen, E. (2001). Multiple family therapy with eating disordered adolescents: Concepts and preliminary results. *European Eating Disorders Review, 9*(1), 33–42.

Shafran, R., Bryant-Waugh, R., Lask, B., & Arscott, K. (1995). Obsessive-compulsive symptoms in children with eating disorders: A preliminary investigation. *Eating Disorders: Journal of Treatment and Prevention, 3*(4), 304–310.

Soyka, L. A., Misra, M., Frenchman, A., Miller, K. K., Grinspoon, S., Schoenfeld, D. A., et al. (2002). Abnormal bone mineral accrual in adolescent girls with anorexia nervosa. *Journal of Clinical Endocrinology and Metabolism, 87*(9), 4177–4185.

Stark, L. J., Jelalian, E., Powers, S. W., Mulvihill, M. M., Opipari, L. C., Bowen, A., et al. (2000). Parent and child mealtime behavior in families of children with cystic fibrosis. *Journal of Pediatrics, 136*(2), 195–200.

Stein, A., Woolley, H., Murray, L., Cooper, P., Cooper, S., Noble, F., et al. (2001). Influence of psychiatric disorder on the controlling behavior of mothers with 1-year-old infants. A study of women with maternal eating disorder, postnatal depression and a healthy comparison group. *British Journal of Psychiatry, 179,* 157–162.

Stein, D. J., Bouwer, C., & Van Heerden, B. (1996). Pica and the obsessive-compulsive spectrum disorders. *South African Medical Journal, 86*(Suppl. 12), 1586–1592.

Stein, M. A., Mendelsohn, J., Obermeyer, W. H., Amromin, J., & Benca, R. (2001). Sleep and behavior problems in school-aged children. *Pediatrics, 107*(4), E60.

Steinhausen, H. C. (1997). Outcome of anorexia nervosa in the younger patient. *Journal of Child Psychology and Psychiatry, 38*(3), 271–276.

Tanner, J. M., & Whitehouse, R. H. (1966). Standards from birth to maturity for height, weight, height velocity and weight velocity: British Children 1965. Part II. *Archives of Disease in Childhood, 41*(219), 613–635.

Trocki, O., & Shepherd, R. W. (2000). Change in Body Mass Index does not predict change in body composition in adolescent girls with anorexia nervosa. *Journal of the American Dietetic Association, 100*(4), 457–460.

Tyrka, A. R., Waldron, I., Graber, J. A., & Brooks-Gunn, J. (2002). Prospective predictors of the onset of anorexic and bulimic syndromes. *International Journal of Eating Disorders, 32*(3), 282–290.

Whelan, E., & Cooper, P. J. (2000). The association between childhood feeding problems and maternal eating disorder: A community study. *Psychological Medicine, 30*(1), 69–77.

White, M. (1989). The externalising of the problem and the re-authoring of lives and relationships. *Dulwich Centre Newsletter,* 3–20.

Wickendon, M. (2000). The development and disruption of feeding skills: How speech and language therapists can help. In A. Southall & A. Schwartz (Eds.), *Feeding problems in children: A practical guide* (pp. 3–23). Abingdon, Oxon, England: Radcliffe Medical Press.

Williams, S. (2000). Body Mass Index reference curves derived from a New Zealand birth cohort. *New Zealand Medical Journal, 113*(1114), 308–311.

Chapter 31

OBESITY AND BODY IMAGE AMONG ETHNICALLY DIVERSE CHILDREN AND ADOLESCENTS

SONIA Y. RUIZ, ALISON PEPPER, AND DENISE E. WILFLEY

Obesity is a major health problem in the United States and is now also recognized as a global problem (James, 2002). Obesity is related to various health problems, including cardiovascular disease, cancers, and diabetes; all are also the major causes of death for all U.S. ethnic minority groups (Kumanyika, 2002). Obesity and obesity-related health problems affect not only the individual but also society. There are direct (medical) and indirect (morbidity and mortality) economic costs associated with obesity (Wolf, 2002). Sadly, overweight and obesity are not just adult health problems—they have affected children too. The prevalence rate for childhood obesity has increased significantly in the past two decades (Gortmaker, Dietz, Sobol, & Wehler, 1987; James, 2002; Troiano, Flegal, Kuczmarski, Campbell, & Johnson, 1995), but most alarming are the rates for ethnic minority children. Most important is the fact that few researchers have systematically examined factors associated with childhood obesity among ethnic minorities. This chapter reviews the literature on childhood obesity among ethnic minority youth, examines the influence of body image on obesity, suggests needed areas for future research using culturally competent research methods, and offers recommendations for prevention and intervention efforts.

PREVALENCE RATES

In December 2001, U.S. Surgeon General David Satcher announced a national plan of action to prevent and decrease overweight and obesity (U.S. Department of Health and Human Services, 2002). This national plan is necessary because, in the United States, obesity has become an epidemic crisis. The prevalence of overweight in children is increasing at such an accelerated rate (Gortmaker et al., 1987) that it doubled in the last two decades (Troiano et al., 1995). Most recent data from the National Health and Nutrition Examination Survey III (NHANES III) showed that from 1988 to 1994, approximately 11% of a nationally representative sample of children ages 6 to 17 were overweight, and an additional 14% were considered at risk for becoming

656

overweight (Troiano & Flegal, 1998).[1] This is a substantial increase among all age, sex, and race groups when compared to data from the following national data reference sets: the National Health Examination Survey (NHES) cycle II (1963 to 1965), cycle III (1966 to 1970), NHANES I (1971 to 1974), II (1976 to 1980), and III (1988 to 1994; Troiano & Flegal, 1998).

While this data illustrate that the prevalence of overweight and obesity has increased in children of all population groups, high rates are also found among children from ethnic minority groups (Rosner, Prineas, Loggie, & Daniels, 1998; Strauss & Pollack, 2001; Troiano et al., 1995). Data from children ages 4 to 12 who were born to mothers enrolled in the National Longitudinal Survey of Youth showed that between 1986 and 1998, overweight prevalence increased fastest among minorities and those living in the southern states (Strauss & Pollack, 2001).[2] Although the relative weight of overweight children increased from 144% to 155%, 12.3% of European American children were overweight compared to 21.5% and 21.8% of African American and Latino children, respectively (Strauss & Pollack, 2001). In addition, data from NHANES I (1971 to 1974), NHANES II (1976 to 1980), NHANES III (1988 to 1994), and the Hispanic Health Nutrition Examination Survey (HHNES, 1982 to 1984) showed that among preschool children ages 2 months though 5 years, the prevalence of overweight[3] was higher in Latinos than in African or European Americans (Ogden et al., 1997).

Differences in the prevalence of overweight between ethnically diverse children parallel earlier research on adolescents. In the largest set of normative height and weight for ethnically diverse children (ages 5 to 11) and adolescents (ages 12 to 17), African American and Latinas ages 12 to 17 had the highest body mass index (BMI) scores (Rosner et al., 1998). Their rates were considerably higher when compared to European and Asian American females, and differences were especially apparent after age 9. For males ages 5 to 17, differences by race were less dramatic. However, Latino boys did have significantly higher BMIs than the other groups. Consistently high obesity prevalence rates were also reported with respect to American Indian children and adolescents (Kumanyika, 1993). Data from 9,464 American Indian schoolchildren (5 to 18 years old) living on or near Indian reservations were compared with two national data reference sets, the NHANES II (1976 to 1980) and the HHANES (1982 to 1984). Although the mean heights were similar, the Native American children weighed more than either population and had significantly higher BMIs for most age and sex groups than the reference populations (Jackson, 1993). The American Indian children had a 39.3% prevalence rate of overweight (BMI > 85th) compared with 15% for all races combined in the NHANES II reference population and 28.6% of the HHANES

---

[1] Troiano and Flegal (1998) classified children and adolescents as at risk when between the 85th and 95th percentile of the BMI cutoffs. The 95th percentile of BMI is used to define overweight.

[2] Strauss and Pollack (2001) defined *overweight* as a BMI greater than the 95th percentile cutoffs.

[3] Ogden (1997) defined *overweight* based on original NCHS weight-for-length (< 2 years) and weight-for-stature (2 to 5) reference growth curves. Prevalence of overweight is defined as the percentage of children whose weight-for-length or weight-for-stature was above the 95th percentile.

population (1982 to 1984; Jackson, 1993; Story et al., 1999). Studies continue to indicate that obesity rates in American Indian children and adolescents are higher than those in all races combined in the United States (Broussard et al., 1991).

Rates of overweight and obesity are particularly prevalent in certain ethnic subgroups. Among U.S.-born Hmong preschoolers attending the Minnesota Supplemental Food Programs for Women, Infants, and Children (WIC) clinics, 23.2% of the 3-year-olds and 22.2% of the 4-year-olds were above the expected 5% of the 95th percentile of weight-for-height (Himes, Story, Czaplinski, & Dahlberg-Luby, 1992; Kumanyika, 1993). Among Latinos, data from the HHANES (1982 to 1984) revealed important subgroup differences in the prevalence of obesity (Kumanyika, 1993; Pawson, Martorell, & Mendoza, 1991). As expected, nearly 5% of the Latino boys and girls and Cuban boys ages 2 to 5 years old in HHANES had BMIs above the 95th percentile. However, Puerto Rican boys and girls had two or more times the expected BMI, and Cuban girls had almost six times the expected 5%. Data for 5- to 12-year-old Latino school-age children in the HHANES population look slightly different (Kumanyika, 1993; Pawson et al., 1991). Particularly, an excess prevalence of obesity was observed in Cuban boys and Puerto Rican boys and girls (including males 12 to 17). Finally, a high prevalence of obesity in Native Hawaiian children and adolescents has also been reported, although mostly in males (D. E. Brown et al., 1992; Kumanyika, 1993).

High rates of obesity have also been identified by tribal and geographical region (Dounchis, Hayden, & Wilfley, 2001; Story, Tompkins, Bass, & Wakefield, 1986). Obesity rates for American Indian schoolchildren ranged from 17% to 23%, which was significantly above the expected 5% based on data from the National Center for Health Statistics, Center for Disease Control (NCHS, CDC; Gallaher, Hauck, Yang-Oshida, & Serdula, 1991). The highest prevalence of obesity is observed in the data for the Pima (Knowler et al., 1991; Kumanyika, 1993). In addition, it appears that weight gain occurs very early in the Pima Indian children (Lindsay et al., 2002). When compared to standard reference values from the NCHS, CDC after the first month of life, Pima children[4] had significantly earlier and greater weight gain (Lindsay et al., 2002). On a population level, overweight prevalence in Navajo adolescents parallels the Pima. In an evaluation of 12- to 19-year-old Navajo adolescents, 35% to 40% had BMIs greater than the 85th percentile (Freedman, Serdula, Percy, Ballew, & White, 1997). The literature contains other reports of high rates of obesity in Mohawk (Potvin et al., 1999) and Cherokee Indians (Story et al., 1986), as well as American Indians in the Aberdeen area (Zephier, Himes, & Story, 1999).

As illustrated in the previous section, childhood obesity is a significant problem in the general population and an even greater problem among ethnic minorities. Most troublesome is that we know very little about the etiology of obesity and even less about the process in ethnic minority children. The most basic model suggests that there is an imbalance between energy intake and expenditure (Andersen, Crespo, Bartlett, Cheskin, & Pratt, 1998; Tucker, 1986). However, other factors have been implicated (e.g., environmental and genetic factors), yet very little is known about this process for ethnic minorities. Because childhood obesity appears to be a greater problem for these

---

[4] Lindsay et al. (2002) based classifications of weight gain on age: < 24 months: weight for length, ≥ 2 yrs: BMI.

children, it is of utmost importance to better understand the underlying causes and develop appropriate prevention and intervention strategies.

RELEVANT CULTURAL VARIABLES

Some key terms discussed throughout the chapter are relevant when including ethnic minority participants in research projects. First, *culture* refers to the shared attitudes, beliefs, norms, roles, and self-definitions (Triandis, 1996). These cultural characteristics can be seen in family roles, communication patterns, ideas about personal control, individualism, collectivism, spirituality, and religion. More specific to social contexts is *ethnicity,* which refers to the sense of "peoplehood," where members of a group share a cultural heritage that gets transmitted from one generation to another (Phinney, 1996). Common behaviors, attitudes, and values are examples of cultural characteristics that are shared among group members. Included in this definition is the shared experience of interdependence of fate or struggles with others in the group. *Ethnic identity* refers to the degree to which individuals identify with their ethnic group and varies from one individual to another (Nagayama Hall & Barongan, 2002). *Acculturation* is the process that occurs when two or more cultural groups come into contact with one another (C. L. Williams & Berry, 1991). Recent research in psychology has focused on the change process that the minority group undergoes in relation to contact with the "host" or majority culture. Last, *generation status* refers to origin of birth of an individual, his or her parents and grandparents, and so on. Rather than simply stating that there are ethnic or racial differences between groups, these terms are used to refer to the experiences of ethnic minorities in the United States and can better help explain why there might be differences among groups.

RISK AND PROTECTIVE FACTORS

One way to target the problem of childhood obesity among ethnic minority children is to focus on the risk and protective processes associated with the development of overweight and obesity status. Risk processes are those features of the environment or the individual that negatively affect the biological, psychological, and/or social capacities of an individual to function and maintain well-being in society (Dalton, Elias, & Wandersman, 2000). For example, it might be helpful to think about those processes and/or factors that increase the likelihood that children overeat, eat unhealthfully, and are sedentary. Protective processes also refers to those features of the environment or the individual that operate to enhance the biological, psychological, and/or social capabilities of the individual to function and maintain well-being in society (Dalton et al., 2000). For example, what must happen for a child to eat more healthfully, control eating behavior, and be more physically active?

Several reviews are invaluable in describing the current state of research among ethnically diverse children and adolescents (Dounchis et al., 2001; Kumanyika, 1993, 2002). In these reviews, variables associated with childhood obesity are identified. The variables range from distal or environmental to more proximal or pertaining to the individual (genetic, psychological, etc.). This section identifies *modifiable* risk and protective processes associated with childhood obesity, as well as needed areas of research. As such, this work can help to identify variables that are important to target in behavioral health interventions and prevention programs for ethnic minorities. In particular, prenatal influences, parental influences, eating behavior, physical activity, education, socioeconomic status (SES), and generation status are examined. Body image is another important variable to consider, but because of its significance in relation to eating symptomatology, it is discussed more fully in the next section. The final analysis should provide us with a better understanding of those variables that are modifiable, treatable, and/or preventable (e.g., relevant to behavioral intervention/prevention).

Prenatal Influences

Mothers with insulin-dependent diabetes or gestational diabetes and infants with high birth weight have all been associated with a greater risk of obesity in childhood (Wilfley & Saelens, 2002). In addition, longitudinal studies of diabetes in the Pima Indian community revealed that the children of diabetic mothers (while pregnant) were more obese, had higher glucose concentrations, and had developed more cases of diabetes at an earlier age than children born to women who developed diabetes after pregnancy or who were nondiabetic (Pettitt, Nelson, Saad, Bennett, & Knowler, 1993).

Parental Influences

Several researchers note the importance of a familial approach to obesity treatment (Epstein, Myers, Raynor, & Saelens, 1998; Golan & Weizman, 2001). However, parental obesity is one of the strongest predictors of child obesity among young children. In contrast, breast-feeding has been found to have a protective influence against later development of childhood obesity (Wilfley & Saelens, 2002), and is also related to lower prevalence of type 2 diabetes mellitus for American Indians (Pettitt, de courten, et al., 1995; Pettitt, Roumain, Hanson, Knowler, & Bennett, 1995). Child-feeding practices were found to explain more variance in total body fat than ethnicity, sex, and SES among African American and European American children (Spruijt-Metz, Lindquist, Birch, Fisher, & Goran, 2002). Parental neglect, disinhibited eating, and high levels of control over children's eating also have been reported to be significantly related to higher weight among children (Costanzo & Woody, 1985; Wilfley & Saelens, 2002).

Eating Behaviors

Ethnic differences in fast-food consumption have been suggested. For example, ethnic minorities may be eating more fast food than other groups (J. D. Williams, Achterberg, & Sylvester, 1993). High rates of television watching, which was significantly correlated with increased dietary fat intake, was evidenced by Latino boys and girls and Asian girls (Robinson & Killen, 1995). Studies also have indicated that Mexican Americans underconsume fruits and vegetables and overconsume sources of fat (Foreyt & Cousins, 1993). It has been suggested that a change in diet for American Indians explains the greater prevalence of obesity among American Indians. For example, Boyce and Swinburn (1993) reported that the composition of the traditional Pima diet of 100 years ago consisted of approximately 70% to 80% carbohydrates, 8% to 12% fat, and 12% to 18% protein. Currently, the composition has been estimated at approximately 47% carbohydrates, 35% fat, 15% protein, and 3% alcohol (Boyce & Swinburn, 1993; Smith et al., 1996).

Physical Activity

The overweight and obesity problem results from the imbalance between energy intake and energy expenditure (Andersen et al., 1998; Tucker, 1986). Increased sedentary behaviors are related to higher rates of obesity among both adults and children (James, 2002). Wolf, Gortmaker, Cheung, Gray, Herzog, and Colditz (1993) reported that Latinos and Asian schoolgirls had the lowest rates of physical activity and the highest rates of sedentary activity (e.g., television viewing). Another study revealed that physical activity levels are lower in African American and Mexican American children than European American children (Anderson et al., 1998). Consequently, physical activity was negatively related to BMIs (Wolf et al., 1993), and increased television watching was associated with increased body fatness (Anderson et al., 1998). Robinson and Killen (1995) reported that although African American girls and boys viewed more television and ate more fatty foods, they were also more physically active than the other ethnic subsamples in this study. Robinson and Killen thus found only a weak association between television viewing and BMI. These results may differ from Anderson et al. and Wolf et al. because these researchers did not find a relationship between physical activity and television watching. Increasing physical activity and decreasing sedentary behaviors is key in combating pediatric obesity (Epstein et al., 1995).

Education

Knowledge of nutrition and healthy diets may be related to obesity. For example, maternal education was reported to be associated with obesity, such that Mexican American mothers with less formal education tended to serve less healthy food and monitored their children's food consumption less than those with more education (Olvera-Ezzell, Power, & Cousins, 1990).

Socioeconomic Status

Socioeconomic status (SES) has been reported to be negatively related to obesity in adult populations (Sobal & Stunkard, 1989). Because ethnic minorities are overrepresented among the low SES groups, this is especially problematic (Gerald, Anderson, Johnson, Hoff, & Trimm, 1994; Kumanyika, 1987, 1994). Knapp, Hazuda, Haffner, Young, and Stern (1988) found that health-related behaviors and values such as education about nutrition were associated with SES. It has also been suggested that weight may affect SES through discrimination (Gortmaker, Must, Perrin, Sobal, & Dietz, 1993) and social mobility (Jeffery, French, & Spry, 1991). However, it is important to note that these studies are correlational; thus, it is not clear what the causal direction may be (Sobal, 1995).

Generation Status

Very few studies reviewed included relevant cultural variables such as acculturation, ethnic minority, or generation status. When and if ethnic minorities are included in studies, usually the *only* information is that there are ethnic differences because other relevant and important variables are not examined. One study did ask this question about generation status, and the researchers found lower obesity rates among Latino and Asian children born outside the United States compared to those born in the United States of immigrant parents (Popkin & Udry, 1998).

Genetic influence is not reviewed here for two reasons. First, this section examines *modifiable* variables, and second, many experts believe that environment or culture explains more of the variance in total body fat. However, the "thrifty-gene" hypothesis has received a lot of attention with regard to understanding the ethnic and racial differences in obesity rates (Neel, 1962). This hypothesis suggests that certain ethnic groups may have a genetic disposition to use food energy more efficiently and to store energy resources in the form of fat (P. J. Brown, 1991). However, most experts believe that the greater prevalence of overweight and obesity in certain ethnic groups has occurred in the past 100 years or so. Most likely, the high prevalence of obesity can be attributed to a change in diet and physical activity levels and not changes in genotype (P. J. Brown, 1991). While there is much that we do not know about the etiology of obesity in general (Hill & Trowridge, 1998), it will be crucial to include diverse samples in the studies as we move forward to better understand the problem of childhood obesity.

In summary, the one definitive statement that can be made based on the previous review of studies is that we do not know much about the etiology of childhood obesity among ethnically diverse children and adolescents. While there has been some work done in this area, more research is needed. It is unfortunate that a health problem of this magnitude has received such little attention from researchers. Despite the paucity of research, it would appear that based on the existing treatment literature for obesity, restoring a balance between energy consumed and expended and learning how to maintain that balance over time are appropriate goals for ethnic minorities *and* nonminorities, alike. While this may be a true statement and some researchers have had some success with their treatment models (Epstein et al., 1998; Golan & Weizman, 2001), too few ethnic minorities have been included to know about the effectiveness with ethnic populations or whether different or modified strategies should be employed. While they did not focus on children, the Diabetes Prevention Program Research Group has targeted diverse individuals (adults) at risk for Type 2 diabetes and have reported great success with an intensive, one-on-one culturally sensitive lifestyle intervention (Knowler et al., 2002). This research is promising for those who are interested in targeting ethnic minorities and providing culturally relevant treatment and intervention. For researchers to develop cultural relevant intervention, some questions to ask might include the following: If ethnic minority children are underconsuming fruits and vegetables, is this more an issue of social class or lack of education? If ethnic minority children are more sedentary, is this because the neighborhoods they live in do not have parks or the parks are not safe? Do ethnic minority children stay indoors more because ethnic minority parents both have to work to support the family and/or do not have the resources for childcare or daycare? In many cultures, a sign of wealth and status is the weight of an individual.

However, when individuals immigrate to other countries, such as the United States, do they start adopting the beliefs of the host culture? If so, when does that happen? Is there conflict between the generations (e.g., grandparents, parents, children)? The answers to these and other questions may help us better understand the obesity epidemic and how to best prevent and treat the problem.

BODY IMAGE

Body image is the perception of a person's current body size (Flynn & Fitzgibbon, 1996) and can play a major role in the relationship between obesity and the development of eating disorders (Dounchis et al., 2001). Because of its possible involvement in the development of obesity, studies that included ethnic minority samples are reviewed. The difference between an individual's perception of his or her current body size to ideal body size is referred to as *body satisfaction* (Dounchis et al., 2001). Having poor body satisfaction can be associated with lower self-esteem, obesity, and an increased prevalence for eating disorders (Guinn, Semper, Jorgensen, & Skaggs, 1997), and it is the single strongest predictor of eating disorder symptomatology (Striegel-Moore et al., 2000). Thus, the risk for eating disorders is heavily influenced by body dissatisfaction (Dounchis et al., 2001). However, there is a dearth of research that examines how body dissatisfaction is influenced by body type preference in ethnically diverse youth. The following section reviews the existing literature on differing body type preferences among ethnic groups, its impact on body dissatisfaction among ethnically diverse youth, and relation to childhood obesity.

Body Type Preference

Body type preference is the ideal body shape that individuals use to compare their own shape or size (Dounchis et al., 2001). Preferences can range from the ultra-thin waif to the voluptuous endomorph, and researchers agree that culture is a powerful determinant (Dounchis et al., 2001; Miller & Pumariega, 2001; Parnell et al., 1996; Sobal, 1995). When comparing body type ideals between African American and European American adolescents, patterns reveal that African Americans generally hold less rigid standards. For example, African American preadolescents (Collins, 1991; Flynn & Fitzgibbon, 1996; Thompson, Corwin, & Sargent, 1997) and adolescents (Botta, 2000; Parnell et al., 1996) selected significantly larger personal ideal body types when compared to European Americans. Also, despite having higher BMIs (Pritchard, King, Czajka-Narins, 1997; Striegel-Moore et al., 2000), African American adolescent females were less likely to view themselves as overweight (Flynn & Fitzgibbon, 1996; Neff, Sargent, McKeown, Jackson, & Valois, 1997), and they had a more positive self-concept than their European American counterparts (Pritchard et al., 1997). In another study, Botta (2000) asked a group of African American and European American adolescents to what extent they saw TV images as realistic ideals, the degree they compared their bodies to these images, and how seeing the images as a realistic ideal and making comparisons impacted their body image disturbance. Botta found that although the adolescents did not differ in how much they compared themselves to TV images, European

American adolescents had much thinner personal ideal body sizes. One possible explanation for this was suggested by Flynn and Fitzgibbon. They suggested that African American females may base their standard of beauty on immediate family members and adult role models (Flynn & Fitzgibbon, 1996) whereas European adolescents may be more likely to internalize messages from the media and their peers (Parnell et al., 1996). In addition, European American females may have more stringent body type preferences because they identify with the European-American culture that is infiltrated with White-waif models and actresses. Meanwhile, African American adolescents allow their individuality, style, and attitudes to determine their self-worth (Dounchis et al., 2001).

African Americans may not be the only minority group with less rigid body type standards than European Americans. Although little research has examined idealistic body types in Latinos, there are some indications that this group also has less rigid standards. In a study that examined how age and degree of exposure to U.S. culture impacts body type preference, overall Latina adolescents and adults chose ideal body types that were significantly larger than European Americans (Lopez, Blix, & Blix, 1995). In another study, after discovering that self-esteem was the most significant determinant of body image among adolescent Latinas, the researchers suggested that Latinas and non-Latinas might have different perceptions of an acceptable body type (Guinn et al., 1997). In the Latino culture, standards for body types are influenced not by commercialized idealism but by realism—Latinos have shorter and heavier statures. Thus, the ethnic predisposition for a greater weight-for-height stature among Latinas may influence their body type ideals and, ultimately, their body image.

However, Flynn and Fitzgibbon (1996) have suggested that culturally sanctioned heavy body image ideals may lead to an increased risk for obesity. For example, evidence from this study suggested that African American and Latino adolescents preferred larger body types than European American adolescents. These results are interestingly consistent with obesity prevalence rates reported earlier in the chapter. That is, in 1998, there were more overweight (i.e., BMI > 95th percentile) African American (21.5%) and Latino (21.8%) children than overweight European American children (12.3%; Strauss & Pollack, 2001). Therefore, researchers must disentangle how culture may serve two purposes: (1) as a protective process against eating disorders and (2) inadvertently contributing high-risk eating behaviors that lead to obesity.

Recent evidence has suggested, however, that ethnic differences in desired body shape may not exist (Gardner, Friedman, & Jackson, 1999a, 1999b; Robinson et al., 1996). Robinson et al. assessed desired body shape among European American, Latina, and Asian sixth- and seventh-grade girls. The three ethnic groups did not significantly differ in their choices of desired body shape. Similarly, in European American and Latino children, Gardner et al. (1999a, 1999b) discovered no significant ethnic differences on perceived or ideal body sizes. The answer to the question of whether there are ethnic differences in ideal body types remains uncertain. Perhaps there is an inconsistency in results because the degree of exposure to U.S. culture operates as a powerful determinant in body type preferences among adolescents (Dounchis et al., 2001). For example, if African American women reject their identity and idealize the European identity, they may be more likely to endorse attitudes about body image that are related to eating disorders (Abrams, Allen, & Gray, 1993). If cultural differences do not contribute to body type preferences, ethnic identity may influence body type preference. For example, on observing the increasing rate of anorexia among Native American girls as they move off their reservations, Yates (1989) suggested the phenomenon might be related to a denial of the traditional Indian woman.

Body Dissatisfaction

Body type preference can influence the degree to which individuals are satisfied with their bodies. Specifically, the difference between a person's perceived and preferred body type is a measure of body dissatisfaction (Dounchis et al., 2001; Dunkley, Wertheim, & Paxton, 2001; Gardner et al., 1999a). Adolescents who accept their weight as ideal will be more satisfied with their bodies than comparable adolescents who desire a thinner shape. Thus, the greater the discrepancy between perceived shape and preferred body type, the greater the body dissatisfaction. Body dissatisfaction is also influenced by the inability to accurately assess an individual's current body size, or perceptual disturbances, as well as by affective and attitudinal beliefs (Gardner et al., 1999a).

Relevant to this discussion is how an individual's body assessments and related attitudes are influenced by cultural standards. This section examines body dissatisfaction among ethnicities. There is evidence to support the idea that body dissatisfaction is higher in minorities than previously assumed, which contradicts the popular belief that body dissatisfaction occurs only among European Americans.

Caldwell, Brownell, and Wilfley (1997) suggested that European American females experience greater cultural pressure to be thin than non-European Americans. Other researchers have referred to eating disorders as *culture-bound syndromes* (Crago, Shisslak, & Estes, 1996; King, 1993; Wildes, Emery, & Simons, 2001) because the U.S. culture is obsessed with physical beauty and surrounded by falsified thin and flawless bodies. Many more White-waif models portray such images, so it is assumed that European Americans are much more susceptible to body dissatisfaction than women of color (Striegel-Moore et al., 2000). Thus, American trends may not be as influential on minority populations as they are for European Americans.

Indeed, several researchers have agreed that African American adolescents are more satisfied with their bodies (Abrams et al., 1993; Botta, 2000; Siegel, Yancey, Aneshensel, & Schuler, 1999; Story, French, Resnick, & Blum, 1995), experience less weight concerns (Thompson et al., 1997), and have a lower drive for thinness (Striegel-Moore et al., 2000; Thompson et al., 1997) than European American adolescents. This may result from the different influences the African and European American cultures have on adolescents. For example, when asked about the factors that influenced their concerns about the female body, African American adolescents reported being more influenced by immediate family members and teachers while European Americans were more influenced by their peers, TV, and magazines (Parnell et al., 1996). As a result, African Americans may embrace a greater range of normal body weights that are heavier than what European American adolescents accept. In fact, despite possessing greater BMIs than adolescent European Americans, African American adolescents are less dissatisfied with their bodies (Pritchard et al., 1997; Siegel et al., 1999; Thompson et al., 1997). Preference for a larger body type may function as a protective factor for eating disorders, after all. African American women were found to be less likely to develop anorexia and bulimia when compared to European American women (Powell & Kahn, 1995). However, at the same time, adherence to a heavier cultural standard may place African American women at an increased risk for obesity (Kumanyika, 1993; Rand & Kuldau, 1990). Yet, it is important not to equate preference for larger body types with obesity. For example, one ethnographic study based on more than 300 societies did not find one society that had an ideal of extreme obesity. Furthermore, more than 81% of the societies did prefer "plumpness" or being "filled out" (P. J. Brown, 1991; P. J. Brown & Konner, 1987).

Studies with Latinas and Asian Americans are few, but their contribution is undeniable. For instance, when comparing a representative sample of European American, Latina, and Asian sixth- and seventh-grade girls, Latina and Asian girls reported significantly greater body dissatisfaction than European American girls (Robinson et al., 1996). Furthermore, studies reporting no significant differences among ethnicities on body dissatisfaction continue to be replicated. European American and Latino children ages 7, 10, or 13 have very similar levels of body image perceptions and dissatisfaction (Gardner et al., 1999b). The majority of rural Latina and American Indian high school girls in one study expressed being concerned about their weight at levels comparable to urban European Americans (Snow & Harris, 1989).

To challenge the belief that body dissatisfaction is restricted to European American females, investigators must demonstrate that an ethnic group does not consistently have higher body satisfaction than European Americans. From the evidence presented previously, investigators have shown that body dissatisfaction is more common than originally assumed in adolescent minorities. Although findings were inconsistent, body image in ethnic minorities may emerge as a significant issue in future research, and more research is needed to understand the cultural influences.

Ethnicity is only one of possibly many influences on body preferences or body dissatisfaction in children and adolescents. Researchers have begun speculating about other variables that may be related to body preference and/or body dissatisfaction. However, no variables have been identified as the leading cause because body image may be associated with many different factors, each contributing only a small portion to the variance (Gardner et al., 1999a). Additional influences on body dissatisfaction that have been suggested as they relate to ethnic differences include BMI (Striegel-Moore et al., 2000), SES (Story et al., 1995; Thompson et al., 1997), and puberty (Siegel et al., 1999; Striegel-Moore et al., 2001). This area needs additional research and may greatly contribute to our understanding of both obesity and eating disorders.

A NEED FOR COMMUNITY PSYCHOLOGY

We have outlined the differences in prevalence rates of overweight and obesity between ethnic minority and European American children, reviewed studies to identify risk and protective factors or processes that may help to explain the greater prevalence among ethnic minority children, and reviewed the body image and body dissatisfaction literature to determine how they may be related to eating disturbance. This final section offers concrete recommendations on addressing the problem of childhood obesity among ethnically diverse children.

There is a great need for the collaboration between childhood obesity researchers and the community health care service deliverers, and the field of community psychology may be one of the answers. In support of this idea, Hill and Trowridge (1998) noted the importance of coordinating efforts among "policymakers, health professionals, community leaders, and parents" (p. 570). As to targeting childhood obesity, very few empirical studies have been conducted with ethnic minority participants. Consequently, there are even fewer studies that have included ethnic minority participants in treatment outcome studies. Ironically, at the local level (state and county), community health care centers are implementing their own child obesity treatment programs. However, rarely do they use empirically validated models of treatment or behavior change. It also becomes difficult to evaluate the effectiveness of their programs because participants are usually not compared to controls nor are they randomly selected to treatment conditions. Thus, there becomes a disparity between what is happening in the community and what is going on in the researcher's *labs*.

One way to address this disparity is to use a community psychology approach. Community psychology is interested in social and community problems and how these social systems affect individuals (Dalton et al., 2000). This can become complex because individuals live in social structures that form their community. For example, an individual can be part of a family, workplace, or school structure. Most importantly, individuals need to be understood within the context of which they live (Dalton et al., 2000). Bronfenbrenner's (1979) ecological model has been used to help understand the various sources of influence on the individual (Dalton et al., 2000). Bronfenbrenner's model examined five levels of analysis—the individual, microsystem, organization, locality, and macrosystem. This model emphasizes the importance of looking at multiple levels of influence on an individual. For example, an overweight child (individual) may be influenced by his or her family, classroom, friendship network, small religious congregation, athletic team, and so on (microsystem), that is influenced by various microsystems such as classes at the school, the school board, larger religious congregations, or larger volunteer community groups (organizations). The next level of analysis is the community, which may include geographic localities such as small towns, urban blocks or neighborhoods, or entire cities (localities). Last are the greater society, culture, government, and economic institutions beyond the local community (macrosystem).

How might looking at these different levels of analysis be helpful in addressing the problem of childhood obesity? Programs have been developed to help individuals and their families (Epstein et al., 1998; Golan & Weizman, 2001). But what we have not seen are efforts directed at the other levels of analysis. For example, researchers have suggested that improving the nutritional content of school lunches or decreasing the amount of fat and saturated fat in foods offered is another way to address childhood obesity (Bronner, 1996). Targeting localities/communities and the macrosystem could be helpful. That is, targeting American Indian reservations, where there is a significant problem with obesity and obesity-related health problems (diabetes, heart disease, etc.), is one example of targeting a locality or community. In a country that likes to super size everything, changing the social norm and advocating moderation is an example of intervening. Promoting the idea of increasing physical activity and decreasing sedentary behaviors could be another social campaign directed at the societal level. Most important, with each of these examples, we need to take into consideration cultural factors that operate in ethnic groups.

Community psychology provides the link for the gap that exists between the researcher and the community. Collaboration among members of a community (e.g., researchers, health providers) is the key for those working within a community psychology perspective. The next section outlines specific issues that need to be addressed when working with ethnically diverse communities and ways to implement research and prevention/intervention programs in culturally diverse communities.

Theoretical Issues

In the past decade, psychologists have become aware of two important issues: (1) the need to address the paucity of research that includes ethnic minority participants and (2) the need to address specific research concerns that involve ethnic minority participants (Cauce, Ryan, & Grove, 1998; Phinney & Ladin, 1998). In particular, more attention needs to be given to theoretical, methodological, and research design issues as they pertain to research with ethnic minority populations (Castro, Cota, & Vega, 1999; Cauce et al., 1998; Knight & Hill, 1998; Roosa, Dumka, Gonzalez, & Knight, 2002).

For example, Castro and his colleagues (1999) reviewed a sociocultural model for program planning, development, and evaluation in health promotion among Latino populations. In their model, it is suggested that culture must be attended to more in depth and with greater understanding than in the past. Language, culturally competent staff, integrating cultural aspects into program services (cultural values such as importance of family, interpersonal relationships, etc.), and adjusting services offered to the levels of acculturation that exist within target population are examples of cultural specifics. In addition, a culturally competent program conducts health promotion research to identify factors that will aid in the health promotion within a culture and may be targeted as mediators (Castro et al., 1999). Incorporating cultural competence throughout all stages, including the planning, design, and implementation of a community health promotion, is of utmost importance.

But what does *culturally competent* mean? According to Castro et al. (1999), *cultural competence* "refers to the capacity of health professional or of health service delivery systems to understand and plan for the health needs of a specific cultural subgroup" (p. 141). Two important principles have been identified that are a good starting point in the development of cultural competence: the principle of relevance (starting where people are) and the principle of participation (eliciting the participation of community residents; Minkler, 1990). More concretely, three recommendations for health promotion programs serving Latinos (but that can also apply to any group not represented in the research literature), as outlined by Castro and his colleagues, include:

1. Take a cultural relativist approach to design and delivery.
2. Establish strong relationships with the community you serve.
3. Involve community leaders or representatives in decision-making processes that govern program operations.

While some may think this is too much work, this is what makes a program *culturally competent* and not just culturally sensitive or aware.

Intervention/Prevention

Roosa et al. (2002) also have made suggestions for the prevention scientist who wants to work within the ethnic minority community. First, prevention researchers must understand the different layers of culture (e.g., beliefs, values, and goals) that motivate individuals in a particular group. Second, it is important to understand the pattern of behaviors and rituals among individuals in a group. Third, researchers need to understand the dynamics of the individual's and group's ecological niche or context (Roosa et al., 2002). Perhaps the most crucial point is that prevention programs should not only help individuals but also help individuals within the context or ecological niche in which they live.

According to Roosa and colleagues (2002), several skills are necessary for the prevention researcher to be effective at the two target levels: individual or family and the ecological niche. These skills include knowledge of cultural values and understanding the dynamics of the local ecological niche. These skills can help in recognizing how to influence the ecological niche to get support for intervention for the families in the target community. Finally, the prevention scientist needs to design and implement interventions for the target community that are culturally competent, including:

1. Establishing credibility in the community (e.g., school district, neighborhood or community associations).

2. Assessment (e.g., understand the needs of the community from *their* perspective).

3. Motivation (or behavior) change methods appropriate for the target community (e.g., family-centered, use of *promotores* or health promoters).

4. Maintenance strategies for the target behaviors (Roosa et al., 2002).

Measurement Issues

If the goal is to better understand health and health problems in ethnic minorities, this can be accomplished only if the instruments being used measure the same constructs equally across groups. Researchers in psychology have become more aware of the need to understand developmental and/or psychological processes with ethnic minority populations (Knight & Hill, 1998). This becomes difficult, however, if the psychological measures that are being used are not equivalent across ethnic and language groups. Most of the psychological measures have been developed and validated with nonminority European American participants. To assume that the conceptual models are the same for samples that were not included in the development or validation studies is faulty. This is not just a psychological issue anymore; the medical field also is becoming more aware of these issues as shown in a recent article from the *Journal of the American Medical Association* that raises concern over the lack of culturally competent measures and treatment for Latino children (Flores et al., 2002).

Various methods for addressing the issue of measurement equivalence have been suggested (Hines, 1993; Hughes, Seidman, & Williams, 1993; Hui & Triandis, 1985; Knight, Virdin, Ocampo, & Roosa, 1994; Knight, Virdin, & Roosa, 1994; Malpass & Poortinga, 1986) and can be categorized into item, functional, and scalar equivalence

(Hui & Triandis, 1985). *Item equivalence* refers to items from a measure having the same meaning across ethnic or racial groups. *Functional equivalence* is achieved when scores on one measure have the same precursors, consequents, and correlates across ethnic or racial groups. *Scalar equivalence* is the most difficult to achieve but the most important. Scalar equivalence exists when a score on a particular measure refers to the same degree, intensity, or magnitude of the construct across ethnic or racial groups (Knight & Hill, 1998). Relevant examples for eating disorder and obesity research include, eating disorder symptoms, body image/preference, and/or beliefs about health and diet. At the present time, there is not enough research being conducted in the area of measurement equivalency; however, this is an area that ethnic minority health researchers will want to focus on in future research.

Recruitment and Sampling

Cauce and colleagues (1998) have illuminated how scarce the research literature is as to the inclusion of ethnic minority participants. In a content analysis of two major psychological journals, these researchers documented that approximately 10% of the articles published between 1990 and 1993 included ethnic minorities in the samples and/or where the focus of the study was on ethnicity. In that content analysis, there was one special issue (a journal) on minority children that accounted for approximately half of the articles in the analysis. Thus, 10% is most likely an overestimation of the degree to which ethnic minorities were the focus and included in those studies. Furthermore, it is disheartening to note that the research picture has not improved over the years (Graham, 1992; Jones, 1983; McLoyd & Randolph, 1984, 1985). Before Cauce et al.'s study, Graham, Jones, McLoyd, and Randolph (1985) all conducted similar studies, and the number of ethnic minorities and the number of studies that focused on ethnicity as a research topic have barely equaled 6% of all the empirical studies conducted in psychology (e.g., social psychology, child psychology, or child development). Based on these findings, it should not have been surprising that when we began our research for this chapter, there was so little research found. For example, our PsychInfo search using terms such as *minorities and childhood obesity* came up with three hits, and only one specifically pertained to ethnic minorities. Because of the obesity epidemic, especially among ethnic minorities, we can no longer afford to neglect the inclusion of ethnic minority participants in our research. This is especially important as we try to understand why there are such dramatic differences in prevalence rates, as well as in the development of culturally appropriate treatment programs.

When conducting obesity research or recruiting participants for treatment programs, the use of culturally competent strategies is imperative. Cauce and her colleagues (1998) offered the following recommendations based on their review of several sources (Capaldi & Patterson, 1987; Ellickson, Bianca, & Schoeff, 1988; Gregory, Lohr, & Gilchrist, 1992; Gwadz & Rotheram-Borus, 1992; McAllister, Butler, & Goe, 1973; Stouthamer-Loeber, van Kammen, & Loeber, 1992; Streissguth & Guinta, 1992). While ethnic minorities were the target of their efforts, Cauce and her colleagues suggested that these strategies can be used with any group. Six *recruitment strategies* are outlined. The first strategy is to pay participants for their research participation. Offering participants a small fee is an effective way to motivate people to participate in research. Length of the interview and traveling distance should be considered when determining the amount for the participant fee. The second strategy suggests using referrals or references from respected others. *Respected others* might be community leaders, school administrators, clergy, or religious leaders. The third recruitment strategy is to use a more personal touch in recruiting participants. In support of the personal touch, Castro et al. (1999) noted that one of the cultural values associated with Latinos is "personalismo," which means that Latinos value interpersonal relatedness. Thus, when deciding on whether to use mass mailings, phone calls, or personal contacts, it might be wise to use a more personal touch, especially when working with ethnic minorities. The fourth strategy recommends that the research go to the participant if the participant is not coming to the research. The researcher and his or her staff might make home visits or find a location in the target community (e.g., recreation center, church hall) to recruit folks. Often in low-income communities, people have to rely on public transportation; thus, if they only have to commute a short distance in their own community or possibly even walk to the research site, this makes it more likely that people will participate. The fifth strategy notes the importance of a name and suggests that the research project's name be a helpful way to recruit participants. For example, because the words *childhood obesity* may not be seen in a positive light, creating a catchy description or name for your project might be better received. The sixth strategy is be persistent. Unless you use the human participant's pool at your university, participant recruitment can be difficult. When working in the community, patience and persistence pays off. One note of caution, however; you should balance number of contacts with unethical and excessive contacts. Thus, you create a phone contact policy, such as allowing for at least three phone contacts with live individuals versus answering machines before terminating contact. If planning home visits, expect to have no-shows or cancellations. To combat the no-shows and cancellations, offering an incentive for those participants who do keep their initial appointments may be helpful.

Once you spend a great amount of time and, most likely, money on recruiting participants, ensure that you keep the participants in the study. The next set of strategies is especially critical for longitudinal studies. Because future obesity research in areas such as weight loss and maintenance is important, longitudinal research designs will be necessary. Five *retention strategies* were outlined by Cauce and her colleagues (1998). First, be prepared and anticipate changes for the long term. If there is a possibility of tracking participants long term, prepare for this in the beginning. That is, obtain key information that will help you find the participants in the future (e.g., correct spelling of names, date and place of birth, place of employment). It is also recommended that you obtain the addresses and phone numbers of two to three family members or close friends who are likely to know how to locate the target family in the future. Other sources available for public viewing that may be helpful in locating families include county marriage records, the crisscross directory, and voter registration files. Second, maintain contact with your participants. This can be done with birthday cards that are sent out to the participants. If the participants have moved, this will be discovered before the next scheduled interview and the research team can begin to locate them. Mailing newsletters and birthday cards or providing an incentive for participants who provide new address information are other options. Third, make sure to reimburse your participants appropriately for their time and commitment to the project. Their initial participation was important, but continued participation is even more important because they cannot be replaced. That is, if you are gathering data at multiple time periods for each of the participants, it becomes imperative to retain the participants. Incentives can be offered that increase in payment for each wave of data collection or a bonus if all waves of data are collected. The fourth strategy refers to the earlier idea of establishing a relationship with the participants. Interviewers and experimenters with good people skills will most likely have high retention rates. Finally, the fifth retention strategy is to make sure that the research participation experience is positive or, at least, not aversive. For example, designing interviews in two parts might decrease fatigue. While there are advantages and disadvantages to doing this, the overall goal is to make sure that the participant's experience is not overwhelming. Cauce et al. (1998) suggested that if your refusal rate is greater than 10%, ask the participants why they are refusing so that you can possibly address the issues that are inhibiting folks from participating.

CONCLUSION

This chapter reviewed the literature on childhood obesity among ethnic minority youth, examined the influence of body image on obesity, and discussed the role of community psychology in future research directed at ethnic minority communities. While it seems that the development of childhood obesity in ethnically diverse children is similar to European Americans (e.g., imbalance between energy intake and expenditure), there are important differences in how that imbalance developed (e.g., SES, acculturation, generation, cultural beliefs). It is crucial to gather more information about these factors and their possible role in the etiology of obesity. Equally important is to start obtaining data on treatment and prevention. Using a community psychology approach will greatly aid in this endeavor. Specific suggestions from experts in the ethnic minority mental health field were offered to provide a greater understanding of the theoretical, methodological, and research design issues relevant for work in the ethnic minority community. It is hoped that this chapter will help in generating more research in a much needed area.

REFERENCES

Abrams, K. K., Allen, L., & Gray, J. J. (1993). Disordered eating attitudes and behaviors. *International Journal of Eating Disorders, 14*(1), 49–57.

Andersen, R. E., Crespo, C., Bartlett, S. J., Cheskin, L., & Pratt, M. (1998). Relationship of physical activity and television watching with body weight and level of fatness among children. *Journal of American Medical Association, 279*(12), 938–942.

Botta, R. A. (2000, Summer). The mirror of television: A comparison of Black and White adolescents' body image. *Journal of Communication,* 144–159.

Boyce, V. L., & Swinburn, B. A. (1993). The traditional Pima diet: Composition and adaptation for use in a dietary intervention study. *Diabetes Care, 16,* 369–371.

Bronfenbrenner, U. (1979). *The ecology of human development: Experiments by nature and design.* Cambridge, MA: Harvard University Press.

Bronner, Y. L. (1996). Nutritional status outcomes for children: Ethnic, cultural, and environmental contexts. *Journal of the American Dietetic Association, 96*(9), 891–900.

Broussard, B. A., Johnson, A., Himes, J. H., Story, M., Fichtner, R., Hauck, F., et al. (1991). Prevalence of obesity in American Indians and Alaska Natives. *American Journal of Clinical Nutrition, 53*(Suppl.), 1535–1542.

Brown, D. E., Severance, C. J., Sako, E. K., Chun, D. Y., Young, L. L., & Johnson, J. L. (1992). Growth of Native Hawaiian school children. II: Body mass indexes and skinfold measurements. *American Journal of Human Biology, 4,* 433–445.

Brown, P. J. (1991). Culture and the evolution of obesity. *Human Nature, 2*(1), 31–57.

Brown, P. J., & Konner, M. (1987). An anthropological perspective on obesity. *Annals of New York Academy of Sciences, 499,* 29–46.

Caldwell, M. B., Brownell, K. D., & Wilfley, D. E. (1997). Relationship of weight, body dissatisfaction and self-esteem in African American and White female dieters. *International Journal of Eating Disorders, 22,* 127–130.

Capaldi, D., & Patterson, G. R. (1987). An approach to the problem of recruitment and retention rates for longitudinal research. *Behavioral Assessment, 9,* 169–177.

Castro, F. G., Cota, M. K., & Vega, S. C. (1999). Health promotion in Latino populations: A sociocultural model for program planning, development, and evaluation. In R. M. Huff & M. V. Kline (Eds.), *Promoting health in multicultural populations: A handbook for practitioners* (pp. 137–168). Thousand Oaks, CA: Sage.

Cauce, A. M., Ryan, K. D., & Grove, K. (1998). Children and adolescents of color, where are you? Participation, selection, recruitment, and retention in developmental research. In V. McLoyd & L. Steinberg (Eds.), *Studying minority adolescents: Conceptual, methodological, and theoretical issues* (pp. 147–166). Mahwah, NJ: Erlbaum.

Collins, M. E. (1991). Body figure perceptions and preferences among preadolescent children. *International Journal of Eating Disorders, 10*(2), 199–208.

Costanzo, P. R., & Woody, E. Z. (1985). Domain-specific parenting styles and their impact on the child's development of particular deviance: The example of obesity proneness. *Journal of Social Clinical Psychology, 3,* 425–445.

Crago, M., Shisslak, C. M., & Estes, L. S. (1996). Eating disturbances among American minority groups: A review. *International Journal of Eating Disorders, 19*(3), 239–248.

Dalton, J. H., Elias, M. J., & Wandersman, A. (2000). *Community psychology: Linking individuals and communities.* Stamford, CT: Wadsworth.

Dounchis, J. Z., Hayden, H. A., & Wilfley, D. E. (2001). Obesity, body image, and eating disorders in ethnically diverse children and adolescents. In J. K. Thompson & L. Smolak (Eds.), *Body image, eating disorders, and obesity in youth: Assessment, prevention, and treatment* (pp. 67–98). Washington, DC: American Psychological Association.

Dunkley, T. L., Wertheim, E. H., & Paxton, S. J. (2001). Examination of a model of multiple sociocultural influences on adolescent girls' body dissatisfaction and dietary restraint. *Adolescence, 36*(142), 265–279.

Ellickson, P. L., Bianca, D., & Schoeff, D. C. (1988). Containing attrition in school based research. *Evaluation Review, 12,* 332–351.

Epstein, L. H., Myers, M. D., Raynor, H. A., & Saelens, B. E. (1998). Treatment of pediatric obesity. *Pediatrics, 101,* 554–570.

Epstein, L. H., Valoski, A. M., Vara, L. S., McCurley, J., Wisniewski, L., Kalarchian, M. A., et al. (1995). Effects of decreasing sedentary behavior and increasing activity on weight change in obese children. *Health Psychology, 14*(2), 109–115.

Flores, G., Fuentes-Afflick, E., Barbot, O., Carter-Pokras, O., Claudio, L., Lara, M., et al. (2002). The health of Latino children: Urgent priorities, unanswered questions, and a research agenda. *Journal of the American Medical Association, 288*(1), 82–90.

Flynn, K., & Fitzgibbon, M. (1996). Body image ideals of low-income African American mothers and their preadolescent daughters. *Journal of Youth and Adolescence, 25*(5), 615–630.

Foreyt, J. P., & Cousins, J. H. (1993). Primary prevention of obesity in Mexican-American children. *Annals of the New York Academy of Sciences, 699,* 137–146.

Freedman, D. S., Serdula, M. K., Percy, C. A., Ballew, C., & White, L. (1997). Obesity, levels of lipids and glucose, and smoking among Navajo adolescents. *Journal of Nutrition, 127*(Suppl.), S2120–S2127.

Gallaher, M. M., Hauck, F. R., Yang-Oshida, M., & Serdula, M. K. (1991). Obesity among Mescalero preschool children: Association with maternal obesity and birth weight. *American Journal of Diseases in Children, 145,* 1262–1265.

Gardner, R. M., Friedman, B. N., & Jackson, N. A. (1999a). Body size estimations, body dissatisfaction, and ideal size preferences in children six through thirteen. *Journal of Youth and Adolescence, 28*(5), 603–618.

Gardner, R. M., Friedman, B. N., & Jackson, N. A. (1999b). Hispanic and White children's judgments of perceived and ideal body size and others. *Psychological Record, 49,* 555–564.

Gerald, L. B., Anderson, A., Johnson, G. D., Hoff, C., & Trimm, R. F. (1994). Social class, social support and obesity risk in children. *Child Care, Health, and Development, 20,* 145–163.

Golan, M., & Weizman, A. (2001). Familial approach to the treatment of childhood obesity: Conceptual model. *Journal of Nutrition Education, 33*(2), 102–107.

Gortmaker, S. L., Dietz, W. H., Sobol, A. M., & Wehler, C. A. (1987). Increasing pediatric obesity in the United States. *American Journal of Diseases in Children, 141,* 535–540.

Gortmaker, S. L., Must, A., Perrin, J., Sobol, A. M., & Dietz, W. H. (1993). Social and economic consequences of overweight in adolescence and young adulthood. *New England Journal of Medicine, 329,* 1008–1012.

Graham, S. (1992). "Most of the subjects are White and middle class": Trends in publishing research on African Americans in selected APA journals, 1970–1989. *American Psychologist, 47,* 629–639.

Gregory, M. M., Lohr, M. J., & Gilchrist, L. D. (1992). Methods for tracking pregnant and parenting adolescents. *Evaluation Review, 17,* 69–81.

Guinn, B., Semper, T., Jorgensen, L., & Skaggs, S. (1997). Body image perception in female Mexican-American adolescents. *Journal of School Health, 67*(3), 112–115.

Gwadz, M., & Rotheram-Borus, M. J. (1992, Fall). Tracking high-risk adolescents longitudinally. *AIDS Education and Prevention* (Suppl.), 69–82.

Hill, J. O., & Trowridge, F. L. (1998). Childhood obesity: Future directions and research priorities. *Pediatrics, 101*(3), 570–574.

Himes, J. H., Story, M., Czaplinski, K., & Dahlberg-Luby, E. (1992). Indications of early obesity in low-income Hmong children. *American Journal of Diseases in Children, 146,* 67–69.

Hines, A. M. (1993). Linking qualitative and quantitative methods in cross-cultural survey research: Techniques from cognitive science. *American Journal of Community Psychology, 21,* 729–746.

Hughes, D., Seidman, E., & Williams, N. (1993). Cultural phenomena and the research enterprise: Toward a culturally anchored methodology. *American Journal of Community Psychology, 21,* 687–704.

Hui, C. H., & Triandis, H. C. (1985). Measurement in cross-cultural psychology: A review and comparison of strategies. *Journal of Cross-Cultural Psychology, 16,* 131–152.

Jackson, M. Y. (1993). Height, weight, and body mass index of American Indian schoolchildren, 1990–1991. *Journal of American Dietician Association, 93,* 1136–1140.

James, W. P. T. (2002). A worldview of the obesity problem. In C. G. Fairburn & K. D. Brownell (Eds.), *Eating disorders and obesity: A comprehensive handbook* (pp. 411–416). New York: Guilford Press.

Jeffery, R., French, S., & Spry, V. (1991). Socioeconomic status differences in health behaviors related to obesity: The Healthy Worker Project. *International Journal of Obesity, 15,* 689–696.

Jones, J. M. (1983). The concept of race in social psychology. In L. Wheeler & P. Shaver (Eds.), *Review of personality and social psychology* (Vol. 4, pp. 117–150). Beverly Hills, CA: Sage.

King, M. B. (1993). Cultural aspects of eating disorders. *International Review of Psychiatry, 5,* 205–216.

Knapp, J. A., Hazuda, H. P., Haffner, S. M., Young, E. A., & Stern, M. P. (1988). A saturated fat/cholesterol avoidance scale: Sex and ethnic differences in a biethnic population. *Journal of the American Dietetic Association, 88*(2), 172–177.

Knight, G. P., & Hill, N. E. (1998). Measurement equivalence in research involving minority adolescents. In V. McLoyd & L. Steinberg (Eds.), *Studying minority adolescents: Conceptual, methodological, and theoretical issues* (pp. 183–207). Mahwah, NJ: Erlbaum.

Knight, G. P., Virdin, L. M., Ocampo, K. A., & Roosa, M. (1994). An examination of the cross ethnic equivalence of measures of negative life events and mental health among Hispanic and Anglo American children. *American Journal of Community Psychology, 22,* 767–783.

Knight, G. P., Virdin, L. M., & Roosa, M. (1994). Socialization and family correlates of mental health outcomes among Hispanic and Anglo American children: Considerations of cross-ethnic scalar equivalence. *Child Development, 65,* 212–224.

Knowler, W. C., Barrett-Connor, E., Fowler, S. E., Hamman, R. F., Lachin, J. M., Walker, E. A., et al. (2002). Reduction in the incidence of Type 2 diabetes with lifestyle intervention or metformin. *New England Journal of Medicine, 346,*(6) 393–403.

Knowler, W. C., Pettitt, D. J., Saad, M. F., Charles, M. A., Nelson, R. G., Howard, B. V., et al. (1991). Obesity in the Pima Indians: Its magnitude and relationship with diabetes. *American Journal of Clinical Nutrition, 5*(Suppl. 1), 1543–1551.

Kumanyika, S. (1987). Obesity in Black woman. *Epidemiologic Reviews, 9,* 31–50.

Kumanyika, S. (1993). Ethnicity and obesity development in children: Prevention and treatment of childhood obesity. *Annals of the New York Academy of Sciences, 699,* 81–92.

Kumanyika, S. (1994). Obesity in minority populations: An epidemiologic assessment. *Obesity Research, 2*(2), 166–182.

Kumanyika, S. (2002). Obesity in minority populations. In C. G. Fairburn & K. D. Brownell (Eds.), *Eating disorders and obesity: A comprehensive handbook* (pp. 439–444). New York: Guilford Press.

Lindsay, R. S., Cook, V., Hanson, R., Salbe, A. D., Tataranni, A., & Knowler, W. C. (2002). Early excess weight gain of children in the Pima Indian population. *Pediatrics, 109*(2), 1–6.

Lopez, E., Blix, G., & Blix, A. (1995). Body image of Latina compared to body image of non Latina White women. *Health Values: Journal of Health Behavior, Education, and Promotion, 19*(6), 3–10.

Malpass, R. S., & Poortinga, Y. H. (1986). Strategies for design and analysis. In W. J. Lonner & J. W. Berry (Eds.), *Field methods in cross-cultural research* (pp. 47–84). Newbury Park, CA: Sage.

McAllister, R. J., Butler, E. W., & Goe, S. J. (1973). Evolution of a strategy for the retrieval of cases in longitudinal survey research. *Sociology and Social Research, 58,* 37–47.

McLoyd, V. C., & Randolph, S. M. (1984). The conduct and publication of research on Afro-American children. *Human Development, 27,* 65–75.

McLoyd, V. C., & Randolph, S. M. (1985). Secular trends in the study of Afro-American children: A review of child development, 1936–1980. *Monographs of the Society for Research in Child Development, 50,* 78–92.

Miller, M. N., & Pumariega, A. J. (2001). Culture and eating disorder: A historical and cross-cultural review. *Psychiatry, 64*(2), 93–110.

Minkler, M. (1990). Improving health through community organization. In K. Glanz, F. M. Lewis, & B. K. Rimer (Eds.), *Health behavior and health education: Theory, research, and practice* (pp. 257–287). San Francisco: Jossey-Bass.

Nagayama Hall, G. C., & Barongan, C. (2002). *Multicultural psychology.* Upper Saddle River, NJ: Prentice Hall.

Neel, J. V. (1962). Diabetes mellitus: A "thrifty" genotype rendered detrimental by "progress"? *American Journal of Human Genetics, 14,* 353–362.

Neff, L. J., Sargent, R. G., McKeown, R. E., Jackson, K., & Valois, R. F. (1997). Black-White differences in body size perceptions and weight management practices among adolescent females. *Journal of Adolescent Health, 20,* 459–465.

Ogden, C. L., Troiano, R. P., Briefel, R. P., Kuczmarski, R. J., Flegal, K. M., & Johnson, C. L. (1997). Prevalence of overweight among preschool children in the United States, 1971–1994. *Pediatrics, 99*(4), 1–7.

Olvera-Ezzell, N., Power, T. G., & Cousins, J. H. (1990). Maternal socialization of children's eating habits: Strategies used by obese Mexican-American mothers [Special issue]. *Child Development, 61*(2), 395–400.

Parnell, K., Sargent, R., Thompson, S. H., Duhe, S. F., Valois, R. F., & Kemper, R. C. (1996). Black and White adolescent females' perceptions of ideal body size. *Journal of School Health, 66*(3), 112–118.

Pawson, I. G., Martorell, R., & Mendoza, F. E. (1991). Prevalence of overweight and obesity in U.S. Hispanic populations. *American Journal of Clinical Nutrition, 53*(Suppl. 1), 1522 1528.

Pettitt, D. J., de Courten, M. P., Nelson, R. G., Fernandes, R. J., Hanson, L., Roumain, J., et al. (1995). Lower prevalence of NIDDM in breast fed Pima Indians [Abstract]. *Diabetes, 44*(Suppl. 1), 6A.

Pettitt, D. J., Nelson, R. G., Saad, M. F., Bennett, P. H., & Knowler, W. C. (1993). Diabetes and obesity in the offspring of Pima Indian women with diabetes during pregnancy. *Diabetes Care, 16,* 310–314.

Pettitt, D. J., Roumain, J., Hanson, R. L., Knowler, W. C., & Bennett, P. H. (1995). Lower glucose in pregnant and nonpregnant Pima Indians who were breast fed as infants [Abstract]. *Diabetologia, 38*(Suppl. 1), A61.

Phinney, J. S. (1996). When we talk about American ethnic groups, what do we mean? *American Psychologist, 51,* 918–927.

Phinney, J., & Ladin, J. (1998). Multiple selves, multiple worlds: Three useful strategies for research with ethnic minority youth on identity, relationships, and opportunity structures. In V. McLoyd & L. Steinberg (Eds.), *Studying minority adolescents: Conceptual, methodological, and theoretical issues* (pp. 112–125). Mahwah, NJ: Erlbaum.

Popkin, B. M., & Udry, J. R. (1998). Adolescent obesity increases significantly in second and third generation U.S. immigrants: The national longitudinal Study of Adolescent Health. *Journal of Nutrition, 128*(4), 701–706.

Potvin, L., Desroriers, S., Trifonopoulos, M., Leduc, N., Rivard, M., Macaulary, A. C., et al. (1999). Anthropometric characteristics of Mohawk children aged 6–11 years: A population perspective. *Journal of American Dietician Association, 99,* 955–961.

Powell, A. D., & Kahn, A. S. (1995). Racial in women's desires to be thin. *International Journal of Eating Disorders, 17*(2), 191–195.

Pritchard, M. E., King, S. L., & Czajka-Narins, D. M. (1997). Adolescent body mass index indices and self-perception. *Adolescence, 32*(128), 863–880.

Rand, C. S., & Kuldau, J. M. (1990). The epidemiology of obesity and self-defined weight problem in the general population: Gender, race, age, and social class. *International Journal of Eating Disorders, 9*(3), 329–343.

Robinson, T. N., & Killen, J. D. (1995). Ethnic and gender differences in the relationships between television viewing and obesity, physical activity, and dietary fat intake. *Journal of Health Education, 26*(2), S94–S98.

Robinson, T. N., Killen, J. D., Litt, I. F., Hammer, L. D., Wilson, D. M., Haydel, K. F., et al. (1996). Ethnicity and body dissatisfaction: Are Hispanic and Asian girls at increased risk for eating disorders? *Journal of Adolescent Health, 19,* 384–393.

Roosa, M. W., Dumka, L. E., Gonzalez, N. A., & Knight, G. P. (2002). Cultural/ethnic issues and the prevention scientist in the twenty-first century. *Prevention and Treatment, 5,* 5. Retrieved August 22, 2002, from www.journals.apa.org/prevention/volume5/pre0050005a.html.

Rosner, B., Prineas, R., Loggie, J., & Daniels, S. R. (1998). Percentiles for body mass index in U.S. children 5–17 years of age. *Journal of Pediatrics, 132,* 211–222.

Siegel, J. M., Yancey, A. K., Aneshensel, C. S., & Schuler, R. (1999). Body image, perceived pubertal timing and adolescent mental health. *Journal of Adolescent Health, 25,* 155–165.

Smith, C. J., Nelson, R. G., Hardy, S. A., Manahan, E. M., Bennett, P. H., & Knowler, W. C. (1996). Survey of the diet of Pima Indians using quantitative food frequency assessment and 24-hour recall. *Journal of the American Dietetic Association, 96,* 778–784.

Snow, J. T., & Harris, M. B. (1989). Disordered eating in South-western Pueblo Indians and Hispanics. *Journal of Adolescence, 12,* 329–336.

Sobal, J. (1995). Social influences on body weight. In K. D. Brownell & C. F. Fairburn (Eds.), *Eating disorders and obesity: A comprehensive handbook* (pp. 73–77). New York: Guilford Press.

Sobal, J., & Stunkard, A. J. (1989). Socioeconomic status and obesity: A review of the literature. *Psychological Bulletin, 105*(2), 260–275.

Spruijt-Metz, D., Lindquist, C. H., Birch, L. L., Fisher, J. O., & Goran, M. I. (2002). Relation between mothers' child-feeding practices and children's adiposity. *Clinical Nutrition, 75,* 3, 581–586.

Story, M., Evans, M., Fabsitz, R. R., Clay, T. E., Rock, B. H., & Broussard, B. (1999). The epidemic of obesity in American Indian communities and the need for childhood-prevention programs. *American Journal of Clinical Nutrition, 69*(Suppl. 1), 747–754.

Story, M., French, S. A., Resnick, M. D., & Blum, R. W. (1995). Ethnic/racial and socioeconomic differences in dieting and body image perceptions in adolescents. *International Journal of Eating Disorders, 18*(2), 173–179.

Story, M., Tompkins, R. A., Bass, M. A., & Wakefield, L. M. (1986). Anthropometric measurements and dietary intakes of Cherokee Indian teenagers in North Carolina. *Journal of the American Dietetic Association, 86*(11), 1555–1560.

Stouthamer-Loeber, M., van Kammen, W., & Loeber, R. (1992). The nuts and bolts of implementing large-scale longitudinal studies. *Violence and Victims, 7,* 63–78.

Strauss, R. A., & Pollack, H. A. (2001). Epidemic increase in childhood overweight, 1986–1998. *Journal of the American Medical Association, 286*(22), 2845–2848.

Streissguth, A. P., & Guinta, C. T. (1992). Subject recruitment and retention for longitudinal research: Practical considerations for a nonintervention model. *NIDA Research Monographs, 117,* 137–154.

Striegel-Moore, R. H., McMahon, R. D., Biro, F. M., Schrieber, G., Crawford, P. B., & Yoorhees, C. (2001). Exploring the relationship between timing of menarche and eating disorder symptoms in Black and White adolescent girls. *International Journal of Eating Disorders, 30,* 421–433.

Striegel-Moore, R. H., Schreiber, G. B., Lo, A., Crawford, P., Obrzanek, E., & Rodin, J. (2000). Eating disorder symptoms in a cohort of 11 to 16-year-old Black and White girls: The NHLBI growth and health study. *International Journal of Eating Disorders, 27,* 49–66.

Thompson, S. H., Corwin, S. J., & Sargent, R. G. (1997). Ideal body size beliefs and weight concerns of fourth-grade children. *International Journal of Eating Disorders, 21,* 279–284.

Triandis, H. C. (1996). The psychological measurement of cultural dyndromes. *American Psychologist, 51,* 407–415.

Troiano, R. P., & Flegal, K. M. (1998). Overweight children and adolescents: Descriptions, epidemiology and demographics. *Pediatrics, 101*(3), 497–504.

Troiano, R. P., Flegal, K. M., Kuczmarski, R. J., Campbell, S. M., & Johnson, C. L. (1995). Overweight prevalence and trends for children and adolescents: The National Health and Nutrition Examination Surveys, 1963 to 1991. *Archives of Pediatric and Adolescent Medicine, 149,* 1085–1091.

Tucker, L. A. (1986). The relationship of television viewing to physical fitness and obesity. *Adolescence, 21*(84), 797–806.

U.S. Department of Health and Human Services. (2002). *Surgeon General launches effort to develop action plan to combat overweight, obesity.* Retrieved August 15, 2002 from www.surgeongeneral.gov/news/pressreleases/obesitypressrelease.htm.

Wildes, J. E., Emery, R. E., & Simons, A. (2001). The roles of ethnicity and culture in the development of eating disturbance and body dissatisfaction: A meta-analytic review. *Clinical Psychology Review, 21*(4), 521–551.

Wilfley, D. E., & Saelens, B. E. (2002). Epidemiology and causes of obesity in children. In C. G. Fairburn & K. D. Brownell (Eds.), *Eating disorders and obesity: A comprehensive handbook* (pp. 429–432). New York: Guilford Press.

Williams, C. L., & Berry, J. W. (1991). Primary prevention of acculturative stress among refugees: Application of psychological theory and practice. *American Psychologist, 46,* 632–641.

Williams, J. D., Achterberg, C., & Sylvester, G. P. (1993). Target marketing of food products to ethnic minority youth. In C. L. Williams & S. Y. Kimm (Eds.), *Prevention and treatment of childhood obesity* (pp. 107–114). New York: New York Academy of Science.

Wolf, A. M. (2002). The health economics of obesity and weight loss. In C. G. Fairburn & K. D. Brownell (Eds.), *Eating disorders and obesity: A comprehensive handbook* (pp. 453–459). New York: Guilford Press.

Wolf, A. M., Gortmaker, S. L., Cheung, L., Gray, H. M., Herzog, D. B., & Colditz, G. A. (1993). Activity, inactivity, and obesity: Racial ethnic, and age differences among schoolgirls. *American Journal of Public Health, 83*(11), 1625–1627.

Yates, A. (1989). Current perspectives on the eating disorders. I: History, psychological and biological aspects. *Journal of American Academy of Child and Adolescent Psychiatry, 28*(6), 813–828.

Zephier, E., Himes, J. H., & Story, M. (1999). Prevalence of overweight and obesity in American Indian school children and adolescents in the Aberdeen area: A population study. *International Journal of Obesity, 23*(Suppl. 2), S28–S30.

Chapter 32

CHILD SEXUAL ABUSE AND EATING DISORDERS

KEVIN M. THOMPSON AND STEPHEN A. WONDERLICH

During the mid-1980s, clinicians and researchers began to consider the possibility that child sexual abuse (CSA) might function as a risk factor for eating disorders (Oppenheimer, Howells, Palmer, & Chaloner, 1985). This link seemed feasible because many CSA and eating disorder patients manifested similar symptoms such as shame, body denigration, and low self-esteem. Nevertheless, before the mid-1990s, there existed a paucity of research on the association between CSA and eating disorders. When Kendall-Tackett, Meyer-Williams, and Finkelhor (1993) published their comprehensive review of the effects of sexual abuse on children, they were unable to include eating disorders as a plausible outcome of CSA because little information was available on the subject.

Since the mid-1990s, a number of investigators have examined whether child sexual abuse might play a role as a risk factor for eating disorders. Indeed, sufficient attention had been paid to this association to facilitate a meta-analytic review in 2002 (Smolak & Murnen, 2002). While this attention suggests that researchers are no longer ignoring this nexus, we continue to need more specific and sensitive information about the processes that mediate and moderate this association. To that end, we review what we know about the association between CSA and eating disorders, propose conceptual models that can be tested, and delineate ideas for future directions in this area.

We restrict our review to the impact of CSA on eating disorders as they affect females for several reasons. First, while some researchers recognize that males may experience similar sexual victimization rates in childhood (Murphy, 1989; Urquiza, 1989), males tend to manifest traits of a more externalizing nature (such as aggression) because of such abuse. Second, the earlier ages for sexual abuse among boys[1] hamper reliable reporting of these incidents. Third, it may be more difficult for boys than girls to disclose acts of sexual abuse to a survey interviewer or social service

---

[1] The National Child Abuse and Neglect Data System (1994) reports that the average age of sexual abuse among boys is between 4 and 6 years while the average age for girls is between 11 and 14.

679

investigator because of cultural roles that reduce the admission of vulnerability characteristics in males. Nevertheless, we believe that future research needs to address the CSA-eating disorder nexus for males if some of these measurement obstacles can be overcome.

PREVALENCE ESTIMATES OF CHILD SEXUAL ABUSE AND EATING DISORDERS

Any discussion of the prevalence of a phenomenon hinges on debates about the proper definition for that phenomenon. Pope and Hudson (1992) noted 10 years ago that the definition of CSA varies among studies, which in turn produces variation in the prevalence estimates of CSA. Variation in the definition of CSA can be found according to whether physical contact constituted a feature of the act and the age difference between victim and perpetrator. Furthermore, definitions and prevalence estimates of CSA continue to remain controversial because of allegations of false reporting in cases involving divorce and child custody (Crosson-Tower, 2002) and the sentiment that many cases are socially constructed through false memory syndrome (Gardner, 1991).

Because of variation in the definition and assessment of CSA, prevalence estimates in the literature are wide ranging. In 1984, Finkelhor reported that between 9% and 52% of females had some sexual abuse exposure as children. However, studies that use common definitions appear to derive fairly stable estimates of CSA regardless of time and social context (Finkelhor, 1994; Finkelhor, Hotaling, Lewis, & Smith, 1990). Many researchers have adopted Wyatt's (1985) definition of CSA as involving (1) any intrafamilial sexual activity before age 18 that was unwanted by the respondent or that involved a family member five or more years older than the respondent, and (2) any extrafamilial sexual activity that occurred before age 18 and was unwanted or that occurred before age 13 and involved another person five or more years older than the respondent. Using this definition, Wilsnack, Vogeltanz, Klassen, and Harris (1997) found that 21%[2] of a nationally representative sample of women were victims of CSA. This rate appears to be in the range of estimates reported in both representative and nonrepresentative samples in which researchers have found that between 17% and 32% of women report being sexually abused in childhood (Vogeltanz et al., 1999).

Estimates for eating disorder behaviors show that bulimia nervosa (BN) affects approximately 2% of adolescent and young adult females (American Psychiatric Association [APA], 1993) while restricting anorexia nervosa (AN) is surmised to affect roughly 1% of this same population (APA, 1993). In recent work with a representative sample of adolescents, Striegel-Moore, Lewinsohn, and Seeley (2001) reported that 1.4% of their sample met a diagnosis for full syndrome AN, and 2.8% of the sample satisfied criteria for full syndrome BN. Larger estimates are typically derived for girls and adult females who self-report on eating disorder symptoms. Samples of adolescent girls and young adult females reveal that between 10% and 55% exhibit symptoms of eating-disturbed

---

[2] This sample was weighted to compensate for a stratified sample and for variations in response rates.

behaviors, making them at risk for eating disorders (Ackard, Neumark-Sztainer, Hannan, French, & Story, 2001; Thompson, Wonderlich, Crosby, & Mitchell, 1999).

CHILD SEXUAL ABUSE-EATING DISORDER ASSOCIATION

Several literature reviews have now been published delineating the association between CSA and eating disorders. Earlier reviews focused on methodological weaknesses in the literature and suggested strategies for more systematic measurement and data collection (see Connors & Morse, 1993; Everill & Waller, 1995; Rorty & Yager, 1996). However, an earlier review by Pope and Hudson (1992) also concluded that evidence suggesting that CSA posed a risk factor for BN was sufficiently weak to justify redirecting our efforts to identify alternative risk factors for eating disorders. However, a later systematic review conducted by Wonderlich, Brewerton, Jocic, Dansky, and Abbott (1997) examined a series of hypotheses as to the relationship of CSA and BN and concluded that it was too early to dismiss CSA as a risk factor for BN. Since the publication of that review, a series of empirical articles has attended to the CSA-eating disorder association. This chapter summarizes the earlier Wonderlich et al. review and offers a review of research published since that time. We include articles that employed some measure of CSA, whether assessed in adulthood or childhood, and eating disorder behaviors. These behaviors could include clinical diagnoses or self-reported subclinical symptomatology. Our review includes studies that measured eating disturbance in CSA and nonabused control subjects, measured rates of CSA in eating disorder subjects and appropriate controls, and examined the association of CSA and eating behavior in community-based samples.

RESEARCH HYPOTHESIS 1: CHILD SEXUAL ABUSE IS SIGNIFICANTLY ASSOCIATED WITH EATING DISTURBANCE SYMPTOMATOLOGY

Wonderlich et al. (1997) Summary

The Wonderlich et al. (1997) review included both broad and narrow criteria for study inclusion[3] and focused specifically on BN for this hypothesis. As to the question of association, the investigators identified 12 studies that met their inclusion criteria. Of the 12 studies, 10 supported the hypothesis that CSA was associated statistically with BN. This meant that (1) the rate of eating disorders among CSA subjects was significantly greater than the rate presented by non-CSA subjects, (2) the rate of CSA in eating disorder subjects was significantly greater than the rate posed by eating disorder subjects

---

[3] Broad criteria was defined as: (1) at least 10 subjects per cell, (2) an eating disorder assessment using the *DSM-III* or *DSM-III-R* or a self-report instrument with adequate reliability and validity, and (3) utilization of a standard CSA definition. Narrow criteria included (1) above, plus an eating disorder based on an interview using *DSM-III-R,* and (3) an interview assessing CSA episodes that involved physical contact.

who were not victims of CSA, or (3) there were associations between CSA and BN in the general population that could not reasonably be attributed to chance.

Post-1995 Review and Summary

Table 32.1 displays the summaries for the 32 studies we identified that examined the association between CSA and eating disorder symptoms using community-based samples, eating disorder subjects, and CSA subjects. Of the 32 studies, 17 studies employed community-based samples. Thirteen of the 17 community-based studies reported significant associations between CSA and some measure of eating disorder symptomatology. Among the four studies where CSA was not significantly related to eating disorder behavior, it either failed to produce a significant bivariate correlation, or its association with eating disorders was eliminated once other forms of childhood maltreatment or recent sexual assault episodes were controlled. Eight studies that employed eating disorder subjects and assessed sexual abuse in childhood were identified. Half showed support for a significant CSA-eating disorder association. Four studies found that CSA was not a significant correlate of eating disorders. Finally, seven studies were identified that compared CSA and non-CSA subjects in terms of eating disorder symptomatology. All seven found a significant association between CSA and eating disturbances. Consequently, we can temporarily surmise that a significant association between these variables appears most likely in samples employing CSA subjects, followed by community-based samples, and eating disorder subjects.

RESEARCH HYPOTHESIS 2: CHILD SEXUAL ABUSE IS MORE HIGHLY ASSOCIATED WITH BULIMIC SYMPTOMS THAN RESTRICTING ANOREXIA SYMPTOMS

Wonderlich et al. (1997)

Six studies met broad criteria for inclusion in this earlier review. Four of six found higher rates of CSA in bulimic than anorexic subjects, thus providing modest support for the idea that CSA was more strongly associated with BN than with restricting anorexia.

Post-1995 Review and Summary

Five studies were identified in which investigators included both BN and restricting anorexia subjects, or in which some measure of bingeing and purging and dietary restriction was employed involving non-eating-disordered subjects. One study (Romans, Gendall, Martin, & Mullen, 2001) found that CSA was associated comparably with AN and BN. The other four studies found that relative to dietary restrictors, CSA was more highly associated with AN-BN subtype or BN purging subtype (Favaro, Dalle Grave, & Santonastaso, 1998; Nagata, Kiriike, Iketani, Kawarada, & Tanaka, 1999), BN (Garfinkel et al., 1996), or binge-purge behavior (Thompson, Wonderlich, Crosby, & Mitchell, 2001). Consequently, these patterns echo the earlier Wonderlich et al. (1997) review in concluding that CSA is more highly associated with symptoms of BN than with symptoms of AN.

Table 32.1   Summary of the Association between CSA and Eating Disorders

Number of Studies Post-1995	Studies Supporting the Research Hypothesis	Studies Not Supporting the Research Hypothesis
Community-Based Samples*		
17	13	4
Comments:	CSA was significantly associated with various measures of eating disorder symptomatology (Romans et al., 2001; Fairburn et al., 1997; Wonderlich et al., 1996; Laws & Golding, 1996; Edgardh & Ormstad, 2000; Petrie & Tripp, 2001; Ackard et al., 2001; Thompson et al., 2001; Bulik et al., 2001; Kendler et al., 2000) and continued to be significant after controls for relevant confounds (Johnson et al, 2002; Thompson et al., 2001; Neumark-Sztainer et al., 2000).	CSA was eliminated as a significant risk factor in these studies after controls for childhood emotional abuse (Kent et al., 1999), childhood physical abuse (Perkins & Luster, 1999), and recent sexual abuse (Kenardy & Ball, 1998). CSA was not associated with eating disorders using the BULIT-R (Korte et al., 1998).
Eating Disorder Subjects		
8	4	4
Comments:	CSA was significantly associated with BN (Welch & Fairburn, 1996; Deep et al., 1999), AN-BP and BN-P groups (Favaro et al., 1998), and AN (Fairburn et al., 1999).	Presence or absence of CSA did not significantly differentiate subjects for bulimia (Steiger et al., 2001; Waller, 1998; Sullivan et al., 1995). BN was associated only with CSA in the presence of borderline personality disorder (Steiger et al., 2001).
CSA Subjects		
7	7	None
Comments:	CSA was significantly associated with various measures of eating disorder symptomatology (Wonderlich et al., 2001a, 2001b, Swanston et al., 1997; Romans et al., 2001; Wonderlich et al., 1996; Wonderlich et al., 2000; Jarvis & Copeland, 1997).	

*Includes two studies that employed samples of twins (Bulik et al., 2001; Kendler et al., 2000).

RESEARCH HYPOTHESIS 3: CHILD SEXUAL ABUSE IS A SPECIFIC RISK FACTOR FOR EATING DISORDERS

Wonderlich et al. (1997) Summary

Wonderlich et al. (1997) identified seven studies that met at least broad criteria for inclusion. None of the seven studies affirmed statistically that CSA was a specific risk factor to the eating disorders. In general, studies concluded that rates of CSA in eating disorder samples were either similar to or less than rates unearthed in various other psychiatric comparison groups and that samples of CSA victims displayed a wide variety of psychiatric disorders beyond eating disorders.

Post-1995 Review and Summary

Seven studies were identified that examined whether CSA posed a unique risk factor for eating disorder symptomatology. Like the Wonderlich et al. (1997) review, all of the studies found that CSA was a risk factor for psychiatric impairment in general. Six studies employed eating disorder subjects and generally found that CSA was associated with an array of psychiatric comorbid disturbances (Anderson, LaPorte, Brandt, & Crawford, 1997; Favaro et al., 1998; Nagata et al., 1999; Welch & Fairburn, 1996). The three studies employing CSA subjects noted that while CSA was associated with eating disorders, it was also significantly associated with other forms of psychopathology, including impulsive and self-destructive behaviors (Swanston, Tebbutt, O'Toole, & Oates, 1997; Wonderlich et al., 2001b).

RESEARCH HYPOTHESIS 4: CHILD SEXUAL ABUSE IS ASSOCIATED WITH GREATER PSYCHIATRIC COMORBIDITY IN EATING DISORDER SUBJECTS

Wonderlich et al. (1997) Summary

This question examines whether the presence of comorbidity is higher in eating disorder subjects who present evidence of CSA compared to eating disorder subjects who were not CSA victims. Five of six studies found evidence of higher comorbidity in eating disorder subjects who were also CSA victims than nonvictims. The lone study that did not reach this conclusion was limited to specific examination of depressive symptoms (Pope, Mangweth, Negras, Hudson, & Cordas, 1994).

Post-1995 Review and Summary

We identified eight studies that employed a sample of eating disorder subjects and also assessed comorbidity differences in CSA and non-CSA subjects. Table 32.2 shows that of the eight studies, seven found some support for elevated levels of comorbidity in eating disorder subjects who experienced CSA versus those who did not. Not all supporting

Table 32.2   CSA and Comorbidity Differences in ED Subjects

Number of Studies Post-1995	Studies Supporting the Research Hypothesis	Studies Not Supporting the Research Hypothesis
8	7	1
Comments:	CSA was associated with greater comorbidity in eating disorder subjects for measures assessing PTSD (Steiger et al., 2001), anxiety disorders (Favaro et al., 1998; Anderson et al., 1997), dissociation (Brown et al., 1999), depression (Anderson et al., 1997), substance dependence (Deep et al., 1999), and general comorbid psychiatric disorders (Sullivan et al., 1995; Steiger et al., 2001).	CSA did not differentiate comorbidity prevalence in eating disorder subjects (Nagata et al., 1999).

studies, however, found uniformly higher rates for all measures of comorbidity in CSA subjects. For instance, Steiger et al. (2001) found that CSA was associated with elevated levels of posttraumatic stress disorder but not major depressive disorder or borderline personality disorder. Favaro et al. (1998) found that CSA differentiated subjects on the basis of anxiety disorder but not dissociation.

RESEARCH HYPOTHESIS 5: CHILD SEXUAL ABUSE IS ASSOCIATED WITH GREATER SEVERITY OF EATING DISORDER SYMPTOMS

Wonderlich et al. Summary

Only three studies met at least broad criteria for inclusion in the review. Of the three, none of the studies provided evidence suggesting that CSA was associated with a greater magnitude of symptoms involving distorted body perception, weight, binge frequency, or eating-related attitudes.

Post-1995 Review and Summary

We eliminated studies in which eating disorder subjects were compared with non-eating disorder subjects on the question of whether the *nature* of CSA affected the severity of eating disorder symptomatology (see Anderson, LaPorte, & Crawford, 2000; Hart & Waller, 2002). Instead, we simply focused on studies that examined whether the presence of CSA was associated with more severe eating disorder symptoms. Of the seven studies we identified, none found that the presence of CSA was associated with greater eating disorder psychopathology (Anderson et al., 1997, 2000; Favaro et al., 1998; Nagata et al., 1999; Steiger et al., 2001; Sullivan, Bulik, Carter, & Joyce, 1995; Waller, 1998).

RESEARCH HYPOTHESIS 6: PARTICULAR FEATURES OF CHILD SEXUAL ABUSE ARE ASSOCIATED WITH THE DEVELOPMENT OF EATING DISTURBANCES

Wonderlich et al. Summary

Five studies were identified in this review that met criteria for study inclusion. Four of the five found support for the hypothesis. Wonderlich et al. also examined studies to determine whether particular aspects of the abuse were related to symptom patterns in subjects with eating disorders. The lone study that included a measure of CSA found that a perceived negative response to disclosure surrounding the incident was associated with more vomiting among eating disorder subjects (Waller & Ruddock, 1993).

Post-1995 Review and Summary

Since the 1997 review, a number of investigators have examined whether the nature of CSA acts as a moderator on eating disorder symptomatology, following Spaccarelli's (1994) contention that the context of the CSA incident can temper the presence and degree of psychopathology. We included studies that examined whether the incident(s) was disclosed, the nature of the reaction to the disclosure, whether CSA was accompanied later on by a rape incident in adulthood, and other measures of the familial environment that could exacerbate or suppress the emergence of eating disorders.

Nine studies were identified that examined possible moderating influences on CSA. Table 32.3 shows that seven of the studies found some support for the idea that the specific nature of CSA is associated with eating disorder symptoms. These studies

Table 32.3 Particular Aspects of CSA and the Development of Eating Disturbance Symptoms

Number of Studies Post-1995	Studies Supporting the Research Hypothesis	Studies Not Supporting the Research Hypothesis
9	7	2
Comments:	Aspects of the CSA incident that moderated eating disorder symptomatology included whether rape occurred in adulthood (Wonderlich et al., 2001b), early menarche (Fairburn et al., 1997; Romans et al., 2001), parental separation (Romans et al., 2001), threat of force (Bulik et al., 2001), disclosure of the incident (Ackard et al., 2001), and severity of the act(s) (Deep et al., 1999; Hart & Waller, 2002; Kendler et al., 2000).	The nature of CSA (e.g., age at abuse, intra vs. extra familial, physical force) was not associated with eating disorder symptomatology (Anderson et al., 1997; Anderson et al., 2001).

employed a variety of moderator measures, including rape in adulthood (Wonderlich et al., 2001b), threat of force (Bulik, Prescott, & Kendler, 2001), early menarche (Fairburn, Welch, Doll, Davies, & O'Connor, 1997; Romans et al., 2001), parental separation (Romans et al., 2001), disclosure (Ackard et al., 2001), and severity of CSA (Deep, Lilenfeld, Plotnicov, Pollice, & Kaye, 1999; Hart & Waller, 2002; Kendler et al., 2000). Two studies failed to find support for the hypothesis using various measures of the nature and scope of abuse (Anderson et al., 1997, 2000).

RESEARCH HYPOTHESIS 7: CHILD SEXUAL ABUSE IS TEMPORALLY PRIOR TO EATING DISTURBANCE BEHAVIORS

This issue was not addressed in the Wonderlich et al. (1997) summary. Since that review, several articles have examined whether CSA preceded the onset of dieting, bingeing and purging, and other eating behavior disturbances. Generally, these studies have been retrospective by design rather than using child subjects in a prospective, longitudinal design.

Studies that have reported jointly on the age of onset of the CSA episode and eating behavior symptomatology have shown that CSA generally precedes the onset of eating disturbances (Anderson et al., 1997; Romans et al., 2001). Wonderlich et al. (2000) reported that CSA preceded the onset of eating disturbance behavior in 93% of their subjects. Two studies that assessed eating disorder psychopathology found that five years separated the earlier CSA episode from the onset of eating disturbance (Anderson et al., 2000; Welch & Fairburn, 1996). Deep et al. (1999) found that CSA preceded AN onset by five years; BN onset, by three years; and BN onset in substance dependence subjects, by one year.

Thompson, Wonderlich, Crosby, Redlin, and Mitchell (2002) recently attempted to establish more precise timing of these incidents/behaviors in a sample of CSA subjects. While CSA preceded time of onset of all of the eating disorder behaviors, the time frame between CSA and the onset of eating disturbance was narrower among women who reported multiple eating disorder behaviors than among women who reported only one eating disorder behavior.

CONCEPTUAL MODELS

Several comprehensive reviews of the potential CSA-eating disorder pathway have been generated in the literature (see Brown, 1997; Spaccarelli, 1994). In addition, more empirical testing of these conceptual schemes is now emerging (see Murray & Waller, 2002; Petrie & Tripp, 2001). Nevertheless, clinicians who treat eating disorders continue to need more precise information about the developmental sequences that emerge following CSA to provide more effective treatment for their patients. The extant literature leads us to surmise that there may be three separate pathways by which CSA might contribute to the probability of eating disorders. In this section, we delineate three conceptual schemes about CSA-eating disorder pathways with the hope that this discussion will spur more extensive empirical testing of these models.

The first model focuses on eating problems as a shame and coping mechanism and seems particularly relevant for explaining intrafamilial abuse (Murray & Waller, 2002). This shame and coping model has been suggested by the work of Kearney-Cooke and Striegel-Moore (1994) and focuses attention on the core mediating processes of coping, bodily shame, and bodily disgust. Others such as Mannarino and Cohen (1996) and Andrews (1995) have extended their work. Under this model (see Figure 32.1), the sexually abused girl begins to feel ashamed of her body as she perceives her body as a disgusting object, tainted by her perpetrator. Because the victim views her body with contempt and disgust, there is an attempt to destroy the body through starvation or ridding herself of consumed food (Brown, 1997). The CSA victim begins to perceive herself as "different," "lacking credibility," and feeling shame about body image (Andrews, 1995, 1997; Mannarino & Cohen, 1996). To cope with this self-perception and associated emotional states, the abused girl begins to diet in at attempt to modify her appearance. Dieting then triggers more extreme coping behaviors such as bingeing and purging to control weight. Another interpretation of the body shame mediating process is that the sexually abused girl is feverishly attempting to regain control through ritualized eating behavior (Schecter, Schwartz, & Greenfield, 1987).

Two other conceptual models appear to have emerged in recent years but have received less empirical testing. One of these models focuses attention on the mediating linkage provided by impulsive and self-destructive behaviors following the CSA episode (see Figure 32.1). This model suggests that CSA victims are vulnerable to a host of impulsive personality traits and self-destructive behaviors following the trauma. In this model, the eating disorder symptoms are likely to emerge as an expression of such predisposing impulsivity-oriented psychopathologies (see C. Johnson & Connors, 1987). Psychopathologies that appear pertinent to this model include borderline personality disorder (Waller, 1993), dissociation (Kent, Waller, & Dagnan, 1999), impulsive self-destructive behavior, drug use, and posttraumatic stress disorder (Wonderlich, Wilsnack, Wilsnack, & Harris, 1996; Wonderlich et al., 2001a).

Support for this model requires that the onset of eating disorder follows the development of impulsive and self-destructive traits and behaviors; therefore, eating disorder onset is dependent on the emergence of these mediational behaviors. Recent research has found support for this sequential scheme (e.g., Nagata, Kawarada, Kiriike, & Iketani, 2000; Thompson et al., 2002). Nagata et al. found that 80% of multi-impulsive eating disorder patients had self-mutilation or suicide attempt history *before* the onset of eating disorder while the majority of normal weight bulimics reported shoplifting before the onset of eating disorders. In another study, Thompson et al. noted that extreme dieting succeeded all measures of self-reported impulsive behaviors, and all of these impulsive behaviors preceded bingeing and purging, save suicide attempt. Furthermore, there is evidence to suggest that such impulsive, self-destructive behavior is associated with CSA (Favaro & Santonastaso, 1998; Wonderlich et al., 2001a).

The third model posits that CSA results in pervasive psychobiological dysregulation that disrupts normal development and leads to a host of psychopathologies (see Figure 32.1), including eating disorder symptomatology. Importantly, this model does not imply that CSA leads to a specific psychopathology that mediates the association between CSA and eating disorders (as in model 2), but instead implies that CSA results in a latent psychobiological disturbance that increases the risk of an array of impulsive,

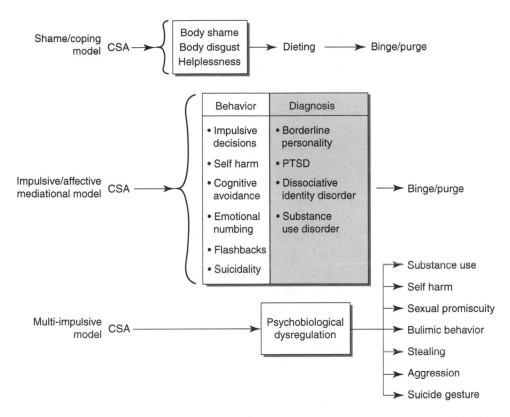

Figure 32.1   Three Models of the Relationship between CSA and Eating Disorders Behavior.

self-destructive behaviors, which are likely to co-occur in a given individual. The finding that CSA increases the risk of "multi-impulsive" bulimia (i.e., Nagata et al., 2000; Wonderlich et al., 2001a) is germane to this model. However, this model also raises the specter that such individuals may be best conceptualized not as eating disordered, but as displaying a multifaceted form of psychopathology that includes disturbances in eating. Some studies suggest that one-fourth to one-third of bulimic individuals show multiple forms of impulsivity, which may represent a unique multi-impulsive syndrome and appears to have a significant relationship to early abuse experiences (Wonderlich & Mitchell, 2001). Future taxonomic studies are needed to clarify whether such behavior represents a distinct syndrome.

Latent structure analysis could be useful for determining the existence of such a taxon and for further identifying how many levels or categories of the taxon are needed to adequately describe the association between the observed measures and psychobiological dysregulation.

SUMMARY

Because researchers have sufficiently attended to this association, we can employ the standardized nomenclature proposed by Kraemer et al. (1997) to assess the status of

CSA as a risk factor for eating disorders. Kraemer et al.'s risk factor typology scheme enables us to cautiously state the following:[4]

1. CSA has been demonstrated to be statistically associated with eating disorder outcome, making it a correlate of eating disorder symptomatology.

2. CSA appears to precede the onset of eating disturbance behavior in retrospective assessment strategies, making it a potential risk factor for eating disturbance behavior. Further, CSA appears to be associated with growth in eating disorder symptoms, controlling for initial symptom level (see J. G. Johnson, Cohen, Kasen, & Brook, 2002)

3. While CSA cannot be altered once it occurs, it is possible to prevent the occurrence of this risk factor and to modify the psychological mechanisms following CSA through treatment. This makes CSA a potential variable risk factor for eating disorders. Beyond this, there have been only a few prospective, longitudinal designs that have examined the association of CSA on eating disorders in girls who are free of eating disorder symptomatology at baseline. Thus, it is risky and premature to posit that CSA is a "causal risk factor" for eating disorders.

4. The absence of any research that suggests that CSA is a necessary and sufficient condition for eating disorders suggests that CSA currently cannot be identified as a "cause" of eating disturbance behavior.

To more clearly account for the estimated risk of CSA as it pertains to the eating disorders, we recommend that researchers employ a prospective, longitudinal design involving a sample of girls who are free of any eating disorder symptomatology. These subjects could be followed longitudinally, beginning in late childhood. Subjects could then be characterized by the presence or absence of CSA and matched on other factors (e.g., divorce, poverty, physical abuse). We recommend that at the least, variables from the various conceptual models be included to determine whether there might exist various subtypes of eating disorder subjects and whether the emergence of these subtypes is a function of the presence and nature of CSA.

REFERENCES

Ackard, D. M., Neumark-Sztainer, D., Hannan, P. J., French, S., & Story, M. (2001). Binge and purge behavior among adolescents: Associations with sexual and physical abuse in a nationally representative sample: The Commonwealth Fund survey. *Child Abuse and Neglect, 6,* 771–785.

American Psychiatric Association. (1993). Practice guidelines for eating disorders. *American Journal of Psychiatry, 150,* 685.

Anderson, K. P., LaPorte, D. J., Brandt, H., & Crawford, S. (1997). Sexual abuse and bulimia: Response to inpatient treatment and preliminary outcome. *Journal of Psychiatric Research, 31,* 621–633.

---

[4] Refer to Figure 32.2 in Kraemer et al. (1997).

Anderson, K. P., LaPorte, D. J., & Crawford, S. (2000). Child sexual abuse and bulimic sympto-matology: Relevance of specific abuse variables. *Child Abuse and Neglect, 24,* 1495–1502.

Andrews, B. (1995). Bodily shame as a mediator between abusive experiences and depression. *Journal of Abnormal Psychology, 104,* 277–285.

Andrews, B. (1997). Bodily shame in relation to abuse in childhood and bulimia: A prelimi-nary investigation. *British Journal of Clinical Psychology, 36,* 41–49.

Brown, L. (1997). Child physical and sexual abuse and eating disorders: A review of the links and personal comments on the treatment process. *Australian and New Zealand Journal of Psychiatry, 31,* 194–199.

Brown, L., Russell, J., Thornton, C., & Dunn, S. (1999). Dissociation, abuse and the eating dis-orders: Evidence from an Australian population. *Australian and New Zealand Journal of Psychiatry, 33,* 521–528.

Bulik, C. M., Prescott, C. A., & Kendler, K. S. (2001). Features of childhood sexual abuse and the development of psychiatric and substance use disorders. *British Journal of Psychiatry, 179,* 444–449.

Connors, M. E., & Morse, W. (1993). Sexual abuse and eating disorders: A review. *Interna-tional Journal of Eating Disorders, 13,* 1–11.

Crosson-Tower, C. (2002). *Understanding child abuse and neglect.* Boston: Allyn & Bacon.

Deep, A. L., Lilenfeld, L. R., Plotnicov, K. H., Pollice, C., & Kaye, W. H. (1999). Sexual abuse in eating disorder subtypes and control women: The role of comorbid substance depen-dence in bulimia nervosa. *International Journal of Eating Disorders, 25,* 1–10.

Edgardh, K., & Ormstad, K. (2000). Prevalence and characteristics of sexual abuse in a national sample of Swedish seventeen-year-old boys and girls. *Acta Paediatrica, 88,* 310–319.

Everill, J. T., & Waller, G. (1995). Reported sexual abuse and eating psychopathology: A re-view of the evidence for a causal link. *International Journal of Eating Disorders, 18,* 1–11.

Fairburn, C. G., Welch, S. L., Doll, H. A., Davies, B. A., & O'Connor, M. E. (1997). Risk factors for bulimia nervosa: A community-based case-control study. *Archives of General Psychia-try, 54* 509–517.

Favaro, A., Dalle Grave, R., & Santonastaso, P. (1998). Impact of a history of physical and sex-ual abuse in eating disordered and asyptomatic subjects. *Acta Psychiatrica Scandinavica, 97,* 358–363.

Favaro, A., & Santonastaso, P. (1998). Impulsive and compulsive self-injurious behavior in bu-limia nervosa: Prevalence and psychological correlates. *Journal of Nervous and Mental Dis-eases, 186,* 157–165.

Finkelhor, D. (1984). Current information on the scope and nature of child sexual abuse. *Sex-ual Abuse of Children, 4,* 31–54.

Finkelhor, D., Hotaling, G., Lewis, I. A., & Smith, C. (1990). Sexual abuse in a national survey of adult men and women: Prevalence, characteristics, and risk factors. *Child Abuse and Neglect, 14,* 19–28.

Garfinkel, P. E., Lin, E., Goering, P., Spegg, C., Goldbloom, D. S., Kennedy, S., et al. (1996). Purging and nonpurging forms of bulimia nervosa in a community sample. *International Journal of Eating Disorders, 20,* 231–238.

Hart, J., & Waller, G. (2002). Child abuse, dissociation, and core beliefs in bulimic disorders. *Child Abuse and Neglect, 1289,* 1–16.

Jarvis, T. J., & Copeland, J. (1997). Child sexual abuse as a predictor of psychiatric co-morbidity and its implications for drug and alcohol treatment. *Drug and Alcohol Dependence, 49,* 61–69.

Johnson, C., & Connors, M. E. (1987). *The etiology and treatment of bulimia nervosa: A biopsy-chosocial perspective.* New York: Basic Books.

Johnson, J. G., Cohen, P., Kasen, S., & Brook, J. S. (2002). Childhood adversities associated with risk for eating disorders or weight problems during adolescence or early adulthood. *American Journal of Psychiatry, 159,* 394–400.

Kearney-Cook, A., & Striegel-Moore, R. H. (1994). Treatment of childhood sexual abuse in anorexia nervosa and bulimia nervosa: A feminist psychodynamic approach. *International Journal of Eating Disorders, 15,* 305–319.

Kenardy, J., & Ball, K. (1998). Disordered eating, weight dissatisfaction and dieting in relation to unwanted childhood sexual experiences in a community sample. *Journal of Psychosomatic Research, 44,* 327–337.

Kendall-Tackett, K. A., Meyer-Williams, L., & Finkelhor, D. (1993). Impact of sexual abuse on children: A review and synthesis of recent empirical studies. *Psychological Bulletin, 113,* 164–180.

Kendler, K. S., Bulik, C. M., Silberg, J., Hettema, J. M., Myers, J., & Prescott, C. A. (2000). Childhood sexual abuse and adult psychiatric and substance use disorders in women: An epidemiological and cotwin control analysis. *Archives of General Psychiatry, 57,* 953–959

Kent, A., Waller, G., & Dagnan, D. (1999). A greater role of emotional than physical or sexual abuse in predicting disordered eating attitudes: The role of mediating variables. *International Journal of Eating Disorders, 25,* 159–167.

Korte, K. L., Horton, C. B., & Graybill, D. (1998). Child sexual abuse and bulimic behaviors: An exploratory investigation of the frequency and nature of a relationship. *Journal of Child Sexual Abuse, 7,* 53–64.

Kraemer, H. C., Kazdin, A. E., Offord, D. R., Kessler, R. C., Jensen, P. S., & Kupfer, D. J. (1997). Coming to terms with the terms of risk. *Archives of General Psychiatry, 54,* 337–343.

Laws, A., & Golding, J. M. (1996). Sexual assault history and eating disorders symptoms among white, Hispanic, and African American women and men. *American Journal of Public Health, 86,* 579–582.

Mannarino, A. P., & Cohen, J. A. (1996). A follow-up study of factors that mediate the development of psychological symptomatology in sexually abused girls. *Child Maltreatment, 1,* 246–260.

Murphy, R. T. (1989). Coercive traps and the risk for child abuse: An analogue study. *Dissertation Abstracts International, 50,* 754.

Murray, C., & Waller, G. (2002). Reported sexual abuse and bulimic psychopathology among nonclinical women: The mediating role of shame. *International Journal of Eating Disorders, 32,* 186–191.

Nagata, T., Kawarada, Y., Kiriike, N., & Iketani, T. (2000). Multiimpulsivity of Japanese patients with eating disorders: Primary and secondary impulsivity. *Psychiatry Research, 94,* 239–250.

Nagata, T., Kiriike, N., Iketani, T., Kawarada, Y., & Tanaka, H. (1999). History of childhood sexual or physical abuse in Japanese patients with eating disorders: Relationship with dissociation and impulsive behaviors. *Psychological Medicine, 29,* 935–942.

Neumark-Sztainer, D., Story, M., Hannan, P. J., Beuhring, T., & Resnick, M. D. (2000). Disordered eating among adolescents: Associations with sexual/physical abuse and other familial/psychosocial factors. *International Journal of Eating Disorders, 28,* 249–258.

Oppenheimer, R., Howells, K., Palmer, R. L., & Chaloner, D. A. (1985). Adverse sexual experiences in childhood and clinical eating disorders: A preliminary description. *Journal of Psychiatric Research, 19,* 357–361.

Perkins, D. F., & Luster, T. (1999). The relationship between sexual abuse and purging: Findings from community-wide surveys of female adolescents. *Child Abuse and Neglect, 23,* 371–382.

Petrie, T. A., & Tripp, M. (2001). Sexual abuse and eating disorders: A test of a conceptual model. *Sex Roles: A Journal of Research,* 17–29.

Pope, H. G., & Hudson, J. I. (1992). Is childhood sexual abuse a risk factor for bulimia nervosa? *American Journal of Psychiatry, 149,* 455–463.

Pope, H. G., Mangweth, B., Negras, A. B., Hudson, J. I., & Cordas, T. A. (1994). Childhood sexual abuse and bulimia nervosa: A comparison of American, Austrian and Brazilian women. *American Journal of Psychiatry, 151,* 732–737.

Romans, S. E., Gendall, K. A., Martin, J. L., & Mullen, P. E. (2001). Child sexual abuse and later disordered eating: A New Zealand epidemiological study. *International Journal of Eating Disorders, 29,* 380–392.

Rorty, M., & Yager, J. (1996). Histories of childhood trauma and complex posttraumatic sequelae in women with eating disorders. *Psychiatric Clinics of North America, 19,* 773–791.

Schecter, J. O., Schwartz, H. P., & Greenfield, D. G. (1987). Sexual assault and anorexia nervosa. *International Journal of Eating Disorders, 5,* 313–316.

Smolak, L., & Murnen, S. K. (2002). A meta-analytic examination of the relationship between child sexual abuse and eating disorders. *International Journal of Eating Disorders, 31,* 136–150.

Spaccarelli, S. (1994). Stress, appraisal, and coping in child sexual abuse: A theoretical and empirical review. *Psychological Bulletin, 116,* 340–362.

Steiger, H., Gauvin, L., Israel, M., Koerner, N., Ng Ying Kin, N. M. K., Paris, J., (2001). Association of serotonin and cortisol indices with childhood abuse in bulimia nervosa. *Archives of General Psychiatry, 58,* 837–843.

Striegel-Moore, R., Lewinsohn, P. M., & Seeley, M. S. (2001). *Psychosocial adjustment of women who have experienced an eating disorder during adolescence.* Paper presented at the annual meeting of the Eating Disorder Research Society, Bernalillo, NM.

Sullivan, P. F., Bulik, C. M., Carter, F. A., & Joyce, P. R. (1995). The significance of a history of childhood sexual abuse in bulimia nervosa. *British Journal of Psychiatry, 167,* 679–682.

Swanston, H. Y., Tebbutt, J. S., O'Toole, B. I., & Oates, R. K. (1997). Sexually abused children 5 years after presentation: A case-controlled study. *Pediatrics, 100,* 600–608.

Thompson, K. M., Wonderlich, S. A., Crosby, R. D., & Mitchell, J. E. (1999). The neglected link between eating disturbances and aggressive behavior in girls. *Journal of the American Academy of Child and Adolescent Psychiatry, 38,* 1277–1285.

Thompson, K. M., Wonderlich, S. A., Crosby, R. D., & Mitchell, J. E. (2000). Sexual victimization and adolescent weight regulation practices: A test across three community based samples. *Child Abuse and Neglect, 25,* 291–305.

Thompson, K. M., Wonderlich, S. A., Crosby, R. D., & Mitchell, J. E. (2001). Sexual violence and weight control techniques among adolescent girls. *International Journal of Eating Disorders, 29,* 166–176.

Thompson, K. M., Wonderlich, S. A., Crosby, R. D., Redlin, J. A., & Mitchell, J. E. (2002). The temporal ordering of childhood sexual abuse, eating disturbances, and impulsive and self-destructive behaviors. In S. P. Shohov (Ed.), *Advances in psychology research.* New York: Nova Science.

Urquiza, A. J. (1989). The effects of childhood sexual abuse in an adult male population. *Dissertation Abstracts International, 50,* 356.

Vogeltanz, N. D., Wilsnack, S. C., Harris, T. R., Wilsnack, R. W., Wonderlich, S. A., & Kristjanson, A. F. (1999). Prevalence and risk factors for childhood sexual abuse: National survey findings. *Child Abuse and Neglect, 23,* 579–592.

Waller, G. (1993). Association of sexual abuse and borderline personality disorder in eating disordered women. *International Journal of Eating Disorders, 13,* 259–63.

Waller, G. (1998). Perceived control in eating disorders: Relationship with reported sexual abuse. *International Journal of Eating Disorders, 23,* 213–216.

Waller, G., & Ruddock, A. (1993). Experience of disclosure of childhood sexual abuse and psychopathology. *Child Abuse Review, 2,* 185–195.

Welch, S. L., & Fairburn, C. G. (1996). Childhood sexual and physical abuse as risk factors for the development of bulimia nervosa: A community-based case control study. *Child Abuse and Neglect, 20,* 633–642.

Wilsnack, S. C., Vogeltanz, N. D., Klassen, A. D., & Harris, T. R. (1997). Childhood sexual abuse and women's substance abuse: National survey findings. *Journal of Studies on Alcohol, 58,* 264–271.

Wonderlich, S. A., Brewerton, T. D., Jocic, Z., Dansky, B., & Abbott, D. W. (1997). Relationship of childhood sexual abuse and eating disorders. *Journal of the American Academy of Child and Adolescent Psychiatry, 36,* 1107–1115.

Wonderlich, S. A., Crosby, R. D., Mitchell, J. E., Roberts, J. A., Haseltine, B., DeMuth, G., et al. (2000). Relationship of childhood sexual abuse and eating disturbance in children. *Journal of the American Academy of Child and Adolescent Psychiatry, 39,* 1277–1283.

Wonderlich, S. A., Crosby, R. D., Mitchell, J. E., Thompson, K., Redlin, J., DeMuth, G., et al. (2001a). Eating disturbance and sexual trauma in childhood and adulthood. *International Journal of Eating Disorders, 4,* 401–412.

Wonderlich, S. A., Crosby, R. D., Mitchell, J. E., Thompson, K., Redlin, J., DeMuth, G., et al. (2001b). Pathways mediating sexual abuse and eating disturbance in children. *International Journal of Eating Disorders, 29,* 270–279.

Wonderlich, S. A., Donaldson, M. A., Carson, D. K., Staton, D., Gertz, L., Leach, L., et al. (1996). Eating disturbance and incest. *Journal of Interpersonal Violence, 11,* 195–207.

Wonderlich, S. A., & Mitchell, J. E. (2001). The role of personality in the onset of eating disorders and treatment implications. *Psychiatric Clinics of North America, 24,* 249–257.

Wonderlich, S. A., Wilsnack, R. W., Wilsnack, S. C., & Harris, T. R. (1996). Childhood sexual abuse and bulimic behavior in a nationally representative sample. *American Journal of Public Health, 86,* 1082–1086.

Wyatt, G. (1985). The sexual abuse of Afro-American and White American women in childhood. *Child Abuse and Neglect, 9,* 507–519.

Chapter 33

MEDIA'S ROLE IN THE PERPETUATION AND PREVENTION OF NEGATIVE BODY IMAGE AND DISORDERED EATING

MICHAEL P. LEVINE AND KRISTEN HARRISON

This chapter extends our reviews of theory and research concerning media influences on weight and body shape in girls and women (Groesz, Levine, & Murnen, 2002; Levine, Piran, & Stoddard, 1999; Levine & Smolak, 1996, 1998; see also Bordo, 1993; Thompson & Heinberg, 1999; Thompson, Heinberg, Altabe, & Tantleff-Dunn, 1999).

Seven basic questions form the skeleton of any body of evidence purporting to establish the validity of media effects:

1. What are "mass media" and what "effects" are we assessing?
2. Do people have extensive exposure to mass media?
3. Could the content of mass media be the basis for the phenomena at issue?
4. What are the principal findings from qualitative, experimental, and correlational studies of media effects?
5. What do we know about the processes by which mass media might exert the influences demonstrated via research?
6. What are the implications of what we know, *and* what we do not yet know, for developing theory and research?
7. What are the implications of what we know for prevention?

This chapter briefly addresses questions 1 through 3 and then concentrates on questions 4 through 7. It is well established that children, adolescents, and adults are immersed in mass media (Arnett, 1995; Harris, 1999; Roberts, Foehr, Rideout, & Brodie, 1999; Singer & Singer, 2001). It is also indisputable that media content is rich with unhealthy messages about gender, attractiveness, ideal body sizes and shapes, self-control, desire, food, and weight management (see, e.g., Currie, 1999; Kilbourne, 1999; Pope, Olivardia, Gruber, & Borowiecki, 1999; Pope, Phillips, & Olivardia, 2000; Silverstein & Perlick, 1995; Spitzer, Henderson, & Zivian, 1999). People have no trouble finding the raw material for maladaptive but *entirely normative* media-based schema (Levine &

Smolak, 1996, 1998; Smolak & Levine, 1996). The "thinness schema" for girls includes beliefs such as:

- Beauty is a woman's principal project in life.
- Slenderness is crucial for success because success means heterosexual attractiveness.
- *Image* is really substance, because it constitutes a technology for being pleasing to males and for demonstrating to a female that she is in control of her life.
- Women are "naturally" invested in the beauty assets that are all important in competition for males.

These principles are readily available for boys as well and are an essential part of the interlocking processes that teach males to objectify females (Smolak & Murnen, 2001).

The "muscularity-power schema" for boys emphasizes the following convictions, for example:

- The ideal shape for an adolescent boy and a "real man" is a mesomorphic build, with a large upper torso featuring well-developed shoulder, arm, and chest muscles, coupled with a slim waist, hips, and buttocks.
- Being "underweight" or "light" or "flabby" is definitely inconsistent with masculinity, because men are defined in part by size, power, and strength.
- A muscular body is impressive and attractive to females.
- A muscular body is a manifest sign of power, success, and potential for success in masculine pursuits such as sports.
- A muscular body guarantees improved health (Labre, 2002; Leit, Gray, & Pope, 2002; Morrison, Morrison, & Hopkins, 2002; Pope et al., 2000; Thompson et al., 1999).

The negative impact of these schematic messages is augmented by many irreconcilable, pernicious contradictions, that is, double binds. For example, women are exhorted to be "fit," "toned," and "in control," while also "feeling free" to "let go," "give in," and "consume" various products, ranging from "slim" cigarettes to high-calorie foods (Bordo, 1993). Moreover, the process of engaging with some mass media, such as television and fashion magazines, is desirable unto itself. Thus, these media are potentially powerful mechanisms for activating emotional processing instead of intellectual elaboration. This in turn makes them ideal for promulgating one-dimensional stereotypes of gender, class, race, and beauty (Comstock & Scharrer, 2001).

MEDIA AND THE MASSES

Definitions

This chapter emphasizes two prominent forms of mass media: magazines and television. A *mass medium* is a deceptively complex form of communication generated by shifting networks of individuals (e.g., writers, photographers, computer specialists, actors) and financial organizations (e.g., communications conglomerates, production companies, advertising agencies; Harris, 1999). Mass media represent many motives: entertainment, marketing, education, socialization, and political influence. Conversely, people select and use media for many purposes, including entertainment, but also exploration of important issues pertaining to popularity, identity, gender roles, and sexuality (Arnett, 1995; Currie, 1999). As multinational and diversified industries, media are motivated to maximize profits by attracting and holding very large, anonymous audiences. Magazines are of particular interest because their marketing is carefully targeted to audiences such as adolescent girls.

The Phenomena to be Explained

The key outcomes of potential media influences are a spectrum of body image problems, unhealthy eating behaviors, and unhealthy forms of managing size, weight, and shape (Smolak & Levine, 1996). At the extremes are the prototypical syndromes of anorexia nervosa, bulimia nervosa, and binge eating disorder, as well as the muscle-focused form of body dysmorphic disorder. The spectrum encompasses negative psychosocial characteristics such as low self-esteem, obsessions, shame, self-loathing, and appearance-focused social anxiety.

Ideally, a theory of media influence would also explain four interrelated phenomena:

1. The pronounced gender difference.
2. The extraordinary prevalence of negative body image and unhealthy eating patterns among girls and women.
3. The explosion of disordered eating and obesity during the latter half of the twentieth century and the early part of twenty-first century.
4. Body image problems and steroid abuse among males (Pope et al., 2000; Silverstein & Perlick, 1995; Smolak & Murnen, 2001).

EVIDENCE FOR MASS MEDIA EFFECTS: SUSCEPTIBILITY STUDIES

Congenitally blind women have a more positive body image and healthier eating patterns than women who lost their sight later in life and women who are sighted (Baker, Sivyer, & Towell, 1998). This is but one of many striking pieces of convergent evidence that the ways in which people experience and express the image of their bodies—in the mirror or in their mind's eye—are strongly influenced by cultural ideals of what a person should look like to be attractive, healthy, and good (Thompson et al., 1999; Thompson & Stice, 2001). In this section, we consider "susceptibility" to media effects, a category of research pertaining to studies of people's orientation toward mass media, their internalization of media-based ideals, and their tendency to compare themselves to those standards.

Exposure and Susceptibility

Interviews of 40 randomly selected Australian adolescent boys ages 12 to 15 indicated that more than half perceived mass media and other more proximal influences, such as family, as having no effect or a positive effect on their body image, eating, or exercise behavior (Ricciardelli, McCabe, & Banfield, 2000). This and similar findings (e.g., Morrison et al., 2002) are in marked contrast to interview and survey studies of adolescent girls, who consistently describe mass media as being a very significant factor in promoting cultural ideals of slender beauty and the desire to be thinner (see, e.g., Field, Carmago, Taylor, Berkey, & Colditz, 1999; Milkie, 1999; Tiggemann, Gardiner, & Slater, 2000).

For example, Jones, Vigfusdottir, and Lee (in press) found that, compared to boys, middle school girls (ages 11 to 14) were significantly more engaged with appearance-related magazines, were more likely to internalize the beauty ideals in them, and had greater body dissatisfaction. A path analysis indicated that, for girls, exposure to appearance-related magazines and to appearance conversations each predicted body dissatisfaction through the mediator of internalization of the slender beauty ideal. The path analytic model for girls explained 48% of the variance, whereas the sociocultural model for boys explained only 21% of the total variance in body dissatisfaction. For boys, exposure to appearance-related magazines was not a significant exogenous variable, and even peer appearance criticism contributed directly to body dissatisfaction without mediation by internalization of a muscular ideal. Jones et al.'s findings are supported by other studies of boys and girls of varying ages (see, e.g., Polce-Lynch, Myers, Kliewer, & Kilmartin, 2001; Ricciardelli & McCabe, 2001).

Internalization of Appearance Ideals

The thin ideal of beauty is ubiquitous in mass media. Internalization of this standard is clearly a *causal* factor for negative body image and disordered eating in females (Thompson & Stice, 2001). Mass media are also one major mode for socializing young adolescent girls to believe that the source of beauty ideals and ideal beauty practices is located outside the self, that is, that boys and consumption of mass media are critical determinants (Peirce, 1990). These facts do not imply that mass media are independent of, or more important than, other social influences such as peer teasing (Smolak & Murnen, 2001).

The most valid measure of assimilation of the slender beauty ideal for females is the internalization subscale of the Sociocultural Attitudes Toward Appearance Questionnaire (SATAQ; Heinberg, Thompson, & Stormer, 1995). Of its eight items, seven pertain to media images and social comparison (e.g., "I wish I looked like a swimsuit model," and "I tend to compare my body to people in magazines and on TV"). Smolak, Levine, and Thompson (2001) administered the original SATAQ to young adolescent girls, while giving young adolescent boys a version focusing on muscularity as the cultural ideal. For girls, the expected factors of awareness and internalization were replicated and validated. The boys' data were best captured by three factors: internalization, awareness, and the perception that most males believe that the more muscular they are, the better they look. For boys, these three dimensions did not predict weight control techniques, although internalization of the muscular ideal was a modest predictor of use of muscle-building techniques (Smolak et al., 2001). Not surprisingly, given the research reviewed (e.g., Ricciardelli & McCabe, 2001), SATAQ total score and the awareness and internalization subscale scores were much stronger correlates of total body esteem and use of weight control techniques for girls than for boys (see also Cusumano & Thompson, 2001).

Keery, Shroff, Thompson, Wertheim, and Smolak (in press) recently developed the Sociocultural Internalization of Appearance Questionnaire-Adolescents. This scale was evaluated in over 200 adolescents (ages 11 to 15) in three countries (USA, Australia, and India). It was found to be highly reliable in all samples and scores on the scale correlated significantly with levels of body dissatisfaction and eating disturbance in all samples. Thompson, van den Berg, Roehrig, Guarda, and Heinberg (in press) also recently reported on the 3rd edition of the Sociocultural Attitudes Towards Appearance Questionnaire (SATAQ-3) in a large sample of college students and an eating disordered sample. Four subscales formed the revision: internalization (general), internalization (athlete), pressures, and information. Regressions indicated that internalization (composite score) and pressures explained variance associated with eating disturbance beyond that explained by information.

Social Comparison

Using very different methodologies, Gurung, Williamson, and Goetzinger (2002) and Milkie (1999) found that young White girls and women want to be thin for the sake of beauty and attractiveness and not because they associate positive characteristics with it. This is consistent with a recent finding by S. S. Posavac and Posavac (2002) that the relationship between self-media ideal discrepancy and unhealthy weight concerns is to a significant extent independent of global self-esteem, at least for college-age women. Milkie's in-depth interviews revealed that most girls ages 14 to 16, and especially Black girls, were aware of, and critical of, the unrealistic beauty ideals conveyed in glamour and fashion magazines. Nevertheless, most girls enjoyed reading those magazines, and the White girls typically used them for self-assessment, that is, for social comparison (Milkie, 1999). Three factors increased the probability most girls would, despite their critical knowledge, engage in unfavorable social comparisons with the unrealistic visual images of slender beauty:

1. The conviction that the pictures are indeed ideals adopted and endorsed by their peers.
2. The juxtaposition of toxic, "perfect" images with compelling text about real girls and their problems.
3. The girls' accurate perception that males' evaluation of them was influenced by media imagery.

Black girls and other minority respondents stated that they did not compare themselves to the images or aspire to be like them, because they were White ideals and because those ideals were too rigid and narrow.

Martin and Kennedy (1993, 1994) have shown that, for a majority of girls ages 8 through 18, reading fashion magazines does indeed activate a process of "social comparison" with the models in the advertisements and fashion layouts. This often results in feeling bad about their own appearance, a tendency that is greater for girls who consider themselves more physically unattractive. Studies of elementary school girls (Field et al., 1999; Taylor et al., 1998), middle school girls (Field et al., 1999; Levine, Smolak, & Hayden, 1994), and young women in college (see Thompson et al., 1999, for a review) confirm that females who read fashion magazines and compare themselves to the models report greater body dissatisfaction and higher levels of disordered eating. Apparently, this comparison tendency is more important than extent of media exposure, and the two variables do not interact (Jones, 2001; Morrison, Kalin, & Morrison, in press).

Martin and Gentry (1997) found that when girls ages 9 through 14 were explicitly instructed to compare their own physical attractiveness to that of models in ads, they immediately felt less attractive. However, the data from conditions emphasizing self-improvement and self-enhancement motives were less comprehensible. This research needs to be extended because it highlights the importance of motivation and information processing in the effects of the thin ideal but offers only mixed support for a simple theory of social comparison motives.

Universalistic social comparison is the tendency for individuals to use celebrities, actors, musicians, singers, and so on as a standard for evaluating their physical appearance (Heinberg & Thompson, 1992). Morrison et al. (in press) found that, although Canadian high school boys were less likely than girls to engage in such comparisons when evaluating their own attractiveness, the boys' universalistic comparisons with the muscular ideal were correlated with negative body image and with trying to gain bulk via eating and steroid use. Similarly, girls' universalistic comparison tendency predicted negative body image, but it also was correlated with dieting to lose weight and with pathogenic weight control.

Jones (2001) examined social comparisons that 7th grade (M age = ~12.5) and 10th grade (M age = ~15.5) girls and boys in the United States make to peers and to models and celebrities. Jones also found that girls were more likely than boys to make social comparisons concerning style, shape/build, and facial attractiveness. With respect to shape (for girls) and build (for boys), both genders were equally likely to use models and peers as the standard for social comparison. With respect to weight, though, boys also preferred same-sex peers as the standard, whereas girls were equally likely to choose models and same-sex peers for comparative self-evaluations related to weight. Consistent with the findings of Morrison et al. (in press), the tendency to make social comparisons to models/celebrities and to same-sex peers on the dimensions of height and weight were positively correlated to body dissatisfaction for boys and girls, but the relationships were stronger for girls. However, in contrast to Morrison et al.'s results, Jones found that social comparisons by boys to either class of target on the dimension of build was not a significant predictor of body dissatisfaction. The process by which girls and boys determine the need for social comparison, select targets, make comparisons, and evaluate the available information is a critically important area for further research on media effects.

EVIDENCE FOR MASS MEDIA EFFECTS: EXPERIMENTAL MANIPULATIONS OF THE SLENDER BEAUTY IDEAL

The Contrast Effect

A meta-analysis by Groesz et al. (2002) of 43 effect sizes from 25 studies (e.g., Stice & Shaw, 1994) indicated that, relative to comparison pictures of larger models or inanimate objects, controlled exposure to a series of images of slender models causes a modest ($d = .31$) immediate increase in a girl's or woman's negative feelings about her body. This contrast effect is slightly larger ($d = .50$) for females who have already internalized the slender standard of beauty and/or who come to the laboratory already feeling self-conscious or bad about their bodies.

One contributor to this effect is the tendency of young women with negative body image to perceive slender models or celebrities (or at least their representations in the media) as being more slender than they actually are (King, Touyz, & Charles, 2000). Another potentially very important factor is the interplay between slenderness and cues for objectification of the female body (Harrison & Fredrickson, in press; Smolak & Murnen, 2001). Lavine, Sweeney, and Wagner (1999) found no difference in effects on actual and ideal body image between presentation of no ads and presentation of the attractive women in nonsexist contexts. The key variable in affecting the immediate body dissatisfaction of males and females was the sexist (objectified, eroticized) versus nonsexist nature of the ads.

Processes

Jansen and de Vries (2002) found that repeated *subliminal* presentation of images of the slender beauty ideal did not affect young college women, regardless of whether participants were high or low in dietary restraint. This research needs to be replicated using more sophisticated tests of implicit attitudes, but it supports Baker et al.'s (1998) suggestion that conscious processing of visual stimulation is necessary for the contrast effect.

Wilcox and Laird (2000) reasoned that young women who focus on the slender models in magazines and defocus attention on themselves are more likely to enjoy the pictures through a process of identification. Conversely, women who focus on the models *and* themselves will be more likely to activate upward social comparison processes that generate negative affect, including negative feelings about their bodies. Two studies provide indirect evidence for this proposition. Wilcox and Laird found that young college women who had a tendency to be influenced by personal (versus situational) cues reported a drop in weight satisfaction and self-esteem following exposure to images of slender beauty (but not images of clothing). Conversely, as predicted, women who reviewed the same slides of slender models but who were more responsive to situations tended to have *greater* weight satisfaction and state self-esteem than those women who saw slides of normal-weight, full-figured women. Along the same lines, E. Henderson-King and Henderson-King (1997) found that women who were low "self-monitors" felt bad about their bodies after exposure to similar images of slender beauty. Low self-monitors are less responsive to the demands of situations and tend to be described by friends as introspective and anxious.

Hargreaves and Tiggemann (2002) postulated that girls ages 15 through 18 would be more negatively affected by the thin-beauty ideal in television commercials if these images activate a set of beliefs and assumptions (i.e., a self-schema) emphasizing the core importance of appearance. Appearance-focused commercials did indeed produce more overall appearance dissatisfaction, especially for girls who had a self-schema emphasizing appearance (see Groesz et al., 2002, as well as D. Henderson-King, Henderson-King, & Hoffman, 2001). This was the case regardless of whether the girls' viewing style was more personal or more detached. Moreover, regardless of initial level of body dissatisfaction, the appearance-related commercials produced greater activation of appearance-related schema, as documented by several measures of cognitive set. Regression analyses demonstrated that, consistent with a cognitive perspective, schema activation was a mediator of part of the effect on appearance satisfaction. In a related study, Lavin and Cash (2001) found that young female college students with a clear self-schema for appearance experienced more body dissatisfaction following exposure to verbal information about appearance-based social stereotyping.

Harrison (2001) demonstrated that different versions of the thin ideal activate different types of self-schema. Adolescents with discrepancies between their perceived actual and ideal bodies felt especially dejected after exposure to a media portrayal of a thin girl being socially rewarded. In contrast, adolescents with discrepancies between their perceived actual bodies and the type of bodies their parents think they ought to have felt especially anxious after exposure to a portrayal of a fat girl being socially punished. Harrison argued that activation of self-discrepancies mediates the relationship between ideal-body messages and the negative emotional reactions—agitation and dejection—seen in anorexia nervosa and bulimia nervosa, respectively.

Situational and Personal Moderators

Although age is not clearly a moderator (Groesz et al., 2002), there is preliminary evidence that very young girls are also susceptible to the contrast effect. Gibbons (1999) randomly assigned prepubertal girls ages 9 through 12 to view either slides of adult models in advertisements (complete with text) from fashion magazines such as *Vogue* and *Glamour,* slides of young girls modeling in the magazines such as *Girl's Life* and *American Girl,* or slides of neutral scenes such as houses or docked boats. Girls exposed to fashionable peers, but not adult models, reported feeling heavier, less happy, less attractive, and less intelligent.

D. Henderson-King et al. (2001) affirmed Harrison's (2001) contention that responses to images of idealized slender beauty are moderated by contextual and individual factors. Young female undergraduates were randomly assigned to view either 40 slides of neutral images or 10 such slides interspersed with 30 slides of idealized slender beauty. A third of the women in each condition saw the slides in the presence of two silent males, while another third viewed the slides in the presence of two males who made brief positive comments about three slides in the series. The contrast effect occurred only in the presence of silent males. When the males commented, the overall effect of exposure to the images was slightly more positive than the effect of neutral images. This counterintuitive finding was replicated in a second study by D. Henderson-King et al. Apparently, conscious processing of appearance-related information helped women to activate a critical stance toward sociocultural messages, rather than priming self-ideal discrepancies, which produce the contrast effect.

In a study of Australian adolescent girls ages 12 to 13 (grade 7) or 15 to 16 (grade 10), Durkin and Paxton (2002) found that, as predicted, the slides of attractive models reduced the girls' current experience of body dissatisfaction. However, 32% of the 7th grade girls and 22% of the 10th grade girls in the model-exposure condition showed an assimilation effect, that is, an increase in state body dissatisfaction (see also Wilcox & Laird, 2000). For the younger girls, the contrast effect (versus the assimilation effect) was predicted by the more concrete measures of actual body mass and a dispositional tendency to feel fat. For the older girls, the predictors of contrast were that same disposition, as well as the more psychological variables of thin-ideal internalization and a tendency to compare their body with others. These results replicate Gralen, Levine, Smolak, and Murnen's (1990) correlational analysis of the predictors of negative body image and disordered eating in middle school and high school girls. In developmental terms, a stable concern with "thin and fat," a growing psychological sophistication, and increased size relative to the slender ideal may combine to render the psychological impact of the thin-beauty ideal and the self-ideal disparity greater for vulnerable girls in middle to late adolescence than for younger adolescent girls (Durkin & Paxton, 2002; Smolak & Levine, 1996).

Males and the Muscular Ideal

Several studies (e.g., Ogden & Mundray, 1996) have shown a contrast effect for males similar to that for females as to feeling fat and feeling dissatisfied with their bodies. Lavine et al. (1999) found that exposure to attractive female and male models in sexist television advertisements caused women to feel heavier and men to feel thinner (and possibly more "lightweight" and puny). As Lavine et al. note, perhaps the self-ideal body image discrepancy for males was activated through an association with the salient female ideal, or the fit, muscular models in the television advertisements may have constituted the activating force. Hargreaves and Tiggemann (2002) found that television commercials emphasizing appearance-related products (e.g., clothes, food) and the female slender beauty ideal tended to activate an appearance schema for adolescent boys but had no effect on their mood or body dissatisfaction. On the other hand, three studies have shown that presentation of the muscular ideal does have an immediate negative impact on body-build satisfaction in young men (Grogan et al., 1996; Gurung, Suchomel, Stowe, Otto, & Goetzinger, 2002; Leit et al., 2002).

EVIDENCE FOR MASS MEDIA EFFECTS: SURVEY RESEARCH LINKING MEDIA EXPOSURE TO BODY COGNITIONS AND DISORDERED EATING

Eating disorders are cognitive-behavioral patterns that develop and are expressed over time. Thus, it is neither possible nor ethical to "induce" an eating disorder in the controlled setting of the laboratory. Consequently, researchers interested in media effects have turned to surveys. For example, surveys conducted in the United States and Australia show that the more adolescent girls and boys feel pressured by the media to be thin, the more likely they are to engage in dieting behaviors (McCabe, Ricciardelli, & Finemore, 2002; Wertheim, Paxton, Schutz, & Muir, 1997; see also Stice, 2001, for a review).

Surveys of children and adolescents also generally show a positive correlation between *habitual exposure* to extremely thin bodies and wanting a thinner body for themselves. Levine et al. (1994) found that the more a group of White female adolescents reported reading thin ideal magazines, the greater their drive for thinness and level of disturbed eating. Harrison (2000a) studied a sample of both female and male adolescents, the majority of whom were also White, and found disordered eating behaviors and cognitions to be correlated with exposure to television programming with fat main characters and with reading of thin-ideal magazines. Once again, the relationships were stronger for females than for males. Botta's (2000) survey of White and African American adolescent girls found that self-reported television viewing predicted increased bulimic symptomatology, but only in White adolescents. Pathogenic dieting methods (e.g., limiting calories to less than 1,200 a day) have also been correlated with beauty and fashion magazine reading among adolescent girls (Thomsen, Weber, & Brown, 2002). This relationship between media exposure and disturbed eating has been shown to emerge even before adolescence. Harrison (2000b) measured overall television viewing, along with disturbed eating and body ideals, in a sample of first-, second-, and third-grade girls and boys. Overall, television viewing was positively correlated with disturbed eating in both girls and boys.

The findings from studies of young women (usually undergraduates) are similar to those done with adolescents and children. Harrison and Cantor (1997) correlated thin-ideal magazine and television exposure to thinness-favoring attitudes and behaviors. Exposure to thin-ideal media, especially magazines, predicted disordered eating among females, as well as thinness-favoring attitudes among males. These relationships remained significant even when selective exposure to thin-ideal media, based on interest in fitness and dieting as media topics, was controlled. In a pioneering study linking media exposure to disordered eating in young women, Stice, Schupak-Neuberg, Shaw, and Stein (1994) demonstrated that thin-ideal media exposure predicted increased disordered eating both directly and through various mediators, including gender-role endorsement and thin-ideal internalization. College students are not the only vulnerable group of young women. When queried about their perceptions of the influence of the media's thin ideal, young female eating disorder patients (who presumably have already internalized the thin ideal) reported feeling more media-influenced than a nondisordered comparison group (Murray, Touyz, & Beumont, 1996).

Along with internalization of the thin ideal (Stice et al., 1994; Thompson & Stice, 2001), self-discrepancies and favorable attitudes toward thin media personalities are important mediators and, over time, moderators. Harrison's (2001) survey of adolescent males and females showed that discrepancies between a person's actual body and his or her ideal body appear to mediate the relationship between thin-ideal television exposure and eating disorder symptomatology, body dissatisfaction, and drive for thinness. This suggests that adolescents with self-discrepancies may be more vulnerable to the effects of thin-ideal media. Moreover, in a survey of female undergraduates, Harrison (1997) reported that interpersonal attraction to thin, but not average-weight or heavy, female media personalities predicted disordered eating cognitions and behaviors. Thus, survey research supports the contention of experimental studies (Groesz et al., 2002) and qualitative studies (Milkie, 1999) that comparison of the self with ultra-thin media personalities is an important element of the relationship between thin-ideal media exposure and discontent with the body.

In summary, it appears the relationship between thin-ideal media exposure and disordered eating is positive, though moderate in size, for both children and young adults. Although Harrison (2000b) reported no sex differences in her sample of first- through third-grade children, studies of older samples generally show that the relationship is slightly stronger for females than males. Further, body image and eating behavior in White girls and women, as compared to people of color, are more vulnerable to the effects of thin-ideal messages in mainstream media (Milkie, 1999). Jane, Hunter, and Lozzi (1999) assessed media exposure and eating attitudes and behaviors in a sample of Cuban American female undergraduates. As was the case in Botta's (2000) survey of African Americans, there was no significant relationship between disordered eating and amount of exposure to the thin-ideal in television and magazines.

Body-Relevant Attitudes and Self-Perceptions

Survey methods have also been used to correlate media exposure with body-relevant attitudes and perceptions. McCreary and Sadava's (1999) study of young men and women revealed a positive correlation between television viewing and participants' belief that they were overweight, independent of their actual weight. Harrison (2003) linked college women's exposure to the ideal body on television with their desire for a smaller waist and hips, but not a smaller bust, and with acceptance of body-change methods such as breast surgery and liposuction. Tiggemann and Pickering (1996) found that viewing soap operas and movies predicted greater body dissatisfaction, whereas sports viewing predicted increased body satisfaction. Borzekowski, Robinson, and Killen (2000) studied ethnically diverse adolescent girls' exposure to various visual media, including television, computer games, and music videos. They found that viewing music videos positively predicted perceived importance of appearance and weight concerns.

Thus, it remains unclear which genres are most influential.

General Social Attitudes about Thinness and Fatness

The survey by Harrison (2000b) showed that the more television elementary school boys reported watching, the more likely they were to negatively stereotype a fat girl (but not a fat boy) as lazy, greedy, mean, and unpopular. For girls, television viewing was unrelated to stereotyping either a fat girl or a fat boy. Internalization of the thin ideal may be conceptualized as another general attitude about thinness and fatness; it represents, in the mind's eye, the "ideal body" as necessarily thin (Thompson et al., 1999). Botta (1999) surveyed adolescent girls about their overall television viewing and their particular viewing of dramatic programs that featured extremely thin characters. Botta found that the tendency to compare the self to thin media personalities (a tendency she calls "body image processing") is important in predicting internalization of the thin ideal from television.

Implications

The survey method has yielded a rich set of data about the relationship between media exposure and beliefs, feelings, and behaviors involved in disordered eating. In summary:

- Small to moderate positive relationships exist
- Where there are sex differences, correlations tend to be larger for females, although among children the relationship appears to be of equal magnitude and direction for girls and boys.
- In the few instances where racial differences have been examined, relationships tend to be larger for Whites.
- The media-disorder relationship remains robust even when selective exposure to thin-ideal media is controlled.

Even for those research participants who profess no interest in fitness and dieting as media topics, exposure is still linked to disordered eating and cognitive aspects of the thinness schema.

Survey-based studies have left many questions unanswered. First, because correlation does not demonstrate causation, we must still address the critical question: Does exposure to ideal-body media cause eating disorders, or do people with eating disorders seek out ideal-body media? Research by Stice (1998, 2001) illustrates this point. In one study, both internalization of the slender beauty ideal and perceived pressure to be thin (emanating from family, friends, dating partners, and media) predicted significant, short-term increases in body dissatisfaction in girls ages 14 to 17. These factors were also concurrently associated with body dissatisfaction, which in turn predicted increases in dieting and negative affect. But another study revealed a different pattern concerning disordered eating. Perceived pressure from media to have a thin body and to lose weight was correlated simultaneously with bulimic symptoms in college students, whereas self-reported exposure to media modeling of unhealthy behaviors was not. However, neither media pressure (social reinforcement) nor media modeling prospectively predicted development of bulimic symptomatology in high school seniors. There is a pressing need for longitudinal research and for prevention studies bearing on the effects of reducing or mitigating media-related risk factors (Stice, 2001). Analyses showing that early media exposure predicts later disordered eating, independent of the extent to which early eating problems predict later media exposure, will help demonstrate the causal impact that has, until now, been only an assumption underlying this line of research.

A second question is exactly what kinds of media seem to be most responsible for the problem. While some researchers (e.g., Stice et al., 1994) have shown that overall television viewing predicted disordered eating symptomatology, others (e.g., Harrison, 2000a) have found this relationship to be significant only for thin-ideal television. This matter is complicated by wide variation across studies in the scales and procedures used to measure habitual media exposure. Whereas many researchers use standard eating disorder measures (the Eating Attitudes Test, for instance), they are continually "reinventing the wheel" when it comes to media measures. Standardization of media measures will be challenging but well worth the effort.

A related question pertains to race and sex differences. Most investigators assess media exposure broadly, focusing on mainstream genres or the most popular television programs and magazines. This means that the current conclusion that people of color and men are somehow less vulnerable to the effects of ideal-body media might be erroneous, however, because minority females and males might well be influenced by media and genres that are not being assessed via a focus solely on the mainstream programs emphasizing mainstream ideals of attractiveness.

Another question that remains unanswered is the degree to which thin-ideal internalization is a necessary part of the media-disorder relationship. As demonstrated previously, there is substantial evidence that perceived media pressure to be thin is correlated with increased weight and body dissatisfaction in girls and boys ages 8 through 18 (Cusumano & Thompson, 2001; Van den Bulck, 2000). There is also substantial evidence that this experience of pressure involves exposure to and internalization of the slender ideal, which then becomes a mediator for subsequent reinforcement of the negative effects (Cusumano & Thompson, 1997; Stice et al., 1994; Thompson & Stice, 2001). Yet, the structural equation modeling by Stice et al. (1994) reveals a direct path from media exposure to disordered eating. In addition, Harrison's (2000b) survey of elementary school children suggests that thin-ideal internalization may not be important until adolescence. In this study, television viewing positively predicted disordered eating but was unrelated to the desire for a thin body. Harrison argued that the link might derive from the fact that dieting messages are ubiquitous on television, particularly in advertising; therefore, dieting to lose weight may be perceived by heavy-viewing children as something healthy and normal, even glamorous. In this way, dieting may be a way of "playing dress-up" rather than a way of meeting an already-internalized personal ideal (see also Smolak & Levine, 1996). Studies are needed to determine at what age children begin to internalize this media-conveyed thin ideal and engage in dieting behaviors to meet this ideal. Similarly, more research is needed on the interaction between media exposure and other influences such as parents, peers, and romantic partners in producing body image problems or disordered eating (Levine et al., 1994; Milkie, 1999; Ricciardelli et al., 2000).

PREVENTION: ACTIVISM AND LITERACY

Media Activism

The prospect of changing the mass media or inoculating individuals against the onslaught of multinational, multibillion-dollar corporations strikes most people as Quixotic. Thinking about mass media and their negative effects typically evokes the question: "What can any of us really *do,* really . . . ?"

In late September 1988, Vivian Meehan, cofounder of the National Association of Anorexia Nervosa and Associated Disorders (www.anad.org), led a successful petition and letter-writing campaign to remove a Hershey Foods Corporation's advertising campaign (for a thin chocolate bar) proclaiming that "You can never be too rich or too thin."

It is inspiring and personally transformative to learn that an ostensibly monolithic "sociocultural factor" such as mass media can be influenced to a small degree (for now) by organized citizen action (Irving, 1999; Wallack, Dorfman, Jernigan, & Themba, 1993). The nonprofit organization, Dads and Daughters, Inc., guided by media-savvy director Joe Kelly, has harnessed the Internet to mount many effective protests through its "Take Action" campaign (www.Dadsanddaughters.org/action/takeaction.htm).

Media Literacy

Another approach to mitigating negative effects focuses on working with the people who use and are affected by mass media. *Media literacy* is a general term for "the process of critically analyzing and learning to create one's own messages in print, audio, video, and multimedia" (Hobbs, 1998, p. 16). These skills are seen as crucial for full citizen participation in a democracy suffused with mass media. Media educators see students as active learners with the capacity to enrich their typically complex understanding and use of mass media and culture; students are not seen as totally naive, gullible, and passive victims of an insidious, monolithic media. Thus, the goal of media literacy is neither media cynicism, nor blanket condemnation of other people's pleasures such as reading fashion magazines, watching auto racing on television, or listening to popular music.

Outcomes of Brief Media Literacy Programs

Wolf-Bloom (1998) arranged a 2.25-hour media literacy workshop for Girl Scouts. Senior Scouts served as peer educators. The program began with a portion of "Slim Hopes" (Kilbourne, 1995) plus an episode of Joan Lunden's "Behind Closed Doors" (original airing, January 27, 1997), featuring a fashion shoot for *Cosmopolitan* and a computer refashioning (to correct "her many flaws") of supermodel Cindy Crawford's image for another layout (Levine et al., 1999). Then the girls practiced critical analyses of media popular with adolescent girls. Finally, the girls discussed the implications of the predictable discrepancy between real girls' bodies and the "perfect" images in the media. Compared to controls, program participants had better body image at follow-up and reduced social comparison to media images. There were no effects for disordered eating or internalization of the slender beauty ideal.

Wolf-Bloom's work, although more than a "one-shot" presentation, is typical of brief programs. It dissects deceptive media techniques (e.g., airbrushing, computer graphics) used to construct the idealized images, and it teaches participants to critically evaluate and resist unhealthy appearance-related messages. Several programs structure their media literacy around the questions posed by Erica Austin's (1993) Message Interpretation Process (MIP) model: Do *real* women look like the models in advertising? Will buying the product being advertised make me look like this model? Does this model look like this because of this product? [and] Does thinness really guarantee happiness and success?

Research with elementary school girls (Kusel, 1999), high school girls (Irving, DuPen, & Berel, 1998), and college women and men (H. D. Posavac, Posavac, & Weigel, 2001; Thompson et al., 1999) also shows that even brief media literacy projects can have positive effects on media skepticism and body image, although the specific outcomes are usually time-limited and somewhat inconsistent across studies (see also Thompson &

Heinberg, 1999). Brief media literacy interventions can affect logical processes involved in the perceived realism of the images and in the perceived similarity between the audience and the models of beauty. But, not surprisingly, one-shot programs are inadequate to affect long-standing attitudes (see also Irving & Berel, 2001).

Stormer and Thompson's program for college students (described in Thompson et al., 1999) included information about media ideals of male attractiveness. The students learned about the very unhealthy ways in which some men try to attain the lean, muscular ideal, for example, fanatical workouts at the gym, steroid use, and obsessive attention to diet. At posttest, there were several positive results for men as well as women; but at three-week follow-up, attrition was high, and only the women sustained a reduction in internalization of the slender beauty ideal (S. Stormer, personal communications, August 13 & 16, 1999).

Outcomes of More Intensive Media Literacy Programs

Neumark-Sztainer, Sherwood, Coller, and Hannan (2000) randomly assigned half of 24 Girl Scout troops (mean age = 10.6) to a control condition, while the remainder received the media literacy program "Free to Be Me." The themes of the six 90-minute lessons were similar to Austin's MIP model. However, "Free to Be Me" also applies social cognitive theory's concept of reciprocal determinism (Neumark-Sztainer, 1996). Thus, the researchers and Scout leaders encouraged the girls to be activists in helping peers and in changing mass media to establish healthier norms. The girls critically evaluated advertisements and then wrote letters to businesses to advocate for healthier images. These letters were posted on the Web site of the National Eating Disorders Association (NEDA; www.nationaleatingdisorders.org) to promote activism and advocacy by other girls.

"Free to Be Me" had several positive effects that were sustained at three-month follow-up (Neumark-Sztainer et al., 2000). Participants were less likely to read *Seventeen* magazine, which promotes the slender beauty ideal and feminine identity based primarily on appearance and fashion (Peirce, 1990). In addition, thin-ideal internalization was reduced, and the girls' belief in their ability to be activists and thus affect weight-related social norms was increased. However, there was no effect on dieting, and there were no sustained effects for the modest pre- to posttest improvements in body-related knowledge and body size acceptance.

Neumark-Sztainer et al.'s work suggests that more intensive media literacy programs offer a great deal of promise as one component of an ecological approach to prevention. This conclusion is supported by outcome evaluations of five separate programs that either emphasized media literacy or incorporated it as a major component of a multifaceted prevention program:

1. NEDA's *GO GIRLS!*™ for high school students (Levine et al., 1999; Piran, Levine, & Irving, 2000).

2. An adaptation of *GO GIRLS!*™ for Australian middle school students (Wade, Davidson, & O'Dea, 2003).

3. The *Full of Ourselves* program designed by the Harvard Eating Disorders Center (Steiner-Adair et al., 2002).

4. The *Body Traps* cultural literacy class at Stanford University (Springer, Winzelberg, Perkins, & Taylor, 1999).

5. A 6.33-hour "media analysis program" developed for women and men at Northern Illinois University (Rabak-Wagener, Eickhoff-Shemek, & Kelly-Vance, 1998).

MEDIA LITERACY AND PREVENTION OF STEROID USE IN MALE HIGH SCHOOL ATHLETES

Sociocultural processes underlying internalization of the muscular ideal and consequent use and abuse of anabolic steroids (AS) are salient in the lives of young male athletes, particularly football players. Goldberg et al. (2000) developed the *Adolescents Training and Learning to Avoid Steroids* (ATLAS) program for male high school athletes (see also MacKinnon et al., 2001; www.atlas.program.com). This intervention is an excellent example of how media literacy could be part of high quality, programmatic research with clear implications for prevention of negative body image and disordered eating in males.

Based on social cognitive theory, as well as several prominent theories about health promotion, ATLAS combines classroom sessions about strength and nutrition with experiences that develop behavioral competence (e.g., strength training). In keeping with the principle of reciprocal determinism, ATLAS also harnesses the influence of peers and influential adults, ranging from coaches to parents to school cafeteria staff. In the media literacy training, peer educators help the athletes to locate and analyze advertisements and articles about AS and supplements, as well as ads for products that "treat" the unspecified adverse effects of the very steroids and steroid-like products advertised in the same muscle-building magazines. In addition, the boys worked together to create, through various types of simulated media (e.g., video, posters, theatrical performances), messages that promoted strength and fitness in healthier ways.

Outcome evaluations strongly suggest that, at one-year follow-up, the ATLAS program has a sustained preventive effect on knowledge, attitudes, and behaviors. Compared to the control participants, over time, ATLAS participants reported less initiation of use of anabolic steroids, "athletic" supplements and other performance-enhancing drugs, and alcohol and other drugs (Goldberg et al., 2000; L. Goldberg, personal communication, August 14, 2002). Regression analyses demonstrated that skepticism about media advertisements was one path through which the program influenced reduced intentions to use AS, as well as increased self-efficacy in strength training (MacKinnon et al., 2001).

PREVENTION: HEALTH CAMPAIGNS, SOCIAL MARKETING, AND MEDIA ADVOCACY

Campaigns using mass media to bring about important social changes have been an integral part of efforts to reform slavery, lack of women's suffrage, child labor, and epidemic cigarette smoking (Rice & Atkin, 2001). Media campaigns are very relevant for addressing eating problems and eating disorders as public health issues, because such campaigns can—at least to a modest degree—educate, advise, advocate, transform, and reinforce change (Derzon & Lipsey, 2002). As this chapter emphasizes, although the continua of negative body image and disordered eating are painful and debilitating in intensely personal ways, these problems are deeply embedded in multiple strands of our fundamental social and cultural fabric. And, so are mass media. If you wanted to change how our society felt about body image, would you rather have access to the curriculum of every ninth-grade health class in the United States or three episodes of the television program *Friends*?

Media advocacy is the strategic use of mass media and other resources of citizens in a democracy to change individual behavior and public policy (Wallack et al., 1993). A related concept is *social marketing,* defined as "use of marketing principles and techniques to influence a target audience to voluntarily accept, reject, modify, or abandon a *behavior* for the benefit of individuals, groups, or society as a whole" (Kotler, Roberto, & Lee, 2002, p. 5; italics added). Could the tools of media advocacy and social marketing be brought to bear on socially desirable changes in attitudes and behaviors toward, for example, body image and eating?

The National Eating Disorders Association worked with the advertising firm Olgivy and Mather to develop the "Listen to Your Body" campaign (Hoff, 2002; click on the *Listen to Your Body* print campaign link at http://www.nationaleatingdisorders.org for more information, including the ads themselves). The target audience for this antidieting campaign is girls ages 12 through 17, so one ad features actor Jamie Lynn Sigler of the television program *The Sopranos* and two others feature Melissa Joan Hart of *Sabrina the Teenage Witch*. As of August 2002, one or both of these ads were placed on NEDA's Eating Disorders Awareness Week 2001 posters and in a large number of magazines, including *Cosmopolitan, Fitness, Nickelodeon, People, Scholastic Science World,* and *YM*. The penetration and effect of these ads are as yet undetermined, but it seems likely they are partly responsible for the upsurge in visits to the NEDA web site and calls to their 800 hotline. In 2002, the number of "hits" on the web site topped 30 million, while the number of calls approached 25,000.

CONCLUSIONS, CHALLENGES, AND FUTURE DIRECTIONS

There is no doubt that mass media are important sources of what we think about, how we evaluate what we think about, what we overlook and ignore, and how we interact with important people in our lives (Harris, 1999; Singer & Singer, 2001). There is also no doubt that media portrayals of attractiveness, gender, and technologies of health both reflect and contribute to body dissatisfaction, unhealthy eating and weight management, and disordered eating in females and males who are vulnerable to these influences. We are gratified to see that many first-rate researchers around the world are turning their attention to the developmental interactions and transactions among mass media, other sociocultural factors, and personal factors that increase vulnerability or resistance. We are now just beginning to understand what normative and abnormal processes lead a person to:

- Seek to evaluate and improve the self in terms of appearance ideals.
- Assimilate that ideal and compare self to it.
- Be highly motivated by the ensuing dissatisfaction to take potentially unhealthy steps, directed in part by mass media, toward weight/shape preoccupation, restrictive dieting, and disordered eating.

REFERENCES

Arnett, J. J. (1995). Adolescents' use of media for self socialization. *Journal of Youth and Adolescence, 24*(5), 519–533.

Austin, E. W. (1993). Exploring the effects of active parental mediation of television content. *Journal of Broadcasting and Electronic Media, 37*, 147–158.

Baker, D., Sivyer, R., & Towell, T. (1998). Body image dissatisfaction and eating attitudes in visually impaired women. *International Journal of Eating Disorders, 27*, 319–322.

Bordo, S. (1993). *Unbearable weight: Feminism, Western culture, and the body.* Berkeley: University of California Press.

Borzekowski, D. L. G., Robinson, T. N., & Killen, J. D. (2000). Does the camera add 10 pounds? Media use, perceived importance of appearance, and weight concerns among teenage girls. *Journal of Adolescent Health, 26*, 36–41.

Botta, R. A. (1999). Television images and adolescent girls' body image disturbance. *Journal of Communication, 49*, 22–41.

Botta, R. A. (2000). The mirror of television: A comparison of Black and White adolescents' body image. *Journal of Communication, 50*, 144–159.

Comstock, G., & Scharrer, E. (2001). The use of television and other film-related media. In D. G. Singer & J. L. Singer (Eds.), *Handbook of children and the media* (pp. 47–72). Thousand Oaks, CA: Sage.

Currie, D. H. (1999). *Girl talk: Adolescent magazines and their readers.* Toronto, Ontario, Canada: University of Toronto Press.

Cusumano, D. L., & Thompson, J. K. (1997). Body image and body shape ideals in magazines: Exposure, awareness, and internalization. *Sex Roles, 37*(9/10), 701–721.

Cusumano, D. L., & Thompson, J. K. (2001). Media influence and body image in 8–11-year-old boys and girls: A preliminary report on the Multidimensional Media Influence Scale. *International Journal of Eating Disorders, 29*, 37–44.

Derzon, J. H., & Lipsey, M. W. (2002). A meta-analysis of the effectiveness of mass-communication for changing substance-use knowledge, attitudes, and behavior. In W. B. Crano & M. Burgoon (Eds.), *Mass media and drug prevention: Classic and contemporary theories and research* (pp. 231–258). Mahwah, NJ: Erlbaum.

Durkin, S. J., & Paxton, S. J. (2002). Predictors of vulnerability to reduced body image satisfaction and psychological well-being in response to exposure to idealized female media images in adolescent girls. *Journal of Psychosomatic Research, 53*, 995–1005.

Field, A. E., Carmago, Jr., C. A., Taylor, C. B., Berkey, C. S., & Colditz, G. A. (1999). Relation of peer and media influences to the development of purging behaviors among preadolescent and adolescent girls. *Archives of Pediatric Adolescent Medicine, 153*, 1184–1189.

Gibbons, J. A. (1999, December). *The effects of exposure to magazine photographs on aspects of body image in prepubescent females.* Unpublished doctoral dissertation, Arizona State University, Tempe.

Goldberg, L., MacKinnon, D., Elliott, D. L., Moe, E. L., Clarke, G., & Cheong, J. (2000). The Adolescents Training and Learning to Avoid Steroids (ATLAS) Program: Preventing drug use and promoting health behaviors. *Archives of Pediatric and Adolescent Medicine, 154*, 332–338.

Gralen, S. J., Levine, M. P., Smolak, L., & Murnen, S. K. (1990). Dieting and disordered eating during early and middle adolescence: Do the influences remain the same? *International Journal of Eating Disorders, 9,* 501–512.

Groesz, L. M., Levine, M. P., & Murnen, S. K. (2002). The effect of experimental presentation of thin media images on body dissatisfaction: A meta-analytic review. *International Journal of Eating Disorders, 31,* 1–16.

Grogan, S., Williams, Z., & Conner, M. (1996). The effects of viewing same-gender photographic models on body-esteem. *Psychology of Women Quarterly, 20,* 569–575.

Gurung, R. A. R., Suchomel, N. N., Stowe, A., Otto, J., & Goetzinger, L. (2002, August). *Physique anxiety, social perception, and mood: A focus on men.* Poster presented at the annual conference of the American Psychological Association, Chicago.

Gurung, R. A. R., Williamson, L. A., & Goetzinger, L. (2002). *The thin, the fit, and the realistic: Effects on social comparisons, body esteem, and mood.* Unpublished manuscript, University of Wisconsin-Green Bay.

Hargreaves, D., & Tiggemann, M. (2002). The effect of television commercials on mood and body dissatisfaction: The role of appearance-schema activation. *Journal of Social and Clinical Psychology, 21,* 287–308.

Harris, R. J. (1999). *A cognitive psychology of mass communication* (3rd ed.). Hillsdale, NJ: Erlbaum.

Harrison, K. (1997). Does interpersonal attraction to thin media personalities promote eating disorders? *Journal of Broadcasting and Electronic Media, 41,* 478–500.

Harrison, K. (2000a). The body electric: Thin-ideal media and eating disorders in adolescents. *Journal of Communication, 50,* 119–143.

Harrison, K. (2000b). Television viewing, fat stereotyping, body shape standards, and eating disorder symptomatology in grade school children. *Communication Research, 27,* 617–640.

Harrison, K. (2001). Ourselves, our bodies: Thin-ideal media, self-discrepancies, and eating disorder symptomatology in adolescents. *Journal of Social and Clinical Psychology, 20,* 289–323.

Harrison, K. (2003). Television viewers' ideal body proportions: The case of the curvaceously thin woman. *Sex Roles, 48,* 255–264.

Harrison, K., & Cantor, J. (1997). The relationship between media consumption and eating disorders. *Journal of Communication, 47,* 40–66.

Harrison, K., & Fredrickson, B. L. (in press). Women's sports media, self-objectification, and mental health in Black and White adolescent females. *Journal of Communication.*

Heinberg, L. J., & Thompson, J. K. (1992). The effects of figure size feedback (positive vs. negative) and target comparison group (particularistic vs. universal) on body image disturbance. *International Journal of Eating Disorders, 12,* 441–448.

Heinberg, L. J., Thompson, J. K., & Stormer, S. (1995). Development and validation of the Sociocultural Attitudes toward Appearance Questionnaire. *International Journal of Eating Disorders, 17,* 81–89.

Henderson-King, D., Henderson-King, E., & Hoffman, L. (2001). Media images and women's self-evaluations: Social context and importance of attractiveness and moderators. *Personality and Social Psychology Bulletin, 27,* 1407–1416.

Henderson-King, E., & Henderson-King, D. (1997). Media effects on women's body esteem: Social and individual difference factors. *Journal of Applied Social Psychology, 27,* 399–417.

Hobbs, R. (1998, Winter). The seven great debates in the media literacy movement. *Journal of Communication,* 16–32.

Hoff, H. (2002). *Listen to Your Body* Campaign. Unpublished document, National Eating Disorders Association. (Available from Holly Hoff, Director of Program, NEDA)

Irving, L. M. (1999). A Bolder Model of Prevention: Science, practice, and activism. In N. Piran, M. P. Levine, & C. Steiner-Adair (Eds.), *Preventing eating disorders: A handbook of interventions and special challenges* (pp. 63–83). Philadelphia: Brunner/Mazel.

Irving, L. M., & Berel, S. R. (2001). Comparison of media-literacy programs to strengthen college women's resistance to media images. *Psychology of Woman Quarterly, 25,* 103–111.

Irving, L. M., DuPen, J., & Berel, S. (1998). A media literacy program for high school females. *Eating Disorders: Journal of Treatment and Prevention, 6,* 119–131.

Jane, D. M., Hunter, G. C., & Lozzi, B. M. (1999). Do Cuban-American women suffer from eating disorders? Effects of media exposure and acculturation. *Hispanic Journal of Behavioral Sciences, 21,* 212–218.

Jansen, A., & de Vries, M. (2002). Pre-attentive exposure to the thin female beauty ideal does not affect women's mood, self-esteem and eating behaviour. *European Eating Disorders Review, 10,* 208–217.

Jones, D. C. (2001). Social comparison and body image: Attractiveness comparisons to models and peers among adolescent girls and boys. *Sex Roles, 45,* 645–664.

Jones, D. C., Vigfusdottir, T. H., & Lee, Y. (in press). Body image and the appearance culture among adolescent girls and boys: An examination of friend conversations, peer criticism, appearance magazines, and the internalization of appearance ideals. *Journal of Adolescent Research.*

Keery, H., Shroff H., Thompson, J. K., Wertheim, E., & Smolak, L. (in press). Development and preliminary validation of the Sociocultural Internalization of Appearance Questionnaire-Adolescents. *Eating and Weight Disorders.*

Kilbourne, J. (1995). *Slim hopes: Advertising and the obsession with thinness* [video]. (Available from the Media Education Foundation, 28 Center Street, Northampton, MA 01060; Web site www.igc.apc.org/mef/mef.html)

Kilbourne, J. (1999). *Deadly persuasion: Why women and girls must fight the addictive power of advertising.* New York: Free Press.

King, N., Touyz, S., & Charles, M. (2000). The effect of body dissatisfaction on women's perceptions of female celebrities. *International Journal of Eating Disorders, 27,* 341–347.

Kotler, P., Roberto, N., & Lee, N. (2002). *Social marketing: Strategies for changing public behavior* (2nd ed.). Thousand Oaks: Sage.

Kusel, A. B. (1999). *Primary prevention of eating disorders through media literacy training of girls.* Unpublished doctoral dissertation, California School of Professional Psychology, San Diego.

Labre, M. P. (2002). Adolescent boys and the muscular male body ideal. *Journal of Adolescent Health, 30,* 233–242.

Lavin, M. A., & Cash, T. F. (2001). Effects of exposure to information about appearance stereotyping and discrimination on women's body images. *International Journal of Eating Disorders, 29,* 51–58.

Lavine, H., Sweeney, D., & Wagner, S. H. (1999). Depicting women as sex objects in television advertising: Effects on body dissatisfaction. *Personality and Social Psychology Bulletin, 25,* 1049–1058.

Leit, R. A., Gray, J. J., & Pope, H. G., Jr. (2002). The media's representation of the ideal male body: A cause for muscle dysmorphia. *International Journal of Eating Disorders, 31,* 334–338.

Levine, M. P., Piran, N., & Stoddard, C. (1999). Mission more probable: Media literacy, activism, and advocacy in the prevention of eating disorders. In N. Piran, M. P. Levine, & C. Steiner-Adair (Eds.), *Preventing eating disorders: A handbook of interventions and special challenges* (pp. 3–25). Philadelphia: Brunner/Mazel.

Levine, M. P., & Smolak, L. (1996). Media as a context for the development of disordered eating. In L. Smolak, M. P. Levine, & R. Striegel-Moore (Eds.), *The developmental psychopathology of eating disorders* (pp. 235–257). Mahwah, NJ: Erlbaum.

Levine, M. P., & Smolak, L. (1998). The mass media and disordered eating: Implications for primary prevention. In W. Vandereycken & G. Van Noordenbos (Eds.), *Prevention of eating disorders* (pp. 23–56). London: Athlone.

Levine, M. P., Smolak, L., & Hayden, H. (1994). The relation of sociocultural factors to eating attitudes and behaviors among middle school girls. *Journal of Early Adolescence, 14,* 472–491.

MacKinnon, D. P., Goldberg, L., Clarke, G. N., Elliot, D. L., Cheong, J., Lapin, A., et al. (2001). Mediating mechanisms in a program to reduce intentions to use anabolic steroids and improve exercise self-efficacy and dietary behavior. *Prevention Science, 2,* 15–27.

Martin, M. C., & Gentry, J. W. (1997). Stuck in the model trap: The effects of beautiful models in ads on female preadolescents and adolescents. *Journal of Advertising, 26,* 19–33.

Martin, M. C., & Kennedy, P. F. (1993). Advertising and social comparison: Consequences for female preadolescents and adolescents. *Psychology and Marketing, 10,* 513–530.

Martin, M. C., & Kennedy, P. F. (1994). Social comparison and the beauty of advertising models: The role of motives for comparison. *Advances in Consumer Research, 21,* 365–371.

McCabe, M. P., Ricciardelli, R. A., & Finemore, J. (2002). The role of puberty, media and popularity with peers on strategies to increase weight, decrease weight and increase muscle tone among adolescent boys and girls. *Journal of Psychosomatic Research, 52,* 145–154.

McCreary, D. R., & Sadava, S. W. (1999). Television viewing and self-perceived health, weight, and physical fitness: Evidence for the cultivation hypothesis. *Journal of Applied Social Psychology, 29,* 2342–2361.

Milkie, M. (1999). Social comparisons, reflected appraisals, and mass media: The impact of pervasive beauty images on black and white girls' self concepts. *Social Psychology Quarterly, 62,* 190–210.

Morrison, T. G., Kalin, R., & Morrison, M. A. (in press). Body-image evaluation and body-image investment among adolescents: A test of sociocultural and social comparison theories. *Adolescence.*

Morrison, T. G., Morrison, M. A., & Hopkins, C. (2002). *Striving for body perfection? An exploration of the drive for muscularity in Canadian men.* Unpublished manuscript, University of Saskatchewan, Red Deer College, Red Deer, Canada.

Murray, S. H., Touyz, S. W., & Beumont, P. J. V. (1996). Awareness and perceived influence of body ideals in the media: A comparison of eating disorder patients and the general community. *Eating Disorders: Journal of Treatment and Prevention, 4,* 33–46.

Neumark-Sztainer, D. (1996). School-based programs for preventing eating disturbances. *Journal of School Health, 66,* 64–71.

Neumark-Sztainer, D., Sherwood, N., Coller, T., & Hannan, P. J. (2000). Primary prevention of disordered eating among preadolescent girls: Feasibility and short-term impact of a community-based intervention. *Journal of the American Dietetic Association, 100,* 1466–1473.

Ogden, J., & Mundray, K. (1996). The effect of the media on body satisfaction: The role of gender an size. *European Eating Disorders Review, 4,* 171–182.

Peirce, K. (1990). A feminist theoretical perspective on the socialization of teenage girls through *Seventeen* magazine. *Sex Roles, 23,* 491–500.

Piran, N., Levine, M. P., & Irving, L. M. (2000, May). *GO GIRLS!™ Preventing negative body image through media literacy.* Paper/workshop presented at the Summit 2000 (Children, Youth, and the Media Beyond the Millennium) conference, Toronto, Ontario, Canada.

Polce-Lynch, M., Myers, B. J., Kliewer, W., & Kilmartin, C. (2001). Adolescent self-esteem and gender: Exploring relations to sexual harassment, body image, media influence, and emotional expression. *Journal of Youth and Adolescence, 30,* 225–244.

Pope, H. G., Jr., Olivardia, R., Gruber, A., & Borowiecki, J. (1999). Evolving ideals of male body image as seen through action toys. *International Journal of Eating Disorders, 26,* 65–72.

Pope, H. G., Jr., Phillips, K. A., & Olivardia, R. (2000). *The Adonis complex: The secret crisis of male body obsession.* New York: Free Press.

Posavac, H. D., Posavac, S. S., & Weigel, R. G. (2001). Reducing the impact of media images on women at risk for body image disturbance: Three targeted interventions. *Journal of Social and Clinical Psychology, 20,* 324–340.

Posavac, S. S., & Posavac, H. D. (2002). Predictors of women's concerns with body weight: The roles of perceived self-media ideal discrepancies and self-esteem. *Eating Disorders: Journal of Treatment and Prevention, 10,* 153–160.

Rabak-Wagener, J., Eickhoff-Shemek, J., & Kelly-Vance, L. (1998). The effect of media analysis on attitudes and behaviors regarding body image among college students. *Journal of American College Health, 47,* 29–35.

Ricciardelli, L. A., & McCabe, M. P. (2001). Self-esteem and negative affect as moderators of sociocultural influences on body dissatisfaction, strategies to decrease weight, and strategies to increase muscles among adolescent boys and girls. *Sex Roles, 44,* 189–207.

Ricciardelli, L. A., McCabe, M. P., & Banfield, S. (2000). Body image and body change methods in adolescent boys: Role of parents, friends, and the media. *Journal of Psychosomatic Research, 49,* 189–197.

Rice, R. E., & Atkin, C. K. (Eds.). (2001). *Public communication campaigns* (3rd ed.). Thousand Oaks, CA: Sage.

Roberts, D. F., Foehr, U. G., Rideout, V. J., & Brodie, M. (1999). *Kids & media @ the new millennium: A Kaiser Family Foundation report.* Menlo Park, CA: The Henry J. Kaiser Family Foundation.

Silverstein, B., & Perlick, D. (1995). *The cost of competence: Why inequality causes depression, eating disorders, and illness in women.* New York: Oxford University Press.

Singer, D. G., & Singer, J. (Eds.). (2001). *Handbook of children and the media.* Thousand Oaks, CA: Sage.

Smolak, L., & Levine, M. P. (1996). Adolescent transitions and the development of eating problems. In L. Smolak, M. P. Levine, & R. Striegel-Moore (Eds.), *The developmental psychopathology of eating disorders* (pp. 207–233). Mahwah, NJ: Erlbaum.

Smolak, L., Levine, M. P., & Thompson, J. K. (2001). The use of the Sociocultural Attitudes toward Appearance Questionnaire with middle school boys and girls. *International Journal of Eating Disorders, 29,* 216–223.

Smolak, L., & Murnen, S. (2001). Gender and eating problems. In R. H. Striegel-Moore & L. Smolak (Eds.), *Eating disorders: Innovative directions in research and practice* (pp. 91–110). Washington, DC: American Psychological Association.

Spitzer, B. L., Henderson, K. A., & Zivian, M. T. (1999). Gender differences in population versus media body sizes: A comparison over four decades. *Sex Roles, 40,* 545–565.

Springer, E. A., Winzelberg, A. J., Perkins, R., & Taylor, C. B. (1999). Effects of a body image curriculum for college students on improved body image. *International Journal of Eating Disorders, 26,* 13–20.

Steiner-Adair, C., Sjostrom, L., Franko, D. L., Pai, S., Tucker, R., Becker, A. E., et al. (2002). Primary prevention of eating disorders in adolescent girls: Learning from practice. *International Journal of Eating Disorders, 32,* 401–411.

Stice, E. (1998). Modeling of eating pathology and social reinforcement of the thin-ideal predict onset of bulimic symptoms. *Behavior Research and Therapy, 36,* 931–944.

Stice, E. (2001). Risk factors for eating pathology: Recent advances and future directions. In R. H. Striegel-Moore & L. Smolak (Eds.), *Eating disorders: Innovative directions in research and practice* (pp. 51–73). Washington, DC: American Psychological Association.

Stice, E., Schupak-Neuberg, E., Shaw, H. E., & Stein, R. I. (1994). Relation of media exposure to eating disorder symptomatology: An examination of mediating mechanisms. *Journal of Abnormal Psychology, 103,* 836–840.

Stice, E., & Shaw, H. (1994). Adverse effects of the media-portrayed thin-ideal on women and linkages to bulimic symptomatology. *Journal of Social and Clinical Psychology, 13,* 288–308.

Taylor, C. B., Sharpe, T., Shisslak, C., Bryson, S., Estes, L. S., Gray, N., et al. (1998). Factors associated with weight concerns in adolescent girls. *International Journal of Eating Disorders, 24,* 31–42.

Thompson, J. K., & Heinberg, L. J. (1999). The media's influence on body image disturbance and eating disorders: We've reviled them, now can we rehabilitate them? *Journal of Social Issues, 55,* 339–353.

Thompson, J. K., Heinberg, L., Altabe, M., & Tantleff-Dunn, S. (1999). *Exacting beauty: Theory, assessment, and treatment of body image disturbance.* Washington, DC: American Psychological Association.

Thompson, J. K., & Stice, E. (2001). Thin-ideal internalization: Mounting evidence for a new risk factor for body-image disturbance and eating pathology. *Current Directions in Psychological Science, 10,* 181–183.

Thompson, J. K., van den Berg, P., Roehrig, M., Guarda, A., & Heinberg, L. (in press). The Sociocultural Attitudes towards Appearance Questionnaire-3. *International Journal of Eating Disorders.*

Thomsen, S. R., Weber, M. M., & Brown, L. B. (2002). The relationship between reading beauty and fashion magazines and the use of pathogenic dieting methods among adolescent females. *Adolescence, 37,* 1–18.

Tiggemann, M., Gardiner, M., & Slater, A. (2000). "I would rather be size 10 than have straight A's": A focus group study of adolescent girls' wish to be thinner. *Journal of Adolescence, 23,* 645–659.

Tiggemann, M., & Pickering, A. S. (1996). Role of television in adolescent women's body dissatisfaction and drive for thinness. *International Journal of Eating Disorders, 20,* 199–203.

Van den Bulck, J. (2000). Is television bad for your health? Behavior and body image of the adolescent "couch potato." *Journal of Youth and Adolescence, 29,* 273–288.

Wade, T. D., Davidson, S., & O'Dea, J. (2003). Reducing risk factors for eating disorders in adolescents using a universal primary prevention approach. *International Journal of Eating Disorders, 33,* 371–383.

Wallack, L., Dorfman, L., Jernigan, D., & Themba, M. (1993). *Media advocacy and public health: Power for prevention.* Newbury Park, CA: Sage.

Wertheim, E. H., Paxton, S. J., Schutz, H. K., & Muir, S. L. (1997). Why do adolescent girls watch their weight? An interview study examining sociocultural pressures to be thin. *Journal of Psychosomatic Research, 42,* 345–355.

Wilcox, K., & Laird, J. D. (2000). The impact of media images of super-slender women on women's self-esteem: Identification, social comparison, and self-perception. *Journal of Research in Personality, 34,* 278–286.

Wolf-Bloom, M. S. (1998). *Using media literacy training to prevent body dissatisfaction and subsequent eating problems in early adolescent girls.* Unpublished doctoral dissertation, University of Cincinnati, OH.

Chapter 34

COSMETIC SURGERY AND COSMETIC MEDICAL TREATMENTS

DAVID B. SARWER, LEANNE MAGEE, AND CANICE E. CRERAND

According to the American Society of Plastic Surgeons (ASPS), 1.9 million individuals underwent cosmetic surgical and nonsurgical procedures in the United States and Canada in 2001 (ASPS, 2002). These numbers include not only cosmetic surgical procedures, such as liposuction and breast augmentation, but also nonsurgical cosmetic treatments, such as chemical peels and Botox® injections to temporarily reduce wrinkling. While these numbers are staggering, they are an underestimation of the number of cosmetic medical treatments performed annually. Physicians from a variety of medical disciplines now offer these procedures. For example, the American Society for Aesthetic Plastic Surgery (ASAPS), which annually releases statistics on the number of procedures performed by board-certified plastic surgeons, dermatologists, and otorhinolaryngologists, reported that almost 8.5 million cosmetic procedures were performed in 2001 (ASAPS, 2002; see Table 34.1). This represents a 304% increase since 1997.

This chapter provides an overview of the psychological literature on cosmetic surgery and cosmetic medical treatments. The chapter begins with a discussion of the possible reasons for the increasing popularity of cosmetic medical treatments. Central to this discussion is an overview of the relationship between body image and cosmetic surgery. The chapter briefly traces the history of psychological studies of cosmetic surgery patients. Next, the relationship between specific forms of psychopathology and cosmetic surgery is discussed. The chapter concludes with a discussion of psychological assessment procedures for mental health professionals who may encounter persons interested in these treatments.

THE POPULARITY OF COSMETIC MEDICAL TREATMENTS

As Table 34.1 suggests, the popularity of cosmetic medical treatments has exploded. Procedures such as liposuction and breast augmentation have doubled in popularity in four years. The newest procedures often eclipse the popularity of the "household names" within a few years. Even before its formal FDA approval in the spring of 2002, botulinium toxin (Botox) injections for facial wrinkling were the most commonly performed

Table 34.1   Cosmetic Medical Treatments Performed in 2001, 2000, and 1997

Procedure	2001	2000	1997	Percent Change 1997 vs. 2001
Abdominoplasty (tummy tuck)	71,123	58,426	34,002	+109
Blepharoplasty (cosmetic eyelid surgery)	246,338	212,133	159,232	+55
Botulinum toxin injection (Botox®, Myobloc®)	1,600,300	1,096,611	65,157	+2,356
Breast augmentation	216,754	203,310	101,176	+114
Breast lift	60,142	45,710	19,882	+203
Breast reduction (women)	114,926	90,042	47,874	+140
Buttock lift	2,813	2,122	1,549	+82
Cellulite treatment (mechanical roller massage therapy)	61,985	51,253	NA	NA
Cheek implants	6,282	7,059	11,040	−43
Chemical peel	1,361,479	630,194	481,227	+183
Chin augmentation	27,123	20,499	27,373	−1
Collagen injection	1,098,519	592,195	347,168	+216
Dermabrasion	66,776	29,905	40,214	+66
Face-lift	117,034	102,842	99,196	+18
Fat injection	78,509	84,724	38,259	+105
Forehead lift	71,653	60,756	55,090	+30
Gynecomastia, treatment of (male breast reduction)	16,512	15,968	11,168	+48
Hair transplantation	22,041	38,978	61,023	−64
Laser hair removal	854,582	487,807	NA	NA
Laser skin resurfacing	122,617	116,901	154,153	−20
Laser treatment of leg veins	142,820	85,907	NA	NA
Lip augmentation (other than injectable materials)	30,781	21,266	NA	NA
Lipoplasty (liposuction)	385,390	376,633	176,863	+118
Lower body lift	4,268	3,362	2,125	+101
Microdermabrasion	915,312	610,705	NA	NA
Otoplasty (cosmetic ear surgery)	26,844	19,452	22,939	+17
Rhinoplasty (nose reshaping)	177,422	135,795	137,053	+29
Sclerotherapy	557,856	525,237	NA	NA
Thigh lift	6,114	10,357	2,895	+111
Upper arm lift	6,048	4,913	2,516	+140
TOTALS	8,470,363	5,741,173	2,099,173	+304

Note: Statistical data courtesy of the American Society for Aesthetic Plastic Surgery (ASAPS).

NA = Not available (was not asked in prior survey).

Final figures are projected to reflect nationwide statistics and are based on a survey of doctors who have been certified by the American Board of Medical Specialties-recognized boards, including, but not limited to, the American Board of Plastic Surgery.

Figures for procedures include, but are not limited to, those performed by ASAPS members. ASAPS members are plastic surgeons certified by the American Board of Plastic Surgery who specialize in cosmetic surgery of the face and entire body.

cosmetic treatments, with 1.6 million individuals undergoing the treatment in 2001 (ASAPS, 2002). Perhaps even more interesting is the case of breast augmentation surgery. In 1992, 32,607 women underwent cosmetic breast augmentation (ASPS, 2002). During that year, following concerns of the relationship between the silicone gel implants and a variety of autoimmune disorders, the FDA banned the use of silicone-filled implants for cosmetic purposes. Many predicted that breast augmentation surgery would plummet in popularity. In 2001, however, 206,354 women underwent breast augmentation with saline-filled implants, a 533% increase since the ban (ASPS, 2002).

How do we explain the dramatic increase in popularity of almost all cosmetic medical treatments? There are at least three potential explanations: the medical community, the mass media and entertainment industry, and the patients themselves.

The Medical Community

There is little doubt that advances in the medical aspects of cosmetic surgery have contributed to its increasing popularity. Almost all of the procedures are safer than ever before. Many procedures can be offered using minimally invasive equipment. Research on wound healing and postoperative wound care has decreased the recovery time for many procedures.

Plastic surgeons once cornered the market on cosmetic medicine. Today, dermatologists, otorhinolaryngologists, and ophthalmologists also offer these treatments. In fact, there is no regulation that prevents a physician of any medical discipline from performing cosmetic procedures. These treatments are typically paid for out of pocket and rarely covered by insurance. Physicians who offer these procedures frequently can offset income lost to declining insurance reimbursements. As a result, it is a rather safe prediction that increasing numbers of physicians will offer these treatments in the future.

Unlike many other medical treatments, cosmetic treatments lend themselves nicely to direct-to-consumer marketing. The ASPS has run nationwide advertisement campaigns that have appeared in national magazines and television commercials. City-based and regional magazines typically are filled with advertisements for physicians who offer cosmetic treatments. Advertisements can be found on bus stops and billboards. One developing trend involves physicians forming relationships with spas, salons, and health clubs to attract new clients.

Mass Media and the Entertainment Industry

The mass media also has likely contributed to the dramatic increase in cosmetic treatments. Stories on cosmetic surgery are frequently featured on talk shows and news magazine programs. Several major cable networks regularly air shows that introduce the viewer to a cosmetic surgery patient preoperatively and follow him or her into the operating room and several months postoperatively. The newest developments in cosmetic medicine are regularly found in the pages of the expanding number of women's and men's health and beauty magazines.

Images of Hollywood stars have long been thought to influence consumers' beliefs about their appearance (Etcoff, 1999). The public has emulated the hairstyles, clothing choices, and body types of popular celebrities for decades. Today, the public is bombarded by mass media images of beauty unlike ever before. In the 1950s, if you wanted to see Marilyn Monroe, you had only a select number of opportunities—her next movie, an occasional television appearance, or the rare magazine cover. Today, if you want to see Julia Roberts, you can wait for her next movie, or you can flip through hundreds of cable channels looking for one of her previous films or a biography of her life. If one isn't on, you can rent one of her movies at a video store. At the bookstore, she will likely appear on the cover of one of an endless number of fashion, style, or entertainment magazines. If you still haven't gotten your fill, you can always search the Internet for pictures of her. It is even easier to see celebrities such as Jennifer Lopez and Britney Spears, whose crossovers from music to movies and back again further increase their exposure. At any point in the day, you are only minutes away from images of the entertainment industry's ideals of beauty.

Perhaps more relevant to the discussion of cosmetic medical treatments is that the nature of these images has changed over time (Sarwer, Grossbart, & Didie, 2002; Sarwer, Magee, & Clark, in press). Although Marilyn Monroe was the definitive beauty ideal of her time, she would be considered overweight by today's standards of beauty (ironically, her zaftig appearance and size 12 figure are similar to that of the average American woman today). Beauty icons such as Miss America and the *Playboy* centerfold have become significantly leaner over the decades (Garner, Garfield, Schwartz, & Thompson 1980; Mazur, 1986), and their body weights have now stabilized at very low levels (Katzmarzyk & Davis, 2001; Rubenstein & Caballero, 2000; Wiseman, Gray, Mosimann, & Ahrens, 1992). Over the past few years, a new ideal has emerged—a lean, muscular, yet full-breasted, woman. This body type rarely occurs in nature without the help of restrictive dieting, excessive exercise, liposuction, and breast augmentation (Sarwer, Magee, et al., in press). All of this occurs before the computer enhancements and airbrushing perfect the image on the movie screen or magazine cover.

The Patients Themselves

Our attitudes about our bodies also have likely fueled the growth of cosmetic surgery. A 1997 survey of *Psychology Today* readers suggested that 56% of women and 43% of men were dissatisfied with their overall appearance (Garner, 1997). In response to this dissatisfaction, we spend billions of dollars each year trying to improve our appearance through a variety of means. For example, it is estimated that Americans spend at least $40 billion each year trying to lose weight (Wicklegren, 1998). Americans spent $8.8 billion on physician fees for cosmetic medical treatments in 2001 (ASAPS, 2002). According to a nationwide telephone survey of 1,000 American households conducted by the ASAPS, 57% of women and 53% of men indicated that they approve of cosmetic surgery. Additionally, 34% of women and 19% of men said that they would consider cosmetic surgery for themselves either now or in the future (ASAPS, 2002). We have grown comfortable seeing our bodies as malleable entities.

The "face" of the typical cosmetic surgery patient is also changing. The stereotypical cosmetic surgery patient is probably an older Caucasian woman interested in anti-aging treatments. In 2001, men and women between the ages of 51 and 64 underwent 25% of all procedures; 44% were performed on "baby boomers" ages 35 to 50 (ASAPS, 2002). Increasing numbers of individuals from a variety of racial and socioeconomic groups now seek cosmetic surgery. Ethnic minorities accounted for 17% of procedures performed in 2001 (ASAPS, 2002).

Perhaps over the past decade, more individuals have figured out on their own something social psychologists have learned through years of research—that, like it or not, our appearance matters. Physically attractive individuals are seen in a more favorable light than their less attractive peers, and they frequently receive preferential treatment from others in a variety of situations across the life span (Eagly, Ashmore, Makhijani, & Longo, 1991; Feingold, 1992; Langlois et al., 2000). Evolutionary biologists and psychologists take this argument one step further, suggesting that our preferences for physical beauty are genetically wired and serve a distinct evolutionary purpose, namely reproduction. Studies across species have suggested that animals are attracted to symmetry, pathogen resistance, and bright color because these features suggest reproductive viability (Etcoff, 1999).

Humans studies have suggested that individuals are more responsive to signs of youthfulness, symmetry, and a lower waist-to-hip ratio (WHR) because they suggest increased fertility and decreased risk of disease (Etcoff, 1999). Several studies have suggested that men rate women with a low WHR (less than .8) as more attractive, younger, healthier, and more feminine looking than women with a high WHR (Singh, 1993, 1995). When WHR is held constant, women with larger breasts are judged as being more attractive than those with smaller breasts (Singh & Young, 1995). Therefore, spending thousands of dollars to undergo cosmetic surgery on a physically healthy body may make a great deal of sense.

In summary, there are likely many potential explanations for the heightened popularity of cosmetic treatments. The increase in the number of physicians who offer these treatments, coupled with improvements in surgical technique, healing time, and safety, have contributed to the rise in popularity. Although somewhat difficult to document, the mass media, from its portrayals of beauty to its fascination with cosmetic surgery, has likely played a role. Finally, changes in our population itself, from an acceptance of these treatments to perhaps a greater awareness of the importance of physical appearance in daily life, have potentially fueled cosmetic surgery's increase in popularity. Regardless of the reasons, there is little to suggest that the popularity of these treatments will wane in the future.

PSYCHOLOGICAL CHARACTERISTICS OF PERSONS WHO UNDERGO COSMETIC MEDICAL TREATMENTS

Over the past 50 years, several plastic surgeons have studied the psychological traits of their patients. Because the benefits of these procedures are often as much psychological as physical, mental health professionals also have become interested in these individuals. One issue of interest to both groups of professionals has been the preoperative appropriateness of patients with specific characteristics. Another issue has been the psychological changes that occur following a change in appearance. These studies have used both paper-and-pencil assessments of psychological characteristics and clinical interviews to assess psychological status. Some studies have focused on preoperative traits, while others have examined postoperative changes in psychological functioning. These studies can be loosely grouped into three generations of research.

First-Generation Studies

The pioneers of the investigations of the psychological characteristics of cosmetic surgery patients were a group of plastic surgeons and psychiatrists at Johns Hopkins University in the 1950s and 1960s. This research, like most of the studies of this era, relied predominantly on the use of clinical interviews of patients conducted by psychoanalytically trained psychiatrists. Perhaps not surprisingly, most studies concluded that a vast majority of patients were highly psychopathological. In one study, 70% were diagnosed with significant psychological disturbance, most commonly described as neurotic depression and passive-dependent personality (Edgerton, Jacobson, & Meyer, 1960). Studies of patients seeking face-lifts and rhinoplasties reached similar conclusions (Meyer, Jacobson, Edgerton, & Canter, 1960; Webb, Slaughter, Meyer, & Edgerton, 1965). These studies also examined changes in psychological status postoperatively. Some reported generally favorable outcomes, whereas others reported some negative consequences (Edgerton et al., 1960; Meyer et al., 1960; Webb et al., 1965).

As a group, this set of studies provided a rich description of the psychological characteristics of cosmetic surgery patients. However, these studies (as well as the majority of interview-based studies to follow) had several methodological problems. The high rates of psychopathology may have been a reflection of the theoretical biases of the psychiatrist-investigators. The nature of the clinical interview used in these studies was not delineated, making validation or replication impossible. Finally, the studies failed to employ uniform diagnostic criteria and control or comparison groups, making it impossible to determine whether patients exhibited levels of psychological disturbance greater than those undergoing general medical procedures or the population in general (Sarwer & Pertschuk, 2002; Sarwer, Wadden, Pertschuk, & Whitaker, 1998b).

Second-Generation Studies

In the 1970s and early 1980s, psychological studies of cosmetic surgery patients began to include psychometric assessment tools. In contrast with interview-based studies of the first generation, most studies that used standardized paper-and-pencil measures found lower rates of psychopathology (Sarwer & Pertschuk, 2002; Sarwer et al., 1998b).

The most widely used psychometric testing tool has been the Minnesota Multiphasic Personality Inventory (MMPI). Essentially normal MMPI profiles have been found in studies of breast augmentation patients (Baker, Kolin, & Bartlett, 1974), face-lift patients (Goin, Burgoyne, Goin, & Staples, 1980), and in two separate investigations of rhinoplasty patients (Micheli-Pellegrini & Manfrieda, 1979; Wright & Wright, 1975). Studies employing alternate measures, such as the California Personality Inventory and the Brief Symptom Inventory, found few differences between cosmetic surgery patients and normal controls, with both groups falling within the norms of the measures (Goin & Rees, 1991; Shipley, O'Donnell, & Bader, 1977). Two additional studies found only modest evidence of psychopathology. A study of rhinoplasty patients using the Eysenck Personality Inventory found increased levels of neuroticism and obsessiveness as compared to controls (Hay, 1970). A study of breast reduction patients that used the Crown-Crisp Experimental Index found only modest elevations in depressive and anxiety symptoms as compared to controls (Hollyman, Lacey, Whitfield, & Wilson, 1986).

In contrast to the conclusions drawn from the interview-based research of the 1960s, the findings of studies that relied on psychometric assessments suggested less psychopathology among prospective patients. In his review of the literature, Wengle (1986) concluded that studies of the 1970s and 1980s suggested that persons who seek cosmetic surgery are predominantly normal and that surgery can have positive psychological benefits. Similar to the first generation of studies, the second generation also had methodological problems. Several studies did not include preoperative assessments, and others failed to use control groups. When comparison groups were included, investigators frequently failed to describe similarities or differences between the groups. Thus, the appropriateness of such comparisons is unknown, thereby limiting the conclusions that can be drawn from the results (Sarwer & Pertschuk, 2002; Sarwer et al., 1998b).

Third-Generation Studies

Many studies of the past decade have sought to improve on the shortcomings of the previous investigations. Interview-based studies have typically used widely accepted diagnostic criteria. Psychometric studies have frequently included both pre- and postoperative assessments using valid and reliable psychometric measures.

Clinical Interview Studies

In 1993, Napoleon revisited the issue of psychopathology among cosmetic surgery patients. Using a clinical interview and behavioral observations of 133 patients, he concluded that 19.5% met diagnostic criteria for an Axis I disorder, predominantly anxiety and mood disorders (Napoleon, 1993). Seventy percent of patients were diagnosed with an Axis II disorder. The use of *Diagnostic and Statistical Manual of Mental Disorders,* third edition-revised (*DSM-III-R*; APA, 1987) diagnostic criteria is an improvement over the first-generation clinical interview studies. However, the use of an unspecified clinical interview, reliance on nonstandardized observations of interactions between patients and staff, and the lack of inter-rater reliability of diagnoses could account for the high rate of Axis II disorders found in this sample (Sarwer et al., 1998b).

A study of cosmetic surgery patients in Japan reported similarly high rates of psychopathology (Ishigooka, Iwao, Suzuki, Fukuyama, Murasaki, & Miura, 1998). Over a 17-year period, 415 male and female cosmetic surgery patients underwent an unspecified psychiatric interview and were evaluated using *International Classification of Disease-10* (World Health Organization [WHO], 1992) diagnostic criteria. Approximately 48% of patients were given diagnoses, the most frequent being neurotic and hypochondriacal disorders. As with the Napoleon study, the rate of psychopathology in the study by Ishigooka and colleagues is significantly larger than would be expected in the general population. It is also inconsistent with the observations made by American plastic surgeons of the daily interactions with their patients.

Psychometric Investigations

Several psychometric studies have significantly improved on some of the methodological problems found in previous investigations. In one study, women seeking a variety of cosmetic procedures completed measures of quality of life, depressive symptoms, social support, and coping preoperatively and at one and six months postoperatively (Rankin,

Borah, Perry, & Wey, 1998). Women reported significant improvements in quality of life and depressive symptoms following surgery. A study of rhinoplasty patients assessed pre- and postoperatively found a decrease in neuroticism and anxiety at eight months and five years postoperatively (Ercolani, Baldaro, Rossi, & Trombini, 1999).

In summary, it is difficult to draw firm conclusions from the three generations of research. Clinical interview investigations, including recent studies that have used formal diagnostic criteria, have categorized patients as highly psychopathological. In contrast, psychometric investigations have found far less preoperative psychopathology and have documented psychological improvements postoperatively. Complicating interpretation of the results are the methodological problems that have plagued the majority of studies. Nevertheless, two tentative conclusions can be drawn (Sarwer & Crerand, 2002; Sarwer & Didie, 2002; Sarwer & Pertschuk, 2002). First, individuals who seek cosmetic medical treatments exhibit a wide range of psychological symptoms. Second, it may be premature to confidently conclude that the majority of patients experience significant psychological improvements postoperatively. A subsequent generation of research is needed to assess the validity of these conclusions.

BODY IMAGE AND COSMETIC MEDICAL TREATMENTS

Body image dissatisfaction is thought to motivate many appearance-enhancing behaviors, from weight loss and exercise to clothing and cosmetic purchases. It also has long been considered to play an important role in the decision to seek cosmetic medical treatments. Individuals who seek cosmetic surgery report increased dissatisfaction with their bodies preoperatively and improvements in body image postoperatively (e.g., Baker et al., 1974; Killman, Sattler, & Taylor, 1987; Schlebusch, 1989; Sihm, Jagd, & Pers, 1978). Pruzinsky and Edgerton (1990) have suggested that cosmetic surgery is, in fact, body image surgery.

As the field of body image exploded in popularity in the 1990s, the relationship of body image to cosmetic surgery began to receive both theoretical and empirical attention. Drawing from previous models of body image, Sarwer and colleagues proposed a model of the relationship between body image and cosmetic surgery (Sarwer et al., 1998b). This model suggested that physical as well as psychological factors (perceptual, developmental, and sociocultural) influence attitudes toward the body. These attitudes consist of a *valence,* defined as the importance of body image to an individual's self-esteem, and *value,* described as the degree of body image dissatisfaction. Ultimately, it is the interaction of body image valence and body image value that is thought to influence the decision to pursue cosmetic surgery. Individuals with a high body image valence and a significant degree of body image dissatisfaction were thought to comprise the majority of cosmetic surgery patients (Sarwer et al., 1998b).

Preoperative Investigations of Body Image

Although body image has been studied in cosmetic surgery patients since the 1970s, only recently have studies included reliable and valid empirical measures of body image. In the initial study of this kind (Sarwer, Wadden, Pertschuk, & Whitaker, 1998a), 100 women seeking a variety of cosmetic procedures completed the Multidimensional Body-Self Relationship Questionnaire (MBSRQ; Brown, Cash, & Mikulka, 1990) and the Body Dysmorphic Disorder Examination-Self-Report (BDDE-SR; Rosen & Reiter, 1996). Results were compared to those of the normative samples for each measure. Prospective patients reported a heightened dissatisfaction with the specific body feature for which they were pursuing surgery. They also reported a greater investment in issues of health and fitness. However, they did not report a greater investment or increased dissatisfaction with their overall body image. Similar results were found in studies of female aging face patients (Sarwer, Whitaker, Wadden, & Pertschuk, 1997) and male cosmetic surgery patients (Pertschuk, Sarwer, Wadden, & Whitaker, 1998).

Women who seek breast augmentation or reduction surgery also have significant body image concerns. As compared to breast augmentation patients, breast reduction patients reported greater dissatisfaction with their breasts and overall body image (Sarwer, Bartlett, et al., 1998). The difference in dissatisfaction with the overall body image may have been a function of body weight because reduction patients were significantly heavier than augmentation patients. Greater than 50% of both groups reported significant behavioral change in response to their breasts, including avoidance of being seen undressed by others and camouflaging the appearance of their breasts with clothing or special bras.

Three studies have compared breast augmentation candidates to women who were not seeking breast augmentation surgery. As compared to an age-matched sample of small-breasted women, breast augmentation candidates reported significantly greater dissatisfaction with their breasts (Nordmann, 1998). Breast augmentation candidates also reported more frequent negative emotions in situations where they were aware of their physical appearance (Nordmann, 1998). A subsequent study comparing breast augmentation patients to physically similar women not pursuing breast augmentation replicated these results (Sarwer, LaRossa, et al., in press). This study also found that breast augmentation patients reported a greater investment in their appearance, more frequent appearance-related teasing, and more frequent use of psychotherapy in the year before surgery. Another recent study suggested that breast augmentation patients are motivated to pursue augmentation by their own feelings about their breasts, rather than direct or indirect influence from romantic partners or sociocultural representations of beauty (Didie & Sarwer, in press).

Summarizing these empirical studies, it appears that persons who seek cosmetic surgery experience heightened body image dissatisfaction. Early investigations, which compared patients to normative samples, found that patients reported increased dissatisfaction with the specific feature considered for surgery. They also reported greater investment in health and fitness but not greater overall body image dissatisfaction. Recent studies of breast augmentation patients using physically similar women as controls have replicated these findings. In addition, these studies have suggested that breast augmentation patients report heightened situational dissatisfaction with their breasts, report a history of more frequent appearance-related teasing, and report more frequent use of psychotherapy.

The clinical significance of these latter findings is unclear (Sarwer & Didie, 2002). For many women, the pursuit of cosmetic surgery to address body image dissatisfaction may be an adaptive coping strategy in a culture that overemphasizes the importance of physical appearance. Alternatively, as suggested by the finding of greater use of psychotherapy by breast augmentation patients, the pursuit of breast augmentation may be influenced by some form of psychopathology, which may be better treated by a mental health professional than a cosmetic surgeon. Additional studies, using appropriate psychometric measures, are needed to further assess the preoperative psychological status of prospective cosmetic surgery patients.

Postoperative Investigations of Body Image

As noted previously, several studies have suggested that cosmetic surgery patients experience improvements in body image postoperatively. Only a handful of studies have assessed changes in body image using paper-and-pencil measures. One suggested that women reported a more positive body image following facial cosmetic surgery (Dunofsky, 1997). The study, however, did not include a preoperative assessment and used an outdated version of the MBSRQ. Glatt and colleagues (1999) found that women who underwent breast reduction surgery reported less dissatisfaction with their breasts compared to breast reduction candidates assessed preoperatively. Unfortunately, the same women were not studied both pre- and postoperatively.

Recently, 45 women assessed preoperatively (Sarwer et al., 1998a) completed the MBSRQ and BDDE-SR on average seven months postoperatively (Sarwer, Wadden, & Whitaker, 2002). These women reported significant improvements in the degree of dissatisfaction with the feature altered by surgery. However, they reported no change in their overall body image. A study that assessed breast augmentation patients pre- and postoperatively found that greater than 90% reported an improved body image and greater than 85% reported an enhanced self-image (Cash, Duel, & Perkins, 2002). Unfortunately, this study did not include widely used measures of body image. An investigation of women who have had their silicone breast implants removed also demonstrated the impact of cosmetic surgery on body image (Walden, Thompson, & Wells, 1997). These women reported less satisfaction with their appearance, fewer positive appearance-related thoughts, and greater discrepancy between their ideal and current (postimplant removal) breast size. Breast implant removal, which is experienced by approximately 10,000 women each year (ASPS, 2002), may have a profoundly negative impact on body image.

Despite a limited number of empirical studies, it appears that cosmetic surgery patients experience body image improvements postoperatively. Nevertheless, additional studies are needed to delineate the relationship between cosmetic procedures and body image.

COSMETIC MEDICAL TREATMENT AND PSYCHOPATHOLOGY

Given the large number of persons who seek cosmetic medical treatment each year, it is likely that all of the major Axis I and II disorders occur among these individuals (Sarwer & Crerand, 2002; Sarwer & Didie, 2002; Sarwer & Pertschuk, 2002). Previous reports have documented cases of mood disorders (e.g., Goin et al., 1980; Schlebusch & Levin, 1983), thought disorders (e.g., Edgerton, Langman, & Pruzinsky, 1991; Knorr, 1972), anxiety disorders (Rankin & Borah, 1997), and personality disorders (e.g., Edgerton et al., 1960; Napoleon, 1993; Webb et al., 1965). Although surgeons have been frequently cautioned about performing cosmetic treatments on patients with these conditions, the relationship between these disorders and postoperative outcome has not been firmly established. Disorders with a body image component, such as body dysmorphic disorder and eating disorders, may occur more frequently in the population of individuals who undergo cosmetic treatments (Sarwer, 2002; Sarwer & Crerand, 2002; Sarwer & Didie, 2002).

Body Dysmorphic Disorder

Although studies have suggested that many cosmetic surgery patients report heightened dissatisfaction with the physical feature considered for surgery, extreme dissatisfaction may suggest the presence of body dysmorphic disorder (BDD). *BDD* is defined as a preoccupation with a slight or imagined defect in appearance that leads to clinically significant distress or impairment in social, occupational, or other areas of functioning (American Psychiatric Association [APA], 1994). BDD has several characteristics that distinguish it from more "normative" body image dissatisfaction seen in the typical cosmetic surgery patient. Any area of the body may become a source of preoccupation for a person with BDD, although the skin, hair, and nose are the most common (Phillips & Diaz, 1997). The preoccupation may consume several hours of the day. Some individuals engage in ritualistic checking of their appearance with mirrors; others practice significant avoidance behaviors and may be unable to maintain employment or relationships. In severe cases, BDD sufferers may become housebound or suicidal (Phillips & Diaz, 1997).

BDD may be difficult to identify among persons who seek cosmetic treatments (Sarwer, Crerand, & Didie, 2003; Sarwer & Didie, 2002; Sarwer & Pertschuk, 2002). Given the newness of BDD to American psychiatry (it was first introduced in *DSM-III-R*), physicians who offer these treatments may be unfamiliar with the disorder. Persons who seek cosmetic medical treatments often seek to improve slight appearance defects that are within the range of "normal." Such defects, however, are frequently judged as observable and correctable by the surgeon. As a result, judgment of a defect as "slight" is highly subjective. The degree of emotional distress and behavioral impairment, rather than the size or nature of the physical defect, may be more accurate indicators of BDD in this population (Sarwer & Didie, 2002; Sarwer & Pertschuk, 2002; Sarwer et al., 2003).

Several studies have suggested that the rate of BDD among persons who seek cosmetic medical treatments may be greater than estimates in the general population. A study of 100 female cosmetic surgery patients that used the BDDE-SR found that 7% of patients met diagnostic criteria for BDD (Sarwer et al., 1998a). Two studies of dermatology patients, which used a different questionnaire, found that 12% to 15% met diagnostic criteria (Dufresne, Phillips, Vittorio, & Wilkel, 2001; Phillips, Dufresne, Wilkel, & Vittorio, 2000). Similarly, 15% of 415 Japanese cosmetic surgery patients were diagnosed with BDD based on a clinical interview (Ishigooka et al., 1998). BDD may not be limited to persons with "slight" appearance defects. A study of individuals with visible deformities undergoing reconstructive procedures found that 16% met diagnostic criteria (Sarwer, Whitaker, et al., 1998). Methodological differences can explain the different percentages found in each study. Nevertheless, it appears that 7% to 16% of persons who seek cosmetic medical treatment may have BDD.

Studies of persons with BDD suggest that they attempt to correct their appearance defects through cosmetic medical treatments with great frequency. Among 250 adults with BDD, approximately 76% reported seeking nonpsychiatric medical treatments such as surgery and 66% have received them (Phillips, Grant, Siniscalchi, & Albertini, 2001). Unfortunately, the majority of patients have not benefited from these treatments. According to one report, 72% of procedures resulted in no change, and 16% led to a worsening of BDD symptoms (Phillips et al., 2001). Veale and colleagues (Veale, 2000; Veale et al., 1996) reported that greater than 75% of persons reported being dissatisfied with the outcome of their cosmetic treatments. There is also concern that individuals with BDD may be more likely to bring legal action and threaten or commit acts of violence against the surgeon and his or her staff (Sarwer et al., 2003). These reports suggest that BDD may contraindicate cosmetic surgery (Sarwer et al., 2003; Sarwer & Didie, 2002; Sarwer & Pertschuk, 2002).

Case Example

The following case describes a patient with BDD who presented for cosmetic surgery.

Frank, a 26-year-old, single Caucasian man, was concerned about a small blemish on his forehead. He worked as a financial analyst for a large company. He was an attractive man who arrived at his consultation fashionably dressed and well groomed. Over the past six months, he had become increasingly concerned with the blemish. He indicated that it had started as a pimple and that he checked in the mirror several times a day. He reported that he frequently touched or rubbed it with the hope that it would go away. Over time, he believed it had become more noticeable and attracted everyone's attention. On questioning by the surgeon, Frank indicated that he was also concerned about several other marks on his body. Frank reported that he rarely socialized or dated because of his concern about his forehead. When he went out in public, he wore a hat to cover the mark. The surgeon indicated that he might be able to remove the blemish, but the result would leave him with a small scar. Before proceeding with surgery, the surgeon asked Frank to see a psychologist to discuss his concerns about his appearance.

Eating Disorders

Individuals with anorexia nervosa or bulimia nervosa typically experience a significant disturbance in body image. As a result, both disorders may be disproportionately represented among persons who seek cosmetic treatments. Case reports have suggested that women with both disorders who have undergone liposuction, breast augmentation, and even facial procedures have experienced worsening of their eating disorder symptoms postoperatively (McIntosh, Britt, & Bulik, 1994; Willard, McDermott, & Woodhouse, 1996; Yates, Shisslak, Allender, & Wollman, 1988). Many women interested in breast augmentation surgery have a body mass index that is low normal or underweight (Sarwer, Bartlett, et al., 1998; Didie & Sarwer, in press). Some may exhibit eating disorder symptoms, although this has yet to be formally studied. A report of five breast reduction patients with bulimia suggested that four of the five women experienced an improvement in their bulimic symptoms postoperatively (Losee, Serletti, Kreipe, & Caldwell, 1997).

Case Example

The following case illustrates a patient with anorexia who presented for cosmetic surgery.

Randi was a 23-year-old, single Caucasian woman who presented for breast augmentation. She was 5'8" with a weight of 118 lbs. and a body mass index of 18 kg/m^2. She worked as a fashion designer. She desired to increase her breast size from a 32A to a 32C. On her medical history form, Randi indicated that she had undergone two rhinoplasties and dermabrasion to treat some mild acne. Randi also noted that she had not experienced her menstrual period in almost a year. The surgeon asked Randi about her eating and exercise habits. She told the surgeon that she exercised for approximately two hours a day, weighed herself several times a day, and was "very careful" with her diet. The surgeon referred Randi to an eating disorders specialist for further assessment.

Summary

Given the increasing numbers of men and women who now seek cosmetic medical treatments, all of the major psychiatric diagnoses likely exist among these individuals. The rate of occurrence of specific diagnoses, with the exception of BDD, is unknown. Studies that use widely accepted diagnostic criteria in combination with standardized assessment procedures are needed to determine the rate of psychiatric disorders among persons who seek these treatments. Studies that explore the relationship between psychopathology and postoperative outcome are also needed because the relationship between most forms of psychopathology and cosmetic treatments is unknown.

PSYCHOLOGICAL ASSESSMENT OF PATIENTS INTERESTED IN COSMETIC MEDICAL TREATMENTS

Mental health professionals may encounter men and women interested in cosmetic medical treatments in one of several scenarios. Individuals with body image concerns in a psychotherapy practice may be considering (or may have undergone) cosmetic procedures. In addition, mental health professionals may be asked by physicians offering these procedures to consult with a patient preoperatively to assess the patient's appropriateness for surgery. Alternatively, mental health professionals may be asked to see a patient to assess and treat psychopathology that may have revealed itself postoperatively.

Pretreatment Consultations

Few, if any, physicians who offer cosmetic medical treatments require patients to undergo a mental health evaluation preoperatively. The majority of individuals who seek cosmetic procedures are thought to have specific appearance concerns and realistic postoperative expectations (Sarwer, 2001, 2002; Sarwer & Didie, 2002; Sarwer &

Pertschuk, 2002). Thus, they are assumed to be psychologically appropriate for surgery. A minority of patients, however, exhibits symptoms that may lead the surgeon to request a psychological evaluation. A consultation with a patient interested in cosmetic medical treatment should incorporate the basic principles of a psychological evaluation. In addition, it should focus on three additional areas: motivations and expectations for surgery, psychiatric history, and appearance concerns and body dysmorphic disorder (Sarwer, 2001, 2002; Sarwer & Didie, 2002; Sarwer & Pertschuk, 2002). Male and adolescent patients also may warrant particular attention because of their relatively infrequent presentation for surgery.

Motivations and Expectations

The motivations of cosmetic surgery patients have been categorized as internal or external (Edgerton & Knorr, 1971; Goin et al., 1980; Meyer et al., 1960). Internal motivations are thought to include improvements in patients' self-esteem or body image. External motivations are believed to capture the "secondary gain" of a surgical change in appearance—that patients will be treated differently following surgery. Preoperative motivations are closely linked to psychological and social expectations postoperatively (Pruzinsky, 1996). Although cosmetic procedures frequently enhance an individual's physical appearance, they may have only modest effects on the social response of others (Cash & Horton, 1983; Kalick, 1979).

When asked, patients often struggle to articulate their motivations for surgery beyond stating, "I want to look better/younger/more attractive." Other patients may be hesitant to discuss their motivations out of fear that they are not the "right" motivations for surgery. To assess the source of patients' motivations, it may be useful to ask: "When did you first think about having this procedure?" or "What makes you interested in surgery now as compared to six months ago?" To assess patients' postoperative expectations, ask: "How do you anticipate your life will be different following surgery?" Patients with internal motivations and those who can articulate realistic expectations are thought to be more likely to meet their goals for surgery as compared to those who are hoping to revive a relationship or receive an overdue promotion.

Psychiatric Status and History

An assessment of current psychological status, as would be done in any mental health consultation, is an important part of the consultation. As discussed previously, it is likely that all of the major psychiatric conditions occur in this population. The presence or history of a particular disorder may not be an absolute contraindication for treatment, particularly if it is unrelated to the procedure. Particular attention should be paid to disorders with a body image component. In the absence of sound data on the relationship between psychopathology and surgical outcome, appropriateness for surgery should be made on a case-by-case basis and involve collaboration between the mental health professional and surgeon (Sarwer, 2001, 2002; Sarwer & Didie, 2002; Sarwer & Pertschuk, 2002).

Most surgeons will not operate on a patient who is actively psychotic, manic, or severely depressed (Sarwer & Pertschuk, 2002). One surgery group, however, has reported successful surgical treatment of patients with significant psychopathology (including several who were described as psychotic and several who may have had

BDD; Edgerton et al., 1991). They suggest that these patients be treated in close collaboration with a mental health professional. While these results are encouraging, this approach to working with patients with significant pathology is uncommon.

A thorough psychiatric history should be obtained on all persons interested in cosmetic procedures. Patients should be asked about both current and past diagnoses. Patients with a history of psychopathology who are not currently in treatment should be assessed for the need for treatment. Patients under psychiatric care should be asked if that professional is aware of their interest in cosmetic medical treatment. These professionals should be contacted to confirm that the patient is presently appropriate for treatment. Unwillingness to allow the provider to be contacted or admission that the patient has not shared his or her appearance concerns with the mental health professional may be indicative of psychopathology.

Appearance Concerns and Body Dysmorphic Disorder

The assessment of body image concerns may be the most important component of the consultation with patients interested in cosmetic medical treatment (Sarwer, 2001, 2002; Sarwer & Didie, 2002; Sarwer & Pertschuk, 2002). Patients should be asked to discuss their appearance concerns, and they should be able to describe them in detail. The consulting professional should be able to see the focus of concern rather easily. Patients concerned with features that look relatively normal or those who are concerned with features not readily visible to the professional may be suffering from BDD.

The mental health professional should inquire about the degree of distress associated with the feature. The amount of time spent thinking about, checking, or fixing the appearance feature should be assessed. It is also important to determine the degree of disruption in daily activity. Patients who report becoming very upset when thinking about their appearance, those who spend more than one hour a day focused on their appearance, and those who report significant avoidance of activity may be suffering from BDD.

Male and Adolescent Patients

Just over 1 million men underwent cosmetic medical procedures in 2001, representing 12% of all patients (ASAPS, 2002). The aesthetic surgery community typically has viewed male patients with a significant degree of skepticism. In the first study of male cosmetic surgery patients, all 18 patients studied were diagnosed as psychotic, neurotic, or personality disordered (Jacobson, Edgerton, Meyer, Canter, & Slaughter, 1960). Although future studies of male patients found few differences as compared to female patients (Hay, 1970; Pertschuk et al., 1998), the perception of male patients as being psychopathological has endured. Given that men still represent a small percentage of persons who seek cosmetic medical treatments, a psychopathological male patient may be more likely to remain in the mind of a surgeon as compared to a problematic female patient (Sarwer & Crerand, 2002).

In 2001, 298,704 individuals under the age of 18 underwent cosmetic procedures (ASAPS, 2002). This represents an increase of approximately 70% since 1999. Many of these procedures treat skin and acne problems common in adolescence. Nevertheless, an increasing number of adolescents are enhancing their appearance with cosmetic medicine. These treatments are somewhat controversial because little is known about the psychological characteristics of adolescents who seek these procedures or the effects of the procedures on their developing bodies (Sarwer, 2001). Because the onset of both BDD and eating disorders typically occurs during adolescence, mental health professionals encountering adolescents interested in these treatments should pay particular attention to these disorders.

Postoperative Consultations

Physicians offering cosmetic treatment typically ask for a mental health consultation postoperatively in one of two scenarios (Sarwer, 2001, 2002; Sarwer & Didie, 2002; Sarwer & Pertschuk, 2002). The treating physician may ask the mental health professional to assess a patient who is dissatisfied with a technically successful surgery. In other cases, the physician identifies psychopathology that was not detected preoperatively. These patients are frequently better candidates for psychotherapeutic or psychiatric care rather than additional surgery. Cognitive-behavioral models of body image psychotherapy (e.g., Cash, 1996; Rosen, 1996) may be useful with these patients. In some cases, diagnosis-specific treatments may be warranted.

CONCLUSIONS

The popularity of cosmetic medical treatments has exploded over the past decade. Safer, minimally invasive procedures, mass media influences, and an increased willingness to alter and enhance our bodies are all factors that may help account for the growth of these treatments. Because the benefits of these procedures are both physical and psychological in nature, research on the psychological characteristics of these patients, particularly their body image concerns, has become an area of increased interest to both medical and mental health professionals. At present, the relationship between psychopathology and the pursuit of these treatments is somewhat unclear. It appears, however, that certain body image-related disorders, such as BDD, may be over-represented among persons who seek these procedures. Thus, both the physicians who offer these treatments and the mental health professionals who consult with them need to be aware of the psychological issues, particularly the body image concerns, of these patients. Additional studies of preoperative psychopathology and its relationship to postoperative outcome are needed to help us better understand this growing population of individuals.

REFERENCES

American Psychiatric Association. (1987). *Diagnostic and statistical manual of mental disorders* (3rd ed., rev.). Washington, DC: Author.

American Psychiatric Association. (1994). *Diagnostic and statistical manual of mental disorders* (4th ed.). Washington, DC: Author.

American Society for Aesthetic Plastic Surgery. (2002). *Cosmetic Surgery National Data Bank—2001 statistics.* New York: Author.

American Society of Plastic Surgeons. (2002). *National Clearinghouse of Plastic Surgery Statistics.* Arlington Heights, IL: Author.

Baker, J. L., Kolin, I. S., & Bartlett, E. S. (1974). Psychosexual dynamics of patients undergoing mammary augmentation. *Plastic and Reconstructive Surgery, 53,* 652–659.

Brown, T. A., Cash, T. F., & Mikulka, P. J. (1990). Attitudinal body image assessment: Factor analysis of the Body Self Relations Questionnaire. *Journal of Personality Assessment, 55*, 135–144.

Cash, T. F. (1996). The treatment of body-image disturbances. In J. K. Thompson (Ed.), *Body image, eating disorders, and obesity* (pp. 83–107). Washington, DC: American Psychological Association.

Cash, T. F., Duel, L. A., & Perkins, L. L. (2002). Women's psychosocial outcomes of breast augmentation with silicone gel-filled implants: A 2-year prospective study. *Plastic and Reconstructive Surgery, 109*, 2112–2121.

Cash, T. F., & Horton, C. E. (1983). Aesthetic surgery: Effects of rhinoplasty on the social perception of patients by others. *Plastic and Reconstructive Surgery, 72*, 543–550.

Didie, E. R., & Sarwer, D. B. (in press). Factors which influence the decision to undergo cosmetic breast augmentation surgery. *Journal of Women's Health.*

Dufresne, R. G., Phillips, K. A., Vittorio, C. C., & Wilkel, C. S. (2001). A screening questionnaire for body dysmorphic disorder in a cosmetic dermatologic surgery practice. *Dermatologic Surgery, 27*, 457–462.

Dunofsky, M. (1997). Psychological characteristics of women who undergo single and multiple cosmetic surgeries. *Annals of Plastic Surgery, 39*, 223–228.

Eagly, A. H., Ashmore, R. D., Makhijani, M. G., & Longo, L. C. (1991). What is beautiful is good, but . . . : A meta-analytic review of research on the physical attractiveness stereotype. *Psychological Bulletin, 110*, 109–128.

Edgerton, M. T., Jacobson, W. E., & Meyer, E. (1960). Surgical-psychiatric study of patients seeking plastic (cosmetic) surgery: Ninety-eight consecutive patients with minimal deformity. *British Journal of Plastic Surgery, 13*, 136–145.

Edgerton, M. T., & Knorr, N. J. (1971). Motivational patterns of patients seeking cosmetic (aesthetic) surgery. *Plastic and Reconstructive Surgery, 48*, 551–557.

Edgerton, M. T., Langman, M. W., & Pruzinsky, T. (1991). Plastic surgery and psychotherapy in the treatment of 100 psychologically disturbed patients. *Plastic and Reconstructive Surgery, 88*, 594–608.

Ercolani, M., Baldaro, B., Rossi, N., & Trombini, G. (1999). Five-year follow-up of cosmetic rhinoplasty. *Journal of Psychosomatic Research, 47*(3), 283–286.

Etcoff, N. L. (1999). *Survival of the prettiest.* New York: Doubleday.

Feingold, A. (1992). Good looking people are not what we think. *Psychological Bulletin, 111*, 304–341.

Garner, D. M. (1997). The 1997 body image survey results. *Psychology Today*, 32–84.

Garner, D. M., Garfield, P. E., Schwartz, D., & Thompson, M. (1980). Cultural expectations of thinness in women. *Psychological Reports, 47*, 483–491.

Glatt, B. S., Sarwer, D. B., O'Hara, D. E., Hamori, C., Bucky, L. P., & LaRossa, D. (1999). A retrospective study of changes in physical symptoms and body image after reduction mammaplasty. *Plastic and Reconstructive Surgery, 103*, 76–82.

Goin, M. K., Burgoyne, R. W., Goin, J. M., & Staples, F. R. (1980). A prospective psychological study of 50 female face-lift patients. *Plastic and Reconstructive Surgery, 65*, 436–442.

Goin, M. K., & Rees, T. D. (1991). A prospective study of patients' psychological reactions to rhinoplasty. *Annals of Plastic Surgery, 27*, 210–215.

Hay, G. G. (1970). Psychiatric aspects of cosmetic nasal operations. *British Journal of Psychiatry, 116*, 85–97.

Hollyman, J. A., Lacey, J. H., Whitfield, P. J., & Wilson, J. S. P. (1986). Surgery for the psyche: A longitudinal study of women undergoing reduction mammaplasty. *British Journal of Plastic Surgery, 39*, 222–224.

Ishigooka, J., Iwao, M., Suzuki, M., Fukuyama, Y., Murasaki, M., & Miura, S. (1998). Demographic features of patients seeking cosmetic surgery. *Psychiatry and Clinical Neurosciences, 52*, 283–287.

Jacobson, W. E., Edgerton, M. T., Meyer, E., Canter, A., & Slaughter, R. (1960). Psychiatric evaluation of male patients seeking cosmetic surgery. *Plastic and Reconstructive Surgery, 26*, 356–372.

Kalick, S. M. (1979). Aesthetic surgery: How it affects the way patients are perceived by others. *Annals of Plastic Surgery, 2*(2), 128–134.

Katzmarzyk, P. T., & Davis, C. (2001). Thinness and body shape of *Playboy* centerfolds from 1978 to 1988. *International Journal of Obesity and Related Metabolic Disorders, 25*(4), 590–592.

Killman, P. R., Sattler, J. I., & Taylor, J. (1987). The impact of augmentation mammaplasty: A follow-up study. *Plastic and Reconstructive Surgery, 80,* 374–378.

Knorr, N. J. (1972). Feminine loss of identity in rhinoplasty. *Archives of Otolaryngology, 96,* 11–15.

Langlois, J. H., Kalakanis, L., Rubenstein, A. J., Larson, A., Hallam, M., & Smoot, M. (2000). Maxims of myths of beauty? A meta-analytic and theoretical review. *Psychological Bulletin, 126,* 390–423.

Losee, J. E., Serletti, J. M., Kreipe, R. E., & Caldwell, E. H. (1997). Reduction mammaplasty in patients with bulimia nervosa. *Annals of Plastic Surgery, 39,* 443–446.

Mazur, A. (1986). U.S. trends in feminine beauty and overadaptation. *Journal of Sex Research, 22,* 281–303.

McIntosh, V. V., Britt, E., & Bulik, C. M. (1994). Cosmetic breast augmentation and eating disorders. *New Zealand Medical Journal, 107,* 151–152.

Meyer, E., Jacobson, W. E., Edgerton, M. T., & Canter, A. (1960). Motivational patterns in patients seeking elective plastic surgery. *Psychosomatic Medicine, 22,* 193–202.

Micheli-Pellegrini, V., & Manfrieda, C. M. (1979). Rhinoplasty and its psychological implications: Applied psychology observations in aesthetic surgery. *Aesthetic Plastic Surgery, 3,* 299–319.

Napoleon, A. (1993). The presentation of personalities in plastic surgery. *Annals of Plastic Surgery, 31,* 193–208.

Nordmann, J. E. (1998). *Body image and self-esteem in women seeking breast augmentation.* Unpublished doctoral dissertation, MCP Hahnemann University, Pennsylvania.

Pertschuk, M. J., Sarwer, D. B., Wadden, T. A., & Whitaker, L. A. (1998). Body image dissatisfaction in male cosmetic surgery patients. *Aesthetic Plastic Surgery, 22,* 20–24.

Phillips, K. A., & Diaz, S. F. (1997). Gender differences in body dysmorphic disorder. *Journal of Nervous and Mental Diseases, 185,* 570–577.

Phillips, K. A., Dufresne, R. G., Jr., Wilkel, C. S., & Vittorio, C. C. (2000). Rate of body dysmorphic disorder in dermatology patients. *Journal of the American Academy of Dermatology, 42*(3), 436–441.

Phillips, K. A., Grant, J., Siniscalchi, J., & Albertini, R. S. (2001). Surgical and nonpsychiatric medical treatment of patients with body dysmorphic disorder. *Psychosomatics, 42,* 504–510.

Pruzinsky, T. (1996). Cosmetic plastic surgery and body image: Critical factors in patient assessment. In J. K. Thompson (Ed.), *Body image, eating disorders, and obesity* (pp. 109–127). Washington, DC: American Psychological Association.

Pruzinsky, T., & Edgerton, M. T. (1990). Body image change in cosmetic plastic surgery. In T. F. Cash & T. Pruzinsky (Eds.), *Body image: Development, deviance, and change* (pp. 217–236). New York: Guilford Press.

Rankin, M., & Borah, G. L. (1997). Anxiety disorders in plastic surgery. *Plastic and Reconstructive Surgery, 100*(2), 535–542.

Rankin, M., Borah, G. L., Perry, A. W., & Wey, P. D. (1998). Quality-of-life outcomes after cosmetic surgery. *Plastic and Reconstructive Surgery, 102,* 2139–2145.

Rosen, J. C. (1996). Body dysmorphic disorder: Assessment and treatment. In J. K. Thompson (Ed.), *Body image, eating disorders, and obesity* (pp. 149–170). Washington, DC: American Psychological Association.

Rosen, J. C., & Reiter, J. (1996). Development of the body dysmorphic disorder examination. *Behavior Research and Therapy, 34,* 755–766.

Rubenstein, S., & Caballero, B. (2000). Is Miss America an undernourished role model? *Journal of the American Medical Association, 283,* 1569.

Sarwer, D. B. (2001). Plastic surgery in children and adolescents. In J. K. Thompson & L. Smolak (Eds.), *Body image, eating disorders, and obesity in children and adolescents: Theory, assessment, treatment, and prevention* (pp. 341–366). Washington, DC: American Psychiatric Press.

Sarwer, D. B. (2002). Cosmetic surgery and changes in body image. In T. F. Cash & T. Pruzinsky (Eds.), *Body image: A handbook of theory, research, and clinical practice* (pp. 422–430). New York: Guilford Press.

Sarwer, D. B., Bartlett, S. P., Bucky, L. P., LaRossa, D., Low, D. W., Pertschuk, M. J., et al. (1998). Bigger is not always better: Body image dissatisfaction in breast reduction and breast augmentation patients. *Plastic and Reconstructive Surgery, 101,* 1956–1961.

Sarwer, D. B., & Crerand, C. E. (2002). Psychological issues in patient outcomes. *Facial Plastic Surgery, 18,* 125–133.

Sarwer, D. B., Crerand, C. E., & Didie, E. R. (2003). Body dysmorphic disorder in cosmetic surgery patients. *Facial Plastic Surgery, 19,* 7–17

Sarwer, D. B., & Didie, E. R. (2002). Body image in cosmetic surgical and dermatological practice. In D. J. Castle & K. A. Phillips (Eds.), *Disorders of body image* (pp. 37–53). Hampshire, England: Wrightson Biomedical.

Sarwer, D. B., Grossbart, T. A., & Didie, E. R. (2002). Beauty and society. In M. S. Kaminer, J. S. Dover, & K. A. Arndt (Eds.), *Atlas of cosmetic surgery* (pp. 48–59). Philadelphia: Saunders.

Sarwer, D. B., LaRossa, D., Bartlett, S. P., Low, D. W., Bucky, L. P., & Whitaker, L. A. (in press). Body image concerns of breast augmentation patients. *Plastic and Reconstructive Surgery.*

Sarwer, D. B., Magee, L., & Clark, V. L. (in press). Physical appearance and cosmetic medical treatments: Physiological and sociocultural influences. *Journal of Cosmetic Dermatology.*

Sarwer, D. B., & Pertschuk, M. J. (2002). Cosmetic surgery. In S. G. Kornstein & A. H. Clayton (Eds.), *Textbook of women's mental health* (pp. 481–496). New York: Guilford Press.

Sarwer, D. B., Wadden, T. A., Pertschuk, M. J., & Whitaker, L. A. (1998a). Body image dissatisfaction and body dysmorphic disorder in 100 cosmetic surgery patients. *Plastic and Reconstructive Surgery, 101,* 1644–1649.

Sarwer, D. B., Wadden, T. A., Pertschuk, M. J., & Whitaker, L. A. (1998b). The psychology of cosmetic surgery: A review and reconceptualization. *Clinical Psychology Review, 18,* 1–22.

Sarwer, D. B., Wadden, T. A., & Whitaker, L. A. (2002). An investigation of changes in body image following cosmetic surgery. *Plastic and Reconstructive Surgery, 109,* 363–369.

Sarwer, D. B., Whitaker, L. A., Pertschuk, M. J., & Wadden, T. A. (1998). Body image concerns of reconstructive surgery patients: An under recognized problem. *Annals of Plastic Surgery, 40,* 404–407.

Sarwer, D. B., Whitaker, L. A., Wadden, T. A., & Pertschuk, M. J. (1997). Body image dissatisfaction in women seeking rhytidectomy or blepharoplasty. *Aesthetic Surgery Journal, 17,* 230–234.

Schlebusch, L. (1989). Negative bodily experience and prevalence of depression in patients who request augmentation mammaplasty. *South African Medical Journal, 75,* 323–326.

Schlebusch, L., & Levin, A. (1983). A psychological profile of women selected for augmentation mammaplasty. *South African Medical Journal, 64,* 481–486.

Shipley, R. H., O'Donnell, J. M., & Bader, K. F. (1977). Personality characteristics of women seeking breast augmentation. *Plastic and Reconstructive Surgery, 60,* 369–376.

Sihm, F., Jagd, M., & Pers, M. (1978). Psychological assessment before and after augmentation mammaplasty. *Scandinavian Journal of Plastic and Reconstructive Surgery, 12,* 295–298.

Singh, D. (1993). Adaptive significance of female physical attractiveness: Role of waist-to-hip ratio. *Journal of Personality and Social Psychology, 65,* 293–307.

Singh, D. (1995). Female health, attractiveness, and desirability for relationships: Role of breast asymmetry and waist-to-hip ratio. *Ethology and Sociobiology, 16,* 465–481.

Singh, D., & Young, R. K. (1995). Body weight, waist-to-hip ratio, breasts, and hips: Role of judgments of female attractiveness and desirability for relationships. *Ethology and Sociobiology, 16,* 483–507.

Veale, D. (2000). Outcome of cosmetic surgery and DIY surgery in patients with body dysmorphic disorder. *Psychiatric Bulletin, 24,* 218–221.

Veale, D., Boocock, A., Gournay, K., Dryden, W., Shah, F., Willson, R., et al. (1996). Body dysmorphic disorder: A survey of fifty cases. *British Journal of Psychiatry, 169,* 196–201.

Walden, K. J., Thompson, J. K., & Wells, K. E. (1997). Body image and psychological sequelae of silicone breast explantation: Preliminary findings. *Plastic and Reconstructive Surgery, 100,* 1299–1306.

Webb, W. L., Slaughter, R., Meyer, E., & Edgerton, M. (1965). Mechanisms of psychosocial adjustment in patients seeking "face-lift" operation. *Psychosomatic Medicine, 27,* 183–192.

Wengle, H. P. (1986). The psychology of cosmetic surgery: A critical overview of the literature 1960–1982-Part I. *Annals of Plastic Surgery, 16,* 435–443.

Wicklegren, I. (1998). Obesity: How big a problem? *Science, 280,* 1364–1367.

Willard, S. G., McDermott, B. E., & Woodhouse, L. M. (1996). Lipoplasty in the bulimic patient. *Plastic and Reconstructive Surgery, 98,* 276–278.

Wiseman, C. V., Gray, J. J., Mosimann, J. E., & Ahrens, A. H. (1992). Cultural expectations of thinness in women: An update. *International Journal of Eating Disorders, 11,* 85–89.

World Health Organization. (1992). *The ICD-10 classification of mental and behavioral disorders.* Geneva, Switzerland: Author.

Wright, M. R., & Wright, W. K. (1975). A psychological study of patients undergoing cosmetic surgery. *Archives of Otolaryngology, 101,* 145–151.

Yates, A., Shisslak, C. M., Allender, J. R., & Wollman, W. (1988). Plastic surgery and the bulimic patient. *International Journal of Eating Disorders, 7,* 557–560.

Chapter 35

FUTURE DIRECTIONS IN EATING DISORDER AND OBESITY RESEARCH

LINDA SMOLAK AND RUTH H. STRIEGEL-MOORE

In the late twentieth and early twenty-first centuries, body image and eating disorders became the focus of numerous research studies. Journals, including the *International Journal of Eating Disorders, Eating Disorders: The Journal of Treatment and Prevention,* the *European Review of Eating Disorders,* and *Body Image,* were founded to accommodate the burgeoning research. All relevant medical and psychological journals, including *American Journal of Psychiatry, Developmental Psychology, Pediatrics,* and *Journal of Abnormal Psychology,* published articles on body image and eating problems. During this same period, rates of obesity grew among children and adults of all ages and ethnicities so that eventually obesity came to be considered a major, perhaps the major, public health problem in the United States.

As this volume and other recent books (Cash & Pruzinsky, 2002; Fairburn & Brownell, 2002; Striegel-Moore & Smolak, 2001; Thompson, Heinberg, Altabe, & Tantleff-Dunn, 1999; Thompson & Smolak, 2001) indicate, considerable progress has been made in understanding, treating, and preventing body image and eating problems. There are, for example, data indicating that internalization of the thin body ideal presented by the media, peers, and parents increases the risk that an adolescent girl will develop an eating disorder (McKnight Investigators, 2003; Thompson & Stice, 2001). We are also beginning to understand the molecular genetics of obesity (Cope, Fernández, & Allison, Chapter 16 in this volume). Evidence further suggests that cognitive-behavior therapy (CBT) is relatively efficacious in treating bulimia nervosa (e.g., Peterson, Wonderlich, Mitchell, & Crow, Chapter 12, this volume). The components of effective prevention programs are being delineated conceptually and empirically (e.g., Levine & Piran, 2001; Levine & Smolak, in press; Stice & Hoffman, Chapter 3, this volume). These examples underscore the diversity of research efforts and successes in the field.

At the same time, there are surprising gaps in our knowledge. In a recent review of more than 100 studies of recovery from anorexia nervosa, Steinhausen (2002, p. 1284) concluded that "There was no convincing evidence that the outcome of anorexia nervosa improved over the second half of the last century." In reviewing the literature on atypical eating disorders, Fairburn and Walsh (2002, p. 173) claim that "there have been no formal descriptive studies in which their psychopathology has been well assessed." Garvin and Striegel-Moore (2001) suggested that even basic epidemiological data are lacking, leaving unanswered, for example, the question of how many individuals in the United States experience an eating disorder. Although epidemiologic data in other countries are available (see Hoek, 2002), studies in Europe or Canada do not include ethnic minority groups. Data are sketchy at best (and, in some cases, nonexistent) concerning atypical eating disorders, men, children, older adults, and ethnic minority groups.

This chapter outlines several important questions that urgently need to be addressed. By necessity, these goals are broadly phrased. We do not offer specific research hypotheses. Furthermore, we have tried to address a wide range of issues covering classification, etiology, treatment, and prevention of body image and eating problems as well as obesity. These issues are raised in the hope of stimulating research that will ultimately allow us to better serve the population of people who are affected by the entire range of body shape and eating-related problems.

CLASSIFICATION AND EPIDEMIOLOGY

The *Diagnostic and Statistical Manual of Mental Disorders,* fourth edition (*DSM-IV*; American Psychiatric Association [APA], 1994), recognizes three eating disorders (ED): anorexia nervosa (AN), bulimia nervosa (BN), and binge eating disorder (BED). BED is considered a provisional category. Franko, Wonderlich, Little, and Herzog (Chapter 4, this volume) remind us of the importance of the definitions we use for these disorders. Franko and her colleagues also point out a number of questions about the *DSM-IV* definitions. We focus on two: What characterizes eating disorders not otherwise specified (EDNOS), and how can typologies better accommodate the heterogeneous clinical presentations of eating disorders? And, are the symptoms of eating disorders culture, gender, or age specific?

Eating Disorders Not Otherwise Specified and Typology

Despite extensive criticism of the *DSM* typology (see Striegel-Moore & Marcus, 1995, for a review), the classification of eating disorders has remained essentially unchanged. Perhaps the most problematic aspect of the current classification scheme is the fact that it leaves unspecified the symptom picture of the majority of individuals who present for treatment due to problematic eating behaviors (Andersen et al., 2001). This large group also is heterogeneous in its clinical presentation. The diagnosis of EDNOS includes several distinct subgroups: individuals whose eating disorder symptoms fail to reach the severity or duration threshold required for a diagnosis of AN or BN, individuals with atypical eating disorders, and individuals whose clinical picture is marked by recurrent binge eating in the absence of the inappropriate compensatory behaviors that characterize BN. The latter clinical picture has been designated provisionally as BED, an eating disorder in need of further study. This designation has had a tremendous impact on research activity, as reflected by the growing number of studies that have focused (in some instances, exclusively) on BED. While few would question that the diagnosis of BED does describe a distinct clinical picture, the question of whether BED should remain a diagnosis separate from BN remains, however, unresolved (Strober, in press). Because the EDNOS category has "secondary" status to the "named" eating categories, few studies have been conducted to better define and examine the various syndrome constellations, other than BED, that may be captured under this designation. Consequently, little is known about the etiology, clinical course, treatment, or prognosis of the EDNOS syndromes.

There is a pressing need to better define EDNOS; nevertheless, as Franko and colleagues (Chapter 4, this volume) illustrate so compellingly, research is needed to reconsider the entire *DSM-IV* eating disorder typology to address conceptual inconsistencies and the clinical reality that the boundaries among the eating disorders are not as distinct as the typology might lead us to believe. Experts have tried a number of strategies, including latent class analysis (Bulik et al., 2000), taxometric analyses (Gleaves et al., 2000; Joiner, Vohs, & Heatherton, 2000), and expanding the focus to include personality profiles (e.g., Wonderlich & Mitchell, 2001) or biological indicators (e.g., Steiger et al., 2001) as a basis for organizing the typology. The scientific merit of these varied approaches will be maximized if investigators can agree on a common assessment protocol of both the core eating pathology and the related dysfunctions (e.g., personality or biological parameters) to permit comparisons across studies or reanalysis of data based on different theoretical frameworks. Finally, almost completely absent in this research is a comprehensive discussion of how best to establish "clinical significance" of various eating pathologies (Striegel-Moore & Marcus, 1995).

Are Eating Disorder Symptoms Culture, Gender, or Age Specific?

There is a question as to whether the current definitions are biased toward the European or North American experience of ED and less applicable to other cultures. Much of this debate centers on the requirement of "an intense fear of gaining weight or becoming fat, even though underweight" in diagnosing AN (APA, 1994, p. 326). As Franko et al. (Chapter 4, this volume) note, many authors consider this "fat phobia" to be the raison d'être of AN. This is, they argue, what sets the weight loss in AN apart from the weight loss in other psychiatric disorders, including somatization disorders and depression.

Yet, other authors suggest that in other cultures and other periods of history a substantial number of women presenting with egosyntonic self-starvation that looks like AN are not fat-phobic (Lee, Lee, Ngai, Lee, & Wing, 2001; Ramacciotti et al., 2002). Indeed, some American women fit this description, too, though they may be categorized as "atypical" rather than AN. This has led several authors to argue that it is either the egosyntonic element or a need for control in the face of conflicting messages or changing environments that is at the core of AN (Katzman & Lee, 1997; Lee & Katzman, 2002; Rieger, Touyz, Swain, & Beumont, 2001). Franko and her colleagues (Chapter 4, this volume) point out that, among American women, research has shown that those suffering from AN without the "fat phobia" component seem to recover more fully than those whose clinical picture includes fat phobia. Research is needed to ascertain whether this is true in other countries also. Research also needs to address the relationship of "fat phobia" to maintaining an egosyntonic perspective on weight loss and to the need to gain control over some part of the individual's life.

Another problematic aspect of the current nosology is that it defines ED in gendered terms. For example, one of the core criteria for AN is amenorrhea, a symptom that only women may experience. In definitions of BN, the emphasis on inappropriate compensatory behaviors has been skewed toward weight control behaviors that are more common among females than males, such as vomiting or using laxatives or diuretics for weight control (Lewinsohn, Seeley, Moerk, & Striegel-Moore, 2002). Excessive exercise for weight control purposes, a behavior that is common among males has not received adequate attention and, as a result, remains poorly defined and measured. Males are less likely than females to experience overeating as "out of control" and, therefore, are less likely to meet criteria for binge eating. Because epidemiological studies typically use an initial question about binge eating and "skip" subsequent diagnostic questions if the respondent denies presence of binge eating, we do not have scientific data to answer the question of whether overeating without a self-reported sense of loss of control should be considered a symptom of an eating disorder. Moreover, the question of whether inappropriate efforts to increase muscle mass should be captured under the category of eating disorders has not yet been considered fully. As McCabe and Ricciardelli document in Chapter 29 of this volume, among males, steroid use for improving physical appearance is as common as vomiting is among females. Furthermore, they describe research documenting the considerable adverse effects of steroid use on health and mental health. Yet, steroid use has not yet received the same type of attention as has been devoted to vomiting. Because of the gendered definition of ED, males with disordered weight and eating-related behaviors have not been studied much. A particularly pressing concern is the fact that the evidence base for the treatment of males with ED is sketchy at best.

BIOLOGICAL FACTORS AND EATING DISORDERS

In beginning her discussion of genetic risk factors, Cynthia Bulik (Chapter 1, this volume) states that the findings concerning genetic influences are "sufficiently strong and adequately replicated to warrant the recommendation that all individuals in the field consider developing at least a passing familiarity with their meaning and their implications for etiology, prevention, and treatment of eating disorders." This recommendation can easily be extended to research focusing on biochemical and pharmacological factors in eating disorders. Future research needs to not only expand our understanding of genetic, biochemical, and pharmacological influences and treatments but also integrate it effectively with extant sociocultural and cognitive knowledge.

Distinctions Need to Be Made among Etiology, Maintenance, and Relapse of Symptoms

The pharmacological literature reviewed by de Zwaan, Roerig, and Mitchell (Chapter 9, this volume) makes it clear that there are distinctions among etiology, maintenance, and relapse. While some pharmacological treatments help in resolving symptoms, others are effective in preventing relapse. Indeed, some treatments that are ineffective in reducing symptoms, perhaps because malnutrition interferes with their absorption, are helpful once more normal eating is restored.

This distinction is important for both future biochemical and sociocultural research. Because of the low base rate of eating disorders, particularly AN, biochemical researchers have often compared women who have "recovered" from eating disorders to women with no history of eating disorders (Kaye & Strober, 1999). One problem with this approach is that eating disorders create biochemical changes that may be more or less permanent. Hence, we may be misled about what biochemical factors contribute to the onset of ED, although we cannot overstate the importance of knowing the biochemistry of the maintenance of and relapse back into ED symptoms.

De Zwaan and her colleagues (Chapter 9, this volume) document the relatively poor performance of antidepressants, including the selective serotonin reuptake inhibitors (SSRIs), in eliminating bulimic symptoms and even in maintaining a reduction of bulimic symptoms. There are many possible explanations for this. One is that our assumptions concerning the role of serotonin in the development and maintenance of BN is problematic. Only prospective research can resolve this issue, and we need such longitudinal data to allow us to distinguish between the biochemistry of the onset, maintenance, and relapse of ED. The biochemical research will, in turn, help us to develop increasingly effective treatments, including, perhaps, very early intervention pharmacology.

Research concerning sociocultural factors faces the same challenge. As Field (Chapter 2, this volume) notes, we need the type of prospective research just described to identify risk factors. The problem so far has been finding a point in development when there is no investment in the thin ideal or no body dissatisfaction. Most research participants are adolescents or adults, so the putative "precursors" to eating disorders need to be controlled statistically. In fact, body dissatisfaction or thin-ideal internalization may be early symptoms of eating disorders. Again, then, researchers need to carefully delineate factors that cause, intensify, or maintain eating disorders and their symptoms.

Equifinality and Equipotentiality

Recent studies of genetic linkage in ED (e.g., Bulik et al., 2003) begin by selecting families in which two or more members suffer from an eating disorder. While risks of developing an eating disorder are certainly higher if a family member suffers from an eating disorder, concordance rates for BN in monozygotic twins are substantially below 50% (e.g., Kendler et al., 1991). Furthermore, as Bulik notes (Chapter 1, this volume), "heterogeneity in a sample can reduce underlying linkage signals." So, genetic research tends to narrow the participant or symptom pool when possible, focusing on restricting AN or on vomiting. This implies that the research is looking at a specific subset of people suffering from eating problems.

The focus on a subset of ED sufferers raises the possibility that the disorders we currently consider eating disorders are a more heterogeneous group than we have acknowledged. This contention is further underscored by the relative effectiveness of cyproheptadine with restricting AN as opposed to purging AN or bingeing (see de Zwaan et al., Chapter 9, this volume). We are seeing evidence, then, of what developmental psychopathology models refer to as *equifinality*. There are multiple pathways to similar symptoms. Research may find that genetics is involved in some forms of eating disorders more than others. Similarly, sociocultural factors may play a larger role in some cases than in others. Stice's (2001) dual pathway model of BN provides an example of a model that considers the possibility of equifinality. In future research, we need to more carefully consider such differences in outcomes as well as in risk and protective factors.

Future research should also more carefully consider equipotentiality, the possibility that a risk factor can contribute to multiple outcomes. One core issue here is distinguishing affective disorders from eating disorders. We must also more effectively distinguish which symptoms are attributable to or maintained by the different disorders. As de Zwaan and her colleagues (Chapter 9, this volume) describe, psychopharmacological research has already begun this process. For example, antidepressants can alleviate the mood problems and obsessive elements accompanying AN even if weight does not improve. Sociocultural research has also increasingly considered equipotentiality as exemplified by Stice and Bearman's (2001) findings that body dissatisfaction is associated with the development of both depression and eating problems. Genetic and biochemical research will need to address these issues in the future.

INTEGRATION WITH SOCIOCULTURAL MODELS

De Zwaan and her colleagues (Chapter 9, this volume) hypothesize that chronic binge eating and vomiting affect the vagus nerve in a way that actually maintains disordered eating. This reminds us of the fact that experience can shape physiological responses—a broadly accepted principle in developmental neuroscience (e.g., McLellan, 2002; Ruda, Ling, Hohmann, Peng, & Tachibana, 2000). There are other examples of this in the ED literature, such as the finding that even moderate dieting by women affects l-tryptophan levels and, hence, perhaps, 5HT. This, in turn, might affect binge eating (Anderson, Parry-Billings, Newsholme, Fairburn, & Cowen, 1990). Genetic researchers have long distinguished genotype from phenotype, a distinction that includes a role for the environment. Indeed, this distinction is the basis of the diathesis-stress model that continues to generate new theories of psychopathology.

Future researchers need to be more effective in integrating biological and sociocultural factors in our models of eating disorders. For example, what distinguishes monozygotic twins who are concordant for BN from pairs that are not? How much might early negative affect, a temperament characteristic that is likely genetically mediated (Bates, 1980), affect the development of ED? As the research of Martin et al. (2000) on this issue suggests, this relationship may be important for understanding the development of eating problems. But their research also raises the intriguing possibility that this is truer for girls than for boys. The question "Why women?" raised almost 20 years ago by Striegel-Moore, Silberstein, and Rodin (1986) returns in a new form: How do biology and culture combine to produce more eating disorders in women than in men? When we suggest that genetics or biochemistry is at the root of eating disorders, we must explain *why* that characteristic would occur or be exacerbated more commonly in women than in men.

TREATMENT

As illustrated by the impressive range of intervention described in this volume, significant advances have been made in the treatment of ED. Although CBT remains the forerunner in an increasingly crowded field of psychological treatments (see Pike, Devlin, & Loeb, Chapter 7, this volume), increasingly, empirical evidence is being accumulated in support of the use of other types of "talking cures." As evidenced by the advances in interpersonal psychotherapy (IPT; Tantleff-Dunn, Gokee-LaRose, & Peterson, Chapter 8), dialectical behavior therapy (DBT; McCabe, LaVia, & Marcus, Chapter 11, this volume), feminist therapy (Piran, Jasper, & Pinhas, Chapter 13, this volume), and several family therapy approaches (Lock, Chapter 10, this volume), many treatments now incorporate an interpersonal focus.

Three avenues are particularly pressing if we wish to advance the treatment of eating disorders: research of the efficacy of treatments of AN, studies identifying why and how treatments work, and effectiveness studies that answer broad implication questions.

Studies of Treatment Efficacy in Anorexia Nervosa

Fewer than a dozen randomized clinical trials (RCTs) have been published on the treatment of AN. A report by the Anorexia Nervosa Workgroup (in press) describes the challenges that have to be overcome in this research. One challenge arises from the fact that AN is relatively uncommon (compared to disorders such as depression, alcohol abuse, or anxiety disorders), making it difficult for investigators to recruit adequate samples within the typical time frame of an RCT study. To cope with this difficulty, investigators increasingly team up with colleagues for multisite trials. The high cost and considerable complexity of implementing multisite trials (Kraemer, 2000) make this approach feasible only for the more experienced investigator. Because research funding always is limited, the push toward multisite trials may lead to a reduction in funding for less experienced investigators.

Another challenge stems from the complexity of the disorder. Because of the often-severe health problems experienced by patients with AN, the treatment requires a multimodal approach. In practice, many treatments for AN share core components, making it difficult to determine which of the components (e.g., behavioral, cognitive, family therapy, medication) is effective and necessary for the overall efficacy of the treatment. Related, experts have called for a discussion of what forms of intervention comprise adequate control groups for RCT studies on AN, given that no or minimal treatment may not be clinically or ethically acceptable.

Why or How Do Treatments Work?

Few studies to date have examined the mechanisms that may underlie central treatment outcomes. As treatment outcome research in ED matures, increasingly, experts call for efforts to move beyond demonstrating that a given treatment works. Understanding for whom or why CBT helps many patients to improve or overcome their eating problems promises to allow us to develop more focused strategies or to specify subpopulations most suited for a particular treatment approach (Kraemer, Wilson, Fairburn, & Agras,

2002). Studies of the mediators of treatment require larger sample sizes, creating added challenges in terms of patient recruitment and project costs.

Effectiveness Studies

This volume illustrates the broad gains that have been made in developing empirically based psychological treatments for ED. While just a few years ago, RCT studies focused primarily on CBT (Whittal, Agras, & Gould, 1999), investigators now are examining the efficacy of other treatment modalities, including IPT (Tantleff-Dunn et al., Chapter 8, this volume), DBT (McCabe et al., Chapter 11, this volume), or family therapy (Lock, Chapter 10, this volume), and of treatments that seek to integrate components of various therapeutic approaches that had been found effective (Peterson et al., Chapter 12, this volume). Despite these encouraging developments, health services studies suggest that there is some cause for concern. Even though empirically validated treatments have been identified, only a minority of individuals with an eating disorder receive these treatments (Spitzer, Kroenke, & Williams, 1999). For example, a survey among health service providers found that only a small number used CBT (or even components of CBT) in their daily clinical practice with ED patients (Mussell et al., 2000). There seem to be two principal reasons for this gap in disseminating proven treatments to those who need them. The first arises from an inability or failure of patients to access treatment specifically for the eating disorder; the second arises from the inability or failure of health services providers to implement the proven treatments. Hence, even patients who access care specifically for their eating disorder are unlikely to benefit from the advances of RCT studies.

Underuse of mental health services results from a complex interplay of multiple determinants ranging from economic to demographic and personal factors (Bijl & Ravelli, 2000; Kessler et al., 1999). Certain population groups, especially men and ethnic minorities, appear to be particularly likely to be underrepresented among those obtaining treatment specifically for the eating disorder (Lewinsohn et al., 2002; Striegel-Moore, Leslie, Petrill, Garvin, & Rosenheck, 2000; Wilfley, Pike, Dohm, Striegel-Moore, & Fairburn, 2001). Studies focusing specifically on barriers to seeking treatment for an ED have included small, female samples of convenience; consequently, the reasons for underuse of treatments among the ED population are not well understood. Preliminary data suggest economic barriers (e.g., treatment is not covered by health insurance) and personal barriers such as lack of knowledge about the availability of treatment or fear of being stigmatized (Cachelin, Rebeck, Veisel, & Striegel-Moore, 2001; Cachelin, Veisel, Barzegarnazari, & Striegel-Moore, 2000). Future studies need to examine more fully the barriers to accessing ED treatment and test strategies aimed at eliminating or reducing the impact of such barriers.

Seemingly paradoxically, studies have shown that even though only a minority of individuals receive treatment specifically for the eating disorder, the population of individuals with an eating disorder tends to use health services more frequently than non-eating disorder individuals (Garvin & Striegel-Moore, 2001). For example, a British study found that patients who had been newly admitted to an ED treatment facility had visited their general practitioner significantly more often during the preceding five years, compared to non-eating-disordered individuals who were matched to the cases on age, sex, marital status, and socioeconomic status (Ogg, Millar, Pusztai, & Thom, 1997). In the United States, Johnson, Spitzer, and Williams (2001) found that women with BN and BED reported significantly more visits to a physician in the past three months, compared to patients with no psychiatric disorder. One reason for the underuse of eating disorder treatments may be the fact that few health service providers know of their patients' eating disorder. For example, a recent study of more than 3,000 primary care patients found that patients with a current eating disorder (7% of participating patients) were particularly likely to go undetected: The primary care physician was aware of the eating disorder in only 10% of all cases (Spitzer et al., 1999).

The underuse of empirically proven treatments for eating disorders is a serious problem because these treatments may reduce the burden of suffering in several ways. Patients treated successfully with these interventions, by definition, will no longer suffer from their eating disorder symptoms. Moreover, it is possible that by shortening the duration of their eating disorder, patients may reduce their risk for secondary health problems. Finally, effective treatment may result in a decrease in cost (cost offset) because total health utilization falls as a result of mental health intervention. There is continuing controversy about whether a cost offset exists for mental health treatments in general (Gabbard, Lazar, Hornberger, & Spiegel, 1997; Yates, 1994), and results vary by disorder (Lave, Frank, Schulberg, & Kamlet, 1998; Von Korff et al., 1998).

Cost Offset and Cost Effectiveness

Finally, little is known about the relative cost effectiveness of empirically proven treatments for eating disorders, leaving unanswered the important question of whether one type of treatment is less expensive than another treatment (Agras, 2001; Mitchell & Peterson, 1997). The eating disorder field has yet to enter into a sustained dialogue about the design issues in this area. In the only cost-effectiveness study published to date, Koran and colleagues (Koran, Agras, Rossiter, & Arnow, 1995) illustrate the complexities of cost-effectiveness analyses by providing several estimates of cost effectiveness using different definitions of outcome (abstinence versus symptom reduction) and of direct costs. Not surprisingly, results vary by outcome cost estimate, but overall, the data suggested that drug treatment was more cost effective than CBT. The authors outline several limitations, including the small number of patients in each intervention arm (four groups of 12 each and one of 23) and the limited assessment of costs. Because the study used self-referred and carefully screened patients to meet inclusion criteria, it is unclear whether results would generalize to samples that are more broadly representative of individuals with BN (Hargreaves, Shumway, Hu, & Cuffel, 1998). Larger and more diverse samples representing a broader spectrum of BN are needed to permit more stable estimates of costs and ensure adequate power for detecting meaningful differences across treatments. The study retrospectively measured the costs directly associated with the treatments and may have missed other treatment costs incurred during the study period or indirect costs of treatments. Experts have noted that medications typically need to be taken long term (Zhu & Walsh, 2002), an obvious factor to be considered in cost-effectiveness research. The study also did not measure the impact of the interventions on subsequent health care costs, information that would be needed for determining possible cost offsets due to the treatment for BN. More studies are needed in this important area of research.

PREVENTION

This book is dedicated to a discussion of the interrelated phenomena of body image disturbances, eating disorders, and obesity. While the precise nature of the interrelationships requires substantial new research, there is no doubt that there are at least some shared etiological and cognitive-behavioral features. Additionally, the chapters by Henderson and Brownell (Chapter 17, this volume) and by Stice and Hoffman (Chapter 3, this volume) explicitly demonstrate the public health costs of these problems. During the past decade, we have seen increasing acceptance of eating disorders as requiring prevention rather than only treatment. The sheer number of studies reviewed by Stice and Hoffman—even with their methodological exclusions—indicates this shift in orientation. Henderson and Brownell make a cogent argument for a similar perspective in the obesity field.

There is a pressing need for prevention programs in body image and eating disturbances as well as obesity. By definition, prevention programs aim to stop the development of a problem, either in the form of inhibiting the introduction of the problem (as vaccinations might do for smallpox) or by stopping early symptoms from developing into full-blown disorders (as cryosurgery might do for precancerous cervical cells). Stice and Hoffman's review (Chapter 3, this volume) indicates that we have made considerable progress in the latter. Targeted eating disorders prevention programs have met with considerable success. These programs reduce symptoms in high-risk women, presumably cutting the likelihood that they will eventually develop eating disorders. Indeed, Stice and Hoffman conclude that targeted programs working with older (> 15 years) samples have been the most successful. They suggest that "It may also be that younger participants have not struggled with body image and eating disturbances long enough for them to be sufficiently motivated to engage in prevention programs." We argue that one of our goals should be to prevent such struggles. These struggles are associated with a range of psychological and physical problems and, in some cases, lead to the dangerous intransigent obesity and eating disorders described throughout this volume. With that in mind, we offer three recommendations for themes in future prevention research.

Continuation of Research on Themes and Delivery Methods

Stice and Hoffman (Chapter 3, this volume) note that it is not completely clear what themes and methods are most effective in preventing eating disorders. They do discuss some interesting evidence suggesting that "There also appeared to be a trend for interventions that were not explicitly presented as eating disorder prevention programs to produce more positive effects." If this trend continues in future research, it bodes well for potentially integrating eating disorders and obesity programs (see following discussion) given that most of these "covert prevention programs" were presented as interventions for weight control or body acceptance.

There is much more research available on eating disorders prevention, and even the specific tact of media literacy, than on steroid abuse or obesity prevention. It is clear, then, that research on delivery systems and themes of prevention programs—in all of the areas covered in this book—is imperative. It is likely that these aspects do impact the effectiveness of programs. For example, the emphasis on cognitive methods to alter body image may partly explain the relative lack of success of prevention programs with elementary school children. Furthermore, both delivery and themes need to take into account the needs of the schools at which they are aimed. This, too, is likely to increase the efficacy of the programs by encouraging teachers, coaches, and other school personnel to more faithfully implement the programs. Delivery techniques also affect costs, so this, too, must be considered. Thus, considerable research is still needed to develop effective programs.

Focus on the Environment, Not Just the Individual

The chapters by Henderson and Brownell (Chapter 17, this volume), Anderson-Fye and Becker (Chapter 27, this volume), and Smolak and Murnen (Chapter 28, this volume) emphasize the *cultural* nature of obesity and eating disorders. The choice of the word *cultural* here is intentional. As Anderson-Fye and Becker detail, research from Asia, Africa, the Middle East, the Caribbean, and Latin America shows that eating problems vary across cultures; that as women move from one culture to another, their rates of eating disorders shift; and that changes in cultural traditions lead to changes in eating disorders. Becker's own research in Fiji is a cogent example of this (Becker, 1995). It is evident, then, that broadly defined cultural differences contribute to eating disorders.

Within American culture, we see evidence of ethnic group, gender, and, at least in terms of obesity, social class differences in body image, eating disorder, and obesity problems. McCabe and Ricciardelli (Chapter 29, this volume), Smolak and Murnen (Chapter 28, this volume), Levine and Harrison (Chapter 33, this volume), and Anderson-Fye and Becker (Chapter 27, this volume) all discuss important gender differences in the expression of body image and eating problems as well as in risk factors for their development. Eating patterns and exercise opportunities may contribute to social class differences in obesity. These and other chapters demonstrate the importance of various levels of cultural and social influences in the development and maintenance of eating disorders and obesity.

Yet, as Stice and Hoffman's chapter (Chapter 3, this volume) in particular evidences, the vast majority of prevention programs have focused on the individual. Girls and women are taught to value their own bodies, to stop dieting, and to resist teasing. Most of the media literacy programs described by Levine and Harrison (Chapter 33, this volume) emphasize teaching girls to critique, question, and resist media images and messages. With the skills they acquire in these prevention and media literacy programs, people are returned to what Henderson and Brownell (Chapter 17, this volume) refer to as "the toxic environment." Many people, perhaps especially young girls who are being exposed to pressure to be thin from family, peers, and media, are not likely to be able to sustain or even implement skills gained in these programs.

Prevention program designers need to acknowledge more clearly the "incontrovertible evidence that social and cultural contexts contribute to the risk for eating disorders" (Anderson-Fye and Becker, Chapter 27, this volume) as well as obesity. Programs need to do more to actually *change* the environment, as some of the media activism programs have done. Such changes, as suggested by various authors in this volume, might focus on peer teasing, objectification of women, or availability of fast food in schools.

Such research will be challenging. First, evaluation will be difficult. The type of experimental, pre-post, control group design appropriately favored in Stice and Hoffman's review (Chapter 3, this volume) will be difficult. Any control group typically should come from a different school (or college) and perhaps a different school district. Imagine, for example, a program that required policy changes and in-service education in terms of coach, teacher, and peer comments about weight and shape. Furthermore, what effects might we expect to find? Process evaluation in terms, for example, of whether negative comments really did decrease to some critical level would be a crucial first step. Only once this had been established might we reasonably expect to see effects on thin-ideal internalization or other risk factors.

How long would it take to see such results? We would almost certainly be looking at a long-term endeavor, one that is not likely to quickly appeal to funding agencies. Yet, it is precisely this type of prevention program that is consistent with a substantial— and growing—body of literature.

Integrate Body Image, Eating Disorder, and Obesity Concerns

Henderson and Brownell (Chapter 17, this volume) point out that obesity is a more costly and deadly public health problem than either alcohol or tobacco. Similarly, Stice and Hoffman (Chapter 3, this volume) outline not only the frequency and costs of eating disorders but also the potential role of body image and weight control behavior in the development of depression and obesity. The extent of all of these problems, coupled with the expense, limited availability, and relatively low success rates of treatment, argues for prevention programs.

But can schools or other organizations afford separate programs for obesity, eating disorders, and body image problems? Moreover, do we need separate programs for different ethnic groups and genders? For example, is a program such as the ATLAS program described by Levine and Harrison (Chapter 33, this volume) needed for boys while one of the girls-only programs described by Stice and Hoffman (Chapter 3, this volume) is implemented for the girls? Schools have neither the time nor the money nor the personnel to implement so many programs (Smolak, Harris, Levine, & Shisslak, 2001).

Obesity, body image, steroid abuse, and eating disorders are related problems. Their prevention programs share common goals of healthy eating, regular exercise, positive body image, and media literacy or activism. They might even share methods, such as encouraging daily exercise opportunities for young children or teaching coaches the dangers of pushing adolescents to achieve a particular weight or size to be successful. Furthermore, many activists have expressed concern that obesity programs might inadvertently encourage eating problems or that eating disorders prevention programs might facilitate obesity. Integrating obesity and eating disorders programs would alleviate some of these concerns.

Such integration efforts will require substantial research. First, more risk factor research is needed to identify shared or at least complementary etiological factors. These data will assist with identification of specific program goals. Second, appropriate target groups need to be identified. Stice and Hoffman (Chapter 3, this volume) present evidence suggesting better effectiveness with high-risk girls. Would this apply to obesity or to steroid prevention programs also? The lack of existing research in these areas makes it impossible to answer this question, even tentatively. Third, we need research looking at delivery methods for obesity and steroid prevention programs.

CONCLUSIONS

The chapters in this volume effectively review a broad range of topics concerning body image, eating disorders, and obesity. Despite the currency and coverage of this work, much is unknown about these phenomena. Indeed, in writing this chapter, we found it difficult to narrow our focus to a manageable set of "future direction" suggestions.

It is self-evident that the needed research outlined here and throughout this book will require substantial amounts of funding from both government and private sources. Currently, body image and eating disorders research are underfunded. Despite proclamations about the epidemic of obesity and its importance as a public health problem, little prevention research has been funded. We need to find ways to change this situation.

This requires at least two approaches. First, we need to find research proposals that appeal to funding agencies. Collaborative projects, ranging from multimodal treatment or prevention efforts to multisite research projects, are likely to hold such appeal. They are more likely to be cost effective, insomuch as they integrate approaches instead of requiring separate research projects for each perspective. Furthermore, at least in the field of prevention, multimodal projects are likely to carry greater appeal to potential users because they are broader in the ways that school districts (or other users) can implement them. Multisite projects also are likely to have greater external validity than are single-site endeavors, particularly in terms of ethnic groups. For studies of relatively uncommon phenomena, such as full syndrome AN, multisite studies enable an adequate number of participants and, hence, sufficient statistical power, particularly in longitudinal studies where attrition is often a problem.

Second, eating disorders professionals need to continue to educate the public in general and funding agencies in particular. Many people are at least somewhat aware of the core symptoms of eating disorders and obesity, yet far fewer are familiar with corollary symptoms, mortality and morbidity rates, the value of treatment, and the possibility of prevention. While the educational efforts are aimed toward increasing funding, they also serve to underscore what this volume shows: We have learned much about body image problems, eating disorders, and obesity. We are ready to move on to researching more nuanced etiological models, promising methods of treatment, and potentially effective prevention programs.

REFERENCES

Agras, W. S. (2001). The consequences and costs of the eating disorders. *Psychiatric Clinics of North America, 24,* 371–379.

American Psychiatric Association. (1994). *Diagnostic and statistical manual of mental disorders* (4th ed.). Washington, DC: Author.

Andersen, A. E., Bowers, W., & Watson, T. (2001). A slimming program for eating disorders not otherwise specified: Reconceptualization of a confusing, residual diagnostic category. *Psychiatric Clinics of North America, 24,* 271–280.

Anderson, I., Parry-Billings, M., Newsholme, E., Fairburn, C., & Cowen, P. (1990). Dieting reduces plasma tryptophan and alters brain 5-HT in women. *Psychological Medicine, 20,* 785–791.

Anorexia Nervosa Work Group. (in press). The development of research priorities for the treatment of anorexia nervosa. *International Journal of Eating Disorders.*

Bates, J. (1980). The concept of difficult temperament. *Merrill-Palmer Quarterly, 26,* 299–320.

Becker, A. E. (1995). *Body, self, and society: The view from Fiji.* Philadelphia: University of Pennsylvania.

Bijl, R. V., & Ravelli, A. (2000). Psychiatric morbidity, service use, and need for care in the general population: Results of the Netherlands Mental Health Survey and Incidence Study. *American Journal of Public Health, 90,* 602–607.

Bulik, C., Devlin, B., Bacanu, S., Thornton, L., Klump, K., Fichter, M., et al. (2003). Significant linkage on chromosome 10p in families with bulimia nervosa. *American Journal of Human Genetics, 72.* 200–207.

Bulik, C. M., Sullivan, P. F., Kendleer, K. S. (2000). An empirical study of the classification of eating disorders. *American Journal of Psychiatry, 157,*(6), 886–895.

Cachelin, F. M., Rebeck, R., Veisel, C., & Striegel-Moore, R. H. (2001). Treatment seeking for eating disorders among ethnically diverse women. *International Journal of Eating Disorders, 30,* 269–278.

Cachelin, F. M., Veisel, C., Barzegarnazari, E., & Striegel-Moore, R. H. (2000). Disordered eating, acculturation, and treatment-seeking in a community sample of Hispanic, Asian, Black and White women. *Psychology of Women Quarterly, 24,* 244–233.

Cash, T., & Pruzinsky, T. (2002). *Body image: A handbook of theory, research, and clinical practice.* New York: Guilford Press.

Fairburn, C., & Brownell, K. (2002). *Eating disorders and obesity* (2nd ed.). New York: Guilford Press.

Fairburn, C., & Walsh, T. (2002). Atypical eating disorders (Eating Disorders Not Otherwise Specified). In C. Fairburn & K. Brownell (Eds.), *Eating disorders and obesity* (2nd ed., pp. 171–177). New York: Guilford Press.

Gabbard, G. O., Lazar, S. G., Hornberger, J., & Spiegel, D. (1997). The economic impact of psychotherapy: A review. *American Journal of Psychiatry, 154,* 147–155.

Garvin, V., & Striegel-Moore, R. H. (2001). Health services research for eating disorders in the United States: A status report and a call to action. In R. H. Striegel-Moore and L. Smolak (Eds.), *Eating disorders: Innovative directions in research and practice* (pp. 135–152). Washington, DC: American Psychological Association.

Hargreaves, W. A., Shumway, M., Hu, T., & Cuffel, B. (1998). *Cost-outcome methods for mental health.* San Diego, CA: Academic Press.

Hoek, J. (2002). Distribution of eating disorders. In C. Fairburn & K. Brownell (Eds.), *Eating disorders and obesity* (2nd ed., pp. 233–237). New York: Guilford Press.

Johnson, J. G., Spitzer, R. L., & Williams, J. B. W. (2001). Health problems, impairment and illnesses associated with bulimia nervosa and binge eating disorder among primary care and obstetric gynecology patients. *Psychological Medicine, 31,* 1455–1466.

Joiner, T. E., Vohs, K. D., & Heatherton, T. F. (2000). Three studies on the factorial distinctiveness of binge eating and bulimic symptoms among nonclinical men and women. *International Journal of Eating Disorders, 27,* 198–205.

Katzman, M. A., & Lee, S. (1997). Beyond body image: The integration of feminist and transcultural theories in the understanding of self-starvation. *International Journal of Eating Disorders, 22,* 385–394.

Kaye, W., & Strober, M. (1999). Neurobiology of eating disorders. In D. Charney, E. Nestler, & W. Bunney (Eds.), *Neurobiological foundations of mental illness* (pp. 891–906). New York: Oxford University Press.

Kendler, K. S., MacLean, C., Neale, M., Kessler, R., Heath, A., & Eaves, L. (1991). The genetic epidemiology of bulimia nervosa. *American Journal of Psychiatry, 148,* 1627–1637.

Kessler, R. C., Zhao, S., Katz, S. J., Kouzis, A. C., Frank, R. G., Edlund, M., et al. (1999). Past-year use of outpatient services for psychiatric problems in the National Comorbidity Survey. *American Journal of Psychiatry, 156,* 115–123.

Koran, L. M., Agras, W. S., Rossiter, E. M., & Arnow, B. (1995). Comparing the cost effectiveness of psychiatric treatments: Bulimia nervosa. *Psychiatry Research, 58*(1), 13–21.

Kraemer, H. C. (2000). Pitfalls of multisite randomized clinical trials of efficacy and effectiveness. *Schizophrenia Bulletin, 26*(3), 533–541.

Kraemer, H. C., Wilson, G. T., Fairburn, C. G., & Agras, S. (2002). Mediators and moderators of treatment effects in randomized clinical trials. *Archives of General Psychiatry, 59,* 877–833.

Lave, J. R., Frank, R. G., Schulberg, H. C., & Kamlet, M. S. (1998). Cost-effectiveness of treatments for major depression in primary care practice. *Archive of General Psychology, 55,* 645–651.

Lee, S., & Katzman, M. (2002). Cross-cultural perspectives on eating disorders. In C. Fairburn & K. Brownell (Eds.), *Eating disorders and obesity* (2nd ed., pp. 260–264). New York: Guilford Press.

Lee, S., Lee, A. M., Ngai, E., Lee, D. T., & Wing, Y. K. (2001). Rationales for food refusal in Chinese patients with anorexia nervosa. *International Journal of Eating Disorders, 29,* 224–229.

Levine, M. P., & Piran, N. (2001). The prevention of eating disorders: Toward a participatory ecology of knowledge, action, and advocacy. In R. Striegel-Moore & L. Smolak (Eds.), *Eating disorders: New directions for research and practice* (pp. 233–253). Washington, DC: American Psychological Association.

Levine, M. P., & Smolak, L. (in press). *The prevention of eating problems and eating disorders: Theory, research, and practice.* Mahwah, NJ: Erlbaum.

Lewinsohn, P. M., Seeley, J. R., Moerk, K. C., & Striegel-Moore, R. H. (2002). Gender differences in eating disorder symptoms in young adults. *International Journal of Eating Disorders, 32,* 426–440.

Martin, G., Wertheim, E., Prior, M., Smart, D., Sanson, A., & Oberklaid, F. (2000). A longitudinal study of the role of childhood temperament in the later development of eating concerns. *International Journal of Eating Disorders, 27,* 150–163.

McKnight Investigators. (2003). Risk factors for the onset of eating disorders in adolescent girls: Results of the McKnight longitudinal risk factor study. *American Journal of Psychiatry, 160,* 248–254.

McLellan, F. (2002). Countering poverty's hindrance of neurodevelopment. *Lancet, 359,* 236.

Mitchell, J. E., & Peterson, C. B. (1997). Cognitive-behavioral treatment of eating disorders. In L. J. Dickstein, M. B. Riba, & J. M. Oldham (Eds.), *Review of psychiatry* (Vol. 16, pp. 107–133). Washington, DC: American Psychiatric Press.

Mussell, M. P., Crosby, R. D., Crow, S. J., Knopke, A. J., Peterson, C. B., Wonderlich, S. A., et al. (2000). Utilization of empirically supported psychotherapy treatments for individuals with eating disorders: A survey of psychologists. *International Journal of Eating Disorders, 27,* 230–237.

Ogg, E. C., Millar, H. R., Pusztai, E. E., & Thom, A. S. (1997). General practice consultation patterns preceding diagnosis of eating disorders. *International Journal of Eating Disorders, 22,* 89–93.

Ramacciotti, C. E., Dell'Osso, L., Paoli, R. A., Ciapparelli, A., Coli, E., Kaplan, A. S., et al. (2002). Characteristics of eating disorder patients without a drive for thinness. *International Journal of Eating Disorders, 32,* 206–212.

Rieger, E., Touyz, S. W., Swain, T., & Beumont, P. J. V. (2001). Cross-cultural research on anorexia nervosa: Assumptions regarding the role of body weight. *International Journal of Eating Disorders, 29,* 205–215.

Ruda, M. A., Ling, Q. D., Hohmann, A. G., Peng, Y. B., & Tachibana, T. (2000). Altered nociceptive neuronal circuits after neonatal peripheral inflammation. *Science, 289,* 628–630.

Smolak, L., Harris, B., Levine, M. P., & Shisslak, C. (2001). Teachers: The forgotten influence on the success of prevention programs. *Eating Disorders: Journal of Treatment and Prevention, 9,* 261–266.

Spitzer, R. L., Kroenke, K., & Williams, J. B. W. (1999). Validation and utility of a self-report version of PRIME-MD: The PHQ primary care study. *Journal of the American Medical Association, 282,* 1737–1744.

Steiger, H., Young, S. N., Ng Ying Kin, N. M. K., Koerner, N., Israel, M., Lageix, P., et al. (2001). Implications of impulsive and affective symptoms for serotonin function in bulimia nervosa. *Psychological Medicine, 31,* 85–95.

Steinhausen, H. (2002). The outcome of anorexia nervosa in the twentieth century. *American Journal of Psychiatry, 159,* 1284–1293.

Stice, E. (2001). A prospective test of the dual-pathway model of bulimic pathology: Mediating effects of dual dieting and negative affect. *Journal of Abnormal Psychology, 110,* 124–135.

Stice, E., & Bearman, S. (2001). Body image and eating disturbances prospectively predict increases in depressive symptoms in adolescent girls: A growth curve analysis. *Developmental Psychology, 37,* 597–607.

Striegel-Moore, R. H., Leslie, D., Petrill, S. A., Garvin, V., & Rosenheck, R. A. (2000). One-year use and cost of inpatient and outpatient services among female and male patients with an eating disorder: Evidence from a national database of health insurance claims. *International Journal of Eating Disorders, 27,* 301–389.

Striegel-Moore, R. H., & Marcus, M. (1995). Eating disorders in women: Current issues and debates. In A. G. Stanton & S. J. Gallant (Eds.), *Women's health book* (pp. 445–487). Washington, DC: American Psychological Association.

Striegel-Moore, R. H., Silberstein, L. R., & Rodin, J. (1986). Toward an understanding of risk factors for bulimia. *American Psychology, 41,* 246–263.

Striegel-Moore, R. H., & Smolak, L. (Eds.). (2001). *Eating disorders: Innovative directions in research and practice.* Washington, DC: American Psychological Association.

Thompson, J. K., Heinberg, L., Altabe, M., & Tantleff-Dunn, S. (1999). *Exacting beauty: Theory, assessment, and treatment of body image disturbance.* Washington, DC: American Psychological Association.

Thompson, J. K., & Smolak, L. (2001). *Body image, eating disorders, and obesity in youth: Assessment, prevention, and treatment.* Washington, DC: American Psychological Association.

Thompson, J. K., & Stice, E. (2001). Thin-ideal internalization: Mounting evidence for a new risk factor for body-image disturbance and eating pathology. *Current Directions in Psychological Science, 10,* 181–183.

Von Korff, M., Katon, W., Bush, T., Lin, E. H., Simon, G. E., Saunders, K., et al. (1998). Treatment costs, cost offset, and cost-effectiveness of collaborative management of depression. *Psychosomatic Medicine, 60,* 143–149.

Whittal, M. L., Agras, W. S., & Gould, R. A. (1999). Bulimia nervosa: A meta-analysis of psychosocial and pharmacological treatments. *Behavior Therapy, 30,* 117–135.

Wilfley, D. E., Pike, K. M., Dohm, F., Striegel-Moore, R. H., & Fairburn, C. G. (2001). Bias of binge eating disorder: How representative are recruited clinic samples? *Journal of Consulting and Clinical Psychology, 69,* 383–388.

Wonderlich, S., & Mitchell, J. (2001). The role of personality in the onset of eating disorders and treatment implication. *Psychiatric Clinics of North America, 24,* 249–258.

Yates, B. T. (1994). Toward the incorporation of costs, cost-effectiveness analysis, and cost-benefit analysis into clinical research. *Journal of Consulting and Clinical Psychology, 62,* 729–736.

Zhu, A. J., & Walsh, B. T. (2002). Pharmacologic treatment of eating disorders. *Canadian Journal of Psychiatry, 47,* 227–234.

Author Index

Subject Index

Reproductive function:
body image dissatisfaction and pregnancy, 470–471
eating disorders and, 104–105
obesity and infertility, 104
Respiratory system, 375, 380
Restraint measures, 121–122
Restricting subtype, anorexia nervosa (ANR), 62
Restrictive eating (childhood/adolescence), 640
Risk assessment, health (obese patients), 384–386
Risk behaviors, health (males), 607–609
Risk factors for eating disorders, 17–29
appropriate inference (implications of study design, sample, and terminology), 20–29
case-control studies, 22–24, 25
choice and implications of study design, 24–26
cohort studies, 24, 25
cross-sectional studies, 20–22, 25
randomized clinical trials, 24, 25, 28–29
case definitions, 26
bulimic behaviors and dissatisfaction with weight and shape, 27–28
full criteria eating disorders, 26
partial criteria cases, 26–27
costs, 29
difference among true risk factors, confounders, and correlates, 17–20
exposure of interest, 28–29
Risk hierarchy form, 146
Role disputes, 170–171
Role transitions, 169–170
Rumination, 636–637

Sample characteristics (as source of observed differences), 23–24
Satiety hormone, 98
Scalar/item/functional equivalence, 669–670
Schools/schooling:
eating problems in childhood/adolescence, 649
obesity prevention policies:
eliminating availability of soft drinks, fast foods, and unhealthy snack foods in schools, 346
eliminating food advertising in schools, 346
weight-related stigmatization in, 353–355
Selective eating, 639
Self, actual/ideal/ought, 250
Self-directed diet and exercise programs (obesity treatment), 424–426
Self-discoveries, 531
Self-discrepancy and mood (in integrative cognitive model of bulimia nervosa), 248–250
Self-esteem, 133, 310
Self-help, 291–292, 427, 428
Self-in-relation model, 270
Self-monitoring, 122–123, 429
Self-regulation, 133, 251–252
Self-report measures:
general eating disorder symptoms, 119–121
Bulimia Test-Revised (BULIT-R), 120
Eating Attitudes Test (EAT), 119
Eating Disorder Diagnostic Scale (EDDS), 120–121
Eating Disorders Inventory (EDI), 119–120
specific eating-related domains:
body image, 122
restraint, 121–122
Self-schemas, 150–151, 518
Self-worth, 133

Sequential treatment, 202–204
Serotonergic neurotransmitter system, 66
Sexual abuse. See also Child sexual abuse (CSA):
body image dissatisfaction and, 471–472
feminist approach to eating disorders and, 594
inpatient treatment model, and patients with history of, 311
Sexual harassment, 594
Sexual orientation, body image dissatisfaction and, 472
Shame/coping model (CSA and ED), 688, 689
Situational Inventory of Body Image Dysphoria (SIBID), 507, 508, 531
Skills training, 241–243, 254–256
Skin:
medical assessment, obese patient, 378
picking (in body dysmorphic disorder), 549
Sleep studies (obesity assessment), 383–384
Social attitudes about thinness and fatness, 705–706
Social comparison theory, 473–474, 699–700
Social consequences of obesity, 350–355
faced by overweight adolescents, 350–351
faced by overweight adults, 352
faced by overweight children, 350
Social context, in feminist therapy, 263–266
Social experiment, 4
Social marketing, 711
Social role theory, 591
Social transformation, 275–276
Sociocultural aspects of eating disorders, 565–581
cross-cultural variation, 567–570
Africa and Middle East, 568–569
Asia, 568
Latin America and the Caribbean, 569–570
small-scale, indigenous populations, 570
cultural factors relevant to disordered eating, 575–576
definitions, 659
differences in beauty ideals and body concerns across cultures, 465
eating disorders among occupational, athletic, and gay subcultures, 573–574
ethnic minority populations, eating disorders among, 570–573
future directions, 740–741
gender and feminist perspectives, 579–580
generation status, 659
global distribution (eating disorders among world populations), 566–567
historical perspective, 565–566
socioeconomic influences, 573
transition: globalization, acculturation, and assimilation, 576–579
Western culture and eating disorders, 574–575
Sociocultural aspects of obesity. See Ethnicity, obesity and body image among ethnically diverse children/adolescents
Sociocultural Attitudes toward Appearance Questionnaire (SATAQ), 507, 508, 619, 698–699
Sociocultural factors:
body dysmorphic disorder, 555
body image dissatisfaction, 464–470, 484
additive effects of multiple sociocultural agents, 469–470
changes in the ideal image of beauty over time, 465–466
differences in the beauty ideals and body concerns across cultures, 465
media influence, 468–469